HISTORY OF THE PANJAB

HISTORY OF THE PANJAB:

FROM THE REMOTEST ANTIQUITY

TO

THE PRESENT TIME

SYAD MUHAMMAD LATIF

GYAN

Published by

Gyan Publishing House
5, Ansari Road
Daryaganj, New Delhi-110002
Phone: 011-47034999, 9811692060
E-mail: books@gyanbooks.com

Distribution Network
gyanbooks.com
India, USA, Canada, UK, Australia

ISBN: 978-93-7014-121-6 (PB)

First Published, 1891

2nd Impression 2025

Printed at: Gyan Press, Delhi.

HISTORY OF THE PANJAB
Author: SYAD MUHAMMAD LATIF

HISTORY OF THE PANJÁB

FROM THE REMOTEST ANTIQUITY

TO

THE PRESENT TIME.

BY

SYAD MUHAMMAD LATIF,

EXTRA JUDICIAL ASSISTANT COMMISSIONER, GURDASPUR,

FELLOW OF THE PANJÁB UNIVERSITY,

AND MEMBER OF THE BENGAL ASIATIC SOCIETY.

Calcutta:

PUBLISHED BY THE CALCUTTA CENTRAL PRESS COMPANY, LIMITED.

5 Council House Street.

1891.

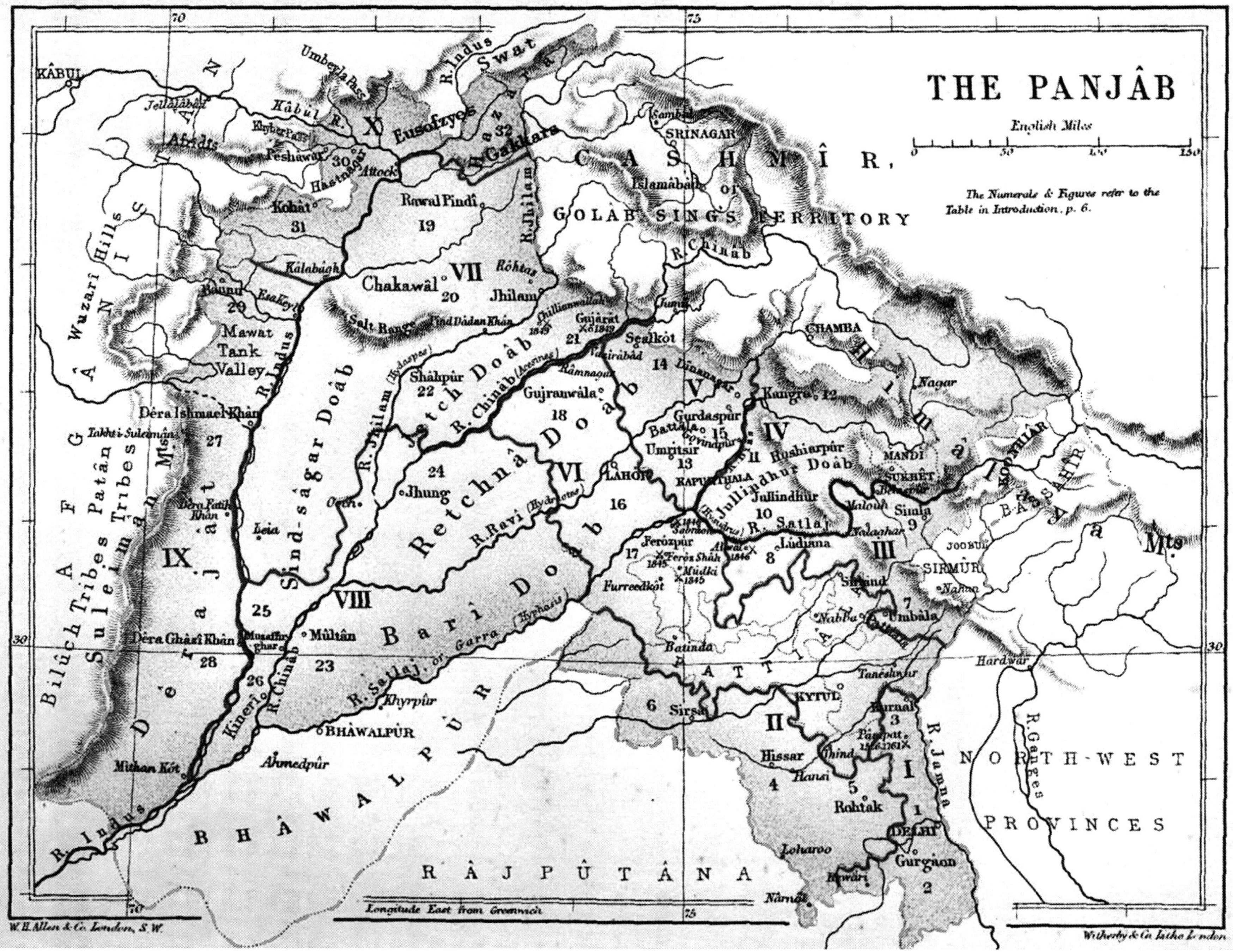
THE PANJÂB
English Miles
0 50 100 150
The Numerals & Figures refer to the Table in Introduction, p. 6.
CASHMÎR,
GOLAB SINGS TERRITORY
KÂBUL
Jellalabad
Khyber Pass
Afridis
Peshawar
Umbeyla Pass
R. Indus
Swat
Kâbul R.
X
Eusofzyes
32
Gakkars
30
Attock
Kohât
31
Rawal Pindî
19
R. Jhilam
SRINAGAR
Islamâbâd
R. Chinab
Kâlabâgh
VII
Chakawâl
20
Rôhtas
Jhilam
Salt Range
Pind Dâdan Khân
Bannu
29
Mawat
Tank
Valley
Wuzari Hills
Dêra Ishmael Khân
27
Takht i Suleimân
Suleimân Mts
Bilûch Tribes
Patân Tribes
IX
Dêra Fatih Khân
Leia
Sind-sâgar Doâb
R. Indus
Jetch Doâb
Shâhpur
22
R. Jhilam (Hydaspes)
R. Chinab (Acesines)
Gujarât
21
Sealkôt
Jumû
CHAMBA
Kangra
12
Nagar
Himâlaya Mts
Gujranwâla
18
Râmnagar
Wazirâbâd
14
V
Gurdaspur
Battâla
15
Umritsir
13
IV
Hushiarpûr
Jullindhur Doâb
MANDÎ
SUKHET
KOONHIAR
BASAHIR
24
Jhung
Retchnâ Doâb
R. Ravi (Hydraotes)
VI
LAHOR
16
KAPURTHALA
Jullindhur
10
R. Satlaj (Hesudrus)
Simla
9
Nalaghar
Ludiana
8
Ferôzpur
17
Sobraon
Furreedkôt
III
JOOBUL
SIRMÛR
Nahan
Sirhind
7
Umbâla
Nabba
Pattiala
Hardwar
Tanêshwar
Batinda
25
VIII
Bari Doab
Mûltân
23
Dêra Ghâzî Khân
28
26
R. Chinâb
Kineri
R. Satlaj or Garra (Hyphasis)
Khyrpûr
BHÂWALPÛR
Ahmedpûr
Mithan Kôt
6
Sirsa
KYTUL
II
Kurnal
3
Panipat
Hissar
Hansi
4
5
Rohtak
I
1
DELHI
Gurgaon
2
Loharoo
Rewari
Narnol
R. Jamna
R. Ganges
NORTH-WEST PROVINCES
BHÂWALPÛR
RÂJPÛTÂNA
Longitude East from Greenwich
W. H. Allen & Co. London, S.W.
Witherby & Co. litho London

PREFACE.

In the pages of History there is probably no story at once so grand, so romantic, and so pregnant with instruction, as that of the British conquest of India and the progress of the British Nation in the East. What deeds of noble daring, what examples of calm resolution and untiring devotion, does it not unfold! Over what fortresses, once deemed impregnable, has not the 'meteor flag of England' waved triumphantly! Through what forbidding mountain passes, what dreary defiles, and what tangled glens have not the notes of her bugles echoed and her bright arms gleamed! In what majestic halls, dainty pavilions, and jewelled domes have not the strains of her martial music and the cheers of her advancing soldiery resounded!

In their submission to her sway, the children of the sun, the founders of the mighty Empires of Kanauj and Ajuddhia, enshrined in the legends of Rámá, feel honoured. Before her might the children of the moon, the founders of the dynasties of Indraprastha and Pataliputra, glorified in the legends of Krishna and the Pandavas, bowed their heads. These were the heroes of the age of Hindu chivalry, and they are, to this day, honoured with the title of Rájputs, or the sons of kings. At Britain's feet lay, equally humbled, the hardy Mahratta, who had so long successfully baffled the power of the Moghal, and the proud Afghan, who, more than a century before, had challenged the might of the stern Nádir.

But in no part of this great Empire was British rule received with more genuine satisfaction than in the country of the Five Rivers. With a manly and calm resignation, the disciples of Govind, beaten in a fair fight, cheerfully submitted to their conquerors. Unlike the Rájput, the Sikh did not seek glory by tracing back his genealogy to the sun or the moon. Nor, like the enthusiastic Musalman, did he pride himself on the heroic deeds of ancestors who, under the impulse of religion, had subverted the mightiest empires on the face of the earth. Nevertheless he was a Singh of the Guru, an earthborn Singh, or lion of his race. The Sikhs owed their position to the strength of their own arms. The very land they ruled was, not many generations back, ploughed by their forefathers.

A peculiar race of people, they flourished in a peculiar country. From the remotest antiquity, an interest has attached to the land of the Five Rivers unequalled by that attaching to any other land of this great Peninsula. Placed, as it is, by Nature in a locality which gives it a crowning position, and serving as the gateway to India, every invader from the North has, by its possession, sought the road to fame. In pre-historic times, it was, presumably, the Panjáb that was first invaded by the Aryans from their camping ground beyond the snowy ranges of the stupendous Himálayas. Here the holy singers composed their Vedic hymns, the great literary memorial of their settlement in the country. The Brahmins, the Rájputs and the Bannias, who form the sacerdotal, military and mercantile classes of the Hindus, are, alike, the descendants of the fairer race, the Aryans of Bactria. The lower and servile dark-skinned classes represent the people they subdued.

The Aryan conquerors of the Panjáb were, in their turn, subdued by the Scythians, or Tartars, of Turkistan, whose hordes, having overrun parts of Asia, found their way into the regions of the Indus. The Scythic, or Northern, form of Buddhism competed with the earlier Buddhism of Asoka, famous for his rock and cave edicts. The Scythian influence in the Panjáb is a historical fact. Alexander made the Panjáb the classic ground of his conquest, and it was in the Panjáb, too, that, in after times, the armies of Islam, after overrunning Asia, Africa and Southern Europe, as far as distant Spain and Gaul, obtained their first footing on Indian soil. For upwards of two centuries did the Hindu masters of the country baffle the power of the Mahomedan invaders. Mahmúd sacked and destroyed the Hindu fanes, broke up their idols, and subjected the land to every conceivable form of misery and degradation, carrying away thousands of the inhabitants into hopeless slavery. The hordes of the great mercenary Tartar leader, Changez Khan, under his brother, inflicted on the Panjáb all the horrors which had been experienced in Hungary, Russia, and Germany, and even on the shores of the Baltic. Tamerlane, the world-renowned conqueror, who left to his descendants twenty-seven crowns, and made Samarkand the mistress of Asia, enriching her with the spoil of a thousand cities, made the Panjáb the scene of his military adventures. The knightly Baber, the hardy Nádir, and the Abdáli, Ahmad Shah, each in his turn, used the Panjáb as the base of warlike operations for conquests beyond its classic rivers. In short, from the time of Alexander to the invasion of Shah Zaman, of unlucky memory, it has served as a bulwark to India against all the invasions from the North and West.

The Panjáb is the home of Sikhism, the religion founded by Nának, who, instead of detailing and sub-dividing divinity, loftily invoked the deity as the one and indivisible God, and appealed alike to the *mullah* and the *pandit*. Here Arjun met his famous martyrdom, and here Govind, consummating the dispensation of Nának, died, declaring his priestly mission to be fulfilled, and the Guruship to rest in the general body of the *Khálsá*. Here did the Sikh confederacies rise under their respective warlike leaders, resulting in the establishment of the doctrine that the Army and State of the *Khálsá* were the substantive power of the Panjáb. Ranjít Singh, of the *Sukerchakia misl*, then appeared on the scene, and became the founder of the Sikh monarchy in the Panjáb; but his descendants lacked the political foresight and wisdom that had characterized his policy, and their incapacity lost to the Sikhs a kingdom which it had taken years of toil and persevering energy on the part of Ranjít Singh to establish.

The aggressive policy adopted by the Sikhs towards the paramount Power of India, compelled the latter to take up arms against them. The country was conquered; but, generosity prevailing over policy, the victors restored to the recognised heir to the throne the territories which they were entitled to hold by right of conquest. The Sikh ministers and Darbár, however, violated the treaty; and the *Khálsá* army, rising up in arms, waged a fierce war to destroy the benefactors of their race, whose clemency alone had saved them from utter annihilation. The violators of the treaty were punished, and the province was absorbed into the British Empire, under the administration of Lord Dalhousie. The conquered nation, whose own acts had invited the conflict which thus terminated in its downfall, was considerately, nay, generously, treated by the victors. British statesmen respected the fallen fortunes of the Sikhs, and, by a policy of combined vigour, and conciliation, achieved those great victories of peace which will ever reflect honour on the British name. The names of the famous Lawrences, worthy choice of Lord Dalhousie's benevolent policy, are inscribed in characters of light on the frontispiece of the History of India, among those of the illustrious British heroes and statesmen to whose energy, talents and diplomatic skill, England owes its possession of her empire. The Lawrences were ably assisted in their task by worthy successors, Sir Robert Montgomery and Sir Donald McLeod, whose names became deservedly great throughout the land. To these and other British statesmen the Panjáb owes a debt of undying gratitude for their services to the country; and their memory will be held in lasting honour. They were the pioneers of the Empire founded by the British, to whose subsequent success in the country they paved the way.

It is the history of a country so situated, thus acquired by the British, and so governed by that nation, that I have attempted to write in the following pages. The want of a complete History of the Panjáb has long been felt. The familiar and able works of McGregor, Cunningham, Malcolm, and Prinsep are histories of the Sikhs from the time of Bábá Nának. They treat of the origin of the Sikh nation and sect, their habits and customs, and describe how they rose to political significance and power. The history of the reigning family of Láhore, by Major Carmichael Smyth, describes the part which the Dogra family of Jammú played in the grand drama of the Panjáb. It aims at describing the secret history of the Sikh court, and gives a vivid account of the intrigues which resulted in the final collapse of the Sikh monarchy. The works of Colonel Steinbach, the Panjáb adventurer, of Major H. M. L. Lawrence, and *The Court and Camp of Ranjít Singh*, by Colonel

Osborne, all treat of the Sikh period. The learned works known as the *Panjáb Rájás* and *Panjáb Chiefs*, by Sir Lepel Griffin, have been devoted to special subjects. None of these works tells us anything of the pre-Sikh period, much less of the Hindu and pre-Hindu periods. The wars with the British are not fully described, and the account of the second Sikh war and of the annexation of the country by the British is entirely omitted. Nothing is said of the subsequent eventful British period, the obvious reason being that many of the works now extant were compiled about the time of the annexation of the country. Moreover, a perusal of these works discloses a want of uniformity in the accounts they severally give of the Sikh period, especially where the authors, having no access to official records, depended on native sources of information. The Urdu history of the Panjáb ascribed to Rai Kanhia Lal contains little that is original. The diary of Maharájá Ranjít Singh, written in Persian by Sohan Lal Súri, would be a useful work of reference, were it not couched in a hyperbolic style and loaded with fiction.

It is to supply a manifest want, then, that the present work has been undertaken. The difficulties with which I have had to contend in prosecuting my task have been great. It has proved not only a work of vast magnitude, but one of great delicacy and responsibility. Fully conscious of my own shortcomings, I was nevertheless deeply impressed with the need for such a work in the interests of my countrymen. There was not a passage of history before the advent of the Brîtish which did not strike me with emotion, or which did not, as we come down from that period of insecurity and spoliation to the period of profound and unbroken peace enjoyed during the British period, disclose the truth that India, under the benign rule of England, has changed from a waste land, full of thorns and brambles, to a verdant garden, resplendent with bright and fragrant flowers. I felt impelled to narrate to my countrymen the story of the land of their birth, from the remotest antiquity to recent times, based on historical truth, and free from party spirit or sectarian prejudice. Colonel Gurwood, in his celebrated work, *The Despatches of the Duke of Wellington*, has said: "The great end of history is the exact illustration of events as they occurred, and there should neither be exaggeration nor concealment, to suit angry feelings or personal disappointment. History should contain 'the truth, the whole truth, and nothing but truth.'" I have endeavoured to act on this motto, and to narrate the facts in their true colours, no matter to what particular nation or creed they related. My difficulties have been twofold. This being a provincial history, much of my material had, in the first instance, to be collated from voluminous works on India, which could not be done without extensive reading, and, secondly, in order to test the truth of my authorities, I had to compare the various accounts given. The result has been that only such accounts have, to the best of my belief, been incorporated in this book as, after the exercise of due diligence and caution, were found to be supported by concurrent testimony, or as seemed to receive corroboration from works which may be accepted as authorities on the subject of Indian history.

My task, however, in spite of its difficulties, and the years of toil bestowed on it, has been to me a labour of love; and, now that it is at an end, I feel that the time employed on it could not have been devoted to a worthier purpose. I have brought the history of the Panjáb down to the present time, in the hope that it may find readers among the friends of civilization and of English progress generally, as well as among students, and at the same time I venture to hope that the learned public may find in it a succinct and comprehensive history of this country.

It has not been thought necessary to append references to historical facts in every instance, as this would have swelled the work with footnotes. Numerous works of Oriental history have been consulted; but my acknowledgments are chiefly due to those of Sir William Jones, Briggs' celebrated translation of *Ferishta*, Sir H. M. Elliot's *Historians of India*, the *History of India*, by the Honorable Mountstuart Elphinstone; the works of Murray, Taylor, Marshman, Mill, Talboys Wheeler, Keene, Fraser and MacFarlane. For the ancient portions of the history, I am indebted to the excellent works of Dr. Hunter, General Cunningham, McCrindle, Dunker, Thomas Maurice, Ludlow, Tavernier, and the Rev. Mr. Hunter. In writing the Mahomedan period, the *Akbarnáma* of Sheikh Abul Fazl, the *Tabakát-i-Akbari* of Moulana Nizám-ud-dín Ahmad, the *Ain-i-Akbari*, by Professor Blochmann, the *Syrul-Muta Akhirin*, of Mír Gholam Husein Khan, translated by Briggs, the *Hadikatul Akálim* of Murtazá Husein, the *Bhadshahnáma* of Mulla Abdul Hamíd, of Láhore, the *Ikbálnáma Jahángíri* of Mutamid Khan, the *Alamgírnáma* of Mahomed Kázim, and the *Moasir-i-Alamgíri* of Mahomed Sákí, were also consulted. For the portion relating to the Sikhs, I am obliged to the works of Sir John Malcolm, McGregor, Cunningham, Prinsep, Smyth, to the *Panjáb Rájás* and *Panjáb Chiefs*, by Sir Lepel Griffin, Dr. Honighbergher's *Thirty-five Years in the East*, Moorcroft's Travels, Burne's Travels, to the narrative of journeys by Masson and Victor Jacquemont, and to Dr. Trumpp's translation of the *Adi Granth*. For the account of the Sikh wars and the Mutiny, I am chiefly indebted to the *History of the Panjáb* by Thornton, Nolan's *British Empire*, Kaye's *Sepoy War*, *The Crisis of the Panjáb* by Frederick Cooper, and *The Panjáb and Delhi in 1857*, by the Rev. J. Cave-Brown. The chapter on the trade and industries of the Panjáb I owe to official reports, especially to the excellent works of Mr. Baden-Powell. In describing the aborigines of the Panjáb and the customs of the Hindus, and for the statistical portion of the history I could not have done without consulting the able official reports drawn up by Mr. Denzil J. Ibbetson. I have also to thank many kind friends who have assisted me by lending me rare books, or with their advice. Dewán Ram Nath most courteously allowed me the use of his learned father Dewán Amar Nath's manuscript history, called the *Khálsá Dewan*, in Persian, I had also the privilege of using Moulvi Din Muhammad's *History of the Panjáb*, in manuscript, which was lent me by his son, Munshi Ghulam Farid Khan, Extra Assistant Commissioner. In sketching the British Period, the official reports were consulted as well as my own notes.

A few words are here necessary regarding the arrangement of the work. Although particular care has been taken to narrate every important fact that I was able to ascertain relating to the Panjáb, I have omitted nothing which was likely to be of interest to the student of history. Though care has been taken to avoid entering into the broad subject of Indian history, many events have had to be mentioned for the sake of their historical value, and the intense interest attaching to them. For instance, while describing the events which occurred in the Panjáb in connection with the invasion of Nádir Shah, or Ahmad Shah, I found it impossible to omit mention of the more important account of the sack of Delhi and the massacre of its inhabitants. Delhi, although the ancient capital of Hindostán, forms now an integral part of this province, and I have treated it as a Panjáb city. Hence, whatever of interest took place there, has been mentioned; for, as it was the capital of the Mahomedan Empire of India, the incidents at the Court materially affected the welfare of the Panjáb and its people. The History of the Panjáb would have lost much of its interest if no mention, however brief, of the political condition of the empire, of which it formed a component part at various periods, had been made. Some events, although, strictly speaking, not relating to the Panjáb, had to be noticed, to render the narrative complete, for without them the link between connected series of important occurrences would have been missing. For instance, while describing the exploits of Mahmúd of Ghazni on the frontier of the Panjáb, I could not see my way to omit mention of his more important victories at Somnath, so celebrated in history, and read with equal interest everywhere. A full life has been given of celebrated sovereigns, conquerors and other personages known to Indian history, who played a conspicuous part in Panjáb politics, such as Alexander the Great, Akber, Nádir, Jahángír and the Empress Nur Jahán. A full life of Maharájá Ranjít Singh, of modern fame, and a fuller account of his interesting reign than has ever yet been published, have been given. The lives of the Sikh Gurus, and an account of the Sikh *misls* will, it is hoped, be found to contain much new and important matter. They will give the reader an idea of the manner in which the Sikh religion and power developed in the Panjáb. The reign of each Mahomedan King has been separately treated, with special reference to the events of the Panjáb and the political changes and condition of the people in that country at various times. The origin of the people has been traced, so far as was consistent with the objects of this work and the religious notions of the people, and their remarkable customs and usages have been described. I have, in short, attempted to trace the Panjábi, from the time when he lived a primitive life, to that in which he claims the highest privileges that could be legitimately conferred upon him; from an age of barbarism to an age of enlightenment, when he shares, with the rest of the Crown's subjects, the benefits and blessings of a civilized Government.

The magnitude of the scheme must be my plea for the brief manner in which I have treated of general subjects, for, had I ventured to deal with them fully, the work would have swelled to an enormous extent, and it was not intended to make it an encyclopædia. I have, in short, endeavoured so to treat of each subject as to bring the work within the compass and scope of a provincial history.

That a competent English scholar would have done more justice to the work, I freely admit. I am neither unconscious of my own shortcomings, and of the many defects in the work which I have ventured to lay before the public, nor, in spite of the care bestowed on the work, am I in a position to claim for it the credit of being a complete history of the Panjáb. It is possible that some mistakes have crept in, for which I ask the indulgence of the learned reader. It is possible, too, that more discerning eyes will find imperfections in my work that are invisible to mine; but, in the words of Mill, "I shall yet appeal from the sentence of him who shall judge of me solely by what I have not done. An equitable and truly useful decision would be grounded upon an accurate estimation of what I have done, and what I have not done, taken together." If that eminent historian of India, with all his great literary talents, thought the plea applied to his case, it will, *à fortiori*, have application to the case of one like myself, who has no pretensions whatever to systematic scholarship. And if I am asking the learned reader to approve of my labours in a field of some difficulty, I do so, not because I am sanguine of their worth, but because I have so much confidence in his indulgence. My reason for attempting the work is simply this: Since no one of higher qualifications had thought of such a work, I conceived that I might make an attempt, however imperfect, to supply what I considered a want, with no ostentatious object, but with a view solely to awakening interest, and inducing more competent persons to complete what I might have left incomplete, and to accomplish what I was not in a position fully to execute.

And now, my dear countrymen, before I close this review, let me say a few words to you, words which I feel you will do well to take to heart. When you have read my history, will you put it on the shelf of forgetfulness, as many books of entertainment are read and put aside after the curiosity excited by them is over? Or will you elect to treat it like some fiction, or some Indian tale, which so many of our young men read for the sake of amusement, and to pass the time? I sincerely hope and trust that you will not do this, for such is not the object of my work. Let me hope that you will weigh carefully and calmly the facts narrated to you; that you will exercise due diligence; and then that, in order to draw conclusions, you will appeal to your reason, your conscience and your good taste. Do not think that the Panjáb of to-day is the Panjáb of forty years back. Do not forget what the condition of your country was forty years ago, or to appreciate heartily the manifold blessings of British rule and the influence of British civilization on your country. It was all very well for Lord Macaulay, in his unrivalled essays on Clive and Warren Hastings, to paint in glowing terms the magnificence and grandeur of the Moghal Court and of its ministers and grandees. Truly has he said that "the innumerable retinues and gorgeous decorations which surrounded the throne of Delhi, dazzled even eyes which were accustomed to the pomp of Versailles. Some of the great Viceroys, who held their posts by virtue of commissions from the Moghal, ruled as many subjects as the king of France or the Emperor of Germany. Even the deputies of these deputies might well rank, as to extent of territory and amount of revenue, with the Grand Duke of Tuscany or the Elector of Saxony." It has been a misfortune to our generation that Lord Macaulay did not write a History of India, for it would have been a work in which he would have taken the most genuine interest. Had the great essayist taken up his pen to write a history of this country, he would not, in all human probability, have omitted to lay before the world the other side of the picture. He would have informed us whence the wealth had come which enabled the Imperial Court to maintain its State, or the Viceroys of Provinces to decorate their palaces and entertain a countless host of retainers, and what means were employed in accumulating these vast treasures for the Imperial Exchequer. Did it ever reach the royal ear how a poor old woman had passed the night even half a mile from the Imperial palace? Was it ever known whether she was oppressed by the Imperial servants, or by a wealthy lord, or by an official exercising authority? Did it matter at all if she passed her night in groans and lamentations, in hunger and privation? Was a lamp lit in her dark, small room to solace her hours of affliction? Did the grand Signor ever care to see what was passing in the cottage of a poor peasant, a short distance from the Imperial city, through the grinding tyranny of those whom he had put in authority? Exceptions, of course, there are; and our country can point with pride to names like those of Asoka, Bikramajit and Akber, brilliant examples of royal enlightenment and munificence, under whom India prospered, and whose example was worthily followed by some others. To the memory of these kings every respect is justly due. Their great names have been handed down to posterity, as benefactors of their people and country. But monarchs of this description have been so few that they can be counted on one's fingers.

I have recounted to you the history of the Great Moghal before he had sunk to the condition of a pensioner and a puppet. What does it disclose? Corruption, degradation and treachery stalked openly through the land. Confusion and disorder of every kind ran riot over the length and breadth of the empire. The country was desolate, and vice, cruelty, extravagance and profligacy overspread its surface. Strife became chronic, and anarchy reared its head everywhere. The money which enabled the Moghal and his Omerahs to embellish their palaces, was wrung from helpless people in the interior of the country. The land was farmed out to contractors who exercised arbitrary power to satisfy their cupidity; and these had, in their turn, to disgorge to the Imperial Treasury a portion of their plunder, if they could not bribe the officers who had access to the throne. Murders of the most horrible type, robberies of a most outrageous and shocking character, were the order of the day. Honour, justice and position were bought and sold. The rulers of the land were sunk in voluptuousness and pollution of the most revolting description, and immersed in an abyss of enfeebling debauchery. They had, in most instances, thrown themselves into the arms of vile panders and parasites, who were slaves of their own sensual appetites. Barbers and fiddlers, pimps, eunuchs and mountebanks, acquired considerable fortunes, and usurped the functions and prerogatives of royalty. Sometimes a puppet king was set up to suit the private ends of the Omerahs. He was either an inexperienced youth, picked up at random from the innermost recesses of the *zanáná*, who was absorbed in the pleasures of the seraglio, and to whom affairs of State were disagreeable interruptions, or a crippled old man, on the brink of the grave, respectable only in his feebleness. The money squeezed out of the poor raiyat was wasted in expensive feasts, pageants and shows; in glittering trappings for horses, or in richly caparisoned housings of costly elephants—in short, in folly and pomp of every conceivable description, not to mention the sumptuous salaries and allowances of a multitudinous host of idle attendants, bands of singers, musicians, dancing girls, and crowds of sycophants and impostors. The court of the king was a hotbed of intrigue. The ministers were divided, and party spirit ran high. Viceroys and satraps of different provinces, farmers of revenue and others in power, sought to build up a sovereign rule for themselves on the basis of plunder and blackmail. The Government was rapacious, tyrannical and hated to a degree. Intestine broils and commotions, incessant bloodshed and anarchy, at length undermined the great house of Tymúr. The court of Láhore, when no longer guided by the genius of Ranjít Singh, fell into a state even worse than that of the corrupt Court at Delhi subsequent to the period of Bahádur Shah, the successor of Aurangzeb. *De mortuis nil nisi bonum* is doubtless an excellent sentiment; but the truth must be told, and told, too, in all its nakedness, that the lesson of history may be learned with profit. *Fiat justitia, ruat cœlum!* The empire founded by the genius of Baber collapsed, and the throne reared by Ranjít on the ruins of Moghal greatness fell, too, in its turn. Where are now the mighty potentates before whom the greatest lords of the land trembled? Where is the Grand Moghal, who, seated on the peacock throne, exacted prostration from the chiefs of the most ancient dynasties of India? Where is his band of tall and brilliantly clad heralds with golden staves in their hands, who made the famous Sewáji bow before Aurangzeb, calling out loudly on each step, as the Mahratta advanced to the royal presence to pay him homage: "Lo, the Asylum of the Universe! lo, the Lord of the Nations! lo, the conqueror of the world! *Shah in Shah Badshah salámat!*" All have crumbled into dust, and nothing remains but the memory of their good or evil deeds! A humane nation from the far West, unrivalled among the nations of the world for its benevolence and sympathy with mankind, has been destined by the mysterious decree of Providence to rule over this vast empire, to vindicate its honour, to shelter God's people, to protect the weak, to punish the tyrant, to do away with the darkness of ignorance, to diffuse the light of learning, and to fulfil its great mission in the world, which is the good of the nations committed by God to its care. The tremendous hurricanes that swept over India, shattered to pieces its sacred temples and stately palaces, destroying its hopes and spreading misery and desolation around, have happily all passed away, and a cheering breeze, accompanied by refreshing showers from the West, has brought on its wings, for the parched land of India, its fertilizing influence and the sweet fragrance of blossom and flower. Once more has the withered tree of hope gathered new life and become laden with sweet fruit. The Hindu, in his pagoda, utters his "*Ram, Ram!*" bowing with the utmost humility before his Devatas; the Mahomedan, in his mosque, with his face turned towards Mecca, repeats his "*Allah, Allah!*" with all the fervour of a true Musalman; and the Sikh, in his Gurudoára, reverentially waves the *chowri* of peacock plumes over the *Granth*, his holy book, and invokes the spirit of the "*Wáh Guru*" to help him in his worldly affairs. What an age of peace and concord is ours! The ages of Naushrvan, the just, and Harun-ul-Rashíd, the magnificent, celebrated in the history of the East, are not to be compared with it.

Should you not, my dear young countrymen—you, who are

the flower of the educational institutions established by the bounty of the British; you who are to take our places when we are gone, and in whom are fixed our future hopes,—should you not, I say, be thankful to God, after you have gone through the pages I lay before you, that the days of calamity of our country are over? Do you still believe that your country was ever a garden of roses, as you see it now? Your country, as you must already know without my telling you of it, is, by its very situation, the most exposed to foreign danger. Is it not now one of the most secure, and has it not become one of the most prosperous and flourishing, of the countries of the globe under the fostering care of the English? The same bands of fanatics, marauders and highway robbers who were once a terror to the people, and who had spread devastation throughout the land, are turned into peaceful cultivators and useful citizens. The same land which was stained with the blood of the innocent, or which was the haunt of the leopard and the panther, now smiles with rich harvests and luxuriant vegetation. The same dwellings where many a widow passed a gloomy life, lamenting, it may be, over a murdered husband, the victim of some strife, or where lived afflicted mothers, grieving over the deaths of their sons, who had, perhaps, fallen bravely defending hearth and home, are now full of life and joy and comfort. No longer are the weak the prey of the strong. Justice is impartially administered. It reaches equally the palace of the Nawáb and the cottage of the peasant. The strong arm of the law established by the British Government is put forth, not to destroy but to protect, to shelter and to guide. The people are happy, contented, peaceable, loyal and prosperous. The revenues of the country are a source of strength to the Government and of advantage to the subject. A financial system, based upon correct principles of political economy, has been instituted. By the introduction of measures of amelioration and a policy at once vigorous and conciliatory, the country of the Five Rivers, instead of being a source of perpetual anxiety and danger, as in times of old, has become a source of real strength to the Government of India. Its brave soldiers have shared with the armies of Great Britain the toils of war and the glories of victory; the sagacious fidelity of its people has materially assisted the Government in preserving and diffusing the blessings of peace. One Imperial policy has bound the princes and people together in a common tie of loyalty to the Crown of England. The various races and nationalities of India, putting aside their religious differences, have become moulded into a united people. Undisturbed in the possession of their hereditary rights, secure in the full enjoyment of their traditional honours, protected in the prosecution of their lawful interests, encouraged in all that is excellent and praiseworthy in their conduct in life, the princes and people of this country have great reason to congratulate themselves on the manifold blessings of British rule.

As you have read in history, favour was, in former times, won by those who made the richest presents to the King, or who pleased ministers and favourites with valuable gifts, which were the spoils of districts, and came out of the pocket of the poor raiyat. The *Amírs* vied with each other who should make richest present. The anniversaries of the King's accession, and the marriages of the members of the royal household, afforded recurring pretexts for extortion. Under the British Government, the servants of the State are forbidden to receive any presents whatever, and the Government itself accepts none without giving an equivalent in return. No longer is prostration exacted on the occasion of the visits of princes and rájás to the British rulers, nor is any one of them treated with insolence or contempt. For the respect shown by them as vassals of the Crown, they are treated with every mark of consideration and honour consistent with the dignity of the Imperial Government, and their hereditary rights and privileges are maintained intact and unimpaired.

We find the British Government prosperous, and the people under it contented and happy, because it acts on the grand motto that "the prosperity of the country is the only true source of wealth." The end and aim of that rule is the welfare of the people, not the personal aggrandisement of the rulers.

Tavernier has said of Shah Jahán (though, according to our notions, Akber had far better claim to the honour) that "he reigned not so much as a King over his subjects, but rather as a father over his family and children." Had that distinguished traveller been alive to-day, he would have clearly seen that what Shah Jahán did for his subjects was, after all, only as a drop in the ocean, compared with what British statesmen have done for the people of this country. The architectural remains of his period, in various parts of India, will ever stand as brilliant monuments to his fame, but, in the eloquent words of the great essayist, De Quincey, in his essay on the British rule in India: "Higher by far than the Moghal gift of limestone or travelling stations or even roads and tanks, are the gifts of security, of peace, of law and settled order." And any one who chooses to look impartially around him may at once verify what this eminent writer has said. The real fame and strength of the British rulers lie in the vast schemes undertaken by them for the good of the people. Witness the gigantic railway projects, and the roads which have connected together all the great centres of population, and become the means of developing the trade and increasing the wealth of the country. Witness the vast public works that have been carried out. Witness the grand schemes of irrigation which have converted thousands of acres of barren land into green smiling plains. Witness the great good done to the country by the numerous charitable institutions that have been established—schools, colleges and hospitals. Witness the blessings of religious toleration and of freedom enjoyed by the meanest subject, a state of things unparalleled in any other country under the sun, the liberty of the press, the efforts of the Government to prevent pestilential diseases, to check famines and to improve conservancy in towns and villages. Witness the unexampled generosity which has placed within the reach of the humblest enquirer after truth the accumulated treasures of Western learning. Witness the great improvements our country has made in her municipal institutions. Witness the mighty undertakings for the defence of the empire, which, in reality, means the defence of your liberty and honour, and the protection of your lives and property.

Remember that we are living in the Victorian age, an age unrivalled in history for the blessings of peace. We have the honour and satisfaction of being the subjects of the Lady Queen, that Great Empress, than whom a more gracious sovereign, a more pious lady, a kinder mother, a more beloved ruler, or a more magnanimous person, the world has not seen. It is she, the ruler of the nation whose flag floats in every quarter of the globe, whose power extends to remotest seas, whose language is spoken over the whole surface of the civilized world, whose possessions comprise a seventh part of the earth's surface, and on whose empire the sun never sets; it is she who has ever the prosperity of her Indian subjects at heart, of whom the late Viceroy said, from his personal knowledge, that, "among her many pre-occupations and anxieties, there is no section of her subjects whose interest she watches with more loving or affectionate solicitude than that of her Indian subjects." The Christian, the Jain, the Hindu, the Buddhist, the Mahomedan and the Sikh share alike the bounty of her reign, and are equally protected by the laws instituted under her beneficent rule. Posterity will glory in the reign of Victoria! Future generations will take pride in her great name. Piety, duty, justice, generosity—these are characteristic of our Great Queen! Long after we shall have sunk into oblivion, that name shall yet be living in the hearts of the people! It shall live as long as the cultivator yokes his oxen to the plough on Indian soil, as long as the weary traveller refreshes himself under the shade of a tree, to protect himself from the burning Indian sun. It has become a watchword with the people. Verily, it is the pride of the brave, the staff of the weak (عصاء پیر), the dread of evil doers. It is loved; it is respected; it is honoured.

Having explained to you the object and scope of my work, let me hope you will follow the example of those whose names shine in history as benefactors of their race, and that you will tread in the path of those who have tried to raise nations in the scale of civilization. Above all, let me hope that you will do your duty to your sovereign. Respect the rulers, the benefactors of your country, and identify yourselves with their interest, for in their interest lies your well-being. Gain their confidence by honest deeds. Think not, under any guise or pretext whatever, of rivalry with your rulers, for that is sure to bring upon you the wrath of God and misfortune. Remember that you are as yet but learning your alphabet in the great School of Progress, that you have only just set your foot on the threshold of that Grand Institution, that you are as yet but on the first step of the ladder which leads to the lofty palace of Human Glory, and that the ambitious ideas of some among you, of equality with the conquerors of the East, however mildly you may desire to express them, or in whatever phraseology you may endeavour to cloak them, will, in the end, redound to your own discomfiture and hurt. Learn, then, to respect your rulers heartily, and look upon the lowest of their rank as your protector and master. Serve them heartily, and, in so doing, forget not what the poet of Shiráz has said :—

تو بندگي چو گدايان بشرط مزد مکن
که خواجه خود روش بنده پروري داند

"Do not serve, like a mendicant, in the expectation of getting a return for your labour ;
For your master himself knows how best to reward his servant."

My last advice to you, young men, is, *Fear God, love mankind, and honour the Empress.* Let this motto be instilled not only into your own minds, but into those of your children, and you will then, let me assure you, be, in your turn, honoured in this world and in the world to come.

And let me now, dear countrymen, pray unto God, the merciful Father of us all, and let all who read this, or hear it read, join with me in the prayer :—

"Long live our Gracious Queen, the Empress of India !"

AMEN !

M. L.

JHANG, *March 20th, 1889.*

CONTENTS.

PART I.—THE EARLY PERIOD.

PART II.—THE MAHOMEDAN PERIOD.

PART III.—THE RISE OF THE SIKHS.

PART IV.—THE LIFE OF MAHARÁJÁ RANJÍT SINGH.

PART V.—PERIOD FOLLOWING THE DEATH OF RANJÍT SINGH.

PART I.—THE EARLY PERIOD.

CHAPTER I.

HYDROGRAPHY OF THE PANJÁB.

Origin of the word Panjáb.

THE Panjáb, the Pentapotamia of the Greek historians, the north-western region of the empire of Hindostán, derives its name from two Persian words, *panj* (five), an *áb* (water), having reference to the five rivers which confer on the country its distinguishing physical features. It is bounded on the north by the vast Himálayan ranges, which divide it from China, Tibet and Káshmír; on the east by the river Jamna, the North-Western Provinces and the Chinese Empire; on the south by Sind, the river Sutlej, which separates it from Baháwalpúr, and Rájputáná; and on the west by the Sulaiman range, which divides it from Bilúchistán, and Afghanistán, which joins the Khaibar. The great network of the lofty Himálayan mountain ranges along the northern line includes the States of Chamba, Mandi, Suket and Náhan, as also the hill stations of Simla, with its smaller mountain States, the famous Kángra, the Nagarkot of Abulfazl, including the valleys of Kúlú, Seoráj, Lahoul and Spiti, and Dalhousie to the farthest north. Along the western line of the range, the Marí hills and the fertile Hazárá valley contribute magnificently to the colossal grandeur of the solemn mountains. The divisions of Delhi and Hissar, in the south-east, which had previously formed part of the territory under the Agra Government, were, for convenience of local administration, transferred to the Panjáb after the mutiny of 1857.

Boundaries.

Remarkable features in the topography of the country.

The most remarkable feature in the topography of the country is found in its rivers, the feeders of the great Indus, which, after traversing for hundreds of miles the mountainous regions of the lofty Himálayas, descend into the plains, fertilizing the soil, and continue their course generally to the south, until, after their confluence with the Indus, the Nile of India, the amalgamated waters fall into the ocean. These rivers run between the Indus and the Jamna, and their names, in succession, eastward from the Indus, are the Jhelum, the Chináb the Raví, the Biás and the Sutlej. With reference to the designation of *Panjáb*, or "Country of the Five Waters," it is to be observed that there are, in fact, six rivers instead of five; but, as the Indus was much dreaded by the religious classes, and was considered the sacred boundary of Hindostán to the far west, the ancients seem to have disregarded it in giving the country its present name. A delineation of these rivers is necessary, not only because they form the principal features in the topography of the Province, but because their importance, from a military as well as from a political and mercantile point of view, has been admitted from the remotest antiquity to the present day.

The five Rivers of the Panjáb.

The Indus.

THE INDUS.

The Indus,* though not itself one of the rivers which give the country the name it bears, claims our first attention, having a common origin with

* The Sindhú (literally meaning *sea* or *collection of water*), or Sindhús of Sanskrit, the Sinthus of the Greeks, the Sindus of the Romans, the Sintow of the Chinese, and the Abisindh of the Persians. Pliny called it Indus. Abul Fazal describes it as follows in the *Ayíní Akbari*:—"According to some, the Sindh rises between Káshmír and Káshghar, while others place its source in Khatta. It runs through the territories of Swát, Atak (Attock), Benares, Chanparah and the territories of the Bilúchís." The Benares referred to here is the "Atak Banaras" of Mahomedan historians, at the opposite extremity of the empire, in contradistinction to "Katak Banaras" in Orissa.

them in the summits of the Himálayas and being the trunk or stock into which the streams of Kábul and the Panjáb flow. From its long, tortuous and circuitous course, no less than from its position in a country inhabited, for the most part, by semi-barbarous races, it has been most appropriately recognised as the great Indian barrier on the north-west. Conquerors from the far west and north have regarded the crossing of this barrier as the first step in the conquest of the fertile regions of Hindostán; while travellers, equally with historians, have testified to its importance in its relations with the countries to the east and west of it. Its loud, rushing stream, together with the broad expanse of its waters, inspired the Hindus with awe, and, believing that the river issued from a lion's mouth, they have called its source *Sinh-ká-báb*, signifying the mouth of the lion.* The river rises in an unexplored region called Kanre, Kangri, or Kantesi, in the Kailása range of the Himálayas, the Olympus of Hindu mythology, the mansion of their gods and Sivá's paradise, 22,000 feet above the level of the sea, in latitude 31°20′ N. and longitude 81°30′ E. Its source is fixed on the northern declivity of Kailás, not far from the Chinese town of Goretope, or Gúri, and within a few miles of Lake Ráwan Hrod. Its course through the mountains has been carefully followed by the European travellers Moorcroft, Trabeck, Vigne and Gerard, while the public is indebted for much valuable information regarding it to the plans furnished by that enterprising traveller, Alexander Burnes, who navigated it from the sea to its mouth at Panjnad. Taking its rise in Tibet, behind the great mountain walls of the Himálayas, its course is first to the north-west, for about 160 miles. In this part of its course, the river is known as Sinh-ká-báb, until it receives, on its left bank, the Ghár river. A short distance lower down it enters the valley of Káshmír, and, continuing a north-westerly course, reaches Leh, the capital of Ladákh. Several large streams and mountain torrents join it in its progress through Ladákh, after which it dashes down a gorge beyond Iskardo in the north-west of Káshmír. Taking thence a southerly direction, it receives, from the north-west, the Gilgit, a considerable river, which joins it about three miles south of Makpani Shagaron. Penetrating then through the lower hills of the great Hindu Kush chain, where, for 120 miles, its furious waters are confined between a succession of rocky gorges and deep and narrow valleys, rugged and difficult of access, it reaches Darband, the north-western angle of the Panjáb, 812 miles from its base, in latitude 34°25′ N. and longitude 72°51′ E.

It is considered the great Indian barrier on the North-West.

The source of the Indus.

Its course.

Entering next the valley of Chuch, in a broad channel, the Indus becomes navigable by rafts, but is of no great depth and forms many sand-banks and islands. About 40 miles lower down it receives from the west the great Kábul † river, which, after draining the extensive basin of Kábul and fertilizing the valleys of the Sufed Koh, the Hindu Kush and Chitrál, meets it amidst numerous rocks. The volume of water in the river Kábul being as large as that of the Indus, and its course as rapid and violent, the confluence is turbulent and attended with great noise. Soon after the river rushes, once more, through a narrow opening in the midst of the branches of the Sulaiman range of mountains, and is fordable at many points during the winter, though the attempt is perilous, from the force and rapidity of the current and the benumbing coldness of the water, while it is liable to

* According to Thibetan notions, borrowed evidently from the Hindus, the rivers of India issue from the mouths of different animals. Thus the Indus issues from a lion's mouth, the holy Ganges from that of a peacock (Mahcha-ká-báb), the Sutlej from that of an elephant (Langchin-ká-báb), and the Tibet river from that of a horse (Sterchuk-ká-báb),—Moorcroft's *Travels*, vol. i, p. 261.

†The Cophas of Strabo and the Cophenes of Arrian.

sudden floods and freshets. On one occasion Ranjít Singh lost a force, variously stated at from 1,200 to 7,000 horsemen, in crossing the river at one of these fords. In 1809, Shah Shújá forded it above its confluence with the Kábul river, but this was considered an extraordinary exploit. The effect of the junction of these rivers and of their tortuous course through the rocks is such that, even when the water is at its lowest, waves and eddies are formed, causing a sound like that of the sea; but the case becomes quite different when the volume of water is increased by the fall of rain and the melting of the snows on the high mountains. A terrific whirlpool is created the roar of which, like the waves of an angry sea, may be heard at a great distance, to the amazement of the traveller whose ears are unaccustomed to such a noise. The swollen stream not unfrequently engulfs boats, or dashes them to pieces on the rocks. There is a story associated with two black rocks, named Kamália and Jallália, which are situated a little below its junction with the Kábul stream; and which, jutting into the river, make the passage dangerous. The rocks are named after the brothers Kamál-ud-dín and Jallál-ud-dín, sons of Pír Roushan, the founder of a sect of Mahomedans, called the Roushnais, in the middle of the 16th century, who were flung from their summits by order of the Emperor Akbar. The doctrine of the sect was that nothing existed but God, whose worship was not necessary. They ignored the Qurán and disbelieved in revealed religion. As the two advocates of the Roushnai heresy had caused such a great destruction of souls, the Mahomedans, who abhorred their doctrines, named these rocks after them, from the danger of their situation and the great loss of life caused by the whirlpools at their base.

The Indus forded by Ranjít Singh and Shah Shújá.

The rocks Kamália and Jallália.

But its vast floods and prodigious rises, coupled with enormous accretions of ice, which, sliding down the lofty mountains, suddenly burst forth from their flanks, make the Indus a most violent and dangerous river. From time to time the barriers formed by landslips and avalanches burst and the accumulated waters rush down with great fury, causing destruction in their course. A debacle or cataclysm, caused by a landslip in 1841, produced terrible devastation along the course of the river, down even to Atak.* On 10th August 1858, the river suddenly rose 90 feet.

A remarkable landslip.

The Kábul river possesses a peculiar advantage over the Indus, above its confluence with the latter, in that it is navigable for forty miles above that point, while a violent and rapid current renders the Indus impracticable immediately above the junction. Gold is found in various places in the vicinity of Atak, along the upper course of the Indus and its tributaries. Reaching Atak† in 33°54′ N. latitude and 22°18′ E. longi-

The Kábul river.

Atak.

* This great catastrophe occurred in the reign of Máhárajá Shersingh. An eye-witness describes it thus:—"For many weeks the course of the river had become very slow owing to a stoppage at some distance above Atak. One day in the afternoon the villagers saw in the north an enormous cloud of a black colour, reaching to the sky. They took it for a storm of wind. The supposed cloud came nearer and nearer, and the ground shook with great violence. People thought it was a tremendous earthquake accompanied by a storm of unusual severity. Immediately after, there was observed a vast sheet of water rolling down with great velocity, extending over miles aronnd and carrying everything before it. People began to fly, but it was now too late. Some ascended to the tops of trees to save their lives. From 5,000 to 6,000 lives were lost, hundreds of villages were destroyed and thousands of people rendered homeless. The fort of Atak was filled with water, which subsided on the third day, after great damage to life and property."

† *Atak*, a Hindi word, means obstacle, restraint or check, signifying that the river was the sacred boundary of Hindostán on the west, and laying the Hindus under the prohibition of crossing it in that direction. The fort of Atak is situated on a commanding height, on the left or east bank of the Indus, and overhanging the river. The fort of Khairábád, built, according to some, by Akbar, and according to others, by Nadir Shah, is situated on the right bank of the river opposite Atak. The fort of Atak was built by the Emperor Akbar in 1583, to command the passage of the river. It was constructed under the direction and supervision of Khwája Shams-ud dín, Khwafi. It is in the form of a parallelogram having the shortest faces about 400 yards long, and the other sides about double that extent. The walls are of

tude, the river, which here assumes that name, is again contracted within narrow limits, varying in width from 260 yards to 100 yards, but the current is deep and rapid. The Indus is crossed at Atak, in the dry season, by a bridge of boats and a ferry. The main trunk road to Peshá-war and Afghanistán crosses it at this point, and a railway has been carried over it on a bridge lately constructed. Lower down, as it enters the hills, its breadth is still more contracted, so that at Níláb, fifteen miles below Atak, it is sometimes only a stone's throw across, but with a current of great velocity. From this point the course of the river is south and south-west, parallel to the Sulaiman ranges and along the western side of the Panjáb. The current, which, for ten miles below Atak, was calm, deep and rapid, between high cliffs of slate rocks, becomes rough, and, as it passes round high perpendicular rocks with great velocity, the surface of the water is lashed into whirlpools most dangerous to navigation. The water in this part of the river is of a dark lead colour, from the blue limestone hills through which it passes, and hence the name Níláb* or "blue-water," given as well to the river as to a town on its bank twelve miles below Atak. Winding among the hills, it reaches Kálábágh, 110 miles below Atak, and then passes through the great salt range, again in a deep, clear and tranquil stream. From Kálábágh to Mithankot, a distance of 350 miles to the south, the banks are generally low, so that, as the inundations advance, the country round is covered with water as far as the eye can reach. The inundations, which originate in the melting of the snow in the Himálayas and the Hindu Kush, commence in spring and diminish on the approach of autumn. Two or three miles below Mithankot, and in N. lat. 28°55′, E. long. 70°28′, the river is joined by the *Panjnad* (the Chináb), which conveys the collected waters of the Panjáb rivers, after

The confluence of the Indus with the Panjnad.

a course of 1,650 miles, the junction being 490 miles from the sea. The arid, sandy nature of the soil, below the confluence of the Indus with the Panjnad, causes much absorption and evaporation, though the wasting of water is not very apparent to the eye, owing to the gradual character of the diminution of the current. Finally, the river empties itself, by many mouths, into the

The great high roads running parallel to the Indus.

Arabian Sea. Parallel to its western bank, runs, for several hundreds of miles, the great north road from Sindh to Bannú, while along its eastern bank lies the road from Múltán to Rawalpindi. The two great frontier districts of Dera Ismáil Khán and Dera Ghází Khán are intersected by

---

polished stone. The fort is very interesting, and its situation is important from both a commercial and military point of view. It has been the route of almost all the invaders of India from the north, and was the point where the armies of Alexander, Taimúr and Nadir Shah crossed the river in three distant ages. The merit of discovering the route is given to Alexander, who, after passing the mountains, encamped at Alexandria Paropamisana, the modern city of Kandahár, and, having subdued the tribes to the west of the Indus, crossed the river at Taxila, the modern Atak, the only place where the stream is so calm that a bridge can be thrown over it. Near Khairábád, on the opposite side, is a fine aqueduct, made by a chief of the Khatak tribe in old days, to irrigate the lands adjoining. To the west of the fort, 50 yards lower down, is the tomb of a Dewán of the Saint Abdul Kádar Gilání. The inscription, in the Túghra character, on a stone on the edge of the grave, gives the name as Shekh Abdúl Rahmán, with the date 1132 H., or 1713 A.D. Facing the north, a white marble slab is fixed on the Láhorí Gate with the following inscription :—

سر شاهان عالم شاه اكبر — تعالي شانه الله اكبر

"Akbar the King is king of the kings of the earth. Great is God and magnificent is his glory."

The inscription is dated 991 H. = 1583 A.D.

During the time of the Moghal Emperors royal troops were cantoned in the fort. Ranjít Singh, with his characteristic trickery, obtained possession of it in 1813 by bribing the Afghan governor, and it remained in the hands of the Sikhs till the British conquest in 1849. It was gallantly defended by Lieutenant Herbert in 1848, and is now occupied by a considerable British detachment and battery of artillery.

* The Nanbilus, or Nanlibe, of Ptolemy.

this river, the one to the east and the other to the west. The width of the river ranges from 480 to 1,600 yards, and during inundations in some parts exceeds a mile, while the depth varies from 4 to 24 feet.

The Indus a most magnificent river.

Notwithstanding all its drawbacks, the Indus is a magnificent stream, a very 'prince of rivers,' as Boileau calls it. Indeed, when the length of its course, the vastness of its volume and many of its special characteristics are considered, it may be reckoned among the greatest rivers of the world. In the time of Aurangzeb it carried a large trade, and Hamilton, who visited Sindh at the close of the 17th century, found the traffic upon its stream considerable. The trade was subsequently destroyed by the oppression and rapacity of the numerous petty chiefs who claimed supreme power over tracts adjoining its course, but the success of the British arms has led to its restoration on a far more extensive scale. The first steamer was launched on the river in 1835, but navigation, whether by steamers or native boats, has considerably decreased since the opening of the Indus Valley State Railway in 1878. A flotilla is now maintained in connection with the Railway Department.

The boats on the Indus.

The boats used on the Indus are *zauraks*, or flat-bottomed boats, *dundhis*, or cargo-boats, *kaunthóhs*, or ferry-boats, and *dúndas*, or fishing-boats. The *jhamptis*, or state barges, of the Mírs, are constructed of teak and are of considerable dimensions. The *duggah*, strongly built, with projecting stern and bow, is used in the boisterous parts of the current above Kálábágh.

Its fishes.

The river abounds in fish and in alligators of the long-snouted species. The *Culpea neowhii* is largely consumed along the coast, the population of which is almost amphibious. The *pala* is caught in large quantities for local consumption and is also dried for export. Crocodiles, otters and turtles are numerous. The boatmen of lower Sindh, like the Chinese, live in their boats. In lower Sindh a *pulla-jar* often conveys passengers across the river, while in Sukkur the *maskh*, or inflated skin, is largely used.

THE JHELUM.

The Jhelum,* which is indentified with the Hydaspes of the ancients, is the second in size, and the most westerly, of the five great streams which intersect the Panjáb east of the Indus.

The source of the Jhelum.

It rises† in the mountains which form the north-eastern boundary of the valley of Káshmír, its fountain head being the Lidur in the remotest hill range, lat. 34°8′, long. 75°48′. Flowing then in a south-westerly direction,

Its course.

it receives in its course the Brang from the south-east, and the Sandren, the Vishan, and several other tributary streams which have their origin

* Its Sanskrit name is Vidasta; in the dialects it is known as Vayat and Bebut; near Jalalpúr, the supposed scene of the battle between Alexander and Porus, it is called Betusta of the *Ayini Akbari*. It is the Hydaspes of Arrian and the Bidaspes of Ptolemy. Sharf-ud-dín, the historian of Taimúr, has called it both Dendan and Gamad.

† "The source of the river Bebat," writes the Emperor Jahangír in his memoirs, "is a fountain in Káshmír called Virnág. The name signifies, in the Hindi language, a snake, and it appears that, at one time, a very large snake haunted the spot. I visited this source twice during the lifetime of my father. It is about 20 *kos* from the city of Káshmír. The spring rises in a basin, of an octangular form about twenty yards in length by twenty in breadth. The vestiges of the abodes of the devotees, numerous chambers made of stone and canes, are in the neighbourhood. The water is so clear that, although its depth is said to be beyond estimation, yet if a poppy seed be thrown in, it will be visible till it reaches the bottom. There are very fine fish in it. As I was told that the fountain was unfathomably deep, I ordered a stone to be tied to the end of a rope and thrown into it, and thus it was found that its depth did not exceed the height of a man and a half. After my accession I ordered its sides to be paved with stones, a garden to be made round it, and the stream which flowed from it to be similarly decorated on both sides. Such elegant chambers and edifices were raised on each side of the basin that there is scarcely anything to equal it throughout the inhabited world. The river expands much when it reaches near the village Pampúr which is ten *kos* from the city."—*Elliot*.

in the Pír Panjál range. The Vishan issues by a subterraneous passage from the Kosab Nug, a small but deep lake in the Pír Panjál, at an elevation of about 12,000 feet above the level of the sea. Here the river gushes out from the foot of the lofty eminence, in a full, strong torrent, and, finding its way through the rocky barrier with which it is surrounded, passes through the picturesque string of lakes in the neighbourhood of Srinagar, draining the lower country and confined by high embankments, which prevent its overflow into the valley. Before entering the Walar Lake, it receives a considerable tributary, the Sindh, which rises in the lofty mountains on the north. The united stream then emerges from the snow-clad hills, by the narrow pass of Barámúlá, and, washing Mozaffarabád, reaches the boundary of Pugli. The pass forms an outlet for the entire basin of Káshmír. A bridge of seven arches crosses it at Barámúlá, and the river is here 420 feet broad. The whole course of the river, from its mouth to the lower end of Barámúlá, is about 130 miles, for seventy of which it is navigable. Two *kos* below Mozaffarabád, or 205 miles from its source, it receives, from the north, the Kishanganga, or Hasara, a stream of equal volume, which rises in Bultistán, or Little Tibet. Taking thence its course in a narrow rocky bed and passing Chand Mukh and Dangli, it skirts the territory of Kukhar in Amirpúr. Pursuing thence a southerly direction, it leaves the mountains, after a course of 255 miles from its source, and emerges into the plains of the Panjáb, near Chindas, a very great stream. From this point it becomes navigable as far as the sea. Higher up, where the river forms the boundary between the Káshmír State and the Hazárá and Rawalpindi Districts of the Panjáb, it is impracticable, owing to numerous rapids, though timber from Káshmír is floated down in large quantities. Its current, in its course through the hills, is very rapid, the breadth of the river being from one to two hundred yards. At the town of Jhelum the breadth is above 450 feet, which is greater than that of the Indus above Atak. Below Jhelum the river turns to the westward, and, washing Jalálpúr and Monga, skirts the plains of Bhera and Khusháb. Resuming then a southerly direction at Girot and Sáhiwál, in the Shahpúr District, it enters the flat open country of Jhang, where it is bounded by the *bár*, or high uplands of the jungle. Heavy rains subject the river to frequent inundations over the low lands, and the effect of the floods is most beneficial, the soil being enriched by the mud left on its surface and its productive power greatly increased. It finally joins the Chináb in lat. 31°11′ N., long. 72°12′ E., after a course of 490 miles, and about 100 miles north of Múltán. The place of the junction of these rivers is called Trimmú, which is ten miles south of Maghiáná.

The river subject to heavy inundations.

The principal towns upon the Jhelum are Káshmír, or Srinagar, Jhelum, Pind Dádan Khán, Bherá, Miání and Sháhpúr. The joint streams, called the Chináb, or Chíná, receive the Rávi, twenty-six *kos* lower down, near Fazilsháh and Ahmadpúr from the east, and, retaining the name of Chináb, pass four miles and a-half to the west of Múltán, and flow southwards to Uch, where, at Shíní Bakri, they are joined by the Ghárá, or Sutlej, which latter river at this point includes the waters of the Biás, 58 *kos* below Múltán and 32 below Babáwalpúr. From this point to Mithankot, 44 *kos* further down, where they finally fall into the Indus, these five streams in one take the name *Panjnad* (five rivers). For some distance the Indus and Panjnad run almost parallel to each other, until all merge in one, the great Indus, which, from the point of confluence majestically takes up a south-westerly direction. The banks of the Jhelum were the scene of the battle between Alexander the Great and Porus. Nearly opposite, on the Gujrát bank, is the modern battlefield of Chilianwálá. The Jhelum abounds

The Panjnad.

Historical associations.

in fish, and crocodiles are more numerous in this than in any other of the Panjáb rivers.

THE CHINÁB.

The source of the Chináb.

The Chináb,* the Acesines of the ancients, is the largest of the five rivers by which the Panjáb is traversed, and rises in lat. 32°48′ N. and long. 77°27′ E. Like that of most of the principal streams of India, its source is in the snowy mountains of the Himálaya in the Káshmír ranges. According to Vigne, it rises in a small lake called Chandra Bhágá, and the river is called Chandra in the upper part of its course. After receiving accessions from Tilbet, the river flows with a steady current through the Ritanka Pass, 13,000 feet above the sea. The Suraj Bhágá, a stream of less magnitude, joins it from the north, at Tándí, where the river assumes the name Chináb. Taking then a north-westerly course for 130 miles, it flows with a full, steady current to Kishtwár, where, 5,000 feet above the sea, it receives a considerable confluent, called the Sinud, from the north. Taking thence a south-westerly direction and passing Akhnúr, above Jammú, where it becomes navigable, it opens on the plains of the Panjáb in the Sialkot District, near the village of Khairi Rihal, under the name of Chináb, literally the river of China, indicating a belief that it has its origin within the borders of China.† Taking a westerly course, it washes Wazírábád, and, passing Ramnagar, enters the desert region of Jhang and joins the Jhelum on its right, at Trimmú, in lat. 31°12′ N. and long. 72°12′ E. The turbulence of the confluence is described by Arrian as having been terrific, but the meeting of the waters is now entirely free from violence or danger even in the middle of summer, when the rivers are usually in flood. The Rávi, or Hydraotes, joins it on the left, 50 miles further down and below Fazilpúr, in lat. 30°33′ N. and long. 71°46′ E., nearly 180 miles from Úch, owing to the windings of the river, and upwards of 53 miles from Múltán. Continuing still a southerly course, but slightly inclining to the west for 110 miles, it is joined by the Ghárá, or the mingled waters of the Biás and Sutlej, in lat. 29°21′, long. 71°6.′ At the confluence the rivers are very tranquil, the red colour of the Chináb being distinguishable on the right, or west, for some miles downwards, from the pale colour of the Ghárá on the left, or east side. Lastly, the combined waters, after a course of 765 miles, lose themselves in the Indus, in lat. 28°55′ N. and long 70°28′ E., being still 450 miles distant from the sea.

Its course.

The Chináb is more rapid than any other of the Panjáb rivers; the banks are low, but open, well-wooded, and copiously irrigated by larger channels of running water. Logs are floated down from the hills, 70 or 80 *kos* higher up, at the Jállalábád ferry. Its junction with the Ghárá, as already observed, is effected without noise or violence, though, according to Arrian, it surpasses the Nile. After receiving the waters of the Panjáb it falls into the Indus by a mouth thirty stadia‡ in width.

THE RÁVÍ.

The source of the Rávi.

The Rávi,§ the Hydraotes and Yarotis of ancient geographers, is the least by far of the Panjáb rivers. It rises in Kúlú, in the Kángra District,

* The Sanskrit Chandra Bhágá, or moon destiny; the Chanderbhaka of the *Ayīni Akbari*; the Acesines of Arrian and Sandabilis of Ptolemy. It is also called Janda Bálá and Shantrú in different portions of its course through the mountains.

† Moorcroft conjectures from this that the Greek name Acesines might have some allusion to this also.—*Travels*, vol. i., p. 196.

‡ Burn's *Travels in Bokhara*, vol. iii., p. 300.

§ The Adris of Ptolemy, the Hydraotes of Arrian, the Hyarotes of Strabo, the Phuadis of Pliny, the Irawadi of the *Ayīni Akbari*, the Iravati of the Sanskrit (this being a name in the Puranic mythology of Indra's elephant), and the Raid of Masudi, the Arabian geographer. It is also the name of a tribe in the Montgomery District.

in the low mountains of Bungall, a short distance west of the Rotang Pass, about lat. 32°26′, long. 77.° Taking a westerly direction, it unites with the Sibkirotar, a rivulet that rises from a spring between Dal Kund and Gouri Kund, near Munimys, or Mani Mohis, regarded as sacred by the Hindus, and the two, swollen by mountain torrents, run south-west with a tortuous current. In these mountain tracts the river is called Raina by the people. Debouching from them, it flows past the city of Chamba, on its right bank, and flowing to Uláns, receives the Liang from Bhaunso, in the Chamba country, 30 *kos* from the capital. Here it is called the Rávi.* It receives the Tavi, which rises in the mountains of Seoj, in the Badarwa territory, 10 *kos* from Jammú, at Trimmú Ghât. The Rávi is crossed by the bridge of Sháh Daula, thirty *kos* lower down, and 15 or 20 from Láhore. It enters the plains near Rajpúr, from which point the *Sháhnahr*, or Royal Canal, was, in old times, dug to Láhore, a distance of about 80 miles. The distance, as the crow flies, from Wazírábád ferry, on the Chináb, to that of Miáni, on the Rávi, is 55 miles. In the vicinity of Miáni the river has many quicksands, and its banks are low but well-wooded. At Mádhopúr, at the head works of the Bári Doáb canal, in the Gúrdáspúr District, the water of the river is much reduced by artificial canals. In the same district the river washes the skirts of the town of Derá Nanak, having, in 1870, carried away the Tálf Sahíb, a shrine of great sanctity with the Sikhs. It still threatens this sacred town of the Sikhs on its banks. After leaving the hills, the general course of the river is south-westerly, and, passing through the Gúrdáspúr and Amritsar Districts, in the same direction, it enters the Láhore District. Near the city of Láhore the river divides into three branches, one of which runs close to the town. Continuing a south-westerly course, but latterly inclining more to the west, it receives its principal tributary, the Degh, on its right bank, in the Montgomery District, and, passing through the Múltán District, finally emerges into the combined waters of the Chináb and Jhelum near Ahmadpúr, in lat. 30°40′ N., after a course of 450 miles from its source and 40 miles above the city of Múltán. Beyond this point the rapidity and breadth of the river, now the Chináb, are particularly noticed by the historians of Alexander and Taimúr.

Its course.

The river is fordable in many points.

The water of the Rávi is redder than that of the Chináb, and it is fordable, in many places, for eight months in the year. The bottom is more muddy than that of any of the other rivers, but the banks are high and firm, and there are only a few places where the breadth exceeds 150 yards. Nothing can, however, exceed its sinuosities, which almost double the distance and are a great impediment to navigation. Thus, Láhore is only 175 miles from the mouth of the Rávi, but the distance exceeds 380 miles by river. A considerable quantity of grain is exported from Láhore by boats, and, in seasons of heavy flood, *deodar* timber is floated down in rafts from the Chamba forests.

From the muddy nature of its bottom (about one-fifth being mud, the remainder sand), the Rávi is a foul river, and is much studded with sand banks, some of which are dangerous quicksands. Near Láhore its banks sometimes rise to a perpendicular height of forty feet; at other places their height is about half that, giving the river much the appearance of a nicely cut canal. In 1661 the encroachments of the river in the direction of the town of Láhore having caused much alarm, the Emperor Aurangzeb had a

The Bandi Alamgiri.

* The place was first visited by Vigne. Compare Vigne's *Travels in Káshmir*, vol. i., p. 153, and Moorcroft's *Travels in the Himálayan Provinces of Hindostán and the Panjáb*, vol. i., p. 127.

massive quay of masonry constructed for upwards of three miles along the banks. The remains of this huge bulwark exist to this day to the north-west of the town.

THE BIÁS.

The source of the Biás.

The Biás* or Biáh, the Hyphasis of Greek geographers, ranks sixth among the Panjáb rivers including the Indus. It rises in the southern slope of the Ritanka Pass, among the snows in Lahoul, in the north-east of the Panjáb, at a point 13,326 feet above the level of the sea, in lat. 32°24′ N., long. 77°11′ E. Abul Fazal, in the *Ayíní Akbari*, names the source of the Biás Abye Kund, rising in the mountains of Kúlú, in the Sultánpúr parganáh of Akbar's time.

Its course.

Taking a southerly course, from the Ritanka Pass, for about forty miles, it flows with a rapid current to the west and, skirting Mandi and Nadáun, enters the Kángra District at Sanghol, at an elevation of 1,920 feet above the sea level, forming the main channel for the drainage of Kángra. Then, taking a north-westerly course for about 80 miles, it debouches into the plains of the Panjáb at Mír-thot Ghât, in 32°5′ N. lat., 70°25′ E. long., being still 1,000 feet above the sea level. Winding round the base of the Siwálik hills in the Hoshiarpúr District, the river takes a southerly and then a south-westerly direction, for a further distance of 80 miles, and, flowing first between the districts of Hoshiarpúr and Gúrdáspúr, touching Amritsar District for a few miles and then forming the boundary between Amritsar and the Kapurthala State, its bright blue waters mingle with those of the turbid Sutlej, 35 miles south-south-east of Amritsar, and three miles above Hari ká Pattan, after a total course of 290 miles from its source. It is crossed by a railway bridge at Wazír Bholar Ghât.

The river is subject to periodical rises and falls, but is fordable in most places during the cold weather. There are many quicksands in its bed, and, when the waters are low, many islands and sandbanks are left exposed. The Biás and the Sutlej, at their junction, are of nearly the same size, the latter being rather the larger of the two. The sources of both the Rávi and the Biás are west of that of the Chináb, though, in the plains, they flow to the east of that river, which, with the Rávi, forms a crescent, or segment of a circle. Near the junction of the Biás with the Sutlej the Kangar, a tributary of the former, forms a *jhíl*, or shallow lake, where the Emperor Akbar built a beautiful and cool summer-house, or shooting-box, with underground apartments, the neighbouring jungle then abounding with beasts of prey and of the chase—tigers, leopards, deer and wild hog. The river is memorable in ancient history as forming the limit of the great Macedonian conqueror's advance in the East, for here he had to turn his back on the inauspicious gods of India, after erecting twelve massive pillars to commemorate the event. In more recent times the British General, Lord Lake, made his famous march to the Biás, in pursuit of Jaswant Raó Holkar, when he sued for peace in 1805, and concluded a treaty on 24th December of that year.

The summer-house of Akbar.

Historical associations.

THE SUTLEJ.

The source of the Sutlej.

The Sutlej, or Setlej,† the Hesudrus of the ancients, is the most easterly of the rivers of the Panjáb. Like the Indus, it rises on the slopes of the

* The Bihasis of Ptolemy, the Hypasis of Pliny, the Hypasis of Arrian, and the Vyasa of the Sanskrit, being the name of a Rishi, or sage, celebrated in the classical literature of the Hindus. The local name is Vipasá, or Beypáshá, Beascha, Bihasis, or Bipasis, Beand and Beah, or Viah.

† The Saranges of Arrian, the Zaradrus, Zadadrus, or Zapádpos of Ptolemy, the Sydrus or Kesidrus of Pliny, the Hypanis of Strabo, the Shetúrder and Seteluj of the *Ayini Akbari*, and the Sittoda, Satadru, or Sútrudra of Sanskrit. The lower mountaineers called it Satadru, the natives of Khanower, Zagti, and the Tartars, Lanying Kampá (Kampá signifying river in general).

sacred Kailás Mountain, its most remote sources being the eastern feeders of the great lakes, Manasarovara and Ráwan Hrod, in lat. 30°8′, long. 81°53′. The source of the Sutlej is near those of both the Indus and the Brahmaputra, the Tsanpu of Tibet, the height of the neighbouring mountain peaks being estimated at 22,000 feet. Abul Fazal, writing in 1582, says that its ancient name was Shetuder, and that its source was in the peaked mountains of Ghablore, in the Chinese empire. The Hindus regard the Kailása as paradise, the seat of Shiva, their deity. Starting from its mountain elevation the Sutlej first enters the vast alluvial tract of Goge. Close to Khab, 188 miles from its source, it receives from the north-west of Leh, or Spiti, a stream larger than itself, 8,592 feet above the sea. The scene of the confluence of the two rivers is described by travellers as sublime, a most stupendous work of nature, and one of the grandest phenomena in the world. The Spiti, issuing from a deep and narrow rocky channel, almost subterranean, its calm blue current mixes with the muddy waters of the Sutlej with a tremendous roar. Below the point of junction the river is so deep and rapid that, even with a ten-pound sounding lead, no bottom could be found. Eighty miles further up, at Ling, the river is crossed by means of iron chains, the breadth being too great to admit of a rope bridge. A short distance below Ling the bed of the river is 10,792 feet above the sea level. The river is here called by the natives Langzhing Khampa; lower down it is called Muksung; again Sanpú; then again Zeungti; lower still Samidrang; yet lower down, in Basahar, Satudra (or hundred channelled), and lower still Sutlej, by which name it is known up to its junction with the Indus. Near Shipki, within Chinese territory, the elevation of the stream is 10,000 feet above the sea. Below Shipki the river is obstructed by rocks, and the torrent, being confined in a narrow channel, is rapid and tortuous. Turning with great velocity it takes a north-westerly direction for about 150 miles, through mountainous regions almost inaccessible to man, after which, turning to the south-west and skirting the outer Himálayas, it bursts into many streams, which unite in one channel as the river approaches the Siwálik range. At Jaure, on the north, or right, bank, springs rising to a temperature of 130° Fahrenheit are found issuing only two or three feet from the river, the waters of which have a strong sulphurous smell. The fall of the Sutlej from Shipki to Rampúr in Basahar is, with little exception, nearly uniform, and about 60 feet in the mile. At Rampúr the river is crossed on inflated skins, during the cold season, while, during the rains, it is crossed by a suspension bridge of ropes termed *jhúlá*.

Its course.

The suspension bridge.

A little below Biláspúr the Sutlej takes a north-westerly course, after which it turns again to the south-west and then flows south-east. A few miles above Rupar, in 30°58′ lat., 76°29′ long., it breaks through the mountain rampart of the Himálaya in the low sandstone range of Jhejwán, and emerges into the plains of the Panjáb as a broad, turbid stream, no more retaining its blue, mountain tinge, but becoming navigable. From Rupar it takes a westerly course and divides into two branches, which reunite before reaching Ludhiáná. From Philour, where the breadth is 2,100 feet, the Sutlej is navigable at all seasons. Pursuing thence its course to Hariká Pattan, it joins the Biás, after completing a course of 570 miles. The united streams, which assume the name of Ghárá below the confluence, join the Chináb at Úch to form the Panjnad at their junction with the Indus at about 29′ N.

The Sutlej abounds in fish, and is remarkable for the coldness of its water, indicating its elevated and distant source. It was the river of the treaty between the English and Máhárájá Ranjít Singh in 1809.

CHAPTER II.

PHYSICAL FEATURES OF THE COUNTRY, ITS AREA, POPULATION, CLIMATE, PRODUCTS AND TRADE.

Extent of the country. Population.

The Panjáb, with its feudatory states,* covers an area of 144,436 square miles, and, according to the census of February, 1891, contains a population of 25,061,956† souls. The Province, which is under the administration of a Lieutenant-Governor, lies between 27°39′ and 35°2′, N. latitude and 69°35′ and 78°35′, E. longitude. The shape, in outline, of the Panjáb proper approaches that of a sector of a circle, the centre being at the confluence of the Panjnad and the Indus, the extreme radii being the Sulaiman range and the River Sutlej, and the arc in the highest latitude close to the 35th parallel. The capital of the Panjáb is Láhore, situated about the centre of the Province, which was itself called by that name during the Moghal dynasty; but by far the most important city, as regards population, art and trade, is Delhi, the ancient metropolis of Hindostán.

Láhore.

Physical features of the country.

The Panjáb is an extensive, flat plain, hemmed in by high mountain walls on the north and west, and open to the south and east. The physical features of the country in the northern and southern parts are very marked.

The north-east angle comprises the Alpine region of Kángra, and the north-west angle the Eusafzai, Pesháwar, Kohát and Hazárá Valleys. The fertilizing influence of the great rivers, the courses and characteristics of which have just been described, contributes mainly to the charming appearance of the sub-montane tract, intersected by green valleys and encircled by snow-clad hills. The southern, or plain, part belongs naturally to the same level table-land as the thirsty desert of Rájputáná and the wild and dry country of Sindh. This plain is divided into Doábs, or intra-fluvial tracts, which form the natural divisions of the country. The Doábs are still popularly known by the names which were given them in the days of the Moghal ascendancy, and are called after the respective rivers which enclose them, by combining the initial letters or syllables of each name; a fact noticed by the historians of Alexander, furnishing proof of the searching nature of their enquiries. "The greater part of the country," says Arrian, "is level and champaign, which is occasioned, as some suppose, by the rivers working down mud during their inundations, so that some of the countries have borrowed their names from the rivers which pass through them." Thus the tract between the Biás and Rávi is called the Bári Doáb, (land of two rivers), that between the Rávi and Chináb the Rechna Doáb, and that between the Chináb and Jhelum the Chaj Doáb. The space enclosed between the Jhelum and Chináb, on one side, and the Indus, on the other, takes its name from the latter river and is styled the "Sindh Ságar" Doáb or "Ocean of the Indus." The tract enclosed between the two last of the Panjáb rivers, the Biás and Sutlej, is called the Bist Jalandar, this

The Doábs of the Panjáb.

---

* Káshmír, which is under the control of the Panjáb Government, is excluded from consideration.

† British territory, 20,805,279; Native states, 4,256,677, excluding Pangi and Lahúl, of which the census has not yet been ascertained. According to the census of February 1881, the population of the Panjáb, including the feudatory States (but excluding Káshmír) was 22,712,120 souls, or one-tenth of the whole area, and one-eleventh of the total population of the Indian Empire. Of the total population of the Province (according to the census of 1881) one-half were Mussalmans, two-fifths Hindus and one-tenth Sikhs. The proportion of each sect to the total population according to the last census, has not yet been ascertained; but it is not likely to have altered very much. It would appear from the figures given above, that the population of the British territory in the Panjáb has increased from nineteen millions in 1881, to twenty-one millions in 1891, while that of the native states exceeds the corresponding figures of 1881 by about 9 per cent. As the resnlt of most districts shows, the aggregate figures in nearly all British India show an increase over the figures for 1881.

being the fifth of the Panjáb Doábs, and comprising the British districts of Hoshiarpúr and Jalandar and the native state of Kapurthala. Of these *Doábs,* the Bári carries off the palm, comprising the central Manjha, or home of the Sikh nation, and the great cities of Láhore, Amritsar and Multán.

Its plains.

The Panjáb, considered as a whole, presents the appearance of a gently sloping plain, leading from the high mountains on the north to the sandy deserts on the south. The slope is regular and gradual, so that even the upper parts are of moderate elevation. Thus the great cities of Láhore and Amritsar are each 900 feet above the level of the sea; the surface slopes regularly to the south-west, and we find Mithankot at an elevation of 220 feet. The unbroken flatness of the surface causes frequent and extensive changes in the courses of the great rivers. Thus one of the *nalás* in the low, sandy country between the Sutlej and Ludhiáná was the bed of the river fifty years ago. The Sutlej is specially apt to change its course, but the tendency to desert their channels is a characteristic of most of the rivers of the Panjáb. Bands of sand traverse the country in a direction north and south, indicating the old beds of the rivers. The Rávi, which 40 years ago flowed under the walls of the city of Láhore, flows now in a channel three miles to the north. The Sutlej, which formerly had its course close to the city of Ludhiáná, now flows seven miles north of it; the Chináb, which flowed by Rám Nagar, is now separated from it by four miles, and the Jhelum has undergone similar changes.

The face of the country presents every variety.

No country in the East presents the same variety of features as does the land of the five rivers. From tracts of the most luxuriant cultivation and extensive green plains the traveller passes to the most arid deserts and bushy jungle. Traversing the northern tracts, he would regard the Panjáb as the garden of India; but, as he approaches the south, the barren sandy plateau to the south-west, the wastes of Hissár to the south-east, and the Bár of the Chaj Doáb present a strange scene to his view. He sees interminable wastes, the wildest prairies overgrown with grass and scrub. The centres of the Doábs, with their inexhaustible pasturage, sustain noble breeds of cattle, buffaloes, sheep, and goats. The camels which carry the main traffic between the Panjáb and Afghanistán, are reared upon these boundless grazing lands. They yield an abundant supply of fodder for the horses of the country, and are the sole source of wood fuel for the railway, the chief towns and cities and the great British cantonments.

Wastes.

Their peculiar aspect.

Here and there in the wilderness a hamlet is found, inhabited by a semi-barbarous people, subsisting on camel's milk. But in these wild tracts, far from the crowded resorts of men, are the remains of ancient cities and the ruins of villages, temples, tanks, wells and water-courses, indicating that the region was once not inferior to the most favoured districts.

Salt range.

The great salt range of the Panjáb, springing from the root of the Sufed Koh, extends eastward to the Indus, which it crosses at Kálábágh, and, continuing its eastward course across the Sindh Ságar Doáb, terminates somewhat abruptly on the right bank of the river Jhelum. It is of no great elevation, there being few places where it rises more than 2,000 feet above the level of the sea. The range contains inexhaustible veins of rock-salt, deposits of chloride of sodium, formed of grass wacke, limestone, sandstone, gypsum and red tenacious clay. To the south stretches the sandy champaign, while to the north is a plateau, abrupt, rocky and precipitous. On the north-eastern frontier, close to the town of Mandi, the lower ranges of the Himálayas contain inexhaustible beds of fossil salt of a reddish colour, very compact and heavy. There are also to be found in these ranges extensive strata of limestone, standstone, gypsum, argillaceous slate and occasionally veins of quartz.

The salt range produces, besides the mineral that gives it its name, antimony, alum and sulphur. Mandi also produces iron and common salt. In the salt range of Makhad and on the left bank of the Indus coal is found. Gold in small quantities exists in the beds of the Chináb, Karo and Soan, and graphite, or plumbago, in the Pír Panjál range, in Káshmír.

The climate of the Panjáb presents extremes of heat and cold. In the regions extending along the southern base of the Himálayas, the south-west monsoon blows, and the rainfall is abundant. But in places distant from both the hills and the sea the heat is excessive and very little rain falls. The Himálayan tract enjoys an annual rainfall ranging from 70 to 120 inches; the submontane zone of Siálkot, Gúrdáspúr, Hoshiarpúr and Ambála, which skirts the foot of the mountains, from 30 to 40 inches; the eastern plains from 14 to 20 inches; the north central districts from 20 to 26 inches, and the western plains from 5 to 11 inches. The monsoon season, upon which depend the autumn crops and spring sowings, lasts from the middle of June to the end of September. The spring harvest depends largely on the winter rains of January. The hot weather proper begins with April. The heat in the summer is intense; scorching winds blow, the earth is parched, vegetation withers, and many trees are shorn of their leaves. In Múltán, in the extreme south-west, the heat is so oppressive as to be proverbial. At Láhore the thermometer has been known to rise to 112° in a tent artificially cooled. Bernier, with his experience of the burning Arabian desert, describes the climate between Láhore and Káshmír at this season as much more distressing, and mentions his dread each morning of being unable to survive till the evening. Some of his companions actually died from the heat, even in the shade. A kind of hot wind which blows in the deserts of Baháwalpúr and Bilúchistán is often fatal to travellers, even though natives, whom accident exposes to its fierce blast. The extreme heat of the summer begins to moderate about the middle of September, and towards the beginning of October the weather changes, and the nights become fairly cool, though the days are still hot. In June, when the heat is intense, great piles of clouds appear and the south-west monsoon bursts with little warning. With thunder and lightning come furious storms of wind, and this war of the elements is followed by heavy torrents of rain, which cool the atmosphere and make the vegetation green. The pleasant showery weather continues for three months. The winter, which even Englishmen find cold, lasts till the end of March. In the beginning of January the weather is cold and bleak; sharp frosts are common, and water exposed to the air freezes at night in all parts of the Province.

Climate. Seasons.

Except in the hills the flora of the Panjáb contains comparatively little that is indigenous. There are no natural forests in the plains; extensive tracts occur covered only with grass, shrubs and bushes, principally *babúls* of the *mimosa* species. Even the date palm is an exotic tree, introduced by the Mahomedan invaders of Sindh in the early days of the *Khalifát.* The wild palm, which produces no fruit, and the *pilu* (*Salvadora Persica*) which bears fruit, largely consumed by the people of the *bár* jungle, are abundant in sandy tracts; as are various species of willow, the *pípal* (*Ficus religiosa*) and the *banian.* The mango is largely cultivated in the south-east of the Panjáb and attains a high degree of perfection about Múltán and Hoshiarpúr. Clumps of trees are found around village sites and in the environs of towns; and diverse species of *acacia* and tamarisk, the *táhli*, called *sissú* in Eastern India, largely used for building purposes, the *ním* (*Melia azadirachta*), the *tulsi* (*Ocymum sanctum*), *madar* (*Tropæa*), *karmal*, or wild rue, *byr*, or jujube (*Zizyphus jujuba*),

Natural productions. Trees.

karil, or *caparis*, and *jawassi*, or camel-thorn, are met with. Cultivated fruit trees are abundant, and among others may be mentioned the orange, pomegranate, apple, peach, fig, mulberry, quince, apricot, almond and plum, the fruit of which is largely consumed by the inhabitants. The Government has done much to extend the planting of timber and in the way of introducing exotics, and extensive groves have been planted round cantonments and public buildings and in other places suited for arboriculture. The sides of roads and the banks of canals have been adorned with shade-giving trees, and forest conservation has of late years done invaluable service in establishing and extending nurseries and plantations, a work which before the annexation of the Province by the British had received little, if any, attention.

Planted fruit trees.

Animals.

The fauna of the Province has the reputation of being richer and more varied than its flora. Elephants are not found in a state of nature; those mentioned by Arrian as having been seen on the banks of the Indus having apparently been turned loose by the Indian troops in the heat of their flight before the Macedonian arms. Tigers are still found in the forests, and the lion was once not uncommon in the jungle. The other beasts of prey are leopards, panthers, hyænas, lynxes, wolves, bears, jackals, foxes, stoats, martens and various other small species of viverræ. There are also nilgais, antelopes and various other kinds of deer, goats, wild boar, porcupines, monkeys, large and hideous vampires, so sacred to the Hindus, and other bats. The feathered tribes include parrots, peafowl, junglefowl, pheasants, eagles, vultures, hawks, quails, pelicans, various kinds of partridges, waterfowl in great numbers and variety, cranes, herons, magpies, hoopoos and doves. The bulbul, sometimes called the Indian nightingale, whose sweet voice and beautiful shape are praised by the poet Háfiz of Shiráz, though of inferior vocal powers to its congener of Europe, is yet greatly admired. Among poisonous snakes the most remarkable are the cobra-de-capello, and a small snake, the sangchur, the bite of which causes instantaneous death. The rivers are infested with alligators, and fish of various species abound. The silkworm is reared with great skill and industry, and bees produce abundant wax and honey. Camels thrive in the hot southern plains, and herds of buffaloes on the grazing lands adjoining the rivers. Horses of excellent quality are reared in the north-east part of the country, and the chiefs who breed them take great pride in their equestrian capabilities.

Birds.

Camels, buffaloes and horses.

Agricultural produce.

Of agricultural products, sugarcane is grown everywhere in the fertile tracts and indigo in the low southern regions, both being largely exported towards Sindh and Kábul. Cotton is produced and exported in large quantities. Wheat and maize are extensively cultivated and of excellent quality. They not only suffice for home consumption but are exported in great quantities. The other articles of produce are buckwheat, rice, barley, millet, *bajra* (*Holcus spicatus*) *joár* (*Holcus sorghum*), *múng* (*Phasæolus mungo*); oil-seeds, such as sesamum and mustard, various sorts of vetches, carrots, pease, beans, onions, turnips, cucumbers, melons, and various kinds of cucurbitaceous plants. The palm and the date-palm are found in clusters in dense groves in the districts of Múltán, Mozaffargarh, Jhang and Deráját. Extensive irrigation is carried on by means of canals, and the Persian wheel is employed to draw water from the wells. Of the above crops, wheat, gram and barley are grown in the spring, and *bajrá*, *joár*, Indian corn, rice, cotton, pulses, indigo and sugarcane in the autumn. Wheat is largely produced in the divisions of Láhore, Amritsar, Jalandhar and Rawalpindi and in the Deráját. The largest areas under cotton

The spring and autumn crops.

cultivation are found in the districts of Láhore, Ambála, Gurgáon, Rawalpindi and Dera Gházi Khán. The chief sugar-producing districts are Siálkot, Gúrdáspúr, Jalandhar, Hoshiarpúr and Ambála. Indigo is almost entirely confined to the districts of Múltán, Mozaffargarh and Dera Ghází Khán. Ambála, Sháhpúr and Kángra have the largest poppy cultivation. Tea is grown in the hill tracts of Simla and Kángra.

The Agri-Horticultural Gardens.

Since 1882-83 the Agri-Horticultural Gardens of the Province have come under the direct management of the Government, and a Committee, presided over by the Commissioner of Settlements and Agriculture, has been established, the functions of which are to distribute plants and seeds, to conduct experiments on behalf of Government, to train skilled gardeners and to maintain the gardens at the head-quarters of the Province.

The Panjáb forests.

The forests and preserves of the Panjáb are rich in trees. *Deodár* (*Cedrus deodara*) is grown in the higher Himálayan ranges of Hazárá, Chamba, Kúlú and Basahar; *chíl* (*P. longifolia* and *P. excelsa*) in the Siwáliks and other hill tracts of the Kángra, Hoshiarpúr, Gúrdáspúr, and Rawalpindi Districts; small *sál* (*Shorea robusta*) at Kalesar in the Ambála District; and *kíkar* (*Acacia Arabica*), *jand* (*Prosopis spicigera*), *jál* (*Salvadora Persica* and *S. oleides*), *phulai* (*Acacia modesta*), *karil* (*Capparis aphylla*), *ber* (*Zizyphus jujuba*) and *dakh* (*Butea frondosa*) in the plain rakhs of the *bár* tracts of the Province.

Manufactures.

The chief markets of the Panjáb are Láhore, Amritsar, Múltán and Delhi, the indigenous manufactures being chiefly silk, carpets and wool. Carpentry, ironmongery and the manufacture of arms have made good progress. No steam machinery has yet been introduced into the Panjáb and the manufactures of the Province are all carried on by hand. The only factories which the Panjáb can boast of are a woollen factory, a silk filature and a sugar mill, but these are under European management and owned by European traders.

Cotton and woollen fabrics.

Pesháwar and Ludhiáná produce cotton fabrics of considerable merit. At Pesháwar are manufactured fine checked *lúngis*, with gold or coloured borders, which are worn as turbans by Musalmans living on the frontier. Their habit in this respect has also been adopted by many respectable Musalmans in the east of the Panjáb. Ludhiáná is noted for the variety of its *patkas* (girdle cloths), *lúngis*, *kheses*, a striped cloth called *gambroon*, twills, jeans, checks of several kinds and thick white twilled *choutáhis*. *Súsi*, a striped cotton fabric, used chiefly for women's clothing, is manufactured at Batála. Jhang is noted for excellent cloths with large dark blue and white checks, and Delhi for its fine muslin. *Ghati*, a fine glazed and close-woven white cloth is made at Ráhon, in the Jalandhar District. Fine cotton pile carpets are made at Múltán and *daris* at Ambála. Amritsar is the centre of shawl weaving, though it does not produce as fine work as Káshmír. Kángra and the Simla States produce excellent checked and plain shawl blankets, often with fringes and coloured borders. Fabrics of goat's hair are also made, and *pattú*, a kind of narrow woollen furred cloth. *Phulkáris*, resembling crewel work, and consisting of floss silk, floral or other patterns worked on dark grounds, are made at Amritsar, Siálkot, Hoshiarpúr, Gujránwála, Hazárá, Rohtak, Hissár and the Wazírí country. Wrappers with work of this description are worn by women. Delhi, Láhore and Amritsar are famous for their gold and coloured silk embroidered work.

Shawl manufactures.

Wood carving.

Excellent wood work is made at Amritsar, Delhi, Bherá, Siálkot, Jhang, Simla, Hoshiarpúr and Bhiwáni, which are also noted for carving and inlaid work on wood. At Hoshiarpúr work consisting of ivory and brass inlay on shisham wood has risen to considerable commercial importance. Brass vessels for household use are extensively manufactured at Amritsar, Pind Dádan Khán, Sáhiwál (Sháhpúr), Riwári, Bhiwáni, Jagádhri, Hoshiarpúr and Kángra. The *nielo* work of Káshmir, the beaten copper work of Amritsar, the cutlery and gunsmith's work of Siálkot and Nizamábád (near Wazírábad), the *koftgari*, or damascene work of Siálkot, Gujrát and Láhore, and the jewellery of Delhi are noted for their excellence. The enamelled work of Káshmír, in shades of blue and green done on silver, gold and copper gilt, is very effective. Múltán produces fair enamelling. The "majolica" ware of Peshávar is peculiar to that place and is glazed by a process known only to the makers. The glazing on pottery of Múltán and Delhi is of frit, or a composition of flint and alkali. A knowledge of hard glazing and of beautiful colours for encaustic tiles is possessed by certain natives of Jalandhar, descendants of the old decorators of the famous mosque of Wazír Khán at Láhore. Similarly stone carvers survive at Delhi who claim to be the descendants of the families who in the fourteenth century adorned the celebrated Kutab Minár. Leather work, embroidered with silk or gold thread, is made at Peshávar, Deráját and Hoshiarpúr. Paper is made at Siálkot suited only for writing with native reed pen.

Brass work.

Glazed work on pottery.

Stone carving.

Imports.

The chief foreign imports consist of British cotton and piece-goods. From other parts of British India are imported sugar, spices and other groceries, woollen, cotton and silk cloths, dye stuffs, metals and metallic utensils of various descriptions, precious stones, ivory, glass, porcelain and cutlery. The imports from countries to the westward consist of gold, turquoises, silver, silk, cochineal, maddar, asafœtida, fresh and dried fruit, safflower, wool and horses. The exports consist chiefly of grain, *ghí*, hides, silk, wool, carpets, cotton fabrics, shawls, indigo, cotton, tobacco, salt and horses.

Exports.

CHAPTER III.

THE ABORIGINES OF THE PANJÁB.

The Panjáb presumably the home of the ancient savage races.

THE position of the Panjáb as the natural gateway of the peninsula of India, and the advantages it possesses in soil and climate, immense fertile plains, rich valleys and abundant water-supply, lead to the belief that its occupation by the original races must have been among the earliest settlements of mankind. This belief is strengthened by the concurrent testimony of modern enquirers that the people first reduced to subjection by the Scythian or Aryan conquerors from the north-west were the aboriginal inhabitants of the Panjáb. In the epic poetry of the ancient Hindus, mention is made of the "black Sudra beyond the delta of the Indus." The population which was subsequently subdued by the Aryans in the valley of the Ganges, is designated by the same name, "Sudra," and when they advanced from the valley of the Indus and the Ganges to the south, they encountered there also populations of a similar character.

The testimony of the Vedas.

The aborigines.

In the regions inhabited by these aborigines they required little or no protection from the elements, so necessary in colder tracts, and their accommodations were rude and imperfect. They lived in natural caves, more or less rounded in form.* The abundance of fruit, herbs and roots, and of beasts of prey, and feathered game, afforded them an easy means of subsistence, and as they possessed no knowledge of the properties of metals, the only weapons they used were stones, clubs, and spears made of wood hardened by fire and tipped with the horns of animals. They spoke rude languages and covered their nakedness with the skins of animals. Living in small numbers and in isolated communities like the families who first wandered into Greece, Italy and the eastern tracts of Europe, they remained ignorant and barbarous. Hunting, which is the first step in the progress of a people after emerging from a state of savagery, seems to have been the earliest occupation of these barbarians. When they multiplied, they formed themselves into small tribes and became owners of flocks. The possession of land was valued and became a subject of dispute between the heads of families, who were thus led to provide themselves with the means of defence. When, at a later period, the properties of metals became known to them, they began to employ iron weapons in their fights and adorned their persons with rude ornaments of copper and gold. They were acquainted with the potter's art, and the vessels made by them were not inelegant in shape.

Their habitation and mode of life.

Their occupation.

Their weapons.

Herodotus, speaking of these aborigines, tells us that they lived in marshes on the banks of rivers and subsisted on raw fish and raw flesh. Their boats consisted of canoes made of reeds. They wore garments of bark, and, when any member of a family fell sick, the rest immediately killed him and devoured the corpse. Those who lived to old age were similarly slaughtered, and the young feasted on their bodies. Some lived only on herbs, others on the produce of the chase. Herodotus speaks of the Indus as the only river, besides the Nile, abounding in crocodiles or alligators. Megasthenes thought it was the largest of all the rivers in the world after the Nile. Ctesias speaks of it as a great river which watered the lands of India, and in which grew tall and stout reeds. He first described the elephant to the Greeks and gave an account of certain Indian birds with red heads, crimson tails, black beaks, dark-blue necks, and some of them with tongues which enabled them to speak Indian, stating that these birds, if taught, would speak Greek.

Their dress.

Megasthenes informs us that the primitive Indians were nomadic, and that, like the Scythians, they did not till the soil, but subsisted on such produce as the earth yielded spontaneously, on the bark of trees, called by the Indians *tala*, or on such wild animals as they could kill. They clothed themselves in the skins of animals, as was the case with the Greeks. Dionysos having then made his appearance, taught the Indians to cultivate the land. He is described as having first yoked oxen to the plough and furnished the Indians with agricultural implements. He taught them what the Greeks call the satyric dance and the use of turbans. He also taught them the worship of the gods with cymbals and drums, which they continued to use till the time of Alexander. Trumpets had not then been invented. He is said to have had in his army a great host of women. According to the Greek writers, when Alexander came to the land of Asvakas he was waited upon by an embassy from the Nysæans, who informed him that their city had been founded by Dionysos, who had given it the name Nysa, and that the neighbouring hill, Meron, was called after the name of that deity.

Their food.

Dionysos believed to have first taught them the use of the plough,

And the worship of the gods.

The aborigines were a black race, and are expressly mentioned as such in the *Rig Veda*, the oldest existing monument of the Hindu language and poetry. Thus, referring to an Asúra, one of the names by which the aboriginal tribes were known, it is stated that "Indra tore off the black skin of the

The aborigines a black race.

* The habitations of the ancient Gauls were circular huts made of reeds and lined with mud. The pile huts of Switzerland were of a similar kind.

aggressor." In another place it is said that "Indra, the slayer of Vrita, the destroyer of cities, has slain the black-sprung servile hosts." They have also been termed Negritos from their physical affinities with the Negroes, being seldom tall, and having coarse woolly hair, short broad noses and thick lips.

Their number.

The number of aborigines in India exceeded twenty millions in 1872, of which 959,720 were returned for the Panjáb. No separate returns for these tribes were furnished in the census of 1881, but they were classed among the low caste Hindus. The true aborigines have left no settlements or fixed habitations in the Panjáb proper, and seem to have been all driven away to the south-east by the Aryan invaders from the north-west. Their remnants in the Panjáb are the Sánsís, or gipsies, a wild-looking people, living in temporary sheds in jungles, and subsisting chiefly on mice and such other small animals as they can catch. There are also other wandering tribes in the Panjáb plains, who form the hereditary criminal classes of the Province, and whose existence is recognised by the Criminal Tribes Act of 1871.

The remnants of the aboriginal races in the Panjáb.

The outcast tribes.

Many of the low and outcast tribes of the Panjáb are believed to have sprung from the aboriginal races. These are the *Churahs*, or scavengers, the *Chamárs*, or workers in leather, the *Lohárs* of the hills, where they perform menial offices, the *Mahtams, Bawarias, Aheris, Thoris, Labanas* and *Kehals*, or jungle and river tribes, the *Sánsís, Pernas, Nats, Bázigars, Pakhiwaras, Hárnis, Gandhilas, Ods* and *Hesis*, or gipsy and vagrant tribes. "Many of them," observes Mr. Ibbetson in his Census Report of 1881, "are almost certainly aboriginal, and most of them have customs, beliefs and worship peculiar to themselves." The practice of magic and sorcery is almost entirely confined to these classes. The scavengers and the Sánsí gipsies invariably bury their dead with the face downwards. This is done to prevent the spirit escaping, as, according to the belief of a section of the Hindus, Churahs and some other low castes become *bhúts*, or devils, after death and trouble people by producing fever and other malignant diseases.* All these tribes are considered to be out of the pale of Hindu society.

They believe in magic and sorcery.

Curious custom of burying dead.

Th aboriginal tribes.

The aborigines are, generally speaking, to be found in dense unhealthy forests along the base of the Himálaya mountains, from the Panjáb to Eastern Bengal. None of them are to be met with in the mountains on the west and north-west boundaries of the Panjáb, that is, west of the river Indus. The principal Sub-Himálayan tribes of the aborigines are the *Garrows* who actually border on Mongolian races, *Nágas, Lushaís, Kukies, Lepchas, Tharús, Kacharis*, and *Boksas*, and they extend till they meet the Thibetan, Chinese and Burmese races. The aboriginal tribes are also to be found scattered over the inaccessible regions of Central and Western India and in the Deccan. The Nairs of South-Western India practise polyandry. Among them property is inherited, not by the issue of the owner, but by the sister's issue. The *Santáls*, a very numerous and powerful tribe, whose insurrection, some years ago, was the cause of some anxiety to the Government, inhabit the Rájmahal hills near Calcutta, and the Khonds,† who until late years performed the horrible rites of human sacrifice, in the mountains

---

* Census Report, 1881, vol. i., p 117, Mr. Ibbetson further adds :—"Riots have taken place, and Magistrates have been appealed to to prevent a Churah being buried face downwards. Should a Churah be burnt instead of being buried, his body is placed in the same position."

† They kidnapped children and adults, and, after fastening them, like cattle, slaughtered them for sacrifice. The victim was fixed against a post, his chest being fitted into the cleft of a branch cut when green. The priest then wounded the victim slightly with his axe, on which the whole crowd threw themselves upon the victim and stripped the flesh from the bones. The possession of a strip of such flesh was considered auspicious. The priest then invoked the Tari Pannu, or the Goddess of Earth, in the following terms :—"You have afflicted us greatly ; have brought death to our children and our bullocks, and failure to our corn, but we do not complain

which divide Orissa from the Deccan. The Khonds are men of a deep black colour, with thick, long, black hair and a peculiar language. They are of pure ancient descent and have preserved their distinctive ancient rites and customs, without intermixture with the Hindus. *Kolis,** *Bhíls* and *Gonds* are confined to the mountain ranges of the Vindhia, Sátpúra and Arávali in Central India. The wilder tribes of Gonds still live in forests and subsist on the chase. Further west are *Minas, Waghars*, and *Mahars*, who all preserve their aboriginal customs and language. The *Mahars, Beydars, Mangs, Whallias, Purias, Wadars*, and others in the Deccan and Mysore, with a few others mentioned below, represent the rest of the aboriginal tribes. Though more or less mixed with the Hindus, they have retained their original superstitions, and have not abandoned the worship of demons, spirits, and natural objects. The *Carambers, Irulars*, and *Paliars* are found among the mountain ranges of Southern India and the Nilgiris, the sanitarium of the Madras Presidency. They live in deep forests and lead savage lives, like the cannibals of the Andaman Islands.

They were driven back from the Panjab plains by the great Aryan race.

The conquest of the aboriginal tribes of India by the great Aryan race from the north-west drove these tribes to the wildest regions of the hills forests and lowlands now inhabited by them, just as, on the conquest of Spain by the Arabs, the Goths withdrew to the Galician and Asturian mountains, or, after the Norman conquest, the Saxon outlaw resorted to distant hills, marshes and fens. Thus, the Aryans did not mingle with the ancient population whom they conquered, but expelled them, and drove them to take refuge in inaccessible mountains and morasses. Those who accepted their civilization were allowed to live in despised and subordinate positions. These formed the mixed races now represented by the working classes, the cultivators, the artisans, the labourers and watchmen, in Hindu village communities. The ancient race of conquerors received in the land of their adoption the appellation of Hindus.

The Hindus.

The primitive tribes were of Scythic origins.

Who are these aborigines, the fragments of prehistoric times, who were subdued by the Aryan invaders from the north more than three thousand years ago? They belonged, no doubt, to one common stock, and that stock was of Scythian origin.† In the remotest ages they lived in the plains of Central Asia, the primitive home of the Mongolians and the Chinese. This is proved not only by their common physiognomy but by the affinity of spoken words in the hills of Eastern Bengal, China and Assam, and by a close resemblance in their religious beliefs, customs and usages.

Flint weapons.

In various parts of Southern India, tools and weapons made of stone, flint knives and axes have been found. The ancient Sanskrit literature bears testimony to the fact that India, like the countries of Europe, had successively its ages of stone, bronze and iron. Thus, the warriors of Rámá are described in the Rámáyana as having fought with stone implements against their enemies. The thunderbolt of Indra is described as a lithic missile.

Sepulchral monuments, made of round or conical stones, huge rocks, or

---

of this. It is your desire only to compel us to perform your due rites and then to raise and enrich us. Do you now enrich us! Let our herds be so numerous that they cannot be housed; let children so abound that the care of them shall overcome their parents, as shall be seen by their burned hands; let our heads ever strike against brass pots innumerable hanging from our roofs; let the rats form their nests of shreds of scarlet cloth and silk, let all the kites of the country be seen in the trees of our village from beasts being killed there every day. We are ignorant of what is good to ask for. You know what is good for us. Give it to us."—*Journal of B. A. S.* for 1852.

* General Briggs thinks it was when Europeans first employed the Kolis as porters that the English gave them the appellation *Kúli*, now universally applied to porters of all races throughout India.

† General Briggs thinks they were of common origin with the Scythian or Central Asian tribes. The same view is held by Mr. Hodgson, late Resident of Nepál.

mounds of earth, cairns, barrows, cromlechs, dolmens, believed to belong to prehistoric times, are found in many places, and iron arms, arrow-heads, spears and pottery have been also found buried in the ground with the ashes of the dead. They are all of Scythian or Turanian pattern, and in their workmanship almost exactly resemble relics of prehistoric times found in various parts of England and Europe. In the Indian Museum in Calcutta there is a collection of stone weapons, chiefly knives, celts and arrow-heads. All these relics of antiquity prove that, at some very remote time, and long before the Aryans had penetrated into India, the country was inhabited by a very ancient race of people who, in their origin, were Turanian or Scythian. These, of course, entered India by a more southerly route, and must not be confounded with the aborigines of the north-west of the Panjáb. In the Kumaun hills, rocks have been found covered with "cup-marks," or holes scooped out in the face of the rock, varying in size from an inch and a-half to six inches in diameter and in depth from half an inch to one inch. Sir J. Simpson, in his *Archaic Sculpturings*, notices such cups and circles found on stones and rocks in Scotland, England and other countries of Europe. According to local tradition, the marks on the Kumaun rocks were the work of *godlas* (herdsmen). The discovery of these cup-marks on rocks in different tracts of India and Europe has led archæologists to important conclusions. All agree in holding that they are not of natural formation, but are artificial and indicate sculptural design. According to Mr. Rivett-Carnac, who minutely examined these marks in the Kumaun hills, the idea that such remains are the work of the *goálas*, or herdsmen, prevails equally in Kumaun and Central India, many hundred miles south. An idea prevails in the Himálayas and many parts of Central India that a *goála* dynasty, a race of nomads, or "shepherd kings," held the country before the advent of the Aryan civilization. Mr. Carnac thinks it probable that "these markings are the rude records of a nomadic race which at an early epoch of the world's history left the Central Asian nursery and, travelling in different directions, have left their traces, in Europe, as in India, of tumuli and rock sculpturings generally to be found in hill countries and inaccessible spots whither, at a later period, they were forced to retreat before the advance of a more civilized and a more powerful race; the one being what are generally known by the somewhat vague term of Scythians, or shepherd kings, and the other the Aryans, descended from the same parent stock and who, later, were forced by the necessities of increasing numbers to emigrate from the common central Asian home to explore and conquer the rich countries far to the west and south."

Similarity of these weapons with the relics of prehistoric times found in various parts of Europe.

Conclusions to be drawn from this coincidence.

Cup-marks on the rocks of the Kumaun hills.

Similar cup-marks on the rocks of Scotland and England.

Conclusions.

Mr. Campbell found artificial circular marks, as indicated above, on the rocks of Kángra in the Panjáb. Dr. A. M. Verchere found small holes or cups in large boulders between Jubbi and Nikki on the Indus. Dr. Charles Race made similar discoveries in America and in Ireland. These markings, of a type common to both Europe and diverse parts of India, unmistakably point to those countries having, in ages gone by, been inhabited by a primitive race of men, one section of which went west, the other south in search of fresh climes and pastures. In other words, they show that a race of nomadic tribes, who at a very early date swept over Northern Europe, penetrated into the Panjáb and India also.

Discovery of artificial circular marks on the rocks of Kángra.

Similar discoveries in America and Ireland.

Several of the original tribes seem to have a tradition of their ancient abode in the northern hills, regarded by them as the gods of their race. "Till lately," observes the learned Dr. Hunter, "the Gonds buried their dead with the feet turned northwards so as to be ready to start again for their ancient home in the north."

The northern hills regarded as the gods of the non-Aryan races.

The non-Aryan races of India are commonly divided into three stocks. The first stock, comprising the Thibeto-Burman tribes, which cling to the skirts of the Himálayas, penetrated into India by the north-eastern passes. The second, styled the Kolarian, entered Bengal also by the north-eastern passes, and the Dravidian, or third stock, found its way into the Panjáb from the north-west.* The three divisions of the non-Aryan races.

The Dravidians now inhabit the southern part of India as far down as Cape Comorin. Their languages are found by philologists to be akin to the ancient Turanian or Scythian. This fact, coupled with the discovery of imperishable prehistoric monuments of Scythian styles, already referred to, proves the settlement of a Turanian or Scythian race in the south of India long before the Aryan conquest of the country. It proves successive waves of invasions by tribes undoubtedly of Scythian origin. Affinity of the Dravidian with the Turani language.

The aborigines who inhabited India at the time of the early Hindu invasion are called in the *Rig Veda Asúras, Rakshasas, Syums, Dasyus, Dasas* or slaves. The Aryans are found in the *Rig Veda* invoking their gods to grant them room against the Dasyus, who are described as a dark-blue cloud, to keep them distinct from themselves, to place the Dasyus on the left hand, to turn aside their arms, to increase the might and glory of the Aryas, to crush the hostile Dasyus, and to bring the "black skins" under the sway of the Aryas. The Dasyus are styled "enemies" and "evil spirits." The Aryan gods are thanked for "having dispersed the slave enemies of black descent." They are described as "flat-nosed" or "noseless" monsters, and despised as a "godless black-faced tribe," without rites or sacrifice. They are described as living in cities and well-built dwellings, a circumstance which makes it clear that, at that remote time, the aborigines had made fair progress in civilization and that they have now greatly degenerated. Thus, the ancient Hindu god Indra is described as "destroying the perennial cities of the Asúras and humiliating their defenders," "destroying the cities of the Dasyus" and "demolishing the hostile and ungoldly cities." He is given the credit of demolishing "a hundred cities of stone for the pious Divodasa." Agni is likewise celebrated as "having destroyed the spacious iron walled cities of the Dasyus" and having slain them. In several places he is described as the "destroyer of the cities." He is praised as having "quickly demolished the strongholds and seven-walled cities of Srukta and other Asúras." He is invoked "to repair to the cities inhabited by the Rakshasas." He is praised as having "bowed down the thunderbolt of the ungodly Asúra," and as "having, with the adamantine thunderbolt, demolished the hundred ancient cities of Sambara," said to be one of the Asúras or aborigines. Sarasvati is praised as "being as firm as a city built of iron." In their Vedic hymns mention is made of the "wealthy Rakshasas" and of their "seven towers" and "ninety forts." There is no means of ascertaining the exact period of their moral and spiritual decay. Yet the perfection of the Tamil language of Southern India, so free from Sanskrit intrusion, and admitted to have attained its maturity before the introduction of Sanskrit, which language it has survived, leads to the inference that, before the descent of the great Aryan race, more than three thousand years ago, the aborigines of India had reached a degree of civilization by no means inferior to that possessed by their conquerors.

Scornful epithets for the primitive tribes in the Vedic hymns.

They are described as living in cities,

And as possessing forts and towers.

Their civilization.

In the Hindi language a tenth of the words used are of other than Sanskrit origin, and the same has been found with regard to a fifth of the

* According to Dr. Hunter, the Dravidians of the north-west and the Kolarians of the north-east crossed each other in Central India, and the Dravidians, advancing in mighty hosts from the north to the south, dispersed the Kolarians to the east and west.

Mahratta words. Yet further south there is a still smaller intermixture of Sanskrit words in the Telegu, Canarese and Malayan languages. The non-Sanskrit words in these languages bear a close affinity to the Tartar, or more properly the Turanian, tongues, which is proof that the first wave of conquest that rolled over India, was from the bleak mountainous regions of Scithi or Central Asia.

Affinity of non-Sanskrit words in Telegu, &c., with the Turanian tongue.

The Turanian Hindus became the great temple-builders of India, and their religious monuments, extant to this day in India, are subjects of admiration in the work of the great writer on Indian architecture, Ferguson. The beautiful rock-cut temple of Kylas at Ellora, the great pagoda at Tanjore, and the temple at Seringhan, are among the architectural erections of the race of men conquered by the Brahmins.

Architectural monuments of the Turanian Hindus.

The aborigines differed entirely from their Hindu conquerors in their mode of life and religious belief. Unlike the Hindus, they observed no distinctions of caste. Indeed, it may be doubted whether any distinctions existed among the earliest Hindus. The religious orders of Yogis and Gosains repudiate caste, and even the Brahmin, on being admitted to that fraternity, gives up that distinction. The Hindus burn their dead. The aborigines buried theirs in the ground, beneath rude circular stones, mounds and perpendicular slabs, like the early inhabitants of Europe. Human remains have been dug out of their graves, from under these slabs. They buried with the dead their arms, ornaments, vestments, and sometimes also their cattle, as among the Scythians, believing that by such a course they would obtain them in the next world. Herodotus mentions that the ancient Scythians buried with their warriors models of their arms. In Poland and the steppes of Tartary, battle-axes, iron bows and arrows have been found in old graves. In Nágpúr (Central India) similar discoveries have been made. All these burial places are of Scythian origin and afford proof of the descent of the people north and south of the great Himálayan range from one common stock of Scythian or Central Asian origin. Hindu widows are forbidden to marry. The widows of the aborigines not only re-marry, but, following the practice of the Scythian tribes, usually marry the younger brothers of their deceased husbands.

No caste among the non-Aryan races.

Their mode of burying the dead.

The modern Hindus, unlike the ancient Aryans, abstain from eating beef. The aborigines feed alike on all flesh. The Dagis, a small tribe in the Panjáb, believed to be the remnants of an aboriginal race, eat beef openly. The Sánsís, or gipsies, the hunting classes and the river tribes of the Panjáb, who are believed to belong to the primitive races, eat foxes and jackals and even lizards and other vermin. The modern Hindu, unlike the Vedic* worshipper, is forbidden to use fermented liquor. The Shastras condemn indulgence in wine as sinful. Among the aborigines no ceremony, civil or religious, is complete without drinking and dancing. The *Mahábhárata* is full of drinking scenes. The people of each caste, among the Hindus, prepare their own food and eat of none which is not prepared by those of their own, or of a higher, caste. The aborigines observe no such restrictions. The Hindus abhor the idea of depriving a creature of life. The aborigines sacrifice living human beings at their altars. They have no Brahminical priesthood. They judge their priest by his mode of life and by the degree of skill he is supposed to possess in magic and sorcery. The civil institutions of the Hindus are all municipal. Those of the aborigines are patriarchal.

The aborigines feed on all flesh.

They use fermented liquors.

Their social customs.

The primeval title of these tribes admitted by the Hindus,

* Not only did the worshippers of Vedic times indulge in wine, but their gods also freely partook of it. Thus, says an Aryan worshipper, invoking the god Indra: "Sit down, Indra, on sacred grass and, when thou hast drunk the soma, go home."

Predial slavery was enforced in nearly every part of India, and such of the aborigines as escaped death, or were not driven to the mountains and deserts, were forced to labour for their Hindu masters. In some places they still work as serfs of the soil, in others they pay heavy rents to the Hindu owners. Yet a remarkable feeling pervades nearly all these aborigines, who consider themselves to be the real proprietors of the land. The Minas of Rájputáná remind each other of their right by the following distich:—

بہاگ را دھن راج ھو — بہوم را دھن ماج ھو

"The Rajah is the proprietor of his share;
I am the proprietor of the land."

The primeval title of these tribes is to this day admitted by the Hindus in a striking manner. When a new Rájá in Mewar takes his seat on the *masnad*, the ceremony of applying the *tilok* on his forehead, as the symbol of royalty, is performed by a Mina. He marks the Rájá's forehead with the red spot, which is the blood drawn from a Mina's toe. The same ceremony is performed by a Bhíl on the installation of the Rájput Rájá of Udaipúr, the most ancient of the Hindu princes. This shows that the inherent right of the aborigines as the original owners of the soil is still admitted by Hindu sovereigns of the first rank, who consider their title to sovereign power incomplete until the original lord of the soil is willing to acknowledge it by shedding his own blood for him. As a conquered race, however, they are despised and doomed to live in servitude and bondage to their conquerors and lords. The Aryans differed from these barbarians in both mind and disposition. They felt this difference most acutely, carefully excluded them from the Indian commonwealth and regarded them as beasts, rather than as human beings. In Chapter X. of the *Institutes of Manú*, the great Hindu legislator, it was ordained that—(1) "Their abodes should be out of towns. (2) Their sole property is to consist of dogs and asses. (3) Their only clothes should be those left by the dead. (4) Their ornaments should be rusty iron. (5) They should wander from place to place. (6) No respectable man should hold intercourse with them. (7) They were to perform the office of executioners in the case of criminals condemned to death by the King. For this duty they might retain the bedding, clothes and ornaments of those executed." Their condition was in every case one of perpetual slavery. In Chapter VIII. Manú says: "The Chandala, or impure, can never be relieved from bondage though he be emancipated by his master. How can he whom God has destined to be the slave of Brahmins ever be released from his destiny by man?" The site of every new building should be carefully cleaned of bones of dead animals, particularly of those of Chandalas, reckoned to be highly injurious to buildings.

But they are despised as a conquered race,

And are excluded from the Indian commonwealth.

They are called *Chandalas*, or impure.

CHAPTER IV.

THE ARYAN CONQUEST OF THE PANJÁB.

ALL authorities agree in pointing to the mountains in the north-west (the direction of the Hindu Kush mountains, the true Caucasus) as the primitive home of the fairer and more powerful race who first migrated into the Panjáb. Bands of these immigrants penetrated into the Panjáb through the Himálayan passes. Being fresh from a cold northern country, they were fair in colour and they called themselves *Arya*, *viz.*, the "noble," the

The primitive home of the Aryans.

"honourable," or the "ruling." The word is derived from a root signifying *ploughing*, from which it is to be inferred that, being given to agricultural pursuits, they adopted the word as their tribal designation. In the *Rig Vedu* the word *Arya* always indicates Brahminical tribes, in contradistinction to the *Anarya*, or "the ignoble" race, who surrounded the *Aryas*, or "the noble."

The remembrance of their mountainous mother country by the Aryans.

The recollections of frost and snow peculiar to their mountainous country seem to have been so pleasing to them that, generations after their migration into this country, they would ask their gods no boon short of one hundred winters. They bore the closest relation to the inhabitants of the tableland of Irán, who also called themselves Arya, Airya or Ariyas. Darius, in one of his cuneiform inscriptions, styles himself "an Aryan and of Aryan descent." The Greeks called them Ariori.

The affinity of the Aryan with the Turanian language.

The language of the Aryas is very closely connected with that of the *Avesta*, the sacred book of the fire-worshippers of Irán, and it bears a close analogy to the language of the monuments of Darius and Xerxes, in the western half of that country. The religious notions of the Iránians and Indians exhibit striking marks of similarity. According to the author* of the *Dabistan*, so often quoted by Sir William Jones in his excellent work, a powerful monarchy had been established in Persia before the accession of Cayumus. It was called the Mahabal, or Meha Beli, dynasty, and it raised the Persian Empire to the zenith of human glory. The Persians, who profess the faith of Hoshang, distinguished from that of Zeratusht, maintain that the first monarch of Irán and of the whole earth was Mahábád (a Sanskrit word), and that he divided the people into four orders, the religious the military, the commercial and the servile, the same as were, in long after times, recognised in India. From these facts, Sir William expresses his firm conviction that the religion of the Brahmins (the ancient Aryas) prevailed in Persia before the accession of Cayumus, whom the Parsís, from respect to his memory, consider as the first of men, although they believe in a universal deluge before his reign. Hundreds of Parsí nouns are pure Sanskrit, and the language of the Zendís is a dialect of the latter language. The characters of the inscriptions on the ancient ruins of the palace, now called the throne of Jamshed, at Istakhar, or Persepolis, the capital of ancient Persia, bear a close analogy to the inscriptions of Indian sculpture at Elephanta in Bombay, and the staff of Firozshah in Delhi. They are all Deva Nágri, or characters very much resembling it, and establish, beyond doubt, the common origin of the Aryas of India and those of Persia.

Brahminism the ancient religion of Persia.

The Panjáb the seat of the early Aryan migration.

The Aryas of India were at first limited to the regions of the Indus and the Panjáb, and, in their ancient scripture, mention is frequently made of the Indus, and not of the Ganges. This fact establishes, beyond doubt, that the fairer races, descending from the heights of the Caucasus, first occupied the country of the Indus and its five tributary streams. Their great rivers were, thus, the Indus and its tributary streams. Their prayer was: "May Sindhu (in Pliny *Sindus, i.e.*, the river, from *syand*, to flow), the renowned bestower of wealth, hear us and fertilize our broad fields with water!" The Greeks got the name of the great river from the Aryans and passed it on to Western Europe. The mention in the *Avesta* of the land *Hafta Hindu* (seven streams) clearly refers to the regions of the Panjáb. In the inscriptions of Darius, the population on the Indus is called *Idhus*. The Greeks render these names as *Indos* and *Indoi*.

The Indus, the great river of the Aryans.

Probable date of their first migration to India.

The period when the Aryans first penetrated into India is uncertain. Some suppose it to have been about the time of the exodus under Moses.

* Muhammad Muhsin Fani, a native of Káshmír, who compiled his valuable work from old authentic Persian records.

According to the internal evidence furnished in the *Rig Veda*, they had not spread beyond the north-west of India fifteen centuries before the Christian era, or some 3,400 years ago.* Sir William Jones traces the foundation of the Indian empire to above 3,800 years from the present time. Dr. Wilson, in his excellent work called *India Three Thousand Years Ago*, computes the period at fifteen hundred years before Christ. We learn from the Hebrew scriptures that, about 1000 B.C., the merchants of Tyre and Israel sailed in ships from Eltah, on the coast of the Arabian Gulf, for the countries of the south, and, after three years' absence, returned laden with gold, silver, precious stones, ivory, sandalwood, peacocks and apes. Now, peacocks and sandalwood belong exclusively to the regions of India, and the Hebrews denote these and other articles by Sanskrit names. The Upper Indus and the upland valleys of the Himálayas are rich in gold, and it follows from this, assuming that the country visited was India, that the Aryans were in possession of that country as early as 1000 B.C. Ptolemy places the land of the Abiria at the mouth of the Indus, and, according to an Aryan poem, this nation possessed cows, camels, sheep and goats. Abiria is identified with the *Ophir* of the Hebrews and the *Ahir* of India, meaning a grazier, and, if this supposition be correct, it proves that a tribe possessing cattle settled on the banks of the Indus anterior to 1000 B.C., and that it could have been no other tribe than the Arya. From these and other data Max Duncker, the eminent German scholar, concludes that the Aryans must have descended into the valley of the Indus about the year 2000 B.C., *i.e.*, "about the time when the Kingdom of Elam was predominant in the valley of the Euphrates and Tigris, when Assyria still stood under the dominion of Babylon and the kingdom of Memphis was ruled by the Hyksos."

About the time when the Aryans invaded India, tribes speaking the same language immigrated into Europe and settled in Greece, different tracts of Scandinavia, Germany and Italy, the seat of Imperial Rome. One of the western offshoots founded the Persian monarchy, while another stock settled in Spain and ancient England. Modern linguistic researches have established the unity of the great Aryan family from Ceylon to Great Britain and Scandinavia, from the farthest north to the equator. The Brahmins, the Rájputs and the English are alike the descendants of the ancient Aryans. The term *Arya* really applies to a race of Brahmins whose abode was situated near the great ranges of the Caucasus. Emerging from the grand school of the Chaldean magi at Babylon, these Brahmins carried their learning and arts northwards as far as the Caspian and Euxine. Mingling, in after times, with the learned colony of Egyptians, they diffused the light of science over the countries to the north and east, namely, Persia, Bactria, Media, Sogdiana, Thibet and Khata.

Unity of the great Aryan family from Ceylon to Great Britain and other European countries.

From the Teutons, one of the branches of the great family of the Aryans, have descended the English, who, though widely separated from the Hindus of India, have a claim to a common ancestry with them. It was, however, long after the introduction of Hindu and Greek civilization that the English nation emerged from a state of utter barbarism.

The descent of the English.

In point of physiognomy the Aryans of India bear a close resemblance to their brothers of the West. Their straight noses and finely-chiselled features and their light colour all bear the noble Caucasian stamp possessed by them in common with the nations of the West. They once spoke Sanskrit in its rude form and are still acquainted with that language. Modern philologists have proved the common origin of the Sanskrit with the learned languages of the West.

Physiognomic analogy between the Aryans of India and those of the West.

*Three hundred years later the *Institutes of Manú* introduced a reform into the religion and government of the Hindus. The Puránas are a compilation of much later date.

Affinity of words in languages spoken in the East and the West.

The mutual relationship of the Aryan, Greek, Latin, Letto-Sclavonian, Germanic and Celtic languages proves, beyond doubt, the affinity of the nations who speak them. The words are our common inheritance, the relics of antiquity, descended to us from our forefathers in ages gone by; and, as coins help us in deciphering the landmarks of ancient history, so do languages and the words which, like coins, we exchange in our daily avocations and the necessary intercourse of life.

Words common in the languages of the East and West.

We have all a common fund of words for the members of the family, for cattle, carts, wagons, boats, implements of husbandry, metals, vessels, tools and weapons. The close resemblance of even modern Indian languages to those of the West is, in some instances, striking. Thus, we recognise, in the Persian word *Panjáb* (the five rivers) the Πέντε of the Greek, the *aber* of modern Welsh; in *doáb* (space between two rivers) the Greek δύο, or the Latin *duo* and the same in Welsh. In *rájá*, Sanskrit, the Latin *rex;* in *badnám*, Persian, the *bad name* of English, almost without change. The *warm* of English is the *waram* of old German, *werm* of old Dutch, *formus* of old Latin, θερμος of Greek, *garm* of Persian and *gharma* of Sanskrit. *Father*, English, is *fáder* in Gothic, *vader* in Dutch, *vater* German, *pater* Latin, πατήρ Greek, *padar* Persian, *pita* Sanskrit, *báp* Urdu. For *mother*, English, we have the Icelandic *môther*, Danish and Swedish *moder*, old Germanic *muotar*, *muatar*, Latin *mater*, Sanskrit *mátá*, Persian, *mádar*, old Sclavonic *mati*, Russian *maty*, Irish *mathaig*, Italian, Spanish and Portuguese *madre*, French *mere*, and Urdu *mán*. The case is the same with *brother*, *sister* and many other words commonly used in daily life. The English word *widow* is derived from two Sanskrit words, *vi* and *dháva* (*vidháva*), *vi* meaning without and *dháva* meaning husband. It is in German *wedewe, wituwa, witawa, witwá;* Prussian *widdewa*, Latin *vidua*, from *viduus*, bereft of a husband. Similarly, the word *daughter* is derived from the Sanskrit word *duhitri*, meaning a 'milkmaid,' that being the special part of the domestic economy which fell to the share of a daughter among the early Aryans. In Dutch it is *dogter*, *dochter*, Icelandic *dottir*, Swedish *dotter* and *dattír*, Gothic *dauhtar*, Persian *dukhtar*. The close similarity between the Dutch and Persian words is most striking. The Indian *deva*, the bright one, from *div*, to shine, is the Latin *deitas*, from *deus* God, or *divas*, *dius* belonging to a deity, Lithuanian *deuas*, French *deite*, Spanish *deidad*, Portuguese *deidade*, Italian *deita*. It recurs as the *Zeus* (*dyaus*) of the Greeks and the *Jupiter* (*dyauspitar*) of the Romans. All employ cognate words for the processes of household industry and domestic economy. *Sewing*, fastening together with a needle and thread, is in Urdu *sína* and in Latin *suere*. There are cognate terms for the divisions of the year according to the moon, the elementary numbers, yards, gardens, citadels, gods, myths, sacrifices and customs. The Osiris and Isis of Egyptian mythology are the *Iswára* and *Isar* of the Hindus, and what is *Mitra* in the Hindu Veda is *Mithra* in the Iránian Avesta. The Aryan *Varuna*, god of the upper air, is the *Ouranos* of the Greeks. The Iránian *Veretra*, chief of evil spirits, is the Indian *Vritra*.

Conclusions drawn from the relationship of words.

What does this mutual relationship of words spoken by nations separated by remote distances from one another prove? It proves two things: *first*, that the nations which possess and use these words have a common descent in both the Continents of Europe and Asia, that they have sprung from a common stock.* The Greek, the Latin and the Teutonic languages

* "There is not an English jury now-a-days," observes Professor Max Müller, "which after examining the hoary documents of language, would reject the claim of a common descent and a legitimate relationship between Hindu, Greek and Teuton."

are related to the Sanskrit and the ancient Iránian exactly in the same way as these European languages are closely related to each other; in other words, they are sister languages. *Secondly*, it proves that, even before these nations had separated, they had attained to a certain degree of civilization; they tilled fields, reared cattle, used tools, built houses, wagons and boats.

The *Rig Veda* (literally "fount of knowledge," or "fount of vision") is regarded by the Hindus as the highest, the most sacred and the most ancient of the Shástras. They claim for it divine revelation, and in its very substance revere it as a portion of the Divine essence, perfect, infallible and containing the primitive truth. Along with the Parsí worship and the Chinese philosophy, it is indeed one of the most ancient things existing in the world. It supplies the oldest evidence concerning the life of the Aryas who settled in the regions of the Indus 2000 years B.C. The Vedas are four in number, the Rig, the Sámá, the Yájar and the Athárvan. The *Rig Veda*, entitled *Mantra*, is a collection of hymns, metrical prayers and invocations, 1,017 in number. In its collective form it is called *Sanhita*, or a collection of poems, and it is in fact the only true and original Veda. It contains 10,580 verses, all addressed to the gods. Indra, the god of rain, who had command over the clouds and brought the showers which filled the streams and rivulets flowing from the Himálayas, received the largest number of songs. Agni (*L. ignis*), the god of fire, who guided people, became the next object of adoration. The Sámá consists of extracts from the *Rig*. The Yájar also borrows much of its materials from the *Rig*. The Athárvan, otherwise known as *Brahmana*, is of a considerably later date than the *Mantra*, or *Rig Veda*, and furnishes directions for performing the sacred rites in which the priestly families sing the hymns and give explanations on various points. The Vedas draw before our eyes a vivid picture of the phenomena of the heavens. They lay before us a charming view of the operations of nature, and teach us to look with awe on everything grand and sublime. The hymns belong to different ages and, before the art of writing was introduced, were preserved by the saintly families, or Rishis, to whom they are believed to have been revealed. In that shape they were handed down for generations from father to son. Some of the poems are written in a very ancient dialect, legible only to the best Sanskrit scholars, and presumably belong to the earliest period of Aryan existence. Others are written in soft poetical language and belong to later times, when the Aryans had made considerable progress in civilization. At every step they disclose imaginative power and liveliness of fancy. They contain no historical facts, but give sacred legends, formulas for public worship, ritual observances and ceremonies. Many of the poems are ascribed to family priests and minstrels, and in some the name of the Rishi, or author, is also mentioned. Thus, it is said: "This song was made by Darghatamas, of the race of Angiras," or, "This new hymn was composed by Nodhas, a descendant of Gautama." The sacred hymns were faithfully preserved by the minstrels, after they had advanced eastward from the land of the Indus.

The Rig Veda. — Its undoubted antiquity. — The four Vedas. — The lively pictures drawn by the Vedas. — The sacred hymns. — Their language.

The earliest hymns fail to furnish any clue to the older abodes and previous fortunes of the race of men who delighted in them. We may, however, gather from a variety of similes and metaphors in them, that the Aryas, who had a common camping ground in Central Asia with the inhabitants of the far West, were a people given more to the keeping and breeding of cattle than to the work of the plough. They were a pastoral people, of nomadic habits. The Gopás, or Gopáls (cattle-keepers) were held in high estimation, and a cowherd was at times called a prince. The Rishis who composed hymns prayed their gods to bestow upon them many cows

The Aryans presumably a pastoral people of nomadic habits.

abounding in milk. The deities were invoked to protect the cows from misfortune, to increase the herds and to make the pastures green. Cattle were the medium of exchange, as are coins in modern times. Payments were made and fines imposed in kine, and one of the war-cries signifies "a desire for kine." Night and day the subject of cows was present to their minds. The cow was pronounced to be the animal favoured of the Almighty, and since it was so useful to man, its preservation became a religious obligation. But veneration for the cow is not confined to the Hindus. The ancient Egyptians and Phœnicians equally venerated this most useful, valuable and gentle animal. The worship of the bull Apis is the leading feature of Egyptian mythology. Besides buffaloes, sheep and goats, the Vedas mention horses, and parched corn was sprinkled at the sacrifices of horses to deities, in the hope that such offerings would promote the breeding of horses. The Aryans also kept humped oxen and camels.

Their veneration for the cow.

Their subsequent division into three tribes.

According to the *Zenda Vesta* of the Iránians, the Aryan community was divided into three divisions, or tribes, of which one lived by hunting, another tended flocks of cattle, and the third followed an agricultural life. This was, of course, when they had attained to a settled state of society.

The hymns of the *Rig Veda* were presumably composed in the Panjáb.

The hymns of the *Rig Veda* were composed in the Panjáb and in the colonies along the Indus. Here (in the Panjáb) the psalmists sang them, invoking their gods for victory against the "black-skinned" Indians, or against the opponents of their own race. The Sindhú (Indus), "the far famed bestower of wealth," is the object of special praise and veneration. Mention is made of the "Sapta Sindhawa,"* or seven rivers, as the dwelling place of the Aryans. These are the Sindhú (Indus), Vitasta (Jhelum), Asicni, or Acesines (Chináb), Irávati (Rávi), Vipása (Biás), and Satadru (Sutlej). The seventh river is the Saraswati, identified with the Sarsúti, near Thanesar, expressly mentioned in the *Veda* as the "seven-sistered." The country was abundantly watered and rich in pastures.

Reasons for this conclusion.

The names of Yamuna and Ganges occur only casually, and the Vindhya Mountains and the Narmadas (Nárbádá) are not mentioned at all. This shows that, at the time when these hymns were composed, the Aryans were still confined to the regions of the Panjáb. One of the famous settlements made by them in that age of heroic song was between the Saraswati (Sarsúti) and the Drishadvati, the modern Ghaggar. The land was created by the gods (*devatas*), and on that account they gave it the name *Brahmavarta*, or "land of the holy singers." The country is still considered sacred, and from it the Aryans gradually spread to the fertile tracts of the Yamuna and the Ganges.

The *Brahmavarta*.

Bloody encounters between the primitive Aryans and the ancient races of India.

The songs of the *Rig Veda* afford ample testimony that the primitive Aryans were not allowed to settle in the Panjáb unmolested. Long and bloody struggles were maintained with the wild and warlike Rakshasas, the Asúras and the tawny-coloured Pishachas. The aborigines dwelt in cities built of stone, and possessed horses, cattle and chariots. They fought desperately for hearth and home, and the numerous invocations for victory in the Vedic hymns prove what difficulties the Aryas had to encounter before they finally subdued the darker race. The fierce Indra, who had the power of bringing on rain storms, is, with his voice of thunder, his sword of lightning and troops of black clouds, invoked to cleave the dark bodies of the "demons," to crush the hordes of "black skins." The gods are invoked to snap the bowstrings of the enemy. The hymns are full of the praises of Vedic warriors and heroes. The mailed warrior is compared

Aryan invocations of victory.

* Identified as the "Hafta Hindu" of the *Avesta* of the Iránians.

with the brightness of a cloud, when he advances into the midst of the battle-field. The strength of his armour is praised, and his bow is described as doing wonders, "conquering all the regions round." "The strong hoofed steeds utter shrill neighings, and with their chariots rush on the enemy, trampling them under their hoofs and crushing them to death." The Aryans fought in chariots drawn by horses. The ancient Greeks adopted the same mode of fighting and, in the Trojan War, immortalized by Homer, which is supposed to have taken place about 1150 B.C., war chariots were used. The Aryans had also infantry soldiers who, however, were inferior to the charioteers. Besides the war chariots and the infantry, swords,* axes, bows, spears, trumpeters, and standard-bearers are mentioned. From the very earliest period the Hindus used the standard as a conspicuous object of display in a central position, to excite feelings of chivalrous devotion in the minds of the warriors. Trumpets and drums were used to excite them to valorous deeds or to convey the orders of commanders. The drum, according to the *Rig Veda*, is the most ancient instrument used by the Hindus. It roused the warlike spirit of the warriors, and was thus invoked :—"War drum, fill with your sound both heaven and earth ; and let all things fixed or moveable be aware of it ; do thou, who art associated with Indra and the gods, drive away our foes to the remotest distance. Sound loud against the hostile host : animate our prowess ; thunder aloud, terrifying the evil-minded ; repel, drum, those whose delight it is to harm us ; thou art the first weapon of Indra ; inspire us with courage. Recover these our cattle, Indra : bring them back ; the drum sounds repeatedly as a signal : our leaders mounted on their steeds assemble. O Indra, may our warriors, riding on their cars, be victorious !" In the *Rig Veda* and the other great epics mention is made of the war-cry, the words used being religious sayings, or the word *jaya* (victory) added to the name of the leader, *e.g.*, "*jaya Rama !*" "victory to Rama !" or "*jayastu Pándúputranám !*" *i.e.*, "success to the sons of Pándú !" The use of elephants in war was as yet unknown, though mention is made of a tame elephant, the property of an Asúra.

Their mode of warfare,

And weapons of war.

The war drum.

It is invoked as a deity.

The war-cry.

In their constitution the Aryans of the Indus were not civic. In their earlier colonies each father was the priest of his own family circle, yet tribal sacrifices were presided over by the "chief of the settlers" (*vispati*); and the Vedic communities were, by degrees, organized into chieftainships or kingdoms. Each community looked on its Rájá or Prince as its ruler, and obeyed him. The Rájás ruled over *grama* (villages) and *pura* (fortified habitations). The minstrels and priests, who formed part of their retinue, sang glorious songs of war and victory. They also offered prayers and sacrifices, and, after a victory over the black Dasyus, or a rival prince, composed poems eulogising the deeds of the heroes in battle. For their poetical compositions they were munificently rewarded by their lords. The rewards were slave women, dresses, cows, gold and chariots. One of these priests praises Svanaya, son of Bavya, as the "unconquerable Prince who dwells on the Indus."

The organization of the Aryans.

The life of the Aryas in the Panjáb was martial and manly. There their warlike character developed, and they adapted themselves to the conditions of a tropical climate, though they seem never to have forgotten their northern home, where, on the heights of the snowy Himálayas and behind its stupendous walls, they placed the paradise of their gods and heroes. They dug channels for the purpose of irrigating their fields, and sowed corn (*dhánd*), beans, barley and sesame. They were acquainted

Their martial spirit developed in the Panjáb.

* The sword is undoubtedly a very ancient weapon of war. The first mention found of it is in the 34th chapter of Genesis, where Jacob's sons use it against the Shechemites.

Their civilization.

with the arts of spinning and weaving and of working in leather. They had among them smiths, carpenters, carriage-makers, ship-builders, goldsmiths and other artisans. They possessed some knowledge of navigation; they had physicians among them who understood the healing properties of herbs, of which mention is made in the Vedic hymns. Frequent mention is made of drinking-houses and of dice, of musicians and of dancers. Gaily-attired females, with "their hair in four knots," and dressed in "beautiful garments," were coveted. Yet monogamy seems to have been the rule, and a prince had to content himself with one wife. A maiden could choose her husband. She was accounted happy "because she could make choice of a husband in the nation." The marriage ceremony was looked upon with solemnity. The husband and wife are described as "rulers of the house."

Social customs.

The contrast between the social customs and usages of the ancient Aryas and the Hindus of the present day is in some instances striking. Woman enjoyed a higher social status in Vedic times than that now accorded her. She was termed "the light of the dwelling." She had the privilege of acquiring knowledge, and some of the most eloquent hymns in the Vedas are attributed to female authors, ladies and queens. Child-marriage, although not absolutely prohibited, was not encouraged. Distinctions of caste were unknown, and Brahminism represented a profession, not a distinct caste. The Brahminical office, indeed, comprehended a variety of avocations, and the members of the fraternity performed military duties, carried on mercantile business, or engaged in agriculture at pleasure. The Vedas did not teach the doctrine of the transmigration of souls. It was firmly believed that the dead went to the regions of heaven to rejoin there the heroes who had gone before them, to live with friends who dwelt in eternal bliss, and to behold their parents, wives, and children. "Enter on the old path in which our forefathers have gone; go to our forefathers; there abide with Yama in the highest heaven and prosper among the people of Yama;* depart thou, depart thou to the world of righteousness; meet the ancients, meet Yama." Such was the Vedic farewell to the dead. An invocation to the god Agni says: "Let him, O Agni, rejoin the fathers, for he drew near to thee with the libations of sacrifice." Yama is then invoked: "Surround him, Yama, with thy protection against the hounds who watch for thee, the guardians of thy path, and give him health and a painless life." The next world is described as "imperishable, unchangeable, where there is eternal life and splendour, where is the sanctuary of heaven, where the great waters flow, where there is ambrosia (*amrita*) with peace, joy and delight, and where all wishes and desires are fulfilled." The Hindu philosophy of successive purgations of the spirit in various states of existence, till it is absorbed into the essence of the deity, was thus unknown in Vedic times. This belief was held by the Druids of ancient Britain and by the priests of ancient Egypt.

Distinction of caste unknown.

Their ideas of future life

And of the next world.

Self-immolation not sanctioned by the Vedas.

The horrible crime of *sáti*, or the burning of a widow on the funeral pile of her husband, was not sanctioned by the Vedas. On the contrary, a widow was exhorted "to return to the world of life," as she had done her duty to her husband. Unlike the Hindus of the present day, the ancient Aryas held beef in esteem as an article of food. There were at one time beef-eating gods and beef-eating worshippers. Agni, the god of fire, is described as "having quickly consumed 300 buffaloes." The haunts of *gaura* and *gaváya* (species of cows) are mentioned, whither Indra has

Beef used as an article of food.

* Yama is believed to have been the first man who, passing through death, became immortal. Having seen the way to the next world, he conducts people there and acts for them as a guide.

recourse "for the food of the pious." The Vedas enjoined the ceremony called *gomedha*, or the sacrifice of cattle, and reference to such sacrifice is made in the *Mahábhárata* and *Rámáyana*.* At the entertainment given to sages and friends, a heifer and a cow were slaughtered and the guest was, on this account, called *goghna*, or "cow-killer." Professor Colebrook observes, in the *Asiatic Researches*, that "a guest entitled to honourable reception is a spiritual preceptor, a priest, an ascetic, a prince, a bridegroom, a friend, or, in short, any one to welcome whose arrival a cow must be tied, for the purpose of slaying her; whence a guest is denominated *goghna*, or cow-killer." In ancient Hindu medical works, such as the *Charaka Sanhita*, which dates from about the fifth or sixth century B.C., beef is recommended for a woman that is *enceinte*. In the chapter on food in this work, the author recommends that the flesh of cows, buffaloes and hogs should not be eaten daily. This clearly shows that beef was then used as an article of food, though it was considered too rich to be used every day. Fish, curds and barley cakes are likewise prohibited for every-day use. The ceremony of sacrificing a cow was called *gava mayana*.

The sacrifice of the cow.

The Aryan settlers of India were a spirit-drinking race and indulged freely in soma beer and wine or spirit. Sages and saints drank the sweet fermented juice of the soma (the *haoma* of Irán) and made an offering of it to the gods. The soma is a plant peculiar to the mountains west of India and the Bolan Pass. The wine made from it was of most ancient origin; the Aryas offered it to the spirits of the sky, even before they had set foot on the land of the Indus. It was an exhilarating liquor, most acceptable to the gods. The soma is described in the Vedas as having been brought from the summit of the hills by a tamed falcon. Its healing qualities are praised; it was believed to prolong life, and it inspired the sacred songs of the minstrels.

The Aryans were a spirit-drinking race.

The soma tree.

Its description in the Vedas.

Like the ancient Aryans of Irán, the Aryans of India buried their dead. The bow, the symbol of honour, bravery and lordship, was taken out of the hand of the corpse and a wall of separation erected between it and the circle of relations and friends present at the burial. "We here and thou there," said the living; "we set this wall of separation for those who live, that no one may hasten to that goal; they must cover death with this rock and live a hundred autumns." Among the fire-worshippers of Irán the custom of burial gave way to the exposure of dead bodies on the mountains, and in the "towers of silence," where they became a prey to the birds. The modern Hindus of India burn their dead.

The burial ceremonies of the ancient Aryans.

CHAPTER V.

THE ANCIENT HINDUS.

After the Aryans had migrated into the regions of the Yamuna (Jumna) and the Ganges, they colonized extensive districts and founded large cities in their newly acquired territory. The period of their immigration into that fertile country is fixed at about 1500 B.C. It brought with it more arduous tasks than had occupied the Vedic heroes in the land of the Panjáb. They not only had to contend against the old population, but they also became involved in wars, among themselves, for the acquisition of the best

* I presume the sacrifice of cows by the ancient Aryans before their gods was due to the sanctity in which that animal was held.

The Aryan immigrants form themselves into large communities or nations.

territories. In these contests for sovereign power, the immigrants attached themselves to their respective leaders or chiefs, and thus large communities or nations were formed. Successful leaders found themselves in possession of extensive territories and became the acknowledged rulers of the people inhabiting those dominions. Petty chieftainships merged, in the course of time, into comparatively powerful sovereignties, and in the long periods of peace which followed, and in which the conquerors applied themselves diligently to the task of organizing the subdued territories, the caste system began to be developed. Preëminent over all other castes were the Brahmins,* who acted as councillors at the courts of different sovereigns. They also acted as minstrels and priests at sacrifices, and sang the sacred hymns which caused the gods to descend. The Brahmin was considered nobler than all the rest of mankind.† He gained a supremacy alike over the king and the people. The predominance of the Brahmin over all the other castes creates a new era in the history of the Hindus. Their system of philosophy was prevalent about the year 800 B.C., when the dynasty of Pradyotas ruled the kingdom of Magadha on the south bank of the Ganges. The land between the Yamuna and the Ganges was called the *Brahmarshidesa*, or "land of the Holy Sages." Here lived the two great ancient Hindu nations, the Kúrús and the Pandús, immortalized by the songs of the *Mahábhárata*, and here were Hastinapúra, Indraprastha, Krishnapúra, holy cities of ancient fame.

Development of the caste system.

The predominance of the Brahmins.

The four castes.

Next to the sacerdotal class, or Brahmins, were the Shatrias, or the military, who protected the people, the Vaisyas, or workers, who tended the herds, tilled the fields and carried on trade, and the Súdras, or servile class, the remnants of the vanquished aborigines, who served the three other orders in menial capacities. The Brahmins were the first-born order; they were nearer to Brahma, or the Holy Spirit, than the others. That the human race might be multiplied, Brahma caused the Brahmins to be created from his mouth, the Shatrias from his arm, the Vaisyas from his thighs, and the Súdras from his feet. The Shatrias were to carry the sword. They were also called Rajnaya, or Rájbansís, which means "connected with the royal dynasty," and are now represented by a class of people known as *Rájputs* (of royal descent). The Vaisyas by degrees mingled with the other classes and have now almost disappeared as a distinct sect.

The Brahmins the first-born order.

The *Code of Manú*.

The doctrine of monotheism.

The Brahmins secured their social supremacy by a compilation of customary laws known as the *Code of Manú*. According to Duncker, this Code was put together about 600 B.C., though others assign to it a much later date. The doctrine of monotheism is recognised throughout the *Institutes of Manú*. It enjoins a true knowledge of "one Supreme Being" whose nature is thus described in the opening passage:—

The Hindu conceptions of the deity, the universe and ourselves.

"This (*i.e.*, the universe) existed only in darkness, imperceptible, indefinable, undiscovered, undiscoverable, as though it were wholly immersed in sleep.

"Then the self-existing Power, Himself undiscerned, but making this world discernible, with five elements and other principles, appeared, with undiminished glory dispelling the gloom.

"He whom the mind alone can perceive, whose essence eludes the external organs, who has no visible parts, who exists from eternity, even He, the soul of all beings, whom no being can comprehend, shone forth in person.

"He having willed to produce various beings from His own Divine substance, first, with a thought created the waters and placed in them a productive seed.

"That became an egg, bright as gold, blazing like a luminary with a thousand beams, and in that egg He was born himself, Brahma, the great forefather of all spirits.

---

* Brahmin, from the root *brah* (to grow) means one who elevates or causes to grow or increase. It signifies the ideal union of all that is sacred and divine.

† *Mahábhárata*.

"The waters are called *Nárá* because they were the production of *Nárá* (the spirit of God), and since they were His first (*ayana*) place of motion, He is hence called Náráyana (moving upon the waters).

"From that which is, the first cause, not the object of sense, existing, not existing, without beginning or end, was produced the Divine Male, famed in all worlds under the appellation of Brahma.

"In that egg the Great Power sat inactive a whole year, at the close of which, simply by an effort of mind, he caused the egg to divide itself.

"And from its two divisions he framed the heaven and the earth; in the midst of the subtle ether, the eight regions and the permanent receptacle of the waters.

"From the Supreme Soul he drew forth mind, existing substantially, though unperceived, by sense, immaterial; and consciousness, the internal monitor, the ruler," &c., &c.*

Such are the Hindu conceptions of the mysteries of the universe, of the Supreme Being and of ourselves. They are held to contain infallible dogmas of divinity, the profoundest maxims of truth.

The *Rámáyana* and the *Mahábhárata*.

The Hindu literature has given birth to two noble epic poems, the *Rámáyana* and the *Mahábhárata*. The incidents related in the former refer to a period about 1000 B.C., but the compilation belongs to a later date. The reputed author is a poet named Válmíki. The subject treated of is the invasion of Ceylon by Rámá, king of Awadh, whose wife, Sítá, had been abducted by Ráwan, the aboriginal or demon prince of Ceylon. A great fight took place and Sítá was rescued.

The great war between the Pandús and the Kúrús, 1200 B.C.

The venerable epic, *Mahábhárata*, deals with a period about 1200 B.C. The composition is ascribed to a sage named Wasaya,† who lived in the second century before Christ. It describes the great war between the Pandús, or the people of the *suria* (solar) race, then represented by their king Yudishtir and the Kúrús, or men of the *chandra* (lunar) race, headed by their king Dhritarashtra. The capital of the Pandús was Indraprastha (Delhi), on the banks of the Yamuna, and that of the Kúrús, Hastinapúr on the Ganges. Yudishtir claimed the kingdom of his rival, and to decide the dispute all the chiefs of the lunar race were marshalled on the plains of Kurúkshetra, near Drishadvati, the modern Thanesar, a battle-field which, in after times, so often decided the fate of the combatants for the Empire of India. The beautiful, steadfast hero, Krishna, who, in his youth, dancing among the rustics, captivated at once milkmaids and princesses by his skill in music, sided with the Pandús. Fifty royal leaders and many tributary and allied princes from the Indus to the Narbáda, and from the bases of the Himálayas to Bengal and Behar, assembled on the field of battle. The whole of Hindostán proper breathed war. Yudishtir, with his armies, advanced to the battle-field, clad in garments of yellow and gold, and took his seat in his state carriage. He was followed by the long-armed Bhima, with his flashing looks and knitted brows, and holding in his hand an iron club, wrought with gold, and brave Arjuna, who carried a great bow with an ape on his banner. As the great armies met, Bhishma, a Kúrú general, waving his banner from his golden chariot on the opposite side, cried to his warriors: "To-day the gates of heaven are opened for the brave; go ye the way by which your fathers and ancestors have gone to heaven by following gloriously. Would ye rather end life on a sick bed in pain? Only on field should a Shatria (soldier) fall." He then blew his horn, and the armies rushed upon each other. Fearful was the slaughter which ensued. The battle-field was strewn

Krishna. Bhima. Arjuna. Bhishma.

* Sir William Jones' Works, vol. iii.

† Wasaya is a term signifying compiler. Some think it is not a proper name, and if this theory be correct, the real name of the author, or authors, is open to doubt.

with the dead. The "harnessed elephants" became unmanageable, and, in their fury, dragged the warriors from their chariots. The contending armies poured showers of arrows upon each other, the painted shields of hide were perforated, and the warriors engaged in a hand-to-hand fight, like "maddened tigers." The battle raged with great fury for eighteen days, and the result was the total defeat of the Kúrús. All their great generals, including the veteran soldier, Bhishma, were slain and their army annihilated. The victors shouted, and blew their horns for joy. Immense treasures in gold, silver, precious stones, rich stuffs, skins and slave girls fell into their hands. The vanquished and aged king, Dhritarashtra, retired into the forests of the Ganges, with his wife Gandhari, and there perished in the flames. The Pandús made their triumphant entry into Hastinapúr, where Yudishtir, having seated himself on the throne, received the homage of the conquered kings. A great sacrifice of horses was offered in which all the allied princes took part. Arjuna then conquered for Yudishtir the Sindhavas, or regions of the Indus, and the Gandháras (Kandahar), the country beyond that river. Yudishtir reigned for thirty-six years and then died.

Terrible carnage.

The utter rout of the Kúrús.

The Panjáb conquered by the Pandús.

Such is the story of the *Mahábhárata*, or "Great War." At the conclusion of the epic we are told: "What the Brahmin is to the rest of mankind, the cow to other quadrupeds, the ocean to the pool, such is the *Mahábhárata* in comparison with all other histories."* Readers and hearers of this book are said to have their home in heaven and all their sins are forgiven.

The Panjáb noted for its noble steeds.

In the *Dhammapadam*, an ancient book on Hindu law, mention is made of the "noble Sindhú horses." The horses bred on the banks of the Indus were considered the best in India. The *Rámáyana* mentions the nation of the Kaikeyas, occupying the upper course of the Irávati (Rávi) and Vipása (Biás). The King of the Kaikeyas was known by the title Asvapati, or the "Lord of Horses." He flourished in the fourth century B.C., and his metropolis is called Girivrájá in the *Rámáyana*. On the left bank of the Indus was the great city of Taxila, invaded in the same century by Alexander of Macedon. The laws of the Brahmins prevailed in those regions, and the duty of executing criminals and burying the dead was performed by the Chandalas, or aborigines.

The Brahmins of the Ganges looked on the people of the Panjáb, their ancient home, with scorn. They called them *Palikas*, *i.e.*, "excluded," and *Vratyas*, or "heretics." "Their women," said they, "wandered through the streets and fields adorned with garlands, intoxicated and undraped. With cries like the neighing of horses, they run to the bathing places." These remarks are, however, much exaggerated and show the arrogance of the Brahmins of the Ganges, who thus wished to ignore the common link between themselves and the Hindu tribes of the Panjáb. All the accounts given of the Panjáb by Western writers unite in bearing testimony to the fact that, in the second half of the third century B.C., the Brahmin philosophy was predominant in the country of the five rivers. The country was thickly inhabited. It was divided into a number of principalities governed by warlike princes and noble families. There were superintendents of cantons and chiefs of cities and districts. There were also free nations possessing fortified towns, and they could alone bring armies of 50,000 into the field. They possessed cities in which 70,000 men could be kept prisoners of war. Both the princes and the free nations possessed

The Panjáb 300 years B.C.

* Duncker.

war elephants and chariots. Their citics were surrounded by brick and stone walls and towers. According to Megasthenes, some of the cities were fortified with broad and deep trenches, filled with water from rivers. The most powerful of these kingdoms was Káshmír, which extended to the land of Abbisara. The country between the upper course of the Vitásta (Biás) and the Asikni (Chináb) was governed by the royal dynasties of the Pauravas.

The splendour of the kings.

The splendour of the kings and princes is described by the Greeks in glowing terms. They lived in sumptuous palaces, adorned with gardens and terraces, and were surrounded with women-servants and body-guards. Their robes glittered with gold and jewels. Even the soles of their shoes were wrought with gold. In their ears they wore rings adorned with jewels of great size and brilliancy. Their necks were encircled with strings of pearls, and they adorned their arms and chests with shining jewels. The golden staff was the symbol of royalty. Their commands were conveyed in writing and stamped with an ivory seal. No one was admitted to an audience of the king without a present. People shewed him the greatest reverence, they knelt before him and even prayed to him, as they did to the Deity. Happy and fortunate events, such as the winning of a battle, the birth of a royal child, the offering of a sacrifice, marriage, visits from illustrious guests, &c., were announced to the citizens by the ringing of bells. On such occasions the streets were thoroughly cleaned, and flowers and garlands hung along them; the roads were sprinkled with sandal water, decked with banners, bunches of flowers and umbrellas, and lined with jars, placed at proper distances, in which frankincense and other perfumes were burnt.

The profound respect paid to the king by the people.

His seraglio.

The king had a numerous seraglio and the influence of the women was great. Anyone daring to cast a look on the king's wife was forthwith dispatched. The king took great care of his life and guarded himself against conspiracies, which were common. Only women purchased from their fathers were trusted for this work, and the king was waited upon by this guard of Amazons. They prepared his food, attended his table, brought wine for him and conducted him to the sleeping apartment. He never ventured to sleep during the day and, to defeat plots against his life, constantly changed his bedchamber at night. His wives did not leave him, even while hunting, and were, in their turn, guarded by the viragos. These argus-eyed women rode, some on chariots, some on elephants and some on horses gorgeously equipped. They were armed with weapons of various kinds, as if they were going to war.* The king hunted in enclosures and discharged arrows from a platform, two or three armed women standing by his side. He was similarly accompanied by women in war. The king never left his palace except to go to war, or to the chase, to offer sacrifice, or to attend a festival. The sight of his equipage was grand and imposing. First, came the kettle-drummers and the blowers of shells. They were followed by elephants with gold and silver trappings, chariots, drawn each by four horses, and some with stout and beautiful oxen yoked to them. Then came the soldiers, handsomely equipped and followed by a procession of trays containing the royal robes, gold and silver utensils set with emeralds and precious stones, water-basins, chairs, tables, &c. These were followed by lions, tigers, panthers, buffaloes and other wild beasts, some in large iron cages, others bound and borne in vehicles and wagons. After these were carried, on four-wheeled wagons, live trees, on which were domesticated birds,

His guard of Amazons.

His hunting-ground.

His equipage.

* The *Sakuntala* describes Rájá Dushyanta as attended in the chase by Yavana women with bows in their hands and wearing garlands of flowers.—*M'Crindle.*

parrots, pigeons, peacocks and other birds valued for the sweetness of their voices or the beauty of their plumage. The king, gorgeously robed, sat on his elephant, or in his state carriage, amid sweet odours and clouds of perfume, surrounded by crowds of women, spearmen being ranged outside the circle. Courtiers and ministers, attended by bands of musicians, followed. The way was marked off with ropes, and it was death to pass within this limit.

Megasthenes' description of ancient India.

Megasthenes, who was sent on an embassy by Seleukos Nikator to Sandrakottos (Chandragupta), the king of the Prasii, whose capital was Palibothra (Patna), has given a vivid account of India. He is believed to have visited the country between 302 and 288 B.C. According to Clinton, he visited India a little before 302 B.C. From the minute accounts he has given, in his Travels, of the rivers of Kábul and the Panjáb, it is clear that he passed through those countries and lived in them. He describes the people as skilled in the arts. The soil produced every species of fruit and vegetable known to cultivation, while in the ground were found numerous veins of all sorts of metals—gold, silver, copper, iron, tin, &c., of which ornaments, utensils, and implements of war were made. Both Megasthenes and Arrian, who wrote an account of the expedition of Alexander in Ionic, speak of two Indian harvests, one in the winter season, when, as in other countries, the sowing of wheat, barley and pulse took place, and the other in summer, when cotton, millet, sesamum, and rice were sown. "India," writes Megasthenes, "has never been visited by famine, and scarcity in the supply of edible grains has never been felt." Those engaged in agriculture were not disturbed by wars. They carried on their work of husbandry unmolested, and cultivated lands were not ravaged or trampled under foot by victorious armies. Agriculture was held sacred, and husbandmen, being regarded as public benefactors, were protected from all injury. They were, in consequence, not provided with weapons of war, and were exempt from all military duties or other State business.

His accounts corroborated by Arrian.

Slavery unknown among the ancient Hindus.

Slavery was unknown to the Hindus, and their law ordained that no one among them should be wholly subject to the will of another. The sages conducted the sacrifices and celebrated the obsequies of the dead. They regulated the calendar and appointed propitious dates for sacrifices and public festivals. In the beginning of each year the king convened a great assembly of these sages, at which they predicted the fortunes of the State, the events, good or bad, of the year, stating whether it would bring copious rains or be dry, and whether it would be healthy or unhealthy. Both the king and the people took measures according to these predictions. If a philosopher erred in his predictions, no punishment awaited him for the first two failures, but anyone who erred three times was bound to preserve absolute silence for the rest of his life. No power on earth could induce a man condemned to silence to utter a single word.

Predictions by Hindu sages and philosophers.

Strange punishment.

Social habits and customs of ancient Hindus.

According to the Greeks, the manners of the Indians were simple, and they lived frugally, never tasting wine except at sacrifices. The rich loved finery and wore ornaments and garments worked in gold and jewels. Truth and virtue were held in esteem. The people were honest in trade and seldom went to law. Theft was of very rare occurrence, and houses and property were generally left unguarded. They trusted each other in lending money, and did not require seals or witnesses to attest such transactions, nor was security wanted. Money was not put out on usury. If anyone failed to recover money or a deposit, he never had recourse to a law suit, but simply blamed himself for trusting a knave and bore the loss with equanimity. Mutilation was punished with mutilation, in addition to the cutting off of the culprit's hand, but anyone who deprived an artisan of an eye or a hand was put to death. Perjury was punished with the loss of a hand or a foot, and for heinous crimes the offenders were flayed by the king's orders. Another punishment, considered infamous to the last degree, was shaving the head.

Their administration of justice.

The Greeks extol the Indians' love of justice. Their magistrates and judges were conscientious and administered equal justice. The king himself paid great attention to the dispensing of justice and sometimes spent the whole day in hearing and deciding cases. While he was so engaged, four attendants rubbed him with cylinders of wood, or ebony rollers, this being the favourite mode of exercising the body.

Polygamy among ancient Hindús.

The Indians, we are told, married many wives. A wife was purchased for a yoke of oxen, and, notwithstanding the low price, she was faithful and chaste. Women were also given as prizes to competitors who excelled in archery, wrestling, boxing, running or any other manly exercise.

Restrictions of caste.

Megasthenes condemns, in the Indians, the want of fixed hours for meals and the practice of partaking of food alone. This, however, only shows their attention to business and their disregard for personal ease and convenience. Their not eating in public was apparently due to the restrictions of caste, which had obtained a firm footing in the country before the Greek invasion.

Government of the country.

According to Strabo, the government of the country was carried on by means of officers whose functions were distinct. These were the civil and the military. The former included collectors of land-taxes, surveyors of lands, superintendents of markets, who also supervised weights and measures, overseers of cities and superintendents of ferries and of irrigation canals. There were officers appointed to supervise artisans, such as blacksmiths, carpenters, miners and sawyers; officers to superintend trade, commerce, manufactured articles and industrial arts; officers who received reports of births and deaths, and officers who superintended roads. A pillar was set up at every ten stadia to show distances. In the great epics mention is made of urban roads, as being wide and spacious, and lined on either side with the shops of traders and merchants and with private houses of great beauty and elegance. The streets were watered, to lay the dust, and were cleansed of rubbish. In the *Rámáyana* mention is made of a grand trunk road from Oudh to the Panjáb. All this is proof that the ancient Hindus led a settled and civilized life.

Civil department.

Attention to strangers.

Due attention was paid to the comfort of foreigners, and special officers were appointed to accommodate them. They are, however, described as careful in keeping a watch over the action of strangers.

Military department.

The military department consisted of officers, foot soldiers and charioteers. The foot soldiers carried bows as tall as a man. The arrow was discharged by placing one end of the bow on the ground, holding it fast by the toes of the foot and drawing the string backwards. An arrow shot by an Indian archer pierced, according to Arrian, the strongest shield and the hardest breastplate. In his left hand the soldier carried a buckler made of hide. All were armed with swords, though some wielded javelins. Cavalrymen carried lances and bucklers of small size on the left arm. There were chariots and war elephants. In the former sat the charioteer and two fighting men beside him. A war elephant carried a driver and three warriors armed with bows and arrows. The chariots were profusely decorated. In the *Rig Veda* mention is frequently made of "golden chariots." This may be due

Infantry.

Cavalry.

The war chariots.

to a lively fancy and poetical imagery, but there is no doubt that the chariots of Vedic times were embellished in a manner befitting the owner's rank. The *Rámáyana* and the *Mahábhárata*, which are of a later date, speak of pearl fringes and jewelled decorations for the chariots of great men.

The golden cars.

The description of ancient Indian cars in the Puránas is still more fulsome. Savitri is described in the *Rig Veda* as "mounted on his high standing chariot decorated with many kinds of golden ornaments and furnished with golden yokes." The "bountiful Indra" is thanked for "the gift of a golden chariot." He is invoked to bestow "handsome golden chariots." A "golden seat," "golden reins," "golden shafts," "golden axles," and "golden wheels" are talked of repeatedly. The passion for chariots does not seem to have been a characteristic peculiar to the ancient Hindus. The Assyrians had painted and highly embellished chariots. Fifteen centuries before Christ, the Egyptians obtained chariots, completely covered with ornaments and inlaid with gold, from the Mesopotamians. A great number of chariots were employed for military purposes. Every battalion of 450 foot soldiers had, according to Amarakosha, 81 cars and 243 horses.

The art of war as known to the ancient Hindus.

Horace Hayman Wilson and Gustav Oppert have written excellent treatises on the art of war as known to the ancient Hindus. The work written by the latter on the weapons, army organization and political maxims of the ancient Hindus, derives its information from two ancient Sanskrit works, the *Nitiprakasika* of Vaisampayana and the *Sukraniti* of Usanas, or Sukracáryá. Vaisampayana is introduced in the *Nitiprakasika* as communicating at Taksasila in the Panjáb to King Janamijaya the nature of the Dhanurveda, or the art of using the bow, the peculiarities of the weapon and all particulars connected with war and the administration of the country.

The officers of the army.

The troops of the ancient Hindus were commanded by generals, who were mostly the king's ministers. The crown prince was generally next in command to the king, and all received their pay regularly every month. The crown prince received 5,000 *varvas** a month; the commander-in-chief drew 4,000 *varvas*. The first charioteer, the *atiratha*, was usually a royal prince, who received 3,000 varvas a month; the *maharatha* 2,000 varvas. The Hindus connect their weapons and arms with metaphysical causes, and a supernatural origin is ascribed to all armour.

The use of firearms and gunpowder.

According to Professor Oppert, the ancient Hindus were acquainted with the use of firearms and gunpowder. They had war machines made of metal or stone, out of which they hurled iron and lead balls at their enemies. These were doubtless discharged by means of gunpowder. The ancient Indians were great adepts in the art of smelting and casting metals. The Arabs, who, in old times, maintained active commercial intercourse with India, received their earliest gunpowder supply from that country and made some improvements on the original manufacture. M. Langhs, in a paper read in the French Institute in 1798, contended very strongly that gunpowder was invented in India, and the same opinion was put forward by Beckmann, in 1811, in his *History of Inventions and Discoveries*. Colonel Tod says, in his *Annals of Rájastán*: "We have in the poems of the Hindu poet Chand frequent indistinct notices of firearms, especially the *nalgola*, or tube ball." When Sultan Mahmúd of Ghazní fought Anandpál, Rájá of Láhore, in 1008, cannon (*tope*) and muskets (*tufang*) were, according to Farishta, employed by the Sultan. In the apocryphal

* The *varva* was an ancient gold coin (*ashrafi*). All the higher officers of State were paid in gold currency, which is proof of the abundance of gold in India in ancient times.

letter which Alexander wrote to Aristotle, he described "the frightful dangers to which his armies were exposed in India when the enemy hurled upon them flaming thunderbolts."

The Sanskrit work *Sukraniti*, previously referred to, states that "the wall of a King's fortress is always guarded by sentinels, is provided with guns and other projectile weapons, and has many strong bastions, with proper loopholes and ditches." In another passage of the *Sukraniti* it is stated that the royal watchmen who are on duty about the palace carry firearms. The *Kamauclakiya*, acknowledged as one of the earliest works on Nitisastra, says that "confidential agents remaining near the king should rouse him by stratagems, gun-firing and other means, when he is indulging in drinking-bouts, among women, or gambling." From this Professor Oppert concludes that the practice of firing guns as signals was in vogue among the ancient Hindus. The word firearm is literally in Sanskrit *agniaster*, a weapon of fire. There is no doubt that gunpowder was known in both China and India at periods far beyond all investigation.

The art of gun-firing known to the ancient Hindus.

There were also the commissariat and naval departments. The former superintended the transport of the accoutrements of war, military requisites and provisions for soldiers by means of bullock-trains, horses, camels, &c. The latter coöperated with the admiral of the fleet. Private persons were prohibited from keeping elephants, which were considered the property of the State.

The commissariat and naval departments.

The Hindus dressed in a cotton shirt reaching below the knee and half-way between it and the ankle. Over this was thrown a mantle, folded round the shoulders and fastened under the right shoulder. The lower part of the body was covered with a cloth reaching to the middle of the leg. This was the common *dhotí*. Rich people wore necklaces, earrings of gold and ivory, and bracelets. They rode in chariots drawn by four horses, and it was considered undignified to ride on horseback without a retinue. Attendants followed, holding umbrellas over them, and everything was done to give their processions an imposing and picturesque appearance. Men allowed their beards to grow and dyed them a variety of colours, red, green, dark-blue and purple. The women were draped; they wore no tight-fitting garments. They stained their hands and feet with *henna*, sandal and lac. Their eyebrows and foreheads were coloured with musk; their hair adorned with flowers. All wore ornaments and jewels, differing in value according to the means of the wearer.

The dress of the ancient Hindus.

Religious ascetics are often spoken of by the Greek writers. They lived in woods, clothed themselves with the bark of trees, and subsisted on leaves or wild fruit. They abstained from all pleasures and remained motionless for days together, till the joints became perfectly rigid, or till the nails grew through the palms of the hands and out at the back. Kings came to them and begged their intercession with the gods, in affairs of State or in matters connected with themselves.

Religious ascetics.

CHAPTER VI.

THE MODERN HINDUS.

THE Hindus of the present day in the Panjáb do not materially differ from their co-religionists in other parts of India, though there can be no doubt that, as regards religious rites and observances, some changes have taken place among them. The whole of their system of theology is professedly founded on the Vedas, and the great objects of worship in the *Mantras* are Indra, or the firmament, Surya, the god of the sun, Soma, the god of the moon, and the gods of fire, air, water, earth, the atmosphere and spirits. The elements and planets are personified. We remember how the Aryans of the Panjáb, in their struggle with the aboriginal tribes, invoked the gods for help. Indra, the god of heaven, thunder, lightning, storms and rain, destroyed the towers and fortresses of their enemies. The warriors in the land of the Indus were urged to follow the victorious chariot of Indra. Indra was invoked to raise up the souls of the warriors, to be with them when the banners of war waved, and to give them supremacy over the black skins. The stature of Mitra, the highest god of light, transcended the sky. He "sustained heaven and earth," "his glory spread beyond earth" and "with never closing eyes, he looked down on all creatures." Varuna was the god of the life-giving water which sprung from the heavens. Agni, the god of fire, "warmed everything with a glance." The Vedas taught belief in "one Supreme Power," "the Self-existing Power," "He whom the mind alone can perceive." By degrees the worship of deified heroes was inculcated, and numberless inferior gods were introduced. About the tenth century of the Christian era, however, these notions about the Deity seem to have undergone a material change, and the Hindu worship has been since chiefly confined to Shiva, Vishnu, Sakti and a few other gods. Rámá, the champion of the famous epic poem, *Rámáyana*, Krishna and other heroes emanating from Vishnu, are worshipped as gods.

The philosophy and religion of the ancient Hindus.

The modern notions regarding the Deity.

The Hindu gods.

It may be interesting to give here a brief sketch of the characteristics of the principal Hindu gods now worshipped.

Brahma.

Brahma, the grandfather of the gods and of the human race, is the chief person of the Trinity, representing the creating, the preserving and the destroying principles, the three mighty forces by which nature works her miracles. He is represented in the form of a man with four faces of gold, dressed in white and riding on a goose. He holds a wand in one hand and a dish for charity in the other. He is the possessor of the most spacious heaven, "the beauties of which could not be described even in two hundred years."

Indra.

Indra, who was so much dreaded and flattered by the ancient Aryans, is now most frequently worshipped by women. He is regarded as the generous bestower of sons, riches, houses and different kinds of pleasure in this world and the next.

Shiva.

Shiva, "the destroyer," "the prince of death and god of war," is represented, sometimes, with five faces and four arms, and, at others, in the natural form of a man, but with an additional eye. He is adorned with a necklace of skulls, and is propitiated as the enemy of mankind. He dances over mangled corpses and drinks blood from the skulls of the slain. Festivals are annually held in his honour, at which horrible ceremonies of self-inflicted torture are performed; such as piercing the tongue, inserting pieces of wood into the wound and such like rites. He is the husband of the goddesses Durga and Kálí.

Vishnu.

Vishnu, "the preserver," is represented in the form of a black man with four arms, one of which holds a club, another a shell, the third a wheel and the fourth a water-lily. His garments are yellow, and he rides on an animal half man and half bird. He is the household god and has power to remove family misfortunes. He is the lord of two wives Lakhshmi, the goddess of fortune and prosperity, and Saraswati, the goddess of learning. Lakhshmi is dressed in yellow garments. She sits on a snake, rides on a bird; her dwelling is in water, but she is constantly moving, and never remains in one place.

Ganesh, represented by a corpulent man, with his elephant head and four hands, sits on a rat. He is the son of the goddess Durga. He has power over civil matters. Go to a banker's and you will find the image of Ganesh painted on the door; go to a *bania's* shop and the figure of Ganesh, on a prominent part of the wall, will be the first object to attract your eye. All men of business keep his image as an emblem of protection. Letters are commenced in his name; a person, when beginning to read, first salutes him, and the title pages of account books are decorated with his likeness in saffron. A traveller, when stepping out of his house to undertake a journey, invokes Ganesh in the words: "O thou who solvest every difficulty, make my journey successful." Ganesh.

The goddess Durga is represented as having ten arms, with which she holds many instruments of war. She is the great destroyer of giants, and with that object took many births. She is also called Sáti and Parváti, and festivals in her honour are very popular. Durga.

Kálí is another lady famous for her military exploits. She is quite worthy of her husband Shiva, being represented as a black Medusa, with snakes for hair and every characteristic of horror and dread. She once obtained a victory over a certain giant, and was so much pleased that she danced till the earth shook to its foundations, and many were killed. Finding, then, that her own husband, Shiva, was among the dead, she was struck with horror, put out her tongue to an enormous length and remained motionless as a statue, in which attitude she is represented. Kálí.

Saraswati, the goddess of learning, is represented as a white woman. She stands on a water-lily and plays on the lute. She has the special gift of making men learned and eloquent, and festivals are held in her honour with great rejoicings. Saraswati.

Among the terrestrial gods may be mentioned Krishna, the famous piper, who enchanted alike milkmaids and princesses. While only a boy of eight, he puzzled the gods of heaven, who, becoming angry with the villagers, had sent terrible storms of hail, rain and wind against them. Men and cattle were dying, when the hero picked up the sacred mountain Goverdhan and held it like an umbrella over the heads of the villagers and their cattle, thus saving their lives. He flirted with sixteen thousand milkmaids at once. This prodigious character was accidentally killed by an arrow which struck him while sitting under a tree. He is regarded, not merely as an incarnation, but as Vishnu himself, and is worshipped by all wealthy Hindus and by nearly all the women. Krishna.

Rámá, one of the incarnations of Vishnu, is the hero of the epic poem *Rámáyana*. *Rám* signifies "happy" or "he who makes happy." The name of this deity is intimately connected with the Hindu conception of divine power, and it is from him that the Hindu salutation, "*Rám Rám!*" meaning "happiness," or "may you be happy," is derived. He is credited with many adventures with Hanúmán, the monkey-god. Rámá.

The *Dhanurveda*, or the knowledge of weapons and arms, personified as a deity, is credited with possessing four feet, eight arms and three eyes. In his four right hands he holds a thunderbolt (*vajra*), a sword (*khadga*), a bow (*dhanu*) and a discus (*cakra*), and in his four left arms a hundred killer (*sataghni*), a club (*goda*), a spear (*sula*), and a battle-axe (*paltisa*). His crest is provided with charms; his body is polity; his armour is a spell; his heart represents charms and spells; his two earrings are weapons and The *Dhanurveda*.

missiles; his ornaments are war tactics; his eyes are yellow; he is girt with the garland of victory and he rides on a bull.

The Hindu objects of worship.

The Hindus, pacific both by creed and habit, seem to have taken their notions of the Deity from the awe inspired in their minds by things grand or uncommon in the universe, by anything terrifying or strikingly beautiful and attractive, or by anything eminently useful. This accounts for their worship of the sun, the moon, the stars and other heavenly bodies, of animals, birds, trees and rivers. Brahmins are fed in honour of *Surajdevata*, and people abstain from eating salt, or from setting milk to make butter, on Sundays. The pious Hindu, while bathing in the sunlight, invariably throws a handful of water in the direction of the sun to cool and refresh the god. The lion, the king of the forest, is worshipped; so are serpents. The elephant, which possesses a gigantic form, is worshipped; but the camel, in spite of its size, is denied this honour, apparently because it does not possess the bulk, or the magnificence and grace which form the principal features of its massive, dark-skinned brother. The beautiful peacock is an object of reverence, and its plumes form fans for gods and kings alike. The *pipal* and *bor* trees are worshipped owing to their great size and the shade they afford to travellers. Their roots are supplied with water, which is supposed to quench infallibly the thirst of departed relatives and friends in the world unseen. The monkey is worshipped under the name of Hanúmán. *Hanú* in Sanskrit means *cheek-bone.* The monkey falling from the sun's orbit broke his cheek-bone, and was called Hanúmán, or the monkey-god. He is immortal and can give long life to men, hence he is worshipped on birthdays.

Hanúmán.

The larger rivers of India are the objects of great veneration. With the ancient Aryans the Scindhus was "the far-famed bestower of wealth." With the modern Hindus, Jamnaji, or Lady Jamna, and Gangamai, or Mother Ganges, represented as female deities, are the chief objects of adoration. Brahmins are fed in honour of the Lady Jamna. The *Puránas* are loud in their praises of Mother Ganges. She is believed to have her source in heaven, whither her waters finally return, after purifying the souls of men upon earth. Her mercies and gifts are boundless, and her virtues and good attributes beyond conception. Bathe in her waters, and all your sins, however heinous, are washed away. Touch them and you are purified. Meditate on them, from however great a distance, and you are sure to obtain instant relief from your trouble. The very sight, the very name, the very thought of "Ganga," carries with it incalculable blessings. It is meritorious to die within sight of the Ganges. Sick persons are taken to its banks, that they may breathe their last by the holy stream and thereby pave the way to heaven. It is the great repository of the bones of the dead. From great distances the bones of Hindus are carried to the river and thrown into the holy waters for the benefit of the souls of the dead. The annual fair of Hardwar is held on its banks during the first fortnight of April, when thousands of votaries flock from all parts of India to bathe in the sacred stream and wash away their sins.

The Jamna.

The Ganges.

The cow.

The Dhartimai.

The cow is the object of the profoundest veneration, and the Dhartimai, or Mother Earth, a most honoured deity. When a cow is milked the first stream is allowed to fall on the ground as an offering to the goddess. Before wine or medicine is taken, a few drops are sprinkled on the ground in her honour. The custom seems to have been the same among the ancient Persians, as the following couplet of the celebrated poet, Háfiz of Shiráz, shews:—

اگر شراب خوري جرعه فشان برخاك
ازان گناه که نفعي رسد بغير چه باک

"When you partake of wine throw a handful on the ground,
For no harm can result from a sin which benefits others."

Certain pools and tanks are considered sacred and are celebrated places of pilgrimage.

Snake worship is very prevalent in the Panjáb, and the festival of *Nág Panchmi* is observed in honour of the snake deity. In Kúlú many temples are dedicated to the *nág*, or serpent, to whom are attributed divine powers.* In the upper Biás valley there are temples dedicated solely to serpents. The *deodár* (from *deva*, divine, and *dárú*, remedy) tree is worshipped in the hills of Kúlú and oblations are offered before it. The deity is propitiated by the offer of a piece of iron. It cures diseases in persons and cattle, protects the flocks of shepherds and gives good crops to husbandmen. The *jand* tree, the product of arid lands, is the "Mother Jand" which blesses people with children. It is presented with wreaths of flowers, fanned and pressed with both hands for hours together, that the kind mother may be propitiated. A marriage procession must go to her, to offer benedictions, if the kind mother is not far. If at a distance, she has yet power to make men and women happy. The astonished spectator may often find a Hindu girl, in the Jhang and Múltán districts, standing before the jandi mother with downcast and tearful eyes, praying in musical tones: "*Jandi de wadde darbár bachra lene aiyán*," "I have come to the grand darbár of Jandi to solicit from her the gift of a child." Another young woman may be found prostrating herself before the goddess, singing:—

جنڈي دي دربار جوتان جاگديان
ميري جهولي رير كهڈا جو تان جاگديان

"The darbár of Jandi is ever brilliant with lamps,
Give me a baby to play in my lap; O Jandi, thy lamps are ever shining."

Stones possessing some peculiarity are worshipped. In Kálánaur, in the district of Gúrdáspúr, there is a black hillock round which thousands from the neighbourhood flock in order to worship it. A grand edifice is built on it, and it is called the seat of *Mahádeo*, or the "Great Deity."

The sainted dead are worshipped. The worship of some of these saints is common to both Hindus and Mahomedans. The tombs of Saint Sakhi Sarwar at Nigahia, in the district of Múltán, Báwá Faríd Shakarganj, at Pákpattan, in the district of Montgomery, Bu Ali Kalandar, at Pánipat, in the district of Karnál, and Mai Hír, at Jhang, are the chief instances of the reverence paid by the Hindus to Mahomedan shrines. Many Hindus have belief in the celebrated Mahomedan saint, the Pír Dastgír of Jílán, and make offerings of sweetmeats in his honour. Similarly, Khwája Khizr, to whom, according to the Mahomedans, the care of travellers and of rivers is confided, is also worshipped by the Hindus. He is the Hindu god of water, and lamps are lighted in his honour on the banks of rivers and canals, or on the brinks of wells.

A belief in the transmigration of souls forms the principal element of the Hindu faith. Until the soul is purified in its essence there can be no deliverance from a future existence; the soul must appear and disappear in the forms of various beings until that degree of purity is attained. The laws of Manú lay down rules for the accomplishment of this object. The chief of

Snake worship.

Tree worship.

The *jand* tree.

Worship of stones.

Worship of the sainted dead.

Belief in the transmigration of souls.

---

* *The Himálayan Districts of Kúlú, Láhoul and Spiti*, by Captain A. F. P. Harcourt, Bengal Staff Corps, Assistant Commissioner, Panjáb. Describing these temples, the author says, "the effigies of serpents are profusely cut either in wood along the lintels of the doorways or iron casts of the same being screwed into the woodwork of the door-posts."

these is subjecting the body to sufferings and privations of all kinds and withdrawing from all worldly concerns. The pious should consciously neither molest nor destroy any living being, lest it should contain the spirit of one whom the living would have been the least inclined to injure, if, like himself, he had been alive. One's future state of being depends entirely on the good or bad deeds of the present life. It is related that a Brahmin once seeing a beautiful cat in the lap of an English lady during her evening drive, stood amazed by the roadside, exclaiming, "Great is Ram! This creature must surely have done good deeds in a former state of existence that it should now enjoy the good luck of occupying the lap of a *Faringan* (English lady)."

The system of caste.

The system of caste has taken such deep root in the social institutions of the Hindus that it now forms the vital part, the very mainstay, of their religion. Religious ceremonies have been associated with almost every civil transaction, and an order of priesthood merging into hereditary sacerdotalism has been established. This may be called modern Hinduism, as distinguished from that of the age of the Vedas. The spiritual power gradually lifted its head and the secular power collapsed. The Brahmins worked on the imaginations and fears of the people so well that, from being active and useful members of society, from being counsellors, magistrates and military commanders, they became an indolent, covetous and superstitious set of people. Like so many tax-gatherers they expect the accustomed fee on ceremonies which have become as numerous as themselves. The occasions are not few on which they must be feasted. Should a man die, bedsteads, horses, dresses, utensils and other articles of use in daily life must be given to the Brahmins, for without these the deceased would be inconvenienced in the next world. With the bedstead must be given a pillow, blanket and other necessaries, for whatever is given to the Brahmin in this world is used by the dead in his future life. He there sleeps a good sleep on the bedstead, rides on the horse and wears all the garments that are here given to Brahmins. The Brahmin is no more than a custodian, an instrument through whom your articles are safely transmitted to your friend or relative in the world unseen. The more you comfort the Brahmin here, the more will your friend be comforted in the next world. Thus do the Brahmins live on the community as privileged pensioners. He who breaks his word with a Brahmin, or inflicts any injury on him, will, after death, be born again in the form of a devil living in a thick forest, doomed to lament for ever and suffer extreme distress. It is related that a monkey, seeing a fox devouring carrion, was seized with compassion for her, and exclaimed: "Dear sister,—I pity you in your miserable condition. You have to feed yourself on such abominations. You must surely have committed the most heinous crimes in your former life." "Alas!" cried the poor fox, shedding tears, "my dear brother, I was once a man. Having made a promise to a Brahmin, I had the misfortune not to fulfil it. This is the punishment I am undergoing for that offence. I am compelled to live this life until my former sins are atoned for." From the moment of birth until the time the soul leaves its earthly tenement, no subject engrosses the attention of the pious more than the sacred Brahmin. The dust of their feet is a cure for diseases, a charm against evil spirits, an antidote to counteract evil. In their pleasure is the pleasure of the gods, in their wrath is the wrath of heaven. They are the "mouth of the gods."

The Brahmins and their prerogatives.

The Mahomedans of India affected by the Hindus in their social customs.

Nor have the Mahomedans in India been able to exclude the effects of the caste system from their community, for, while in Turkey, Arabia and Egypt Mahomedans eat and drink with Christians, the Indian Musalman would neither dine with a Christian nor eat food prepared by him. The Mahomedans of India, as far as the common people are concerned, are an exclusive community. Respectable tribes marry only in their own class, and are much restricted as to giving their daughters in marriage to persons of an inferior tribe or caste, or receiving daughters of such families. In Mahomedan countries other than India such distinctions are unknown. The habit of ages has made caste prejudice inherent in the people. It has, as it were, become their common law. Buddhism, which professes a common brotherhood among mankind, waged a war of centuries against caste, but was not accepted by the people, who relapsed into caste. In Ceylon, where the faith of Buddha has survived, caste is found side by side with it. The great Nánák preached social equality of all races and tried to unite all creeds by one common tie, but his followers, after struggling for years to establish the doctrines of their leader, have now surrounded themselves with a fence of caste more or less impassable.

Caste in India not a new thing.

The caste system is only technically bad. It may be said to be morally bad if it created hatred and abhorrence of one another among people, from pride or an affectation of superiority. But, generally speaking, it has not that effect in India. It is to the Hindus simply what in Western countries are the social ties and restrictions observed by people who enjoy the benefit of a superior education. The distinction observed by the ancient Romans between patrician and plebeian was essentially a caste distinction. The hereditary distribution of employments among the ancient Egyptians bore a close analogy to caste. What, however, in India is known as the caste system is rather an unwritten law of nations by which they bind themselves to one another in matters social and religious. Everybody in Europe, everybody in Arabia and Persia sets up his separate table. Persons of a certain standing in society ordinarily marry only among people of position equal to their own. They shrink from the idea of forming alliances, or even of mixing, with people of inferior social status to themselves, lest their dignity, or their influence, should decline, or be lost. This is virtually the observance of a custom analogous to the caste system of India, with only this difference that the Hindus have carried their system too far; they have made it too rigid. Caste, then, properly speaking, is not peculiar to India.

Policy of the Government in regard to diverse castes and religions prevalent in India.

The Government of India, which tolerates all religions, has not interfered with the caste system of the country. Yet, so far as its own action is concerned, it has wisely ignored caste. The streets of a town are open equally to Brahmins, Saiyads, *chamárs* and sweepers. Education in schools is given equally to the sons of princes and of *baniás*, of nawábs and of *dhobís*. All sit on the same bench, or the same floor, and are instructed by the same tutor. In jails, as in hospitals, all are treated alike. No preference is given to the people of one class over those of another. State appointments are open to all. The son of a shopkeeper or of an oilman, if he possesses the necessary qualifications, is as eligible to fill the highest appointment open to a native as is the son of a nawáb or a prince. Certain sections of the community have already planted their foot on the social ladder. As education spreads, as people appreciate the system of a free, enlightened and impartial Government more thoroughly, the rigid distinctions of caste will be quietly, calmly and imperceptibly removed, although, as long as the sun shines on the soil of India, as long as the cultivator ploughs his land, as long as the flower imparts its sweet odour to the garden, so long will the caste system remain in India. It is the sacred

Probable future of the caste system of India.

pledge given by the members of the great Indian nation to one another. It is the backbone of Indian society. It is the great inheritance bequeathed to them by their forefathers. It is founded on the law of nature, the law of nations. The Persian poet says:—

کند هم جنس باهم جنس پرواز
کبوتر با کبوتر باز با باز

"Every bird takes wing with one of its own species;
Pigeons keep with pigeons, hawks with hawks."

Change of customs among the Hindus.

Some of the changes that have taken place among the Hindus of the present day are remarkable. The old Hindu dress is changed. It is now worn only by the Brahmins. Under the civilization of the ancient Hindus, women enjoyed full liberty. They were not condemned to live in seclusion, nor were they treated as inferiors. A woman was poetically called "the light of the house." Women were not bought with money, as were Egyptian and Chinese women, but they were treated on terms of equality with men. "Where the females are honoured," said the ancient Hindu sages, "there the deities are pleased; but when they are dishonoured, then all religious rites become useless." Influenced by the Mahomedan custom, Hindu women in many families are not allowed to appear in public; though the *purda* custom among them has never been very rigidly observed. The marriage of widows was not prohibited. The king was the guardian of all widows and unmarried women. A woman was the sole owner of property brought by her to her husband's house; and it was inherited by her daughter. She could dispose of it at her pleasure without any restriction. Hindus, in ancient times, never lent money for gain. The taking of interest now forms the principal part of Hindu money transactions. Following the Mahomedan custom, the rule of monogamy has been relaxed among the wealthier Hindus.

Influence of Mahomedan social customs on Hindu society.

Social customs of the Hindus.

As an indispensable duty, a Hindu must wash before meals. For the purpose of ablutions a running stream is preferred to standing water. Men and women go to the riverside to bathe early in the morning, and on their return bring a brazen vessel filled with water, the use of which at home is considered most auspicious. If through old age, infirmity or sickness, a man cannot go to a stream to bathe, he must perform the necessary ablutions at home. Hindus repeat their prayers with their faces turned towards the east. Their mythology, side by side with the Egyptians, is the oldest in the world, and it reaches the profoundest depths in its efforts to sound the mysteries of the universe. In its purity it breathes a spirit of sublime devotion and adoration to one immortal spirit, it inculcates benevolence to mankind, gentleness to all living creatures, and a spirit of self-denial and indifference to this transient world. Some passages in the *Code of Manú*, giving a description of mortal beings, of the woes and sorrows of this world, and of the happiness of the world to come, are of singular beauty, and I quote them here from the excellent work of Sir William Jones. Speaking of the present state of being, the writer says:—

The Hindu mythology full of glimpses into the profoundest truths.

"A mansion with bones for its rafters and beams; with nerves and tendons for cords; with muscles and blood for mortar; with skin for its outward covering; filled with no sweet perfume, but loaded with excrements;

"A mansion inhabited by age and sorrow, the seat of malady, harassed with pains, haunted with the quality of darkness, and incapable of standing long; such a mansion of the vital soul let the occupier always cheerfully quit;

"As a tree leaves the bank of a river, or as a bird leaves the branch of a tree, thus he who leaves his body is delivered from the ravening shark of the world."

On the same subject the writer says :—

"Giving no pain to any creature, let him collect virtue by degrees for the sake of acquiring a companion to the next world, as the white-ant by degrees builds his nest.

"For in his passage to the next world neither his father, nor his mother, nor his wife, nor his son, nor his kinsmen will remain in his company; his virtue alone will adhere to him.

"Single is each man born, single he dies; single he receives the reward of his good, and single the punishment of his evil deeds.

"When he leaves his corpse, like a log or a lump of clay on the ground, his kinsmen retire with averted faces, but his virtue accompanies his soul.

"Continually, therefore, by degrees, let him collect virtue for the sake of securing an inseparable companion; since with virtue for his guide he will traverse a gloom, however hard to be traversed!"

The following passage illustrates the nature of asceticism.

"Restrain, O ignorant man, thy desire of wealth, and become a hater of it in body, understanding and mind; let the riches thou possessest be acquired by thine own good actions; with those gratify thy soul.

"The boy so long delights in his play, the youth so long pursues his beloved, the old so long brood over melancholy thoughts, that no man meditates on the Supreme Being.

"Who is thy wife, and who thy son? How great and wonderful is this world; whose thou art and whence thou camest, meditate on this, my brother, and again on this.

"As a drop of water moves on the leaf of the lotus, thus, or more slippery, is human life! The company of the virtuous endures here but for a moment,—that is the vehicle to bear thee over the land and ocean.

"To dwell in the mansion of gods, at the foot of a tree, to have the ground for a bed and a hide for vesture; to renounce all ties of family or connections; who would not receive delight from this devout abhorrence of the world?

"Day and night, evening and morn, winter and spring depart and return. Time sports, age passes on, desire and the wind continue unrestrained.

"When the body is tottering, the head gray and the mouth toothless; when the smooth stick trembles in the hand which it supports, yet the vessel of covetousness remains unemptied."

A Hindu becomes unclean on the birth in his house of a child in the direct line, or on the death of a person related to him. The touch of a dead body also causes uncleanness, and a man is considered to a certain extent impure while on a bed of sickness. As soon as he bathes and shaves, he becomes clean. While he remains impure, he is interdicted from performing any religious ceremony, and is forbidden to shave his head or cut his nails. A man who kills a cow, even by accident, commits a great crime, and forthwith becomes unclean, and he cannot be purified without going to the Ganges, and performing there certain ceremonies. While on the way to the sacred river, he must carry with him a stick, with the tail of a cow fastened to it, as a mark that nobody is to touch him. In the Kúlú hills, if a cow dies while fastened to anything, the person who tied her up becomes unclean, and nobody will eat at his hands until he is purified. Cleaning the teeth is forbidden on the anniversary of the death of a father or mother. The teeth are cleaned with a small piece of newly-cut green wood, called *dátún*, and the following prayer is said at the time :—"God of the forests, I have cut from your branches a bit of wood to clean my teeth with. Grant to me, by this act which I am about to do, a long life, strength, honour and intelligence; and bestow upon me many cows, much riches, prudence, judgment, memory and power."

Uncleanness.

Cleaning the teeth.

Ghosts, spirits and fairies are held in the utmost dread by women and children. Scavengers are believed to become ghosts after death, and the chief agents in producing fever and other diseases. The effect of a malevolent spirit is removed by the charm of a faquír or a bhagat, and divination and exorcism have become professions with both men and women in

Belief in ghosts and spirits among ignorant people.

towns and villages. Amulets are worn by women and children as a protection against the evil eye, and a tiger's claw and a shell fastened to a string and worn on the breast or neck is a sure remedy for counteracting a covetous or evil look. Iron possesses the quality of frustrating the evil eye in a pre-eminent degree, and garlands of siras and mango leaves are also powerful protectives when fastened over gateways and arches. On the birth of a male child various ceremonies are observed to ensure his long life and immunity from small-pox and evil spirits. Charms are fixed to the wall and fires burnt night and day to prevent the approach of evil spirits.

Ceremonies on the birth of a child.

The Díwálí festival.

Feasts and festivals are, for the most part, rigidly observed. At the Díwálí festival there is not a shop or a house that is not cleaned, fresh plastered and lit up with lamps. It is on that night that the souls of ancestors are supposed to visit their living relations, and no pains are spared by the latter to comfort them. The god Krishna, the celebrated cowherd and piper, is worshipped on that night with a variety of ceremonies.

CHAPTER VII.

BUDDHISM IN THE PANJÁB.

When the original purity and simplicity of the Hindu religion had become debased by the introduction of idolatry; when the worship before rendered to one Supreme Being, the Creator of the Universe, had been extended to terrestrial gods; when the influence of the Brahmins and the caste system were supreme, there arose a reformer, whose object was to emancipate the people from their errors and prejudices and awaken them to a sense of their responsibility and duty to God and man. This was Buddha, the celebrated sage and hermit prince, whose religion has been accepted by nearly half the human race. His original name was Sidhartha, and he was the son of Suddhodana, who reigned over Kapilavastú, the capital of a kingdom of the same name, at the foot of the Nepál mountains. He was born in the year 622 B.C., and belonged to the family of the Sakias. He received his education from Brahmin tutors, but from his boyhood he was given to contemplation, and his father, wishing to draw him to a more active life, married him at the age of sixteen to Gopa, an accomplished princess. Besides her, the prince had two other wives and a number of concubines, with whom he lived a life of luxury and pleasure in his palaces. But he continued to be of a reflective turn of mind, and would say to himself: "Life is like the spark produced by the friction of wood; it is lighted and is extinguished," and he would discourse of the instability of life and the deliverance of the soul. In this manner he lived till his twenty-ninth year, when one day, while driving out, he saw a decrepit old man, with bald head and trembling limbs, covered with incurable sores, and again a corpse on a bier with the friends of the deceased weeping round it. What profit, he asked himself, could there be in youth, which was subject to so many diseases, to age and to death? Woe to this life of misery and sorrow, a life which is but the sport of a dream and the sound of a lyre! Woe to the earth, which is a vale of misery, and to the world, which is full of pain! Sidhartha then resolved to retire from the world, and, leaving his palace, his wives and children (among whom was a son

Birth of Buddha, 622 B.C.

His retired and solitary habits in his youth.

His reflections on the type of old age, infirmity and death.

just born to him), he escaped by night, eluding the guards who had been placed by his father to watch him. He subjected himself to the severest penances, enduring hunger, thirst, heat, cold and storms; but, having failed, after six years of continual mortification and austerities, to discover the truth, he gave himself up to meditation, and at last conceived that he had arrived at the knowledge necessary to enable a man to disregard the evils that flesh is heir to. In this knowledge were included four sublime truths: pain; the creation of the pain; freedom from pain; and the means of its annihilation, which is the attainment of eternal bliss. All living creatures, he maintained, were without exception subject to torments and pain. Their knowledge of the existence of evil leads to their striving to liberate themselves from it. He called himself Buddha, the "enlightened," and preached the doctrines of his religion to his fellow-creatures. He commenced his public ministry at the age of thirty-six. He used to dress in dingy yellow robes, and, with his head shaved, and a bowl in his hand, like Paul, the great Christian missionary, who traversed the whole length of the Roman Empire, he travelled about for forty-four years, visiting distant parts of the country and converting peoples and princes. The principal scenes of his life, Ajuddhia, Gáyá and Rájgarh, are now places of pilgrimage and the favourite resorts of the followers of his creed. He spent his last night in preaching, and after bidding farewell to his pupils, sank into meditation, and died calmly, at the advanced age of eighty, in a grove and under the shadow of a sál tree, where a bed had been prepared for him by his faithful disciple Ananda. His last words were, "Nothing continues," indicating plainly that beyond death there is nothing but extinction and absorption into the Divine Being. His ashes were buried in Kasia, in the Gorakhpúr District, amid a great concourse of mourners.

His great renunciation.

His doctrines.

His enlightenment.

His preachings.

His death, 548 B.C.

His last words.

Buddha did away with the ceremonies of the Hindus, set aside the Brahmin priesthood, abolished sacrifices and dethroned the gods of the Indians. He condemned the desires of the flesh and recommended self-torture, with a view to bringing the body into subjection to the spirit. His life-long object was universal propagandism and the reduction of mankind to a state of spiritual thraldom. His religion spread over the whole of India, but, after a hard contest for fifteen hundred years, it finally gave way to Brahminism, which has outlived its formidable rival. In the abstract, it was atheism, coupled with a system of rigid self-mortifications and penances; it shunned the very idea of a future state and declared annihilation, or nothingness (*niruáná*), to be the end of present existence. A religion so barren in its results proved distasteful to the lively and imaginative people of India, and was discarded by them. Atheism never was, and never will be, a religion. Yet we find that, banished from its native home, Buddhism, as a religion, has won greater triumphs in its exile, spreading over the whole of further Asia, including Ceylon, Burma, Siam, Japan, China, Cochin China, Mongolia, Manchuria, Thibet and the Eastern Archipelago. It has left a voluminous literature in Sanskrit, Chinese, Pali and other languages.

Buddhist influence on Hinduism.

The religion was discarded by the Hindus.

Several Chinese pilgrims toiled through Central Asia into India, to visit the birthplace of their religion. The first of these was Fa-Hian who entered the Panjáb from Afghanistán, in 399 A.D. He found Buddhist monks and temples side by side with Hindu temples. Hieuan Tsiang, another Chinese pilgrim, visited the Panjáb, by the Central Asian route, in the first half of the seventh century. He found Buddhist monasteries and monks scattered over the country. In Káshmír, the king and the people were all orthodox Buddhists, and the kingdom of Afghanistán was ruled by a Buddhist king. The monuments of Asoka and Kanishkha, the two

The Chinese pilgrims in the Panjáb, 399 and 630 A.D.

great Buddhist kings, were to be seen on the Panjáb frontier. He spent fourteen months in the ancient town of Chinapati, ten miles, according to General Cunningham, west of the Biás, where Kanishka, the royal founder of Northern Buddhism, had kept his Chinese hostages. The pilgrim, who has left a full and interesting record of his travels, traversed the Panjáb and reached the mouths of the Ganges. He met with both Hindu and Buddhist temples, but subsequently Hindu revivals, headed by various reformers, resulted in the gradual overthrow of Buddhism and its final extinction, between 700 and 900 A. D.

Buddhism now a defunct religion in the Panjáb.

In Spiti, in the Kángra District, the only religion at the present day is Buddhism. In Láhoul the religion is essentially Buddhism, and Buddhist monasteries are maintained. In the higher parts of Pangi, in Chamba, the Lámánism of Thibet prevails. In the valleys of Bhágá and Chandra Buddhism is the dominant faith. Except in these hill territories, Buddhism is a defunct religion in the Panjáb.

Asoka, the Buddhist king.

Buddhism attained its greatest extent and influence in India under the benevolent reign of Asoka, or Priyadási, grandson of Chandragupta, who ascended the throne of Magadha in 275 B.C. His kingdom extended from the mouth of the Ganges on the east to the Indus on the west. He was a man of singular ability, and possessed great powers of observation. Renouncing the Hindu faith, he became a convert to Buddhism, and by his zeal extended the doctrines of his new faith by sending political missions to China, Thibet, Burma, Siam, Ceylon, Cambodia and Java. He maintained friendly relations with the sovereigns of Greece, Syria and Egypt, and introduced the useful sciences and arts of those countries into his own. He had a great taste for architecture and sculpture and his monumental remains, rock and cave temples, monasteries and pillars, to this day bear testimony to the excellence of his character, his public spirit and wisdom, and are the admiration alike of linguists, palæographists and historians, to whom they unfold forgotten chapters of history. They are scattered from the Bay of Bengal and the southern slopes of the Vindhia mountains to the Khaibar Pass, beyond the Indus. One of these is the rock of Kapúrdagarhi in Eusafzai, forty miles from Peshávar, discovered by General Court, the inscriptions on which were deciphered by the traveller Masson, about fifty years ago. The great Asoka tolerated Hinduism and preached peace and fellowship among men. His inscriptions, which are more interesting than those of Darius, the son of Hystaspes, inculcate maxims of moral excellence and self-denial and afford indubitable proof of the noble soul of their author. One of them runs as follows:—"For those who differ from him in creed, that they, following his example, may with him attain eternal salvation." Another contains the following ordinance :—"He desires that all unbelievers may everywhere dwell (unmolested) as they also wish for moral restraint and purity of disposition. For men are of various constitutions and desires."*

His missionary efforts.

His rock and cave edicts.

His rock inscriptions.

JAINISM IN THE PANJÁB.

Jainism is, properly speaking, a compromise between Hinduism and Buddhism, for while, on the one hand, it condemns sacrifices, denies the divine origin of the Vedas, rejects the Hindu doctrine of immunity from punishment through almsgiving and the invocation of gods, and attaches no importance to the rites observed for the repose of the spirits of the dead, it, on the other hand, recognises the priestly institutions of the Brahmins,

* Pillar edict, VI, and Rock edict, VII, in the work of General Alexander Cunningham, called the *Corpus Inscriptionum Indicarum*, vol. i.

adheres rigidly to the Hindu system of caste, so repugnant to Buddhists, and has rules connected with purification, weddings, death, inheritance, the worship of gods, closely analogous to those of the Hindus. The Jains revere the cow, keep fasts and consider the killing of any living creature an unpardonable sin. The Jains in the Panjáb belong to the *Vasaya*, or mercantile class, and are generally educated. They are divided into two sects, the *Saráogis* and *Aswals*. The great mass of the Jain population is to be found in the eastern districts of Delhi, Rohtak and Hissár.

CHAPTER VIII.

INVASION OF THE PANJÁB BY OSIRIS, KING OF EGYPT.

Egypt the Misrasthán of the ancient Hindus.

THE ancient Hindus called Egypt Misrasthán,* from its being first inhabited by Misraim, the son of Ham. This is the appellation given to it in Scripture, and the name Misra is preserved to this day at Cairo, the capital of the country, which surpasses all the kingdoms of Asia in antiquity. Menes, its earliest ruler, was regarded as the first sovereign of the human race; and the credit of having been the first invader of India is also given to one of its earliest kings. The name of this monarch was Osiris, who was considered by the writers of antiquity to be the original Dionysius, or Bacchus. His genealogy is lost in fable; but he is acknowledged to have flourished at a period long before the Greeks emerged from barbarism, and is praised not only as a great warrior, but as a zealous promoter of the useful arts. Accounts of his memorable expedition to India have been given by Herodotus, Diodorus, Siculus and Strabo, who had all visited Egypt, and derived their information from its priests, as well as from Plutarch. The tradition is that, after founding the city of Thebes and conferring on the Egyptians the blessings of civilization and the useful sciences, he directed his attention to the conquest of the East. He is said to have been accompanied in his expedition by his mail-clad sons, Anulus and Macedo, and to have had in his train Apollo and Pan,† Triptolemus, skilled in husbandry, Maro, a planter of vines, and the Muses skilled in music. He conquered Ethiopia and Arabia, in which countries he instituted various measures of reform, among others the construction, in the former, of vast embankments which prevented the overflow of the Nile and saved the surrounding country from desolation. Having completed his conquests in those regions, he marched at the head of his forces in the direction of India, and entered the Panjáb‡ by the Persian frontier. According to the writers already

Its undoubted antiquity.

Osiris supposed to be the original Dionysius or Bacchus.

His celebrated expedition to the East

His march to India.

---

* *Sthán*, in Shástri, means a place. Thus, the word Misrasthán signifies the "place of Misraim." Misr, مصر, a Hebrew word, means "large city." In the Puránas the names of large towns invariably end in *sthán*, which is tantamount to the modern *púra* or *púr*. Thus, Mecca, in Arabia, is called Mochoasthán, from its being the place of Mocsh-Iswárá, an ancient deity, and Bactria, the modern Balkh, Varnisthán.

† They subsequently came to be worshipped as gods.

‡ The Greek writers do not expressly mention the Indus as the region invaded by the Egyptian king; but, from the facts that he entered India by the Persian route, that he first crossed the mountains, and that he visited the vine groves, it is natural to conclude that the regions of the Indus were the chief scene of his exploits. Again, the Greeks tell us that he pushed his conquests as far as the source of the Ganges. Others say that he was stopped in his career only by the bounding ocean. This also points to the north as the gateway whence he made his descent into the fertile plains of the Panjáb. The vine, the cultivation of which is attributed with so much emphasis to Dionysius, is unquestionably the product of Kábul and other Himálayan regions north-west of the Panjáb.

mentioned, he found the Indians leading a primitive, pastoral life, wandering in the plains and mountains, unacquainted with tillage and unaccustomed to the art of war. The Indians assembled in immense numbers, from all quarters, to defend their country, and with their rude weapons opposed the progress of the invading army. Among the attendants at the court of Dionysius were a number of female devotees, who acted as priestesses. These, under the impulse of inspiration and divine phrensy, made the plains resound with the acclamation, "Io! Bacche, Io! Triumphe." They, as well as the soldiers of the army, were furnished with lances and spears. The Indians offered but a feeble resistance, and their ranks being soon broken, the plains of the Panjáb fell, for the first time, into the possession of a foreign conqueror. The invader pushed his conquests to the mouth of the Ganges and, after a three years' stay in India, returned to his native land. He is said to have erected pillars to commemorate his victory, and to have left monuments descriptive of his triumphs; but these have not survived the wreck of time.

The Panjáb conquered by foreigners.

I have already said that, when Dionysius entered India, he found the people in a state of ignorance and barbarism. He taught them the art of cultivating the ground and the worship of the Gods. For the blessings he conferred on the people of India he obtained immortal honour in that country and was worshipped as a god. Cities were founded in his name, and Megasthenes tells us that places were pointed out to him in the country which this benefactor of the human race had visited. Plutarch, in his treatise on Isis and Osiris, informs us that, to commemorate the far-famed expedition of Dionysius to India, those games were established which in Egypt were called Pamylia, in Greece Dionysia and in Rome Bacchanalia. His work establishes beyond dispute that the Egyptian Isis and Osiris are the Isu and Iswárá of the Hindus. His worship has spread extensively and his festivals are celebrated with music and song.

Osiris teaches Indians the art of ploughing land.

He is worshipped as a god.

INVASION OF THE PANJÁB BY SEMIRAMIS, QUEEN OF ASSYRIA.

Semiramis succeeds to the throne of Assyria, 900 B. C.

When the ancient empire of Babylonia was absorbed in that of Assyria, Ninus, the founder of Nineveh, is recorded to have become its first sovereign. On his death, about the ninth century B. C., Semiramis, his queen, succeeded to the vast monarchy which his valour had acquired. She was endowed with martial talents as well as great beauty. Impelled by ambition and tempted by the immense riches of India, by the unrivalled beauty of its scenery and the luxurious fertility of its soil, she undertook her celebrated expedition to this country, an expedition which, from the exaggerated nature of the accounts that have been given of it by historians, is regarded as romantic and fabulous. Yet, according to Diodorus, the particulars of this great enterprise were extracted by Ctesias from the archives of Babylon. Moreover, the various forms in which it has been narrated by classical writers, and the great fame which, from a remote antiquity, has attached to it, when put to the test of recent investigations, bear unequivocal testimony to the fact that the expedition was really undertaken. Semiramis is believed to be the Sami Rámá of the Hindu Puránas and is worshipped by the Hindus as a deity. Her favourite dwelling is the sacred *soma* tree, round whose fires the Devatas exult. She is described as having made her first appearance at Aschalansthán in Syria. The classical writers of the East represent her as having been fed by doves in a desert and having departed from the earth in the form of a dove. According to the Puránas, the dove itself was a manifestation of Sami Rámá. The dove is an emblem of Assyria in

Her expedition to India.

She is believed to be the Sami Rámá of the Hindu Puránas.

the warlike insignia; it is equally the emblem of the goddess of peace and prosperity in India, under the altered name of Máhá Bhágá, or the prosperous goddess. The festival of Semiramis is still held in India about the month of October, when lamps are lighted under the soma tree, and an offering of rice, flowers and liquor is made. Songs in praise of the deity are sung, and she and her favourite residence, the tree, are worshipped.

She was contemporary with Virasena, the king of India.

About the time when Sami Rámá flourished in Assyria, there ruled in India a king of great piety named Virasena. He visited Mochoasthán (Mecca) to pay his benedictions to Mosch-Iswárá, otherwise known as Mathadena, and after a long series of ardent devotions (*ugra tapasia*) the deity was pleased to make him king over Sthavaras, or the immoveable part of the universe. He was hence called Sthavarpati (the Staurabates of the Greeks) and he had under his jurisdiction the hills, the earth, trees, plants and grass. His kingdom lay near the sea, apparently the regions of the Indus. Being incensed at an insult offered to his authority by Sami Rámá, queen of Vahnisthán, Sthavarpati invaded her country with a large army and routed the Bactrian forces. The proud Assyrian queen was humbled and paid her homage to the mighty king of India by acknowledging him as the son of Mahadeva.

Hindu version of the story.

The above legend, given in the Shastras, is wrapped in fiction, yet, when compared with the Greek accounts, it is found to be based on historic truth, with only this difference that, whereas by the accounts of the Western writers, the queen of Assyria is represented as having invaded India, the Indians make the king of India the aggressor. As to the names of the kingdoms concerned, the contending parties, the scene and the result of the contest, both accounts are in perfect accord.

Account of the expedition given by the classical writers.

From the accounts of this expedition, as given by the classical writers, it does not appear that the Assyrians penetrated far beyond the western frontier of the Panjáb. The principal scene of their memorable exploit was the region bordering on the Indus. Having extended her dominions widely over Western Asia, their great queen, Semiramis, determined on the conquest of India, renowned, even in those early times, for its great wealth and populousness. The great obstacles to the execution of her ambitious design were, it is said, chiefly two, the presence of a wide and turbulent stream on the north-west of India, which formed a barrier on its frontier, on that side, and the superiority of the Indians in possessing war elephants, which, by their unwieldy forms and the vastness of their strength, spread terror and consternation in the battle-field. To overcome these difficulties she employed the whole resources of her mighty empire.

Artificial elephants.

She caused a large number of counterfeit elephants to be constructed out of the hides of beasts, which were stuffed so as to represent those animals, the motive power introduced in them being camels. Naval architects from Phœnicia, Cyprus and other maritime districts bordering on the Assyrian dominions, were, at the same time, employed in Bactria to construct vessels suited for the navigation of the Indus, and the whole forest was cut down to facilitate the project. It took three years to complete these mighty preparations, and the enormous structures fabricated were conveyed from Bactria overland. The Assyrian army, consisting of the bravest and most experienced soldiers, accompanied by maritime adventurers, marched to the frontier of India headed by the queen herself and her famous general, Dercetæus.

Her mighty preparations for the expedition.

Staurabates, the Indian monarch, who claimed descent from the Surájbans, or race of the sun, with a numerous army and a mighty host of elephants, advanced to meet the invader. He also launched on the Indus a large number of boats, made of the bamboo canes so abundant on the marshy banks of that river. The superior naval arrangements of the Phœnicians, combined with their skill in navigating the fleet, enabled them to inflict a terrible defeat on the Indians. More than a thousand boats belonging to them were sunk, and immense numbers of them were taken prisoners. The Indian king nevertheless succeeded in rallying his forces and retired to some distance from the river.

The defeat of the Indians.

Elated with this success, Semiramis ordered a great bridge to be constructed over the Indus, by means of which she crossed that rapid stream. A guard of sixty thousand men was appointed to defend the bridge. The counterfeit elephants were arranged in the van of the battle, and the sight of them took the Indians by surprise. But their astonishment was soon changed into contempt, when they were told by deserters from the Assyrian army that the objects of their wonder were only fabrications of the inventive genius of the Assyrian queen. The Indian king moved forward with resolution, and a sanguinary fight ensued, in which the Assyrians were completely routed, their sham elephants were trampled upon by the enraged living elephants of the Indian army, and a great number of their fighting men were slain on the battle-field. Semiramis is described as having fought with the heroism which characterized all the actions of her life. Dressed in military attire, she animated her troops by her example, as well as by her voice. She was conspicuous in every stage of the battle; and is said to have ultimately engaged in a hand-to-hand encounter with her royal male foe, who twice wounded her, once with an arrow that pierced her delicate arm, and the second time with a javelin that struck her in the shoulder. Wounded in body and afflicted in mind, the Queen effected her retreat to her native land, though not without considerable loss to the remnants of her army, thousands of whom found a watery grave in recrossing the river, while thousands were cut down by the pursuing Indians. Some say that Semiramis herself perished in the fight, but certain it is that the Assyrians, after suffering this disaster, thought no more of the conquest of India.

Another hard contested battle.

Heroism displayed by the Assyrian queen.

Final rout of the Assyrians.

INVASION OF THE PANJÁB BY SESOSTRIS, KING OF EGYPT.

According to Eusebius,* the Cæsarean, acknowledged to be the father of ecclesiastical history, Sesostris flourished on the throne of Egypt in the eighteenth century before the Christian era. He was a powerful king both by land and sea, who greatly extended the bounds of his empire and enriched Egypt with many noble edifices and wise institutions. Having overrun the whole province of Asia and the spacious provinces of higher Asia, and having passed the eternal snows of the Caucasus and penetrated the wild deserts of Scythia and Thrace, this great legislator, warrior and conqueror, bent his attention towards the conquest of India. He is described as having led his army, by the usual route, into Northern India, or the Panjáb, and, continuing thence his progress eastward, he extended his sway as far as the Ganges. There, according to Diodorus and the geographer, Dionysius, he erected pillars, descriptive of his conquest and glory, and inscribed with symbols indicative of the attitude displayed by the conquered people in defending their country. In every other country the conqueror is said to have erected similar pillars, some of which survived to the time of Herodotus, who saw them in Palestine, while others were seen by Strabo in

* He was born in Palestine about 264 A.D. He took the surname of Pamphili from his friend Pamphilius, Bishop of Cæsarea, to whom he was much attached.

Æthiopia and Arabia. In every city of his vast empire he built and dedicated temples to the special deity of the place.

Discoursing on the subject of the Indian zodiac, Sir William Jones informs us, in the *Asiatic Researches*, that "the practice of observing the stars began, with the rudiments of civil society, in the country of those whom we call Chaldæans, from which it was propagated into Egypt, India, Greece, Italy and Scandinavia before the reign of Sacya (identified with Sesostris), who, by conquest, spread a new system of religion and philosophy from the Nile to the Ganges." The system referred to by Sir William was essentially that materialism which, twelve hundred years after, was propagated in India by Buddha and his followers.

IRRUPTIONS INTO THE PANJÁB OF THE ANCIENT SCYTHIANS, OR TARTARS.

According to Abul Ghazí, the authentic historian of the Tartars, quoted by Sir William Jones, the history of that nation begins with Oghaz, as that of the Hindus begins with Rámá. He was contemporary with Caiumeras, the first regular king of Persia, of the Pashadadian family, being the grandson of Moghal, or Mungal Khan, the direct descendant of Japhet.* This hero and patriarch of the Scythians is described as having lived to a great age and employed his early years in re-establishing the religion of Japhet in the kingdoms of Thibet, Tangat and Kitay. He afterwards made war on Persia, during the minority of Hushang, grandson of Caiumeras, and besieged and conquered Khorásán. He next carried his arms into the provinces of Irák, Azarbajan and Armenia, which he rendered tributary. He then advanced to Kábul and Ghazní and reduced Northern India, including Káshmír. Jagma, the ruler of Káshmír, and descendant of an ancient race of Hindu kings, offered a stout resistance, but the determined valour of Oghaz surmounted every obstacle, and, after a severe struggle of a year, Káshmír was reduced, Jagma was massacred, and a considerable number of the inhabitants of Káshmír were put to the sword.

Oghaz, the first great king of the Scythians.

He conquers Northern India.

After achieving these brilliant victories, Oghaz returned to his hereditary dominions by way of Badakshan, the country of the ancient Massagetae and Sogdiana. On his return home, he is said to have given a grand banquet in honour of his victories in foreign countries. The entertainment was given in tents adorned with pomegranates of gold and precious stones. The Tartars regard the numeral *nine* as sacred. In this national feast nine thousand sheep were slaughtered, together with nine hundred horses. All the articles of food and drink, such as the bottles of wine (of which the ancient Tartars were extravagantly fond), and the jars of mare's milk (which was considered wholesome), were regulated by the same auspicious numeral.

It is not certain how far the descent of the Tartars under Oghaz extended into the Panjáb. It included, in its course, the Hydaspes, or Jhelum; and, as it was undertaken more with the object of plunder than for the purpose of permanently occupying the country, it does not seem to have left any traces behind it.

Extent of his conquest.

The next irruption of importance of the Tartar hordes into the Panjáb was undertaken in the time of Cyaxares, the first sovereign of Media, the most powerful kingdom that sprung from the ruins of the ancient Assyrian empire, overthrown by Arbaces. The invasion took place about the middle

Next irruption of the Tartars into the Panjáb, 650 B.C.

* Gog and Magog, the *Yajuj* and *Majuj* of the Arabian historians, are descendants of Japhet. Magog was Japhet's second son, and it clearly gives the origin of the word "*Moghal*."

of the seventh century B.C. Vast hosts of human savages, descending from the heights of the Caucasus and its neighbourhood, spread over the countries of Upper Asia, including the regions of the Panjáb bordering on the Indus. These northern tyrants were, however, repulsed with great slaughter by Cyaxares. A considerable portion of the routed army of the Scythians settled in the Panjáb, and a race of them, called Nomardy, inhabited the country on the west bank of the Indus. They are described as a nomadic tribe, living in wooden houses, after the old Scythian fashion, and settling where they found sufficient pasturage. A portion of these settlers, the descendants of Massagetae, were called the Getes, from whom sprung the modern *Játs*. These Scythian barbarians were known in the Panjáb by the appellation of Huns; and the violent contests between the Indians and the Huns are not only testified to by Sanskrit writers, but are also proved by inscriptions on pillars in a most ancient Sanskrit dialect. The following inscription, deciphered by Mr. Wilkins, occurs on a pillar near Buddál:—

The origin of the *Játs*.

"Trusting in his wisdom, the king of Gaur (Bengal) for a long time enjoyed the countries of the eradicated race of Utkal (Orissa), of the Huns of humbled pride, of the kings of Dravir (a country south of the Carnatic), and Gujar (Gujrát) whose glory was reduced, and the universal sea-girt throne."

The original settlements of Getes, or *Játs*, in the Panjáb.

The Getes, or Játs, in ancient times inhabited the whole valley of the Indus down to Sindh. In the works of Pliny and Ptolemy they are called Játii and in that of Strabo, Zamthii. According to Dr. Hunter, a branch of these Scythian hordes, having overrun Asia about 625 B. C., occupied Patálá on the Indus, the modern Hyderabad in Sindh. They were all, in subsequent times, called *Játs*, and now form a most numerous, as well as the most important section of the agricultural population of the Panjáb.

The Takka tribe originally a Scythian.

When Alexander the Great invaded the Panjáb, in the fourth century B. C., he found the Ráwalpindi District inhabited by a tribe called Takkas, or Takshaks. They belonged to a Scythian host who had migrated into the Panjáb about the 6th century B. C., and they gave its name to the great city of Taxila, invaded by Alexander, and then the capital of the Panjáb, the site of which has been ascertained to have been between the Indus and the Jhelum. Taki, derived apparently from the same name Taxila, and identified by General Cunningham with the modern Asrúr, forty-five miles west of Láhore, was the capital of the Panjáb in the 7th century A.D. The Takka tribe is, to the present day, found in the Panjáb, in the Delhi and Karnal Districts.

The White Huns.

That a race called Tue Che, or White Huns, had established themselves in the Panjáb and along the Indus, in the first century of the Christian era, has been confirmed, not only by the ancient writers, Arrian, Strabo and Ptolemy, but by coins and inscriptions of Scythian origin recently discovered, and by the names of Indian tribes, such as the Sakás, Hans and Nágás, who are all of Scythian origin. Vikramaditya, one of the most popular and enlightened of the Indian Rájás, who ruled over the kingdoms of Mágadha, Málwá and Central India, in 56 B.C, and whose reign forms the Augustan age of Hindu literature and science, defeated the Huns in a great battle; but they were never quite driven out of the country, and they held Western India for about 250 years afterwards, though their fortunes rose and fell at intervals, during the first six centuries after Christ. The great battle of Korúr, near Múltán, in which the Scythians sustained a severe defeat, was fought about the middle of the sixth century A.D. This battle is declared to have "freed India from the Huns."

The migration of vast hordes of Scythian plunderers and conquerors into the Panjáb, and, indeed, into the whole of India as far as Bengal and Behar, had its effect both dynastic and religious. A Scythic monarchy had been established in the Panjáb by Kanishka, who held the fourth Buddhist Council, in 40 A.D., and established the Northern or Thibetan form of Buddhism in the country, as distinguished from the Buddhism of Asoka, which was in full vigour in Southern India. But Scythian influence and civilization had been gaining ground long previously, and the establishment of Buddhist sovereignty in the Panjáb, in the first century of the Christian era, of which Chinese travellers give further proof, was the result of a contest which had raged between Hinduism and Northern Buddhism for a long series of years before.

A Scythic dynasty established in the Panjáb.

PERSIAN CONQUEST OF THE PANJÁB.

According to the Persian historian, Mír Khond, quoted by Sir William Jones, in his *History of Persia*, the first recorded invasion of India by the Persians was under Farídún, son of the great Jamshed,* the founder of Isthákar, or Persepolis, and the fifth monarch of the Pashadadian dynasty, who flourished about 750 B.C. Feeling the weight of years upon him, he divided his vast empire among his three sons, to the eldest of whom, Lalun, he allotted Syria, while to the second, called Túr, he gave the country lying between the Oxus and the Jaxartes, and to the youngest, Irage, the district of Khorásán. The countries now known as Irán and Túrán derived their names from Túr and Irage, the sons of Farídún.

Farídún.

No details are given as to how far the empire of Farídún extended in India, but it certainly included the Panjáb, as, according to the *Mahábhárata*, India was, for a long time before Cyrus, who died in 529 B.C., subject to the king of Persia. Xenophon, in his work entitled *Cyropædia*, informs us that Cyrus made the Indus the eastern boundary of his empire. Other writers treat of the whole of the Panjáb as a conquered country of the Persians, and make its most eastern river the boundary.

The empire of Farídún included the Panjáb.

The empire of Cyrus extended to the Indus.

The Indians, from the time of Farídún, were accustomed to pay tribute to the Persian monarchs Shangal, their Rájá, called by Ferishta Shinkol, who reigned at Kanauj, refused to pay tribute, whereupon Afrasiab, king of Persia, being enraged, sent his general, Pieran, at the head of fifty thousand chosen horse, to chastise the Indian monarch. Being routed by the Indians, this general shut himself up in the hills, and the Persian monarch, hearing of this disaster, hastened to his relief, at the head of a hundred thousand horse. A great battle was fought between the Persians and the Indians, in which the latter sustained a severe defeat, and Afrasiab, pursuing the enemy, put thousands of them to the sword. Shinkol fled to Bengal and from thence to the mountains of Tirhút. Soon afterwards Shinkol sent his agents to Afrasiab, praying that "he might have the honour of kissing the feet of the lord of nations." His request having been granted, Shinkol was admitted into the audience of his Persian majesty, with a sword and a coffin, which he carried. Afrasiab placed Rhoat, the son of Shinkol, on the throne of India, and took the defeated king with him to Turán as a State prisoner. Rhoat remitted the fixed tribute, including a large amount of money for the use of his father in Persia.

Afrasiab invades India.

Darius I, the son of Hystaspes, who was elected king of Persia in 521 B.C., is mentioned as the next Persian sovereign who attempted the conquest of India. Having fitted out a great naval armament, he put it under the command of Scylax, of Caryandria, a city of Caria, in Greece, the

*Jamshed first introduced among the Persians the use of the solar year, in honour of which he instituted the celebrated festival of *Nauroz*, when the sun enters Aries.

object of the expedition being to determine the exact point at which the Indus meets the ocean, and to explore the western provinces of India. Scylax, who was the most distinguished naval commander of that early age, accomplished this tedious and hazardous voyage in a period of two years and a-half, and, returning to the Court of Susa, furnished the required information to Darius. No detailed accounts have been preserved of this celebrated naval expedition, or of the subsequent conquest of the western regions of India effected by the Persian monarch. But it is recorded that he drew from India a larger revenue than had ever been remitted to any Persian king before his time. India is said to have been but one of the twenty countries subject to Persia during the reign of Darius, but the tribute of the newly conquered province amounted to nearly a third part of the revenue of his other possessions. According to Herodotus, this tribute was paid in gold, the reason assigned by Mr. Rennel, in his memoirs, being that the "eastern tributaries of the Indus, as well as some other streams that descend from the northern mountains anciently yielded gold-dust." The description of the country given by Herodotus leads to the conjecture that the regions conquered by Darius comprised the modern provinces of Múltán and Láhore, and possibly Gujrát. It establishes, beyond doubt, that those provinces were, even in those early times, most populous and highly cultivated.

The naval expedition of Scylax under Darius I.

The regions conquered by Darius.

Nausherván.

Nausherván, who ruled the Persian empire when Muhammad, the Prophet of Arabia, was born, styled himself "King of Persia and India." There are no records left to show that he ever crossed the Indus; but it is possible that his supremacy was acknowledged by the monarchs of Hindostán, for Sir Edward Sullivan mentions it as a fact that, when Bahrámgor, Jing of Persia, came to India in disguise, in 330 A.D., to study the wise laws and regulations of the country, "he was discovered by the extraordinary feat of shooting an elephant dead with an arrow in the head, and he was received with great homage by Básdeo, king of Kanauj."

CHAPTER IX.

INVASION OF THE PANJÁB BY ALEXANDER THE GREAT, KING OF MACEDON.

It fell to the lot of Alexander to attain such world-wide renown as no other king has enjoyed, from the remotest antiquity to the present day. His fame as a conqueror has spread alike over the continents of Europe and Asia, and his name is familiar to every tyro in history and every schoolboy. He was the son of Philip of Macedon and Olymphias, the daughter of Neoptolemus, of Epirus, and was born at Pella in 356 B. C. An account of his short but eventful life was written by two of his companions, but both these accounts were lost. They were, however, well known in Macedon and the countries adjoining and had been read by learned people. Among those who had studied these original works were Arrian and Quintus Curtius, and it is to them that the world is indebted for complete histories of the life of this remarkable man, written in the fifth century after his death. To the graphic descriptions of these elegant scholars we also owe our knowledge of the condition of India twenty-one centuries ago. It is rather startling to find that upwards of 300 years before the Christian era, when Western Europe

Birth of Alexander, 356 B.C.

had not as yet emerged from a state of barbarism, Alexander met on the banks of the Indus tribes who had made great progress in the arts and sciences.

His education.

The education of Alexander was first confided to a maternal relation, Leonidas, then to Lysimachus, and, finally, to Aristotle, of whom it is justly said that the master was worthy of the pupil and the pupil worthy of the master. Withdrawing him to a distance from the court, this great philosopher instructed his pupil in every branch of learning, especially in the arts of government and war. He inspired his mind with military ardour and invigorated his body by athletic sports. At an early age Alexander greatly distinguished himself in war against the Thebans. His father, Philip, embracing him after the victory, said: "My son, seek for thyself another kingdom, for that which I have is too small for thee." A quarrel took place between the father and the son, when the former repudiated Olympias. Alexander took his mother's side and fled to Epirus, to save himself from his father's vengeance, but was soon after restored to favour and accompanied Philip in his expedition against the Trihalli, when he saved his father's life in the battle-field. On the assassination of Philip, Alexander ascended the throne, in 336 B.C., at the early age of twenty. With the exception of the Jews, all the nations of the world were at that time idolaters. The empire of Persia, founded by the great Cyrus, comprised the whole of Asia then known, besides Egypt, and was governed by Darius, called, before his accession, Codomannus, the great-grandson of Darius II, commonly called Nothos. It was divided into one hundred and twenty provinces ruled by satraps, and the limits of the empire included the portion of the Panjáb lying on both sides of the Indus, though the country had never been thoroughly subjugated. The people of Persia professed the religion of Zoroaster. The small but powerful country of Greece was divided into several States which were constantly at war with each other. Soon after his accession to the throne, Alexander conquered Thrace and reduced Thebes, which, in consequence of its refusal to surrender, he razed to the ground, putting six thousand of the inhabitants to the sword and carrying away thirty thousand men as slaves. In his celebrated march across the Hellespont, he defeated an army of 110,000 Persians, on the banks of the Granicus, with an army of less than half that number, killing with his own lance the son-in-low of Darius. He conquered city after city in Asia Minor, and inflicted a great defeat on the Persians at Issus, in which all the treasures, as also the family of Darius, fell into the conqueror's hands, by whom they were treated with great tenderness. Darius twice made overtures for peace, offering all Asia up to the Euphrates to the conqueror, but Alexander refused to accede to his terms, saying: "Darius must recognise me as the ruler of Asia and the lord of all his subjects." Upon this Parmenio, one of Alexander's generals, referring to the advisability of accepting the Persian offer, exclaimed: "I would do it if I were Alexander." "So would I," replied the king, "if I were Parmenio."

Quarrel between him and his father.

Alexander ascends the throne of Macedon, 336 B.C.

The Persian empire.

Panjáb a part of that empire.

Alexander's celebrated march across the Hellespont.

Defeat of the Persians at Issus.

He now turned his arms against Syria and Phœnicia, occupied the great city of Damascus, and conquered all the cities on the shore of the Mediterranean. Tyre, the western emporium of commerce, resisted his arms, but was reduced and destroyed after a seven months' siege. By the monopoly of the trade of this city Alexander became the arbiter of the destinies of the world. He then marched to Jerusalem and received the submission of Palestine, after which he delivered Egypt from the Persian thraldom, restored its old institutions, and founded, on the coast of the Mediterranean, the city of Alexandria, which he used as a grand depôt for arms. Marching then to the Libyan desert, he visited the temple of Jupiter Ammon, and was saluted by

Conquest of Tyre.

Submission of Palestine.

the high priests as a son of Jove. Turning then northwards, he entered Messopotamia, the seat of the earliest kingdoms, and crossing the Tigris, entered Assyria, on the return of spring. On the plains of Arbela, washed by the Tigris on the west, and about sixty miles east of the ruins of the celebrated Nineveh, a great battle was fought between Alexander and Darius, in which the latter was defeated and his army dispersed with great slaughter. Alexander was anxious to see his enemy alive, but the latter had been pierced by the javelins of the invaders and died of his wounds, before his wish could be fulfilled, in the fiftieth year of his age. The victor mourned over his unfortunate rival and sent his body to Persia, there to be interred in the mausoleum of his royal predecessors. He pursued Bessus, the powerful satrap of Bactriana, who aspired to the throne of Persia, but the rebel was surrendered to him by Spitamenes, the satrap of Sogdiana (Bokhara). According to Curtius, Bessus was led, stark-naked, with a chain encircling his head, into the presence of the Macedonian sovereign, as a savage unworthy to wear the garb of a man. Alexander had his nose and ears cut off, and he was subsequently put to death with arrows.

Persepolis put on fire.

In a fit of drunkenness, and at the instigatien of Thais, an Athenian courtezan, Alexander set fire to the far-famed Persepolis, the capital of Persia and the wonder of the world, and reduced that magnificent city to a heap of ashes. He then overthrew the Scythians and conquered Sogdiana (Bokhara), where he married the beautiful Roxana, the daughter of Oxyartes, brother of Darius, said to have been the handsomest of the virgins of Asia. He conquered Susa, where he found extensive treasures, entered Hyrcania, the modern Mazindran, marched through Khorasán and, invading Bactria, conquered the kingdom of Marcanda, the modern Samarkand. Wherever Alexander went, he subdued nations, built strong forts and founded new cities, though the sites of many of them cannot without much difficulty be now traced.

Conquest of Asiatic countries.

Having then conquered Drangiana, Archosia, Gedrosia and Seistan and reduced the western part of Kábul lying between Ghazni and Kandahár, Alexander crossed the Hindu Kush, in ten days, by the same route which he had pursued in following Bessus, the rebel satrap. He had previously collected his information concerning India at Bactria, from the Indian fugitives in that country, who told him what prospects of success India presented to an invader. He was thus fully informed of the magnificence of the country and of its riches in gold, gems and pearls. Even the shields of Indian soldiers, so the Macedonian monarch was told, glittered with gold and ivory. He grounded his claim to the Empire of India on the right of the ancient monarchs of Persia, whose dynasty he had subverted. It is highly interesting to trace the events which happened in the Panjáb and on its north-western border more than two thousand years ago. The names of the places visited by the armies of Alexander, in his great expedition to India, have changed since that time; but eminent scholars and travellers like Burnes, Wood, Morier, Smith,* Abbot, Archdeacon Williams, General Cunningham, Rennel, D'Anville, Wilson and others, have taken much pains to identify them with modern names. The peculiar character of the country visited and the general faithfulness of the accounts given by the Greek writers leave little doubt as to their identity, notwithstanding the length of time that has elapsed since these memorable events took place.

His information respecting India.

Tribes on the north-west border of the Panjáb.

The tribes on the border of the Panjáb and in the neighbourhood of Kábul were as wild and rude then as they now are, and Alexander had to

* See Smith's *Dictionary of Greek and Roman Geography.*

encounter and reduce them before entering the luxuriant plains of the Panjáb. Having advanced to the Cophenes (or the Kábul river), he sent his generals Hephaestion and Perdiccas, at the head of considerable detachments, to make a survey of the surrounding country and prepare a bridge of boats on the Indus for the transport of his army. Having then taken a north-easterly direction, with a band of archers and half his army, he crossed the Choes and marched against the Aspii, or Apasii, a considerable tribe inhabiting the southern foot of Paropamisidæ, the modern Hindu Kush mountains. The mountaineers offered a vigorous resistance, and Ptolemy was sent to encounter them at the head of a large force. The brave people, despairing of defending their capital, abandoned it, after first setting it on fire, and retired to the high mountains. The Grecian general attempted to expel them from this position, but the mountaineers advanced to meet the invaders, and the fight which ensued between the two armies was most sanguinary. Ptolemy struck the chief of the tribe with his spear, but it failed to penetrate the solid breastplate and armour worn by him. The brave Grecian general then hurled another spear at his enemy with such force that he was killed on the spot. The fight now became thickest around the body of the slain chief, to which the hardy mountaineers flocked with great fervour, and it was not until Alexander had himself opportunely arrived, with a large reinforcement, that the enemy was repulsed. According to Arrian, forty thousand men were killed in this battle on the side of the vanquished.

Fight with the Aspii.

Alexander then marched through the territory of the Guraaei, the modern Ghazní, and the people, terrified at the fate of the Aspii, tendered their submission to the invader.

Conquest of Ghazni.

The next people subdued on the west of the Indus were the Assaceni, whose capital was Magassa, a strongly fortified town washed, towards the east, by a rapid river, and strengthened, on the west and south, by rocks of stupendous height. The king of this tribe having recently died, the queen-mother governed the country on behalf of her infant son. Alexander blockaded the town in force, and while reconnoitring the fortifications, he was wounded in the leg by an arrow fired from the rampart, which tortured the brave king to such a degree that he could not avoid exclaiming: "While I am hailed as a deity and the son of Juptier, the agony of this wound too plainly demonstrates to me that I am still but a mortal." Alexander advanced his battering engines, from the tops of which his Macedonians discharged showers of arrows on the besieged. The fight continued with great severity for three days. On the fourth day the besieged surrendered on honourable conditions. The queen came out from the gates, at the head of her female attendants, carrying golden goblets full of wine, which were offered as an oblation to Alexander, as to a deity. Curtius admires the beauty of the queen and declares that she presented Alexander with her infant son.

Subjugation of the Assaceni.

After reducing the Assaceni, Alexander marched to Ora and Bazira, identified as the modern Bajour. The former was ruled by Abissarus, a powerful Indian prince, who having opposed the progress of the invader. with his warlike countrymen, the Macedonians scaled the walls of this hitherto impregnable fortress with great skill, and took it by storm. Bajour was then conquered, but not without severe loss on the side of the Indians.

Conquest of Bajour.

The next place of importance reduced was the castle of Aornus, on the right bank of the Indus, identified by Major Abbot as the Máhabád (or mighty rock) of the Hindus. It is supposed to be near the town of Amb, in the Eusufzai country. The place was captured after an obstinate fight,

Capture of the castle of Aornus.

and the rock resounded with the acclamations of the victors. Alexander on taking possession of this celebrated rock, offered magnificent sacrifices and erected on it altars to Minerva and Victory.

Reduction of Pakhli.

Turning then to the north-east, Alexander marched to Pucela, or Peucelaotis, the capital of the district now known as Pakhli. His generals, before his arrival, had been occupied for thirty days, in endeavouring to reduce the place but, on the approach of the king, the Indians submitted and hastened to pay homage to the conqueror, who restored the territory to them.

The ancient city of Nysa.

Being anxious to glean some knowledge of the customs of the Indian tribes, Alexander despatched Nearchus and Antiochus, at the head of large detachments of troops, to collect information about the country and to seize some of the natives to help the Greeks in their march into the interior. Troops were, in the meanwhile, sent in the direction of the Indus, to level a road for the passage of the army. After these preparations, Alexander entered that part of the country of the Assaceni, in the Western Panjáb, beyond the Indus, where the ancient city of Nysa, known in Sanskrit as Naishádá, sacred to Dionysius, or Bacchus, was situated. As soon as the Nysians were apprised of his arrival, they sent a deputation consisting of their chief, named Akonphus, and thirty elders, to solicit his protection. The deputies expressed their earnest belief that the king would extend his protection to them, out of respect to the memory of Dionysius, who had founded that city, as a monument of his victories and as an asylum for those veterans in his army, who were prevented by age or infirmity from returning to their home and had settled there. The surrounding country was called Nysa, and the town Nysa was founded after the name of the conqueror's nurse. The delegates further informed Alexander that to the neighbouring mountain Dionysius had given the name of Meros, from the circumstance of his having been fabulously born from the thigh of Jupiter. Alexander, pleased with the address of the deputies, acceded to their request and confirmed to them their liberties, provided they furnished him with a contingent of three hundred horsemen and furnished a hundred of their best citizens as hostages. At the last demand Akonphus smiled, and Alexander enquiring of him the reason, he replied: "We could have well afforded to part with that number, nay double that number, of *bad* men in Nysa, but how can any city be governed which is deprived of one hundred of its best citizens?" The answer pleased the king, and the condition regarding the furnishing of hostages was dispensed with.

Alexander waited upon by a deputation of elders.

The liberty of the Crysians restored.

Submission of Taxiles, the Indian king

The country between the Indus and the Hydaspes (Jhelum) was governed by a powerful Indian prince named Taxiles, of that ancient Turanian race which, at that time, inhabited the Ráwalpindi District. On reaching the Cophenus (the Kábul river), Alexander despatched a herald to Taxiles and other Indian princes west of the Indus, calling on them to meet him on their respective frontiers, as he approached their territories, and tender their submission to him. In obedience to this command, Taxiles, having crossed the Indus, paid homage to Alexander, presenting him with two hundred talents of silver, three thousand oxen, above ten thousand sheep and thirty elephants, and supplying him with a reinforcement of seven hundred Indian troops. He also made himself personally serviceable to him in the prosecution of his future plans regarding India. Plutarch has given an interesting account of the first meeting between the two kings, and the following is the substance of the dialogue which ensued. "What occasion is there," asked the Indian king of his contemporary from the far west, "for war between you and me, if you are not come to take from us our bread and other necessaries of life, the only things that reasonable men will take up arms for? As to

Dialogue between Alexander and the Indian king.

gold and silver and other possessions, if I am richer than you, I am willing to oblige you with a part of what I have; if I am poorer, I have no objection to share in your bounty." Charmed with the frankness, no less than with the address, of the Indian king, Alexander answered: "Think you, then, with all this civility, to escape without a conflict? You are much deceived, if you do. I will dispute it with you to the last, but it shall be in favours and benefits, for I will not have you exceed me in generosity." Alexander kept his word faithfully. He made more valuable presents to his Indian ally than those he received from him and showered royal favours on him, adding new territories to his dominions, which tended substantially to increase his strength. Alexander was, on his march to the Indus, accompanied by Taxiles and other princes of the country, who carried out all the orders given them with the utmost promptitude. Astes, King of Pencealotis, who resisted, was seized and slain, the whole of his country having been conquered after a severe struggle, which lasted a full month. On reaching the Indus, Alexander came to a thick wood which grew on its banks. A large quantity of timber was cut, and with it two large vessels with thirty oars were constructed, besides many rafts to carry the supplies. A halt was made here for thirty days, which were spent in recreation, in sacrifices to the gods and in gymnastic exercises. A bridge of boats had already been constructed by Hephaestion and Perdiccas, who had been previously sent with that object, and sacrifices having been again offered up, the passage of the army was effected, without loss or opposition, in May 327 B.C. The whole army under Alexander at this time numbered 135,000 men, including 15,000 cavalry, levies from the hills west of the Indus, under Ambisaras, their Chief, and 5,000 Indian auxiliaries, under Mophis of Taxila. The Macedonian army crossed the Indus at Attock, where the politic Akbar, in after ages, founded the fort of that name, commanding the passage of the river. The troops having reached the opposite bank in safety, Alexander's first care, according to his custom, was to offer sacrifices to the gods of Victory and War, after which the usual athletic games were held.

Defeat and death of the king of Pencealotis.

The Macedonian army crosses the Indus at Attock, 327 B.C.

Sacrifices to the gods.

At the period of Alexander's invasion the country east of the Indus was ruled by three sovereigns of the Hindu race. The kingdom of Taxiles as before observed, lay between the Indus and the Hydaspes (Jhelum), that of Porus, denominated Panrava in the Sanskrit, and Fur in the Persian of the Sikandar Namah, extended from the last-named river to the Acesines (Chináb). The dominions of Abisares lay among the mountains. All these rájás were subordinate to the supreme máhárájá of Magadha, whose kingdom lay on the south bank of the Ganges. The name of this máhárájá was Chandra Gupta, called by the Greeks Sandracottus, who had been raised to the throne of Magadha by Chancaya, a passionate and vindictive Brahmin, after the murder of the celebrated Rájá Nanda, the last king of the renowned dynasty of the rájás of Bihár, who had, for a long series of years, ruled the kingdom of Magadha.

The three principal monarchies of the Panjab at the time of Alexander's invasion.

Proceeding on his journey, Alexander arrived at Taxila, the capital of Taxiles, described as a wealthy and most populous city, between the Indus and the Jhelum. Taxiles and his subjects accorded the most cordial reception to the Macedonian king, and, in grateful acknowledgment of this treatment, the king assigned to him a great part of the adjoining country. The Greeks describe the country as being more fertile than Egypt. As to the identity of Taxila, various suggestions have been made. Wilson identifies it with the Takhsasila of the Hindus; Smith considers that it is represented by the vast ruins of Mankyala; General Cunningham, with more precision, identifies it with the ruins of Deri Sháhán. Taki (the modern Asrúr), between

Taxila the capital of Taxiles.

Taxila identified with Deri Sháhán.

Láhore and Pindi Bhattian, was the capital of the Panjáb in 633 A.D. At Taxila, Alexander was met by the ambassadors of neighbouring kingdoms, among whom were the delegates from Abisares, the sovereign of the northern hills, inhabited by a powerful and warlike mountain tribe, called by the modern Indians the Ghakkars, and Doxareus, who ruled one of the districts in the plains. The Macedonian king received their submission favourably, and, in return for the presents made by them, loaded them with princely gifts.

Porus refuses to yield.

Porus, however, who had vast military resources at his command, and who, on this account, was feared on every side, refused to yield tamely to the foreign invader, and resolved at any cost to himself to maintain the independence of his country and the nation. In answer to the herald sent to demand tribute and a meeting, on the border of his dominions, as a proof of his submission to the Macedonian conqueror, the king, so says Curtius, replied that he would certainly meet Alexander on his frontier, though not as a vassal, but in arms, which alone could decide the fate of empires.

Having placed a Macedonian garrison at Taxila, and appointed Philip to be the governor of the province, Alexander moved towards the eastern bank of the Jhelum, where he was informed that Porus was encamped with his army, to dispute the passage of the stream. The army which Porus had brought into the field at this time numbered, according to Strabo, thirty thousand efficient foot, seven thousand horse, three hundred armed chariots and two hundred war elephants. These huge animals, like lofty towers, were ranged along the opposite bank in an imposing array. Plutarch, the historian of Alexander, has given a lucid account

Alexander wages war on him.

of this memorable battle, from Alexander's own letters. The Grecian army advanced along the main road leading from Attock to Jalálpúr. The rainy season was then at its height, and the floods were augmented by the melting of the snows by the summer heat on the hills. Alexander, finding the river much swollen by the floods and rain, caused the vessels on the Indus to be taken to pieces, and transported them to Jhelum overland. In the meanwhile he amused Porus by constantly manœuvering his army so as to make it appear that he had neither the intention nor the means of readily crossing the river, the fords of which were moreover carefully guarded

The military tactics of Alexander.

by the enemy, a report being also sedulously circulated that the enterprise had been abandoned till the rainy season was over. Deceived by these stratagems, Porus relaxed his precautions and Alexander, taking advantage of a dark, tempestuous night, crossed the river at a point, fourteen miles west of the modern battle-field of Chíliánwálá, and about thirty miles south-west of the town of Jhelum.* As soon as Porus was informed of this movement, he despatched his son, at the head of a force, to check the invader's passage, but, before the young prince could arrive at the selected spot, Alexander had safely landed all his troops on the eastern shore. He now at once charged the Indians vigorously with his cavalry and defeated them, their

The son of Porus slain in the battle-field.

leader, the son of the king, being, slain and four hundred of their troops falling with him in the action. The death of his brave son had a painful effect on Porus, who was marching in person to encounter the invading army of the

Sanguinary battle.

Greeks. The engagement is described as having been a most severe one, and the defeat of the Indians as most complete. According to Arrian, twenty thousand of their infantry and three thousand of their cavalry

Defeat of Porus.

were killed. All their chariots were lost and the elephants either killed or incapacitated by wounds, while Porus was himself wounded in the battle. He is described as most majestic in person, being 7ft. 6 in.

---

* Hunter's *Indian Empire*, Ed., 1886, p. 164.

in height, yet well proportioned and of pleasing demeanour. Alexander sent Meroe, his bosom friend, to conduct the vanquished king to his tent with all the honour due to his rank. As the Indian king reached the royal pavilion, Alexander, accompanied by his high officers, advanced to meet him, and, as he drew nearer, he was deeply impressed with the grandeur and nobility of his form, as well as with his kingly bearing. His wonted loftiness of spirit had not forsaken him even in the midst of the utter wreck of his power which he had just sustained from the Macedonian arms. Alexander asked the fallen king what he would wish him to do for him. "To treat me," replied Porus, "like a king." The Macedonian king, smiling, rejoined: "That I would do for my own sake, but tell me what I may do for thee. "All my wishes," answered the Indian monarch, "are summed up in my first reply." The nobility of these answers so much pleased Alexander that he numbered Porus among his intimate friends, and he not only replaced him on the throne of his ancestors, restoring to him all his dominions, but added extensive territories to his former kingdom.

Meeting between the two kings.

Alexander reinstates Porus.

The obsequies of the brave men who had fallen in the battle-field, on the side of the Greeks, were performed with great splendour, and the most costly sacrifices offered to the gods in honour of the important victory achieved. The event was also commemorated by the founding of two cities, one on the western bank of the Chináb, where the Grecian army had encamped, which Alexander called Bucephalus, after his favourite charger, which had died there of old age, after being his faithful companion in all his battles, from his youth up, and the other on the battle-field, east of the river, which he called Nicæa (Victory). The ruins of Bucephalus have been traced near the modern town of Jalálpúr and the town of Nicæa has been identified with the modern Mong, east of the Chináb.*

Obsequies of the fallen soldiers on the side of the Greeks.

Cities founded by Alexander in honour of the victory.

Having spent a short time in resting his army, and having appointed Craterus to superintend the building of the new cities alluded to above, Alexander made a survey of the whole country between the Jhelum and the Chináb, called, in after times, the Chenut Doab. It is described by the Grecian writers as a flat but beautiful country, densely populated and very rich. It contained, according to Arrian, thirty-seven cities, the smallest of which had not less than five thousand inhabitants, and a large number of villages. The same authority mentions that a third city was built by Alexander, on the bank of the Acesines (Chináb), which the conqueror crossed by means of boats and inflated hides. The country between that river and the Hydraotes (Rávi) was ruled by a king, whose name also happened to be Porus, and who was constantly at war with his rival of the same name, who ruled the country west of the Acesines. This second Porus, terrified at the approach of Alexander, fled beyond the Hydraotes, and the whole of his country was seized by the conqueror, and made over to his rival.

Country between the Jhelum and the Chináb.

Porus the Second.

His flight on the invader's approach.

The passage of the Hydraotes was effected without difficulty. According to Major Rennel, whose opinion is confirmed by other authorities, Alexander crossed the Hydraotes "near the place where the city of Láhore now stands." The country on the left bank of the river was inhabited by a powerful and martial tribe called the Cathaei,† or the modern Cathiá, whose capital, Sanghálá, is mentioned as being a strong city, well fortified by nature and art. Rennel

Alexander crosses the Rávi at a point near Láhore.

Sanghálá, the capital of Cathaei.

* Alexander built another city in the Panjáb in memory of his favourite pet dog Peritas, but the site is not known.

† Some scholars maintain that they were the Khatris, a branch of the Kshatrya, or warrior caste. Compare Rennel's *Memoirs* with the work of Mr. R. N. Cust, called *The Pictures of Indian Life*, published in 1881.

places Sanghálá in a direction south-west of Láhore, at a distance of three days' march. Burnes found the remains of a city answering to Sanghálá in the vicinity to the south-east of the modern capital of the Panjáb. Mr. Cust, in his *Notes on Indian Life* says: "The site of this town is not known, but it must have been somewhere in the Bári Doáb;" while Wilford identifies it with Kálánaur, in the Gúrdáspúr District, and Masson with Haripa. The exact site, however, is not clearly known. "Yet there can be no doubt," observes Mr. Thornton, in his interesting little work on the antiquities of Láhore, "that Alexander crossed the Rávi in the vicinity of Láhore and must, in all probability, have passed the site of the modern city."

Position of Sanghala.

Coalition formed against Alexander by the Panjáb tribes.

A coalition was now formed against Alexander by the Cathians, the Malli, or people of Múltán (the Mallisthán of the Hindus), and the Oxydracae (identified with the people of modern Úch), so called by the Greeks from their *sharp sightedness.* All these three nations were most valiant and skilful in war, and the reputation they enjoyed for bravery only induced Alexander to apply himself the more resolutely to the task of reducing them. The city of Sanghálá is thus described by Arrian. "It was situated on an eminence, though not a very lofty one. An extensive lake washed it on one side, while the other sides were defended by high walls flanked with strong bastions." Alexander lost no time in investing the city with his own troops. He posted large bodies of cavalry on the border of the lake. His battering rams shook the walls to their foundations and the Greeks took the town by storm. The weapons employed by the Indians on this occasion were bows and arrows and hand missiles, which had very little effect on their well-disciplined foes well clothed in armour. The consequence, according to Arrian, was that seventeen thousand Indians fell in this battle, while seventy thousand of their number were taken prisoners. A vast booty fell into the hands of the victors, including three hundred chariots and five hundred horses. The city of Sanghálá was razed to the ground and the conquered territory made over to Porus, the elder, who was present in the action with a levy of five thousand troops. Two other cities, adjoining Sanghálá, were deserted by their inhabitants, and five thousand people who had been left behind were butchered by the Macedonians in cold blood. The entire country between the Hydraotes (Rávi) and the Hyphasis (Biás) was reduced. According to Curtius, the country adjoining the river last mentioned was inhabited by a people remarkable for the superior beauty of their person. The writer also praises them for the wisdom of their legislative code and for the excellence of their morals. They were ruled by a king named Sophites, who, on the approach of Alexander, threw open the gates of his chief city and went out to meet the invader, accompanied by two beautiful youths, his own sons, and a long procession of nobles. On seeing the conqueror, the Indian king laid at his feet the royal insignia, studded with glittering diamonds. The king was dressed in a long garment with embroidery of gold on a purple ground, which descended to his feet. His sandals were made of rich gold brocade studded with pearls and rubies. His ears glittered with two pendent gems of uncommon size and of the purest water. Alexander received him with every mark of honour and girded on him his sceptre with his own hand. Having rested his army at the capital of this prince, Alexander pursued his march to the Hyphasis (Biás). A king, named Phegeus by Diodorus, governed the country bordering on the western bank of this river, and he met the conqueror with magnificent presents. The soul of Alexander was fired at the intelligence which was brought to him daily of the

The capture of Sanghálá.

The country between the Biás and the Rávi.

Its king.

He submits to the Macedonian king.

Alexander's march to the Hyphasis.

dazzling wealth and great fertility of the regions of the Ganges, of kingdoms overflowing with riches and of treasures accumulated for ages, and his desire was to plant the triumphant flag of Macedon on the extreme eastern limit of Asia, where it was bounded by the ocean. He had now reached the Hyphasis (Biás) at a point conjectured to have been below its confluence with the Sutlej. The historians of Alexander make no mention of the Sutlej, though they allude to a desert beyond the Hyphasis which existed below the junction of the two rivers. Here his soldiers were told that the the kings of the Gangarides and Parasians had formed a confederacy to check the progress of the Macedonians with an army of eighty thousand cavalry, two hundred thousand infantry, two thousand armed chariots and three thousand war elephants. They heard of the warlike resources and power of Palibothra, the Indian Babylon, of the might of the royal lunar race that adorned the throne of Magadha, and of the military strength of the Hindu towns of Indraprastha, Hastinapúr and Mathúra. Above all, they were told that, after they had crossed the Hyphasis (Biás,) their direct line of march would lie through a dreary desert of eleven days' journey, at the end of which they would reach the Ganges, described as a very broad, deep and rapid river. These appalling accounts filled the Grecian soldiers with consternation, and they refused to march further, on the plea of fatigue and exhaustion, caused by the hardships they had undergone in the late wars, carried on in countries so difficult of access and so remote from their beloved home. The ambition of Alexander, moreover, was boundless, and there was no knowing where he might lead them.

The Grecian soldiers dismayed at the appalling accounts heard by them of the regions of the Ganges.

Their refusal to march further.

In vain did Alexander appeal to the valour and zeal of the Macedonian soldiers. In vain did he seek to win the sympathy of his veteran officers for his projects. In vain did he remind them of their past glorious career, and of the great victories they had gained on the plains of Arbela and in Bactria, Sogdiana and other places, auguring future triumphs still more glorious. He urged upon them further that retreat would be untimely and disgraceful, and that, having advanced thus far towards their goal, they should not relinquish the dazzling prize. All his eloquence had no effect on the toil-worn soldiery, whose desire to revisit their native country was insuperable, and retiring to his tent in disgust, he shut himself up for three days in sullen solitude, refusing to see even those who had the privilege of his intimate friendship: but when, on his again appearing in public, he found the soldiers as obstinate as before, the conqueror of the world, fearing that the disaffection might result in open sedition, at length yielded a reluctant assent to the wishes of his army.

Alexander exhorts them to continue their march.

The soldiers insist on a retreat.

Alexander yields a reluctant assent.

Before, however, commencing his retrogade march, Alexander raised twelve magnificent altars of hewn stone, fifty cubits in height, on the eastern bank of the Hyphasis (Biás) below its confluence with the Hesudrus (Sutlej) as an enduring monument of his labours and victories, and upon them sacrifices to the gods were offered, with due solemnity, followed by the customary festivities and equestrian games. According to Arrian, these altars were equal in height to fortified towers, but far exceeded them in bulk. Plutarch, in his *Vita Alexandris*, informs us that these colossal altars remained standing in his time, and that "the Indians from beyond the Ganges used to come and sacrifice upon them." Mr. Prinsep, writing on the expedition of Alexander, in the *Journal of the Asiatic Society of Bengal*, says: "Appollonius Tyaneus saw these altars, in the first century of the Christian era, when a king of Greek race, named Pharaotes, was reigning in the Panjáb." Burnes made a diligent search for their remains below the junction of the Biás and the Sutlej, but could find none.

The altars of Alexander.

Return of Alexander to the Bias and the Rávi.

Alexander recrossed the Hyphasis and the Hydraotes (Biás and Rávi) and came to the eastern bank of the Hydaspes (Jhelum), where a large flotilla had been prepared to transport his army down the Indus. Two thousand boats of various sizes had been built of timber found in the mountain forests and consisting of firs, pines, cedars and various other trees. As Alexander embarked on board his vessel, he offered sacrifices to the maritime deities, and, standing on the prow, poured from a golden cup a libation into the river invoking the deities of the stream. The army was divided into four divisions; the first, under Craterus, marched along the right bank; the second, comprising the major part of the forces under Hephaestion, on the left. Nearchus commanded the river fleet, as admiral, and Philip followed the rest of the forces. The restless spirit of Alexander and that insatiable desire for new conquests and knowledge which marked the whole of his career, impelled him repeatedly to disembark and to compel all who failed to make voluntary submission to submit to his rule. The most formidable of the tribes which refused to acknowledge his sovereign power were the Malli, or people of Múltán, the Mallisthán of the Hindus, inhabited by Brahmins, and the Oxydracae, or people of Úch, in the vicinity of Múltán. Having crossed the intervening desert, Alexander marched along the left bank of the Acesines and reached a small stream which separated him from the Malli. Several of their cities were taken, and the inhabitants put to the sword. On the southern bank of the Hydraotes, a considerable distance above its confluence with the Acesines, stood a town of the Malli, described as being "strongly fortified by nature and art." It was almost wholly inhabited by Brahmins. On passing the river, the Macedonians slew a vast number of the inhabitants and took many prisoners. The citadel, which was besieged, was bravely defended by the Brahmins, who repulsed the first attack made by the Greeks. Alexander led the storming party himself, and was the first to mount the scaling ladder. Animated by their leader's zeal and example, the Grecian soldiers climbed the wall one after another. The Brahmins, seeing their case hopeless, collected their wives and children, and, after their ancient custom, setting fire to their own houses, perished in the flames, while many thousands fled to the desert, or concealed themselves in the deep recesses of the forest, rather than submit to the rule of the stranger. The Malli were a free Indian nation and had enjoyed their independence from the time of the conquest of India by Bacchus. No nation in the Panjáb was naturally more averse to yielding to a foreign yoke than the Malli.

The retrograde movement of his army.

He makes a war on the Malli.

And lays siege to their citadel.

The storming of the capital.

Alexander now marched to the capital of the Malli, where the people of the surrounding country had taken refuge, and where, by one decisive stroke, he hoped to gain a complete victory over that numerous and valiant tribe. The army was formed into two divisions, the one led by Perdiccas and the other by Alexander himself. An impetuous assault was made on the walls of the city, headed by Alexander himself, and one of the gates was burst open. The Indians, despairing of defending the town, retired to the citadel, which they resolved to hold to the last. The citadel was now closely besieged, and the king gave orders that the walls should be at once scaled. These orders not having been put into execution as quickly as Alexander wished, he snatched a scaling ladder from one of the soldiers, applied it to the wall, and, covering himself with a shield, rapidly ascended. He was closely followed by three of his most distinguished officers. Having gained the summit, Alexander entered into a personal conflict with numbers of his adversaries. Being recognised by the brilliancy of

Alexander's reckless bravery.

his armour, the king formed a conspicuous mark for the archers who were stationed on the adjoining battlements. Some of his assailants he killed with his sword, others he hurled headlong down the ramparts. Some of his soldiers, seeing their king in danger, attempted to scale the wall with ladders; but such was the pressure upon them that they gave way in the confusion. In the meanwhile, the fierce and dauntless spirit of Alexander induced him to adopt a still more reckless measure. Observing that he could not long retain his dangerous situation on the battlement, he gallantly leaped into the fortress, followed by three of his officers, and stood fighting among the thickest of the foe, resolving to conquer, or die a hero's death. The commander of the Indian army rushed upon him sword in hand, but was run through the body by Alexander. Many others who renewed the attack shared the samo fate. Alexander and his companions, planting themselves against a wall, repelled every attack. His eyes glowed fiercely, and such was the awe which his majestic deportment and terrible features inspired, that at length none dared approach him. The brave Abreas, who, with dauntless spirit, was fighting by the side of his sovereign, was struck with an arrow through the temple and expired at the feet of his royal master. Another arrow, three feet in length, piercing Alexander's breastplate, entered his body and wounded him severely in the breast. A great deal of blood flowed from the wound, but Alexander retained his equanimity, and, despising death, continued fighting with undiminished ardour; but at length his strength failed him, and, a dizziness seizing him, he fell forward on his shield, and his two surviving companions covered his body with their shields. They, too, were both severely wounded, but they forgot their own misfortunes in the sufferings of their royal master. In the meantime, the excitement on the other side of the wall was great. All chance of scaling the walls by ladders having been destroyed, iron pins were driven into the walls which were made of brick, and the soldiers, mounting on one another's shoulders, gained the top. Great was their excitement on seeing their king lying wounded, and, with a terrible outcry, the devoted soldiers, rushing down from the walls, formed themselves into a rampart round his prostrate body; portions of the wall being soon dismantled, the bulk of the army forced their passage into the heart of the citadel. A tremendous carnage now ensued among the Malli, the infuriated soldiery sparing neither age nor sex. Alexander was borne to his tent on a shield, and the greatest anxiety was felt for him. The arrow, which had penetrated his chest, had caused a great effusion of blood. It was extracted from the body, with much skill, by Critodemus, a physician of Coos. A report of the king's death having, in the meanwhile, been spread, intense alarm prevailed in the camp and every face exhibited the utmost solicitude. To remove the apprehension of his soldiers, Alexander appeared before them, and waved his right hand to salute his faithful followers. He then ordered his horse to be brought, and rode through the ranks, to the great joy of the whole army; and the neighbouring woods resounded with the acclamation: "Long live Alexander; health and prosperity to the conqueror of Asia!"

A startling feat.

Alexander wounded.

Intense excitement among the Grecian soldiers.

A tremendous carnage.

Both the Malli and Oxydracae, or people of Uch, sent heralds to Alexander with tenders of unconditional submission; Alexander accepted the submission of both, and appointed Philip satrap of his newly acquired dominions. The people of Uch sent him one thousand men, the bravest and noblest of their race, as hostages, besides five hundred war chariots, with their charioteers and horses, fully equipped. Alexander was much gratified by this mark of respect shown by the Oxydracae, and returned

Submission of the Malli and Oxydracae.

their hostages, keeping the chariots with their horses and drivers. While Alexander was under medical treatment, his army was employed in enlarging his fleet, by the construction of new ships, near the confluence of the Hydraotes (Rávi) and Acesines (Chináb). At Panjnad, in the southern extremity of the Panjáb, he built a city which he called Alexandria. It was furnished with docks and was intended to facilitate commerce and navigation, as well as to overawe the surrounding nations, but no vestige of it now remains. On resuming his voyage, Alexander received the submission of the Alastain, or Avasthanas, an independent Indian tribe, who had been conquered by his general Perdiccas, and he also subjugated the Ossadians. His fleet next sailed down to the capital of the Sogdi, the modern Bhakkar, whose king, Musicanus,* tendered his submission, presenting Alexander with a large train of elephants and presents of immense value. Alexander entered his capital, the beauty and magnificence of which he greatly admired. Musicanus was permitted to retain possession of his country, and a fortress was built in his chief city, under the superintendence of Craterus, to be garrisoned by Macedonian troops. It was the wish of Alexander to establish a chain of forts along the whole line of the Indus, for commercial and political purposes, and this scheme was put into execution by the construction of new military posts and towns along the banks of the Indus, and at the junctions of its tributary streams along the south-western line. Burnes identifies the ancient capital of Bhakkar with Alore, four miles distant from the modern town of Bhakkar.

Alexander's naval and commercial arrangements.

The king of Bhakkar tenders his submission to Alexander.

Military posts and towns established along the line of the Indus.

Alexander next proceeded on board his ship, accompanied by his entire navy, to the adjoining country of Oxycanus, who had failed to send ambassadors and presents to him when the Greek troops entered his territory. Two of his principal towns were carried by assault and plundered, the king himself being taken prisoner and put to death. He next marched against Sambus, the sovereign of Sindomana, identified with the modern province of Sindh. The king, terrified at the approach of the Greeks, fled to the neighbouring mountains, but the leading men of the town opened the gates to Alexander, and, by pacifying that monarch with magnificent presents, saved their city from plunder. About this time a coalition was formed by the Brahmins to expel the foreign invaders, who had violated their sacred soil by their encroachments; Musicanus, the king of the Sogdi, in spite of the favour with which he had been received, joining the confederacy. Alexander appointed Peithon to crush the insurgents, and the Greek general defeated the rebel tribes with great slaughter. Musicanus was himself brought in chains before Alexander, by whose order he was publicly crucified, together with a large number of priests and Brahmins who had been conspicuous in inciting the insurrection. The voyage having been resumed after these events, the fleet entered the delta, where the Indus divides into two great branches. The chief city of this place was called Patalla, and the territory was ruled by a prince of the name of Mocris, who, arriving in Alexander's camp, made him a voluntary offer of his treasures and kingdom. Alexander restored to him the sceptre, which he had presented as a mark of submission, and sent him back to his territory with honour. General Cunningham identifies Patalla with Hyderabad in Sindh. This place was strongly fortified, and a harbour was constructed with docks sufficient to accommodate a large fleet. Leaving his fleet with Nearchus, Alexander marched with his

Coalition formed by the Brahmins.

Their defeat and punishment.

Submission of the chief of Patalla.

---

* Mr. Thornton conjectures that the termination *canus*, in names like these, is probably the title of *Khan*, and that *Musicanus* may be *Musa Khan*. But we are told, by the Greek and native authors, that the Malli and the Sindomanni were governed by Brahmins. Musa Khan could never have been a Hindu name.

army to Persia and Susa, by way of Gedrosia (Mekrán), and Karmania (Kermán), in September, 326 B.C. It has been calculated that from the day he left Pella, the capital of Macedon, till his arrival in Babylon, the distance traversed by him exceeded nineteen thousand English miles, a wonderful feat indeed in those days. He had conquered the whole of the then known world. In every part of the world visited by his arms he founded magnificent cities, constructed large fleets and devised measures for the development of trade and commercial intercourse. He subdued the most powerful nations, and conquered the mightiest kingdoms and empires. He reduced to ashes the proudest cities, and levelled to the dust their loftiest towers, fortresses and palaces. He had no opponent left, and he was making preparations for still more extensive schemes, both of conquest and civilization, one of which was the complete subjugation of the whole peninsula of India, when he was cut off, still in the prime of life. He died in his palace at Babylon on the 13th of June of the year 323 B.C., in the 32nd year of his age, after a reign of twelve years and eight months, from a fever contracted by his indiscreetly bathing in the river after excessive indulgence in strong spirits and other pleasures of the table. His body was deposited in a golden coffin at Alexandria, and divine honours were paid to him in Egypt and other countries. He appointed no heir to his extensive dominions; but to the question put to him as to who should inherit them, he replied: "The most worthy." The death of this great conqueror, at so early an age, furnishes a memorable instance of the transitory nature of all that concerns human life and human greatness! Within a few years of his death, his wives, his child and his mother were all killed, and his vast empire divided among his generals, so that nothing remained of him but his name.

Alexander leaves India, 326 B.C.

His vast schemes of conquest and civilization.

His death, 323 B.C.

It will be observed from the above narrative that Alexander established no system of government in the Panjáb. The policy he adopted in that country was to make alliances with the native kings, subjugating by force of arms those who opposed him, and making over their territories to such as were friendly to him. He founded new cities and established military and naval posts in the Panjáb, along the course of the Indus. He left behind him detachments of troops at various places in the Panjáb and Sindh, which indicated a design on his part to return to the country at no distant date; but this design, as we have seen, was not destined to be carried into execution.

Policy adopted by him in the Panjáb.

CHAPTER X.

FROM THE DEATH OF ALEXANDER TO THE MAHOMEDAN INVASION.

On the partition of the empire, which followed Alexander's death, Seleucus Nicator, governor of Babylon, not only retraversed and reduced to subjection that country and Bactria, but subjugated the whole country beyond the Euphrates, and crossed the Indus, B.C. 305, to attack Sandracottas (Chandragupta), king of Magadha, or Bihár, who had already succeeded in expelling the Greek garrison from the Panjáb principalities and had compelled the inhabitants to acknowledge his supremacy. Immediately on the departure of Alexander from Indian soil, the Indians rose in revolt, and the Macedonian governor left by him in the country was slain, while

Seleucus Nicator.

The Indians rise in revolt against the Greeks.

his mixed force of Greeks and Indians were either put to the sword, or otherwise dispersed. The result of this proceeding was a massacre of the Indians by the Macedonian contingent, King Porus the First being put to death by the new governor sent by Alexander, notwithstanding that that monarch had given many practical tokens of friendship towards the Macedonians at the time of Alexander's invasion. The governor, however was himself despatched on the approach of Chandragupta, who had established a new power in India. This prince, a mere adventurer, had followed Alexander's camp, in the Panjáb, after his exile from the Gangetic valley, in the hope of securing his aid in recovering his lost provinces, and, after the departure of the conqueror, he not only managed to recover the Gangetic regions, but expelled the old Nanda dynasty and seized Páliputra, the modern Patna. Seleucus, after crossing the Indus, inflicted several defeats on Chandragupta; but, on a rebellion breaking out in Babylon, he was compelled to leave the Panjáb in order to protect his own territories. Previous to his departure he concluded a treaty of peace by which the Panjáb, with the valley of the Indus, as far as Peshâwar, was ceded to the Indian king, who, in return, presented the Greek general with five hundred elephants and a hundred war chariots. In order to cement an alliance with the Indian king, Seleucus gave his daughter in marriage to Chandragupta, and left Megasthenes, the learned Greek, who subsequently wrote his famous account of India, as his ambassador at the court of Magadha. Although, from this time, the power of the Greeks ceased to be dominant in the Panjáb, there is no doubt that commercial relations of some sort continued to be maintained between India and Syria, coins of Seleucus Nicator having been found in Balkh and Bokhara. In the year 206 B. C., the Panjáb, according to Greek and Roman historians, was invaded by Antiochus, the grandson of Seleucus Nicator, called by the Hindus Antiyako Yona Rájá*. At that time the Panjáb was ruled by Asoka, grandson of Chandragupta, a zealous Buddhist, whose edicts, engraved in stone, are found at Sháhbáz Garhi (in the Peshâwar District), the modern name of Súdána, a very ancient Buddhist city, so called from a Buddhist prince. His stone pillars and granite blocks, with inscriptions recorded thereon in the Pálí language, have been traced from Orissa and Kutch to a region beyond Kábul, and the world is indebted for the collection and translation of these inscriptions to the talents and labours of Mr. James Prinsep, the eminent Oriental scholar, to whom also is due the credit of having first discovered a key to the ancient Pálí characters. Antiochus concluded a treaty of peace with Asoka, and Greek influence was thus maintained in the Panjáb. Further proof of this fact is furnished by the discovery of Greek coins on the frontiers of the Panjáb and Afghanistán.

Chandragupta, 326 B. C.

Treaty between the Greeks and the Indian king.

Invasion of the Panjáb by Antiochus, 206 B. C.

The great inscription of Asoka

The great inscription of Asoka is on a large trap rock to the north-west of the present village of Shahbaz Garhi, and contains the names of five Greek princes, namely, Antiochus of Syria, Ptolemy Philadelphus of Egypt, Antigonus Gonatos of Macedon, Magas of Kyrene, and Alexander II of Epirus. The whole circuit of Sudana (Shahbaz Garhi), which General Cunningham has identified with the Polushá, or Fo-Sha, of the Chinese pilgrims, Fá-Hien and Huen-Thsang, and with the Bazari of Arrian, is four miles in extent, and the spot is to this day pointed out outside the eastern gate of the city, where Asoka gave his daughter and son as alms to a Brahmin, who sold them into slavery.

Invasion of the Panjáb by Eneradites, the great king of Bactria, 165 B. C.

Eneradites, the great king of Bactria, invaded the Panjáb in the year 165 B. C., reducing the country as far as Patálá, the modern Hyderabád, in Sindh, while he also sent an expedition to Kach and Gujrát. His

* Namely, Antiochus, king of Greece.

successors, Menander and Appollodotus, ruled the Panjáb from the year 126 B. C. to the year 110, B. C., coins of the former being found from Kábul to Mathúra, on the Jamna. The Græco-Bactrian kingdom was subverted in the year 127 B. C., but its offshoots continued to reign over the Panjáb, the valley of the Indus and Kábul, to the commencement of the first century B. C., as is proved by the discovery of coins of Greek mintage with Aryan inscriptions on the reverse.

The deductions drawn by Professors Lassen and Wilson from the inscriptions on the coins of Parthian princes found in the Panjáb, show clearly, I think, that the Panjáb was in the possession of those princes from 90 to 60 B. C. This is further evidenced by the fact recorded in history that, on the dismemberment of the vast empire of Eneradites the Great, which followed immediately on his death, India was invaded by Mithridates, a Parthian monarch, about 140 B. C.

Invasion of Mithridates, the Parthian king, 140 B.C.

About the year 110 B. C. the Scythic element was predominant in the Panjáb. According to Chinese historians, the You-ti (Getes or Jits), who occupied a vast tract of land between China and the Teen-shan, or the Celestial Mountains, having been driven out of that country after many bloody campaigns with the Huns, emigrated in great hordes to Afghánistan and to the borders of the Panjáb, and firmly established themselves in that part of the country. They wrested the kingdom of Taxila from the Manas in the year 105 B. C., and their kings, Ayes and Azilises, were in possession of the whole country of the five rivers, as has been proved by coins recently discovered.

Scythic element predominant in the Panjáb, 110 B.C.

The Scythian kings were expelled from the Panjáb by the great Indian sovereign, Vikramaditya, in the year 56 B. C., but on his death the country was overrun by fresh hordes of Scythians, who established in it a dynasty of kings bearing the name of Kadphises. These were, in their turn, subverted by a fresh swarm of Scythian invaders, to whom belonged the dynasty of the Kaneski kings. That these dynasties continued to rule the Panjáb up to the fifth century of the Christian era, is proved by the discovery of Kadphisic and Kaneski coins in the Panjáb, Bámian and Kábul; by the evidence furnished by the Chinese traveller, Fá-Hien, who crossed the five rivers of the Panjáb early in the fifth century; by the inscriptions on a temple near Kotah, in Rájputáná, dated 409 A. D., bearing a memorial of a Jit prince of Salpúra, and by the evidence collected in the *Annals of Rájputáná*. Colonel Tod, the author of these annals, observes with reference to the Jit princes, that "these Jit princes, of Salpúra, in the Panjáb, were the leaders of that very colony of the Yuti from the Jaxartes who, as recorded by De Guignes, crossed the Indus in the fifth century and possessed themselves of the Panjáb." Gold, silver and copper coins of Græco-Scythian type, all Kaneski and Kadphisic, mixed with coins of the Sassanian monarchs of the third and fourth centuries of the Christian era, were found in the ruins of Manakyálá,* half-way between Atak and Jhelum, in 1830, by Generals Ventura and Court, then in the service of Máhárájá Ranjít Singh.

Vikramaditya, the Indian sovereign, 56 B.C.

The Kadphisic and Kaneski dynasties of Scythian kings, 500 A.D.

The northern part of Eusufzai was known to be very rich in ancient remains, the principal groups of ruins being Shahbaz Garhi, Takhti Bai, Shahri Bahlol, Jamal Garhi, Kharkai, Swáldher and Ránigát, east of Mardán.

In the beginning of the fifth century A. D., the dynasty of Kadphises was subverted by the White Huns, or Ephthalites, who were subdued in 555 A. D. by the Turks.

The White Huns subverted by the Turks, 555 A.D.

* A large tope, eighty feet high and about 320 feet in circumference, supposed by some to be the capital of the country of Taxiles. Fifteen smaller topes exist in the same locality. Coins were found in all of these.

The Panjáb ruled by the kings of Káshmír, 613 A.D.

Portions of the Panjáb were also, from time to time, conquered by the kings of Káshmír, and when the Chinese pilgrim Huen-Thsang visited that country, in the year 613 A. D., he found the territory between the Indus and the Jhelum ruled over by a Káshmír king of the Nágá, or Karkota, dynasty.

The Indian embassy to the Roman emperor, 20-22 B.C.

In 20-22 B.C., according to Orosius, Porus, an Indian prince, sent an ambassador to the Emperor Augustus of Rome, to court his friendship. The Roman emperor received the embassy in Spain, and, a considerable time having been spent in fruitless negotiations, another embassy was sent by the Indian king to try and arrange affairs. These ambassadors, who had been reduced to three, the rest having died of fatigue at Antioch, were seen by Nicolas of Damascus, and were the bearers of a friendly letter, written on parchment, or vellum, in Greek. It is said that Porus ruled over six hundred kings, and was anxious to cement a friendship with Cæsar, to whom he would have been glad to render any service that might have been required of him. The ambassadors had a large retinue, and were the bearers of valuable presents from their king, being accompanied by a Brahmin, Zarmanochagos, who subsequently burnt himself on a pile at Athens, as Kalanos had done before him at Pasargadae, a great and ancient city of Persia, on the river Cyrus. The following inscription was engraved on a monument which was raised to his honour :—"Here lies Zarmanochagos, an Indian of Bargosa, who voluntarily terminated his life in conformity with the custom prevailing among his countrymen."

Greek influence in the Panjáb.

The fact that the credentials of the Indian sovereign were written on a skin indicates plainly how far Grecian influence had operated on Hindu prejudices. In the Panjáb, where the Greeks had settled in considerable numbers, their influence was great. The architecture of the country owed its first impulse to Grecian art, and the Buddhist monasteries abound with statues and figures chiselled after the fashion of the Greeks. These monuments of Buddho-Grecian art have been excavated from various parts of the Panjáb border, and now form a beautiful collection in the Láhore Museum.

PART II.—THE MAHOMEDAN PERIOD.

CHAPTER I.

EARLY MAHOMEDAN INVASIONS.

WHEN the deluge of barbarism had overspread the west; when the eastern nations of Asia, Syria and Egypt had lost all manly spirit and sunk under the weight of despotism, vice, cruelty and immorality in their worst form; when the Roman empire had lost all its real greatness and the empire of Persia its internal vigour and strength; in short, when the darkness of ignorance prevailed throughout the greater part of the known world, a new religion sprang up in the world which materially affected the political history of the nations. This was the religion of Islám, founded by Muhammad, an Arabian of the tribe of Kuresh, who announced to his countrymen a divine revelation which he was commanded to promulgate with the sword. He assumed the sacerdotal office in Medina and, seated on a rough and unadorned pulpit in a mosque, and with his back against a palm tree, he declaimed to his idolatrous countrymen against the worship of Al-Lata and Al-Uzzah, and received in a camp without the walls the ambassadors from Mecca, a respect never paid before to the Chusroes of Persia or the Cæsars of Constantinople. He called the latent passions and talents of the Arabs into activity and animated them with a new spirit. Armed with the Qurán and the sword, and supported by the enthusiastic ardour of his followers, he waged a war with the civil and religious institutions of the world, and, introducing new politics and new manners, changed the political and moral condition of things. By the force of his persuasive eloquence and extraordinary zeal and energy, this great Arabian reformer converted a race of wandering shepherds into the founders of mighty empires, and kindled new aspirations in more than one-fourth of the population of the globe. With a rapidity to which there is no parallel in the history of nations, the empire of the Saracens extended itself from the Straits of Gibraltar on the west to India on the east, and from the shores of the Atlantic to the borders of China, diffusing in the countries subdued their learning and arts. Within the short period of a century from the establishment of the Mahomedan era,* the warriors of Islám overran Egypt, Syria, Northern Africa and part of Spain on the west, and Persia and Central Asia on the east. Almansur, of the family of Abbas, the conqueror of Persia, made Bagdád the seat of his Government. Forty years later, Harún-ul-Rashíd, the Magnificent, made Bagdád the chief emporium of merchandise between East and West Asia, and extended his dominions from the Mediterranean to the frontiers of Hindostán.

Promulgation of Islam.

Its rapid success.

Muhammad propagated his religion by the sword. "The sword," said he, "is the key of Paradise and Hell. A drop of blood shed in the cause of God, a night spent in arms, is of more avail to the Faithful than two months of fasting and prayer. Whoever falls in battle is forgiven his sins; in the day of judgment his wounds shall be resplendent as vermilion and odoriferous

The holy crusades.

---

* The Muhammadan era commenced in 622 A.D., the date of the flight of Muhammad from Mecca to Medina, and any given year of it is designated *Hijri*, signifying 'of the Hijrat' (or Hijra), 'departure or flight.'

as musk; and the loss of his limbs shall be replaced with wings of angels and cherubim." He who perished in a holy war went straight to Heaven. In Paradise nymphs of fascinating beauty impatiently waited to greet his first approach. There the gallant martyrs lived for ever a life of happiness and bliss, free from all sorrows, and liable to no inconvenience from excess. They would possess thousands of beautiful slaves, and get houses furnished with splendid gardens, and with all the luxuries of life, to live in. Such liberal promises of future happiness, added to an immediate prospect of riches and wealth, were enough to kindle the frenzy of the desert population of Arabia. Their martial spirit was roused, and their sensual passions were inflamed. As early as 589 A.D., in the 31st year of the Hijra, the Mahomedans penetrated into the extensive province of Khorásán, comprising the greater part of the original dominions of the imperial family of Ghazni, under Abdulla, son of Amír, one of the generals of Caliph Usmán, and thirteen years later they conquered Kábul in the south of Persia. Caliph Umr founded Basra, from which place expeditions against Sindh and Bilúchistán were undertaken.

Expeditions against Sindh and Bilúchistán.

The immense and fertile territory of Mávar-un-Nahr, the Transoxiana of the ancients, though invaded by Abdulla, the son of the famous Zeiad, governor of Basra, in the time of the Caliph Moáviá, in the 53rd year, Hijri, was not completely conquered by the Mahomedans till the 83th year, Hijri, when the great cities of Bokhára and Samarkand were conquered by the Arab general Katiba. In the year 711 A.D., the Governor of the Hijaz despatched a considerable army, under his nephew Kásim, to obtain the restitution of an Arab vessel which had been detained at the mouth of the Indus by Rájá Dahú, the prince of the country. The Hindu rájá assembled a numerous force, but Kásim carried by storm a celebrated temple held in great sanctity by the Brahmins, where a large booty fell into the hands of the Mahomedan invaders. The Hindus were panic-stricken and fled, their rájá having perished in the field of battle. Elated with this triumph, the youthful Arab general advanced to the capital of Dahú, Brahminabád, which was gallantly defended by the Hindu queen. In an attack made by the Mahomedans, this lady, with her Rájput bodyguard, perished, and the whole country was at the mercy of the invaders. Kásim then marched to Múltán, which was carried by assault, and a few more victories of less importance completed the conquest of Sindh. The conqueror now turned his attention towards the consolidation of his dominions, and the conciliation of the people, when a circumstance happened which abruptly terminated his useful career. The rájá had two beautiful daughters, who, on the death of the monarch, were sent to Damascus by Kásim for the harem of his sovereign, the Caliph. On presentation before the Grand Seignior, one of the damsels burst into tears, declaring her unfitness for the high place that was about to be accorded to her in the royal seraglio, in consequence of her having been dishonoured by Kásim before she had left India. The anger of the king was roused, and a mandate was issued to sew the body of the conqueror of Sindh in a raw hide and send it to Damascus. When the body arrived, the Hindu princess acknowledged the innocence of Kásim, but rejoiced at having had the death of her father avenged. Both ladies were, on this, instantly beheaded by order of the Caliph, who vainly lamented the death of his brave and able general. By the death of Kásim the Mahomedan Government of Sindh sustained a blow which it was never afterwards in a position to retrieve. His successors ruled the country for about forty years, but the Rájpút tribes of Sumera, having expelled them, became masters of the land.

Kásim, the Arab general.

First conquest of Sindh and Multan.

Death of Kásim.

CHAPTER II.

GHAZNIVIDE DYNASTY:

ALAPTAGÍN.

During the successive dynasties of the Imperial families of Moávià and the sovereigns of the house of Abbasi, who succeeded to the Khalifát, the Arabian empire retained its full vigour, but after the death of the great Harun-ul-Rashid, its temporal power began to show signs of gradual decay. The satraps of different provinces threw off their allegiance and assumed the title of royalty, while the government of the Khalifát became confined to the province of Bagdád and its dependencies, and the authority of the Caliph was considered supreme only in matters of religion. The Tahirites, or successors of Tahir, who was the first to assume independence, established themselves in the great provinces of Khorásán and Transoxiana. They were, in 872 A. D., succeeded by the Sofarides, a dynasty of kings founded by Yakúb, a brazier of Sistan, who had obtained great celebrity by his military adventures. These were, in their turn, subverted, in 903 A. D., by the Samanís, the founder of which dynasty was one Ismail, who assumed the royal title in the 263rd year of the Hijra. He had a great reputation for justice and humanity, and reigned in Bokhara, Máwarul Nahr, Khorásán, and a great part of the Persian empire. The family of Samanía reigned in tranquillity for 120 years. The fifth prince, Abdul Malik, died at Bokhárá, leaving a minor son, Mansúr. Alaptagín, a Turki slave of the late king, who governed the vast province of Khorásán, declared for the uncle of the young prince; but Mansúr was raised to the throne by the opposite faction. Offended with Alaptagín, the young monarch ordered him to Bokhárá; but the governor marched with a considerable army from Nishápúr, the capital of Khorásán, to Ghizni, and after gaining several victories over the royal troops, assumed the insignia of sovereignty.

The power of the Khalifat on the wane.

The family of Sámánía.

Alaptagin, a Turki slave.

He assumes the insignia of royalty.

Alaptagín frequently employed his armies, under his general, Sabuktagín, for the reduction of the provinces of Múltán and Lamghán, and thousands of the inhabitants of those provinces were carried away as slaves to Ghizni. Jáipal, the rájá of Láhore, finding his troops unable to withstand the armies of the northern invaders, formed an alliance with the rájá of Bhatia,* but the confederate armies failed to prevent the assailants from carrying away great spoils from India each time they attacked the country.

His general, Sabuktagin.

Jaipal, rájá of Láhore.

Alaptagín reigned in peace for fifteen years, and on his death, in 976, was succeeded by his son Abu Ishác; but, the latter dying in less than two years, Sabuktagín, the general of Alaptagín and originally his slave, who had married his daughter, was, by the unanimous voice of the army, installed on the throne of Ghizni.

Death of Alaptagin, 796 A. D.

AMÍR NASIR-UD-DÍN SABUKTAGÍN.

According to Minhájús Siraj, Sabuktagín was a slave† of Turkish extraction. Nusar Hájí a merchant, having purchased him while a boy, brought him from Turkistan to Bokhárá, where he sold him to Alaptagín.

The descent of Sabuktagin.

* Bhatia has been identified with modern Bhatner. The State was, in the Hindú period, a tributary of the rájá of Láhore.

† Though a Turki slave, Sabuktagín claimed illustrious descent from the royal family of Yezdijerd, the last of the Persian kings, who, his army having been routed during the reign of Caliph Usman, was murdered at a water-mill, near the town of Merv. His family, who took up their abode in Turkistan, formed connections with the people, and became Turki.—*Farishta.*

Sabuktagín was educated and taught the use of arms with the other slaves of Alaptagín. He was, at first, a private horseman in the service of that prince, and, being of a vigorous and active disposition, used to hunt for him in the forest. At an early age he gave promise of future greatness, and his patron, appreciating his talents, entrusted him with the conduct of considerable military expeditions, and soon raised him to important posts in the army, till at length, on assuming sovereign authority at Ghazni, he conferred on his protegé the high title of *Amír-ul-omera* (chief of the nobles), *Vakíl-i-mutlak* (sole representative). Sabuktagín, on his accession to the throne, assumed the title of Nasír-ud-dín, or Conqueror of the Faith, and styled himself *Amír*, or noble. Having subdued and annexed Kandahar, and taken the fortress of Bust, the capital of Zabulistán, where he met the famous Abul Fath, whom he made his chief secretary, on account of his great learning and wisdom, he resolved upon a war with the idolaters of India, who as yet had known only the worship of Brahma and Budh. The Panjáb was at that time ruled by Jaipál, the son of Haspál, whose territory extended from the Indus to Laghmán on the one side, and from Káshmír to Múltán on the other. Having marched eastwards, with a considerable army in 977 A.D., he reduced certain forts, caused mosques to be built, and, with a large booty, returned to Ghazni.

His assumption of regal power.

He marches on the Panjáb frontier.

Jaipál, who at this time resided in the fort of Bhatinda, finding that the reiterated attacks of the Mahomedans seriously affected the peace of the country, levied a great army, and brought together numerous elephants, with the view of attacking them on their own ground. He crossed the Indus and marched to Laghmán, where he was met by Sabuktagín. In the skirmishes which ensued, Mahmúd, the son of Sabuktagín, though then but a boy, gave signal proofs of heroism and soldiership. A furious storm of hail and wind, which occurred during the night, spread terror and destruction around. The troops of the rájá of Láhore suffered heavily, and great numbers of his cattle perished. The rájá finding his army dispersed, the next morning made overtures for peace. Sabuktagín was disposed to accede to the Hindu rájá's request, but the influence of the youthful Mahmúd, who was an ambitious warrior, prevented him from accepting the terms offered. Upon this Jaipál sent other ambassadors to the king to explain to his majesty that the custom of the Rájput soldiers was, if driven to extremities, to "kill their wives and children, set fire to their houses and property, let loose their hair, and, rushing in despair among the enemy, drown themselves in the crimson torrent of revenge." Sabuktagín, unwilling to reduce the conquered rájá to despair, consented to make terms, the rájá agreeing to give up one million *dirams* and fifty elephants as the price of peace. The rájá being unable to pay the whole of this sum in camp, persons of trust were sent with him to Láhore to receive the balance, while hostages were left with Sabuktagín for their safety. Finding himself secure in his capital, however, the rájá, acting on the advice of his Brahmin counsellors, repudiated the agreement and threw the Mahomedan officers into prison. Sabuktagín, who had by this time reached Ghazni, was exasperated on hearing this, and at once set about retracing his steps to Laghmán at the head of a numerous army to avenge the insult offered to him by the Hindu rájá.

Conflict with Jaipál, rájá of Láhore.

The rájá sues for peace.

The terms of peace.

Jaipál prepared to meet the coming storm. He entered into an alliance with the neighbouring kings of Delhi, Ajmere, Kallinjer and Kanauj, and the confederate armies, which are represented as having consisted of 10,000 horse and a considerable number of infantry, the flower of Indian chivalry, arrayed themselves on the confines of Laghmán to hurl back the Mahomedan

Coalition among the Hindu rájás.

invaders. Sabuktagín, having ascended a neighbouring hill, beheld the vastness of the Indian host, which in extent is described as having resembled a boundless ocean. Encouraging his chiefs with the hope of glory, and appealing to their valour, he gave each his commands, and, dividing his soldiers, who were few in number, into squadrons of five hundred, directed them to make successive attacks on a weak point of the Hindu army. This manœuvre made it appear as if bodies of fresh troops were being constantly sent forward against the wearied cavalry of the Hindus, whose ranks were broken, causing confusion and consternation to spread among their forces. Taking advantage of this disorder, Sabuktagín ordered a general assault, and the Hindus, worsted at every point, fled and were pursued by the victorious Mahomedan troops to the banks of the Niláb. The victor levied heavy contributions on the countries west of the Indus, and, making Pesháwar and Laghmán the eastern boundary of his dominions, appointed one of his officers, with ten thousand horse, to the government of the conquered country, and retraced his steps to Ghazni.

Dexterous movements of Sabuktagín.

His victory.

He returns to Ghazni.

For the rest of his life, Sabuktagín was engaged in military exploits to the north-west of his dominions. He died at Tamruz, near Balkh, in August, 997 A.D., in the fifty-sixth year of his age and the twentieth of his reign, his remains being carried to Ghazni for interment.

His death, 997 A. D.

Sabuktagín was a prince who, in addition to uncommon bravery and prudence, was endowed with a sense of equity and moderation. His wazír was Abul Abas Fazil, a minister of great talent in the management of affairs of State. It is said of Sabuktagín that, when out hunting one day, he saw a deer grazing with her young fawn. Putting spurs to his horse, he pursued and seized the fawn and, laying it across his saddle with its legs bound, took his way homewards; but, happening to look back, he beheld the afflicted mother following him at full speed. The heart of Sabuktagín melted with pity and he set the young fawn at liberty, to the great joy of the mother, who often turned to gaze on him with tears in her eyes. He is said to have seen, that night, in a dream, the Prophet of God, who said to him: "The generosity and compassion which you have this day shown to a distressed animal have been appreciated by God, and the kingdom of Ghazni is marked as your reward; let not greatness undermine your virtue, but thus continue your benevolence towards mankind."

His character.

Anecdotes.

According to the author of *Madsir-ul-mulk*, Mahmúd, the son of Sabuktagín, having built a splendid house in his pleasure garden, invited his father to a magnificent entertainment. The taste, beauty and skill displayed in the structure of the royal edifice tempted the young prince to seek the opinion of his father regarding it. But Sabuktagín, to the great disappointment of his son, said that he looked on it all as a bauble which any of his subjects might raise by means of wealth; it was the business of a prince, he said, to erect more durable monuments of fame, which might stand for ever, like pillars of glory, such as good deeds that were worthy of imitation, but difficult to be surpassed by posterity. The poet, Nizám Urazi, of Samarkand, observes upon this: "Of all the magnificent palaces built by Mahmúd, there remains not one stone upon another, but the edifice of his fame still triumphs over time and remains a lasting monument of his greatness."

SULTAN MAHMÚD, GHAZNAVI.*

When Sabuktagín died, his eldest son, Mahmúd, was at Nishápúr. The second son, Ismail, being by his father's side in his last moments, obtained

*Surnamed Butshikan, or the Iconoclast. His titles were *Amín-ul-Millat*, "Asylum of the Faith," and *Yamín-ud-Daulat*, "the Right Hand of the State."

The throne contested between Mahmúd and his younger brother Ismail.

Defeat of Ismail.

his consent to his own succession, and, on the death of his father, was crowned with great solemnity at Balkh. Mahmúd, however, asserted his right to the throne and offered Balkh and Khorásán to the younger brother as an independent monarchy, if he abandoned his pretensions to the rest, but Ismail declined the offer. Mahmúd, upon this, made war on Ismail, supported by his uncle Boghraz and his own younger brother, Amír Nasír-ud-dín Eusuf. The troops of Ismail were supported by a row of elephants, and the two armies engaged with great fury near Ghazni. After a desperate struggle Ismail acknowledged himself defeated and delivered up the keys of the fortress and treasury to his brother, Mahmúd, who kept him in honourable restraint for the rest of his life.

Mahmúd ascends the throne of Gházni

And declares his independence.

He receives robes and titles from the khalif of Bagdád.

His assumption of the title of Sultan.

Mahmúd was thirty years of age when he ascended the throne and was in the prime of life. Having been the constant companion of his father in military expeditions, and entrusted by him with independent military commands, he had gained a large experience in the art of war, while in the arts of peace he possessed all the qualities of a great prince. His first act, after ascending the throne, was to send an ambassador to the court of Bokhára to tender his allegiance to the royal house of Samáni, but soon afterwards he threw off that allegiance and declared his independence, in 999 A. D. Mahmúd now employed himself in reducing to order the provinces of Balkh and Khorásán, and, his fame reaching the court of Bagdad, the Caliph Alkadar Billah, of the house of Abbas, sent him a rich honorary dress and bestowed upon him the dignified titles of *Amin-ul-Millat*, or "Asylum of the Faith," and *Yamin-ud-Daulat*, "the Right Arm of the State." He assumed the title of Sultan, and received in marriage the daughter of Elik-han, emperor of Bokhára, the usurper of the Samáni dynasty.

His zeal for the propagation of Islam.

Mahmud's first invasion, 1001 A. D.

His war with Jaipal, rájá of Láhore.

His victory.

Jaipal abdicates and dies on the funeral pile.

Mahmúd had long heard accounts of the wealth and splendour of the countries to the east of his frontier, and had made a vow that, if blessed with tranquillity, he would turn his arms against the idolaters of Hindostán, extirpate idolatry from that country, and introduce, in its stead, the worship of the one true God. Mahmúd was himself familiar with the parts of India bordering on the banks of the Indus, and his zeal for the propagation of Islam, as well as the confidence he reposed in the bravery of his troops, soon impelled him to undertake an invasion of that country. Accordingly, in the month of August, 1001 A.D., he marched from Ghazni to Peshávar, at the head of ten thousand chosen horse. Here Jaipál, the rájá of Láhore, met him with 12,000 horse and 30,000 foot, supported by 300 elephants. An action took place between the two armies, and the Hindus fought desperately, but they had at last to give way before the disciplined cavalry of Mahmúd, and were completely routed, five thousand of their number being slain on the field of battle, and Jaipál with fifteen of his principal chiefs being taken prisoners by the victors. The victory achieved by Mahmúd acquired for him great fame and wealth; and among the spoils gained there were sixteen necklaces inlaid with precious stones, that worn by Jaipál alone being valued at £82,000. After this victory Mahmúd marched to Bhatinda, the fort of which he invested and reduced. In the following spring he released Jaipál, on his stipulating to pay an annual tribute, but he put to the sword the Afghan chiefs who had opposed his march to the Panjáb. The aged Hindu king, Jaipál, feeling himself disgraced by the defeats sustained by him and considering himself disqualified to rule, abdicated the throne in favour of his son Anangpal,* and, having mounted a a funeral pile, which he had himself raised, sacrificed himself to his gods.

* Farishta calls him Anandpal, but in the *Rájputáná Chronicles* and the *Puránas* he is called Anangpal. *Anang*, in [illegible] means 'incorporeal' or 'unsubstantial.'

On his return from a military expedition into Sistan, in 1004 A.D., Mahmúd found that the tribute from Hindostán had not been fully paid. Anangpal, the rájá of Láhore, had paid his share, but a tributary prince, Biji Rai, rájá of Bhatia, had withheld his quota, and, being bitterly hostile to the Mahomedans, was molesting the Mahomedan Governors whom Mahmúd had established in India. Mahmúd entered the rájá's territory by the Múltán route, and found Bhatia fortified with a high wall and surrounded by a deep broad ditch. The Rájá drew up his Rájput army in order of battle, and the Indians charged the Mahomedans so desperately that the latter were repulsed in several engagements during three successive days. All the strong positions were held by the Hindus, and so severe was the loss sustained by the Mahomedan troops that they were on the point of abandoning the field. At length, on the fourth day, Mahmúd, prostrating himself towards Mecca, in sight of his army, with his hand outstretched in prayer, and shouting that the Prophet had given him the victory, led the main attack himself. A loud shout from the soldiers rent the air, and the Mahomedans pressed forward with such impetuosity that the enemy were driven back to the gates of the city. The following morning, the fort of Bhatia was closely besieged, and in a few days the surrounding ditches were all filled up. Biji Rai, finding it impossible to maintain his position, abandoned the citadel, leaving a small garrison to defend it, and took refuge in a wood on the banks of the Indus with the rest of his troops. He was pursued in his forest retreat by a detachment of Mahmúd's army, which attacked his position and reduced him to great straits. His best friends deserted him, and he was on the point of being taken prisoner, when he fell on his own sword and thus put an end to his life. His followers, who attempted to avenge the death of their master, were, for the most part, put to the sword. Bhatia was taken by assault. Two hundred and eighty elephants, with a large number of slaves and other spoils, fell into the hands of the king, who returned triumphant to Ghazni.

Second Invasion, 1004 A. D.

Fight against the rája of Bhatia.

A furious onset.

Suicide committed by the raja.

Shekh Hamid Sadi, the first Mahomedan ruler of Múltán, acknowledged allegiance to Amír Sabuktagín and paid him tribute. After him his grandson Abul Fath Dáúd, the son of Nasir, acknowledged himself the vassal of the Sultan of Ghazni, but he shook off his allegiance in 1500 A.D., in collusion with Anangpal of Láhore. Mahmúd now formed the design of reconquering Múltán, and in the beginning of the spring marched with a large army to that place. In the hills of Pesháwar he was opposed by Anangpal's troops, which were signally defeated and pursued by the Ghazni army to the town of Sodra,* on the bank of the Chínab.

Third Invasion, 1005 A. D.

Anangpal, deserting his capital, fled to Káshmír. Mahmúd marched to Múltán by way of Bhatinda and laid close siege to it for seven days. Dáúd at length surrendered and was pardoned, on a promise to pay an annual tribute of 20,000 gold dirams. The Sultan would probably have prolonged his stay in India, but news of the invasion of his western territories by his father-in-law Elek Khan, King of Kashgar, compelled him to retrace his steps to Ghazni, leaving the affairs of India in the hands of Sewakpal, a Hindu prince who had become a convert to Mahomedanism under the influence of Abu Ali, Governor of Pesháwar.

Conquest of Múltán.

A rebellion on the part of Sewakpal, the deputy, who expelled all the officers of the Sultan from their respective departments, again brought Mahmúd on the soil of India in 1005-6. He sent forward a part of his cavalry in advance, and the troops, coming unexpectedly in sight of the Hindu army,

Fourth Invasion, 1005-6 A. D.

Rebellion of Sewakpal, a renegade Hindu raja.

* The modern Wazírábád on the left bank of the Chínab.

inflicted a signal defeat on them. Sewakpal was imprisoned, compelled to pay a fine of 400,000 dirams, and kept a State prisoner for the rest of his life.

Fifth Invasion, 1008 A. D.

But the treacherous conduct of Anangpal, in supporting the rebellion at Multán, rankled in the breast of Mahmúd, who was resolved on inflicting severe chastisement on him. Accordingly, early in the spring of 1008 A. D., he marched to India with great expedition, at the head of a large army. Anangpal, conscious of the power of the Mahomedans, and remembering former disasters, appealed to the religious zeal of the Indian rájás to drive the common enemy from their sacred soil. The appeal was responded to, and the rájás of Ujjain, Gwálior, Kanauj, Delhi, Ajmere and Kalanjar, collecting all their available forces, marched to the Indus. The greatest army that had yet assembled on the soil of the Panjáb appeared in sight of the plains on the confines of Peshávar, and its numbers continued to increase daily. Money was supplied from all quarters for the conduct of the operations, and so great was the patriotism displayed that Hindu women in distant parts melted their ornaments, and sent in silver and gold to provide resources for the national cause. The Ghakkars, a powerful hill tribe in the north-west of the Panjáb, joined the confederate armies with 30,000 fighting men, and the Mahomedan troops, being surrounded on all sides, and fearing a general assault, were obliged to entrench themselves.

Anangpal.

His appeal to the Hindú rajas for help.

They respond to his call.

For forty days the two armies lay inactive and face to face, each side hesitating to advance. At length the spell was broken by the Hindus, who took advantage of an opportunity given by the Mahomedans who had sent six thousand archers to the front, to provoke the enemy to advance against the entrenchments. The archers were attacked by the wild Ghakkars, and, notwithstanding the Sultan's exertions and presence in their midst, were repulsed. The Hindus penetrated into the Mahomedan position with great fury, and dreadful was the carnage which ensued, five thousand Mahomedans being put to the sword in a very short time. A determined rally on the part of the Mahomedans, however, had the effect of checking the advance of the Hindus, a great number of whom were slain. Meanwhile an event happened which proved disastrous to the Hindu cause. The elephant on which the prince of Láhore, commanding the Indian armies, was mounted, became unruly, owing to the sound of the naptha balls and the shower of arrows, and took to flight. This spread terror and confusion among the Hindus, who, thinking themselves deserted by their king, retreated in great disorder. Availing themselves of the confusion thus caused, the Mahomedans, with Abdullah Tai at the head of 6,000 Arabian horse, and Arsala Jazib with 10,000 Turks, Afghans and Khiljis, sallied out from their entrenchments, and pursued the enemy with great slaughter. Immense booty, with 30 elephants, fell into the hands of the victors.

Panic in the Hindu camp.

Defeat of the Hindus.

The passion for propagating the faith of Islám and destroying Hindu idols, fermented in the mind of Mahmúd, who, soon after the victory, marched against the sacred town of Nagar Kot, and, for the first time, broke their idols and levelled their temples with the ground. Having devastated the country round with fire and sword, he laid under close siege the famous fort of Bhím, one of the holy shrines of the Panjáb, and a repository of great wealth, situated on the summit of a steep mountain, from which issued flames, known in modern times as Jwála Mukhi, of effulgent countenance, or the holy burning fountain. It was the strongest fortress in the north of Hindostan and contained a most superb temple, roofed and framed with precious metal, and a celebrated college for the study of the Shástras. The garrison had left the fort to take part in the campaign, and the Brahmin

The fort of Bhim taken by storm.

priests within were little accustomed to war and bloodshed. They therefore made overtures to capitulate, and opening the gates of the temple fell upon their faces before the conqueror and begged for mercy, which was granted. Immense booty in gold and silver ingots, jewels, pearls, corals, diamonds and rubies, which had been collected in this temple from the neighbouring kingdoms since the days of Bhím, fell into the hands of the victor, who returned, with this vast treasure, to Ghazni. In the year 1009 A.D., the Sultan held a great meeting on the plain outside his capital, at which he displayed to his *omeras* (nobles) and the astonished people, the enormous wealth, in golden thrones, precious stones, and rich ornaments, which he had brought away from the Panjáb, bestowing kingly presents on all the officials of state according to their rank and deserts.

Immense booty obtained.

In the year 1011 A.D., Mahmúd resolved on the conquest of Thanesar, which was represented as being held by the Hindus in as great veneration as Mecca is by the Mahomedans. In vain did Anangpal offer the king the revenues of Thanesar, with a promise to remit the same annually to the royal treasury, to reimburse him for all the expenses of his expedition, and to present him, beside, with fifty elephants and jewels of considerable value, for Mahmúd was determined to root out idolatry from all India. Disdaining the offers made to him, he captured the town, plundered the inhabitants, destroyed its great temples and broke its idols to pieces. The principal of these idols, called Jagsoom, and believed to have existed since the creation, was broken up into innumerable fragments and sent to Ghazni, Mecca and Baghdad, to be trodden under foot in the street. Two hundred thousand prisoners are said to have been carried off on this occasion by Mahmúd, to Ghazni, so that their camp appeared like an Indian town, and the booty taken away was again enormous.

Sixth Invasion, 1011 A.D.

The temple of Thanesar plundered.

In the year 1013, Mahmúd marched with an army against Nanduna, situated in the mountains of Buluat, and, having invested the place, compelled the garrison to capitulate. Jaipál II, who had succeeded his father, Anangpal, seeing that he was no match for the Sultan, withdrew with his armies to Káshmír. Mahmúd, leaving a governor appointed by himself in the hill territory, moved without delay to Káshmír, on which the rájá of Láhore abandoned the province and fled to the hills. Mahmúd plundered Káshmír of all its great wealth, and, having compelled the inhabitants to embrace the religion of the Prophet, returned to his capital with rich spoils.

Seventh Invasion, 1013 A.D.

The sack of Kashmir.

Two years after, the Sultan revisited Káshmír for the purpose of punishing certain rebel chiefs and reducing some forts which could not be attacked in the previous expedition. The principal of these was Lokot, famous for its height and strength. All the efforts of the Sultan to reduce the place during the summer failed, and he was compelled to abandon the enterprise on the approach of winter, and return to Ghazni.

Eighth Invasion, 1015 A.D.

Unsuccessful attempt on Lokot.

In the spring of 1017 A.D., Mahmúd marched to Kanauj with an army of 100,000 of horse and 20,000 foot, his route lying through the mountains north of Káshmír. The Rájá of Kanauj, Kamar Rai, affected great state and splendour, but, being unprepared for defence, he sued for peace. He then marched to Mirath, the prince of which place, Hardit, also submitted, and then to Mahawan, on the banks of the Jumna, which he reduced. The Rájá, Kiel Chand, having in despair first slain his own wife and children, turned the point of his sword against himself and caused his own destruction. He then set out for the rich city of Mathura, consecrated to Krishen Basdeo and, meeting little opposition, gave it up to plunder. All the idols were broken or burned, most of the temples were destroyed, and an enormous amount of silver and gold was carried away. Mahmúd stayed at Kanauj for

Ninth Invasion, 1017 A.D.

Conquest of Kanauj, Mirath and Mathura.

Destruction of temples and idols.

twenty days, during which time the city suffered greatly from fire and pillage. Having subdued some petty Rájput princes, the Sultan returned to Ghazni, laden with spoil and encumbered with captives, the private plunder of his army being not less than that gathered into the public treasury.

The Sultan's return to Ghazni.

The king, during his stay in India, was struck with the beauty of Indian architecture. On his return to his capital, he erected a magnificent mosque of marble and granite, which he furnished with rich carpets, candelabra and furniture of silver and gold, and called the "Celestial Bride." The example was followed by the nobles of his court, who vied with each other in embellishing the capital with magnificent private palaces and public buildings. In the neighbourhood of the royal mosque, Mahmúd established a grand university, a vast library of books by learned authors, and a museum of natural curiosities and works of art, at an enormous expense to the State.

Architectural embellishments of the capital of Mahmúd.

The taste for architecture increased, and, in a short time, the capital of Mahmúd was decorated with beautiful mosques, pavilions, fountains, reservoirs, aqueducts and cisterns, unequalled in design and workmanship by any work of the kind in previous ages. In 1019 the Sultan forwarded an account of his victories to Alqádir Billah, the Caliph of Baghdad, who had it read out at a grand assembly of the Mahomedans of that city who celebrated with great rejoicings the victories which the Moslem arms had gained in distant parts of the globe.

Tenth Invasion, 1021 A.D.

A confederation of the Hindu princes having, in 1021, attacked Kowar Rai, Rájá of Kanauj, for entering into an alliance with Mahmúd, the Sultan again marched into India, but before he could arrive, Kanauj had been reduced by Nanda Rájá, of Kalinjar in Bundelkhand, who had put Kowar Rai and a number of his chiefs to death. To avenge his death, the Sultan proceeded to Kalinjar and put Nanda Rai to flight. After this victory, Mahmúd marched to Káshmír, investing, by the way, the impregnable fort of Lokot.

Láhore sacked.

He then entered Láhore and ordered his troops to sack the city, in revenge for Anangpal's having joined the confederacy against the Rájá of Kanauj. Here enormous wealth fell into his hands, and the Rájá, finding himself unequal to his adversary, fled to Ajmere for protection. In the spring of the same year, Mahmúd, appointing his own satraps to the charge of the conquered provinces, returned to Ghazni.

Malik Ayaz left in charge of Láhore.

He left Láhore in charge of his favourite counsellor and general, Malik Ayaz, whose name is associated with many anecdotes and sayings of his royal master. The Malik built the walls and citadel of Láhore and enlarged and beautified the town. During the incumbency of this popular Ghaznivide governor, Láhore became a seat of learning, and men from Ghazni came and settled there, among them being Makhdum Shekh Ali Ganj Baksh, Hujweri, whose mausoleum, known as Data Ganj Baksh, outside the city, is held in great reverence by the Mahomedan population.*

Láhore called Mahmudpúr.

Mahmúd called Láhore, after his own name, Mahmúdpúr, and he struck coins at Láhore which bore the following inscription in Arabic and Hindi:—

Reverse (in *Kufi* characters).

القادر بالله

لا اله الا الله محمد الرسول الله

Coin struck by Mahmúd at Láhore.

يمين الدوله و امين الملة محمود

بسم الله ضرب هذا الدرهم به محمود پور سنه ثمان عشرة واربعمائة

---

* A fair is held here every Friday. The tomb of Malik Ayaz by the Taxali Gate, or old Mint, is still revered by the people as the burial place of the founder of Láhore.

"Al Kadar Billal *
There is no God but God, and Mahomed the Prophet of God.
The Right Hand of the State, the Asylum of the Faith, Mahmúd.
In the name of God this Dirham was struck at Mahmúdpúr, in 418 A.H."

Obverse (Hindi).
Abyak tamak, Mahammad Avatar, Nri pati Mahmúd.
"The invisible is one.
Mahmúd incarnation.
King Mahmúd."—

Margin (Hindi).
"In the name of the invisible this Tanka was struck at Mahmúdpúr in 418."†

Two years after this, Mahmúd again marched to India with the object of chastising Nanda Rai, Rájá of Kalinjar, who had escaped punishment in the preceding expedition. He moved against him by way of Láhore, and, passing Gwalior, laid siege to the fort of that place; but the rájá tendered his allegiance and was spared. Nanda Rai also averted the calamity which awaited him by tendering a timely submission and valuable gifts, and, these having been accepted, he was confirmed in the possession of his territories.

Eleventh Invasion, 1023 A.D.

The rájá of Kalinjar tenders his allegiance.

Mahmúd had long heard accounts of the sanctity and wealth of the celebrated temple of Somnáth, a town on the sea coast of Kaithiawar, which was frequented by devotees from all parts of India. The god Soma, after whom the temple was called, was believed to possess absolute power over the souls of all. He was believed to regulate the successive transmigrations, and to have power to bless or curse dismembered souls. The temple was a most splendid one, and was held in great veneration by all the votaries. Determined to destroy such a notorious centre of idolatry, he marched from Ghazni, in September 1024, accompanied by 30,000 volunteers, the youth of Turkestan and the neighbouring countries, who followed the king without pay, with the express object of destroying this temple. Having crossed the desert of Múltán, he arrived at Ajmere, which he sacked, and, reducing other fortresses, he reached Somnath, by rapid marches, without opposition. The fortress of the temple was strongly defended by the Rájputs, and for three successive days the assaults of the Mahomedans were repulsed with great loss. Mahmúd at length leaped from his horse, and, prostrating himself on the ground, implored the help of God. Remounting and taking Abul Hassan, his Circassian general, by the hand, by way of encouragement, he cheered the troops on with such enthusiasm that they stormed the fortress and laid 5,000 of the garrison dead at their feet. The remainder of the enemy embarked in boats to save their lives, but were followed by the Mahomedans, who sank many of the boats. Mahmúd now entered the temple, accompanied by his sons and a few of his *Omerahs* and chiefs. As he entered the great hall, he saw before him a stone idol,‡ nine

Twelfth Invasion, 1024 A.D.

The temple of Somnáth.

Mahmúd resolves to destroy this temple.

The garrison put to the sword.

* It would appear that the name and title of the Caliph of Baghdad, the Supreme Pontiff of Islam, preceded the Sultan's own name, out of the reverence in which he was held by the whole Moslem world.

† Thomas' *Pathan Kings of Delhi*, p. 48.

‡ The temple of Somnáth was a superb edifice, built of hewn stone. The rájás of various parts of India had bestowed the revenue of 2,000 villages for the maintenance of its establishment, which comprised chiefly Brahmin priests. The offerings made at the shrine by the pilgrims who visited it from all parts of India at particular festivals, were enormous. At the eclipses from 200,000 to 300,000 worshippers used to attend the temple. The idol was washed twice a day with water from the Ganges, which was brought for the purpose from a distance of 1,200 miles, and which alone was considered worthy of being employed in its daily ablutions. A great bell, supported by a golden chain, and weighing 200 maunds, called the devotees to worship. The establishment consisted of 2,000 Brahmins, 500 dancing girls, 300 musicians and 300 barbers, who shaved the devotees before they were admitted into the temple. Shaven priests prostrated themselves before the great idol, and dancing girls, adorned with jewels, made their performances before it. It was customary with the rájás, at one time, to devote their daughters to the service of this great religious institution, in order to obtain the blessings of the gods. There were, in this temple, besides the idol of Somnáth, hundreds of small images wrought in gold and silver, which were all melted down by Mahmúd, and the gold and silver they produced carried away to Ghazni.

The image broken to pieces.

feet in height. The Sultan, approaching the image, struck off its nose with a blow of his mace. He then ordered two pieces of the idol to be taken to Ghazni, one to be thrown on the threshold of the grand Mosque and the other at the court door of his own palace. Two more pieces were at the same time taken away to be sent to Mecca and Medina. The Brahmins offered to give the Sultan a large quantity of gold if the image were spared, and even the courtiers of Mahmud represented to him that the destruction of one idol would not abolish idolatry; but Mahmud scorned the idea, remarking that, if he were to spare the idol for the sake of gain, his name would be handed down to posterity as an "idol seller," whereas his object was to be known rather as the "idol destroyer." The image was forthwith broken in pieces, and its interior was found to contain a quantity of precious stones far exceeding in value the amount which had been offered by the priests. After a short stay at Somnáth, the Sultan conquered Gandawa, in Katch, and Anhalwárá, a magnificent city, and, having bestowed the kingdom of Gujrat on a prince of the country, returned to Ghazni by way of Sindh. The expedition to Somnáth and the campaign in Gujrát occupied two years and a half.

Vast booty obtained.

Thirteenth Invasion, 1027 A.D.

Campaign against the Játs of the Indus.

Mahmúd's last expedition to India was undertaken in 1027. The campaign was directed against the Ját tribes living on the banks of the Indus who had molested the Mahomedan army on its return from Gujrát. The tribes were reduced, and no further invasion of India on a large scale was contemplated.

Death of Mahmúd, 1030 A.D.

His burial.

His person.

Mahmúd soon after became seriously affected with stone, and died on the 29th April, 1030, in the sixty-third year of his age and the thirty-third of his reign. He was buried by torchlight, amid the tears of his people, in Kasr Firozi at Ghazní. In person he was of middle height and well made, vigorous and hardy beyond his fellows, so that few in his army could wield his mace or throw his spear. His face was deeply pitted from the effects of smallpox. Having one day looked in his looking-glass, he said to his wazir: "I have resilvered my glass, and, looking in it, I see so many faults in my face that I easily overlook those of others. The face of a king should brighten the eyes of all beholders; whilst mine appears the picture of misfortune." The wazir replied, with Eastern obsequiousness: "It is not one in ten thousand that sees your countenance, but your virtues are diffused over all."

His character.

Of the private life of Mahmúd but little is known. His favourite wife was Haram Núr, or the Light of the Harem, called also from her exquisite beauty Mihr Shighil, the Sun of Beauties. She was the beautiful daughter of Elek, the Uzbek king of Káshghar, the inveterate foe of Mahmúd; but the Sultan solaced his leisure with other charms than those of Haram Núr and freely partook of the forbidden juice of the grape, notwithstanding his orthodox proclivities. He was a sincere friend to learning and literature, and, according to the famous Abul Fazl, no king ever had more learned men at his court, maintained a finer army, or displayed more magnificence.

His administration of justice.

His justice was inflexible, and it has been metaphorically stated that in his reign the wolf and the lamb drank together at the same fountain. Two days before his death he ordered his whole wealth in gold, precious stones, jewels, &c., to be exhibited to him. He looked on all the works his hand had wrought and on the labour he had gone through, and saw that all was vanity and vexation of spirit. He shed tears at parting from these treasures and ordered them to be taken back to the treasury, without suffering his officers to distribute any portion of that which was shortly to pass altogether from his hands. The following day he commanded a review of his army

His last sight of his treasures and army.

elephants, horses, camels and chariots, which he inspected on a travelling throne. One hundred thousand foot, 50,000 horse and 1,300 elephants passed in review before him as the dying hero reclined on his couch, and when he had feasted his eyes on all, he burst into tears and retired to his palace full of mortification and grief.

At the time of his death, Mahmúd left an empire far exceeding that of any monarch then living. His sway extended from Káshmír to Ispahán and from the Caspian to the Ganges. He was looked upon by all the Mahomedan world as its chief. He was one of the greatest monarchs who have ruled over the destinies of an Asiatic country, and there are few of the world's conquerors who have established a reputation equal to his.

Extent of his monarchy.

Three miles south of Ghazní may still be seen the cupola that surmounts the grave of Sultan Mahmúd. The world-renowned sandalwood gates of Somnáth, which the great warrior carried to Ghazní, were erected by his followers to adorn his grave. Forty-six years ago they were brought back to Hindostán by the armies of a nation whose name even was not known in the East when the gates were carried away, and they are now objects of curiosity in the British Museum in London. To this day the priests of the Mahomedan faith read the Qurán over the tomb of the famous Sultan of Ghazní.

The mausoleum of Sultan Mahmúd.

The gates of Somnáth.

SULTAN MASÚD I.

Sultan Mahmúd left two sons, Muhammad and Masúd, who were twins. The latter, at the time of his father's death, was in Ispahán, and Amír Ali, son of Kazil Arslán, the father-in-law of Mahmúd, installed Muhammad on the throne of Ghazní. Muhammad had, however, reigned only five months when he was deprived of his sight and deposed by Masúd, who was proclaimed Sultan of Ghazní.

Muhammad succeeds Mahmúd, his father.

But is blinded and deposed by his brother Masúd, 1033 A. D.

Having subjugated the Saljuk Tartars, Masúd turned his attention to the affairs of India, and, in the year 1033 A D., made an attack on the fort of Sursuti, in the Káshmír hills. The garrison offered a bold resistance, but Masúd caused scaling ladders to be applied to the walls, and the fort was carried after a bloody fight. The entire garrison were put to the sword, except the women and children, who were carried away as slaves. The intelligence of the defeat of his general by the Saljuks compelled Masúd to return to his wetsern dominions to restore order. He retraced his steps to India in 1036, reduced the fort of Hansi, the ancient capital of Savalak, deemed to be impregnable, and then marched to Sonipat near Delhi, which was also reduced, the governor, Dipál Hari, having fled to the woods, abandoning all his treasures, which fell into the hands of the conqueror. On his return to Láhore the Sultan, having conferred the insignia and title of royalty on his son Maudúd, entrusted to him the government of that province, and, leaving with him Khwája Ayáz, his favourite counsellor and minister, himself returned to Ghazní. He was, however, hard pressed by the Saljuk Turkmáns in 1042, and, being much discouraged by the perfidy of his generals, he collected all his wealth from the stronghold of Ghazní, and, loading it on camels, withdrew to Lahore the same year, with the determination to live in India for the rest of his life. On reaching Láhore he sent his son, Prince Maudúd, to Balkh, as governor of that province; but on the banks of the Jhelum his soldiers and slaves mutinied and deposed him, raising his blind brother, Muhammad, whom he had brought with him, to the throne. Masúd was kept in close confinement, but was soon after assassinated by his cousin, Sulaiman. Masúd reigned nine years. He was a prince of a warlike temperament, possessed of much courage,

Masúd invades India, 1033 A. D.

Maudúd entrusted with the government of Láhore.

Sultan Masúd deposed by the army and put to death.

He is succeeded by Muhammad.

The character of Masúd.

but at the same time affable and generous. Like his great father, he was a patron of learning, and built many handsome mosques and palaces* and endowed colleges and schools.

SULTAN MAUDÚD.

Maudud, son of Masúd assumes the crown and marches on Láhore.

Maudúd, hearing of his father's murder, repaired in all haste to Ghazni where he was crowned Sultan amidst the acclamations and rejoicings of his people. He then immediately marched to Láhore to avenge his father's death. Muhammad, who was blind, having appointed his younger son, Prince Námi, to the government of Pesháwar and Múltán, marched in person to the Indus to give battle to Maudúd. An action was fought at Dhantor between uncle and nephew, when victory declared for Maudúd. Muhammad, with his sons and several officers who had taken part in the deposition of Masúd, being taken prisoners, were, with the exception of Abdul Rahim, the son of the blind king Muhammad, put to the sword. At the spot where he had gained the victory, Maudúd founded a town which, from the triumph he had gained, he called Fathábád. The remains of Masúd and his family were carried to Ghazni, to be interred in the family vault. Prince Námi, the son of the blind king Muhammad, having mutinied at Múltán, a force under the Wazír Ahmad was sent to reduce him to subjection, and the prince was defeated and slain. Maudúd had now no rival left except Mádúd, his own brother, then in charge of Láhore, who was not disposed to yield to him. Accordingly, Maudúd marched with a large army to reduce him; but before any decisive action could be fought, Mádúd was, on the morning of the Íd Kúrban festival, found dead in his bed, and hence all opposition ceased.

Muhammad put to death.

Insurrection of the Hindu rájás, 1043 A.D.

In the year 1043, the Hindu rájás of Northern Hindostán availed themselves of the absence of Maudúd at Ghazní, where he had gone to subdue a fresh Saljuk insurrection, to form a confederation, and, having retaken Hansi and Thanesar with their dependencies, re-established the temple of Nagarkot in great splendour. This success inspired the rájás of the Panjáb with such confidence that three of them advanced to invest Láhore, at the head of 10,000 horse and a numerous body of foot. Siege was laid to the city, and the dilapidated walls were soon laid in ruins; but the Mahomedan garrison within defended the town, street by street, and fought desperately in defence of their faith, children and property, so that, for a period of seven months, all the efforts of the Hindus to reduce the town failed. No succour having, however, arrived, and the garrison being reduced to sore straits by famine, the brave defenders at length resolved either to win a victory or to die the death of martyrs. Accordingly they made a sortie and fought with such resolution that the Hindus fled and were pursued with great slaughter. This victory had the effect of breaking up the Hindu confederation, and the Indian possessions of the Ghaznivide dynasty remained in peace for the rest

They advance and lay siege to Láhore.

But are defeated.

---

* One of these palaces was built at Ghazní in the year 1036. It contained a magnificent hall, in the midst of which was placed a throne of gold, studded with jewels of enormous value. Over it was suspended, with a golden chain, a crown which emitted lustre from numerous precious stones, forming a canopy for the King, when he sat in state to give the public audience.—*Farishta.*

Mr. Rodgers found the coins of Masúd I. in the city of Amritsar. They were of the horse and bull type with the name مسعود Masúd over the horse. Some had on them مسعود محمد Masúd Muhammad and مسعود محمود Masúd Mahmúd.

Mr. Rodgers believes these coins were struck by Masúd at Lahore.—*Journal of Asiatic Society of Bengal*, No. 1, January 1881.

Mr. Thomas, at page 58 of his work on the Pathan Kings of Delhi, gives a woodcut of the coin of Masúd in Kufi letters clearly legible above the horse's head.

of Maudúd's life. Maudúd was soon after siezed with a severe bowel complaint and died at Ghazni, on December 24th, 1049, having reigned upwards of nine years.*

Death of Maudúd, 1049 A.D.

SULTÁN ABUL HUSEIN.

Masúd II.

On the death of Maudúd, his son, Masúd II., a child four years old, was raised to the throne by the party of Ali Bin Rubea; but the troops of the latter were worsted by Alaptagin Hájib, who had espoused the cause of Abúl Husein, a son of the Emperor Masúd I., and, the infant king having been deposed, after a nominal reign of six days, Abúl Hasan was proclaimed emperor of Ghazni.

Abúl Husein proclaimed emperor.

Ali Bin Rubea, the rebel officer, having plundered the royal treasury at Ghazni and brought over to his side a portion of the household troops, fled to Pesháwar, and, coalescing with the inhabitants, raised a large army, with which he reduced Multán and Sindh and subdued the Afghans, who, taking advantage of the disorder that prevailed in the country, had declared their independence. Abúl Husein, who was unable to restore order in the Panjáb, was, towards the end of 1051, defeated and deposed by Abdúl Rashíd, a son of Sultán Mahmúd, after reigning a little more than two years.

He is deposed 1051 A.D.

Accession of Sultán Abdúl Rashíd.

SULTÁN ABDÚL RASHÍD.

The first act of the new Sultán was to prevail on Ali Bin Rubea, who had usurped the Indian possessions of the Ghaznivides in the north-west, to return to his allegiance; and peace was restored on the frontier of the Panjáb. Nashtagin Hájib received the rank of *amír*, and, having been appointed governor of the provinces east of the Indus, was sent with a large army to Láhore. Nagarkot had again fallen into the hands of the Hindus; but the Mahomedan troops laid siege to it, and, scaling the walls, on the sixth day of the siege, carried the town. Abdúl Rashíd reigned one year, at the end of which he was assassinated by Toghral, usurper, and an *amír* of Maudúd's Court, who forcibly married a daughter of the late Sultán Masúd. The usurper was, in his turn, assassinated by Amír Nashtagin

Nashtagin Hájib appointed governor of the Panjáb.

Assassination of Sultán Abdúl Rashíd, 1052 A.D.

---

* Maudúd struck coins at Láhore bearing the following inscription:—

عدل
شهاب الدولة
وقطب الملة
ابوالفتح مودود

"The Just, the Star of the Faith, the Valiant Maudúd."

According to Mr. Rodgers, the principal authority on Panjáb coins, these coins were of four distinct types. They all had the bull on one side, and over it was the inscription in Hindi, *Sri Samanta Deva*. In these coins Láhore is spelt لوهور Lohor. Albiruni calls Láhore لوهاور (Loháwar).

Coins of Maudúd.

Mr. M. L. Dames, C.S., obtained a gold coin of Maudúd from a banker of Dera Ismáil Khan who had bought it from a Povinda merchant. It had the following inscription:—

[*Obverse.*]

لااله الاالله محمد الرسول الله وحدهٗ لا شريک لهٗ

"There is no God but God, and Muhammad the Prophet of God. He is One; no one is His partner.

[*Reverse.*]

القايم بامرالله شهاب الدوله مودود سنة

"The Star of State, Maudúd, who rules by the command of God. Year .

Hájib, on the fortieth day of his accession, while stepping up to the throne to give a public audience.*

SULTÁN FARAKHZÁD.

Death of Farakhzád, 1058 A.D.

Farakhzád, the son of Sultán Masúd I., was raised to the throne of Ghazni by Nashtagin Hájib, who was made Prime Minister to the new king. The Indian possessions of the Ghaznivides remained in peace during the reign of this Sultán, which lasted six years, at the end of which he died and was succeeded by his brother, Ibráhím.

SULTÁN IBRÁHÍM.

Sultán Ibráhím.

He captures Ajudhiah, 1079 A.D.

And Rúdpál,

And marches on Dera.

The town is reduced.

Having settled the affairs of the Saljuks, Sultán Ibráhím marched to the Panjáb, to conquer those parts of the country which had not before been visited by the Mahomedan arms. Accordingly, in 1079, he captured Ajuddan, now called Pák Patan, in the Montgomery District. He then invested Rúdpál,† situated on the summit of a steep hill. The clearing of the surrounding wood was a work of great difficulty, and thousands of pioneers were employed in its execution. The miners then carried their galleries under the walls, which coming down in the course of time, the Hindu garrison surrendered. The Sultán then marched to Dera, a town inhabited by a race of people who originally came from Khorásán, whence they had been banished by King Afrasiáb for rebellion. Dera was found to be well fortified, and the Sultan had the road cleared with infinite labour, in order to lay siege to the place; but, the rainy season preventing him from putting his warlike plans into execution, he was compelled to remain inactive for three months. No sooner, however, had the rains abated, than he called on the inhabitants to surrender and embrace the faith of Islám. His proposal was rejected, and the siege of the town was renewed and lasted for some weeks, with great loss on both sides. The town was at length taken by assault, and considerable booty fell into the hands of the victors, who carried away 100,000 persons, as slaves, to Ghazni.

Death of Sultán Ibráhím, 1098 A.D.

His character.

Sultán Ibráhím died in 1098, having reigned 42 years. He was blessed with 36 sons and 40 daughters by various wives. The daughters he gave in marriage to learned and religious men. He was a religious devotee, but this did not prevent his paying due attention to the affairs of the kingdom. He caused the fast of Ramazán to be observed during the months of Rajab and Shabán and kept the entire three months sacred with great strictness. He wrote an ornamental hand, and sent two copies of the *Qurán*, in his own handwriting, as a present to the Caliph of Baghdád, by whom they were sent as valuable contributions to the libraries of Mecca and Medina. He was a regular attendant at the lectures on religion delivered by Imám Eusuf Shujamandi, and was so humble that the Imám was permitted to reprove his sovereign without check. He was succeeded by his son Masúd III‡.

---

* The inscription on his coin was follows :—

عدل عزالدولته امين الملته

ابوالمنصور عبدالرشيد

"The just, prosperous, guardian of the faith, the victorious Abdúl Rashíd."—*Journal of B. A. S.*

† Ferishta describes this place as a fort surrounded on three sides by a river, thus forming a peninsula, which is connected with other hills. It was covered with an impenetrable jungle and infested with venomous serpents. The identity of the place has not yet been established.

‡ Sultán Ibráhím struck coins in the Panjáb bearing the following inscription :—

عدل السلطان المعظم ابوالمظفر ابراهيم لوهور

"The great and just king, the victorious Ibráhím, Lohor."—*Journal of B. A. S.*

SULTAN MASÚD III.

Sultán Ibráhim was succeeded on the throne of Ghazni by his son, Masúd III. He possessed a martial spirit and was distinguished for his love of justice and benevolence. He revised all the existing laws of the State and compiled a new code of law founded on better principles than had previously obtained. Having appointed Hájib Toghantagin general of his army and viceroy of Láhore, he sent him thither at the head of a large force. The General crossed the Ganges and carried the Mahomedan arms further than had been previously done, except by the great Mahmúd. He plundered many rich cities and temples and returned to Láhore laden with enormous spoil. Sultan Masúd III. Hájib Toghantagin appointed viceroy of Láhore.

During the reign of this emperor, Láhore became the real capital of the Ghaznivide dynasty, which having been deprived of most of its territory in Irán and Turán, the royal family were compelled to reside in India, where their possessions had now become consolidated. After reigning sixteen years without domestic troubles or foreign wars, Masúd died in 1118 A. D. Láhore becomes the real capital of the Ghaznivide dynasty. Death of Masúd III, 1118 A. D.

SULTAN ARSLAN.

Arslan, a son of the late king, having ascended the throne, imprisoned his brothers; but Sanjar, the Sultan of the Suljuks, having espoused the cause of the princes who had been put aside, gave Arslan battle, and the latter was defeated and put to flight. Arslan came to the Panjáb, and, collecting his Mahomedan troops, returned to recover his capital, but Sultan Sanjar again took the field in person and, a second time, expelled him from Ghazni. The defeated king took refuge with the Afgháns, but was hotly pursued and taken prisoner. He, soon after, met a violent death at the hands of his brother Bahrám, in the twenty-seventh year of his age and the third of his reign. Súltan Arslán. His death, 1121 A. D.

SULTAN BAHRAM.

Sanjar, the Sultan of Saljuks, placed Bahrám, the brother of Arslan, on the throne of Ghazni. Muhammad Bhylim, the Viceroy of Láhore, on the part of his brother Arslan, having refused to tender his allegiance to the new king, Bahrám marched from Ghazni to reduce him. An action was fought between the royal troops and those of Bhylim, the Láhore viceroy, in which the latter was defeated and taken prisoner, on 5th December 1118. Bhylim, however, swore allegiance, and the Sultan, after reinstating him in the government of the country, returned to Ghazni. Bhylim, subsequently to the departure of Bahrám, strengthened his position in the Panjáb, and, having built a new fort at Sawalik, conveyed thither his whole wealth, family and effects. Having then enlisted numerous recruits in his service from the Arabs, Persians, Afghans and Khiljis, he committed great depredations in the territories of the independent chiefs, and at length aspired to sovereign power. This brought Bahrám a second time on the soil of the Panjáb. Muhammad Bhylim had ten sons, to each of whom he had assigned the command of a province. They all joined their father with the whole of their resources, and the confederate troops met the advancing army of Bahrám at Multan. An obstinate fight took place, in which Bhylim and his sons were defeated, and in their flight they sank in a deep quagmire, in which they all perished. After this victory, the Sultan appointed Salar Hasan, son of Ibráhim Alvy, to the government of Láhore and himself marched back to Ghazni. Bahrám. Bhylim, viceroy of Láhore. He aspires to independence. His defeat and death.

Bahrám, soon after, having publicly executed his son-in-law, Kutb-ud-dín Muhammad, an Afghán of Ghor, involved himself in a struggle with Saif-ud-dín Suri, Prince of Ghor and brother of the deceased. Saif-ud-dín was surrounded by the perfidious Ghaznivide troops, who had apparently embraced his cause, and brought a prisoner to Bahrám, by whom he was executed in a barbarous manner. Álá-ud-dín, the brother of Saif-ud-dín, now Sultan of Ghor, marched to avenge his brother's death, and, after a bloody contest, took possession of Ghazni, which he gave up to indiscriminate plunder. Most of its noble edifices were razed to the ground, and, for seven days, the city was abandoned to fire and sword. Insatiate of revenge, Ala-ud-dín, who acquired the appellation of Jahánsoz, or "the incendiary of the world," carried a number of the most venerable and learned men in chains to Koh Firoz, to celebrate his victory, and there ordered their throats to be cut. Bahrám, after this defeat, fled to India, but died on the way of a broken heart, in the year 1152, after a reign of thirty-five years.

Death of Bahrám, 1152 A. D.

SULTAN KHUSRÁU.

Khusráu, his son, succeeds.

Khusráu, the son of Bahrám, having left Ghazni, arrived safely at Láhore, where he was saluted king. When Álá-ud-dín had retired to Ghor, Khusráu marched from Láhore, with the object of recovering his lost kingdom, but on the way he heard of the death of Sultan Sanjar, on whom he relied for help, and of the invasion of Ghazni by the Turkomans of Ghiza. He was therefore compelled to retrace his steps to Láhore where he reigned in peace for seven years. He died at Láhore in 1160, leaving his dominions to be inherited by his son, Khusráu Malik.

Dies at Láhore, 1160 A. D.

SULTAN KHUSRÁU MALIK.

Khusráu Malik.

Khusráu Malik, the son of the late Sultán Khusráu, ascended the throne and ruled with justice and moderation. He was destined to be the last of the great Ghaznivide dynasty who ruled in India. The kingdom of Ghazni was, during his time, invaded and conquered by Sultán Shaháb-ud-dín Muhammad Ghori, the brother of Ghiás-ud-dín, Sultán of Ghor, who had succeeded his cousin, Saif-ud-dín, the son of Ala-ud-dín. Not satisfied with that acquisition, he marched an army into the Panjáb and overran the provinces of Pesháwar, Afghanistan, Multan and the Indus. In the year 1180, he invested Láhore, which, being strongly fortified by Khusran Malik, all the attempts of the invader to take it failed, and peace was at length concluded between the contending parties. Muhammad Ghori retired from the country, carrying with him Malik Shah, the son of the emperor, a child of four years of age, as a hostage.

Ghazni conquered by Shahab-ud-din Muhammad Ghori, the Sultan of Ghor.

His first Invasion of the Panjáb, 1180 A. D.

Four years later, Muhammad Ghori again invaded the Panjáb and laid seige to Láhore, but, failing to capture the town, he laid waste the open country and slew many of the inhabitants. Then, after establishing a strong garrison at Sialkot, to command the country between the Rávi and the Chináb, he returned to Ghazni. On the departure of Muhammad, Khusráu Malik, in conjunction with the Ghakkars, besieged the fort of Sialkot, but a stout resistance being offered by Husain Firmáli, the Governor, and all the attempts of the besiegers to carry it by assault failing, the seige was raised.

Second Invasion, 1184 A. D.

Shortly after, or in 1186, Muhammad Ghori advanced against Láhore for the third time. He averted suspicion, however, by giving out that the expedition was intended to chastise the Saljuks, and, to prove that this was his object, he sent back Malik Shah, the son of the Sultan, to Láhore, with a magnificent escort. Khusráu Malik, being impatient to see his son, from whom he had long been separated, and suspecting no treachery, marched from Láhore with a small retinue to meet him, but Muhammad Ghori turned to the mountains, by rapid marches, at the head of 20,000 cavalry, and,

Third Invasion, 1186 A. D.

taking Khusráu's small force in the rear, cut off his retreat in the direction of Láhore and surrounded his camp at night. Khusráu awoke in the morning only to find himself a prisoner in the hands of his adversaries. Having thus secured the person of the Emperor, Muhammad Ghori demanded instant possession of Láhore. The gates of the city were thrown open, and Muhammad Ghori took possession of the capital of the Panjáb, unopposed, in the name of his brother, the Sultán of Ghor. Thus the great Ghaznivide dynasty, which had lasted from 962 to 1186, or for 224 years, ceased to exist, and the empire passed from the house of Ghazni to that of Ghor. Khusráu Malik, with his family, was sent to Ghor, and there kept in confinement. He reigned twenty-eight years.

A skilful manœuvre.

Láhore conquered by Muhammad Ghori.

CHAPTER III.

THE GHORI DYNASTY.

MUHAMMAD GHORI.

Ghias-ud-din, having succeeded to the throne of Ghazní, on the death of his cousin, Saif-ud-dín, appointed his brother, Shabáb-ud-dín Muhammad, commonly known as Muhammad Ghori, his general. In the year 1176, this last illustrious leader conducted an army against Múltán, which he completely subdued. He then marched to Uch, the scene of Alexander's memorable assault, and the place where he was so severely wounded after scaling the walls. The Rája of Uch shut himself up in the fort, which was closely invested. Muhammad, finding the fort impregnable, opened private negotiations with the rájá's wife, and promised to marry her if she would make away with her husband. This base woman returned for answer that her own days were spent, but that she had a young and beautiful daughter whom she would be glad to marry to the Sultan if she were left in undisturbed possession of the country and the wealth it contained, and that, on the Mahomedan general agreeing to these terms, she would immediately despatch the rájá. Muhammad agreed to this proposal, and the wicked woman found means of putting her husband to death. The gates of the fort were opened by the rani, and Muhammad took possession of it without trouble. Agreeably to his promise Muhammad married the rájá's daughter, on her embracing Islám; but he had no hesitation in breaking his promise with the mother, for, instead of entrusting her with the government of the country, he sent her off to Ghazní, where she soon after died of remorse and vexation. Nor did the daughter survive her long, for, in the short space of three years, she also fell a victim to a broken heart. Having conferred the government of Múltán and Úch on one Ali Kirmání, Muhammad returned to Ghazní.

Muhammad Ghori conquers Múltán and Úch

The perfidy of a rájá's wife.

Muhammad's expeditions to Láhore in 1180, 1184 and 1186 have been described in the preceding chapter. Having settled the province of Láhore, he entrusted the government to Ali Kirmání, and himself retired to Ghazní. His campaigns in the provinces of Hindostán are matters of Indian history. In the year 1193 A.D., the great battle of Naráin was fought on the banks of the Sarsuti. In this battle the chosen champions of the soil and the best representatives of Áryan chivalry were arrayed on the side of the Hindus, and it virtually decided the fate of Hindostán. Pirthi Ráj, the rájá of Ajmere, the head of the Chohan Rájputs and the descendant of one

Ali Kirmani appointed governor of the Panjáb.

The great battle of Narain, 1193 A. D.

of the princes of mount Abú, was taken prisoner and afterwards put to death; while Chawand Rai, the king of Delhi, a descendant of the Tomára rájás, and many other Princes, were slain on the field. Thousands of the inhabitants were put to the sword, and incalculable wealth fell into the conqueror's hands. In the course of the same year, Qutb-ud-dín Ebak, the general of Muhammad, took the fort of Mirath and the town of Delhi from the family of Chawand Rai. Delhi henceforward became the seat of the Mahomedan government in India, and the inhabitants of all the surrounding districts were compelled to embrace the faith of Islám.

Delhi conquered and made the seat of the Mahomedan empire of India, 1193 A.D.

Meanwhile the Ghakkars,* a tribe in the mountains of the Panjáb, having raised the standard of revolt, committed great depredations, laying waste the country between the Jhelum and the Chenáb. These wild people overran the whole of the Panjáb and even captured Láhore. Muhammad Ghori, who was now at Ghazní, hearing this, marched into the Panjáb. He first attacked Múltán, which had also revolted, and, being joined by many friends, he defeated Zirak, the traitor who, having assassinated Amir Dáud Hasan, the kings's viceroy at Múltán, had usurped the province a short time before. He then ordered his general, Qutb-ud-dín Ebak, to attack the Ghakkars on the east, while the king personally engaged them from the west. The Ghakkars now found themselves between two fires. They were defeated with great slaughter, and most of their number were converted to the faith of Islám. Láhore having been recovered from their hands, Qutb-ud-dín returned to his government of Delhi.

Láhore captured by the Ghakkars.

Who are defeated with great slaughter by Qutb-ud-dín Ebak.

Having settled the affairs of India, the Sultan, on his way to Ghazní, encamped near the village of Rohtak on the bank of the Indus. Here a body of Ghakkars, who had lost some of their relations in the late wars, entered into a conspiracy to take his life. The tents in which the king slept were allowed to remain open to admit fresh air from the riverside. This enabled the assassins to see into the sleeping apartments, and, eluding the sentinel placed at the door, they found their way into the tent. Two slaves, who were fanning the king, on seeing the assassins, stood petrified with horror, and the assassins immediately plunged their daggers into the Sultan's body and killed him, inflicting on him no less than twenty-two wounds. This event took place on 14th March, 1205.

Assassination of the Sultan, 1205 A. D.

Thus fell Sultan Shaháb-ud-dín, surnamed Muhammad Ghori, one of the greatest Mahomedan kings that ever ruled an Asiatic empire. His remains were carried in mournful pomp to Ghazní, in a hearse, and there interred in a new vault which had been constructed for his daughter. He reigned thirty-two years from the commencement of his rule over Ghazní and three years from his accession to the throne, and left no issue. Like his great ancestor Mahmúd, he had to encounter combinations of the Hindus; and while Mahmúd came to conquer, to plunder, and to return laden with spoils, Muhammad came to conquer, retain the country conquered, and die in it. Thus he laid the foundation of a subsequently great Mahomedan empire in India.

He laid the foundation of the great Mahomedan empire in India.

* According to Farishta, the Ghakkars were a race of barbarians, inhabiting the country along the banks of the Niláb, up to the foot of the Seválik Hills. They professed no religion or morality, and committed great cruelties on the Mahomedans. The baneful custom of infanticide had its origin in this tribe. As soon as a female child was born, the father would take her to the door of the house, and, holding the child in one hand and a knife in the other, proclaim that if any one wanted a wife, he was at liberty to take her away; if nobody came forward, the poor infant was immediately put to death. Thus, among the Ghakkars the number of males predominated over that of the females, and polyandry existed. Muhammad Ghori converted the chief of this tribe to the faith of Islám, released him from confinement, and, having conferred on him a dress of honour, restored him to the chiefship. His followers were easily induced to adopt the tenets of the faith and most of the inhabitants of the hills between Ghazní and the Indus became converted to Mahomedanism,—some by force, others by persuasion.

CHAPTER IV.

THE TARTAR, OR SLAVE DYNASTY.

KUTB-UD-DÍN EBAK.

ON the death of Muhammad Ghori, his nephew, Mahmúd, assumed the royal title at Ghor. Desirous of securing his friendship, and being in no position to oppose him successfully if he should refuse to acknowledge his sovereignty, the new king, immediately after his accession, sent all the insignia of royalty, a canopy, standards and drums, a throne and a warrant of investiture as king, to Kutb-ud-dín Ebak, his uncle, viceroy of Northern India. Kutb-ud-dín, who received these marks of royal favour with profound respect, was crowned as the first Mahomedan king at Láhore, on July 24th, 1205 A.D.

Kutb-ud-dín Ebak crowned as the first Mahomedan king of Láhore, 1205 A. D.

In his childhood, Kutb-ud-dín had been brought from Turkistan to Neshapore by a merchant, who sold him to Kázi Fukhr-ud-dín, son of Abdúl Azíz Kufí. The Kazí, finding that the lad was intelligent and endowed with genius, sent him to school, where he made considerable progress in knowledge and science. On the death of his patron, he was sold as part of his estate to a merchant, and by him presented for sale to Muhammad Ghori, who, having purchased him, gave him the nickname *Ebak*, from his little finger being broken. Ebak conducted himself so well that he was shortly afterwards appointed master of the horse, and then to the command of an army. His natural talents now finding full scope for action, he soon gained the reputation of being a brave soldier, a consummate general, and a prudent administrator.

The ancestry of Kutb-ud-dín.

Taj-ud-dín Yelduz, governor of Kirman and Shirwan, whose daughter Kutb-ud-dín had married, now marched to Láhore at the head of an army, and, aided by the treachery of the governor, whom he afterwards expelled, took possession of the city. Kutb-ud-dín, on hearing of this event, advanced from Delhi to recover Láhore, at which place a battle was fought in the latter end of 1205, when Taj-ud-dín Yelduz was defeated, expelled the city and compelled to retrace his steps to Kirman. Kutb-ud-dín pursued Yelduz to Ghazni, where he was crowned king, but, being unable to hold the city, he returned almost immediately to India. Here he spent the rest of his life in consolidating his dominions and regulating the finances of the empire. He died in 1210 from a fall from his horse in a match at *chowgan*, a sort of racing game. He had reigned five years and exercised sovereign powers for upwards of twenty years under the title of commander-in-chief and viceroy to his patron, Muhammad Ghori. He was a man of great genius and bravery, and raised himself from the position of a slave to that of one of the most powerful kings that ever controlled the destinies of an empire. He was loved for his social virtues, while his generous liberality became proverbial. The celebrated Kutab Minar at Delhi, with a splendid mosque, commenced by Kutb-ud-dín and completed by his successor Shams-ud-dín Altmash, still towers high in its proud majesty to commemorate the conquest of Delhi by the first Mohamedan general who ruled the ancient capital of India.

Láhore is invested by Yeldus, governor of Kirman.

But is retaken by Kutb-ud-dín after a fight.

Death of Kutb-ud-dín, 1210 A. D.

His character.

He builds the celebrated Kutab Minar at Delhi.

ARAM.

Weak government of Aram. *Many districts of the Panjáb are lost to the empire.* *He is deposed by Shams-ud-dín Altamash, 1210 A. D.*

On the death of Kutb-ud-dín, Aram, his only son, succeeded him on the throne. He was wanting in courage and resolution, and, owing to his weakness, Nair-ud-dín Kubácha, one of the adopted slaves of Muhammad Ghori, made himself independent, and, marching thither at the head of an army, established his authority in Sindh, Multán, Uch, Shirwan and other districts of the Panjáb. Other chiefs, following his example, also asserted their independence. Upon this, a deputation of the Omerahs waited upon Shams-ud-dín Altamash, the son-in-law and adopted son of the late king, and invited him to assume the sovereignty of the kingdom. Shams-ud-dín readily acceded to their request, and, having defeated Aram in a battle within sight of the city of Delhi, took possession of the throne. This event happened the same year, 1210, in which Aram was crowned king.

SHAMS-UD-DÍN ALTAMASH.

Ancestry of Shams-ud-dín.

Shams-ud-dín was the son of one Elam Khan, of the Albery tribe, and his mother belonged to a noble family of Khata. He was sold as a slave by his brothers to a company of travelling merchants, who carried him to Bokhara, where they sold him to a relative of Sadar Jahán, prince of that country. He received a good education at Bokhara, and, on the death of his master, was sold to a merchant, who again sold him to another. With the permission of Sultan Muhammad Ghori, he was ultimately purchased for fifty thousand pieces of silver by Kutb-ud-dín Ebak, who, later on, gave him one of his daughters in marriage.

He defeats Taj-ud-dín Yelduz, king of Ghazni, 1215 A. D., *And repels Jalal-ud-dín of Khwarzm.* *His conquests in Hindostán.* *Death of Shams-ud-dín Altamash, 1236 A. D.*

Altamash, now the son-in-law of his master, daily rose to favour, being first created general-in-chief and soon after appointed viceroy of Northern India. Four years after his accession to the throne, Taj-ud-dín Yelduz, king of Ghazni, having been defeated by Khwarzm Shah, king of Khwarzm, turned his attention towards the conquest of the east. In the year 1215, he seized the Panjáb and occupied Thanesar. Shams-ud-dín Altamash, having collected his troops, gave him battle on the plains of Naráin, defeated him, and took him prisoner. In the year 1217, Altamash attacked Nasir-ud-dín Kubáchá, his brother-in-law, who had become independent in Sindh, and gained a complete victory over him at Manserarah; on the banks of the Chináb. Four years afterwards, the Tartars, under their great leader, Changez Khan, having overrun the country of Khwarzm and penetrated as far as Ghazni, Jalál-ud-dín, son of the late Sultan of Khwarzm, was compelled to retreat in the direction of Láhore, where Altamash gave him battle and compelled him to retreat. The same year, Altamash finally reduced Sindh, with the co-operation of his wazír, Nizám-al-mulk* *Junedi,* Jalál-ud-dín *Kubácha,* his old adversary, having been drowned while attempting to cross the Indus. Shams-ud-dín Altamash reduced Malwa and Ujjain, and re-established his authority over the province of Bengal, which had assumed independence. At Ujjain, one of the most famous and ancient Hindu cities in India, he destroyed all the great temples and conveyed the images of Mahakáli and Vikramaditya, from whose death the Hindus reckon their era, together with many other figures of brass, to Delhi, to be broken at the door of the grand mosque. In the year 1236 he marched an army towards Multán, but fell sick on the road, and, returning to Delhi, died on the 30th April 1236, after reigning twenty-six years. He was another model of self-elevation by the force of genius, and during his reign the Mahomedan empire in India extended and gained materially in strength.

* This was the first wazír in Hindostán who received the title of Nizám-ul-mulk. The title seems to have been very generally adopted afterwards, and the descendants of the last Nizám ul-mulk are to this day the reigning Nawábs of Hyderabád State.

RUKN-UD-DÍN FEROZ.

Rukn-ud-dín crowned king, May 1st, 1236 A.D.

After the reduction of Gwalior, in 1231 A.D., Rukn-ud-dín Feroz was appointed by his father, Shams-ud-dín Altamash, viceroy in the Panjáb. When the emperor died, Rukn-ud-dín happened to be at Delhi, and was there crowned king. But he soon gave himself up to licentious excesses and neglected the affairs of state, which were mainly conducted by his mother, Shah Turkan, a cruel woman, who put to death all the women of the Emperor Shams-ud-dín's harem. Malik Ala-ud-dín Khán was at that time governor of Láhore, and Malik Kabír Khán, viceroy of Multán. A coalition of the chiefs was formed at Láhore to depose the king, and was joined by all the nobles of the northern and western provinces. The king marched against the confederates, but was deserted by some of his principal chiefs, who retired with their followers to Delhi and raised Sultána Razia Begum, eldest daughter of Shams-ud-dín, to the throne, Shah Turkan, the king's mother, being put in confinement. Rukn-ud-dín was defeated by Sultána Razia Begum, delivered up to her, and died in prison some time afterwards, after reigning only six months and twenty-eight days.

Combination of the chiefs against him.

He is defeated and deposed by his sister Sultana Razia Begum, November, 1236 A. D.

SULTÁNA RAZIA BEGUM.

Razia, a talented Princess.

Sultána Razia Begum, called *Malikai Dowran*, was endowed with all the qualifications necessary for the ablest kings. She was no ordinary woman, and the most severe critics of her actions could find no fault with her, but that she was a woman. She was possessed of valour, determination and courage in an eminent degree, and her remarkable talents and habit of close application to business enabled her, in the time of her father, to make herself familiar, not only with the routine of current business, but also with the art of politics. She was the constant companion of her father, and, while the king was engaged in the reduction of the fort of Gwalior, he appointed her his regent at the capital during his absence. When the Omerahs asked him the reason of his appointing his daughter to conduct the affairs of Government, in preference to any of his sons, he replied that "he observed his sons gave themselves up to wine, women, gambling and wind (flattery), and that he thought the government too weighty for them, while Razia, though a woman, had a man's head and heart, and was better than twenty such sons." She was well educated and could read the Kurán with correct pronunciation.

Her application to business.

Razia, after her assumption of imperial authority, changed her apparel, assumed the royal robes, gave public audience from the throne daily, and transacted all the business of state in public, revising and confirming the laws of her father and dispensing justice with equal hand.

The confederate Omerahs, who had met at Láhore, marched to Delhi, but the queen so skilfully sowed the seeds of dissension among the leading chiefs that they soon broke up their camp and dispersed. The queen conferred the office of prime minister on Khwaja Mahdi Ghaznavi, with the title of Nizám-ul-mulk, while Kabír Khan was made viceroy of Láhore. All the disturbances were now quelled, and the governors of distant provinces tendered their submission to the queen. Some of the malcontents having been executed and the rest reduced to submission by milder measures, peace and prosperity once more reigned throughout the land. Unfortunately for the queen, who was unmarried, she displayed the frailty of her sex by taking into her confidence an Abyssinian slave, named Jamál-ud-dín. Royal favours were daily showered on this individual. He was raised at once from the office of master of the horse

Kabír Khan, viceroy of Láhore.

Jamál-ud-dín the Abyssinian slave.

(*Mír Akhor*) to that of Amír-al-umrah, or the chief of the nobles. Such was the familiarity that existed between the queen and her slave, that, when she rode out, Jamál-ud-dín was in the habit of lifting her to her saddle by raising her up under her arms. This behaviour excited at once the disgust and envy of the nobles and Omerahs, who were much incensed, alike with the favours shown, and the liberties permitted by their sovereign, to an Abyssinian slave

The behavior of the Láhore viceroy.

The first to give open expression to his discontent was Malik Kabír Khan, the viceroy of Láhore, who threw off his allegiance and made himself independent. The queen marched against him at the head of an army to chastise him, and succeeded in reducing him to submission. The Malik conducted himself on this occasion with such humility that the empress, either believing in his sincerity, or desirous of securing his co-operation, not only reinstated him in the government of Láhore, but conferred on him, in addition, the governorship of Múltán, lately vacated by Malik Karaguz.

Revolt of Altúnia, the Turkish chief,

Who marries the queen.

She is defeated,

And put to death, 1239 A.D.

During the same year, Malik Altúnia, a chief of Turkish origin, governor of Bhatinda, revolted. The queen gave him battle, but, the Turkish chiefs in her army mutinying, she sustained a defeat, and her Abyssinian favourite was killed. The queen was herself taken prisoner and brought to Altúnia, who kept her in confinement in the fort of Bhatinda. The Turkish officers raised her brother Behram, a son of Shams-ud-dín Altamash, to the throne. Altúnia soon after married the queen, who raised an army of Ghakkar Jats and marched on Delhi, where a severe action was fought, in which the queen was defeated and fled to Bhatinda. The queen, having once more rallied her scattered forces, made a second effort for the crown, but she was again defeated on the plains of Kythal, on the 24th October 1239, and both she and her husband were taken prisoners. She was assassinated on the 14th November of the same year, after reigning three years and a half.

MOIZ-UD-DÍN BEHRAM SHAH.

Behram Shah, brother of Razia Sultana, ascends the throne, 1239 A.D.

Moghal irruption into the Panjáb, 1241 A.D.

Láhore plundered by the Moghals.

The king imprisoned and put to death, 1241 A. D.

When the empress, Razia Begam, was incarcerated in the fort of Bhatinda, Moiz-ud-dín Behram Shah ascended the throne, on the 21st of April 1239, and Malik Karaguz was again appointed Viceroy of Láhore. The peace of the empire was disturbed by internal discords and dissensions, while it was at the same time threatened by a formidable invasion from without. The hosts of the great mercenary leader, Changez Khan, having swept over the countries of Central Asia, made incursions into the Panjáb. They carried fire and sword wherever they went, and, advancing from Ghazni, seized Láhore on the 22nd of November 1241. The viceroy, finding his troops mutinous, was compelled to fly in the darkness of night. The Moghals gave up the city to indiscriminate plunder, and thousands of the inhabitants were carried away prisoners. The king, on hearing of this disaster, sent the Wazír Ikhtiar-ud-dín at the head of some troops, to drive the invaders out; but the danger had already passed away, and the invaders had retired from the country, after completing their work of devastation. Meanwhile, the wazír mutinied, and, a plot having been formed against the king, he was deposed, taken prisoner, and put to death in 1241, after a reign of little more than two years.

ALA-UD-DÍN MASÚD.

Accession of Ala-ud-dín Masúd.

Moiz-ud-dín Behram Shah was succeeded on the throne by Ala-ud-dín Masúd, son of Rukn-ud-dín Feroz. During his reign the Panjáb was invaded by the Moghals from Kandahar and Talikhan, under the command of Mangu Khan. The Moghals advanced as far as the Indus and laid siege to Úch. The king, putting himself at the head of his troops, marched to meet the enemy in person. He had advanced as far as the Biás, when, hearing that the enemy had been repulsed by the local authorities, he retired to his capital. On his return to Delhi, the king gave himself up to debauchery, and neglected the affairs of the empire. The nobles, wearied of his excesses and cruelties, determined to depose him, and invited his uncle, Nasír-ud-dín, from Baraich to ascend the throne. When Nasír-ud-dín arrived, he found the imbecile king already deposed and in prison, where he subsequently died, having reigned only four years and one month.

He is deposed by his uncle Nasír-ud-dín and put in confinement, 1246 A.D.

NASÍR-UD-DÍN MAHMÚD.

Nasír-ud-dín Mahmúd crowned king of Delhi, 1246 A.D.

Nasír-ud-dín Mahmúd, who was crowned king of Delhi on the 10th June, 1246, was the youngest son of Shams-ud-dín Altamash, and was appointed by him viceroy of Bengal. At his father's death he was thrown into confinement by the cruel queen, Sháh Turkán, and remained a prisoner until the accession of King Masúd, who conferred on him the governorship of Baraich.

Ghias-ud-dín Balban, wazír.

Nasír-ud-dín, on ascending the throne, conferred the office of minister, with the title of Alagh Khan, on Malik Ghias-ud-dín Balban, originally a slave of Shams-ud-dín Altamash, who subsequently gave him his daughter in marriage. Ghias-ud-dín's nephew, Sher Khan, having received the title of Moazzam Khan, was appointed to the government of the Panjáb, including Múltán, Bhatner and Sirhind. Sher Khan was one of the most renowned men of his age. He possessed all princely qualities, was a good soldier in the field, and a talented counsellor at court. He rebuilt the forts of Bhatner and Sirhind, and maintained a standing army to watch the hostile movements of the Moghals, who had now become masters of Ghazní, Kábul, Kandahar, Balkh and Herat.

Sher Khan, governor of the Panjáb.

Punishment of the Ghakkars, 1247 A.D.

In July, 1247, the king marched in person, at the head of his army, in the direction of Múltán, and encamped for some time on the banks of the Indus. He then visited the provinces of the Indus, with the view of chastising the Ghakkars for their continued inroads, and for the assistance rendered by them to the Moghals in their incursions into the Panjáb. Thousands of these Ghakkars, of all ages, and both sexes, were captured and carried away into confinement.

The emperor marches to Múltán, 1248 A.D.

In the year 1248, Nasír-ud-dín married the daughter of his wazír, Ghias-ud-dín Balban, and in the year following he marched to Múltán at the head of an army. Sher Khan, the viceroy of Láhore, nephew of the wazír, joined him on the banks of the Biás with twenty thousand chosen horse. The king remained at Múltán for a few days, and, having appointed Fyz-ud-dín Balban to the government of Nagore and Úch, and restored order in those districts, he returned to Delhi. In the year 1250, Sher Khan, the talented viceroy of Láhore, equipped an army and marched towards Ghazní, which he annexed once more to the empire of Delhi, driving the Moghals from the country. Coins were struck in the name of Nasír-ud-dín, and he was acknowledged king of all the territories in that province. Two years later, the king again marched to Múltán, where several forts had been lost in consequence of the attack of a large body of insurgents from Sindh. The rebellion was quelled, and the government of Múltán was conferred on Arsula Khan. Towards the latter end of 1257, a Moghal army, having crossed the Indus, committed depredations in the Panjáb; but the emperor marched against them, and the Moghals, hearing of his approach, retired.

Ghazní annexed to the empire of Delhi, 1250 A.D.

Arrival of an ambassador from Halaku Khan, 1258 A. D.

Death of the emperor, 1266 A. D.

His character.

In March 1258, the Panjáb was visited by an envoy from the court of Halaku Khan, grandson of Changez Khan, the celebrated Tartar. He paid a visit to Delhi, where he met with a most magnificent reception. In the year 1264, the emperor fell ill, and, after lingering for a long time, expired on the 18th of February, 1266, after a reign of more than twenty years.

Nasír-ud-dín Mahmúd was one of the ablest and most amiable and generous kings of Hindostán. His personal habits were most simple, and he avoided all ostentatious display. When the envoy of the Tartar king, Halaku Khan, visited Delhi, the court was attended by twenty-five princes from Asia, who, with their numerous retinue, had sought protection at Delhi from the armies of Changez Khan. Many tributary Indian rájás and chiefs also stood with folded arms before the throne. Amidst all this display of grandeur and magnificence, the king sat on the throne in a quiet unassuming manner and in plain dress. While in prison, he earned his livelihood by making copies of the Kurán, and refused to receive the State allowances. He often used to say that the man who did not know how to earn his bread did not deserve it. He kept up the occupation of earning his livelihood by copying the Kurán after his assumption of sovereign power. Unlike his predecessors, he never kept any concubines, and had but one wife, whom he obliged to do all domestic work single-handed. When she complained, upon one occasion, that she had burnt her fingers in baking bread for him, and asked that she might be allowed a female servant to assist her, the king exhorted her to persevere, observing that by so doing she would obtain her reward on the day of judgment, and adding, at the same time, that the public money was a trust given to him by God for God's people, and that he was bound not to squander it in needless expenses. One day a nobleman of the court was inspecting a copy of the Kurán in the handwriting of the king in his presence, when he pointed out a letter, which he said had been written twice over. The king, having looked at it, smiled and drew a circle round it. When, however, the critic had left the court, his majesty began to erase the circle. A bystander begged to know the king's reason for doing this, to which his majesty replied "that he knew the word was originally right, but he thought it better to erase it from a paper than to touch the heart of a poor man by bringing him to shame." This is only one proof among many of the virtues of his private life, though, as a sovereign, he ruled the country with vigour, and was not wanting in that zeal and personal bravery which are the real characteristics of a king, in evidence of which we may point to his many victories on the north-west frontier of his dominions, as well as to his brilliant successes over the Hindu states of India, a detailed notice of which does not fall within the province of this work. The *Tabakati Nasíri*, dedicated to Nasír-ud-dín Mahmúd, was compiled during his reign by Minhajussiráj Jurjání.

The virtues of his private life.

His public career.

GHIÁS-UD-DÍN BALBÁN.

Origin of Ghias-ud-din.

Ghiás-ud-dín, like many other great men of his time, was originally a Turki slave. He was a native of Kara Khata, and belonged to the tribe of Albery. He was bought at Bagdad by Khwájah Jamal-ud-dín, of Bassora, and conveyed by him to Delhi, where he was sold to Shams-ud-dín Altamash. He was first appointed superintendent of the royal falconry, in the duties of which office he was well versed, and, having by his dexterity and devotion gained the favour of his royal master, was soon created a noble. He had successfully administered the Panjáb during the reign of Rukn-ud-dín Feroz, was advanced to the dignity of Amír Hajib, or lord of requests, in the time of Ala-ud-dín Masúd, and raised to the office of grand wazír in the late reign of Nasír-ud-dín Mahmúd. Having settled the affairs of Bengal, the king paid his first visit to Láhore in 1266. The city had suffered greatly from the incursions of the Moghals, and his majesty having ordered it to be placed in a proper state of defence, the city walls were repaired. After constructing some public buildings, the king returned to Delhi.

The emperor visits Láhore, 1266 A. D.

In the following year, 1267, Sher Khan, the energetic viceroy of Láhore, who had most ably repelled the incursions of the Moghals, died, and was buried at Bhatuer, in an extensive mausoleum which he had himself constructed for the purpose. The emperor appointed his eldest son and heir, Prince Muhammad, surnamed Tájul Mulk, Sher Khan's successor. The prince was a youth of great talents, with a fine taste for literature, being himself a polished and profound Persian and Arabic scholar. On establishing his court at Láhore, he brought with him all his learned men who adorned the capital of Hindostán, and, amongst others, the prince's favourite tutor, Amir Khusrow, the poet-laureate, and Khwájah Hassan. He was visited at Láhore by Sheikh Osman Turmuzi, the most learned man of his time, but he soon after left for his native land, Turán. According to Ferishta, one day, when the Sheikh was reading his poems in Arabic in an assembly of literary men, presided over by the prince, the beauty and excellence of the odes was such that all the poets present were moved, and the learned prince could not himself repress his tears. During the prince's residence at Multán he invited the celebrated Sheikh Sadi of Shiráz twice to his court, but the Sheikh begged to be excused on the ground of his advanced years, and it was not without persistent solicitations that he was at length persuaded to accept some presents which had been sent him. In return, Sadi sent the prince copies of his works, and spoke in eulogistic terms of the attainments of Khusrow.

Death of Sher Khan, 1267 A. D.

Prince Muhammad the heir-apparent, appointed viceroy of the Panjab.

His court becomes the resort of famous authors and learned men.

At the command of the emperor, his youngest son, Kara Khan, surnamed Nasír-ud-dín, recruited and organised an army to watch the movements of the Moghals; and a place of rendezvous was formed on the river Biás, in the event of an invasion from the north-west, where the two princes could join the imperial army in expelling the enemy. The emperor was absent from his capital for three years, on account of a great rebellion in Bengal in 1279, when the viceroy, Toghral Khan, had assumed the title of king. After suppressing this rebellion, the emperor returned to Delhi, where Prince Muhammad paid him a visit. He had not been with his father three months when news reached him of the invasion of Multán by the Moghals. He hastened back to Múltán, and, marching at once against the enemy, defeated and drove them back with great slaughter. All the territories which had been lost to the kingdom were recovered.

The Moghals are driven back from Múltán.

But another disaster was yet awaiting the Panjáb. Persia was at this time ruled by Arghan Khan, son of Ebak Khan, and grandson of Halaku Khan, who had conquered the empire about the year 1258 A.D. The eastern provinces of Persia, from Khorasan to the Indus, were ruled by Tymúr Khan,* of the family of Changez Khan, who, about this time, invaded the Panjáb at the head of 20,000 horse, to avenge the slaughter of the Moghals which had taken place during the former year. The whole country about Depalpore and Láhore was ravaged, and the villages depopulated. The court of the Láhore viceroy was then at Multán. Having heard of these depredations, Muhammad hastened to Láhore and prepared for a vigorous resistance. Tymúr Khan, having advanced to the Rávi, observed the vast hosts of the Indian army on the opposite bank; the gallant Muhámmad,

Tymúr Khan, general of Arghan Khan, invades the Panjáb, 1258 A. D.

* This king must not be confounded with Amír Tymúr of Gorkan, commonly known as Tamerlane.

desirous of engaging with the renowned Moghal chief on equal terms permitted him to pass the river unmolested. The two armies, being drawn up in order of battle on the bank of the river, engaged each other in an action in which both commanders greatly distinguished themselves, each performing prodigies of valour. At length the Moghals gave way, and were hotly pursued by the Indians. Prince Muhammad, becoming tired of the pursuit, separated from the main body with 500 attendants, and, halting on the bank of a stream, became absorbed in prayer. At this juncture, however, a Moghal chief, who had concealed himself in an ambush at the head of 2,000 horse in a neighbouring wood, with his detachment, suddenly fell on the prince's party which was unprepared to meet it. The gallant prince, immediately mounting his horse, cheered on his small band to the fight; and a desperate conflict took place, in which he was overpowered by superior numbers, and at length fell, mortally wounded, but not before he had three times obliged the Moghals to retreat. A detachment of the Indian army were now seen coming to the rescue, but too late to save their leader. Many prisoners fell into the hands of the Moghals in this conflict. Amir Khusrow, the prince's favourite and tutor, who so graphically describes the way in which he obtained his release, in his celebrated poem called "Khizr Khani," being among the rest.

The Moghals are routed,

But the heir-apparent is killed.

The news of the death of his beloved son quite prostrated the old king, now upwards of eighty years of age, and he sank rapidly under the weight of his affliction. He sent Ke Khusrow, his grandson, son of the deceased prince, to take the command at Láhore and Múltán, in the place of his lamented father, and a few days afterwards expired, in the year 1286, after a reign of twenty-two years.

Ke Khusrow, grandson of the emperor, appointed governor of the Panjáb.

Death of Ghias-ud-dín Balban, 1286 A.D.

During the reign of Ghiás-ud-dín Balbán, Delhi became the chief seat of learning and literature and the resort of learned and holy men. There flourished during his time, in Delhi, the celebrated Sheikh Faríd-ud-dín *Masúd*, entitled *Shakarganj*, Sheikh Baha-ud-dín Zakaria, Sheikh Badr-ud-dín *Arif* of Ghazní, the most venerable Khwája Kutb-ud-dín Bakhtiár Kúkí, the celebrated saint, and Shidi Moula.

The learned and holy men of his time.

The deceased monarch's court was the most magnificent and dignified in Asia, and, during his reign of twenty-two years, he admitted no one to public office who was not a man of merit and family, while he most scrupulously excluded all men of low birth from his court. Not less than fifteen sovereigns from Asia, who had been driven from their homes by the arms of Changez Khan, sought an honourable asylum at his court, and to each a sumptuous establishment was allowed. When the emperor gave audience from the throne, they all stood on the right, according to their rank, with the exception of two princes, the relations of the Caliph of Bagdad, who, on account of their holiness, were allowed a seat on either side of the *Masnad*.

The etiquette of his court.

The etiquette of his court was very strict, and its appearance most imposing, while such was the solemnity and grandeur of the royal presence, that none could approach the throne without mixed feelings of awe and admiration. Nor was Balbán less splendid and gorgeous in his cavalcades. His state elephants were caparisoned in purple and gold trappings. His horseguards, consisting of a thousand brave Tartars, attired in splendid and glittering armour, were mounted on the finest steeds of Persia and Arabia, with bridles of silver and saddles of rich embroidery. Five hundred chosen foot, in rich liveries, with drawn swords, preceded him, proclaiming his approach and clearing the way before him. The Omerahs then followed, according to their rank, with their various equipages and attendants. In his early youth he was addicted to wine, but on his accession to the throne, he

His cavalcades.

became the deadly foe of this luxury, prohibiting the sale and manufacture of liquor throughout his dominions under the severest penalties.

MOZ-UD-DÍN KEKUBÁD.

On the death of his grandfather, Kekubád, son of Nasír-ud-dín Kara-Khan, at that time viceroy of the province of Bengal, then in his eighteenth year, ascended the throne by the title of Moz-ud-dín. He was a handsome and engaging youth, and had been brought up with great rigour by his father, but he soon gave himself up to licentious habits, leaving the executive power of the State entirely in the hands of the wazír, who, for his own private ends, encouraged the riotous debauchery of his master. The only event of importance which occurred in the Panjáb during his short reign was an invasion of the districts of Láhore by the Moghals. The king sent an army against them, under Malik Yar Beg *Birlas* and Khan Jehan. The Moghals were defeated near Láhore, and a great number of them were brought prisoners to Delhi, where, shortly afterwards, all the Moghal officers in the service of the State were executed on the pretence of their collusion with their countrymen.

Kekubád crowned emperor, 1288 A.D.

Fresh incursion of the Moghals.

Massacre of the Moghal officers.

The feeble monarch neglecting the affairs of the State, the executive power was assumed by three nobles of the court, of whom Malik Jalal-ud-dín Feroz, of the Khiljai tribe, was the chief. At his instance, the king was assassinated in his country palace, while lying sick and helpless on his bed. The event happened in 1288, and with it the slave dynasty of kings, which had reigned from 1205 to 1288, a period of eighty-three years, came to an end. Kekubád had reigned a little more than three years. On his death, Jalal-ud-dín Khiljai was proclaimed king.

Kekubád murdered, 1288 A.D.

CHAPTER V.

THE KHILJAÍ DYNASTY OF THE TARTARS.

JALAL-UD-DÍN FEROZ.

When Changez Khan was on his way back to Turán, from the pursuit of Jalal-ud-dín Khwarzm Sháh on the banks of the Indus, his son-in-law, Khalíj Khan, a descendant of the Khulich or Khalíj, with his tribe, amounting to thirty thousand families, settled in the mountains west of the Panjáb, where they still remain. The Ghiljais belonged to a martial race, and, being of warlike disposition, they entered the service of the kings of Ghazní and India, and among them some obtained opportunities of holding posts of distinction and trust under their respective governments. Jalal-ud-dín, a descendant of Khalíj Khan, rose into favour with the late king, but was himself seventy years old when he ascended the throne.

Origin of the Khiljái kings.

During his reign, in the year 1291, Abdulla, a grandson of Halaku Khan, the grandson of Changez Khan, having invaded the Panjáb at the head of a hundred thousand horsemen, Jalal-ud-dín Feroz collected a large army and marched in person to meet him. A general action was fought on the plains of the Panjáb, in which, after a very severe contest, the Moghals were defeated, many of their chiefs slain and a large number of them taken

Panjáb invaded by Abdullah, a grandson of Haláku Khan, 1291 A.D.

prisoners. The king, who was noted for his clemency, at length granted peace to the invaders with permission to withdraw from the country. At this time Oghlú Khan, a grandson of Changez Khan, with three thousand followers, joined the king, who gave him his daughter in marriage. These Moghals all became converts to Mahomedanism. The emperor, having appointed his son, Arkally Khan, viceroy of Láhore, Múltán and Sindh, and having left with him a strong force, departed for his capital.

Arkally Khan appointed viceroy of the Panjab.

Jalal-ud-dín was assassinated at the instance of his nephew, Ala-ud-dín, on 19th July, 1295, after reigning for a period of seven years. He was celebrated for his many amiable qualities, particularly for his humanity and benevolence. He appointed Amír Khusrow his librarian, and, having raised him to the rank of an Omerah, permitted him to wear white garments, a distinction usually confined to the blood-royal and to the highest nobles of the court.

Jallal-ud-din murdered 1295 A.D.

ALA-UD-DÍN KHILJÍ.

On the murder of the late king, the queen-dowager placed her youngest son, Kadr Khan, on the throne, the eldest son, Arkally Khan, being in his province of Múltán and having declined to come to the capital. Ala-ud-dín, who had formed the project of establishing an independent kingdom in Oudh, abandoned the idea, and hastened to Delhi, where he was opposed by the young king; but the latter, seeing the troops of Ala-ud-dín drawn up in order of battle, retired to the city in despair, and was deserted by a number of his nobles. Ala-ud-dín entered the city with great pomp, and was crowned king in the latter end of the year 1296. The young king, with his mother, his harem, his treasure, and a few of the Omerahs who had remained faithful to the last, set out for Multán, where he joined his brother. Ala-ud-dín, finding his position secure, began to concert measures to extirpate the issue of his late uncle Jalal-ud-dín Feroz. With this view, he despatched a force of forty thousand horsemen to Múltán under the command of his brothers, Alaf Khan and Zaffar Khan.

Ala-ud-din crowned king, 1296 A.D.

He despatches a force to Multán.

Múltán was laid under a siege, which lasted two months, but the citizens and the garrison betrayed the cause of the princes, who were surrendered on promise of general safety, of which the most solemn assurance was given. Under orders of Ala-ud-din, however, the princes were blinded on the way, put in confinement in Hansí, and subsequently put to death.

Two of the royal princes blinded and put to death.

In the second year of his reign, advices reached the king that an army of a hundred thousand Moghals, under Amír Daud, king of Mawalunahr, was advancing towards the Panjáb with the object of conquering Múltán, Láhore and Sindh, and was carrying everything before him with fire and sword. Ala-ud-dín sent his brother Alaf Khan to check the progress of the invaders, and the two armies came into contact in the district of Láhore. A most sanguinary battle ensued, in which the Moghals were defeated, with a loss of twelve thousand men and many of their principal officers. A large number of persons of all ranks were taken prisoners, and subsequently put to the sword, no clemency being shown even to women and children captured in the Moghal camp.

The Moghals invade the Panjab, 1297 A.D.

The Moghals are defeated in the district of Lahore.

Undismayed by their previous disaster, the Moghals, under Kutlugh Khan, son of Amír Daud Khan, king of Mawalunahr, again invaded the Panjáb in the year 1298. Their army on this occasion, according to Ferishta, consisted of two hundred thousand horse, and, having occupied all the countries beyond the Indus, they advanced to the very gates of the capital, and encamped on the banks of the Jumna. The king put himself at the head of his troops and gave the invaders battle, when, after a most bloody engage-

A fresh irruption of the Moghals, 1298 A.D.

ment, the Moghals were compelled to retreat and to evacuate India as rapidly as they had advanced towards it. Elated with this success, Ala-ud-din now formed a project of founding a religion of his own, in order that his name might be carried down to posterity in company with those of other great men, and he also proposed to undertake the conquest of the world, like Alexander the Great, leaving a viceroy in India; but his wild projects were soon after abandoned.

They are compelled to retreat.

The king's ambitious projects.

In the year 1303, the king was engaged in expeditions to Warangal, the capital of Telingana, and Chittor in Rájputáná. Intelligence of these remote expeditions having reached Mawalunahr, Turghay Khan, the Moghal chief, thinking that the emperor would be absent a long time, invaded India with a body of twelve thousand horse. He reached Delhi unopposed, and plundered the suburbs. At this juncture, however, the Moghal army, from whatever cause, whether seized with a sudden panic, or, as is probable, sated with plunder, retired precipitately to their own country.

A renewed Moghal invasion, 1303 A.D.

Their unexpected return.

In the following year, 1304, they made another irruption into India, under Ali Beg, a descendant of Changez Khan and Khwájah Tásh. Forty thousand Moghal horsemen having passed north of Láhore, penetrated as far as Amroha in Rájastán. Toghlak Khan, governor of the Panjáb, was deputed to oppose them with a large force. He inflicted a signal defeat on the enemy, who lost seven thousand men in killed and wounded. Nine thousand of their troops were made prisoners and sent in chains to Delhi, where, according to Ferishta, they were all put to death, Ali Beg and Khwájah Tásh being trampled under the feet of elephants.

The Moghal invasion of 1304 A.D.

Victory of the governor of the Panjáb.

Nine thousand Moghals slaughtered.

In the year 1305, the Moghals again invaded the Panjáb, under Elak Khan, a general of Amír Daud Khan, in order to avenge the death of Alí Beg and Khwájah Tásh. Multán was ravaged; but Ghazi Beg Toghlak formed an ambuscade on the banks of the Indus, and, when the Moghals, enriched with spoil, were on their way to their country, suddenly fell upon them, and defeated them with great slaughter. Most of the survivors, being exposed to the hot winds and the burning sand, perished in the deserts of Central Asia. Three thousand captives, with Elak Khan, the chief of the Moghals, were sent to Delhi, where they were all put to the sword by the king's order, a pillar being constructed of their skulls. The Moghal women and children, taken prisoners in this war, were sent to different parts of India, to be sold as slaves in the markets. But these repeated disasters did not deter the Moghals; for they again invaded the Panjáb the same year, under Yakhalmand, a chief of considerable reputation, and were again defeated by Toghlak, several thousand of them being sent as captives to Delhi, where, according to the custom of the time, they were all put to death. Toghlak, on this occasion, pursued them as far as Cábul, Ghazní and Kandahar, and laid the inhabitants under heavy contribution. These excursions were repeated by Toghlak each year, so that the Moghals remained on the defensive and for many years to come gave up all idea of invading Hindostán.

Another Moghal invasion defeated 1305 A.D.

They renew the attack and are pursued to Kábul and Ghazní, 1305 A.D.

The reign of this emperor is noted for many reforms effected by him in the civil administration of the country. He enhanced the revenue demand on land to half the value of the produce; fixed the price for grain, cloth, horses, cattle, and grocery. He issued loans from the public treasury, by means of which merchants were enabled to import cloths from neighbouring countries. But he prohibited the exportation of a fine kind of manufacture, and no one was permitted to wear such stuffs without special authority from the king, which was given only to men of rank. The use and manufacture of spirituous liquors were prohibited under pains of the severest kind. Re-

The civil administration of Ala-ud-din.

gulations for the army were made, and the pay of military men of all ranks was fixed. His authority was dreaded by the greatest men in the land, and his will alone was the law. Becoming suspicious of the Moghals, who had entered the royal service after embracing the faith of Islam, he dismissed them all, and, not content with this, he, for some unaccountable reason, had fifteen thousand of these unhappy creatures butchered in the streets of Delhi in one day, while all their wives and children were enslaved. No one dared to remonstrate with the king for such barbarous cruelty. Though at first illiterate, he applied himself assiduously to the acquisition of knowledge, and became able to read, write, and study books. He built magnificent palaces, mosques, mausoleums, and colleges, and became a patron of learning. Among the holy men of his time were Nizám-ud-dín *Oulia*, of Delhi, Sheikh Ala-ud-dín, the grandson of the celebrated Sheikh Fariddin *Shakarganj*, Sheikh Rukn-ud-dín, the son of Sadr-ud-dín Arif, and grandson of the famous Baha-ud-dín Zakaria of Múltán. Among the poets of the time were Amír Khusrow, Amír Hassan, Sadr-ud-din Ali and Mouláua Aríf.

Fifteen thousand Moghals in the royal service put to death.

The learned men of his time.

Ala-ud-dín died on the 19th December 1316, after a reign of twenty years and some months.

The king's death, 1316 A.D.

KUTB-UD-DÍN MOBÁRAK SHAH.

After the death of Ala-ud-dín Khiljaí, Malik Kafúr, the eunuch slave, who had been purchased by the late king at Cambay and had risen to high rank and favour, having assembled the Omerahs and produced a spurious document of the deceased king, acknowledging his youngest son Omar as king, placed him on the throne. The prince was then only seven years of age, and Kafúr himself began to administer the affairs of the kingdom as regent. He put out the eyes of Khizr Khan and Shádí Khan, the elder sons of the king, and, however ridiculous it may appear, the eunuch, nevertheless, married the mother of Prince Omar, the late emperor's third wife. A band of assassins was then sent to assassinate Mobarak Khan, the king's third son, but the prince had the presence of mind to throw his jewels before them. The ruffians quarrelled about the division of the prize, and information of the affair reaching the commander of the royal guards and his lieutenant, they, with their men, entered the eunuch's apartments and put him to death. Mobárak then assumed the sovereign power, but was not crowned king until the 22nd March, 1317.

His youngest son, Omar, succeeds.

The royal princes are blinded.

Malik Kafúr put to death.

Mobárak ascends the throne, 1317 A.D.

Mobárak's first measures were just and beneficial. He released a large number of convicts, and had all the exiles recalled by proclamation. To gain popularity, he made a present of six months' pay to the troops, and restored lands which had been resumed during the last reign. He removed all obnoxious taxes and tributes, and the restrictions on commerce which had been imposed by his late father, and commerce again flowed in its accustomed channels. He, however, abandoned many of the wise institutions of his father, and gave himself up to licentious revelry; vice and lust became the fashion of the day, and most people were infected by his example. The king committed the most villainous excesses that can disgrace human nature, and became infamous for every vice. He was murdered on the night of the 9th March, 1329, by a body of ruffians hired for the purpose by Malik Khusrow, originally a Hindu slave, who had risen into high favour with him.

He gives himself up to licentiousness.

Mobarak Khiljaí murdered, 1329 A.D.

Malik Khusrow ascended the throne the following day with the title of Nasír-ud-dín. Everybody having any pretension to relationship with the late king, was murdered in cold blood. The king took to himself Dewal Devi, the beautiful wife of Khizr Khan, the brother of his master

Malik Khusrow usurps the throne.

Extirpation of the royal family.

and sovereign. Ghazi Beg Toghlak, the able and brave viceroy of Láhore, having heard of the shocking revolution brought about by Khusrow, marched from the Panjáb at the head of an army to deliver the oppressed subjects from the hands of the usurper. Most of the governors of provinces joined Toghlak with their troops. Moghaltagin, the governor of Múltán, who was unwilling to act in concert with him, was killed by Behram Abia, a Moghal chief of note, who put the whole Multán army at the disposal of the Láhore viceroy. The confederate armies, having advanced to Delhi, were met by the royal troops on the banks of the Sursuti, but the latter were so effeminate and so enervated by idleness and debauchery, as to be no match for the hardy veterans of the frontier, who were thoroughly practised in war and had repeatedly beaten the Moghals in the field. Malik Khusrow was defeated and put to flight, but was subsequently found concealed in an old tomb, whence he was dragged forth and at once executed on the 22nd August, 1321.

Ghazi Beg, viceroy of Láhore, marches on Delhi,

And defeats Malik Khusrow,

Who is put to death 1321 A.D.

The following day, the nobles and Omerahs of the city waited on the victor to pay him their respects and to lay before him the keys of the city. Ghazi Beg made his triumphant entry into the city. As he came in sight of the *Hazár Minar*, or palace of thousand minarets, he wept bitterly, and, addressing the public, said that he considered himself only as one of their number, that he had unsheathed his sword to rid the world of a monster, and that, if none of the royal race survived, he would most willingly serve anyone who might be selected by the nobility to be their king. The multitude cried out with one voice that none was so fit to reign as he himself, who had shielded them from the vengeance of the Moghals and had freed them from the grinding tyranny of an usurper; and, thereupon lifting him up, they carried him to the great hall of public audience and, seating him on the royal throne and bowing before him with folded hands, hailed him as "Shahjehan" (King of the Universe). Ghazi Beg, however, on assuming the sovereign power, contented himself with the more modest title of "Ghiás-ud-dín." Thus, the dynasty of the Khiljaís, after reigning from 1288 to 1321, passed away amidst a chaos of revolts, bloodshed, and outrages of the most horrible nature.

Ghazi Beg Toghlak elected king.

CHAPTER VI.

THE TOGHLAK DYNASTY, 1321 TO 1398.

GHIAS-UD-DÍN TOGHLAK.

GHIAS-UD-DIN Toghlak was crowned king amidst the enthusiastic acclamations of the multitude. Muhammad Kásim Ferishta writes, in his interesting work, that, when deputed by his sovereign, Ibrahím Adil Shah, of Bijápur, to the court of the Emperor Jehangír, then at Láhore, he enquired from persons well versed in history what they knew of the origin of the Toghlak dynasty. Though unable to produce any written authority on the subject, they all agreed that Toghlak was the name of Ghiás-ud-dín's father, that he was a Turki slave of Ghias-ud-dín Balbán and had married a wife of the Jat

The origin of Ghazi Beg Toghlak.

tribe in the vicinity of Láhore, by whom he had issue, a son, Ghází Beg, who, on his accession to the throne, assumed the title of "Ghiás-ud-dín, or "Asylum of the faith."

He assumes the title of Ghiás-ud-dín.

His previous career.

Ghiás-ud-dín had for many years acted as viceroy of Láhore, which then included all the frontier provinces from the Himálayas to Sindh. He was a person of mature age and possessed of considerable tact and judgment. As already noted, he had successfully repelled the repeated incursions of the Moghals, and even attacked them in their own country. He now adopted Behram Abia as a brother, in return for his having effectually aided him with an army from Multán in the late crisis, and put him in charge of all the provinces on the banks of the Indus. In the meantime he strengthened his western frontiers by building new forts and establishing garrisons on the borders of Kábul. Further incursions of the Moghals were thus effectually prevented. He regulated the affairs of his kingdom to the entire satisfaction of his people, reformed the laws, encouraged commerce, patronized men of literary ability, and constructed public buildings. He built a new citadel at Delhi, which he called Toghlakábád. He was killed by the fall of a roof of a pavilion in Delhi, in February 1325, after a reign of four years and some months. The poet, Amir Khusrow, who lived to the end of his reign, wrote his history, under the title of *Toghlak Namo.*

His new beneficent schemes.

He is accidentally killed, 1325 A.D.

MUHAMMAD TOGHLAK.

He is succeeded by Alaf Khan or Muhammad Toghlak.

Character of the new king.

On the death of Ghiás-ud-dín Toghlak, his eldest son, Alaf Khan, ascended the throne under the title of Muhammad Toghlak. He was one of the most accomplished men of his age. His views were generous and his policy was conciliatory. The fame of his liberality induced learned men from Asia to resort to his court, and he lavished his bounty on his courtiers to a degree unsurpassed in previous times. He founded hospitals for the sick and established almshouses for the widows and destitute. He was eloquent in speech, and his writings in Persian and Arabic were models of elegant style and composition. He had made history his favourite subject of study, and was well versed in the sciences of physics, logic, astronomy and mathematics. In remarkable cases, he visited the patients himself, and noted, with much interest, the progress of their complaints. He studied the philosophy of the Greeks, and held discourses on metaphysical subjects with the learned men of the time, Assed *Mantaki*, or "the logician," Obed, the poet, *Maulana* En-ud-dín *Shirazi*, Najm-ud-in *Jutishar*, and other eminent scholars of the day.

Invasion of the Panjáb by Turmushrin Khan Moghal, 1327 A.D.

The first great event of his reign was a formidable irruption of the Moghals, who now aspired to the complete conquest of Hindostán. In the year 1327 Turmushrin Khan, a chief of the Chaughattai tribe, and a Moghal general of much celebrity, invaded the Panjáb at the head of a great army. Having subdued Multán, Laghman and the northern provinces, he advanced to Delhi by rapid marches. The emperor, who had not yet settled his government, and who was ill-prepared for an action, thought it best to preserve his dominions by the payment of an enormous sum of money to the invaders, who, gratified by the present, which was almost equal to the price of a kingdom, withdrew. Their retreat was through Gujrát and Sindh, which countries they plundered to the uttermost of their power, carrying off with them thousands of the inhabitants as slaves.

Their retreat on payment of ransom.

Wild schemes of the emperor.

Attempt to conquer China, 1337 A.D.

In the year 1337, the king embarked on the wild project of conquering China and despatched 100,000 horse through the Nepál hills, under Malik Khusrow, his sister's son, to subdue that country. The troops entered the Himálaya Mountains, and small forts were built by them at intervals for the purpose of securing their communications. On reaching the Chinese border, the Indians were opposed by a numerous army. The rainy season now set in, and the low country was completely inundated, while the mountains were covered with impervious woods, and, to crown the distress of the Indians, a severe famine soon began to decimate them. In the midst of these calamities a large number of the invading army were cut off by the Chinese troops, while, during their retreat, the mountaineers plundered them of their baggage. The whole army thus fell victims to the king's ambition, and, as Ferishta says, scarcely a man survived to relate the fate of the expedition, except those who had been left behind in the garrisons.

Failure of the expedition.

In 1340 Malik Behram Abia, the old friend of the king's father, raised the standard of insurrection. The king had removed the seat of his government from Delhi to Deogarh, which he called Dowlatabád, and had given stringent orders to all his Omerahs to remove to the new city with their families. Ali, a confidential servant of the king, was sent to Behram, viceroy of Multán, with the same message; but he proving unwilling to comply with the king's requisitions, Ali had recourse to insolent threats. High words passed between the messenger and the viceroy's son-in-law; and, blows ensuing, the messenger's head was struck off by one of Behram's attendants. The king, hearing of this disrespect to his authority, forthwith put his army in motion and arrived before Múltán. Malik Behram drew up his forces in order of battle, and an engagement took place between the two armies, attended with great bloodshed on both sides. Behram's troops were at last defeated and put to flight. The King, who was much incensed, gave orders for a massacre of all the inhabitants of Multán, but the holy saint Rukn-ud-dín mediated with him and persuaded him to refrain from so bloody a deed. The vanquished army was pursued by the victors, who overtook Malik Behram, and, killing him, brought his head as a trophy to the king, who, after these events, returned to Delhi, having appointed Behzád Khan his viceroy at Múltán.

Revolt of Behram Abia, governor of Múltán 1340 A.D.

The king moves in person to chastise him.

Behram is defeated and put to death, 1340 A.D.

About the year 1341, Sháhú, a powerful chief of the Afghán Mountains, ravaged the countries north of the Panjáb and invaded Múltán. The governor, Behzád Khan, appeared with his army to oppose him, but was defeated with great slaughter and put to death. The invader laid waste the whole province, and its inhabitants were reduced to great straits. These tidings having reached Delhi, the emperor moved towards Múltán at the head of an army, but Sháhú, on his approach, fled to his hill fastness, and, the danger being thus averted, the king retraced his steps to his capital.

Invasion of Múltán by Sháhú the Afghan chief, 1341 A.D.

His flight.

In the year 1341 the Panjáb was once more invaded by the Ghakkars, under their chief malik Hyder Khan. Tatar Khan, the viceroy of Láhore, opposed the enemy, and, in a battle which was fought, the Láhore army was defeated and the viceroy killed. On news of this disaster reaching the court at Delhi, the emperor despatched Khwája Jahán at the head of a large army against the Ghakkars, who were put to flight and expelled from the country.

The Panjáb invaded by Ghakkars, 1341 A.D.

Who are finally defeated and repulsed.

In the year 1351, the emperor, having been joined by Altún Bahádur, at the head of 5,000 Moghal horse, went on an expedition to Tata, to chastise the Sumera prince of Sindh. The Moharram festival coming on, he halted within sixty miles of the city to pass the first ten days of the month. During the halt he partook of fish in excess and contracted a fever. Before he had recovered, he embarked in a vessel for Tata, but expired within 30 miles of of that town, on 20th March 1351, after a reign of twenty-seven years.

Expedition to Sindh, 1351 A.D.

Death of Muhammad Toghlak, 1351 A.D.

The historian, Zia-ud-dín Barm author of the history of Firoz Shah, flourished in the time of Muhammad Toghlak, and accompanied the emperor on many of his expeditions. The emperor, notwithstanding his education, proved himself a tyrannical despot before he had been long on the throne. During his residence at Delhi he once set out with his army on a hunting expedition. On arriving in the district of Bairam, he told the officers that he had come, not to hunt beasts, but men, and he barbarously caused the inhabitants to be massacred. Thousands of their heads were brought to Delhi and hung over the city walls. On another occasion, writes Ferishta, he made an expedition in the direction of Kanauj and put the inhabitants to the sword. The country was laid waste for many miles round, and desolation and terror spread over the land. The king once entertained the project of conquering the Persian empire, and raised 370,000 horse for the purpose, thereby impoverishing the resources of the country; but the scheme had to be abandoned as impracticable. Of his expedition to China we have already given an account. A curious incident is described by Ferishta of the emperor's whims and caprice, which has led Mr. Elphinstone to speculate whether he was not strongly tainted with insanity. During a journey to Malabar, which had rebelled, he fell dangerously ill, and, entrusting Imad-ul-mulk with the command of the army, returned to Dowlatabad, his favourite habitation. Being afflicted with a violent toothache on the way, he lost one of his teeth. This tooth was buried in Bír with great ceremony, and a magnificent stone mausoleum was constructed over it which exists to this day, a monument of the king's vanity. The king entertained the greatest reverence for the Caliph of Baghdád, whose ambassador, Haji Syad Hurmuzy, was received with great ceremony by him in 1344. The king advanced twelve miles from the city on foot to receive him, and put the Caliph's letter on his head. On his return to the city, a grand festival was held, and the king's fancy carried him so far that he caused the Caliph's name to be inscribed on all the royal robes and furniture. Shekhúl Shayukh Misri, the Caliph's envoy, who arrived in 1162, was received with the same distinction, and subsequently, when a prince of the house of Abbasi arrived, he was always seated on the king's right hand at court, and the king was at times seen even sitting on the carpet below him.

His cruel propensities.

Projected conquest of Persia.

His whims and caprice.

His reverence for the Caliph of Bagdád.

FIROZ TOGHLAK.

On the death of Muhammad Toghlak, his cousin Firoz, whom he had declared his successor on his death-bed, being absent with the army, Sadr Jahán, a relation, placed a boy six years old on the throne. Firoz advanced to Delhi at the head of his troops, and the pretensions of the boy being withdrawn, he ascended the throne on September 14th, 1351, under the title of Firoz Toghlak. He visited Kalanaur, then in the district of Láhore, on a hunting excursion, in 1353, and had a splendid palace built on the banks of the Sarsuti. The year 1354 was rendered memorable by the king founding a new city adjoining Delhi, to which he gave the name Firozabád. He then marched to Depálpúr, and, on July 12th, opened the great canal, forty-eight kos in length, which he had had constructed for the purpose of irrigation from the Sutlej to the Kaggar rivers. Another canal, constructed in 1356, carried the waters of the Jamna to the wastes of Hansi and Hissár, where he built a strong fort which he called Hissár Firoza. A third canal, connected with the Kaggar and Sarsuti, extended to the village Peri Khera, where he founded a city which he called Firozabád after his own name.

Firoz Toghlak crowned king, 1351 A.D.

He visits Kalanaur, 1353 A.D.

And founds Firozabád, 1354 A.D.

His canal projects.

He founds Hissár Firoza and Firozabád.

In the year 1358 the Moghals invaded the Panjáb as far as Depálpúr. Kábul Khan, the lord of the privy chamber, was sent with an army to meet them, but the invaders, having taken much booty, retired to their own country before the royal troops could arrive.

Moghal incursions into the Panjab, 1358 A.D.

The name of Nasir-ul-mulk, the youngest son of Mardan Doulat, is mentioned by Ferishta as the governor of Láhore during the reign of the Emperor Firoz. Few incidents of local interest occurred in the Panjáb during his reign. In 1379 the emperor marched to Samana, Ambála and Shahabád, and having levied tribute from the rájá of the Sarmor hills, returned to his capital.

Nasir-ul-Mulk, governor of Láhore.

Firoz died on October 23rd, 1388, at the advanced age of ninety, after reigning thirty-eight years. The date of his death (790 A. H.) is derived from the words وفات فیروز (death of Firoz) according the *Abjad* calculation. Firoz was a liberal and just prince, beloved alike by his soldiery and subjects of all ranks. He was a learned man and the author of the work known as *Futuhat Firozshahi.* Zia-ud-dín Barni lived at his court, and, in his work called the "*Tawarikh Firozshahi,*" has written a history of his reign. He introduced many new laws, abolished the practice of mutilating criminals, reduced the demand on cultivators within reasonable limits, in consequence of which the landholders flourished and the State revenue increased, and encouraged learned men. He was seldom seen in his capital, but undertook frequent tours, inspecting his dominions and giving orders conducive to the welfare of his people on the spot. He applied the public money in the construction of works of public utility, and the local historian, Zia-ud-dín Barni, enumerates 50 dams across rivers to promote irrigation, 40 mosques, 30 colleges, with mosques attached, 20 palaces, 100 caravanserais, 200 towers, 30 reservoirs or lakes for irrigating lands, 100 hospitals, 5 mausoleums, 100 public baths, 10 monumental pillars, 10 public wells and 150 bridges, besides numerous gardens and pleasure-houses, built and founded by him. For the maintenance of all these public buildings, lands were assigned rent-free.

Feroz Toghlak dies, 1388 A. D.

His character.

His laws.

His public works.

After the death of Firoz Toghlak, his grandson, Ghias-ud-dín, succeeded him. This youth gave free rein to his youthful passions and lusts, and, after a brief reign of five months, was put to death along with his Wazír Firoz Ali, by a faction headed by Rukn-ud-dín, who supported the cause of his brother and cousins. This occurred on February 18th, 1389.

He is succeeded by Ghias-ud-din his grandson, 1388 A. D.

Who is put to death 1389, A. D.

Ghiás-ud-dín was succeeded on the throne by Abú Bakr, another grandson of Firoz Toghlak; but he reigned only till November 29th of the same year, when he was deposed by Muhammad, son of Firoz, who had fled from the capital on the abdication of his father and was now recalled by the unanimous consent of the Omerahs.

Abú Bakr succeeds, 1389 A. D.

But is deposed the same year.

NASIR-UD-DÍN MUHAMMAD TOGHLAK II.

Prince Muhammad, on ascending the throne of his ancestors, assumed the title of Nasir-ud-din Muhammad. This was, however, not until August 1390, when the rival claimant, Abu Bakr, having been finally defeated, had fled from the capital to Mewát. In the year 1391 advices reached the king that the Wazír Islam Khan, to whom he owed his elevation to the throne, had made preparations to retire to Láhore and Multán at the head of a large number of troops, with the design of exciting a revolution in those provinces. The emperor charged him with treason, and, on the evidence of his relations, condemned him to death. In the year 1394 the Ghakkars rebelled under their leader, one Shekha. The emperor sent his son, Húmayún, to crush the rebellion, but died of fever at Mahomedabad on February 19th, 1394, after a reign of six years and seven months. His remains were interred in the same vault in which his father had reposed.

Nasir-ud-dín Muhammad ascends the throne, 1390.

Rebellion of the Ghakkars, 1394.

Death of the emperor, 1394.

Nasir-ud-dín Muhammad Toghlak was succeeded by his son Húmayún, who, on ascending the throne, assumed the title of Sekandar; but he was

Húmayún succeeds and dies.

attacked by a violent disease and died suddenly, after a brief reign of forty-five days.

MAHMÚD TOGHLAK.

Mahmúd succeeds.

Distracted state of the empire.

On the death of Húmayún, the succession was violently contested; but Mahmúd, a youth and the son of the late king Nasir-ud-dín Muhammad, was at length raised to the throne. The kingdom was, however, distracted by dissensions among the nobles, and factions were formed in the Court which encouraged the viceroys of different provinces to revolt and assert their independence. Khawja Jahan, the wazír, assumed the title of Malikushshark, or the king of the East, and asserted his independence in a portion of Bengal. The Ghakkars were in revolt in the Panjáb, Gujrát had become an independent kingdom, and Malwa and Khandes had long ceased to acknowledge their dependence on the Court of Delhi. The Panjáb, however, was not lost to the emperor, for the governors, for a time at least, remained firm in their allegiance to him, while confusion and dissensions reigned supreme everywhere in India.

The Ghakkárs defeated by Sárang Khan governor of Depálpúr.

Sárang Khan, the governor of Depálpúr, having collected a large body of troops in the province of Multán and the north-west of the Panjáb, marched against the Ghakkars, and a severe battle was fought on the plains of Ajuddhan, twenty-four miles from Láhore. The Ghakkars were defeated with great loss, and their chief, Shekha, fled and sought refuge in the hills of Jammu. After this victory Sárang Khan returned to Depálpúr, leaving his younger brother, Adíl Khan, at Láhore.

The revolt of Sarang Khan, 1395.

His defeat.

In the year 1395, differences having arisen between Sárang Khan, governor of Depálpúr and Khizr Khan, governor of Multán, war was declared between them. Several engagements took place with varying success, but victory at last declared for Sárang Khan, who, having captured Múltán, enlarged his power and resources. Elated with this success, Sárang Khan, the following year, advanced on the capital itself, but Tatar Khan, the governor of Pánipat, and Almás Beg, gave him battle and signally defeated him on October 4th, 1396, and compelled him to fly to Múltán.

The Moghals under Prince Pír Múhammad, grandson of Tymur invade Multan 1396.

In the year 1396, Mirza Pír Muhammad the grandson of Tymúr, commonly known as Tamarlane, having constructed a bridge-of-boats over the Indus, crossed that river at the head of an army and laid siege to Úch. Malik Ali, the governor of Úch, was reduced to great straits when Sárang Khan, the governor of Múltán advanced to relieve and reinforce him. Mirza Pír Muhammad, hearing of this advance, moved to the Biás and out-flanking the Múltán troops fell on them just as they were crossing the river. The troops were taken by surprise and driven into the stream, in which large numbers of them were drowned. Many were put to the sword, and only a small number succeeded in effecting their retreat towards Múltán. The prince pursued them to the gates of Múltán, and Sárang Khan shut himself up within the citadel, which was beseiged by the Moghals.

Sárang Khan is compelled to capitulate.

The beseiged held out for six months, when, provisions failing, Sárang Khan was compelled to capitulate with his entire garrison. Pír Muhammad lost most of his horses and articles of transport in this protracted campaign, and the rainy season setting in, he was unable to undertake further operations.

India invaded by Tymur, 1398 A.D.

In the meanwhile two factions had been formed at the court of Delhi, one under Ikbál Khan, and the other under Mokarrab Khan. The king was a mere puppet in the hands of the former, who succeeded in expelling Mokarrab Khan and his partisans from the city. Peace was being restored in the capital when another calamity befell the Indians. This was the invasion of Tymúr Beg Gorkan, who, having been informed of the disturbed condition of the country, had conceived the design of subduing the whole of India.

CHAPTER VII.

INVASION OF TYMÚR.

INTELLIGENCE of the civil wars in India and the general distractions and disorders of the empire having reached Tymúr, or Tamerlane, at Samarkand, in 1396, he despatched an army under his grandson, Pír Muhammad, who overran the countries west of the Indus. Tymúr followed in person, and, crossing the Indus on September 12th, 1398, advanced by forced marches on Láhore. An advanced guard was despatched under Shekh Núr-ud-dín to subdue Shaháb-ud-din Mobárak Khan, governor of the Panjáb, who had advanced to the Chináb in order to check the progress of the invader. Mobárak Khan, took up an isolated position on the bank of the river, and, throwing round it a deep ditch, with fortifications, prepared to defend it to the last. Repeated attacks were made by the Indians and repulsed each time by the Moghals, until at length Tymúr came up with his whole force. Mobárak Khan, overcome with fear at the approach of so large an army, secretly embarked with his family and treasures, and sailed down the river, leaving to their fate the Indian garrison, who, finding their leader gone, surrendered unconditionally.

Tymúr crosses the Indus, 1398.

Mobárak Khan, governor of the Panjáb, checks his progress at the Chináb.

But is repulsed.

Tymúr now proceeded along the river bank to the junction of the Chináb with the Rávi. His army crossed by a bridge-of-boats thrown across the river for the purpose, and encamped outside the town of Talamba. Provisions failing, a sally was made into the town for the purpose of obtaining them, but the impatient soldiery began to plunder the town, and the inhabitants, resisting them, were mercilessly massacred. Without waiting to besiege Talamba, which would have retarded the progress of the invading army, Tymúr marched to Shahnawaz, where he was opposed by a Ghakkar chief. This chief he slew, and, having seized as much provisions as he could carry off, set fire to the rest of the town. He then crossed the Biás and sent a reinforcement of 30,000 horse to his grandson, Mirza Pír Muhammad, who, as already stated, had conquered Multán, and was now much harassed by the inhabitants, who cut off his supplies and followed him up closely. Tymúr soon after joined the prince in person. Ajuddhan (Pákpattan) was spared, out of reverence for the memory of Shekh Farid *Shakarganj*, whose tomb is situated there, though the place had been almost entirely deserted by the inhabitants on the approach of the invaders. Tymúr now marched to Bhitner, the chief of which place had been the principal source of the prince's troubles. Here the people of Depálpúr, and the adjoining places, had assembled in large numbers to protect themselves against the advancing army of the Moghals. The town not being sufficient to accommodate such a large number of people, most of them were obliged to take shelter under the walls. But few of them escaped the sword of Tymúr's troops, who attacked them and slew many thousands. The Governor of Bhatner offered a faint resistance, but Tymúr in person

Talamba plundered. Massacre of the inhabitants.

Tymúr crosses the Biás,

And marches to Bhitner,

pressed the enemy so hard that he drove them back, and captured the city gates. The enemy were hunted from street to street, and in a few hours Tymúr was master of the whole city. The garrison now surrendered at discretion, and the governor, having presented Tymúr with 300 Arabian horses, was favoured with a dress of honour. Soliman Shah and Amir Alladád were ordered by Tymúr to take possession of the gates of the citadel and to put all to the sword who had shown opposition to Prince Pír Muhammad. Accordingly 500 persons were massacred by the Moghals in a few minutes.

Which city he captures.

The people in the fort, all of whom were witnesses of this tragedy, were panic-stricken at the sight, and, despairing of their own lives, slew their wives and children, set fire to the place, and, seeking only an honourable death, fell with the energy of despair on the blood-thirsty Moghals, thousands of whom fell by their hands. Being, however, unaccustomed to regular warfare, they were soon overpowered by the disciplined army of Tymúr, and were, in the end, cut off to a man. The scene was horrible in the extreme. Thousands lay dead on both sides. Tymúr, called by Ferishta "the fire-brand of the universe," was inflamed to such a degree at the conduct of the inhabitants that not a life was spared by him in Bhatner. All the inhabitants were massacred and the city reduced to ashes.

Desperate fight.

Horrible massacre.

Tymúr then marched on Sarsuti, the inhabitants of which were butchered and the town pillaged. The district of Fatehabád was then visited and ravaged, as were the neighbouring towns of Rájpúr, Ahrúny and Tuhana. From the latter place, Tymúr reconnoitred the country in person, sending out 5,000 horse under Hakím *Iráki*, who attacked and captured Samana. His troops were distributed under different chiefs, who ravaged the entire provinces of Láhore and Multán, carrying fire and sword wherever they went. Tymúr then crossed the Jamna by the route of Pánipat, and, taking the fort of Loni by assault, massacred its garrison. While he was reconnoitring in the direction of Delhi, the Emperor Mahmúd Toghlak, with his wazír, Ikbál Khan, sallied out of the city with 5,000 horse and foot and 27 elephants. A skirmish ensued in which the Indian troops were driven back and their chief officer, Muhammad Sef Beg was taken prisoner and beheaded by the order of Tymúr. After these operations the victor returned to his camp. In Tymúr's camp there were no less than 100,000 prisoners captured by him since he crossed the Indus. It happened that, on the day when he was attacked by the Delhi emperor, these unfortunate men made certain demonstrations of joy at the prospect of their misfortunes being brought to a close. On news of this being conveyed to Tymúr, he ordered all above the age of fifteen to be put to death. The order was immediately carried into execution and nearly all of them were massacred in cold blood.

The provinces of Multán and Láhore ravaged.

Tymúr marches on Delhi.

One hundred thousand prisoners put to the sword.

On January 13th, 1399, Tymúr forded the Jamna unopposed, and entrenched himself on the plains of Ferozabád, adjoining Delhi. Hundreds of buffaloes were picketed out in the ditch with their heads facing the enemy, and after them were drawn up lines of infantry at proper intervals. The astrologers declared the 15th of January to be unlucky, but Tamerlane, caring little or nothing for their prediction, and putting his trust in God, formed his line of battle. The advance was made by the Indian troops, commanded by the Emperor Mahmúd in person, assisted by the wazír, Ikbal Khan. The first charge so terrified the elephants on the king's side that they became quite unmanageable and fled to the rear of the Indian columns, spreading confusion among them. The veteran army of Tymúr, taking advantage of the situation, made a determined attack on the enemy, and the Indians were completely routed and pursued to the very gates of Delhi. The king and the wazír escaped in the night, the king making his way to

The battle of Fyzábád, 13th January, 1399.

Defeat of the Indians.

Gujrát. The chief men of the city now crowded round the conqueror, who gave them protection on condition of their paying tribute. On the following Friday, the Mahomedan sabbath, Tymúr was proclaimed emperor of Hindostán and the *Khutba* was read in his name in all the mosques.

Tymúr proclaimed emperor of Hindostán.

The Delhi troops had been routed and the king had fled; but a greater calamity still awaited it. It seems that Tymúr had entrusted the task of levying contributions from the towns-people to the chiefs and magistrates of the city. Certain nobles and rich merchants refused to pay their share of contribution. Upon this the Amir sent troops to Delhi to help the magistrates to collect the money. In the meantime, Tymúr, according to his custom after a victory, held a grand banquet in the camp, in which he entertained his grandees and Omerahs.

The troops sent to the city created the utmost disorder, and, getting beyond control, began to plunder the place. None dared to acquaint Tymúr with this circumstance, in the midst of his festivities, and the brutal soldiery continued their excesses unrestrained. Hindu females were outraged and their property seized and even the Mahomedans were not spared. The patience of the citizens being exhausted, they at length resolved to face the disaster which had befallen them, like men. They closed their gates, put their own wives and children to death, set their houses on fire, and, with such weapons as they could lay hands on, rushed on their enemies. A general massacre ensued. The whole city was in flames and nothing was to be seen in the streets but heaps of dead and the blood of the victims. Great was the havoc which took place, and the horrors which ensued were quite unprecedented. The courage of the men at Delhi at last failed them before the hardy and merciless Tartars, who now drove them before them like sheep, enormous booty falling into the hands of the victors.

General massacre and pillage at Delhi.

Tymúr halted fifteen days at Delhi. He was much struck with the elegance displayed in the architecture of the superb mosque built by the Emperor Feroz, and read with much interest and admiration the inscription on this monument of Toghlak's reign, describing the history of his times and the regulations enforced under his government. He carried architects and masons from Delhi to Samarkand to build a mosque there on a similar scale. After these events, Tymúr set out to return to his own country. Mírut was taken by storm and the garrison put to the sword. Khizr Khan, governor of Multán, who, it will be remembered, had been worsted by Sarang Khan, governor of Depálpúr, in 1396, and, on the approach of Tymúr, had concealed himself in the hills of Mewat, now came in and made submission to the Amír, by whom he was graciously received. The Amír took many forts on the route, and, on his arrival at Jammu, compelled the rájá to embrace the Mahomedan faith, after a severe combat, in which the latter was wounded. Jasrat, the brother of Shekha Ghakkar, opposed Tymúr, but was defeated and put to flight. Shekha severely reproved his brother for his conduct, and the matter having been represented to Tymúr, he was admitted into his presence and taken into favour. During the Amír's absence at Delhi, Shekha, availing himself of the confused state of affairs, took possession of Láhore and refused to submit to the Amír, when he was encamped at Jammu. The Amír accordingly sent a detachment of his army to Láhore, which was besieged and captured after a few days, and Shekha was brought in chains to Tymúr and instantly beheaded by his orders. During his stay at Jammu, Tymúr appointed Khizr Khan his viceroy for the provinces of Láhore, Multán and Depálpúr and returned to Samarkand by the Kábul route.

Submission of Khizr Khan, governor of Multán.

The principality of Jammu reduced.

Shekha Ghakkar rebels at Láhore, but is seized and beheaded.

The victor's return to his country.

After the departure of Tymúr, Delhi remained in a state of anarchy for a space of two months, when it began to be re-peopled. It was seized by Prince Nasrat Shah, son of Fettah Khan, a cousin of Mahmúd, with 2,000 horse from Mírut, but he was expelled by the Wazír Ikbál Khan, who resumed the administration of affairs. Being joined by Behram Khan, governor of Samana, Ikbál Khan marched to Multán to reduce Khizr Khan. The united armies were encountered at Talamba by Rai Dáúd, Kamál Khan and Rai Habhú, the son of Rai Ratta, chiefs of the Northern Provinces, but their troops were routed and they themselves taken prisoners. Khizr Khan massed his armies of Multán, Láhore and Depálpúr and gave Ikbál Khan battle at Ajuddan. The two armies met on the 18th of November 1405 A.D., when Ikbál Khan was slain and his army repulsed with slaughter. News of this having reached Delhi, Doulat Khan Lodi and Ikhtiár Khan, who held military commands there, invited Mahmúd Toghlak from Kanauj, and placed him once more on the throne. He contracted a fever, of which he died at the capital in February 1412, after an unfortunate and inglorious reign of twenty years, and with him fell the dynasty of the adopted slaves of the Emperor Shaháb-ud-dín Ghori.

Affairs of the Panjáb after the departure of Tymúr.

The King Mahmúd returns to Delhi.

His death, 1412.

CHAPTER VIII.

THE DYNASTY OF SYADS.

SYAD KHIZR KHAN.

Doulat Khan succeeds, 1412.

AFTER the death of Mahmúd Toghlak, the nobles elected Doulat Khan Afghan Lodi, originally a private secretary, who, after the death of Ikbál Khan, had been raised by the late King to the dignity of wazír, with the title of Aziz-ul-Mamálik. Doulat Khan ascended the throne in April 1412, and had coins struck in his name. But the capital was invaded, in the name of Tymúr, by Khizr Khan, viceroy of Láhore, who, with an army of 60,000 horse, invested the citadel, and, after a siege of four months, compelled Doulat Khan to surrender, on the 4th of June, 1416. Doulat Khan was confined in Hissár Feroza, where he subsquently died.

But he is expelled by Khizr Khan, viceroy of Láhore,

Khizr Khan was a Syad and the son of Malik Suleman, a man of considerable repute and the adopted son of Malik Mardan Doulat, governor of the province of Multán in the time of the Emperor Feroz Toghlak. On the death of Malik Mardan Doulat, he was succeeded in the government of Multán by his son, Malik Shekh, who, in his turn, was succeeded by Malik Suleman. On the death of Malik Suleman, the office of viceroy of Multán descended to his son Khizr Khan.

We have already related how Khizr Khan was driven from Multán after his struggle with Sárang Khan, and how, on the invasion of Tymúr, having gained his favour, he was reinstated in his government of Multán, to which were added those of Láhore and Depálpúr. This enabled Khizr Khan to strengthen his hands in the north-west, and finally to pave his way to the throne. However, on his accession to power, he thought it more politic not to assume royal titles, but to govern the country in the name of his more formidable predecessor, the Amír Tymúr, the memory of whose bloody career was yet fresh in the minds of the people. Accordingly he caused

Who rules the country in the name of Tymúr.

coins to be struck and the *Khutba* read in the name of that conqueror. When Tymúr died, the name of his successor, Shah Rukh, was substituted in the *Khutba*, and tribute was remitted to him at Samarkand. By this measure he disarmed the jealousy of the nobles of the late government, to whom the name of Tymúr was still fraught with terror. He appointed Malik Tohfa his wazír, under the title of Taj-ul-mulk, and conferred the government of Multán on Abdul Rahím, the adopted son of his father, whom he honoured with the title of Ala-ul-Mulk.

During the reign of Khizr Khan the Panjáb remained at peace. He died on May 20th, 1421 A. D., after a reign of seven years and a few months. He was an active and successful ruler, and by his energy and resolution recovered most of the provinces which had been lost to the empire. The people had become deeply attached to him, and, as a mark of respect to his memory, the inhabitants of Delhi wore black garments for a space of three days.

Death of Khizr Khan, 1421.

His great popularity.

SYAD MOBÁRAK SHAH.

On the death of Khizr Khan, his son, Mobárak, ascended the throne with the title of Moiz-ud-dín Abdul Fatah Mobárak Shah. He conferred the government of Láhore and Depálpúr on Malik Rajab. The Ghakkars under their leader Jassa, the brother of Shekha, became a powerful tribe in the Panjáb. This chief, after committing great depredations in Tata, had gone to Jammu in the course of the preceding year, and had there defeated Ali Shah, King of Káshmír, whom he made a prisoner. He now aspired to the sovereignty of the whole of Hindostán, and with that view assembled an army to invade Delhi. He recalled Malik Toghan, chief of the Turks, from the hills, and appointed him amír-ul-omerah, or general-in-chief of his troops. The first operations were directed against the Panjáb. Láhore was seized. Jalandhar was then reduced, and the Moghal governor, Zirak Khan, cast into chains. The Ghakkars then fell on Sirhind, the fort of which they besieged, reducing the governor, Islam Khan, and his garrison to great straits.

Syad Mobárak succeeds, 1421.

Revolt of the Ghakkars, under Jassa their chief.

They capture Láhore, 1421,

And fall on Sirhind.

The rainy season had now set in; but this did not prevent the Emperor Mobárak Shah from advancing at the head of his troops from Delhi to repulse the enemy. His army marched to Sirhind; but on its approach Jasrat raised the siege and fled to Ludhiána. The royal army pursued, but Jasrat had cleverly withdrawn all the boats from the river Sutlej; and the emperor was thus compelled to halt until the stream became fordable. By this time, Zirak Khan had managed to effect his escape and had joined Mobárak Shah. On October 8th, 1421, the river was forded by Malik Sikandar, the wazir, Zirak Khan, Mahmúd Hussan, Malik Kálu, and other Omerahs, and by the emperor himself, followed by the main army. In an action fought between the royal troops and the Ghakkars, the latter were completely routed, vast numbers of them being slain, and their baggage captured. Jasrat crossed the Chináb and fled to the mountains, and, being pursued by the king's troops to Bisál, a strong fort in which he had concealed himself, again took refuge in flight. It being now the month of Moharram (January 1422), the Emperor Mobárak Shah visited Láhore, where he spent some time in superintending the repair of the palaces and fortifications which had been seriously damaged in the late wars, after which, having appointed Mahmúd Hussan viceroy, he retired to his capital.

They are defeated.

The Emperor Mobárak Shah visits Láhore, 1422.

Scarcely had he reached his capital, when Jasrat, descending from his hill fastness, appeared again on the scene. He laid siege to Láhore for six months, the town being strongly fortified and well and bravely defended. All his

Fresh incursion of the Ghakkars, 1422.

Their attempt to reduce Láhore fails.

attempts to reduce it having failed, he raised the siege and retired to Kálánaur. From that place he invaded Jammu, the rájá of which had, in the previous campaign, conducted the king's army to Bisál. Being, however, unable to make any impression on the rájá and his dominions, Jasrat retreated to the Biás to recruit his army. In the meantime Láhore was reinforced with fresh troops under the Wazír Malik Sekandar, who formed a junction with Malik Rajab, governor of Depálpúr, and Islam Khan, governor of Sirhind, at the head of their respective troops, when the confederate armies marched against Jasrat, who was driven with considerable loss across the Chináb and forced to retire again to his mountain retreat. The Ghakkars, who were left without a leader, were now pursued by the vigilant wazír, who, skirting the Rávi, reached Kálánaur, and, being joined by the rájá of Jammu, discovered vast numbers of the Ghakkars, who had concealed themselves in various places, and put them all to the sword. After these transactions the wazír with his troops returned to Láhore. The emperor, highly pleased with the gallant conduct of the Wazír Malik Sekandar, appointed him viceroy of Láhore, and Mahmúd Hussan was recalled to Delhi.*

The wazír Malik Sekandar appointed viceroy of Láhore.

Incursions into the Panjáb by the Ghakkars.

No sooner had the royal troops withdrawn, than Jasrat Ghakkar again appeared in the field. Collecting an army of 12,000 Ghakkars, he defeated and slew Rai Bhim, rájá of Jammu, and ravaged the provinces of Láhore and Depálpúr. The governor, Malik Sekandar, marched against him from Láhore, but Jasrat, on his approach, again fled to the hills with the spoil which he had collected. Malik Abdul Rahím Ala-ul-mulk, governor of Multán, having died in the meantime, Malik Mahmúd Hussan was sent with an army to Multán. About this time also Amír Shekh Ali, a Moghal chief in the service of Shah Rukh Mirza, governor of Kábul, at the instigation of Jasrat, invaded Bhakkar and Tata.

Their defeat.

In September, 1427, Jasrat Ghakkar laid siege to Kálánaur, and having inflicted a defeat on Malik Sekandar, compelled him to retreat to Láhore. The emperor sent reinforcements under Zirak Khan, governor of Samana and Islam Khan, governor of Sirhind; but before they could join the armies of Láhore, Malik Sekandar inflicted a severe defeat on Jasrat, and deprived him of all the wealth which he had collected by plundering the country.

Invasion of the Panjáb by Amír Seikh Ali, governor of Kábul, 1429.

In the year 1429, the Panjáb was invaded by Amír Shekh Ali, governor of Kábul, on behalf of Shah Rukh Mirza. He was joined by the Ghakkars and committed great depredations in the Panjáb, On reaching Láhore, he imposed a tribute equal to one year's revenue on Malik Sekander, the governor, and then marched to Depálpúr, ravaging the country as he went. According to Ferishta, 40,000 Hindus were massacred on this occasion. An attempt made by Imád-ul-mulk, governor of Multán, to surprise Shekh Ali at Talamba failed. Marching along the bank of the Rávi, the Moghals advanced to Kherabád, and from thence to Multán, which was assaulted on 29th May, 1430. The assault proving unsuccessful, Multán was closely invested. Reinforcements in the meantime arrived from Delhi under Fatteh Khan, son of Mozaffar Khan Gujráti, and a sanguinary battle was fought between the armies of the Moghals under Amír Shekh Ali, and those of Delhi and the Panjáb under Imád-ul-mulk. At the outset the

Massacre of the Hindus.

A bloody battle fought at Multán, 1430.

* This fact establishes the importance which was always attached to the Panjáb as the north-west frontier of India. The post of wazír at the seat of government was, it seems, treated as of secondary importance to that of the Láhore viceroy. Indeed, as has already been shown, the power of the Syads could have never become supreme in India had they not been the fortunate possessors of this important province, which eventually paved the way to their future greatness.

Moghals gained some advantage, but the death of Fatteh Khan, of Gujrát, inspired the Indians with a thirst for revenge, and they fought with such determination that the Moghals were defeated. They were closely pursued by the victors, and their whole army was either put to the sword or drowned in an attempt to cross the Jhelum. Amír Shekh Ali, with a few of his attendants, fled to Kábul.

Defeat and flight of Amír Shekh Ali.

In 1432 Nasrat Khan *Gurgundaz* was appointed viceroy of Láhore, and the Panjáb was, in that and the following year, invaded by Malik Jasrat and Amír Shekh Ali. These attacks were, however, successfully repulsed by the imperial troops. After Nasrat Khan, Aladád Lodi was for a time appointed governor of Láhore, but the government of the country was eventually conferred on Imád-ul-mulk. Syad Mobárak Shah was murdered by conspirators, while at worship in a mosque which he had lately built in the new city. This event took place on January 28th, 1435. He had reigned thirteen years and three months.

The king murdered, 1435.

SYAD MUHAMMAD.

On the same day on which Mobárak Shah was assassinated and laid in his grave, his son, Syad Muhammad was installed on the throne of Delhi. The wazír, Sarwar-ul-mulk, whose perfidy had resulted in the murder of the late king, received the title of Khan Jahán, with the supreme control over the whole ministry.

Syad Muhammad succeeds, 1435.

In the year 1436, a serious insurrection broke out in Multán among the Afghans, called Lunga. About the same time also Láhore was captured by Behlol Lodi, who, after the death of his uncle, Islam Khan, had usurped the government of the province of Sirhind. He took possession of Depálpúr and made himself master of the whole country as far as to the south of Pánipat. He was, however, soon reconciled to the king, who, at his instance, put Hissam Khan, the deputy wazír, to death, and deprived Kamal-ul-mulk of the office of wazír, both steps fraught with danger to the empire, the downfall of which was now predicted. The governors of the provinces aspired to independence, while the zemindars, foreseeing the commotions, which were likely to follow, withheld payment of the revenue. Ibrahim Shah Sharki, king of Jaunpúr, took possession of several districts in the neighbourhood of his dominions, while Sultan Mahmúd, king of Málwá, made an attempt on Delhi in 1440. Behlol Lodi, at the instance of the king, marched to oppose him with 20,000 horsemen arrayed in armour; but the feeble king gave himself up to alarm and sent ministers to his rival to propose terms. This act of pusillanimity on the part of his sovereign induced Behlol to aspire to the throne, and, pursuing Sultan Mahmúd on his own account, he defeated and put him to flight. The king, unaware of his designs, rewarded his services by conferring on him the title of Khan Jahán, and, to show his favour still more, he even adopted him as his son.

Insurrection at Multán, 1436.

Behlol Lodi appears on the scene.

Weak state of the empire.

In the year 1441, the king confirmed Behlol Lodi in the government of Láhore and Depálpúr, which he had already usurped. He also permitted him to attack Jasrat Ghakkar; but Behlol, instead of making war on him, secured his friendship, and, thus strengthening his hands, enlisted numerous bodies of Afghans in his service. He also attacked Delhi and invested it for some months, but the design was for the present abandoned.

The power of Behlol on the ascent.

Syad Muhammad died a natural death in 1445, and was succeeded on the throne by his son Ala-ud-dín.

Death of Syad Muhammad, 1445.

SYAD ALA-UD-DÍN.

Ala-ud-dín succeeds.

Syad Ala-ud-dín, having succeeded his father Syad Muhammad, took up his residence in Búdaon, where, instead of directing his attention to the affairs of his kingdom, which had become distracted, he employed his time in building pleasure-houses, laying out gardens and giving entertainments. At this time the empire of Hindostán was divided into several independent kingdoms; and the provinces of the Dekkan, Gujrát, Málwá, Jaunpúr and Bengal had each its own king. The Panjáb, including Depálpúr and Sirhind, as far south as Pánipat, was in the possession of Behlol Khan Lodi, and the authority of the king was confined to the city of Delhi, with a small tract of the adjoining country. The king was duped by his councillors to such a degree that, acting on their advice, he imprisoned and disgraced his wazír, Hamid Khan, and even entered into a plan to assassinate him. The wazír found means to effect his escape from confinement, took possession of the king's effects, and sent the females of the royal harem out of the city. While the king's attention was absorbed in quelling these domestic feuds, Behlol Khan Lodi quietly entered the capital and was proclaimed king in 1450. The King Ala-ud-dín adopted him as his son, and, formally abdicating the throne in his favour, withdrew to Búdaon, where he died in 1478, after having reigned in Delhi for seven years and lived in retirement at Búdaon for about twenty-eight years.

Abdicates the throne, 1450.

And dies, 1478.

CHAPTER IX.

THE LODI DYNASTY.

BEHLOL LODI.

The ancestors of Behlol.

THE ancestors of Behlol were a commercial tribe of Afghans who carried on trade between India and Persia. Malik Behrám, the grandfather of Behlol, having abandoned his occupation in the time of Firoz Toghlak, entered the service of Malik Mardan Doulat, governor of Multán. He had five sons, the eldest of whom, Malik Sultan, fought with distinguished bravery against Ikbál Khan, the Delhi wazír, in an action in conjunction with Khizr Khan, viceroy of Multán, in which he had the good fortune to slay the wazír with his own hands. Pleased with this gallant conduct, Khizr Khan appointed him governor of Sirhind, with the title of Islam Khan, while his brothers were honoured with high posts. On one of these brothers, Malik Kaly, the father of Behlol, Khizr Khan bestowed a district. The wife of Malik Kaly was killed by the fall of a house, while *enceinte*, but, by a surgical operation, the child, who subsequently received the name of Behlol, was brought into the world alive. Malik Kaly was shortly afterwards killed in action, and the young Behlol grew to manhood under the care of his uncle, Islam Khan, governor of Sirhind, whose daughter he married, and whom, on his death, he succeeded in his command. How Behlol seized the government, at a time when its dissolution seemed imminent, in the reign of the last and imbecile king of the Syad dynasty, has been already narrated. Behlol governed the empire with a firm hand and re-incorporated the kingdom of Jaunpúr with the dominions of Delhi, the

Shirki dynasty of kings having become extinct during the struggle. In the year 1451 the king made a tour through the Panjáb, and visited Multán, where he re-organized the army and settled the affairs of his western provinces. The following year, the viceroy of Multán rose in rebellion, but, on the king marching in that direction, the disturbance was quelled and order restored in the Panjáb. The king suffered from chronic disease, of which he died in 1488, after a long and prosperous reign of thirty-eight years and eight months.

His tour in the Panjáb, 1451.

His death, 1488.

Ferishta relates that, in his youth, Behlol used to pay his benedictions to Sheda, a celebrated darvesh of Samana. One day, while the youth was present, the darvesh, in a fit of enthusiasm, exclaimed: "Who will give Rs. 2,000 for the kingdom of Delhi?" Behlol said he had only Rs. 1,600 which he had saved in his life, and had it brought before the darvesh. The holy man accepted the present, and, laying his hands on Behlol's head, called out "*Shah bash, Beta,*" literally meaning "Be thou king, my son." The friends of Behlol ridiculed the idea of his wasting his money thus, but Behlol observed: "If matters should turn out as the darvesh has foretold, I have made a cheap bargain; if not, the blessings of a holy man can do no harm."

Anecdote.

Behlol was a liberal, mild and just prince. He treated his courtiers as his friends, and could seldom be induced to mount the throne, as he said: "It is enough for me that the world knows that I am a king; no object could be gained by my making a display of my royalty."

The character of Behlol.

SIKANDAR LODI.

On the death of Behlol, his son, Nizám Khan, ascended the throne, under the title of Sikandar Lodi. No event of interest to the Panjáb is recorded in his reign. He reduced the Hindu Rájás of Bundelkhand and Northern Málwá, and maintained the reputation of his father by his administration of the country. He was in the midst of preparations for the invasion and reduction of Gwalior, when he was seized with an attack of quinsy, to which he succumbed, expiring on the 14th of December, 1617, after a reign of twenty-eight years and five months.

Nizám Khan ascends the throne, under the title of Sikandar Lodi.

His death, 1617.

A prince of high literary attainments, and himself a poet of more than ordinary merit, Sikandar was ever the munificent patron of all literary men.

His character.

Among the works compiled in his reign is the *Farhang Sikandari*. He bestowed liberal allowances on religious men, and distributed alms and food to needy people every Friday. He encouraged charity, and whenever he heard an instance of a generous act done by any of his nobles, never failed to commend it, saying: "You have laid foundation of a virtue; you will never repent it." He destroyed the temples of idolatry, and in Muttra had mosques and bazaars built opposite the bathing stairs leading to the river. The shaving of beards and heads by barbers on occasions of Hindu pilgrimages was prohibited during his time.

His encouragement of charity.

His intolerance to the Hindus.

IBRAHIM LODI.

Sikandar Lodi dying at Agra, his son, Ibrahim Lodi, ascended the throne. He caused his own brother Jalal Khan to be imprisoned, and subsequently put to death. His acts of cruelty and severity procured for him numerous enemies, and general dissatisfaction arose among the nobility. The governor of Behar declared his independence and defeated the king's troops in several engagements. Doulat Khan Lodi, viceroy of Láhore, also revolted, and reduced all the country as far south as Delhi. Prince Ala-ud-dín, uncle of

Ibrahim, his son, succeeds, 1517.

Discontents and rebellions.

Ibrahim Lodi, who had fled to Kábul, appeared in the field at the head of an army of 40,000 horse, and being joined by Doulat Khan, proceeded to Delhi to expel the king. The battle which ensued seemed to be favourable to the prince at the outset, as most of the king's officers deserted their master and joined him, but the following day the fortune of war changed, and the troops under Ala-ud-dín having dispersed in search of plunder, the king rallied his forces, and, collecting a large number of elephants, made an attack on the enemy's position, which, after great slaughter on both sides, resulted in the rout of his troops, who fled in confusion and were slaughtered in considerable numbers during the pursuit. After this defeat Prince Ala-ud-dín retreated to the Panjáb.

Doulat Khan Lodi invites Baber to India.

Dissatisfied with the court of Delhi, Doulat Khan Lodi, viceroy of the Panjáb, now sent his agents to Kábul to urge Baber, the Moghal prince, a son of a great-grandson of Tymúr, to attempt the subjugation of the empire of Hindostán, in imitation of his ancestor's conquests. Baber, accordingly invaded India in 1526, and a battle was fought between the Moghals and the Indians on the plains of Pánipat, a battle-field on which the fate of India has so often been decided. This memorable battle, which was fought on April 21st, 1526, resulted in the victory of Baber. Ibrahim Lodi, the last of the dynasty, was slain on the field, and by his death a new dynasty under the Moghals was established. The reign of Ibrahim Lodi had lasted twenty years, and the dynasty to which he belonged seventy-six years in three successions, from 1450 to 1526 A.D.

Baber invades India, 1526.

Defeat and death of Sultan Ibrahim, 1526.

CHAPTER X.

THE MOGHAL DYNASTY.

ZAHIR-UD-DÍN BABER.

Parentage of Baber.

BABER, the son of Omer Shekh Mirza, was the sixth in descent from Tymúr. His mother, Kutlugh Negár Khanam, was a Moghal of the race of Changez Khan. He was the most singular person in Oriental history. While but yet a boy twelve years of age, he was placed by his father in charge of the kingdom of Judiján. Omer Shekh Mirza having met with an accidental death by a fall from a pigeon-house, the nobles of the court elevated Baber, his son, to the throne of his ancestors. The new king, on his accession assumed the title of Zahir-ud-dín. At the age of fifteen, Baber conquered Samarkand, the capital of his ancestors, but, being too young to retain his conquest, he was deprived of it, and even his own dominions slipped from his hands. After various vicissitudes, Baber, seeing his position secure in the western countries, deemed the opportunity favourable for the invasion of India, which he had long contemplated, with a view to establishing an empire there in virtue of his ancestors' conquests. He made his first advance upon India in 1519. Marching with his army to the Indus, he crossed the river and reached Bhera in the Panjáb, where instead of plundering the country, he imposed a contribution of 4,00,000 *shahrukhis* on the inhabitants, by way of ransom. From Bhera, he sent his envoy, Moulana Murshed, to the Court of Ibrahim Lodi, intimating that the dominions of the Panjáb had so frequently been in the possession of his ancestors that it behoved the

His early life.

His adventures.

His views on India.

His first campaign, 1519.

Bhera laid under contribution.

king of Delhi to give up his pretensions to that province, and thus avert the calamities of a war. Here he received the happy tidings of the birth of a son, whom, from his having been born while he himself was preparing to invade Hindostán, he named Hindal. Having subdued the countries as far as the Chináb, and appointed Hussan Beg Atka governor of the conquerred territories, he advanced at the head of his army to chastise the Ghakkars. The fort of Birhala was invested, and the Ghakkars were defeated in a sally by Dost Beg, the Moghal general. Baber at the same time cutting off their retreat in person, they were compelled to fly to the mountains, and a considerable number of them were killed in the flight. The fort of Birhala, with all its treasures, fell into the hands of the victor, who, leaving Muhammad Ali as his lieutenant, retraced his steps to Kábul.

Birth of Hindal Mirza.

Advance to the Chináb.

The Ghakkars chastised.

The latter part of the same year witnessed another invasion of India by Baber, who this time contemplated the reduction of Láhore. The Eusafzies endeavoured to check his advance, but they were defeated and repulsed. On reaching Peshawár, he caused the fort to be put in thorough repair, and, having settled the affairs of the border, marched to the Indus. News was, however, brought to him of the invasion of Badakhshan by Sultan Syad, king of Káshgar, and he was compelled to return, leaving a blood relation, Muhammad Sultan Mirza, with 4,000 horse, to conduct affairs in India.

Second campaign, 1519.

The Eusafzies defeated.

In 1520, he again marched into India, chastising the Afghans on his way. Siálkot capitulated, and the inhabitants were saved from massacre and plunder. But Syadpúr was less fortunate, for, the inhabitants having opposed the invader, the entire garrison was massacred in cold blood, while the inhabitants were carried off into slavery. In the midst of these events, intelligence was brought to Baber of the invasion of Kábul by an army from Kandahar. He was therefore compelled to retreat to his own country, where he not only succeeded in expelling the invaders, but reduced Kandahar, driving out Shah Beg Arghún, who was compelled to seek refuge in Bhakhar, the capital of Sindh. He then conferred the government of Badakhshan on his eldest son, Húmáyún, and that of Kandahar on his second son, Kamran.

Third campaign, 1520.

The capture of Siálkot.

Massacre of the inhabitants.

In 1524, a deputation from Doulat Khan Lodi, viceroy of the Panjáb, waited on Baber at Kábul inviting him to the Panjáb and offering to place Láhore in his hands should he condescend to march to this country. In the meantime the emperor of Delhi, suspecting the loyalty of Doulat Khan Lodi, had expelled him from Láhore, and the ex-governor was compelled to take refuge among the Bilúchís. Baber advanced to the Panjáb at the head of his army, and, while passing through the country of the Ghakkars, was opposed by the imperial officers of the Panjáb, named Behar Khan Lodi, Mobárak Khan Lodi and Bhikan Khan Lohani, at the head of a considerable army. A sanguinary battle was fought on the plains of Láhore, in which the Panjáb army was defeated with great slaughter and put to flight. Baber made his triumphant entry into the city of Láhore, and, after the fashion common to his tribe, set fire to the houses. After remaining here four days, he marched against Depálpúr, the garrison of which having offered a desperate resistance, he assaulted the place, and put the entire garrison to the sword. At Depalpúr, Baber was joined by Doulat Khan Lodi and his three sons, who had taken refuge among the Bilúchís. He was honourably received, and the government of Jalandhar, Sultanpúr and other districts of the Panjáb was conferred on him. Doulat Khan, however, subsequently deserted the cause of Baber, and fled to the hills with his family. This very much affected Baber's interests in India, and he now thought it advisable to return to Kábul without prosecuting his plans further in Hindostán. Accordingly, he

Fourth campaign, 1524.

Baber's negotiations with the viceroy of Láhore.

He invades Láhore which he conquers,

And sets the streets on fire.

His arrangements of the conquered country.

marched to Láhore, and there made the following arrangements for the administration of his newly-acquired territories. Mir Abdul Aziz was appointed governor of Láhore, Khusrow Gokaltash governor of Sialkot, Bábá Khushka, governor of Depalpúr, under the orders of Sultan Ala-ud-dín, the disaffected brother of the king of Delhi, and Muhammad Ali Tajak, governor of Kálánaur. After adopting these measures, Baber returned to Kábul.

Fifth campaign, 1525.

During the absence of Baber from India, Ala-ud-dín, assisted by Doulat Khan and his son, Ghazí Khan, marched to Delhi at the head of 40,000 horse and invested that city. They were, however, defeated and returned to the Panjáb. Baber, hearing of this defeat, made his fifth invasion of Hindostán. He was on this occasion joined by his son Húmáyún from Badakhshan, and Khwája Kalán from Ghizni. He crossed the Indus on December 15th, 1525, at the head of only 10,000 chosen horse. He marched upon Delhi with an army of 13,000 horse, and was met at Pánipat by Ibrahim Lodi, at the head of 100,000 horse and 100 elephants. The hardy sons of the mountains, under the guidance of their brave and experienced leader, fought desperately. The Afghans, ignorant of the art of warfare, drew up their columns in extended lines, and at the outset the cavalry made a charge. The Moghals steadily repulsed the advancing columns, and, before the enemy could reach their lines, threw them into confusion. In their retreat, the Afghans found themselves surrounded. The emperor now gallantly advanced in person and fell on the enemy's centre, but the Afghans were totally routed and 5,000 of their number cut off, the king, Ibrahim Lodi, being among the slain. Sixteen thousand Afghans were slain in this battle and the rest all fled. Immediately after the battle, Baber deputed Muhammad Sultan Mirza and three of his generals to occupy Delhi, while he sent Prince Húmáyún to occupy Agra. The Moghal king made his own triumphant entry into Delhi, on 22nd April, 1526, when the *Khutba* was read in his name by Shekh Zia-ud-dín, of Delhi. Having then made his benedictions to the tombs of saints and heroes, the king proceeded to Agra.

He marches on Delhi.

The battle of Pánipat.

The emperor of Delhi is defeated and slain.

Baber enters Delhi as a conqueror, April 1526.

His gifts and presents.

On 9th May of the same year, Baber opened the public treasury and made a present of Rs. 3,50,000 to his son Húmáyún and one of Rs. 2,00,000 and four handsome shields to his cousin, Muhammad Sultan Mirza. Rich presents were also made to all his chiefs, and even the merchants who had followed his camp were rewarded. A great part of the treasure was sent to Kábul to be divided among persons who deserved a reward, and large sums were sent to Samarkhand, Khorásán, Kashghar, Irak, Mecca, Medina, Kerbela, Najaff, Mashed and other holy places, in aid of the religious institutions there. For these acts of generosity people gave Baber the name of *Kalandar*, that is, one who usually spends what he has and keeps nothing for to-morrow.

His warlike operations in Hindostán.

In 1519, Baber defeated and took prisoner Muhammad Khiljae, king of Málwá. He then reduced Rájputáná, and placed Mahomedan garrisons in strong positions. He waged war on Muhammad Lodi, who, assuming the title of Sultan, had occupied Benares with 100,000 men, and defeated and expelled him. Bengal and Oudh were reduced, and in less than four years most of the ancient possessions of the empire of Delhi were recovered. Baber died at Agra on 26th December 1530, in the fiftieth year of his age, having reigned thirty-eight years. It is said that, some time before the death of the king, Húmáyún became seriously ill, and his life was despaired of. When the physicians declared his case to be hopeless, the affectionate father walked thrice round his bed and prayed that the illness of the prince might be transferred to him. A short time afterwards he was heard exclaiming: "I have borne it away." From this time the king continued to sink, till, at last, he expired. However pleasing to the credulous the story may appear, the

His death, 1530.

fact is that immense personal exertions in various wars, a life of luxury, and the climate of India, had much to do with the weakness of frame and the disorders which at length ended in the dissolution of this extraordinary prince. According to his will his body was carried to Kábul and interred in the sepulchre by a sparkling stream which he had himself selected as the place of his final rest. The tomb is surrounded with beautiful gardens and is a favourite resort of the people of the town and of travellers. The date of his death is given in the words—

بهشت روزي اش باد

"May heaven be his lot."

The date of the year of his birth is comprised in the words شش محرم "6th of Moharram," and by a strange coincidence he died on the same date as the poet says:—

بروزشش محرم زاد آن شهه مکرم

تاریخ وفاتش هم آمد شش محرم

"On the 6th of Moharram died that illustrious king;
The date of his birth was also the 6th of Moharram."

Baber was one of the most accomplished princes that ever adorned the throne of an Asiatic empire. A born soldier, nature had gifted him with a genius which combined in itself the qualities of a consummate general, a vigorous administrator, a talented poet, and a true lover of all that was grand and sublime in the universe. He wrote his own *Memoirs* in the Turki language with a beauty and elegance seldom surpassed by the best Oriental writers. It is a most delightful record of the king's unassuming habits, good taste, wit, humour, cheerful boon-companionship and sense of enjoyment of the gifts of nature. The work was translated into Persian by Mirza Abdul Rahim Khan-i-Khánán during the reign of Akbar, Baber's illustrious grandson. With indomitable bravery, he possessed a persevering energy and a resolution which never failed him in his greatest misfortunes. Hardly an Asiatic prince, known to history, experienced more vicissitudes of fortune than did Baber. At one moment he was seen installed on the throne of a great kingdom; at another he could hardly find a hut to afford him shelter. Now he was the general of a large army; now a private individual with scarcely an attendant to follow him. He was the knight-errant of Asia, and the romances of the heroes of the Middle Ages truly applied to him. In person he was handsome; in address engaging and unaffected; in disposition light-hearted, open, and generous, and in countenance pleasing. In his commentaries he compares his own conquest of Hindostán with that of Mahmúd of Ghazni and Sultan Muhammad Ghorí, and points out how differently situated he was from those conquerors, and what difficulties, at home and abroad, he had to contend with before he founded the Moghal empire of Hindostán. Notwithstanding his vast schemes of conquest and self-aggrandizement, he indulged in nocturnal revels and festive entertainments with jovial comrades, in which great excesses were committed. Ferishta relates that, on occasions of such orgies, he used to fill a reservoir with wine in his own beautiful flower garden, and on it was inscribed the following ode:— His character.

"Give me but wine and blooming maids,
All other joys I freely spurn;
Enjoy then, Baber, while you may,
For youth once past will ne'er return."

NASÍR-UD-DÍN HÚMÁYÚN.

HIS FIRST REIGN.

Húmáyún succeeds.

Húmáyún, who succeeded his father, Baber, to the throne of India, was an amiable and accomplished prince. He was remarkable for his affability, tender disposition, and love of social intercourse. He made the science of astronomy his favourite object of study, wrote works on the nature of the elements, and fitted up seven halls of audience, named after the planets, and transacted business in each of these once a week. The audience was given according to the planet of the day; military chiefs being received in the hall of Mars, judges and ministers in that of Mercury, ambassadors, poets and travellers in the palace of the Moon, and civil officers in that of Venus. Each hall was painted and decorated so as to exhibit some symbol peculiar to the planet, and the attendants were similarly attired.

His taste for astronomy.

Húmáyún had hardly occupied his seat on the throne when his brother Kámrán Mirza, governor of Kábul and Kandahar, formed the design of making himself master of the Panjáb. With that view he marched from Kábul, giving out that his object in proceeding to Hindostán was to offer his congratulations to his brother on his assuming the sovereignty of that country. Húmáyún, however, perceiving his designs, sent him delegates and appointed him viceroy of the Panjáb, Peshávar and Laghmán, and the prince was thus appeased.

Kamran Mirza appointed governor of the Panjáb.

Operations in Hindostán.

Húmáyún waged wars on the Hindu Rájás of Bundelkhand, reduced Chenár, marched against Bahádur Shah, sovereign of Gujrát and the countries of Málwá as far south as Ahmadnagar, defeated him and fought bloody engagements with Sher Khan Pathan, who had established an independent monarchy in Bengal and Behar. After recovering various lost provinces and suppressing rebellions, Húmáyún might have expected to reign in peace, but his brothers, Kamran and Hindal Mirza, gave him fresh trouble, and in 1539 the former marched from Láhore, at the head of 10,000 horse, to seize on Delhi, while the emperor was engaged in a war with Sher Khan at Rohtas. He was, however, foiled in his attempt by Fakhar-ud-dín Ali, the commandant at Delhi, and, after a faint attempt on Agra, returned to Láhore.

Treason of his brothers.

He is discomfited by Sher Khan Sur.

His retreat to Láhore, 1540.

The following year the emperor was discomfited by Sher Khan and obliged to abandon his capital. He retreated to Láhore, and was, in July, 1540, joined in the Panjáb by many of his Moghal officers, who had been dispersed in previous battles. Sher Khan still continued his pursuit, and, having crossed the Biás near Sultánpúr, compelled the emperor, in November, to cross the Rávi and retreat to Tatta and Bhakkar. In his marches across the western desert, Húmáyún endured the severest calamities which ever fell to the lot of an Eastern monarch. His wanderings in the burning sands of the deserts, almost destitute of water or the shade of a tree, were marked by extreme misery and privations, and most of his followers perished from exhaustion and thirst. The emperor had his harem with him and the Sultana was far advanced in pregnancy. Such wells as there were in the wilderness were fortified and guarded with the utmost jealousy by hereditary freebooters and marauders. They were so deep that the man driving the bullocks which pulled the bucket of water fastened with a rope, had to be informed of the reaching of the bucket at the top by a beat of drum. One of these wells was reached by the party after four days' toil and wandering. When the bucket was drawn up, the thirsty crowd rushed to it so impatiently that the rope broke and the bucket fell

Horrors of his march through the desert.

into the well, and, with it, several unfortunate beings who had struggled with one another for the first drink. At one place the king's horse dropped dead from exhaustion, and 'the asylum of the world' could not find another until a trooper caused his own aged mother to dismount from her horse, which the king rode. In the midst of these miseries the Sultana, Hamida Bano Begam, gave birth to a son, the Prince Akbar, destined to be one of the greatest sovereigns of the East. The hostile rájás were still in pursuit of Húmáyún, who, leaving his family under the care of the Rana of Amarkote, fled to Sistan, but the treacherous chief delivered over the infant child to Kámrán, the king's brother and mortal enemy, who carried him to Kandahar. Húmáyún for the present gave up all idea of re-establishing the Moghal empire in Hindostán.

Birth of his son Akbar, 14th October, 1542.

Húmáyún retreats to Sistán.

CHAPTER XI.

THE SUR DYNASTY.

SHER SHAH SUR.

Sher Shah, whose original name was Farid, was the son of Hassan, himself the son of Ibrahim Khan, of the tribe of Sur, a native of Roh in Peshâwar, who came to Delhi, in the time of Behlol Lodi, in search of military employment. In consequence of Hassan having little regard for his wife, Farid quitted his protection and entered the service of Jamal Khan, governor of Jaunpur, as a common soldier, under whose patronage he applied himself diligently to the study of history and poetry and became a profound scholar. He subsequently joined Bahádur Khan, son of Daria Khan Lohâni, who having subdued Behar, had assumed royal titles under the name of Muhammad Shah. On one occasion, when that monarch was on a hunting expedition, Faríd slew a tiger with a single blow of his sabre. The king was so much pleased with this act of skill and bravery that he conferred on him, on the spot, the title of Sher Khan, or the lion-knight, by which name he was ever after distinguished. On the death of Muhammad Shah Lohani, his wife Sultana Lado acted as regent for his minor son and appointed Sher Khan her minister; but, she, too, dying soon after, Sher Khan succeeded to the administration. By his subsequent marriage to Lado Malika, the beautiful widow of Taj Khan, late governor of Chunar, he secured to himself that impregnable fort and its dependencies. While the Emperor Húmáyún was engaged in Gujrát, Sher Khan reduced the whole of Behar and Bengal, and, after the defeat of the Moghals at Gour, in Bengal, formally assumed the sceptre of royalty and was crowned king of Bengal in 1539, with the title of Sher Shah. The next year he marched against the Emperor Húmáyún, who was advancing on Agra at the head of 100,000 troops. The battle which ensued, and in which Húmáyún was defeated, decided the fate of the empire of Hindostán for the time, and Húmáyún was pursued by Sher Shah in person to the Panjáb. The flight of Húmáyún to Sindh, and the disasters which he encountered have been described in the preceding chapter. Sher Shah, having appointed his trusted and able general, Khawás Khan, to the government of the Panjáb, returned to Agra.

The origin of Sher Shah Sur.

How he rose to power and independence.

The battle of Agra, 1540.

Khawás Khan appointed governor of the Panjáb.

The emperor reduced to subjection the rebellious Hindu States of Central India, invaded Márwár and conquered Chittor, which surrendered. Shortly afterwards he moved his army towards Kalanjar, the rájá of which place refusing to surrender, the fort, one of the strongest in India, was closely besieged. Mines were sunk under the rocks and batteries for artillery constructed to blow up the walls. The emperor, seeing that the siege had made much progress, ordered a general assault, when a shell, bursting in the battery where he stood, set fire to a magazine and blew up several gunners together with the king and many of his chiefs. The king was so scorched that he was carried for dead to his tent, but he survived, and, though, breathing with much distress, he continued to encourage his troops to prosecute the attack with all their might. He was in his death agonies when news was brought to him of the final reduction of the fort. With a cheerful countenance he exclaimed: "Thanks be to the Almighty God!" and immediately expired. The event took place on May 22nd, 1545, when he had reigned as emperor of Hindostán for about five years.

Sher Shah killed at Kalanjar, 1545.

His character.

Sher Shah was a man of great military talents, and if the Moghals for a time lost their empire in India, it was due to the strategical skill and tactics of this Pathan king. By his energy and perseverance he had raised himself from the position of a common soldier to the dignity of a king of a mighty empire. He extended the limits of the empire in every direction and applied himself diligently to the civil administration of the country. From the Ganges to the Indus, a distance of 2,000 miles, he constructed a highway, bordered with fruit-trees, which afforded shelter to the weary traveller. Every two miles a well was dug, and at every stage a caravanserai was established for the accommodation of travellers, at the expense of the State. Magnificent mosques were built on the highways, and readers of the *Koran* and *Mullahs* provided for them. Horse-posts were established at convenient distances, to facilitate the conveyance of Government messages, as also to benefit the trading classes and the public. Similar arrangements were made from Agra to Mandu, a distance of 450 miles. General security reigned throughout the country, and there is every reason to think that, if the life of this military adventurer had been spared longer, India would, under his munificent reign, have enjoyed the blessings of peace and prosperity. Ferishta relates that Sher Shah, on being one day told that his beard was growing white, replied: "It is true, I have ascended the throne in the evening of my life, a circumstance I always deplore, as it has left me so short a time to make myself useful to my countrymen and to promote their welfare." Sher Shah's remains were carried to Sasseram in Behar and interred on his family estate in a magnificent mausoleum erected to his memory, which exists to this day in perfect condition, surrounded by a beautiful reservoir of water, and is admired by travellers as one of the noblest pieces of architecture constructed by the Pathan kings of India.

His internal improvements and reforms.

Anecdote.

His last resting-place.

SALEM SHAH SUR.

Salem Shah supplants his elder brother, 1545.

On the death of Sher Shah, the officers of the army elected his younger son, Jalál Khan, to be their emperor in preference to the elder Adíl Khan. Jalál Khan was a brave soldier, and, having always taken an active part in his father's campaign, had become extremely popular with the army. He was crowned emperor of Hindostán in the fortress of Kalanjar on May 25th, 1545, three days after his father's death, by the title of Islam Shah, but was more familiarly known as Salem Shah.

Heibat Khan, viceroy of Láhore, known by the title Azim Húmáyún, with whom Kutab Khan had sought protection after plundering the countries in the neighbourhood of the Kamáon hills, displayed a spirit of independence and disregarded the summons of the imperial court, requiring his attendance at Delhi. He was joined by his brother, Said Khan, from Agra, Khawás Khan, a trusted noble of Sher Shah, and by other disaffected chiefs. The Emperor, Salem Shah, marched to Láhore at the head of his army, and was met at Amballa by the confederate forces, which were more than twice as numerous as his own. The troops were drawn up in order of battle and advanced against the insurgents. Fortunately for the king, a dispute had arisen the previous night among the confederate chiefs as to the choice of a future king. Khawás Khan, who still entertained a respect for the family of his patron, Sher Shah, was in favour of the election of Prince Adíl Khan, while Azim Húmáyún had views of his own to advance, affirming that "the kingdom was no man's inheritance, but belonged to him who wielded the sharpest sword." Factions formed, and the following day, when the troops on both sides were in motion, Khawás Khan withdrew with his contingent. This circumstance tended so much to weaken the enemy that they offered but a feeble resistance, and Salem Shah gained a decisive victory.

Rebellion of the Láhore viceroy.

His defeat.

About the year 1548, Kámrán Mirza, having been put to flight by his brother Húmáyún, joined the Ghakkars in the Panjáb. Húmáyún crossed the Indus immediately afterwards, and was advancing to the Panjáb. Salem Shah had just had leeches applied when the news of this reached him. . He instantly rose from his bed, called out his army and was in camp six miles off the same evening. As the bullocks were grazing in the country, and could not be collected in time to carry the heavy artillery to the Panjáb, the assiduity of the king procured two thousand men to drag the unwieldy weapons, and the king arrived at Láhore with great expedition. Húmáyún, however, retreated, and Salem Shah returned to Delhi and eventually retired to Gwalior. He paid another visit to Láhore, shortly before the celebrated Shekh Alai was condemned to death, on a charge of personating Imam Mahdi and founding a sect called Mahdavi. The Shekh was tried by a body of learned men, and, with the king's approval, stripped and whipped to death.

The emperor visits Láhore twice.

The king had been long afflicted with a painful disorder, of which he died in his palace at Gwalior in 1553, after a reign of about nine years. It is worthy of remark that Mahmúd Shah, king of Gujrát, and Barham Nizám Shah, king of Ahmadnagar, died during the same year. In commemoration of this remarkable circumstance a poet wrote a short epitaph in which the words—

His death, 1553.

A remarkable coincidence.

زوال خسروان

" The ruin of kings " represent the date, *i.e.*, 961 or 1553 A.D.

MUHAMMAD SHAH SUR ADILI.

On the death of Salem Shah, his son, prince Firoz, then twelve years of age, was raised to the throne by the Omerahs of the Sur tribe; but he had not reigned three days when Mubariz Khan, the son of Nizám Khan, nephew of the late Sher Shah and brother-in-law of Salem Shah, entered the female apartments, and, dragging the young prince from the arms of his mother, Sultana Bibi, his own sister, slew him with his own hand, and, ascending the throne, assumed the title of Muhammad Shah Adili.

Muhammad Shah Adili murders his nephew and usurps the throne, 1553.

Muhammad Shah could neither read nor write, and was addicted to the company of low people. He raised one Hemu, a common shopkeeper, who was superintendent of markets in the time of Salem Shah, to the post of prime minister. The king, neglecting the affairs of his kingdom, became a profligate libertine, and under him the court of Delhi became the resort of men of low birth, who had nothing but flattery to recommend them. The king began to squander his wealth even in the streets among the populace, shooting arrows of gold worth Rs. 10 or 12 each, as he rode, for the pleasure of seeing the multitude fight with one another for the possession of the gold so heedlessly lavished. Hemu proved to be a man of much spirit and energy, and became the mainstay of Muhammad Shah Adili. Brawls among the rough Pathans became the order of the day, and the king proved quite incapable of checking these disorders. Jealous of the increasing popularity and influence of his own brother-in-law, Ibrahim Khan Sur, he gave private orders for his arrest. But Ibrahim's wife, the king's sister, informed him of this design in time, and he fled to Chunar. The king sent Isa Khan Niazi in pursuit of him, at the head of an army, but in an engagement which ensued Isa Khan was defeated and compelled to fall back. Elated with this success, Ibrahim Khan raised a considerable army, and, while the king was absent in Chunar, seized on Delhi, and, ascending the throne, proclaimed himself emperor. Muhammad Shah made a feeble attempt to suppress the insurrection, but finding his rival too strong for opposition, he agreed to an arrangement by which he obtained the government of the eastern provinces, while Ibrahim Khan was allowed to retain possession of the western. The empire of Hindostán was thus virtually divided between rival claimants.

His vices and incapacities.

Hemu, a shopkeeper, made Prime Minister.

He proves a man of capacity.

Ibrahim Khan Sur proclaims himself emperor.

The empire of India parcelled out.

SEKANDAR SHAH SUR.

Scarcely had Ibrahim Khan Sur assumed the regalia of royalty, when another candidate appeared for the throne. This was Ahmad Khan Sur, a nephew of Sher Shah, whose sister was married to Muhammad Shah Adili. Having won over some of the leading chiefs of the western districts to his side, among whom was the powerful Hebat Khan, a noble of the court of Salem Shah, he assumed the royal titles in the Panjáb which he began to rule under the title of Sekandar Shah Sur. He then marched to Agra at the head of 12,000 cavalry, with the view of expelling Ibrahim Khan from his western dominions, and encamped at Kera, 20 miles distant from that city. Ibrahim Khan marched out to oppose him, with an army of 70,000 horse. Some idea of the magnificence and splendour of his train may be formed when it is mentioned that 200 chiefs and officers occupied tents lined with velvet, and that each of them had the privilege of keeping a musical band, called *Nobat-nakara*, while the gorgeous equipage of the king filled the spectators with admiration and awe. A battle ensued between the two armies, in which the imposing hosts of Ibrahim Khan were signally defeated, and the king himself retreating to Sambhal, the conqueror took possession of both Agra and Delhi.

Revolt of the Panjáb under Sekandar Shah Sur.

Splendor of the king's equipage.

Sekandar Shah takes possession of Delhi and Agra.

Sekandar Shah did not long enjoy the fruits of his conquest, for Húmáyún, after his long exile, invaded India, and Sekandar Shah was compelled to repair to the Panjáb to oppose the invader. He was defeated near Sirhind by Behram Khan and the young Prince Akber, and compelled to fly to the Sewalik mountains. He afterwards returned to Bengal, where he died, after reigning a short time. With his death, the date of which is not given, the dynasty of the Sur Pathans became extinct.

Húmáyún marches to recover India, 1555.

Defeat of Sekandar Shah.

His death.

CHAPTER XII.

THE MOGHAL DYNASTY—(RE-ESTABLISHED).

NASIR-UD-DÍN HÚMÁYÚN.

HIS SECOND REIGN.

AFTER his reverses in Sindh, Húmáyún repaired to Persia by way of Sistan and Herat. He was conducted to the capital of Sistán by Ahmad Sultan Shamlu, who treated him with the utmost consideration, and furnished a number of female attendants for the Sultana. At Herat he was hospitably received by Prince Muhammad Mirza, the eldest son of Shah Tamasp, king of Persia. On arrival at Kazwin, he deputed his general, Bahram, to the court of Ispahan to negotiate with the Shah for an interview. The Shah invited the royal fugitive to an interview and received him with the most magnificent hospitality, enabling him to maintain the outward forms of state. The familiarity between the two kings increased. In the course of conversation, the Shah one day asked the Moghal sovereign how his weak enemy had triumphed over him. To this Húmáyún replied: "Through the enmity of my brothers." His Persian Majesty, upon this, observed: "But you have not treated your brothers as they deserve." The subject was renewed one day, when the monarchs were at dinner, and after they had done, Prince Bahram Mirza, the brother of Shah Tamasp, approached the latter with a wash-hand basin and a pitcher. When the Shah had washed his hands and the prince had retired with the utensils, the former, resuming the dialogue, said: "This is the way you ought to have treated your brothers." This remark reached the prince's ear, and he was the more offended on account of Húmáyún's ready assent to what the Shah had hinted. From that moment the prince began to entertain hostile feelings towards Húmáyún, and did every thing in his power to slander him. He would often hint to his royal brother that Persia was in no way concerned in advancing the interests of a prince of the house of Tymúr in so remote a country as India, and his influence led the grandees of the court to share the same view. Húmáyún was very much disappointed in his expectations. His royal host neglected him and at one time he became even apprehensive of his life. In this difficulty he secured the sympathy and friendship of the king's talented sister, Sultana Begum, Kazi Jahan *Kazvini*, and Nur-ud-dín, the physician and counsellor. They combined to use their influence with the Shah in order to restore confidence between the two kings, and to reinstate Húmáyún in the Shah's favour. To effect this object the wit of the royal lady was exerted. She composed a poem in praise of Ali, the true and rightful successor of the Prophet Muhammad, according to the belief of the Siahs, to which sect the Persian king belonged, and at the end inserted Húmáyún's name as the author of the ode. She then placed a copy of it before her royal brother, who seeing the devotion of Húmáyún to Ali, was pleased, and expressed a hope that the Moghal king might be induced to embrace the Shia doctrines, and, on his return to Hindostán, enforce them among the people of that country, adding that, if he undertook to do so, he would assist him to recover his throne. The Sultana informed Húmáyún of this, and the latter appropriately replied: "I have always privately inclined to the Shias, and, indeed, this, to a certain extent,

Húmáyún's reception at the court of Persia.

Dialogues between His Persian Majesty and His Indian Majesty.

The Shah neglects Húmáyún,

Who gains over the Shah's sister.

Confidence restored between the two kings.

accounts for the ill-feelings which my brothers entertain towards me." The Shah furnished Húmáyún with a contingent of 10,000 cavalry, under the command of his younger son, Murád Mirza and General Budagh Khan Kajár.

The Shah assists Húmáyún with troops.

On reaching Kandahar, Húmáyún was joined by his old generals, Muhammad Sultan Mirza, Alugh Mirza, Kasim Husain, Sultan Mirza Mirak, Sher Afgan Beg, Fazil Beg and others, who, having quarrelled with Kamran Mirza, the emperor's brother, had left his service. After protracted wars with his brothers, Húmáyún became undisputed master of the whole of Afghanistán.

Húmáyún conquers Afghanistán.

It is related that, in one of these wars, when siege was laid to Kábul, Kamran Mirza, who was in possession of the city, exhibited, on the ramparts of the citadel, the boy Akber, then four years old, bound to a funeral pile, meaning that the child would be forthwith put to death if the father advanced. Húmáyún, however, disregarded the threat, and, unmoved by the painful sight, pressed the siege and compelled the garrison to retreat. He found his boy safe in the arms of the Sultana, and, taking him up in his arms, kissed him, exclaiming that, though, like Joseph, he had been put to extremities through the envy of his brothers, yet he hoped, by the grace of God, to reach the summit of glory, and he prayed that his son might reach the same degree of power and magnificence. Askari Mirza was, after these transactions, released from his confinement in Badakshan and permitted to proceed to Mecca, but he died, while crossing the deserts of Arabia, in 1554. Hindal Mirza, another brother, lost his life in an attack on the Khaibar. The third brother, Kamran, was blinded, and eventually obtained permission to go to Mecca, and, after residing there for three years, died a natural death.

Exhibition of the boy Akber on the ramparts of the Kábul citadel.

In the year 1553, Húmáyún, having taken up his residence in Kábul, sent his son Akber, then about twelve years of age, to the government of Ghazní under the charge of the Wazir Jalál-ud-dín Muhammad. The same year, another son having been born to Húmáyún, he was named Muhammad Hakím Mirza. About this time the civil wars in Hindostán had distracted the whole empire. The representatives of the Sur family were fighting with one another for supremacy, and Omerahs and viceroys of various provinces had raised the standard of revolt. The people had become wearied of the ill-cemented Pathan rule and of the Pathans themselves. The friends of Húmáyún wrote to him from Agra and Delhi, inviting him to return and take possession of the country, which, they asserted, would fall an easy prey to his enterprise. The king felt considerable hesitation in yielding to their request. Unlike his father, who, contrary to the advice of his astrologers, had directed his first attack against Delhi on a day pronounced by them to be unlucky, Húmáyún was a believer in divination, and, feeling melancholy on the subject, was advised to try an experiment.

Distracted state of the empire of India.

Recourse to an old method of divination.

Accordingly, three messengers were sent in different directions and told to come back with the names of the first persons they met. The messengers returned. The first was met by a traveller named *Daulat*, or "Wealth," the second by a man who called himself *Morád*, or "Good Fortune," and the third by a villager whose name was *Sa-ádat*, or "Object of Desire." The omens, says Ferishta, were declared propitious and preparations for a march were forthwith made.

The king could muster only 15,000 horse. Leaving Monim Khan in charge of the government of Kábul, and making over to him his minor son, Muhammad Hakím Mirza, Húmáyún marched from Kábul in December, 1554. On the Indus, Bahram Khan, *Turkman*, his veteran general, joined him, with a body of chosen troops from Ghazní and Kandahar. He appointed Bahram

Húmáyún marches on Peshawar,

Khan, his general-in-chief, and directed him to advance with Khizr Khan, Tardi Beg Khan, Sikandar Khan *Uzbak*, and Ali Kuli Khan *Shibáni*. At Pesháwar, the king was joined by his younger son, Akber.

Bahram Khan, having crossed the Indus at the head of his army, first encountered Tártár Khan, the Afghan viceroy of Láhore, whom he surprised and defeated. Tártár Khan, abandoning the fort of Rohtas, fled, and was hotly pursued by the Moghal general to the walls of Láhore, which was also evacuated. Húmáyún entered Láhore unopposed, and halted there for some days, to make the necessary arrangements for a further advance. From this place he sent Bahram Khan to Sirhind, and the whole country up to that point was occupied. Intelligence being at the same time received that the Afghans had collected in large numbers at Depálpur, under Shahbaz Khan and Nasir Khan, Pathan commandants, he sent a strong detachment against them, under Shah Abul Maáli, a Sayad of great sanctity, and originally a resident of Kashgar, to whom the king had shown great condescension, by calling him his son. The Sayad routed the enemy and returned with enormous booty to Láhore.

And enters Láhore.

Operations in Depálpur.

Meanwhile Sikandar Shah's army of 30,000 horse, under Tartar Khan and Kábul Khan, was advancing against Húmáyún from Delhi. Bahram Khan, with Prince Akber, marched to check the Indian army. The weather was cold and the Afghan soldiers had kindled great fires in their camp, on the opposite bank of the Sutlej, to warm themselves at night. Bahram Khan, taking advantage of their situation, crossed the river at night with the whole of his army, which, falling upon the Afghans on all sides, routed them at Machiwárá. The whole of the elephants and baggage and a number of horses belonging to the Afghans fell into the hands of the Moghal general, while the detachments sent out by him occupied the country almost up to the walls of Delhi. Húmáyún was so pleased with the bravery displayed by his general that he bestowed on him the title of Khan-i-Khánán.

Defeat of the Afgháns in Machiwárá.

Sikandar Shah was now advancing to meet the invader, at the head of 80,000 horse and a large number of guns and elephants. Bahram Khan, too weak to hazard an action in the open field, retired into the fort of Naushera, where he laid in a stock of provisions and prepared it for a siege. From this point he made repeated sallies on the enemy's position and inflicted heavy loss on them. At the same time he sent urgent messages to the emperor at Láhore begging him to join him, which Húmáyún did without delay.

The 18th of June, 1555, is memorable in the annals of India, for, on that day, was decided the fate of the empire in respect of the nation that was to govern it for the next three centuries. The young Prince, Akber, was, in the early morning, inspecting the pickets of the camp, when the Afghans, under Sikandar Shah and Tartar Khan, advanced and offered battle. The Moghal army met the advancing columns, and a fierce battle, worthy of the great prize for which the two claimants fought, took place. The young Akber, who was in the thickest of the fight, greatly distinguished himself by his feats of valour. He led the troops in a grand charge and inspired them with such ardour that nothing could resist them. The battle raged with great fury, and, for a time, the issue was doubtful, but the Afghans were at last defeated with great slaughter and took to flight. Their king, Sikandar Shah Sur, fled to the Siwálik mountains, leaving the whole country in the hands of the invader. Troops were sent in advance to Delhi and Agra, which were occupied without opposition. Húmáyún re-entered Delhi in July 1555, and ascended the throne of his father, after an exile of

The decisive battle of Sirhind, 1555.

Young Akber gains his first laurels in this battle.

Húmáyún re-enters Delhi, 1555.

Sháh Abul Maáli the first Moghal viceroy of Láhore.

fifteen years. He appointed Shah Abul Maáli his viceroy of the Panjáb with instructions to hunt out the fugitives. Bahram Khan Turkoman received the highest honours in the State; Tardi Beg Khan was appointed governor of Delhi, Sikandar Khan Uzbak, governor of Agra, and Ali Kuli Khan of Mirath and Sanbhal.

The accident to Húmáyún which cost him his life, 1556.

Húmáyún ascended the throne of Hindostán only to die in possession, for, in less than a year, he met with an accident which cost him his life. On the evening of January 21st, 1556, he was walking on the terrace of his library, in the new citadel built by him, to which he had given the name *Din Panáh** (the Asylum of the Faithful) for the purpose of recreation, when he sat down to inhale the fresh breeze from the river side and the open plain opposite. As the time for evening prayer approached, he descended the steps to go below and offer up prayers. While he was in the act of descending, the *Moazzan*, or "Crier," announced the hour in the usual manner from the royal chapel. The emperor paused to repeat the creed, and sat down on the second step, till the call to service was over. When the Crier had done, he endeavoured to rise, with the assistance of the staff which he usually carried, but the pointed end of the staff slipped along the marble pavement, as the king was leaning on it, and his majesty fell headlong over into the palace below. He was picked up unconscious and placed in his bed, and, although he recovered his speech, the injuries he had received were mortal, and, after some days of suffering, he died on January 25th, 1556.† He was buried in the new city, on the banks of the Jamna, and the splendid marble mausoleum raised over his remains by his son, Akber, is in perfect preservation to this day and admired by travellers as one of the most beautiful and elegant architectural monuments of early Moghal times in India. Húmáyún was fifty-one years old when he died and he had reigned fifty-five years in Kábul and India.

His burial.

His character.

Though inferior in capacity to his great father, Baber, he was yet endowed with a natural goodness of heart, generosity and candour, and his simple and genial habits, good humour and courtesy, won for him the affection and esteem of all around him. In person he was of a bronze complexion and of elegant figure. He was himself a poet and was fond of the company of learned men. He professed the Sunni persuasion and was strict in his devotions and ablutions, so that he never uttered the name of God without first performing the latter ceremony. Ferishta narrates that once, having occasion to call out to one Mir Abdul Hye, he called him only "Abdul," omitting the word "Hye" ("God"), because he had not performed his ablutions, and when the man came, the king apologised to him, giving reasons for having so acted.

Húmáyún was not without military talents, and his many reverses in India and Afghanistán were partly due to his clemency to his brothers, who ill-deserved it. He was passionately fond of his wife and child. It is greatly to the credit of Húmáyún that in his numerous victories not a single instance can be found of his having tainted his hands with blood, and if he blinded his ungrateful brother, Kamran, after the fashion of the time, it was after repeated trials and merely to save him from death. The history of few Eastern kings exceeds in interest that of the noble-hearted Húmáyún. His early misfortunes, the reverses which he met with in Sindh, his adventures

* This citadel was built by Húmáyún on the banks of the Jamna in 1533, before his expedition to Sarangpúr and Málwá.

† The words "همایون بادشاه از بام افتاد," "King Húmáyún fell down from the terrace," give the date of his death.

in the countries bordering on the Indus, his vicissitudes of fortune in Kábul, create deep sympathy; and the fortitude and resignation which he displayed under the severest trials deserve praise.

Had Húmáyún's life been spared, there is every reason to believe he would have ruled India with moderation, prudence and energy, but Providence had reserved such a career for the long, prosperous, and eventful reign of his illustrious son, Akber.

CHAPTER XIII.

JALAL-UD-DÍN AKBER.

According to Shekh Abul Fazl, when Húmáyún met with his fatal accident, Akber, with his tutor, Behram Khán, was employed in the Panjáb. The express, Ali Kuli Khan, who had been despatched by the Moghal Omerahs from Delhi, communicated the intelligence to him at Kalanaur, where Akber was then residing. On hearing the news, Behram Khan and other officers present at once installed Akber on the throne, on February 15th, 1556.* Thus, Akber was only thirteen years and nine months old when he commenced his reign. He conferred the high office of minister on Behram Khan, whom he called by the affectionate title of *Bábá*, or father, and his first act of benevolence was an order from the throne prohibiting the collection of the *Nazrána* which was levied on the occasion of a royal installation.

Coronation of Akber at Kalanaur, 1556.

Behram Khan created Prime Minister.

Akber, on ascending the throne, did not find his position quite secure. The party of Muhammad Shah, *Sur Adili*, was still in the ascendant in the eastern provinces; Sikandar Shah, *Sur*, though defeated, was yet in the field at the head of a strong body of Pathans; the Hindu princes of Rajputáná and Central India had not yet acknowledged the new Mahomedan Government of Delhi as the paramount power, and, above all, the grandees of Húmáyún's court were discontended respecting the estates and allowances conferred on them. To enter upon a detailed account of these events, however, is not within the province of this work, and the reader is referred for them to the excellent works of the Honourable Mounstuart Elphinstone, Murray and Taylor. Suffice it to say that the energy and talent displayed by Akber enabled him speedily to overcome all these difficulties. From the commotions which disturbed the country, the Panjáb was not exempt. The governor, Shah Abul Maáli, the boon companion of Humáyun, having shown a disposition to assume independence, was seized in his palace at Láhore and placed in confinement under the immediate charge of Pahlawáu Gulzár, the *Kutwál*, or chief police officer, of the town. The Shah found means of escape, and his custodian, dreading the shame of the charge of treason likely to be brought against him, put an end to his existence. The king led his army towards the hills near Ambala and defeated Sikandar Shah, who fled to the hills. He then subdued the mountain tribes of the

The difficult task which lay before Akber.

He overcomes it.

Seditious conduct of the Láhore governor.

The emperor defeats Sikandar Shah Sur near Ambala.

*The platform on which the ceremony of installation took place, is still preserved at Kalanaur, but the surrounding edifices were all destroyed for the sake of the bricks, and where grandees stood with folded hands before a mighty monarch, the cultivator now drives his plough. It is to be regretted that these architectural monuments of so much interest to antiquarians should have been destroyed in recent times during the British rule.

Panjáb near Nagarkot. The rainy season having then set in, he took up his residence in Jalandar. About the same time Khizr Khan, husband of Sultana Gulbadan Begum, the king's aunt, was appointed governor of Láhore.

Khizr Khan appointed governor of Láhore.

Hemu, the active Hindu minister of Muhammad Shah, *Sur Adili*, had, in the meanwhile, taken possession of Agra after a short siege, and, advancing upon Delhi, occupied it, expelling the Moghal governor, Tardy Beg Khan. He commemorated this event by assuming at Delhi the title of Rájá Vikramajit, and was now advancing to the Panjáb with a large army. The Moghal force was small, and its officers were panic-stricken. Akber was advised by a council of war, convened by him, to desist from hazarding an action against an enemy as numerous as locusts, and to retire to Kábul; but the voice of his faithful and gallant general, Behram Khan, prevailed and the sentiments of Akber being in unison with his, hostilities were determined upon. Pánipat, which had so often decided the fate of the empire since the old days of Muhábhárata, was chosen as the battle-field, and Hemu advanced with a considerable army. The king offered battle on the morning of November 5th, 1556. Hemu had brought a large number of elephants to terrify the Moghals, and these were so galled by flights of lances, arrows and javelins, that they became furious and quite unmanageable, and charged amongst the ranks of the Afghans, who were thus thrown into confusion. Hemu was conspicuous by being mounted on an elephant of prodigious size, and commanded a detachment of 4,000 horse, the best of the old Pathan chivalry. He urged these to the attack with great bravery, but, in the midst of the fight, his eye was pierced by an arrow and he sank back in his *howda* from pain. His troops, believing that he was dead, took to flight; but the gallant Hindu, notwithstanding the intense agony of the wound, raised himself, drew the arrow from the socket of the injured eye, and, binding his head with a handkerchief, put himself at the head of the fight, with the few men who still adhered to him. His elephant was at last surrounded by a body of horse, and he was carried prisoner to the emperor. When Hemu came into the royal presence, Behram Khan proposed to his majesty to kill the infidel captive with his own hand, so that he might be ranked among the Ghazis, or champions of the Faith. Akber, feeling reluctant to perpetrate the horrible deed, contented himself by touching Hemu's head with his drawn sword, while the furious Behram, drawing his sabre, severed the captive's head from his body at a single blow. Thus an end was put to the career of a Hindu who, by the force of his genius, had risen from an insignificant position in life to the dignity of minister of an empire. He was the first Hindu who had risen to the highest distinction under the Mahomedan government of India. He proved himself fully worthy of the confidence reposed in him, and, if the Afghans were enabled to contest the empire of India with the bravest of the Moghal leaders, it was due mainly to the intrepidity and warlike talents displayed by this able Hindu general.

Hemu, the shopkeeper, assumes the title of Rájá Vikramajit.

And advances towards the Panjáb.

Battle of Pánipat, 1556.

Defeat and death of Hemu, 1556.

His character.

During the action at Pánipat the Moghals captured 1,500 elephants and Akber's victory being complete, he marched from Pánipat and took possession of Delhi without opposition. About this time Khizr Khan, viceroy of the Panjáb, having been defeated by Sikandar Shah, *Sur*, was obliged to fly to Láhore. Akber, on receiving this intelligence, marched to the Panjáb, expelled Sikandar Shah from Kalanaur to which he had advanced, and compelled him to retreat to the fort of Mankot, built by the Emperor Salem Shah, *Sur*. The emperor stayed at Kalanaur for a period of three months, and was there joined by his mother and other ladies of the royal

Campaign in the Panjáb.

Submission of Sikandar Shah Sur.

seraglio from Kábul. Muhammad Hakím Mirza, the king's step-brother, with his mother and sister, were allowed to remain at Kábul in charge of the government of that country, under the tutelage of Mowjim Khan. Mankot surrendered after a siege of six months, and Sikandar Shah was permitted to retire to Bengal, leaving his son, Abdul Rahman Khan, as hostage in the royal camp. The king, with Behram Khan, his regent, then reached Láhore. In the month of April, 1558, the marriage of Behram Khan with Sulema Sultana Begum, niece of the late Emperor Húmáyún, was celebrated at Jalandar amidst great rejoicings and festivities, and the emperor honoured the nuptials with his presence.

Hostile proceedings of Shah Abul Maáli.

Shah Abul Maáli, the favourite noble of the late Húmáyún, who, it will be remembered, had effected his escape from confinement at Láhore, having now joined Kamál Ghakkar, marched on an expedition to Káshmír, but they were repulsed with great slaughter. Shah Abul Maáli then repaired to Depalpúr, and, having joined Bahádur Khan, *Sistani*, excited a revolt, but was unsuccessful and fled beyond the Indus, and from thence to Gujrat and Jámpúr, but was seized by Khan Zamán and sent a State prisoner to Agra.

Difference between Akber and his minister Behram Khan.

A difference now arose between the Emperor and Behram Khan Turkman, his able minister and general. The ward had treated his protector with the utmost consideration, and endowed him with the highest powers. But the protector insulted the prerogatives of royalty and committed excesses to which the young Akber, sensible of his obligations to the minister, feigned to tolerate. Thus, on one occasion, during the emperor's absence on a hawking party, Behram Khan, without even the ceremony of taking the king's orders, caused Tardy Beg Khan, governor of Delhi, one of Húmáyún's earliest and most devoted followers to be beheaded. Other persons were also summarily executed by order of Behram Khan, to the great disgust of the Chaghattai nobles. He also removed from office Mullah Pir Muhammad, the king's preceptor, and appointed another person, devoted to his own interests, in his place. One day, in an elephant fight, one of the royal elephants, pursued by its antagonist, rushed through the ropes of the minister's tents, and the accident was taken by him as a personal affront, but he was appeased on protestations being made by the king that no indignity was intended. On another occasion, a royal elephant, having become unmanageable in the rutting season, attacked and killed another belonging to the minister, who ordered the keeper of the former to be put to death, much to the annoyance of the king. Soon after this, another of the royal elephants ran furiously against a barge in which the minister was taking his pleasure and almost upset it. Behram Khan thought this was actually a design against his life, and caused the driver, who had been made over to him by the king, to be put to death. These transactions tended to widen the breach between the emperor and the minister, who, finding himself out of favor, marched against the Afghans of Bengal with a view to establishing himself in that quarter. Before proceeding far, however, he altered his plans and proceeded to Nagore, with the object of making a pilgrimage to Mecca, but he gave up the notion and collected a force with the view of establishing himself in the Panjáb.

Arrogance of Behram Khan.

The king at last made an effort to deliver himself from the thraldom in which he lived, and resolved to assert his rights by carrying on the government of the country himself.

His fall.

Accordingly, he sent Mír Abdul Latif Kazwini, his preceptor, to Behram Khan with the following message: "Till now, our mind has been taken up with our education and the amusements of youth, and it was our royal will that you should manage the affairs of our empire. But it being our intention henceforward to govern our people according our own judgment, let our well-wisher withdraw from all worldly concerns, and, retiring to Mecca, far removed from the toils of public life, spend the rest of his days in prayer." Behram Khan sent the ensigns of his rank, banners, kettle-drums and his elephants to the king, and proceeded as far as Bikaner, on his way to Mecca, but changed his mind and returned to Nagore. He soon after returned to the Panjáb, where he raised the standard of revolt. He was pursued by Pir Muhammad Khan, and driven to Bhatinda, where Sher Muhammad Khan, one of his old adherents, expelled his escort, and, contrary to his expectations, appropriated his whole property to himself. The ex-minister then proceeded to Depálpúr, governed by Darvesh Mahomed, *Uzbek*, one of his old adherents. The Governor put in confinement Khwaja Muzaffar Ali who was sent by the minister to wait on him, and sent him to the king. All hopes of success being thus at an end, the ex-minister marched to Jalandar, and, proceeding thence to Machiwara, was encounted and routed by Muhammad Khan Atka, the Moghal General. Akber now proceeded in person to Láhore, and had reached Ludhiáná when he heard of the total defeat of Behram Khan near the Sewalak mountains. The exiled minister, now in the greatest distress, sent his confidential agent, Jamál, to his royal master, representing his unfortunate condition and imploring pardon. The king despatched Mullah Abdulla, a native of Sultánpúr, to the minister, with assurances of forgiveness, and sent his principal nobles to conduct him to the court. The repentant minister's reception by his generous master presented a most impressive scene, which is thus described by Ferishta. "When Behram Khan entered the royal tent, he hung his turban round his neck, and, advancing rapidly, threw himself in tears at the foot of the throne. Akber, stretching forth his hand, caused him to rise, and seated him on his right hand, in his former station, at the head of the nobles. A splendid dress was now brought, and the king addressed the fallen minister in the following words :—"If Behram Khan loves a military life, the governments of Kalpi and Chanderi offer a field for his ambition. If he choose rather to remain at court, our favour shall not be wanting to the benefactor of our family ; but should he be disposed to seek devotion in retirement, let him perform a pilgrimage to Mecca, whither he shall be escorted in a manner worthy of his rank." Behram Khan replied, "The royal confidence being once shaken, how can I wish to remain in the royal presence ? The clemency of the king is enough, and his forgiveness is more than a reward for my former services. Let me, therefore, turn my thoughts from this world to another, and be allowed to proceed to the holy sepulchre." Akber assented. A pension of Rs. 50,000 was settled upon him, and Behram Khan proceeded to Gujrat to seek means of transport to Arabia, but was stabbed to the heart in the suburbs of Pattan by an Afghan whose father he had slain in battle with his own hand during the reign of Húmáyún. Thus ended the career of this great minister and soldier, and Akber, now 18 years of age, was left henceforth to rule alone. The widow of the deceased, and his son, Mirza Abdul Rahim, then only four years old, were escorted to Agra, where they were amply provided for by the emperor.

Behram tries to create disturbances in the Panjáb,

But his troops are routed.

Perplexity of Behram.

His repentance,

And pardon.

His assassination, 1561.

Akber his own master at eighteen.

About this time Muhammad Khan Atka, governor of the Panjáb, repaired to court, according to orders, with suitable presents. In 1561 A.D., Raja Puran Mal gave his daughter in marriage to the king, and he and his son, Bhawáni Das, were enrolled among the grandees of the court. In 1562, Adam Ghakkar having disturbed the peace of the Panjáb, the officers of the province reduced him to submission with the aid of Kamál Ghakkar and the Moghals

Akber marries a Hindu princess.

and made him prisoner. In 1563 an attempt was made on the king's life by one Kutlegh Fouládád, a slave of Mirza Sharf-ud-din Husein, who, having joined the king's retinue, lodged an arrow, a span deep, in Akber's shoulder. It was with some difficulty extracted, and Akber displayed great fortitude in enduring the pain. The assassin was immediately put to death by the king's attendants.

Attempt on the king's life. Unsuccessful.

In 1566, Muhammad Hakím Mirza, half brother of Akber, having been expelled from Kábul by Suleiman Mirza, Chief of Badakhshan, marched to Láhore in conjunction with Fredún Khan, *Kábuli*, with the object of establishing himself there. The officers of the Panjáb, Kutab Khan *Atka* and Pir Muhammad Khan, made preparations to defend the city. Muhammad Hakím Mirza, arriving before Láhore, tried by every art to gain over the local commanders, but was foiled in his attempts. Meanwhile, Akber lost no time in marching to the Panjáb in person, which he did with great expedition. Hakím Mirza retreated precipitately with his troops towards Kábul, and peace was restored in the Panjáb. The king advanced slowly to Láhore, where he spent some days in hunting.

Rebellion of Hakím Mirza the king's half-brother. He invades the Panjáb, 1566. Peace restored in the Panjab.

On September 2nd, 1569, the favourite Sultana was delivered of a son, who was called Salem. The emperor, on this occasion, performed a pilgrimage on foot from Agra to the shrine of Khwaja Moin-ud-dín *Chishti* at Ajmere, and returned to Agra by way of Delhi. The following year he took the daughter of Rájá Kalian Mal in marriage, and, marching from Nagore to Ajudhan, paid his benediction to the shrine of Shekh Farid-ud-dín *Gunjshakar*. His majesty then proceeded to Depálpúr, where the governor, Mirza Aziz *Koka*, presented him with many valuable articles, products of the country.

Birth of Salem, afterwards called Jahángír, 1569.

In 1575, Khan Jahan was appointed governor of Láhore, but in 1579 that office was conferred on Rájá Mán Singh, one of the king's most trusted generals and administrators. During the latter end of the same year, Muhammad Hakím Mirza, taking advantage of the insurrections in Bengal and Behar, made another attempt on Láhore. He sent Shádmán *Koka* at the head of a thousand cavalry, in advance; but that officer, on crossing the Indus, was attacked by Rájá Mán Singh and put to flight. On Muhammad Hakím reaching Rohtás, Rájá Mán Singh retreated to Láhore, to which the prince laid siege on February 15th, 1579. The city was gallantly defended by Rájá Mán Singh, Sayad Khan and Rájá Bhagwan Dass; but the king marched from Agra to the relief of the province, and Hakím Mirza, hearing of his approach, retreated to Kábul. The imperial army crossed the Indus in boats, whereupon Hakím Mirza's officers fled from Peshávar. On reaching Jallalabad, Prince Salem was left in charge of the main army, while Prince Murád proceeded in the direction of Kábul with the advanced guard. On March 6th, 1579, Hakím Mirza gave Prince Murád battle, himself leading the attack. Kanwar Mán Singh and Tuzak Khan *Atka* opened fire from the elephant swivels, and Hakím Mirza, with his troops, was defeated and put to flight. Intelligence of his victory reached the king at Surkhaband. His majesty entered Kábul without opposition on March 11th, 1579. Hakím Mirza fled to Ghorband, and thence sought forgiveness, which was readily granted, and the government of the country restored to him, the army returning to Agra. The emperor, on his return to the Indus, ordered the fort of Attock to be built. He arrived at Láhore on October 13th, 1579, and, having conferred the governorship of the Panjáb on Rájá Bhagwan Das, marched back to Agra.

Second irruption of Hakím Mirza into the Panjáb, 1579. Láhore laid under siege. Hakím Mirza retreats to Kabul, And from thence to Ghorband. Fort of Attock constructed, 1579. Rájá Bhagwan Das appointed governor of the Panjáb.

In the year 1585, the daughter of Rájá Bhagwan Das was married to Prince Muhammad Salem Mirza, the emperor's eldest son. The following year,

Death of Hakim Mirza, 1580.

Prince Muhammad Hakím Mirza, the king's half-brother, died at Kábul, and Kanwar Mán Singh, son of Rájá Bhagwan Das, was invested with the chief authority at Kábul. The appointment of a Hindu Rajput as governor over the Afghan population was one of the many proofs of Akber's daring, yet wise, policy. The emperor now proceeded to the Panjáb, sending an escort to Kábul to bring the children of Muhammad Hakím Mirza to Láhore. During his stay at Láhore, Akber organized military expeditions against Káshmír, Swát and Bajour. A force was also detached under the command of Kanwar Mán Singh to punish the Roshnai Afghans, known by the appellation of Zandaka Kafars. These were followers of a native of Hindostán who, assuming the title of Pir Roshnai, converted a large number of people to his creed. On his death, his son, Jalala, succeeded him, and, after staying at the court of Akber for a short time, fled to the country of the Afghans, where he raised the standard of revolt and interrupted the communications between Kábul and India.

The emperor's stay at Láhore.

The Roshnai sect.

The expedition to Swát and Bajour, 1586.

The expedition to Swát and Bajour was placed under the command of Zen Khan *Koka*, who was reinforced by troops under Syad Khán Ghakkar, Sheikh Fezi, Mullah Sheri and Sheikh Akil. Hakím Abdul Fatah *Gilání*, with several other officers of note, was also sent in the same direction at the head of troops; but notwithstanding these precautions, the Afghans fought so desperately that the imperial army sustained a signal defeat, and eight thousand of the troops were killed, including Rájá Bir Bal, the great minister, Mullah Sheri, and other officers of distinction. Zen Khan *Koka* and Hakím Abdul Fatah succeeded in joining the king's camp at Attock with great difficulty.

Ill success.

Rájá Bir Bal killed in the action.

Kanwar Mán Singh, who had been detached against the Roshnai Afghans, met with better success. He defeated the insurgents at the Khyber Pass, and put them to flight with great slaughter. The emperor, after these events, returned from Attock to Láhore, whence he despatched Kanwar Mán Singh to Kábul to assume the government of that country. The same year, the prince royal, Muhammad Salem Mirza, was married to the daughter of Rai Singh, a Rajput prince.

Matrimonial alliance with a Hindu princess.

Expedition to Káshmír.

The expedition to Káshmír, sent under Shah Rukh Mirza, Rájá Bhagwan Das and Shah Kuli Khan Mahram, succeeded so far as to secure the monopoly of saffron, and the privilege of coining money in the king's name, but the army suffered greatly from the snow and heavy rains. The emperor sent fresh contingents under Amirul Bahr Muhammad Kásim Khan of Kábul, and the country was completely reduced.

Conquest of Káshmír, 1586.

During the emperor's residence at Láhore he received the visit of Suleiman Mirza, grandfather of Shah Rukh Mirza, from Kábul, and an ambassador from Abdullah Khan Uzbek. In the year 1586, the peace of the Panjáb frontier was again disturbed by Jalala, the leader of the Roshnai sect, who defeated Kanwar Mán Singh in an action, and compelled him to fly to Bangash. The emperor sent reinforcements under Abdul Matálib Khan, Muhammad Kuli Beg and Hamza Beg Turkman, who inflicted a severe defeat on the enemy, and put them to flight with heavy loss. The same year, a son was born to the prince royal at Láhore by the daughter of Rájá Bhagwan Das, and was named Sultan Khusrow. Great rejoicings were made by the emperor on the occasion. In February, 1589, Kanwar Mán Singh was recalled from Kábul to Láhore, and Zen Khan *Koka*, the king's foster-brother, was sent to the former place to assume the government of the country. Syed Eusuf Khan Mashhedi was, in the meantime, appointed to the government of Káshmír in the place of Muhammad Kasim Khan, who was recalled. The king now resolved to pay a visit to his newly acquired kingdom of Káshmír. Accordingly, he left Láhore for Bhimber on

Birth of Sultan Khusrow, 1586.

The king visits Káshmír,

April 27th, 1589, and, having reached Srinagar, the capital of Káshmír, staid there a few weeks to make arrangements for the proper government of the country. From Káshmír the emperor proceeded to Kábul, where he staid for two months. On his way to Kábul, Hakim Fathulla Gilani died at Dhamtor and was buried at Baba Hasan Abdul. A force was despatched from Attock under Shah Báz Khan Kamboh to reduce the Eusáfzai Afghans, who were defeated and dispersed. At Kábul intelligence reached the king of the death, at Láhore, of Rájá Todar Mal, his great finance minister, and Rájá Bhagwan Das, which caused him sincere distress ; and he left for Láhore on November 19th, 1589. The court was held for some years at Láhore in consequence of the threatened attack on Kábul by Abdullah Khan Uzbek.

And Kábul, 1589.

Death of Rájás Todar Mal and Bhagwan Das, 1589.

In the year 1590, Eusuf Khan Mashhedi, governor of Káshmír, having left his younger brother, Mirza Yádgár, in charge of the government of that country, himself repaired to court. Yádgár Mirza, having, during the absence of his brother, married the daughter of a wealthy zemindar of Káshmír, raised the standard of insurrection and caused the Khutba to be read in his own name. The local commanders, Kazi Ali, the collector of revenues, Husein Beg, and Sheikh Umar Badakhshi, collected troops and opposed the insurgent chief, but Kazi Ali was slain in action, and the remainder of the Moghal officers fled from Káshmír. The emperor, having received advices of these events, sent Sheikh Farid Bakhshi at the head of a force to recover the province of Káshmír. Yádgár Mirza appeared within sight of the king's troops, but he was seized by stratagem by Sadak Beg and Ibrahim Khan Koka, officers of the Moghal forces, who put him to death and produced his head before Sheikh Badakhshi. The whole province of Káshmír was thus reduced a second time under the Imperial Government of Akber. The emperor himself marched to Káshmír shortly afterwards, and remained there for forty days. Syed Eusáf Khan Meshhedi having been appointed to the government of Káshmír, the emperor marched to Rohtas, where he received the visits of the chiefs of Tatta and Sindh.

Insurrection in Káshmír, 1589,

Is quelled.

In the year 1591, Akber sent an expedition from Láhore, where he himself was at the time, to Sindh, under Mirza Khan, *Khan Khanan*, with several officers, a train of one hundred elephants and a pack of artillery, with the object of recovering that province for the Delhi sovereignty; but the imperial general was foiled in his attempt to conquer the province. The Emperor sent another detachment, which having entered Sindh by the way of Amarkot, the province was reduced, and the chief of Sindh was appointed a noble of high rank at court.

Conquest of Sindh, 1591.

In 1593, Jalala, the chief of the Roshnai Afghans, created disturbances in the valley of Khaibar. Jafar Khan Kazwini, surnamed Asaf Khan, was sent to reduce him. Jalala was defeated, and he and his brothers were sent prisoners to court.

Defeat of Jalala, chief of the Roshnai sect, 1593.

One of the most memorable exploits of Akber in Hindostán was the the siege of Chittor. The besieged maintained an obstinate resistance; but the imperialists, by erecting batteries and by mining operations, gained possession of the walls, and the war elephants and cavalry, rushing furiously into the fort, completed the work of destruction. More than thirty thousand Rajputs were slain in this battle, and the few who escaped owed their life to stratagem. The fame acquired by the capture of this hitherto impregnable fortress, facilitated Akber's conquests in Gujrát, Behar, Rajputáná, and Bengal, though it took him fifteen years to reduce the insurrectionary Afghans of the eastern provinces. Another memorable event of Akber's reign was the siege, in 1594, of Ahmadnagar in the Dekkan, and its most gallant defence by Chánd Bibi, the daughter of Hosein Nizam Shah. This

The siege of Chittor, 1567,

And of Ahmadnagar, 1594.

The celebrated Chánd Sultáná.

extraordinary woman, the most able politician of her age, had been the queen and dowager-regent of the neighbouring kingdom of Bijapúr. The royal troops were under Prince Murád Mirza and Mirza Khan. The besieging party having opened their trenches, raised mounds, erected batteries and sank mines. The explosions caused great consternation among the besieged, but the princess defended the breach with masculine bravery. She appeared with a veil over her face, and, she having caused the guns to be brought to bear on the besieging party and stones to be hurled on them, these active measures resulted in the repeated repulse of the assailants. The siege lasted three months, at the end of which period scarcity of provisions prevailing in the Moghal camp, Prince Murád Mirza thought it advisable to open negotiations with Chánd Bibi. Berar was retained for Akber, while Ahmadnagar, with its dependencies, remained in charge of the minor Bahádur Shah, the grandson of Burhan Nizam Shah II.

In the year 1596, Abdulla Uzbek, who had long threatened an invasion from the north, having died, Akber returned from Láhore to Agra. In the year 1602 the whole province of the Dekkan, including Asir, Burhanpúr and Ahmadnagar, was annexed to the empire of Delhi, and Akber assumed, by proclamation, the title of "Emperor of the Dekkan" in addition to his other titles. The same year, Sheikh Abul Fazl was recalled from the Dekkan, but the learned Sheikh was attacked and cut off by banditti near Orcha in the district of Márwár, to the intense grief of the emperor.

Murder of Abul Fazl, 1602.

The religious notions of Akber.

Akber was a lax Musalman and celebrated the Persian festival of Nauroz or New Year's Day. He endeavoured to form a new religion, which was merely a pure deism, founded on the great doctrine of divine unity. The forms and ceremonies of this religion were chiefly derived from the ancient Persians, who professed the religion of Zoraster. Every morning he exhibited himself at a window, and the multitude knelt down before him. The water of his feet was used to cure diseases, and he professed to work miracles. Women made vows to him in the hope of becoming mothers, and on their bringing him presents when their object was gained, the king used to accept them. Other people asked for lasting bliss, for strength of body, for reunion of friends, increase of wealth, elevation in rank, and many other things. The king gave satisfactory answers to every one and suggested remedies. Not a day passed but people brought cups of water on which the king breathed, and which were used as a remedy for the sick. He worshipped the sun with the Brahmin, discoursed with the Christian, prostrated himself before the crucifix, as he did to the sun, while he respected with equal impartiality the tenets of the Jews, and with great patience weighed or refuted the arguments of the rival priests or sages.

He professes to work miracles.

Akber had fixed his capital at Agra, but his favourite residence was at Fattehpúr Sikri, twelve miles from that city. The interval between the two places was occupied by a bazar. In 1582, Akber resolved on moving his court from Fattehpúr to Láhore, and, from that year to 1598, he apparently made the latter city his head-quarters. He had been visited at Fattehpúr by three Christian fathers, Ridolfo Aguaviva,* a man of great learning, Monserrate and Enriques, a Persian by birth, who acted as interpreter. They presented him with a Polyglot Bible in four languages, which the great Moghal placed on his head, and the images of Jesus and the Virgin Mary, which he kissed, to the great delight of the Portuguese missionaries. The Christian fathers accompanied the emperor's camp to Láhore, and the greatness of his army and the splendour of his equipage excited their intense

Láhore made the head-quarters of Government, 1582-1598.

The Moghal Court visited by the Christian fathers, December 1568.

They accompany the emperor to Láhore.

Their description of his equipage.

* Abul Fazl calls him Padri Radif.

wonder. Five thousand elephants marched in the rear of the army, their heads were covered with iron plates, their trunks decorated with swords, and their tusks armed with daggers. The Portuguese missionaries, in their journal, describe Láhore as a "Delightful City." On arrival there, they were taken to the imperial residence, situated "on an island in the river," and introduced to his majesty, whom they describe as "a man about 50 years old, white like a European." The missionaries entertained hopes of being able to Christianize the king, but had eventually to return in disappointment to Goa.

Second mission of the Portuguese Jesuits, 1591.

Third mission, 1595.

Akber styled the Jesuits of Goa *Dánáyán-i-Frang* or "the wise men of the Franks," and in 1582 wrote them to send him translations of the Pentateuch, the Psalms and the Gospels, and also some person who could explain to him the mysteries of religion. A mission was sent to him in 1591, but the members of it did not stay long in India. A third mission was sent under Father Jerome Xavier, who had two companions, Benedict of Goes in Portugal and Emmanuel Pignero. They joined the emperor at Láhore in May 1595, and staid with him for several years. Xavier and Benedict also accompanied the emperor and his son, Prince Salem, to Káshmír. Xavier was a good Persian scholar. At the request of the emperor, he wrote his *Life of Christ* in Persian. As he mentions in the preface, the Persian version was made by him in conjunction with Moulana Abus-Sanárín, of Láhore.

Discourses in Láhore on religious subjects.

The Ibadat Khana.

The Khyrpura.

The Dharmpura.

It was during his stay at Láhore that Akber appears to have introduced those principles of religious toleration which have rendered his name so conspicuous in the annals of eastern potentates. There he seems to have reached the height of human greatness, and "As happy as Akber" passed into a proverb. Religious discussions were held in the *Ibadat Khana* on Sabbath evenings, at which learned men were invited to attend. The emperor and the grandees of the empire were present at these meetings. Abul Fazl started the questions and expounded the views of his master. The king's court was the resort of learned men of every creed, who came from various countries and were admitted to converse with him. Profound points of science, the subtleties of revelation, the curiosities of history, and the wonders of nature were freely discussed. The king listened with majestic gravity to all that was said, and passed through the most diverse phases of thought, adopting all sorts of religious practices and sectarian beliefs. Two buildings were erected outside the city of Láhore for the purpose of carrying on religious controversies. One of these called Khyrpura * was intended for the Muhammadans, Jews and fire worshippers, and the other called Dharmpura for the Hindus. The debates sometimes created fatal discords, and in one of them a learned Shia, Mullah Ahmad, author of the *Tarikhi Alfi*, was assassinated in the streets of Láhore by Mirza Fouládd. The assassin was subsequently condemned to death, and executed by being bound alive to the leg of an elephant.

Akber's public and private life.

His tenderness for animals.

Akber gave public audience every day in two spacious halls, in each of which was set up a royal throne. He seldom sat on the throne, but stood by it, passing verbal orders. He was very fond of hunting, and took great delight in the performances of wrestlers, fencers, dancers and actors, and in fights between buffaloes, rams, elephants, cocks and harts. He recollected the name of each of his elephants, and gave names to his horses, wild beasts and pigeons. In his youth he was passionately fond of leopards and hunting with leopards. A thousand leopards were collected in his park. The best

* The building was in the vicinity of Dárá Nagar on the left of the road leading to Mián Mír.

leopard belonging to him was known by the name of Samand Marak, and was carried with much pomp in a *Chandol*, with drums beating in front, and attendants fully equipped running at his sides. He kept his elephants obedient to his command, and mounted them by putting his foot on the tusks even when they were in the rutting season. He was fond of the *Siahgosh*, or *Felis caracal*, for hunting purposes, and imported dogs of excellent breeds and quality from all countries. He hunted with hawks and falcons, and amused himself by watching the conflicts between spiders and flies, and particularly the attempts of the latter to escape. In fulfilment of a vow made by him before the birth of his eldest son, Akber never hunted on Fridays.

He possessed an inventive genius.

Akber was possessed of an inquisitive mind. He sent an expedition to explore the source of the Ganges, and tried to discover what was the first spoken language. He had twelve infants brought up by dumb nurses, and when they grew up, caused them to be brought into his presence. They were unable to speak a word, and could express themselves only by signs. The experiment was a failure. He was skilled in various mechanical arts. He invented extraordinary carriages for travelling and carrying loads, designed water-wheels and carts, and a machine for drawing water from a well which at the same time moved a mill stone. He invented a wheel which cleaned sixteen barrels in a very short time. He had workshops for making guns and casting ordnance within the precincts of the palace. He invented elephant gear and introduced the brand system known as the Dagh-o-mahalli law.

His system of horse posts.

Akber delighted in Indian fables. He had the fables of Mír Hamza, consisting of 360 stories, copied in beautiful handwriting and illustrated by appropriate pictures. Throughout his dominions he established the system of posts and had two horses and a set of footmen stationed at every stage of five kos distance.

His knowledge of physiognomy.

Akber took great care in entering into details (*Kasrat*) with the object of understanding the whole (*Wahdat*), and this, according to Sheikh Abul Fazl, was the secret of his success. The Sheikh praises Akber as a good physiognomist. According to Badáoní, Akber learnt the art from the Jogis. He saw through men at the first glance.

His measures of reform.

He abolished the tax called *Karmi*, or contributions from pilgrims who visited the holy shrines, and remitted the *Jazía* or poll-tax upon the Hindus. In the 25th year of his reign, he took a census of all the inhabitants throughout his empire, and imperial mandates were issued to jagirdars, shikdárs and daroghas, directing them to draw up lists of the people of all sexes, village by village. He appointed inspectors to stop widow burning among the Hindus, and he restricted polygamy amongst the Musalmans. He imposed stringent restrictions on prostitution* and inflicted severe punishment on seducers. He interdicted beef, and to touch beef was considered a sin. Influenced by the Hindu princesses of the harem, he foreswore beef, garlic, onions and the wearing of the beard. The shaving of the beard was considered as the highest sign of friendship and affection for his majesty, who scarcely admitted a bearded person into his presence. The use of wine was allowed if required for strengthening the body, and if prescribed by doctors, but intoxication was severely punished. Marriages

His Hindu proclivities.

Restriction as to early marriage.

* His Majesty himself summoned some of the principal prostitutes and asked them who had deprived them of their virginity. On receiving exact information, he punished, censured or put in long confinement in fortresses, the men concerned, some of whom were men of renown and grandees. *Ain-i-Akberi.* A separate quarter was assigned to prostitutes outside the town, and the place was called Shaitanpúra (Devil's Villa). A Darogha and a clerk were appointed to register the names of those who resorted to them. No one could take a dancing girl to his house without permission.—*Tarikh-i-Badaoni.*

of boys before 16 and of girls before 14 were prohibited, because the offspring of early marriages was weakly.

Akber assumes the position of a religious reformer.

In devising his new religion called the *Din-i-Ilahi*, or the Divine faith, Akber proposed to inculcate the reverence of God according to the knowledge of him derived from reason. He recommended the adoration of the sun, the planets, or fire, symbols of the Divinity, and as a means of obtaining a true knowledge of Him and His wisdom. He gave his religious system the name of *Tauhi-di-Ilahi*, or divine monotheism. He introduced his reforms and innovations by degrees, and, before promulgating them, obtained the legal opinion of the principal Mahomedan lawyers. Thus it was that he was acknowledged to be the head of the church, the Pope, or Caliph of Islam.* As the supreme spiritual guide of Islam, he had the right to govern its members according to his own judgment, and under his authority it was declared that "there is no God but one God, and that Akber is his Caliph." He ordered the words "*Alla ho Akber*" to be engraved on his seal. It was also declared that Akber was the 12th Imam, the regenerator of the world, the reconciler of the seventy-two sects of Islam. The idea originated in Abul Fazl, the chief tool of Akber and his inseparable companion. Lastly, Akber was adored as God, though he himself does not seem to have laid claim to supernatural illuminations. The following odes of Fezi may be cited in proof of this:—

His new religion.

He assumes ecclesiastical supremacy,

And is worshipped as a deity.

شاهي كه بفضل ذوفنون خوانيمش — از راه خداي رهنمون خوانيمش
هر چند كه سايهٔ خدا يند شهان — او نور خداست سايه چون خوانيمش

"He (Akber) is a king whom on account of his wisdom we call *Zúfanún* (professor of the sciences),
And our guide in the path of religion;
Although kings are the shadow of God on earth,
He is the emanation of God's light; How then can we call him a shadow?"

At another place says the same poet:—

خواهي كه چو من راه هدي بشناسي — نشناخته شاه را كجا بشناسي
اين سجدهٔ ناقبول سودت ندهد — اكبر بشناس تا خدا بشناسي

"If you wish to acquire the knowledge of the path of righteousness as I have done,
You cannot do it without acquiring the knowledge of the king;
This unaccepted prostration is of no advantage to you,
Have knowledge of Akber, and you will have knowledge of God."

The study of Arabic was prohibited, and that of astronomy, mathematics, medicine and philosophy encouraged. Names like Muhammad and Ali were disused. Circumcision before the age of twelve was prohibited. The Hejra era and the Arabian months were abolished, and a new era introduced, of which the first year was the year of the emperor's accession. The months were named after those of the ancient Persians. The ordinary salutation, "*Salam-alekum*!"

Innovations in the Mahomedan religion.

* It having been represented to the king that the Prophet and his four successors used themselves to preach, that the Abbasi Caliphs observed this tradition, and that in later times Amir Tymúr, the *Sahib Kiran* and Mirza Ulagh Beg followed the example set, the king felt it his duty to follow the custom observed by the Caliphs and Imams. Accordingly, on Friday, the 1st Jamadi-ul-awal, he went to the grand mosque of Fatehpúr, and, mounting the pulpit, thus opened his discourse:—

The Lord to me the kingdom gave,
He made me prudent, strong and brave,
He guided me with right and truth,
Filling my heart with love of truth;
No tongue of man can sum His state,
Alla ho Akber! God is great.

He cited verses from the Koran, offering thanks to God for His benevolence and mercies; then repeating the *Fatiha*, he came down from the pulpit, and read his prayers.—*Tabakat-i Akberi*, the 25th year of Akber's reign.

(Peace be unto you) was abandoned, and for it was substituted "*Alla ho Akber*" (God is most great), to which the answer was given, "*Jalli Jalalahu*" (May his brightness shine forth). These innovations gave great offence to the Mahomedans.

Translation of Sanskrit works into Persian.

Akber ardently desired the cultivation of knowledge and encouraged every kind of learning. With this view, he established schools at which the Hindus and Mahomedans received education according to their turn of mind and circumstances in life. He specially directed his attention to the cultivation of Indian literature. Under his direction Fezi translated from the Shastras, the *Nala* and *Damyanti*, an episode of *Mahábhárata*. He also compiled versions of the *Bija* and *Ganita*, and *Lilawati* of *Bhaskara Acharya*, the well-known Hindu works on algebra and arithmetic. Besides Fezi, the Sanskrit translators of his court were Abul Kadir Badaoni, Mullah Shah Muhammad, Nakib Khan, Haji Ibráhím, Sultan Haji, Mullah Shesi and others. Abul Kadir, among other works, translated the *Rámáyana* and *Singhásan Battisi*. The translation of the *Mahábhárata* and the *History of Káshmír* were made under the superintendence of Fezi. Haji Ibrahim Sirhindi translated the *Atharva Veda*, a Hindu work, noted for the difficulty of its style and the abstruseness of its meaning.*

The remodelling of the revenue system.

The old system of revenue collections.

The improvements effected by Akber.

The survey of lands.

The government demand.

At the instance of his distinguished counsellor, Rájá Toodar Mal, the great financier of the age, Akber remodelled the revenue system of his empire. A multitude of cesses that pressed most heavily on industry were abolished. At first the revenue was levied by the viceroys of different provinces, who, wholly ignorant of finance, farmed them out to Hindu bankers, who varied the assessment, and tortured the cultivators at discretion, in order to make up the stipulated sum. From the monies thus collected, the viceroy paid the troops and remitted the balance to the imperial exchequer. Akber changed the system at once, by requiring the viceroys to remit the revenue to the imperial exchequer, and issuing the pay of the troops from the royal treasury. He caused all the lands, whether in town or country, cultivated or uncultivated, to be measured according to a uniform standard, and with the most perfect survey instruments. The State demand was limited to one-third of the annual produce, and commuted to payments in money. The system was, in fact, a continuation of a plan devised and partially introduced under Sher Shah, the Pathan king; and Todar Mal, the principal agent in the reform, only strove to re-establish the ancient principles of native finance. The state demand, in the time of Sher Shah, was fixed at a fourth of the produce. Akber, as already stated, reduced it to one-third.

Officers of land revenue.

The collectors of *Khálsá* lands and the jagirdars realized the revenue (*mál*) and cesses (*jihát*) according to a fixed code of law called the (*Dasturul-amal*). There were *ámils* for the collection of revenue, and they had two subordinates, a *karkun* (manager) and a *khas nawis* (accountant).† The *ámil* was known by the native name *pattel*, or chief (like the Mairi in France and the Alcalde in Spain). The patwari of each village was to apportion lands of each description, and the collectors were to remit cash to the treasury under the seal of the patwari. They were to be vigilant to prevent oppression and to treat each individual according to his desert. The pyke was the watchman and head of the police. Besides these essential personages, there were the money-changers, who were the silversmiths; the priest or mullah, who was the schoolmaster; the astrologer, the smith, the carpenter

* The Mahomedans obtained a knowledge of Sanskrit not long after the establishment of their faith, and Indian works on astronomy, music, astrology, Hindu theology, agriculture, physiognomy, and palmistry, were translated into Arabic during the early periods of the Caliphs.

† *Akbar Nama*, 27th year of the reign.

the potter, the leather worker, the tailor, the barber, the washerman, the physician, the musician and the dancing-girls, who were all paid an allowance out of the general funds of the village. Every tract of land calculated to produce one crore of tankas yearly, was placed under the charge of an officer called *karori*. The Aín-i-Akberi, or the laws and regulations of Akber, set forth in detail the reforms in the revenue administration introduced by Akber which tended materially to replenish the public treasury.

The village general funds.

The court of Akber was the most splendid ever held in India, and his style of living was of a most sumptuous character. Every establishment was maintained on a scale of imperial magnificence, and regulated in its minutest details by the personal directions of the emperor. He never had fewer than 12,000 horses and 5,000 elephants in his own stables, independently of those required for hawking, hunting and war. His camp was a great moving city, and furnished with an equipage that provided for him, even in a desert, all the pomp and luxuries of an imperial palace. A vast space was enclosed by tents, surmounted with gilt cupolas and by screens of red canvas, and enriched with the most gorgeous ornaments, gilt globes and spires that dazzled the sight,—all forming a wall within which were erected a great number of splendid and richly furnished pavilions, some of which were used as rooms of state, some as banqueting halls, and others for retirement or repose, while an inner enclosure contained the apartments of the ladies, all fitted up in the most costly and elegant manner. This enclosure occupied an area of full five miles in circumference.

The splendour of the Imperial court.

His camp.

There was always a grand display of wealth and magnificence on the emperor's birthday. A large space, about two acres in extent, near the capital, was covered with superb tents, that of the emperor being conspicuous by the splendour of its decorations. The nobility had similar pavilions, where visits from one to another were paid and received, and where they were sometimes honored by a visit from the king himself. The whole space was covered with carpets of gold and silk tissue, hangings of velvet, embroidered with gold, pearls and precious stones. At the upper end was placed the royal throne, on which his majesty sat to receive homage from the Omerahs and nobles, who were honored with rich dresses, jewels, horses, elephants and other gifts. The emperor was weighed in golden scales against gold, silver, perfumes and other substances in succession, which were distributed among the spectators who crowded the plain. The emperor showered gold and silver nuts, almonds and other fruit with his own hand, which were eagerly scrambled for by the gravest of the courtiers.

The emperor's birthday.

The emperor is weighed against gold, silver, &c.

On the great festival of the Vernal equinox, the emperor, surrounded by the grandees of the realm, sat on the throne, wearing high heron plumes and sparkling with diamonds, rubies and emeralds. Many hundred elephants, all richly adorned, passed before him in procession, the leading elephant of each company wearing large gold plates on its head and breast. Trains of horses, gorgeously caparisoned, followed, after which came, in succession, rhinoceroses, lions, tigers, panthers, hunting leopards, hounds and hawks, the procession winding up with a vast host of cavalry, resplendent with cloth of gold.

The festival of Now Roz.

By the sack of Hindu towns and places of worship, as well as the plunder obtained from the citadels of the Mahomedan rulers whom Akber had subdued in war, he had accumulated an incredible amount of treasure. Jahángír, his son, mentions that the great Tymúr never collected a tenth of the amount. At Agra four hundred pairs of scales are said to have been at work, weighing gold and jewels, and the total could not be made in five months. Eight large vaults were filled with jewels, coins, gold and silver idols, plates,

Enormous wealth of the king.

brocades, tapestries, bullion, and manuscripts, valued at nearly seventy

The king's crown.

millions sterling. The crown resembled a Persian diadem. It had twelve points, surmounted by diamonds of the purest water, and of the most brilliant colour, the centre being set with a pearl of extraordinary size

The royal throne.

and value. It was valued at above two millions sterling. The throne was reached by silver steps, on which four silver lions supported a canopy of gold, adorned with jewels, the whole valued at thirty millions of English money.

The last days of Akber embittered by the refractory conduct of the Crown prince.

The last days of Akber were embittered by the profligacy of Salem, the Crown prince, and an influential body of the grandees, among whom was Rájá Mán Singh, formed the design of elevating his son Khusrow, a minor, to the throne; but Akber nipped the project in the bud. A melancholy event occurring about the same time, the emperor sank fast under the weight

Death of Prince Dániál, 1605.

of his grief. This was the death of Prince Dániál, in the town of Burhanpúr, from excessive drinking, on April 8th, 1605. His majesty, finding that

The emperor's last moments.

his last moments had come, summoned all his Omerahs to his bed-side. When they were assembled round his couch, he delivered to them a suitable speech, and, wistfully looking round at them, asked them to forgive any offence of which he might have been guilty towards any of them. He then gave them a sign to invest his son Salem with the turban and robes which had been prepared for him, and to gird him with his favourite scimitar. He entreated his son to be kind to the ladies of the family, and never to neglect or forsake his old friends and dependents. The grandees prostrated themselves before their dying lord and did him homage. The dying sovereign bowed himself also. The priest was then introduced. The king repeated the confession of faith, closed his eyes, and died in all the forms of a pious

His death, 1605.

Musalman. This happened on October 13th, 1605. Akber had reigned fifty-one years and some months. The words

فوت اکبر شاه

"The death of King Akber"

His burial-place.

give the date of his death. He was buried at Sekandra, near Agra, in a mausoleum that had been commenced some time before.

His character.

Akber was the contemporary of Queen Elizabeth, and, like her, was endowed by nature with the wisdom and insight which enables its possessor to collect able statesmen round the throne. The main features of his life bore a strong resemblance to those of Asoká, the Buddhist prince, who had ruled India eighteen centuries before him. He was a born statesman and soldier. He had never received an education, or even learnt to read or write. But he had pondered over histories, and grand ideas seethed in his majestic and philosophical mind. He was endowed with a marvellous memory, judicious forecast and deep judgment. He ignored distinctions of race and creed, and wished to mould the Rájput and Musalman into one imperial system. By taking the daughters of Rájput princes in marriage, his policy was to break the Rájput league which had existed for twenty centuries, and to hold the empire together by cementing a political alliance between Musalmans and Hindus. He married the daughters of the rájás of Jeypúr, Jodhpúr and Bikanír, was much attached to his Hindu wives, and, on their account, joined in the Brahminical worship and sacrifices. He was handsome

His person.

in his person and engaging in his manners; of rather more than middle stature, and stout of body; his complexion was a ruddy nut brown; his eyes were full and dark and his eyebrows meeting; his forehead was open He was possessed of prodigious strength, which was probably due to the great breadth of his chest and to his long sinewy arms and hands. On the left side of his nose there was a fleshy wart, about the size of a small pea, which physiognomists considered very auspicious. His voice was loud and his speech sweet and elegant. His manners were fascinating and his features full of dignity. He was possessed of remarkable courage, and, while yet a boy, performed prodigies of valour. Even in sports he displayed conspicuous courage and agility, and his daring encounters with tigers and wild beasts, and his amusements with unbroken horses and elephants, are an indubitable proof of the extraordinary strength he possessed. He took intense delight in all manly exercises, and would walk thirty or forty miles, or ride sometimes a hundred miles, in a day. On one occasion he rode from Ajmere to Agra, a distance of 220 miles in two successive days. He was a most expert marksman and had a favourite gun* which he used in shooting thousands of game. In his youth he indulged in wine and merry festivities, but he soon became abstemious and refrained from animal food on particular days.

A generous and merciful ruler, a kind master, a forgiving father, a sincere friend, a generous foe, a brave soldier, a talented statesman, Akber is the ideal sovereign of India, and has left behind him one of the brightest names in the history of the world, a name familiar to all civilized nations, and one which to this day is on the lips equally of the Hindus and Mahomedans that inhabit this vast empire.†

CHAPTER XIV.

NÚR-UD-DÍN JAHÁNGÍR.

Jahángir crowned emperor of Hindostán, 1605.

NÚR-UD-DÍN, surnamed Salem, on ascending his father's throne, assumed the sounding title of Jahángír, "Conqueror of the World." He was crowned in the fort of Agra on October 12th, 1605, in the 38th year of his age. The event was commemorated by an inscription on the sand stone panel, in the Delhi gate of the fort, where it is still to be seen, concluding with the prayer: "May our King Jahángír be the king of the world!"—1014. The new king distributed costly gifts on the occasion, and handsomely rewarded the poets who composed congratulatory poems. The following poem of Maktub Khan, the librarian and manager of the royal Nakkash Khána, giving the date of the accession, is cited by the emperor in the Tuzuk Jahángír:—

صاحب قران ثاني شاهنشه جهانگير
با عدل و داد بنشست برتخت كامراني
اقبال و بخت و دولت فتح و شكوه و نصرت

---

* This was the first of his majesty's private guns and was known by the name of Sangrám —*Ayíní Akberi.*

† Akber used the *Iláhí* year and Persian months on his coins, instead of the year of *Julus* or the accession to the throne. His gold coin bore the following inscription:—

مهر مهر شاه اكبر آبروي اين زر است — ضرب آگره

تا زمين و آسمان را مهر انور زيور است — اسفندارمز ۴۰ الهي

"The sun of the seal of King Akber is the honour of this gold coin.
So long as the earth and the sky are adorned with the luminous sun."
"Struck at Agra. Isfandármiz, 40 Ilahi."

پیشش کمر بخدمت بسته بشان مالي
سال جلوس شاهي تاريخ شد چو بنهاد
اقبال سر بپاي صاحب قران ثاني

"When the second Sáhib-i-Qirán,* the Emperor Jahángír,
Sat on the throne of prosperity with justice and moderation,
Glory, prosperity, wealth, victory and pomp,
Girded their loins for service before him.
It is in the year of the royal accession that
Glory has laid its head at the foot of the second Sáhib-i-Qirán."

He restores the Mahomedan ritual.

He confirmed most of his father's ministers in their posts, but removed from office all those who had favoured the religious innovations of Akber, and restored the forms and ritual of the Mahomedan religion to their former supremacy. He raised Sharif Khan, his boon companion, to the dignity of prime minister, and appointed Said Khan Moghal, viceroy of the Panjáb. He issued some ordinances for the benefit of his subjects. He abolished the duties called Tamgha and Mir Bahri. He caused sarais, wells and mosques to be built on the highways that were infested by robbers. He passed a law forbidding the bales of merchants to be opened without their consent, and directed that no soldiers or servants of the state should locate themselves in private houses. The use, manufacture and sale of every sort of intoxicating liquor was prohibited, though Jahángír had been himself notoriously in the habit of taking wine. The jágírdárs and officers of the Khálsá were forbidden to take lands of the *rayats* by force, or to form connections with the people without permission. He established hospitals in large towns, and appointed doctors to attend the sick at the expense of the state. The slaughter of animals on certain days was prohibited, as in the days of Akber. The old Tartar ceremony of prostration before the sovereign was exacted from all who had an audience of the king, and his majesty, like his father, appeared every morning at the "jharoka" (window) to exhibit himself to the multitude below, and receive their blessings. He introduced a measure which afforded complainants special facilities for obtaining easy access to him. A chain of gold was attached to a battlement of the fort, with the other end affixed to a stone column on the bank of the river. It was called "the chain of justice." It was 30 yards long and had sixty golden bells on it. It communicated with a cluster of golden bells within the King's own apartments, and every person oppressed was allowed to shake it, and appeal to the king to grant redress, in spite of the officers interested in keeping back the information.

His beneficent measures at the commencement of his reign.

The ceremony of prostration in audience before the king renewed.

The "chain of justice."

The rebellion of the emperor's eldest son, Khusrow.

In the spring of 1606, or six months after the accession of Jahángír, his eldest son, Khusrow, having broken into rebellion, fled to the Panjáb, where he collected a body of upwards of 10,000 troops. He plundered the country as he went, and, having invested Láhore, set one of the gates of the city on fire. The city was gallantly defended by the imperial officers, Mirza Husain, Diláwar Beg Khán, Husain Beg, Diwán, and Núr-ud-dín Kuli, Kotwál, who repaired the breaches in the wall of the city that had been caused by the fire of the besiegers. Said Khán, who was deputed to Káshmír, having heard of the seige of Láhore by Khusrow, repaired from the Chináb with his contingent and joined the royal troops in the fort. In the meantime Jahángír was on his march to Láhore, and the imperial vanguard, under Sheikh Farid Bokhári, appearing within sight of the city, Khusrow drew up his troops in order of battle. A sanguinary engagement took place between the two

He lays siege to Láhore,

* Sáhib-i-Qirán literally means one born under an auspicious conjunction of two or more planets. It was a title of honor given by the historians to Taimúr. Jahángír is here styled the equal of Sáhib-i-Qirán.

armies, the result of which was the total defeat of Khusrow's army and his flight in the direction of Kábul.

But is defeated and captured, 1606.

The Prince was crossing the Chináb by night, when the ferry-boat in which he had embarked ran on a sand bank. He was arrested by the King's officers, who were in pursuit, and brought before his majesty in the garden of Mirza Kamran, on the Rávi, handcuffed and fettered. He was led up from the left side according to the practice of Changez Khán. On his right was Husain Beg, and on his left Abdul Aziz. "The Prince," writes Jahángír in his memoirs, "stood between them, trembling and weeping. Husain Beg, suspecting that he would be made the scapegoat, began to speak sorrowfully, but he was not allowed to continue. Khusrow was placed in custody.

Barbarous punishment of Khusrow's principal advisers.

I then ordered the two villains to be inclosed in the skins of a cow and an ass respectively, and to be put on asses, their faces towards the tails, and to be paraded in this manner round the city. Husain Beg, who was inclosed in the cow's skin, lived only to the fourth watch, as the skin of that animal dries quickly, and then died. Abdul Aziz, who was in the ass's skin, which is less affected by moisture, survived a day and a night, when he died."

Rewards for good services rendered.

Sheikh Farid, in recognition of his services, received the title of Múrtazá Khan and the zemindars of the Chináb, who had helped in the arrest of the rebel Prince were rewarded with jágírs. Foremost among these was Kelan, son-in-law of Kamál Choudri of Lodhra, who was specially favoured by his majesty. The emperor remained in the garden of Mirza Kamran from 1st Zil Hij to 9th Moharram, 1015 A.H. (1607 A.D.) on account, as he says, of bad weather.

The emperor's description of a horrible scene of cruelty.

"On the 9th of Moharram," continues the royal writer, "I entered the castle of Láhore, where I took up my abode in the royal pavilion built by my father on the principal tower, from which to view the combats of elephants. Seated in the pavilion, and having directed a number of sharp stakes to be set up in a double row, from the garden of Mirza Kamran to the gates of Láhore, I caused the 700 traitors who had conspired with Khusrow against my authority, to be impaled alive upon them. There cannot be a more excruciating punishment than this, since the wretches lingered a long time in the most agonising torture before they died, and the spectacle of their agony was most frightful." Along the ghastly avenue the wretched Prince was borne on an elephant to witness the writhing and shrieking, in agony, of these victims to his father's fierce revenge and his own ambition. The mother of Khusrow poisoned herself, preferring to die rather than live and see the misery and affliction of her son.

Punishment of Arjan Mal, the fourth Seikh Guru.

The celebrated Guru Arjan Mal, the fourth Guru of the Sikhs, and the compiler of the *Adi Granth*, was charged with having assisted the rebel Prince Khusrow with spiritual aid. He was put in close confinement, and his death is attributed to the torture to which he was subjected. Tradition, however, asserts that he disappeared in the Rávi, as he plunged into the water to bathe. He is regarded by the Sikhs as their first martyred Guru, and his death changed them from a peaceful to a warlike nation.

The emperor's march to Kabul.

Intelligence having reached the emperor at Láhore that the Kazal Báshis had laid siege to Kandahar, he sent a force in that direction under the command of Ghází Beg Khan. A few days afterwards, the emperor himself marched to Kábul, leaving Khilj Khan, Mirán Sadar Jahán and Mír Sharif Amli in charge of Láhore. Having crossed the Rávi, he alighted in the garden of Dilamez and staid there for four days. "On the fifth day," continues the emperor, "I marched from the garden to the village called Harípúr, three-and-a-half *kos* from the city. On Tuesday flags waved in Jahángírpúr, which was a hunting ground of mine. Near this village I had a minaret erected over the remains of an antelope of mine, which I had called Ráj. It was the best fighter I possessed, and was the best decoy for wild ones. A marble stone affixed to this minaret contained the following inscription of Mulla Muhammad Husain of Káshmír, well known for his excellence in the art of caligraphy:—'In this delightful spot, an antelope was caught by the Emperor Núr-ud-dín Muhammad Jahángír, which, in the space of one month, became quite tame and was considered the best of all the royal antelopes.' The tombstone was carved in the shape of a deer. Out of regard for this animal, I prohibited the hunting of antelopes in this forest. On Thursday, the 14th of Zil Hij, we encamped in the pargana of Chandwála, and on Saturday reached Háfizábád, where we put up in the buildings constructed under the superintendence of Mír Kiran-ud-dín, the *karori* at that station." On 21st Zil Hij, the emperor reached Gujrát. When the Emperor Akber was on his march to Káshmír, he built a fort on the other side of the river, and had it inhabited by Gujars, who had hitherto lived on plunder. The place was, in consequence, named Gujrát and formed into a separate pargana. On the first of Moharram the emperor marched to Rohtás. "The fort of Rohtás," writes the emperor, "was built by Sher Khan, the Pathan king. The fort is constructed in ravines, most difficult of access. It was built with the object of overawing and keeping in check the turbulent race of the Ghakkars, who inhabited the adjoining country. Sher Khan died leaving the work incomplete. It was completed by his son and successor Salem Khan. On one of the gates the cost of the building is engraved on stone, and it amounts to 16,10,00,000 dáms, which is equal to 34,25,000 rupees of Hindostán coin. The camp moved to Hassan Abdál on the 12th. About a *kos* to the east of this place is a cataract which flows with much rapidity. On all the road to Kábul there is no cascade like this, though on the road to Káshmír there are two or three of the same kind. In the middle of the basin, whence the water flows, Rájá Mán Singh has built a small edifice. It abounds in fish from a quarter to half a yard long. I staid three days in this attractive spot, and partook of wine with my companions. I also had the pleasure of fishing there. Hitherto I had never thrown the *bhanwar jál* (net) so common in India. It cannot be thrown without some difficulty; but I tried it with my own hands, and succeeded in catching ten or twelve fish. Having strung pearls in their noses, I let them go again in the cold water. I asked the inhabitants and people acquainted with history who Bábá Hassan was, but no one could give any definite information. The most noted spot in this locality is a spring which issues from the foot of a small hill. The water is exceedingly pure, delicious and fragrant, and the following verse of Khusrow well applies to it:—

A favourite antelope.

Foundation of Gujrát.

The emperor's description of the fort of Rohtás,

And of Hassan Abdál.

His fishing at the lake.

درتہہ آبش زصفا ریگ خُرد
کور تواند بدل شب شمرد

"The water is so transparent that a blind man in the middle of the night could count the particles of sand at the bottom."

Khwája Shams-ud-dín Muhammad Khan, who was for a long time the minister of my father, had a summer house * erected there, and a cistern excavated, into which the water of the spring flows, irrigating the fields and

* Sir Henry Elliot thinks it probable that this is the place now occupied by the Sikh Granthís, who have set up there the *panja*, or hand, of Bábá Nának, and have established the cistern as a sacred spot where they feed fat fish. "Considering at how late a period this place came under the dominion of the Sikhs, it is curious," remarks Sir Henry, "that popular feeling should concur in the new belief that Bábá Nának visited the spot and performed the miracle ascribed to him, which is recorded by our modern travellers who have visited the spot."

gardens. Close to it he built a dome to be used as his tomb, but it so happened that he was not buried there, and the spot was used as the burial place of Hakim Abul Fath Giláni and his brother Hakim Himam, by order of my father."

The king then reached Amardi, described as a most extraordinarily green plain. At this place there were seven or eight thousand horses of the Khatars and Dilazaks, who were highway robbers and practised every kind of oppression. The emperor gave orders to Zafar Khan, son of Zen Khan Koka, to march the whole of the Dilazaks to Láhore before the return of the royal camp from Kábul, and to seize the chiefs of the Khatars and keep them in prison.* At Pesháwar the emperor put up in the garden of Sirdar Khan and received the respects of the Eusafzai chiefs. The governorship of Pesháwar was bestowed on Sher Khan, an Afghan. On his way to the Khaibar Pass, his majesty encamped at Ali Masjid and reached Kábul. The siege of Kandahar was raised. The whole of the year 1606 the emperor passed pleasantly in Kábul and Káshmír, returning to Agra in the beginning of 1607.

The emperor at Pesháwar.

His return to Agra, 1607.

THE HISTORY OF NÚR JAHÁN.

Jahángír is the only Mahomedan sovereign whose reign was influenced by a passion which, in other countries, has so often decided the fate of empires, operating more forcibly than even ambition or avarice. The object of his love was Núr Mahal, a Persian lady, famed for her unrivalled beauty and brilliant accomplishments. The life of this lady is full of romantic interest. She obtained a complete ascendancy over the emperor's mind, and for sixteen years the history of Núr Jahán is the history of Jahángír and of his empire. Her original name, from the parents' side, was Mihr-ul-nisa. She was the daughter of Mirza Ghiás Beg, son of Khwája Muhammad Sharíf, an Uzbek Tartar noble of Tehrán. The Khwája was governor of Khorásán, during the reign of Muhammad Khan Tuklú, and, on the latter's death, was appointed wazír of Yazd by King Thamasp of Persia. When Húmáyún sought refuge in Tehrán, after his disastrous flight from India, King Thamasp specially appointed Muhammad Sharíf to look after the comfort of his royal guest. The Khwája had two sons, Aga Tahir and Mirza Ghiás Beg. Ghiás Beg was married to the daughter of Mirza Ala-ud-dín, and the result of the union was two sons and two daughters, the younger of these being Mihr-ul-nisa.

The parentage of Núr Jahán.

After the death of his father, Ghiás Beg, being reduced to poverty, travelled to Hindostán with his wife, his two sons, and a daughter. The family was in such distress that the Mirza's wife, who was then in an advanced stage of pregnancy, was carried on a cow which followed a caravan, the rest of the party walking on foot. On the way to the city of Kandahar was born the future empress of the country to which the distressed parents were journeying in search of a livelihood. She was born in a desert, where the poverty of her parents, and their inability to maintain the mother, so as to admit of her nourishing the infant, compelled them to leave her at the foot of a tree to the chances of the road. The mother fainted with anguish as the spot where the infant lay receded from her view. The father, returning, found the infant encircled by a hideous serpent, which he forthwith killed. The distressed condition of the mother and child excited the compassion of Malik Masúd, the chief merchant of a caravan which happened to be

Mirza Ghiás Beg her father.

The extreme poverty of the family.

Her birth.

The merchant Malik Masúd.

* These orders appear to have been faithfully executed, for there are now no Dilazaks here. Of the Khatars there are still several villages, and the fertile plain of Khatar is still called after their name.—Sir Henry Elliot's *History of India.*

travelling by the same route. He was struck with the child's beauty, and, taking her up, resolved to educate her as his own daughter. He treated the family with the utmost kindness during the rest of the journey, and employed the child's mother as her nurse. He found the father a polished and refined man, and, on reaching the capital, took him into his employ.

Ghiás Beg introduced to Akber.

Through the medium of this merchant, who was known to Akber, Mirza Ghiás Beg obtained an audience of the emperor at Fathpúr. He narrated to Akber how his father had served the emperor's while a guest of the Shah in Persia, and thus obtained a share of royal patronage. His majesty was so much pleased with the Mirza's graceful manners and business-like habits, that he raised him to the dignity of dewán, or treasurer of the royal household, and conferred upon him the exalted title of Itimádud Daula. The Mirza soon became known for his genial habits and generous disposition. He had studied the old poets and was a good poet himself, and wrote the *shikasta* in a bold and elegant style. His leisure hours were devoted to the study of poetry and style. According to Mirza Muhammad Hadi, the historian of Jahángír, the Mirza was so charitably disposed that no one ever left his doors dissatisfied, but, in the taking of bribes, he was most unblushing and fearless.

His high literary attainments.

The early education of Núr Jahán.

The girl who had been the unconscious cause of the introduction of her father to so kind a benefactor, received all the educational advantages which life in the capital of India could afford. As she grew up into a woman, her exquisite beauty, surpassing goodness, and unequalled elegance became the subject of attraction and universal admiration. The wife of the Lord High Treasurer, the mother of the young Mihr-ul-nisa, was in favor with Mariam Zamáni, the wife of Akber, a Hindu princess, the daughter of the Rájá of Jaipúr and mother of the heir-apparent, Prince Salem, and she used to visit the royal lady, accompanied by her daughter, and a procession of women in palanquins with closed curtains. The young Mihr-ul-nisa, happy in mind, and endowed with all the charms of beauty and unstudied grace of movement, used to amuse the kind-hearted queen with the dances of her native land and the songs of the mountains of Balkh. She had a tall, slight, statuesque figure, regular features and a small oval face. Her head was small and was set on gently sloping shoulders. Her eyes were dark and almond-shaped. She had a thousand charms, a thousand attractions. While she was dancing, one day, Prince Salem entered the royal apartment. The eyes of the two met. Salem was fascinated by the graces of her person, no less than by her sprightly wit. The attachment was mutual. But the young lady's hand was already plighted to one of the emperor's nobles, Ali Kuli Beg. This youth, a nobleman of Irák, was previously in the employ of Ismail II, king of Persia, as superintendent of the royal kitchen. While Abdul Rahim, surnamed Khán-i-Khánán, was carrying on war against the Thatta tribe in the neighbourhood of Múltán, Ali Kuli Beg entered the Imperial service, and, having distinguished himself by deeds of valour in the field, became a favourite with the minister, who introduced him to the emperor during his majesty's stay at Láhore.

The Empress Mariam Zamání.

The maiden Núr Jahán.

Her wit and charms.

She fascinates Salem.

Ali Kuli Beg the Turkomán noble.

Salem had met Mihr-ul-nisa several times at her mother's house, and found opportunities of courtship. His behaviour so much exasperated the mother of Mihr-ul-nisa that she spoke of it to the Queen Mariam Zamáni, and, through her the matter reached the ears of Akber. Salem, entranced by the beauty of the Turkomán lady, vowed to marry her, and petitioned his father to annul her engagement with the Persian noble. Akber was too honorable a man to commit such an injustice. He remonstrated with his son, and, refusing to annul the engagement, managed to keep his treasurer's

Akber remonstrates with his son for his behaviour.

daughter out of the prince's sight. He also recommended her mother to marry her to her betrothed on the first opportunity. Mihr-ul-nisa, with all her great ambition and strong attachment for the heir-apparent, had no voice in her own destiny. In vain did she warn her parents and her brother that, by refusing the marriage, they would incur the wrath of Salem, who was cruel in his revenge. In vain did she plead that his whole happiness depended on this marriage, as did hers. In vain did she point out that she had no fear of Jodh Bai, Prince Salem's principal wife, and that she would mould Salem like wax in her fingers. She was at last married to Ali Kuli Beg. According to custom, the newly-wedded pair saw each other for the first time through a looking-glass. The Turkomán, looking into the glass, beheld a face singularly beautiful, but angry and pale, and at once became deeply enamoured of her. But his own face did not in the least interest his affianced bride. "How frightful to the sight is thy tall sheep's-skin Persian cap!" were the first words uttered by Mihr-ul-nisa. The mother rebuked her for her peevish speech; but the bridegroom gently answered: "A blow from the hand of my beloved is as sweet as a grape." The marriage ceremony being over, the young but dangerous beauty was removed to a distance from her royal lover, the bridegroom taking her away to his manor in Bardwan.

The marriage of Mihr-ul-nisa with Ali Kuli Beg.

Time passed and the good old Akber died. Jahángír came to the throne. Twelve years had elapsed since he had first set eyes on Mihr-ul-nisa. She was now thirty, and no longer in the prime of her youth. But she preserved her grace of manner, and her beauty was as captivating as ever. Her memory had taken deep root in the mind of her royal lover, who was greatly affected by her marriage with another. No sooner had Jahángír assumed sovereign authority, than his passion for her revived. He became the implacable enemy of Ali Kuli Beg, and resolved upon gratifying his criminal propensity at the cost of an execrable crime. It was to remove his rival from the scene. Ali Kuli Beg was a wealthy and highly-esteemed Amír. He was brave and fearless. He had married Mihr-ul-nisa with all the knowledge of Salem's intimacy with her, and cared little for the enmity of the heir to the throne. The emperor durst not openly put his powerful antagonist to death. He therefore found it necessary to have recourse to the meanest stratagem. He first determined upon persecuting him. These persecutions were so severe that, had they not been attested by eye-witnesses and contemporary writers, they would appear incredible. In the first instance, he was compelled to engage unarmed in an encounter with a tiger under circumstances which seemed to leave little doubt of his fate. But, in the conflict, which took place in the presence of the king, the hero extricated himself, and came off victorious after a display of dexterity and valour seldom equalled. The emperor, apparently pleased with the almost supernatural strength displayed by him, conferred upon him the flattering title of *Sher Afgan*, or destroyer of lions. His wounds had not yet quite healed when, at the emperor's instance, a furious elephant was let loose on him as the wounded man alighted from his palanquin. With a single stroke of his sword did Sher Afgan sever the trunk of the huge animal, and thus save his life. On another occasion forty assassins, employed by Jahángír, suddenly attacked Sher Afgan in his bed-room. He beat off half the number, and the rest fled. Finding all these expedients of no avail, the emperor appointed his foster brother, Kutb-ud-dín, a corpulent but resolute man, viceroy of Bengal, on condition of his endeavouring to induce Sher Afgan to divorce his wife, and, in case of his refusal, putting his hated rival to death. The viceroy represented the matter to the husband who, however, not only rejected the

Jahángír, on coming to the throne, resolves on securing the object of his passion.

His persecution of his rival.

He confers on him the title of Sher Afgan.

The emperor charges his foster brother to remove his rival from the scene.

dishonourable proposal with disdain, but resigned his command, and left off wearing arms, as a token of freedom from the king's bondage. The viceroy subsequently took occasion to visit the estates of Sher Afgan and invited his attendance. Sher, suspecting something wrong, waited on him with a dagger concealed in his dress. On the viceroy's renewing the subject, high words passed between him and Sher, who plunged his dagger into the bulky person of the governor, so that his bowels gushed out. The wounded Kutb-ud-dín called aloud to the guards to prevent the assassin's escape, on which Pír Muhammad Khan, Káshmíri, a brave officer, charged Sher Afgan and dealt him a blow with his sword on the head, but Sher returned it so dexterously that his assailant was killed on the spot. The guards now rushed forward against the solitary rebel, and four more men fell beneath his avenging dagger. Seeing that he must succumb to superior numbers, he proposed to his assailants to come forward one by one to single combat, but the invitation was not responded to. The courage of the hero did not fail him even in this extreme hour. Turning his face to Mecca, he threw some dust over his head by way of ablution and stood firmly to meet his fate. His body was perforated by bullets and he at last fell a victim to the basest treachery. His assailants had not the courage to approach him until they saw that he was in his last agonies.* The murder of his foster brother gave Jahángír a pretext for taking proceedings against Sher Afgan's family. The whole of his property was confiscated. The lovely widow was sent under custody to Agra, as an accomplice, but was not prosecuted. On her arrival at the court, Jahángír offered her marriage; but she was so deeply affected by the death of her brave husband, that she turned a deaf ear to the king's addresses, notwithstanding her early attachment to him. The repugnance shown by her disgusted Jahángír, whose mind was, moreover, so tortured with remorse at the base and impolitic deed committed by him that he took no notice of his dearly bought prize for four years, and Mihr-ul-nisa remained neglected in the seraglio as an attendant on the king's mother. She received an allowance of two shillings a day to support herself and her female attendants, and the smallest and most uncomfortable apartment in the harem was allotted to her. There she supplemented the small allowance she received by needle-work and painting, and managed to adorn her rooms so beautifully that everything that artistic instincts, inventive genius and exquisite taste could produce was to be found in her little habitation, which was crowded by the ladies of the harem, who came to consult her about fashions and styles, and make purchases of her painted silk and admirable needle-work.

A severe but unequal combat.

Prodigies of valour performed by Sher Afgan.

His fall.

The emperor's remorse at what had been done.

Mihr-ul-nisa is neglected,

And lives in seclusion,

On a New Year's Day (the Mahomedan Now Roz) festival, as Jahángír entered the royal seraglio, he happened to cast his eyes on Mihr-ul-nisa, his old love, who now lived in solitude and seclusion. She was dressed in plain white muslin, which enhanced her loveliness and fascinating beauty. This one view acted like magic on Jahángír, and the flame of love was rekindled in his heart. He instantly threw round her neck the necklace he wore, containing forty pearls, each valued at £4,000, and she was removed to the king's quarters and installed as his Sultana. In 1611 their marriage took place with unusual pomp. Her ascendancy over Jahángír was unbounded, and her influence at the court paramount. She was consulted by the emperor on all affairs of importance, and his Majesty resigned to her the direction of his imperial household. Mihr-ul-nisa managed it with magnificent pomp and with due regard to economy and order. The emperor's chief con-

But is eventually married to Jahángír, 1611.

Her great influence over the emperor.

* A handsome domed mausoleum in the neighbourhood of Bardwan still stands and marks the grave of the hero.

solation was derived from her company, and his sole happiness seemed to consist in exalting his new wife, and in surrounding her with honors. From Mihr-ul-nisa (sun of women) she was surnamed Núr Mahal (the light of the harem), and shortly after came to be styled Núr Jahán Begum (the light of the world). Her father, who had already been created Itimád-ud-Daula by Akber, was now elevated to the dignity of grand wazír, while her elder brother, Abul Kassan, was appointed Master of Ceremonies with the title of Itimád Khan. Dil-árám, nurse of Núr Jahán, was appointed head of the royal seraglio, which consisted of six thousand women, including female slaves and women soldiers and guards, among whom were Chinese, Abyssinians, Hindus, Circassians, and Mahomedans. The Sadr-ul-Sadúr was forbidden to issue any stipend to any member of the harem without Núr Jahán's seal.

She receives the title Núr Jahán, light of the world.

The emperor's description of her influence over him.

Núr Jahán exercised a great influence over Jahángír, directed, it is believed, by the sage counsels of her father. She effected a most beneficial change in his cruel disposition and put a check on his savage outbursts of temper. She prevented his indulgence in wine in the day time, and moderated his evening potations. The emperor in his autobiography alludes most touchingly to the good influence of Núr Jahán and her family, and ascribes much of his prosperity to their prudent counsels. "At the period," declares the emperor, "in which this is written (about the fourteenth year of the emperor's reign) I may say that the entire possession of my treasure, whether of gold or jewels, is under her. Of my unreserved confidence, indeed, the Princess is in complete possession, and I can truly say that the whole fortunes of my empire are in the hands of this highly endowed family." The elevation of the old man, Núr Jahán's father, to the coveted office of wazír created no envy. He possessed all the qualities that adorn that exalted rank, and he proved one of the ablest ministers that ever ruled at an Eastern court.

She assumes the royal prerogative.

In a few years matters reached such a pitch that, according to Muhammad Hadi, the compiler of Jahángír's memoirs, his majesty was king only in name. Núr Jahán differed from the emperor as to her stately functions, only in the fact that her name was not read in the *khutba*. The emperor conferred upon her rights of sovereignty and government. In all matters that attracted her attention, her will alone was law. She presented herself every morning at the balcony of her palace (jharoka), below which all the grandees and Omerahs were assembled to pay her homage and receive orders. Coins were struck in her name with the superscription :—

بحکم شاه جهانگیر یافت صد زیور   بنام نورجهان بادشاه بیگم زر

"By order of the King Jahángír gold has a hundred splendours added to it by receiving the impression of the name of Núr Jahán the Queen Begum."

Her seal bore the following inscription :—

نورجهان گشت بفضل اله   همدم و همراز جهانگیر شاه

"Núr Jahán became, by the grace of God, the consort and partner of King Jahángír."

All orders were issued with the following title, bearing the name of Núr Jahán :—

حکم علیة العالیة نورجهان بیگم بادشاه

"By Order of Her Exalted Majesty, Núr Jahán Begum, Queen."

The emperor was so enamoured of her that he could not bear to part with her for a moment; and it is said that, while his majesty was seated in public darbár, a curtain was hung next to the throne, behind which sat Núr Jahán. His majesty used to say, "I have made over the kingdom to Núr

Jahán Begum, the sole consolation of her royal husband. For myself I want nothing more than a pound of meat and two pints of wine." In another place Jahángír says, "My wife has wit enough in her little finger to rule the whole kingdom without my troubling my head about it." For twenty years Núr Jahán held this despotic monarch under her sway. For her sake the emperor even consented to dispense with a custom strictly observed by the Mussalmáns. Sir Thomas Roe, who was sent to India as ambassador by the king of England, mentions that Jahángír used to drive in the streets of Agra with Núr Jahán, unveiled, in a bullock cart, drawn by small oxen called *gahnis*.

Her high accomplishments.

Both eastern and western writers bestow high encomiums on Núr Jahán. She was undoubtedly the most accomplished woman of her age. According to oriental writers, she was an asylum for the oppressed and a fountain of high virtues and goodness.

The queen readily bestowed dowries on the daughters of such poor parents as chose to beg for them, and, it is said, that, in this way, her bounty enabled five hundred girls to get married.

She contrives many improvements.

The court of Jahángír owed many reforms to her good sense and judgment. Under her excellent management, it not only became more magnificent and decorous, but was maintained with greater economy than before. Her taste and skill were manifested chiefly in reforming the ladies' dresses, in which she introduced many improvements more becoming than any before her time. She was the author of the modern bodice and inner shirt, and contrived many articles of female dress which are in use to this day. She also contrived improvements in the furniture of apartments. She planned public edifices and gardens, from the produce of which she is said to have first extracted the attar ("otto," properly *itr*) of roses. By her orders many cities were embellished with fine mosques, pleasant gardens, sarais, reservoirs and fountains, most of which stand to this day, a monument of her public spirit and artistic genius. Her private rooms, and her balcony, with its white marble pillars, still stand in the castle of Agra.

Her dexterity in sports.

She was a good rider and well skilled in hunting. Seated on an elephant, she once shot four tigers with her own hand. Of her dexterity in the sports of the field a poet has thus humorously written:—

نورجہان گرچہ بظاہر زن است

درصف مردان زن شیرافگن است

"Although Núr Jahán is a woman in appearance, yet in the ranks of men she is a woman who can destroy a lion (Zan-i-Sher* Afgan)."

Her facility in composing extempore verses.

She was herself skilled in poetry, and one of the causes of her having charmed Jahángír is said to have been the promptitude with which she composed extempore verses. She composed excellent Persian poems and wrote, like Salema Sultan Begum and Zibun Nisa Begum, under the assumed name of *Makhfi*. She was ready-witted and good at repartee. On one occasion Núr Jahán happening to be by when the emperor saw the new moon, his majesty looking at her said:—

هلال عید براوج فلک هویدا شد

"The new moon has appeared high up in the sky."

Núr Jahán forthwith replied:—

کلید میکده گم گشته بود پیدا شد

"It is the key of the cellar which was lost and has been found."

* If the word 'zan' (slayer) here used be interpreted 'wife,' the expression 'Zan-i-Sher Afgan,' which also means lion-slayer, would mean wife of Sher Afgan. The author has in this verse shown that Núr Jahán was originally the wife of Sher Afgan.

Thus the couplet was completed. The second line alludes to the emperor's fondness for wine and the permission to indulge in it, at *Id* after the fast of Ramadán.

Being herself a poetess, she became a patroness of learning, especially in those who were well skilled in the art of poetry, and always gave them munificent rewards.

Anecdotes.

Numerous stories are told of the love existing between Jahángír and Núr Jahán and of the incidents which led to it. One of these stories may be here cited. It is said that Jahángír, while yet a youth, was walking about in a fancy fair, at which the ladies of the harem were present to sell the articles of their handicraft. The garden, coupled with the lovely articles for sale, the beauty of the visitors and their holiday costumes, presented a picturesque and lively scene. The prince held two pigeons in his hands, and, taking a fancy to some pretty flowers, determined upon plucking some of them. This necessitated his making over the pigeons to a bystander. Núr Jahán happening to be near, the prince made over the pigeons to her, placing one in each of her hands. After the prince had made his collection of flowers, he asked Núr Jahán, then in the prime of her youth, for the pigeons, but, to his surprise, he saw that she had only one. The youthful prince asked the girl what she had done with the other pigeon.

"It has flown away," was the reply. "How?" inquired the prince half excited, half amazed. "So," was the reply of the lovely girl, who forthwith set the only pigeon in her hand at liberty. The gay and sprightly tone in which the youthful lady expressed herself, and the winsome frankness and fascinating simplicity of her manner had an enchanting effect on the mind of the prince. Indeed Núr Jahán's success at the fair was beyond all precedent, for a single word from her lips had fetched for its price the heart of the future monarch of India.

Her daughter Lado Begum.

Núr Jahán bore no children to Jahángír. She had a daughter by her first husband, Sher Afgan, called Lado Begum, whom she married to Shahir Yár, the fourth son of Jahángír.

The emperor's family.

The emperor's eldest son was Khusrow, who was still in confinement in charge of Auna Rae, a Rájput. The second son, Perwaz, was a drunkard like the father and his two uncles, Morád and Dániál, who had both died of excessive drinking. He was in command of the troops in the Dekkan. To the third son Khurram, afterwards Shah Jahán, was married to Arjumand Bano Begum, surnamed Mumtáz Mahal, the beautiful daughter of Asaf Khan, and niece of Núr Jahán. He was a successful general, and had already distinguished himself in a war with the Ráná of Udaipúr in Marwar. It is worthy of note that, after the defeat of the imperial troops in the Dekkan, under the best Moghal generals, Prince Khurram, by his perseverance and valour, succeeded in reducing to submission this powerful Hindu chief. The prince, pursuing the policy of his illustrious grandfather, not only accepted the offerings made by the Ráná in token of submission, but, the moment that chief made his salutation, raised him by the hand, seated him by his side and treated him with the utmost consideration and respect. The whole of the territory conquered in Marwar, since the days of Akber, was restored to the Ráná, whose son was raised to the dignity of Amír in the imperial court.

Victories of Shah Jahán (prince Khurram) in Marwar, 1613.

His moderation.

Death of Rájá Mán Singh.

About this time Rájá Mán Singh died in the Dekkan. The Raushnais broke into rebellion, and the outbreak was suppressed on the death of their spiritual leader Ahdád, the grandson and successor of Bayazid.

Mission of Captain Hawkins, 1608.

In the autumn of 1608 the emperor received at his court a British officer, Captain Hawkins, who was the bearer of a letter from his sovereign, James I.

The letter was translated to his majesty by a Portuguese Jesuit, one of several who were at the Moghal court. The emperor treated the envoy politely and conversed with him freely in the Turkish language. He was, however, advised by his courtiers that if the English were permitted to trade in his dominions, the Portuguese, who were a stronger power, would be displeased, and would cease to visit the Indian ports for the purpose of trade, which would result in loss to the imperial revenue. The emperor, on this, summarily dismissed the British officer. In December, 1615, a regular embassy under Sir Thomas Roe came to Ajmere to negotiate a treaty of amity with the emperor. His majesty received the ambassador with unusual honour, and not only confirmed former grants, but accorded permission for the location of resident English agents at some of the principal towns in India. Sir Thomas Roe has left a vivid description of the court of Jahángír, and his journal contains much information which may even now be read with great interest.

The embassy of Sir Thomas Roe, 1615.

The pestilence of 1616.

The year 1616 was memorable for a severe pestilence which broke out in the Panjáb after two years drought. It is described as having been contagious and lasted eight years. From the Panjáb the disease travelled to Sarhind and to the Doáb of Hindostán, as far as Delhi. In Láhore its ravages were so great that houses full of dead were left locked, and no person dared enter for fear of his life.

Prince Khurram receives the title of Shah Jahán, 1616.

During the same year Prince Khurram received the rank or peerage of "twenty thousand," with the title of *Shah Jahán*, or "King of the World," as a compliment to the great talents displayed by him in the war. He had also the privilege of sitting on a chair placed by the side of the imperial throne. A grand expedition, organized against the Dekkan, was put in charge of the prince, and, the army having been put in motion, Jahángír himself followed, in order that he might be at hand to support the prince in case of need. Malik Ambar was defeated and obliged to abandon Ahmedabád, while Ibrahim Adil Shah, of Bijapúr, swore allegiance to the emperor.

Sir Thomas Roe's account of Shah Jahán.

Sir Thomas Roe, who accompanied the emperor on his march to Mandu, had the opportunity of forming the acquaintance of Shah Jahán. The prince was then not more than twenty-five. He was grave and discreet beyond his years. The ambassador, with reference to his demeanour, observes that "he never saw so settled a countenance, or any man maintain so constant a gravity, never smiling, nor by his looks shewing any respect or distinction of persons, but entire pride and contempt for all."

Death of Prince Khusrow, 1622.

On his return from Káshmír, in October 1622, Jahángír held his court at Láhore. The same year, the unhappy Khusrow died in custody, and this circumstance seemed to complete the security of the succession of Shah Jahán. About this time also died Ghiás Beg, the father of Núr Jahán. From this time the empress, who was deprived of the benefit of her parent's wise counsel, began to exercise a pernicious influence over the destinies of the empire. She embittered the closing years of her husband's life by intrigues and open warfare. The emperor's health had been greatly impaired by a serious illness in 1621, and the ambitious empress determined that his youngest son, Shahir Yár, who had married her daughter by her first husband, should succeed him. The report reached the ears of Shah Jahán, who had just received a command to recover Kandahar from its Persian conquerors. After a fruitless interchange of messages between the emperor at Láhore and his discontented son at Mandu, Shah Jahán, with a view to counteract the designs of his step-mother, openly raised the standard of

Intrigues of the Empress.

The rebellion of Shah Jahán, 1623.

* *Ikbal Náma Jahángírí.*

revolt against Jahángír. The emperor on this marched against him from Láhore. On the approach of the emperor, Shah Jahán retired to the hills of Mewat, and from thence to Talingana. He then repaired to Rájmahal, engaged the governor, and, defeating him in a pitched battle, took possession of Bengal and Behar. He was, however, followed by the imperial commanders, and, having been deserted by his own troops, surrendered his last strongholds and made submission to the king.

He submits to the emperor.

The empress now became jealous of Mohábat Khan, the chief commander of the army, and the ablest general in the emperor's service, whose success in the field and growing influence at court gave her cause for apprehension. In obedience to the summons from the court, he set out for the imperial camp, then on its way to Kábul, attended by a body-guard of five thousand Rájputs, on whose fidelity he could safely rely. Jahángír was on this occasion accompanied by an immense retinue of troops and servants, to the number of thirty thousand. Before his arrival in the camp, Mohábat Khan had betrothed his daughter to a young nobleman, namely Barkhurdar, without waiting for the emperor's permission, which it was customary for a person of his rank to obtain. Mohábat Khan sent the bridegroom to the emperor to make his excuses. As the young nobleman entered the royal camp, he was forced to dismount from his elephant. He was disrobed and compelled to clothe himself in dirty rags. He was then cruelly stripped and beaten with thorns, in the presence of the court, and conducted bare-headed and backwards, on a sorry jade, through the camp, amid the shouts of the whole army. The whole of his dowry was seized and his property sequestrated. When Mohábat himself approached the royal camp, he was refused admission. Incensed at this treatment, Mohábat broke one morning into the tent where the emperor lay asleep. His majesty awoke to find himself a prisoner and cut off from his troops across the bridge-of-boats on the Jhelum, which was guarded by the Rájput soldiers of his captor. Recognising Mohábat Khan, he exclaimed, "Traitor, what means this?" Mohábat knelt before his sovereign with due humility, declared that he meant no treason, and that, being afraid of his own life, he had thrown himself at his majesty's feet. He then begged the emperor to mount an elephant, that the people might see that he was safe. The emperor saw the necessity of complying with his request, and was conveyed to the tents of his general, surrounded by a guard of Rájput soldiers. One of Jahángír's personal attendants was allowed to mount with his master, and a servant, with a bottle and goblet, so essential to Jahángír's existence, was allowed to accompany him.

Breach between the emperor and Mohábat Khán.

Brutal treatment of his son-in-law by the emperor.

Mohábat seizes on the emperor's person, 1626.

Núr Jahán made a desperate attempt to recover her lord. The bridge-of-boats on the Jhelum had been burnt by the Rájputs. She was therefore compelled to cross the stream by a ford which was discovered lower down the river. The ford was full of dangerous pools, and her advance was opposed by the Rájput troops. Núr Jahán, on her elephant, was the first to cross, and exposed herself in the thickest of the conflict. Her elephant was surrounded by the valiant Rájputs, who showered their balls and arrows round her howdah. The empress emptied four quivers of arrows with her own hand. The infant daughter of Shahir Yár in her lap received a wound from an arrow, which was with difficulty extracted by the empress, whose elephant, having received a wound on the trunk, was carried down by the stream. After making several plunges into deep water, it succeeded in reaching the shore. Núr Jahán's women came lamenting and shrieking as they saw her howdah stained with blood and herself the mark for numerous arrows. A body of her troops penetrated into the minister's rear, and

Núr Jahán attacks Mohábat's camp.

Her spirited conduct.

almost reached the emperor's tent, but the Rájputs, headed by Mohábat Khan, drove back the imperialists, and gained a decisive victory, and Núr Jahán, was compelled to retreat to the strongly fortified city of Láhore. Asif Khan, the brother of Núr Jahán, was driven to Attock and compelled to surrender. Núr Jahán, seeing no hopes of recovering the person of the emperor by force, consented to join her husband in his captivity. Mohábat took the royal captive to Kábul, where he set him at liberty, being influenced by the unwearied exertions of his devoted wife.

She is repulsed.

She joins the emperor in his confinement,

And procures his release.

The emperor, after his deliverance, returned to Láhore, by way of Rohtas, and rewarded Asif Khan for his loyal services by conferring on him the viceroyalty of the Panjáb and the ministership of the empire. The winter being over, his majesty set off on his annual visit to the valley of Káshmír, and celebrated the Now Roz of 11th March 1627, in his camp, on the banks of the Chináb. Some time after his arrival in the happy valley, Prince Shahir Yár was taken dangerously ill and conveyed to Láhore for the sake of its warmer climate. About this time Mirza Khan, *Khan-i-Khánán*, son of Behrám Khan, died, in the seventy-second year of his age. The emperor's own health began to fail rapidly, and he had a severe attack of asthma, an old complaint of his. He became so weak that he was obliged to give up horse exercise, and was carried about in a palanquin. A severe attack of rheumatism supervening, he despaired of life, the despondent expressions to which he gave vent causing intense grief to all. His appetite was gone, and he rejected opium, which he had been accustomed to take for forty years. He felt inclined for nothing but a little wine. Great fears being entertained for his life, an attempt was made to convey him to Láhore. On reaching Berám Killa, the pleasant hill scenery revived his love for sport. He ordered a drive of deer, and himself sat on the bank of a stream, with a loaded rifle ready to shoot the game as it passed before him. A deer being driven to the place where the emperor was seated, his majesty fired at and wounded the animal, which fell. A beater who followed it, missed his footing and fell down a precipice, a mangled mass, near the emperor's feet. His majesty's nerves were shattered by the shock. He repaired to the camp, and, sending for the mother of the deceased, spoke to her a few words of consolation and made her a gift of money. But he became restless, and his condition showed no improvement. He continued his march to Rájouri, and, journeying from thence, at the close of the day, he called for a glass of wine, but was unable to drink it. He was carried towards Bhimbar, but expired early in the morning of 28th October, 1628, in the fifty-ninth year of his age and the 22nd of his reign. The funeral ceremonies were performed at Bhimbar, and the corpse was sent, under an escort, to Láhore, where it was interred in the garden of Núr Jahán, who built a splendid tomb over the remains of her lamented husband.

Asif Khan created viceroy of the Panjáb.

Illness of the emperor.

His death, 1628

His burial.

Jahángír is described by English travellers as a monarch with an easy, courteous, and sociable manner. He was contemporary with James I. of England, and, by a strange coincidence, not only were their reigns of the same duration, but they resembled each other in their character, being both given to favourites and drink. He issued an edict against tobacco in 1617, in unconscious imitation of his Western brother, the use of that plant for smoking being then a novelty in both England and India. Like the great Akber, he repeatedly pardoned the misconduct of his officers, as is shown in the instances of Mán Singh and Khan-i-Khánán, and he freely pardoned his rebel son, Khusrow.

His character.

In person Jahángír was tall and handsome, with a broad chest and long arms. His eyes were strangely keen and piercing, and his complexion

His person.

was a ruddy nut-brown. A peculiar feature about him was that he wore small gold earrings, in token of bondage to the great saint Sheikh Salem, *Chishti*, to whose prayers, his parents believed, they owed his birth, and after whom they had also named him Salem.

With the death of her husband and the capture of Shahir Yár, her son-in-law, whom she tried to raise to the throne, the influence of Núr Jahán expired. After the latter event she retired into privacy, and lived at Láhore for twenty years, with her daughter, Prince Shahir Yár's widow. A pension of twenty-five lakhs of rupees per annum was allowed her out of the public treasury. She wore the plain white dress of a Moghal widow, secluded alike from amusement and business, and gave herself up to study and retirement, cherishing the memory of her husband. She died at Láhore at the age of seventy-two, on 29th Shawal, 1055 (1646 A.D.), and was buried in an elegant, sepulchre-like *baradari* (summer-house), which she had herself built near her husband's mausoleum.

Núr Jahán a widow.

She fixes her residence at Láhore.

Her death, 1646.

Jahangír struck various coins in Hindostán, Kábul and Kandahar. The following couplet is seen on several rupees coined at Láhore in the 14th year of his reign :—

The coins of Jahángír.

زنام شاه جهانگیر شاه اکبر پور ۱۴
هميشه باد آبروي سکه لاهور ۱۰۱۸

"Through the splendour of the name of King Jahángír, the son of King Akber, may the coin of Láhore be ever brilliant! 1018, 14th year."

According to *Tuzak-i-Jahángíri*, when the emperor ascended the throne, the amir-ul-omerah, in commemoration of the event, presented him with the following couplet. Rupees were coined in Láhore, Káshmír and Kandahar with the following inscription :—

روي زررا ساخت نوراني چو رنگ مهر و ماه
شاه نورالدين جهانگير ابن اکبر باد شاه
۱۵ ضرب لاهور

"The King Núr-ud-dín Jahángír, the son of King Akber, has rendered the appearance of gold as brilliant as that of the sun and the moon. Struck at Láhore in the year 15."

Several rupees bear the following inscription :—

لاآله الاالله محمد الرسول الله
نورالدين محمد جهانگير بادشاه

"There is no god but God, and Muhammad is the Prophet of God. Núr-ud-dín Muhammad Badi Shah."

The *Tuzak* informs us that Asif Khan was ordered to have the following couplet inscribed on gold coin :—

بخط نور بر زر كلك تقدير
رقم زد شاه نورالدين جهانگير

"In the character of splendour the divine decree has inscribed on coin the name of King Núr-ud-dín Jahángír."

The following coin was struck at Kábul :—

سکه زد در شهر کابل خسرو گيتي پناه
شاه نورالدين جهانگير ابن اکبر بادشاه

"The Asylum of the World, King Núr-ud-dín Jahángír, the son of Akber Shah, has struck this gold coin at Kábul."

The Kandahar coin bore the inscription :—

سکه قندهار شد دلخواه
از جهانگیر شاه اکبر شاه

"The coin of Kandahar became beautiful through King Jahángír, son of Akber Shah."

Mr. Rodgers, in the *Journal of the Bengal Asiatic Society*, mentions several coins of the Láhore mint.

The following coin was struck in 1019, the 5th year of the reign :—

زر لاهور شد درماه بهمن چون مه انور — سنه ۵
بدور شاه نورالدین جهانگیر ابن شاه اکبر — ۱۰۱۹

"In the month of Bhaman, the gold of Láhore became like the luminous moon in the reign of Núr-ud-dín Jahángír, the son of Akber Shah. 1019 A.H., 5th year."

Another coin, struck during the same year, has the following inscription :—

در اسفندار مزاین سکه درلاهور زد بر زر
شهنشاه امم .شاه جهانگیر ابن شاه اکبر

"In the month of Isfandar Múz, the monarch of the people, Shah Jahángír, the son of Akber Shah, stamped this coin on gold at Láhore. 1019, A.H., 5th year."

The following coins of Láhore, mentioned by Mr. Rodgers in his excellent article in the journal above referred to, are too interesting to be omitted :—

مه اردي بهشت این سکه در لاهور زد بر زر
شهنشاه زمان شاه جهانگیر ابن شاه اکبر

"In the month of Tír, the king, the defender of the faith, Shah Jahángír, the son of Akber Shah, stamped this coin on gold at Láhore."

بماه تیر در لاهور زد این سکه را بر زر
پناه دین ملك شاه جهانگیر ابن شاه اکبر

"In the month of Urdi Bahisht, the monarch of the age, Shah Jahángír, the son of Akber Shah, stamped this coin on gold at Láhore."

A remarkably fine rupee has the following inscription :—

بدهر باد روان تا فلک بود در دور — ۱۳
بنام شاه جهانگیر سکه لاهور — ۱۰۲۷

"May the coin of Láhore be current in the world in the name of Jahángír Shah as long as the heavens revolve ! 1027 A.H., 13th year."

A rupee in the possession of Mr. J. D. Tremlett, mentioned by Mr. Rodgers, has the following couplet :—

بفروردین زر لاهور شد رشك مه انور — ۱۰۲۰
زنور سکه شاه جهانگیر ابن شاه اکبر

"In the month of Farwardín, the gold of Láhore became an object of jealousy to the bright moon through the resplendence of the stamp of Jahángír Shah, the son of Akber Shah, 1020 A.H., 6th year."

The multiplicity of coins of various denominations struck in the royal mint of Láhore is sufficient proof of the popularity of that town during the reign of Jahángír, and his fondness for the capital of the Panjáb.

Mr. Rodgers mentions only one coin of the Delhi mint. It had the following couplet for its inscription :—

زر فتح و نصرت جهانگیر شاه ۲۱
بدهلي زد از فیض لطف آله ۱۰۳۵

"Through the abundance of the favour of God, King Jahángír struck the coin of victory and triumph at Delhi. 1035 A.H., 21st year."

The two following inscriptions on coins are very striking :—

شبیهہ حضرت شاہ جہانگیر
قضا بر سکه زر کرد تصویر

"The fates have drawn a representation of His Majesty King Jahángír on a gold coin.

حروف جہانگیر و الله اکبر
ز روز ازل تا ابد ہے برابر

Mr. Rodgers rhymes it thus—

"The letters in Jahángír's name,
And those of God the Greatest,
From the first day have one value had,
And shall have to the latest."

CHAPTER XV.

SHÁHAB-UD-DÍN SHAH JAHÁN.

IN his will, Jahángír had declared Prince Shahir Yár successor to the throne. Asif Khan and the soldiery at once declared for Shah Jahán, who was then in the Dekkan. Asuf Khan, in concert with Iradat Khan, *Khan-i-Azim*, resorted to the stratagem of proclaiming Dáwar Bakhsh (also called Mirza Bolaki), son of Khusrow, of unlucky memory, in order, on the one hand, to prevent disturbances, and, on the other, to defeat Núr Jahán's arrangements and secure Shah Jahán's succession. Accordingly, Dáwar Baksh having been seated on horseback, the royal canopy was raised on his head and the *khutba* read in his name near Bhimbar. The royal retinue, with the puppet sovereign, then moved to Láhore. Dáwar Bakhsh proclaimed emperor.

Meanwhile, Prince Shahir Yár had crossed the Jhelum, with a body of horse, to secure Láhore. On reaching Láhore, he was urged by his intriguing wife to assume the royal title. He seized the royal treasury and everything belonging to the State which was in Láhore, and was joined there by Sultans Hoshang and Tymúr, sons of Dániál. Shahir Yár at the same time assumes royal titles at Láhore.

On the other side, Asif Khán, with the mock king, Dáwar Bakhsh, advanced. The opposing forces met about three *kos* from Láhore; but the raw troops of Shahir Yár broke and fled, almost without striking a blow. He had taken no part in the engagement himself, but had retired, with a body of 2,000 cavalry, to the vicinity of Láhore, to await the course of events. Hearing of the rout, he shut himself up in the fortress of Láhore, which was invested the following day by the armies of Asif Khan and Azim Khan. Azim Khan effected his entry into the fort at night, and the next morning all the other Omerahs followed him. Shahir Yár, deserted by his friends, hid himself in a cellar of the female apartments. There he was discovered by a eunuch, dragged out and led bound into the presence of Dáwar Bakhsh. He was kept in confinement for two or three days and afterwards blinded. In the meantime Shah Jahán reached Agra, and ascended the throne on February 4th, 1628, under the title of Abul Mozaffar Sháhab-ud-dín Muhammad. At the same time he was proclaimed emperor at Láhore and the *khutba* was read in his name in all the mosques. Dáwar Bakhsh, whom the supporters of Shah Jahán had set up as a matter of policy, was now placed in confinement, and, The forces of the two princes meet at Láhore. The defeat of Shahir Yár. He is captured and blinded. Shah Jahán ascends the throne at Agra, 1628. He is proclaimed at Láhore.

along with Shahir Yár, he was shortly after strangled at Láhore, by order of the new king. Shahir Yár possessed singular beauty of person, but was not gifted with corresponding mental power. Hence the nickname *Nashudani*, '*Femi-raut*,' given to him by the oriental historians. Hoshang and Tymúr, sons of the drunken Dániál, two sons of Murád and two sons of Parwez were publicly executed, their bodies being buried in a garden at Láhore, and their heads sent as trophies to the new king at Agra.

Massacre of the royal princes at Láhore.

Having been born at Láhore on the 30th Rabi-ul-awal, 100 A.H. (1592 A.D.)* by the daughter of Ude Singh, son of Rájá Máldeo, Ráná of Marwár, commonly known as Jagut Gosáin, Sháh Jahán was 37 years of age when he was proclaimed emperor of Hindostán. On ascending the throne, he raised Mohábat Khan to the post of commander-in-chief, and appointed Asif Khan his wazír, with a salary of a million sterling a year. His daughter, Mumtaz Mahal, niece of Núr Jahán, was the sole and dearly loved wife of Shah Jahán. She had a dazzling white complexion, and she fascinated Shah Jahán by her beauty, as her aunt, before her, had fascinated Jahángír.

Influence of Mumtaz Mahal.

Shah Jahán's first acts.

Among Shah Jahán's first acts was the restoration of the lunar month of Islam in ordinary correspondence. His Mosalmán proclivities induced him to capture the Portuguese settlement of Hughli and make 500 or 600 Christians prisoners. The Cathedral Church, built in 1599, was demolished, as were the fortifications and other places of worship. The prisoners were carried to Agra, where some were circumcised, and made converts to Mohamedanism, while others suffered death. Some of the Portuguese women were placed by the emperor in his own harem, while others were distributed among the harems of the nobility.

Ill-treatment of the Portuguese.

The emperor's passion for magnificence.

To his military talents Shah Jahán added a strong love for splendid pageantry and architectural grandeur. His expensive entertainments and costly upholstery were marked by a profusion and display of wealth which were unparalleled even in those days of eastern luxury, and have surrounded the name of the great Moghal with a halo of romance. The first anniversary of his accession cost him £1,600,000 sterling, and a suite of tents was prepared for the occasion in Káshmír which, according to the historian Khafi Khan, it took two months to pitch. He adorned the principal towns of the empire with handsome edifices and superb palaces, and his example was followed by the nobles and chiefs of the country. The old city of Delhi, which extended for more than thirty miles along the banks of the Jamna, having become desolate through repeated depredations, Shah Jahán founded a new Delhi in 1631, and called it, after his own name, Shahjahánabád† or the city of Shah Jahán.

His first anniversary.

He founds new Delhi, 1631.

The new city, which was bounded by the river and a wall, or rampart, of red granite seven miles in circumference, was adorned with the noblest streets, palaces, gardens, mosques and aqueducts. The waters of the Jamna, near Delhi, being strongly impregnated with nitre, and the water in the interior of new Delhi being unwholesome, a canal was constructed which drew its supply from that of Feroze Shah, at a distance of seventy miles, and supplied the principal streets of the town with clear and wholesome water. Another canal, 135 miles in length, ran opposite the palace, on the left bank

* Tozak-i-Jahángírí.

† On founding new Delhi Shah Jahán struck the following coin :—

سکه شاه جهان آباد رایج درجهان

جاودان بادا بنام ثاني صاحب قران

"May the coin of Shahjahánabád be ever current in the world, by the name of the second Sahib-i-Quiran."

of the river. Both canals were constructed by Ali Mardan Khan, formerly Governor of Kandahar, under the king of Persia, who, dreading the tyranny of his master, sought an asylum in the court of Shah Jahán. Subsequently, in 1820, the British Government cleared out the canal and re-opened it in the city, on which occasion the inhabitants went out to meet the stream, and cast sweetmeats and flowers into it, as a manifestation of their joy.

The canals o Ali Mardan Khan.

The palace of Delhi.

At the new city the king built a fortified palace of red granite, a mile and a half in circuit, described by Bishop Heber as one of the noblest pieces of architecture he ever saw, and far surpassing the Kremlin at Moscow. It is surrounded by a wall of red sandstone, forty feet high and flanked with turrets and cupolas. The interior was decorated with spacious courts, pavilions of white marble, surmounted by golden domes and cupolas, with pillars and arches exquisitely carved and ornamented with arabesques, gilt and stucco work, and ceilings most elegantly adorned with a rich foliage of gold and silver filigree work; a simple and chaste mosque with marble arcades, a marvel of Mahomedan art; bath houses and beautiful gardens, planted with fragrant flowers and cooled with fountains and cascades. The mosaic paintings are now mostly destroyed. The silver filigree ceiling, the estimated value of which was £170,000, formed part of the spoil of the Mahrattas in 1759, by whom it was melted down.

The famous peacock throne.

In the centre of the hall of special audience, or 'House of Lords,' stood the famous peacock throne, so called from its having the figures of two peacocks standing behind it, with tails expanded, and the whole so inlaid with precious stones of appropriate colours as to represent life. The throne was six feet long and four feet broad, composed of solid gold, inlaid with rubies, emeralds and diamonds. It was surmounted by a gold canopy, supported by twelve pillars, all richly emblazoned with costly gems. Around the canopy hung a fringe of pearls. Between the two peacocks stood the figure of a parrot carved out of emeralds. On each side of the throne stood an umbrella, the symbol of royalty, formed of crimson velvet richly embroidered with gold thread and pearls, with handles eight feet long of solid gold studded with diamonds. This unparalleled achievement of the jeweller's art was executed by Austeu de Bordeau, who, after defrauding several princes of Europe by means of false gems, which he fabricated with great skill, repaired to the Imperial Court of Shah Jahán, where he made his fortune and was in high favour with the emperor. Tavernier, a Frenchman, and himself a professional jeweller, who inspected it, estimated the value at six millions of pounds sterling. This glittering ornament of the court of the Great Moghal was subsequently carried away by the Persian conqueror, Nádír Shah.

The grand mosque, built, 1658.

In 1658, the last year of Shah Jahán's reign, he built the great Jama Masjid, the chief mosque of Dehli, and one of the most beautiful mosques in the East. It rises majestically from a rocky eminence, overlooking the city, with a square platform of 450 feet, approached by magnificent flights of steps. It is surrounded by open arcades, and has three domes of pure marble placed upon drums, out of which they emerge in a curve, and two lofty towers each 130 feet high. Its construction is said to have employed a daily average of 5,000 workmen for a period of six years. The cost of the building was £100,000 of English money.

The Táj Mahal.

But the best known of all the architectural works of Shah Jahan is the celebrated mausoleum of the empress at Agra, raised in honour of Mumtaz Mahal, his favourite queen. She died in childbirth of her eighth child, in 1629, at Burhanpúr, whither she had accompanied her royal husband, on his campaign in the Dekkan against Khan Jahán Lodi; and the emperor, like Edward I, his brother of England, carried the remains of his consort to the metropolis and laid them in a spot in the garden, still pointed out close to the grand mosque, where they remained during the long period of eighteen years that the sepulchre was being erected for their reception. The mausoleum stands on an elevated terrace, and is built of white marble inlaid with precious stones. Its vast and soft swelling dome is surrounded with many turrets of white marble, the whole fabric being supported by four great arches, the mould of which is enriched with beautiful engravings of Arabic characters in black marble. Tavernier, who witnessed the commencement and the completion of this great work, remarks that it employed twenty thousand men daily for twenty-two years, a fact from which some idea of its excessive costliness may be formed. The building is said to have cost £750,000. The emperor, according to the same authority, began to make his own sepulchre on the other side of the river, and intended to connect the two tombs by a magnificent bridge, but his war with his son Aurangzeb and his subsequent captivity prevented the carrying out of his design, and, when he died, his remains were buried close to those of his beloved wife.

The emperor's march to Káshmír, 1633.

In 1633, Shah Jahán proceeded, *viâ* Láhore, to Káshmír, where he remained for the summer. Compensation for damages done to cultivation on the march was paid.

Recovery of Kandahar, 1639.

In 1639 A.D., Kandahar, of which a precarious possession had been held by the Moghal sovereigns from its first conquest by Baber, and which had been in the occupation of the Persians since the 17th year of Jahángír's reign, was surrendered to the Emperor Shah Jahán by the governor, Ali Mardan Khan, who, having been driven to revolt by the tyranical proceedings of his Persian master, Shah Safi, gave up the city to the Moghal emperor and himself joined the imperial court at Láhore, where he was received with great honour by the emperor. Ali Mardan Khan was a man of great talents and energy, and he distinguished himself very highly under his new sovereign, who raised him to the post of amir-ul-omerah, or premier noble, and intrusted him with important military commands beyond the Indus. His skill and judgment in the execution of works of public utility, to which the celebrated canal of Delhi, known after his name, still bears ample testimony, and the taste and elegance which he displayed on all occasions of public festivities and shows, excited universal admiration at the court.

Ali Mardan Khan joins the emperor at Láhore, 1637.

He is created viceroy of the Panjáb, 1639.

In 1639, Ali Mardan Khan was made viceroy of the Panjáb. He inaugurated his appointment by the construction of a canal which brought the waters of the Rávi to Láhore to irrigate the country between the city and the Himálayas. The court spent the summer at Káshmír, and the winter was passed at Láhore. Láhore was visited at this time by Father Manrique, an Augustinian prior, who, in his memoirs, published in Rome in 1653, has given a graphic account of the Moghal court and the mode of living there. By the intervention of a Jesuit priest, Father Joseph Da Castro, he obtained an interview with the prime minister, Asif Khan, at his magnificent palace at Láhore, described as gorgeously decorated and profusely adorned with paintings. The minister received the father with great distinction, and gave him an entertainment at which the Christian priest dined with the minister, and which the emperor himself and several of the ladies of the royal seraglio graced with their presence. The banquet was served with great splendour and attended by many ladies of the harem, who made their appearance unveiled. The minister presented the priest with a gift of Persian melons and a bag of money. An imperial decree was passed, sanctioning the restoration of some places of worship, recently destroyed, and

Láhore visited by Father Manrique, the prior of Hughli.

He is entertained by the prime minister in his palace of Láhore.

the liberation of Father Antonio Da Cristo, the prior of Hughli, who was in confinement.*

Death of the Wazír Asif Khan, 1641.

On the 10th November, 1641 (17th Shabán 1051 A. H.), Asif Khan died at Láhore, in his seventy-second year, the same age at which, four years after, his celebrated sister, Núr Jahán died at the same place, and was buried north of Jahángír's tomb. He was the father of Mumtaz Mahal, the favourite wife of Shah Jahán, and received from him the title of *Yamin-ud-doula Khan-i-Khanan Sipah Salar*. He was commander of 9,000. Besides his magnificent palace at Láhore, where Manrique, the Jesuit Father, visited him, he left a colossal fortune.†

Invasion of Balkh, 1644.

In 1644, Ali Mardan Khan carried the Moghal arms into Balkh and Badakshan, and ravaged the country far and wide; but the severity of the winter eventually compelled him to retreat. Fourteen thousand Rájputs under Jagat Singh, eldest son of Rájá Mán Singh, were sent to reinforce the general, and it is interesting to read how these brave Hindu warriors, sympathising with a tolerant Mahomedan government, and disregarding their prejudices, stormed the stupendous mountain passes, covered with snow, and exerted themselves in constructing redoubts, the rájá himself wielding an axe, like others, and encouraging his men to deeds of valour against the fierce Uzbaks in those frozen regions. Never did the chivalry of that ancient martial race shine more conspicuously than in this remote enterprise. Despite the severity of the climate many splendid victories were achieved. The emperor himself moved to Kábul in support of his generals, but, perceiving the waste of life and substance which these fruitless campaigns in distant regions involved, was constrained to make over the province to Nazar Muhammad, at whose inducement he was originally tempted to undertake the expedition. The retreat of Aurangzeb from Balkh to Kábul was very disastrous, and a great portion of the Indian army perished in the snow.

The disastrous retreat of Aurangzeb.

Kandahar lost to the Indian empire, 1649.

About the end of 1649 A.D., Kandahar was retaken by the Persians, after a siege of two months and a-half. Aurangzeb and the wazír, Allami Saádullah, hastened from the Panjáb to drive out the invaders, but arrived too late to save the city, owing to the severity of the climate and to the mountain passes being covered with snow. Shah Jahán followed Aurangzeb to Kábul. The prince and the wazír invested the place for four months at the head of 60,000 horse and 10,000 infantry, but were foiled in their attempt to recover the city. After the siege had been raised, Shah Jahán marched from Kábul to Láhore.

The expedition to Thibet, 1650.

In 1650, the court remained at Láhore, and, a fresh campaign having been undertaken in Thibet, Skardo was captured. In 1651, the court returned to Kábul, and, the following year, Prince Aurangzeb and Wazír Allami Saádullah, renewed the siege of Kandahar with a numerous and well-equipped army, supported by a siege train. After exhausting every resource, the prince was again compelled to return to Kábul unsuccessful, and was sent as viceroy to the Dekkan. Dara, the eldest son of the emperor, now volunteered to undertake a fresh expedition to Kandahar, and a splendid army, far exceeding that previously employed, with a fresh train of ordnance, was placed under his

Second attempt on Kandahar, 1652.

Its failure.

Great expedition under Dara Shakoh.

* Keene.

† The real name of Asif Khan was Mirza Abul Hassan. As commander of 9,000, he was in receipt of a salary of sixteen karors, twenty lakhs of dams, or 40,50,000 rupees. He had besides jagirs yielding a revenue of five millions of rupees. His property at his death was valued at twenty-five millions of rupees consisting of jewels worth thirty lakhs, gold mohars of the value of forty-two lacks, silver valued at twenty-five lakhs, silver utensils worth thirty lakhs, and other property valued at twenty-five lakhs. His palace at Láhore, which had been built at a cost of twenty lakhs of rupees, was, on his death, given to Prince Dara Shakoh, and twenty lakhs of rupees in cash and valuables were distributed among his three sons and five daughters. The rest was escheated to the Crown. Blochman's *Ain-i-Akbari*.

command. The armies assembled at Láhore in the winter of 1652 and commenced their march in the spring of the following year, the emperor himself following the army to Kábul. The operations were commenced at the hour prescribed by the royal astrologers as the most auspicious. The siege was prosecuted with great vigour for five months, but was destined to end in the same disappointment as had been experienced twice before. Dara, after losing the best of his troops, was compelled to return with no greater success than had been achieved by his brother. This was the last attempt of the Moghals to recover Kandahar, which thenceforward ceased to be an appendage to the court of Delhi.

The siege of Kandahar, 1652.

Failure and retreat of Dara Shakoh.

It was about this time that the court of Shah Jahán was visited by the Italian physician, Manucci. He describes the emperor as a man of about sixty years of age, fond of gaieties, but of enlightened ideas and majestic and stately deportment. The peacock throne was still surrounded by the members of the royal family, and the most perfect harmony reigned between them and the emperor. His majesty had lost his valuable ministers, Asif Khan and Mohábat Khan, but this only induced him to become more active in the discharge of his public functions. He had four sons, all accomplished and well fitted to adorn the throne of the greatest of empires. The eldest son, Dara, the favourite of the aged monarch, was kept about his person and admitted to a considerable share of the government. He was a high-spirited, liberal prince, a free-thinker, like his great-grandfather, with a taste for the cultivation of Hindu learning and for European manners and modes of thought. Shuja, the second son, viceroy of Bengal, professed the *Shiá* creed. He was greatly addicted to pleasure and, though of a mild disposition, was yet brave, and from his youth accustomed to civil and military command. He corresponded with the Shah of Persia, and maintained a secret understanding with the leading Hindu *rájás*. The third son, Aurangzeb, viceroy in the Dekkan, possessed a character quite different from that of any of his brothers. He was able, cautious, ambitious and designing. He maintained a reserved deportment, and, shunning pleasure, applied himself closely to business. He held religious discourses with pious men and affected to be more ambitious of obtaining a reputation as a *faqír*, or saint, than as a great lord. He spent his time mostly in meditation, prayer, and reading the Qurán, and went even so far as to pretend that he subsisted on the earnings of his manual labour. He subsequently declared his resolution of renouncing the world and proceeding on a pilgrimage to Mecca, but was deterred from doing so by his father, who was quite unconscious that the crafty young man would afterwards prove himself a dangerous opponent. Aurangzeb concealed his ambitious designs behind the veil of religion. Morád, viceroy of Gujrát, was magnificent, proud, brave and generous. By the same wife (the lady of the Táj), who was the mother of the four sons, the emperor had also two daughters, both unmarried and living with him at the time of the visit of Manucci, the Italian physician. The eldest, Jahanara, called the Shah Begum, or the princess royal, was devotedly attached to her imperial father. She is described as being over thirty years of age. She possessed fascinating beauty and great accomplishments, and was the supporter of the interests of Dara Shekoh. The younger, Roushanara, less attractive, was most subtle and astute in her knowledge of the secrets of the harem, and was of great use to Aurangzeb in keeping him informed of the transactions of the palace in most critical times.

The visit of the Italian physician, Manucci.

His account of the emperor.

Shah Jahán's four sons.

Dara.

Shuja.

Aurangzeb.

Morád.

The emperor's two daughters.

Jahanara.

Roushanara.

The emperor suffered an irreparable loss in the death of Allami Saádullah Khan, which took place on 9th April 1656. He was the most able and upright of ministers India had produced since the days of the tolerant

Death of Allami Saádullah Khan, 1656.

Akber. His son, though only eleven years of age, was handsomely provided for by the emperor, and, according to Khafi Khan, his descendants held offices of trust and distinction in his time, nearly a century after their ancestor's death.

Death of Ali Mardan Khan, 1657.

On the 16th of April, 1657, the emperor sustained a severe blow in the loss of another able and faithful servant, the premier lord, Ali Mardan Khan, universally regarded as the most talented officer both in field and court. He died on his way to Káshmír and was buried in the environs of Láhore.

The Hindu propensities of Shah Jahán.

Notwithstanding his Mahomedan proclivities, the Hindu origin of Shah Jahán (who had very little Chúghattai blood in his veins, his mother as well as his grandmother being both Hindus) manifested itself in many ways. Early each morning he appeared at the jharoka window, overlooking the plain, where he offered his devotions to the rising sun. People of all ranks, who stood at this time below, paid him homage. This mode of showing oneself is called in the language of the country *darshan* (view), and was in imitation of a usage existing in the times of ancient Hindu sovereigns. In conformity with the practice of the Jamshed kings of Persia, the emperor gave a grand banquet on New Year's Day, called the Now Roz, when he was weighed against gold, silver and jewels, which were lavished among the grandees of the court. Dishes full of gems and gold were waved over his head on these occasions, and emptied on the floor, to be scrambled for by the courtiers, who all forgot their dignity at the time. Akber had taken a golden sun, fashioned of jewels, as the symbol of sovereignty, and placed it on his throne. Shah Jahán took the image of a peacock, made of gold and jewels, as the ensign of royalty. It was the ensign of the ancient Buddhist, Brahmin and Rájput rájás. Following the custom of the Hindu rájás, Shah Jahán laid the foundation of public buildings in human blood. When the foundations of the new palace and the city were laid at Delhi, several criminals were slaughtered and their blood was shed on them. Two stone statues of Rájputs were mounted on two stone elephants and placed at the grand entrance facing the great square of the palace. This was in imitation of the old custom of the Hindu rájás, who placed colossal images of elephants at the entrance of their palaces and temples, as their guardian deities. The palace was guarded by Rájputs. Shah Jahán, than whom no prince was ever fonder of luxury, spent the cold weather at Agra and the summer in the lovely vale of Káshmír, where he beguiled the time in a succession of varied enjoyments. Láhore, though no longer the capital of the empire, was still a town of considerable importance. The emperor was attached to it as his birthplace, and held his court there on his marches to Káshmír and back. It was the arsenal and rendezvous of the armies that marched beyond the Indus, and it continued to increase in size, wealth and splendour. He enlarged and beautified the palace under the superintendence of Asif Khan, and built the *Samman Burj*, or the "palace of mirrors." Here the emperor showed himself every morning, through a lattice window, to the multitude assembled beneath, and to the grandees who came to receive the commands of his imperial majesty.

The jharoka window. The festival of Now Roz. The ensign of royalty. The stone elephants. Shah Jahán fond of Láhore. He enlarges and beautifies the Láhore palace.

The fancy fair.

On every New Year's festival, a fancy fair was held at the palace, at which the wives and the daughters of the amírs opened shops of needle and other handicraft work and exposed their beautiful wares for sale. The begums and the ladies of the royal household attended the fair, and his majesty and his harem played the part of purchasers.

The emperor's harem.

The mahal, or harem quarter, of the king, a paradise of pavilions and gardens, covered an immense area of the palace between the royal bath and the jharoka window. It consisted of numerous halls and arched chambers

His female Tartar guards.

opening into gardens and fountains. The king was guarded by a force of Amazons, consisting of a hundred Tartar women. These fair guardians of the royal person were commanded by a woman who received the pay of an amír of the empire. Each queen and princess had an establishment of her own, consisting of bands of damsels and female slaves. The damsels played on musical instruments, sang and danced before the ladies of the harem and the padshah. The harem consisted of two thousand women, and none knew anything about them except the eunuchs, the lady visitors and the padshah. It was a network of intrigue which brought to the ladies of the harem presents from the nobles of the court and the viceroys. Tavernier mentions the case of the viceroy of Sindh, of whose tyranny and extortion there were loud complaints. He was recalled to Agra, and people expected that he would be strangled for his misconduct. He, however, paid the Begum Sahib, as the elder daughter of the king was called, twenty thousand, and the king fifty thousand, gold mohurs; and not only was his fault forgiven, but he was made viceroy of Allahabád, a richer province.

The establishment of the princesses.

The harem-a network of intrigue.

Dangerous illness of the emperor, 1657.

The conduct of his sons.

In August, 1657, the emperor, who was residing at Delhi, was seized with a severe and sudden illness. He remained unconscious for several days, and his recovery was deemed hopeless. Dara, as the regent of the state, took the administration into his own hands, and thus became a cause of jealousy to the other brothers. Shuja was the first to take the field. He marched from Bengal at the head of a large army towards the capital. Morád, viceroy of Gujrát, seized the public treasure and proclaimed himself emperor. Aurangzeb, a perfect master of the art of dissimulation, acted with caution. He feigned to resign in favour of Morád, telling him in his letters: "I have not the slightest wish to take any part in the government of this deceitful and unstable world; my only desire is that I may make the pilgrimage to the temple of God." These professions induced Morád to join his forces to those of the dissembler, and the confederate armies put Dara and Shuja to flight. Aurangzeb, by a stratagem, then made Morád prisoner and removed him to the fort of Gwalior, where he was executed. Shah Jahán recovered sufficiently to resume the administration of the government, but the flame of civil war had been kindled, and could not be suppressed now, even by the king's own efforts. The emperor wrote letters to Shuja with his own hands, commanding him to return to his government; but that prince continued his march on Agra until he was met by Suleman Shakoh, son of Dara, on the banks of the Ganges. He was defeated and compelled to return to Bengal. In the beginning of June 1658, Dara marched from Agra to oppose his brothers, but was totally defeated at Chambal, and compelled to fly to Delhi with a handful of followers. The old emperor adhered to the cause of Dara; but Aurangzeb, after the flight of Dara to Delhi, took immediate possession of the city of Agra and made Shah Jahán a prisoner in his palace. The governor of Delhi closed the fortress against Dara, who then rapidly marched on Láhore. Here he seized the public treasury, which contained a large sum of money. Shah Jahán sent him ten camels laden with silver and gold coins, and with these Dara began to collect his shattered army and to raise new levies, but the vigilant Aurangzeb, after settling the affairs of Delhi, advanced on Láhore, and Dara, on hearing of his approach, fled from Láhore, with 3,000 or 4,000 horse, and took the road to Multán on his way to Sindh. In the meanwhile Shuja was advancing from Bengal to Benares at the head of 25,000 horse and a numerous train of artillery. Aurangzeb gave him battle at Kajwa, midway between Allahabád and Etawa, and completely routed him. Dara, leaving his baggage at Bhakkar, on the Indus, proceeded to Gujrát in the

The hypocrisy of Aurangzeb.

The civil war, 1657-58.

Aurangzeb enters Agra,
And makes Shah Jahán a prisoner in his palace, 1658.

Flight of Dara Shakoh to Láhore.

Defeat of Shuja.

Dekkan, where, having been joined by the governor, Shah Nawaz Khan, he was acknowledged as the supreme authority in the whole province, including Surat and Broach. Aurangzeb, who was now at Jeypúr, having heard of the proceedings at Gujrát, marched in that direction, and attacked and defeated Dara, who fled in great distress towards Sindh. He then pursued his march to Kandahar, but, in the small territory of Jun, on the eastern border of Sindh, he lost his faithful wife. He sent her remains, with a small escort and two of his most confidential servants, to Láhore, to be there interred, and, after the period of mourning was over, prosecuted his journey to the Indus. He was, however, betrayed by the chief of Jun, and with his son, Siphr Shekoh, was delivered up to Aurangzeb. He was brought to Delhi, loaded with heavy chains, and was there, by the king's special orders, made to ride on a sorry elephant, without housing, and, having been thus conducted through the principal streets, was tried by a mock tribunal, which pronounced him an apostate from the faith. Both father and son were kept prisoners in the ancient fort in old Delhi, guarded by the Afghans who had betrayed Dara. Dara was condemned to death by the lawyers, and the sentence was, with apparent reluctance, confirmed by Aurangzeb. A personal enemy was directed to carry out the sentence. Dara and his son were preparing lentils at the time. Seeing the executioners, Dara made a stout resistance with the small knife then in his hands, but, being overpowered by numbers, he fell and was beheaded. His body was exhibited on an elephant to the populace, while his head was brought to Aurangzeb, who had it wiped and washed in his presence, and, being satisfied of its identity, shed tears. It was then interred in the tomb of Húmáyún. Siphr Shekoh was sent to Gwalior and there kept as a State prisoner. Shuja, after his defeat by Mír Jumla, fled to Dacca, whence he made his way to Arrakan, accompanied by his wife, two sons and three daughters. The rájá of Arrakan received the unfortunate prince hospitably, but demanded one of his daughters in marriage. The request was revolting, and Shuja formed a plot to usurp the throne of Arrakan with the help of the Mahomedan subjects. The plot being discovered, Shuja fled to the mountains, and nothing more was heard of him. The princes were beheaded by the rájá with blunt axes and the princesses were starved to death. Such was the miserable end of Dara and Shuja.

Dara flies to Sindh in great distress.

Is betrayed by the chief of Jun, and delivered to Aurangzeb,

Who cruelly puts him to death, 1659.

Shuja flies to Arrakan.

Uncertainty of his fate.

After his deposition by his son, Aurangzeb, Shah Jahán, who did not die till the 23rd of January, 1666, lived for eight years. A palace, strongly guarded, was assigned for his residence in Agra, and he was treated with the utmost respect for the remainder of his life. He exercised complete authority within the palace and was allowed an ample establishment. He withheld the imperial jewels from his undutiful son, and when the latter made a demand for them, he threatened that the hammers were ready to pound them into dust if an attempt were ever made to enforce such a demand. Aurangzeb had the forbearance to withdraw his demand. At another time Aurangzeb solicited the daughter of Dara in marriage for his son Akber. Shah Jahán refused to allow the removal of the young lady, who kept a concealed dagger with her, declaring that she would rather put an end to her own life than give her hand to the son of her father's murderer. Aurangzeb thereupon quietly desisted from his solicitation. The deposed emperor was solaced in his captivity by the affectionate attentions of his favourite daughter, Jahanara. His last moments were cheered by the sight of the mausoleum of the wife of his youth from the window of his bed-room.

Shah Jahán in his prison.

Some time before his death, Aurangzeb had sent submissive letters to

Shah Jahán, who was induced to send some of the crown jewels to his son. Aurangzeb, as an acknowledgment of this act of kindness, sent a European physician to treat the old king. The name of this physician is not stated, but he had been employed in more than one work of poisoning, and had been advanced to high office in the state. The death of Shah Jahán was soon announced. It happened during the night, when Aurangzeb was ready to march for Káshmír with a contented mind. The suspicion was never removed that the aged king had been removed by poison. Fakhr-un-nissa, the eldest daughter of Aurangzeb, congratulated her father on the occasion. The funeral ceremonies were performed with great splendour. The entire troops at Agra, in mourning costume, formed the procession, and Aurangzeb followed the funeral car in solemn sadness, and with tears in his eyes, to the celebrated mausoleum of his mother, where the remains of the unhappy monarch were interred by the side of those of his beloved wife. So died Shah Jahán, the most magnificent monarch who ever ruled the destinies of the Indian empire. He was seventy-four years old when he died, and had reigned thirty years.

Death of Shah Jahán, 1666.

Grave suspicion that Aurangzeb was guilty of parricide.

The funeral.

All historians agree in speaking in eulogistic terms of the high prosperity of India during the reign of Shah Jahán. The presence, in the heart of the city of Láhore, of a splendid mosque, such as that of Wazír Khan, is a proof of the existence of much public as well as private wealth. Shah Jahán made many costly additions to the palace of Láhore and laid out the elegant Shálámár gardens of Láhore and Káshmír celebrated in Moore's *Lalla Rookh.* It was he who founded modern Delhi and adorned it with a castellated palace and a magnificent mosque, the finest in the East. To him India is indebted for that splendid edifice, the Táj of Agra, a monument of historical significance, unequalled by any other edifice in the world for the mysterious fascination which attaches to it. It is the admiration of the world, and the architectural pride of India. As a financier, Shah Jahán had the reputation of managing his extensive establishment with great circumspection. In spite of the costly campaigns carried on from the borders of the Carnatic to the frontier of Balkh and Thibet; in spite of his magnificent shows and expensive entertainments; in spite of all his expenditure on public works, which were of such magnitude as had never before been undertaken by a single monarchy; in spite of his periodical expeditions to Káshmír and his expenses in maintaining a standing army of 200,000 horse, he left at the end of his reign a treasure estimated at twenty-four crores of rupees, besides vast accumulations in wrought gold and silver and in pearls.

Great prosperity of India under Shah Jahán.

His economy.

Tavernier, the French traveller, who constantly visited most parts of India during the reign of Shah Jahán, speaks of him as having "reigned not so much as a king over his subjects, but more as a father over his family and children." Describing the great prosperity and security enjoyed during his reign, Tavernier says: "He was a great king, during whose reign there was such a strictness in the civil government, and particularly in the security of the highways, that there was never any occasion to put any man to death for robbery." "Nor was this prosperity," says Elphinstone on the authority of European travellers,* "confined to royal residences; all travellers speak with admiration of the grandeur of the cities, even in remote provinces, and of the fertile and productive countries in which they stood." We have also the testimony of the Italian physician, Manucci, who came to India in 1649,

Testimony of European travellers.

* Mandelslo for Gujrát; Graaf and Burton for Bengal, Behar and Orissa; and Tavernier for most parts of India. Pietro Della Valle, writing in 1623, the last year of Jahángír, says: "Here generally all live after a genteel way, and they do it securely as well, because the king does not persecute his subjects with false accusations nor deprive them of anything when he sees them live splendidly and with appearance of riches."

and lived there for the long time of forty-eight years. His memoirs contain a full description of the family and court of Shah Jahán as an eye-witness. John Albert de Mandelslo, who had served as a page to the Duke of Holstein, came to India in 1638, the tenth year of the reign of Shah Jahán, and he speaks highly of the flourishing condition of the empire, and the riches and attractions of its great cities. He has given a vivid description of the imperial palaces and mode of life. Francis Bernier, who, with more political insight, travelled in India during the year 1655-1667, gives an interesting account in his travels of the state of India during the reign of Shah Jahán. Rai Bahara Mall Darás, accountant, and Khafi Khan, the historian of the time of Aurangzeb, both extol Shah Jahán for his justice and care of the people.

CHAPTER XVI.

MUHY-UD-DÍN AURANGZEB.

Aurangzeb ascends the throne, 1658.

AURANGZEB was in his fortieth year when he deposed his father. He ascended the throne of Delhi, in 1658, but did not assume the title of emperor until October 1660, or two years after, when the *khutba* was read and money coined in his name. The title of sovereignty which he adopted was *Alamgír*, "Conqueror of the World," the same that had been engraved by Shah Jahán on a sabre which he had sent him as a present at Agra, together with an autograph letter, in the preceding year.

He assumes the title of "Alamgír."

His coin.

The superscription on one side of the coins, consisting of the creed and the names of the first four Khalifs, was omitted, on the ground that the coins were liable to pass into the hands of infidels and be placed in impure spots. The inscription was changed into the following couplet bearing the emperor's name.

سکه زد درجهان چو بدرمنیر   شاه اورنگ زیب عالمگیر

"The Emperor Aurangzeb Alamgír has struck coin in the world like the brilliant moon."

The above inscription appeared on silver coin. For the gold coin the words بدر منیر (brilliant moon) were changed into مهر منیر (brilliant sun).

His first measures.

He abolished the New Year festival of March, as an imitation of the fire worshippers, and restored the Arabic lunar months, in conformity with Mahomedan usage. He issued an edict prohibiting the use of wine, and punished all Mahomedans convicted of drinking spirituous liquors with the deprivation of a hand or a foot.

Gambling houses suppressed.

He suppressed all gambling-houses and issued an edict abolishing singing, dancing and buffoonery. The singers and musicians attached to the palace were all discharged. Special officers were appointed to enter any house where music was heard and to burn the musical instruments. These were collected in heaps and destroyed. Hundreds of musicians were thus reduced to starvation.* All dancing girls were to be either lawfully married or banished from the king's dominions.

Musicians suppressed.

* One Friday afternoon, as the emperor was proceeding to the grand mosque to offer prayers, attended by his body guard, he saw a large concourse of people following a bier and filling the air with loud lamentations and screams. On enquiry as to the cause, he was told that the remains of "Music," the mother of the mourners, were being taken to her last resting-place. The emperor cried: "Bury her deep; she must not rise again."—*J. Talboys Wheeler*, on the authority of *Manucci*. Compare also *Khafi Khan*.

Dismissal of State astrologers and poets.

A system of the strictest economy introduced.

The spy system.

Harsh measures against the *Shias*.

Edict against moustaches.

Destruction of the Hindu temples.

Astrology was forbidden, and all astrologers attached to the court were removed. The office of the royal poet was likewise abolished, and the allowances of poets, who in previous times had been honoured, were discontinued. The emperor introduced a system of the strictest frugality and the most minute supervision, and professed to provide for his own subsistence by embroidering caps with his own hands. He brought the spy system to such perfection that his great knowledge of all that went on was attributed by the credulous to supernatural agency. He professed to be a *Sunni* of the strictest type, and, having resumed the lands of the *Shiá* grandees, expelled them to Káshmír, there to live on such pensions as were assigned to them. He used to say about the *Shias:* "They are united to us by the Qurán, but they have separated themselves by errors regarding the succession to the Khalifát, so they must be separated from us altogether." He issued an edict prohibiting the *Shiás* from wearing long moustaches, and appointed officers to measure their moustaches and clip them if they exceeded the orthodox standard. He discouraged the teaching of the Hindus, burnt to the ground the great pagoda near Delhi, and destroyed the temple of Bishnath at Benares, and the great temple of Dera Kesú Rái at Mathúra, said to have been built by Rájá Narsingh Deo, at a cost of thirty-three lakhs of rupees.* The gilded domes of this temple were so high that they could be seen from Agra. On the site of the ruined temple, he built a vast mosque at a great cost. The richly decorated idols of the temples were removed to Ágra and placed beneath the steps leading to the mosque of Nawáb Begum. The name Mathúra was changed into Islámábád, and was so written in all correspondence and spoken by the people. Aurangzeb had resolved that the belief in one God and the Prophet should be, not the prevailing, but the only religion of the empire of Hindostán. He issued mandates to the viceroys and governors of provinces to destroy pagodas and idols throughout his dominions. About three hundred temples in various parts of Rájputáná were destroyed and their idols broken. The emperor appointed múllahs, with a party of horse attached to each, to check all ostentatious display of idol-worship, and, some time afterwards, he forbade fairs on Hindu festivals, and issued a circular to all governors and men in authority prohibiting the employment of Hindus in the offices of state immediately under them, and commanding them to confer all such offices on Mahomedans only. About the year 1690, the emperor issued an edict prohibiting Hindus from being carried in palanquins or riding on Arab horses. All servants of the state were ordered to embrace the Mahomedan religion, under pain of dismissal, those who refused were deprived of their posts. A large number of jogis, sanniasis and other religious men were driven out of the king's dominions. The emperor reduced the duty on merchandise belonging to Mahomedans to one-half the amount paid by Hindus, and remitted a number of other obnoxious taxes.† Following the tradition of his house, he, in 1661, married his son, Moazzam, to the daughter of Rája Rúp Singh. In the 22nd year of his reign, he renewed the *Jazia*, or poll-tax, on Hindus, throughout his dominions. The Hindus of Delhi gathered in large numbers beneath the jharoka window, on the banks of the river, and implored his majesty to remit the obnoxious tax; but the emperor was inexorable. The Hindus adopted the expedient of closing the shops in the city, and all business came to a standstill. They thronged the bazars from the palace to the grand mosque, one Friday, with the object of seeking relief. The crowd increased every moment, and the king's equipage was interrupted at every

All ostentatious display of idol-worship stopped.

Hindu fairs suppressed.

Exclusion of Hindus from the public service.

They are deprived of the rights of citizenship.

Banishment of the Hindu ascetics.

Renewal of the *Jazia*.

* Ma-ásiri Alamgíri.

† *Muntakhibul Lubah* of Khafi Khan.

step. He stopped for a while to hear them, but the multitude held their ground. At length, under orders from the emperor, war elephants were directed against the mob, and, the retinue forcing its way through, numbers were trodden to death by horses and elephants. After this the Hindus submitted without further demur.

Aurangzeb introduced changes in the mode of saluting him and abolished the long-established custom of appearing at the balcony of the palace, thus depriving the people of an innocent pleasure. The royal appearance at the jharoka abolished.

The long reign of Aurangzeb was chiefly occupied in the final subjugation of the Dekkan. He conquered the kingdoms of Golconda and Bijápúr, and had the satisfaction of seeing his dominions extended to the farthest limits of the Carnatic. The period which marked the death of Shah Jahán, was the most prosperous of Aurangzeb's long reign. His governor of Káshmír had brought Little Thibet under subjection, and the viceroy of Bengal had added Chittagong, on the eastern shore of the Bay of Bengal, to his dominions. Throughout the Mahomedan world, the emperor was held in the highest respect, and his capital was attended by ambassadors from the sherif of Mecca, the princes of Arabia, the Khan of the Uzbeks and the king of Abyssinia. Even the Shah of Persia sent a complimentary embassy to the court of Aurangzeb, who in return sent an embassy of unusual splendour from India to Persia; but some questions of etiquette which arose created such a difference between the king of Delhi and Shah Abbas, that, under the orders of his Persian majesty, the beard of the Indian envoy was set on fire by a page. The emperor's wrath on the return of the beardless envoy knew no bounds. He reproached him bitterly for not having stabbed the Shah to the heart, and executed him the same day by having him bitten by a venomous snake.*

The emperor's conquests in the Deccan.

His power held in respect throughout the Mahomedan world.

During his summer visits to Káshmír, Aurangzeb appeared to be quite a different man from what he seemed in the hot palace of Delhi. In the cool retreats of the happy valley, he indulged in the society of his ladies, who pleased him with flattery and caresses. The summer retreats to Káshmír.

He was fascinated by a Christian lady, a native of Georgia, named Udepúri. When a child she had been sold to Dara, the elder brother of Aurangzeb, by a slave dealer, and she grew up to be exceedingly handsome. On Dara's death, she infatuated Aurangzeb and became his favourite queen. She was the mother of Kám Baksh, the emperor's youngest son. The Udepúri Begum.

In 1672, the Afghans beyond the Khaibar, who were the most refractory subjects of the king, rebelled. Amín Khan, the son of Mir Júmla, and governor of Kábul, who resided at Pesháwar, entered the plains of Kábul at the head of an army to punish the insurgents, but the whole of his army were cut to pieces, his chief wife was slaughtered, and his mother, sister and daughter were carried away as slaves. The following year, the emperor proceeded to the seat of war in person and obtained some successes, but tidings of disturbances in the neighbourhood of the capital compelled him to retrace his steps to Delhi. The Santa Rámis, a sect of Hindu devotees had risen in revolt and committed great excesses. The royal troops defeated the insurgents and massacred in cold blood the male inhabitants of the localities where the insurrection had broken out. Women and children were seized and sold as slaves. The emperor, in the meantime, recalled Amín Khan, and appointed one Kasim Khan in his place. Kasim Khan was an experienced chief, and won the hearts of the Afghans by his seeming

The expedition against the Afghans of the Khaibar, 1672.

Ill success.

Revolt of the Santa Rámis.

A tragedy.

* This mode of execution was not uncommon under the Moghal Government. Shah Jahán was once told that the *Kotwal*, or Police Magistrate, of Delhi had taken a bribe. He had the offender bitten by a cobra, and he died in a few hours.

courtesy and friendship. He entertained the Afghans at a grand banquet held at Peshâwar in honour of the circumcision ceremony of his son, and gave them a splendid feast in the grand square of the city. Horse-racing, elephant-fights, games and exhibitions were the order of the day. In the midst of these rejoicings Kasim Khan suddenly left the assembly, which was a signal for a massacre. Bodies of armed men, who had been concealed in the neighbouring houses, poured volleys of musketry on the Afghan guests, who had attended the feast without a suspicion of treachery. There was a general massacre of the Afghans, and it spread consternation throughout Kábul. The Afghans were paralysed and gave no further trouble for the rest of Aurangzeb's reign.

Massacre of the Afghans at Peshâwar.

The imperial camp.

The imperial camp of Aurangzeb was quite a moving city, being as large and populous as Delhi itself. He was fond of camp-life and seldom lived in his palaces in the towns. The ladies of the harem, seated on glittering howdahs and veiled, accompanied him. They were attended by a multitude of women on horseback, cloaked from head to feet. The king's establishment, consisting of cooks, Abyssinian slaves, mace-bearers and criers, was numerous. Provisions in abundance were carried with the camp. Drinking water from the Ganges was carried on the backs of camels. The imperial treasure was carried on elephants and carts. The king's pavilions consisted of magnificent courts, halls and chambers, and every approach was guarded by cannons. There were hosts of cavalry and infantry, camp-followers and servants, victuallers, foragers and others, with luggage, tents and horses.

Death of Aurangzeb, 1707.

Aurangzeb died in his camp at Ahmadnagar, in 1707, at the advanced age of eighty-nine, and in the fiftieth year of his reign. Ever suspicious of all around him, he studiously kept his sons at a distance to defeat any possible attempt at plotting on their part. Before his death, he seems to have felt strongly that his dissolution was near, and the letters he dictated to his sons in his last days are sufficiently indicative of the intense remorse he felt for the past. He writes:—"I came a stranger into this world and a stranger I depart. I know nothing of myself, what I am, and for what I am destined. My back is bent with weakness and my feet have lost the power of motion. The breath which rose is gone and has left not even hope behind it. I resign you, your mother and your son to God, as I myself am going. The agonies of death come upon me fast. Udepúri, your mother, has been a partner in my illness, and wishes to accompany me in death; but everything has its appointed time. I go. Whatever good or evil I have done has been done for you. Come what may, my vessel is launched on the waves. Farewell! Farewell! Farewell!" Shortly before his death he wrote a will giving the northern districts of his empire to Moazzam, the southern to Azam, and the kingdoms of Golconda and Bijápúr to the youngest son, Kám Baksh. Thus died Aurangzeb, one of the greatest and least happy of the Tartar sovereigns that have ruled an Eastern empire. In marked contrast to his predecessors from Baber downwards, he was sober and abstemious. Under him the Moghal empire reached its greatest limits. He applied himself assiduously to business, and evinced a keen interest in the administration of his country. He was of small stature, with a long nose, a round beard, and an olive skin. He usually wore plain white muslin, and had a large emerald affixed to his turban. Gemelli Carreri, who saw the emperor in his seventy-eighth year, says: "The emperor stood amidst his grandees leaning on a staff; he received petitions personally; read them without the aid of spectacles, and endorsed them with his own hand. He did all this with a cheerful, smiling countenance and seemed pleased with his duty."

His letters to his sons.

His will.

His character.

His person.

His attachment to Mahomedanism seems to have been sincere; but his bigotry and intolerance towards Hindus revived religious animosities between the various classes of the population; and the disintegration of races to which his hypocrisy gave rise, paved the way for the speedy dismemberment of the once powerful Moghal monarchy in India.

His bigotry towards the Hindus.

Its fatal consequences to the empire.

CHAPTER XVII.

KUTB-UD-DÍN MUHAMMAD MOAZZAM, SHAH ALAM BAHÁDUR SHAH.

Contest for sovereignty among the sons of the deceased emperor.

THE injunctions of Aurangzeb regarding the succession, though just in the abstract, were unheeded by his sons. At the time of his death, Moazzam, the eldest son, was viceroy of Kábul. Azam was encamped near him, and Kám Baksh, the youngest and most beloved of his sons, was in his kingdom of Bijápúr.

Moazzam assumes the royal diadem.

Moazzam, on hearing of his father's illness, had marched from Kábul with his two younger sons, Khajasta Akhtar and Rafi-ul-kadr, and he was on his route when tidings reached him of his father's demise. He immediately assumed the royal diadem and ascended the throne. The ceremony took place on the first Wednesday of Moharram, 1119 A.H. (March 1707 A.D.), precisely at midnight, this being the hour declared to be auspicious by the astrologers, the sun at that time entering the sign of Leo. Azam proclaimed himself emperor* in his camp, and, ordering the imperial music to strike up, took command of the army. At that time Monim Khan, an able and well-intentioned officer, son of Sultan Beg Birlas, a Turkomán noble, was viceroy of the Panjáb. While Moazzam was a prince, Aurangzeb had appointed Monim Khan to be his dewán, and he had managed well the prince's jagírs in the province of Láhore. On that account, as well as for his activity in the cabinet, and unbending integrity, he was held in great esteem by Moazzam. At the present juncture he was most active in constructing bridges over the various rivers and collecting large supplies at Láhore.

Monim Khan, viceroy of the Panjáb.

Moazzam effects a junction with Monim Khan at Láhore.

Moazzam, descending from Kábul, effected, a junction with Monim Khan at Láhore, while his son Moz-ud-dín, viceroy of Multán, joined him with all the available troops and a powerful train of artillery. The prince encamped at Láhore in April, and the nobles in his retinue presented their offerings and paid their homage.

Money was coined and the *khutba* read in his name in Láhore. The new rupee was increased half a *masha* in weight. Having remained at Láhore till after the new moon of *Saffur*, the combined armies marched to Agra, and a battle was fought for the throne of Delhi at Tajo, in which Azam was defeated and slain with his two sons. Their bodies were conveyed to Delhi and buried in the precincts of Húmáyún's mausoleum. The emperor em-

Action between Moazzam and Azam.

Victory of Moazzam, henceforward Bahádur Shah, 1707.

---

* Azam Shah, on assuming sovereign authority, struck coin bearing the following inscription:—

سکه زد درجهان بدولت و جاه

باد شاه ممالک اعظم شاه

"The monarch of the dominion, Azam Shah, struck coin in the world with prosperity and glory."

braced Monim Khan for his gallantry in the field, presented him with an unprecedented gift of a *karor* of rupees, and elevated him to the office of wazír, with the title Júmlat-ul-mulk.

Shah Alam, on ascending the throne of Delhi, assumed the title of Bahádur Shah. He received the submission of the Amírs of Irán and Túrán, the former headed by Asad Khan and his son, Zulfikar Khan, and the latter by the blind veteran, Ghazi-ud-dín Firozejang, and his mighty son, Chin Kalich Khan, who had been created *Khan-i-douran* by Azam, and was the founder of the Nizám dynasty in the Dekkan. On Chin Kalich Khan was conferred the tittle of *Jalil-ul-kadr*, and he was raised to the dignity of Vakil-i-mutlak, or lord lieutenant of the empire.

The grandees of the empire.

Revolt of prince Kám Baksh.

No sooner had Prince Kám Baksh heard of the death of his brother, Azam, and his nephews, than he made preparations for war. In vain did the mild emperor try to pacify him, as the overtures sent served only to strengthen his defiance. Provoked by his arrogance, the emperor was obliged to take the field against him, and a battle was fought near Hyderabád in which the army of the insurrectionary prince was routed and he himself mortally wounded. The benevolent monarch ordered his wounded brother to be brought into his camp, where European surgeons were appointed to attend him. Towards evening Bahádur Shah himself went on foot to his brother's tent to pay him a visit, and, covering his head with his own mantle, exclaimed: "Alas! I never desired to see my brother in this condition." "Nor did I ever desire," rejoined the proud dying man, "to see you in the condition you now are." The rash prince refused all nourishment and expired the same night, his body being sent to Delhi to be interred in the cemetery of the race.

His defeat.

His death, 1708.

The victory over Prince Kám Baksh and his ultimate fate put an end to all competition for sovereignty in Hindostán. About this time (1709-10) the Sikhs, a class of eclectic sectaries, who had sprung up in the Panjáb, overran the provinces of Sirhind, Saháráupúr, and part of Mozaffarnagar, and committed great excesses on the people. Having been driven across the Jamna by the imperial troops, they fell back on the Jalandar Doáb. Their forces by this time exceeded seventy thousand. Shams-ud-dín Khan, the Moghal governor of Jalandar, collecting all the available troops, gave the Sikhs battle at Ráhon, where they were repulsed with great loss.

Rise of the Sikhs.

Their defeat at Ráhon.

The Moghal capital removed to Láhore, 1710.

The atrocities committed by the Sikhs in the Panjáb induced Bahádur Shah to remove his capital from Delhi to Láhore. Asad Khan, lieutenant-general, who had entered the mountains to blockade the Sikhs, having died at Láhore, the office was conferred on Hidayatulla Khan, son of Inayat-ud-dín Khan; and Rustam Dil Khan was sent to the hills to chastise the Sikhs. The emperor in the meantime encamped on the banks of the Rávi. A short time after, Rustam Dil Khan quitted his command in the hills and repaired to Láhore. He was punished with the forfeiture of his jagír and his command, and put in confinement in the citadel of Láhore. Muhammad Amín Khan was sent to the hills to take the command of the imperial army. The Sikhs were forbidden to enter into the city of Láhore, and they now came to the suburbs at night by swimming the Rávi, and retired before day-break.

Punishment of the Sikhs.

They are forbidden from entering Láhore.

Bahádur Shah was fond of the society of learned men, and took great delight in discourses on the topics of law and divinity. He was a Mahomedan of the *Shiá* persuasion, and, on his arrival at Láhore, he assembled the learned men of the town, most of them staunch *Súnnis*, and wished to get them by force of argument to acknowledge the justice of Ali's succession to the Khalifát, in preference to the three first khalifs. The learned men

Bahádur Shah a Shiá.

His religious discourses with the Ulemas of Láhore.

were defeated in argument, and the emperor ordered that the word *wusi* (heir) should be added to the attributes of Alí in the public prayers and the *khutba*. The innovation proved very unwelcome to the *Súnnis*. Jan Muhammad and Haji Yar Muhammad, the most eminent learned men of Láhore, accompanied by other scholars and a large multitude, waited on the Kazi and the Sadr and remonstrated with them openly on the use of the word *wusi* in the *khutba* and the prayers. The emperor's eldest sons, Azím-ush-shan and Khajasta Akhtar, were both zealous *Súnnis*, and they suffered the *Shiá* minister who had been sent to the chief mosque to repeat the *Shiá* creed, "and Alí is the saint of God," to be dragged from the top of the pulpit by the congregation and hewn in pieces before he had time to utter the offensive words. Haji Yar Muhammad, Muhammad Múrád Khan and a few other learned men waited upon his majesty in his oratory. After much disputation, hot words ensued between the king's supporters and Haji Yar Muhammad. The emperor, seeing him excited, asked him if he was not afraid to speak so boldly in the audience of a king. The Haji replied: "I had wished four things from my Creator,—first, acquisition of knowledge; second, preservation of my creed; third, pilgrimage; fourth, martyrdom. Thank God, I have been gifted with the first three. Martyrdom remains, and I hope to get it now through the kindness of your majesty." The whole of the inhabitants of the city, together with a party of Afghans, were bent on resisting the innovation with all their might and fortunes, and the Sadr, not long after this event, presented a petition to the king, in which his majesty was invited over to their principles. On this petition the emperor wrote with his own hands that the *khutba* should be read in the form used in the reign of Khuld Zami Aurangzeb. After this concession by the throne the agitation ceased.

Innovation in the public prayers.

Murder of the Shia pontiff in the grand mosque of Láhore.

The Sunni form of *khutba* restored.

The emperor had passed his seventieth lunar year when a change became perceptible in his mind. He was then encamped on the Rávi, in the suburbs of Láhore. In the early part of February, 1712 A.D., he took it into his head to give orders to kill all the dogs in the city of Láhore, as well as his camp. He was all at once seized with fainting fits, which continued without intermission till 21st Moharram, 1124 A.H. (19th February 1712, A.D.), when, about two hours before night, he breathed his last. The princes and ladies of the harem made loud lamentations round his bed.* The nobles left the royal camp in the darkness of the night to join the parties of their respective princes, while many of the camp-followers, greatly alarmed, retired to the city with their families. The following day there was great agitation in the city, and the streets were crowded with multitudes of noisy people who gave free rein to their imagination as regards the succession to the monarchy. The body of the late emperor was conveyed to Delhi, where it was buried within the precincts of the mausoleum of the Saint Kutb-ud-dín. He died in the seventy first lunar year of his age and the fifth of his reign.

Change in the emperor's temper, 1712.

His death, 1712.

A great bewilderment follows.

Bahádur Shah was a generous, munificent and an excessively good-natured prince. His tolerance and amiability were a great contrast to the bigotry and hypocrisy of his predecessor. Brought up in the school of adversity,† he had grown up mild and affable to such a degree that people called him the saint king. Before taking up arms against his brother, Sultan Muhammad Azam, he wrote to him that if he would be satisfied with the Dekkan, which was an extensive kingdom, and which the deceased emperor had set apart for him, he would desist from warlike operations. But these overtures were disregarded by Muhammad Azam, and the emperor

The character Bahádur Shah.

* *The Memoirs* of Irádat Khan.

† He was kept in confinement by his father, Aurangzeb, for seven years.

was compelled to wage a war which proved disastrous to his defiant brother. When Rustam Dil Khan, commander of Shah Alam's escort, ascending the incapacitated elephant of Muhammad Azam in the battle-field, cut off that prince's head with his sword and hastened to the camp of his master with his prize, in the exulting hope of great reward, the compassionate Shah Alam, seeing the head of his slaughtered brother, shed tears of affection and bestowed upon Rustam Dil Khan nothing but reproaches. He forbade the march of victory to be beaten, and treated the ladies of the harem and the young princes with the utmost respect and tenderness.

His court.

His family.

Seats in the durbar.

His court vied in splendour and magnificence with that of Shah Jahán. The peacock throne was surrounded by seventeen princes of the blood-royal. Jahándar Shah, the eldest son, with his three sons, his third son, Rafi-ush-shan, with his three sons, and Bedar Dil, son of his nephew, Bedar Bakht, sitting on the right of the throne; and his second son, Azím-ush-shan, with his two sons, Jahan Shah, his fourth son, with his son, Ali Tabar, the only surviving son of Azam Shah, and the two sons of Muhammad Kám Baksh, being seated on the left. Behind the royal princes, on the right, stood the sons of conquered sovereigns, such as Sikandar Ali Shah, of Bijápúr, and Kutb Shah, king of Golconda, from the rank of seven to three thousand, such as were allowed to be on the platform between the silver rails.* It was customary with the emperor to distribute betel and perfumes, on the *Íds* and other important festivals, to his grandees with his own hand, according to rank, and the recipient received the gift with bows and salutations. According to his historian, his gifts in jewels and rich dresses were truly royal. In his dress in private he was plain, like a devotee, and he never omitted to read prayers in company. He took much interest in presiding over the Friday service himself in the great tent of audience, and repeated the Qurán "with a tone and sweetness which captivated the most eloquent Arabians."

Munificence of his gifts.

Bahádur Shah a devotee.

His popularity in the Panjáb.

Notwithstanding his religious innovations at Láhore, which, it must be remembered, were unattended by a single act of oppression, he was most popular in the Panjáb, and one of the gateways † of Láhore, the Shah Almi gateway, was called after his name. "The fact," according to Thornton, "is some testimony of the popularity of this prince." It has been truly observed that had Bahádur Shah, and not Aurangzeb, succeeded Shah Jahán on the throne of the Moghal, the dynasty of that race would not have become extinct as soon as it did.

CHAPTER XVIII.

MUHAMMAD MOZ-UD-DÍN JAHÁNDAR SHAH.

The struggle for sovereignty.

THE death of Bahádur Shah was followed by the usual struggle for sovereignty among his four sons. The first and second had already, during the lifetime of the emperor, manifested signs of grave suspicion towards each other. One day, as they were in attendance on their royal father, and sitting close to his bed, Azím-ush-shan, esteemed at the time for his warlike

* *Memoirs of the Moghal Empire*, by Irádat Khan.

† It was formerly called the Bherwala gateway.

talents, perceived a dagger of exquisite workmanship under the corner of a pillow. He took it up, and, drawing it from the scabbard, began to admire the beauty of the jewels with which it was adorned and the water of the blade. No harm was apparently meant, but such was the terror felt by the effeminate prince, Moz-ud-dín, that he immediately sprang up from his seat, and, his turban falling off, fled precipitately in the direction of the door of the tent with bare head, and, forgetting his slippers at the entrance, fell over the ropes. It was not until the servants had assisted him to rise that he adjusted his dress, and rode to his camp with as much speed as possible.

The effeminate character of Moz-ud-dín.

Azím-ush-shan, the favourite of his father, and the ablest of the princes, acted as his lieutenant and had command of the household. Being already in possession of the imperial camp, treasury and jewels, and having a large army in his pay, he raised the royal canopy over his head and received the homage of the ministers of state and the crown officers. Amír-ul-omerah Zulfikar Khan embraced the cause of Moz-ud-dín, who was joined by the two other brothers, Rafi-ush-shan and Khajasta Akhtar, on the understanding that there should be an equal division of the empire and treasures after victory had been gained over Azím-ush-shan. The three allied princes encamped near the city of Lahore, but Moz-ud-dín's camp was immediately under the walls, and the greater part of his train occupied the houses of the nearest streets. Azím-ush-shan encamped on the plain, with the river in his rear. The confederates, acting on the advice of Amír-ul-omerha, drew all the artillery from the citadel, and planting it on a rising ground, arrayed their united forces in one line, with their rear resting on the city. A continuous cannonade was kept up on both sides for four days. On the fifth day, Azím-ush-shan marched out from his camp in order of battle. Khajasta Akhtar moved forward steadily, in slow order, to oppose the enemy, and fighting with varied success was kept up for three days. On the eighth day a brisk attack was made on the enemy's entrenched position by Zulfikar Khan and Rustam Dil Khan. They met with a hot resistance from Azím-ush-shan's troops, who were, however, overpowered and compelled to fall back. Two Hindu rájás, Muhkan Chand, *Khatri* and Ráj Sing, *Jat*, were killed on the side of the defeated army, after performing deeds of great valour. At that very moment Suleman Khan, *Peni*, came with a fresh body of horse to support Azím-ush-shan's forces; but the gallant leader fell killed by a musket ball. His body, out of respect for his courage, was sent to the city by the victors. Out of a body of sixty or seventy thousand troops in Azím-ush-shan's army, there only remained now ten or twelve thousand, and these, towards evening, retired to the city of Láhore in great confusion.

The civil war at Láhore, 1712.

Two Hindu rájás killed.

Next morning, the number of Azím-ush-shan's troops was reduced to two or three thousand only, the rest having all deserted or fled. Undismayed by this circumstance, the prince resolved to advance, and sent for the elephant on which he usually rode; but the animal refused to kneel, in spite of the driver's attempt to compel him. The prince sent for another; but by this time the number of his troops was still further reduced. He was soon joined by Rájá Jay Singh with little more than a thousand cavalry; but hardly had the action commenced when a violent storm of wind sprung up and put in motion all the sands of the Rávi. Clouds of dust arose, and this, added to the smoke of the powder discharged by the guns of the confederate armies, spread consternation in the enemy's lines. A cannon-ball struck Azím-ush-shan's elephant on the root of the proboscis and made him furious. The prince himself, after receiving many wounds from arrows and musket-balls, sank down fainting in his seat. The animal turned about in great fury and ran to the water-side, and his driver, losing his seat, fell to the

Azím-ush-shan routed.

He is drowned in the Rávi.

ground. Jalál Khan Lodi, who sat behind the prince, slid down the ropes and fled. Amín-ud-doula and several other nobles made an attempt to stop the animal, but it rushed into the river with the wounded prince, Azím-ush-shan, and sank never to rise again. His son, Muhammad Karím, descending from his elephant, mounted a horse and took to flight, but he was pursued by the victors and slain.

Defeat and death of Khajasta Akhtar.

Dissensions now arose among the three confederate brothers, and confusion and bloodshed ensued. Khajasta Akhtar, in accordance with the terms of the treaty, wished to divide the imperial treasures, consisting of eighty cart-loads of gold coin (*ashrafis*) and a hundred cart-loads of rupees, into three equal parts, of which Jahándar Shah was to receive one, but, through the machinations of Zulfikar Khan, only two-fifths were allotted to the two brothers, while three-fifths were appropriated by Jahándar Shah. This very much exasperated Khajasta Akhtar, who forthwith proclaimed himself king by the title of Jahán Shah. He was joined by several officers of rank, and, collecting a large army, gave Jahándar Shah battle, but was defeated and slain. His son, Farkhunda Akhtar, a prince of most promising attainments, who sat behind his father on the same elephant, descended and fought sword in hand, but fell dead covered with wounds.

Conflict between Moz-ud-dín and Rafi-ush-shan.

Artifices of Zulfikar Khan, the premier noble.

Azím-ush-shan defeated and killed.

There now remained only two rivals for the throne, Moz-ud-dín and Rafi-ush-shan. The latter placed implicit reliance on the fidelity and oaths of Amír-ul-omerah Zulfikar Khan, who, during the lifetime of the late emperor, had supported that prince against Khan-i-Khánán. The prince and the Amír-ul-omerah had also exchanged turbans, and the latter had been called 'uncle' by the former. Placing the most implicit reliance on the friendship of the Amír-ul-omerah, Rafi-ush-shan had resolved to remain a spectator till one of his rivals should fall, when, with the assistance of his supporter, he would rush on the survivor and dispose of him. He communicated his design to his followers, and, ordering the great kettledrum to be beaten, made an immediate advance against Moz-ud-dín. Nor was Rafi-ush-shan ill prepared for action, but, much to his surprise, he saw his sworn friend, the Amír-ul-omerah, ranging the army of his rival in battle array and conducting the whole of the operations. The prince advanced at full gallop and charged the enemy with heroic valour; but in the midst of the action he was betrayed by his badakhshi, who, in pursuance of a private arrangement with the Amír-ul-omerah, turned his arms against his master. Seeing this, the spirited prince threw himself from his elephant, and, drawing his sword, penetrated singly into the thickest of the fight. He performed great feats of valour, but fell covered with wounds. Three of his sons, Muhammad Ibrahim, Rafi-ud-doula and Rafi-ud-darajat, were wounded, but escaped with their lives. Elated with his triumph over his only rival, Moz-ud-dín ordered the march of victory to be sounded. He permitted the mangled bodies of his brothers to lie on the field of battle for three days, exposed to the view of the public. They were afterwards conveyed to Delhi and interred, without ceremony or pomp, in the mausoleum of the Emperor Húmáyún, the general receptacle of murdered princes of the race.

Accession of Moz-ud-dín under the title of Jahándar Shah, 1712.

Murder of the princes royal at Láhore.

Moz-ud-dín, now in undisputed possession of the crown, ascended the throne by the title of Jahándar Shah. The first act of the new emperor, after coming to power, was to pollute his hands with the blood of the princes royal, a crime which had become characteristic of the race of Tymúr on assuming the imperial diadem, from the times of the latitudinarian Jahángír. Sultan Karím-ud-dín, the eldest son of Azím-ush-shan, was seized

---

* *Memoirs of Iradat Khan.*

at Láhore, through the agency of Hidayat Kesh Khan, and beheaded in the emperor's presence. Ali Tabar, son of Azím Shah, *Ferozmand*, the two sons of Kám Baksh, and other princes of the blood were all murdered. After these transactions the emperor marched from Láhore and made his entry into Delhi with all the pride of a conqueror.

The incapacity of Jahándar Shah.

Jahándar Shah was a weak and indolent prince, effeminate, licentious and fond of ease. He was addicted to low vices, unworthy of royalty, and he made himself the abject slave of the whims of a public courtesan. This woman, named Lál Kaur, obtained such an ascendancy over the king that he became her tool, and, forgetting his own dignity and decency, surrendered himself entirely to her society and influence. She received the title of Imtiyaz Mahal Begum (the most accomplished of the ladies), and an annual allowance of two *karors* of rupees for her household expenses, exclusive of her clothes and jewels. She also received the distinction of riding close to the emperor on an elephant covered with a canopy, a privilege enjoyed only by princes of the royal blood. The emperor's foster brother, Gokal Tash Khan, was raised to the dignity of Amír-ul-omerah, or lord premier, with the title of Khan Jahán Bahádur. Her brother, Khushál, was made commander of seven thousand horse, and her uncle, Niamat, received the command of five thousand. A woman named Zohra, keeper of a vegetable stall, one of Lál Kaur's particular friends, was promoted to high rank, with a suitable jagír. She shared in the sweets of her friend's elevation, and appeared in the streets on an elephant, richly caparisoned, with a retinue equal to that of the first noble of the empire, which she established close to the apartment of the royal ladies. The grandees and courtiers who sought favour, sent their presents to the royal favourite through Zohra. The emperor frequently rode with Lál Kaur in a chariot through the streets, where they purchased sometimes jewels, gold, silks and fine linen, and at other times greens, fruits and the most trifling articles. The detestable jaunts of the emperor and his mistress at last reached such a pitch, that, on a certain night, after spending the whole day in merriment and roaming in different gardens near the capital, they retired to a tavern, where they became insensible. After rewarding the tavern-keeper with a large sum and the grant of a village, they returned to the palace in a state of intoxication, But only the mistress entered the apartments, where, neglecting her sovereign, she slept heavily. The coachman, who had shared in the carousal of his royal master, without examining the coach, carried it to the stable. The next morning, the officers of the palace, not finding the emperor, were alarmed, and a search was made for his majesty, who, to the amazement of all, was found fast asleep in the arms of Zohra, one of his companions of the night, in the wagon, two miles from the palace. This scandalous event gave great offence to the nobles, but it excited only laughter in the weak Jahándar Shah and his abandoned favourites. The emperor became so dead to all feelings of shame and honour, that, in passing through the streets, he seized the wives and daughters of the lowest tradesmen, who were quite helpless. Once, in accordance with a vulgar superstition, he went, with his mistress, to bathe in the tank of Charaghi Delhi, in the hope that this ceremony would promote pregnancy. The mistress had the insolence to insult Zeb-ul-nissa, the learned daughter of the Emperor Aurangzeb, because she would not pay her compliments to her. She complained of this to the emperor, but the royal lady rejected the proposal of the base monarch with scorn, and resolutely maintained her own dignity.

He becomes the slave of a dancing girl.

Zohra, the keeper of a vegetable stall.

The emperor a perfect libertine.

A scandal.

Insult offered to Zeb-ul-nissa, the learned daughter of Aurangzeb.

The paramount power of Zulfikar Khan.

While the king abandoned himself to dissoluteness and indulged in most revolting vices, the Amír-ul-omerah, Zulfikar Khan, exercised the paramount power in the State. His will became absolute in all matters connected with the administration of the country; and his pride, according to Irádat Khan, was such that "even Pharaoh and Shadád could not have obtained admission to his threshhold." In the midst of this scene of disorder and imbecility, it was reported that Farrukhseer, son of Azím-ush-shan, the

Revolt of Farrukhseer.

favourite son of Bahádur Shah, assisted by the Sayads, Abdulla Khan, governor of Behar, and Husain Ali Khan, governor of Allahabád, both brothers was preparing for war at Patna, where public prayers had been read for him in the mosques and money coined in his name. A powerful army, under Az-ud-dín, the emperor's son, and Khwája Ahsan Khan, Khan-i-douran, brother of Gokal Tash Khan, was sent to oppose his progress, but was defeated. On this the emperor left his capital with an army of 70,000 horse, a numerous body of infantry and a train of artillery, with the

The battle of Agra, 1712.

Amír-ul-omerah, Zulfikar Khan, in the chief command. The two armies confronted each other on 30th December, 1712, on the plains of Agra. A fierce attack made by the Sayads threw Jahándar's army into confusion, and,

Defeat of the emperor.

the best of his generals having been slain, among them being his foster brother, Gokal Tash Khan, the thoughts of the craven emperor turned to his mistress, Lál Kaur, and, mounting her elephant, he retreated to Agra in the dusk of the evening. Zulfikar Khan maintained his ground until the first watch of the night, but, seeing that matters were past remedy, he left the field at the head of his troops, but in good order. The emperor, having shaved his beard and whiskers like a Hindu, and disguised him-

His flight to Delhi.

self by a change of dress, fled to the capital, in the night, with his mistress and a host of singers, eunuchs and people of all sorts attached to his person. On arriving at Delhi, instead of going to the citadel, he went to the house of the old wazír, Asad-ud-doula, who immediately seized him and placed him in confinement. Farrukhseer applauded the wazír's conduct, and Jahándar Shah was placed in the custody of Sayad Abdulla Khan, and

He is confined in Salemgarh.

kept in close confinement in the palace of Salemgarh. Thus ended the reign of the weak Jahándar Shah,* after a duration of only eleven months. Zulfikar Khan reached his father's palace in Delhi soon after Jahándar Shah.

Mr. Rodgers, in the *Journal of the Bengal Asiatic Society*, mentions the following inscriptions on the coins of Jahándar Shah :—

در آفاق زد سکه بر مهر و ماه   ابوالفتح غازی جهاندار شاه

"Abul Fath Ghazi Jahándar Shah put his stamp on the sun and moon throughout the world."

Another coin had the following inscription :—

بزد سکه بزرد چو صاحب قران   جهاندار شه باد شاه جهان

"The victorious Emperor Jahándar Shah struck coin in his dominions like the sun and moon."

The *Miftah-ul-Tawarikh* gives the following inscription :—

بزد سکه در ملک چون مهر و ماه   شهنشاه غازی جهاندار شاه

"The victorius Emperor Jahándar Shah struck coin in his dominions like the sun and moon."

CHAPTER XIX.

MUHAMMAD FARRUKHSEER.

Farrukhseer ascends the throne, 1713.

FARRUKHSEER was still on the battle-field when he ascended the throne at daybreak on 1st January 1713 A.D., and gave public audience. Entering Delhi on the 9th of that month, he commenced his reign of terror. Sayad Abdulla Khan received the dignity of wazír, with a rank of 7,000, and the title "Kutb-ul-Mulk Yári Wáfádár Zafarjang." His younger brother, Husein Ali Khan, was raised to the office of commander-in-chief, with a rank of 7,000 and the title "Amír-ul-omerah Ihtamam-ul-mulk." Muhammad Amin Khan was created "Itimad-ud-doula," and Chin Kilich Khan was honoured with the title of "Nizám-ul-mulk Bahadur Fattehjang" and invested with the viceroyalty of the Dekkan. Zulfikar Khan, having bound his hands together with his turban, presented himself before the emperor with his old father, Asad Khan, and implored pardon. His majesty, with every appearance of kindness, commanded Zulfikar Khan's hands to be released and presented him with robes and jewels. He then ordered Asad Khan to return home, and desired Zulfikar Khan to wait in an outer tent. Here the ex-minister was surrounded with a number of nobles and their servants, who taunted him for having been the cause of the death of Azím-ush-shan, the emperor's father, and Muhammad Karím. But he returned rough and sharp answers, and thereupon a leathern thong was thrown round his neck and pulled tight. He strove to disentangle the cord, but was assailed by a number of men with daggers and instantly despatched. The same day, Jahándar Shah was taken out of the small and dark room in the *Tirpolia* in which he was confined, and strangled. The emperor then directed that Jahándar Shah's head should be stuck upon a spear and carried through the most frequented parts of the city on an elephant, with the body of the late emperor thrown across the animal. The body of Zulfikar Khan was tied to the tail of the elephant, with the head downward, while the venerable old man, Asad Khan, attended by all the ladies of his family, in veiled carriages, followed the elephant on a palanquin. After being thus paraded through the whole city, the bodies were thrown down at the gate of the fort. The body of the late emperor was sent to the burial place of the family within the precincts of Húmáyún's tomb. On account of his old age Asad Khan's life was spared, but he was confined for life in Khan Jahán's palace, and all his assets and those of his son were sequestered. Most of the princes of the blood and the nobles of the old court were murdered in cold blood, and Az-ud-dín, son of Jahándar Shah, Wala Tabar, son of Muhammad Azim Shah, and Húmáyún Bakht, younger brother of Farrukhseer, a boy ten or eleven years old, were deprived of their sight by red-hot needles being drawn across their eyes. The tongue of Rájá Soba Chand, Zulfikar Khan's treasurer, who had exercised too much freedom in his speech, was cut off.

The rise of the Sayad brothers, Abdullah and Husein Ali.

The humiliation of Zulfikar Khan.

His tragic and cruel death.

Jahándar Shah executed.

Barbarous acts of the new emperor.

Murder of the princes royal.

Barbarous punishments.

The empire did not prosper under Farrukhseer. He was weak and timid, destitute of morals and capacity, and lavished favours on low people. The Wazír Abdulla Khan, on attaining power, gave himself up to pleasure

The power of the Hindu, Ratan Chand.

and left all the affairs of his high office in the hands of a Hindu named Ratan Chand, once a retail shop-keeper, but who now exercised uncontrollable authority over all Hindostán in the name of his indolent master.

The Sikhs become turbulent in the Panjáb.

The Sikhs, in the meantime, became turbulent in the Panjáb, and, emerging from the hills, laid waste the whole country between the Sutlej and Láhore. Abdul Samad Khan, *Dilerjang*, a Turrani nobleman, leaving Arif Khan, his lieutenant, in Káshmír, marched against the Sikhs, with Kamar-ud-dín Khan, Muhammad Amín Khan and Asghar Khan. The emperor himself moved towards the Panjáb with a large army. The Sikhs, blockaded and pressed by hunger and deprivation, surrendered at discretion. Two thousand of them were massacred and their guru, Bandá, sent in chains to Delhi, with his associates, where they were all tortured and put to death.* Abdul Samad Khan, having humiliated the Sikhs and caused the destruction of their leader Bandá, now took vigorous steps to destroy their power and to extirpate the race. A royal edict was issued to put all who professed the religion of Nának to the sword, and a money reward was offered for the head of every Sikh. The irritated Mahomedans gave them no quarter, and wherever a Sikh was found he was butchered unmercifully. In order to give full effect to the royal mandate, Mahomedans and Hindus were strictly enjoined to clip their hair short. The Hindus were ordered to shave their heads, and any Hindu found with long beard or hair was immediately slain. These extreme measures of resentment and persecution spread terror and consternation throughout the whole Sikh nation. Those who remained of them fled to the mountains to the north-east of the Panjáb, or concealed themselves in remote jungles. Many who could not abandon their homes changed their external appearance, had their beard and moustaches clipped, and gave up their outward form of worship.

Punishment of the Sikhs.

Death of the old veteran, Asad Khan, 1716.

During the sixth year of Farrukhseer's reign, or in 1716 A.D., the venerable Asad Khan, father of Zulfikar Khan, who had been in the public service since about the twentieth year of Shah Jahán, died in the ninety-fifth year of his age. He was a member of Mír Jahán's family, and, with a lofty spirit and indomitable courage, nevertheless possessed a placid disposition and a charitable heart. He never stooped to the nobles of the new court, but lived with dignity, and preserved his influence throughout the empire to the very last. The old man on his death-bed prophesied the fall of the Delhi empire. He said to the messenger who had been sent by the emperor on a visit of condolence on his part: "Now the day of retribution seems at hand; the emperor is full in its way; and I much fear, from the appearance of the general disaffection throughout the kingdom, that ruin sits beneath the columns of the throne of Tymúr." These words were ominous, as the event proved; the fate of the empire was indeed sealed.

He prophesies the fall of the house of Tymúr.

Breach between the emperor and the Sayad brothers.

The emperor considered the yoke of the Sayad brothers burdensome, and became anxious to strip them of their power. Husein Ali, one of the brothers, was sent on a war with the Mahrattas. The imperial troops under him having been distracted, he entered into a convention with Rájá Sahuthe, Mahratta, by which the claims of the latter to independent sovereignty were recognized, and other concessions given to the Mahrattas. The emperor refused to ratify this disgraceful treaty, and the breach between him and the Sayads became wider. The minister, making common cause with the Mahrattas, advanced upon Delhi with his own army and a force of 10,000 Mahratta auxiliaries, and took possession of the city, after some opposition. Considerable sympathy towards the emperor was shown by the citizens of

Husein Ali, assisted by the Mahrattas, takes possession of Delhi, 1718.

* For a full account of these proceedings see the *Life of Bandá Guru*.

Delhi, among whom he was popular, and several of the Turkish nobles and courtiers tried to strike a last blow for the defence of their emperor. They even succeeded in driving out the Mahratta guards of the city gates and killing fifteen hundred of the enemy's troops; but irresolution on the part of the emperor demoralized his supporters, and he was compelled to conceal himself for safety in the recesses of the seraglio. A body of negroes and armed Abyssinians, Georgian and Calmuc women, always guarded the king's chamber. The resistance offered by them having been overpowered, the soldiery penetrated within the gate, and every apartment was searched for the emperor. The women and the guard of Amazons were tortured to compel them to point out the place of his retreat, and he was at length dragged from his concealment. At this sight a number of the princesses and ladies of the first rank, among whom were the emperor's mother, wife and daughter, ran to his assistance, crying and wailing, and, forming a circle round his person, entreated the Afghan soldiers to liberate him. He was, however, disengaged from the women, thrown into a dungeon on the top of the *Tirpolia*, and partially deprived of sight. The chronogram commemorating this event is found in the sentence:

The emperor is seized and blinded, 1718.

فاعتبروا يا اولي الابصار

"Take warning, ye that have eyes."

Suddenly it was announced to the citizens that Shams-ud-dín Rafi-ul-darajat, the younger son of Rafi-ul-kadr, and grandson of Bahádur Shah, had assumed the regalia of the empire, and that Farrukhseer had ceased to reign. The kettledrums thundered forth at the palace gates, the heralds sounded from the porticoes of the court halls, the salutes boomed through the morning air. The young prince, a stripling of twenty, was taken out in haste from the State prison of Salemgarh, adjoining the palace, and placed on the throne. He had no time even to bathe and clean himself, and was thrust upon the throne in the clothes that he had on when he got out of his bed. Abdulla Khan had just time to take off his neck a string of large pearls and throw it over the robe of the prince. Farrukhseer, after suffering all the agonies of a lingering death, was flung into his solitary cell. A leathern thong, or the bowstring, was strained round his neck. The prince tried to keep it off his neck, by holding it with both his hands, and struggled desperately with his hands and feet. He gave vent to his feelings by reproaching the wazírs and even the Divine justice which suffered such wicked men to live. But there was no escape, and the unhappy prince had the misfortune of suffering dint of blows in addition to a painful death caused by a dagger. The event happened on 16th May 1719. His body was carried to the sepulchre of the Emperor Húmáyún and buried there with due pomp and magnificence.* He had reigned six years and four months.

Rafi-ul-darajat ascends the throne, 1719.

Cruel execution of Farrukhseer, 1719.

---

* The funeral was attended by a large crowd of leading citizens, but no sooner had the procession quitted the suburbs of the town than the chief mourners were hooted and assailed with stones, bricks and clods of earth.—*Syrul Mutakherin.*

The inscription on the coin of this emperor was as follows :—

سکه زد از فضل حق بر سیم و زر — باد شاه بحر و بر فرخ سیر

"Farrukhseer, the monarch of the land and sea, put his stamp on silver and gold through the grace of God."

The mischievous children of Delhi parodied the couplet thus—

سکه زد بر گندم و موتهه و مٹر — باد شاه دانهه کش فرخ سیر

"The greedy King Farrukhseer struck coin on wheat, lentils, and pea."

CHAPTER XX.

SHAMS-UD-DÍN ABUL BARAKAT RAFI-UL-DARAJAT.

A GENERAL amnesty having been granted on the accession of Rafi-ul-darajat he received the congratulations of Kutb-ul-mulk Sayad Abdulla and other grandees of the empire. The poll-tax on the Hindus, which had been revived during the reign of the late emperor, at the instance of his secretary, Inayatullah, was abolished, and assurances of security and protection were given to the people throughout the country. The two Sayad brothers Kutb-ul-mulk Abdulla and Amír-ul-omerah Husein Ali, governed the empire, but the puppet king died of consumption within three months of his accession.*

RAFI-UD-DOULA, SHAH JAHÁN II.

On the death of Rafi-ul-darajat, the Sayad brothers, the king-makers, raised his younger brother, Rafi-ud-doula, to the throne, under the title of Shah Jahán II. Like his deceased brother, he had no part in the government of the country and was placed under the direction of Himmat Khan, an amír who directed all his affairs, public and private, and arranged for his food and clothing. He was not allowed to go to the mosque for prayers on Friday, or to go hunting, or even to talk to any of the grandees of the court, except in the presence of one of the Sayads or his guardian. Neko Sere, younger son of

Insurrection at Agra.

Prince Akber and grandson of Aurangzeb, assisted by the officers of Agra and the militia of the neighbourhood, assumed independence and proclaimed himself king. Amír-ul-omerah Husein Ali gave him battle and made him prisoner. At the fort of Agra immense treasures, consisting of jewels and valuables, fell into the hands of the victor. Among the rest were the effects

The effects of Núr Jahán Begum and Mumtaz Mahal.

of Núr Jahán Begum and Mumtaz Mahal, amounting to two or three *karors* of rupees. There was a sheet of pearls prepared by Shah Jahán for his beloved queen, Mumtaz Mahal, which was spread over his tomb on the anniversary of her marriage and on Friday nights. There was also the ewer of Núr Jahán and her cushion of woven gold and precious pearls, with borders of valuable garnets and emeralds. The booty created a quarrel between the Sayad brothers, and it was not until Ratan Chand, the minister of Abdulla, had intervened that, four months after, Husein Ali grudgingly surrendered twenty lacs of rupees to his brother as his share of the spoil.

After a nominal reign of three months and some days, Rafi-ud-doula died of dysentery and mental disorder. Like his brother, he was buried within the precincts of the mausoleum of Khwája Kutb-ud-dín.

---

* According to Mr. Rodgers, this king struck coin with the following inscription :—

زد سکه بهند با هزاران برکات
شاهنشه بحر و بر رفیع الدرجات

"Rafi-ul-darajat, the monarch of land and sea,
Struck coin in India, with thousands of blessings."

CHAPTER XXI.

ABUL FATHA ROUSHAN AKHTAR NASÍR-UD-DÍN MUHAMMAD SHAH.

On the death of Rafi-ud-doula, the Sayad ministers called Roushan Akhtar, son of Khajasta Akhtar Jahán Shah, one of the sons of Bahádur Shah, then in confinement, to the throne. Since the death of his uncle, Jahándar Shah, this prince, with his mother, Mariam Makani, a princess of uncommon spirit and tact, had lived in obscurity in the fort of Delhi. He was born on Friday, the 23rd of Rabi-ul-awal, 1114 A.H., or 5th August A.D. 1702, in the neighbourhood of Ghazni; and, at the time of his being called to the throne, was a handsome youth of eighteen. Great care had been bestowed on his training, and his benevolent countenance seemed to prognosticate future greatness. Availing himself of a fortunate hour, he ascended the throne on 15th Zikaád, 1131 A.H. (October 1719 A.D.), and assumed the title of Abul Fatah Nasír-ud-dín Muhammad Shah Badshah Ghazi.* Brought up in the school of adversity, and fully sensible of the delicacy of his situation, the young emperor had the forbearance to conform to the guidance of the two rival politicians to whom he owed his elevation. But it was not long before he felt their yoke burdensome and formed a plot to get rid of them. While Husein Ali was marching an army towards the Dekkan to subdue a refractory chief, a hired assassin, by name Mír Hyder, a Calmuc, approaching his palanquin, attracted his attention by waving a petition in his hand. The minister was then going to his tent. He made a sign to his servants to allow the man to approach, and, taking the petition from his hand, began to read it, when Hyder dexterously plunged his dagger into his heart. The blow was fatal, and the minister rolled over a corpse from the opposite side of his litter.† He had only time to say "Kill the emperor," thereby showing his suspicions of his sovereign's complicity; and his nephew made a desperate attack with his troops on the emperor, in deference to the dying injunctions of his uncle, but was himself shot in an attempt to penetrate the king's tents, and his followers dispersed. Abdulla, hearing of his brother's fate, marched against the emperor, at the head of a large army, but he was defeated and taken prisoner. Muhammad Shah, now a free sovereign, entered his capital amidst the shouts of his people. Three years after his fall, Sayad Abdulla died in obscurity, on 19th September, 1723.

The princess Mariam Makani.

Birth of Muhammad Shah, 1702.

He ascends the throne, 1719.

The new emperor feels the burden of the Sayad brothers' yoke.

Assassination of Husein Ali, October, 1720.

Abdullah taken prisoner, 1720.

Death of Sayad Abdullah, 1723.

---

* The Lord of Victory, the Champion of the Faith Muhammad Shah, the King Hero (literally one who fights against the infidels).

Muhammad Shah being very handsome at the time of his accession to the throne, a poet composed the following verse in commemoration of this event :—

روشن اختر بود اکنون ماه شد — یوسف از زندان برآمد ماه شد

"It was a bright star, now it became the moon. Joseph came out of prison and was king."

Note.—The eastern poets call Joseph, the moon of Egypt. Muhammad Shah is here compared to Joseph, and the prison has reference to the king's confinement before coming to the throne.

† The assassin was instantly cut to pieces by the fury of the attendants.

Death of Badshah Begum, 1721.

In the month of Zilhij, 1133 (September 1721), died Badshah Begum daughter of Aurangzeb, called also Zinet-ul-nissa Begum.

Revolt of Husein Khan, the Afghan chief of Kasúr.

Nawab Abdul Samad Khan, *Dilerjang*, viceroy of the Panjáb, had kept the Sikhs well in check. He was now called upon to take the field against the Pathans of Kasúr, south of Láhore, who had raised the standard of revolt under their leader Husein Khan, an Afghan, and taken possession of some fertile districts about Kasúr and Láhore. The Afghan commander, expelling the collectors and officers of the crown, assembled troops, with which he gave battle to Kutb-ud-dín, the general sent by the viceroy of Láhore to chastise him, and succeeded in dispersing his cavalry, slaughtering the commander and carrying off all his baggage. He soon found himself at the head of eight or nine thousand horse, by whose aid he levied contributions in the surrounding country. The viceroy of Láhore marched against him at the head of seven or eight thousand troops. The two armies met at Chúnian. The centre of the Láhore army was commanded by Kerim Kuli Khan; the right columns were placed under Jani Khan and Khwája Rahmatulla, two of the viceroy's relations, and the left under Arif Khan, his lieutenant, and Akgar Khan, the whole being under the command of Hafiz Khan, brother of Khan Mirza. The advance guard was composed of one thousand Rohilla Afghans, while the viceroy posted himself in front of the left column. On the side of the enemy, Mustafa Khan, own nephew of Husein Khan, was placed in the first line, together with Rahmat Khan, Seid Khan and other Pathan commanders, all mounted on elephants. A desperate fight took place, in which the viceroy of Láhore was on the point of being borne down, when Akgar Khan rushed upon the enemy with his corps of Durranís, and the example set by him to his men at once changed the state of affairs. Husein Khan's army was thrown into confusion. His elephant driver fell dead from his seat. Shahbaz Beg, his religious preceptor, who always took a seat on his right hand, was also killed, while a musket ball, discharged by Hafiz Ali Khan, having pierced Husein Khan's forehead, he too fell and was immediately despatched by the sword of the brave Afghan warriors. The Pathan troops, now considerably reduced, fled in disorder, and the drums of victory were beaten in the imperial army. The battle took place in the time of the Sayad ministers, who sent letters of congratulation to Abdul Samad Khan, and conferred upon the Láhore governor the additional title of *Sef-ud-doula*, or "Sword of State."

The battle of Chúnian.

Defeat of the Afghans.

Disturbances in Káshmír.

Abdul Nabi, the Káshmírian, otherwise known as Mohtawi Khan.

Peace was scarcely restored in the Panjáb when religious disturbances of a most serious character took place in the neighbouring country of Káshmír. One Abdul Nabi, a Káshmírian *Mullah*, otherwise called Mohtawi Khan, having assembled a large number of disorderly Mussalmans, demanded that henceforward Hindus should be interdicted from riding on horses, from wearing white robes (*jámas*), from putting on turbans and armour, from going on excursions in fields and gardens except at stated hours, and bathing on certain days. The whole Hindu quarters of the city were plundered and set on fire, and many Hindus were mercilessly killed. Mír Ahmad Khan, the viceroy of Káshmír, who had refused to sanction the proposed reforms of the bigoted *Mullahs*, was attacked in his place with stones and brickbats. Seid Wali, the governor's nephew, and Zulfikar Beg, the Kotwal's deputy, were slain by the mob. The governor opposed the seditious insurgents with regular troops, but was defeated. Elated with this success, Mohtawi Khan began to subject the Hindus to the grossest oppression and torture. Many had their noses and ears cut off, others were forcibly circumcised, and in some instances they were horribly mutilated. After these acts of wanton barbarity, Mohtawi Khan, having repaired to the great

Illtreatment of the Hindus in Káshmír.

The bigoted Mullahs.

The Hindus frightfully tortured.

mosque at the head of a grand throng, deposed the imperial governor and proclaimed himself ruler of Káshmír with the title of Dindár Khan. News of the outbreak in Káshmír having reached Delhi, Momin Khan was deputed to restore order in that country. Mohtawi Khan repented, but it was now too late. The bellies of his two young children, who always accompanied him, were ripped open before his eyes, and he was himself subsequently killed with all the tortures which resentment could prompt. The followers of Mohtawi Khan avenged the death of their leader in a fearful way. They hacked to pieces about three thousand of the inhabitants in the *Shiá* quarters of the city, blinded many, seized and carried away a vast number of women and children, and plundered property amounting to several lakhs of rupees. Among the slain were a large number of Moghal travellers, who fell with their wives and families. They then proceeded to the house of the Kazi and Shah Nawáz Khan, the Bakshi general of the Moghal army. The latter remained concealed in his house, but the Kazi, having changed his dress, made his escape. The infuriated mob razed the Kazi's house to the ground, leaving not a brick on the spot. It was only after great exertions and much bloodshed that the Imperialists were able to restore order in Káshmír.

Mohtawi Khan proclaims himself ruler of Káshmír.

He is defeated and slain.

His death is revenged.

Shocking barbarities.

Peace restored in Káshmír.

Abdul Samad Khan died at Láhore in June, 1737. The emperor, on hearing of his death, bestowed a *khilat* of condolence on his brother, the Wazír Kamr-ud-dín Khan. Other robes of condolence from his majesty were received by the family of the deceased at Láhore. Zakaria Khan, the eldest son of the deceased, who received the title of Khan Bahádur, as a distinction, was appointed to the governments of Láhore and Múltán. The new governor ruled the Panjáb with vigour and conferred the appointment of prime minister on Lakhpat Rai, Khatri, of Láhore, who had been the trusted dewán of his father. His brother, Jaspat Rai, acted as secretary and counsellor. The title of rájá was conferred on both brothers, but, out of modesty, they never assumed the appellation. Zakaria Khan took active measures for the repopulation of the towns and villages which had been devastated by the ravages of the Sikhs, and made *takávi* advances to the agricultural classes to induce them to resume the cultivation of the land. He sent detachments of troops to guard the highways and protect travellers from the predatory incursions of the Sikhs. Munificent rewards were offered for the arrest of notorious Sikh robbers and plunderers, and they were daily brought in chains and executed in the streets of Láhore. These vigorous measures had the desired effect. Peace and tranquillity reigned in the Panjáb, the Sikhs were completely vanquished, and were not to be seen even in Mánjha, the country chiefly inhabited by them, and the Panjáb enjoyed peace for twenty-one years preceding the invasion of India by Nádir Shah in 1738.

Death of Abdul Samad Khan, 1737.

Zakaria Khan, Khan Bahádur, appointed governor of Láhore and Multán.

The brothers Lakhpat Rai and Jaspat Rai.

Active measures of Zakaria Khan.

The Panjáb at peace.

Khan Bahádur exercised absolute authority in the Panjáb, and the weakness of the court at Delhi raised him to the rank of satrap. He constructed spacious palaces for his private residence, and also a fine mosque at Begumpúra, three miles from the modern Láhore, where he passed his days in ease as an indifferent spectator of the concerns of the court of Delhi and of the progress and rise of the Mahrattas.

The Panjáb Viceroy assumes the position of a satrap.

The grandees of foremost rank about the court at this time were Saádat Khan, a Persian adventurer, viceroy of Oudh, and Chin Kilich Khan, a Turkish noble, viceroy of the Dekkan, who afterwards laid the foundations of independent monarchies in their respective provinces, but who now resided at the court. Saádat Khan was a *Shiá*, and Chin Kilich Khan, a *Sunni*. Their mutual rivalry gave rise to party spirit among the Omerahs of the court, and this materially affected the government of the country, which was

Party factions created at court.

Saádat Khan.

Chin Kilich Khan.

The grandees of the empire.

already manifesting signs of decay. Amín Khan, the Turráni noble, was made wazír; Kamr-ud-dín obtained the household, and Mír Hyder Khan, a military adventurer of the Chughattai race, and Hyder Kúli Khan, important commands in the military department.

The emperor resigns himself to pleasurable pursuits.

The emperor, freed from the thraldom of the Sayad brothers, resigned himself to ease and pleasure. His favourite counsellors were dissolute young men like Amír Khan, who was created Umdat-ul-mulk, and some other young nobles of lively temper and disposed to good fellowship. His mistress, named Cowki, daughter of Shah Ján Muhammad, a darvish, had such an ascendancy over him that he put her in charge of his private signet, which she used at her discretion. She also signed, "by order," answers to petitions on State affairs, which she carried within the seraglio. Disgusted with these proceedings, and finding himself overlooked, Asif Jah (the nizám), who had assumed the office of wazír on the demise of Amín Khan, withdrew from the court, as also did the Persian immigrant, Saádat Khan. Public business was neglected, and disorders multiplied. The Mahrattas had overrun the whole country between Ajmere and Gwalior, and, pushing forward to the very gates of Agra, struck terror into the hearts of the populace. Meanwhile, a formidable riot took place in the imperial capital, which was not suppressed until the Wazír Kamr-ud-dín Khan, by his personal exertions, dislodged the riotous Hindus from the cathedral mosque which they had seized, using rockets against them. Again, a great pestilence broke out and ravaged the country from Patna to Láhore. It was in the midst of these troubles that another storm, by far the severest that had ever been experienced in India since its invasion by Tamerlane and Babar, burst upon the country, now reduced to a state of hopeless wreck and decay. The Persian conqueror, Nádir Shah, a prince of the same stamp as the Tartar Changez Khan, or the Chughattai Tymúr, having made himself master of the whole country from the Tigris to the Indus, invaded Hindostán under circumstances which will form the subject of a separate chapter.

Distracted state of the empire.

The rise of Nádir Shah.

CHAPTER XXII.

THE INVASION OF NÁDIR SHAH.

Before proceeding with our narrative of the events connected with the invasion of India by this great Asiatic conqueror, it may be interesting to give here a brief sketch of his life.

Birth and parentage of Nádir Kúli, afterwards known as Nádir Shah.

Nádir Kúli belonged to the Afshars,* a Turkomán tribe, and was born, in December 1688, in the castle of Dastgarh, fifty miles north of Mashhad, the capital of Khorásán. From a petty freebooter and highway robber, he became the greatest warrior and conqueror Persia has ever produced, the deliverer of his country, and the terror of the whole of Asia. His father, Imám Kúli, was chief of the Afshar tribe, and governor of the fortress above-

* The Afshar are a clan of the Tartar tribe, who had formerly removed from the Trans-Oxus provinces to avoid the oppression of the Moghals, their time being divided between war and pastoral work. Like the nomadic Arabs, they changed their quarters as frequently as circumstances demanded. Nádir was of humble origin. Mirza Mahdi, his private secretary and biographer, makes an apology for the obscurity of his extraction by saying, "he was a precious pearl which owed its excellence and brightness to its own intrinsic value, and not to the river which gave it birth."

named, where a guard was kept to prevent the Uzbek Tartars from making incursions into Khorásán. The father of Nádir Kúli dying during his minority, his uncle took command of the fortress, which had been hereditary in the family, in the name of the minor, bnt when Nádir came of age, he refused to deliver the trust to him. The youthful Nádir, being thus deprived of his birthright, went to Mashhad, a city famous for the sepulchre of Imám Ali Razá, and there entered into the service of Beglerbeg,* as one of the under-masters of ceremonies. In this office he behaved so well that the prince soon gave him the command of a troop of horse. When seventeen years old, he was taken prisoner by the Uzbek Tartars, with whom he had had frequent skirmishes, but, after remaining in slavery for about four years, he effected his escape. Being now reduced to poverty, he was forced to borrow small sums of money of any who would lend them to him, to procure the common necessaries of life. He led a life of adventure for some years, and, collecting armed followers around him, he at length made his power supreme in his native province.

He enters the service of a prince of Mashhad.

Is taken prisoner by the Uzbek Tartars.

When the Afghan *Khiljis*, the greatest of the western tribes who inhabit the country round Kandahar, expelled Shah Husein, the last of the once powerful line of the *Safvi* kings who ruled over the destinies of Persia for two hundred years, and Mahmúd, the son of Mír Weis, the *Khilji*, having put to death Husein with all his family, except one son named Thamasp, became ruler of Persia (October 1722), that empire was assailed by the Turks and Russians, who had entered into a confederacy for the purpose of dismembering the kingdom. The western provinces were conquered by the Porte, and the northern, comprising Gilan (the ancient Hyrcania) and other places bordering on the Caspian Sea, by the Muscovites, under the Czar Peter. Thamasp, the son of the vanquished monarch of Persia, fled to the Caspian and took protection with a pastoral tribe called Kajar, who occupied the elevated plains which extend over a great part of Persia. He was there joined by Nádir Kúli, then in the prime of his youth, at the head of a body of hardy and warlike shepherds, animated with patriotic feelings. Nádir, in one of his first exploits, seized Mashhad, and then recovered Khorásán from the Abdális. The rule of the Afghans under Ashraf, the son of Mahmúd, the *Khilji*, had become intolerable on account of the new king's grinding tyranny and oppression, and had produced in the mind of every Persian a deadly hatred of the very name *Afghan*, a feeling which exists to this day. He waged a war against the *Khiljis* under Ashraf, and completely routed the Afghans, who were killed in great numbers in the battle, or perished in the desert on their way home (1828). Ashraf was assassinated by a Bilúch during his retreat from Kirman to Kandahar, 1729.

Nádir Kúli joins Thamasp, prince of Persia,

And wages a war against the *Khiljis*,

Whom he defeats, 1728.

The adventurer, Nádir Kúli, placed the diadem on the head of the rightful heir, Thamasp, who, for his services, conferred on him the viceroyalty of Khorásán, Mazindaran, Sistan, and Kirmán. Nádir, who had hitherto made no pretensions to sovereign power, assumed the title of Thamasp Kúli (or the slave of Thamasp), with the addition of that of "Khan." He then marched against the Turks and recovered from them the province of Tabrez.

His wars against the Turks and the Abdalis.

A party of the Abdális had by this time overrun Khorásán and laid siege to Mashhad, then held by Ibráhim, Nádir's brother, whom they defeated in a pitched battle. Nádir again engaged the tribe, and, completely subduing it, recovered the lost territories. The Abdális, under Zulfikar Khan, the brother of Ahmad Shah, and son of Zamán Khan, were driven

* A title signifying, in the Turkish language, "Lord of Lords."

Lays siege to Herát, 1731.

back to their own territory with great slaughter. In the beginning of 1731 Nádir laid siege to Herát, a task even more arduous than that of reducing the Abdális, and took it after a most obstinate resistance, which lasted ten months. At this juncture, both the Abdális and the *Khiljis* entered into a combination against the invader. After this conquest, the victor banished the leading Saddozais to Múltán, and compelled a large force of the Abdális to join the army. It was about this time that Nádir relinquished the *Shiá* faith of his ancestors and embraced *Sunniism*, thus enlisting the sympathy of the Abdális, who subsequently became his most powerful allies and devoted followers.

He renounces the *Shiá* and adopts the *Sunni* faith.

In 1731, Nádir defeated the Turks in Hamdán and regained the Armenian provinces, which had been seized by the Turks during the reign of Ashraf, but on his return he was annoyed with his sovereign for entering into a disadvantageous treaty with the Turks, and, having deposed him, deprived him of sight. The wary general did not, however, yet venture to occupy the vacant throne himself, but, ordering the king's son, who was then in his cradle, to be brought out of the seraglio, placed the royal diadem on his head, and proclaimed him king, under the name of Abbas III, 1732. The puppet king died in 1736. The way to the throne was now clear for Nádir. He had a firm hold on the affections of the soldiery and on the fears of the nation. But even now this sagacious politician did not give up his characterstic caution. At Murgháb, he summoned all the grandees of the kingdom, the civil and military officers, the governors of provinces and magistrates, and, amidst an assembly of 100,000 persons was, by popular acclamation, saluted as the king of the Persians, under the name of Nádir Shah. Like Cæsar, he went through the form of refusing a proffered crown. He thanked them for the honour they had done him, which was contrary to his intention in calling them together, yet he looked on the voice of the people as the voice of God, and, with seeming reluctance, and on the condition that the *Shiá* sect be abolished, and that of the *Sunnis* established throughout the kingdom, he at last agreed to accept his elevation to the throne, and was crowned king, February 26th, 1736.* He married his eldest son to the sister of Shah Thamasp, thereby allying his own family with that of the Safvian kings, who still commanded the respect of the people. It was his policy, while usurping the possessions of other sovereigns, thus to unite his own family by marriage ties with those of the vanquished monarchs; and he subsequently formed such alliances with the emperor of Bokhára, a

Deposes and blinds his own sovereign.

His cautious measures.

Is saluted king of the Persians amidst acclamations, under the name Nádir Shah, 1736.

Affiance with the Safvian family.

---

* Nádir Shah, on being proclaimed king, struck coins in his name bearing the following inscription :—

سکه بر زر کرد نام سلطنت اندر جهان   نادر ایران زمین و خسرو گیتی پناه

"The coins of Nádir of Persia, protector of the world, have proclaimed his empire throughout the earth."

On the reverse, in a cypher, was the inscription :— الخير في ما وقع

Meaning, "What is past is best." The mumerical value of the letters of this motto make up 1148, the year of his elevation to the throne.

At Kandahar he struck coins, which had the word السلطان نادر "The Sultan Nádir," on one side, and the words خلد الله ملكه - ضرب في قندهار "May God perpetuate his reign. Struck at Kandahar," on the other.

After his victory at Karnál, he struck the following coin in India :—

هست سلطان بر سلاطين جهان   شاه شاهان نادر صاحب قران

"The King of Kings on the Earth and the Lord of Lords is Nádir, the Blessed."

On the reverse—

خلد الله ملكه - ضرب دار الخلافه شاه جهان آباد

"May God prolong his reign : struck Shah at Jahánábád, the capital, 1152."

descendant of Changez Khan, and with Muhammad Shah, the emperor of Delhi.

His policy in such a union.

He required the people to take an oath of submission and fealty, to which they tamely and readily submitted. The *Múllah Báshi*, or high priest, had the audacity to address the king thus: "As to matters of religion, we have the law of God and the traditions of his Prophet, Muhammad, to guide us; it is not for princes to make innovations therein, and, therefore, I humbly hope your majesty will not begin your reign by attempting to overthrow the established religion." These words were too bold to be borne by the high-spirited Nádir, who immediately ordered the múllah to be strangled. Collecting then the Mahomedan priests, he asked them how they employed the vast income allowed them by the State. They answered that it was spent on religious objects, such as the maintenance of colleges, the salaries of the priests and the attendants on a large number of mosques, in which prayers were hourly offered for the success of the arms of their prince and the prosperity of the empire of Persia. He told the múllahs, that experience had made it quite clear that their prayers had not been heard, for the empire had been on the decline for the past fifty years, and had been almost ruined by invasions and rebellions until, by the command of God, his victorious armies had come to defend the lives and property of the people; that it was his royal pleasure that those poor priests (meaning his soldiers) who had followed his standard to give liberty to the Persians, should be first provided for, and that, therefore, the greater part of the church lands and revenues should be confiscated and appropriated for the support of the army. This order was carried out, and it was found, on computation, that an income of 10,00,000 tomans, or £3,000,000 per annum was thus saved to the State. The priests were directed to find other means for their subsistence. Nádir then published an edict ordering all his subjects to conform to the *Sunni* religion, on pain of his royal displeasure. This edict directed that, at the time of calling to prayers and standing up at prayer, the words *Ali, Wali-Ullah* علي ولي الله '*And Ali, the friend of God*,' which were always added to the *Kalima* by the *Shias*, be omitted.* It being also usual with the governors in their assemblies after *Fatiha and Takbír*† to say in the prayer, "May the king from whom all our fortunes flow live for ever," Nádir Shah ordered that the practice of using such expressions at prayers should be discontinued. He observed: "As a *Takbír* for prolonging the life of a mortal man is vain and of no effect, I expressly order that every Khan who is master of a *Tabal*‡ and ensign, say it in this manner: 'Thanks be to the true king for all benefits.'" The edict concluded in the following words: "Henceforward all persons must observe these settled regulations and written orders; for whoever deviates therefrom will incur the displeasure of the king of kings. Written in the royal resid-

The impudence of a *Múllah Báshi*.

Allowances to the priests abolished.

Edict forbidding the use of the *Kalima* as used by the *Shias*.

Prayers for the long life of the king discontinued.

* The *Kalima* is thus read by the *Shias*:—

لااله الاالله محمد الرسول الله و علي ولي الله

"There is no god but God, and Muhammad is the Prophet of God, *and Ali, the friend of God*." Nádir Shah ordered the words in *italics* to be struck out of the *Kalima*.

† The *Fatiha* is a prefatory prayer, which is generally the first *sura* or chapter of the *Quran*. *Takbir* is repeating three times the words الله اكبر *Allah-o-Akbar*, "God is greatest," before the *Kalima*,

لااله الاالله محمد الرسول الله "There is no god but God, and Muhammad is the Prophet of God."

‡ The *Tabal* is a small drum which general officers fix to their saddles. The possession of it is a mark of rank.

ence of Ispahan in the month of Saffar, 1149" (June 1736 A.D.). The edict was received with great joy by most of the king's subjects, particularly by his soldiers, who, being all *Sunnis*, became personally attached to him.

Resumption of war with the Turks.

He resumed war with the Turks and recovered the whole of the territory which had been occupied by the Porte and the Russians, making peace with both powers.

Conquest of Kandahar and Balkh.

Nádir now embarked on his great enterprise, the subjugation of the *Khiljis*, and the restoration of Kandahar to the Persian kingdom. He marched with an army of 80,000 men and was joined by the Abdális, now his staunch allies. The *Khiljis*, under Husein Khan, the governor of Kandahar, made a desperate resistance, but after a siege which lasted about eighteen months, Kandahar fell into the hands of the Persians (1738), and the whole country surrounding it was annexed to the kingdom of Persia. Zulfikar Khan and his brother, Ahmad Shah, were made prisoners in Kandahar during the siege of that city. Nádir released the brothers and sent them to Mazindarán, in command of a force of their own tribe. While the blockade of Kandahar was going on, the Shah's son, Raza Kuli Mirza, conquered Balkh, and achieved a great victory over the king of Bokhára in person, on the banks of the Oxus.

Victory over the king of Bokhára.

Embassies to the court of Muhammad Shah.

During the siege of Kandahar, a large number of Afghans fled to the territory of the Indian emperor and sought protection there. Nádir Shah, who was determined to extirpate the whole race of Afghans, sent his confidential agent, Ali Mardán Khan, as ambassador to the court of Muhammad Shah, the emperor of Hindostán, to prevent the influx of Afghan fugitives into his territory near Ghazni, and to expel those who had already found an asylum in his dominions. The emperor received the envoy with every mark of respect, and dismissed him with an assurance that active measures would be taken to intercept the Afghan rebels, and that fresh supplies of troops would be sent to the Persian borders. Nothing, however, came of the emperor's promise, and a second embassy, under Muhammad Khan Turkomán, was sent to India with the same request as before, and returned with renewed assurances of help on the part of the Indian sovereign. Shortly after this, however, the Afghans fled in troops from the newly subjugated province of Kandahar, and found an asylum in Kábul and Ghází, and still no steps were taken by the Indian sovereign towards intercepting the progress of the fugitives. Nádir Shah was greatly incensed at the apathy of his perfidious ally, who had thus harboured the most dangerous enemies of the Persian monarchy. He therefore sent a third embassy, under a Persian nobleman, with instructions not to stay at Delhi for more than forty days, but the ambassador was detained at Delhi for about a year, without a reply being given him. The Shah issued stringent orders for the envoy to quit the capital of the Moghal immediately, which he did, without even now receiving an answer from the emperor or his ministers. The Moghal was at this time engaged in a contest with the Mahrattas, and his court was divided,—one faction being led by Khan-i-Dauran Khan, the commander-in-chief of the Indian armies, favored by the emperor, and the other by Chin Kilich Khan, surnamed Asaf Jáh, who was at this time subadar of the Dekkan. Probably the Indian emperor did not attach any importance to Nádir Shah's demand, and the great Moghal thought it below his dignity to recognise Nádir as the legitimate sovereign of the Persian empire. The energies of the Moghal were absorbed in the settlement of the difficulties created by the incursions of the Mahrattas, and no troops could probably be spared for the purpose of guarding the Indian frontiers, which then extended to Ghází and Kábul. However that may be, the Persian

Muhammad Shah's breach of faith.

His detention of the Persian ambassador.

The Moghal engaged in a contest with the Mahrattas.

monarch was greatly irritated by the disingenuous and insidious conduct of the emperor of Hindostán, and considered it a direct insult to his sovereign authority. About the same time letters were received by the Shah from Nizám-ul-Múlk and Saádat Khan, the disaffected Omerahs of the Moghal court, inviting him to march to India, extirpate the family of Tymúr, and assume the reins of government himself. To redeem the honour of his empire, and encouraged by the representations he received from India, Nádir Shah resolved upon an invasion of that country, and, with an army of 1,25,000 horse, Kazil-báshis, Georgians, Turks, Khorasánis, Balkhis, &c., all inured to fatigue and hardships, he set out from Kandahar in May 1738 A.D. (about the vernal equinox of 1149 Hijri). He passed the rivulet called the Mákhur, which was then the boundary between the Persian and Indian empires, and took the road to Gházní, the capital of Zabulistán. The governor of that city, with the chief residents, came out to meet the king, with rich presents, and offered his submission. The Persian army advanced like the waves of an angry sea, which the governor thought it beyond his power to resist. The gates of the city were opened for the Persian king, who, having garrisoned it with his own men, continued his march on Kábul. Sherdil Khan, an amír, 70 years of age, was the Moghal governor at Kábul at the time. His assistant, Násir Khan, had left Kábul for Peshάwar before the arrival of Nádir Shah. The principal inhabitants of Kábul came out to salute the king in a body, and gave him a reception suitable to his dignity, but the governor, Sherdil Khan, offered an obstinate resistance, and closed the gates of the city against him. Neither fair promises nor threats could induce the wily old man to open the gates. The town was closely besieged by the Persian troops for six weeks. The besieged made a gallant and desperate defence, and old Sherdil Khan, with his two sons, maintained his position with great firmness and resolution. A general assault made by the Persians was unsuccessful. Recourse was now had to a stratagem which succeeded, and Sherdil came out of the city to enter into a compact with a supposed friend who had given him to understand that he was at the head of an army against Nádir. The traitor seized Sherdil and put him in confinement. His sons still gallantly held the town, but the garrison being struck with terror and confusion, deserted their posts on the ramparts of the city. Nádir Shah, taking advantage of the panic, forced open the gates and took possession of the city, the inhabitants of which were put to the sword. One of Sherdil's sons was killed, while defending the gates, and the surviving son, with the gallant old man, his father, was inhumanly put to death by the avenging Nádir.

Indignation of Nádir Shah.

He is invited to invade India.

Sets out from Kandahar, 1738.

Submission of Ghazni.

Nádir Shah marches on Kábul.

Resistance of the governor.

Unsuccessful assault.

Seizure of the governor by stratagem.

Capture of the town.

The victor found in the Kábul treasury two million five hundred thousand rupees and effects to the value of two millions more, in which were included four thousand complete suits of armour, inlaid with gold, four thousand of polished steel, four thousand coats of mail for horses, and a great quantity of fine tissue and dresses, which had been deposited there by the Emperor Shah Jahán.

Treasure found in Kábul.

The king remained at Kábul for seven months, the whole of which time was occupied by him in maturing his plans for the invasion of Hindostán on the basis of intelligence furnished him by the treacherous Omerahs in the Court of the Moghal, and his emissaries in other places of importance in India, west of the Jamna. In the meanwhile another envoy, who had been sent with several Kábul chiefs to the court at Delhi, with an ultimatum to the great Moghal, was killed, on his way to India, by Mír Abbás, the governor of Jallálábád, and the chiefs were compelled to return to Kábul. Nádir, highly incensed at this, marched to Jallálábád,

The king remains in Kabul seven months.

Murder of the king's envoy by the governor of Jallalabád.

Capture of Jallálábád.

took the fort and town by assault, and killed Mír Abbás, with all the Indians who had sided with him. His family were sent in chains to the royal camp.*

Advance on Peshá-war.

After subduing Bámián, Ghoreband and other provinces of Afghanistán, under the Indian empire, the victor set his army in motion, and, at the head of ten thousand chosen Kazil Báshi † horse, advanced towards Peshá-war. The Moghal governor at Peshâwar at this time was Násir Khan, a pious man, who spent much of his time in hunting, or in devotion and in reading the *Qurán*. He had in vain written repeatedly to the Moghal Government for a supply of troops, reminding the emperor that he was himself 'but as a rose bush, withered by the blasts of autumn, while his soldiery were no more than a faded pageant.' The intrigues at the Court of Delhi prevented all hopes of succour from that quarter; yet the governor, closing the Khaibar Pass against the invader, opposed him with a body of seven thousand Afghans and Indians, whom he had assembled around him. Sarwar Khan, a Barakzai chief, rendered Nádir important aid, which enabled him to cross the Khaibar by the old route used by Tymúr in invading India. The Persians fell suddenly upon the troops collected by Násir Khan. After a short engagement the courage and resolution of the Indians wholly forsook them, their ranks were broken, and those only escaped the sword of the victor, who beat a precipitate retreat. When Násir Khan saw that his whole army had either been put to the sword, or fled panic-stricken, and that further resistance was fruitless, he surrendered himself prisoner to the king of the Persians (20th November 1738). Several Indian chiefs were at this time taken prisoners and their camps pillaged. The monarch soon after took Násir Khan into favour and appointed him one of his courtiers.

Passage of the Khaibar.

Defeat and surrender of Násir Khan, governor of Peshâwar, 1738.

Before crossing the Atak, Nádir Shah sent the following letter to the emperor of Hindostán, which was received in the beginning of Jamádiul Awwal, 1151 H.:—

Letter of Nádir to the Moghal emperor.

"Be it clear to the enlightened mind of your High Majesty, that my coming to Kábul and possessing myself thereof was purely out of zeal for Islám and friendship for you. I never could have imagined that the wretches of the Dekkan could have imposed tribute on the dominions of the king of the Musalmans. My stay on this side of the Atak is with a view. that, when these infidels move towards Hindostán, I may send an army of victorious Kazil Báshis to drive them to the abyss of hell. History is full of the friendship that has subsisted between our Kings and your Majesty's predecessors. By Ali Murtaza I swear that, excepting friendship and a concern for religion, I neither had, nor have, any other views; if you suspect the contrary you may, but I always was, and will be a friend to your illustrious House."

---

* A Kazil Bash noble in Nádir Shah's camp at Jallálábád, in a letter written by him to a friend in Delhi, gave the following particulars regarding that monarch :—

"After morning prayers, he sits on a throne, the canopy of which is in the form of a dome and of gold; 1,000 young men with royal standards of red silk and lance tops, from which hang tassels of silver, are disposed regularly and at proper distances; 500 beautiful slaves, from 12 to 20 years old, stand, one half on his right hand and the other half on his left; all the great men stand confronting him, and the arzbegi stands between, in readiness to represent whatever is desirable, and everybody has his cause decided at once. Bribery is not so much as known here. He has particular information given him of everything that passes; all criminals, great or small, rich and poor meet with immediate death. He sits till noon, after which he dines and then reposes a little. When afternoon prayers are over, he sits till evening prayers, and when these are over, he shoots five arrows into the *Khak Toda* (a heap of rubbish) and then retires into the women's apartments."—*Fraser*.

† The Kazil Báshis are an order of soldiers among the Persians, as the Fenizaris are among the Turks. The word signifies, in the Turkish language, *Redheads*, from the red caps they wore when first organized by Shekh Haidar, the father of Shah Ismail, the first king of the Safvi family.

At Atak Nádir Shah put on an Indian dress and sat on the throne after the manner of Indian emperors.

Nádir Shah now crossed the Indus, which, at that season of the year, was swollen by the rains and flowed with a rapid current. On entering the Panjáb, he commanded his army to ravage the country, and to freely use both fire and sword in all places. The consternation and desolation caused by his troops throughout the Panjáb soon spread over the whole of India. The whole country was seized with terror, and his victories and brutalities became the topic of all circles.

Nádir Shah enters the Panjab.

He then, at the head of his Turkomán army, crossed the Jhelum, and after that, without boats or rafts, the Chináb at Shahdaula, "furious as the ocean or as an arm of the destructive sea," in the words of Mirza Mahdi. Kalandar Khan, an amír in the service of the Moghal, and naib of the viceroy of Láhore, was in charge of Emanábád, subordinate to Láhore, with a body of ten thousand horse. Amír Khan, one of the dependants of Násir Khan, who had now submitted to Nádir Shah, made a night attack on Emanábád with his own people and a large body of Kazil Báshis. Kalandar Khan having been killed in the action, Amír Khan garrisoned the place with his own troops. Zakaria Khan, the viceroy of the Panjáb, who had advanced ten *kos* from Láhore, with an army of twenty thousand horse, had no sooner heard of this than he retreated to his capital. The Persian army pillaged all the towns and villages on its way to the capital and massacred the inhabitants. On the first of Shawal, the Persian monarch reached the banks of the Rávi, which he forded, and his troops coming up in sight of the Láhore army, a battle ensued, in which the Láhore governor was completely routed and repulsed with great slaughter.* The conquerors were so close upon the heels of the conquered in the pursuit, that they at once obtained possession of the gates of the town. Zakaria Khan, on returning to the citadel, put it in a state of defence, mounting cannons on the ramparts and strengthening his position by all available means. The king of Persia crossed the Rávi on the fourth day, and pitched his tents in the Shalámár gardens.

Crosses the Jhelum and Chináb.

Emanábád captured on his behalf by Amír Khan.

Defeat of the governor of Láhore.

The Shah puts up in the Shalámár gardens.

The viceroy of Láhore, Azuddaula Nawab Zakaria Khan, surnamed Khan Bahádur, sent an officer of rank to implore the clemency of the Shah, promising the completest submission. On the part of his Persian Majesty, Kifáyat Khan, an amír of his Court, was commissioned to settle the terms. On the 12th of Shawal, the viceroy was met by Wazír Abdul Báki, and by him conducted into the presence of the Shah. His majesty received the viceroy with great courtesy and consideration, and presented him with a *chapkan* of gold brocade, a jewelled dagger and a horse. On the 14th, the viceroy having been again introduced to the Shah at the royal camp in the gardens of Shalámár, he, according to the terms settled, laid before the throne of the conqueror twenty lakhs of rupees, a portion of which had been taken from the State coffers, and the remainder raised by contributions from the wealthiest inhabitants, and a large number of elephants. The present was graciously accepted by the Persian monarch, and Láhore was thus saved from the horrors of a massacre and spoliation. Zakaria Khan, having been confirmed in his government of Láhore, departed in all honour. The Shah took into his service Hayátullah Khan, the second brother of Azuddaula, and appointed him to the command of five hundred horse. Fakhr-ud-doula

The city spared, on payment of tribute.

* According to Anand Rám, *Mukhlis*, author of the "Tazkara," the fighting was renewed the next day, and "the plain was strewed with the slain." Anand Rám was an eye-witness of much that passed during Nádir Shah's stay in India, and suffered from his exactions. Five lakhs of rupees were extorted from him.

Amín-ud-dín Khan was at the same time appointed subadar of Káshmír, and sent thither with a considerable number of troops. Having thus settled the affairs of the Panjáb, the monarch quitted Láhore for Delhi on 29th December. He struck a gold coin at Láhore on the obverse of which was the inscription نادر السلطان "Nádir, the Sultan," and on the reverse ضرب دارالسلطنت لاهور ١١٥١ خلد الله ملكه: "Struck at the capital of Láhore, 1151, May God preserve his reign!" On the bank of the Biás, the tyrant ordered one thousand and seven State prisoners, whom he had kept in close confinement during his journey from Pesháwar to Láhore, to be inhumanly put to death. The order was promptly executed.

Nádir leaves for Delhi.

Coins money at Láhore.

Nádir Shah continued his march towards Delhi, and on 14th February reached the plains of Karnál. The emperor of Delhi at the head of his troops, had reached the town two days previously, and was joined by Burhán-ul-Mulk, Saádat Khan, the viceroy of Oudh, Khán-i-Dourán Khan, the commander-in-chief, Asif Jáh Nizám-ul-mulk, the viceroy of the Dekkan, and Kamr-ud-dín Khan, the ground wazír. The Moghal and the Persian armies were divided by the canal of Ali Mardán Khan, and the former had thrown up intrenchments, and redoubts mounted with 500 pieces of artillery. The Indian army consisted of 150,000 horse, exclusive of irregular cavalry, and was divided into three divisions which extended to an amazing length. The Indians also brought with them a great many elephants, as a bombastic show to overcome the Persian invader, forgetful of the fact that these huge animals, and the enormous pieces of ordnance, would impede them in their movements. The Persian soldiers, though far inferior in numbers, were trained to arms and thoroughly disciplined, being well accustomed to endure severe hardship under the stern training of their leader. Saádat elected to risk an engagement in the field with the veteran armies of the Persian king, who remained on the defensive. The folly of taking the offensive against an invading army is obvious. The effeminate Indian army soon proved itself quite unable to cope with the valour of the hardy Turkománs, and Saádat was the first to give way, after a scene of havoc and confusion, which lasted for five hours. He was joined in the battle by the Khán-i-Dourán, who maintained his ground with great firmness and resolution. The Indians at last gave way. Saádat was taken prisoner by the Persians, and Dourán, who was wounded in the action, was taken to his camp, where he died. A fresh attack was made on the Persians by Muzaffar, the gallant brother of Dourán, under whom were Ali, his son, Raja Gagar Mal, and several officers of rank. Muzaffar held his ground firmly, and a desperate fight took place, resulting in the slaughter of ten thousand Indian troops. After this disastrous conflict, the remainder of the Indians retired to their intrenchments. In this battle ten Indian princes of eminent rank, with one hundred nobles and officers of distinction, and thirty thousand soldiers, were slain on the field.

Defeat of the Moghal army at Karnál.

The victor now took possession of all the strong posts round the camp of the Delhi emperor, which he subjected to a strong blockade, thus cutting off all his supplies.

Camp of the emperor blockaded.

The third day after the defeat and rout of the Moghal armies, Muhammad Shah resolved upon resigning his crown to secure the clemency of the conqueror. Having, therefore, previously acquainted Nádir Shah with his intention, he set out on the morning of the twentieth for the Persian camp on his travelling throne, attended by the viceroy of the Dekkan, the grand wazír and other nobles, and a small retinue. The king of Persia, hearing of the approach of the Delhi emperor, sent his son Nasrulla Mirza to conduct His Majesty to his camp. The prince met the emperor at the limits

Muhammad Shah determines to resign his crown.

His meeting with Nádir.

of the camp. Muhammad Shah alighted from his travelling throne, embraced the prince and seated him by his side. When the party reached the royal tent, Nádir Shah received the emperor at the door. Both their majesties embraced each other, and, holding one another by the hand, they entered the audience tent, where they sat down together on the same *musnad*. A repast was prepared, and a waiter having first offered coffee to Nádir Shah, the latter, with his own hands, courteously offered it to Muhammad Shah, saying: "Since your majesty has done me the honour of coming here, we are brothers, and may you remain happy in the empire of Hindostán." The remains of the repast were given to Umdat-ul-Mulk, Amir Khan Bahádur, Mutamidud Doula, Muhammad Ishák Khan Bahádur, Bihráz Khan and other nobles who had accompanied Muhammad Shah. The conference lasted for several hours, and nothing which courtesy and friendship required, was omitted by Nádir Shah. He expressed his regret at the action of the Delhi emperor in allowing the *chauth* to the Mahrattas, and permitting foreigners to invade his dominions. On this latter point the Delhi emperor remarked to his victorious companion: "If I had not been dilatory in complying with your majesty's request, I could not have secured the pleasure of seeing your majesty to-day." This facetious remark of the Delhi monarch elicited a smile from the stern Nádir.

Courtesy of Nádir Shah.

The Delhi emperor was treated as a guest in the Persian camp, and received every mark of respect. After retiring to another tent, Nádir Shah had a long consultation with his wazír as to the future policy to be adopted. He then returned to the royal tent, and made it formally known to Muhammad Shah, that, as the imperial house of Tymúr had given no cause of offence to the Persian empire, it was far from his wishes to make India a part of his kingdom, provided the Indian emperor would pay him an indemnity for the war. To this Muhammad Shah agreed, as also to Nádir's troops remaining in the capital to recover from the fatigues of the campaign, until such time as the money should be paid.

The emperor a guest in the Persian camp.

Agrees to pay an indemnity.

The emperor was permitted to send for his harem, and, with all his family members and Omerahs, remained in honourable confinement, being constantly guarded by Persian horsemen. The Indian army was left without officers, and the Persians seized upon the ordnance, the military chest, the jewel office, the wardrobe and the armoury. The keys of all the establishments in the fort of Delhi were politely demanded by the Shah, and quietly made over by the emperor, being sent through Thamasp Khan to Latfullah Khan, the Delhi *Killadar*, or commandant of the fort. The officers of the Persian king thus put themselves in possession of the fort and of all within it.

Remains in confinement in the Persian camp.

Keys of the Delhi fort surrendered to the invader.

The two kings then marched towards Delhi. The emperor was conducted by a rear guard of ten thousand Persian horsemen. His army was divided into two irregular columns and marched on both flanks of the Persians. Arrived at Delhi, Nádir Shah encamped in the luxuriant gardens of Shalámár. Muhammad Shah obtained leave to enter the city in order to prepare his palace for the reception of the victor; and, on the following day, Nádir made his victorious entry into the city at the head of 12,000 horse.

Nádir enters Delhi.

He distributed his army over all the quarters of the town and the fort, placing the gates of the city and the citadel under guards of his own men. He gave orders that his troops should not in any way interfere with, or molest, any of the emperor's subjects under pain of being deprived of their ears.

His army distributed through the town.

Muhammad conducted his vanquisher to a magnificent apartment in the royal palace, which was profusely decorated for the occasion. Nádir Shah demanded twenty-five *karors* of rupees as the war indemnity. Muhammad opened the imperial treasury and stripped it of its most valuable

Nádir demands an indemnity of twenty-five *karors*.

jewels and curiosities, that had been accumulated for ages, and brought them as presents to the conqueror. He laid, at the feet of the conqueror, vast heaps of gold and silver in coin and ingots, valuable vases set with diamonds, rubies and other precious gems, with a great variety of sumptuous furniture, diadems and thrones, including the famous peacock throne, inlaid with pearls and precious stones, which had been constructed by Shah Jahán at a cost of six millions and a half sterling, according to the valuation put on it by Tavernier. The Omerahs and grandees of the court followed the example of their emperor, and presented the conqueror with gifts valued at millions of rupees. Nádir now, being master of vast treasures, paid his army their arrears. These payments, according to Jones Hanway, were made in his own coin, which was struck upon this occasion.*

The treasury stripped of its most valuable articles.

Khutba read in the name of Nádir.

The Íd festival came on at this time, and the *khutba* was read in the grand mosque of Delhi in the name of the Persian King, Nádir Shah. The king treated the subjects of the Delhi emperor with moderation, and adopted measures to protect the inhabitants from outrage, the strictest discipline being observed.

His moderation.

An unfortunate incident.

All went on smoothly, until an unfortunate circumstance occurred in the city which compelled Nádir Shah to taint his victory with those horrid deeds of bloodshed and spoliation which to this day have associated his name with ideas of terror and dread. The day following the Id, a great tumult arose among the mob in the streets, owing to a Persian soldier forcibly seizing some pigeons that were exposed for sale in the market. The man to whom the pigeons belonged gave out, in a fit of frenzy, that Nádir Shah had ordered a general pillage. This was sufficient to inflame the infatuated mob, who had borne the intrusion of the strangers with gloomy discontent. Maddened with rage, they rushed upon the Persians, who were in various parts of the city, guarding different quarters, and killed many of their number. To add to this, some of the inhabitants having raised a cry, to the effect that Nádir Shah was dead, the suppressed fury of the populace burst forth. The report spread like lightning over the town. A great tumult arose, and the inhabitants fell upon the Persians, and cut to pieces all they could find. The night was dark; the mob broke into the royal stables and put to death the keepers of the elephants. Three thousand Persians were killed in the city, the rest retiring into the citadel. About midnight the officers of Nádir Shah represented the state of affairs to his majesty. The Shah, annoyed at being roused, said angrily: "My men maliciously accuse the people and wish me to slaughter them and to give the signal for plunder." On the matter being again urged, he ordered his men to act wholly on the defensive during the remainder of the night. At daybreak, Nádir Shah rode forth from the palace and appeared in the Chandni Chauk Street, hoping that his presence would overawe the people and put a stop to their fanaticism. The first objects that met his eyes in the streets were the dead bodies of his countrymen who had been killed in the night by the mob. He sent a strong party to suppress disorder; but the mob, instead of being appeased, became bold and insolent, and began to discharge arrows and firearms at the Persians. Nádir Shah repaired to the mosque of Raushan-ud-doula (then recently built) and there summoned into his presence Nizam-ul-mulk, Sarbuland Khan and the grand wazír, Kamr-ud-dín Khan, and threatened to put them to immediate death, charging them with having fomented the sedition. The Omerahs immediately swore on the *Qurán* that they were innocent, and they were pardoned. But now came the fatal hour which brought utter

The populace rise against the Persians.

Three thousand of them killed.

Nádir's unsuccessful efforts to allay the tumult.

* *History of Nádir Shah.*

ruin on the magnificent city that had so long been the mistress of India and the pride of the East. At daybreak, a person from the neighbouring terrace designedly fired upon the king of Persia. The shot, missing him, killed one of his immediate attendants, who fell dead before his eyes. The fierce spirit of the Shah was now roused to the utmost fury, and unsheathing his sword he ordered a general massacre of the inhabitants of the unfortunate town. The tumult had by this time subsided, but the orders of Nádir Shah were executed with such rigour that till midday the streets of Delhi ran with blood. Guns were ordered out and the streets swept with grape. The incensed Persians destroyed all before them, demolishing every building they came to, and levelling to the ground the loftiest and most spacious edifices of the metropolis of the Indian empire. In the midst of this horrible work of death and destruction, the bloodthirsty Nádir sat in gloomy solitude in the little mosque of Raushan-ud-doula, gloating with vengeance on the work of devastation going on before his eyes. The bloody scene extended from *Sarafa Ardui*, in front of the fort, to *Idgáh*, which is three *kos* distant, and from *Chitli Kabar* as far as the tobacco market and *Pul Mithai*.* The whole of the Dariba Bazaar ran red with the blood of bankers and merchants. Neither sex nor age was spared. Before two o'clock in the afternoon, it is computed, between 120,000 and 150,000 were slaughtered, though not a third part of the population were visited by the sword of the avengers. So great was their dread of the Persians that the wretched Indians bent down their heads before them like sheep to be slaughtered, and one Persian soldier is said to have butchered a whole family of ten, men, women and children, without encountering any opposition whatever. Thousands of Hindus burnt themselves alive with their wives and daughters, while thousands more threw themselves into wells. The work of destruction was carried on in the most diabolical spirit. The Chandni Chauk, the fruit market, the Dariba Bazaar and the buildings around the Jama Masjid were set on fire and reduced to ashes. The flames of the burning houses reached the skies, and the crackling of the falling edifices deafened the ears and filled the streets with *debris*. The streets were strewn with corpses, which lay about as thickly as leaves after a storm. While this dreadful scene was going on, the destroyer, as before mentioned, sat calmly in the masjid. His countenance was fierce and terrible, his eyes glared with fury, and none but the slave attending on his royal person durst approach him. At length the wretched emperor, attended by his nobles, forced his way into the presence of the Shah. He stood, like a statue, in the attitude of a suppliant, with downcast eyes and tears streaming down his cheeks. The nobles, who ventured to approach nearer, bowed down their foreheads to the ground. Nádir Shah asked them sternly what they wanted. "Spare the city," was the unanimous cry.† Nádir Shah granted the request, and, sheathing his sword, ordered an immediate cessation of the massacre. His words were no sooner uttered than they were obeyed; the massacre ceased and every sword was sheathed. The Persian heralds proclaimed peace throughout the city. Nádir Shah then returned to the citadel, where, under his orders, several of the Omerahs, who

The king fired at.

General massacre of the inhabitants ordered.

Horrible bloodshed.

The streets set on fire.

The emperor and his Omerahs beg for mercy.

Cessation of the massacre.

---

* So called from the shops of confectioners there.

† The implorers of mercy, addressing the tyrant Nádir Shah, said metaphorically, trembling and frightened :—

کسي نماند که ديگر به تيغ ناز کشي — مگر که زاده کني خلق را و باز کشي

"Not a soul has been spared by thy avenging sword. If it be thy wish to carry on the work of destruction any further, infuse life into the dead and renew the slaughter."

were suspected of being accomplices in the late treason, were beheaded. The tyrant's thirst for blood was, however, not yet satiated. On some trivial excuse he put to the sword six thousand of the inhabitants of Moghalpúra, while thousands were slain in the villages adjoining Delhi. In the royal market, where the tumult had first arisen, he had the noses and ears of seven hundred persons, who were indiscriminately seized, cut off.

Slaughter of the people living in the neighbourhood of the capital.

Nádir Shah, satiated with the carnage, now proceeded to take possession of all the moveable treasures in the town, by this time to a great extent in ruins. He seized upon the regalia of the Moghal emperor and the public treasure, in which were found concealed jewels, specie and rich robes, the accumulation of ages, which the Moghal emperors had been most diligent in procuring by every means in their power, many of the articles being of unrivalled beauty. These, together with elephants, horses and everything valuable belonging to the royal house of Tymúr were seized. The victors then plundered the nobles and wealthy citizens, and by threats, torture and every severity, compelled them to produce their hidden treasures and valuables. Contributions were then levied upon the citizens. The gates of the city were closed, and the citizens tortured with a view to making them disgorge their wealth. Great numbers of the inhabitants died of this treatment, while many, to avoid suffering, shame and poverty, destroyed themselves. Sleep and rest forsook the people, lamentations proceeded from every house having inmates, and death was sought rather than avoided.

Nádir seizes on the regalia of the Moghal Empire.

The citizens put under contribution.

Dreadful tortures.

Large contributions were also levied on the governors of provinces, and the total wealth carried away by Nádir is described by historians as being between eight and thirty *karors* (£8,000,000 and £30,000,000) of money, exclusive of jewels, rich stuffs and other valuable property, among which was included the famous *Kohinúr* diamond, now forming part of the British regalia. He also carried away a large number of elephants, horses, camels and valuable furniture, and the most skilful workmen and artisans, numbering several hundreds.* He married his son, Nasrullah, to the daughter of Azíz-ud-dín, the son of Kam Baksh, and a grandson of Aurangzeb. The Shah himself felt a violent desire to make the beautiful daughter of Muzaffar, the brother of Khan Douran, his queen, but he was prevented from carrying out his wishes by one of his wives, who possessed the art of controlling his temper, which the rest of the world so much dreaded. The week following the marriage of Nasrullah was spent in public entertainments, banquets, shows, pageants and other amusements, among which were the combats of wild beasts. Nádir then amply rewarded his troops for their hard and faithful services, and every private soldier got a largess of above twelve pounds.

The wealth carried away by Nádir.

He marries his son to a princess of the house of Tymúr.

Entertainments.

The last act of Nádir was to convene an assembly of all the Omerahs and chiefs of State, in which he replaced the imperial diadem on the head of Muhammad Shah with his own hands, and helped him to ascend the throne of his ancestors. A treaty was drawn up ceding all the territories northwest of the Indus, together with Sindh and Tatta, to the king of Persia. The Shah then spoke at length to the Moghal Emperor about his future policy, and enjoined on his Omerahs the necessity of obedience to their sovereign and a regard for his welfare. After these transactions the king left Delhi, on his

Muhammad Shah restored.

All the country west of the Indus ceded to Nádir Shah.

* Fraser gives a long list of the wealth carried away by Nádir Shah from India. He is stated to have carried away jewels from the emperor and the Omerahs, treasure, goods and assets of the value of seventy *karors*; his officers and soldiers carried away ten *karors*, and he spent twenty *karors* more on the maintenance of his army in India, giving them arrears of pay and a gratuity. He carried away 1,000 elephants, 7,000 horses, 10,000 camels, 100 eunuchs, 130 writers, 200 smiths, 300 masons, 100 stone-cutters, and 200 carpenters.

way back to his country. The *Mullah Báshi*, standing at the door of his royal master's residence, in a loud voice, made the following proclamation:—"Soldiers! the King of Kings, the Lord of Benevolence, our Master, the Protector of the world, conquered the country of Hindostán and has restored it. To-morrow our victorious banners move to Irák. Be you prepared!" Before leaving the metropolis, the Shah ordered Haji Shídi Fouládd Khan, the *kotwal*, or superintendent of police, to see that none of the Persians remained behind on any account whatever. Delhi had suffered the fate of Nineveh and Babylon at the hands of Nádir Shah, though her residents were not carried away as slaves. It took them some time to awake from their lethargy and resume business.

The conqueror's return home.

As the time of his departure from Delhi approached, Nádir Shah sent his minister, Nawab Abdul Baki Khan, with Hayátullah Khan, son of Azaddaula, Nawab Zakaria Khan, to Láhore, with orders directing the latter to collect and remit to the Persian treasury a contribution of one *karor* of rupees. The messenger met the Nawab in the Shalámár gardens, and was honourably received. Zakaria Khan, on his return to the city, called a meeting of all the principal residents, merchants, bankers, and wealthy people, and explained to them that the Shah wanted to save Láhore from ruin. The amount of one *karor* of rupees was collected, and the messenger, with this money, departed and joined the main army of the Shah, now on its march.*

He takes a ransom from Láhore.

As the whole country along the Láhore road had been desolated by the Persian army on its march to Delhi, Nádir Shah resolved to take the route by Siálkot. On 9th Rabiulawwal (May 1739, A.D.), his camp reached Kalúwál on the banks of the Chináb. A heavy fall of rain, the preceding night, had carried away the bridge-of-boats, but another small bridge was constructed, by means of iron cables, at a narrower part, close to the village of Akhnúr. On the 14th, the Persian camp at Kalúwál broke up, and began crossing the river at Akhnúr. Only a portion of the army had effected its passage when, by the force of the current, the bridge was swept away, and two thousand Kazil Báshis were hurled into a watery grave. The Shah, mounting on *Maha Sundar*, the powerful elephant that had been bestowed on Zakaria Khan, made a search for a ford, but, none being found, it was resolved that the army should be ferried over in boats. The whole army and the baggage having landed on the opposite bank, Zakaria Khan, who had accompanied the royal camp, was permitted to depart. The districts of Gujrát, Siálkot, Pasrúr, and some districts forming the zemindari of Khudáyar Khan Abbási, of Múltán, were put in charge of Zakaria Khan, on condition of his paying twenty lakhs of rupees per annum, as revenue, into the Persian treasury. At the Chináb the Shah ordered Abul Husein Beg, the Yakah Báshi, to place trustworthy persons at the ferry to examine all persons before they crossed the river, and to seize all valuables which might be discovered on them, and send them to the royal treasury. On the publication of this order, many soldiers, of their own accord, presented what jewels they possessed and were handsomely rewarded by the king. Others, who had concealed their booty in packs and in the saddles of their horses, mules and camels, were compelled to deliver them up. Some had buried their treasures in the ground, hoping to dig them up again, but they remained in the bowels of the earth, as not a soul was allowed to recross the river. Others, out of rage, threw what they had into the river. All the Hindostáni prisoners in the Shah's camp were now released, and made over to Zakaria Khan, to be sent back to their respective homes.

The Persian camp on the banks of the Chináb in its retrograde movement.

Part of the Panjáb annexed.

A search of the person of all Persian soldiers ordered.

Release of Hindostáni prisoners.

---

* Fraser.

The Shah on the banks of the Jhelum.

In spite of the heavy rain which fell almost incessantly, the Shah, by a succession of rapid marches, reached the banks of the Jhelum. In the midst of the swollen river a camel, laden with gold plates, slipped and fell off the bridge-of-boats with its load, and was drowned. Here the Persian Shah sent back Muhammad Shah's artillery, and made the gunners a present of the gold plates that had sunk in the river. The men tried their best to recover the lost property, but only wasted their time and energies, as nothing was found except a brass basin and an ewer. Marching along the borders of Ráwalpindi, the king passed Hasan Abdal, and, after subduing the Afghans of Eusafzai, proceeded by quick marches to Jallálabád, and arrived at Kábul on 20th November, 1739, A.D. The same year, he marched his army into Sindh, which he subdued, reducing Khudáyár Khan, the governor, to great straits. At Sindh he summoned Nawáb Zakaria Khan, the governor of Láhore, to help him in conducting the campaign against the Bilúchis. He celebrated the festival of the New Year at Larkanah in Sindh, with great pomp and splendour, and bestowed considerable presents on his army. To the officers of the first rank he gave five hundred mohurs each, to others from one to three hundred mohurs and to every private soldier two mohurs.* After these transactions, Zakaria Khan was sent back to Láhore, and Nádir Shah, at the head of his troops, proceeded to Kandahar.

His march to Sindh, 1739.

Zakaria Khan, the Láhore viceroy, summoned.

The Shah's gifts to his army.

Departure for Kandahar.

After his departure from Sindh, Nádir waged war against Tartary, which he completely subdued, and successfully fought against several other eastern countries. He had taken with him a band of musicians and dancers from Delhi, in order to instruct the people of his own country in Indian music, which he much admired. He was bountiful in his rewards, and had it proclaimed through all the provinces of Persia that his subjects were exempted from the payment of taxes of all kinds for a period of three years. He made a grand display at Herat of the curiosities he had brought from Hindostán, and several days were spent in pageants, shows and entertainments. He was so pleased with the peacock throne of Shah Jahán, that he ordered his jewellers to make another after the same pattern, and of like splendour, together with a pavilion equally rich and magnificent. He called this the *Takhti Nadiri*, or "Throne of Nádir," and placed it in his *Díwánkhana*, or public hall, at Herat, with the peacock throne brought from Delhi, and various beautiful and costly thrones of other monarchs subdued by him. His wealth of jewels enabled him to make arms of every description, richly inlaid with precious stones, as well as harness, chairs and other articles ornamented with jewels. By his express orders his *Moabir Báshi* (quarter-master-general) had a large tent prepared by the best workmen that could be procured. It was lined with green satin, but the jewels with which it was decorated did not appear to advantage, and by the king's orders it was taken to pieces and a new one made, the top of which, for convenience of transport, was separated from the sides. The new tent was displayed to his majesty on his return from the Turán expedition. The outside was covered with fine scarlet; the linings were of violet-coloured satins, on which were representations of birds and beasts, trees and flowers, the whole made of pearls, diamonds, rubies, amethysts and other precious stones, the tent-poles being decorated in like manner. On either side of the tent was a screen on which were the figures of two angels in precious stones. The tent-pegs were of massive gold, and the whole tent, with its walls and poles, formed the burdens of seven elephants. This magnificent specimen of oriental grandeur was displayed at all festivals in the *Díwánkhana* at

Grand display at Herat.

The *Takhti Nadiri*.

The decorations of a royal tent prepared.

* The mohur was a Hindostáni coin worth Rs. 24.—*Memoirs of Khwája Abdul Karim.*

Herát, during the remainder of Nádir Shah's life.* His taste for splendour induced him to have these elegant articles finished in the highest perfection of art, which exhibited at one view the richest and the finest pearls and precious stones, that were once the pride of the Great Moghal.

Nádir Shah extended the empire of Persia as far as the Oxus on the north and the Indus on the south. He had conquered province after province and subdued many warlike nations. He was now old, and wished for rest by placing the diadem on the head of his son, Nasrullah, as soon as the completion of his military projects should enable him to resign it. He fixed upon the castle of Kelát as the place of his retreat, and furnished it with a sumptuous palace, elegant baths, aqueducts and spacious houses for his grandees and Omerahs. As he advanced in years, he lost all power of mind, which became distracted and weak. Once he entered into a religious controversy with the *mullahs* of Bagdád, and spent many idle days in religious disputes, a strange circumstance in one of his active nature. At another time, in a fit of rage, he had his son Raza Kuli's eyes torn out. He repented his hasty passion; and remorse, anguish and despair followed, and produced a disorder of the mind. His madness increased, and, with it, his tyranny. Allavi Khan, the royal physician, in prescribing medicine for him, had the courage also to administer wholesome advice. The *hákim Báshi* also corrected the impetuosity of his temper for the benefit of mankind. By this skilful treatment, his disposition so far improved, that for a fortnight he did not think of ordering anybody to be deprived of his sight or life. But, on the departure of Allavi Khan, his morbid humours again got the upper hand, and he returned to his old courses. For the most trifling offences, he would order people to be deprived of their eyes and others of life. The governor of Fars revolted, and his example was followed by the governors of some other provinces. This drove Nádir Shah to a degree of fury which can scarcely be conceived; he put to death a great number of his governors and Omerahs on the slightest suspicion; not satisfied with taking the lives of the leaders of the rebellion, he depopulated whole cities, and a great number of his subjects sought refuge in mountains and deserts to avoid torture and death. He had further resolved to cause a general massacre of his Persian troops at the hands of the Afghans and the Uzbeks, in whom he reposed the most implicit confidence. But the tyrant's own end was now near. The very night preceding the morning on which he had determined to put his bloody scheme into execution, he was himself murdered. A plan was formed by his nephew, Ali Kuli Khan, who aspired to the throne, and coveted the vast treasures of his uncle, to put an end to his life. Nádir Shah was then encamped at Fathábad, in the neighbourhood of Mashhad, with the view of carrying out his schemes. Fatigued with a long march, he had retired early to his tent, and slept quietly till midnight of the 8th June, 1747. At the instigation of his nephew, Muhammad Kuli Khan, Ardemi, a relation of the Shah, and *Khushki Báshi* (commanding officer of the body-guard), with seventy of the khusheks, or guards, had bound themselves by an oath to assassinate Nádir Shah that very night. When the appointed hour came, fifty seven of their number were seized with a panic, and refused to join in the execution of the plot. The other thirteen, however, tore down the *Sera parda*,† and entered the harem. The eunuch on guard resisted them, but he was cut down. The assassins at first in-

Nádir fixes on Kelát as the place of his retreat.

His mind distracted.

He puts out the eyes of his son,

And becomes a despotic tyrant.

Revolt of provinces.

Conspiracy to put an end to the tyrant's life.

* Gladwin's *Memoirs of Khwája Abdul Karim.* The author informs us that, after the death of Nádir Shah, his nephew, Adil Shah, and his grandson, Shah Rukh, took the tent to pieces and dissipated the materials.

† The curtain or veil of a tent.

voluntarily drew back, on hearing the old king's challenging voice, at which the fiercest of men trembled; but they soon regained courage, and one of the assassins aimed a blow at the king with a sabre. The king fell, and, on his endeavouring to raise himself, the conspirators rushed on him, and, repeating their blows, destroyed a life which had been devoted to destroying the lives of others. Thus fell, at the age of sixty years, Nádir Shah, the terror of Asia, the pride and deliverer of his country, the restorer of its freedom, and the conqueror of India, who, from an humble station in life, raised himself to a dignity which few monarchs have attained by birth.

Assassination of Nádir Shah, 8th June 1747.

At daybreak, the Omerahs found the body of Nádir Shah lying headless on the ground. The ladies of the harem had been previously sent off to Kelát, with their effects, under charge of Nasrullah Mirza. An old woman who remained behind, was seen bewailing over the head of her royal master, which lay at a distance from the trunk. Nine days after the assassination, Ali Kuli Khan ordered the body to be removed to Mashhad, where it was buried in the mausoleum which Nádir Shah had prepared for himself.*

His body buried in Mashhad.

* Having traced this great Asiatic conqueror to his last resting-place, we give below extracts from an interesting paper written on the personal description and character of that sovereign by an English gentleman † who knew Nádir Shah personally and was his companion for years in his exploits.

The character of Nádir Shah.

"Nádir Shah is about fifty-five years old, upwards of six feet high, well-proportioned, of a very robust make and constitution, his complexion sanguine, and inclining to be fat, but the fatigue he undergoes prevents it; he has fine large black eyes and eye-brows; and, in short, is one of the most comely men I ever beheld. The injury the sun and weather have done to his complexion only gives him a more manly aspect. His voice is so uncommonly loud and strong, that frequently, and without straining it, he gives orders to his people at above a hundred yards distance. He drinks wine with moderation, but is extremely addicted to women, in which he affects great variety, and yet never neglects his business on their account; his hours of recreation among the ladies are but few, seldom entering their apartments before eleven or twelve at night, and is up and in public by five in the morning. His diet is is simple, chiefly *pillao* and plain dishes; and, if public affairs require his attendance, he neglects his meals and satisfies his hunger with a few parched peas (of which he always carries some in his pockets) and a draught of water. In the camp or in the city, he is almost constantly in public, and, if not, he may be sent to, or spoken with, by any person. He musters, pays, and clothes his army himself, and will not suffer any perquisites to be taken from the soldiers by his officers on any pretence whatever. He has monthly accounts transmitted to him of the state of affairs in all parts of his dominions, and holds a correspondence with his several private spies in every place; besides, in every province and city there is a person called *Ham Kalam* appointed to inspect the governor's actions and keep a register of them. No affair of any consequence can be transacted, but in the presence of that officer who, besides the accounts the governor is obliged to send monthly, transmits his journal by a separate conveyance whenever he thinks proper, without permitting the governor to peruse it; he has no settled salary or gratuity for his trouble, but is rewarded or punished just as Nádir Shah finds he deserves. This extraordinary caution, in a great measure, prevents the governor's oppressing the people or entering into conspiracies or rebellions against him. He is extremely generous, particularly to his soldiers, and bountifully rewards all in his service who behave well. He is at the same time very severe and strict in his discipline, punishing with death those who commit a great offence; and with the loss of their ears those whose transgressions are of a slighter nature; he never pardons the guilty of what rank soever, and is highly displeased, if, after he has thoroughly examined the affair, any person presumes to intercede in their behalf, before which they may give their sentiments with freedom.

When on a march, or in the field, he contents himself with eating, drinking and sleeping like a common soldier, and enures all his officers to the same severe discipline. He is of so hardy a constitution that he has been often known, of a frosty night, to repose upon the ground in the open air, wrapped up in his cloak, with only a saddle for his pillow, especially when upon an extraordinary enterprise which required expedition, he has been obliged to outmarch his baggage, by which means he has fallen upon the enemy when they least expected him. He is never happy but when in the field, and laments the time when he is obliged to stay in a city to refresh his troops, in which (as in all things else) he uses the utmost despatch. His meals are over in less than half an hour, after which he returns to business, so that the servants, who attend him standing, are changed three or four times a day. He never indulges himself in any kind of pleasure in the day time, but constantly at sunset retires to a private apartment where, unbending himself at once from business, he sups with three or four favorites and drinks a quart, or, at most, three pints, of wine, behaving all the time in the freest and most facetious manner. In his private conversation no person is allowed to mention anything relating to public business; nor, at other times, must they presume upon his intimacy to behave with more familiarity than their equals. Two of his evening companions

† According to Fraser, this gentleman resided for years in Persia, spoke the language, and had been frequently in the company of Nádir Shah.

THE REIGN OF MUHAMMAD SHAH.

(PERIOD FOLLOWING THE INVASION OF NÁDIR SHÁH.)

FORMATION OF THE SIKHS INTO CONFEDERACIES.

THE commotions which followed the invasion of Nádir Shah, and the confusion into which the province of Láhore was thrown, were favourable to the Sikhs, who, impoverished by long extortion, took again to rapine and plunder. They fell upon the peaceful inhabitants of the Panjáb and plundered them of what property they were carrying to the hills to save themselves from the rapacity of the Persian conqueror. They infested the whole country between the Rávi and the Biás, as well as the Mánjha jungles, harassed the routes of communication, and, moving about in small armed parties, began to plunder villages. At first they established secret associations and contented themselves with petty acts of depredation, but the impunity which attended these initial forays now encouraged them openly to resort to the holy tank of Amritsar, where they held councils among themselves. Their number daily increased, those who had retired to hill fastnesses returning, and others joining their standard in multitudes for the sake of rapine and plunder, which were considered lawful. Sikh horsemen were seen riding at full gallop towards their favourite shrine at Amritsar, the

The Sikhs again become troublesome.

Their number increased, and with it their audacity.

---

happening to transgress on that point, by taking the liberty to advise him in public, he immediately ordered them to be strangled, saying, 'such fools were not fit to live, who could not distinguish between Nádir Shah and Nádir Kuli.' He has been very kind to those who please him in private conversation, and behave with a becoming decency and deference in public, where they are taken no more notice of, nor have they any more influence over him than others of the same rank.

His mother, who was living in the year 1737, (at the request of some who were attached to the royal family) intreated Nádir Shah, some time after he had seized a king, to restore him, not doubting but His Majesty would make him sufficient amends by creating him generalissimo for life. He asked her whether she really thought so? She told him she did. Upon which he smiled and said, 'If I was an old woman, perhaps I might be inclined to think so too,' and desired her to give herself no trouble about state affairs.

He was married to Shah Thamasp's aunt, the youngest sister of Shah Sultan Husein, by whom he had one daughter. He has several young children by his concubines, and two sons by a woman he married in his obscurity. The eldest Raza Kuli Mirza, is about twenty-five years of age. He was trained up from his childhood in the army, where from a subaltern he has been gradually advanced to the rank of a general and appointed Viceroy of Persia during his father's expedition to India. The second son Nasrallah Mirza, who is about twenty-one years of age, is nominal governor of Mashhad and the province of Khorásán, having a person to direct and manage for him.

His eldest son, when ranked as a lieutenant, had only that pay to subsist on, and in all other stations had no more than his commission entitled him to. His fatner regarded him no more than he did the other officers, and permitted him to associate with them, giving him to know that if he was guilty of any crime or breach of duty, he should be punished with as great rigour as any of the rest. On his behaving well, he not only promoted him, but increased his paternal affection for him.

Among Nádir Shah's extraordinary faculties, his memory is not the least to be admired, there being few things of moment that he ever said or did, but what he remembers; and can readily call all the principal officers in his numerous army by their names. He knows most of the private men who have served under him at any time and can recollect when and for what he punished or rewarded any of them. He dictates to one or two secretaries, and gives orders about other affairs at the same time with all the regularity and promptness imaginable.

In time of action, I am told, he is equally surprising, it being scarce credible how quick he is in discerning the odds on either side, and how active in succouring his troops. If any of his general officers give ground without being greatly overpowered, he rides up and kills him with a battle axe (which he always carries in his hand) and then gives the command to the next in rank. In all the battles, skirmishes and sieges, he has been engaged in (although he generally charges at the head of his troops), he never has received the least wound or scar, and yet several horses have been shot under him and bullets have grazed his armour."

Another eye-witness who saw him later, says about his age and description: "From the appearance of his countenance, the strength of his limbs, and the vigour of his faculties, he did not seem to be above fifty years age." But on his death he must have been about sixty, for the same authority says later on: "His beard was quite white, and he used to have it dyed black regularly twice a week. Having lost all his double teeth, he seldom ate food that required much mastication, and when he did, he swallowed it without chewing. His front teeth were all sound and firm in his head."—*Memoirs of Khwája Abdul Karim.*

pilgrimage being no longer performed in secret or in disguise as before. The wealthiest of them purchased horses and mounted their followers, while the more adventurous sought celebrity by daring exploits and aspired to military honours.

Enquiry of Nádir Shah about them.

Nádir Shah, when he passed through the Panjáb, on his return from Delhi, asked the governor, Zakaria Khan, what sort of people the Sikhs were who had plundered the rear of his army, which was laden with spoils, and, from a contempt of enemies, travelled without any order. He said they were a crowd of disorderly *faqírs* who visited the tank of Amritsar every six months. Nádir asked where their abode was, to which the governor replied: "Their houses are their saddles." The conqueror smiled and said: "Surely they ought to be crushed and their country seized."

They build a fort of Dalíwál.

The Sikhs now presented an organized, martial appearance, and built a small fort at Dalíwál on the Rávi. Their associations increased in number and strength, and their ravages were not now confined to the open country, but extended to the very neighbourhood of Láhore.

Death of Nawáb Zakaria Khan, governor of Láhore.

Shortly after the assassination of Nádir Shah, Nawáb Zakaria Khan, the viceroy of Panjáb, died at Láhore. The following is his genealogy:—

- **Muhammad Amín Khan, Itimad-ud-doula.**
  - **Nawáb Abaul Samad Khan, Diler Jang.**
    - **Azad-ud-doula Nawáb Zakaria Khan, Khan Bahadur.**
      - **Yahya Khan.**
      - **Hayátulla Khan, surnamed Shah Nawáz Khan.**
    - **Khaneja Abdulla Khan.**
  - **Nawáb Kamr-ud-dín Khan, Itimad-ud-doula, Nasrat Jang.**
    - **Mír Muínul Mulk, surnamed Mír Mannú married, Morád Begum.**
      - **Amín-ud-dín Khan, died a minor.**
    - **Intizam-ud-doula, Khan-i-Khánán.**

Nawáb Zakaria Khan was for many years governor of Láhore. He was married to the daughter of his uncle, Nawab Kamr-ud-dín Khan. He had a high character for probity and uprightness, and his justice was proverbial.

His great popularity at Láhore.

He was popular with all classes of the community, and he liked the people of Láhore, as he was liked by them. In those days the bigoted *mullahs* of Láhore were in the habit of provoking quarrels with the Hindus on religious subjects, and used to subject them to much annoyance. The Khan always tried to settle these disputes amicably, and never shewed undue favour to any particular sect.

A story of his justice.

In illustration of his justice, the following story is narrated by a contemporary historian of Láhore, who had opportunities of forming an opinion of his public career. A Hindu of Láhore had the misfortune to possess a beautiful wife. A Moghal residing in the same locality became enamoured of her, and tried to secure her affections, but the modest woman remained loyal to her husband, and rejected the Moghal's overtures with scorn. The latter thereupon resolved to obtain by stratagem what he had failed to do by persuasion. He contrived that garments such as are worn by a Mahomedan bride should be secretly introduced into the woman's apartments and, from their being found in them, on a search being instituted at his instance, endeavoured to establish the fact of a secret alliance with her. But his wiles were laid bare by the governor, who, in the disguise of a faqír, himself ascertained the actual state of affairs, and ordered the Moghal to be put to death. Several other anecdotes of the justice of Nawáb Zakaria Khan are related by the people.

On the death of Zakaria Khan, the subedári of Láhore was conferred on Mír Momin Khan, but, shortly after, Yahya Khan, the eldest son of Zakaria Khan, was appointed governor, through the interest of the wazír, Kamr-ud-dín Khan.

Yahya Khan appointed to the government of Láhore.

The Sikh marauders had now grown so bold that they plundered the *dhobís* on their way to the Rávi, to wash clothes. An armed band of these ruffians proceeded to levy contributions at Emnabad, a town to the north of Láhore, and captured a large number of flocks and herds in its vicinity. Yahya Khan sent out a small detachment of troops, under Dewán Jaspat Rai, to disperse the insurgents, but the latter, falling upon the troops with fury, overpowered and repulsed them, killing the leader Dewán Jaspat Rai. The disastrous end of this expedition exasperated the viceroy, who now sent a large force against them under the command of Lakhpat Rai, the prime minister. The dewán fully avenged his brother's death by defeating the insurgents with great slaugther, and driving them to the north-eastern corner of the Panjáb. To complete his revenge, he brought with him a thousand Sikhs in irons to Láhore, and having compelled them to ride on donkeys barebacked, paraded them in the bazars of Láhore. They were then taken to the *nakhas khána* or horse market, outside the Delhi Gate of the city, and there beheaded one after another, without mercy. The place has since been called by the Sikhs *Shahídganj*, or place of martyrdom, in commemoration of the event. The scene of the execution is marked by a *samadh*, or shrine, erected in honour of Bhái Tárá Singh, the chief martyr, and an old companion of Govind Singh, who, though offered a pardon on condition of his renouncing his faith and consenting to have his long hair cut, persistently refused, and was thereupon beheaded,* 1746, A.D.

The Sikhs lay Emnabad under contribution.

They are defeated by Lakhpat Rai, the dewán.

Executions at *Shahídganj*, Láhore, 1746.

The governor, Yahya Khan, now issued a proclamation for a general massacre of all Sikhs, wherever they could be found. Death was to be the punishment of all persons who invoked the name of Guru Govind, and a reward was offered for the heads of Sikhs. Thousands were put to death daily and their heads brought before the subadár of Láhore for the reward. As usual with the votaries of the Guru on such occasions, many had their long hair cut short, and their flowing beards clipped, to avoid detection and consequent death, while others concealed themselves in the jungle or fled across the Sutlej.

Order to kill all Sikhs found in the Panjáb.

Reward offered for their heads.

It was about this time that the viceroyalty of Láhore was contested between Yahya Khan and his younger brother, Hayátulla Khan, on whom the title of Shahnawáz Khan had been conferred by Nádir Shah, in the expedition against the Afghan Núr Muhammad Khan Leli. Shahnawáz Khan bore a high character for courage and talent, and his principal business in the Panjáb since the invasion of Nádir Shah had been to quiet the districts and increase the revenue. He now refused to give his elder brother his share of the vast effects left by Zakaria Khan. Shahnawáz Khan held the governorship of Multán and, at the head of a large number of troops, marched to Láhore and encamped in the neighbourhood of Shalámár, where his father's tomb now is. Negotiations were carried on through Dewán Súrat Singh. On the day of the Íd festival, the brothers attended the *Idgáh* for divine service. When the service was over, an altercation ensued between the brothers, resulting in a rupture. Yahya Khan's followers were slain, and he was himself taken prisoner by Shahnawáz, who, proceeding to Láhore, took possession of all his deceased father's estates, and proclaimed himself viceroy, without waiting for the orders of the imperial government at

Difference between Yahya Khan and Shahnawáz Khan.

The latter marches to Láhore at the head of an army.

* "The hair, the scalp and the skull," said the old follower of Govind, "have a mutual connection: the head is linked with life, and I am prepared to yield it with pleasure."

And defeats and imprisons Yahya Khan.

Delhi, which was, indeed, too weak or indifferent to interfere. With Yahya Khan all his officers of state were put in chains, including the old dewán, Lakhpat Rai.

Shahnawáz Khan assumes the governorship of Láhore.

Shahnawáz Khan, on assuming the governorship of Láhore, erased from his own seal the words فدوي جان نثار محمد شاه "Devoted servant of Muhammad Shah," and substituted in their stead the following verse:—

His State seal.

"O Lord, thou art witness of my intentions; since my heart inclines to good, bestow good upon me."

The old seal in its border had the names of the emperor's ancestors commencing from Tymúr; in the new seal, he caused the names of the twelve *Imáms* to be engraved, having relinquished the *Sunní*, and adopted the *Shiá*, faith. The new governor conferred the office of prime minister on his dewán,* Koura Mal, whom he sent for from Multán and put at the head of affairs. He left Adína Beg Khan,† the active governor of the Jalandar Doáb, who had risen during the time of his father, Khan Bahádur, and had administered that turbulent province with much vigour and ability, in charge of that tract of country. He settled the revenues of the country and extorted large sums of money from his father's officers. The Delhi wazír, Nawáb Kamr-ud-dín Khan, used both threats and entreaties to induce Shahnawáz to liberate his brother, Yahya Khan, but without avail. Shortly afterwards, however, Yahya Khan was enabled to effect his escape, through a contrivance of his aunt, assisted by other ladies of the seraglio. Yahya Khan, having been packed up in a hamper, was placed on a tray and covered over with cloth. The tray was carried out on the head of a page, as if containing victuals, and the Khan, having thus regained his liberty, repaired to Delhi, assisted by Ahmad Yár Khan, a powerful Pathan of Kasúr. Shahnawáz Khan, when he discovered the trick, punished all the accomplices in the plot. As he vented his wrath upon his aunt, the old woman made the following sensible and affectionate remarks:—"Had the circumstances been reversed, and you, the prisoner, instead of Yahya Khan, I should have exerted all my endeavours to have you set at liberty, for the heart of a parent feels most affection for the child who is in adversity. I am now in your power; dispose of me as you think proper." These sagacious words, prompted by goodness of heart, had the effect of magic on Shahnawáz, who gave the old lady no further trouble. Yahya Khan, presenting himself before the emperor at Delhi, laid his grievances before his majesty, through his uncle, Kamr-ud-dín Khan. Fearful of the consequences of his own acts, and of the presence of his discontented brother at the capital, Shahnawáz Khan opened a secret correspondence with Ahmad Shah, Abdáli, who had become master of Afghanistán after the assassination of Nádir Shah, in June 1747.

He appoints Koura Mal his prime minister.

And leaves Adína Beg Khan in charge of the Jalandar Doab.

Yahya Khan's escape to Delhi.

Secret negotiations of Shahnawáz Khan with Ahmad Shah, Abdáli.

Early history of Ahmad Shah, Abdáli.

Ahmad Khan, the son of Zaman Khan and grandson of Daulat Khan, belonged to the Saddozai sub-division of the Abdális. The family originally resided at Multán, but Abdulla Khan, the son of Hayát Sultan, the ancestor of Ahmad, settled in the neighbourhood of Herat in 1129 Hijri, and was

* Koura Mal was originally a corn chandler, and could hardly earn his bread, but he had now become possessed of immense riches, and had the privilege of using kettle-drums and flags. He was at this time governor of Multán.—*Farhatún Nazirin* of *Muhammad Aslam.*

† The name of Adína Beg Khan will frequently occur in these pages. He was the son of Channú, an Aiám of Sharakpúr, Tahsíl Láhore. He received his training in a Moghal family, and having remained at Bajwára in Hoshiarpur, for some time, emigrated early to Allahabád, where he began his career as a common soldier. The chief object of his study was the revenue work, and his interest in the finances induced him to give up his military occupation and return to the Panjáb where he succeeded in obtaining the appointment of collector (corresponding, in the present day, to the post of patwárí) in the village of Kanak near Ludhiáná. The tact and judgment which he displayed in the revenue work, soon obtained for him the governorship of Sultánpur under the viceroy of the Panjáb, and he held this appointment at the time of Nádir Shah's invasion.—*Ahwál-i-Adína Beg Khan.*

acknowledged as the head of the Abdális, who inhabit the mountainous country near Herat. The Saddozais are held in religious veneration, and this fact, combined with the activity and personal bravery which young Abdulla possessed, materially tended to his rise. His aspirations to sovereign power led to his imprisonment by Abbas Kuli Khan, *Shamlu*, the Herat governor of Shah Husani. *Safví*, king of Persia; but when the kazalbáshis expelled Abbas from Herat, Abdulla found an opportunity of making his escape from confinement. Having collected the people of his tribe, he defeated and imprisoned Jáfar Khan, who had become governor of Herat, and took possession of the whole tract of country known by that name. When Nádir Shah rose to power and subdued Herat, he found Zulfikár Khan, Abdáli, and his brother Ahmad Khan (afterwards Ahmad Shah) captives of the Ghilzais. Having liberated the brothers, he conferred upon them new honours, and sent them to Mazindaran to live in peace,* though he kept a watchful eye over them. Nádir Shah had great respect for Ahmad Khan, and, on his expedition to India, took him to that country. Ahmad Khan, on attaining power, changed the name of his tribe, from some superstitious motive, from Abdáli to Durráni, by which it has ever since been known. Having fought his way through the greater part of Khorasán, and overrun the neighbouring countries of Kandahar (where a treasure of 30 lakhs of rupees, which was being escorted to the treasury of Nádir Shah, fell into his hands) he, at the age of 23 years, was crowned king of Kandahar, in 1747, under the name of Ahmad Shah, with the assistance of the Durráni, Kazalbáshi, Bilúchi and Hazárá chiefs.† Having

He accompanies Nádir Shah to Hindostán.

His conquests.

Is crowned king of Kandahar, 1747.

* There is no authority for the statement made by Dow and Prinsep that the Durráni king was originally a mace-bearer of Nádir Shah's. He was the chief of his own tribe, the Saddozais, and Nádir Shah, after his conquest of Kandahar, had sent him to reside with honour in Mazindaran, his object being to keep the enterprising youth at a distance. But all accounts agree that Ahmad Shah accompanied Nádir Shah to Hindostán.

† Ahmad Shah, on assuming sovereign power, caused a coin to be struck in his name which bore the following inscription :—

حکم شد از قادر بیچون باحمد بادشاه سکه زن بر سیم وزر از موج ماهی تا بماه

"God, the inscrutable, commanded Ahmad, the king, to impress his name on silver and gold from the bottom of the sea to the moon."

A coin struck in Káshmír had the following inscription :—

سکه بر زر بزد بفضل اله
شاه عالم پناه احمد شاه

"Through the Grace of God, Ahmad Shah the king, the Asylum of the World, struck gold coin."

According to Mr. Rodger's he struck a coin at Láhore bearing the following inscription :—

در دران احمد شاه بادشاه
ضرب دارالسلطنت لاهور
جلوس میمنت مانوس احد

i.e., "King Ahmad Shah, the pearl of the Durráni: struck at the capital of Láhore in first auspicious year of the reign."—*Journal of B. A. Society*.

His seal was in the shape of a peacock, and had the following inscription on it :—

الحکم لله یا فتاح — احمد شاه در دران

"By the command of God, the Bestower of victory, Ahmad, the king, became the pearl of the Durránis."

Ahmad Shah entertained a great veneration for his spiritual guide, Sábar Shah of Láhore. He was often seen lying naked by the side of Ahmad on his throne, rubbing the king's ears, the king not uttering a word. It is said that, on Nádir Shah's death, the faqir, putting on Ahmad's head a chaplet of grass, saluted him king.—*Memoirs of Abdul Karim Ulvi.*

The king had the highest esteem for the issue of Nádir Shah. Thus, he left Shah Rukh Mirza, the son of Raza Kuli, and grandson of Nádir by Fatima Sultan Begum, daughter of Shah Husein, *Safvi*, in the government of Mashhad, and married his son Tymúr Shah to the daughter of Shah Rukh Mirza.—*Ibid.*

spent the winter in Kandahar, in setting the affairs of the conquered districts and arranging his plans for future expeditions, he left it, in the spring of 1748, at the head of 12,000 Durráni fighting men. He reduced the Khilzáis, and put to flight Nádir's governor at Gházni. His eyes were fixed on India, as the source of wealth and the most productive field of conquest and glory, and, having reduced Kábul and Peshávar, and expelled the Governor Násir Khan,* who had declared for the Great Moghal, he, with incredible celerity, crossed the Indus, expelling from Atak and Chach the imperial officers, whose feeble resistance was well chastised.

He fixes his eye on India.

Crosses the Indus.

Shahnawáz Khan forsakes the cause of the Abdáli.

In the meantime, the usurping viceroy of Láhore had been taunted with treason by his uncle, the grand-wazír at Delhi, who, appealing to his nephew's sense of honor, urged upon him the necessity of standing firm in his allegiance to the hereditary sovereign of their family and country. The young man's pride was touched, and, generosity prevailing over policy, he resolved upon opposing the arms of the invading Durránis. Uza Khan, an amír of the Durráni king's, who had been deputed by his master to Láhore, to settle terms with the Láhore governor, finding that the wind had ceased to blow in his favour, returned in despair to Atak, without waiting for the king's instructions. Not discouraged by the unfavourable issue of his first negotiations with the Láhore governor, Ahmad Shah now sent his family priest, Bába Sábir Shah, to renew them, hoping that his saintly position would enable him to win over the governor to his side. Sábir Shah, on coming to Láhore, endeavoured to intimidate the governor into a surrender, but lost his life in the arrogant attempt. The particulars were thus related to Khwája Abdul Karím by Muhammad Yár Khan, Ahmad Shah's minister, who was intimately acquainted with the darvesh.†

Sábir Shah, the family high priest of Ahmad Shah.

He is sent as a plenipotentiary to the Court of Láhore.

His high reputation as a faqír.

His prognostication.

Bába Sábir, a handsome youth, was the son of a farrier of Láhore. From an early age he had an inclination to abandon worldly concerns, and leaving his own country, while yet very young, he travelled to Kábul, Kandahar and Herat. A short time before the assassination of Nádir Shah, the youthful darvesh was seen pitching a small tent, and they asked him, "Faqír, what do you mean by this?" He replied: "The empire of Nádir Shah has ceased to exist; I am setting up the tent of Ahmad Shah." As predicted by him, Ahmad Shah became king, and this is said to have greatly increased the influence of Sábir Shah with the Abdáli king. It was on the advice of Sábir Shah that Ahmad Shah, on assuming sovereign authority, adopted the title of *Durri Daurán*, or the "Pearl of the Age," whence he and his Abdáli descendants were called Durránis. When the faqír came to Láhore, the spies of Shahnawáz Khan informed him that the magician of Ahmad Shah had come with the object of bewitching all the guns. His person having been seized, he was brought into the presence of Shahnawáz Khan, who, however, at the intercession of Adína Beg Khan, and knowing that he had been sent as the agent of the Abdáli king, received him in open darbár, with the civility and respect to which his rank entitled him. But the holy man, puffed up with the idea of his religious greatness, and of his being the plenipotentiary of the Durráni sovereign, looked on all around him with scorn, and began to address Shahnawáz Khan as a subordinate. He censured him for his conduct in first inviting the

The faqír's insolence to the Láhore governor.

* Jahán Khan, the commander-in-chief of the Afghans was, at this time, joined by Abdul Samad Khan, Muhammadzai of Iskinagar, 16 *kos* north of Peshávar. Násir Khan, being unable to encounter the Shah's army, crossed the Atak and fled to Chach Hazárá. Sardar Jahán Khan was sent to pursue him with a detachment of troops, and he expelled the chief from Hazárá. Násir fled to Láhore and his valuables and munitions of war fell into the hands of the Afghan commander.—*Memoirs of Abdul Karím Ulvi.*

† *Memoirs of Khwája Abdul Karím.*

Durráni king to the Panjáb, and then seeking the degradation of defection from his allegiance, and threatened that, if he failed to tender his submission to the Shah, he would be severely punished. These remarks, made publicly, exasperated the young governor in the highest degree. He ordered the insolent faqír and his colleague, Muhammad Yár Khan, to be committed to prison. The next day, Shahnawáz Khan's courtiers persuaded him that he would bring a great calamity on himself and the whole Indian nation, if he allowed Sábir Shah, the magician, to live. The governor, on this, gave orders that the priest be immediately put to death, and the executioner's sword sent the holy ambassador's head rolling on the floor. Muhammad Yár Khan was set at liberty at the intercession of some of the Omerahs. Shahnawáz now made preparations for an active resistance to the invading army. He collected all the troops of the neighbouring districts, and put the city and fort in a state of defence, strengthening the gates and the principal positions with artillery, and mounting cannons on the ramparts of the fort. Ahmad Shah was greatly incensed at the murder of his high priest and ambassador, and immediately crossed the Rávi. The governor of Láhore sent a force under Zi!a Khan, a Pathan of Kasúr, to oppose him, but the Khan went over to the enemy with all his troops. Áhmad Shah then attacked the governor under the walls of Láhore, where the latter had intrenched himself. After a feeble opposition, the Indian troops were disastrously defeated in sight of Láhore and fled in great confusion and terror, their defences having been all carried by the Durránis. Shahnawáz Khan fled to Delhi with all his jewels and valuables, Moharram 1161 H. (January 1747). Kamr-ud-dín Khan was so much enraged at his previous conduct that he instantly put him in confinement. Moghalpúra, then the richest and most populous *mohalla* in the city of Láhore, outside the present town walls, was pillaged by the invaders, and the Omerahs of state who lived there, were also plundered. The Abdáli conqueror then made his triumphant entry into the city, the resources of which, now all at his disposal, materially tended to strengthen his arms. He found there a large quantity of artillery and small arms. A heavy contribution was levied on the city, and it was some time after that Momín Khan, the Kasúr Afghan, and Lakhpat Rai, the dewán, having paid their *quota* of the contribution, obtained their freedom. The zemindars of the Panjáb paid him homage, and the hill rájás sent their agents to him with presents and tendered their submission. The king stayed at Láhore for above a month, to arrange the affairs of the Panjáb, and to prepare himself for the great expedition which was the chief object of his visit to this distant land.

The murder of Sábir Shah.

Active warlike preparations of the Láhore governor.

First invasion of Ahmad Shah, January, 1747.

Defeat of the Láhore governor.

The sack of Moghalpúra, the wealthiest quarter of the city of Láhore.

Ahmad Shah enters Láhore,

Which he subjects to a heavy contribution.

Having been joined by fresh contingents from Kábul, and having conferred the governorship of Láhore on Dewán Lakhpat Rai, and the dewáni on Momin Khan of Kasúr, the Abdáli king continued his march to the Sutlej. Muhammad Shah, on hearing this, sent for his son Ahmad, kissed him in open darbár, gave him a copy of the *Qurán*, and then dismissed him, with instructions to march and check the progress of the invader. The prince had, at his command, a powerful army consisting of 80,000 horse, and was accompanied by the grand wazír, Kamr-ud-dín Khan, Abul Mansur Khan, Safdar Jang and Saiyad Salabat. The grand wazír had in his train Abdulla Khan and Faizulla Khan, sons of Alí Muhammad Khan, the Rohilla chief, who were staying at Delhi with their contingent. The Durráni force did not exceed 12,000 men. The Moghal troops took up an entrenched position at Manaura, nine miles from Sirhind, and were joined by Rájá Isar Singh, the son of Jai Singh of Jaipúr, and other Rájputáná chiefs who came with their respective *quotas*, as well as by some powerful zemindars. The Abdáli

Advance to the Sutlej.

The emperor sends the heir-apparent, Ahmad, to oppose the invading army of Ahmad Shah.

crossed the river at a ford, and, the Indian troops having been left in the rear, he obtained possession of Sirhind, where a large quantity of baggage and ammunition, together with a number of cannons, with which the Abdáli was before entirely unprovided, fell into his hands. He then successfully cut off the convoys of the Delhi army, and intercepted the communication of the imperialists with the capital. The energy displayed by the Durránis intimidated the Delhians. Various skirmishes took place between the detachments of the two armies located at different points, but nothing decisive occurred for about a month. The Durráni king was in the meantime enabled to advance some pieces of artillery, and a heavy cannonade was kept up for several hours on the flank of the imperial army.

The Abdáli occupies Sirhind.

Desultory skirmishes.

One evening, as the aged wazír, Kamr-ud-dín Khan was engaged in prayer, a cannon ball from the Durráni artillery struck him in the knee, from the effects of which the good old wazír expired during the course of the night. The wazír was esteemed and loved by all the troops, who had the greatest confidence in his wisdom and bravery. His death was concealed by the heir-apparent, Mirza Ahmad, and his son Mír Mannú,* a brave and intrepid soldier. The prince called together some of his principal sardars, and it was resolved, in a council of war, that the body of the wazír should be placed in a sitting posture in the howdah of his own elephant, supported by pillows, and early next morning the battle be renewed. The young prince Ahmad led the attack early the following morning with great valour, supported by the youthful Mannú, who performed prodigious acts of personal bravery. The fight was a most sanguinary one, the Durránis maintaining their ground with great resolution. They were, however, overwhelmed by superior numbers, and were on the point of flight when another unfortunate circumstance happened. Isar Singh, the Jaipúr rájá, who commanded a body of 20,000 horse, approached the wazír's elephant to solicit orders, when he found that the wazír was dead. Struck with panic, he left the field† with his troops, and his example was followed by the imperial troops. The Abdáli, taking advantage of this confusion, pressed the imperial troops hard. The youthful Mannú, however, stood firm, and by his personal exertions not only rallied the troops of Safdar Jang and other Indian allies, but renewed the charge with such vigour as to break the centre of the Durránis, and spread the utmost confusion throughout their ranks. In the meanwhile, the Afghans, ignorant of the use of Indian rockets, which they had seized in large numbers at Láhore, in the arsenals of Shahnawáz Khan, used them in such a manner as to cause the greatest injury among their own people. Their flanks were enveloped in smoke and the panic and confusion which ensued may be better imagined than described. Mannú took immediate advantage of the confusion in the Durráni lines, and, making a grand charge, became complete master of the field, which was strewn with the Durráni dead and wounded. The Durránis fled, and were pursued for ten miles beyond their entrenchments, which were all demolished by the imperial elephants. The loss on both sides was equal, but the surprising feats of valour displayed by the youthful Mannú enabled the Moghals to carry the day.

Wazír Kamr-ud-dín Khan killed by a cannon ball.

The Rájputs desert the imperialists.

The bravery displayed by the youthful Mannú, son of the deceased wazír.

The Abdáli king is defeated,

Such was the blow inflicted on the Durránis by the gallant Mannú that the Abdáli king, relinquishing all his designs against the Indian empire, pre-

And compelled to march off homewards, March, 1748.

*The gallant Mír Mannú, on seeing his father dead, rent his clothes and began to weep bitterly, but Ahmad Khan who held the command of 5,000 troops in the imperial army, reminded him that it was no time to weep like a child, but that he should act like a man and drive the foreigners from the country.—*Tárikh-i-Ahmadi.*

†The Rájputs were, on this occasion, dressed in yellow. A Rájput when so dressed in the battle field, has sworn not to turn his back to the field, yet the troops under Isar Singh fled so precipitately, that they did not stop until they had reached Jaipur.

cipitately recrossed the Atak, without making any further effort to effect the object of his invasion.

The Sikhs harass his rear.

Mír Mannú appointed governor of the Panjáb under the title of Moín-ul-Mulk.

The watchful Sikhs harassed the king's rear, and, the Panjáb having been thus recovered for the Moghals, Mír Mannú, the son of the late wazír, was, for his conspicuous gallantry in the field, appointed governor of Multán and Láhore by the imperial government at Delhi, under the title of Moín-ul-Mulk.

The emperor's grief on the loss of his wazír.

The emperor had a sincere attachment for his wazír, Kamr-ud-dín Khan, on whose counsel he chiefly relied, and in whom he reposed the most implicit confidence. When the news of the wazír's death reached the emperor, he wept bitterly, and, retiring to his chamber, passed the whole night in a state of restlessness. Next morning, as he mounted the throne as usual, the Omerahs of state came to condole with him on the death of the wazír, and began to speak highly in praise of the deceased, in order to flatter the emperor, whose grief was thus renewed. He exclaimed: "Cruel fate! thus to break the staff of my old age. Where now shall I find so faithful a servant?"* He was thus afflicted when he breathed his last, on the morning of 14th April 1748, in the thirty-first year of his reign.

Death of the emperor Muhammad Shah, 1748.

His person and character.

Muhammad Shah, in his youth, was of a robust make and possessed good intellect. He was fond of hunting, and of the sport now known as "Polo," but had a tendency to heart disease. In the latter part of his life, the constant use of opium, together with other excesses, shattered and debilitated his whole frame.

His issue.

At the time Muhammad Shah died, the heir-apparent, Prince Ahmad, was with his army at Sirhind. Malika Zamáni, one of the emperor's widows, who was the daughter of Farrukhseer, in order to prevent commotions, enjoined Ghazí-ud-dín Khan and other Omerahs to keep the event secret until the return of the prince. The corpse was put into a long wooden packing case for European clocks, and, having been wrapped in a sheet procured from the steward, on the pretence that it was required for the dinner table, was temporarily buried in Hayát Baksh's garden.† The emperor left one son, Mirza Sultan Ahmad, and one daughter, Hazrat Begum. Prince

* Dewán Amar Nath, author of *Tárikh-i-Khálsá*, a MS. work lent to me by his son Dewán Rám Nath, notices the death of Nawáb Kamr-ud-dín Khan in the following interesting passage, which I take from his excellent work :—

نواب قمرالدین خان دران زمانیکه بوظائف باد حق مواظبت داشت بضرب

١١٦١ ١١٦١

گلوله جان بحق سپرد - آه وزیرالممالك بها در شهید گردید - دهلي خراب شده

١١٦١ ١١٦١

و قمر عالم رفت - زهي نواب قمرالدین خان - تاریخ وفاتش یافتند - و محمد

شاه حینیکه این خبر شنید این بیت هندي بدیهه بر زبان آورد بن جنکي همکو

نیند نه آتي تهي سوگئي - جو دیکهه همکو هنستے تهي سو آخر کو رو گئي

"Nawáb Kamr-ud-dín Khan was struck by a cannon ball while engaged in prayer and surrendered his life to the Almighty. The era of his death is obtained from the words:—'Alas! the gallant minister of state is dead;' 'Delhi has been ruined;' 'The moon of the world has set;' 'Alas! Nawáb Kamr-ud-dín Khan.' The King Muhammad Shah, when he heard this intelligence, repeated the following verse extempore :—

"He without whom I had no rest is no more: he who was cheered on beholding me has departed."

† The corpse of Muhammad Shah having been subsequently disinterred from the garden of Hayát Baksh, was buried in state in the precincts of the mausoleum of Nizám-ud-dín. Prince Ahmad, on ascending the throne, gave his parent the title of *Hazrat Firdaus Arámgáh*.

Sultan Ahmad, on receiving intelligence of his father's death, set out immediately for Delhi, leaving Nizám-ul-Mulk in charge of the affairs of the Panjáb.

CHAPTER XXIII.

MOJÁHID-UD-DÍN ABUL NÁSIR AHMAD SHAH.

Ahmad Shah proclaimed emperor, 1748.

In less than a week after his father's death, Ahmad Shah, having assumed the imperial umbrella and all the insignia of royalty, was proclaimed emperor under the title of *Mojáhid-ud-dín Abul Násir Ahmad Shah Gházi*. The ceremony of inauguration took place at Pánipat on 2nd Jamadi-ul-awal, 1161 H. (or April 18th, 1748). Abul Mansúr Khan *Safdar Jang*, nephew and son-in-law of the late Saádat Khan, viceroy of Oudh, assumed the titular functions of wazír, though the power was, to a great extent, exercised by the empress-mother. She was a Hindu dancing girl, and, having been introduced into Muhammad Shah's harem in the beginning of his reign, received the title of Udham Bái. She was afterwards called "Báíjiá Sáhiba," and then "the parent of the pure, the lady of the age, Sáhibjee Sáhiba, on whom be peace." On becoming the mother of the heir-apparent, she assumed the title of Nawáb Kudsia Begum. She was entirely governed by the head eunuch, Jáwed Khan, a man about fifty years old, who could neither read nor write. He was created "Nawáb Bahádur," with a *Mansab*, or rank of 6,000, and in concert with Ahmad Shah's mother, undertook the management of the realm. The new emperor, who had been brought up in the recesses of the seraglio, and had no experience of public business, became absorbed in youthful pleasures, and gave up the whole of his time to pastimes, sport and debauchery, frivolities inherited by him on both sides. He extended his *zanáná* so that it occupied a space of a mile. He lived in gardens for one and two months at a time, and would remain without seeing the face of any male being for a week together.

He confers the office of wazír on Safder Jang.

The empress-mother.

The power of the eunuch, Jáwed Khan.

The new emperor gives himself up to the pleasures of the harem.

Mír Mannú governs the Panjáb with vigour.

During the early period of Ahmad Shah's reign, the Panjáb continued to enjoy peace and prosperity. The new governor of the province, Mir Moin-ul-Mulk, was a man of vigour and activity. He confirmed Koura Mal as judicial dewán and his deputy, and retained the services of the experienced Adína Beg Khan, who governed the Jalandar Doáb with much tact and judgment. The Sikhs, in the meantime, again became troublesome. The invasion of the Abdáli was a matter of all-absorbing interest, upon which the attention of the whole empire was concentrated, and it afforded the ever vigilant Sikhs a favourable opportunity of springing up in numbers and renewing their acts of depredation. They again began to pay visits to the holy tank and shrines at Amritsar, and had even the audacity to throw up a fort of mud which they called Rám Rouni, and which is now called Rámgarh, in the vicinity of Amritsar. Jassa Singh, the *Kalal*, one of their number, rose into power and ventured to proclaim that the "Dal" of the "*Khálsá*," or the army of the theocracy of "Singhs," would be the new power that should govern the State. Fanatic confederacies of the Sikhs were now seen roving in all directions, ravaging the country and devastating the very suburbs of Láhore. Firmly established in his authority, Mír Mannú considered the best mode of chastising the Sikhs. His first act

But the Sikhs reappear with increased strength.

And proclaim the birth of a new power in the State.

Mannú adopts measures to chastise them.

was to storm the fort of Rám Rouni which he captured and reduced. He then stationed detachments of troops in all parts infested by the Sikhs, with stringent orders to shave their heads and beards wherever they might be found. These measures, being rigorously enforced, inspired public confidence, checked the progress of Sikh proselytism, and compelled the votaries of the Guru to conceal themselves in the mountains or jungles. Mír Mannú issued strict orders to the hill rájás to seize the Sikhs and send them in irons to Láhore. These orders were obeyed, and hundreds of Sikhs were brought daily to Láhore and butchered at the *Nakhas*, or *Shahídgunj*, outside the Delhi Gate, in sight of multitudes of spectators. The young Mannú became an irreconcilable foe of the Sikhs, and was determined to extirpate the nation; but the influence of his minister, Koura Mal, who was himself a Sikh of the *Khálsá* sect, withheld him from carrying out his resolution. His plans were also secretly thwarted by Adína Beg Khan, the artful governor of Jalandar Doáb, who saw in the turbulent tribe a means of advancing his own interests, and took care not to reduce them altogether, but to confine their excursions within such bounds as to give them internal security, without affording them an opportunity of ostensibly coming in contact with the ruling authority.

The Sikhs are dispersed.

They are butchered in large numbers at *Shahídganj*, Láhore.

Artful contrivances of Adína Beg Khan.

Abdáli Ahmad Shah had retreated across the Indus with no inclination to relinquish his designs on Hindostán, whose glittering gold had dazzled his eyes when he had first visited India in the train of his more formidable predecessor, Nádir Shah. He was not then an inattentive observer of the vast resources of the Indian empire, and a single defeat was not enough to induce him to give up his plans of conquest and aggrandizement. At the close of the rains of 1748, he re-crossed the Indus, at the head of a considerable army, and disturbed the peace which the Panjáb had enjoyed since the assumption of power by the vigorous Mannú. In vain did the young goveror ask for re-inforcements from the distracted court at Delhi. Thinking that further delay might prove disastrous, Mannú, at the head of his troops, moved from Láhore to repel the danger as best he could. He pitched his camp at Sodhárá, on the south bank of the Chináb, where he threw up three entrenchments. Ahmad Shah, having crossed the Jhelum and Chináb, arrived within six miles of his camp. Some smart skirmishes took place, but Moin-ul-Mulk, seeing the superiority of the enemy's forces, wisely refrained from hazarding a general action. The Durránis laid waste the country around Láhore. Moin-ul-Mulk at length despatched agents to the Durráni camp to arrange terms of peace. Ahmad Shah's own administration had not yet been firmly established on the other side of the Indus, and the bold front assumed by Mír Mannú, who had effectually checked his progress at Sirhind, made a deep impression on his mind. He, therefore, thought it prudent to withdraw on the condition that the revenues of the four districts of Pasrúr, Gujrát, Siálkot and Aurangabád, the most fruitful principalities of the Panjáb, should be assigned to him, as they had been to Nádir Shah, from whom he pretended to have inherited his power and title. The governor further agreed to hold the government of the Panjáb in the name of the invader, and to remit the tribute, before mentioned, regularly to the Shah.

Second invasion of Ahmad Shah, 1848.

Mannú marches from Láhore to repel the invasion.

The country around Láhore ravaged.

Mannú sues the Durráni king for peace.

The terms of peace.

Ahmad Shah retires across the Indus.

The affairs of the Panjáb being thus satisfactorily arranged, the Abdáli king retraced his steps to Kandahar. On his way he settled the districts of Dera Ismáil Khan, Dera Gházi Khan and Shikárpur and the southern Afghan tribes acknowledged him as king.

The southern Afghan tribes acknowledge him as their king.

The praise awarded to the young Mannú for his success in averting the coming storm, aroused a feeling of intense jealousy against him among

Intrigues against Mannú at the court of Delhi.

the Omerahs in the Imperial Court at Delhi, who contrived to throw him into disfavour by proposing to the puppet king that the governorship of Multán should be conferred on Shahnawáz Khan. The Omerah who most dreaded Mannú's power was the Wazír Safdar Jang, who was forming plans for asserting his own independence in the province of Oudh. Mír Mannú was deprived of the governorship of Multán, which was conferred on Shahnawáz Khan. Mannú was not a man who would allow himself to be calmly superseded by his nephew, whom he had himself supplanted in Láhore. Relying on his own resources, and being fully aware of the imbecility of the Delhi Emperor and of his weakness, he resolved on a rupture with the new governor and detached his minister, Koura Mal, to resist him by force of arms. Shahnawáz Khan, having collected all his troops, came on to the frontier of Multán to give the dewán battle. Several skirmishes took place with varied success, and for about six months the new governor of Multán maintained his ground, but at the end of that period a decisive battle was fought which determined his fate, and he was himself slain and his whole army dispersed. Elated with the success which had attended his follower's arms, the viceroy of Láhore conferred on Koura Mal the title of rájá, and created him the subadar of the province of Multán.

He is deprived of his charge of Multán, which is made over to Shahnawáz.

Mannú resists.

Shahnawáz is defeated and slain.

Koura Mal created subadar of Multán, with the title of rájá.

Mír Mannú, now in the height of his glory, thought he was as much independent of the imperial court at Delhi whose authority he had successfully baffled, as of the Abdáli monarch, whom his diplomacy and prowess had kept in check. He had subdued the turbulent Sikhs and cleared the Mánjha and the Doáb countries from the inroads of these mercenaries. He therefore audaciously withheld from the Abdáli Shah the revenue of the four districts which he had stipulated to pay him, thus affording him a pretext for again crossing the Indus, which he did in the season of 1751-52. Having advanced to the right bank of the Chináb, he sent his agent, Dewán Sukh Jiwan Mal, to the Láhore governor, to demand the arrears of revenue. Mír Mannú denied his liability to pay anything in the shape of subsidy to the Abdáli Shah, adding that he had agreed to pay it previously under stress of circumstances, but he did not consider the condition bound either party, and held that each was always at liberty to act according to circumstances. As, however, the Shah had taken the trouble of coming to the Panjáb, he would be glad to pay him such arrears as might be found due, provided he forthwith retraced his steps to Kábul, as the zemindars had all fled in consternation on hearing of the approach of the Abdáli King, and it was impossible to levy a tax of even a pice upon the people of the country as long as the Durráni troops remained where they were. None knowing better than Mannú himself that the reply made by him to the Abdáli King was neither satisfactory nor reassuring, he followed Sukh Jiwan Mal himself to the Chináb, at the head of a large number of troops, to show a bold front, expecting that the invader might thus be induced to retire. He also requested Rájá Koura Mal, Názim of Multán, and Adína Beg Khan, Bahrám Jang, governor of the Jalandar Doáb, to join him at the Chináb with their respective forces. He sent his mother and family to Jammu, where they would be safe and out of reach of all pursuit. Ahmad Shah, without risking a battle, crossed the Chináb, and encamped between Sodra and Wazirábad. Marching then towards the Rávi, he halted at a short distance from the suburbs of Shahdará. Mír Mannú crossed the Rávi at the head of a considerable force, and pitched his tents opposite those of the invader. Here he took up an intrenched position, and continued firing was kept up on both sides for several days, but with no perceptible advantage

Mannú withholds tribute from Ahmad Shah.

Third invasion of Ahmad Shah, 1751-52.

Mír Mannú marches to the Chináb to oppose the progress of the invader.

Ahmad Shah proceeds to Láhore without risking battle.

to either. The whole country between the Rávi and the Chináb was devastated by the Durránis. At length the invaders suddenly broke up their camp and proceeded to invest Láhore, having crossed the river at a ford higher up on the east. Ahmad Shah encamped at the Shalámár gardens, the favourite pleasure ground of kings and conquerors. Mír Mannú marched back to the city in alarm, barricaded the streets, and, having strengthened the interior posts, took up a strong intrenched position under the walls of the city, and remained strictly on the defensive. Skirmishes took place every day, and for four months did the gallant Mír Mannú maintain his position, baffling all attempts of the invading army to conquer it. The Durránis subjected the intrenched posts of Mannú to a strict blockade, cutting off all communications from without. Famine now prevailed in the Láhore camp to such an extent that the only fodder for horses and cattle consisted of chopped straw from the roofs of thatched houses, while the provisions for the men were completely exhausted. A council of war was now convened, consisting of Rájá Koura Mal, Adína Beg Khan and other Omerahs. They unanimously agreed that a *sortie* was imperatively necessary, and that it would be impossible for the troops to hold out much longer in a state of starvation. Rájá Koura Mal differed from this view, on the ground that the Indian troops were no match in the field for the hardy Afghans, and that it would be mad to run the risk of such an unequal combat. The hot weather, he urged, was setting in, and in a fortnight more the hill veterans of the Shah would find it trying for them to stand the scorching heat of the sun, and would either raise the siege, or attack the besieged in their intrenched posts, to their own disadvantage. The surrounding country had been devastated and scarcity of forage and provisions would as seriously affect the Durráni camp as the Indian. On the whole, urged the rájá, the foreigners will be placed at a considerable disadvantage if the beseiged continued quietly to hold their own under their present trying circumstances. This was, of course, the best policy that could, under the circumstances, be adopted, but the patience of all was exhausted, and the prudent counsel of the experienced Hindu was not heeded. Preparations were made for an attack on the enemy's position, and early on the morning of 12th April, 1752, the impetuous Mannú sallied out with his right and left wings, and took up his position on the elevation of an old brick kiln near the village of Mahmúd Buti. The Abdáli king made immediate preparations for an advance with his cavalry. His artillery moved into action, and a heavy cannonade was kept up till midday on both sides. The battle was a desperate one, and the result seemed at first doubtful, when some confusion taking place among the Indian troops, the Shah ordered an immediate charge of his Durráni horse. So impetuous was the attack that the Indians gave way, and the tide of victory at once turned in favour of the Afghans. Mír Mannú was compelled to fall back within his own lines in the intrenchments. Rájá Koura Mal, at the head of a chosen body of cavalry, came to the rescue of his master, and so determined were his followers that the scale would have once more inclined the other way, had not an unfortunate incident happened which cost the life of the gallant rájá. The elephant on which he rode accidentally trod on an old grave, the earth of which sank under the feet of the huge animal, which fell down with its rider. Before the animal could be extricated by the driver, the rájá was overtaken by a Durráni horseman, who at once severed his head from his body, and carried it as a trophy to the Abdáli Shah. The death of this brave general spread consternation throughout the whole of his troops who fled in dismay. Adína Beg Khan also withdrew, and such was the

And lays siege to Láhore.

Protracted war operations.

Distress in the Láhore camp.

A council of war convened.

Mannú sallies out of his intrenched position,

But is defeated and compelled to fall back.

Rájá Koura Mal killed in the action.

panic, that the viceroy, seeing that a prolonged contest would be ruinous, prudently retired into the citadel.

The city fortifications were tottering, and wholly unfit for defence. The troops had just received a shock which had disheartened them. To expect reinforcements or other help from Delhi in time was a vain hope. The citizens were worn out with the prolonged seige. Under these circumstances Mannú thought that his best policy was to submit to the conqueror.

Mannú tenders his submission to the Shah,

He accordingly notified his intention to the Shah, and sent some influential Omerahs of his court to his camp in the Shalámár gardens. The negotiations were conducted through Shah Wali Khan, the grand wazír. The Abdáli was only too glad to close the campaign, and sent his principal officer, Jahán Khan, to the city to conduct the viceroy to his camp.

Who receives him with honour.

He received Mír Mannú with all the honours due to his rank, and bestowed on him a high eulogy for the courage and bravery displayed by him on all occasions, and for his skill and dexterity as a warrior, and tact and judgment as a counsellor.*

The viceroy laid at the victor's feet fifty lakhs of rupees, eleven horses, with gold and silver trappings, and two elephants, with howdahs wrought with silver and gold. The Shah conferred on him a rich *khilat*, with a jewelled sword and a horse, and re-instated him as his viceroy in the Panjáb.

Conquest of Kashmir.

The Shah now re-crossed the Rávi and encamped at the mausoleum of Jahángír. From this place he sent a Durráni, Amir Abdulla Khan, at the head of a strong detachment, to seize Káshmír, and expel the Moghal governor of that province. The delegate penetrated into the valley, and reduced the province to subjection without encountering any opposition. The Kábul Khatri, Sukh Jiwan Mal, was appointed the Shah's governor in Káshmír.

The country as far east as Sirhind is ceded to the Abdáli,

During the same campaign the Shah, by negotiation, obtained from the Delhi emperor a cession of the country as far east as Sirhind. Abdulla Khan, in the meanwhile, rejoined the king at Shahdará, and, the rainy season being about to set in, the Shah re-crossed the Indus, and conducted his army back to Kábul.†

Distracted state of the Panjáb.

The Sikhs appear again on the scene.

After the departure of the Abdáli invader, the Panjáb remained in a distracted state. A war extending over a period of half a year, carried by strangers in the heart of the province, had necessarily enfeebled the administration, and the Sikhs were not slow to take advantage of this state of things. They extended their depredations on all sides, and laid waste the country lying between Amritsar and the hills. The viceroy of Láhore ordered Adína Beg Khan, whose inaction at Láhore was not altogether above suspicion, to inflict on the seditious Sikhs a severe chastisement. Adína Beg Khan watched for an opportunity to destroy the Sikh union, and to bring them to order.

But are defeated by Adina Beg Khan, 1752.

During a festival at Makhowál, their holy place of worship, while thousands of Sikhs had repaired thither on a pilgrimage, he suddenly

* An interesting anecdote is related here by Abdul Karím Ulvi, the historian of Ahmad Shah. When Mír Mannú presented himself before the Abdáli conqueror, the Shah sarcastically asked him, "How is it that you did not present yourself before the threshold of your lord before this to do him homage?" "Because" replied Mír Mannú, "I had another lord to serve." "And why," rejoined the Durráni Shah satirically, "did not your lord and master succour you at this moment of your distress?" "Because," answered the youthful Mannú boldly, "he was sure that his servant would take care of himself." "And supposing," continued the Shah, "I had fallen into your hands, what treatment would you have shown to me?" "I should have severed your majesty's head from your body and sent it to my king," was the reply. "And now that you are at my mercy, what do you expect of me?" "If you are a merchant," said Mannú, "sell me; if an executioner and tyrant, cut off my head; but if you are a king, show me kingly generosity and pardon my life." The Shah was struck with the address and dauntless spirit of his youthful adversary, and conferred upon him the title of *Farzand Khan Bahadur Rustami Hind*.

† On his return to Kandahar the Shah laid the foundation of a great city, which he called after his name, Ahmad Shahí.

fell upon them and defeated them. He was, however, careful to desist from wholly extirpating them, as he thought their utter annihilation would, to a great degree, strip him of his own importance as the manager of a turbulent province. He, therefore, came to an understanding with them that their exactions should be moderate, while their payments to the State should not be excessive. He also entertained many of them who had a love for arms, in his service, thus checking their mischief, and at the same time making good use of them. One of these mercenaries was Jassa Singh, a carpenter, who subsequently became a leader of considerable importance. Thus did the shrewd governor of the Jalandar Doáb put a check for a time upon the depredations of this restless and ambitious sect.

Who, nevertheless, from motives of his own, refrains from reducing them to insignificance.

Jassa Singh, the carpenter.

At Delhi, Ghazi-ud-dín, the grandson of Chin Kilich Khan, became Amír-ul-Omerah, or captain-general, but, dying in October 1752, he was succeeded in the office by his son, Shaháb-ud-dín, under the same title as that borne by his father. Safdar Jang, the titular wazír, being jealous of the growing influence of the eunuch, Jáwed, at the Court, and of the favours shown him by the emperor and his mother, procured his assassination in a banquet to which he had invited him. This outrage exasperated the emperor, who took the office of wazír from Safdar Jang, and conferred it on Khan-i-Khánán Intizam-ud-doula, son of the late Kamr-ud-dín Khan. This event took place in 1753. Safdar Jang, not being disposed to submit, raised the standard of insurrection, and was resisted by Ghazi-ud-dín the younger. Mír Moin-ul-Mulk, the governor of the Panjáb at this critical moment, sent a party of veteran Afghans to aid his kinsmen of the Durráni faction at the capital, and the result was a civil war which lasted for a period of six months. Ghazi-ud-dín called in the Mahrattas to his aid, and expelled Safdar Jang, who retired to his possessions of Allahabád and Oudh. The irresolute emperor was now more disgusted with Ghazi-ud-dín for his arrogance, than he had ever been with Safdar Jang. He marched out of his capital with as strong a force as he could collect, to give battle to Ghazi-ud-dín, and to shake off his tyrannical yoke by force of arms. Ghazi-ud-dín sent his Mahratta confederate against the emperor, and his troops, falling unexpectedly on the imperialists at Sikandra, seized the camp. The pusillanimous king, leaving the ladies of his harem to be stripped of their ornaments by the enemy, fled precipitately to Delhi, where he took refuge in the palace. His ladies were sent to Delhi in country carts. Ghazi-ud-dín repaired to Delhi, and, having invested himself with the official robes of wazír, deposed the king, and put out his eyes, as well as those of his mother. This occurred on 5th June, 1754. Intizam-ud-doula was stripped of his wealth and dignity, and subsequently put to death. Safdar Jang died soon afterwards, and was succeeded in his provinces by his son, Jalal-ud-dín Hyder, surnamed Shujá-ud-doula Bahadur. The unhappy Ahmad Shah was molested no further; but remained a State prisoner in Salemgarh, and died a natural death in 1775, after reigning six years.

Affairs at the Court of Delhi.

Discontent of the wazír Safdar Jang.

He assassinates the emperor's favourite, Jáwed.

Ghazi-ud-dín the younger.

He calls in the Mahrattas and expels Safdar Jang.

The emperor is disgusted with Ghazi-ud-dín, and makes war on him,

But is defeated, blinded and deposed 1754.

Death of Ahmad Shah, 1775.

CHAPTER XXIV.

ÁZ-UD-DÍN ALAMGIR II.

After the battle of Sikandra, Nawab Malkai Zamání (Queen-dowager), Názir Rozafzún Khan and other Omerahs of the court, voted for the installation of Muhammad Áz-ud-dín, son of Moz-ud-dín Jahándar Shah, on the throne. Nizam-ul-Mulk Asaf Jáh Ghazi-ud-dín Khan holding the same view, Áz-ud-dín was called to the public hall of audience, and placed on the throne with the title of *Abul-Adl Áz-ud-dín Muhammad Alamgir Sáni Bádshah-i-Ghazi*. The new emperor was an elderly man of fifty-five, having been born in 1699 A.D., in the 43rd year of the reign of Aurangzeb. He had five sons, the eldest of whom was twenty-eight years old. He had devoted his hours to the study of theology and history, and he eschewed every kind of pleasure. He never missed his prayers at the five appointed times, and read them in the congregation, and on the sabbath he never failed to attend the *Jama Masjid*, or the wooden mosque within the palace. So devout a man was unlikely to take interest in the administration of the country, and the youthful king-maker, Ghazi-ud-dín, exercised absolute authority. But a deathblow had, by this time, been struck at the prestige of the Great Moghal by widespread anarchy in the country, and the dominions of Akber had fallen into a pitiable condition. The Mahratta name had become a terror, or a beacon, throughout southern India; Oudh and Allahabád were held by Shujá-ud-doula; the country south of Agra had been seized by the *Jats*; Bengal, Behar and Orissa were swayed by the dynasty of Allawardi Khan; Malwa and Ráj-putáná had ceased to pay tribute; and the Panjáb had become tributary to the new Durráni Kingdom of Afghanistán, established by the Abdáli, Ahmad Shah. Only the country around Delhi, and a few districts north of the Sutlej, remained under the direct sway of the descendants of Tymúr. Mír Mannú, or Moin-ul-Mulk, regent of the Panjáb, did not long survive the re-establishment of his authority as the viceroy of a new king. He was killed in a shooting excursion, by a fall from his horse, in 1756 A.D. His widow, Murad Begum,* a woman of vigour and activity, proclaimed her minor son, Amín-ud-dín, a child three years old, viceroy under her own guardianship. She professed submission to both the Delhi court and the Abdáli king, and her appointment as regent to the infant viceroy was ratified by both.† Murad Begum, on attaining power, honoured her late husband's ministers and courtiers, whose counsel she sought on all State matters, and on whose advice she entirely depended. She had now established her authority firmly, when another calamity happened to her. The child in whose name she was governing, died of small-pox before ten months had expired. The spirited Begum thereupon took up the administration in her own name and proclaimed herself vicegerent of the Panjáb. The Omerahs at the court of Láhore, who entertained great respect for her deceased husband, acknowledged her supremacy, and, agents having been sent to the courts of Delhi and Kábul, royal *firmans* were obtained, recognising the lady as the viceroy of the Panjáb.

Alamgir proclaimed Emperor, 1754.

The new emperor a devout man.

The enfeebled state of the empire.

Death of Mír Mannú, viceroy of the Panjáb, 1756.

Murad Begum, widow of Mír Mannú, governs the Panjáb in the name of her infant son.

Murad Begum proclaims herself viceroy of the Panjáb.

Firmly established in her government, Murad Begum displayed the frailty of her sex. She began to look with distrust upon the Omerahs of her husband's court, to whom she owed her magnificence and her elevation to power. Mír Bikhári Khan, son of Raushan-ud-doula Turre Báz Khan, prime minister to the late viceroy ‡ and chief secretary of the Begum's darbár, once her great favorite, was seized in the *zanáná* interior apartments, and beaten so severely with shoes and sticks by the female servants, under the Begum's orders, that he expired under the punishment. The Mír's only fault is believed to have been that he had given the lady some personal disappointment of a kind never forgiven by her sex. This

Mír Bikhári Khan.

His cruel death.

* Also called Mughlani Begum—*Tarikhi Ahmadi*.
† Compare Cunningham's *History of the Sikhs*, p. 104.
‡ He built the Láhore Golden Mosque or *Sunahri* Masjid.

act of cruelty, prompted by personal pique on the part of the Begum, disgusted all the old Omerahs, who were themselves ignominiously treated. Almost all gave up attending the darbár, where not only honor but life was at stake, and petitions were sent to the Court at Dehli, complaining of the conduct of the Begum. At the same time, the enfeebled and distracted state of the government of Láhore encouraged the Sikh associations to raise their heads again and renew their acts of depredation. These bearded freebooters traversed various parts of the province, laying waste the country, depopulating villages and towns and carrying off flocks and herds. All order, both civil and military, was at an end. Not a pice could be levied from the zemindars on account of government demands. Disorder, anarchy and confusion prevailed throughout the country. Ghazi-ud-dín, the Dehli wazír, who had some respect for his intended* mother-in-law, deputed Sayad Jamil to help the Begum in the administration of the country, and the Sayad, arriving at Láhore, introduced some measures of reform, but the lady became jealous of his power, and begged Ghazi-ud-dín to remove him. The young wazír was inflexible. The incensed lady, who had a thirst for authority, thereupon sent her agents to the Abdáli king, complaining of the encroachments of the Delhi Court, and the slight she had received at the hands of the imperial officers. Her duplicity being soon discovered, Ghazi-ud-dín marched from Dehli, accompanied by Mirza Ali Gohar, Alamgir's eldest son, at the head of a large army, in the beginning of 1169 Hijri. The force had reached Machiwárá, seventy *kos* from Sirhind, when the wazír opened negotiations for the marriage, and, with a handful of followers, advanced to Láhore as if to celebrate the nuptials. When all suspicion had been completely lulled, he surprised the town by a stratagem, and surrounded the house of the Begum, who found herself a prisoner in her own bed. When he perceived that all his entreaties failed to obtain her consent to the marriage, he unscrupulously seized her, and placing her in close confinement, deprived her of her rank and liberty, and, carried her to Dehli as a State prisoner. The government of Láhore was given by the wazír to Adína Beg Khan for a tribute of thirty lakhs of rupees. Prince Ali Gohar was annoyed by the complaints of the widow, and tried to persuade Ghazi-ud-dín to re-instate her, but the young minister paid no regard to his remonstrances, and annoyed the lady in every possible way. On her way to Dehli, the incensed mother-in-law reproached Ghazi-ud-dín for his treachery in the most poignant diatribes, and prophesied the fall of the Indian empire, the destruction and the ruin of the country, and the massacre of its people by the Northern invader, who, she maintained, would, on no account, forgive the ungallant act of the officers of the imperial Government towards her. The unabashed minister married her daughter, and bore the brunt of his mother-in-law's rage as best as he could. The old lady's prediction was soon realised, for, no sooner did Ahmad Shah hear of the occupation of Láhore by the Dehli Government, and the outrage committed on his regent, than he left Kandahar, in the season of 1755-56, crossed the Indus, drove Adína Beg Khan, the governor, out of Láhore and garrisoned the place with his own troops. Adína, unable to resist, fled to the north of Láhore and sought protection under the hill rájás.

The Sikhs renew their depredations in the Panjab.

Sayad Jamil sent to Láhore as deputy governor.

The heir apparent Ali Gohar marches to Láhore.

Ghazi-ud-dín's treacherous seizure of Murad Begum, 1756.

Adína Beg Khan appointed Viceroy of Láhore.

Fourth invasion of Ahmad Shah 1755-56.

Flight of Adína Beg Khan.

Ahmad Shah then hastened to Dehli, through Sirhind, and reached the neighbourhood of the capital without encountering the least obstacle, Nawáb Najib-ud-doula, who is believed to have been in secret correspon-

* It seems that Mír Mannú, to strengthen his interest at the Court of Dehli, had, before his death, promised his daughter to Ghazi-ud-dín, who still held out hopes of securing the young lady, though, after the viceroy's death, both she and her mother were extremely averse to it.

dence with the invader, came as far as Karnál to pay homage to the Abdáli Shah, while the Emperor Alamgir II, with Imad-ul-Mulk Ghazi-ud-dín Khan, the wazír, came to meet the king at Narela, ten *kos* from Dehli, on the Sirhind road. Ahmad Shah received the king with great distinction, and both monarchs entered Delhi together, Alamgir having previously decorated the Moghal palace for the reception of his illustrious visitor. Ghazi-ud-dín was frightened on the visit of the Abdáli king to the capital, and by the good offices of prince Ali Gohar ingratiated himself with the widow of Moin-ul-Mulk. She interceded on the wazír's behalf with the invader, who, pleased with his address, pardoned him and confirmed him in his rank and office on condition of his paying a heavy tribute. The Abdáli now commenced laying heavy contributions on the Omerahs of the capital. He demanded ninety lakhs of rupees from Nawáb Intizam-ud-doula Khan-i-Khánán, son of Kamar-ud-dín Khan, and Sardar Jahán Khan was appointed to realise the money. The Omerah expressed his inability to pay such a heavy contribution. Mahram Khan, Khoja Sarai (eunuch) was thereupon ordered to search the nawáb's house for money and valuables. The order was obeyed, and more than three times as much as the Shah demanded was discovered hid in the ground, in the treasury, and in various parts of the house. The houses of all the other Dehli Omerahs and nawábs were similarly searched and excavated, and incalculable wealth fell into the hands of the Abdáli king. Thus, on the information supplied by Murad Begum, the widow of Mír Mannú, the house of Sholapuri Begum, the wife of Kamar-ud-dín Khan, was searched, and cash, ornaments and jewels worth several lakhs of rupees were found and seized. The avaricious Shah's thirst for riches and wealth was not yet satiated, and greater calamities were in store for the unfortunate people of Delhi. Having extorted all he could from the Omerahs of State, he ordered the town to be pillaged, and nearly all the horrors which had been experienced at the time of Nádir's invasion, were repeated. The Shah remained at Dehli for two months, during which time the unfortunate capital was systematically plundered. He formed an alliance with the Dehli emperor by marrying his son, Tymúr Shah, to the daughter of Ahmad Shah son of Muhammad Shah. He then laid seige to Balamgarh, a strong fort, and put the garrison to the sword. Proceeding then to Mathra, he surprised the sacred city whilst the people were solemnising one of their religious festivals, slaughtered, unsparingly, the unfortunate votaries, put the inhabitants to the sword for the enormous crime of defending their faith and honour, razed to the ground rich and spacious temples, and carried hundreds of the Hindus into slavery. The tyrant next advanced to Agra, to which city he laid siege, and, being exasperated at the repulse sustained there by the Durráni troops at the hands of Fazil Khan the Moghal governor, he spread death and devastation through the territory of the *Jats*.

Ahmad Shah enters Delhi.

Exactions.

Pillage.

Massacres.

Slavery.

After these promiscuous slaughters and scenes of barbarity, the Shah, having suffered much from the heat, returned to Delhi. He himself now formed a matrimonial alliance with Hazrat Begum, younger daughter of Muhammad Shah, by his wife Sahib Mahal. Having then levied a heavy contribution on the emperor Alamgir, he reinstated him on the throne of his ancestors. He appointed Intizam-ud-doula Khan-i-Khánán, son of Kamar-ud-dín Khan, grand wazír, and Najib-ud-doula Amír-ul-Omerah Bakhshi, or commander-in-chief of the empire, and, after these transactions, returned to Kandahar (A.D. 1757). The emperor of Dehli was compelled to cede the Panjáb and Sindh to Tymúr Shah. Thus, the spoliation and ruin which Nádir Shah had commenced, were pretty well completed by Ahmad Shah. On his way to Láhore, the Sikhs plundered his baggage, and cut off the stragglers of the

Alamgir restored on the throne of Delhi.

Panjáb and Sindh ceded to Prince Tymúr Shah.

Afghan army. Ahmad Shah was much incensed at these daring acts of depredation, and threatened to punish the insurgents, but, as he was in a hurry to set out for Turkistan in order to suppress a rebellion, he ordered his son, Tymúr Shah, to punish the Sikhs for the excesses they had committed.

The conqueror left his son, Tymúr Shah, in charge of the provinces on the left bank of the Indus, including the territory of Multán and Láhore, under the guidance of his able general and confidential officer, Jahán Khan. The forces left with the prince were of no considerable strength, and consisted of a few Durráni and Persian guards, with a detachment of troops raised in the country. Abdul Samed Khan Muhammad Zie was appointed governor of Sirhind, Sarfráz Khan Afghan Faujdar of Doábá, or the country between the Sutlej and Biás, and Buland Khan, Saddozie, a native of Multán, subadar of Káshmír.

Arrangements for the government of the country.

After the departure of Ahmad Shah, prince Tymúr governed the Panjáb with vigour and ability, and for one year peace and tranquillity reigned in the province. The insurgent Sikhs were punished, their armed bands were thoroughly dispersed, and they were put under proper restraint.

Able administration of Prince Tymúr.

Adína Beg Khan, who had assisted the Dehli minister in recovering Láhore, and who, on the appearance of Ahmad Shah, had fled to the hills, now appeared again on the scene. Opposed to the Afghan interest, he established himself in the Jalandar Doáb, and began to enlist the Sikhs in his service. His forbearance and connivance encouraged the Sikhs to create fresh disturbances and give renewed trouble. They swarmed the country between the Biás and the Sutlej, and carried on their depredations as far as Amritsar, where Jassa Singh, the carpenter, had the audacity to restore the Ram Rouni. Sikh bands were also seen ravaging the country around Kalanaur and Batála.

The Sikh element again predominates.

Connivance of Adína Beg Khan.

Tymúr's first act was to summon Adína Beg Khan to Láhore, as a dependant of his government. The wary veteran evaded compliance, alleging, as his excuse, that the turbulent Sikhs were watching for a favourable opportunity, and that, were he to absent himself from his post, they would seize the country and secure a permanent hold on it. Not satisfied with this excuse, the Abdáli prince sent a detachment of troops under Murad Khan to punish the chief and take possession of the Doáb country. Sar Buland Khan and Sarfráz Khan, Afghans, accompanied the general in his expedition. Murad Khan crossed the Biás at the head of the Afghan troops. Adína Beg Khan, collecting his Sikh troops, advanced to give battle to Murad Khan, and a fight ensued in which the Láhore troops sustained a signal defeat. Sar Buland Khan, one of the Afghan generals, being slain, Murad Khan, and Sarfráz Khan, seeing no recourse left them but flight, retraced their steps to Láhore with the remnants of their troops.

He is summoned to Láhore,

But evades compliance.

Troops sent against him

Are defeated.

The wazír, Jahán Khan, now marched in person from Láhore, at the head of a considerable army, to inflict chastisement on the insurrectionary chieftain. At Batála he was met by Murad Khan, whom the old wazír suspected of treason and complicity with the enemy. Under his orders, Murad Khan was executed at the tank of Shamsher Khan in Batála. Adína Beg Khan, on hearing of the approach of the wazír with a large Afghan army, retired into the northern hills, his usual place of shelter.

Wazír Jahán Khan marches against Adína Beg Khan.

The latter retires to the hills.

The young Afghan prince and his wazír, Jahán Khan, now directed their attention to punishing the increasing audacity of the Sikhs. Their stronghold at Amritsar, called the Ram Rouni, was attacked and levelled with the ground; the sacred reservoir was filled up, and all their places of worship were defiled. This outrage on the sacred city of the *Khálsá* provoked the whole Sikh nation to such a degree that they assembled in

Tymúr expels the Sikhs from Amritsar,

great numbers and determined to defend their religion with the sword. They ravaged the whole country round Láhore, which swarmed with Sikh horsemen. Jahán Khan came out against them and succeeded at first in dispersing them. The Sikhs, however, assembled in larger numbers, and were strong enough not only to cut off communication between the fort and the country, but also to collect the revenues of the country around Láhore and dispose of it as they liked. The Afghan Prince engaged them on several occasions, but was worsted each time in consequence of the superiority of their numbers. In a desperate engagement which took place between the Pathans and the Sikhs, the latter fired a volley, every bullet of which took effect. A great number of Pathans fell, and the rest fled. The Sikhs kept up the fire with great vigour, and in the heat of the action, Jahán Khan's horse, being wounded, fell with its rider. The Sikhs rushed forward, to kill the Khan, with the loud war cry, "*Wáh Guru-ji-ki-fateh*," but the Khan fled on foot, and was protected by his men. The Pathans were completely routed, and this was the first decisive victory on record achieved by the Sikhs over the Afghans.

But the Sikhs rally and defeat him.

About the same time, serious disturbances broke out in the Jalandar Doáb, instigated by Adína Beg Khan, who had fled on the prince's approach, but who now excited the chiefs against the Afghans, and with their aid defeated a division of the Afghan troops under Sarfráz Khan at Jalandar. The whole Panjáb was now in a state of commotion. The Afghan prince and his guardian, seeing that all their attempts to disperse the Sikhs had failed, and that the numbers of the insurgents were daily increasing by thousands, and aware that the forces at their own disposal, however well-armed and disciplined, were too few in number to stand before them, considered it prudent to evacuate Láhore and retreat towards the Chináb. They retreated in the night, unknown even to their own Hindostáni troops, whom they distrusted, and in such haste that the royal family fell into the hands of the enemy, though they were subsequently released. This took place about the middle of 1758. The triumphant Sikhs occupied Láhore under their celebrated leader Jassa, the Kalal, or carpenter, who had declared the *Khálsá* to be a "State" (or a political body united under one government), and who now assumed the sovereignty of the country. Thus did the Sikhs become, for the first time, masters of Láhore. They used the mint of the Moghals to coin a rupee with an inscription :—"Coined by the Grace of the *Khálsá* in the country of Ahmad, conquered by Jassa Singh, the Kalal."

Disturbances in the Jalandar Doáb.

The Afghans retire.

The Sikhs occupy Láhore,

And coin money, in the name of the *Khálsá*, 1756-58.

The Sikhs, who, in no small degree, owed their rise to power and freedom to the courtesy and forbearance of their ally, Adína Beg Khan, now forgot their debt of gratitude to him. They expelled from Láhore, with disgrace, Khwaja Mirza Jan, the agent of Adína Beg Khan, but that old and wily chief was, in his turn, not wanting in energy to checkmate them. Shaháb-ud-dín, styled Ghazi-ud-dín, had called in the aid of the Mahrattas to support his authority against Najib-ud-doula, the Rohilla chief, who, it will be remembered, had been installed in the office of commander-in-chief at Dehli by the Abdálí king, as a reward for his joining his majesty at Karnál, and was looked upon as the Abdáli's agent. The royal fort at Dehli was laid under siege by Ragho Nath Rao, better known under his familiar appellation of Raghobá, and, after a month's defence, Najib-ud-doula escaped. The helpless emperor once more fell under the control of Ghazi-ud-dín. At this juncture Adína Beg Khan invited the Mahratta chiefs to enter the Panjáb and extend their arms to the Indus. He stipulated for the payment of a daily * sum for

Disagreement between Adína Beg Khan and the Sikhs.

Adína invites the Mahrattas to the Panjáb.

* One lakh of rupees for a march, and fifty thousand for a halt.—*The Memoirs of Moulvi Din Mohamad of Batála.*

the expenses of the invading Mahratta troops during their march, and held out to them hopes of enriching themselves by plunder. The expedition was undertaken by the Mahrattas with alacrity, and Raghobá and Malhar Rao, the Mahratta chiefs, marched towards the Panjáb at the head of a considerable army. They were joined at the Sutlej by Adína Beg Khan, who put at their disposal the Sikh troops which he still retained in his employ. The Mahrattas entered Sirhind and defeated Abdul Samad Khan the Durráni general, who was stationed in that town with a body of twenty thousand Rohillas, horse and foot. The city had no sooner been evacuated by the Afghans, than the Sikh followers of Adína Beg Khan subjected it to a general pillage. This incensed the triumphant Mahrattas, who considered the booty their exclusive privilege, and who, jealous of the Sikhs, resolved upon punishing them for their wanton outrage. The children of the *Khálsá*, however, taking advantage of a dark night, fled with their prize, and put themselves beyond the reach of the pursuing Mahrattas.

The Mahrattas march to the Panjáb.

The Mahrattas occupy Sirhind.

After the fall of Sirhind, the Mahrattas advanced rapidly to Láhore, accompanied by their ally, Adína Beg Khan. Sardar Jahán Khan, with Prince Tymúr Shah, pitched his tents at Kachhi Serai, where, taking up an intrenched position, he prepared for action. A battle ensued, in which the Durránis were defeated, and Jahán Khan retired across the Attak with two hundred horse, leaving his property and treasure to be plundered by the invaders, and Láhore was occupied by the Mahrattas. This event took place in May, 1758. Adína Beg Khan had this victory celebrated at Láhore by beat of drums, and great rejoicings took place. As a reward for his services, the Mahrattas installed Adína Beg Khan in the office of viceroy of the Panjáb, with Khwaja Mirza as his deputy at Láhore. Sahib Pátil, a Mahratta general, marched to the fort of Attak at the head of ten thousand troops, in pursuit of Tymúr Shah, while Shamaji Rao was appointed governor of Multán. The power of the Mahrattas had at this time reached its zenith, and the prophecy of Sivaji, the founder of their monarchy, was fulfilled, that they should water their horses in the Indus and in the Hughli. They had traversed the country from the Dekkan to the Indus, had overrun the metropolitan provinces of Dehli and Agra, were masters of the Panjáb, had concerted with Ghazi-ud-dín the Dehli wazír a plan for annexing Oudh to their conquests, and now openly aspired to the subjugation of the whole of Hindostán. It was not until the great battle of Pánipat that their power declined.

Defeat of the Afghans at Kachhi Serai.

Láhore occupied by the Mahrattas, 1758.

Adína Beg Khan appointed viceroy of the Panjáb.

The power of the Mahrattas in its zenith.

Nothing in the shape of order or discipline prevailed in the Panjáb during the short time the Mahrattas held the reins of government. The Sikhs committed depredations in all parts of the country, unchecked by the foreigners, who were nominally rulers, and the zemindars resisted by force the demand of the government for revenue. Perplexities and commotions in Hindostán and the Dekkan soon compelled the Mahrattas to abandon the country which they did in the same year in which they had subdued it, leaving a detachment at Láhore. They left Adína Beg Khan as their governor there, on the condition of his remitting to their treasury an annual tribute of seventy-five lakhs of rupees. The Rohillas mutinied, under one Qutab Shah, and the Afghans of Malerkotla raised the standard of rebellion under their chief Jamal Khan. The insurgent forces collected in large numbers in the neighbourhood of Phillour, where Adína Beg Khan gave them battle. The engagement was a sanguinary one. The Afghans and the Rohillas greatly outnumbered the viceroy's forces, whose loss in killed and wounded was great. Desertions had commenced in the viceroy's army, when Jamal Khan's elephant coming close to the viceroy's, Mohamad

The Mahrattas eventually evacuate the Panjáb, 1758, leaving Adína Beg as their governor of Lahore.

Trouble given by the Rohillas and the Afghans of Malerkotla.

Taufiq, the chela of Khan Bahadur, who worked as the *mahâwat* of Adína Beg Khan's elephant, fired at him with his musket. This killed Jamal Khan, and, no sooner had he fallen, than the insurgent troops, struck with panic, fled, a great number of them being slain by the pursuing troops of the Láhore viceroy.

They are defeated by Adína Beg.

This victory over the insurgent tribes tended greatly to strengthen the position of Adína Beg Khan in the Panjáb, and spread terror throughout the whole province. He fixed his head-quarters at Batála, and appointed his own governors for the provinces of Multán, Thatta and Láhore.* The hill rájás tendered their allegiance to him; the zemindars made their submission, and Rájá Sef Ali Khan, of Kangrá, paid him his homage. The Dehli Court conferred upon him the title of Zafar Jang Bahadur, treating him as an independent chieftain.

Who now exercises sole authority in the Panjáb, and fixes his head-quarters at Batála.

The Sikhs of the Mánjha country become troublesome.

The Sikhs of the Mánjha country now began to give trouble, and, collecting in large numbers, carried on their depredations in the surrounding districts. Mir Aziz Bakhshi was sent to chastise them, and he brought 12,000 Sikhs as prisoners to Batála, where the viceroy resided at the time with Nidhán Singh *Randháwá*, their head. The rising had been scarcely suppressed when a greater and more serious one took place in Ramgarh (then known as Rám Nomi) under the Sikh leaders Jai Singh, Kanhia, and Jassa Singh Ramgarhia. Troops were sent to suppress this insurrection; but the end of the viceroy, who now aspired to complete independence in the Panjáb, was near. He was attacked with cholic in his palace, in the town of Batála, and was laid in his grave on 11th Moharram, before the end of 1758. His body was, according to his own will, conveyed to Khánpúr, in the neighbourhood of Jalandar, and interred there.

More Sikh insurrections.

Death of Adína Beg Khan, 1758.

His previous history and character.

Adína Beg Khan had long played a very conspicuous part in the diplomacy of the Panjáb. From an humble position in life, he advanced till he was made Kardár of Sultánpúr, and the Nawáb Zakaria Khan, viceroy of Láhore, subsequently appointed him governor of Bahrampúr in the Gurdáspúr district. The nawáb once put him in close confinement for default of payment of goverment revenue, but the Omerahs interceded, and he was reinstated. He was a master of Indian diplomacy; for, amidst storms of confusion and anarchy, raised by parties with conflicting interests, who aspired to political supremacy, he maintained his position intact. By his tact, address and judgment, he raised himself in the estimation of each successive viceroy of Láhore, who looked upon him as a source of strength. His management of the Jalandar Doáb was highly successful. He was shrewd and crafty. The Sikhs he amused, the Delhi Court he despised, the Afghans he bewildered, and the Mahrattas he effectually influenced in his favor to break the power of both the Sikhs and the Afghans and to obtain his own independence. He turned every change to his own advantage; and while the interest of everybody else suffered from the disorder that prevailed, he never allowed his own to be sacrificed. He was unscrupulous and sometimes cruel. Once he ordered a confectioner who had refused to supply him with preserves, to be boiled alive. The poor wretch's life was saved through the intercession of some of the bystanders.†

The state of Láhore under Adína Beg Khan.

Láhore was never prosperous under him. Scarcity of provisions prevailed, and no edible grain could be imported into the city without his leave. He left no issue or successor, though the thriving town of Adína-

* *Farhatun Názirin.*

† Boiling seems to have been the torture in use at this period.

nagar, which he founded in the Gurdáspúr district, with its gardens and palaces, still perpetuates his memory, which is held in respect by both the Sikhs and the Mahomedans, as that of the last Moghal Governor of Láhore. On the death of Adína Beg Khan, Jankú Rao, the Mahratta chieftain, who was stationed in the vicinity of the metropolis at the head of a formidable army, entrusted the goverment of Láhore to a Mahratta chief called Shámáji, whom he despatched in that direction. Sadiq Beg Khan, one of Adína Beg Khan's followers, was appointed by the Mahratta chief, to the administration of Sirhind, while the management of the Jalandar Doáb was given to Adína Beg Khan's widow. Shámá, on reaching Láhore, applied himself diligently to the task of government, and pushed on his troops as far as the Indus. But the Sikhs, who had been kept in check by the able administration of Adína Beg Khan, now renewed their depredations in the Panjáb. They subjected the Mahomedans to the greatest hardships and severities. The sacred tank of Amritsar, which had been filled in by Tymúr Shah, was again cleared out, and the task of taking out the rubbish and filth from the sacred pool was forced upon the Mahomedans, who were prodded with bayonets, and struck with the butt-ends of muskets, to expedite them in the work. The news of Tymúr Shah's disastrous retreat from the Panjáb, and the successes of the Mahrattas and the Sikhs in that country, having reached Ahmad Shah, Abdáli, he sent his General, Nur-ud-dín Khan, a Bamizie chief, at the head of an army, across the Indus. The general advanced to Jhelum, and without opposition occupied the country between that river and the Indus, at that time inhabited by the Ghakkars, the Kantars and the Jonds, all Mahomedan tribes, the original residents of the country who were favorably inclined towards the Afghans. The general then marched to the Chináb, where he awaited the arrival of the Abdáli Shah.

Arrangements of the country on his death.

Shámáji Mahratta appointed governor of Láhore.

The Sikhs, now unrestrained, renew their ravages in the Panjab.

Nur-ud-dín Khan, the general of Ahmad Shah Abdáli.

Having settled his affairs with Násir Khan, the independent chief of Bilúchistan, Ahmad Shah, with a numerous army, crossed the Indus in the winter of 1759, and advanced to the Chináb by the Jammu road. He continued his march through the north of the Panjáb to avoid the swollen rivers, and, on reaching Láhore, defeated with great loss the Mahratta commander who fell back upon Dehli. The Shah, after this victory, appointed Karim Dád Khan, an Afghan, governor of the province of Láhore, and Zen Khan, governor of Gujrát. Having effected a junction with Najib-ud-doula who assisted him with supplies, the Shah marched in the direction of Jamna.

Fifth invasion of Ahmad Shah, 1759.

Defeat of the Mahratta commander at Láhore.

The Shah advances to the Jamna.

In the meanwhile, the perfidious Delhi wazir, Ghazi-ud-dín, dreading the effect of the restoration to power of the harmless old emperor by the Abdáli, and suspicious of his uncle, Intizam-ud-doula, the former Khan-i-Kánán, who sided with the emperor in sympathising with Najib-ud-doula, resolved on putting them both to death. He caused Intizam-ud-doula to be slaughtered, while that noble was in the act of reading his prayers. The emperor was fond of visiting religious men and *derveshes*. Taking advantage of this weak point, Imad-ul-Mulk caused a report to be spread abroad that a saint of prodigious sanctity from Kandahar had arrived in the city, and taken up his quarters in the ruined Kotla of Firoz Shah. The helpless devotee, desirous of seeing the hermit, repaired to the Kotla in a palanquin, almost unattended. As he reached the door of the chamber, he saw a curtain which was raised for his reception. Shortly after he had entered the room, a cry for help was heard. Mirza Baber, son-in-law of the emperor, who had been made to stay outside, suspecting foul play, drew his sword and wounded several men, but the conspirators, who were headed by Mahdi Ali

Affairs at Delhi.

Murder of Intizam-ud-doula.

Khan, the Káshmíri, put him in a palanquin, and sent him back to the city under a strong guard. The supposed hermit, who proved to be a savage Uzbek, named Bala Bash Khan, then, on a signal given, jumped up, and, with the help of three others, inflicted repeated wounds with daggers, and brought the old man to the ground. The assassins then stripped the body of its rich robes, and threw the trunk from the top of the parapet on to the sands at the foot of the Kotla. After lying on the ground for eighteen hours, the body was taken up by order of Mahdi Ali Khan, and interred in the sepulchre of the emperor Húmáyún. The tragedy occurred on 30th November, 1759. Alamgir II * was sixty years of age when he died, and had reigned about six years.

Tragic murder of the emperor Alamgir II, November 1759.

CHAPTER XXV.

ALI GOHAR SHAH ALAM II.

WITH the murder of Alamgir II, the great empire of Delhi had virtually ceased to exist. The wazír, Imad-ul-Mulk, raised to the nominal throne Mohi-ul-Millat, grandson of Prince Kám Baksh, but he was never acknowledged, and Ali Gohar, the prince imperial, who was a fugitive in Bengal, subsequently ascended the throne, under the pompous title of Shah Alam, or "king of the world," when, in fact, all that remained actually in his possession was a few districts around the capital. The rest had been all lost to the empire, either by usurpation of the viceroys, or by foreign conquest. Imad-ul-Mulk, finding his position untenable, took himself to the protection of the *Jats*. He then moved to the Dekkan, and lived in obscurity until 1800, when he died.

Shah Alam succeeds to the throne, 1759.

Ahmad Shah, the Durráni king, crossed the Jamna opposite Saharanpúr, and then fought those bloody battles which have been surpassed by few in India in havoc and carnage. The people of the country were exasperated by the depredations of the Mahrattas, and the re-appearance of the Abdáli Shah was hailed by a large party in India. The Mahratta detachments retired from Lahore to Delhi on the approach of the Shah, who was joined by the celebrated Najib-ud-doula, Hafiz Rahmat Khan, the Rohilla chief, and many other Mahomedan families. Continued skirmishes took place between the Durránis and the Mahrattas, before the latter, under the command of their General Dataji Sindhia, crossed the Jamna, and reached Badli near Delhi. Here both armies lay intrenched for several days. The Shah cut off the enemy's supplies, and the Mahrattas, being put to great straits for want of provisions, came out to give him battle. They advanced with great resolution, and a sanguinary battle was fought, the first shock of which was severely felt by the Rohilla contingent of the Shah. The Rohillas were on

Ahmad Shah crosses the Jamna.

The people become tired of the Mahrattas.

Confederacy of the Mahomedan chiefs.

The battle of Badli.

---

* Beale, in his *Miftahul Tawarikh*, gives the following inscription of the coin of this emperor :—

بزر زد سکه صاحب قراني — عزيز الدين عالمگير ثاني

"Áz-ud-dín Alamgir the Second, struck coin on gold like the Sahib Qurán."

Another coin bore the following inscription :—

سکه زد برهفت کشور همچو تابان مهر و ماه — شه عزيزالدين عالمگير غازي بادشاه

"The valiant king Áz-ud-dín Alamgir put his stamp on the seven climes like the shining sun and moon."

foot, and were hard pressed by the diminutive but active, Mahrattas, who were mounted on small ponies. The Shah ordered his *zamhurchies*, or fusileers, mounted on camels, to surround the Mahratta detachment which had engaged the Rohillas. They fired a volley from the backs of the camels on which they rode, and were promptly assisted by the Shah's bodyguard, which by this time had crossed the Jamna and appeared in the field. But the day was carried by Ahmad Khan, *Bángash*, of Farakhabad, the Pathan chief of the Doáb, who charged the flanks of the Mahrattas with ten thousand horse; and so vigorous was the attack made by him, that the scale of fortune turned in favour of the Durráni Shah. The Mahrattas were driven from the field with great slaughter; their army of 80,000 was completely destroyed, their leader, Dataji Sindhia, was slain, and all their generals vanquished; except Malhar Rao Holkar, who had fled when the first charge was made.

Doubtful issue of the campaign.

Ahmad Khan, *Bangash*, carries the day.

Defeat of the Mahrattas.

Ahmad Shah next surprised the division under Malhar Rao Holkar, near Sikandra, and so effectually routed it, that the Mahratta general was himself compelled to fly naked, with a handful of his faithful adherents. The Abdáli then entered Delhi, and the unfortunate capital was again given up to plunder. The Shah remained a few days at Delhi, where he received delegates from the rájás of Jeypur, Marwar, &c., who, came with *nazárs* to pay him homage. He cantoned for the rainy season at Anúp Shahar, on the border of Oudh, where he succeeded, after some negotiation, in securing the alliance of the powerful Shujá-ud-doula.

The battle of Sekandra.

The Mahrattas are routed.

Ahmad Shah occupies Delhi,

Which is given up to pillage.

The Mahrattas, though humbled by their disasters at Badli and Sikandra, never lost their spirit, and, after making fresh exertions to repair their losses, resolved upon a great and decisive action to maintain their supremacy in Hindostán. A formidable army of that nation accordingly left the Dekkan, commanded by Wiswas Rao, the heir-apparent to the Peshwa, or Supreme Prince, Sada Sheo Rao, his famous nephew, commonly known in India under the name of Bhau Janku Rao, Malhar Rao, and Shamsher* Bahadur, another son of the Peshwa. All the great Brahmins and the principal Mahratta chiefs accompanied these princes, who were joined by Suraj Mal, with a body of 30,000 *Jats*, and reinforced by many other Rájput chiefs. The force easily occupied Delhi,† where the small Durráni garrison, who held it, was cut to pieces after a spirited defence, the *killadar*, Yáqúb Ali Khan, effecting his escape with difficulty. Kunjpúrá, on the Jamna, 60 miles north of Delhi, was next besieged, and the whole Durráni garrison was put to the sword, including Najabat Khan, the head of the Pathan family who held the place. The Shah was encamped on the left bank of the Jamna, which was swollen by rains, and which divided the two armies. The massacre of the Kunjpúrá garrison, within sight of the Durráni camp, exasperated him to such a degree that he ordered his army to cross the river at all hazards.‡

The Mahrattas resolve on a decisive action.

They are joined by Suraj Mal *Jat* and other Rájput chiefs.

The slaughter of the Durráni garrisons at Delhi and Kunjpúrá.

The Shah's bold passage of the Jamna.

---

* Shamsher Rao was a Mahomedan, being the son of the Peshwa by a Mahomedan wife. A Mahomedan wife is allowed to the Peshwa.

† The Bhau on this occasion gave full vent to his cupidity by doing those deeds of depredations which mark the conquests of the barbarians. He destroyed beautiful tombs and shrines, carried away their riches, and defaced rich Moghal palaces for the sake of their ornaments and precious stones. The silver ceiling of the great hall of audience of the magnificent emperor Shah Jahán was taken down, and the silver which had cost seventeen lakhs of rupees melted. The royal throne was seized, and so were the rich ornaments in the palace of the Moghal, who, though shorn of his old splendour, yet possessed such immense fortune and riches as few eastern empires could boast of.

‡ The Shah is described at first as having repeated some verses of the *Qurán*, and, having blown them on an arrow, discharged it from his quiver into the river. Raising then the cry *Bismillahi allaho-akbar* "in the name of God, the great God," he plunged into the river, followed by his bodyguard, numbering four thousand slaves. The rest of the troops followed the Shah.—*Tarikhi Ahmadi*.

The brave troops plunged into the waters of the Jamna, which was crossed on 23rd October, partly by fording and partly by swimming. The passage was effected with some loss; but the daring spirit displayed by the Durráni king, and the alacrity with which his army crossed the swollen and rapid stream, spread dismay through the camp of the Mahrattas, who, feeling themselves unable to cope with the hardy veterans of the Shah in the open field, retired to Pánipat, where they intrenched themselves and mounted the parapets with all the ordnance they could collect. The troops under the Mahrattas numbered 300,000 men, including the cavalry in their regular pay, which numbered 55,000, predatory Mahratta horse, regular infantry, and the contingents from allied States. They had also three hundred pieces of cannon. The troops under the Abdáli consisted of 40,000 Afghans and Persians, 13,000 Indian cavalry and 38,000 Indian infantry, with about 70 pieces of cannon borrowed from Indian allies. The Shah was unremitting in his energy in cutting off the enemy's supplies and keeping a strict blockade on their intrenched position. Govind Rao Bundela, collecting 10,000 or 12,000 horse on the lower Jamna, spread these troops over the country, so that the Afghan camp was deprived of all means of communication and began to suffer severely for want of provisions. At length Atai Khan Popalzie, nephew of the grand wazír, with Haji Karim Dád Khan Durráni, fell suddenly on Govind Rao's camp, early one morning, and succeeded in completely destroying it, Govind being himself slain in the action. The treasure and provisions which he was conveying for the Mahrattas fell into the hands of the victorious Afghans. Shankar Rao, the Mahratta killadar of Delhi, fell in this action. By the overthrow of his detachment, the Durránis made themselves masters of the surrounding country, and the difficulties which they experienced in procuring supplies for their camp were now removed. But the main body of the Mahrattas maintained their position intact in the intrenchments, and, though desultory engagements and skirmishes* occurred from time to time, the Mahrattas carefully refrained from hazarding a general action in the open field. This state of affairs lasted for three or four months. The two armies lay close to each other, and the patience of both was nearly exhausted. Yet the Shah's troops reposed in their leader the greatest confidence, and the Indian allies had the highest respect for his opinion. Every hardship was borne with patience, and such was the dread of the Shah that none dared to utter a word† against his commands.

The Mahrattas retire to Pánipat.

The number of the Mahratta troops.

Force under the Abdáli.

Partial actions.

The war is protracted.

The severest distress and pressure were now felt in the Mahratta camp for want of supplies. The town of Pánipat was within their lines, and they

* In the last of these actions the Mussalmans sustained a heavy defeat, about six thousand Rohillas under Najib-ud-doula being killed and five hundred infantry wounded. This victory seems to have encouraged the Mahrattas to risk a battle in the open field.

† Kanshi Rao, a contemporary historian, has given a vivid picture of the transactions of this period and the principal actors of the scene. The Durráni king, Ahmad Shah, had a small red tent pitched for himself about a mile and a half in front of his camp. Early each morning, after reading his morning prayers, he came out of it on horseback accompanied by his son, Tymúr Shah, and forty or fifty horsemen. He personally examined all his posts and reconnoitred the enemy's position. He rode forty or fifty *kos* every day, returning to his camp at noon, when he dined, either in the small red tent, or the royal camp in the lines. At night time bodies of Durráni and Hindostáni horsemen, 5,000 strong each, patrolled the camp and remained under arms the whole night. The Shah was constantly seen among them. He used to say to the Hindostáni chiefs: "Do you sleep, I will take care that no harm befalls you." Every day the artillery were engaged in firing at long distances, and skirmishes were carried on, the parties withdrawing to their respective quarters towards sunset. Three very severe actions took place, but none was decisive. This state of affairs continued for over three months. At length the Hindostáni chiefs, whose patience was exhausted, begged of the Shah to put an end to their toils and hardships by attempting a pitched battle. To this the Shah replied: "This is a matter of war with which you are not acquainted. In other matters do as you please, but leave this to me. Military operations must not be precipitated; you shall see how I will manage this affair; and at a proper opportunity will bring it to a successful conclusion."

consumed everything in the shape of provisions in it. Surrounded by carcasses of animals, dying cattle, hungry followers, and hemmed in in their camp, their embarrassments were becoming unendurable. A foraging party, sent by them under a strong guard into the country, was discovered by the Afghans and put to the sword. At length the great Mahratta chiefs, wearied by extreme distress, surrounded the Bhau's tent and entreated him to put an end to their miseries by a sortie. In this last extremity the Bhau wrote a short note with his own hand to Kanshi Rao, and sent it to the Durráni camp by his confidential servant. The words of this note were these:—

Distress in the Mahratta camp.

"The cup is now full to the brim, and cannot hold another drop. If anything can be done, do it, or else answer me plainly at once: hereafter there will be no time for writing or speaking."

The patience of the Mahrattas is exhausted.

Kanshi Rao communicated this note to Nawáb Shujá-ud-doula at three o'clock in the morning (7th January 1761). Information soon reached the nawáb that the whole body of the Mahrattas had marched out of their lines to attack the Durránis. The nawáb immediately went to the Shah's tent and asked the eunuchs to awake his majesty. The Shah at once appeared, and, without changing his dress, mounted his horse which always stood ready at the door of the tent. The troops were ordered out as he went along. It was a little before daybreak. They had advanced a *kos* and a half when the booming of artillery was heard from the advancing lines of the Mahrattas. The Shah immediately called his grand wazír, Shah Wáli Khan, and his ministers, Shah Pasand Khan and others, and making over the Persian *kallian*, which he smoked sitting on his horse, to his eunuch, went in full gallop in the direction of the enemy. The two armies met. The Shah's centre was composed of the Rohillas and the Durránis, commanded by the grand wazír. He kept the reserve for himself, with the flower of the Afghan army. The Mahrattas had their artillery in front, and their infantry followed close behind. The artillery suddenly opened fire, and Ibrahim Khan,* Gardi, a Mussalman deserter from the French service, with his brother, Fateh Khan, desperately and successfully charged the flank of the Shah's army. This laid open the right of Shah Wáli Khan. The charge here was the fiercest and closest. Attai Khan, the grand wazír's nephew, fell by the side of his uncle. The Durránis, hard pressed, were compelled to give way. The Bhau and Wiswas Rao, both mounted, were encouraging their people and stimulating them to action. The war cries of the Mahratta warriors—*Har Har Jae Mahadeo*—were borne on the breeze, and the greatest fervour prevailed throughout their ranks. Everything was apparently favourable to the Mahrattas. Nawáb Shujá-ud-doula, whose division was near, was unable to see, on account of the clouds of dust with which he was enveloped. The grand wazír then, in full armour, galloped into the midst of his flying forces, and, in extreme rage and despair, reproached them for deserting him, saying, "Our country is afar off, my friends, whither do you fly?" Shujá kept his ground well, but desisted from advancing to help the wazír.

They march out of their camp.

The battle of Pánipat, 1761.

The Shah was not unaware of these transactions, and, finding that the time had come for an advance in person with the reserve of his army, he gave signal for a general charge. The attack was a furious one. The Mahrattas were taken in flank, and fought desperately hand to hand, but the bold and resolute stand made by the Durránis, so daunted them, that they at once turned tail, leaving the field covered with innumerable dead and

* He had obtained great fame for his bravery in the Dekkan, and his troops were drilled after European fashion of warfare.

dying. They were pursued in every direction by the victorious Afghans, who gave them no quarter. Great numbers fell in the pursuit, which was kept up for fifteen or twenty miles in all directions. Wiswas Rao and Bhau, it need hardly be said, were among the slain. Almost all the great Mahratta chiefs were killed or wounded, and the remnants who fled to the Dekkan owed their lives to the swiftness of their horses. Among the refugees were Malhar Rao Holkar, Madhoji Sindhia, who afterwards became the founder of a great State, but who was lamed for life by a gun shot in the flight. Shamsher Bahadur also effected his escape, but died shortly afterwards from the effects of a wound in the neck. According to the best accounts, the number of slain on the side of the Mahrattas amounted to 200,000, while 22,000 prisoners, 50,000 horse and an immense booty fell into the hands of the victors.

The defeat of the Mahrattas, and the destruction of their army, January 1761.

Despondency of the Mahrattas.

This great battle, which has been surpassed by few in carnage, with its disastrous issue for the Mahrattas, sealed the fate of that aspiring nation. Dismay and despondency preyed on the whole people, and Bálájі, their Peshwa, or king, died soon after of grief and disappointment. They evacuated their acquisitions in Hindostán and retired beyond the Narbadá, never to recover their power.

Ahmad Shah returns to the Panjáb.

After the victory of Pánipat, the whole of Hindostán lay at the mercy of the Abdáli conqueror. But he had no wish to ascend the vacant throne of the Moghals; so, after remaining at Delhi for a few days and arranging the affairs of India, he returned to the Panjáb, which had been already ceded to him, and with which he appeared contented.

The Sikh confederacies or associations.

During the absence of Ahmad Shah at Pánipat, the Sikhs had again become troublesome in the Panjáb. The king had called away Karim Dad Khan, Subadar of Láhore, and Faujdar Khan, the Governor of Pasrur, for service in the field. Sar Buland Khan was left as Governor of the Jalandar Doáb and Amír Muhammad Khan in charge of the Suba of Láhore. While the attention of all the Mahomedan chiefs was absorbed in the affairs of Hindostán, the Sikhs ravaged the country far and wide. A great number of them assembled at the Baisákhi festival at Amritsar, where Jassa Singh, Ahluwalia, Chet Singh, Kanhia, Hari Singh, Bhangi and Lahná Singh, assisted by other Sikh sardars, formed a confederacy to pillage Láhore.

They plunder the suburbs of Láhore,

A large number of Sikh horsemen swarmed round Láhore, pillaging the residents who lived outside the city walls and setting their houses on fire. Hundreds of lives were lost, while the damage done to private property was beyond estimation. Amír Muhammad Khan, the naib subadar, shut himself up in the city. The Sikhs surrounded the town on all sides, and demanded a heavy sum of money for *Karha* Parshád*, to induce them to withdraw.

And lay the city under contribution.

The naib subadar offered Rs. 30,000, as the price of sweetmeats for the children of the *Khálsá*, who then withdrew. Ahmad Shah, on his return from Pánipat, took no steps to chastise the Sikhs, or to remedy the disorders that then prevailed in the Panjáb, but, appointing Khwajá Obed Khan, governor of Láhore, Sar Buland Khan, governor of Multán, and Zen Khan to the charge of Sirhind, returned to Kábul in the spring of 1761.

Ahmad Shah returns to Kábul, 1761.

On 12th August, 1765, the Emperor Shah Alam ceded in perpetuity the dewáni or revenue management of the provinces of Bengal, Behar and Orissa to Lord Clive, the British Governor-General in Calcutta. The provinces contained a population of 25,000,000 and yielded a revenue of 4,000,000 sterling. In August, 1788, the Emperor was blinded by Gholám Kádar, the Rohilla chief, who treated the whole royal family with horrible

The emperor Shah Alam blinded and deposed by Gholám Kádar the Rohilla 1788,

* A sort of sweetmeat made of sugar, flour and ghi.

indignity. On the approach of Sindhia, who was the emperor's supporter, the Rohilla chief fled, but was discovered and executed. The blind emperor was once more seated on the throne, but the whole of the imperial dominions in India had now lapsed to Sindhia, and nothing remained of the Moghal royalty but the name. Shah Alam II* died in 1807 A.D., at the advanced age of eighty one years, and was succeeded by his son Abul Násar Moin-ud-dín Akber Shah II, who died in 1821.

But is reinstated by the Mahrattas.

His death, 1807.

It would be foreign to the object of this work to trace the conquests of the British in India; and, the Moghal power having collapsed at this period, we proceed with our narrative of another race which was gaining political strength and organization in the Panjáb. This will form the subject of a separate volume.

Dissolution of the Moghal empire.

---

* He struck coin bearing the following inscription :—

سکه زد بر هفت کشور سایه فضل اله

حامی دین محمد شاه عالم بادشاه

"The shadow of God's mercy, the defender of religion, Muhammad Shah Alam, the emperor, put his stamp on the seven climes."

Another coin had the inscription :—

سکه صاحب قرانی زد زتائید اله

حامی دین محمد شاه عالم بادشاه

"Shah Alam the emperor, through the favour of God, struck coin like that of Sahib Qurán."

PART III.—THE RISE OF THE SIKHS.

CHAPTER I.

THE HISTORY OF THE SIKH GURUS.

1.—GURU NÁNAK.

Birth of Nának, 1469 A.D.

NÁNAK * was born at Talwandi, a village on the Rávi, above Láhore, in the Sharkpur Tahsil, in the Samvat year 1526 (1469 A.D.), at the time when the Emperor Bahlol Lodi ruled India. He was the son of Kálu, a shopkeeper of Talwandi, and belonged to the Bedi sub-division of the *Chhatris*. The tract between the Rávi and Chináb is called the Richná Doáb. This vast delta, during the period immediately preceding the establishment of the Sikh religion, was inhabited by the *Jats* and *Bhattis*. The latter were a nomadic tribe, but had settled down here, after having embraced the Mahomedan religion, at the time of the Mahomedan incursions from the districts north of the Oxus. With the exceptions of a few small fields cultivated by the *Jats*, the entire country was dreary and void. Great jealousy and hatred existed in those times between the Hindus and the Mahomedans, and the whole non-Musalman population was subjected to persecution by the Mahomedan rulers. The tract between the two rivers was called the Bár, and is still known by that name. The village Talwandi was in those

* The incidents of the life of Nának, the founder of the religious system of the Sikhs, have been fully described in his *Janam-sakhis* or narratives of his life, but these are so full of fictions and fabrications, as to render it almost impossible to distinguish between the imaginary and the real; hence the history of the Sikhs during this period is involved in a haze of mystery. The most authentic of these narratives was found in an ancient manuscript believed to belong to the latter part of the time of Guru Arjan, from the fact that its characters and the idioms in which it was composed were obviously ancient, and that the phraseology agreed with the known diction of the Guru. A copy of this manuscript was presented to the library of the East India House by the celebrated H. P. Colebrook, and it has been translated *verbatim* into English by Dr. Trumpp, and incorporated in his valuable translation of the "*Adi Granth*" of Bábá Nának. This *Janam-sakhi* is written in the most bombastic and hyperbolical language, picturing the preposterous performances attributed to Nának in the highest colours; but it may nevertheless be considered a sober composition when compared with the works of the same kind of later origin. I have carefully compared the *Janam-sakhi* of the India Office library, translated by Dr. Tumpp, with the current *Janam-sakhis*, and find much in the latter which is omitted in the former. This fact clearly proves, I think, that the additions are of a later date and deserving of little credit. On the other hand, as observed by Dr. Trumpp, every point in the old *Janam-sakhi* which throws an unfavourable or doubtful light on Nának has been carefully passed over in the latter *Janam-sakhis*. In my sketch of the life of Bábá Nának I have adopted what seemed to me the safest course, namely, that of mentioning all facts which are found both in the old *Janam-sakhi* alluded to above, and in the latter *Janam-sakhis*, including those of which an epitome appears under mark B. in Dr. Trumpp's compilation, since these facts receive corroboration from all available sources. Fabulous stories have been avoided as far as possible, and an attempt has been made to describe facts in their nakedness. Yet it should be remembered that the original writers were men who occupied a very low position in the scale of civilization, and whose education and mode of life were far inferior to those of the growing generation. If some accounts appear to be coloured, it is because they are so in the text; and, however, phantastic they may appear, there can be little room for doubt that some of them are, at least, in their substance, true, while they present to the mind of the reader an exact idea of the veneration and awe in which the name of the great Sikh reformer is still held by thousands upon thousands of his zealous followers and admirers, and express the true notions which they to this day entertain of his genius and mental power.

The *Janam Patri* of Bábá Nának was written, at the instance of Guru Angad, by *Paira Makha Khatri*, of Sultánpúr, as orally dictated to him by Bala, a Sindhu *Jat*, the companion of Nának in his travels. It was written in 1582 Samvat.

times held by one Rai Bulár, of the Bhatti tribe. The house in which Nának was born, is now a place of public worship, and is called Nankáná. Close to it is a tank where Nának used to play in his boyhood, known as Lalkera.

Nának's father was a weighman, or dharwaí, who also acted as patwari of the village. Though not wealthy, he was a respectable man, and was treated by the village people as their head. His father's name was Sewa Rám, and his mother's Binasi. His father's parentage.

Nának founded the religious system of the Sikhs. He was a man of a philosophic turn of mind, adapted to the age in which he lived, and was destined to introduce, with singular success, those measures of reform, toleration, and enlightenment which were the principal wants of his time. In his boyhood, he was of reserved habits, and seldom or never spoke to his associates, except on the occasion of some pressing necessity. He ate but little, and always seemed gloomy and thoughtful; he was endowed by nature with a pious disposition and a contemplative turn of mind. Kálu, who believed that the boy's birth was the result of the prayers of a certain faqír, who had prophesied that his son would become a great man in the world, took him to a physician and asked him to prescribe medicine for him. The youth, however, said to the physician: "Certainly, nothing can cure one who suffers from separation from the great Being who has given him life, vigour and the power of speech, and who alone governs the universe." The physician was deeply affected by the speech and address of the little boy, and he commended them, giving his affectionate father to understand that the best remedy for the boy was to leave him to himself, to be the free agent of his own will. Nának's boyhood. Nának and the physician.

While yet a boy of seven, Nának was taken to the village school, and, when the schoolmaster began to teach him the rudiments of his religion, the youthful scholar politely asked him what proofs could be given of the existence of God. The master was informed that his pupil was the gift of a faqír, and it is said that, renouncing the world, he became a faqír himself. Nának in school.

When his teacher laid before Nának the alphabet to read, the scholar asked the teacher the hidden import of the first letter of the alphabet, which is a straight stroke denoting singleness, and regarded even by the vulgar as implying the unity of God. A firm and irrevocable belief in the unity of the Creator seems, thus, to have been deeply implanted in the nature of the pious Nának while he was yet a mere boy. His sublime notion of the deity.

According to the author of *Serul Mutakhirin*, Nának received his education from a Musalman Moulvie named Syad Hassan, who resided close to his father's house in Talwandi, and was thoroughly versed in the Mahomedan law books. His education.

The greater portion of his time was spent in seclusion and religious contemplation. During the early part of his career, he used frequently to conceal himself in the woods for days together, away from the busy throng, and studiously avoided contact with his fellow-beings. His parents were on several occasions led to believe that he had been lost in the wilderness, or that he had been devoured by ferocious beasts; but, on search being made, he was discovered in the garb of a faqír, indifferent alike to the concerns of his own person and to the cares of the outside world. He spends his time in seclusion and meditation.

When Nának reached his ninth year, his father, following the custom of the Hindus, convened an assembly of all his relations and friends to invest him with the Brahminical thread. Nának was purified in the usual way; and, all the preliminary ceremonies having been gone through, the priests called upon him to wear the thread, preparatory to his being declared a Hindu; but Nának contended that his status would not be Refuses to wear the Brahmanical thread.

improved by wearing the thread, and that he thought the ceremony was quite uncalled for. The guests were much disappointed at the attitude assumed by the young, but talented, Nának, and the Brahmans were without an answer to his philosophical treatment of the matter, of which long accounts are given in the Sikh books. He observed :—

نائين منّي پت اوپ جي صالاهي سچ سوت

درگاه اندر پاي تگ نه تُوتس پوت

"Man is dignified by repeating the name of God. His praise is the strongest thread. This thread once put on, a man can be admitted into the presence of God, and this cannot, my son, ever break down."

Disappoints his father in trade business.

When he was fifteen years of age, his father, with the view of training him in the art of trade and shopkeeping, sent him to a village to purchase salt to the amount of Rs. 40, and to sell it in another at a higher price. Bálá, a servant of the family, was sent with the boy. On his way to the village, Nának met a party of faqírs who were so hungry that they had lost all power of speech, and could not make their wants known except by signs.

His feeding the hungry faqírs.

Nának's compassion was aroused for the destitute and hungry faqírs, and, having purchased provisions worth Rs. 40, he fed the faqírs. The faqírs having satiated their hunger and refreshed themselves, Nának held a long religious discourse with them, and derived particular pleasure from seeing them relieved of their distress. Bálá rebuked the youth for what he thought a waste of money; but Nának observed: "I have made a bargain the profit of which shall be reaped in the world to come. A bargain with God is much more profitable than any transaction with men."

Nának, on returning home, concealed himself in the branches of a tree, from fear of his father, who was informed of what his son had done. The father was in a great fury and began to beat little Nának, but Rai Bulár, who understood the lad, appeased his anger by the payment of Rs. 40 from his own purse.

The "*Khárá Soudá*."

The place where Nának fed the hungry faqírs is known as *Khárá Soudá* (or unalloyed bargain). The tree in which he is reputed to have concealed himself, exists to this day, with its branches bowed down to the

The "Mál Sahib."

ground on all sides, and is called "Mál Sahib" by the people. Notwithstanding the chastisement he had received for his liberality with his father's money, he invariably made a practice of giving the needy whatever he could lay his hands upon in his father's house, and was punished as often as he was discovered in these acts. His father once provided him with a shop at Sultanpúr, furnishing it with articles of merchandise, but, instead of turning them to any account, he gradually bestowed all in charity upon faqírs to the great disappointment and disgust of his father. The spot

The "Hat Sahib."

where Nának opened his shop is called "Hat Sahib," and the weights and measures which he used exist to this day, and are objects of worship and veneration to his disciples.

When Nának reached the sixteenth year of his age, his parents, thinking that a matrimonial alliance would have the effect of turning his mind

Nának's marriage with Sulakhni.

to worldly affairs, got him married. He was married to Sulakhni, the daughter of one Mulá, a Chhatri, resident of Lakhoki, in Batála, Zilla Gurdaspur, but the marriage had not the desired effect, and Nának did not re-

His sister Nánki.

nounce his wandering habit and his love for faqírs. Nának had a sister named Nánkí, who was married to Jay Ram, a Hindu in the service of Nawab Doulat Khan Lodi, a grandee and relation of the reigning emperor of Delhi, Sultan Bahlol. The nawáb held extensive jágírs in Sultanpúr near Kapúrthalá. Sultanpúr lies on the old Grand Trunk Road between Láhore and Dehli, provided with minárs and serais at short distances, and was a place of importance in Nának's time. Nának was sent to Jay Ram to find employment under the nawáb. The nawáb put the almshouse (*Modi Khana*) under the young man's charge, and it is said that Nának distributed charity to the poor with such a liberal hand that in a short time the funds and provisions of the establishment were completely exhausted. Nának was charged with defalcations by the nawáb's servants, but when the nawáb inspected the *Modi Khana*, and examined the accounts and the articles, he found everything in its proper place, and the reports made to him merely trumped up. He, therefore, conferred new honours on Nának; but, some days after, the young man was again similarly charged, and, on enquiry, the accusation being again proved groundless, he left the service of the nawáb, notwithstanding his ardent entreaties that he would remain in his employ.

His employment under Nawáb Doulat Khan Lodi.

Nának became a public preacher at an early age. His sister Nánkí, after repeated admonitions, persuaded him to live in his house, and, while he was in the service of Nawab Doulat Khan, and in the thirty-second year of his age, a son was born to him who was named Srí Chand. After four years and a half, Nának was blessed with another son, who was named Lakhmi Dás.

Becomes a public teacher.

Nának's two sons, Srí Chand and Lakhmi Dás.

Lakhmi Dás was a babe when Nának abandoned all his worldly connections, and, putting on the garb of a faqír, started on a tour. His companions in his travels were Mardaná, the family mirásí, or musician, a skilful performer on the *rubáb* or harp; Lahná, who afterwards became his successor; Bálá,* a Sindhú Jat, and Ram Das, surnamed Budhá, or the ancient.*

His companions, Mardaná Lahná, Bálá and Budhá.

Whatever verses Nának composed in praise of the Divine Being, and the sayings which he uttered to his votaries by way of admonition, were played by Mardaná on his *rubáb*, a stringed musical instrument like a guitar.

He travelled over the whole of India; visited Persia, Kábul and other parts of Asia, and, it is said, even Mecca. A story is related by both Hindus and Mahomedans in connection with Nának's visit to Mecca. It is said that, while at Mecca, Nának was found sleeping with his feet to the *Kaabá*, before which the Mahomedans prostrate themselves when performing their devotions. The Kazi, Rukn-ud-dín, who observed this, angrily remarked: "Infidel, how dare you dishonour God's house by turning your feet towards it!" "Turn them, if you can," replied Nának, "in a direction where the house of God is not."

His travels.

Nának at Mecca.

Nának was sometimes seen in the garb of a Mahomedan dervesh. Meeting a party of Mahomedan faqírs at Multán, he told them that he was but as the stream of the Ganges, which had entered the ocean of holiness, referring, presumably, to the sanctity in which Multán is held by the Mahomedans, in consequence of the presence in it of numerous mausoleums of saints and devotees and of its being the resort of holy men.

At Multán.

Having devoted some years to travel, Nának came to Emnabad in Gujránwálá, and there lived with one Lálú, a carpenter. Mardaná, the *rubábí*, went home to visit his family. The chief of Talwandi, Rai Bulár, who had already been impressed with Nának's talents, hearing of his recent travels, became anxious to see him, and sent him a message to that effect through

His return home.

* Dr. Trumpp believes that Bálá was not a companion of Nának in his travels, because his name does not occur in the old *Janam-sakhi* believed to belong to Arjan's time. I do not consider this a sufficient reason for holding that the later accounts which associate Bálá's name with the travels of Nának, are untrustworthy, particularly since all authors, European or native, agree that Bálá was a companion of Nának from his youth.

He disregards the advice of his kinsmen to return to worldly affairs.

Mardaná. Nának resolved to visit the chief, and shortly afterwards started for Talwandi. Here his father, mother, father-in-law, uncle, and other relations assembled, and once more they tried to persuade him to renounce his wandering habits and the faqír's garb which he had adopted. They exhibited to him his little children, and begged of him, for their sake and that of the mother, to discontinue his itinerant habits. The sighs of his father and the tears of his mother and wife availed nothing with the inflexible and resolute Nának, who answered the assembly in the following admonitory verses :—

کہما هماري ماتا کہئے - سنتو که همارا پتا - ستو همارا چا چا کہئے - جن سنگ
منو رجتیا —

"Forgiveness is my mother, patience my father, and truth my uncle: with these, as my companions, I have controlled the mind."

سن لعلو گن ایسا - سگل لوگ بندهن کے باهندي - سو کن کہئے کیسا

He inculcates in their minds maxims of truth.

"Hear, O Lálú! this admonition:—Can they be called happy who are bound with worldly ties?"

بهاؤ بهائي سنگ همارے پریم پوت سوهاچا
رهي هماري دهیرج کہیئي اس سنگ هم راچا

"Affability, my brother, is my companion: true love is my own son: endurance is my daughter; in the company of these I am happy."

شانت هماري سنگ سهیلي ست هماري چیلي
ایهو کولنب همارا کہیئي مانس مانس سنگ کہیلي

"Assuagement is my constant female friend, and chastity my slave girl; these you may call my kin and kith, who are my associates every moment."

ایک اونکار همارا خاوند جس هم بنت بنئي
اوسکو تیاگ اور کولاگے نانک هوں کهه پاي

"The only God who gave me existence is my master. He who forsakes him and seeks another, O Nának, shall suffer."

Rai Bulár was much pleased with all that he saw of Nának and his vast learning and persuasive eloquence, and, with a view to induce him to remain at Talwandi, offered him lands; but Nának was quite indifferent to such an offer. After a few days' residence in Talwandi, he made preparation for another journey. His uncle Lálú offered him money to enable him to trade in horses, but Nának rejected the offer and addressed his uncle thus:—

Prepares for another journey.

سن شاستر - سوداگري ست گهوڑي لے چل - خرچ بنه چنگائیاں مت من جاي گل
نرنکار کے دیس جانا یا سکه لے محل

"Hear the Shastras and deal in the horses of truth; have good deeds for your provisions; do not consider this a vain story, and prepare your way to the country of God that you may have everlasting bliss."

Visits Bengal.

Nának this time visited Bengal and its hills. He suffered many hardships in this expedition, in consequence of his preaching to the Mahomedans and Hindus, the strange doctrines of his religion which were extremely distasteful to them, and which they opposed by every means in their power; but nothing could dissuade Nának from prosecuting the task which he had imposed upon himself in the cause of truth. While travelling in the hills, he had an interview with the famous *jogi*, Gorakh Nath, whose homilies are well known throughout India, and whose followers have a long cut through the lobe of their ear. He had a long discourse with the *jogi*,

His interview with Gorakh Nath.

full particulars of which appeared in an account of his travels. Nának is also said to have visited certain islands.

While on his travels in Afghanistán, he lost his faithful servant Mardaná, the harper, who was originally a Mahomedan, but who had become a convert to Nának's new doctrines and was burnt, according to his own wish, in Khulm, where he died. He returned to Batála, and thence proceeded to Talwandi. By this time Kálu, his father, and Rai Bulár, the chief of Talwandi were dead. Taking with him Sajádá, the son of Mardaná, he went to Talamba, near Multán. Here Sajádá, was imprisoned by a notorious thug, and Nának, by the force of his eloquence, obtained his release, and made the thug a convert to his faith. He then marched to Kábul and Kandahar. On his way, he is said, by interposing his hand, to have prevented a landslip. The hill received the impression of Nának's hand, which exists to this day, and the place is called "Panja Sahib." On his return from Kábul, he again lived with his old friend, Lálú, the carpenter of Emnabad.

Travels in Afghanistán.

The "Panja Sahib."

By this time the number of Nának's followers had greatly increased, and he was now looked upon by the people as a saint and a patriarch. With the lapse of years his mode of life also changed, and he now no longer hated society or family. Having left Lálú the carpenter, he went with Bálá to witness the famous Gurchatter fair, held in Multán. Here he preached openly to people of all denominations and creeds who had assembled at the fair. The Kardars of the Delhi Emperor, Ibrahim Lodi, the successor of Bahlol, informed his majesty that a faqír whose tenets were different both from the Koran and the Vedas, was openly preaching to the people, and the importance which he was assuming might, in the end, prove serious to the State. By an imperial order, Nának was brought to the emperor, who admitted him to an interview, and, after hearing his ideas on religion, ordered him to be kept in close confinement. Nának was kept in prison seven months and had to grind corn the whole time. His distress came to an end in consequence of the victory gained by the Emperor Baber over Ibrahim, and the latter's death in the great battle at Pánipat, in which the Moghal troops gained a decisive victory.

Change perceptible in Nának's mode of life.

He is taken prisoner at Multán by the imperial Kardars.

Nának now went on his travels to Sindh, and, on his way to that province, visited the mausoleum of the saint, Bawa Farid Shakarganj, at Pákpattan.

Travels in Sindh.

Visits Pákpattan.

Here he had a religious discourse with a learned Mahomedan named Behram, a descendant of Bawa Farid, and composed his book known as "Asá."

Nának, in his travels, is said to have also visited Ceylon. Siv Nábh, the rájá of that place, became a convert to his faith, as also did a number of others. He remained in Ceylon for two years and five months, and composed there his book called "Práu Sangli." The rájá tried to persuade Nának to settle in Ceylon permanently, but to no purpose; for Nának, shortly afterwards, returned to his native land.

Travels in Ceylon

A story is related of Nának's visit to Stamboul, and his interview with the Sultan of Turkey, who was noted for his cupidity and his extreme oppression of his subjects. Nának's admonitions had a great effect on the Sultan, who is said to have bestowed his hoarded treasures on the faqírs and the needy, and to have discontinued his tyranny over his people. Nának settled on the banks of the Rávi towards the latter part of his life and built houses there. He lived as the head of his family, and his residence was a great resort of people of all nations. Though a faqír in name and appearance, he exercised great influence over vast numbers, who looked upon him as their spiritual leader. His expenses were like those of a king, and

And Turkey.

Settles on the banks of the Rávi.

he established an alms-house where thousands of helpless and poor people were fed. The place of his residence still exists on the banks of the Rávi and is known as Derá Bábá Nának. He built there many houses, which were given free to his disciples.

The sect of Udásís.

Of Nának's two sons, Lakhmi Chand and Srí Chand, the former became a man of the world and had two sons whose descendants remain to this day. Srí Chand became a faqír and was the founder of a sect called Udásís. These wear their hair long, binding it on the head like a turban. They do not use trousers, but wear a cloth, a yard long and a span broad, which they pass between their legs to conceal their nakedness, and give it the name of *langoti*. They rub ashes over the body and go unshaved, the application of a razor to any part of their body being strictly prohibitted. The descendants of Srí Chand are called *Nánakpotras*, or descendants of Nának, and also *Sahib Zádas*, or sons of masters. Some call them kirtáris, or holy men devoted to the worship of God.

The *Nánakpotras*.

Nának founds Kirtárpúr.

Nának also founded the town of Kirtárpúr in the Jalandar district, a place of great sanctity and veneration among the Sikhs, and built there a dharmsálá which exists to this day.

Death of Nának, 1538.

Nának lived a long and useful life, and died at the age of 71 years in 1538 A.D. He reigned as Guru sixty years, five months, and seven days. He died at Kartárpúr, a town founded by himself on the Rávi, about forty miles above Láhore. A tomb, or samadh, was erected to his memory, where large crowds used to assemble to commemorate the date of his death, and perform certain religious ceremonies; but it has since been washed away by the Rávi, though a piece of Nának's garment and his other relics are still exhibited to the pilgrims at a dharmsálá, or temple, erected in commemoration of his decease.

His doctrines.

The doctrines of Nának were those of pure deism. He believed in the unity of God, the one invisible God, and strictly prohibited idolatry, and the worship of images. He maintained that true and pure religion was one, and that men were all equal. The numerous religions and castes which had sprung up in the world, were, he said, the device of men. He said, he had read the *Qurán* and the Puránás, but true religion he could find in neither. Yet he respected both, and advised his followers to pick out, and to act upon the truths which each contained. His best endeavours during his long public career, were directed towards removing, or reducing to a minimum, those religions and social differences which had sprung up between the two great sects of India, the Hindus and the Mahomedans, and to reconciling them both; and to a great extent he was successful. His tenets were misunderstood after his death by his zealous followers, who, from a host of faqírs, turned into warriors, though, as will be explained further on, they were driven to such a course by circumstances peculiar to the times they lived in. He viewed with disfavour the intolerance of the Musalmans towards the Hindus, and the precepts of his religion inculcated peace to all mankind, brotherly love to one another, and living virtuously and harmoniously.

His mental struggles for improving the condition of his countrymen.

His notions of the mission of Mahomed and of the Hindu incarnation.

Nának believed in the holy mission of Mahomed and the Hindu incarnation. He admitted that Mahomed was the messenger of God sent to instruct mankind and to lead them to the path of righteousness. But, unlike the Arabian prophet, he never claimed that what he himself preached or addressed to the people was inspired or revealed to him from Heaven; nor did he ever boast of being gifted with supernatural powers, or attribute any of his acts to a power not at the command of other men. He said he was a man among men, mortal as they were, and sinful. "He was a faqír," said he, "before the threshold of God." "Thou art the incorporeal Creator, and Nának is thy slave:" "*Tuí hae Nirankár Kirtar, Nának bandá terá,*" was the theme of the good-hearted, pious Nának. He took particular delight in causing this theme to be played on the *rubáb* by his favourite actor and the companion of his toils, Mardaná. His doctrine was that God was all in all, and he taught all to believe in the Creator, the Lord of Lords, the one God, self-existent, incomprehensible, omnipotent, without beginning and everlasting. Good deeds were nothing in themselves, but the knowledge of the true God was the only way to salvation. No prophet or holy teacher has the power to do good or to do evil to anybody. Everything comes from God, who alone must be depended upon for all our wants. Holy men can only tell and interpret His commands. They are nothing of themselves. He was a believer in the transmigration of souls, and maintained that, after undergoing the prescribed course of punishment for the sins committed by man, the soul shall find its blissful home with God. Although he was taken for an ascetic in his early life, in consequence of his absenting himself from his family, and his dislike for the society of men, yet that was in the ardent search for truth. Nának laboured for years as an enquirer after truth, and passed a considerable portion of his life in travels in India, and beyond its limits; but, after he had seen enough of the world and gained much by his great and varied intercourse with mankind, he became a worldly man himself, and lived in his family and with his people as a patriarch. He then taught his followers that abandonment of the world was quite unnecessary, and that God treated all with equal favour, whether travellers or home dwellers, and that, between the hermit in his cell and the king in his palace, no difference was made in respect of the kingdom to come. The doctrines of this great Hindu reformer have been handed down in the famous book called the "*Granth,*" or holy book, written by himself. It is called the *Adi Granth*, to distinguish it from the second part, composed by Guru Govind, a successor of Nának, who greatly modified the tenets of his predecessor, and infused into his followers ideas of war and conquest, turning them from peaceable subjects into a contentious tribe.

His favourite theme.

His doctrine.

Believes in the transmigration of souls.

Discourages asceticism.

The "*Granth,*" or holy book.

As mentioned before, Nának never professed to possess miraculous powers, or pretended to do supernatural deeds, though his credulous followers attributed such powers to him. They think Nának the incarnation of God, and repeat his name as their saviour, or lord, in their prayers. There are various stories current about his miracles, some of which may, with advantage, be cited here as showing the ideas and notions which his followers entertain of his character. A voice was one day heard by Nának from above, calling upon him to approach. Nának, surprised at hearing the voice, said: "What power have I, O God, to stand in thy presence?" The voice directed Nának to close his eyes. Nának closed his eyes and advanced. He was then told to open his eyes and look. He did so, and heard the word "*Wah*" or "Well done" repeated five times, and then "Wah, Gurují," or "Well done, teacher." Nának then entered into conversation with God, who informed him that he had been sent into the world as a teacher of mankind in the Kalíyug, or dark age, and that he was to lead them into the paths of righteousness and virtue.

Nának disclaimed miraculous powers;

Nevertheless his followers believe he was gifted with such powers.

Origin of the national anthem, "Wah, Guru."

One day Nának, becoming thirsty, asked Budha, who was attending his cattle near a village, to bring some water in a vessel from a tank close by. Budha said there was a tank, but it was dry. Nának said, "Go and see; the tank is not dry." Budha went, and to his astonishment saw that the tank was full of water, although it had not a drop in it in the morning. He brought water for Nának, and became his disciple. At this place

The tank of Amritsar.

Guru *Arjan* constructed a new tank, and called it "Amritsar," or the "Water of Immortality."

The story of the serpent and Nának.

While quite a youth and tending his cattle, the days being hot, Nának went to sleep under the shade of a tree. The sun, declining towards the west, threw its rays on Nának's face. A black serpent, seeing this, approached and spread its broad hood over Nának's face to protect it from the rays of the sun. Rai Bulár, the chief of Talwandi, saw this, and gave Nának's parents the happy tidings that their son was to be a leader of men, and had a great future in store for him. Kálu contemptuously observed that "God's matters were known only to God." The place where this happened is called "*Kírá Sahib*," and a large building has recently been constructed on it by the Sikhs to commemorate the event.

Nának at the prayers of a Mahomedan congregation.

Nawáb Doulat Khan once argued with Nának, that, since he (Nának) forbade idolatry, acknowledged the unity of God, and believed in the mission of Mahomed, he was a Moslem, and, this being the case, there was nothing to prevent his professing the Moslem creed openly. He therefore took him to a mosque, and Nának apparently expressed his readiness to join in the prayers. The Hindus were much alarmed at hearing that Nának had resolved to embrace Mahomedanism, though they knew perfectly well that he was not a Hindu himself in their sense of the word. When, however, the prayers were being read, Nának kept aloof, and did not join the congregation. The nawáb was disappointed, and asked Nának the reason of his not joining in the prayers. Nának said: "The prelate (*Imám*) was uneasy in his mind about the indisposition of his son, and feared that his calf might fall into the well as it had not been properly tethered. The nawáb was thinking of purchasing horses from Kandahar. These thoughts prevailing, how could I read prayers after such men." The *Imám* admitted that what Nának said was really true, and that his attention was divided while he was conducting the prayers. The nawáb also admitted that he was thinking of making a bargain for horses at Kandahar, while apparently engaged in prayers. This astonished the whole congregation; and the Hindus, whose minds were much perplexed, were glad that Nának had not openly embraced the religion of the Prophet. Yet an idea generally prevailed among the Mahomedans that Nának was a true follower of the Prophet, as would seem to be the fact from the following account. At the time when Nának breathed his last, a dispute arose between the Hindus and the Mahomedans regarding the disposal of his body, each party claiming the right to perform the funeral obsequies according to the form of their own religion. The Hindus said that, Nának being a Hindu, his body should, after the fashion of that creed, be burnt, while the Mahomedans maintained that the deceased was a Musalman, and that his remains should therefore be buried according to the rites of the Mahomedans. A quarrel arose between the two parties, and swords were drawn, but through the mediation of more thinking men, it was resolved that the body should be neither burnt nor buried in the grave, but thrown into the river. When the people entered the room where the body was supposed to lie, they found, to their great astonishment, on raising the sheet with which it had been covered, that it was not there. In all probability, it had been secretly removed by one of the contending parties, but only the sheet was, as a matter of fact, found stretched on the ground, with some flowers underneath, instead of the body of the deceased. The Mahomedans took half of this sheet and buried it, with the ceremonies observed on the death of their co-religionists, while the Hindus burnt the other half which fell to their lot.

Dispute on his death between Hindus and Mahomedans regarding the disposal of his body.

The place at Emnabad where Nának slept for some time in the jungle, is called "*Rori Sahib,*" owing to its having been originally a heap of gravels and stones, which Nának used as an altar, and before which he prayed. He stood in the waters of the Biás, near Sultanpúr, for three successive days, neither eating nor drinking anything, and passing the whole time in prayer and meditation. The tree under which he stood is called "*Bábá ki ber,*" the place where he used to perform his ablutions being known as "*Sant Ghât.*" Nának's religious penances.

In one of Baber's expeditions into the Panjáb, Nának, with a number of his followers, among whom was Mardaná, was apprehended at Emnabad and brought before the emperor. Baber, who was himself a very good Arabic and Persian scholar, and also a poet, was much pleased with the conversation which he held with Nának, and with the information given to him on many interesting topics. His interview with Baber, the Moghal emperor.

The Emperor ordered rich presents to be bestowed on the faqír, but Nának refused them, observing that his best reward was the inward pleasure derived from the worshipping of the Creator, and that as his aim in life was to please that Lord of Lords, he had no concern with the kings made by Him. A drug, richly prepared, was brought to the emperor by his slave. His majesty partook of it, and ordered some to be given to the faqír, but Nának requested to be excused, saying: "On a man who is ever intoxicated with the recollection of God, this drug can have no effect." It is strange that Baber makes no mention of the founder of the Sikh religion in his memoirs; but this is probably due to the fact that Nának was not at that time a man of sufficient note and importance to attract the attention of the emperor when engaged in drawing up an account of his own life and exploits.

On one occasion Nának saw a party of Brahmans who were pantomimically going through the performance of baling out water from a river with their hands, as if to irrigate their fields, their faces being turned to the east. This ceremony was being performed in the superstitious belief that the thirst of their dead co-religionists would, by virtue of the act, be quenched. Nának, who was standing on the opposite bank, saw this, and began to mimic their actions, but with his face turned to the west. The Brahmans evidently considered Nának, whom they took for a faqír, to be out of his senses, and indignantly asked him the meaning of his insane performance, informing him that all his labours were in vain, and that he could not hope to relieve the thirst of the departed by such heretical actions. Nának replied: "I am not furnishing water to my dead, but irrigating my fields in Kartárpúr to prevent them drying up by the scorching heat of the sun." "Watering your fields in Kartárpúr! Such a long distance? How can this handful of water benefit your fields which are such a long way off?" rejoined the Brahmans in an excited and indignant tone. "How can, then, your waters," replied the pious, but vexed, Nának, "reach the next world and quench the thirst of your dead? If the water cannot benefit my crops, which are in this world, how can it benefit your dead in another?" Nának never thought that the office which he had created would become hereditary. When he saw that his last end was approaching, he named Lahná, one of his faithful disciples, his successor. The sons and other disciples envied him, but he gave proofs of his faith and devotion. Seeing the dead body of a man lying on the roadside, Nának said: "Ye who have confidence in me partake of this food." All shrunk back, including the Guru's son; but simple Lahná, Nának's most staunch ally and follower, jumped over the dead body, and was about to devour the dead, when he was embraced by Nának, who declared that from that moment his own spirit had gone into Lahná's body, and that he must be regarded as Nának himself. His name he changed from Lahná to "Angi Khud," or "Angad," meaning Nának and a party of Brahmans. He names Lahná as his successor. Proof of Lahná's fidelity.

He is believed to have inherited the spirit of Nának.

"my own body." The belief common among the Sikhs is that the spirit of Nának is inherited by each successive Guru.

2.—GURU ANGAD.

Lahná, on succeeding to the *Guruship*, assumed the title of "Angad," an epithet applied to him by his illustrious predecessor, in consideration of his proved loyalty and devotion. Angad was born in 1504 (1561 Samvat) in the village of Khadúr, his residence on the river Biás, near Gowindwal, in the Tirhún subdivision of the *Chhatris*. The Sikh religion, would, in all probability, have gradually completely died out and sunk into oblivion, as has been the lot of many others, had it not been for the foresight and wisdom of its founder, in establishing an apostolic successorship, and thereby creating a spirit of aspiration and ambition in his followers which insured, to a great extent, its perpetuation.

Nának founds an apostolic successorship.

His motives in so acting.

Nának devoted his life to the instruction of man in the path of virtue and righteousness. His motives were quite unselfish, and he had at his heart the good of the nation and the prosperity of the people among whom he lived. He, therefore, delegated his office neither to any of his sons, nor to any of his early followers, who were probably not with him at the close of his life, but to Angad, who had joined him not long before his death, and whom he considered the most fit. Angad gained his livelihood by the work of his own hands, twisting *van*, or coarse twine made of *munj*.

Early occupation and religious belief of Angad.

He had great reverence for the *Deví* at Jawála Mukhí, near Kángrá, and used to pay her homage every year, travelling on foot. On becoming a disciple of Nának, he gave up his periodical pilgrimages to the *Deví*, being convinced that service to the Guru was more beneficial to him, both here and hereafter, than the performing of pilgrimages to the *Deví* and the worshipping of her effigy.

He upholds the principles of Nának.

Angad was strongly attached to Nának and was his most fervent server and staunch ally. He was hardly possessed of any merits of his own, but he spread the religion of his Guru by following studiously in the path which Nának had paved out for his successors.

Collects the sayings of his predecessor.

He committed to writing* much about his great predecessor, both that which he himself remembered, and that which was narrated to him by Bálá, the old companion of Nának.

He also recorded the results of his own devotional observations which have been incorporated in the *Granth*.

Angad had two sons, both of whom became men of the world. He removed his head-quarters from Derá Bábá Nának to his own village of Khadúr. His feet were afflicted with a severe complaint, to which he fell a victim in 1552, the thirteenth year of the reign of Akber, having reigned as a Guru for fifteen years. His tomb was erected in his native village.

Dies, 1552.

3.—GURU AMAR DÁS.

Amar Dás succeeds.

A cultivated mind, or scientific attainments, do not seem to have been the qualifications which rendered a man eligible for occupying the *masnad* of a Guru. What was looked for in a successor, was moral courage and devotion to the reigning Guru. Amar Dás, on whom the choice of successorship fell, was the most faithful follower of Guru Angad, and a constant attendant on his person. He was a *Chhatri* of the *Bhalla* clan, and was born at Vásarki, a village in the Amritsar district, in 1509. He was, like his predecessor, a man of humble parentage, and supported himself by the proceeds

His parentage and early occupation.

* Angad had the *Janam Patri* of Nának translated from Shastri to Gurmukhi by Paira, caste Mokha, of Sultánpúr.

of his occupation, which was that of carrying goods from place to place on a pony, the only property which he possessed. Having become fond of the society of faqirs, he came to the village of Khadúr and made Guru Angad his spiritual guide. He served him with all his heart, and sacrificed his own comfort for that of the Guru. Yet he never ate anything from the Guru's storehouse, but supported himself by small sums of money which he earned by trading in salt and oil in the market. Every night he used to bring fresh water from the river of Gowindwal, about two *kos* distant from Khadúr, for the ablutions of his Guru. His reverence for the Guru was so great that he never turned his back towards him, and in his midnight journey to the river he used, on all occasions, to walk backwards, *i.e.*, with his face towards the Guru's house. One dark tempestuous night, in the midst of rain, thunder and lightning, as Amar Dás was returning from the river with an earthen jar full of water for the Guru, he accidentally fell into a ditch near a weaver's house, and the jar was smashed to pieces. The weaver, perceiving from the noise that some one had fallen into the pit, said to his wife: "What miserable scoundrel can that be roving about at this time of night? it must be that wretched vagabond Amrú." Amrú managed to scramble out of the hole without assistance, and, having procured another jar, set out again and brought water afresh for his religious preceptor, who enjoyed the bath without knowing anything of the misfortune which had befallen his faithful Amrú. The next day, the Guru was informed by somebody of what had happened on the preceding night, and he was told that people called Amrú the homeless one. The Guru was convinced of his disciple's devotion and sincerity, and, holding him by the neck, said: "Amrú is not homeless, but the home of the homeless; he who will follow him shall find his home with the Lord." He was forthwith declared to be the successor of Angad, who bowed down to him, and then presented him with five pice and a cocoanut, after which he was paid homage to by all.

His reverence for his Guru.

Who declares him to be his successor.

On the death of Angad, Amar Dás established himself at Gowindwal. He was successful as a teacher, and his zeal and activity in preaching, combined with his genial habits and affable disposition, secured for him many converts to the new faith. He was a just and wise Guru, humble and patient. He composed beautiful verses, which have been incorporated in the *Granth*, and are much liked for their simplicity of diction and purity of idea. He found a patient listener in the high-minded Akber. He separated the inert and torpid sect of Udásís, founded by Srí Chand, from the active and worldly Sikhs, and thus prevented the former from being lost in oblivion as a distinct creed.

The new Guru separates the Sikhs from the *Udásís*.

Following the policy initiated by Nának, he disapproved of *satti*, which was sanctioned by the usage of ages, and encouraged the re-marriage of Hindu widows, maintaining that the woman who, bereft of her husband, nobly supported herself under the trial, was a true *satti*, and not the suicide who deliberately ended her existence on the pyre. This was the mild form in which the wise Guru denounced the baneful practice of *satti*.

He denounces the *Satti*.

From the offerings made by his disciples, Amar Dás was enabled to build at Gowindwal a *báoli*, or large oblong tank, the descent to the brink of which is reached by eighty-four steps, with landing places, and covered chambers for travellers to rest in and take refreshments during the heat of the day. The Sikhs believe that whoever bathes on these eighty-four steps one by one, repeating the *Japjí* to the last step, is made free from the eighty-four lakhs of forms of metempsychosis and enters heaven. A grand fair is still held at this *báoli* every year, to which the Sikhs flock from all directions to do homage to the memory of the departed Guru.

Builds a *báoli* at Gowindwal.

Sends out missionaries to preach to the people the faith of the Guru.

Amar Dás sent twenty-two of his chosen disciples to visit various parts of the country, and spread the religion of Nának by peaching and discussion with the people.

He had a son, Mohan, and a daughter Mohaní, *alias* Bheni. When the *báoli* of Amar Dás was in course of construction, a great number of masons and other workmen were employed on it, and a large multitude of spectators used to assemble to see how the work progressed. Among these was a lad named Ram Das, a *Chhatri* of the *Sodhí* sect, and a lineal descendant of Sodhí Ráo, who bequeathed the throne of Láhore to Kalpat Ráo, his uncle. The boy had come from Láhore, and used to sell provisions to the workmen. He was a handsome youth, and Bheni, the daughter of Amar Dás, seeing him, became enamoured of him. He was finally married to Bheni, and this united the family of the *Bhalas* and the *Sodhís*.

Fixes his choice for successorship on Ram Dás his son-in-law.

Amar Dás, was particularly fond of his daughter Mohaní for her filial love and obedience, for which reason he passed over his son, Mohan, and all his other disciples, and bestowed the apostolic blessing upon his son-in-law, Ram Dás, who became his successor in the Guruship.

Dies, 1574.

Amar Dás died in Gowindwal, on 14th May, 1574, having reigned as a Guru for a period of twenty-two years. His tomb was erected at Gowindwal, but has since been washed away by the river.

4.—GURU RAM DAS.

Ram Das succeeds.

'Guru Ram Das, the *Chhatri* of the *Sodhí* clan, was a native of Láhore. His parents moved to Gowindwal, where, in consequence of their poverty, Ram Das had recourse to selling boiled grain, on the proceeds of which he managed to support himself and his poor parents. He was a man of considerable merit, well worthy of the choice of his master, and the affectionate regard of his wife. He was of a quiet and peaceful disposition; and his piety and devotion, combined with his eloquence and energy, ranged hundreds of disciples round his banner. He gave himself up to literary pursuits; and his poetical effusions, in which he has expounded his doctrines, have been incorporated in the *Granth*.

Akber bestows a grant of land on him.

The Guru restores an old tank which he names "*Amritsar*,"

And builds a Harmandar.

In his time, the voluntary offerings of the Sikhs, or disciples, immensely increased, and he was enabled to live in state. At Láhore, he had an interview with the tolerant Akber, who was highly pleased with his accomplishments, and, as a mark of esteem and approbation, granted him a piece of land, which, from its being of a circular shape, was named Chakkar Ram Das. Here Ram Das splendidly restored an old tank which he called "*Amritsar*," or the "*pool of immortality*," and in the midst of which he built a temple, which he named Harmandar, or the mandar of Hari.

He founds the town of Amritsar.

Around this tank were built the huts of faqírs and smaller temples, and the disciples and followers of the Guru came and settled here. The Guru came himself occasionally from Gowindwal to live here, and in time this new town, from *Guru ká Chak*, came to be called Amritsar (the nectar tank), the name given by the founder, by which name it is known to this day.

The boon obtained by him from Akber.

At an interview, Ram Das represented to the Emperor, Akber, that, owing to the long stay of his majesty with his retinue and camp-followers at Láhore, the price of food had risen greatly, and that now, as the Court had left the place, it would fall and the raiats suffer in consequence. He therefore begged his majesty to remit a year's rent to the poor raiats. Akber granted this request, and was strongly impressed with the Guru's sympathy for the poor. The representation made by the Guru to the emperor, prompted as it was by purely charitable motives, and the success which attended it, is said to have immensely increased the popularity of the Guru among the *Jats* and the zemindars, who flocked around him from all sides, thus contributing, in no small degree, to his power and fame. Gains for him great popularity among the zemindars.

In founding the town of Amritsar at a central spot, the Guru laid the foundation of the future greatness of the Sikhs as a nation, for they were enabled now to rally at a common place of worship, conveniently situated, both as regards distance and fertility of the soil. Peaceful in mind and gentle in their behaviour, following yet the mild and pure tenets laid down by their first leader, they learnt to unite together and to foster and engender those feelings of brotherly love which tended to strengthen the national tie, and paved the way to the formation of a commonwealth on true patriotic principles. He lays the foundation of the future greatness of the Sikhs.

Ram Das had three sons by the daughter of Amar Dás. The first, named Mahadeo, became a faqír; the second, Pirthi Dás, turned out a worldly minded man, and the third, Arjan, or Arjan Mal, who was a favourite with his father, succeeded him in the Guruship. From this time the succession to the *gadi* became hereditary, which materially contributed to the growth of the Sikh power, for henceforward the Guru was looked upon by his disciples not only in the light of a spiritual guide, but also as a worldly lord and a ruling sovereign. His three sons. The Guruship becomes hereditary.

Ram Das died in March, 1586, having reigned as a Guru for seven years, and a tomb was erected on the banks of the Biás in honour of his memory. Death of Ram Das, 1581.

5.—GURU ARJAN.

Bheni, the daughter of Amar Dás, aspired to become the mother of all future Gurus, and, with this object in view, she endeavoured to please her father, in whom she believed was the power of granting her desire. Her father was sensible of the great love which Bheni, on all occasions, manifested towards him, and determined to reward her to the utmost of his ability. He, accordingly, asked her, on one occasion, how he could reward her for the great love which she invariably bore him, upon which the sagacious young lady demanded that the Guruship be made hereditary in her offspring. On the death of her husband, her wishes were accomplished, and her son, Arjan, the youngest child of Ram Das, ascended the *masnad* of Guruship in 1581. Arjan, on assuming the dictatorship, established himself at Amritsar. He was the first of the Gurus who laid aside the rosary and the garb of a faqír, and dressed himself in costly attire and converted the saintly *gadi* of his pious predecessors into a princely rostrum. He kept a numerous retinue, fine horses and elephants, and lived in splendour. He was an energetic and aspiring Guru, and his aims were high. He organized the Sikhs into a community, and devised measures for extending his spiritual authority. Arjan succeeds, 1581. He established himself at Amritsar. Lives in state.

His first consideration was to ascertain whether the teachings of the great Nának were equally suited to the multifarious religious denominations and societies that then existed. He attempted to raise the followers of Nának in the scale of society, and, with a view to uniting them by one common religious tie, he gave them a religious code, which they held in the greatest veneration. In this code he incorporated the sayings and verses of Nának, the compositions of his predecessors, and his own, and the choicest literary productions of other religious reformers of those times, whose memory was still fresh in the minds of the people. This code he called the "*Granth*," or the holy book, and it was handed over to the Guru's successors with an assurance that all it contained was pure and binding on all true disciples. A copy was kept in the Harmandar, or holy temple, and recited each day to the crowds who came to bathe in the sacred tank. Hymns were sung in praise of the Lord by bands of musicians, Compiles the "*Granth*," or holy book.

and the incidents of the life of Bábá Nának were repeated with great fervour. Thus was a new spirit infused into the minds of the followers of the Guru.

Organizes a system of taxation.

He organized a system of taxation and appointed delegates, or deputies, for the purposes of collecting it from his followers throughout the country. These contributions, or *nazránás*, from the faithful were collected in all districts by means of the deputies abovementioned, and presented by them to the Guru in an annual assembly. Thus were the Sikhs accustomed to a regular system of government, and, having been formed into a community, gradually developed into a real power. To increase the commonwealth, Arjan also sent his disciples to foreign countries for the purposes of trade, dealing principally in Turkistan horses.

He completed the construction of the grand tank at Amritsar, and built another splendid tank in the same place, called *Kaulsar*. He also built the celebrated tank called "*Taran Taran*" in the Amritsar district.

Builds "*Taran Taran*."

Feud with Chándu Shah.

Arjan refused to betroth his son, Har Govind, to the daughter of Chándu Shah, the financial minister at Láhore, in the times of the Emperor Jahángír, and is said to have returned the betrothal presents sent by Chándu Shah. The Minister, who had himself given the Guru cause for offence, by calling him a beggar and comparing him to the drain of a house and himself to the upper storey, went in person to soothe the Guru with a lakh of rupees; but it was too late; for the Guru declared:—"My words are engraved on stone, and cannot be effaced. If you give me the whole world as a dowry with your daughter, my son will not marry her." The minister was greatly abashed and vowed to destroy the Guru. He calumniated him to the Emperor Jahángír, who was then at Láhore. Arjan was charged with treason, in having offered prayers for the success of Khusrow, the emperor's rebel son, who was in temporary possession of the Panjáb. He was thrown into prison, and the emperor wished to extort a large sum of money from him, which the Guru was unable to pay. He was tortured and died of heat apoplexy, while in confinement near Láhore, in 1606, the second year of the reign of Jahángír. He reigned as a Guru for twenty-four years. His tomb now stands opposite the fort of Láhore, near the mausoleum of Maharájá Ranjít Singh.*

Arjan charged with treason.

Imprisonment and death of Arjan, 1606.

Gúr Das the author of *Gian Ratnaoli*.

The celebrated Gúr Das flourished in the time of Arjan. He was a great writer, and composed the well-known work *Gian Ratnaoli*, consisting of forty chapters, in which he describes the character of Nának. The Sikhs are enjoined by Arjan to read this book. The writer, who was a disciple of Arjan, gives Nának a lofty place in the history of the world, and regards him as the successor of Viasa and Mahomed, sent by God into the world to accomplish a holy mission and to redeem mankind.

The death of Guru Arjan is a great turning point in the history of the Sikh nation, for it inflamed the religious passion of the Sikhs, and it was at this time that those seeds of hatred of the Musalman power were sown which took such deep root in the minds of all the faithful followers of Nának.

6.—GURU HAR GOVIND.

Har Govind succeeds.

Arjan died leaving a minor son and heir, Har Govind, a boy eleven years of age. Taking advantage of his minority, his uncle, Pirthi Mal, urged

* The tradition goes that Chándu Shah had suggested to the emperor that the Guru should be sewed in the hide of a cow.

When the hide was brought before him, the Guru asked permission to bathe in the Rávi. He was sent thither with a strong escort, but, having once plunged into the running water, never appeared again.

McGregor puts Arjan's death in the time of Shah Jahán, and ascribes the feud between him and Chándu to his period. This shows how inaccurate McGregor's accounts generally are.

his own right to succeed to the *gadi;* but the Sikhs deserted him in disgust, suspecting him of intrigue with the hated Chándu Shah, and Har Govind was acknowledged as the Guru.

Har Govind combined the qualities of a warrior, a saint and a sportsman. While Nának abstained from animal food, Har Govind took delight in hunting and in eating flesh. He was the first Guru who organized a military system, and, arming his followers, made them buckle on the sword, and prepared them for action in the field. He was induced to resort to arms in order to chastise his enemy, Chándu Shah, and, having secured the confidence* of the emperor, obtained possession of Chándu's person, and was thus able to avenge himself as he thought best. Har Govind took him to Amritsar, and there had him dragged through the streets with a rope round his feet, and made to sit on heated frying-pans and hot sand, as he had done with Arjan. Thus he died in the most excruciating pain.

He resents the enmity of Chándú Shah.

Har Govind surpassed his predecessor in splendour and state. He maintained a large establishment, which he was enabled to do by the daily increasing income derived from the offerings which were now levied in the form of a tax from the faithful throughout the country, under the system introduced by the politic Arjan. He had eight hundred fine horses in his stables, and kept a numerous, gorgeous and well-equipped retinue. He built the town of Hargovindpur on the banks of the Biás, to serve, in case of an emergency, as a place of retreat.

Becomes a military leader.

Builds Hargovindpur.

His warlike talent led him to enter the service of Jahángír as a military leader, and he even accompanied the imperial camp on its journeys to that paradise of Hindostán, Káshmír; but he fell in the estimation of the emperor through appropriating to his own use the pay of the contingent, through admitting into his service criminals and fugitives, and through his failure to pay the balance of the heavy fine that had been imposed upon his father Arjan. He was placed in confinement in the fort of Gwalior, where he was kept a prisoner for twelve years in a state of semi-starvation. The faithful flocked round the fort and bowed themselves before its walls, to worship the living saint who was undergoing persecution at the hands of the powerful Moghal. At length, roused by pity, rather than affected by the demonstrations of the Sikhs, the emperor ordered the release of the Guru.

Incurs the displeasure of Jahángír.

Is imprisoned in the fort of Gwalior.

His release.

The Emperor Jahángír died in 1628, and Hár Govind entered the service of his successor, Shah Jahan. He raised himself in the estimation of the emperor's eldest son, Dárá Shekoh, the governor of the Panjáb, who in those days lived at Láhore. Dárá was an abstemious prince, simple in heart and manners, and particularly friendly to the faqírs. He and Har Govind became great friends; and, for Dárá's sake, the Guru used to pass a considerable portion of his time in Láhore. He also used to go with the prince to Káshmír on pleasure trips. But he soon fell into fresh difficulties with the imperial government, and circumstances arose which compelled him to make armed resistance. A certain disciple of the Guru was taking a fine Turkistání horse to Amritsar for presentation to the Guru. The horse was

The Guru gains the confidence of Prince Dárá Shekoh.

Quarrels with the king.

* During the emperor's residence at Láhore, Har Govind was admitted to an audience. He presented a rosary of amber to his majesty, who was highly pleased with its splendour, and asked the Guru whether he could procure more pearls of the same kind as were contained in the rosary. The Guru submitted to his majesty that the rosary consisted of a complete set of a hundred pearls, but Chándu, his dewán, had taken most of them, and the ornament was therefore incomplete. The emperor asked the Guru how the pearls had fallen into the hands of the dewán. Upon this, the Guru burst into tears and narrated to the king the whole story. The king was greatly enraged at hearing of the treatment which Arjan had met with at the hands of the dewán, and orders were passed for the person of Chándu Shah to be handed over to Har Govind to avenge himself on him in any manner he chose for his father's death.

seized at Láhore by the officers of the king and presented before his majesty, who, being struck with its beauty, ordered it to be sent to the royal stable, and the price to be paid to the owner. The Guru, hearing this, was much annoyed, but was powerless. The horse became lame and was given over by the king to the chief kazi, or judge of Láhore, who had it properly treated and cured. The Guru pretended to purchase the horse, and, having fixed the price at Rs. 10,000, received it from the kazi, but left Láhore for Amritsar the next day, without paying the money or ever intending to do so. In the meanwhile, a hawk belonging to the emperor was seized by one of the Guru's followers, and a concubine of the kazi's harem, named Kaulán, who, it is said, had become enamoured of the Guru, was abducted. These provocations induced the Mahomedan government to send an armed force against the Guru, with orders to seize him and disperse his followers. Mukhlis Khan marched from Lahore at the head of 7,000 troops, who were, however, signally defeated near Amritsar, their leader being killed in the engagement. The defeated army returned to Láhore after losing many in killed and wounded. This was the first combat in the annals of the Panjáb which was fought between the Mahomedans and the Sikhs.

An army sent against him from Láhore.

The royal troops defeated.

The success, however, did not elate Har Govind with pride. Conscious of the strength and resources of the ruling power and his own comparative weakness, he retired to the jungles of Bhatinda, fifteen miles from Khadúr, south of the Sutlej, to avoid a further encounter with the imperial army. In the meantime, Prince Dárá Shekoh, the friend of Har Govind, exercised his influence with his royal father much to the benefit of the Guru, and matters went on smoothly until fresh troubles arose under the following circumstances.

The Guru retires to the wastes of Bhatinda.

While in the jungles of Bhatinda, Har Govind converted great crowds to the faith of Nának, among them being one Buddhá, a notorious free-booter, known afterwards as Bábá Buddhá, a complimentary title given him by the Sikhs. This man stole two of the emperor's best horses from the imperial stable at Láhore and brought them to the Guru. This behaviour inflamed the king with violent anger, exasperated as he already was by the Guru's previous conduct. Kamar Beg and Lal Beg were sent out from Láhore at the head of an army which crossed the Sutlej; but want of provisions and the difficulties of the march had a disastrous effect on the imperial troops. The army was reduced to great straits, and, being defeated by the Sikhs, fled to Láhore, leaving its commanders slain on the battle field. Har Govind, having twice beaten the Moghal army in the open field, now began to entertain some degree of confidence in his own power, and in the prowess of his followers, He therefore crossed the Sutlej and established himself at Kartárpúr, where he collected a large army, and patiently awaited a favourable opportunity for renewing hostilities.

Another cause of quarrel between the king and the Guru.

The royal troops again defeated.

The Guru establishes himself at Kartárpúr.

Paindá Khan, a Pathan, was the foster brother of Guru Har Govind and his bosom friend. The Guru consequently treated him most liberally. A serious quarrel, however, occurred between the Guru and the Khan over a valuable hawk belonging to the Guru's eldest son, which the Khan had appropriated to himself, the bird having by chance flown to his house. Paindá Khan was beaten in the Guru's tent and turned out of it with disgrace. He went to the emperor at Delhi and complained of the treatment to which he had been subjected. The emperor furnished him with a powerful army, with which he marched to the Panjáb and encountered the Sikhs under their Guru. There was desperate fighting on both sides, and for a long time victory was equally balanced between them. Har Govind exhibited great bravery, despatching with his own hand many Mahomedans, and his perseverance and

Quarrels with his foster brother Paindá Khan.

A third battle with the royal troops.

skill were finally crowned with victory, the Moghal troops being completely defeated and Paindá Khan himself falling in a hand-to-hand combat with his foster brother and playmate.

Har Govind gains the victory.

In the course of the struggle a brave soldier frantically rushed on the Guru with drawn sword; but he skilfully warded off the blow and laid his courageous antagonist dead at his feet, exclaiming: "You have not the knack of using the sword; this is the way to wield it." He was looked upon by the Sikhs, not only as a divine messenger, but as an accomplished swordsman, a hero, and a thorough master of the art of war. A general stampede of the imperial army followed the death of their commander.

Feats of valour performed by the Guru

Har Govind had to contend with innumerable difficulties in his time, but generally surmounted them by the aid of his faithful followers, who were always ready to rally around his banner on the approach of danger.

Towards the close of his life he withdrew to the hills, and resided with his friend, Bábá Buddhá, at Kartárpúr (near Anandapur) where he died in peace, in 1645, after having nominated his grandson, Har Rai, as Guru. He reigned as Guru thirty-one years and six months. His death was considered a national calamity, and the estimation in which he was held by the Sikhs, may be judged from the fact that a great many of them volunteered to burn themselves on his funeral pile. Two of his followers, one a Rájput and the other a *Jat*, jumped into the flames of the burning pyre and continued moving round the corpse, and finally fell and expired at the Guru's feet. Others were ready to follow the example set them, but were forbidden by Har Rai. The Guru's tomb was erected at Kartárpúr.

Death of Har Govind, 1645.

Self-sacrifices on his pyre.

Har Govind had three wives, by whom he had five sons. Gurditta by Mussamat Damodri, Tegh Bahadur by Mussamat Nánkí; and Surat Singh, Amrat, and Atal Ram by Mussamat Mardání. Gurditta, the eldest son, predeceased his father, leaving a son Har Rai, for whom Har Govind had great affection, and whom he appointed his successor. Mussamat Nánkí, the mother of Tegh Bahadur, was greatly dissatisfied with the decision of her husband; but the Guru is said to have pacified her by foretelling that her son would ultimately ascend the *gadi* of the Gurus. He entrusted his arms to Tegh Bahadur's mother, telling her to deliver them to Tegh on his attaining the age of discretion.

The Guru leaves five sons.

7.—GURU HAR RAI.

Har Rai, on succeeding to the apostleship, established himself at Kartárpúr on the banks of the Sutlej. He was a quiet and contented man, affable in his habits, and with no taste for war. The military spirit of the Sikhs, which had been so much fostered by the two preceding Gurus, continued to flourish in his time, for although the Guru took particular care not to meddle with politics, circumstances were not wanting under which the Sikhs were compelled to exert their power and energy to strengthen factious feuds. Thus, the Kahlúr Rájá was reduced to obedience, and Prince Dárá Shikoh, who always maintained a close alliance with the Gurus, was enabled, through the effectual assistance rendered by Har Rai, to keep up the struggle, with his brother, Aurangzeb, for the throne of India. Dárá was, however, defeated and put to death by the ambitious Aurangzeb. After this event Har Rai prudently withdrew from the scene and retreated to Kartárpúr. Aurangzeb, on ascending the throne of the Moghals, issued orders demanding the presence of Har Rai at the imperial court of Delhi, but the Guru submitted a mild petition to his majesty, representing that he was a faqír and would pray for the health, success and long life of the king, in his hut, but, as faqírs had no business at the royal palace, he hoped that his presence would

Har Rai succeeds.

The Guru allies himself with Dára Shikoh.

Aurangzeb resolves to punish him.

be excused. He made Rám Rai, his eldest son, the bearer of this letter to the Imperial Court.

But keeps Rám Rai the Guru's son as hostage at his Court.

Aurangzeb was quite satisfied on receiving this letter, and remarked: "There is no doubt of Har Rai's being a mere faqir," but he kept Rám Rai at his court, as a hostage, and treated him with distinction.

Death of Har Rai, 1660.

After a reign of thirty-three years and six months, Har Rai died in tranquillity at Kartárpúr, in 1661.

8.—GURU HARKISHAN.

Harkishan succeeds, 1661.

Har Rai had two sons, Rám Rai and Harkishan. The former, about fifteen years of age, was detained as a hostage in the imperial Court at Delhi. Being the offspring of a handmaid, and not of a wife of equal rank, and being, moreover, not liked by his father on account of his independence of character, he being in the habit of making his own disciples, his father invariably made it a rule to speak of Harkishan, his younger son, in public, as his apostolic successor, though at the time he was a minor about six years of age. The news reaching the youthful Rám Rai, at Delhi, he was greatly exasperated. A violent contest arose among the Sikhs regarding the succession, and the question was referred to the arbitration of the Moghal emperor, who issued a mandate to Harkishan to repair to Delhi without delay.

Is summoned to Delhi.

The infant apostle reached Delhi, attended by a numerous retinue, and put up in a serai. He was taken to his majesty's *zenáná* as an object of curiosity, and the emperor tested his intelligence and character by asking the boy to recognize the empress among a number of ladies, who were similarly arrayed. The boy pointed out the empress with his finger, and his majesty, pleased with his sagacity, declared his right to succeed to the office of Guru to be indisputable. The infant Guru was, however, attacked by small-pox, and died on 14th March, 1664, at Delhi, where a tomb was erected to him.

Dies, 1664.

When Harkishan was on his deathbed at Delhi, the disciples asked him who should be their spiritual leader after him. The Guru paused for some time, and then, bowing his head before five pice and a cocoanut which he placed on the ground, said: "Go; your Guru is in the village Bakála, near Govindwal, on the Biás." There Tegh Bahadur, with his mother, lived, as also several followers and relations of Guru Har Govind, who had been left there on the latter's way to the hills.

9.—GURU TEGH BAHADUR.

After the death of Harkishan, dissensions arose among the Sikhs as to the succession to the office of *Sat* Guru, or spiritual leader. Tegh Bahadur, son of Har Govind, after a long stay at Patna and many wanderings, had established himself at Bakálá, near Govindwal, where two factions arose, one supporting the claims of Tegh Bahadur, according to the will of the last Guru, and the other supporting the faction of the Sodhis, who had set up a Guru of their own.

Dispute regarding the succession.

Rám Rai, the nephew of Tegh Bahadur, remained at Delhi and aspired to the Guruship. Makhan Shah, an apostle of Har Govind, who was at this time living at Delhi, and exercised considerable influence over the Sikh community, supported the cause of Tegh Bahadur. He left Delhi for Bakála, where he was surrounded by all the Sikhs and the Sodhis. He carried his presents to Tegh Bahadur, who was unwilling to receive them, and said: "Give them to one who is a king." At length Tegh Bahadur was prevailed upon by his mother and Makhan Shah to ascend the *gadi* of the Gurus. The arms left with his mother were now delivered to him. The Guru said he was unworthy to wear his father's sword, and, on seeing the arms, he ordered them

Makhan Shah supports the cause of Tegh Bahadur,

Who succeeds as the ninth Guru of the Sikhs,

to be taken away, telling them that they were mistaken if they took him for "Tegh Bahadur," the "gladiator," and that the title which he aspired to was "Degh Bahadur," or "hero of the cooking pot," meaning that he was a cherisher of the poor and supporter of the hungry. This opportune remark was hailed with feelings of intense joy and satisfaction by the whole Sikh community, who thenceforward looked upon Tegh Bahadur as the defender of their faith and the supporter of their honor. Numerous followers flocked to his banner, and he became a greater Guru than his renowned father Har Govind.

And becomes a greater Guru than his predecessor.

Quarrels with the Sodhis.

Tegh Bahadur resolved upon the extirpation of the Sodhis, by whom he was looked upon as a usurper; but Makhan Shah persuaded him to put his sword in the sheath. He lived with splendour and kept in his employ one thousand armed horsemen. With the immense offerings of his disciples he commenced building a strong fort at Kartárpúr, where he established his ecclesiastical court. This afforded Rám Rai a good opportunity of injuring Tegh Bahadur, by representing to the emperor that his designs were detrimental to the State, and suggesting that immediate measures should be taken to check his ambition. Warrants were accordingly issued from the Court for the arrest of Tegh Bahadur, as a pretender to power and a disturber of the public peace. Tegh Bahadur was brought to the capital with his family and lodged in the house of the rájá of Jaypur. The rájá interceded in his behalf with the emperor, and assured his majesty that Tegh Bahadur was a peaceful faqír and aspired to no political power, that he preferred the life of a recluse, and had resolved upon visiting holy places on a pilgrimage. Tegh Bahadur accompanied the rájá to Bengal, and took up his residence at Patna, where he founded a college for the Sikhs. Here he lived with his wife and kindred for five or six years, and, by his wife Gujri, had a son, Govind Singh, who received his secular education from the pundits of Hindostán. He gave up his time chiefly to devotion and meditation, in places away from human habitations, and visited the sacred Hindu places in Bengal. Finally, he resolved to leave Patna and return home. He came to Anandapur, and bought a piece of ground from the Kahlúr Rájá, named Devi Mádho, for Rs. 500. On this land he built the town of Makhowál, which exists to this day on the banks of the Sutlej, close to Kartárpúr, the chosen residence of his father, and is a place of great sanctity among the Sikhs.

Is summoned to Delhi as a pretender to power.

Retires for a time to Bengal.

Birth of Govind.

The Guru returns to the Panjáb.

Builds Makhowál.

From a devout *Udási* (indifferent to the world) in Bengal, the Guru seems to have turned out a regular freebooter on his return to the Panjáb. He is said to have taken to a predatory career, and to have laid waste and plundered the whole country lying between Hansí and the Sutlej. He formed a league with a Mahomedan fanatic, named Adam Hafiz, and, while this zealot levied blackmail on the Mahomedans, the Sikh apostle did the same on rich Hindus. Predatory incursions were made into the agricultural districts, and to a large number of well-armed disciples were added rural clans, to whom promises of large payments and rich booties were made. To add to the criminal conduct, the confederates afforded a ready asylum to all the fugitives from the Moghal State who sought protection with them. The imperial troops were sent after them, and they were at last captured and brought before the emperor. The Musalman saint was banished, but the Emperor Aurangzeb, whose efforts were directed to converting the whole world to the Mahomedan faith, urged the Sikh Guru to embrace Mahomedanism. The Guru, before leaving for Delhi, is said to have sent for his son, Govind Singh, then fifteen years of age, and, girding upon him the sword of Guru Har Govind, hailed him as the future Guru of the Sikhs. He told Govind that he was going to die, but begged him not to leave his body at Delhi, to become a prey to dogs. He then enjoined upon Govind, as his

Insurrectionary proceedings of the Guru.

He is captured and taken to Delhi.

His address to his son Govind.

worthy son and successor, the necessity and the honour of avenging his death. Having then embraced and kissed the youthful Govind, he left for Delhi. The emperor had in those days thrown hundreds of Brahmans into jail, in the hope that, if they first embraced the religion of the prophet, the rest of the Hindus would readily follow their example. The emperor had many religious disputations with Tegh Bahadur, and asked him to show miracles, if he was a true Guru, or to embrace Islamism. The Sikh, being unable to satisfy his majesty one way or the other, was, by the king's order, thrown into prison, and, on his persistently refusing to become a convert, was subjected to bodily tortures. Tired of his life, he expressed his readiness to show a miracle in proof of the alleged divinity of his mission. He was arrayed before the emperor, all the Omerahs of the State being present to witness the miracle he was about to perform. The Guru said, before the assembly of the Omerahs, that the duty of man was to pray to the Lord, but since he had been commanded by his majesty to show a miracle, he had resolved upon complying with the king's orders. He wrote on a piece of paper, which he said was charmed, and then, having tied it round his neck, declared that the sword would fall harmless on it by the effect of the charm which was written upon it. The executioner was now summoned to test the miraculous charm. The blow was given and the head of the Guru rolled on the floor to the amazement of the court. The paper was then read and contained these words: "*Sir diá, Sar ná diá*"—meaning, that he had given his head, but not his secret. His life was extinct, but the memory of his priestly virtue remained in the world for ever. When the courtiers, tinged with superstition, saw what had occurred, they were struck with horror and surprise. The emperor himself was disgusted and displeased, and ordered the crowd to be dispersed. Such is the account given by a wonder-loving people, though it is more probable that the Guru was executed as a rebel against Government. The catastrophe occurred in 1675, in the thirty-fifth year of the reign of Alamgir. Tegh Bahadur reigned as a Guru for 13 years, 7 months and 21 days. The stern Aurangzeb had the body publicly exposed in the streets of Delhi. The head was burnt at Delhi by the Sikhs, who erected a tomb over the place where the cremation was performed which was called *Sir Gang* (head stack). Through the aid of Makhan Shah, who had been the first to hail the deceased as Guru, the body was brought to Anandapur by some *Mazhbi Sikhs*, or sweepers, and, the funeral rites having been performed over it by the youthful Govind, a great shrine was erected there in memory of the martyred Guru.

Is asked by the emperor to show a miracle.

Ingenious device.

The Guru is slain, 1675.

The *Sákhis* published by the Sikh authors represent Tegh Bahadur as by no means a harmless spiritual instructor. He was a valorous Guru, and although the Sikhs never attained under him any real degree of power as a nation, yet the example set by him contributed, in no small degree, to make his disciples a martial people. The sword of Har Govind was revered by all true disciples, and his arrows were made objects of public worship by all good believers. The Guru was at this time universally acknowledged among the Sikhs as "*Sachá Badsháh*," or veritable king, who guided the soul to salvation, while a temporal monarch guided merely man's worldly actions and controlled his finite faculties. Thus, the aspirations of the Sikh Guru were high, and, though suppressed by the stern Aurangzeb, were fully exhibited during the latter part of the Guru's life, as manifesting kingly, rather than priestly, aims, changing, eventually, inoffensive quietists into fanatical warriors.

The Guru is called "*Sachá Badsháh*," or true king.

10.—GURU GOVIND SINGH.

After the death of Tegh Bahadur, the martyred pontiff, his only son, Govind Singh, then but fifteen years of age, succeeded to the apostleship. The followers of Rám Rai declined into a mere sect of dissenters. Being surrounded on all sides by enemies, the new Guru retreated to the mountains which rise on either side of the Jamna, and occupied himself with the chase and archery. He was fond of hunting tigers and the wild boar, and he became a skilful archer. He made no attempt to study Sanskrit, but acquired a good knowledge of Persian and Hindi. His youth is described in the beautiful verses of *Vichittra Natak*, or "The Wonderous Tales." Govind lived in seclusion during his early manhood, and gave himself up to study and reflection. Having stored his mind well with historical, mythical and legendary lore, he, at the age of thirty-five, embarked on his great enterprise, that of abolishing the distinctions of caste among the Hindus; of admitting converts from all tribes; of arming the whole population; of making worldly wealth and eminence objects to which Hindus of every rank and denomination might aspire, and of making this equality a fundamental principle of his sect. Henceforward a new leaf opens in the history of the Sikhs. It is no longer the record of a sect who, following the peaceful tenets of their founder, desired merely to protect themselves, and had no wish to injure others, but that of a race which, actuated by a deep sense of the wrongs done by a persecuting Government, strove to make itself prominent in the world by those deeds of valour and patriotism which make nations great and glorious.

Govind succeeds, 1675.

His early education.

His high aims.

He resolves on reforming the sect of Nának.

The violent and miserable end of the martyred Guru, and his last injunctions, had made such a strong impression on the mind of Govind, that he longed to wreak vengeance on the murderers of his father and the persecutors of his race, and became the inveterate and irreconcilable enemy of every Mahomedan. He called upon his followers by all the ties and feelings which were dear to them; he urged them in defence of their injured honour and manhood; he conjured them in the name of their murdered Guru, promising them rewards both in this world and the next, to exchange their ploughs and rosaries for swords and daggers. He used all the eloquence of his persuasive genius in demonstrating to them that this was now the only means by which they could hope to regenerate their fallen race. Awakening his countrymen to a new and noble life, and arousing their latent energies to a sense of common duty, he blended the undaunted courage of the soldier with the enthusiasm of the devotee, and inspired the peaceful ploughman with ideas of military glory and national aggrandizement. Composed in mind and matured in experience, he resolved to reform religious corruptions and to put an end to social abuses and depredations. Being acknowledged as the *Sat* Guru of the Sikhs, his well-stored mind conceived, for the first time, the noble idea of transforming the degenerate Hindus into an aspiring race and of moulding the Sikh nation into a religious and military commonwealth, and, in the words of Mr. Elphinstone, "he executed his designs with the systematic spirit of a Grecian lawgiver."

His address to his followers.

Govind combines the qualities of a soldier and a devotee.

And attempts to institute a religious and military commonwealth.

Govind had matured his plans during his retirement in the hills, but, before embarking on his great enterprize, he resolved to secure for himself the aid of the goddess *Durga*, his special object of devotion and adoration. He accordingly sought advice from a Brahman of Benares, famous for his piety and learning, and had him brought to Makhowál, where he was treated with great honour. It was resolved to offer a *hom*, or burnt offering, to the goddess mother. The summit of a hill named *Nainá Devi*, six *koss* distant from Anandapur, was chosen as the site for the performance of

He asks the aid of the goddess *Durga*.

A great offering to the goddess.

the austere rite. A large bonfire was prepared and kept burning for months. Hundreds of maunds of *ghi*, raw sugar and molasses were consumed on this altar, which was not allowed to die down day or night, and when, in course of time, the preparation was pronounced complete, Govind was invited to undergo the horrible trial. It is stated that the terrible goddess appeared to the astonished gaze of her worshipper, and that the Guru was terror stricken at the awful sight; he, however, presented his sword to her as a token of homage. The deity left a mark on the handle and disappeared. The Pandit said it was a propitious omen, and declared that thenceforward the Guru's *panth*, or tribe, would predominate, conquer the country, and become the masters of the land. He added, however; that the rite had remained incomplete, owing to the fear of the Guru at the appearance of the goddess, and that the defect could be remedied only by his sacrificing one of his sons at the Devi's feet. Govind had four sons, Zujar Singh, Ajit Singh, Fatah Singh, and Zoráwar Singh. He sent for his mother Gujri, and asked her to spare one of his sons, that he might sacrifice him as an offering to the deity. Gujri flatly refused. The Guru was now thoroughly bewildered and knew not how to proceed with the burntoffering. Upon this the Pandit declared that the head of one of his followers might be offered as a substitute. Five* disciples sprang forward and offered to lay down their lives for the Guru's sake. One of them was immediately decapitated and his head thrown into the burning fire. The ceremony was now complete in every respect, and the Kanshi Pandit was laden with presents and dismissed. The deity, according to the legend, appeared in armed state and said: "Go; thy sect will prosper in the world."

Legend regarding her appearance.

The sacrifice of a disciple at the altar.

The deity blesses the Guru and his sect.

The inauguration of the *Páhal* ceremony.

It was, according to the Sikh accounts, on the occasion of the voluntary offerings of the five chosen disciples, previously mentioned, for self-sacrifice, that the initiation ceremony known as the *Páhal*, or Sikh making, was inaugurated by Guru Govind Singh. It was no invention of the Guru, but was a renovation of the old Sikh rite which had long ceased to be observed. They were taken into a room, and, having performed the ablutions, were seated one after the other. He then announced to them that, as they had proved themselves to be the true disciples of their Guru, he would bestow on them the *Páhal* of the true religion. He then poured water into a vessel, and mixing refined sugar with it, stirred it with the double-edged dagger or the sacrificial sword, rendered sacred by the touch of the goddess *Devi*. As he was performing the ceremony, his wife by chance passed with some confectionary of five different kinds in her hands. This was hailed as a propitious omen, as the accidental visit of a woman was considered to be a sign that the Sikh nation would live and multiply like the leaves of trees. The Guru then recited some verses and made the surviving four disciples, and another faithful disciple, drink some of the syrup. Part of it was poured on their heads and the rest sprinkled on their body. Then, patting them with his hand, he cried in a loud voice: "Repeat the *Khálsá* of the *Wáh Guru!* Victory to the holy *Wáh Guru*." The faithful disciples were then hailed as "Singhs," or lions, and declared to be the *Khálsá*, or purified and unalloyed. He then had himself inaugurated by the *Páhal* in the same way and exclaimed:—

The disciples are declared to be *Khálsá*, or pure.

> "*Khálsá Guru se aur Guru Khálsá se hoe:*
> *Ek dusre ká tábidár hoe*"—

meaning, that "the *Khálsá* arose from the Guru and the Guru from

* The names of these five have been carefully preserved, though the name of the poor victim whose head was offered to *Naina Devi* is not mentioned. They are Dharm Singh, Sukha Singh, Dia Singh, Himmat Singh, and Makhan Singh. All reports agree on this point, and there can hardly be any doubt that this horrible human sacrifice was offered.

the *Khálsá*. They are the mutual protectors of each other." All the rest of the Guru's disciples were similarly inaugurated, and declared Singhs, or champions of war. The Guru was further pleased to make the announcement that thenceforward, wherever five Sikhs should be assembled together, it should be considered as if the Guru Govind Singh was himself present. In a work written by himself, called "*Rahmat Námá*" or "Rule of Life of Govind," he assured his followers that those who wished to see the Guru would behold him in the "*Khálsá*." It was also declared at the same time that whoever wished to be the true follower of the Guru, must not be without five things, all commencing with the letter K., namely, *kangi* (comb), *kachh* (breeches reaching to the knee), *kard* (knife), *kes* (long hair of the head), and *kirpán* (sword); whoever was without these, would not be considered a true disciple.

And are hencefor-ward to be called Singhs, or loins of God.

Five essential requi-sites of a true Singh of the Guru.

The Guru now embarked on his great enterprize, that of entirely remodelling the Hindu religion and abolishing the distinctions of caste, by trying to bring all men, without distinction of race or descent, to the adoration of that Supreme Being before whom all men, he argued, were equal. He summoned into his presence all Sikhs, and passed stringent orders that every house inhabited by four adult males should contribute two men for service under him. In less than a fortnight 80,000 Sikhs flocked to Makhowál in obedience to the commands of the Guru, and, when all had assembled, the martial Guru, seating himself on a golden chair, delivered an eloquent address, which made a deep impression on the minds of his hearers. He commenced by praising God, whom he described as the Omnipotent, Almighty, invisible and merciful. God must be worshipped, said he, in truthfulness and sincerity, and no material resemblance must degrade him. The Lord could only be beheld by the eye of faith in the general body of the *Khálsá*. He then announced to them the great object of his mission, and declared that he had been sent as a messenger of the Lord, the inheritor of the spirit of Nának, transmitted to him as one lamp imparts its flame to another, to save and liberate the *Khálsá* and to unite all Sikhs in one common chain of brotherhood. "There must be no caste among you," said he, "and you must all be equal, no man greater than the other." The four tribes of the Hindus, the Brahman, the Chhatris, the Vaisya and the Sudra, must all become one, and like *pán* (betel leaf), *chuna* (lime), *supárí* (betel nut), and *kath* (terra japonica, or catechu), the constituents of a masticatory given customarily to visitors, become all of one colour. All must eat at the same table and drink from the same cup; caste must be forgotten; the idols destroyed; the Brahman's thread broken; the graves of the so-called saints abandoned; and the *Quráns* torn to pieces. The only way to salvation was initiation by him into the *Páhal* of the *Sat* Guru, a true belief in the holiness and purity of the *Khálsá*, and the ascription of praise and glory to the Creator. Their words must be in accordance with the deeds,* which are *Karatnass*, *Kulnass*, *Dharmnass*, *Karmnass*, *Ritnass* and *Hatnass*, the total abandonment and forsaking of hereditary occupation, family ties and affection, religious belief, or a belief in the transmigration of soul, ceremonies and social ties, and the adoption, in their stead, of the true religion of the *Sat* Guru.

The great gathering at Makhowál.

The Guru's address.

A new dispensation vouchsafed.

Distinction of caste abolished.

The mode of salvation.

From this time Govind tied up his hair in a knot (or *kes*), thus himself setting an example of his commandments in regard to the keeping of the five articles commencing with the letter *kukka*, or the Persian *káf*, and changed his name to Singh. He similarly changed the name of his followers from Sikh to Singh, or lion, an honourable title exclusively assumed by the Ráj-

The general Sikhs feel themselves elevated in rank.

* Articles of their belief.

puts, the first military class of the Hindus. Thus, the Sikhs felt themselves at once elevated to rank with the highest, and their leader opened to them the dazzling prospect of earthly glory, rousing their military valour and inciting them to deeds of courage. The equality thus given to all Sikhs dissatisfied some of the Brahmans and *Chhatris*, who deserted the Guru; but his chief strength consisted in the lower orders of the Hindus who flocked to his banner and received the *Páhal* initiation. All were allowed to bathe in the sacred pool, and to assemble in the holy temple of Amritsar to offer prayers and hear the *Granth* of the great Nának.

They form the main strength of their leader.

The injunctions of the Guru.

The disciples of Govind, to whom he gave the name of the "*Khálsá*," were required to dedicate themselves from birth, or initiation, to arms, always to keep steel with them in some shape, to allow their hair * to grow, to wear a blue dress, † to refrain from wearing red clothes or eating or smoking tobacco. All prohibitions relating to food and liquors were abolished. They were enjoined to salute each other with the phrase "*Wáh Guru ji ká Khálsá; sri Wáh Guru ji ki Fateh;*" which means "The *Khálsá* is of the Lord! Victory attend the Lord!" Some of these rules, such as the propriety of wearing a blue dress, seem to have originated in a desire to give the Sikhs a distinct national character, and, a spirit of opposition to Hinduism, as the Hindus generally have an aversion to blue. A Brahmanical devotee keeps his head carefully shaved, and this may account for the Sikh prohibition of clipping or removing the hair from any part of the body. The object of the other institutions, such as the principle of devotion to steel, and the exclamation of "*Wáh Guru,*" is obvious, for the steel made them vowed soldiers, while the repetition of the phrase, "*Wáh Guru,*" revived every moment religious fervour in their mind, and constantly awaked them to a sense of their duty and obligations to the community of which they had become members.

The mode of salutation.

The object of unshorn locks and other institutions.

The exclamation, *Wáh Guru!*

The Guru becomes an object of adoration.

Guru Govind had by this time become an object of adoration. His followers worshipped him like a deity; but his plans of military aggrandizement had yet to be matured. He organized his followers into troops and bands, and established forts along the skirts of the hills between the Sutlej and the Jamna, besides military posts and strongholds on the plains lower down the Sutlej, to protect himself against the attacks of his hill neighbours. He got into difficulties with the hill rájás of Náhan, Indore and Nálágarh; but his vast military resources enabled him to rout them all. The Guru himself describes the several actions in which he was engaged, and the personal bravery and military skill displayed by him show that he combined the qualities of a religious teacher and military commander. In the action with the rájá of Nálágarh he routed the Pathan auxiliaries and killed Hari Chand, the rájá, with his own hand. Govind now strengthened his position at Anandapur and allied himself with Bhím Chand, the rájá of Kahlúr who had refused to pay the usual tribute to the imperial authorities at Kangrá, and successfully resisted them by arms. The example set by the Kahlúr Rájá was followed by other hill chiefs, who, countenanced by the Guru, also refused to pay tribute to the imperial treasury. An attack was made on the position of the Guru by the Mahomedan forces, but was completely repulsed. Govind now subdued the country around him, and extended his conquests as far as Rúpar, on the left bank of the Sutlej.

His plans of military aggrandizement.

He quarrels with the hill rájás,

And defies the imperial authorities at Kangrá.

* The Guru venerated Durga Bhawani, the goddess of courage, by whom he was directed to unloose his hair and draw his sword. The Guru, in consequence, vowed he would preserve his hair, as consecrated to that divinity, and directed his followers to do the same.

† The Akális, or never dying (a most remarkable class of the devotees of the Sikh sect), still wear blue chequered dress.

Aurangzeb sends an army against him, 1701.

This caused some anxiety to the Mahomedan Government, and the hill rájás, who had suffered at the hands of the Guru, and who were alarmed lest he should expel them from their dominions, and seize upon their territories, petitioned the emperor to extirpate the power of one who called himself the "True King" (*Sachá Badsháh*). Aurangzeb directed Zabardast Khan, the Governor of Láhore, and Shams-ud-dín Khan, the Governor of Sirhind, to march against the Guru. The Guru made a desperate resistance, but was at last defeated and besieged in the fort of Makhowál. His mother, Gujri, and his two sons, Zoráwar Singh and Fatah Singh, effected their escape to Sirhind, where they concealed themselves in the house of a Hindu disciple.

The Guru is reduced to straits.

Kuljas, the dewán of Wazír Khan, the governor of the province, produced them before the governor, who, being an orthodox Mahomedan, spared their lives, in accordance with the Mahomedan law, which forbids the slaughter of unbelievers who are minors or belong to the female sex. The dewán bore some personal grudge to Govind Singh, and repeatedly entreated Wazír Khan to kill the widow and the two sons of the object of his envy, reminding him that they were the offspring of one who was the inveterate foe of all Mahomedans, and were sure to follow the footsteps of their father. Wazír Khan told him that he would on no account violate the rules of his religion, which prescribed that a son must not suffer for the wrongs done by his father, and that every one was responsible for his own actions. One day, as the two sons of the Guru were sitting in the governor's darbár, he was much pleased with their graceful appearance and seemingly good looks, and said to them with kindness: "Boys! what would you do if we were to give you your liberty?" The boys answered: "We would collect our Sikhs, supply them with implements of war, fight with you and put you to death." The governor said: "If you were defeated in the fight, what would you do then?" The boys replied: "We would collect our armies again and either kill you or be killed." The governor was enraged at this intrepid and haughty reply,

His two minor sons are put to death.

and ordered Kuljas to remove the boys from his presence and to despatch them at his home. The boys were accordingly put to death by Kuljas. Some say he put the children under the foundation of a wall and closed the place up, and thus buried them alive.

His mother dies of grief.

Gujri died of grief at the sad end of her grandchildren.

When all the provisions in the fort of Makhowál were exhausted, Govind, with forty of his faithful adherents (the rest all deserted him or were killed in the action), effected his escape to the fort of Chamkáur below Rúpar.

The Guru flies to Chamkaur.

He was hotly pursued by the imperialists, who surrounded the little place.

His two surviving sons, with their mother, are slain.

His two surviving sons, Jojhar Singh and Jit Singh, with their mother, Sundrí, were slain before his eyes. The Guru himself behaved with great bravery, killing with his own hand Náhar Khan, the commander of the imperial troops, and wounding the other, Khwája Mahomed. It was, however, a combat of a handful of men against overwhelming numbers. The devoted little band fought to the last, but the Guru, taking advantage of a dark night, and accompanied by five of his disciples, threaded his way to the outskirts of the camp in disguise.

His escape from Chamkáur.

The intrepidity of one of his sons.

An interesting anecdote is told here of the undaunted courage of Jit Singh, the son of the Guru. Khwája Mahomed and Náhar Khan, the commanders of the imperial troops, sent a messenger to the Guru, reminding him that he had not the paltry and undisciplined troops of petty hill chiefs to contend with, but was pitted against the invincible armies of the great Moghal, "The King of Kings, the asylum of the poor, the protector of the world, Alamgír Aurangzeb;" that it was madness for him to attempt impossibilities; that it would be well for him to cease hostilities, make his immediate submission, renounce his infidelity and embrace the Islamic faith. The youthful Jit Singh, drawing his scimitar, exclaimed to the bearer of this message: "Utter another word and I will smite your head from your body and cut you to pieces, for daring so to address our chief!" The blood of the envoy boiled with rage, and he returned to the imperial camp with this defiance. When the news of the death of his two sons reached Govind, he received it with the utmost resignation and fortitude. His followers, dressed in mourning costume, came in great numbers to condole with him. Many of them began to weep, for which he gently reproved them, reminding them that these bereavements were the will of God. He drew two paralle lines on the ground with his finger, then rubbed them off with his hand and said to them: "Brother Sikhs! there was no joy when these lines came into existence, and there could be no grief when they were effaced. As these lines were transient, so are the affairs of this sorrowful world transitory. God makes a thing, and unmakes a thing; who are we to grumble since the rein is in His hand? Rely, then, firmly on His will, for He is the Almighty. What are we poor mortals before him?" These words had the effect of magic upon the minds of the Guru's disciples, who, seeing the Guru so firm in temper, laid aside all their grief, and commenced the task before them of fighting with the enemies of their faith with redoubled zeal.

Govind confronts his adversity with resolution.

Govind, with his five adherents, had travelled some miles, when he was met by two Pathans, Náme Khan and Ghaní Khan, who recognizing the Guru resolved to take him to the governor Wazír Khan. The Guru entreated and promised them a munificent reward if they saved his life. They had in former times received kindness at the hands of the Guru, and they now conducted him safe to Bahlolpur in the Ludhiáná District, where the Guru sought protection with his Persian tutor, Pír Muhammad, a quazi. After meeting various reverses and experiencing great calamities, he reached the wastes of Bhatinda, where his disciples again rallied round him. After a short stay in the village of Ráipur and Kahlúr to recruit his health and strength, the Guru journeyed to Muktesar in the Ferozepur District, where all the Sikhs who had deserted him again assembled. Govind was enabled here to collect twelve thousand fighting men, including horsemen and foot soldiers. The news reaching the governor of Sirhind, he sent a body of seven thousand imperial troops to disperse the Guru's forces, and a battle was fought between the imperialists and the Sikhs at Muktesar, in which the latter were victorious. The Guru harangued his soldiers, complimenting them on their bravery in the field and encouraging them to renewed exertions and fidelity. Great numbers fell on both sides in this action. The tank called Muktesar, in the Ferozepur District, was constructed by the Guru on the field of battle, and is held in great reverence by the Sikhs, who believe that whoever bathes in it, obtains salvation. Hence the name "Muktesar," given to it by the Guru, meaning "the tank of emancipation." A great fair is held at Muktesar on the first of Mágh, every year, to commemorate the events which took place there, and the Sikhs from all parts of the Panjáb assemble there.

The Guru in his flight to the Ludhiáná district.

The Sikhs rally around him at Muktesar.

He is pursued by the imperial troops,

Whom he defeats in an action fought at Muktesar.

He constructs the tank Muktesar.

The Guru then went to Malwá and lived there in peace for some time, occupying himself chiefly in making proselytes to his religion, not a difficult task, considering that the people about that part of the country were in a state of lamentable ignorance. He built here a spacious house for his residence, which he called the *Damdamá*. A great fair is annually held here. After the building was completed, the Guru declared that henceforth whoever visited the place, however ignorant he might be, would, by virtue of the

He rests at *Damdamá* near Bhatinda,

pilgrimage, become eminent for his learning, that all his undertakings in this world would be crowned with success, and that blessings would be abundantly showered upon him in the world to come. Many of the credulous Sikhs, in the hope of becoming admirable crichtons, make annual excursions to the place, and such is the force of imagination, that these simpletons are looked upon by their fellow ignoramuses as scholars and philosophers, and their opinions are solicited on all occasions, and their decisions accepted with the greatest deference. The place is inhabited by sádhs and faqírs, who, after travelling about the country, settle there, and it is not to be wondered at if a man attains some wisdom by a visit to Damdamá, after journeying from his own country, and mixing in the society of the aged sádhs of that place. Gurmukhí in its best style is written there.

And gives the place his blessings.

Proceeds to Sirhind.

The Guru then came to Sirhind, the place where his two youngest sons had been brutally killed under the orders of the Mahomedan governor. The Sikhs cherished a hatred of the most bitter kind for this town, and with joined hands submitted to the Guru, "O true king! give us your orders to burn this town to ashes, for we cannot bear the sight of it. It was here that your two beloved sons were assassinated!" The Guru observed that the city itself had done no harm, and that the death of his sons would not be avenged if it were destroyed. The Sikhs, who were greatly exasperated, made repeated representations, but the Guru declined to accede to their request, and prudently so, for he knew very well that a rash attempt like that suggested to him, would entail on him the wrath of the emperor and entangle him in fresh difficulties. He, however, compromised the matter with his agitated followers by saying to them in a loud voice: "Whoever is my Sikh, let him do one thing when he happens to pass by this way to the Ganges. He must pull down two bricks from the city and throw them into the river Sutlej in detestation of the crime committed here on innocent children. My Sikhs will not call it by the name of Sirhind, but by that of *Guru Már*, or the place where Gurus were killed." The ceremony is still observed, and the pilgrims to the Ganges, when they pass through Sirhind, either going or returning, take out two bricks and throw them into the river. The mention of the name of Sirhind in the morning is considered as unpropitious. The Sikhs built there a great shrine, which is still visited by crowds of pilgrims.

Detestation of the Sikhs for this place.

The Guru is summoned by Aurangzeb to the Dekkan.

Towards the close of the reign of Aurangzeb, the Guru lived in peace at Anandapur. But the king, who was then in the Dekkan, always felt anxious about him. He, therefore, issued a mandate summoning the Guru to his preence. When the messenger reached Govind and delivered the royal firman to him, he kissed it and placed it on his head in token of respect. He treated the messenger with the greatest honour, and told him that he regarded himself as a dependent and vassal of the "king of kings," and that to obey his majesty's command would be an honour to him, but that, before accompanying the messenger, he would like to submit his grievances to the emperor in writing. He, therefore, composed a poem in the Persian language, comprising fourteen hundred stanzas, in which he gave a vivid picture of the reverses of his own fortune and the calamities to which he had been subjected at the hands of the Imperial Government. He said he had been rendered childless, motherless and homeless; he had lost all his family, and his dearest friends had been torn from him; the day of reckoning would at last come, when the oppressor would have to account before the Creator for the wrongs done by him to the helpless and oppressed; that for himself he despised death and was weary of his life; that he feared no one, and was willing to die, but that, if he died, his death would be revenged.

He replies to the emperor in a denunciatory poem, composed by himself, in Persian.

The letter, having been sealed, was delivered to the messenger, who was dismissed laden with rich presents. Along with this letter was sent the Guru's agent, Bhái Diyá Singh. The emperor was pleased with the contents of the letter, and the appearance and dress of the Bhái who had accompanied it. He bestowed dresses of honour on the agent, and dismissed him with a letter and valuable presents for the Guru. In this letter the Guru was again desired to repair to the emperor's presence, in which case he would be received kindly. The Guru * accordingly set out to visit Aurangzeb, but, on his way, he heard of the aged monarch's death, 1707.

The emperor is appeased, but nevertheless asks the Guru to repair to his Court.

The Guru departs for the Dekkan.

The death of the emperor, 1707.

When Govind reached the Dekkan, he saw Bahádur Shah seated on the throne of his ancestor. The new emperor received the Sikh Guru with distinction, and bestowed on him presents, consisting of valuable tents, elephants and horses, and appointed him to the command of five thousand men in the army, thus utilizing the services of an insurrectionary leader to the benefit of the State.

The Guru enters the imperial service.

It was during his stay in the Dekkan that Govind took into his employ a Pathan to whom he showed great consideration, purchasing through him a number of fine horses. The Guru was dilatory in payment of the price. The Pathan became impatient and used intemperate language towards the Guru, who, being provoked, drew his sword and severed his head from his body. The Guru repented the loss of his servant and friend, and, sending for his sons and widow, bestowed on them money and presents. But the Pathan lads entertained revengeful feelings against the murderer of their father, and watched for a favourable opportunity to avenge his death. One day they succeeded in stealing upon the Guru's retirement and plunged a dagger into his stomach. Thinking he was dead, the lads ran away. But the Guru was not dead. The dagger had not penetrated sufficiently into his abdomen, though a portion of his entrails escaped through the small wound he had received. The Guru, seeing the wound, cried out: "O brother Sikhs, I am dead!" All the Sikhs assembled. People ran in all directions and the ruffians were seized and brought into the presence of Govind. The Guru, however, told his disciples not to molest the young Pathans, as they had done well in avenging the death of their father, and he ordered that they should be released uninjured.

Is stabbed by assassins.

The wound was sewed up, and to all appearance was healing, but it seems that the Guru, distracted in mind and overwhelmed with grief at the sorrowful end of his children and friends, was bent on dying. One day a strong bow was brought to him for his inspection. He bent it with all his force, and the effect of it was that the stitches of his wounds, which had not yet quite healed, gave way. The bowels again protruded and blood began to flow profusely. The wounds were again sewed up by the surgeon,

Becomes tired of life.

---

* Dr. Trumpp believes that Govind never obeyed the summons of the Emperor Aurangzeb to attend the imperial camp, but he has given neither authority nor reasons for this belief. The whole purport of the *zaffarnámá* composed by Govind, in which he exposes the wrongs of the Moghal Government, tends to show that he proceeded on his journey to visit the emperor. Dr. Trumpp has relied apparently on Sikh accounts only. But it must be remembered that the Sikh authors are always cautious in concealing the weak points of their religious leaders and in giving prominence to anything which redounds to their glory. Thus, they freely acknowledge that Govind rendered material aid to Bahádur Shah in the war which that emperor waged against his rebel brother Kám Baksh, and even own that the Guru took the field of action. But they carefully ignore the fact of the Guru's accepting employment under the emperor. The fact of his taking employment under the Moghal Government is fully confirmed by various writers. *Vide* Sir J. Malcolm's sketches of the Sikhs; Forester's Travels, page 263. The latter author states that Guru Govind had a small command in the Moghal service, which is confirmed by Khapí Khan. Similarly, the Sikh authors throw the whole blame of the murder of the Guru's two youngest sons on Wazír Khan, the Mahomedan Governor of Sirhind. But they deliberately ignore the fact that the instigator of the crime was a Hindu, Kuljas, the Governor's dewán who bore a personal grudge against Govind. The Mahomedan writers may, on points of difference, be safely consulted, as it is very unsafe to rely implicitly on all that the Sikh historians have said.

who had been sent for from Delhi, but the Guru was restless. He mounted a palanquin, and in the same state travelled to the south for change of air and refreshment. When he reached the town of Náder, he became much exhausted and asked his followers to stop there. He then told them that the hour of his death was approaching, and that, as medicine was of no avail, they should distribute alms to the poor and perform a *jag*.* In obedience to the Guru's command, thousands of Brahmans were feasted, and money was distributed to them as alms. The Guru then ordered preparations to be made for his cremation. His Sikhs wept in sorrow at seeing that the dissolution of their spiritual leader and master was near at hand, and in the intensity of their grief, with joined hands, they said to him: "O true Guru! Who will inspire us with truth and lead us to victory and salvation when thou art no more?" The Guru answered that the appointed ten had done their mission, and that he would now entrust his beloved *Khálsá* to the care of God, the never-dying. "I entrust," said the dying apostolic hero, "my *Khálsá* to the bosom of the everlasting divine being. Whoever wishes to behold the Guru, let him offer *karáh parshád* worth Re. 1-4 or less, and bow before the *Granth* and open it, and he shall have an interview with the Guru. Whatever you will ask shall be given you. The *Granth* shall support you under all your troubles and adversities in this world, and be a sure guide to you hereafter. The Guru shall dwell with the society of disciples, the *Khálsá*, and wherever there shall be five Sikhs gathered together, there shall the Guru be also present." The Guru also gave them sundry warnings, telling them that there were impostors in the world who would try to dissuade them from the right path, but that his disciples should be on their guard against them and give no ear to what they say. They must have firm belief in one God and look on the *Granth* as His inspired law. Feeling faint and exhausted, he said to his disciples, "Bathe me and put new clothes on me. Arm me with my weapons, and when I breathe my last, do not take away either my clothes or my arms, but burn them with me." The Guru then himself mounted the funeral pyre, and looking towards the heavens and with great love, he uttered the following Saviyá† :—

The sorrow of his disciples on his approaching end.

The Guru commits the *Khálsá* to the care of God.

His last moments.

پائي گہے تمري جب تے تب تے کچھہ آنکھہ تيري نہين آئيون
رام رحيم پران قران اينک کہين تب ايك نه مانيون
سمرتہه شاستر و بيد سوئي به بهيد کہي هم ايك نه مانيون
سري اسپان کرپا تمري کرسي نه کہيو سب توهي پچھانيون

"Since I touched thy feet, I have fixed my eyes on thee. *O Rám*, *O Rahím* (merciful), the Purans and *Quráns* teach various systems, but I have minded them not. The Smriti,‡ the Shastras and Vedas, all teach various ways, I did not recognize any of them.
O holy God! thy mercy is such that though I have not perceived Thee by the touch of hand, yet I have fully recognized Thee."

He then closed his eyes and began to pray, and expired in the performance of his devotions.

His death, 1708.

Such was the end of the great Sikh reformer, Govind Singh, the tenth and the last Guru of the Sikhs. He died in Sambat 1765, corresponding to 1708, A.D. at Náder, on the banks of the Godavári, in the forty-eighth year of his life, having reigned as Guru 30 years and 11 months. The Sikhs assembled

* A kind of feast given to the Brahmans and the poor.
† The translation of this Saviyá given by Dr. Trumpp in his *Adi Granth* is misleading.
‡ There are 18 *Smritis*, 4 *Vedas*, and 6 *Shastras*, namely, Níái, Bisheshkh (philosophy) Sankh (science of nature), Patanjil (miracle), Mimansa (acts), and Bedánt (or knowledge of God).

from all quarters, and there was a loud cry of "*Jai, Jai Kar*" (victory) which vibrated through the air. Flowers were showered on the pyre. Hymns were sung. The *rabábis* played on the *rebeck* and the *sádhis* performed their *bhajans*. This national calamity was mourned by all his followers, and some are even reported to have expired in consequence of their grief. The tombs of the martyrs were erected and beautiful Dharmsálás built. Among these was constructed the Guru's tomb, which to this day is a great place of worship. The tomb is half a mile from the city of Náder. The Sikhs call it Abchal or Abkálnagar, 'the immoveable city.' A large number of swords, shields, spears, &c., were placed there, and the Sikhs worship these weapons as having belonged to their great Guru. A great number of *pujáris* or devotees are attached to this shrine. Whenever these devotees stand in need of money, they issue letters to the Sikhs abroad. The letter is called Hukamnámá, and every Sikh pays something according to his means and circumstances. It bears on it Govind's own seal in possession of the *pujáris*, which contains the following inscription in the Gurmukhí characters :—

It is considered a national calamity.

His tomb at Náder.

The Hukamnámá of Abkálnagar.

The seal of Guru Govind.

"There is only one God. By the favour of that glorious God, Govind Singh received from Nának the Guru (spiritual guide), hospitality, sword (valour), victory and success undoubted. May the exalted Immortal Being stretch a helping hand !"

Whenever a dispute arises among the true believers, it is settled according to the instructions contained in the Hukamnámá, of Abkálnagar, which is eagerly applied for and obtained by the faithful.

The character of Guru Govind.

Historians agree in eulogizing the great merits of Guru Govind Singh. In him were united the qualities of a religious leader and a warrior. He was a lawgiver in the pulpit, a champion in the field, a king on his *masnad*, and a faqír in the society of the *Khálsá*. He was the right man for the needs of the time. Sikhism in the beginning, namely, in Nának's time, would soon have been extinguished, had its founder adopted the same plan as that recommended by Govind, *viz.*, the free exercise of the sword in defence of religion. The *Adi Granth* of Nának was confined to instilling into the minds of the Sikhs a spirit of meekness and humility. But a crisis was now at hand. Govind perceived that the times had changed, and was consequently determined to keep pace with them. He saw that the passive conservatism of his ecclesiastical predecessors was not suited to the time and did not tend to the diffusion of the religion. He therefore instituted a new code of law which not only treated of religious subjects, but infused a spirit of valour and emulation into the minds of his followers and inflamed them with zeal for deeds of heroism and bravery in the field. He incorporated in it a narrative of his own exploits in a glowing and even hyperbolical style. He placed the

The reforms of Govind as compared with the teachings of Nának.

His new code of law.

four great sects of the Hindus on the same level, and declared that none was greater than the other, thus adding materially to the strength of his nation. He laid the foundation stone of that vast fabric which the Sikh nation was, not long after, enabled to build on the ruins of the Mahomedan power in the Panjáb and emancipated his tribe from foreign thraldom and persecution, giving it the character and rank of a military nation. He instituted the "*Guru Mátá*" or "State council" which met at Amritsar. To this State council, the Sikhs of all denominations were admitted, and an opportunity was given them of expressing their opinions on political matters as a federative republic. His aims were high and the task which he had undertaken was great. Though he died broken-hearted, tired of life, far from the scenes of his exploits, yet the credit is due to him of having founded a political community of no mean order, for he taught a vanquished people how to obtain political ascendancy and national freedom. His persevering endurance in the midst of calamities and disasters was equal to his bravery and valour in the field, and, although he did not live to see his great ends accomplished, yet it is acknowledged on all hands that the conversion of a band of undisciplined *Jats* (given to rapine and plunder or to agricultural pursuits) into a body of conquerors and a political corporation, was due entirely to the genius of Govind, whose history is closely interwoven with that of the Sikhs as a nation.

He institutes the "*Guru Mátá*" at Amritsar.

His death untimely, but labours not in vain.

The modifications introduced by Govind into the institutions of Nának, are fully described in the *Ráhatnámá*, or book of guidance, composed by him. The principles inculcated by the Guru, by which the Sikhs were forbidden to follow the doctrines of the Vedas, Shástras, Purans and *Qurán*, were the following:—They were not to follow the advice of Moulavis and Pandits, nor were they to perform shrádhs or the ceremonies of the anniversaries of the dead (except in the manner prescribed in the *Granth*); they were not to wear the Brahminical thread; the rosary; the bodi, or top knot; they were not to worship tombs or places of cremation; they were to feed none but their own people; they were not to go about bareheaded; they were not to use tobacco; nor were they to cut the hair of any part of their body; they were not to covet other peoples' wives or property; they were not to repeat the Vedas on occasions of joy or sorrow; nor were they to keep the company of the Dhirmalis, or the descendants of Dhirmal, or of the Rámrais, or the follower of Rám Rai, or of the Minás, an aboriginal tribe of cut-throat robbers scattered over the tract of land between the Sutlej and the Jamna, now not much dreaded; or of the Masands, or those who cheat and rob in the name of the Gurus: or of the Sargams, or those who are Nástaks, Saráogís and Jáins. They were to implicitly obey the Guru and to closely study the japji. Those who in any way violated the law prohibiting intercourse with the Dhirmalias, Rámrais, Minás, Masands, and Sargams, rendered themselves liable to a fine of Rs. 2-4, with which *karáh parshád* (a kind of sweetmeat) was purchased and distributed among their co-religionists. The *Granth* was to be repeated on occasions of marriage and death. The bones of the dead, if not carried to the Ganges, were to be thrown into the environs of Amritsar, which are as holy as the Ganges.

The principles inculcated by him.

It was the intention of Govind to modify the code of Nának as laid down in the *Adi Granth*, and with that object he sent his men to the Sodhis of Kartárpúr to bring to him the *Adi Granth* signed by Guru Arjan, which was at that time in their custody, but as the Sodhis were averse to the religious belief of Govind, and did not acknowledge him as their Guru, they declined to lend the book to Govind, making the touching remark that, if the Guru, who styled himself the "true king," had the genius of a lawgiver, he would do well to make a *Granth* of his own. This incensed the Guru, and he resolved upon making his own code. He occupied himself in composing the new *Granth* in his retreat at Damdamá, and finished it there on Sunday the 8th Bhadon, Samvat 1753-1696 A.D. It was named by him the "*Daswan Badshah ka Granth*" or "The Book of the Tenth King." It is composed in old Hindi Bhasha idiom, and in a difficult style, and treats of the knowledge of God, and the way to salvation. It raised the dormant energies of the Sikhs, who, at that time were a vanquished race, and urged upon them the necessity of leading an active and useful life. The author infuses into it his own fervour and spirit, kindling the mind of the reader with lofty ideas of social freedom, and inflaming them to deeds of valour. It describes the cunning and the wiles of women, and admonishes the reader to be on his guard against their tricks. Govind possessed a poetical mind, and his description of the heroic deeds of warlike men, lays before the reader a vivid and sprightly picture of the fields of battle in ages gone by, and animates him with ideas of military glory, and national honour and ascendancy.

His book the "*Daswan Badshah ka Granth.*"

His genius as an author and poet.

It is said that, after initiating his followers into the *Páhal*, the Guru resolved to prosecute a religious war, and threw some of the most valuable articles with him into the river Sutlej to excite them to action. It seems to be an odd way of inducing people to manly pursuits, yet, taking into consideration the fact that Govind had to deal with an unenlightened people, the story told by McGregor may be believed, that the Guru once threw a bracelet worth Rs. 25,000, brought to him by a Sikh from Sindh, into the river, and, when asked by the diver, who was promised Rs. 500 for its recovery, to point out the place where he had thrown it, he took off the other bracelet and threw it into the river, adding: "That is the place." All the by-standers, so the story goes, were struck with astonishment at the Guru's contempt for wealth, and search for the ornaments, costing Rs. 50,000, was given up. The same author mentions that, on another occasion, a Sikh arrived from the Dekkan, bringing with him valuable presents, namely, a sword, an elephant, a white hawk, a rich tent with gilded poles and an Arab horse. The Guru ordered the tent to be pitched, the elephant to be decorated with a costly howdah, and the horse to be saddled and bridled. The hill rájás, who happened to be present, became jealous of this display of wealth, and coveted them. Bhím Chand, of Phillour wishing for the tent and the elephant, and Hari Chand of Hindor for the horse, sword and hawk.

His contempt for wealth.

He is strict in maintaining his dignity and state.

Anecdote.

The wish of the rájás was communicated to the Guru, who answered:—"My disciple has brought these things for me, and I am willing to part with them, provided you agree to my terms, which are, that I first sit in the howdah with the hawk in my hand, the sword girded on my side, and the horse led before me. I shall afterwards sit in the tent, and you will then be welcome to all." The reply was evasive, and the rájás took it as an insult. The seeds of enmity were sown; the fanatic Sikhs abused the rájás for their having dared to ask for the articles for which their Guru had so much liking, and were ready to take action; but Govind advised them to desist, reminding them of his prophecy, while mixing refined sugar with water at the ceremony of initiation (*Páhal*), that 'the Singhs would be a sweet-tongued nation.' It was with much difficulty that a rupture was avoided and peace restored. Subsequent events (already narrated), however, show that the peace was not of long duration, and that several actions were fought between the hill rájás and the Guru in which the latter was successful. The Guru used to wear an aigrette, or plume, on his head, and, when on horse-back, carried a hawk on his left hand. He was always armed with a bow and arrow, a sword and a shield. One day, as he went to visit the Emperor Bahádur Shah in the fort of Agra, accompanied by five of his Sikhs, who were, like himself, dressed and armed, he was prevented by the royal guard at the gate from entering the fort, and told that if he wished to go in, he must lay down his arms. The Guru refused to lay his arms aside. The matter having been reported to the emperor, his majesty, who was noted for his affability and amiable disposition, gave orders for the Sikh Guru's admisson into the fort, and into his presence, with arms, whenever he thought proper to visit him. The emperor always talked to him on the subject of hunting, of which the Guru was particularly fond. The Darbáris held free discourse with the Guru on religious subjects, and the emperor always took pleasure in these conversations.

His attire.

His visits to the king, and his darbár.

The masands, or hereditary deputies of the Guru, had become most obnoxious to the people. They persecuted the people in collecting taxes and put them to great straits. The intolerant practice of this class of tax-gatherers was brought to the notice of the Guru, in the form of a play; and the Guru, thoroughly understanding the object of the players, dissolved this institution by excommunicating them. Others who were found guilty of cruel treatment were thrown into dungeons, or into boiling oil. The mimics who had performed this play with great courage and skill, were handsomely rewarded by both the Guru, and the people who had been delivered from oppression.

He suppresses the system of tax collection by a class of people known as masands.

The Guru was one day preaching at Chamkaur to a body of his disciples, when a Sikh presented his youthful son to him saying: "This lad always remains dull and gloomy and refuses to marry. Would the Guru be pleased to give him some good advice?" The Guru asked the lad what he wanted, and why he was keeping aloof from worldly men. The lad repeated the following verses of Nának, and told the Guru that it was this which had induced him to abstain from worldly affairs:—

The Guru in his preachings.

ایهه کولنب جو تو دیکهداهي چلے نه تیري نال
نال تیري چلن ناهین تس نال کیون چت لائے
ایسے کم بهولي نه‌کرئي جت انت پچهوتائي
گرودا اپدیش سن توهوي تیري نال
کهه نانک سن پیاري توهدا ہے سمجهائے

"The friends whom you see in this world will not accompany you (in the world to come). Those who cannot go with you, why attach your heart to them?

"An act which ultimately results in disappointment should not be done even by mistake.

"Hear the admonition of Nának who always tells the truth, and act upon it that you may become virtuous."

The Guru, who was a good Persian scholar, upon this, read the following verse of Saádí of Shiráz:—

در عمل کوش هرچه خواهي پوش
تاج بر سر نه ِ وعَلَم بر دوش

"Try to do good deeds and then wear what you like; either put the crown on your head or wear an ensign of victory on your arm."

He told the boy, illustrating what he said with examples, that a person may not break his worldly ties and connections, and yet be dear to God. The admonitions of the Guru had a good effect on the mind of the young visitor.

CHAPTER II.

THE HISTORY OF BYRAGI BANDÁ.

Early acquaintance of Guru Govind with Bandá.

It was during his stay in the Dekkan that Guru Govind Singh formed his first acquaintance with Bandá, an ascetic of the byragi order. He had hundreds of followers in his train, and lived in princely fashion.

Govind and Bandá soon became intimate friends, and the former, by his persuasive eloquence and religious zeal, made such a deep impression on the mind of Bandá that he was initiated into the *Páhal*, and became a disciple of the Guru. Bandá, by his dexterity and devotion, soon inspired the Guru with confidence, and became his most staunch ally and adherent. Though he was not acknowledged as the Guru's successor in the apostleship, yet the Guru declared that, after himself, the Sikhs would look upon him as their leader and protector. His dying injunctions to him were that he should remain a warrior, and avenge the blood of his father, as well as of his innocent sons. He told him that he must not fear death, and, taking five arrows from his quiver, and delivering them to Bandá, as emblems of victory, he then added: "Do not approach a woman, if you are my true disciple, and keep these five arrows with you. So long as you follow my instructions, no misfortune will happen to you; if you forget them, or disregard them, you shall answer for the non-performance with your life." Bandá received the arrows with profound reverence, and solemnly promised to obey the commands of the dying Guru.

The Guru's dying injunctions to him.

The Sikhs began to disperse when their commanding spirit was no more; resuming their former occupation, and employing themselves in agricultural pursuits and trade. Bandá, having yet to carry out the dying wishes of the Guru, determined to redeem to the very letter the promise given by him to avenge the wrongs of his late leader. He now, in order to accomplish his design, issued orders to the Sikhs (in the name of Guru Govind Singh), to prepare for hostilities, and assemble at a place appointed by him, for the purpose of overthrowing the Mahomedan rule. The Sikhs broke from their retreat and flocked in numbers round the banner of Bandá, who assumed the title of Guru. Inspired by a bitter feeling of revenge, and taking advantage of the absence of the Emperor Bahádur Shah, surnamed Sháh Alam, in the Dekkan, the Sikhs, under Bandá, appeared in the north-west and ravaged the country far and wide, plundering the people and laying waste the villages and towns. Wazír Khan, faujdar or governor of Sirhind, being informed of this, sent a detachment of troops to punish the marauders; but they were repulsed with great slaughter. Wazír Khan now marched in person, with a large army under his command. A sanguinary battle was fought in the neighbourhood of Sirhind, in which the imperial army was totally defeated, and Wazír Khan himself killed by an arrow which pierced his breast. Bandá now entered Sirhind, (the place where Guru Govind's two sons were murdered) and punished the city in a vindictive and barbarous manner. He commanded it to be fired, and all the inhabitants to be put to death. While the city was in flames, the followers of this fanatic carried on the work of carnage in the most diabolical spirit. They slaughtered the inhabitants indiscriminately without regard to age or sex. They butchered, bayoneted, strangled, hanged,

Bandá assumes the title of Guru.

Proceeds to the north-west.

Defeats the imperial troops at Sirhind.

Captures the town and sets it on fire, 1709-10.

The massacre of the inhabitants.

Dreadful atrocities.

shot down, hacked to pieces, and burnt alive, every Mahomedan in the place. Nor was this all. The dead, too, were made to contribute their share towards gratifying the rage of these voracious vampires. The corpse of Wazír Khan was hanged on a tree, and left to the tender mercies of the crows and vultures. The sanctity of the graveyards was violated, and corpses were exhumed, hewn to pieces, and exposed as carrion for the wolves, jackals, and other nocturnal visitants to these abodes of the dead. The mosques were polluted and burnt down, and the mullas, moulvis and hafizes subjected to the greatest indignities and tortures.

Bandá crosses the Sutlej.

Slaughters the inhabitants.

Elated with his success at Sirhind, Bandá crossed the Sutlej, carrying fire and sword wherever he went. Towns were devastated and the inhabitants plundered, and driven into the wilderness, or put to the sword. Some of the towns were razed to the ground. At Samáná ten thousand men and women were mercilessly put to the sword.*

Approaches Batála.

The Sikhs then crossed the Biás and marched to the city of Batála, now in the Gurdáspúr district. Two leading Mahomedans, both Sayads, lived in the town at the time, Mahomed Fazl Giláni, and Shekh-ul Ahad. On the approach of the murderous and incendiary troops, the former, with a body of his faqírs, fled to Sultanpúr, in the Jalandar Doáb. The latter encouraged the people to fight and prepare for a siege.

Shekh-ul Ahad gives him a fight. Is slain.

Bandá sets Batála on fire.

Destroys its college and puts the inhabitants to the sword.

The Sikhs proceed to Láhore.

The Mahomedans assemble at Láhore to give battle to the Sikhs.

Bandá, with his army, encamped by a tank two miles from the city. The gates of Batála were closed by the inhabitants and Shekh-ul Ahad, with a body of chosen men, went out to meet Bandá. An encounter took place, when the Shekh made a bold stand, but was at last killed, and his followers were dispersed with great slaughter. The body of this brave man was carried to Wazirábad and there interred. His descendants live at Batála to the present time. Bandá then burst open the gates, entered the city, and set it on fire, beginning with the house of Kazi Abdullá, whose wife and children were massacred in cold blood. Batála had been celebrated from a remote period as a great seat of learning, and a college flourished there at the time. This institution was fired, and the whole city given up to pillage and indiscriminate massacre. Having destroyed this beautiful city, the Sikhs, under their leader, proceeded to plunder the neighbourhood of Láhore. They had greatly increased in number at Batála, Kalanaur, and other towns on this side of the Biás, which they plundered and destroyed. At Sirhind immense military stores had fallen into their hands, and by this time they had at their disposal vast treasures, which they had collected from all parts. Great alarm was felt at Láhore, and in the whole country around, at the approach of the Sikhs. The emperor was at Ujjein, busy in suppressing the Rájput rebellion. The viceroy of Láhore, Syad Islám Khan, with the assistance of his Dewán Kázim Khan, put the city in a state of defence, mounting cannon on the ramparts and strengthening it by all other possible means. He solicited the aid of the whole of the Mahomedans in defending the city against the incursion of the Sikhs. The Mahomedans, knowing that their religion, honour and lives were at stake, readily answered his appeal. The leading Mahomedans of the time, Mahomed Taki, Musa Beg, Haji Syád Ismail, Syád Inaitulla and Mulla Pír Mahomed Waiz, with numerous followers, among

* "It is unnecessary," observes Sir John Malcolm, "to state the particulars of this memorable incursion which, from all accounts, appears to have been one of the severest scourges with which a country was ever afflicted. Every excess that the most wanton barbarity could commit, every cruelty that an unappeased appetite of revenge could suggest, was inflicted upon the miserable inhabitants of the provinces through which they passed. Life was only granted to those who conformed to the religion and adopted the habits and dress of the Sikhs."

The fight at the Idgáh of Láhore.

whom were also many * Hindus, assembled at the Idgáh, and were joined by the viceroy of Láhore. The patrolling parties of the enemy were cut off, and a desperate fight ensued, which lasted from morning till evening. Thousands fell on both sides, and success was, in the first instance, doubtful; but at last the Mahomedans gave way before superior numbers, and at sunset they retreated towards the city. They assembled once more under Syád Inaitulla, Mahommed Taki, and Mahommed Zamán, but were again defeated with great slaughter. Láhore, owing to the strength of its fortifications, was not molested, and the people of the town were safe from danger to life and property; but the outskirts, as far as the garden of Shalámár, were ravaged. From within two or three days' march of Delhi to the environs of Láhore the whole country was ravaged. Mosques and tombs were razed to the ground. Horrible crimes were committed. Treachery and cruelty stalked through the land; friend betrayed friend, and every one looked to the safety of his own life and cared not for others. The bearded ruffians forbade the shaving of the hair of the head and beard, and they were joined by thousands of low-caste Hindus. The emperor, having heard of the ravages committed by the Sikhs in the Panjáb, marched with a large army from the Dekkan. At Ajmere thousands of people who had been rendered homeless, and had emigrated from Sirhind, presented themselves before his majesty, who was greatly moved by their miserable and helpless condition. Bandá, having learnt that the emperor, with his whole force, was advancing against him, retreated to Daber, a fort situated in the Himalayás, at the entrance of the Siwálak mountains, which could be reached only by certain dangerous passes and ravines.

Defeat of the Mahomedans. They rallied, but were again worsted.

The whole country ravaged by the Sikhs.

The emperor marches towards Láhore.

Bandá retreats to Daber.

Feroz Khan Mewátí and Mahábat Khan, *Sipahsalar*, were sent in advance of the main troops to check the progress of the Sikhs, while Bayazid Khan, an Afghan of Kasúr, the governor of Jammún, who was at that time at Pánipat, and his nephew Shams-ud-dín Khan, the governor of Jalandar, with their troops, entered Sirhind and commenced the task of repopulating the devastated country. Isa Khan, a rich *zemindar*, was ordered to restore tranquillity in the Jalandar Doáb. The officers of his majesty had no easy task to perform. Towns had been depopulated by the ravages of the Sikhs. Tigers and other fierce beasts roamed about in the neighbourhood of abandoned towns and villages, the re-peopling and the rebuilding of which was a work of no small magnitude. The Sikhs, in the meantime, dispersed and took refuge in their hill fastnesses.

Measures of the imperial government to repopulate the devastated districts.

Bahádur Shah, with all his resources, now made preparations for a march to the Panjáb. The occurrence is fully described by Irádat Khan, a nobleman of his majesty's court, who was with the imperial camp at the time, and an eye-witness of the memorable events that happened. We take the following interesting passage from the memoirs of this nobleman. "About this time, *i.e.*, during the Dekkan and Rajputáná disturbance, intelligence was received of the Sikh rebellion. These infidels were also known by the name of Nánkia and Guru, or followers of Nának, and had been for a long time established in the Láhore district. The present chief † was a descendant of Nának, and exercised such influence over the people that great numbers of all ranks flocked to him at his summons, cheerfully resigning their lives and property into his hands. He now determined to shake to its very basis the true religion of Islam. He engaged Wazír Khan, the faujdar of Sirhind, who was killed in the action with numbers of his followers; after which the Guru possessed himself of the town of Sirhind, and

The historian Irádat Khan's account of these measures.

* *Múntakhibúl-Lúbab* of Khafi Khan.

† The author means Bandá, who, however, was no descendant of Nának.

many districts of the Doáb, as far as Buria, Sahàranpur, and Sadhoura, on both banks of the river Jamna, where he committed unlimited excesses, razing all public edifices, such as mosques, colleges, mausoleums and palaces, killing or taking prisoners the faithful of every age and sex, and plundering with the most cruel severity. The oppression of these wretches was every day increasing, and there was no nobleman daring enough to march from Delhi against them. Asif-ud-doula Asad Khan, the governor of the capital, was greatly alarmed, and behaved in a most pusillanimous manner, and the inhabitants were seized with terror and fled for shelter, with their families, to the Eastern provinces. All this, and a great deal more, was reported to the emperor in hyperbolical language. His majesty deemed it advisable to chastise the rebels in person. He accordingly determined to postpone for the present his design of extirpating the Rájputs. He found it more to his purpose to connive at their faults and to acknowledge their loyalty for the time being, but was determined to punish them when a more favourable opportunity occurred. The emperor now set out for Láhore with the greatest despatch, without visiting either Agra or Delhi. In a short time he arrived at Sirhind, which the rebels deserted on his approach, retiring to Daber, the original residence of their Guru or chief, where they fortified themselves as strongly as possible. Though this insurrection was not of such importance as to disturb the general repose of the empire, yet his majesty, defender of the faith, hearing that the malice of the rebels was directed against the religion, thought it his duty to engage them in person; following the example of Alamgir, who, in the latter part of his reign, appeared at the siege of every fort belonging to unbelievers. A prince or noble, with a Muslim army, would have been enough to extinguish every spark of the rebellion, and to have given Sikhism its quietus. What infatuation could have urged this miserable and disorderly rabble to declare war against so illustrious a monarch?"

The imperial army soon arrived within sight of the Guru's camp, which lay round the walls of Daber on different heights commanding the passes to that fortress, situated on the summit of a hill, surrounded by craggy rocks and glens. Shah Alam's orders to his Omerahs were to the effect that they were not to attack the Sikhs in their strong posts, under any pretence, but were to use every means in their power to induce them to sally forth from the forts. After the contending parties had remained inactive for some days, Khan-i-Khánán, sallied forth, with a number of his troops, to reconnoitre his adversary's position. When, however, he had arrived within cannon shot of their position, the enemy opened fire on the royal troops, while their musketeers and archers, who occupied some of the surrounding elevations, volleyed in their messages of death in quick succession.

The imperial army arrives at Daber.

The war against the Sikhs.

The imperial troops could no longer be held in check. The order was given to advance to the attack. Khan-i-Khánán, dismounted from his horse and led his troops on foot up the most difficult heights, driving the enemy from them with great slaughter. This scene passing within sight of the royal camps, the chiefs and soldiers, emulous of glory, waited not for orders, but hastened to join the attack in great numbers, while the emperor and the four princes who accompanied him, were eager spectators of the whole scene. The imperial troops carried all before them, driving the enemy from the heights surrounding the fortress. The Sikhs were compelled to retreat to the central fort, which had only narrow approaches, difficult of access, to recommend it, without affording good means of resistance. The defenders fought desperately, but would have been completely annihilated, had not the darkness of night given them a further reprieve by rendering

The Sikhs are defeated.

friends and foes undistinguishable to each other. The attack was renewed about dawn, and the fort taken after a short struggle. The Sikh chieftain effected his escape during the night by a narrow path leading from the fort to the hills, which had escaped the general's notice, and retreated into the wildest parts of the snowy range of the Himalayás. The Guru knew well how to disguise himself, and so dexterous was he in this accomplishment, that his most intimate acquaintances were unable to recognize him when he wished to evade detection. When he wished to be known, he appeared as a prince in the richest and most showy garments. When secrecy was his object, he generally took the guise of a jogi or sanniasi.

Bandá effects his escape.

After this success, Shah Alam returned to Láhore, where he died A.D. 1712. The death of the emperor was followed by the usual struggle for power among his sons, and anarchy and confusion again prevailed. These commotions were favourable to the Sikhs, who descending to the plains, bordering on the Indus, again united and flocked around the banner of their fanatical leader.

Bahádur Shah dies at Lahore, 1712.

The Sikhs again rally around their leader.

At this time they built for themselves a large fort called Gurdáspúr, between the Biás and the Rávi, the Lohgarh of the ancients, according to Forster and Malcolm. Islám Khan, the viceroy of Láhore, marched with the view of arresting their progress, but was defeated in a pitched battle. The Sikhs then advanced to Sirhind, and Bayazid Khan, the governor of the province, marched from the town to encounter their army, but was defeated and stabbed by a fanatic follower. The Mahomedan troops fled, but the city, on this occasion, was not subjected to pillage, as on the former occasion of the Guru's visit. The emperor Farrukhseer, who ascended the throne of Hindostán after killing his uncle, Moiz-ud-dín Jahándár Shah (1713 A.D.), now determined on the extirpation of the Sikhs. He ordered Abdul Samad Khan, surnamed Diler Jang, a Turani nobleman, governor of Káshmír, and a general of great reputation, to assume the command of the Panjáb, and punish the insurgent Bandá and his fanatic followers.

They build the fort of Gurdáspúr,

And advance to Sirhind.

The emperor Jahándár Shah determines on extirpating the Sikhs.

Abdul Samad Khan marched from Káshmír with several thousands of his own brave countrymen to Láhore, and was there joined by Mohamed Amin Khan, whom the emperor had sent with a large number of chosen troops from the eastern districts.

Abdul Samad Khan Diler Jang, is sent to chastise them.

Bandá, hearing of the approach of the imperial army, again fled to his hill fastnesses, where he concealed himself. The imperialists followed him with all speed; but he managed to escape, though, in the hurry and bustle of the flight, he was forced to abandon a great part of his treasures, which fell into the hands of the pursuing army and were divided by them among the poor and afflicted persons who had been rendered homeless through the atrocities and devastation committed by the Sikhs. Quiet having apparently been restored, Mohamed Amin Khan was recalled to Delhi, while Abdul Samad Khan Diler Jang was ordered to go to Láhore to restore order in that province which had so seriously suffered from the ravages of the fanatic Sikhs.

The Sikhs disperse on his approach.

After a year's respite, the Sikh chieftain again appeared on the plains of Gurdáspúr and took possession of Kalanaur and Santokh Garh. He summoned the Sikhs from the haunts to which they had temporarily retired, and in less than two months thirty-five thousand warriors* joined his standard.

They assemble again under the leadership of Bandá,

Sheik Mahomed Dáem, the Faujdar of Ambála, encountered the Sikh army, but he was defeated and fled in dismay to Láhore. Upon this Abdul

And defeat the Imperial Faujdar of Ambála.

* According to Rai Kanhia Lal, 50,000.

Samad Khan, the viceroy of Láhore, with his Durráni warriors and train of artillery, marched from Láhore and was reinforced by the imperial troops under Mír Ahmad Khan, the Faujdar of Aurangabad. The Sikhs strengthened their position in the fort of Logharh (Gurdáspúr) and surrounded it by a moat which they filled from the neighbouring canals.

Abdul Samad Khan proceeds against them.

A desperate action was fought in which their leader Bandá showed great valour, but he had to give way to superior numbers, and the discipline of the imperial army, though not without a fierce and desperate struggle, in which he inflicted severe losses on his opponents.

The fight at Gurdáspúr.

Bandá and his followers were driven from place to place by the imperialists, and finally took refuge in the fort of Logharh, which was thoroughly adapted for the purposes of defence, and here he was closely besieged for a long time. All communication from without was cut off, and nothing could be conveyed to the besieged inside. All the provisions in the fort were consumed and its military resources exhausted.

The fort laid under siege.

At length the besieged began to suffer the utmost extreme of hunger and fatigue, and were reduced to eating horses and asses. The small band of followers who had adhered to Bandá faithfully throughout his checkered career, now began to desert him, in consequence of the hunger and hardships to which they were subjected. These people concealed themselves in caves, jungles, deserted villages and other places; but the Mahomedans were indefatigable in unearthing them and putting them to death.

The besieged are put to great straits.

Seeing now that there was no chance of escape, and that he had to chose between surrender and starvation, Bandá elected the former, and sent a message to Abdul Samad, begging him to intercede with the emperor for a free pardon for him, on condition of his leading a peaceful life in future. The nawáb promised to mediate, on which Bandá surrendered, with all his chief councillers, officers and men. He and his associates, having been all put in chains, were sent to Láhore. Many were bound hand and foot and made over to the imperial troops, who, under orders of the nawáb, carried them to the banks of the Rávi, and there, having beheaded them, threw their bodies into the river. After these executions, Abdul Samad Khan made his triumphant entry into Láhore with a long train of Sikh officers and men, headed by Bandá. They were mounted upon lame, worn out hungry asses and camels, each of them having a paper cap on his head. In this condition they were led into the streets of Láhore, followed by a mob which jeered and cursed them. As they were being thus paraded through the streets, the old mother of Bayazid Khan, who had been killed by a Sikh named Báz Singh, while in the act of performing his afternoon devotion, avenged herself for the death of her son, by lifting a large stone and letting it fall on the head of her son's assassin from a terrace overlooking the street. The stone killed Báz Singh on the spot. The whole city of Láhore was at this moment in a state of intense agitation, and the general, apprehending that the prisoners would be killed by the infuriated mob, conveyed them to a place of safety where they were concealed in the trappings of elephants. The following day the general left the city at daybreak with the object of presenting Bandá and his associates alive to the emperor. The prisoners were put under charge of his own son, Zakaria Khan, and Kamrud-dín Khan, under a strong escort. Of the whole number that had been taken prisoners, seven hundred and forty men were taken to Delhi. Bandá was confined in an iron cage.* At Delhi the prisoners were treated with the

Bandá surrenders.

Executions of the Sikhs.

Barbarous display of the Sikh prisoners in the streets of Láhore.

The death of the governor of Sirhind avenged by his mother.

The prisoners, with Bandá, their chief are sent to Delhi.

* According to McGregor, the Mussalman soldiers maintained that Bandá was a magician and would make his escape on the road. One of the Moghals rose and said: "Tie us together on the same elephant, and if he attempts to escape, I will plunge this dagger into his body." Bandá was accordingly tied to this man, and in this manner conveyed to Delhi.

greatest ignominy. In order to give them a contemptible and ludicrous appearance, they were forced to dress themselves in sheep skins, and were then mounted on asses and camels, and exhibited in all the thoroughfares and places of public resort of the city.

Their cruel death, 1760.

Bandá was placed on an elephant, with his face smeared with black, and a woollen cap placed over his head, and an executioner standing over him, sword in hand. He was made to take the lead, as their mock chief. One hundred of them were publicly beheaded that day amidst the jeers and taunts of the mob.

Each succeeding day a similar number were executed, until the whole had paid the penalty of their crimes. They met their doom with the utmost indifference; nay, they even clamoured for priority of martyrdom. Bandá's execution was reserved for the last day. He was dragged from his cage, like a wild beast, and then dressed in a princely robe, embroidered with gold, and a scarlet turban. He was now arraigned before a tribunal who had already doomed him. The heads of his followers, who had been previously executed, were paraded on pikes all round him. The executioner, with drawn sabre, stood behind him, in readiness to carry out the sentence of his judges. All the Omerahs of the court tauntingly asked him why he, a man of such unquestionable knowledge and abilities, had committed such villainous and outrageous offences, which nothing but a lengthy stay in his Satanic Majesty's abode could expiate. He retorted that he was a scourge in the hands of the Almighty for the chastisement of evil-doers, and that that power was now given to others to chastise him for his transgressions. His son was now placed in his lap, and he was ordered to cut his throat, a knife being handed to him for that purpose. He complied with the command without the slightest hesitation. His body was then torn to pieces with red hot irons, "his sable spirit" (according to Mahomedan historians) "taking its flight to the regions of the damned for which it was so well fitted." The Guru suffered this just retribution of heaven in 1760 A.D. Though bravery is a qualification which is highly meritorious, and in all cases one which is handed down to posterity, yet the audacious achievements of this monster are an exception to the rule. His triumphs are not remembered as heroic acts, but as malicious and cold-blooded atrocities. His ruling and insatiable passion was that of pouring out Mahomedan blood. At the present day his name is never mentioned in any part of India unaccompanied with maledictions on his savagery and bloodthirsty propensities. His memory is held in the same detestation by the Sikhs as by the Mahomedans. His policy was directly opposed to that of Nának and Govind, his predecessors. His innovations were forced upon his followers, and those who showed the slightest scruple in accepting them were tortured as unmercifully and cruelly as the Mahomedans. He tortured and put to death many of the staunchest adherents of Govind, because they had refused to comply with his new-fangled doctrines, which were, in direct contravention of the tenets of their religion, as established by their founder. He was so proud of his achievements in his pontifical capacity, that he actually wished his followers to adopt a livery of his own invention, (in supersession of the blue dress which Nának had ordered them to wear) in order that his power as a spiritual leader might be better known to the world. He also changed their war-cry, from "*Wáh Guru ji ka Fateh,*" "*Wáh Guru ji ka Khálsá,*" which had been enjoined by Govind, to "*Fateh Dharam, Fateh Dharsam,*" which latter means, "Success to piety, success to the sect." He also desired his followers to abstain from meat and intoxicating beverages. The Akális, or the never-dying, the true and uncompro-

His memory is not revered.

His innovations in the institutions o Nának and Govind were resisted.

mising followers of Govind, opposed these innovations with the greatest obstinacy, and preferred dying as martyrs in the cause of their religion to living and adopting new modes of life and changing the tenets and precepts of their great Guru. On the byragi's death, all the institutions of Nának and Govind were restored, though the blue dress, which was previously worn by all the Sikhs, become from that time the privileged colour of the Akális, who had proved themselves truly worthy of this distinguishing mark of a true Sikh by the courage and bravery with which they had resisted the innovations of Bandá. A sect called Bandáis, who follow the doctrines of Bandá, still exists in the Panjáb, and its members live in Multán, Tata and other towns on the banks of the Indus. They recieve the *Adi Granth* of Nának, but not the *Daswan Badsháh ká Granth* of Guru Govind Singh.

His distinguishing characteristics.

Devoid of all the better qualities of his illustrious predecessor, Bandá had nothing to commend his memory to posterity, save an undaunted spirit. Govind's selection of Bandá, as his successor, does not appear to have been the result of any very great opinion he had formed of his piety, or of his ability to propagate the religion of which he had been so long the leader, but rather to have been made with a view to his avenging the death of his father and two sons, for which purpose he could not have singled out a better instrument than this ruthless bloodsucker.

CHAPTER III.

THE POLITICAL ORGANIZATION OF THE SIKHS INTO A THEOCRATIC CONFEDERATE FEUDALISM.

Distracted state of the Panjáb after the departure of Ahmad Shah in 1761.

On the departure of Ahmad Shah from Hindostán in 1761, disorder and confusion prevailed throughout the Panjáb. The absence of all regular Government and the turbulent state of the country which followed the commotions at Pánipat, increased the power of the Sikhs. The king concerned himself little about the disorder that had overtaken the internal administration of the province, and his governor at Láhore was in no better position than the military commander of an outlying post. The Sikhs grew more daring and rapacious than ever, laying waste the surrounding country and levying contributions upon the villages. All the principal sardars appropriated lands to themselves, calling the tracts under their jurisdiction after the names of their native villages, such as Ramgarhia, Ahluwalia; while others were named according to the habits of the people, such as *Bhangi*, from their being addicted to the use of bhang, *Cannabis Indica*. They built strongholds and fastnesses for the purpose of better securing their persons and property against the Mussalman invasions, and to serve as the basis of military operations against their opponents. These active measures contributed much to the strength and resources of the Sikh nation. One of the chiefs who laid the foundations of the political greatness of the nation, was Charat Singh, ancestor of Ranjít Singh,* the future Maharájá of the Panjáb. He appeared early in the field, and, by his activity and enterprize, soon acquired the reputation of being a good soldier and a successful leader.

The Sikhs increase in strength.

The rise of Charat Singh, Sukerchakia.

* For a more detailed account of Ranjít Singh's family, see the *History of the Sukerchakia misl*.

The family possessed no ancestral distinction, or antiquity, to boast of, and the first of the family to embrace the Sikh religion was one Desu *Ját*, a petty zemindar of the Sansi tribe, who live in Sakarchak, a village in the Mánjha country. He owned three ploughs and a well, with which he managed to eke out a living for himself and his family. He had a son, Nodh Singh, who married the daughter of Guláb Singh, a zemindar of Majithia. Nodh Singh, after his marriage, abandoned his agricultural pursuits, and became a soldier and commander in the Fyzulpuria *misl*, under the leadership of Kapur Singh, of Gujrát.

Desu a Ját of Sansi.

Nodh Singh, his son.

Nodh Singh died in 1752, and Charat Singh, his son, disdaining to serve in any subordinate capacity, established a party of his own, in which his brothers-in-law, Dal Singh and Jodh Singh, ranked next to him, and, with their assistance, he enlisted in his service a number of armed men, whom he employed in predatory excursions, himself heading the operations. With the money thus collected he was enabled to build a small mud fort in his wife's village, called Gujraoli, north of Láhore. It served as a rendezvous for his troops, and as a store-house for the booty obtained by him from his predatory excursions. It was conveniently situated, being close to Láhore, and serving as a rallying point for the other Sikh confederacies having in view the common object of crushing the Mahomedan power.

A military post established at Gujraoli.

The wisdom of the Abdáli King in contenting himself with the possession of the country that had been previously ceded to him, was now apparent, for, far from being able to maintain a hold on the country across the Sutlej, he found it no easy task to retain a footing in the Panjáb, where the Sikh power was now in the ascendant. Hearing of the success of this people, the Shah, in the beginning of 1762, sent his general, Nur-ud-dín Khan Bamizie, at the head of 7,000 horse, to disperse the Sikh insurgents. The general was repulsed with great loss by the combined forces of Charat Singh, Sukerchakia and other Sikh sardars, and compelled to seek refuge in the fort of Siálkot, where he was closely besieged by the Sikhs. At length, provisions failing, Nur-ud-dín Khan sought protection with the Jammu rájá, where he was joined by the remnant of his troops and officers. The Sikhs, after this success, became still more turbulent, and cut off all communication with Láhore. Jey Singh, Kanhia, and Jassa Singh, Ramgarhia, made themselves masters of Batála and Kalanaur respectively, while Gujar Singh and Charat Singh laid waste the country round Emnabad, in the neighbourhood of Láhore. At length, the Durráni Governor, Khwajá Obed, marched out with all his forces to reduce Charat Singh, and oust him from his new post at Gujraoli. The Sikhs made common cause, and from all directions rallied round the fort which they determined to defend to the last. The Afghan Governor besieged them in their mud fort and cut off all their supplies. The Sikhs were joined by Gujar Singh and Jhánda Singh, who advanced, with their auxiliaries, from Emnabad to the aid of their co-religionists. Some Sikhs serving in the army under the Mahomedan governor, clandestinely entered into a correspondence with their brethren of the Garhi. By these means the Sikhs were enabled to surprise the Afghan camp by night, completely routing the Afghans, and leaving many dead on the field. At this juncture, according to a previous secret arrangement, all the Sikhs in the employ of the Moghal Governor deserted in a body and joined the enemy. The Khwajá himself fled in dismay, leaving his baggage to be plundered by the Sikhs, and shut himself up within the walls of Láhore.

Nur-ud-dín Khan, the Afghan general.

He is besieged at Siálkot.

His flight to Jammu.

Khwajá Obed, the Láhore governor.

He besieges the Sikhs at Gujraoli,

But is defeated and shuts himself up in Láhore.

Elated with their success over the Mahomedan governor of Láhore, the Sikhs began to devastate the whole country, and, in retaliation for the treatment they had received at the hands of the Mahomedans, subjected them to many outrages, indignities and hardships. The votaries of the Guru, the *Dal* of the *Khálsá*, assembled at Amritsar on the Dewáli festival, and publicly performed their ablutions in the sacred tank, and for the first time a regular *Guru Matta*, or assembly of chiefs and followers, was held on the occasion. It was then resolved to invest Jandiálá, a place held by Mohant Akil Dass, who had tendered his submission to Ahmad Shah, and, having rendered him important services in connection with the war at Pánipat, had incurred the displeasure of the followers of Govind. The possessions of Hingan Khan, chief of Malerkotla, were ravaged, and other Mahomedan chiefs, such as Murtaza Khan of Baroach and Kasim Khan, *Aral*, were harassed.* Sirhind was invested; but the Mahomedan governor Zen Khan, assisted by the neighbouring chiefs, was more successful in holding his ground.

The Sikhs assemble at Amritsar, and hold a national council.

Certain Mussalman principalities ravaged.

The report of these disasters having reached the restless Ahmad Shah, he determined to take the field in person, and appeared on the Indus in November 1762, and with a body of his chosen troops made some of those rapid marches for which he was celebrated. The Sikhs were still engaged in the siege of Jandiálá when the king arrived within sight of their camp, by two forced and rapid marches from Láhore, by way of Ludhiáná. The insurgents, being apprised of the Shah's approach, broke up their camp and fled in all directions, the majority retiring to the south of the Sutlej, with the view of assisting their brethren who had invested Sirhind. The Shah established his head-quarters at Láhore and issued orders to the Mussalman jágírdars and chiefs of Baroach, Malerkotla and other military stations, to join the governor of Sirhind with their respective contingents. His temporary absence from the field induced the Sikhs to believe that he had entirely abandoned the further prosecution of the war. But the Shah soon convinced them of this error. While he was at Láhore, he completed all his plans for surprising the enemy, and then sallied forth at the head of his troops with the utmost precaution and secresy. The next evening, he crossed the Sutlej and bivouacked at Ludhiáná. After a few hours halt, he again set out with his army for Sirhind, which he reached before sunrise. His opportune arrival was of the utmost importance to the favourable issue of the war. Zen Khan, the governor of Sirhind, had for some time been holding out against superior numbers with great heroism, but it was plain that the unequal contest could not be prolonged for many more days. The timely appearance of the Shah, however, infused a spirit of courage into the hearts of the besieged troops. He engaged the enemy, who were estimated at between 50,000 and 60,000 strong, at Kot Rahira, south of the Sutlej, and gained a complete victory over them. In this engagement the mountaineers and the Shah's bodyguard were particularly conspicuous for their bravery, the latter being distinguished by the peculiarity of their head-dress, which consisted of conical shaped, woolly sheepskin hats. The field was contested with great determination; but suddenly a panic seemed to seize the Sikhs, and a general stampede followed. The victorious troops pursued the discomfited army in a westerly direction as far as Hariana and Burala. Historians variously estimate the loss of the defeated army in killed and wounded at from 12,000 to 30,000.† Those who escaped the avenging sword of the victors, either made for

Sixth invasion of Ahmad Shah, 1762.

The great defeat of the Sikhs at Kot Rahira near Ludhiáná, February 1762.

---

* *Memoirs of Abdul Karim Ulvi*, page 17.

† According to the *Tárikh-i-Ahmadi*, the loss on the side of the Sikhs was 30,000 killed, though, according to Captain Murray, it did not exceed 12,000. According to Rai Kanhia Lal it amounted to 24,000. Sir John Malcolm says the Sikhs lost upwards of 20,000 men. I think the figure given by Rai Kanhia Lal may be taken as approximately correct. All, however, who have written on the subject, admit that the number of killed and wounded was very considerable.

The Sikh call their defeat Ghulá Ghará or the bloody carnage.

the neighbouring hills, or became prisoners of war. The Sikhs characterised their great disaster by the name of *Ghulá Ghará* or "the sanguinary visitation."

Ala Singh, chief of Patiálá.

Ala Singh, chief of the *Phul* family, and founder of the Patiálá Raj, was made a prisoner at Burala and brought in chains to Láhore, but, through the intercession of Shah Wali Khan, the grand wazír, he was released, on condition of his paying tribute. A *nazráná* of four lakhs of rupees was paid to the Shah by Ráni Fattú, wife of Ala Singh, and the king was so much gratified with the manly deportment of the Sikh chieftain, that he conferred upon him a rich *khilat* and despatched a *firman* to the subedar of Sirhind, on receipt of which he was immediately to restore to him all his jágírs. Ala Singh was, on this occasion, honoured with title of "*rájá*," and he struck a coin bearing the name of the Shah, as the bestower of the kingdom over which he then ruled.

The Shah summons certain chiefs of the Panjáb, and levies nazráná on them.

The Shah then summoned to his presence, at Láhore, Ranjít Deo, rájá of Jammu, Raí Birham of Kapurthala, Ghamand Chand, rájá of Katoj, Nidhan Singh *Randháwá*, the rájá of Kangrá, Mirza Mír Muhammad of Kádián, and other chiefs, and, having received from them suitable *nazráná*, bestowed upon them dresses of state, and dismissed them with honour.

He visits Amritsar,

The Dewáli festival then coming on, the Shah paid a visit to Amritsar, where he spent several days in shooting and recreation, in the company of the Omerahs. He signalized his stay at Amritsar by committing those ravages and atrocities on his vanquished enemies of which the history of eastern countries affords so many examples. The Sikh temple of Harmandar at Amritsar was blown up with gunpowder, and the sacred reservoir again choked with its ruins, and polluted with the blood and entrails of cows and bullocks. Kalandar Khan, a Durráni chief, was appointed to carry out these arrangements. Numerous pyramids were made of the heads of those who had suffered decapitation.

And defiles the holy places of the Sikhs.

The sacrilegious outrages committed by the Sikhs on the Muslim mosques and shrines were now avenged by the demolition of the most sacred edifices in their most sacred city. The law of retaliation was carried out to the letter. The indignities offered to the Mahomedan religion, were, in this instance, as in the others, repaid with compound interest. The outrages suffered by the Mahomedans could not have been atoned for except by the blood of the offenders. Moreover, nothing could have proved so gratifying and satisfactory to them as the carrying out of the work of iconoclasm, since their Unitarian faith cannot tolerate idolatory.

There can be no doubt that the Abdáli acted in strict conformity with the law of his religion, and was actuated by a sense of duty, when he undertook the destruction of the sanctuaries of the Sikhs. Having now completely vindicated his religion, he turned his attention to the affairs of Káshmír. At this time, the governor, Sukh Jiwan, thought proper to administer and govern Káshmír as an independent chief. He expelled the Afghans from Káshmír, refused to pay tribute, and, in short, threw off the yoke of the Shah. The Abdáli had no alternative but that of bringing the governor to his senses, which he did by despatching a large force into the country under the command of Nur-ud-dín Khan, Bamizie, with orders to apprehend and convey him to Láhore. In this expedition the Shah's general was accompanied by Ranjít Deo, the rájá of Jammu, whose co-operation greatly facilitated his arrival at his destination. When the army reached Pir Panjál, the village in which the rebellious governor had fortified himself, they immediately attacked it, and after a slight resistance, Sukh Jiwan was captured, loaded with chains and conducted to Láhore, where he was first sentenced

Sukh Jiwan, the Afghan governor of Káshmír, rebels.

Is defeated and put to death.

to have his eyes put out, and, after this decree had been executed, was put to death. Sur Buland Khan was now sent as governor to Káshmír, and Nur-ud-dín Khan was recalled. In the meanwhile, news of disturbances at Kandahar having reached the Shah, he hastened to Kábul at the end of 1762, leaving a Hindu, named Kábuli Mal, as his governor in Láhore.

Ahmad Shah retires to Kábul, end of 1762.

Kabuli Mal governor of Láhore.

The severe chastisement inflicted by the Shah on the Sikhs, for the indignities to which they had subjected the Mahomedan mosques and shrines was not of a nature to be easily forgotten; thirst for revenge rankled in their breasts, and, now that an opportunity occurred for carrying their cherished desire into effect, they convened a *Guru Matta*, or cabinet council, and determined their future plan of operations. The Muslim troops had scarcely reached the Chináb when the Sikhs concentrated their forces at Amritsar and marched upon Kasúr, a Pathan settlement, which they surprised and plundered, and from which they carried off considerable booty. They then captured and sacked Malerkotla, and slew their old enemy, Hingan Khan, its veteran chief. Elated with these successes, they aimed at acquiring territory, and, with a well equipped force of forty thousand men, they attacked Sirhind in December 1763. The Court at Delhi being incapable of rendering any assistance to the governor of Sirhind, or perhaps being indifferent to Sikh supremacy, Zen Khan, the Afghan governor, was obliged to sally forth to attack the Sikhs. A battle was fought at Pir Zen Múnera, a village seven miles east of Sirhind, between the Sikh and Mahomedan forces, which ended in the complete defeat of the latter, and in which Zen Khan and the Muslim leaders were killed. The whole country from the Sutlej to the Jamna was occupied by the victors without opposition. The town of Sirhind itself was sacked and its buildings were either razed to the ground or set on fire. This being the place in which the mother and children of Govind had been murdered by order of Wazír Khan, Aurangzeb's general, they were determined upon retributive justice. Not a house was left standing, and a custom exists to this day, by which it is considered a meritorious act for every Sikh to carry away a brick from the place and throw it into the Sutlej, to mark his detestation and abhorrence of the place.* The Sikhs divided the plains between the Sutlej and the Jamna among themselves, establishing military posts at important places. Ala Singh, the Patiálá chief, purchased the ruins of Sirhind from the Sikhs for a sum of Rs. 25,000. The seller was the Jumla chief Bhái Budh Singh, an old companion of Govind, to whom the town had been assigned unanimously by the Sikh confederates, who had captured it.

The Sikhs appear again on the scene.

They plunder Kasúr,

And sack Malerkotla.

The Afghans defeated at Sirhind, December 1763.

Zen Khan, the Afghan governor, killed.

Sirhind destroyed and permanently occupied by the Sikhs.

Now that the Sikhs had tasted the fruits of their conquest, their longing for dominion and power became insatiable. They crossed the Jamna and suddenly appeared under the walls of Sahâranpúr; but the appearance of Najib-ud-doula, from the *Ját* country, prevented them from becoming permanently masters of the place.

The Sikhs had by this time, by force of their audacity, become complete masters of the country between the Sutlej and the Jamna. The Hindu governor of Láhore, left by the Abdáli Shah, with Khwajá Obed as his assistant, possessed no control over the people beyond the city walls. Every one feared the Sikhs, whose power was supreme. Out of the regard which, as Hindus, they have for the sacred cow, they now insolently demanded of Kábuli Mal, the subedar of Láhore, the surrender of all the beef butchers in the city. The Hindu governor of Láhore was on the horns of a dilemma. To surrender himself to the Sikhs was not altogether in accord with his

The Sikhs masters of the country between the Sutlej and the Jamna.

Punishment of the beef butchers at Láhore.

* The account given by Sir John Malcolm represents the Sikhs as having also made themselves masters of Láhore at this period; but it is quite unconfirmed.

humour, while to deliver over the Mahomedan butchers to their tender mercies was to incur the displeasure of the Shah, his master. Under these circumstances he thought it advisable to compromise matters by chopping off the ears and noses of some of the butchers and expelling them from the town. Kábuli Mal, no doubt, considered this a meritorious act, for, being a Hindu, he looked upon all butchers, as an abomination and pest.

The success of the Sikhs at Sirhind, and the confusion into which the Panjáb had fallen, brought the Abdáli, Ahmed Shah, again on the scene.

Seventh invasion of Ahmad Shah, 1764.

Having crossed the Indus, he entered Láhore in January 1764, this being his seventh invasion of Hindostán. His appearance on the plains of India, was a signal for the votaries of Govind again to hide their heads in their jungles and hill fastnesses, for they dreaded his very name. Rájá Ala Singh, of Patiálá, was confirmed by the Shah in his tenure of Sirhind, on the recommendation of his grand wazír, Shah Wali Khan. The Shah was much moved by the disorders he saw on all sides. He despatched his troops in every direction to seize the insurgent Sikhs; but they were beyond his reach, having taken refuge west and south of Patiálá and Nabha. After a short stay at Láhore, the Shah proceeded to the Sutlej, where he levelled the houses of the Sikh chiefs to the ground. In numerous villages the standing wheat crops were burnt, or otherwise destroyed, and the Sikh places of worship plundered or desecrated. For two months he continued to ravage the countries south of Láhore, when, hearing of fresh disturbances in his native provinces,

His speedy retirement to Kábul.

he retraced his steps somewhat precipitately to Kábul, without having either effectually punished the atrocities of the Sikhs, or completely recovered the lost province of Sirhind. He acknowledged Ala Singh as governor of the province on his behalf, on condition of his paying a tribute of three and a half lakhs of rupees. He was harassed in the neighbourhood of Amritsar by the Sikhs, and petty engagements were of constant occurrence in which the Afghans suffered greatly. He then crossed the Rávi, and sent his general, Jahán Khan, to Gujrát and Rohtas, at the head of 10,000 Kazalbashes, to punish the Sikhs.

While the Abdáli was moving about the country, the Sikhs, acting upon the adage that "Prudence is the better part of valour," considered it advisable to keep out of his reach, but no sooner had he turned his back, than they burst forth like the smouldering embers of a fire that is stirred, and, overrunning the country,* laid it waste in all directions. They besieged and took

Láhore in the hands of the Sikhs, 1764 A.D.

Láhore. Kábuli Mal, the governor, hurried off to Jammu and claimed the protection of Ranjít Deo, one of the hill rájás. The governor's nephew, (sister's son), Amír Singh, was surprised and arrested, while enjoying himself at a dancing party, and immediately loaded with chains. All the men of his family were made prisoners, and the whole of his property was confiscated to the *Khálsá*.† The city was given up to indiscriminate plunder‡ and was parcelled out by the captors into three lots. South of Láhore, as far as Niáz Beg, was assigned to Sobha Singh; the eastern portion, including

The three Sikh rulers of Láhore.

Kábuli Mal's haveli, was made over to Gujar Singh, and the rest, with the fort and the *Badshahi masjid*, to Lahná Singh. A contemporary poet has given the following chronogram of the capture of Láhore by the Sikhs, giving the Hijrí year 1181, corresponding to 1764 A.D.:—

* For a full account of the proceedings of this period between the Láhore viceroy and the Sikhs, *vide* the *History of the Bhangi misl.*

† The family of Kábuli Mal were released by the three rulers of Láhore, on payment of a *nazrdná*, of 25,000 rupees and sent to Jammu.

‡ At this time there lived at Láhore a faqír of great sanctity named Nathu Shah. The people requested him to ask the invaders to have mercy on the town, and through his intercession the lives of the citizens were spared.—*Umda Tul Twarikh* of Sahan Lal, page 163, vol. I.

جہانے خراب شدہ

"A world has been devastated."

The Sikh chiefs and their followers now partitioned among themselves the whole country between the Jhelum and the Sutlej. Kot Mohy-ud-dín Khan, near the Pathan colony of Kasúr, was closely besieged, and a strong detachment of the Sikhs, compelled Jahán Khan, the Moghal governor of Gujrát, to effect his escape from Rohtas to Siálkot, where he was besieged and put to great straits. Numerous mosques were razed to the ground, and the Afghan prisoners who were in chains, were compelled to smear the débris with the blood of hogs. The Sikh confederates then held a national meeting at Amritsar, their sacred rendezvous, and, by a decree of the *Khálsá*, proclaimed their own sect as the dominant power in the Panjáb, and their own religion as supreme. The assumption of sovereignty by the Sikhs was marked by the striking of a coin bearing the inscription, "Guru Govind had received from Nának *Degh*, *Tegh* and *Fatteh*—grace, power, and victory."

The Sikhs assemble at Amritsar.

And proclaim their own sway by striking a coin.

For two years the Sikhs continued tranquilly to enjoy their supremacy, the chiefs acting independently of one another, and being loyally aided by their followers in all their undertakings. Notwithstanding the multiplicity of chieftains, and their independence, they one and all, considered it a paramount duty to act unitedly in the defence of their religion and country, and thus they formed themselves into a commonwealth. God on their head, the steel of Govind under their arms, and the book of Nának in their hands, these were the safeguards of each true disciple who was a substantive member of the confederacy. They held an annual meeting at Amritsar, after the monsoon, to mature their plans of conquest and aggrandizement. A sort of blackmail, or tribute, called the "Rákhi," literally, "protection money," was levied upon the inhabitants of the subdued tracts of country, and in this manner a regular form of government was introduced.

They resolve themselves into a feuderal confederacy.

The Sikhs, now unchecked, became masters of the whole open country as far west as the Jhelum, while their possessions to the east extended to the plains of Karnál. While they imagined themselves perfectly secure in the enjoyment of their conquests, Ahmad Shah's final invasion in 1767 threw them into a state of consternation and frenzy. The Abdáli, having fully made up his mind to wreak his vengeance upon the rebellious Sikhs, crossed the Indus in the early part of the same year, at the head of his invincible troops, and, encountering the enemy on the banks of the Sutlej, obliged them to retreat precipitately to the woods and mountains south of Jagráon. He found a useful ally in the chief of Katoch, a Rájput veteran, whom he made his lieutenant in the Jalandar Doáb and the adjoining hills. At Kará Báwana, twenty-four miles south of Ambála, on the banks of the Sutlej, he received Amar Singh, who had just succeeded his grandfather, Ala Singh, in the sovereignty of Patiálá, and was pleased to invest him with the title of "Rájá Rajgán Mahandar Bahádur," permitting him at the same time to use the colours and drum as the insignia of royalty. He was also allowed to strike a coin in his own name, which he did, and which bore the following Persian inscription :—

The extent of their possessions.

Eighth invasion of Ahmad Shah, 1767.

The Sikhs retreat to the south of Jagráon on his approach.

The title of Maharájá bestowed on Amar Singh of Patiálá.

حکم شد از قادر بیچون باحمد پاد شاہ - سکہ زن بر سیم و زر از اوج ماهي تا بماه

"By the command of God the Inscrutable, Ahmad, the king, struck coin on silver and gold, from the bottom of the sea to the height of the moon."

He coins money at Sirhind in the name of the Shah.

On the reverse was the inscription :—

سنه جلوس میمنت مانوس ضرب سرهند

"Coined at Sirhind in the auspicious year of the reign."

In recognition of the privilege conferred on him by the Durráni Shah, the rájá presented him with a *nazár* of a lakh of rupees, and, in commemoration of the event, the king, on his part, was pleased to release all prisoners of war taken in the neighbourhood of Sahâranpúr.

The Shah's declining health.

The declining period of Ahmad Shah's life may be said to have set in about this time. He had been suffering the most excruciating pain from cancer of the nose ever since 1764, and now old age appeared to be creeping upon him; for the loss of his martial spirit and activity were very perceptible, and were the common topic of conversation with both his friends and his enemies; the former looking forward with anxiety to the dissolution of their leader, and the latter regarding with great satisfaction the approaching demise of their dreaded chastiser. During the latter days of his stay in India, he adopted a policy of reconciliation where armed resistance was of little avail, and, acting upon that policy, he secured the regard of the Malwa Sikhs by the recognition of Amar Singh as the independant ruler of Patiálá, and the co-operation of the Rájput chiefs of the Jalandar Doáb. He sent a present of fruits to Lahná Singh, the Bhangi chief of Láhore; but the latter returned it to the king, with a message to the effect that fruit was a luxury worthy of an emperor, the asylum of the poor, and that for an humble peasant like himself grain was the best food. The Shah was greatly pleased with the humility displayed by the chief, whom he confirmed in his possessions in the neighbourhood of Láhore.

His policy of reconciliation.

The Shah appointed Sarfráz Khan, the governor of Káshmír, as his lieutenant at Rohtas. He then visited Sirhind, and was much grieved to see it in the ruinous condition to which the Sikhs had reduced it. Returning thence to Láhore, he appointed Moulvi Obedulláh his governor of Láhore, with Dáúd Khan as his deputy. His plans were, however, frustrated by 12,000 of his Durráni troops deserting him and marching back towards Kábul. The Shah thought it prudent to follow them, but was harassed in his retreat by the ubiquitous Sikhs, who cut off his baggage train and plundered his camp followers. As soon as the Shah had crossed the Indus, the Sikhs, under Charat Singh, the grandfather of Ranjít Singh, the founder of the Sukerchakia *misl*, blockaded the stronghold of Rohtas. Láhore was again besieged by three rulers, Lahná Singh, Gujar Singh and Sobha Singh, who had fled on the Abdáli's approach. The Mahomedan governor, Obedulláh Khan, closed the gates of the city, and for two months a guerilla warfare was carried on. At length the gates were opened without much bloodshed. Obedulláh was pardoned, out of consideration for his learing, but Dáúd Khan was cast into a dungeon in the fort, where he remained till he was released, two months after, through the mediation of the citizens. Láhore was now in the possession of the three rulers, and the whole country, as far as Ráwalpindi and the Khanpur valley, was occupied by the Sikhs, unopposed by the Ghakkars, the warlike race who had resisted so desperately the arms of the once powerful Moghals.

Moulvi Obedulláh appointed Afghan governor of Láhore.

Ahmad Shah retires to Kábul.

The Sikhs masters of the country as far as Ráwalpindi, 1768.

Ahmad Shah did not long survive these events. After suppressing a rebellion in Khorasán, he returned to Kandahar, where his malady increased. At Murgháb, in June 1773, Ahmad Shah, probably the most intrepid, active, successful and accomplished general and military genius of the age, breathed his last, in the fiftieth year of his reign. If we compare him with

Death of Ahmad Shah, Abdáli, June 1773.

His character.

the majority of Asiatic rulers, we find him more lenient and less grasping than those whom he subdued; to his subjects, considerate and just to a degree; to those whom he admitted to his society, affable, hilarious and free; to those who suffered in his cause, or in any way aided him, bountiful and generous; to the poor and needy, ever friendly and charitable; and to the rebellious more severe than the severest. As a conqueror, his sceptre extended from Khorasán to Sirhind and from the Oxus to the Persian Gulf. His enemies trembled and his friends took fresh courage at the mention of his name. He courted the society of learned men, and showed the greatest respect to the leaders of religion. He was himself highly educated, and he encouraged learning in others, wherever he found it practicable. He maintained his dignity in public with all the solemnity and grandeur of an Asiatic potentate, and was very punctilious in all State ceremonials. That he often had recourse to fraudulent means and bloodshed, in order to attain his end, may be admitted; but at the same time, we must look to the usages of the times, and judge of his conduct by the prevailing customs of contemporary Asiatic monarchs, who, we find, employed treachery in all their dealings. With all his faults, we cannot but admire the man for his undaunted spirit, military talent and indefatigable energy.

Tymúr Shah, son of the deceased, proclaimed king of Kábul, 1773.

On the death of Ahmad Shah, his grand wazír, Shah Wali Khan, placed his son-in-law, prince Sulemán Shah, second son of the deceased, on the Kábul throne. Tymúr Shah,* the eldest son, who was educated at his father's court, and was his companion in most of his expeditions, was at the time at Herat. Hearing of the wazír's treachery, he marched to Kandahar with a large force of Durránis and Emaks. Sulemán, on hearing of Tymúr's approach, vacated the throne, and Tymúr Shah was at once universally accepted, and duly proclaimed the lawful heir and successor of Ahmad Shah, by the principal chiefs and supporters of his clan in A.D. 1773.†

His administrative measures at home.

The first act of Tymúr Shah, after establishing himself in undisturbed and undisputed possession of his father's throne, was to procure the assassination of Shah Wali Khan, together with his two sons and two cousins. He next proceeded to confer the high dignity and office of grand wazír on Kázi Fyzullah, a Mullah of Doulat Shahi family, and to raise Abdul Latif Khan, of Jám in Khorasán, and Mullah Abdul Ghaffar,‡ to high offices in the State. He reposed the greatest confidence in the loyalty and prowess of his Durráni troops, and he enlisted in his army the Persians and the Tájaks, who were unconnected with the Afghans, and entirely devoted to his person. His mind and mental disposition were those of a financier rather than a warrior, economy appearing to be his special forte, and his policy was based on the conviction that internal peace was the surest means of effecting this end.

He wages war against Sindh.

Tymúr waged war against the Talpur family of Sindh. The possessions of the Sikhs about this time in the Panjáb extended from Saháranpúr in the

* He was born at Mashhed in the month of December 1746, A.D.

† Tymúr Shah, having ascended the throne, struck a coin in his name with this inscription:—

چرخ مي آرد طلا و نقره از خورشيد و ماه – تا زند بر چهره نقش سکهٔ تيمور شاه

"Heaven has borrowed gold and silver from the sun and moon that the coin of Tymúr Shah be struck on its face."

The following was the inscription on his seal:—

علم شد از عنايات الهي — بعالم دولت تيمور شاهي

"Through the grace of God, the kingdom of Tymúr Shah became conspicuous in the world."

‡ The Mullah was a native of Láhore and son of a Hindu Kalál. He was made a convert by Ahmad Shah Abdáli, and under his care became an eminent Arabic scholar.

But refrains, for the present, from meddling with the affairs of the Panjáb.

east, to Attock on the west, and from Multán and Sindh in the south, to Kangrá, Jammu and Bhimber on the north. Tymúr Shah found it beyond his power to settle the affairs of the Panjáb, or to check the progress of the Sikhs by force of arms, the Sikh chiefs freely utilizing the services of the zemindars who had revolted from the Durráni king, and being thereby considerably strengthened in the prosecution of their exploits of rapine and plunder. The independent Sikh sardars became complete masters of their own districts, exercising supreme power over, and for the benefit of, the clans to which they were respectively attached.

The formation of Sikh confederacies.

The various clans under their respective chiefs were leagued together, and formed a confederacy, which they denominated *misl* or "similitude," thereby implying that the chief and followers of one clan were equal to those of another. As the chieftains administered the country according to the law laid down by the founder of their religion, and as they were bound, by this law, to aid one another in support of their religion and country, a law which they scrupulously obeyed, this *misl* may be aptly termed a theocracy. To such a form of government, it was essentially necessary that some person should be appointed to the head of affairs, and they accordingly agreed by common consent to be guided in all matters in which united action might be requisite, by the spiritual head of their church. This personage was appointed, from time to time, by the popular voice of *Khálsá*. A national league was also established at Amritsar by the Akálís.

The national league at Amritsar.

The *Akális* or immortals.

The business conducted at these conventions.

The holy cakes.

It was the duty of this convention, aided by their spiritual preceptor, in the interpretation of the "*Daswán Badshah ka Granth*," or, "The Book of the Tenth Guru," to look to the administration of home and foreign affairs; to arrange and plan expeditions; to avert national danger, and to educate the people in the doctrines of their religion. Holy cakes were distributed on this occasion in commemoration of the injunction of Nának, saluted by the assembly and eaten. All bowed their heads before the sacred book, the *Akálís*, the *Khálsá's* own heroes, exclaiming, "*Wáh Guru ji ka Khálsá; Wáh Guru ji ki Fatteh* ("The *Khálsá* is of the Lord; Victory is to the Lord"). During this ceremony the *rubabis* sang the national anthem, and the musicians played martial and sacred tunes for the diversion of the assembly.

The system of military service explained.

All booty was equally divided among the chiefs, and these, in their turn, subdivided a portion of it among their dependents. The fighting members, however, received their pay from a national fund, to which they contributed by means of plunder and fraud. They received no fixed salary, but were paid according to the state of the aforesaid fund, and were quite at liberty to abandon the profession of arms or to transfer their military allegiance from one chief to another. Many of the boldest of these adventurers, succeeded in establishing parties of their own. Those who were fortunate enough to raise large and powerful bands were acknowledged as independent chiefs, by their compatriots, while those who were less successful, amalgamated their retinues with those of other chiefs. It behoved the chiefs, on all occasions, to be very assiduous in their attention to the wants and wishes of their followers, for it was only by such means that they could hope to retain them in their service, the slightest show of indifference exhibited by a chief to the interests of his fighting men, invariably ending in the latter going over to another chief.

The chiefs and fighting men.

Their mutual relations how regulated.

This system of volunteering their services for national emergencies and plunder, with liberty to leave the profession of arms whenever they might chose to do so, was, at least, beneficial to themselves, if not to the State, for they were sure of having their interests and welfare attended to by their superiors, since neglect on the part of the latter, in these matters, would be the seal of their own ruin.

The Sikhs attributed all their victories to Govind, for they believed they were invisibly led on by him against the enemy. Whether they plundered, robbed, killed, mutilated, or committed any other species of outrage upon their enemies, they invariably called upon the name of Govind. For Govind they fought with the utmost fanaticism; for Govind they died with the calmest resignation. As Singhs, or lions, they lived, fought and died, and, as Singhs, their memories are cherished by their successors.

They all fought in the name of Govind.

During the period of which we are writing, it was customary to build towns and villages on elevations surrounded by walls,—primarily as watch-towers, and secondly, as forts in case of emergency.

Persons were not considered to have attained manhood, or to have any just claim to their wives and children, goods and chattels, &c., &c., until such time as they could prove their rights by the argument of the sword or lance. The agriculturist found, by experience, that the sword and musket were as necessary implements of his calling as the plough, for he dared not attend to his work unarmed. None could hope for membership in the *Khálsá* or governing body, without proficiency in equitation and arms.

Proficiency in arms an essential quality for becoming a member of the predominating *Khálsá*.

When the Mahomedans were the predominating power in the Panjáb, they treated the Sikhs with little consideration, and it was now their turn to suffer. They were employed by the ruling race in the most menial capacities, agriculture being about the most honourable profession in which they were allowed to engage, and, in this, only as tenants.

Treatment of the Mahomedans by the Sikhs.

They were persecuted in every conceivable manner, their mosques being desecrated and turned into pigsties, and their men into swineherds. The grandest of their shrines were utilized as magazines and arsenals. In the meanest of the mosques (which were in a dilapidated condition previous to the Sikh ascendency), the Muslims used to assemble secretly to offer up prayers; but even in these they dared not pray aloud, for fear of their enemies falling upon and annihilating them. They were forbidden the use of beef as an article of food, and those who showed any predilection for it were despatched precipitately to the next world, (the cow being considered the most sacred animal of this world by the followers of Govind).

They were treated as a despised race and deprived of their liberties.

The Mazhabi Sikhs, *i.e.*, those Mahomedans who had embraced the religion of Govind, fared very little better than those who adhered to the faith of their fathers. They were not appointed to any post of trust under their conquerors, and were little better than serfs. The majority of the well-to-do Mahomedans emigrated into British territory, and claimed the protection of its rules. Here they were allowed to follow their religion unmolested. The *muazzan* could now fearlessly summon the faithful to the performance of their devotion, and his stentorian voice gladdened the hearts of those who had so long been in bondage, and who had been prevented by their idolatrous and infidel masters from performing their religious duties according to their divine law. Politics and religion could here be discussed freely; subjects of which they could only dream while under the control of the *Khálsá*.

Most of them consequently emigrated to British India, where they enjoyed the blessings of freedom.

The country at this time in possession of the Sikhs comprised almost the whole of the Panjáb, including a portion of Multán, and most of the territory lying between the Jamna and the Sutlej, and bounded on the north and west by the Indus, on the east by the territories of the rájás of Jammu and Nadaon, and on the south by the territories of the British Government, and the sandy deserts of Jesalmer and Hissar. A general estimate of the value of this country may be formed from the fact that, in

Sikh possessions in the Panjáb at this time.

addition to other countries, it comprised the whole province of Láhore which, according to the calculation made by Bernier, produced, in the reign of Aurangzeb, two hundred and forty-six lacs and ninety-five thousand rupees, or two millions four hundred and sixty-nine thousand five-hundred pounds sterling.

The different denominations of the Sikhs explained.

Before proceeding with our narrative of the Sikh *misls*, or confederacies, it may be interesting to note here the different denominations by which they were known in the country, and give a brief account of the form of their government and their mode of living. First of these are the *Malwa* Sikhs, so called for their extraordinary gallantry under the Byragi Bandá, who, when pleased with their deeds of valour, was said to have foretold, in the joy of victory, that their country would be as rich as Malwa, a province of Hindostán, formerly under Doulat Rao Sindhia, and famous for its salubrious climate, fertility and great population. These Sikhs were originally the Hindus of the *Ját* and Gujar tribes, and inhabited the country between the Sutlej and the Jamna. The most powerful among the Malwa Singhs were Sahib Singh of Patiálá, Bhangá Singh of Thanesar, Bhág Singh of Jhind, and Bhalel Singh of Kythal. Sirhind was also situated in their territories, but was, during the period of which we are writing, only the shadow of its former grandeur. Its once royal palaces, magnificent edifices and majestic mosques, of which any city might have been proud, were no longer gazed upon with curiosity, wonder and amazement by sightseers, the spoliation of the former capital of this country having been completed by the Byragi Bandá.

The *Malwa* Sikhs.

The *Doába* Sikhs.

Next came the *Doába* Singhs, who inhabited the country between the Sutlej and the Biás, called the Jalandar Bist, or Jalandar Doáb, foremost among them being Tara Singh, a chief of considerable power and influence. The country was the richest of the Sikh possessions, and well-known for its healthy climate and fertility.

The *Mánjha* Sikhs.

The *Mánjha* Singhs inhabited the county between the Biás and the Rávi called the Bari Doáb. The great cities of Láhore and Amritsar were in this province, and consequently it was the great centre of the Sikh power. The principal chiefs of this country were the ancestors of Ranjít Singh, who afterwards became the founder of the Sikh monarchy, Fatteh Singh, Ahluwalia and Jodh Singh, Ramgarhia.

The *Dharapi* Sikhs.

The *Dhanigheb* and *Naki* Sikhs.

The Sikhs who inhabited the country between the Rávi and the Chináb, were called the *Dharapi* Singhs from the country being called Dharapi. The Sikhs between the Chináb and the Jhelum were called *Dhanigheb*, and those who resided in Multán, the *Naki* Singhs. The Sikhs on the borders of Sindh, and those settled on the Jhelum, delighted in picking quarrels with the Mahomedan chiefs on their borders, with a view to making predatory excursions into their country, the result of which was that skirmishes and petty engagements between these parties were of constant occurrence.

The weapons of the earlier Sikhs.

The majority of the Sikhs were good horsemen. When equipped for the field, they generally carried sword, spear and musket. The archers used the cross-bow, the weapon of their forefathers. The infantry were generally utilized in garrisoning the forts. The cavalry may be said to have been constantly on field service, for they were always on the lookout for plunder, and were continually watching the movements of their enemies on the borders. The use of cannon was unknown among the early Sikhs, and was gradually introduced as their resources increased and their civil and military power developed. It is believed that in 1800 A.D. the Sikhs had only 40* pieces of field artillery.

* *Life of George Thomson*, by Franklin.

They were addicted to bhang.

The Sikhs used opium and also indulged freely in the use of *bhang*,* which they called *sukha*,† from its supposed comforting and soothing effect. The use of tobacco was unknown to them, and it is still forbidden, except in the case of such Sikhs, the followers of Nának, as reject the institutions of Govind. They also indulged to excess in the use of spirituous liquors, and in justification of their so doing, quoted the following passages from the *Adi Granth*, which say "Eat and give unto others to eat. Drink and give unto others to drink. Be happy and make others happy." The Hindu Shastras were also quoted in support of excess in drinking.‡

And indulged in the use of spirituous liquors.

Their food.

The Sikhs, with the exception of the converts from the Brahmans and *Chhatrias*, ate all kinds of animal food but beef (the slaughtering of cows being looked upon as an act of sacrilege). They ate pork, the use of which, as human food, was prohibited by Nának, whose policy was to reconcile the Hindus with the Mahomedans, and to do away with all formal differences of caste, agreeably to his doctrine of peace and good-will to all men.

Their code of law.

The Sikhs had no code of law to guide them in the administration of affairs or the dispensation of justice to the people, their scriptures, which inculcate general maxims of justice, being seldom acted upon and having no legally binding force. In fact their strict application, or a wilful departure from them, were simple matters of convenience, and such questions were dealt with in reference to the circumstance of each case, and the exigency of the moment, rather than with any regard to the teachings of their leader, as laid down in the *Granth*, or sacred book.

Their administration of civil and criminal justice.

The administration of civil and criminal justice was vested in a *panchayet*, composed of elders, or in a sardar or chief of the tribe, the decision of one or the other being binding. As in the Middle Ages, crimes and tresspasses were expiated by money, the fines being without limit, and estimated, not so much according to the gravity of the offence as the means of the offender. These amercements helped to enrich the chief, or sardar, in whose territory the crime was committed, and, as a rule, they were inflicted for this very purpose. In the event of the fine so inflicted not being paid, all the criminal's relations were seized and cruelly punished along with him, with a view to making them disgorge the amount. The most cruel measures were adopted to elicit confessions, and to extort money for real or supposed injuries. If the offender managed to obtain an acquittal, he paid a *shukráná*, or a present of thanksgiving; if he was convicted, he paid a heavy *jarmáná* or fine; if he did neither, he was thrown into a *Taikháná*,§ or dungeon, and remained there until he satisfied the cupidity of the chief, or until he was removed by death. Capital punishment was unknown, the murderer being, in every case, made over bodily to the relations of the deceased to be lynched. However a murderer might be treated by the relations of the murdered person, whether hanged, drawn, quartered, stoned, suffocated, drowned, staked, decapitated, flayed, roasted, or toasted, it was regarded simply as retributive justice. The most heinous offences were punished with the loss of sight, mutilation of the hands, or deprivation of the nose‖ or ears, though

Punishment of the murderers.

---

* *Cannabis stiras*, an inebriating drug.

† *Sukha* in Bengal is a term generally applied to *dry tobacco*, which is used with the *bhang*. The latter is usually rubbed into a ball (wet) in the palm of the hand, and a small quantity of the former is then added, in order to make it dry enough to smoke. *Bhang* is used as a beverage in the Panjáb.

‡ Liquor inspired manly deeds, courage and resolution. The goddess Durga used it, and was under its influence when she slew Mahishasúr.

§ Called also *bora* or dugeon in the Panjábi.

‖ Mutilation does not appear to be the peculiar characteristic of eastern nations. Statutes were passed in the reigns of Henry the VIII., Edward the VI., Elizabeth, and James I., direct the most incorrigible culprit was, in most instances, let off on payment of a heavy fine.

Mode of disposing of cases of larceny.

In cases of larceny, the party injured, had first to pay the magistrate, or *thanadar*, a sum of money equal to one fourth of the value of the article stolen; the money so paid becoming the property of these functionaries. Without this preliminary, no steps could be taken for the recovery of the property. In the event of the property being recovered, the culprit was handed over to lynch law, though in most cases a *mahar khái*, or approver, stipulated for a full pardon if the delinquent offered a handsome *nazráná*, or present of gratitude, to the chief and magistrate, which was considered as their due, and divided equally among them. The sufferer was kindly advised to keep on his guard, and take good care of his property in future, and, with this satisfaction for the wrong done him, he was dismissed.

Theft

In cases of theft of cattle the rules as to tracks *khoj,** or *surágh*, were strictly followed, so far as the detection of the thief was concerned, and when stolen cattle were tracked into another's ground, the latter was compelled to show the track beyond the boundary of his own land or village, or to pay the value of the stolen cattle.

And highway robbery.

In cases of highway robbery and burglary, the injured parties usually adopted similar means to the aggressor's for the recovery of their property or its equivalent. Unless restitution was made previous to the aggrieved parties arming, blood was sure to be spilt in the settlement of the dispute. The chiefs themselves harboured thieves and robbers and participated in their booty.† Their share of the spoil was known by the term *kundi*, namely, such portion of the plundered property as, by division, fell to the share of the chief.

Boundary disputes.

Boundary disputes among zemindars were, in most cases, attended with bloodshed, which was atoned for by the gift of a daughter in marriage to the nearest relation of the deceased, or the payment of a heavy sum of money, or the surrender of 125 bighas of land.

Duty on land

The Sikhs levied revenue in kind for the grain, half of which was the share of the chief, or sardar, under whom the *raiyat* served, while the other went to the proprietor. All other produce, such as sugarcane, cotton, poppy, indigo, melons, &c., was paid for in cash. Heavy duties were levied on merchandise by each chief as it passed through his dominions; the result of this being that traders were never safe, and suffered much. Every chief exercised the power of taxing trade by prescription. The shawl trade was carried on between Jammu, Srinagar and Nadaon, but the merchants preferred adopting the difficult mountainous routes to reach India, so as to avoid the unjust demands of the Sikhs. The charge of the *caravans* was most frequently given to *Nánakputras* or descendants of Nának, who, owing to the sanctity of their persons, enjoyed certain privileges, and were less exposed to the lawlessness of the Sikh custom houses. They had the reputation of being a mild and inoffensive race, and were revered by all the followers of the Guru, who considered it a sacrilege to molest the race

And merchandise.

The *Nánakputras*.

---

ing the loss of the sight and left hand and of an ear for heinous offences. "An eye for eye, and a tooth for tooth," is the Mosaic law. This law is the law of retaliation. The penalties of mutilation passed during the reign of the British monarchs, as quoted, were for heinous offences. But with Asiatic monarchs it is frequently resorted to in order to gratify a whim, and in the absence frequently of all crime.

* It would thus appear that the law as to tracks now followed in the courts of the Panjáb, was the law which the ancient Sikhs followed. Its success in most cases of cattle-lifting in districts abounding with jungle Bár, where the offence is of frequent occurrence, is quite marked.

† Not an uncommon practice even now with the headmen of villages in the jungle Bár.

of the founder of their faith. They never carried arms, and pursued peaceful occupations, generally as travelling merchants.*

Revenue defaulters.

Revenue defaulters and debtors, absconding to the territory of another chief, and seeking his protection, were not molested, the pettiest chief invariably refusing to deliver up any person claiming his protection. The delinquent was, however, given to understand that he would have to discharge his debt in full as soon as the opportunity occurred for his so doing.

The Sikhs believed in witchcraft.

The Sikhs were all believers in witchcraft and sorcery. If any member of the community was attacked with a severe and sudden illness, vomited blood, or suffered anything unusual, the nature of which could not be readily understood, it was attributed to necromancy, or an evil spirit, or the machination and malice of an enemy. The possession of a waxen image or dough effigy, half burnt human bones, or an amulet, or charm wrapped up in paper and labelled, found in the house or on the person of the suspected individual, was regarded as unmistakeable proof of witchcraft. It was not an uncommon practice to bring charges of sorcery against persons in the courts of justice, and there have even been instances of such prosecutions being instituted in British courts in early times, while it was invariably only with considerable difficulty that the prosecutors were persuaded to withdraw their absurd complaints.†

The *Satti* rites.

Cases of *satti*, or women burning themselves with the corpse of their husbands, were of frequent occurrence among the Sikhs. In all cases, however, they were understood to be willing victims, a slow, reluctant promise exacted from, or made by, the wretched woman, under the influence of grief, being considered sufficient warrant for immolating her upon the funeral pyre of her deceased lord. A multitude immediately assembled round the house of the miserable creature, and a host of females surrounded her person ; noise and uproar, confusion and clamour ensued ; hopes were held out of embracing the departed husband in paradise after the hour of trial was over, and that both would live there in perpetual peace and happiness ; no time was given for reflection ; she was hurried off to the altars of her lord and to the land of promise.

Forced labour.

Another barbarous practice of the Sikhs in those days was that of compelling people to work without payment or compensation of any kind. This was called by them *kar begar*, and was very oppressively felt by the poorer classes.

It is now necessary to give a brief outline of each of the Sikh *misls* or confederacies referred to in this chapter, as they materially contributed to the establishment of the Sikhs as a power in the Panjáb.

---

* When that illustrious British commander, Lord Lake, entered the Panjáb in 1805, the principal chiefs requested general protection for *Ndnakputras*, on account of their religious sanctity, which, it was said, enabled them to move about uninjured where the most deadly conflicts existed. The request was graciously granted.

† Such charges have certainly been brought into the courts in England, and many instances are on record of persons being sentenced to be burnt to death. Thus, Mathew Hale, I believe, was the last judge in England who passed such a sentence for such an offence. The Bible gives instances of witches ; see the following passages ;—

Exodus,	22nd	chapter,	18th	verse,
1st Samuel,	15th	„	23rd	„
Deuteronomy,	18th	„	10th	„
2nd Kings,	9th	„	22nd	„
2nd Chronicles,	33rd	„	6th	„
Micah,	5th	„	12th	„
Nahum,	3rd	„	4th	„

The *Qurán*, too, gives many instances ; see the 113th Sura, entitled "Daybreak," and innumerable other instances.

CHAPTER IV.

THE HISTORY OF THE SIKH *MISLS*.

I.—THE BHANGI *MISL*.

Chajjá Singh founds the confederacy.

CHAJJÁ Singh, *Ját*, a native of Panjwár, eight miles from Amritsar, was initiated into the *Páhal* of the Guru by the Byragi Bandá, on whose death, he converted three other *Játs*, his relations, named Bhím Singh, known also as Bhímá Singh, an inhabitant of Kasúr, Mallá Singh and Jagat Singh. These three, becoming great friends, began to co-operate for purposes of plunder, and were joined in their marauding excursions by Mihán Singh and Guláb Singh of Dhousá, six miles north-east of Amritsar, Karur Singh of Choupal, Gurbaksh Singh, a Sindhú *Ját* of Roránwálá, Agar Singh, *Gangora*, and Sánwan Singh, *Randháwa*, who all became Sikhs of the Guru, receiving their *Páhal* from Chajjá Singh, who was revered as a Guru. The members of the confederacy were much addicted to the use of *bhang*, an intoxicating drug, which is manufactured from hemp, whence they were denominated the Bhangi *misl*. Numerous Sikhs joined the *misl* from all sides, and the armed ruffians began to make night attacks upon villages, carrying away everything of value which they could lay hands on. The success with which they met in their first plundering excursions, was so encouraging, that they now determined to try what the force of their arms could do as regards territorial acquisitions. They thought the time had now arrived when they could look for the fulfilment of Govind's prophecy, which was to the effect that, at no distant date, his followers would make themselves masters of the country. Chajjá Singh, on his death, was succeeded by Bhím Singh, who gave the confederacy an organized form, and who may be called the real founder of the powerful Bhangi *misl*. After Nádir Shah's invasion, Bhím Singh, with the assistance of his allies Mallá Singh and Jagat Singh, recruited his forces from the neighbouring clans, and thus made himself the head of by far the most powerful section of the confederacy.

His associates in his exploits.

The members of the confederacy are addicted to *bhang*.

Chajjá Singh on his death is succeeded by Bhím Singh.

On the death of Bhím Singh, his nephew and adopted son, Hari Singh, became chief of the Bhangi *misl*. He had all the spirit of a daring freebooting chief. He organized large bands of robbers, with which he overran the country, destroying and plundering the towns and villages. Not only did the *misl* increase in numerical strength under him, but its daring exploits, often attended with rich booty, made it the wealthiest of all the *misls*. The fighting strength of the Bhangi *misl* about this time was 20,000 men, who were distributed over various portions of the country. He fixed his head-quarters at the village Gilwáli, in the Amritsar district, capturing Siálkot, Kariál and Mirowál. He extended his ravages to Chiniot and Jhang, and made war on the Abdáli king, Ahmad Shah. In the year 1762, he fell on Kot Khwajá Said, two miles from Láhore, where Khwajá Obed, the Afghan governor of Láhore, had a large magazine, containing arms, ordnance and munitions of war, the whole of which Hari Sing carried off.

Who is succeeded by Hari Singh, his nephew.

Hari Singh establishes himself in Gilwáli.

His conquests.

The Sikhs under Hari Singh next swept over the Indus and the Deraját country. Their generals conquered Ráwalpindi, subdued the Malwa and the Mánjha countries, sacked Jammu, at the head of 12,000 cavalry, made Ranjít Deo, the Rájput Rájá of Jammu, their tributary, and penetrated into the Káshmír Valley, where, however, they were repulsed with loss. On the Jamna, Rai Singh, Bhangi, and Bhagat Singh Karor Singhia, harassed the old Najíb-ud-doula, who aimed at checking the progress of these federal chiefs through the aid of the combined forces of the Rohillas and Mahrattas, in which he would probably have succeeded, had not his death at this critical period put an end to his project.

In 1763 Hari Singh joined the Kanhias and Ramgarhias in an attack on Kasúr, and the following year he fought Amar Singh of Patiálá, but was killed in the action.

He joins the Kanhias and the Ramgarhias.

Is killed in a battle, 1764.

Hari Singh had two wives, by one of whom, the daughter of Choudhri Malla, of Panjwár, near Taran Taran, he had two sons, Jhandá Singh and Gandá Singh, and by the other Charat Singh, Diwán Singh and Bassu Singh. Jhandá Singh succeeded his father in the leadership of the confederacy, which reached its zenith under him. He and his brothers associated themselves with many illustrious chiefs, Sahib Singh, of Siálkot, Rái Singh of Buriá, Bhag Singh of Hallowál, Sudh Singh Dodia, and Nidhán Singh Attu.

Jhandá Singh, his son, succeeds him.

In 1766 Jhandá Singh, at the head of a large force, marched towards Multán, and declared war against Shujá Khan, the Mahomedan governor, and the Dáúdputras, who had emigrated from Sindh during the commotions which followed the invasion of Nádir Shah, and had settled in the country now known as Bahávalpur. A battle was fought on the banks of the Sutlej, with no decisive results; and a treaty was at length concluded between the invaders and Mobárik Khan, the Dáúdputras chief, and the Multán governor, declaring Pákpattan the line of demarcation between the possessions of the Sikhs and the Mussalmans.

He marches to Multán, 1766.

Treaty of peace concluded.

Jhandá Singh next directed his attention towards the Pathan colony of Kasúr, which he subdued, and then, disregarding his treaty with the Multán chief, he made a fresh invasion into their territories in 1771. The fort was besieged for a month and a half, but the Dáúdputras and the Afghan force under Jahán Khan, compelled the Sikh general, Majjá Singh, to raise the siege, and repulsed him with great loss.

Jhandá Singh subdues Kasúr.

Invades Multán a second time, 1771.

Ill-success of the campaign.

In the next year, (1772) Jhandá Singh, joined by Lahná Singh and other Sikh sardars, marched again on Multán, under more favourable circumstances, and consequently with better success. A quarrel arose between the successive governors of Multán, Shujá Khan, Sharif Khan, *Saddozie*, and Sharif Beg *Taklú*. The lastnamed chief sought the aid of Jhandá Singh, which was very readily given. Jhandá Singh appeared at Multán with his brother, Gandá Singh and general Lahná Singh, at the head of a well equipped and powerful army, and immediately attacked Shujá Khan and the Dáúdputras, over whom he gained a complete victory, the defending forces suffering heavy loss. The victors seized Multán for themselves, and divided it between Jhandá Singh and Lahná Singh, who appointed one Diwán Singh, *Chhachowalia*, as *killádar*, and garrisoned the place with their own troops. Sharif Beg, having been thus deceived, fled to Kheyrpur, where he died of a broken heart.

Third invasion of Multán, 1772.

The Sikhs conquer Multán, 1772.

On his return from Multán, Jhandá Singh subdued the Bilúch country which he pillaged, and, capturing Jhang, conquered Mánkhera and Kálá Bagh. He, however, failed in an attempt to carry Shujaábád, built by the Afghans after the loss of Multán. He next visited Amritsar, where he built a brick fort, which he named the Bhangi killa (the ruins of which are still to be seen behind the *Loon Mandi*) and laid out fine bazars. He then

Jhanda Singh overruns the Bilúch country and captures Jhang, Mánkhera and Kálá Bagh.

Visits Amritsar, 1772.

Founds the Bhangi killa.

Recovers the Bhangi *top*.

proceeded to Ramnagar, where he recovered the famous *zamzama*,* or Bhangi gun, from the Chattas. After this he marched on Jammu, at the head of a large army, and made war on Jay Singh, the rising leader of the Kanhia *misl*, and Charat Singh of the Sukerchakia *misl*, for their having aided Brij Ráj Deo, the rival claimant of the Jammu chiefship, against his ally and tributary, Rájá Ranjít Deo, father of the refractory chief. The fighting was carried on for several days without any decisive result. At length Charat Singh, Sukerchakia, was accidentally killed by the bursting of his own matchlock. At one time the Bhangis appeared likely to win the day, but the death of Jhandá Singh, (who was shot by a Mazabhi Sikh, one of his own followers who had been bribed to do so by Jay Singh), decided the contest in favour of the Kanhia *misl*.

Wars with Jay Singh the Kanhia, and Charat Singh the Sukerchakia.

Is assassinated, 1774.

Succeeded by Gandá Singh his brother.

After the assassination of Jhandá Singh, Gandá Singh, brother of the deceased, was unanimously appointed to the leadership of the *misl*, now in the zenith of its power. Gandá Singh collected a large number of workmen, completed the works of improvement which had been commenced by his brother at Amritsar, finished and strengthened the Bhangi fort, and enlarged and beautified the town with many noble edifices.

Who enlarges and beautifies the town of Amritsar.

The treachery of the Kanhias, which had brought about the death of his brother, rankled in the mind of Gandá Singh, and a pretext for giving vent to his injured feelings was not long wanting. Jhandá Singh had bestowed Pathankot, on one of his *misldárs*, Nand Singh, who died about the same time as his chief, leaving a widow and a beautiful daughter. The widow gave her daughter in marriage to Tárá Singh, brother of Hakíkat Singh, Kanhia. She also gave the Pathankot jágír to her son-in-law. Both these acts very much annoyed Gandá Singh. He asked the Kanhias to deliver Pathankot over to him, but they insisted upon holding it as their rightful possession. Thereupon Gandá Singh, collecting a large army, and taking with him the Bhangi gun, proceeded to Pathankot, *viâ* the Batála road, and was joined by many of the Ramgarhia sardars. Tárá Singh and Hakíkat Singh were joined by the Kanhia *misl*, under Gurbaksh Singh, son of Jay Singh, Kanhia, and Amar Singh Bhuggá. The two armies met at Dína-nagar, and fought for several days, without decisive result. Hostilities ceased after ten days' incessant fighting, in consequence of the sudden death of Gandá Singh, from illness. His son, Desa Singh, being a minor, the soldiers elected his nephew, Charat Singh, to the command of the *misl*. In one of the early engagements, however, Chárat Singh was killed at Pathankot. His death spread dismay among the troops of the Bhangi *misl*, who fled, leaving Pathankot and the surrounding country in the hands of the Kanhias. The Bhangis then elected Desa Singh, son of Gandá Singh, as their leader, and returned to Amritsar, with Gujar Singh, the new minister of Desa Singh. It was hardly to be expected, however, that the chiefs who had been inured to campaigning, and whose pride it was to lead their forces against the enemy, under Sardars Hari Singh and Jhandá Singh, would tamely submit to be governed by a stripling. Many sardars became independent, among them being Bhág Singh, Hallowalia. The tribute from Jhang was stopped, and Multán was soon after lost. Muzaffar Khan, son of Shujá Khan, assisted by his ally, the Báháwalpur chief, made an attempt to recover Multán in 1777. He was, however, repulsed by Diwán Singh, the governor of Jhandá Singh, though not without great

Wars against the Kanhias.

Marches against Pathankot.

Dies.

Charat Singh, his nephew, succeeds.

Is killed.

Desa Singh succeeds.

* This was the large gun captured by Sir Henry Hardinge at the head of Her Majesty's 80th Foot and 1st European Light Infantry at Ferose Shahr, on the night of 21st December 1845. It is still at Láhore, being placed in front of the gate of the Central Museum, an object of great historical interest to the curious visitor.

Tymúr Shah invades the Panjáb.

He is betrayed by general Fyzullah Khan.

Terrible massacre at Peshávar.

loss on the side of the latter. And now a greater calamity was awaiting the Sikhs. Tymúr Shah, who had succeeded his father, Ahmad Shah, on the throne of Kábul, determined to recover his lost territories in the Panjáb. He accordingly, sent his general, Fyzulluh Khan, to Peshávar, to levy troops, to make an attack on the Panjáb. The general assembled a considerable * number of the Afghans, chiefly from the Khaibar tribes, with the avowed object of punishing the Sikhs, but entered into a secret plot with Mian Mohamed, son of Shekh Omer, the Sahibzada of Chamkanni, a declared enemy of the Shah, to put an end to the king's life. He marched his troops to the citadel of Peshávar on pretence of parading them before the king; but when they reached the fort, they cut to pieces the guards at the gates and forced their way in. Tymúr Shah ascended the upper story of his palace, and made his situation known to the guards. The Gholám Sháhis, the king's own body guards, and the Durránis, attacked Fyzullah's men, and a terrible slaughter ensued, ending in the arrest of Fyzullah and his son who were both tortured to death.†

Tymúr Shah sends troops against Multán.

The Sikhs repulse the Afghans, 1777-78.

The prince marches to Multán in person, 1778-79.

The Sikhs are defeated in a battle.

Tymúr Shah appoints Shujá Khan to the government of Multán.

The Afghans overrun Báháwalpur and Sindh.

Tymúr Shah now took vigorous steps to prosecute his plans regarding Sindh, Báháwalpur and the lower Panjáb. In the season of 1777-78 he sent two detachments of Afghan troops to expel the Sikhs from Multán, but without success. The Afghans were repulsed with great loss, and Haini Khan, who commanded the expedition, was tied to a cannon and blown away by the Sikhs. In the winter of 1778-79, the incensed Shah marched in person to chastise the Sikhs. Gandá Singh, the Bhangi chief, was at this time embroiled with the leaders of the rival *misls*, and the operations of the Shah against Multán were successful. A desperate fight took place. The Shah's troops numbered 18,000, consisting of Eusafzies, Durránis, Moghals and Kazalbáshes, all under the command of Zangi Khan, the Durráni chief. After a stubborn fight in the field, the hill veterans of the Shah carried the day. The Sikhs fled in great disorder, pursued by the victorious Afghans, who put a large number of them to the sword. The generals who conducted the battle on the side of the Shah, were Zangi Khan, *Kamálzie* and Bahádur Khan son of Fyz Talab Khan *Mahomedsie*. About 3,000 Sikhs were killed in this battle, while 2,000 were drowned in their attempt to cross the river. The heads of several thousand Sikhs laden on camels, were sent to Peshávar as trophies, and exhibited there to the terror and astonishment of the people. After this victory, Tymúr Shah bestowed the governorship of Multán on Shujá Khan, father of Mozaffar Khan, surnamed Safdar Jang, who retained it until expelled by Ranjít Singh. The Shah then subdued Baháwal Khan‡ the Abbási chief of Báháwalpur. The town of Báháwalpur was pillaged, and many of its edifices were burnt. The Nawáb's arsenals, together with a portion of the fort, were blown up. The Nawáb was at length compelled to pay an annual tribute, and the Afghan troops withdrew. The Shah then reduced to subjection the Tálpurs of

---

* According to the memoirs of Abdul Karim *Ulvi*, 25,000 troops were collected by Fyzullah Khan on this occasion.

† According to the author of *Tárik-i-Ahmad Shahi*, 6,000 men were slaughtered by the Jamshedi, the Kalmak, the Gholam Shahi, and the Durráni troops of the Shah. Elphinstone says no distinction was made between the innocent and the guilty in the slaughter which followed. The courtyard of the palace and the royal harem were covered with the bodies of the dead, and many *ulemas*, or learned men, of Peshávar were put to the sword.—*Tárikh-i-Ahmadi*, page 19.

‡ His name was Rukun-ud-dín, surnamed "Mahomed Bhawal Khan Bahádur Nasrat Jang Hafiz-ul-Mulk," a title given to him by the Delhi emperor. He was a *Hafiz*, that is, he could repeat the *Qurán* by heart, and was well versed in Mahomedan law. He was the nephew of Bhawal Khan I., who founded Baháwalpur, and extended his conquest from Bikaner to the Lakhi jungles.

Sindh, who agreed to pay him subsidy. On the Tálpurs agreeing to pay the revenue, the Shah appointed Mir Fateh Ali Shah his viceroy in Sindh.

Desa Singh marches to Chiniot.

Is killed, 1782.

After these incidents Desa Singh marched to reduce Chiniot, and had many skirmishes with the Sukerchakia chief, Mahá Singh, son of Charat Singh, but was killed in action in 1782, having been eight years the head of the Bhangi *misl*.

Gurbaksh Singh, a general of Hari Singh, Bhangi.

He adopts Lahná Singh Saddhawállá as his son.

The latter quarrels with Gujar Singh, son of Gurbaksh's daughter.

Compromise between the two sardars.

One of the bravest men under Hari Singh, Bhangi, was Gurbaksh Singh of Aura, an associate of Bhím Singh, the founder of the *misl*. He was a great warrior, owned about forty villages of his own, and used to scour the country far and wide with bands of horsemen. Being childless, he adopted Lahná Singh (son of Dargáhá, a Kahilar *Ját* of Saddhawállá, in the Amritsar district), as his son. On the death of Gurbaksh Singh, Lahná Singh succeeded him, and he and Gujar Singh, son of Gurbaksh's daughter, quarrelled about the estates left by the deceased. After a fight between their armies, an arrangement was come to between the two sardars by which the estates were equally divided between them. The sardars became the most powerful of the Bhangi confederacy, and, though they joined Jhandá Singh and Gandá Singh, successors of Hari Singh, in many of their expeditions, they have a history of their own.

Kábuli Mal, the Afghan king's governor of Láhore.

Lahná Singh and Gujar Singh resolve on expelling Kábuli Mal from Láhore.

Flight of Kábuli Mal from Láhore.

When Ahmad Shah had left India after his last expedition but one, leaving a Hindu named Kábuli Mal as his governor of Lahore, sardars Lahná Singh and Gujar Singh formed a design to expel the Shah's representative from Láhore and capture the city for themselves. The Sikh horse about this time became more daring, and plundered the country up to the walls of the capital. The governor of Láhore was weak, timid and tyrannical, and, as such, was hated by the people. On receiving intelligence of the plot of the Sikhs, he became alarmed and fled, though, not without first plundering the city. He robbed the shroffs and the rich people of the city, carrying away everything which fell into his hands, and leaving his nephew, Amar Singh, in charge. The Sikhs who had pillaged all outside the city walls and its suburbs, entered the city on the second day after the departure of Kábuli Mal, and the city was given up to indiscriminate plunder, the conquerors dividing the booty equally among themselves. Kábuli Mal sought protection with Ranjít Deo, rájá of Jammu. On his way to the hills, he was roughly handled by some of the malcontents who had abandoned Láhore in consequence of the governor's grinding tyranny, but the escort sent by the Jammu rájá saved his life. He was sent to Ráwalpindi, where he was protected by a detachment of Ahmad Shah's army, stationed there, but died soon after.

His death.

Lahná Singh and Gujar Singh, Bhangis, capture Láhore, 1765.

They are joined by Sobha Singh.

Lahná Singh and Gujar Singh captured Láhore without difficulty. The victors were next morning joined by Sobha Singh, nephew of Jay Singh, Kanhia, who was allowed to participate in the spoils. Other Bhangi and Kanhia sardars followed, and last of all came in Charat Singh, Sukerchakia, who was presented by the new masters of the city with the famous *samzama* gun, which the sardar carried to Gujránwálá. The city was then divided between Lahná Singh, Gujar Singh and Sobha Singh, as was mentioned in the preceding chapter. In 1765 Gujar Singh proceeded north of the Panjáb to make new territorial acquisitions.

Irruption of Ahmad Shah into the Panjáb, 1767.

Sobha Singh and Lahná Singh remained in peace in Láhore for two years; but the spell was again broken in 1767, when the great Durráni leader made his final descent into the Panjáb. The conqueror drove before him all the new Sikh chiefs, for the very name Afghan was dreaded in those days, and the prevailing idea in military circles was that the Sikhs were no match for the Afghans in the open field. Such was the fear of the Afghans, that the proverb of those days is still remembered by the people,

کہا دا پیتا ما ڈا — رهندا احمد شاه دا

meaning, "What we actually eat and drink is our own; the rest is all Ahmad Shah's." Ahmad Shah, according to the popular belief, left nothing for the people, except what was actually in their mouths, but swallowed up everything himself. The joint-governors of Láhore, alarmed at the Shah's approach, fled to Panjwár. But the Shah returned to Kábul soon afterward, confirming, as already stated, Lahná Singh in his possession of Láhore.

The Bhangi sardars vacate Láhore on his approach,

But are subsequently restored.

For thirty years following these events, the joint governors of Láhore reigned in peace; but in 1797, Láhore was invaded by Shah Zaman, who had succeeded to the Kábul throne in 1793. His mind was full of the notion, however absurd, of founding an Indian Empire. In December 1793, the king marched to Pesháwar at the head of a large army, and advanced unopposed as far as Hassan Abdál. From this place he sent his generals Ahmad Khan, *Shahanchi*, and Bahádur Khan, *Mahomedzie*, at the head of 7,000 horse, to conquer the country between the Jhelum and the Chináb. His plans were, however, frustrated by a fresh disturbance at Herat, caused by his brother Mahmúd, and he was compelled to return to his country and abandon his favourite project of invading India. Suffice it to say that his troops, under Ahmad Khan, *Shahanchi*, were defeated and put to flight by the Sikhs, with great loss.

Invasion of Shah Zaman, 1793.

His troops routed by the Sikhs.

Shah Zaman's second invasion of the Panjáb was commenced at the close of the year 1795. Having crossed the Indus by a bridge of boats at Attock, he entered Hassan Abdál, from which place he detached his *shahanchi*, at the head of a large force, to occupy Rohtas. That general took possession of Rohtas without difficulty, and was joined by the Ghakkars, the *Játs* and other Panjáb Mussalman tribes, the Sikhs having fled in dismay to the mountains, or the country beyond the Biás. The king had, however, been only a week in Hassan Abdál, when intelligence of the invasion of Western Khorasán by Aghá Mahomed Khan, *Kajjar*, king of Persia, reached him, and he immediately left the Panjáb for the defence of his dominions, arriving at Pesháwar in January 1796.

Second invasion of Shah Zaman, 1795.

After settling his affairs with Aghá Mahomed Khan, who was compelled to retreat to Teheran, the Shah's infatuation for Indian expeditions brought him again, for the third time, on the confines of the Panjáb. About this time the princes of Upper India, being hard pressed by the English and the Mahrattas, had entered into negotiations with Shah Zaman to bring about another Durráni invasion of India. Thus, Gholám Mahomed, the defeated usurper of Rohilkhand, and the agents of Nawáb Asif-ud-doula, the Oudh wazír, crossed the Panjáb in 1795-96, to urge upon his majesty the necessity of an invasion, assuring him that the Mahomedan world would gladly hail his appearance on the soil of India, as the deliverer of its people. The Shah, having assembled a force of thirty thousand men, half of whom were Durránis, resumed his march to India at the end of November 1796. His army forded the Chináb and marched on to Shah Dera, on the banks of the Rávi, by the Emnabad route, and pitched their camp in the enclosure of Jahángír's mausoleum. From this place he despatched his grand wazír, Hafiz Sher Mahomed Khan, surnamed Mukhtar-ud-doula Wafadar Khan, to Láhore, at the head of twenty thousand troops to occupy the town. The wazír, with his troops, crossed the Rávi by boats. Before his arrival, Lahná Singh and Sobha Singh, the joint governors of Láhore, delivered the keys of

Third invasion of Shah Zaman, 1796.

the citadel to Mian Shah Cherágh, a descendant of the famous saint, Abdul Qadir, *Jilani*, and one of the leading Mahomedans of the city, and retired. The Shah subsequently advanced unopposed to Láhore, which he entered on the 3rd of January 1797.

Shah Zaman enters Láhore, January 1797.

The city was illuminated for three successive nights in honour of its occupation by the Durráni. Some Hindu shopkeepers, who wilfully neglected to light up their shops on the fixed dates, were punished with the payment of *jazia*. The deserted houses in the city were all occupied by the Afghan sardars and nobles, while the parade ground, fronting the palace, swarmed with the followers of the Afghan army. Following the policy adopted by his grandfather, Ahmad Shah, the invader despatched *chapals*, or light parties, in different directions into the country to attack the Sikhs in their retreat by rapid marches, to seize their cattle, destroy their grain, and harass them in other ways. Such forts as were within the reach of these flying columns were reduced. As, however, times had changed since the invasion of Ahmad Shah, and the Sikh power was now in the ascendant, he thought it fit to adopt a policy of mixed conciliation and menace, and great encouragements were held out to all Sikhs who should submit. This led to many of the Sikh chiefs tendering their submission to the Shah, to whom they paid homage at Láhore. The Mahomedans looked upon him as the champion of their faith, and the deliverer of their country. The leading Mahomedans of the Panjáb, Jalal Bhatti, Nizám-ud-dín Khan of Kasúr and others joined him; but the advance of the Durráni army, and the occupation of the capital of the Panjáb by the grandson of the famous Abdáli king, Ahmad Shah, had caused a profound sensation throughout India, however ill-prepared the Shah, and ill-designed and inopportune his plans may have been. Encouragements were held out to the Shah by a refugee prince of Delhi and Tippú Sultan. An interchange of deputations also took place between Shah Zaman and Sindhia, the envoys of the latter having passed through Baháwalpur (as in the instance of the mission of the wazír of Oudh, previously alluded to). Intrigues were set on foot in many parts of India to assist the king, with the object of eventually restoring the house of Tymúr to power. The weakness of the Mahrattas, and the distracted state of the Nawáb Wazír's country of Oudh, induced every able-bodied Mahomedan in Hindostán to arm in defence of his religion and country. The Rohillas, too, were armed *cap-á-pie*, and determined to assist the Shah in his endeavours to conquer India, while even in the Dekkan the advent of the royal hero was hopefully and anxiously awaited by every Mahomedan. How visionary these hopes were, appeared, however, soon after. Intelligence was received of the rebellion of the Shah's brother, Prince Mahmúd, at Herat, and he was compelled forthwith to retrace his steps to Kábul, leaving Ahmad Khan, Barakzie, to look after the affairs of the country between the Jhelum and Sindh, Bahádur Khan, *Mahomedzie*, Bostan Khan, Durráni, and Nurullah Khan, Khatak, at the head of 7,000 horse, 100 zamburas and 4 guns, being left to protect the country.

Rejoicings at Láhore.

Proceedings of the Shah in the Panjáb.

Intrigues in India to restore the house of Tymúr.

Fallacy of the notions entertained.

The Shah retires to his own country.

After the departure of Shah Zaman, Lahná Singh and Sobha Singh returned to Láhore and occupied it. The same year, 1797, Lahná Singh died, and was succeeded by his son Chet Singh, and, about the same time, Sobha Singh died, and was succeeded by his son Mohar Singh. The new governors of Láhore possessed neither the talents nor the capabilities to rule over the country which they inherited, and the subjects entrusted to their care. Chet Singh was an imbecile, while Mohar Singh exercised little influence over the people. Ranjít Singh, the powerful sardar of the Sukerchakia *misl*, formed a plan to capture Láhore, and, with this view, entered

The Bhangi sardars reoccupy Láhore.

Death of Lahná Singh and Sobha Singh, 1797.

They are succeeded by Chet Singh and Mohar Singh.

Incapacity of the new governors.

Ranjít Singh, Sukerchakia, castes his eyes on Láhore.

into collusion with the adherents of the Bhangi chiefs of Láhore, *Hákim* Hákam Rae, Bhai Gurbaksh Singh and Mian Ashik Mahomed. These three wrote to Ranjít Singh, inviting him to enter the city, and promising their support against the joint governors. Chowdhri Mohkam Dín of Kot Nawan, the confidential agent of Chet Singh, prevented his master by persuasions from marching against Ranjít Singh, when the latter entered Anarkalli at the head of a large force, and when Ranjít Singh approached the city, he opened to him the Láhori Gate, of which he had charge. Chet Singh and Mohar Singh fled, and Ranjít Singh thereupon made himself master of Láhore. This was in July 1799. He occupies Láhore, 1799.

We must now revert to the history of the misldars of the Bhangi confederacy. Desa Singh, son of Gandá Singh, was, on his death, succeeded by his minor son Golab Singh, who guided the affairs of the *misl* through his cousin, Karam Singh. Golab Singh enlarged the city of Amritsar, where he resided, and, on attaining years of discretion, overran the whole Pathan colony of Kasúr, which he subdued, the Pathan chiefs of Kasúr, Nizám-ud-dín Khan, and Kutb-ud-dín Khan, brothers, entering the service of the conqueror. In 1794, however, the brothers, with the aid of their Afghan countrymen, recovered the whole of Kasúr from the possession of the Sikhs, and the repeated attempts of Golab Singh to expel the Afghans failed. Golab Singh, in consequence of his debaucheries, was a debilitated and idiotic ruler, possessing neither force of character nor influence sufficient to protect his interests against the intrigues of the rival chiefs whose power was now in the ascendant. Ranjít Singh, having taken possession of Láhore in the year 1799, his successes filled the Sikh chiefs with alarm. The following year a cabal was formed against him, the leading spirits of which were Golab Singh, Bhangi, Sahib Singh son of Gujar Singh, Bhangi, Jassa Singh, Ramgarhia, the famous carpenter, and Nizám-ud-dín Khan of Kasúr. The allied troops of the sardars met the army of Ranjít Singh at Bhasin, between Láhore and Amritsar, and a few petty engagements were fought between the contending parties, which generally proved disastrous to the caballing chiefs. Ranjít was now left complete master of the field. During the time these troops were in the field, the chiefs vied with each other in debauchery, revelry and riot, and Golab Singh, Bhangi, died suddenly of *delirium tremens*.

Desa Singh, Bhangi, on his death, is succeeded by his minor son, Golab Singh, 1782.

A cabal formed against Ranjít Singh.

Death of Golab Singh.

He was succeeded, on his death, by his son, Gurdit Singh, a child, 10 years old, who conducted the affairs of the *misl* through his mother and guardian, Musammat Sukhan. Ranjít Singh was now anxious to possess Amritsar, the stronghold of the Bhangis, where the remnants of the *misl* still held power and influence. In order to create a quarrel, he demanded the famous *zamzama* gun, and on Musammat Sukhan's refusal to part with it, he declared war. The Bhangi fort was attacked by Ranjít Singh, assisted by his ally, Fatteh Singh, Ahluwalia, and, after about five hours fighting, he won the day. All the possessions of the Bhangis were seized by Ranjít Singh, and Gurdit Singh, with his mother, Sukhan, fled to Ramgarh.

He is succeeded by his son, Gurdit Singh.

Ranjít Singh seizes on the possessions of the Bhangis.

It will be remembered that, after the capture of Láhore by the three Bhangi sardars, Gujar Singh had marched northwards with a view to further conquests. His schemes were successful, and he became a far more powerful chief than either Lahná Singh or Sobha Singh had been in their time. He took Gujrát from Sultan Mokarrab Khan, the Ghakkar chief, whom he signally defeated under the walls of the city in 1755, capturing both the city and the adjoining country, and making Gujrát his head-quarters. Next year he overran Jammu, seized Islamgarh, Punch and Deva Batála, and reduced Garura, on the banks of the Chináb, where he seized the property of Rahmat

Proceedings of Gujar Singh, Bhangi.

He conquers Gujrát,

Overruns Jammu,

Khan and Hashmat Khan, and extended his territory as far as the Bhimber hills and the Mánjha country. He, however, fled to Ferozepur on the appearance of the Durráni King, Ahmad Shah, but as soon as the Shah had turned his back on the Panjáb, he again appeared on the scene with a large force and recovered his lost territories without much difficulty. Soon afterwards he laid siege to the famous fort of Rohtas, held by the Ghakkars, with the assistance of Charat Singh, Sukerchakia, who was on the most amicable terms with him, and gave his daughter Raj Kour in marriage to Sahib Singh, son of Gujar Singh.

And captures Rohtas.

His three sons, Sukhá Singh, Sahib Singh and Fatteh Singh.

Gujar Singh had three sons, Sukhá Singh, Sahib Singh and Fatteh Singh. The first two quarrelled and fought, Sukhá Singh being killed. The second son, Sahib Singh, insulted and dishonoured his father, to oblige his brother-in-law, Mahá Singh, the result of which was that the aged Gujar Singh, surrendering all his possessions in favour of the youngest son, Fatteh Singh, retired to Láhore, where he died* in 1788. The following year, the brothers-in-law, Mahá Singh and Sahib Singh, quarrelled, in consequence of the former supporting the claims of Fatteh Singh to succeed to the possession of the territories left by Gujar Singh. An attempt made by Raj Kour, sister of Mahá Singh, to bring about a reconciliation between the two sardars was without avail. For two years the sardars exhibited the greatest hatred and hostility towards each other, till, at length, in 1792, a decisive battle was fought. At this juncture Mahá Singh was deserted by his trusted friend, Jodh Singh, of Wazirábad, while Karam Singh, *Dulú*, responding to the call of Sahib Singh, promptly came to his assistance with a large force. A desperate engagement was now fought between the two armies, the result of which was at first doubtful. It so happened that Mahá Singh became ill during the contest, and fainted on his elephant. The *mahávat*, seeing the chief so ill, turned the elephant from the field, to bring his master to the camp, for the purpose of temporary repose. Mahá Singh's leaving the field was looked upon by his followers as a signal to discontinue the conflict and retire, which they did in the greatest disorder. The siege of the Sodhra fort, where Sahib Singh was shut up, was raised, and Mahá Singh was taken to Gujránwálá, where he died three days afterwards. An attempt was made by his adversary, Sahib Singh, to carry away his body, but it failed through the timely help rendered by Kádar Baksh and Ghouse Khan, who, with their artillery, succeeded in dispersing the Bhangi men.

His death, 1788.

Quarrel between Mahá Singh, Sukerchakia and Sahib Singh, Bhangi.

The battle of Sodhra, 1792.

Defeat and death of Mahá Singh, Sukerchakia, 1792.

Fourth invasion of Shah Zaman, 1798.

After settling affairs with prince Mahmúd, Shah Zaman again had leisure to turn his attention to the Panjáb, where his cause had suffered during his absence. No sooner had the Shah turned his back on the Panjáb, than the Sikhs, as was usual with them on such occasions, emerged from their hill retreats, and other places of retirement, and began to retaliate on the Mahomedans for the cruelty and hardships which they had sustained at the hands of the Durránis. The Sikhs had also cut off a party of five thousand Afghans, which, under the command of a Durráni general, was advancing to Jhelum. The king, having left Peshávar on the 25th of October 1798, entered Láhore without opposition. Sahib Singh, following the example of the Láhore Bhangis, Lahná Singh and Sobha Singh, on the occasion of the previous invasion of the Shah, retired to the hills on his approach. The king renewed his measures of mixed threats and conciliation, and all accounts agree that no outrage of any kind was committed on the people of the Panjáb during this campaign. Many of the Sikh sardars paid their homage to him, and all the Mussalman chiefs and zemindars attended his court at Láhore. He found

He reoccupies Láhore, October 1798.

* The tomb of Gujar Singh, Bhangi, is situated near the Summan Burj of the Láhore fort.

an able ally in Nizám-ud-dín Khan, the Pathan Chief of Kasúr, who exercised great local influence, and employed him in harassing such of the Sikh chiefs, including the youthful Ranjít Singh, as pertinaciously held aloof. The policy adopted by Shah Zaman had already borne fruit. Most of the chiefs of the Panjáb had paid him homage, in person or by proxy, among the former being the young Sikh chief, Ranjít Singh.

Towards the latter part of 1798, news of the invasion of Khorásán by Fatteh Ali Shah, king of Persia, with the intention of supporting Shah Mahmúd's claim to the throne, reached Shah Zaman, which necessitated his quitting Láhore in the early part of January 1799, leaving his general, Shahanchi Khan, at the head of affairs, with a large number of troops. The general was instructed to watch over the interests of the Shah in the Panjáb, and see that the Sikhs lived as peaceful subjects in towns, and harmless zemindars in villages. He was also instructed to use all means in his power to prevent the Sikhs from assembling together in armed parties, and where such parties succeeded in assembling, to disperse them as soon as practicable. Shahanchi Khan, having heard of the gathering of the Sikhs in large numbers, under Ranjít Singh, at Rassulnagar (then known as Ramnagar), immediately proceeded thither. Ranjít Singh called to his aid Sardar Milkha Singh, Pindiwálá, Budh Singh and Ram Singh of Serác Káláwálá, Jodh Singh, Attariwálá and Dharam Singh Jalalia, and a desperate engagement ensued between the Afghans and the Sikhs, which terminated very ruinously for the former. The siege of Rassulnagar was raised, and Shahanchi Khan proceeded thence to Gujrát, with the object of expelling Sahib Singh Bhangi, who, after the departure of the Shah, had returned to that district, and taken possession of the town and its suburbs. The Afghan commander entered into an alliance with the Mahomedan tribes of the Jhelum; but Sahib Singh, on his return, secured the co-operation of the Sikh chiefs, Jodh Singh of Wazirábad, Karam Singh, *Dulú*, and Wazír Singh of Attari. The troops under Shahanchi Khan at this time numbered twelve thousand. A severe fight took place between the two armies, in which the Afghan commander received a bullet wound in the chest, which terminated his existence. The Pathans lost heart on seeing the death of their commander, which led them to beat a hasty and disorderly retreat, and contributed to considerably enlarge the list of casualties. The general's grave is still to be seen four miles east of Gujrát.

Quits Láhore, January 1799, leaving his general, Shahanchi Khan, to look after the affairs of the Panjáb.

The Sikhs defeat Shahanchi at Rassulnagar,

And again at Gujrát.

The general is killed.

About this time Shah Zaman was again assiduously employed in making preparations for another invasion of Hindostán, and made his appearance at Peshávar, when the news of the fall of Kandahar called him to his senses, and he returned to Kábul, giving up all idea of conquering India. Certain it is that had Shah Zaman remained content with his Afghan possessions, and not coveted India, he would not have lost the kingdom of his ancestors. His untimely absence from the seat of his government, and from the theatre of action, afforded an opportunity to his rivals and enemies of hatching plots against him.

Shah Zaman again appears at Peshávar,

But returns to his country soon after.

It was during Shah Zaman's fourth invasion of India, in 1798, that the genius of Ranjít Singh, as a soldier and administrator of uncommon tact, seems to have first attracted the attention of the Durráni Shah, and made an impression, not only on his majesty, but also on other Sikh chiefs. The Afghan monarch had been compelled to hasten his retreat from the Panjáb, by the intelligence of plots in Persia. In consequence of the Jhelum being flooded, great difficulty was experienced in carrying over his ordnance. It was not considered advisable to delay his march to Kábul. He therefore resolved to leave the guns, and reach his destination as expeditiously as

Ranjít Singh's first acquaintance with Shah Zaman.

possible. The Shah now sent a firman to Ranjít Singh, informing him, that, in the event of his taking care of his ordnance, and having it conveyed to Kábul as early as practicable, he would be pleased to consider favourably his aspirations with regard to Láhore. Out of twelve guns which had sunk in the bed of the river, eight were readily extricated and forwarded to Kábul. As a reward for this service, Ranjít Singh got from the Kábul king what he desired, namely, a royal investiture of the capital of the Panjáb. Thenceforward the history of the Sikhs merges in that of their great Maharájá. The remaining four guns, which were taken out in 1823, were placed in the arsenals of Láhore.

He obtains a cession of Láhore from the Afghan sovereign, 1799.

The collapse of the Bhangi confederacy.

Sahib Singh, whose career had been hitherto marked by energy and enterprise, now became an indolent debauchee and drunkard. He quarrelled with the rival chiefs and sardars, and, his power being thus weakened, Ranjít Singh seized upon all his possessions, which were merged in the new kingdom which he was now forming. In 1810 the Maharájá, at the intercession of Mái Lachmi, mother of Sahib Singh, granted him a jágír worth one lakh of rupees, which he held until his death, which occurred in the following year. Ranjít Singh had, by this time, conquered Multán, and married two of the widows of the deceased, Dya Kour and Rattan Kour, by the rite of chádarandazí. Dya Kour gave birth to Peshorá Singh, and Rattan Kour to Multána Singh, the reputed sons of the Great Maharájá. Fatteh Singh, the youngest son of Gujar Singh, went to Kapurthalla and took up service under the Ahluwalia chief, but died soon after, leaving a son, Jymal Singh, who resided in Ramgarh, without pension or estate, and thus the great Bhangi confederacy collapsed.

2.—THE RAMGARHIA *MISL*.

This *misl* took its name from Ram Rouni, or 'Fortalice of God,' at Amritsar, converted into Ramgarah, or 'Fort of the Lord,' by Jassa Singh the celebrated *thoká*, or carpenter. The founder of the *misl* was Khoshal Singh, a *Ját* of Mouza Gugá, in the vicinity of Amritsar, and a follower of the Byragi Bandá. He took his *Páhal* from Bandá, and, on the death of the latter, became a notorious robber and commander of an armed force. When he died, one Nodh Singh, of Sahangi, near Amritsar, succeeded him. As a freebooter, he was more notorious than his predecessor, and always had a greater number of followers. The most daring and intrepid among these were the three brothers, Jassa Sing, Malla Singh or (Mali Singh) and Tárá Singh, sons of Bhagwána *Giani*, carpenters of Mouza Sarsang, in the Láhore district, who, giving up their profession, took up the new one of robbery under the leader Nodh Sing. Jassa Singh took to the profession of arms, and subsequently became very famous among the Sikhs as a brave and intrepid warrior.

Khoshal Singh founds the *misl*.

Nodh Singh succeeds him on his death.

Jassa Singh, the carpenter.

Jassa Singh, with his two brothers, fought on the side of Adína Beg Khan, when that chief entered into hostilities with the Abdáli king, Ahmad Shah, and his gallantry was so conspicuous that Adína Beg gave him the command of his own troops, which, at that time, were chiefly Sikhs. When, being hard pressed by the Afghans, Adína Beg, had fled to the hills, Jassa Singh joined Jay Singh, Kanhia and Amar Singh, Kingrá, in their war against the Pathans, and greatly distinguished themselves. On the departure of Ahmad Shah from India in 1757, and the return of Adína Beg Khan from his hill retreat, the latter made a vow to extirpate the Sikhs, who had become troublesome, and made common cause against the Mussalmans. The Mahrattas, who had, at this time, swept the Panjáb, elevated Adína Beg Khan to the viceroyalty of Láhore. The new viceroy, after reducing Kutab

He supports Adína Beg Khan against the Afghans.

Proceedings of Adína Beg Khan against the Sikhs.

Shah, the Rohilla chief, laid siege to Batála and captured it. Mir Aziz Bakshi, in command of a strong body of cavalry, was sent to the Mánjha country with orders to attack and chastise the Sikhs wherever they could be found. Four thousand pioneers* accompanied the Mir, with their sharpened tools, for the purpose of clearing the jungle where the Sikhs had concealed themselves. Thousands of Sikhs were thus hunted down and mercilessly butchered. The more adventurous fled and sought shelter within the mud fort of Ram Rouni. The principal refugees were Nodh Singh, the head of the Ramgarhia *misl*, his lieutenants, the brothers Jassa Singh, Malla Singh and Tárá Singh; Jay Singh, Kanhia and Amar Singh, Kingrá. Mir Aziz Bakshi, hearing of the retreat of the Sikhs towards Amritsar, proceeded thither and besieged Ram Rouni. The Sikhs, finding that the Mir's troops were more than a match for them in the open field, resorted to sallying forth at night and attacking the outposts of the besieging party, and retiring again to their fort before allowing the Afghans to recover from their surprise. By this means they managed to reduce considerably the number of their enemies. After suffering many hardships and fighting with the courage of lions, the Sikhs were obliged to effect their escape as best they could, which they accomplished one night, after having battered down the walls of Ram Rouni, which had so long sheltered them from their foes. They were pursued in their retreat by the Afghans, and many of them fell under the avenging sword of the Muslims. Those who escaped this slaughter were styled Ramgarhis by their fellow-countrymen, as a compliment to the sacred place where they had sought shelter, and this, more appropriately, gave the *misl* the designation which it bears.

Slaughter of the Sikhs.

Mir Aziz Bakhshi lays siege to Ram Rouni.

The Sikhs disperse.

After the death of Adína Beg, in 1758, the ever-vigilant Sikhs became as troublesome as before. Jassa Singh, about this time, took command of the confederacy, and, aided by the Kanhia *misl*, besieged Dinanagar, Batála, Kalanaur, Srihargovindpur, Kadian, Ghamman and many other towns and places in the districts of Amritsar and Gurdáspúr, yielding a revenue of between six and ten lakhs of rupees. Ahmad Shah came to chastise the Sikhs, and blew up their Harmandar at Amritsar with gunpowder. It was about this time that the *Gullúghárá* battle was fought between the Durráni king and the Sikhs, which for ferocity and brutality surpassed all other battles between the Mahomedans and the Sikhs.

When Nodh Singh died, he was succeeded in the sardari of the *misl* by Jassa Singh. After the departure of Ahmad Shah, this Jassa Singh, with his brothers, Malla Singh and Tárá Singh and Jay Singh, Kanhia, emerged from their jungle retreat, and, collecting their followers, ravaged the country far and wide, and built forts and established military outposts. When Khwajá Obed, the Láhore governor, attacked the Sikh fort at Gujránwálá, he was opposed by the united forces of the Ramgarhias and the Kanhias, and the guns, ammunition and treasure left by the governor, were equally divided by the leaders of the two *misls*.

Nodh Singh on his death is succeeded by Jassa Singh,

Who joins the Kanhias against the Afghans.

A year after this, Ahmad Shah again appeared on the scene, and, crossing the Sutlej, advanced as far as Rohtas and Jandiálá, carrying fire and sword wherever he went. The Sikhs, as usual, fled and concealed themselves in deserts and hills, but no sooner had the Shah started for Kábul, than the Ramgarhias made themselves masters of Batála and Kalanaur, expelling Khwajá Obed, the Afghan governor, and seizing on the surrounding country. The fort of Ram Rouni was again secured by Jassa Singh, who constructed

Captures Batála and Kalanaur.

Restores Ram Rouni.

* The *Memoirs of Moulvi Mahomed Din* of Batála, a contemporary historian.

a large street close to it. Ghamand Chand, the deputy of Ahmad Shah, in Katoch, and other Rajput chiefs of the hills, became his tributaries, and his possessions now comprised almost the whole country between the Sutlej and the Biás towards the hills, including a vast tract of the Bist Jalandar.

Extends the possessions of the Ramgarhias.

Tárá Singh and Malla Singh, the brothers of Jassa Singh.

Jassa Singh, now in the height of his power, gave Batála, with the neighbouring country, to his brother Malla Singh, and Kalanaur to his other brother, Tárá Singh, keeping the rest himself.

War between the Ramgarhias and the Kanhias.

A quarrel arose between the Kanhia *misl*, headed by Jay Singh, Kanhia, and the Ramgarhia *misl*, regarding the division of the revenue of some lands. Batála was besieged by Gurbaksh Singh, son of Jay Singh. Malla Singh, who held charge of the city, was a great tyrant, and, in consequence, was disliked by the people, who supplied the invading Kanhias with provisions and money to prosecute their plans. He was arrogant and haughty, and often killed people for mere amusement. One day, during a terrific storm of thunder and lightning, Malla Singh vauntingly sent a bullet whizzing through the elements, when a stone, falling from the clouds, struck him on the head. He retreated to the fort, but was turned out by the indignant multitude, who opened the gates to the besiegers. Malla Singh fled. Gurbaksh Singh was put in charge of the city by Rájá Singh, and Deva Singh, the governors of the district, and Tárá Chand, the Brahmin. The Kanhia *misl*, under Gurbaksh Singh, soon after this, took possession of Kalanaur, expelling Tárá Singh and wresting the whole country to the Sutlej from the Ramgarhias.

Batála and Kalanaur lost to the Ramgarhias.

Jassa Singh, by his bravery and skill, recovered Batála, where he established a police post, and surrounded the city with a brick wall, 30 feet high and 21 broad. But an attempt to recover Kalanaur failed, as Jeymal Singh, son of Hakikat Singh, Kanhia, made a stout resistance. The fight between the Ramgarhias and the Kanhias continued unabated, and thousands were killed on both sides. Armed bands of the Sikhs preyed upon the country, and the rival *misls* carried off cattle, sheep and goats from each other's territory. Jassa Singh was at last overpowered by Jay Singh, and driven to the other side of the Sutlej, where he collected a large body of irregular horse, and, carried on his old profession of freebooting. Here he was aided by Amar Singh, *Phulkia*, and, establishing himself in the country of Hissar, extended his ravages up to the very walls of Delhi. Once he penetrated into Delhi itself, and carried off four guns from the Moghal arsenal. The Mirath Nawáb agreed to pay him Rs. 10,000 a year on his consenting to leave his district unmolested. He sacked Hissar, to punish the governor, who had forcibly carried away two daughters of a Brahmin, and had the girls restored to their father. A war subsequently broke out between Jay Singh and Maha Singh, the rising chief of the Sukerchakia *misl*, which induced the latter to call to his aid, Jassa Singh from the country across the Sutlej. A bloody battle took place between the allied forces of the Sukerchakias and Ramgarhias on the one side, and the Kanhias on the other, the result of which was the overthrow of the last named *misl*. Gurbaksh, son of Jay Singh, was killed in the battle. Jassa Singh's possessions were restored, and for several years he enjoyed the fruits of his adventures in peace. On the death of his brothers, Malla Singh and Tárá Singh, Jassa Singh retired to Rabela on the Biás.

Jassa Singh is driven across the Sutlej.

He ravages the country up to Delhi.

War between the Kanhias and the Sukerchakias.

The latter call Jassa Singh to their aid.

Jassa Singh recovers his lost possessions.

Dies, 1816.

Jodh Singh succeeds,

And is, on his death, succeeded by Hira Singh.

Jassa Singh died in 1816, leaving two sons, Jodh Singh and Bir Singh, the former of whom succeeded him. Jodh Singh was a man of no activity, and his possessions were encroached upon by his more active cousin, Dewán Singh, son of Tárá Singh. Jodh Singh died, leaving a son, Hira Singh, but all the possessions of the *misl* were now seized by Ranjít Singh, son of

Mahá Singh, who, on his return from Kangrá, in 1808, imprisoned Bir Singh, Dewán Singh and Hira Singh. The Maharájá, taking the road to Rabela, went to Amritsar, and laid siege to the fort of Ram Rouni, which he took. The Maharájá took city after city, and razed to the ground the strongholds of the Ramgarhias to the number of a hundred and fifty, all within a very short time. Adequate pensions were provided for Dewán Singh and Jodh Singh, the remnants of the once powerful Ramgarhia *misl*, which, like the other *misls*, collapsed, and fell before the all-absorbing power of the future Maharájá of the Panjáb.

The rise of Ranjit Singh.

Collapse of the Ramgarhia *misl*.

3.—THE KANHIA *MISL*.

The head of this *misl* was Jay Singh, of Mouza Kánhá, 15 miles east of Láhore, which gave the *misl* the name it bears. One Khushali, a Sindhú *Ját* of Ghanni, who passed his days in extreme poverty and indigence, had three sons, Jay Singh, Jhandá Singh and Singha, the first of whom went to Kapúr Singh of Fyzullahpur, near Amritsar, and was initiated by him into the *Páhal* of the Guru. Leaving Kapúr Singh, he joined Amar Singh, *Kegra*, of Kháná Kacha, in the Mánjha country, a robber who had numerous followers. The most daring of his retainers were Jay Singh, his brother, Jhandá Singh, Amar Singh, *Bhugga*, and Hakikat Singh. They were famous for the manner in which they carried on their predatory excursions, and for the amount of booty which they carried off. They established themselves in the dense *dhák* jungles near Begwál, on the Amritsar road. Neither life nor property was secure against these ruffians, who infested the whole country, from the foot of the hills to the neighbourhood of Láhore. In 1763, after Ahmad Shah had retired from the Panjáb, these plunderers attacked Kasúr, and, after a month's siege, captured the town and carried off all the jewels, silver, gold, shawls and carpets which they could lay their hands upon. Jay Singh, who now became the leader of the *misl*, joined Jassa Sing, the carpenter of the Ramgarhia *misl*, and, as previously mentioned, their united forces opposed the arms of the Abdáli King, Ahmad Shah. He then embellished the city of Amritsar, by building in it a spacious *katra* or quarters.

Jay Singh founds the *misl*.

His parentage.

His associates in his exploits.

He joins the Ramgarhias.

Embellishes Amritsar.

Jay Singh declared war against Jhandá Singh, Bhangi, assisted by Charat Singh, Sukerchakia, whose interests were opposed to those of the Bhangi *misl*, through his support of the claimant to the Jammu chiefship. Having had the satisfaction of seeing his powerful rival, Jhandá Singh, removed, he entered into an agreement with Jassa Singh, Ahluwalia, to expel the other Jassa Singh, Ramgarhia. The chief, last mentioned, was ultimately driven to the wastes of Hariana, where he lived as a robber.

Wars against Jhandá Singh, Bhangi.

Contrives to expel Jassa Singh across the Sutlej.

Jay Singh then marched to Sirhind, ravaging the country as he went, and was present at the great battle of Sirhind, in which Zen Khan was defeated and slain. He next invaded Garota, at the foot of the hills, and after a desperate fight, reduced Ezad Baksh, the chief of that place, to subjection. He then led an army to Hajipur, which he annexed to his possessions, and made the hill chiefs of Nurpur, Datarpur and Saepah his tributaries. Next he conquered Mukeria, where he was strongly opposed by the Mussalman Awans, who, after great slaughter, submitted to his authority. Mukeria was pillaged by the Sikhs, who mercilessly put the inhabitants to the sword.

Overruns Sirhind.

Conquers Nurpur

And Mukeria.

Nawáb Sef Ali Khan, the killadar of Kangrá, was a nominal deputy, in the hills, of the declining Moghal. He had devised to remain in subjection to the Delhi throne, and his possessions were coveted by the aspiring chief of Katoch, Sansar Chand, grandson of Ghamand Chand.

Sansar Chand chief of Katoch.

Several times this chief attacked the famous stronghold of Kangrá with a strong force, but was always repulsed. Having heard of the daring exploits of the Kanhia chief, Jay Singh, and his undaunted courage, he prevailed upon that chief to assist him in subduing the imperial fort. Jay Singh marched to Kangrá, at the head of a numerous body of troops, and the fort was taken. The old Mahomedan governor died a natural death in 1774, and this removed all difficulties in the way of the conquerors. Jay Singh bribed Jewan Khan, son of the deceased nawáb, to vacate the fort, and allow the Sikh troops to enter it. Jay Singh kept the prize for himself, much to the disappointment of the Katoch chief, who, conscious of his own inferiority, saw no alternative but to submit. Being thus strengthened by his new and valuable acquisition, Jay Singh usurped the possessions of the surrounding rájás and thakurs, who paid tribute to Jassa Singh, Ramgarhia, the predatory carpenter chief.

Invites Jay Singh to assist him in his operations against Kangrá.

Jay Singh conquers Kangrá, but retains the conquest for himself.

Jay Singh, being now assisted by the other Misldars, Jassa Singh, Ahluwalia, Tárá Singh, Gheba, and Khoshal Singh, Fyzulpuria, proceeded towards the Pathan colony of Kasúr, which was weakly defended by the Mahomedan chief, Alif Khan. The Pathans defended themselves in their houses and fortifications, but Alif Khan, instead of remaining on the defensive, fell, with his followers, on the besieging party, and the result was so disastrous to the Pathans, that a great number of them were killed, and the rest took to flight, followed by the Sikhs, who, entered the city and plundered it. The pillage was continued with great severity for several days, and the property previously alluded to carried off. The city was destroyed and the fort seized and parcelled out among the chiefs of the *misls*. The fort and the city were, however, re-occupied by Nizám-ud-dín Khan, and the Pathans remained in possession of them until finally expelled by Ranjít Singh.

Sack of Kasúr by the allied confederacies.

Jeymal Singh, son of Hakikat Singh, the deputy of Jay Singh, Kanhia, at Kalanaur.

Hakikat Singh, the deputy of Jay Singh in Kalanaur, died, and his son Jeymal Singh, picked a quarrel with Fatteh Singh, son of Mahtáb Singh. After severe fighting on both sides, Fatteh Singh was made prisoner by Jeymal Singh; but the wife of the former, assembling a large force, attacked Jeymal, and effected the release of her husband. Fatteh Singh died soon after, and by his death, Jeymal Singh was left in undisturbed possession of Kalanaur, which he improved. He reigned peacefully for a long time in Kalanaur, and, unlike his father, under whom the country had been almost desolated, was beloved by both the Hindus and the Mahomedans. He married his daughter, Chand Kour, to Kharak Singh, the eldest son of Ranjít Singh; the nuptials being performed with great pomp and magnificence in the town of Fattehgarh.

His popularity.

He marries his daughter, Chand Kour, to Kharak Singh.

Jay Singh's power paramount in the Panjáb.

Jay Singh now possessed Kot Kangrá, and levied tribute from the hill rájás. He had driven Jassa Singh, Ramgarhia, across the Sutlej, and his influence was paramount in the Panjáb. He took the youthful Mahá Singh, son of Charat Singh, into his care, and assisted the aspiring chief in capturing Rassulnagar, on the Chináb, from a Mahomedan family, Having obtained a footing of his own, Mahá Singh, threw off his allegiance to Jay Singh, and made politics a special subject of study. He plundered Jammu, by which he enriched himself, and increased his influence in the neighbouring mountainous districts. He now quarrelled with Jay Singh, his patron, who claimed a share of the Jammu spoils, in consideration of his having paved the way for the success of the young sardar's plans of aggrandizement. He called to his aid Jassa Singh, Ramgarhia, who gladly availed himself of the opportunity of recovering his lost possessions on this side of the Sutlej. The co-operation of Sansar Chand, grandson of Ghamand Chand,

His quarrel with Mahá Singh, Sukerchakia,

Who calls Jassa Singh, Ramgarhia, to his aid,

chief of Katoch, who had been disappointed at the hands of Jay Singh in the Kot Kangrá affair, was easily secured. In the meantime, the Mahomedan subjects of Batála had suffered hardships and indignities under Jay Singh, who oppressed them, and burnt the houses of many leading Mussalmans. Among the rest, Gholam Ghous was imprisoned, but he effected his escape, and was on his way to Kábul, when he was brought back by Mahá Singh, who promised to re-establish him in Batála. Jay Singh called to his aid Gurbaksh Singh, *Dúia*, and sent him, at the head of a force, in the direction of the Sutlej, to prevent Jassa Singh entering the Panjáb. Gurbaksh Singh crossed the Sutlej and engaged Jassa Singh near Patiálá, when the latter was victorious. Gurbaksh Singh was killed in the battle and his army routed. Various skirmishes took place outside the walls of Amritsar between the Kanhias and Mahá Singh, assisted by his allies, without any decisive result. At length the allied forces met the enemy at Achal, about eight miles from Batála, and a severe fight took place between them and the Kanhias, headed by Gurbaksh Singh, son of Jay Singh. Gurbaksh greatly distinguished himself in this battle, but his army gave way before superior numbers, and Mahá Singh and Jassa Sing carried the day. The death of Gurbaksh Singh, from an arrow wound in the breast, disheartened his followers, who fled in all directions. When Jay Singh saw that his gallant son had fallen in the engagement, after a hand-to-hand combat with his adversaries, he burst into tears, emptied his quiver of its arrows, and, dismounting from his horse, exposed himself to the enemy's fire. Such was the respect for the old veteran that none dared approach him in his grief, and all quietly withdrew. The victorious troops then advanced to Riárki and seized it.

And secures the co-operation of the Katoch chief against the Kanhias.

War between Jay Singh, Kanhia, and Mahá Singh, Sukerchakia, near Batala, 1785.

Gurbaksh, son of Jay Singh, is killed in the action.

Fall of Batála and defeat of Jay Singh, Kanhia.

Thus was the old sardar, Jay Singh, effectually humbled, by this double sorrow, arising from the signal defeat sustained, and the loss of his gallant son. He erected a monument over the remains of his son to the north of the city of Batála. From the fall of Batála may be reckoned the beginning of the decline of the Kanhia confederacy. Pressed by the Ramgarhias, Jay Singh fled to Pathankot, with Jeymal Singh and Tárá Singh. His daughter-in-law, Sadá Kour, the widow of Gurbaksh Singh, who had remained behind, had also to effect her escape barefooted through fear of the enemy, and went to Saiyán. The city was taken possession of by Jassa Singh, Ramgarhia, who put Bagh Singh and Hakikat Singh, his lieutenants in charge of it, expelling Dharam Singh, the chief police officer of Jay Singh, who narrowly escaped by climbing over a wall. The Ramgarhia chief, Jassa Singh, had his possessions restored to him.

Jassa Singh, Ramgarhia, the ally of Mahá Singh, Sukerchakia, takes possession of Batála.

Kangrá still remained tributary to Jay Singh, and, as Sansar Chand had always hankered after its possession, he made war against the former chief to secure this much-coveted territory. He, therefore, fell on Hajipur, and seized the whole country between that town and the hills, including Mukeria. The fort of Atalgarh was gallantly defended by a slave girl of the Kanhia sardar, named Dasser, who, for four months, successfully repulsed the attacks of the enemy, and held the place for her master. This heroine obliged Sansar Chand to raise the siege. War between Sansar Chand and Jay Singh was carried on for a period of three years, when Sadá Kour, the widow of Gurbaksh Singh, who was a shrewd and enterprising lady, devised a plan for securing the alliance of the now rising Sukerchakia chief by a marriage tie. Accordingly, she betrothed her daughter, Mahtáb Kour, to Ranjít Singh, son of Mahá Singh, the leader of the Sukerchakia *misl*. She proceeded to Jawálá Mukhi, and the negotiations between her and Raj Kour, wife of Mahá Singh, were there brought to a conclusion. Sansar Chand, however,

War between Jay Singh, Kanhia, and Sansar Chand of Katoch.

Instance of a feminine bravery.

Alliance by marriage between the Kanhia and the Sukerchakia families.

eagerly and persistently demanded Kot Kangrá, and, the matter having been referred to arbitration, it was finally decided that Jay Singh should abandon Kot Kangrá, and Sansar Chand on his part vacate Hajipur and Mukeria. Further, it was agreed, that, in the event of a war between the Ramgarhia and the Kanhia *misls*, the Katoch chief was to be on the side of the latter.

Compromise between the contending parties.

Jay Singh attempts to recover Batala.

Jay Singh, being now joined by Mahá Singh, Sansar Chand, and the rájás of Nurpur and Chamba, marched against Batála and besieged it. Jassa Singh had, however, made his position so strong in the city, supported by the inhabitants, who had been persecuted by Jay Singh, that all the efforts of the besiegers to carry the place failed. The siege was raised after an engagement of twenty-one days, and Jassa Singh held undisturbed possession of Batála and the surrounding country.

Fails.

Mahá Singh died in 1792 in the village Dharíwál. His death was greatly lamented by his old ally, Jay Singh, who, four years afterwards, gave his granddaughter, Mahtáb Kour, in marriage to Ranjít Singh, the son of the deceased. The nuptials were performed at Batála with a pomp and magnificence worthy of the names of Mahá Singh and Jay Singh, the heads of the Sukerchakia and Kanhia *misls*, respectively; and, as Ranjít Singh was then quite a youth, he was completely under the influence of his able and diplomatic mother-in-law.

Marriage of Ranjít Singh with Mahtáb Kour, granddaughter of Jay Singh, Kanhia.

Jay Singh dies, 1798.

Jay Singh died soon after, A.D. 1798, leaving two sons, Nidhan Singh and Bhág Singh, who were both unfit to govern the *misl* of which the deceased had been the head. They retired, with their mother, Raj Kour to Hajipur and Saiyán, while Mahtáb Kour governed the *misl* and established herself in Batála, where she built a large tank outside the city walls. Having then collected her troops, she fought with Jassa Singh the Ramgarhia. On the death of Mahtáb Kour, in 1800, Ranjít Singh seized on the possessions of the Kanhia *misl*. He first captured Adínanagar, then held by Golab Singh, the son of Chandá Singh, to whom he gave a village in jágír, and then Sujanpur, which belonged to Budh Singh, son of Amar Singh, one of the original founders of the Kanhia *misl*, on whom he bestowed Dharamkot as jágír. Hajipur was next wrested from Jay Singh's widow. Nidhan Singh and Bhág Singh, the surviving sons of Jay Singh, died soon afterwards, and no legitimate heir to the Kanhia *misl* now remained.

Rise of Ranjít Singh.

In 1811, Ranjít Singh went to Batála to reduce the remnants of the *misl* and encamped at the tank of Shamsher Khan. He seized Mukeria, and, returning to Láhore, put her mother-in-law, Sadá Kour, in confinement. Summoning all the zemindars of the Kanhia *misl* into his presence, he declared the collapse of the *misl*, which finally merged into his own power. Batála, the chief stronghold of the Kanhia power, having thus fallen, Shah Din, son of Aziz-ud-dín, was appointed the Maharájá's governor of the place.

Extinction of the Kanhia *misl*.

4.—THE NÁKAI *MISL*.

Hira Singh founds the *misl*.

The principal sardar of this *misl* was Hira Singh, son of Choudhri Hemráj, a *Ját* of the Sindhu *Got*, or clan, and a resident of mouza Bharwál, parganá Faridabad, now included in the Chúnian tehsil of the Láhore district. The country was called Nikka, and lay south-west of Láhore, bordering on Multán; hence the name *Nákai* given to the *misl*. Hira courted the society of the lowest blackguards. Starvation had afflicted him to such a degree that he, and the family who surrounded him, often endured hunger and fasted from necessity. Seeing that the Sikhs had become the terror of the people, and that the adoption of the religion of Nának led to worldly eminence and fame, he took the *Páhal* of the Guru, and his example was followed by his relations and friends. He, like the rest of the chiefs, had a weakness for coveting the property of other people, which led to his becoming a notorious robber. Petty acts of dacoity could not satisfy the ravenous appetite of this knight of the highway. A more savoury and appetising banquet was required for the insatiable maw of this brigand. His success in his petty foraging expeditions, daily attracted large numbers of horsemen to his banner. With these he was enabled to acquire considerable territory. He levied tribute and blackmail upon all the villages he subdued or passed through, which considerably increased both his wealth and his influence. Complaints having been brought to him of the existence of the practice of cow-slaughtering in the territory under Shekh Subhán, the *Sajjada Nishin* of the famous shrine of the Mahomedan saint, Farid, surnamed *Shakarganj*, in Pákpattan, he resolved upon attacking his jágír. Having collected a large number of troops, he proceeded to Pákpattan, where he was opposed by the Mussalmans, under the Shekh, the guardian of the shrine. In this engagement, Hira Singh's plundering career was brought to a close by a bullet-wound in the head. The Sikhs were dispersed with great loss, and returned to Bharwál. Shekh Subhán pursued them with 4,000 cavalry, killing a great number of them. On the death of Hira Singh, his son, Dal Singh, being a minor, his nephew, Nahar Singh, son of Natha Singh, became the head of the *misl*. Nahar Singh occupied the *masnad* of chiefship for nine months, but was killed in a fight at Kot Kamalia in 1768, and was succeeded by his younger brother Ran Singh.

His rise to power.

He fights with Shekh Subhán, the hereditary guardian of the shrine of Farid, *Shakarganj*, in Pákpattan.

Is defeated and slain.

Is succeeded by his nephew, Nahar Singh.

Nahar Singh killed, 1768.

Ran Singh became a powerful chief. The territory under his control was worth nine lakhs of rupees per annum, and comprised Chúnian, part of Kasúr, Sharakpur, Gugera, and, at one time, Kot Kamalia. The confederacy could muster for service in the field two thousand horsemen, besides camel swivels, and a few guns. He fought Kumár Singh of Sayadwálá, which he subdued, and died in 1781.

Ran Singh succeeds.

Dies, 1781.

Ran Singh was succeeded by his eldest son, Bhagwán Singh, who married his sister, Musammat Raj Kour, to Ranjít Singh, son of Mahá Singh, Sukerchakia. Wazir Singh, brother of Kumár Singh, recovered Sayádwálá from Bhagwán Singh, who was himself killed in an action, being succeeded by his brother Gian Singh. The death of Bhagwán Singh was avenged by Dal Singh, son of Sardar Hira Singh, who killed Wazir Singh, but was afterwards himself assassinated, at Bharwál, by a servant of Wazir Singh, who had resolved on avenging his master's death. Gian Singh died in 1807, leaving a son, Sardar Kahan Singh. At length Ranjít Singh, on attaining power, subdued the Nákai *misl*, and seized all the possessions of the family, a jágír of Rs. 15,000 per annum being given to Kahan Singh, the representative of the family in the neighbourhood of Bharwál. Kahan Singh recently died at Láhore at a very advanced age.

Bhagwán Singh succeeds.

Is killed.

Gian Singh succeeds.

Dies, 1807.

Ranjít Singh seizes all the possessions of the family.

Collapse of the *misl*.

5.—THE AHLUWALIA *MISL*.

This *misl* derived its name from the village Ahlu, five *kos* to the east of Láhore, founded by Sadáo Singh a *Ját*, *kalál*, or distiller. He had four sons, Gopal Singh, Hammú, Sekandar and Chàká, and the only thing known about them is that the three younger brothers lived at Láhore, where a street built by Chàká still exists. The eldest, Gopal Singh, had a son, Dewa Singh, who had three sons, Gurbaksh Singh, Sadr Singh and Badr Singh. Badr Singh married the sister of one Bhág Singh, or Bhágú, a distiller of the Tulsi. This man Bhágú (as he was originally called) lived in very indigent circumstances, and, having removed his business from Ahlu, settled in Mohalla Telpura, in the environs of Láhore, close to

Sadáo Singh founds the *misl*.

His four sons, Gopal Singh, Hammú, Sekandar and Chàká.

Badr Singh, son of Gopal Singh, marries the sister of Bhág Singh, a distiller.

the modern village of *Ganj*. Finding no relief here, he went to Fyzullapur, and was there initiated into the *Páhal* of the Guru by Kapúr Singh, the head of the Fyzulpuria *misl*, who, from Bhágú, changed his name into Bhág Singh. Bhág Singh soon became a man of note. Robbers and cut-throats were not scarce in those days in the Panjáb, nor were they slow in recognising those talents in Bágú which so well fitted him to become a leader of these desperadoes. All who desired to enrich themselves at the expense of their neighbours, rallied round his standard, and, with him, plundered the country in all directions.

Jassa Singh is the result of the union.

He is blessed by Mái Sundri, the widow of Guru Govind Singh.

Bhág Singh had great respect for Kapúr Singh, and never did anything contrary to his wishes. Badr Singh married Bhág Singh's sister, who presented him with a son, Jassa Singh, in 1718. When the boy was five years old, Badr Singh died. The widow then took the boy to Mái Sundri, widow of Guru Govind Singh, the Guru having died before Jassa Singh's birth, and the Mái blessed the little boy, and presented him with a silver mace, predicting that he would become a great man, and that he and his descendants would have mace-bearers to attend them. The mother and the child lived at Jalandar with Bhág Singh. Once, when Kapúr Singh went to Bhág Singh's house, he was greatly pleased at seeing the latter's widowed sister playing on the *rubáb*, with her long loose hair dishevelled, singing ballads in adoration of the Guru, her beautiful little son, Jassa Singh, playing by her side. Kapúr Singh blessed her for her devotion to the faith, and asked her to give him the little boy, whose features gave promise of a brilliant future. The mother, acceding to the wishes of the Sikh chief, gave him charge of the boy, and from that moment Kapúr Singh treated Jassa Singh as his own son. When he grew up, Kapúr Singh conferred on him high office, and he distinguished himself so greatly under that chief, that he soon came to be looked upon as a political leader. He also conducted the business of his uncle, Bhág Singh, who, however, was killed soon after in a fight with the Imperial troops at Hariana.

Is adopted by Sardar Kapúr Singh, Fyzulpuria, as his son.

Becomes a political leader.

Succeeds to the chiefship of the misl.

Bhág Singh having died without issue, the sardari of the *misl* devolved on his sister's son, Jassa Singh, as the only person fit to be the head of the confederacy. Jassa Singh, being a man of great enterprise, and possessing a knowledge of military tactics, soon acquired a great reputation. His political talents, religious zeal and lofty aspirations combined, rendered him one of the most powerful federal chiefs of the Panjáb. The Sikhs regarded him as their religious leader. Most of the leading sardars of the time took their *Páhal* from him, among them being Amar Singh, son and successor of Alá Singh, the chief of Patiálá. He claimed descent from the Rájputs of Jasselmer (though called a *kalál*, or distiller), and became the founder of the Kapúrthalla reigning family, which to this day is known by the title of the Ahluwalias. Like his predecessor, he respected the possessions of the Fyzulpuria chief, and joined him in many of his expeditions.

Is regarded as a religious preceptor.

Founds the Kapúrthalla reigning family.

On the invasion of Nádir Shah, Jassa Singh fled, and, with the other Sikh chiefs, took refuge in Muktesar, in the Ferozepur district; but, on the Shah's return, he appeared again and built the fort of Dalíwál on the bank of the Rávi, where he established his head-quarters. In 1743, he, with a large body of horsemen, attacked Dewán Lakhpat Rai, the deputy of Nawáb Zakaria Khan, commonly known as Khan Bahádur, son of Nawáb Abdul Samad Khan, who was carrying treasure from Emnabad to Láhore, put the dewán to death and carried off the treasure. The Láhore viceroy ordered Adína Beg Khan, governor of Bist Jalandar, to punish the Sikhs. Jassa Singh thereupon fled to the Sutlej; but the Sikhs were defeated with great slaughter, and hundreds of them were brought in chains daily

Establishes his head-quarters at Daliwál on the Rávi.

Is defeated by Adína Beg Khan, 1743.

to Láhore and beheaded at the Nakhaskháná, or horse market, now known as Shahidganj, in the Landa Bazar of Láhore. When these persecutions were over, Jassa Singh appeared on the banks of the Sutlej, where he seized on an extensive territory. At the same time the Bhangi *sardars*, Hari Singh and Jhandá Singh, were devastating the country by their marauding excursions. The Láhore viceroy sent Lachmi Narain, an officer of the darbár, with a large force to punish the Sikhs, who were again defeated with great loss, A.D. 1745, Jassa Singh taking refuge in the hills north of the Sutlej. Zakaria Khan died the same year, and two years after, Jassa Singh, assisted by other chiefs, made a raid on Kasúr, but their attention was diverted by the advance of Ahmad Shah, Durráni, who inflicted on the Sikhs a signal defeat in the neighbourhood of Sirhind.

Slaughter of the Sikhs.

The Sikhs are again defeated near the Sutlej, 1745.

Death of Zakaria Khan, 1745.

The Sikhs defeated by Ahmad Shah near Sirhind, 1747.

Ahmad Shah had scarcely left the frontiers of the Panjáb, when Jassa Singh attacked Rájá Gurdit Mal, deputy of Mir Mannú, commonly known as Nawáb Moin-i-ul-Mulk, viceroy of Láhore, near Hoshiarpur, but was repulsed. He then marched into Amritsar and slew Salábat Khan, the governor, and captured a great portion of the district. In 1749, Jassa Singh assisted Koura Mal, the dewán of Mir Mannú, in expelling Shahnawáz Khan, who had been appointed, by the Delhi emperor, viceroy of Multán. A closely-contested battle was fought between the troops of the dewán and those of Shahnawáz Khan in the neighbourhood of Multán, in which the latter was killed, and his troops were completely routed. Jassa Singh returned with his share of the booty, and honours were conferred upon him by the Láhore viceroy.

Jassa Singh assists Koura Mal in seizing Multan, 1749.

In 1753, Jassa Singh defeated Aziz Khan, commander of the Láhore forces, and, two years afterwards, he gained a decisive victory over Adína Beg Khan, Governor of the Jalandar Doáb, at Kadr, compelling the Khan to cede to him Fattehabad on the Biás. A eunuch in high favour with the Láhore court, was one Umed Khan, who was sent at the head of troops against the Kalál chief. Jassa Singh killed Umed Khan in action, and, soon after this, completely defeated Aziz Khan, the commander whom Adína Beg Khan had sent against him. When Ahmad Shah was engaged in his great campaign against the Mahrattas at Pánipat in 1761, Jassa Singh was not idle. He plundered Sirhind and Dialpur, seized Dogar, and Nypal in the Ferozepur district, where he built fortified posts, and captured Jagráon and Kot Isa Khan, on the other side of the Sutlej from Kádar Baksh Khan. About the middle of the same year, he seized Hoshiarpur, Bhiroz and Naraingarh in Ambála, and levied tribute from Rae Ibrahim Bhatti, chief of Kapúrthalla. He then penetrated into Jhang, south of Láhore, but was unable to obtain a footing there, in consequence of the bold front shown by Ahmad Khan, the Sial chief. After the departure of Ahmad Shah, in February 1761, Jassa Singh, with other Sikh sardars, again attacked Sirhind, when Obed Khan, the Láhore governor, was shut up within the walls of the latter city. He then took Laliana, Govindwal, Saliala and Bhopala, and extended his conquests as far as Taran Taran. Having then crossed the Biás, he captured Sultanpur and Talwandi. After the great battle at Barnálá, called by the Sikhs *Gullúghárá*, in which the combined forces of the confederacies were thoroughly defeated by Ahmad Shah on the 10th of February 1772, an expedition was made by the Durráni king against Jassa Singh, who, with the assistance of the *Phulkias* and *Nishanwálás*, had expelled his garrisons from Sirhind and was desolating the country. The Sikhs were completely defeated in this battle, and Jassa Singh, with the other Sikh chiefs, fled to the Kangrá hills.

Hostilities with the Mahomedan government, 1753-55.

Jassa Singh's conquests.

He is defeated by Ahmad Shah.

And escapes to Kangrá.

After the departure of Ahmad Shah, Jassa Singh, with the Bhangi,

Reappears and falls on Kasúr,

Ramgarhia and Kanhia *misls*, sacked Kasúr, defeating Alif Khan, the Pathan leader, and killing Kamal-ud-dín Khan and Hassan Khan, his lieutenants. The territory of Kasúr was made over to the Bhangi *misl*, who retained it till 1774. The confederacies then, collecting an army of 23,000 men, made an expedition to Sirhind, which they razed to the ground, killing the Afghan Governor, Zen Khan, and his deputy Lachmi Narain, the second in command. This was the most important victory gained by the Sikhs, who, on the fall of Sirhind, made themselves masters of all the surrounding country. Jassa Singh then returned to Amritsar, where he built the Ahluwalia Bazar, which exists to this day, the most attractive part of that commercial capital of the Panjáb, and assisted in the restoration of the golden temple, or Darbár Sahib, which Ahmad Shah had defiled with the blood of the sacred cows. In 1768, Jassa Singh overran Gháziuddinnagar and Anúp Shahr, in the neighbourhood of Delhi, and defeated the Moghal General, Mirza Sukhan, who was sent against him. In 1771 he seized Raikot, then held by the Pathans and Rájputs of Barwál, and, six years afterwards, captured Kapúrthalla from Rae Ibrahim Bhatti, and made it his head-quarters.

Which is made over to the Bhangis.

Fall of Sirhind.

Victory gained over the Moghal general in the neighbourhood of Delhi, 1768.

Extent of Jassa Singh's possessions.

Thus, the Kalál Ahluwalia became the greatest sardar among the Sikhs of the Bist Jalandar. His possessions extended on both sides of the Sutlej and also to the east. He was the first to proclaim the sway of the army of the new theocracy, or the *Dal* of the *Khálsá*, the army of the soldiers of God, and was called *Badsháh* (king) by his dependants and followers, though not by the Sikhs generally. He struck a coin in his name bearing the following inscription :—

He is called *Badsháh*, or king, by his followers.

His coin.

سکہ زد در جہان بفضل اکال — ملک احمد گرفت جسا کلال

"Jassa, the *Kalál*, having seized on the country of Ahmad, struck coin in the world through the grace of the Immortal."

His policy.

He possessed immense wealth and military resources. His policy was liberal, and he was friendly to the Mussalmans, many of whom held offices of trust under him.

He joins a coalition against the Ramgarhias, 1776.

In 1776, Jassa Singh entered into a league with Jay Singh, Kanhia, the Bhangis, Sukerchakias and other sardars, to expel Jassa Singh, Ramgarhia, from the Panjáb, so as to avenge an attack made on him by the Ramgarhias. A severe fight took place between the Ahluwalias, assisted by other confederacies, and the Ramgarhias, the result of which was disastrous for the lastnamed *misl*, for their chief was compelled to fly to Hariana, and his possessions north of the Sutlej were seized by the Ahluwalias.

His death, 1783.

Jassa Singh died at Amritsar in 1783, at the age of 65. A monument was erected to his memory in Dera Baba Attal, in the Amritsar golden temple, near that of Nawáb Kapúr Singh Fyzullapuria. The Sikh authors have praised the sardar highly for his saintly and generous disposition. He was a successful general in the field, and, though never acknowledged by the Sikhs generally as their king, yet was invariably intrusted with the command of the combined forces of the confederacies, when a joint action against the enemy was contemplated. His influence among the Sikhs was great, in consequence, chiefly, of his saintly position and orthodoxy, and the greatest sardars considered it an honour to be baptized by him.

His character.

His personal appearance.

In person, Jassa Singh was tall and handsome. It was, indeed, his noble features and attractive looks which, in his infancy, captivated Nawáb Kapúr Singh, who brought him up as his own son, which helped him on throughout his future career. His arms were of unusual length, and he was a good marksman with matchlock and bow. His liberality to the poor made him extremely popular. It is said that he never wore a suit of clothes a second time, but gave it to his attendants. Once, when Ahmad Shah was returning to Kábul, he took with him a body of two thousand Hindu women from the Panjáb to serve as slave girls for his countrymen. Prompted by a sense of duty to his fellow-countrymen, he fell on the Shah's troops one night and rescued the innocent creatures from the clutches of the hardy Afghans. He then liberally provided them with money and sent them all under proper escort to their respective homes. This act of courage and patriotism won for Jassa Singh the affectionate regard of all his countrymen, and tended to increase his influence and popularity among all classes of the people.

His generous disposition.

Jassa Singh, who, like his predecessor, left no male issue, was succeeded in the sardari of the *misl* by Bhág Singh, his second cousin, then in his 38th year. He twice made an attack on the Ramgarhias, and quarrelled with the Bhangi chief, Golab Singh. Sardar Jassa Singh, Ramgarhia, allied himself with Rájá Sansar Chand of Kangrá, and in 1801 routed the Ahluwalias under Hamir Singh, who was severely wounded. Bhág Singh, hearing of this reverse, collected the remainder of his forces, and marched in person to Phagwara against the enemy. He was there, however, taken ill and carried back to Kapúrthalla where he soon after died in 1801.

Bhág Singh succeeds.

His wars.

His death, 1801.

Bhág Singh was succeeded by his only son, Sardar Fatteh Singh, who formed an alliance, offensive and defensive, with Ranjít Singh, the great sardar of the Sukerchakia *misl*, who had just made himself master of Amritsar. The young chiefs swore perpetual friendship on the sacred *Granth*, and exchanged turbans in token of brotherhood. The expedition of the allied chiefs against the Pathan colony of Kasúr having failed, Fatteh Singh recrossed the Biás (1802-1803) and was engaged for the next two years in consolidating his dominions.

Sardar Fatteh Singh succeeds.

He forms an alliance with Maharájá Ranjít Singh.

Jaswant Ráo Holkar, the Mahratta chief, after meeting with reverses in his own country, entered the Panjáb in 1805, to form an alliance with the chiefs of the Cis-Sutlej States against the English. By a treaty concluded between the English and Sardar Ranjít Singh and Fatteh Singh on the 1st of January 1806, the sardars agreed to expel the Mahratta chief 30 *koss* beyond Amritsar, pledging never afterwards to have any concern with Holkar. Lord Lake pursued Holkar as far as the Biás, and presented Fatteh Singh with a leopard, as a mark of esteem and friendship, while the sardar presented the British General with a hawk.

The expedition of Holkar to the Panjáb.

Treaty between the British government and the Sikhs sardars.

Fatteh Singh proved a valuable friend and ally to Ranjít Singh, and accompanied the latter on his expeditions to the south of the Sutlej in 1806, and to Jhang the year following, when the fort was captured, and Ahmad Khan, the Sial chief, expelled, after a campaign which lasted several months. When Sir Charles Metcalfe came to Láhore in 1808, on a visit to the Maharájá, as the plenipotentiary of the British Government, Ranjít Singh sent the sardar and his confidential dewán, Mohkam Chand, to Kasúr, at the head of 2,000 horsemen, to receive the distinguished visitor. Fatteh Singh's friendship with the Maharájá was sincere, and, in the words of Sir Charles Metcalfe, Ranjít Singh was indebted for his extraordinary rise to this alliance. "The quiet character of Fatteh Singh," he says, "who was the equal, if not the superior, in rank and power, of Ranjít Singh, has yielded to the bold commanding spirit of the other, and he has been the ladder by which Ranjít Singh has mounted to greatness." He was present at the signing of the treaty between the British Government and the Maharájá, at Amritsar, whereby the former engaged not to interfere with the Maha-

Fatteh Singh co-operates with Ranjít Singh in his warlike operations of 1806.

The mission of Sir Charles Metcalfe to Láhore, 1808.

Sir Charles's opinion of Sardar Fatteh Singh.

The sardar accompanies the Kangrá expedition, 1809,

rájá's possessions north of the Sutlej, while the latter agreed not to make further encroachments south of that river. Fatteh Singh accompanied the Maharájá in the expedition to Kangrá in 1809, and, when Ranjít Singh marched to Multán in the spring of 1810, he left Fatteh Singh in charge of Láhore and Amritsar. The following year, he accompanied Ranjít Singh on his visit to Sultan Mahmúd, brother of Shah Sujáh at Ráwalpindi, where Mahmúd was then staying on his way to Káshmír, then tributary to the Kábul Government. The same year he reduced Sardar Budh Singh of Jalandar, accompanied by Dewán Mohkam Chand and Jodh Singh, Ramgarhia. Budh Singh fled across the Sutlej, and his estates, worth Rs. 3,00,000 per annum were confiscated to the Láhore darbár. He gallantly fought Fatteh Khan, the Kábul wazír, at Haidrú in 1813, on the side of the Maharájá, and the general was defeated and expelled from the Panjáb. He served the Maharájá in the Báháwalpur, Rajori and Bhimbar campaigns, was present at the famous siege of Multán in 1818, remained in charge of the capital during the campaign at Káshmír in 1819, and, two years later, assisted the Maharájá in the reduction of the fort of Mánkhera.

And helps Ranjít Singh in defeating Budh Singh of Jalandar, 1811.

His war services in the Panjab.

But the avaricious Maharájá now coveted the possessions of his ally, who had so often served with his contingent, and rendered him so much material help in his various expeditions. About this time, as before stated, the Sutlej was declared to be the boundary between the dominions of the Maharájá and those of the British Government, but the Maharájá inwardly disliked the terms of the treaty, and tried to find excuses for altering it. Fatteh Singh's confidential agent, Kadar Baksh, was in attendance on the Maharájá in the Láhore darbár, for the management of his affairs. He proved a traitor to his master, and Ranjít Singh, acting in concert with him, sent two battalions of the Láhore army, under Fakir Aziz-ud-dín and Anand Ram, *Pindari*, to Bist Jalandar, to seize the Ahluwalia possessions. Alarmed at the advance of the Láhore troops, Fatteh Singh, with the whole of his family, fled across the Sutlej, and concealed himself in Jagráon. The Maharájá's officers occupied the sardar's Trans-Sutlej territory, and expelled his garrison. In the meantime, the traitor, Kadar Baksh, who was staying with the Maharájá at Amritsar, died there (it is said, a painful death), and the Maharájá bestowed Talwandi on his sons. The sardar asked for British interference for the security of his Trans-Sutlej possessions, but this was impossible for the British Government to grant, as, under the treaty of 1809, they had expressly engaged not to interfere with the Maharájá's proceedings north of the Sutlej. But the expressed sympathy of the government with the sardar, on the Maharájá's confiscating Phagwara, one of the sardar's earliest possessions, had the effect of leading to an amicable settlement of the matter in dispute between the chiefs. Fatteh Singh returned to the Jalandar Doáb, where he was reinstated in his possessions by Nou Nehal Singh, and Desa Singh, on the part of the Láhore darbár. The whole of the sardar's possessions in the Bári and the Bist were restored. Fatteh Singh put the traitor, Kadar Baksh's sons in chains, and demanded large sums of money from them. Thenceforward he lived in Kapúrthalla in peace.

The Maharájá covets Fatteh Singh's possessions.

Confidence restored between Fatteh Singh and the Maharájá.

The death of Sardar Fatteh Singh, 1837. His character.

Fatteh Singh died in October 1837. He was possessed of an amiable and liberal disposition. Sir Charles Metcalfe called him "mild and good natured, seemingly simple, and undoubtedly wanting in energy." He had the greatest number of military troops under him, and was the largest landowner of all the chiefs in Ranjít's army, and he took seniority over them all. "This is the chief," says Sir Charles, "who was in Lord Lake's camp on the banks of the Biás. He there acquired a respect for the British character which causes him to look to the British Government with the hope of obtaining from it a release from the overbearing tyranny of Ranjít Singh." Notwithstanding the encroachments of the Maharájá on his territory, his feelings towards him were sincere, and he proved true to the bond of friendship which had been formed between him and the Maharájá. He beautified and enlarged Kapúrthalla. He was exceedingly fond of horses, and, in memory of a black charger, for which he had taken a fancy, he erected a beautiful tomb, which exists to this day at the entrance of Kapúrthalla city.

Nehal Singh succeeds.

Fatteh Singh was succeeded in his estates by his eldest son, Nehal Singh. He was fond of architecture, and constructed in Kapúrthalla, the head-quarters of his government, many beautiful edifices which exist to this day, a monument to his memory and public spirit. A quarrel took place between him and his younger brother, Amar Singh, who had been encouraged by the Láhore darbár to entertain hopes of the expulsion of his elder brother in favour of himself. A plot was hatched against the life of Nehal Singh by a number of conspirators, who attacked him, on one occasion, as he was coming out of his female apartments, but he defended himself gallantly and escaped with little injury. These would-be assassins contrived, however (shortly after their failure on his life), to seize and arrest him, and then obliged him to assign a liberal maintenance to his rival, Amar Singh. But the feud between the brothers did not end here. During the reigns, both of Ranjít Singh and of his successor, Kharak Singh, the quarrel remained unabated, and Amar Singh, by his residence in Láhore, secured the favour of Sher Singh, the new Maharájá, hoping to realise his object through the support of that monarch. In all probability his efforts would have been crowned with success, had not an accident occurred which cost Amar Singh his life. On the 28th of March, the Maharájá went on a boating excursion to the Rávi, attended by his courtiers, Rájás Dhian Singh and Hira Singh, Jamadar Khushal Singh, Sirdar Attar Singh, Kalianwala, Rae Kesra Singh, Bhái Gurmukh Singh and Sirdar Amar Singh, Ahluwalia. The boat was seen suddenly to fill with water and sink. The elephants upon which the party rode to the river, were immediately driven into it to the rescue, by which means all were saved, with the exception of Amar Singh. This incident left Nehal Singh in undisturbed and undisputed possession of his dominions in the Jalandar Doáb.

His quarrel with his younger brother, Amar Singh.

The life of Nehal Singh is attempted.

Death of Amar Singh.

When Lord Auckland visited the Panjáb in 1838, Sardar Nehal Singh rendered him important aid in collecting supplies, and otherwise assisting the British troops in their march to Kábul. Two years later, he sent a contingent to Kábul, though his troops had to march only as far as Jallálábád. His conduct was, at least, questionable during the first Sikh war of 1845. In spite of repeated requisitions from the military authorities, he failed to supply provisions to the British troops, which he was bound to do by the treaty of the 25th of April 1809, and afforded no assistance of any kind till after the Sikh army had been defeated. He was ordered to cross the Sutlej and join the British without delay, but he failed to do so, notwithstanding friendly warnings. On the 31st of November news was received by Major Broadfoot to the effect that the Ahluwalia subjects and agents had all joined the enemy, and they fought against the English at Aliwál and Buddowál. The rájá, in extenuation of his pusillanimous and treacherous conduct, pleaded his inability to act otherwise, in consequence of the mutiny of his troops. It, however, appeared to the British Government, after careful investigation, that the rájá's object was to keep aloof as long as the struggle for supremacy between the contending parties was undecided,

Nehal Singh's services to the British Government during the first Kábul war, 1838.

His unsatisfactory conduct during the first Sikh war of 1845.

and then to throw in his fortune with the more powerful side on the cessation of hostilities. As a punishment for his conduct, his territories, south of the Sutlej, estimated at Rs. 5,65,000 a year, were confiscated by the Government. This punishment had a wholesome effect on the sardar, who, in the second war, rendered valuable services to the British Government in collecting supplies. He offered to supply a contingent of troops for service in Multán, but advantage was not taken of their services. When the war was over, the Governor-General honoured the capital of the Ahluwalia chief with his presence, and created Nehal Singh a rájá.

His punishment.

His conduct during the second Sikh war satisfactory.

His reward.

He is created a rájá.

Nehal Singh died in September 1852, and was succeeded by his eldest son, Randhir Singh, then in his twenty-second year. Randhir Singh was an accomplished and enlightened prince. He rendered conspicuous services to the British Government during the Mutiny of 1857. In Jalandar, his troops guarded the civil station, the treasury and the jail, and he employed the whole of his cavalry in the pursuit of the mutineers. In July, Hoshiarpur was strengthened by his troops, consisting of cavalry, infantry and two guns. Both in the Jalandar Doáb and Cis-Sutlej, he and his brother, Prince Bikarma Singh, rendered important services. The number of their troops employed during the Mutiny in the British interests was 1,200 infantry, and 200 cavalry with five guns.

His death, 1852.

Rájá Randhir Singh succeeds.

His services during the Mutiny of 1857.

The services of his brother Bikarma Singh.

The services of the rájá and his brother were most warmly acknowledged by the British Government. This rájá paid an annual tribute of Rs. 1,23,000 in commutation of military service, but in recognition of the loyalty displayed by His Highness during the Mutiny, the Viceroy and Governor-General was pleased to remit a full year's tribute, and, in addition, to reduce the annual sum by Rs. 25,000; *khilats* worth Rs. 15,000 and Rs. 5,000 were awarded to the rájá and his brother respectively. The rájá's salute was increased, and he got the honorary title of *Farzand Dilband Rasikhal Itikad*, while Prince Bikarma Singh was honoured with the title of Bahádur. The rájá and his brother, Bikarma Singh, rendered valuable service to the British Government in Oudh during 1858, and, in the words of the Governor-General, fought "with conspicuous bravery." Their troops engaged the enemy on six different occasions, and captured nine guns. These indefatigable brothers continued for full ten months in the field at the head of their troops. For his devoted services in this part of the country, the rájá was most liberally rewarded. Two rich estates, called Boundi and Bithouli, in Oudh, which yielded Government one lakh of rupees per annum, were granted to the rájá, on *istimrari* tenure, at half rates. Prince Bikarma Singh received an estate worth Rs. 45,000 a year in the Bharaech district. The estates in the Bári Doáb, estimated at Rs. 26,300 per annum, which had been resumed on the death of Nehal Singh in 1852, were restored to the rájá, and finally he received the most highly valued of the privileges, that of adoption, by a *sanad* granted by Lord Canning, Viceroy and Governor-General of India. On the recommendation of the Chief Commissioner of Oudh, the Government of India was also pleased to confer on the rájá the honorary title of Rájá-i-Rájgan, or Rájá of Rájás, which title, however, was intended to have local force in Oudh only, in order to place him above the Oudh talukdars, many of whom were inferior to the Kapúrthalla chief, although called Rájás or Maharájás, such as Maharájá Mán Singh, Maharájá Dirg Biji Singh of Balrampur and others.

Their reward.

Services in Oudh, 1858.

The rewards for their services.

The grant of estates.

In October, 1864 Randhir Singh was invested with the insignia of the most exalted order of the "Star of India," at a darbár held at Láhore on the occasion, and attended by the Maharájás of Káshmír and Patiálá, the Rájás of Jhind, Faridkot and other independent Panjáb chiefs. On this occasion

The rájá is invested with the order of the "Star of India," 1864.

the Governor-General, Lord Lawrence, addressed the rájá, in Hindostáni, to the following effect:—

"Rájá Randhir Singh, Rájá of Kapurthalla,—it is with much satisfaction that I find myself empowered by Her Most Gracious Majesty, the Queen of England, to confer on you so great a mark of her favour as that of the Star of India. This honour has only been granted to those princes and chiefs who unite high rank with great personal merit. It rejoices me to instal you among the chosen number. The speech of Lord Lawrence.

"Your grandfather, Sardar Fatteh Singh, was a chief of considerable renown. He was the well-known leader of the Ahluwalia confederacy, and the companion-in-arms of the great Maharájá Ranjít Singh. Your father, Rájá Nehal Singh, was an old friend of mine, when you were yet a youth. When he passed away, your highness succeeded to his duties and responsibilities and have worthily discharged them. When the Mutiny of 1857 broke out, you were one of the foremost chiefs of this country to do your duty, and ranged yourself on the side of the British Government. After the fall of Delhi your highness headed your troops, conducting them to Oudh, and there assisted in recovering that province. For these services you received, at the time, much praise and liberal rewards; and now, to crown all, you are about to obtain a most signal mark of honour from Her Majesty the Queen of England and India. In the name, then, of the Queen and by Her Majesty's commands, I now invest you with the honourable insignia of the Star of India, of which most exalted order Her Majesty has been most graciously pleased to appoint you to be a knight. I have addressed you in Hindostáni, in order that the princes and chiefs now present may, the more readily, participate in this ceremony, and that your relatives and friends may be more highly gratified; otherwise I should have spoken in English, for I know that you thoroughly understand my language. This circumstance, no doubt, has operated as a bond of union between your highness and my countrymen."

The rájá was a good English scholar, and had long been desirous of paying a visit to England. He accordingly left for England in March 1870, but died at Aden on the 2nd of April, from an affection of the liver, which had much impaired his health. His body was conveyed to Bombay, and there received by his son, Kharak Singh. The cremation ceremonies were performed at Nasik, the sacred city of the Hindus, and his ashes were conveyed to Harduár. Rájá Randhir Singh was succeeded by his son, Kharak Singh, who died a premature death, leaving a minor son.* Death of Rájá Randhir Singh, 1870. Rájá Kharak Singh succeeds. His death.

6.—THE DALÍWÁLIA *MISL*.

This *misl* was so denominated from the village Dalíwál, near Dera Bábá Nának, on the Rávi, east of Láhore, where the original founder, Golába, a *Chhatri*, resided. Having been initiated into the *Páhal* of the Guru, and having changed his name from Golába to Goláb Singh, he became, like the rest, a robber, and the immense riches which he collected, enabled him to maintain a large body of cavalry with which he scoured the country in search of plunder. In his acts of depredation he was joined by a shepherd named Tárá Singh, who received the nickname *Gheba*, from the ingenious manner in which he conveyed his flocks across the mountain glens. He became Goláb Singh's chief associate, and, on his death, succeeded him to the sardari of the *misl*. He joined the Bhangis in their expedition into Kasúr and amassed a great† fortune by the plunder of One Golába, a *Chhatri*, founds the *misl*. Tárá Singh his associate in his exploits. He succeeds Golába.

* This prince, having attained his majority, is now the ruling sovereign of Kapurthalla.
† According to Rai Kanhia Lal, he acquired ornaments worth four lakhs of rupees, besides cash and other valuable property.

that rich Pathan city. He converted Gohar Dass, the influential *Choudhri* of Gang, to the Sikh religion, and the *Choudhri's* example was followed by the whole people over whom his influence was exercised. Thus strengthened, Tárá Singh attacked Sirhind, with the other Sikhs, and helped in the devastation of that town, which had been re-populated after the great havoc committed by the Byragi Bandá. He conquered Fattehábad and the whole country east of the Sutlej, the troops under his control numbering between 7,500 and 10,000. When Ranjít Singh was in the zenith of his power, he sent an expedition, under the command of Fatteh Singh, Ahluwalia, against the Dalíwálias. The result of this invasion of the territories of the Dalíwália chief was that his entire possessions were confiscated; that his *misl* ceased to exist any longer as a body, and that he himself became a refugee. On the death of Tárá Singh, certain villages east of the Sutlej were bestowed in jágír on his sons, Duswandha Singh and Chandá Singh, but these were finally included in the jágír of Bikarma Singh Bedi, the spiritual leader of the Sikhs, and thus the *misl* collapsed.

The military expeditions of Tárá Singh.

Ranjít Singh reduces the *misl*.

7.—THE NISHÁNWÁLÁ *MISL*.

Origin of the *misl*.

This *misl* was founded by Sangat Singh and Mohar Singh, *Játs*, the standard-bearers of the *Dal*, or assembled *Khálsá* army, whence the name Nishánwálá, given to the *misl*. They committed their depredations on the other side of the Sutlej, and carried their predatory inroads to the remotest parts of the country. Once they fell on the populous town of Mirath and pillaged it, considerably enriching themselves thereby. Their chief town was Ambála, where they kept their military stores and supplies, the number of troops under their control being 12,000. Mohar Singh became the head of the *misl* on the death of Sangat Singh. Mohar Singh died without issue; and Ranjít Singh, who was then encamped on the other side of the Sutlej, hearing of his death, deputed his dewán, Mohkam Chand, at the head of an army, to reduce the *misl*. Ranjít's troops soon drove the Nishánwálás from the field, terminating the existence of this *misl*. Their treasures, goods and effects were taken possession of by Mohkam Chand. After the treaty with the British, when the Sutlej was declared to be the line of demarcation between the Sikh and British dominions, Ambála lapsed to the British Government, while Shahábad, belonging to subordinate chiefs, remained under protection, and thus the *misl* became extinct.

Its military strength.

Mokham Chand, the general of Ranjit Singh, reduces the *misl*.

8.—THE FYZULPURIA *MISL*.

Kapúr Singh founds the *misl*.

This *misl* is also called Singhpuria. The founder of the confederacy was Kapúr Singh, a *Ját* zemindar, who wrested the village Fyzullapur, near Amritsar, from its Mahomedan founder, Fyzullah, and, conquering the country round, gave the chief village the name of Singhpuria, whence the name given to the family Singhpuria, though it is frequently called Fyzulpuria. The *Dal* of the *Khálsá*, or the army of the theocracy of Singhs, whose foundation was laid in the times of Farrukhseer, reached the height of their power under the leadership of Kapúr Singh, who really organised this *Dal*, or multitude of soldiers. He was undoubtedly the most distinguished of the Sikh leaders who paved the way for the greatness of the nation as an independent ruling power. His followers, who numbered thousands, gave him the title of nawáb, as a compliment to his genius, this being almost the only instance of a Sikh assuming a Mahomedan title. He converted a large number of people, *Játs*, carpenters, weavers, *Jhiwars*, *Chhatris* and others to the persuasion of Govind, and the religious respect in which he

His great influence over the people of his sect.

He is by them called nawáb.

was held was so great, that initiation into the *Páhal* of the Guru with his hands was considered a great distinction. He used to pride himself upon having killed 500 Mahomedans with his own hand, and, as he had fulfilled the commands of Govind, who enjoined on all true disciples the necessity of revenge upon Mahomedans, he consoled himself with the idea that his heavenly reward would be very great for so meritorious a deed. He had under his control 2,500 armed retainers, and this force, though small, was the fiercest and most dreaded of all the Sikh soldiers for its bigotry. Kapúr Singh scoured the country up to the walls of Delhi, and his possessions extended east and west of the Sutlej. He was certainly the most illustrious and most dreaded of the Sikh sardars before the days of Jassa Singh, Ahluwalia, and Ala Singh of Patiálá. Nawáb Kapúr Singh died at Amritsar in 1753, bequeathing the honours which he enjoyed in the *Khálsá* army, to the Ahluwalia sardar. He called Jassa Singh to him on his death-bed, and, making over to him the steel mace* of Govind, the last great Guru, hailed him as the future leader of the *Khálsá*, and as his successor to the influence which he exercised over the community of the Sikhs.

His zeal for his religion.

His military strength

And possessions.

His death, 1753.

On the death of Nawáb Kapúr Singh, his territory descended to his nephew, Khushál Singh, who equalled his uncle in wisdom and bravery, and extended his conquests on both sides of the Sutlej. His possessions included Jalandar, Nurpur, Bahrámpúr, Bharatgarh, and Patti, and he wrested Banor from the Patiálá chief. Like his illustrious predecessor, he made a great number of converts, and Ala Singh, the rájá of Patiálá, had the honour of initiation into the *Páhal* by him. His hatred of the Mahomedans was equalled only by his undaunted courage, and the cavalry man who shot dead Nawáb Zen Khan, the Mahomedan subadar of Sirhind, in 1763, was his own follower. He seized Ludhiáná, but had subsequently to give half of the district of Banor to Patiálá.

Khushál Singh succeeds.

His conquests.

Khushál Singh was, on his death, in 1795, succeeded by his son, Budh Singh; but the confederacy fell before the rising power of Ranjít Singh, who seized the whole of the Jalandar territory, and the sardar was compelled to take up his residence to the north-west of Ambála, between Kiratpur and Machiwara, under British protection. Budh Singh died in 1816.†

His death, 1795.

Budh Singh succeeds.

Ranjit Singh seizes on the *misl*.

9.—THE KARORA SINGHI *MISL*.

This *misl* is also called *Panjgarhia*, from the village of their first chief, one Karori Mal, a *Ját*, who, on initiation into the *Páhal*, changed his name into Karora Singh, and became a robber like the rest. He founded the *misl* with two companions, Mastán Singh and Karam Singh. Karora Singh left no heir, and was succeeded by Bhagel Singh, who, after the assassination of Zen Khan, subadar of Sirhind, became the most formidable of the Sikh leaders. He made Chiloundi, 20 miles from Karnál, on the Jagádhri road, his head-quarters, and extended his conquests to the banks of the Sutlej, on the east, and the Jalandar Doáb. He had under his control 12,000 fighting men.

Karora Singh founds the *misl*.

Bhagel Singh succeeds him on his death.

His conquests.

The Sikhs having risen against Mulla Ahmad Dad, the Moghal Faujdar of Sirhind, defeated and slew him, in the year 1778. They had also conquered the Málwa country from the Mahomedans. On receipt of this intelligence, Shah Alam, the Delhi emperor, deputed Abdul Ahad Khan, surnamed Nawáb Majad-ud-doula, with an army, under the command of Prince Jawán Bakht (known also as Farkhunda Bakht and Akbar), to chastise the

He aids the Imperial troops of Delhi against the rebel Sikhs.

* In the Akál Bunga, at Amritsar, this weapon of much historical interest is yet to be seen.

† The family is now represented by Sardar Jai Singh, of Manoli, who is in receipt of a jágír from the British Government.

Sikhs. The imperial host, 20,000 strong, with an efficient siege train, reached Karnál without the slightest opposition, and was joined there by Bhagel Singh, *Karora Singhia*, Sahib Singh, *Khundawálá*, and Karam Singh, *Shahid*. The sardars of Kalsia, the most powerful of the *misl*, were represented by Desú Singh of Kythal, who had joined the imperial party at Delhi. The insurgent Sikhs were forced to pay a fine of three lakhs of rupees to the nawáb, and pledged themselves to the payment of an annual tribute. The minister, having been joined by the Sikh troops at Karnál, proceeded northwards; but his progress was checked by Amar Singh, the rájá of Patiálá, who was joined by the Phulkian chiefs, Jhind, Nabhá, Bhador and Malod, the Kanhias and Ramgarhias. The united forces of the Sikh confederacies made a general onset on the imperial army, which offered but a faint resistance. The victorious Sikhs, after this disasterous campaign, which

The campaign of 1878-79.

took place in the winter of 1778-79, poured into the upper Doáb and plundered it. In the whole of this expedition, Bhagel Singh, Karora Singhia, figured prominently on the side of the Imperial army.

In the days of anarchy, when the once powerful Moghal empire was rapidly sinking, the Mahrattas looked on the Panjáb as the richest field for plunder. The expedition of Dhara Mahratta into Patiálá was a complete success. The spring of 1788 witnessed the incursion of another Mahratta

Bhagel Singh joins the Mahrattas, 1788.

adventurer, named Amba Rao, who penetrated into the Panjáb, supported by the famous Rohilla chief, Gholam Kadar, son of Zábita Khan. The first Sikh chief who welcomed the invader was Bhagel Singh, Karora Singhia, who tendered his submission to him, and became one of his most devoted followers.

Dies.

Jodh Singh succeeds.

On the death of Bhagel Singh, Jodh Singh, the son of his friend and associate, Sardar Gurbaksh Singh, the founder of the Kalsia family, was acknowledged as the head of the Karora Singhia confederacy, though his widows, Ram Kour and Ráj Kour, held Chiloundi for many years; and on their death, the estate lapsed to the British Government in September, 1845. Jodh Singh was a man of great ability. He conquered Chichroli, and took possession of Dera, Bassi, Lotab and Achrak. He made encroach-

His conquests.

ments on the Patiálá and Nabhá territories, but was prevented from a repetition of these incursions by Rájá Sahib Sing of Patiálá giving his daughter in marriage to his son, Hari Singh, in 1803. At the siege of Naraingarh, in 1807, the sardar rendered valuable services to Maharájá Ranjit Singh, and was handsomely rewarded by jágírs. He died after the

His death, 1818.

The confederacy is absorbed into the Kalsia family.

siege of Multán, in 1818, and the Karora Singhia confederacy was absorbed into the Kalsia family, whose chief, Bishan Singh, has now an estate yielding Rs. 1,30,000 per annum, with a population of 62,000, and takes precedence over all Cis-Sutlej chiefs, expect Patiálá, Jhind, Nabhá, Malerkotla and Faridkot.

10.—THE SHAHID AND NIHANG *MISL*.

Origin of the *misl*.

The *Akális* or immortals.

This *misl* was headed by persons who claimed to be descendants of the honoured martyrs and zealots beheaded by the Mahomedans at Damdamá, west of Patiálá. The *Akális*, or immortals, were fanatic priests at the temple of Amritsar, who, along with their fanaticism, had a weakness for appropriating to themselves the property of their neighbours. The class of these devotees was founded by Guru Govind, whose institutions it firmly maintained against the innovations of the Byragi faqír, Bandá. They always exclaim *Akál, Akál** in their prayers, wear blue chequered clothes, put

* *A*, Sanskrit prefix, meaning negation; *kal*, death. Thus the compound word, *Akál*, means never-dying, or immortal, and is one of the names of the divinity.

bangles of steel round their wrists, and a circular, sharpened, bright sword round their head.

The heads of the confederacy were Karam Singh and Gurbaksh Singh, whose possessions extended east of the Sutlej, and who had two thousand horsemen under their command. The possessions of the *misl.*

11.—THE PHULKIA *MISL.*

The head of this *misl* was *Phul*, a *Ját* of the Sindhu tribe, thirtieth in descent from Jesal,* the founder of the family, and the state and city of Jesalmir, in Rájputána, who, like almost all other *Játs*, was a Bhatti Rájput. He was the second son of Rúp Chand, by his wife, Mái Umbi, and was born in Mouza Bedowáli, or Mehráj, in 1619 A.D. He founded a village five miles distant from Mehráj, which he called, after his name, *Phul.*† The Delhi Emperor, Shah Jahán, by a *firman*, confirmed him in the office which his ancestors had held. He fought the Bhattis near Phakkarsar in Bhatinda, under Hayat Khan, the Rájput chief, who, meeting with a signal defeat, fled to Bhatner. He was soon after defeated by Isa Khan, Rájput, the founder of a village of that name, this side of the Sutlej, near Ferozepur, assisted by Nawáb Husein Khan, the Pathan chief of Kasúr. The village of *Phul* was plundered by Isa Khan, and the chief, *Phul*, was compelled to retire to his old residence in Mehráj. Having gained in strength, *Phul* declared war against Doulat Khan, the father of Isa Khan, whom he defeated, and, having expelled Mula Singh, the Rájput agent at *Phul*, he recovered possession of that place. After this he attacked the Bhatner chief, Hayat Khan, whose nephews, Mohabat Khan and Mahbub Khan, he slew. *Phul* became a powerful sardar and withheld the payment of revenue to the Imperial Governor of Jagráon, whom he defeated and put in confinement; but every mark of respect was shown to him while under arrest. The prophesy of Guru Har Govind, that *Phul* would become a great man, was fulfilled, for *Phul* had seven sons who became ancestors of the reigning families of Patiálá, Jhind and Nabhá, called after his name the *Phulkias*. The houses of Bhador, Malod, *Landgarhia*, and the family of Jiandan, sprang from his issue, and attained to great wealth and power.

Phul founds the confederacy.

As also the village of that name.

His defeat by the Mahomedan chiefs.

He is expelled from his village.

His subsequent successes.

He becomes a man of great note. The prophesy of Har Govind fulfilled.

The death of *Phul* is said to have occurred under somewhat mysterious circumstances. It is said that he was educated by a celebrated *jogi*, named Samerpuri, who taught him the art of suspending the breath (*habsidam*).‡ The Governor of Sirhind had placed him in confinement for his failure to pay the Government revenue, and *Phul* feigned death by suspending his breath. His custodians, believing him to be dead, made his body over to his relatives. It happened that one of his wives, who alone knew the mysterious power possessed by her husband, was absent at the time. His other relations, ignorant of the circumstance, immediately proceeded to cremate his remains. This took place in Bahádurpur, near Dhanola, in the territory

The death of *Phul*, 1652.

---

* Jesal flourished in the time of Prithi Raj, the king of Ajmir and Delhi, the most powerful of Indian monarchs. His son, Hembel, was expelled by the Ghorian Sultan of Delhi, Shaháb-ud-dín, but was again received into favour and intrusted with the government of Sirsa and Bhatinda (including the country between the Sutlej and the Jamna). He built a strong fort near the town of Hissar, founded by Feroz Shah, where he died in 1271 Samvat. He was succeeded by his son Jaudra, remarkable for being the father of twenty-one sons. The ancestors of the houses of Kythal, Jhumba, Arnowly, Sadhowal, the sardars of Attari, and the rájás of Faridkot, are, like the *Phulkia* family, the descendants of Jandra, the grandson of Jesal.

† The village is now situate in the territory belonging to the Rájá of Nabhá.

‡ Mention of this art is made in the Shastras and the *Granth*, under the name Puranayam. The Hindus maintain that the breath is contracted into the brain, believed to be the seat of life.

of Nabhá, in A.D. 1652, in the seventieth year of the deceased's age. Certain, however, it is that *Phul* died of apoplexy, contracted while a prisoner of the Mahomedan Governor of Sirhind.

Rámá succeeds.

His victories over the Mahomedan chiefs.

Phul was succeeded in the sardari by his second son, Rámá, or Ram Chand. He was constantly overrunning the Bhatti country, and he defeated Hassan Khan, the chief of the tribe, near Chándab, carrying away much plunder, money, horses and cattle. He then made a raid into the territory of Isa Khan, his father's old enemy, defeated him, and carried away everything of value on which he could lay his hands. He waged war with the Mahomedan chief of Kot, and, after a desperate fight, defeated him, and then plundered his camp, which was immensely rich. He was at length assassinated, in the seventy-fifth year of his age, by the sons of Chen Singh, his own sardar, in Malerkotla, in 1714 A.D., in avengement of the death of their father.

Is assassinated, 1714.

Ala Singh succeeds.

He defeats the Rai of Kot, 1731.

His troops slay the imperial general.

Rámá was succeeded by his third son, the famous Ala Singh, the founder of the Patiálá ráj, born in 1695. He rebuilt Barnálá, which had fallen into ruins, and made it the capital of his dominions. He then fought the Rai of Kot, who had collected a large force, assisted by several chiefs, among others, Jamal Khan, chief of Malerkotla, and Nawáb Saiyad Asad Ali Khan,* the Imperial faujdar of the Jalandar Doáb. After a hard contested engagement, the Sikhs carried the day. Asad Ali Khan was slain; his troops fled, and their example was followed by the rest. A large number of the enemy's troops were killed and many were made prisoners. This victory was gained in 1731.

His fame increases.

This brilliant success over the combined forces of the Rájputs and the Pathans, spread terror throughout the neighbouring country, and tended materially to strengthen the position of Ala Singh. The Sikhs across the Sutlej flocked to his standard, and the number of his followers rapidly increased. He conquered many villages and built new ones. His fame reached Delhi, and the emperor, Mahomed Shah, deputed the viceroy, Mir Mannú, and Sami Yar Khan, with a *firman* (dated 21st Ramzan 1137 H.), asking Ala Singh to assist in the management of Sirhind, and promising him the title of ráját if he acquitted himself to the satisfaction of the Imperial court.

He makes war on the Bhattis.

Founds the fort of Bhawánigarh, 1749.

Ala Singh now made war on his hereditary foes, the Bhattis, under Mahomed Amir Khan, son of Hassan Khan of Bhatner. He then joined Ali Mahomed Khan,† the Rohilla faujdar of Sirhind, but was ultimately thrown into prison, and would have perished in neglect had not one of his devoted followers arranged for his release. In 1749 he built the fort of Bhawánigarh, and three years afterwards, Gurbaksh Singh, *Kabka*, one of his sardars, and his brother-in-law, conquered for him the district of *Sanáwar*,‡ also known as *Chourasi* (eighty-four), from the number of villages

* His cousins, Nawáb Saiyad Fakir-ullah Khan and Nawáb Sultan Ali Khan, were faujdars of Thara and Ludhiáná, respectively. The descendants of the family still flourish in the town of Jagráon, in the Ludhiáná District, and are respected for their Arabic learning. Saiyad Rájab Ali Khan *Arastu Jah*, Mir Munshi to the late Board of Administration, was a great-grandson of Nawáb Fakir-ullah Khan. He died in September, 1869, and his two sons, Sharif Hassan and Sharif Hussein, are alive at this moment.

† Ancestor of the Nawáb of Rampur, in Rohilkhand. According to the author of *Serul Mutakharin*, he was found on the roadside, when a baby of 18 months. Daud Khan, an Afghan Omerah of the time of Aurangzeb, picked this child up and adopted him, giving him the name of Ali Mahomed Khan. He succeeded Daud Khan on his death, and became the chief man in Bundelkhand. He fought Har Nand, the faujdar of Moradabad, and defeated him, the faujdar being killed in this engagement. Nawáb Kamr-ud-din Khan was then sent to chastise him. He was then imprisoned, but was again released, and restored to his dignity, on engaging to serve loyally the imperial house.

‡ A town three miles south of Patiálá.

comprised in the district. One of these was Patiálá, now the capital of the territory, where Ala Singh the following year (1757 A.D.) built a small mud fort, called *Sodhion ki Garhi*,* from the Sodhis living in that quarter. Mahomed Sallah, *Khokar*, the chief of Sanáwar, made his submission to Ala Singh. Ala Singh then conquered a great portion of Samana† after a battle with the Rájputs, in which Farid Khan, their chief was killed. He made war on the Bhattis who had been assisted by Nawáb Násir Khan, the Moghal Governor of Hissar, and, after eight days' hard fighting, dispersed them with great loss, 1757. This victory tended much to consolidate Ala Singh's power and increase his influence.

Conquers Sanáwar and builds Patiálá, 1757.

Defeats the Bhattis a second time, 1757.

In the year 1762 A.D., Ahmad Shah invaded Barnálá, then the chief town of Patiálá, to punish the audacity of the Sikhs, who had given trouble to Zen Khan, governor of Sirhind, after his departure from India in the previous year. The Sikhs made common cause against the Mahomedan invader, and the *Phulkia* chiefs, the Ahluwalias under Jassa Singh, the Fyzulpurias, the Singhpurias, the Bháis of Kythal, and many other chiefs formed a league to oppose him. A great battle was fought near Barnálá, which ended in the complete overthrow of the Sikhs, whose loss was estimated at 20,000 men. The Pathans plundered Barnálá, and seized Ala Singh, who was taken a prisoner before the Shah. Ráni Fatto, wife of Ala Singh, obtained the release of her husband by paying to the imperial treasury a present of four lakhs of rupees. A dress of honour was conferred on Ala Singh by the Shah, who embraced him, and, in a *firman*, signed by his wazír, Shah Wali Khan, to the address of Zen Khan, the subadar of Sirhind, enjoined the latter to treat his dominions as separate, and to respect his independence. Ala Singh now laid the foundation of a masonry fort at Patiálá, and directed his attention to the improvement of that town.

The battle of Barnálá.

Defeat of Ala Singh and his associates in arms, 1762.

Ala Singh is taken a prisoner by the troops of Ahmad Shah, Abdáli,

But is subsequently released and pardoned.

The Durráni king again invaded India the next year, and created Ala Singh *Chakladar*, or lessee, of the province of Sirhind, on condition of his paying three-and-a-half lakhs of rupees a year as revenue. The Shah was also pleased to confer on Ala Singh the title of rájá and a dress of honour. Ala Singh accompanied the Shah to Láhore, but, on his return, was laid up with fever at Patiálá, where he died after a short illness of two days, in the seventeeth year of his age, on the 22nd of August, 1765.

Is created a rájá.

His death, 1765.

Ala Singh was succeeded in the ráj by his grandson, Amar Singh. The Durráni king, Ahmad Shah, during his last invasion of India, in 1767, honoured Amar Singh with the title of Rájá-i-Rájgan Bahádur. At Kara Bowana, 24 miles south of Ambála, an interview took place between the king and the rájá, when valuable presents were given to the latter with a flag and a drum, the insignia of an independent prince. He was also permitted to strike coin in his name, he in his turn presenting the king with a *nazráná* of a lakh of rupees.

Rájá Amar Singh succeeds.

Privileges conferred on him by the Durráni sovereign.

Amar Singh made war on the Afghans of Malerkotla, whose chief, Jamal Khan, the Sikhs killed in battle. He made successful attacks on Mani Májrá and Kot Kapurá, captured *Sefabád*, a strong fort, north of Patiálá, expelling its Mahomedan masters, seized Fattehábad and Sirsa, and invested Ránia, a strong fort, eight miles west of Sirsa, held by Mahomed Amin Khan, Bhatti. The Imperial troops were repulsed before Jhind, and Ránia was captured. Faridkot was then overrun, in 1777, but no attempt was made to take formal possession of the territory. He conquered Bhatinda, after a severe

His conquests.

* Traces of this *Garhi* are yet to be seen. It is not the site of the present fort of Patiálá.

† A town, fifteen miles south of Patiálá, with 13,000 inhabitants. It was governed by Jalál-ud-din Feroz, Khilji, who ascended the throne of Delhi, in 1198 A.D., after the death of Sultan Moz-ud-din Kykubad.

fight of four months, and gave Sukh Chen, the chief of the territory, twelve villages as maintenance. The rájá died in February, 1781, of dropsy, brought on by excessive drinking, in the thirty-fifth year of his age.

His death, 1781.

Succession of Sahib Singh. And of Rájá Karam Singh. The adventurer, George Thomas.

Amar Singh was succeeded by his son, Sahib Singh, a child six years of age, and he by Karam Singh. Patiálá was ravaged by the English adventurer, George Thomas,* originally in the service of the famous Zebul Nissa, commonly called the Begum Samrú; but a peace was concluded between him and the Sikhs, in A.D. 1801, the adventurer retiring to his fort in Hansi. For many years Patiálá was under the influence of women of courage, wisdom and activity, such as Ráni Hukma, Ráni Khem Kour, Bibi Pardhan, the grand-aunt of Sahib Singh, and Ráni Rajandar of Phagwara, a first cousin of Rájá Amar Singh, who, at the head of a considerable force, marched to Patiálá, and, releasing Nannú Mal, reinstated him in his office of minister. Ráni Sahib Kour, sister of Sahib Singh, fought heroically against the Mahrattas under Abta Rao and Lachman Rao, when those chiefs crossed the Jamna, and invaded Patiálá. In a brisk engagement which took place between the two armies, near Mardánpur, a few miles from Ambála, the Sikhs, who were no match for the disciplined troops of the enemy, began to give way before superior numbers. The Ráni, seeing that retreat would be disastrous to their cause, at once jumped out of her chariot, and, drawing her sword, exclaimed to the soldiery: "Soldiers! I have resolved not to retreat. It would be a shame for the Sikh nation, if, at this moment, they left a woman, the sister of their sovereign, to be slain by their enemies." The gallantry displayed by this extraordinary woman put the Sikhs to so much shame, that they resolved to conquer or die. They attacked the Mahrattas furiously, but were replused. At length a night attack was resolved upon, and this threw the Mahrattas into such a state of consternation that they retired precipitately, and in great disorder, towards Karnál.

Eminent women connected with the Patiálá house.

The gallantry of Ráni Sahib Kour.

She defeats the Mahrattas.

Death of Rájá Karam Singh, 1845. Rájá Nirandar Singh succeeds. His services during the war with the Láhore State, 1847.

Karam Singh died, in December 1845, and was succeeded by his son, Nirandar Singh, then twenty-three years of age. Nirandar Singh rendered valuable service to the British Government during the war with the Láhore State, and his services were duly acknowledged in a *sanad* granted him by the Governor-General, in September 1847. Renewed assurances of protection, and a guarantee of his rights in his former possessions, were given to the rájá, who, on his part, bound himself to the suppression of *satti*, infanticide and dealings in slaves within his territories.

His reward.

Conspicuous services in 1857-58.

During the great Mutiny of 1857-58, no prince in India stood so boldly and heartily on the side of the British Government as the Maharájá of Patiálá, who was the most conspicuous for his loyalty and attachment to the paramount power. He acted with a resolution, courage and devotion worthy of the name of his illustrious ancestors, which has endeared his memory, not only to all Englishmen, but also to all those Indians who appreciate loyalty to a Government under whom they enjoy the blessings of peace, prosperity and freedom. During the darkest days of the Mutiny, when less sincere friends shrank back, he came forward with redoubled zeal, and put all his resources, unreservedly, at the disposal of the British authorities. The king of Delhi sent him a letter, asking his aid against the British Government, and promising rewards; but the Maharájá for-

* George Thomas came to India in 1781. For several years he was in the service of the Begum Samrú, but was reduced in rank for some misconduct. He took service under Apa Khandi Rao, a Mahratta chief, and instructed the Mahratta troops in the European system of drill. The district of Jhajjar was assigned to him in jágír, but Thomas soon afterwards became independent and rose to power. He ruled the country about Hansi and Hissar. For his military adventures, see the *Memoirs of George Thomas*, by W. Franklin, Calcutta, 1803.

warded the letter in original to the British authorities. He sent a contingent to Delhi under Sardar Partáb Singh, which did excellent service during the siege and assault of that town, the hot-bed of the mutineers. The assistance rendered by the Maharájá was warmly acknowledged by General Wilson. He despatched his troops for the protection of Karnál, Thanesar and Ambála and guarded the Grand Trunk Road from Karnál to Phillour. He sent his mules, elephants, camels and carts to Kálká for the purpose of transporting European troops from the hill stations of Dagshái, Sabbatu and Kasouli to Ambála. The detachments sent by him, under the command of General Van Courtland, were of great service in restoring order in Sirsa, Rohtak and Hissar. His troops fought the mutineers at Ferozepur, Sahároanpur and Jagadhari. He sent a detachment to Alipur, which did good service under General Napier. A contingent of 2,000 troops, sent by him under the command of Dewán Jag Desh Singh and Nehal Chand, restored tranquillity in the Dhoulpur State. He also sent troops to Jhajjar, Oudh and Gwalior, and they were of great service in restoring order and punishing the insurgents. His troops further guarded the ferries on the Chambal river, while the Maharájá, in his own territories, made effectual arrangements for furnishing supplies and carriage, and keeping roads in repair for the transport of British troops. The refugees from Hissar, Rohtak and Sirsa, were looked after with the greatest attention, and munificently supplied with all the comforts of life. The Maharájá expressed his earnest desire to go to Delhi in person, but was dissuaded by the civil authorities and the Commander-in-Chief, as his presence in the Panjáb was of great importance. He also advanced a loan of five lakhs of rupees to the Government, and expressed a desire to double that amount, but the Government wanted no more.

Rewards for the services rendered.

The Maharájá's loyal services during the Mutiny were warmly acknowledged and magnificently rewarded by the British Government :—

1. The Narnol territory of the Jhajjar dominions the Nawáb of which, Abdul Rahmán Khan, had rebelled against the Government, yielding a revenue of two lakhs a year, was ceded to him in perpetuity with full sovereign powers.

2. The Bhádor State, with an income of 80,000 rupees, per annum, which had been long the subject of dispute between the Maharájá and the British Government, was made directly tributary to the Patiálá ráj, with all the rights and privileges which the British Government exercised.

3. The magnificent house of Zinat Mahal, Begum of the ex-king of Delhi, was granted to the Maharájá.

4. The *Phulkian* chiefs, namely, the Maharájá of Patiálá and the rájás of Jhind and Nabhá, were permitted, in all cases of failure of male issue, to adopt an heir from among the descendants of their common progenitor *Phul*, and, in case of such heir by adoption not being named before the decease of any one of the three, permission was given to the surviving rájás to elect a successor from the same stock. The titles of the Maharájá in 1857 were :—

Maharájá Dhiraj Rajeshar Maharájá-i Rajgán Narindar Singh Mahandar Bahádur."

These were increased as follows in 1858 :—

The Maharájá's new titles.

Farzandi Khás Doulat-i-Englishia, Mansuri Zamán, Amirul Omerah, Maharájá Dhiraj, Rajeshar Sri Maharájá-i Rájágan Nirandar Singh Mahandar Bahádur."

Meaning :—

"Choicest son of the British crown, bravest amongst the brave, most grand amongst the grandees, the great rájá over all other rájás, the holy Maharájá of the Rájás, Nirandar Singh Mahandar Bahádur."

Right of adoption granted.

Other concessions were also made; but the most valued of all these was that of the right of adoption, which was also most liberally extended to other chiefs of the Panjáb, Sikhs, Rájputs and Mahomedans. This much-prized boon at once convinced the Panjáb rájás and chiefs that, far from coveting their dominions, the British Government sincerely desired the long and prosperous existence of their States.

Death of Maharájá Nirandar Singh, 1862.

The Maharájá did not live long to enjoy the honours which he had so deservedly won. He fell ill of fever, and died in 1862, in the thirty-ninth year of his age, and the seventeenth of his reign.

Maharájá Mahandar Singh succeeds.

He was succeeded by his son Mahandar Singh, then only ten years old, and the affairs of State were intrusted to a Council of Regency, provided for in 1858.

His education.

In February, 1870, the Council of Regency was dissolved, and the Maharájá, having completed his eighteenth year, was invested with full administrative powers. His education was conducted by Ram Chandra, the great mathematician of Delhi, and, in May 1870, he was created a knight of the most exalted order of the Star of India.

His death, 1876.

Maharájá Rajandar Singh succeeds.

Mahandar Singh was an enlightened prince, and introduced many measures of reform in his State. In May 1870, he presented the Panjáb University College of Láhore with a donation of Rs. 70,000, of which Rs. 20,000 were intended for founding a scholarship in honour of the visit of the Duke of Edinburgh to the Panjáb. He visited Simla and Calcutta, and subscribed large sums to charitable institutions in those places. On the 15th of October of the same year, he formally opened the Sutlej bridge at the request of Sir Henry Durand, Lieutenant-Governor of the Panjáb. He died in April 1876, in the twenty-fourth year of his age, of diseases contracted through excessive use of alcoholic liquors, and was succeeded by his son, Rajandar Singh, a child of four years of age. The affairs of State were again intrusted to a Council of Regency, nominated by the rájás of Jhind and Nabhá, in pursuance of the treaty with the Patiálá State. The Maharájá has been recently invested with powers, and promises to be a most enlightened ruler.

THE JHIND FAMILY.

Tiloka becomes the head of the family.

Gajpat Singh, his grandson.

His conquests and reverses.

He assumes independence, 1772.

The family of most importance among the *Phulkias*, next to the Patiálá House, is that of Jhind. The founder of the family was Tiloka, eldest son of Choudhri *Phul*, the founder of the *Phulkia* dynasty. Gajpat Singh, the grandson of Tiloka, after the defeat and murder of Zen Khan, the Afghan Governor of Sirhind, in 1763, seized a large tract of country, including the districts of Jhind and Safidon, which extended to Pánipat and Karnál. But he paid the revenue to the emperor of Delhi, and acknowledged himself as his vassal. Having once fallen into arrears, he was taken a prisoner to Delhi by the minister, Najib Khan, and was kept in confinement for three years, at the end of which period he was set at liberty, on leaving his son, Mehar Singh, as a hostage. On reaching Jhind, he arranged to pay three-and-a-half lakhs of rupees to the Imperial treasury, by which he not only affected the release of his son, but was created a rájá by the Emperor, Shah Alam, by a *firman*, or royal grant, dated 25th Shawal 1185 A.H. (1772 A.D.). He assumed independent power, and struck coin in his capital.

Rájá Sarup Singh. His action during the war of 1845-46.

In the campaign of 1845-46, Rájá Sarúp Singh, sixth in descent from Rájá Gajpat Singh, was called upon by the British authorities to supply 150 camels for the use of the Sirhind Division. This the rájá neglected to do, in spite of repeated promises and assurances. As he had always received the most liberal treatment at the hands of the British Government, who recognised his claims, which could hardly be said to have any legal foundation, the Government was dissatisfied with his conduct, and Major Broadfoot inflicted upon him a fine of Rs. 10,000. To wipe out this disgrace, the rájá acted with so much zeal and devotion, that he was soon again received into favour. He made himself very useful in providing supplies and carriage, and furnished a contingent which served with the British troops. Another detachment accompanied the Patiálá contingent under Captain Hay, and did good service. The rájá also sent a detachment of his troops to Káshmír, to assist the British officers in suppressing the rebellion of Shekh Imám-ud-dín against Maharájá Goláb Singh. These services were duly rewarded by the British Government, and not only was the fine of Rs. 10,000, imposed by Major Broadfoot, remitted, but lands of the value of Rs. 3,000 a year were granted to him, and the Government engaged never to demand from the rájá or his successors tribute or revenue, the rájá on his part undertaking to place all his troops at the disposal of Government in all cases of emergency, to keep military roads in thorough repair, and to suppress slavery, infanticide and *satti* in his dominions. He further abolished transit duties in the Jhind territory, and, in consideration thereof, the British Government was pleased to confer upon him further lands worth Rs. 1,000 a year.

Warning given.

The Rájá's subsequent good services.

He is amply rewarded for those services.

The Rájá's engagements with the British Government.

The rájá rendered important service to the British Government during the Mutiny of 1857. He was present at the siege of Delhi, and his troops, under Commandant Káhan Singh, fought side by side with the English, when that town was assaulted and the city walls were scaled. The services of the rájá and his troops in connection with the fall of Delhi were prominently noticed by General Wilson in his despatch of 22nd September, 1857, when he said: "Not only have they discharged harassing duties in constant escort of convoys, but they aided the General on more than one occasion in the field, and finally participated in the capture and assault of Delhi." A contingent from Jhind joined the British camp at Alipur, and behaved so well in the battle of Badli Serae as to receive (in the field) the thanks of the Commander-in-Chief, who, moreover, showed his appreciation of the rájá's services by presenting him with a captured gun. The rájá sent his troops to Karnál and Pánipat, where they aided materially in maintaining order and discipline. A detachment sent by the rájá secured from destruction the bridge of boats at Bághpat, 20 miles north of Delhi, and thus enabled the British troops from Mirath to cross the Jamna and join Sir Barnard's forces. Insurgents from the Hansi, Hissar and Rohtak districts had crept into some of the Jhind villages, and stirred up the people, but the rájá was on the spot and the disturbance was promptly quelled.

The rájá's services during the Mutiny of 1857.

The rájá's services to the British Government were splendidly rewarded. The Government of India, in a notification dated 5th November 1857, was pleased to declare that his steady support called for the special thanks of the Government. The territory of the nawáb of Dadri, comprising 575 square miles, 20 miles south of Jhind, with an income of Rs. 1,03,000 per annum, which had been confiscated in consequence of the nawáb's rebellion, was conferred upon the rájá. The territory was capable of great improvement, and the revenue has now almost doubled. Thirteen more villages near Sangrúr, worth Rs. 13,813 per annum, were ceded to him in perpetuity. The confiscated house of Mirza Abubakar, the rebellious prince of Delhi, was also granted to the rájá, as a mark of favour, and the number

He is munificently rewarded.

His titles.

of his salutes and trays of presents increased. The honorary title, *Farzand Dilband Rasik-ul-itikád Rájá Sarup Singh Bahádur Wali Jhind*, was bestowed upon him, and many other concessions were granted him. The Bádrukhán chiefs, near Sangrúr, were made his feudatories, and provision was made for the succession in the event of a minority, or death of a chief without having appointed a successor. He was nominated Knight Grand Commander of the Star of India in September, 1863, but died of acute dysentery on the 26th of January, 1864. He was succeeded by his son Raghbhir Singh, a fine soldier and a man of great tact and judgment.

His death, 1864.

THE NABHÁ FAMILY.

The Nabhá family, with that of Jhind, has descended from the same ancestor, Tiloka, eldest son of *Phul*. Hamir Singh, grandson of Tiloka, a brave and enterprising chief, founded the town of Nabhá in 1755. He conquered many villages, and joined Ala Singh of Patiálá in his expedition against Zen Khan, the Afghan governor of Sirhind, who was slain in action, the tract of country known as Amloh, having fallen to his share. In 1776 he conquered Rori from Rahím Dád Khan, the Moghal Governor of Hansi, and coined money in his capital.

Hamir Singh founds Nabhá, 1755.

His conquests.

Hamir Singh's successes and popularity about this time were due greatly to the ability of his dewán, popularly known as *kubba*, or the hunchbacked. But he did not live in perfect security, owing to the insatiable avarice of his predatory neighbour, Gajpat Singh, the Rájá of Jhind. The latter, in 1774, found some pretext for invading the Nabhá territory, took Hamir Singh prisoner, and wrested from him the important town of Sangrúr, which was never afterwards restored.

He is taken prisoner by the Rájá of Jhind, 1774.

Hamir Singh died in 1783, leaving a son and heir, Jaswant Singh, eight years old. During his minority the affairs of the State were conducted by his mother, Mái Desu, who died in 1790. She was a woman of great courage and resolution, and, during the imprisonment of her husband, recovered most of his territory, which had been forcibly seized by the Jhind rájá. Jaswant Singh entered into an alliance with the British Government, when Holkar, the Mahratta Prince, was advancing northward to Láhore, and refused to aid the latter in any way. Perceiving also that friendship with Ranjít Singh, the grasping Maharájá of the Panjáb, was dangerous, he put himself under British protection, along with the other chiefs of Malwa and Sirhind, 1809. A *sanad*, signed by the Governor-General, was granted to him, exempting him from payment of all tribute, and confirming him in the enjoyment of all ancient privileges. All the other chiefs of the Cis-Sutlej States had the same privileges conferred on them by the proclamation dated 3rd May, 1809.

His death, 1783.

His widow, Mái Desu, acts as regent for her minor son Jaswant Singh.

Jaswant Singh puts himself under British protection.

In September 1810, Mahomed Akber Shah, emperor of Delhi, conferred on the rájá the title of *Bárár Báns Sármour Malvindra Bahádur*. The rájá was a faithful ally of the British Government. When Holkar, the Mahratta, halted at Nabhá, in 1804, and demanded the rájá's aid against the British Government, he had the firmness to refuse all assistance to him, pleading frankly his engagements with the latter Government. He assisted the British in the Gorkha campaign, and in the expedition to Bikaner, and, during the march of the British troops to Kábul, advanced the Government a loan of six lakhs of rupees. The rájá died on the 22nd of May 1840, in the sixty-sixth year of his age, and was succeeded by his son, Devindar Singh.

His services.

His death, 1840.

Devindar Singh succeeds.

Devindar Singh did not promise to be a successful ruler. From boyhood he was surrounded by flatterers and parasites, who impressed upon his

His incapacity.

weak mind false notions of his importance and dignity—he introduced the most absurd forms of etiquette * into his court;—while the Brahmins, who recited *sloks* before him every evening, extolling his virtues and exalting his dignity far above all others, intoxicated him with the belief that the power of the English was on the wane, and that the day was fast approaching when Nabhá would alone reign supreme in the Panjáb.

His conduct in the campaign of 1845. *His punishment.*

When the war between the British and the Láhore Government broke out in 1845, the rájá not only showed his sympathy with the Láhore darbár by overt acts, but intentionally failed to provide supplies on the road from Kálká to Rahana, or to comply with other requisitions of the British Agents for supply. As a punishment for this wilful negligence, the estates of Dehrarú and Amloh, belonging to the Nabhá territory, were confiscated, and, at the close of the war, the rájá was not permitted to attend the Viceregal Darbár at Ludhiáná, where all the other protected chiefs paid their respects to His Excellency the Governor-General. A formal inquiry was subsequently instituted into his conduct, and Rájá Devindar Singh was ordered to be deposed, and his eldest son, then a boy of seven, installed on the *gadi*, under the guardianship of Ráni Chand Kour, his step-grandmother, assisted by three other officers of State. The ex-rájá was deported to Mathra, but, being troublesome there, was removed to Láhore in December 1855, and kept under surveillance in Maharájá Kharak Singh's house, where he died in November, the following year.

He is removed to Láhore, 1855. *And dies there, 1856.* *Rájá Bharpur Singh succeeds.* *His services during the Mutiny.*

Rájá Bharpur Singh, who succeeded his father, while yet a child, attained age of discretion a few months only after the Mutiny broke out in 1857. The youthful rájá, on this occasion, acted with a sincerity and devotion worthy the name of the great *Phulkian* family. He was desirous of operating against the mutineers in person, and of proceeding to Delhi, where the rebels were assembled in great force, and was prevented from carrying out his wish by the British Government only, in consequence of his youth and the onerous nature of the duty. But a small detachment of 300 troops was accepted from him for service in Delhi, and this rendered efficient help during the siege. The rájá's troops also did good service in Ludhiáná, in maintaining order, and a detachment of them was of great use in Jalandar, in destroying a bridge and opposing the passage of the mutineers, when a great number of the mutineers were killed, and several of the rájá's men shared the same fate. Another detachment, supplied by the rájá, formed an escort to the siege trains which accompanied the Commander-in-Chief from Phillour to Delhi. He advanced the Government a loan of two lakhs and a half of rupees at a time when money was very scarce, and was of infinite use in furnishing supplies, carriage and camels. He also performed every other duty which was required from him with the greatest promptitude and willingness.

His rewards.

For these services, he was most liberally rewarded by the British Government. The Commissioner had recommended for him the grant of a territory in the Ludhiáná, or Ferozepur District, valued at Rs. 30,000 per annum, and certain other privileges, such as an increase in the number of pieces in a *khilat*, his treatment on terms of equality with the Rájá of Jhind, his being received under salutes at military stations,

* He required his courtiers to prostrate themselves when they paid their compliments, or spoke to him, and he pressed them to show the most slavish humility in speech and manner. He denied the Rájá of Jhind any title of honour, on the plea of his being only collaterally related to the late rájás, and he would style the Maharájá of Patiálá only as rájá. He refused to see the Lieutenant-Governor of Bengal beyond his own territories, and desired to omit all titles due to officers of the British Government.

or at the Governor-General's darbár, and the return of his visits to the Governor-General by the Foreign Secretary to the Government of India. The Government was also pleased to confer upon him substantial gifts of far greater value. A portion of the confiscated Jhajjar territory, with an income of Rs. 1,06,000 a year, was granted to the rájá in perpetuity, with independent powers and privileges, as in his ancestral estates, on the condition of good behaviour and service, military and political, in all cases of emergency. His *khilat* was more than doubled, and his salute was increased. The right of adoption was conferred upon him by a *sanad*, granted in May, 1860; his honorary titles* were increased; his visits to the Governor-General were ordered to be returned by the Foreign Secretary, and he was invested with powers of life and death. The gifts were truly royal and well deserved.

The address of Lord Canning at the Ambála darbár, 1860.

In the darbár held at Ambála, on 18th January 1860, Lord Canning, Viceroy and Governor-General, addressed the Nabhá chief as follows, in the presence of all the Cis-Sutlej chiefs :—

"You have been equally forward and equally earnest, with other chiefs of your ancient race, in your support of the authority of the British Government.

"The assistance which you gave to the Queen's army in the transport of its heavy artillery from the Sutlej to Delhi was a signal and valuable service.

"Your loyalty and zeal have, as in the case of your fellow-chiefs, been marked by rewards and honours, which will assure you of the high esteem in which your conduct is held by the Government.

"Additions have been made to your possessions, and the grant will be formally confirmed to yourself and your descendants. If these should fail you, your adoption of an heir from amongst the members of the *Phulkian* House will be legally recognized.

"It is the desire of the Queen's Government that the power and dignity of your loyal family should endure and flourish."

Death of Rájá Bharpur Singh, 1863.

Lord Elgin, Viceroy and Governor-General, gave Rájá Bharpur Singh a seat in the Legislative Council in September 1863; but the rájá died on the 9th of November of the same year, of a severe fever contracted from over-exertion. He left no son, and was succeeded by his younger brother, Bhagwán Singh, the fixed *nazráná* in accordance with the terms of the *sanads* of 1860 and 1862, equal to one-third of the gross annual revenue of the State, being paid to the Government on the occasion.

Rájá Bhagwán Singh succeeds.

12.—THE SUKERCHAKIA *MISL*.

THE ANCESTORS OF MAHARÁJÁ RANJÍT SINGH.

The last, but by far the most important, of the Sikh confederacies, whose members were destined to rule over the fortunes of the whole of the Panjáb, was the Sukerchakia *misl*. Ranjít Singh, afterwards known as the Maharájá, belonged to this *misl*. An account of the descent and family of this extraordinary man will, it is hoped, be of particular interest to the reader. The following is the genealogy :—

The genealogy.

* His honorary title was *Farzand Arjumand Ekidat Pywand Doulat-i-Englishia Barar Bans Sarmour Rájá Bharpúr Singh Mohandar Bahádur of Nabhá*.

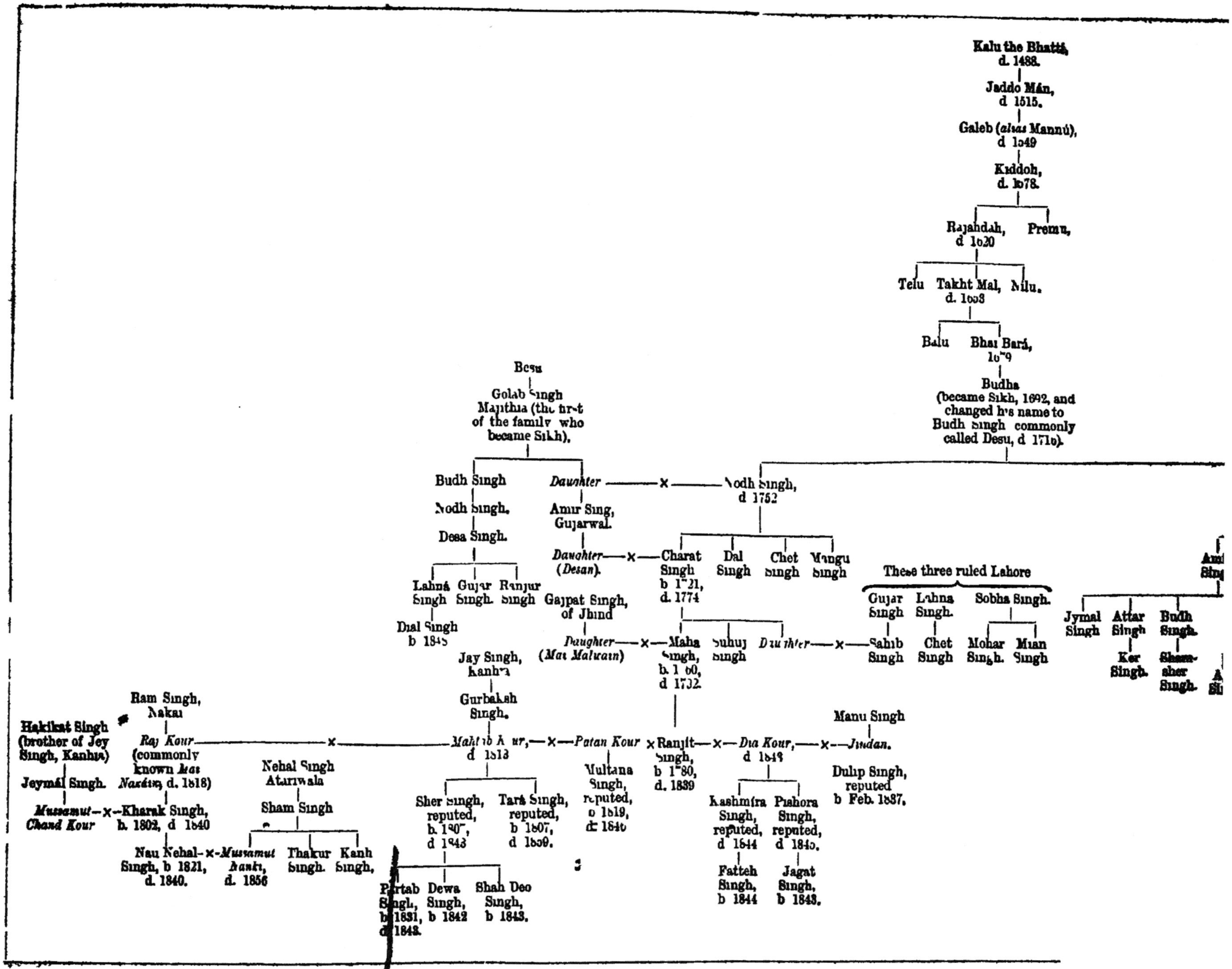
Kalu the Bhatti, d. 1488.
Jaddo Mán, d. 1515.
Galeb (alias Mannú), d. 1549
Kiddoh, d. 1578.
Rajahdah, d. 1620
Premu,
Telu
Takht Mal, d. 1658
Nilu.
Balu
Bhai Bará, 1679
Budha (became Sikh, 1692, and changed his name to Budh Singh commonly called Desu, d. 1716).
Besu
Golab Singh Majithia (the first of the family who became Sikh).
Budh Singh
Daughter
Nodh Singh, d. 1752
Nodh Singh.
Amir Sing, Gujarwal.
Desa Singh.
Daughter (Desan).
Charat Singh b. 1721, d. 1774
Dal Singh
Chet Singh
Mangu Singh
Lahná Singh
Gujar Singh.
Ranjur Singh
Gajpat Singh, of Jhind
Dial Singh b. 1845
Daughter (Mai Malwain)
Maha Singh, b. 1760, d. 1792
Suhuj Singh
Daughter
These three ruled Lahore
Gujar Singh
Lahna Singh.
Sobha Singh.
Sahib Singh
Chet Singh
Mohar Singh.
Mian Singh
Jymal Singh
Attar Singh
Budh Singh.
Ker Singh.
Shamsher Singh.
Jay Singh, Kanhia
Gurbaksh Singh.
Ram Singh, Nakai
Hakikat Singh (brother of Jey Singh, Kanhia)
Raj Kour (commonly known Mai Nakáin, d. 1818)
Mahtab Kour, d. 1813
Patan Kour
Ranjit Singh, b. 1780, d. 1839
Dia Kour, d. 1848
Manu Singh
Jindan.
Jeymál Singh.
Nehal Singh Atariwala
Mussamut Chand Kour
Kharak Singh, b. 1802, d. 1840
Sham Singh
Sher Singh, reputed, b. 1807, d. 1843
Tará Singh, reputed, b. 1807, d. 1859.
Multana Singh, reputed, b. 1819, d. 1846
Kashmira Singh, reputed, d. 1844
Pishora Singh, reputed, d. 1845.
Dulip Singh, reputed b. Feb. 1837.
Nau Nehal Singh, b. 1821, d. 1840.
Mussamut Nanki, d. 1856
Thakur Singh.
Kanh Singh.
Partab Singh, b. 1831, d. 1843.
Dewa Singh, b. 1842
Shah Deo Singh, b. 1843.
Fatteh Singh, b. 1844
Jagat Singh, b. 1843.

Kálú the common ancestor, 1470.

He lived an obscure life.

His death about 1488.

Kálú, a Hindu *Jat* of the Baraech *Got*, lived an obscure life with his family, in Mouza Pindi Bhattian, 40 or 50 miles south-west of Láhore, about the year A.D. 1470. The family had lived there for three generations. Having quarrelled, early in life, with the men of his family in Pindi Bhattian, Kálú left the place, with his wife, with whom he travelled through the low countries. He finally settled down in a village called Sánsri, near Rájá Sansi, the present patrimonial jágír of the Sindhianwálá family, 4 or 5 *kos* west of Amritsar. This was the resort of the wandering tribe known as *Sansis*, who lived in tents or huts made of reeds, and, forming themselves into bands of robbers, plundered the country in all directions. The couple took shelter in a *Sansi* hut, and shortly afterwards Kálu's wife gave birth to a son, who was named Jaddoman, styled the *Sansi*, consequent, it is said on his being treated by the *Sansis* as their adopted son. Another story, is that he was the real son of a *Sansi*, and that Kálú was his reputed father. Kálú subsequently removed, with his wife and only child, to Sand, about a *kos* and a half from Dhrounkal, and four *kos* from Wazirábad, and died there about 1488.

His son, Jaddoman.

His death about 1515.

In consequence of Jaddoman being brought up in the *Sansis* camp, he exhibited a strong inclination to follow the profession of those with whom he had associated in early life. He accompanied the *Sansis* in all their plundering expeditions, and was eventually killed upon one of these occasions. This was about 1515.

His son, Galeb.

He becomes a great robber.

Dies, about 1549.

His son, Galeb, possessed all the thieving proclivities of his freebooting ancestors, and his associates nicknamed him "Mannu," from his ingenious method of driving large herds of cattle from the banks of the Chináb and Jhelum across the Rávi, and there disposing of them. He successfully headed gangs of *Sansi* plunderers, and carried his depredations into the Mánjha country. He died at Sand, about 1549, from the effects of a wound received in one of his marauding excursions.

His son, Kiddoh.

Removes to Sukerchak, 1555.

Leads a peaceful life.

Acquires small landed property.

Dies, about 1578.

Kiddoh, the only son left by Galeb, removed from Sand, first to Kiáli and then, about 1555, to Sukerchak, then a small village, a *kos* and a half south of Gujranwálá. He brought with him a large number of cattle, which he inherited from his father, and, unlike him, led a peaceful and quiet life. The *Sansis* and others of his country, denominated him "Ramthal," or the man devoted to God, on account of his peaceful and quiet nature. By his industry and perseverance he became the owner of several small plots of land in Sukerchak, which he cultivated, and by which he supported himself and his family. He died about the year 1578, leaving two sons, Rájádab and Premú.

Rájádab, his son.

Dies, about 1620.

Rájádab followed the quiet and steady habits of his father, and, in addition to his agricultural pursuits, opened a small grocer's shop in Sukerchak. He made himself familiar with the Landá, or Gurmukhi, characters, and was able to read and write them. He died about 1620, leaving three sons Telú, Takht Mal and Nilú.

Takht Mal his son.

Dies, about 1653.

Telú and Nilú died young. Takht Mal extended his small business by money-lending and shopkeeping. He also took on lease several small plots of land in Mouza Sukerchak and Kiáli, and was regarded as one of the leading men of the village. He died about 1653, leaving two sons, Bálú and Bárá, known also as Bú Bárá or Bhái Bárá.

Bárá, son of Takht Mal.

Bálú became a brigand, and was killed at the age of eighteen, in one of his nocturnal marauding attacks on a village. Bárá, in consequence of his religious temperament, and of his becoming the disciple of a pious devotee in Gujranwálá, obtained the sobriquet of Bhái, or the "peaceful brother." He learnt to read the *Granth*, or the holy scriptures of the Sikhs, and at the age of 25 set out for Amritsar to receive the *Páhal* or Sikh baptism, but met with an accident which prevented him from effecting his object. He, however, assumed the character of a religious fanatic, and is known to have kept his head unshaven, and to have preached the religion of Nának in the villages adjoining Kiáli and Sukerchak. While promulgating the precepts of the Guru, and assuming the character of a saint, he was too shrewd to neglect his own interests, for he soon became possessed of half the lands in Sukerchak. He did not keep a shop, like his father, but reading the holy *Granth* and telling his beads were his chief occupations. Although accident had prevented him from formally embracing the religion of Nának himself, he enjoined on his son, Buddhá, the necessity of being initiated into the *Páhal*, and of visiting Amritsar for that purpose. His dying injunction to his son was that he should read the holy *Granth* and become a Sikh, and, with this his last advice to him, he died in 1679.

He becomes a religious fanatic.

His death, 1679.

His son Buddhá.

Buddhá was only nine years of age when his father died. He remembered his father's dying advice, and, on attaining the age of discretion, which was about the year 1692, he set out for Amritsar, the sacred city of the Sikhs, with several of his new friends, and was there, with his companions, initiated into the *Páhal* of the Guru. Buddhá was, therefore, the first man of the family who adopted the Sikh religion. He was, however, not a man of peaceful disposition, as his father and grandfather had been, but was courageous, enterprising and sagacious. He associated himself with the plundering gangs of Sikhs and *Sansis*, and accompanied them in their predatory excursions, which, however, were confined to carrying away herds of cattle from distant districts of the south. The daring adventures performed by Buddhá Singh, and the success which attended his exploits, soon won for him the reputation of being the boldest and the most resolute of the Sikh freebooters in the country. He built a large house for himself at Sukerchak, which he made his head-quarters, and where he was respected by the people, who gave him the title of *Choudhri*, or headman of their village. The cattle which he carried away, he either appropriated to himself, or sold near Amritsar and Láhore. He thus became possessed of wealth, and was looked upon as a man of some importance.

He becomes a Sikh, 1692.

He becomes a notorious freebooter.

The mare on which Buddhá Singh used to ride was a piebald, and was as famous in the country as its rider. People called this mare Desi; hence the nickname Desú given to Buddhá Singh. It is said he swam across the Jhelum, the Rávi and Chináb fifty times on this mare. He was a brave and courageous man, and is said to have received, during his lifetime, twenty sword cuts and nine matchlock wounds, without his physical strength failing him. He was good humoured, ready witted, and merciful to the oppressed. An anecdote is related of his returning a poor widow all her cattle, which he had seized in ignorance of her helpless condition, without even letting the woman know his name. He died of apoplexy in 1716. His wife, overwhelmed with grief at his death, ran a sword through her heart. The bodies of the husband and wife were burnt together. They left two sons, Nodh Singh, and Chandá Singh, from the latter of whom the Sindhianwálá branch of the family, related to the Maharájá on the mother's side, sprang.

His adventures.

His death, 1716.

Origin of the Sindhianwálá family.

According to the ideas prevailing at the time when Nodh Singh lived, cattle-lifting was considered mean and less profitable, while the business of a *Dhárwi*, or highway robber, was looked upon as an honourable and lucrative profession. Having abandoned the former occupation, Nodh Singh adopted the latter, and was soon enabled to amass a large fortune by his marauding expeditions. He became a notorious highway robber, and

Nodh Singh, the son of Buddhá Singh.

was much dreaded by the people from the borders of Ráwalpindi to the banks of the Sutlej. His influence and standing among the Sikhs, *Játs* and Sardars increased simultaneously with his wealth, and in 1730, Goláb Singh, son of Besú, a Sansi *Ját* of Majithia, married his daughter to him. Goláb Singh, and his brother, Amar Singh, also became Dharwais, and, by the wealth they amassed, became important men and were looked upon as the chiefs of Majithia, where they lived. Nodh Singh joined the Fyzulpuria *misl* of Nawáb Kapur Singh, about the time of the first invasion of the Abdáli King, Ahmad Shah, and, by plundering the baggage and the stragglers of the invading army, enriched himself and his associates. He was now looked upon as the chief of Sukerchak, where the spoils gained were carefully amassed. In 1747, Nodh Singh had an affray with some Afghans, and received a gun-shot wound in the head. It did not prove fatal, but the accident incapacitated him from leading an active life. He lingered for five years without interfering in the affairs of the country, and died in 1752, leaving four sons, Charat Singh, Dal Singh, Chet Singh, and Mangi Singh.

His alliance by marriage with the Majithia family.

He is acknowledged chief of Sukerchak.

His death, 1752.

The youngest son, Mangi Singh, assuming the character of a religious fanatic, began to preach the *Granth*, and was called a Bhái. He died without issue. Charat Singh, born in 1721, kept aloof from the Fyzulpuria *misl*, and soon after persuaded his two younger brothers to do the same. He had his own views of self-aggrandizement, and he truly laid the foundation of the greatness of the *misl*. On account of family dissensions, he removed his head-quarters to Rájá Sansi, near Amritsar; but in 1752, or the year following, he collected around him a number of *Mazbis*, *Sansis*, and other wandering robbers, and, having organised them into a separate body, led them into the adjoining tracts of country on plundering excursions. The success which attended the exploits of the little band, soon made it the terror of the people. The neighbouring chiefs were inspired with confidence in the prowess of the Sikhs, and the impression became so firmly rooted, that Mahomed Yár, the headman of Kiáli, entrusted Charat Singh with the management of his States in Kiáli, and himself joined the band, with fifteen horsemen. Milka Singh, of village Marliawálá, near Gujranwálá, also joined Charat Singh, about the same time, with twenty mounted followers. Thus, the band, originally small, increased to 150 armed horsemen, and with their help Charat Singh, becoming irresistible, took forcible possession of all the villages in the neighbourhood of Gujranwálá, including Katchi Serae, where he established his head-quarters.

His son, Charat Singh, born, 1721.

The successes of his marauding excursions.

He takes forcible possession of the villages in the vicinity of Gujranwálá.

The sardar most intimate with Charat Singh, about this time, was Amir Singh of Gujranwálá, the grandson of Sún Náth, a *Sansi*, whose conviction of the truth of the Sikh religion had induced him to receive his *Páhal* at the advanced age of one hundred years. Like Charat Singh, this Amir Singh belonged to the Fyzulpuria *misl*, but, having dissolved his connection with it, he began to plunder on his own account, and became a notorious robber. His depredations extended from the banks of the Jhelum to the walls of Delhi; and, having acquired large territorial possessions in Gujranwálá, he was looked upon as the chief man of the district. He had three sons and two daughters, the eldest of whom was married to Charat Singh about the year 1756. This marriage tie united the wealth and strength of the two sardars, and led to the formation of a separate *misl*, which, after the place where they resided, was named the Sukerchakia *misl*. The allied chiefs, under one banner, headed the confederacy, though Amir Singh, on account of his age, was never able to take a prominent part in its affairs. They fell on Emnabad, plundered the city, killed the Moghal faujdar, and

Sardar Amir Singh of Gujranwálá.

His eldest daughter is married to Charat Singh, 1756.

The formation of the Sukerchakia *misl*.

The allied chiefs plunder Emnabad.

carried away much booty and munitions of war from the arsenals there. In 1777, the sardars, considering the Katchi Serae ill-adapted to meet their wants, began to build a mud fort, better suited for the purpose; but their attention was diverted by an attack on their possessions by the Mahomedan chiefs of Láhore, who, jealous of the rising power of the Sikhs, had moved with a strong force to destroy their strongholds and disperse their bands. The Sikhs united together and defended their property against the Mahomedans, an account of which has been given in the beginning of the preceding chapter. Suffice it to say, the invading army was completely routed, and its chiefs narrowly escaped with their lives, leaving their military stores and ammunition in the hands of the enemy. From this time the audacity of the Sikhs increased, and they began to organise themselves into a still more compact and formidable body under Charat Singh, who, as his fame increased, established his power as the head of the Sukerchakia *misl.*

And repel an invasion made on their territory by the Mahomedan Governor of Láhore.

Charat Singh becomes the head of the confederacy.

On the appearance of Ahmad Shah, the Abdáli, with his Afghan troops, in 1762, Charat Singh, conscious of his own inability to oppose the disciplined army of the Shah in the open field, and afraid of a direct conflict with the main body of the invaders, sent his family to Jammu, where he concealed all his property, but he was never quiet himself. At the head of a band of chosen men, he harassed the march of the Afghans, cut off the stragglers of their army, and plundered their baggage. The Afghans, on their side, levelled to the ground the mud fort which the Sikhs were building at Gujránwálá.

He harasses Ahmad Shah's troops on their march through the Panjáb.

On the departure of Ahmad Shah, Abdáli, from the Panjáb, Charat Singh, being joined by Bakhshish Singh, his brother-in-law, sacked Wazirábad, and, driving out the Moghal officials, took possession of the city, which he gave to Bakhshish Singh. He then conquered Ahmadábad, which he gave to Dal Singh. At Ahmadábad news reached him that the Hindu subjects of Rohtas were much oppressed by Nur-ud-dín Khan Bamizie, the general of Ahmad Shah, who was stationed there with some troops, and who had permitted cows to be slaughtered. He repaired to Rohtas at the head of his *misl*, and engaged and defeated Nur-ud-dín. Charat Singh plundered Rohtas, and then proceeded to Dhanni, which he conquered. Chakwál and Jalalpur next fell, and escaped the rapacity of the invader only on payment of a *nazráná* or present. He then subdued Pind Dádan Khan, whose governor, Sahib Khan, had his life spared on condition of his paying a heavy fine. He left Budh Singh and Gor Singh, two of his sardars, in charge, and ordered them to build a fort in the place. Proceeding onwards, he conquered Kot Sahib Khan and Rájá-ká-kot, two large towns, and then returned to Gujarwál. The successive victories won by Charat Singh, and the power and resources at his command, made him an object of jealousy to the rival misldars, who all looked upon him with great suspicion, and thought (not without ground) that their own positions were not safe before his vast schemes of conquest and aggrandizement. None, however, became more apprehensive than the sardars of the Bhangi *misl*, who had from the first entertained hostile feelings towards the rising Sukerchakias. But a cause for open conflict was no longer wanting, for circumstances arose in a border hill State, involving a general rupture between the various *misls*.

Sacks Wazirábad.

Captures Ahmadábad.

His conquests west of the Jhelum.

His position is envied by the rival Misldars.

It was during his retreat to the Jammu hills that Charat Singh formed his first acquaintance with the rájás of that State. Ranjít Deo, the rájá, had some misunderstanding with his eldest son, Brij Ráj Deo, whom he desired to deprive of the right of succession, in favour of the youngest son, Mián Dalel Singh. Brij Ráj Deo applied Charat Singh to help him in

Rival claimants of the Jammu Raj.

securing his hereditary right, and agreed to pay the Sukerchakia a large annual tribute if he succeeded in deposing his father. Charat Singh, who entertained an old grudge against Ranjit Deo, acceded to the wishes of the heir apparent of the Jammu Ráj, and, having been joined by Hakikat Singh and Jai Singh, of the Kanhia *misl*, marched towards Jammu, in 1774, at the head of a considerable force. Ranjit Deo was helped by auxiliaries from Chambá, Kangrá, Nurpur and Basehar, and also by a contingent from the Bhangi *misl*, under Jhandá Singh and Gandá Singh, sons of Hari Singh. In the winter of the same year the two armies met on the banks of the Basanti river. Several engagements took place with no decisive results, till at length, in one of these, Charat Singh was accidentally killed by the bursting of a matchlock in the hands of one of his own followers.

Charat Singh takes the side of one of them. Marches to Jammu.

Is killed in the action, 1774.

His character.

Charat Singh was a man of high aims, and far more advanced ideas than his contemporaries of the *misl*. He it was who laid the foundation of the greatness of the family. By his industry, economy and perseverance, he extended his estates, and throve upon the disorder which followed on the overthrow of the Láhore governor, Khwajá Obed. He appeared early in the field as an enterprising leader, and soon rose from a common *Dhárwi*, or highway robber, to the sardari of a confederacy, and contributed materially to the strength of the Sikhs as a nation. The territory left by him on his death is computed to have yielded about three lakhs of rupees annually, and was inherited by his eldest son, Mahá Singh, then ten years old. Charat Singh left another son, Sahaj Singh, and a daughter Ráj Kour, who was married to Sahib Singh, son of the famous Gujar Singh, Bhangi. Mahá Singh being too young to take upon himself the responsibility of governing the *misl*, his mother, Desán, assumed immediate charge of the affairs of State, assisted by Jay Singh, Kanhia. She rebuilt the fort at Gujránwálá, which had been destroyed by Ahmad Shah Abdáli.

The territory left by him on his death.

His minor son Mahá Singh succeeds, under the tutelage of his mother Desan.

An attempt was made by several subordinate sardars of the *misl* to shake off their dependence on Mahá Singh, the chiefs either mistrusting his youth, or being dissatisfied with the regent widow, who had fallen in love with one Jay Rám Missar, a family priest. Prominent among these was Dharm Singh, who openly rebelled. The discontented sardars were, however, greatly disappointed when, contrary to their expectations, no succour came from the Bhangi's quarters; and they were all effectually punished. The opportunity was now taken of celebrating the nuptials of Mahá Singh with the daughter of Gajpat Singh of Jhind, to whom the sardar had been previously betrothed. The ceremony took place with the pomp and grandeur worthy of the name of the *misl* to which the sardar belonged. The bride was ever after called Mái Malwain, or the Málwá mother.

Unsuccessful attempt to overthrow the minor's power.

His marriage with the daughter of Gajpat Singh of Jhind.

Shortly after this, Mahá Singh engaged in an undertaking which gained for him great celebrity as a warrior and conqueror. Rassulnagar, now called Ramnagar by the Sikhs, situate on the east bank of the Chináb, was held by a powerful tribe of Mahomedans called *Chattas*, also known as *Manchuriás*, the head of the tribe at that time being a Mussalman *Ját*, named Pír Mahomed. Mahá Singh, assisted by Jay Singh, Kanhia, made an attack on this town at the head of 6,000 troops, the pretext being the famous *zamzama* gun of Ahmad Shah, which Jhandá Singh, Bhangi, after his conquest of the *Chattas*, had left with Pír Mahomed in deposit, from its being too heavy to be taken across the Chináb. Mahá Singh now claimed it as the property of the *Khálsá*, or the general assembly of the Sikhs. The town of Rassulnagar was besieged, and the blockade continued for four months. The whole of the surrounding country

The battle of Rassulnagar, 1778-79.

belonging to the *Chattas* was depopulated, and, to use the expression of a contemporary historian, not a grain of wheat was left in the house of a zemindar. The *Chattas* in vain sought the aid of the Bhangi chiefs, as they were at this time employed in plundering and conquering Multán and Báháwalpur. The besieged had now no alternative but to sue for peace, and Mahá Singh put his seal on the *Granth*, binding himself not to molest Pír Mahomed if he surrendered his person. The Mahomedan chief, on receiving this assurance, came out unguarded, but was treacherously put under arrest by Mahá Singh. His sons were tied to the mouths of guns and blown to pieces by the orders of the victor, and the town of Rassulnagar was given up to plunder. Mahá Singh's fame spread throughout the length and breadth of the country, owing to his having captured Rassulnagar, and the reputation for valour obtained by him was so great, that many sardars who had hitherto been dependent on the Bhangi *misl*, now acknowledged the Sukerchakia sardar as their chief, and transferred their allegiance to him, and deemed it an honour to fight under his banner. The name of Rassulnagar was changed into Ramnagar, and that of Alipur into Akálgarh. The governorship of the newly acquired territory was given to Dal Singh, a lieutenant of Mahá Singh. The relics of the prophet Mahomed, which fell into the hands of the victors in their sack of Rassulnagar, were removed by Mahá Singh to Gujránwálá, and deposited there in proper custody.

Victory of Mahá Singh and capture of Rassulnagar by the Sikhs.

The relics of the prophet Mahomed.

Birth of Ranjít Singh, 1780.

Two years after the fall of Rassulnagar, on the 2nd November 1780, his wife, Mái Malwain, presented him with a son to whom he gave the name Ranjít Singh. The occasion was marked by great rejoicings and festivities to which all the Sikh sardars were invited. Thousands of rupees were given away to the poor as alms. The child, at a very early age, was afflicted with small-pox of a very virulent type, by which his life was greatly endangered. The father distributed alms to the poor and needy most lavishly, fed multitudes of Brahmins to secure their prayers for the recovery of the boy, and sent rich presents to the sacred temples of Kangrá and Jawálá Mukhi. The child recovered, though with the loss of one of his eyes, while his face was so much disfigured from the marks of the disease, that it rendered him, for ever after, a very repulsive looking person. That this ugly-looking, one-eyed, or *káná*, boy, as he was called, was destined to rule over the country of the five rivers, no one, of course, knew at the time.

Mahá Singh makes war on the Bhangis.

Mahá Singh now began to think of the advisability of extending and enlarging his dominions. The power of the Bhangi *misl* was effectually broken by the invasion of Tymúr Shah, son of Ahmad Shah. The Sikhs, under the Bhangis, were expelled both from Multán and Báháwalpur. Mahá Singh made the downfall of the other *misls* the foundation of his own power. Taking advantage of their weakness, he marched to Pindi Bhattian, pillaged that country, attacked Sahíwál, seized Isá Khel and Musá Khel, and finally sacked Jhang. All these places belonged to the Bhangi sardars, and Desá Singh, the misldar, being a drunkard and a debauchee, was unable to retain them. He was then joined by his brother-in-law, Sahib Singh, Bhangi, son of Gujar Singh, Bhangi, one of the three rulers of Láhore. In the meantime, this Sahib Singh quarrelled with his elder brother, Sukha Singh, and, with the assistance of Mahá Singh, attacked his brother, who was killed in the action. Gujar Singh was much afflicted at hearing of his son's death, and, being very indignant at Sahib's act, determined to wrest his possessions from him. He accordingly marched from Láhore at the head of a large army, and, having crossed the Rávi and

Fight between Sukha Singh and Sahib Singh, sons of Gujar Singh, Bhangi.

Mahá Singh embraces the cause of Sahib Singh.

the Chináb, laid siege to Gujrát. After a brief and feeble resistance on the part of Sahib Singh, Gujar Singh took possession of the town. Sahib Singh, now in open revolt, shut himself up in Islámgarh, but at length sought his father's forgiveness and was pardoned.

Capture of Kotli.

Mahá Singh next invaded Kotli, in the neighbourhood of Siálkot, well known for the manufacture of matchlocks, and compelled the inhabitants to pay a heavy indemnity. During his stay here, he performed one of those acts of barbarous treachery which ever after made his name a terror to all the chiefs and sardars of the province. Under pretence of holding an important consultation, he invited a very large number of sardars; and upon their complying with his invitation, he seized and imprisoned twenty-two of the principal chiefs among them. Charat Singh, Kalálwálá, Dia Singh, nephew of Sahib Singh, Dhanná Singh and Mihán Singh, Wadalia were of the number thus apprehended. These sardars obtained their release only on payment of heavy *nazránás* according to their rank and wealth. He preyed remorselessly upon the country in which he lived, humbled many powerful sardars and reduced to subjection many towns and cities. His power was so much dreaded that none dared oppose him. He now discovered, in another quarter, a very tempting and savoury banquet upon which to gorge his insatiable avarice.

Mahá Singh pre-eminent among the Sikhs, 1785-92.

Ranjít Deo, the rájá of Jammu, was dead, and his son Brij Ráj Deo, who succeeded him, was unable to hold the reins of government, being more fond of debauchery than of attending to affairs of State. Upon ascending the *gadi*, he closely imprisoned his younger brother Mián Dalel Singh. His courtiers and his subjects in general were very discontented, and this encouraged the aspiring Sukerchakia chief to pick a quarrel with him.

He picks a quarrel with Brij Raj Deo of Jammu.

Another cause for interfering with Jammu affairs was the following: the Bhangis had taken possession of some of the territory belonging to the Jammu rájá. Brij Ráj Deo, on ascending the *gadi*, wished to win back this last territory, and applied to Jay Singh and Hakikat Singh, Kanhias, for aid. Karianwálá was recovered for the Jammu rájá, after a pitched battle, and the Kanhias deserted their ally, and went over to the Bhangis. The Sikhs not only succeeded in recovering Karianwálá, but invaded Jammu under Hakikat Singh, Gujar Singh and Bhág Singh, Ahluwalia. The Jammu rájá called to his assistance Mahá Singh, Sukerchakia, but was signally defeated, and agreed to pay a tribute of 30,000 rupees to Hakikat Singh. Six months after the above agreement had been entered into, Hakikat Singh (in consequence of the money not having yet been paid) concluded that Brij Ráj Deo intended to evade the payment thereof; he therefore proposed to Mahá Singh to join him in an attack upon Jammu. The Sukerchakia chief, forgetting his promise of perpetual friendship with the Jammu rájá, readily agreed to the proposal of Hakikat Singh. He marched to Chaprál, while Hakikat Singh took the Zaffarwál road. No declaration of hostilities was made against the rájá of Jammu by the turban brother.

Another cause for interference.

Mahá Singh marches to Jammu, assisted by the Kanhias.

Jammu was at this time noted for its prosperity and wealth. The state of anarchy which prevailed in the Panjáb rendered it very unsafe for merchants and traders to carry on their business there; they, therefore, moved to the Jammu hills, where they were able to carry on their business in peace and safety. Consequently, Jammu had become the most flourishing State north of the Panjáb. Mahá Singh, having organized his troops, marched to Jammu, and Brij Ráj Deo, the effeminate rájá, having heard of his movement, fled to the Trikotá Devi mountains, leaving his country at the mercy of the invader. The principal residents of Jammu came out to

Prosperous condition of Jammu at this time.

Flight of the Jammu rájá on Mahá Singh's approach.

meet the Sukerchakia leader with large presents, but this did not satisfy the avaricious chief. He ordered his troops to plunder the place, an order which they carried out with the greatest alacrity. The city and palace of Jammu were then burnt. They laid waste the whole country, so that, in a short time, a most grievous famine broke out, which extended throughout the length and breadth of the land. Nor did the young Sukerchakia sardar keep faith with his new ally, Hakikat Singh. Now that the rájá was out of the way, he perceived that it would be an easy matter for him to undertake the sole management of the operations. This idea was no sooner conceived than it was carried into effect, to the surprise and disgust of Hakikat and his party. Hakikat Singh died shortly after this affair, and the thirst for revenge died with him.

Ravages committed.

Mahá Sing puts off Hakikat Singh.

The Dewáli festival then coming on (1784), Mahá Singh visited Amritsar, to perform his ablutions in the holy tank of Darbár Sahib, which had been restored by the Ramgarhias. The wealth accumulated by Mahá Singh at Jammu greatly irritated the Bhangi sardars, who longed for an opportunity to take advantage of the weakness of the Jammu family, and excited a strong jealousy in the mind of Jay Singh, Kanhia, once the guardian and ally of Mahá Singh. The youthful chief had every apparent regard for his old mentor, but the hoary-headed sardar, like a vulture, had scented a carcass, and nothing short of dining on it would satisfy him. Mahá Singh, to pacify the old man, even assumed the demeanour of an inferior, and approached him with a tray of sweetmeats in his hands, but the Kanhia sardar would not receive him. He instantly stretched himself out on his couch, and drawing a sheet over him, shouted: "Go away, you *Bhagtia* (dancing boy); I don't want to hear your sentimental talk." This was too much to be borne in silence by so haughty and impervious a young chief as Mahá Singh was. He withdrew in great indignation at the rude treatment shown him by the Kanhia chief, and resolved upon revenge, but he knew that Amritsar, where the Kanhia's power reigned supreme, would be no appropriate place for the accomplishment of his object. He accordingly managed to effect his escape from the sacred city, attended by a few *sawars*, and, having returned home in safety, sent his agents to Jassa Singh, Ramgarhia, who had fled across the Sutlej after his defeat by the allied forces of the Kanhia and Ahluwalia *misls*. The sardar was invited to co-operate with him, in his action against the Kanhias; and hopes were held out to him, of his recovering his lost possessions on this side of the Sutlej in case of success in the venture. Jassa Singh was at that time living in the wastes of Hánsí and Hissar, as a very successful freebooter, and, being convinced of the sincerity of Mahá Singh's offer, he lost no time in returning to the Panjáb with as large a force as he could collect.

Breach of friendship between Mahá Singh and Jay Singh, Kanhia.

An insult offered to the Sukerchakia chief.

Who invites Jassa Singh, Ramgarhia, from across the Sutlej to his aid.

What the old Kanhia chief was doing in the interim, deserves a passing notice. As soon as he had heard of the fall of Jammu, and the death of Hakikat Singh, he prevented Jeymal Singh, son of Hakikat Singh, from proceeding to Gujránwálá, whither he had been summoned by Mahá Singh. The Sukerchakia chief was threatened with vengeance. In 1783 Jandiálá was attacked, and this was followed by the sack of Rassúlpur and Mandiálá. The possessions of Wazir Singh and Bhagwán Singh, the Nákai chiefs, the connections of Mahá Singh, were then attacked, and the sardars were compelled to submit. But, in a struggle which took place about the same time, near Majithia, between the Sukerchakias and the Kanhias, Jay Singh was less fortunate. Not only were his troops routed, but he was compelled to fly from Majithia and take refuge across the Biás. He was making preparations on an extensive scale in the Jalandar Doáb, to renew war

The proceedings of the Kanhia chief.

He makes an attack on the Sukerchakia possessions.

Is defeated near Majithia.

with the Sukerchakias, when Mahá Singh invited to his help Jassa Singh, Ramgarhia and Sansar Chand, rájá of Katoch.

The battle of Batála, 1783.

The particulars of the battle which took place, within a few miles of Batála, between the allied forces of Mahá Singh and Jassa Singh on the one side, and of Jey Singh on the other, need not be repeated here, as they have been already noticed in the account of the Kanhia *misl*. Suffice it to say, Mahá Singh was joined on that occasion by a number of disaffected tributaries of the Kanhia sardar, who had been stirred up by his allies. The heroic Gurbaksh Singh, at the head of 8,000 horse, very imprudently exposed himself to the enemy's fire. The fighting was continued for six hours, till an arrow, shot by one of Guru Sundar Das's men, struck him in the breast and killed him. The Kanhias, seeing their leader dead, fled, leaving their adversaries masters of Batála.

Utter rout of the Kanhias.

They are again defeated at Naushera.

Jay Sing, though humbled, never lost his spirit, and the determination to take vengeance on Mahá Singh still burned in his breast. He collected the remnants of his troops and again attacked Mahá Singh at Naushera, but was repulsed with great loss, and fled precipitately to Nurpur, where he shut himself up on the approach of the enemy.

Marriage of Ranjit Singh with the grand-daughter of Jay Singh, Kanhia.

Sadá Kour, the widow of Gurbaksh Singh, now exercised the greatest influence over her old father-in-law, whose whole affections were centred in the family of his deceased son. This heroine regulated the affairs of Batála in the interest of herself and her only daughter, Mahtáb Kour. She now proposed the betrothal of the girl to the young son of Mahá Singh, hoping thereby to unite the Sukerchakia and Kanhia families in a permanent bond of friendship, and thus to secure for herself the sardari of the Kanhia *misl* upon the demise of her father-in-law. The proposal was readily agreed to by Mahá Singh; the contract was signed in 1785, and, at the close of the following year, the marriage was performed with great pomp. This union proved very fortunate for the interests of the country, Mahá Singh's reign in the Panjáb, for many years after this marriage, being one of peace and prosperity.

War between Mahá Singh and Sahib Singh, Bhangi.

After the death of Gujar Singh, Bhangi, in 1788, Mahá Singh, coveting his possessions, supported the cause of his younger son, Fatteh Singh, against the elder, Sahib Singh, the result of which was that war was declared between Mahá Singh and Sahib Singh, without the slightest regard being paid to the relationship which existed between them by virtue of their intermarriages. Mahá Singh was determined to effect his aspiring and ambitious plans at any cost, and a recourse to arms was thus rendered inevitable. An account of this fight and its issue, has already been given in the notice of the Bhangi *misl*. It is sufficient to say here that Mahá Singh, at this juncture, asserting his own superiority over Gujrát, demanded tribute from Sahib Singh, which was, of course, refused, on the ground that Gujar Singh had never fought under the standard of the Sukerchakia *misl*, but was an adherent of the Bhangi *misl*.

Sahib Singh shut himself up in the Sodhra fort, which was besieged. The siege was continued for three months, during the whole of which time Mahá Singh remained in a state of *delirium tremens*, which eventually led to his being removed from the field, and to the breaking up of the camp. Upon the siege being raised, he was conveyed to his fort at Gujránwálá, where he expired in 1792.

Defeat and death of Mahá Singh, 1792.

His character.

Mahá Singh was brave, enterprising and prudent beyond his years; and the age in which he lived highly favoured his ambitious schemes. So distracted was the state of the country, so small the influence of the *Guru Matta*, or national Sikh assembly, and so rife was intrigue among the ambitious chiefs, that everything favoured the adventurous spirit and ambitious designs of the young Mahá Singh. Such being the case, it may well be surmised that he would not allow so favourable an opportunity to slip by unprofitably to himself. His early feats in arms had acquired for him so great a reputation that many influential independent sardars joined his banner. His rapid successes gave him an ascendancy over all the Sikh chiefs. His military genius, undaunted courage, stern temper and rigid observance of the rules of delicacy and honour, at times involved him in serious trouble, but he honourably acquitted himself on all such occasions. At an early age, he shook off the trammels of his mother's guardianship, to pave the way for his own greatness. In the winter of 1778, he put his mother, Mái Desán, to death with his own hands, because he had long suspected one Hakikat Singh of criminal intimacy with her, though he had taken no serious notice of it, and adopted no measures to put a stop to it. It happened that Mahá Sing had received into his favour one Khodadad Khan, son of Rahmat Khan, of Jalalpur, near Gujrát, who, having fled from his home, had joined the Sukerchakia sardar with some fifteen or twenty horsemen. This man had killed his own mother on the mere suspicion of her attempting to have criminal intercourse with another. Some two years after, at an entertainment, in which both the sardar and Khodadad Khan, his friend, and associate, were present, jocular remarks were passed between the two, and, in the course of conversation, Mahá Singh, asked Khodadad Khan about the circumstances under which his mother had met her death. The matricide was annoyed at this enquiry, and tauntingly replied that he ought to be ashamed to put such a question to one who had killed his mother on mere suspicion of an attempt to engage in an intrigue, while his own (Mahá Singh's) mother was daily committing adultery with the full knowledge of her shameless and insensate son. This retort rankled in the breast of Mahá Singh, but he thought it advisable to remain silent for the time being. He, however, watched for an opportunity to kill his mother; and, one day, finding her alone in her apartment, shot her dead. He then cut off one of her hands with his sword, and, calling Khodadad Khan to the spot, showed him her body and the bloody sword, expressing his hope that the world would now acknowledge that he had done his duty in redeeming the honour of his family, and vindicating his own character, which had been stained by the conduct of his mother. Hakikat Singh, the supposed paramour of the murdered Mái, who was a member of the Kanhia confederacy, seeing this tragedy, fled to Wazirábad, his jágír, at the head of 300 horsemen. After all, it was ascertained that the real paramour of Mái Wazirábadia, as the mother of Mahá Singh was called, was one Jey Ram, a Brahmin, and a family priest, who fled to Pesháwar in precipitate haste to avoid a similar fate to that of his mistress. In other well-informed quarters, it was reported that the Mái had more than one lover. After this matricidal tragedy, Mahá Singh took to heavy drinking in order to drown the unpleasant thoughts which arose in his mind in consequence of the bloody act. This hard drinking greatly impaired the tone of his nervous system; but persons were not wanting who attributed his uneasiness and nervousness to other causes. They said that, from the first day of his marriage, he had had no faith in the fidelity of his own wife, the mother of Ranjít Singh, and regarded one Lakhpat Rae, dewán, his father's minister, a man of engaging manners, as his rival in the affections of Mái Malwain, as the mother of Ranjít Singh was called. Mahá Singh possessed all the qualities of a sardar, and left behind him a high reputation for wisdom and bravery amongst his nation.

How he put his own mother to death.

His grief at his rash act.

PART IV.—THE LIFE OF MAHARÁJÁ RANJÍT SINGH.

CHAPTER I.

FROM HIS ASCENDANCY AS RULER OF LÁHORE TO THE SUTLEJ TREATY, 1799 to 1808 A.D.

His mother, Mái Malwain, acts as regent for the minor sardar, Ranjít Singh.

RANJÍT SINGH, the only son of Mahá Singh, was in his twelfth year when his father died. His mother, Mái Malwain, assisted by the minister of her husband, Lakhpat Rai, dewán, a *Chhatri* of Noushera, was nominated regent, and ruled the confederacy in the name of the minor; though Sadá Kour, the young chief's mother-in-law, widow of Gurbaksh Singh, Kanhia, had also much to do with the conduct of affairs. The wisdom and energy of this extraordinary woman, Sadá Kour, one of the most artful and ambitious of her sex that ever figured in the Sikh history, conduced materially to the success of Ranjít Singh in his early exploits, and it is truly said of her that she was the ladder by which Ranjít Singh reached the summit of his power. By affiancing her daughter, Mahtáb Kour, to the youthful Ranjít Singh, she hoped to secure the support of the Sukerchakia chief in her instalment in the sardari of the Kanhia *misl* on the death of her father-in-law, Jay Singh, to the exclusion of his two surviving sons, Bhag Singh and Nidhan Singh, and to play thus a prominent part in the history of the Panjáb. These objects were fully attained on the death of Jay Singh, Kanhia, which occurred in the year following the demise of Mahá Singh, *viz.*, in 1793, and by which she gained the entire control of the Kanhia *misl*.

Sadá Kour his mother-in-law.

Her politic views.

Ranjít Singh received no kind of education.

Little care had been bestowed on the early education of Ranjít Singh, who spent his days in hunting, indulging in every kind of excess, and gratifying his youthful passions and desires. He was never taught to read or write, and, while yet a minor, under the guardianship of his mother and mother-in-law, became the husband of another wife, Ráj Kour, daughter of Ram Singh, the Nákai chief. On attaining the age of seventeen, Ranjít considering himself as well, or better, qualified to manage public affairs than the triune regency of Lakhpat Rai, Mái Malwain and Sadá Kour, he, like his father, gave them to understand that their supervision in the control of the State would, for the future, be dispensed with. He then took upon himself the sole responsibility, and appointed, as his prime minister, Dal Singh, maternal uncle to his father, Mahá Singh, who, shortly before his death, had entrusted the young chief to his care, binding the turban of sardari on Ranjít's head. Acting under the advice of Dal Singh, Ranjít sent Lakhpat Rai on an expedition to Ketas, where the suspected lover of his mother was easily despatched. All accounts, however, agree that the late dewán was not the only paramour upon whom the Mái Malwain lavished her favours. One Láik Missar was also suspected of entertaining an amorous passion for her. Ranjít Singh, following the example set him by his father, put both his mother and her lover to death with his own hand. For several months preceding this tragedy, the young chief was desirous of convincing himself of his mother's guilt by

He appoints Dal Singh, his father's maternal uncle, his prime minister.

Assassinates Mái Malwain, his own mother.

personal observation and ocular testimony. Early one morning a confidential servant informed him of Láik Missar's presence in his mother's bed-chamber. On hearing this, Ranjít immediately entered the apartment, and there found that his informant's report was only too true. Without uttering a word, he hurried into an adjoining room to provide himself with a sword, with the avowed object of despatching both his mother and her paramour. He returned immediately, sword in hand, but the Missar, hearing some noise, had fled, before the youthful avenger entered the chamber. The Mái was sitting upon her bed, half naked, with her hair dishevelled. The fugitive, in the hurry of the moment, had left his shoes and a portion of his dress in the lady's bed-room. This redoubled the rage of the assailant, who tauntingly asked the lady where her paramour was. She replied with a torrent of abuse, and cursed her son for being so disloyal and shameless as to cast upon an elderly woman like herself, his own mother, an unmerited slur, declaring at the same time that her conduct was as pure as he or anybody could expect. The altercation lasted for some time, till at length the fiery youth, driven to madness by the reproaches of his mother, struck her with his drawn sword. She now, with clasped hands, craved for mercy, but it was too late to suppress the bloody passion with which her shameful conduct and subsequent behaviour had inflamed the youth, and she paid the penalty of her offence with her life. Ranjít Singh, performed the funeral ceremonies of his mother with all the pomp and grandeur expected from a sardar of his standing, but he never showed any sorrow for what he had done, and whenever mention was made of Mái Malwain's death, he merely remarked that she had received her just and proper punishment for her wickedness, and that he was rejoiced that his mother's life was cut short, for, had she lived longer, her sins would have increased, and death was by all means to be preferred to a life of guilt and shame. Láik Míssar managed to effect his escape to Amritsar and threw himself on the mercy and protection of Sadá Kour, Ranjít's mother-in-law, but was treacherously made over to Ranjít by that artful lady, and despatched by him.

Láik Missar.

About this time the Panjáb was frequently invaded by the Durráni King, Shah Zaman, grandson of the Abdáli Ahmad Shah, who cherished the idle hope of founding an Indian Empire. Five times had the king made his preparations for an invasion of India, and as many times, had the exposed state of his western dominions rendered his departure from the country an imperative necessity. Twice had the Shah occupied the capital of the Panjáb, without meeting any opposition, but each time he was compelled to retrace his steps to his hereditary dominions, west of the Indus, without making any arrangement for the permanent occupation of the country. The Sikhs at this period, though powerful as a nation, were strangers to the art of disciplined warfare, and, moreover, the successes of the Abdáli king, Ahmad Shah, which were still fresh in their memory, had made the Afghan name a terror to the people. As already mentioned, the Sikhs concealed themselves in hills or jungles, and fled to countries beyond the reach of the invaders, when the Afghan King approached, and reappeared in large numbers as soon as he had withdrawn.

Shah Zaman, the Durráni king.

Condition of the Sikhs at this time.

Among those who retired before the Durráni invader, was Ranjít Singh. He formed a coalition with other *misls*, circumstanced like his own, and while the Shah was busy with his Láhore affairs, he availed himself of the opportunity to cross the Sutlej, reducing to subjection the districts through which he passed, and exacting tribute from the people. Upon the Shah's retirement, the authority of Ranjít Singh had gradually become predomi-

Ranjít's power gradually developed.

nant among the Sikhs, and his rising fortune made him an object of envy to his contemporary sardars. One Hashmat Khan, chief of the *Chatta* tribe, whose possessions lay on the banks of the Chináb, undertook the hazardous task of taking the young chief's life, and thus removing him from the scene. One day, as Ranjít was returning from a hunting excursion on horseback, his followers having been left behind, Hashmat, who lay concealed in ambush on the way, suddenly sprang up and attacked the youthful sportsman. The blow missed him, and struck the bridle, which it severed in two. Ranjít Singh, coming upon his guard, fell violently on his intended assassin, and with one blow of the sword severed his head from his body. On the death of their chief, the *Chattas* submitted to Ranjít Singh, who annexed a great portion of the estates of the deceased to his own.

An attempt on his life

Fails.

The intended assassin put to death.

The *Chattas* subdued.

The Ramgarhias encroach on the possessions of the Kanhias.

The Ramgarhias having begun to encroach on the possessions of Sadá Kour, widow of Jay Singh, Kanhia, Ranjít Singh, on her application, marched to Batála at the head of a body of cavalry. The town of Miání, the capital of the dominions of Jassa Singh, Ramgarhia, was besieged. The siege lasted for six months, and various skirmishes took place, without any decisive result. At length the rainy season set in, and, the town being surrounded with water, the siege was raised and the troops were withdrawn.

Ranjít Singh interferes.

His designs on Láhore.

Ranjít Singh now began to entertain ideas of making himself master of Láhore, and he was encouraged in his views by Sadá Kour, a woman as ambitious and enterprising as her son-in-law. He thought the time most opportune for the undertaking, as he had no fear of the Durráni's interference, his late services to Shah Zaman, in recovering the lost guns from the bed of the Jhelum river, and forwarding them to Kábul in safety, having, as already narrated, obtained for him a formal grant of it.

Favourable circumstances.

His old enemy, Jassa Singh, Ramgarhia, was advanced in years, and too infirm to take any active part in conducting the affairs of his *misl*.

Golab Singh, Bhangi, was incapacitated by a fall from his horse, and most of the other Sikh sardars were too weak to enter the lists against the redoubtable Ranjít.

The triumvirate government of Láhore.

Láhore was, about this time, governed by the three rulers, Lahná Singh, Gujar Singh, and Sobha Singh. They were unscrupulous, drunken, profligate and tyrannical. How these men rose to power and obtained possession of Láhore, has been fully described in the sketch of the history of the Bhangi *misl*. The chiefs were now dead, but their sons were alive. Lahná Singh had a son, Chet Singh ; Gujar Singh, a son, Sahib Singh, and two other sons, Sukha Singh, and Fatteh Singh ; and Sobha Singh a son, Mohar Singh. The Mahomedans who exercised the greatest influence in the town about this time, were Mian Ashak Mohamed and Mian Mohkam Dín. Their opinion was taken on all important matters connected with the city and its neighbourhood, and they were known as the *Choudhris* of the city. Mian Ashak Mohamed's daughter was married to another equally opulent and influential *Choudhri* of the city, named Mian Badr-ud-dín, who happened to have a quarrel with some of the *Chhatris*, in the town. These *Chhatris*, wishing to avenge themselves on Badr-ud-dín, went to sardar Chet Singh, one of the hákims of Láhore, who at that time resided in the *Summan Burj*, or Palace of Mirrors, in the fort of Láhore, and complained to him of what they represented to be the revolting conduct of Badr-ud-dín whom they charged with holding clandestine correspondence with Shah Zaman, the ruler of Kábul. Certain forged papers were adduced in support of the story told by them, and so many persons corroborated the charge that the sardar was convinced of Badr-ud-dín's gilt. Without giving him an opportunity of offering an ex-

Mian Ashak Mahomed and Mian Mohkam Din.

Mian Badr-ud-din.

His quarrel with the *Chhatris* of the town of Láhore.

planation, and without even having an interview with him, he ordered him to be instantly seized, and he was heavily ironed and cast into a dungeon.

He is seized by Chet Singh.

Mian Ashak Mohamed, the father-in-law of the unfortunate man, and his colleague, Mian Mohkam Dín, were much distressed at hearing this, and, taking with them *Choudhri* Kukka, Ashraff Khan, and many other influential Mahomedans of the city, went in a body to Chet Singh to convince him of Badr-ud-dín's innocence, and obtain his release. They failed, however, to obtain a hearing, and were summarily dismissed from the presence of the sardar, who, with an air of arrogance, had recourse to insulting language. The chiefs returned, greatly disappointed and highly incensed at the haughty conduct of the sardar, and swore vengeance against Chet Singh and his friends the *Chhatris*, the originators of the trouble. Negotiations were kept up for nearly a month to obtain Badr-ud-dín's release, but without avail. All attempts to obtain redress having failed, it was at length resolved to have recourse to other means. A petition was drawn up, signed by Hakím Hákam Rai, Bhái Gurbaksh Singh, Mian Ashak Mohamed, Mian Mohkam Dín, Mohamed Bákar, Mohamed Tahir, Mufti Mohamed Mokarram, Mir Shadi and other leading citizens of Láhore, to the address of Ranjít Singh, describing at full length the conduct of the three governors of Láhore, and the discontent which prevailed in the town, consequent on their ill-treatment of the people. The few troops which were retained, were insufficient for the protection of the town and citadel, the people were oppressed, and their administration was detested. The suburbs of the city, it was represented, had been completely devastated, not a house being left with a roof, the rafters and beams having been all burnt or taken away by those in authority. Within the city walls, nearly half the town had been deserted, and many streets and *mohallas* were depopulated; the governors were habitually carousing, and were constantly in a state of semi-inebriety, and in order to support these Bacchanalia, they were obliged to plunder the citizens.

Failure of a deputation to Chet Singh to obtain Badr-ud-dín's release.

The citizens of Láhore invite Ranjít Singh to occupy the city.

The Sukerchakia chief was, on these grounds, invited to come and occupy Láhore; only his presence, it was said, was required at the capital, the petitioners engaging to do all that was necessary for securing the object in view. One of their number took this letter to Ranjít Singh, who was at the time at Rasulnagar, otherwise known as Ramnagar. A similar message was sent by the Láhore citizens to Sadá Kour, Ranjít's mother-in-law, at this time at the head of the Kanhia confederacy, inviting her co-operation, and requesting her to join in the enterprise. Ranjít Singh, on receiving this letter, deputed his agent Kazi Abdul Rahman, a native of Rasulnagar, to go to Láhore and open negotiations personally with Mian Ashak Mohamed, Mian Mohkam Dín, manager for Chet Singh, and other principal Mussalman inhabitants, and to let him know the result as expeditiously as possible. These preliminaries being over, and an assurance being given to Ranjít Singh that, on his approach, one of the gates of the city would be opened to him, he made all the necessary preparations for war. Having assembled all the troops he could collect, he repaired to Batála to consult his mother-in-law, Sadá Kour. She joined her son-in-law with all her available troops, and to these were added a large number of Akális and Mazbis. The united forces then marched to Amritsar, headed by Ranjít Singh and his mother-in-law, it being given out that the Sukerchakia chief was going on his usual visit to that city to perform his ablutions in the holy tank. From Amritsar, he proceeded in one march to Láhore, at the head, in all, of about five thousand men, who were chiefly stragglers.

A similar message sent to Sadá Kour.

Ranjít, accompanied by Sadá Kour, marches to Láhore.

He put up in the Barádari of Nawáb Wazír Khan, now the Panjáb Public Library, locating his troops on the site of the present Government Post Office in Anarkalli.

The three Láhore sardars, being informed of Ranjít Singh's approach, made preparations to oppose him. The only gates kept open for public business during the administration of the three sardars were the Delhi, the Láhori and the Roshnai gates; all the rest had been closed with masonry walls. Ranjít Singh saw the difficulty of effecting his object. Mian Ashak Mohamed and Mohkam Dín sent him word that all that was necessary to effect his easy entrance into the city had been done, and a large breach opened in the city wall between the Khizri and Yekki gates, to enable him to enter silently. Ranjít Singh, unwilling to act upon the information, and suspecting treachery, determined upon making a triumphant entry by one of the gates of the city. A body of armed men, ridiculously small (about two hundred), who had come out of the city to oppose Ranjít Singh, were beaten and fled back to the city, five of their number having been killed in the conflict which ensued. It was at length resolved, as the result of secret negotiations between the invader and Mian Ashak Mohamed and Mohkam Dín, that Ranjít Singh should advance at 8 o'clock on the morning of 13th Saffar, 1215 H. (1856 Samvat or 1799 A.D.) towards the Láhori gate of the city, which would be opened on his approach. Acting on this resolution, Ranjít marched on to the Láhori Gate, at the appointed time, at the head of a thousand of his chosen men; and, before Sardar Chet Singh was aware of his intention or presence, the gate was opened to him, and he had effected his entrance. The rest of Ranjít Singh's troops followed immediately after, and mounted the ramparts of the city. While these proceedings were going on, Chet Singh was purposely misinformed that the besiegers had appeared at the Delhi gate, which had been shut against them, and that the men in charge of the gate were ready to encounter them. Chet Singh, on hearing this, forthwith left the fort by the eastern gateway, at the head of the five hundred horse, to join the guards in possession of the Delhi gate, and assist them in opposing the advance of the enemy. He had not proceeded far in the direction of the Delhi gateway, when his retainers informed him that the enemy had already entered the city by the Láhori gate, which had been treacherously opened to them, and that, if he wanted to save his life, he should re-enter the fort and prevent its occupation by the invader. Chet Singh now, seeing that he had been purposely misled, the object of the manœuvre being to give Ranjít a fair opportunity of entering the city, immediately turned towards the fort and arrived at the Hazúrí Bagh Gate, just in time to close it against the advancing cavalry of the invader, led in person by the youthful Ranjít Singh. Two or three gate-keepers were shot dead in their attempt to close the gates, by Ranjít's cavalry, who had galloped their horses close up to the gate. Chet Singh shut himself up in the fort. The two other sardars, it need hardly be said, fled from the city before they had heard of Ranjít's entry. Ranjít now opened a desultory fire on the fort, which was promptly answered on Chet Singh's side by his matchlock men inside. This continued for twenty hours.

Cautious measures of Ranjít Singh.

He occupies Láhore, 1799.

Chet Singh outwitted.

He shuts himself up in the fort.

Ranjít Singh now determined to lay siege to the fort, but Sadá Kour prevented him from carrying his determination into effect, urging that the besieged, having no provisions within, and their communication, from without, being cut off, would soon be compelled to surrender. This opinion was borne out by events. The next morning, Chet Singh, finding treachery at work against him on all sides, surrendered, on condition of being allowed to leave the town unmolested, and provided with a suitable allowance for the subsistence of himself and his family. These terms being gladly acceded to by Ranjít Singh, the fallen chief withdrew from the fort. But subsequently surrenders to the victor.

Ranjít Singh treated him with every mark of consideration, and granted him a large village as jágír. Under express orders from him, the city and citizens were to be treated with the greatest consideration by the conquerors, and any acts of plunder and ill-usage on the part of his troops were to be severely dealt with. Notwithstanding these orders, the wealthiest of the citizens closed their places of business and retired to their respective homes. Ranjít, however, soon convinced them that his intentions were honest towards them, and they were induced to re-open their shops and resume business. Mild measures of Ranjít Singh towards the citizens of Láhore.

An order was issued giving protection to all subjects, and promising them shelter from all outside aggression and internal disorder. As an inducement for the artizans to renew their work, a large number of unserviceable guns and military stores that were accumulated in the citadel, were made over to them for repairs, for which they were paid handsomely. These measures had the desired effect. The people were reassured, and in a few days the town became as busy as ever.

The political situation of the Panjáb about this time may here be briefly described. Kasúr, a considerable town, 25 *kos* south-east of Láhore, peopled chiefly by Pathan emigrants, was ruled by Nizám-ud-dín Khan, a powerful Mahomedan chief. Chak-Guru, now known as Amritsar, was in the hands of the Bhangis, under Golab Singh; Multán was governed by Muzaffar Khan, Saddozai, son of Shujá Khan, who claimed common descent with the Abdáli King, Ahmad Shah, and whose ancestors, coming from Kandahar, occupied Multán in the disturbances following the accession of Nádir Shah to the Kábul throne. Daera was occupied by Abdul Samad Khan; Mankera, Hot, Bannú, and the neighbouring country, by Mohamed Shahnawáz Khan Moin-ud-doula, the successor of Nawáb Mahomad Khan, and Tank by Sarwar Khan Katti Khel. These were all Afghan usurpers who, originally governors of the Kábul Government of the Panjáb, had become independent rulers of the countries under their charge, owing to the enfeebled state of the Durráni Government. Dera Ghází Khan, including Báháwalpur, and a tract of country adjoining Multán, was ruled by the Dáúdpotra, Baháwal Khan; Jhang by the Sial, Ahmad Khan; Pesháwar by Fatteh Khan, Barakzai, the nominal vassal of Mahmúd Shah, and Káshmír by his brother, Azim Khan. The fort of Attock was in possession of the Wazír Khels, under Jahándad Khan; the Kangrá hills were under Rájá Sansar Chand; Chambá was under Rájá Charat Singh, and the country from Hoshiarpur to Kapúrthalla under Fatteh Singh, Ahluwalia, afterwards the turban brother of Ranjít Singh. The territories Trans and Cis-Sutlej were governed by independent Sikh sardars, and their confederacies, called *misls*, and other independent chiefs, and so were Wazirábad, Dhanni, Khoshab and Pákpattan, the seat of the great shrine of Bawa Farid, in whose honour it is said— Political situation of the Panjáb at this time.

تاکه قایم بود زمین و زمن — باد آباد خاک پاک پٹن
کاندران روضهٔ جنان آمود — شیخ با و افرید قبله من —

"As long as the earth and the world endure,
So long may the country of Pákpathan flourish;
For in its environs, which resemble paradise,
Rests the Saint Sheikh Bawa Farid."

Firmly established in Láhore, Ranjít Singh occupied himself in consolidating his dominions and making arrangments to secure his

The contemporary Sikh chiefs envy the position of Ranjít Singh.

And form a coalition against him.

authority. The success which had hitherto attended his arms, and now the capture and possession of the capital of the Panjáb by him, rendered him an object of envy, hatred, and uncharitableness among his contemporary chiefs. In order to wrest Láhore from him, a powerful coalition was formed between Jassa Singh, Ramgarhia, Golab Singh, Bhangi, of Amritsar, Sahib Singh, Bhangi, of Gujrát, Jodh Singh of Wazirábad and Nizám-ud-dín Khan of Kasúr. The confederate forces, several thousand strong, left Amritsar for Láhore in the early part of 1800 A.D., under the command of their respective chiefs. Jassa Singh, Ramgarhia, owing to infirmity and old age, was unable to join the expedition personally, but he sent his sons to conduct affairs on his belalf. Ranjít Singh went out to meet them, taking with him as large a force as he could collect from Láhore, as also the contingent furnished by his active mother-in-law, Sadá Kour. The troops of both parties lay encamped opposite each other in Mouza Bhasin, ten *kos*, east of Láhore, for a period of two months; and various fruitless skirmishes took place, without either party gaining the advantage. These procrastinations led the Bhangi sardars to forget the object which had prompted them to take joint action against the common foe. The greater portion of both night and day was spent in carousing and rioting to the entire prejudice of their armies and their cause. This hard drinking proved fatal to Golab Singh, Bhangi, who died suddenly one night in a fit of *delirium tremens*. The death of this sardar spread consternation throughout the camp of the Bhangis, and, it being felt that the Sukerchakia chief was inflexible and well prepared to keep the field, the army of the confederate sardars broke up, and Láhore was ever after left in the undisturbed possession of Ranjít Singh.

The confederate armies meet at Bhasin.

Ranjít Singh maintains himself against the confederacy, 1800.

Near, Batála a battle was fought between Sadá Kour, and Jodh Singh, son of Jassa Singh, Ramgarhia. Ranjít Singh aided the former, and the result was the total discomfiture of the Ramgarhias. After these events, Ranjít Singh, now lord of Láhore, made his triumphant entry into that city. He was received with great honour by the leading citizens, who presented *nazárs* and received rich *khilats* from their new sovereign. In the same year, 1857, Samvat (1800, A.D.), Ranjít Singh proceeded to Jammu. He first seized Mirowál, and then Narowál, the chief of which place presented him with a tribute of 8,000 rupees. He then laid siege to the fort of Jassarwál, and, having reduced it, put the defenders to the sword. Advancing then with his army, he encamped within four miles of Jammu, where the rájá visited him, and thereby averted the calamity which threatened his capital, by presenting him with Rs. 20,000 in cash and an elephant. The invader, having restored the country to him, and presented him with a dress of honour, marched to Siálkot, which he reduced. He then proceeded against Diláwargarh, at that time in possession of Bawa Kesra Singh, Sodhi. Jodh Singh Wazirábádia, who had come to assist the Bawa, fled in dismay, abandoning the cause of his ally, who, after several encounters, seeing that prolonged resistance would avail him nothing, and that his cause was hopeless, delivered himself up to the victor, and was pardoned. Diláwargarh was taken possession of by Ranjít Singh, who gave Shahdera to the Bawa, as jágír, for his maintenance. After these victories, Ranjít Singh returned to Láhore, where, shortly after, he was visited by Eusaf Ali Khan, agent of the British Government, who had come with a friendly letter from that Government, and presents for the Láhore chief valued at 1,000 rupees. The agent was received with due honours, presented with a *khilat* of five pieces, and dismissed with valuable presents, the produce of the country, for the British authorities.

His triumphant entry into Láhore, 1800.

Ranjít Singh marches to Jammu, 1800,

And receives *nazrána* from the Jammu chief.

Reduces Siálkot and Diláwargarh.

Receives an Agent of the British Government at Láhore, 1800.

Assumes the title of Maharájá, 1801.

The following year, 1801, Ranjít Singh formally assumed the title of Maharájá, or Rájá of Rájás, and, in a public darbár held on the occasion, declared that, in all public correspondence, he should be styled "*Sarkar*," signifying power and state. The darbár was attended by all the chiefs, sardars, choudhris, lamberdars, and other dignitaries who owed their submission or allegiance to Ranjít Singh. When all had assembled, the family Purohat, or priest, applied the *tilak* to the Maharájáh's forehead, as a token of his investiture with the sovereignty, and henceforward Ranjít Singh, from being the chief of a tribe of roving plunderers, assumed the power and functions of the sovereign of a nation and the title of Maharájá. The *Ulemas*, the learned men of the town, and poets, recited poems in honour of the occasion; and the whole of the festivities in connection with this great historical event were celebrated with the greatest pomp and splendour. An order was issued for the establishment of a mint at Láhore, and a coin was struck in the name of the Maharájá, bearing the following inscription :—

Strikes coin in his name.

دیگ و تیغ و فتح و نصرت بیدرنگ — یافت از نانک گورو گوبند سنگ

meaning, "hospitality, the sword, victory and conquest unfailing to Guru Govind Singh from Nának."

On the reverse was inscribed the era and place of coining. The ceremonies connected with the opening of the mint were gone through the same day, and the new rupees which were struck and presented, on the following day, for the Maharájá's inspection, were given away in alms to the poor. Following the example of the Mahomedan emperors, the offices of the hereditary *kazis* and *mufties* in the town of Láhore were recognized. Thus, *Kazi* Nizám-ud-dín was presented with a *khilat*, and permitted to decide disputes relating to marriage and divorce among the Mahomedans, and *Mufties* Mahomed Shahpur and Sadulla Chishti, having been similarly honored with *khilats*, were permitted to draw up title deeds relating to transfers of immoveable property, as they had been accustomed to do during the period of the Mahomedan rule. The old *mohalladari* system was re-established, and each *mohalla*, or quarter, of a town, was put under the charge of one of its members possessing more influence than the rest. The office of *kotwal*, or chief police officer, was conferred on Imám Baksh, whose nick-name was *Kharsawar*, or the donkey-rider. New guards were placed at the gates of the citadel, and the military regulations were revised and new ones instituted. The office of hakím, or physician in ordinary to the Maharájá, was conferred on Nur-ud-dín, the younger brother of Aziz-ud-dín. For the better protection of the city, one lakh of rupees were given to Moti Ram, afterwards dewán, to build fresh walls and a moat round it. About this time Sahib Singh, Bhangi, of Gujrát, made an attack on Gujránwálá. Ranjít Singh, accompanied by his mother-in-law, proceeded against the Bhangi chief. Through the intercession, however, of Sahib Singh, Bedi, the descendant of Bábá Nának, who was held in great veneration by the Sikhs, on account of his high family descent, a reconciliation was effected, and the Maharájá returned to Láhore. An electuary medicine (*májún*) the confection of a fish known in the Arabic language as *Sakan kur*, supposed to possess wonderful virile qualities, was prepared by the Hakím, Baghdádi, for the Maharájá, who, much pleased with its effect, conferred on him a jágír of Rs. 20,000 per annum. The Maharájá next proceeded against Nizám-ud-dín Khan of Kasúr, who had entered into an alliance with Sahib Singh, Bhangi, but his attempts to reduce the Pathan chief to subjection were unsuccessful, and he returned to Láhore, though not before he had burnt and pillaged the suburbs.

Appoints *kazis* and *mufties* to settle disputes relating to the Mahomedan law.

Re-establishes the old *Mohalladari* system.

The chief superintendent of city police, Láhore.

The brothers Nur-ud-dín and Aziz-ud-dín.

The city walls rebuilt.

A rupture with the Bhangis avoided.

An unsuccessful attempt on Kasúr.

The Bhangi chief, Sahib Singh, and the Kasúr Pathan, Nizám-ud-dín Khan, again raised the standard of revolt. Ranjít Singh deputed Sardar Fatteh Singh, Kaliwálá, to take the command at Kasúr, and marched in person to reduce Sahib Singh. On the approach of the Maharájá's troops, Sahib Singh shut himself up in the fort of Gujrát, which was closely besieged by the Láhore troops. There was heavy firing on both sides, and several breaches were made in the wall of the fort. At length, Sahib Singh, finding himself no match for the sovereign of Láhore, entered into negotiations for peace, which was agreed to on condition of the Bhangi chief paying a large *nazráná* to Ranjít Sing. This *nazráná* having been paid, and assurances of future submission and good behaviour given, the Maharájá returned to Láhore.

Ranjit Singh marches on Gujrat.

And secures the submission of Sahib Singh, Bhangi, 1801.

The success of a fresh expedition to Kasúr, 1801.

Nizám-ud-dín Khan, against whom an expedition had been sent under Sardar Fatteh Sing, Kaliwálá, was compelled to submit to the terms proposed to him. He repented of his rashness, and, acknowledging himself a feudatory of the Láhore ruler, sent his brother, Kutb-ud-dín Khan, to pay his respects to the Maharájá. The Pathan chief further bound himself to furnish a quota of troops under his brother, to follow the sovereign of Láhore, and, as security for carrying out these stipulations, two Pathan chiefs, Haji Khan and Wásal Khan, were sent to Láhore as hostages. Kutb-ud-dín Khan was then dismissed with a present of an elephant and a horse from the Maharájá.

Ranjit imprisons Dal Singh of Akálgarh by a stratagem.

News reached Láhore that Sardar Dal Singh (the associate of Sardar Mahá Singh, father of Ranjít Singh) had allied himself with Sahib Singh, Bhangi, of Gujrát, and that both sardars were again collecting troops to advance on Láhore. Ranjít Singh sent a friendly letter to Dal Singh, in which he reminded the latter of the cordiality which had existed between him and his father, and assured him that, on that account, he held the old sardar in great esteem, and that the world would laugh at the idea of friends fighting as enemies. He, therefore, with every show of sincerity and goodwill, proposed to the Sardar to come to Láhore, in order that they might conjointly start on conquering expeditions and marauding excursions, as in the good old days of Mahá Singh, and divide the fruits of their combined labours, equally between them. The sardar, being assured of the sincerity of Ranjít's proposal, gave up the Bhangi chief's cause, and repaired to Láhore. Ranjít Singh received him with the honours due to his rank, and furnished him with a spacious house in the fort. During the night, however, he placed a strong guard over the residence of the sardar and put him in confinement. Soon afterwards, the Maharájá marched to Akálgarh, at the head of his troops, to take possession of the captive sardar's territory, but was opposed by Tehjú, the sardar's Ráni, a brave and sagacious woman, who came out in person with her forces to give him battle. Several skirmishes took place with no decisive result. Information was, in the meanwhile, given to Ranjít Singh that the Ráni had opened communications with Sahib Singh of Gujrát, and Jodh Singh Wazirábadia, and that she was about to be joined by their troops. Ranjít Singh, seeing that all his attempts to conquer the Ráni were fruitless, and that his prolongation of the contest would be prejudicial to his interests, deemed it advisable to withdraw, but not without first attempting to impair the power of Sahib Singh. A friendly letter to Jodh Singh of Wazirábad, reminding him of all the favours that had been conferred on him by the late Mahá Singh, and promising his own cordial support in furthering the sardar's views of aggrandizement, was a sufficient inducement for the Wazirábad sardar to desist from taking part with Sahib Singh

And lays siege to Akálgarh,

But is compelled to raise the siege.

Fresh invasion of Gujrát.

Ranjit secures the co-operation of Jodh Singh, Wazirábadia.

against the ruler of Láhore, who now moved to Gujrát with all his available troops. Sahib Singh met him two miles from the city, and a severe fight took place between the two forces, lasting from night till late in the evening. Great numbers were killed on both sides, and the battle was continued pertinaciously on the second and third day. On the fourth day, Sahib Singh shut himself up in the fort, which Ranjít Singh subjected to a heavy cannonade. At length the venerable patriarch, Sahib Singh, *Bedi*, again effectually exercised his influence in bringing about a compromise. A peaceful settlement was arranged, and the siege raised, on Sahib Singh's agreeing to pay a large *nazráná* to the invader, together with a war indemnity. Another condition of the peace was that Dal Singh of Akálgarh should be set at liberty. Ranjít, with his troops, returned to Láhore, and his first act, in pursuance of the terms of the treaty, was to liberate Dal Singh. The old chief, however, had scarcely reached Akálgarh when he expired. Ranjít showed not the smallest regard for treaties and promises. He entered into them, or violated them, as best suited his schemes. Forgetting the conditions of peace, so recently entered into, he coveted the deceased sardar's possessions, and lost no time in marching to Akálgarh. When he arrived within four miles of the place, he sent his agents to Dal Singh's widow, informing her that he had been deeply affected by the death of her lamented husband, and his own valued friend, and that, in consideration of the relations of amity that existed between his father and the late sardar, and more especially to give proof of his own sincerity after the late treaty, he had come to condole with her in her recent bereavement (as it would have been opposed to all the known rules of the etiquette, so strictly enjoined by the custom of the *Khálsá*, which was composed of one brotherhood, if all the other sardars had come to condole with her in her present misfortune, and the Sukerchakia chief had not). The Ráni was at first alarmed on hearing of Ranjít Singh's approach, but when she had heard the agents of the Maharájá at full length, all her suspicions were removed, and she said to her people: "The venerable *Bedi*, the descendant of our great Guru, is between me and the Sukerchakia chief. Let him, then, come and sit on the floor of mourning where others sit." When Ranjít Singh heard this, he was exceedingly pleased. He entered the city with all his troops, and his first act was to put the unfortunate Ráni in close confinement, and her children and relations under a strong guard. Consternation rapidly spread through the whole of the army, on their hearing of her arrest, and a general stampede followed, in which every one looked to his own safety. Ranjít Singh then took possession of the treasures and military stores of the deceased sardar, which were stated to be enormous. Two villages were given to Dal Singh's widow for her maintenance. Ranjít Singh then returned to Láhore.

Compromise effected.

Dál Singh released.

Dies.

Ranjit Singh takes possession of Akálgarh by an artifice.

Intelligence having about this time been received from Batála, of an attack on Ráni Sadá Kour's territory by Sansár Chand, Rájá of Kangrá, who had descended into the plains and plundered some of the Ráni's villages, Ranjít Singh despatched his troops thither, with instructions to Sardar Fatteh Singh, Ahluwalia, to join the troops at Batála. The Maharájá himself followed. The rájá's *kárdárs* on hearing of the Maharájá's approach fled, and the Ráni obtained possession of all the territory that had been wrested from her. The Maharájá seized Noushera, a portion of the Kangrá Rájá's dominions, and gave it to Sadá Kour, with all its revenues. He then marched to Núrpur, which he subdued, the hill Rajá, Sansár Chand, having fled to the Kangrá hills on hearing of his approach.

Encroachments on Sadá Kour's possessions by Sansár Chand of Kangrá effectually stopped.

Núrpur reduced, 1801.

On his return from the hills, he levelled to the ground the fort of Sujánpur * near Patháukot, where Budh Singh and Sangat Singh, two Sikh sardars, had made themselves conspicuous by their military aggressions. He extorted from them the four large pieces of ordnance which they possessed, and having established a police post at Sujánpur, seized the neighbouring districts of Dharmkot, Sukálgarh and Bahrámpur, the old seat of the Patháns. From thence the Maharájá proceeded to Pindí Bhatian, which he subdued, and bestowed upon Fatteh Singh, Ahluwalia; besieged the fort of Band, which surrendered after two months, made the Dhanni country (famous for its breed of horses) tributary to him, and then returned to Láhore with 400 fine horses, the result of his excursions into Pothowár and Dhanni.

Pindí Bhatian, Pothowár and Dhanni taken.

At Láhore news reached the Maharájá of the rebellion of Uttam Singh, Majithia, in charge of Sitpur fort. Troops were sent out to punish the insurgent, and, the fort having been reduced, the sardar was conveyed to Láhore in chains. He was, however, forgiven and reinstated on payment of a heavy fine. Haji Khan and Wásal Khan, the Kasúr hostages, were permitted to return to their homes after being presented with *khilats* (consisting of horses, necklaces of pearls and valuable shawls). In Bysakh of the same year, the young chief having gone to bathe in the holy tank of Guru Ram Dás at Taran Táran, met Sardar Fatteh Singh, Ahluwalia, and, conceiving a friendship for him, exchanged turbans with him, a ceremony symbolical of brotherhood. An agreement of perpetual friendship was recorded on the Granth, to which the young Maharájá and the Ahluwalia sardar fixed their respective seals. The father of Fatteh Singh having died, the same year, Ranjít Singh went to Kapúrthalla to condole with him.

The Maharájá forms a friendship with Sardar Fatteh Singh, Ahluwalia, 1801.

Birth of Kharak Singh, 1802.

The year 1802 was marked by the birth of an heir-apparent to the Maharájá, by his wife Ráj Kour, daughter of the Nakai Sardar, Khazán Singh. The occasion was celebrated with great rejoicings. Valuable *khilats* were bestowed on the sardars of the darbár, and each soldier in the capital received a present of a necklace of gold in commemoration of the happy event. Karam Singh, Toshakhánia, by the Maharájá's orders distributed large sums of money among the poor of the city, and Láhore was the scene of festive merriment for several weeks. The astrologers having been consulted, the infant was named Kharak Singh, and put in charge of Bhái Rám Singh, the family priest.

The Maharájá reduces Daská, 1802,

After the festivites were over, Ranjít Singh, accompanied by his ally, Fatteh Singh, Ahluwalia, marched to Daská, the fort of which place was reduced, the killadar, or officer in charge, having fled in dismay, leaving all to be plundered by the invader. A police post was established at Daská, and the allied chiefs returned to Láhore. Complaints having reached Ranjít Singh, from Pindí Bhatian, of the excesses committed on the zemindárs of that place by Jassa Singh, Bhangi, son of Karam Singh, Dúllú, who held the fort of Chiniot, the Maharájá forthwith proceeded thither at the head of an army. Jassa Singh shut himself up in the fort, which was closely besieged by the Maharájá, and taken after some resistance. A small stipend was allowed to the expelled chief.

And conquers Chiniot, 1802.

* McGregor, at page 156, describes the incident thus "Bágh Singh, Bhangi, who was now at the head of the Káuhia *misl*, died; and his son, who succeeded him, made war on Sadá Kour. She asked for assistance from his son-in-law, who proceeded to join her. He ravaged the country about Batala, and besieged Sujánpur. He at length effected peace between Sadá Kour and her opponent and returned to Láhore." The account is wholly inaccurate. No man by the name of Bágh Singh was ever at the head of the Bhangi confederacy, and how could he have headed the Káuhia confederacy? As is well known, Sadá Kour was herself the head of the Káuhia confederacy. The incident evidently relates to the encroachments of the Kangra chief upon the territory of Sadá Kour bordering the hills. To ascribe the hill chief's actions to the Bhangi is an anomaly which will hardly stand examination.

The Maharájá had scarcely returned from Chiniot, when intelligence reached him of a fresh disturbance raised by Nizám-ud-dín Khan of Kasúr. The Patháu chief had collected a large force of the Afgháns and pillaged two villages within the boundary of the Láhore territory, and was preparing to do further mischief. The Maharájá, much enraged, wrote to Fatteh Singh, Ahluwalia, to repair to Kasúr with all haste, bringing with him as many troops as he could collect, as the Mahomedan chief had repeatedly broken his engagements, and he (the Maharájá) had determined to punish him severely for his breach of treaty. Ranjít Singh himself followed at the head of his chosen troops. The Pathán, who was well prepared, met the confederate army of the Sikhs, and a severe battle was the result, in which both the youthful Ranjít and his ally distinguished themselves by acts of great personal valour. The Patháns, finding themselves unable to cope with the enemy in the open field, retired to the fort. After great slaughter on both sides, the fort was taken, and the remnants of the garrison were put to the sword. As the majority of the buildings of Kasúr were in blocks, or groups, the invaders had little difficulty in reducing each *ábadi*. The city was completely plundered, and a large number of the inhabitants, consisting of men, women and children, were made prisoners of war. Nizám-ud-dín Khan, seeing that his cause was helpless, presented himself before the victor with every sign of humility, and was reinstated, on promise of future submission, and payment of a large *nazráná*, together with the expenses of the war. After this victory, the Maharájá returned to Láhore and distributed large sums of money as alms among the poor, as a thanksgiving offering for the victories gained by him at Chiniot and Kasúr.

Third invasion of Kasúr, 1802.

The city is conquered and given up to plunder,

But is finally restored to its chief.

The Maharájá soon after marched into the Jalandar Doáb, plundering and making annexations as he went along. During this march he heard that the rich widow of a Hindu *Chatri*, named Chuhar Mal, was in possession of the town of Phagwára, and aspired to independence. Ranjít Singh marched into the town, seized Phagwára, and compelled Chuhar Mal's widow to retire to Hardowar. All her property, which was considerable, was confiscated, and given to Sardar Fatteh Singh, together with the whole of the Phagwára territory. On his return from this expedition, the Maharájá, at the express request of Fatteh Singh, visited Kapúrthalla for recreation and amusement, and spent a few days in hunting in the jungles of Sultánpur. News having reached this place of the fresh descent of Rájá Sansár Chand, of Kot Kangrá, into the plains of Jalandar, where he had possessed himself of Bijwára and Hoshiárpur, the Maharájá immediately set out for the place, and, expelling the hill chief from both these towns, established military posts in them. Sansár Chand fled to Kangrá, and Ranjít Singh seized many villages below the hills, and, in a long tour which he made, exacted tribute, or exorted presents in money, from old Sikh chiefs and sardars, among them being Tárá Singh, Gheba, Dharm Singh, of Amritsar, and Budh Singh, of Fyzullapur. In the meantime, Sardar Bhag Singh, Bhugga, having died, all his estates, by the order of the Maharájá, lapsed to Ráni Sadá Kour. The forfeitures and resumptions with which Ranjít Singh systematically visited the family of each chief who died, filled the Sikh sardars with great alarm; yet they were so divided and jealous of each other, that they could devise no means of relieving themselves from his arbitrary exactions.

Ranjít wrests Phagwára from a Hindu widow, 1802.

Fresh troubles with Sansár Chand, of Kot Kangrá.

Military post established at Bijwára and Hoshiárpur.

Exactions and forfeitures.

The return to Láhore was marked by gaieties and festivities, in which the Maharájá indulged to excess. He fell in love with a beautiful damsel, named Morán, and his passion for her was so irresistible, that for a

The Maharájá marries a Mahomedan damsel, 1802.

time he forgot all State affairs, and gave himself up entirely to her company. He, at length, married her according to the Mahomedan rites, and the nuptials were celebrated with great pomp and splendour in a *haveli*, specially purchased for her, between the Shahabin and Láhori gates, called the *Ghobarchion ka katra*, close to which Morán resided.

And coins money in her name.

She obtained a great ascendancy over the Sikh chief, and under his sanction money was coined at Láhore, bearing the inscription of Morán, as the favourite queen of Ranjít Singh. On one occasion the Maharájá appointed Ilahi Baksh, a tape-maker, to the supreme command of his artillery, for no other reason than that he was an adept in the exercise of the clubs, of which the Maharájá was fond.

Pilgrimage to Hardowar.

The negligence into which he had fallen through the fascinations of his newly married wife at last came to an end. He resumed his wonted attention to the affairs of State; performed a pilgrimage to Hardowar (in which he was accompanied by Morán); received the homage of Fatteh Singh, Ahluwalia, and other chiefs; was presented with *nazránás* in cash by the sardars whose territories he passed through, and distributed a lakh of rupees to the poor of Hardowar.

The assassination of Nizám-ud-dín Khan, of Kasúr, 1802.

On his return from the Ganges, news reached him of the assassination, in a domestic fued, of Nizám-ud-dín Khan, of Kasúr, by his brother-in-law Wásal Khan, Haji Khan and Najíb Khan, the two former of whom were recently hostages at the court of Láhore. The cause of the quarrel was the resumption of the jágírs of the murderers by Nizám-ud-dín Khan. The occasion appeared to favour the designs of Ranjít Singh, who, with a large force of confederated Sikhs, marched against the new chief, Kutb-ud-dín, brother of the deceased. He was also joined in his expedition by his ally, the Ahluwalia chief. Kutb-ud-dín was thoroughly prepared for Ranjít's advance, and boldly resisted it. He fortified the whole of his strongholds, stationed his Afghán troops in ambush about the country, and did everything in his power to frustrate the Maharájá's designs, and in this he succeeded so far that, for several months, the invaders gained no advantage over the besieged. Ranjít now had recourse to his old plan of trying to persuade the Afgháns that all was for their benefit, and that it would be to their advantage to surrender. This ruse having failed, he determined to cut off their supplies, by which means he ultimately succeeded in gaining the day. Famine caused many deaths among the besieged, and eventually forced them to capitulate. As the Maharájá had no desire to protract the siege, he readily consented to receive a war indemnity from Kutb-ud-dín Khan, as the penalty of his rebellion, and retired from the country.

Fourth invasion of Kasúr, 1802.

The Patháns offer a stout resistance.

The Maharájá retires on receiving a war indemnity.

The Maharájá marches to Multán.

Before the troops had well recovered from the fatigues of the recent campaign, the indefatigable Maharájá set out for Multán at the head of his army. The chiefs and other dignitaries of his court endeavoured to dissuade him from carrying out his intentions with regard to Multán at that time, representing that the troops were weary and exhausted with their recent exertions, and that they could not be expected to resume the arduous duties of war for some time. Ranjít regarded these counsels as effiminate and untimely, and consequently rejected them. His sole idea was the prize upon which he had set his mind. Multán was rich, and Multán he must have at any cost, and this determined him to start on the expedition without delay. When the troops entered the nawáb's dominions, Muzaffar Khan sent his confidential agents to the Sikh chief to induce him to withdraw on receipt of a *nazráná* and promise of future submission.

And receives tribute from the nawáb, 1802

The nawáb met Ranjít thirty miles from the city. The Maharájá received him with honour, and, having exacted a large tribute from him, retraced his steps to Láhore.*

Ranjít Singh makes himself master of Amritsar, expelling the last representative of the Bhangi confederacy, 1802.

The Maharájá, in December 1802, resolved upon the total reduction of the remnants of the Bhangi *misl*, who still held power in Amritsar. The affairs of this once most formidable confederacy, which was always at enmity with Mahá Singh, when alive, and had once taken the lead in trying to recover Láhore, were at this time governed by Ráni Sukhan, widow of Goláb Singh, in the name of her minor son, Gurdit Singh. The Ahluwalia chief was ordered to join the Maharájá at Amritsar, with all his available troops, and Ranjít Singh himself moved from Láhore, at the head of his forces, accompanied by his mother-in-law.

When the confederate armies reached Amritsar, the Ráni closed the gates of the town, and, mounting the ramparts of the city with heavy ordnance, gave the invading army a warm reception. Sardar Fatteh Singh, Ahluwalia, commenced his operations in front of the Bridge Gate, and the Maharájá opposite the Lohgarh Gate of the town. At length, the gates having given way before a heavy cannonade, the invading troops entered in triumph, with the Maharájá at their head. The troops would have plundered the city, had not the Maharájá prevented them, out of reverence, it is believed, for a place held so sacred to the memory of the Sikh Guru, Ram Dás. The fort of Lohgarh was then besieged and reduced without difficulty, as the Bhangis were much weakened. It rained heavily that day, and the widowed Ráni, with her infant child, had no place to shelter them. At length they found their way to the *haveli* of Sardar Jodh Singh, Ramgarhia, who, pitying their helpless condition, gave them an asylum. On the recommendation of the Ramgarhia sardar, Ranjít Singh allowed a small jágír for the maintenance of the reduced Bhangi Chief, and thus the confederacy collapsed. Ranjít Singh then, entering the holy temple, bowed his head before the Harmandar, and performed his ablutions in the sacred tank. He also increased the stipends of the worshippers of the great Sikh institution, and, as usual with him, on such occasions, gave away large sums of money as alms to the poor as he passed through the bazars of the town.

The affairs of Afghanistán.

The civil war in Afghanistán, carried on by the four sons of Tymúr Shah, Húmáyún, Mahmúd, Shah Zamán and Shah Shujá, between themselves for ascendancy, had ruined that empire, and the once dreaded power of the Afgháns in India was now looked upon everywhere with contempt. The ever-vigilant Ranjít Singh found the time most opportune for extending his conquests in the regions east of the Indus, once the focus of Afghán influence and power.

The Maharájá invades Jhang, 1803.

After the Dasahra festival, which was kept with more than the usual excesses at Láhore, Ranjít Singh sent his agents to Ahmad Khan, the powerful Sial chief of Jhang, demanding tribute, and a promise of future submission as the only alternative to war. Preparations were at the same time made for marching into Jhang, with a thoroughly equipped force. The agents, of course, returned with an evasive answer, which decided Ranjít Singh's declaring war against him, and he set out for Jhang at the head of his troops in 1803, attended by the Ahluwalia chief. The new battalions

* Rai Kánhia Lal, in his *History of the Panjáb*, writes a long account here of a battle having been fought between the troops of Muzaffar Khan and those of Ranjít Singh, in which the latter was victorious. He represents that the Sikhs entered the city, and indiscriminately plundered the inhabitants, but the nawáb at length sued for peace, and his request was granted. I have been unable to corroborate this account from contemporary historians. All that really occurred has been given above. See Dewán Amar Náth's *History of Láhore* (manuscript edition), and compare it with McGregor, page 156, and *Panjáb Chiefs*, page 483.

known as Najibwálá, together with the Maharájá's own artillery, formed part of the expedition. Every village through which he passed was plundered, though not without some resistance on the part of the zemindárs, which frequently resulted in considerable loss of men on the Maharájá's side. Orders were therefore issued prohibiting the troops from visiting the villages, till they had reduced the power of the Sial Chief. Ahmad Khan had collected around him a large number of the Mahomedan tribes, consisting of Sials, Kharals, Bharwánás and others. He had also with him two pieces of artillery, but they were manned by novices. The battle lasted from noon till evening, when Ahmad Khan retired to the city with his two guns. The casualties on both sides were very great. Ranjít Singh besieged the city by night, and cut off the communication of the besieged. The next day the fighting was continued with the same pertinacity as before. Ahmad Khan superintended his artillery personally, and managed to send a shot through Ranjít's tent, which, however did very little mischief. The siege lasted three days. Desertions now commenced on the side of the nawáb, and many of the people who had come from the country to render aid to their chief, returned to their homes. The Hindu population sent a petition to the Maharájá, couched in the most humiliating terms, and promising to render him all the aid in their power immediately on his entering the city. The nawáb's own servants deserted him, and all fled, except Nasrat Khan, Siál. Ahmad Khan, seeing his cause hopeless, fled with his family to Multán. The Maharájá entered the city and took possession of the immense wealth which the Sial chief had been accumulating for so many years. The *Choudhris* of the town sued for protection from plunder, which was promised, and orders were issued accordingly. As the troops had gained nothing in the last three campaigns, little notice was taken of the orders issued prohibiting their plundering. They were determined to make what they could out of this victory, and accordingly eased the inhabitants of all that they could by any means remove. In vain was redress sought from Ranjít Singh, who declared himself powerless to suppress the disorder that prevailed. Ahmad Khan having agreed to pay a tribute of Rs. 60,000 a year to the victor, returned to Jhang. The Maharájá now crossed the Tirmu, attacked Uch, and exacted a large tribute from the chief of that place, Nág Sultán, a Bokhári Syad. The towns of Sáhíwál and Garh Maharájá were then visited, and the Baloch Mussulman chiefs of those places were forced to satisfy the cupidity of the Maharájá with money and horses, with the alternative of having the Sikh army let loose in their city to supply their own wants.

The battle at Jhang.

Defeat and flight of Ahmad Khan, Siál.

The sack of Jhang.

The Maharájá seizes Uch, Sahíwál, and Garh Maharájá, 1803.

Renewed ravages by Sansar Chand of Kot Kangrá.

He is compelled to retreat, 1804.

Sansár Chand again left his hill possessions in 1804, and renewed his ravages on Hoshiárpur and Bijwára, but when Ranjít Singh approached, with the confederated armies, the hill Rájá was compelled to retreat. About this time the Gorkhás aspired to the sovereignty of the whole peninsula of India, and the hill chief soon after became involved with these people.

Discussion on the word "Shalámár."

The "Shalámár Gardens" (or the famous gardens of the emperor, Shah Jahán at Láhore), became the subject of an animated discussion between Ranjít and some of his suite. The Maharájá was of opinion that the literal meaning of the word was "God's Curse," from *Shala*, "God," in the Jhang dialect, and *mar*, a Hindi word meaning "curse." He, therefore, resolved to change the name for some other more appropriate term, whereupon it was explained to him that *Shala* was a Turki word, meaning *pleasure*, and *mar* meant *place*, in that language, so that the words really meant "a place of pleasure," and this name was given to several gardens similarly founded by the Chughattai emperors in Hindostán, after the fashion in vogue in Turkistán, their native country. Ranjít was not the man to be easily convinced of the truth of an interpretation which he himself did not wish to be put upon the word. He asked them, if the word really meant what they said, how it was that Mirza Mahdi, the biographer of Nádir Shah, called it "*Shálá mah*" (شعلهٔ ماه) or "the blaze of the moon," in his description of the life of his royal master, the date of whose advent in India is derived from the chronograms Choghad Kadan چغد قدم (entrance of an owl) and *Ghami ám* غم عام (universal mourning). The arguments of the courtiers in favour of the Turki signification of the word failing to make any impression on Ranjít Singh, he gave his own name to the garden, and called it "*Shahla Bagh*" شهلا باغ, "*Shahla*" meaning in Persian "sweetheart" with dark gray eyes and a shade of red, and "*Bagh*" meaning "garden." The courtiers present passed high eulogies on the Maharájá's ingenuity in selecting so charming a name for the famous gardens of Láhore, and it was ordered, accordingly, that henceforward the gardens be called by that name, and written so in all public correspondence. A few days after, the Sikh monarch visited the Harmandar at Amritsar, and, at a grand review of his troops, bestowed the following honours on military sardars:—

The Maharájá prefers to call it "Shalá Bágh."

Visit.

Honours bestowed.

Sardar Desá Singh, Majithia, to be commander of 400 *sawars;* Hari Singh, Nalwa, from being a menial attendant, to become a sardar with the command of 800 infantry and cavalry; Hukam Singh, *Chamni,* to be superintendent of artillery with the command of 200; Ghouse Khan to be commandant of artillery with the command of 2,000 *sawars;* Roushan Khan and Sheikh Ibadullá, of Hindostán, to be commandant of 2,000 *najibs;* Báj Singh to be styled Bábú Bhag Singh, Moraliwálá, and to be commander of 500, with a jágír; Milkhá Singh to be commander of 700 at Ráwalpindi; Nodh Singh to be commander of 400 with a jágír of Parganá Ghep; Attar Singh, son of Fatteh Singh, Dhari, to be rasaldar of 500 infantry. Mit Singh, Bharania, to be commander of 500 cavalry; Kurba Singh to be commander of 1,000; Nehal Singh, Attariwálá, to be commander of 500.

All the above were created sardars, while the following were made honourary commanders of the forces specified opposite their names, which they were to produce in time of war:—

Jassa Singh, son of Karam Singh, Sahib Singh son of Gujar Singh, Chet Singh, son of Lahná Singh, Bhag Singh, Hallowalia, and the sons of Nar Singh of Chammari, 10,000 troops; the Kánhia sardars, 5,000; the Nakáis, 4,000; the Ráis of the hills, 5,000; the sardars of the Doábá, 7,000.

Treaties with the Mahomedan chiefs of Chináb and Jhelum, 1805.

In the early part of 1805 the Maharájá entered into treaties with the Mahomedan chiefs and families about the Chináb and the Jhelum. The Court of Kábul was no longer regarded as the royal and highest tribunal of India. The chiefs of the Panjáb looked upon the Maharájá Ranjít Singh as the greatest and most powerful chief of India; to him they did homage; to him they looked for advancement, and around his standard they rallied in cases of national danger, or of any great emergency. In February of that year the Maharájá returned to Láhore, and celebrated the Holi festival with the greatest libertinism, as was usual with him. He then, like a pious Hindu, proceeded to Hardowar, with a small retinue, to bathe in the holy Ganges, and wash away, as it were, the sins he had accumulated. Well may the Hindostáni couplet be applied to the character of the eccentric Sikh Ruler:

کہیں عابد بنا کہیں زاهد — کہیں رندوں کا پیشوا دیکھا

"Now a devotee, now a monk, and now a leader of libertines."

He returned from his pious pilgrimage early in June, just as the rainy season began to set in, and immediately set about the management of his financial affairs. He farmed out the revenues to the highest bidders, who were always sure of collecting sufficient for his coffers, as the lives of defaulters were at their mercy.

The farming of the revenues.

Ranjít's next expedition was into the districts which had been conquered by Ahmad Shah in Hindostán. By this time Shah Zamán had had his eyes put out, and had been deposed by Shah Mahmúd, who, in his turn, was supplanted by Shah Shujá, a third brother, afterward the well-known exile of Ludhiáná. Ranjít made a good impression on the Durráni governors of districts, and they, for the most part, elected to make their submission to him. He then led his army into the Mahomedan country between the Chináb and the Indus, and the nawáb of Jhang was again pressed to settle an annual tribute, which was now raised to 1,20,000 rupees. A fresh attack on Multán was resolved upon; but when the Maharájá's advanced guards had reached Mohátma, a village 20 miles north of Multán, the nawáb, who had no wish to fight with the Sikhs, paid 70,000 rupees as ransom to Ranjít Singh, who then departed, after having bestowed a valuable *khilat* on the nawáb. In the midst of this career of victory, he was, however, recalled by intelligence that a large body of fugitive Mahrattas, hotly pursued by the British army, under General Lake, was approaching his eastern frontier. This was no welcome news for the ruler of Láhore, who had no interest in seeing the Panjáb converted into a battle field for two foreign nations. The Mahratta chief, Jaswant Rao Holkár, having been utterly routed by Generals Lake and Fraser, at Fattehgarh and Dig, and, after in vain attempting to raise a new army south of the Jamna, set out for the Panjáb, in the expectation of obtaining assistance from the Sikhs against the British. His hopes were probably strengthened by the fact that certain minor Sikh chiefs of the Trans-Sutlej, such as Gurdit Singh, Ládwá, Bhanga Singh of Thanesar, and others, had already fought on the side of the Mahrattas at Delhi against the English. There was also this circumstance to be taken into consideration that, during his stay at Patiálá, he had obtained large contributions from Rájá Sahib Singh and Ráni Aus Kour. Forgetful, however, that Ranjít Singh was a totally different person to deal with, he reached the neighbourhood of Amritsar at the head of an army of 15,000* men, accompanied by Amir Khan, the Rohilla chief, after successfully evading the detachment of the British army that had been sent to intercept him. But General Lake, who was in his rear, pursued him into the Panjáb with five regiments of cavalry and four of infantry. On hearing of this, Ranjít first summoned Fatteh Singh, and then hastened to Láhore, where Holkar's agents met him with presents from their master, and explained to him the objects of the Mahratta chief's visit. Ranjít Singh repaired to Amritsar † in person, and had an interview with the fugitive, who asked for help against the British, and threatened to continue his march to Kábul, if he obtained no help from the Panjáb. Lord Lake had, in the meantime, crossed the Biás, and encamped at Jallálábád. Great was the contrast between the Hyphasis of that day and the Hyphasis of two thousand one hundred years previously. The river then formed a barrier to the further advance of Alexander the Great, whose Macedonians erected twelve massive

Expeditions to Mahomedan districts.

The Jhang tribute raised to Rs. 1,20,000.

Second expedition to Multán, 1805.

Holkár, the Mahratta fugitive, in the Panjab, 1805.

He asks the Maharájá's aid against the British.

He is hotly pursued by General Lake.

* Native historians have very much exaggerated the strength of Holkar's troops on this occasion. Rai Kánhia Lal has put down the number at 40,000, and Dewán Amar Náth at two lakhs. The number, however, did not exceed 15,000.—Major Thorn's *Memoirs of War*, &c.

† Smyth says Ranjít Singh received the Mahratta chief, Jaswant Rao, at Láhore. It is, however, certain that the Mahratta chief never visited Láhore. Compare Murray and Cunningham's *Histories* with those of Kánhia Lal and Amar Náth.

altars as a memorial on its banks. The inauspicious Indian gods had turned the Macedonian conqueror back, but they had little effect on the illustrious British General, who was as much a stranger in the land of the Five Rivers as the renowned Macedonian had been.

The wonder of the natives at the sight of a European military camp.

Thousands of people assembled on the banks of the Biás, to gaze upon the British troops with wonder. Their eyes were unfamiliar with the sight of a British military camp, its white soldiers (*gorás*) dressed in their military costume, their warlike music, their discipline, their mode of living, and their general appearance; but blessed be the nation to which they belonged, and for whom Providence had destined the sway of these lands. Had it been the march of an Asiatic conqueror like Tymúr the Tartar, Mahmúd the Gháznani, or any other freebooter of their kind, the case would have been very different for the countries invaded. But how did the British General, the conqueror of the metropolis of the Indian Empire, the deliverer of Agra, the city of Akber, the "hero of the land," the "Lord of the age," as the blind Shah Alam called him, conduct his marches into this country? The strictest discipline was observed. Not a grain of wheat was taken without payment; no man, however small or insignificant, was molested; no work, however trifling, was forced upon the people without the payment of liberal wages, and no wrong was done to any person on any account.

The demeanour of the British soldiers towards the natives.

The spectators soon learnt to admire the men of the British army, and were always ready to render them whatever assistance they could in purchasing their goods. The most scrupulous regard was paid to the property of the inhabitants, and as all supplies were punctually paid for, the British troops wanted for nothing that the country could produce. Ranjít Singh, though he would have proved a valuable auxiliary to either of the contending parties, was sensible of his own inability to render any material assistance to either of them, in the confused state of his own kingdom, yet in its infancy; and as his whole policy was directed to giving unity to the scattered Sikh elements, and to moulding the entire nation into one State or commonwealth, he, on the approach of the foreigners, held a council of the Sikh confederacies that still depended upon him for advice or support. It was unanimously resolved in this council, that the chief of Láhore and the Sikh nation should interpose as mediator between the fugitive Mahratta chief and the British Government. On the 19th of December, the Maharájá sent his vakíl to the British camp, and the negotiations were soon concluded. Holkár, finding his whole dominions closed against him, and himself totally helpless, sued for peace; and, on the 11th of January 1806, a treaty was concluded between him and the British Government, by which he had to renounce all his possessions in Northern India, Ranjít, on his part, agreeing to give the Mahrattas no assistance. Thus was the evil which Ranjít dreaded averted, and his Sikhs blessed their stars that they had not been entangled in war with the foreigners. Friendly relations were further strengthened between the British commander and Ranjít Singh, and the Ahluwalia Chief, and, in the course of the same month, the armies which had inspired so much alarm in the Panjáb, retraced their steps to Hindostán. Ranjít Singh had heard many particulars regarding the British from the Mahratta chief, Jaswant Rao, and expressed his astonishment at their warlike exploits. Ever after this, Ranjít dreaded the power of that Government, and determined to be at peace with it. The Holi festival was then celebrated at Láhore with rejoicings, commensurate with the embarrassments which had perplexed the Sikhs during the past few months, and Ranjít Singh, with his mind at rest, freely indulged in all kinds of excesses.

Ranjít Singh convenes a council of the Sikh confederacies.

Treaty of peace concluded between the British and the Mahrattas, 1806.

The foreign armies leave the Panjáb.

The Maharájá's visit to Katás, 1806.

In Bysakh (April) 1806, he proceeded to bathe in the holy tank in Katás, on the banks of the Indus, and reduced the zemindárs in the vicinity of that river to subjection. On his return from this journey, he was seized with a violent illness, brought on by his own indiscretion, and was compelled to break his journey at Miáni, on the Jhelum, until he had recovered his health. The rainy season was spent at Láhore in carrying out local improvements and inaugurating financial measures. The Shalámár gardens were repaired, and the canal of Ali Mardán Khan, which watered them, was re-opened. This measure was productive of a twofold benefit, first, by restoring the splendid gardens, and, secondly, by improving the adjoining lands, which soon yielded an increased revenue.

Repair of the Shalámár gardens, 1806.

Dewán Mohkam Chand appointed chief of the Sikh army, 1806.

In the same year, 1806, Ranjít Singh, appreciating the talents of a *Chhatri* named Mohkam Chand, formerly in the employ of Sahib Singh, of Gujrát, made him the chief of his army, much to the annoyance of the Sikh sardars. He proved an able general, and fully justified the confidence reposed in him by his new master. Ranjít's success throughout the most eventful period of his life was, to a great extent, due to the choice he made of his servants of State, as his subsequent career abundantly shows. The same year, having crossed the Sutlej at the head of an army, he seized Zirá, expelling the widow of Sardar Mohar Singh, Nishanwálá, who held the place against the invader for some time. Being then assisted by the traitor, Sodhi Jawahr Singh, father of Guru Goláb Singh, of Manawar, he captured Muktesar and Kot Kapurá, possessions of Sardar Jagat Singh, Buria. He then fell on Dharmkot, which he reduced; subdued Mári, expelling Hari Singh and Arbel Singh, brother-in-law of Tárá Singh, Gheba, and then marched to Farídkot, the chief of which place averted the danger of an attack by the timely payment of a handsome tribute.

Capture of Zirá, Muktesar, Kot Kapurá, Dharmkot and Mari, 1806.

Farídkot overrun.

Quarrel between Rájá Sahib Singh of Patiálá and his wife Ráni Aus Kour.

A violent dispute arose about this time between Rájá Sahib Singh of Patiálá, and his wife, Ráni Aus Kour, the mother of the regent prince, Karm Singh. She was an ambitious and intriguing woman, and was devising plans to set aside her husband in favour of her minor son, or to secure for herself a separate territory. She was greatly encouraged in her designs by the Mahratta chief, Jaswant Rao, during his stay at Patiálá, as the latter wanted to make his own fortune out of the struggle. The approach of Lord Lake, however, compelled the Mahratta to cross the Sutlej, and leave matters to be settled between the husband and the wife. It, however, happened that the Patiálá rájá was, about this time, also at enmity with the chief of Nabhá, the subject of the dispute being a village named Doladhi, twenty miles north of Patiálá and two miles west of Nabhá, which the rájá of the latter place claimed. With the connivance of Jaswant Singh, Rájá of Nabhá, Bhái Tárá Singh, the Patiálá official in charge of Doladhi, was murdered. Rájá Bhág Singh, of Jhínd, embraced the side of the Nabhá chief, and sardar Bhanga Singh of Thanesar, his nephew, Sardar Mahtáb Singh, and Bhái Lal Singh of Kythal, that of Sahib Singh, the Patiálá rájá.

The factions formed lead to a fight,

Various skirmishes took place during a period of two months between the contending parties, attended with much bloodshed, till, at length, in one of these fights, Sardar Mahtáb Singh of Thanesar was killed. On hearing this news, the Patiálá rájá was greatly incensed, and it ultimately led to a severe fight between him and the Nabhá Rájá, at Nirwáná, six miles from Nabhá, in which Rájá Jaswant Singh, being defeated, fled to Nabhá. One hundred and fifty men were killed on both sides in this engagement. The contending parties invited Ranjít Singh to decide their disputes, and that wily chief was only too glad to avail himself of an opportunity

In which the Rájá of Nabhá is defeated.

The contending parties appoint Ranjít Singh as their arbitrator.

to interfere.* The Dasehra was no sooner over, than the ruler of Láhore crossed the Sutlej, on 26th July, 1806, with 20,000 horse, having in his train Sardar Fatteh Singh, Ahluwalia, Gurdit Singh of Ládwá and many other chiefs. Having received large *nazránás* from Sardar Budh Singh of Jalandar, and Sardar Dharm Singh of Phillour, and, having reduced Nakodar, he entered the Patiálá territory on the third day, and at once seized Doladhi, the possession of the Patiálá rájá, and the subject of dispute between him and the Nabhá chief, driving the Patiálá troops out of the town. From Doladhi, the Maharájá proceeded to Mansúrpur, in Patiálá, which he invested. The rájás of Jhínd and Nabhá, who had induced the Maharájá to make the attack, were in his train. But the Patiálá troops, on this occasion, greatly out-numbered those of the Láhore chief who were engaged in the field. Mir Zulfikár Ali, nephew of Mir Maksúd Ali, commandant of the Patiálá artillery, personally superintended the firing of the heavy ordnance. He managed, during the engagement, to send a shot through the howdah of the elephant on which Rájá Bhág Singh was seated. Ranjít Singh viewed all this through his telescope from a distance, on his elephant, whence he saw the overwhelming number of the enemy's troops. In the meanwhile, Chen Singh, the agent of Rájá Sahib Singh, of Patiálá, arrived with fresh messages on behalf of his master. The next day peace was concluded between the Rájá of Patiálá and the Maharájá of Láhore, who restored Doladhi to the Patiálá chief. The Maharájá then levied a *nazráná* of Rs. 50,000 from Rájá Jaswant Singh, of Nabhá.

He crosses the Sutlej for the first time, July, 1806.

Nakodar reduced 1806.

Ranjít Singh enters the Patiálá territory,

And engages with the Patiálá troops.

Peace concluded.

The visit of the Láhore sovereign, at the head of so large an army, to the Trans-Sutlej States, was the subject of a correspondence between the British Resident at Delhi and the Rájá of Jhínd, and it was considered advisable to strengthen the British garrison at Karnál, to provide against any unforeseen emergency, though Ranjít Singh had his hands quite full enough just then with the affairs of the territories which he had recently visited, and under the circumstances had no wish to give the British Government any cause of offence.

Strengthening of the British garrison in Karnál.

Ludhiáná was at this time held by Núrunnissa and Lachmi, the widows of Rai Ilias Khan,† a Mussalmán Rájput of Raikot, whose family had held it for two hundred years. The declining Mahomedan family had sought the protection of the adventurous George Thomas. Ranjít had no weakness for generosity. His policy was self-aggrandizement at any price. Might was right with him. With him the weak were sure to go to the wall, and their ruin was the foundation upon which he built his greatness. Expelling the helpless widows, he made himself master of Ludhiáná, together with the surrounding villages, the whole of which he bestowed upon his maternal uncle, the Rájá of Jhínd. He also wrested Parganá Thárá, in the Basiá talúk, from the widow of Mian Ghous, and gave it in jágír to Mohkam Chand, his favourite general. Jhandálá, Raikot, Jagráon, Baddowál, Talwandi, Dháká and Basia, all originally possessions of Rai Ilias, next fell into his hands, and were divided among the Rájás of Jhínd and

Ranjít wrests Ludhiáná from the widows of Rai Ilias and gives it to the Rájá of Jhind, 1806.

Usurpations and rewards.

* A strict policy of non-interference, inaugurated by Lord Cornwallis, prevailed at this time in British India, and all connection with the powers beyond the Jamua was avoided. This may account for the fact of Ranjít's arbitration being sought in preference to that of the English.

† Rai Ilias Khan was a Mussalmán Rájput and a man of great importance in Ludhiáná towards the close of the 17th century. His great ancestor, Tulsi Dás, coming from Jesselmír, settled in Farídkot in 1323, and became a convert to Mahomedanism. His son, Gopál, founded Shahjahánpur, in the Ludhiáná district, and Rai Kálá, one of his decendants, became the founder of Talwandi in 1478. This Talwandi is still know as *Rai ki Talwandi*. The family reached the zenith of its power in 1620, when it mastered the town of Ludhiáná, which, 140 years previously, had been founded by two Pathán Lodhis, named Eusaf and Nihang. Hence the name Ludhiáná or Lodhiáná was given to the town. In the beginning of the present century Raikot, Talwandi, Jandálá or Jandiálá, Buddowál, Jagráon, Ludhiáná, Basiá, &c., towns of some importance, were in possession of Rai Ilias Khan's widows.

Nabhá, Sardar Fatteh Singh, Ahluwalia, Dewán Mohkam Chand, Sardar Basáwá Singh and Sardar Bhanga Singh. During the same campaign, he conquered the district of Ghamgrama, expelling the owners, Ját Singh, Gujar Singh and Kábil Khan, and dividing their territories between the Nabhá chief, Jaswant Singh, and Gurdit Singh, chief of Ládwá. He made no advance further south than Ambála, and, after celebrating the Dewali festival at Thanesar, and performing his ablutions in the holy tank there, he recrossed the Sutlej. Little was done by him in this campaign towards improving the relations between the rájá of Patiálá and his wife, though both, in their turn, had presented him with large sums of money and precious jewels to secure his goodwill.

Nothing done to restore confidence between the Patiálá Rájá and his Ráni.

Taking route by Rahon, the residence of Tárá Singh, Gheba, Ranjít Singh proceeded to pay his superstitious devotions to the holy fires, the natural flames of Jawálá Mukhi. Intelligence was brought to him there by Sardar Fatteh Chand, younger brother of Rájá Sansár Chand of Kangrá of the encroachments on the hill rájá's territory by Amar Singh, Thapa, the general of the Nepál army, who, after subduing and ravaging the mountain districts from the Ganges to the Sutlej, had fallen on Kangrá with the determination to subdue it. He had levied tribute from the hill chief of Garhwal, and reduced the young chief of Nálágarh, who had, however, offered a gallant resistance. The neighbouring states of Sarmor, Basihar, and Bhagat had all fallen in succession, and the invader had now laid siege to the Kangrá fort. The sardar, therefore, asked for help against the invading Gorkhás, on condition of his paying a large *nazráná*. Ranjít Singh gladly acceded to his request, and, on arriving in the neighbourhood of Kangrá, was visited by Zoráwar Singh, a confidential agent of General Amar Singh, who, on his master's behalf, offered a *nazráná* of double the value of that promised by Sansár Chand, on condition that the Maharájá would withdraw with his troops. The Maharájá declined the offer, on the ground that he had given his word to the Kangrá chief, though his policy was to expel the strangers (who were likely to disturb the peace of his own kingdom) from the borders. A pestilence, however, broke out among the Gorkhá troops, causing great mortality in their camp, and this necessitated their withdrawal with the utmost expedition. On his return from the hills, with the promised *nazráná* from the hill rájá, Ranjít Singh stationed one thousand troops at Nadaon, and instructed Sardar Fatteh Singh, Kalianwálá, to remain at Bijawar with his troops, to watch the future motions of the Gorkhá commander.

The Gorkhás of Nepál invade Kangrá, 1806.

The interference of Ranjít Singh is sought.

But the Gorkhás withdraw, 1806.

The beginning of 1807 was marked by the death of Nar Singh, an old Sikh sardar, and the consequent collapse of Pasrúr and Chamára, extensive territories held by the sardar. A small jágír was conferred on the son of the deceased sardar, as maintenance. Kutb-ud-dín Khan, of Kasúr, the successor of the able Pathán, Nizám-ud-dín Khan, had again become trouble some. The Maharájá, by removing such a thorn in his side as Kutb-ud-dín Khan, from his vicinity, was anxious to strengthen his own position. The opinion was also rightly held by him that the acquisition of the mythological rival of Láhore from its Mahomedan owners, and the subjugation of the Pathán colonists would tend materially to the advancement of his own prestige and popularity amongst the *Khálsá*. A formidable expedition was organised, headed by himself and Jodh Singh, the son of his father's old ally, Jassa Singh, Ramgarhia, the famous carpenter. The territory was invaded in February 1807. It contained many small forts, all of which were well stored with munitions of war and provisions. The invader invested the town, cutting off all communications from without. The siege

Annexation of Pasrúr and Chamára, 1807.

Fifth invasion of Kasúr, 1807.

lasted for a month, by which time the besieged had consumed all their store of provisions, and had begun to live on the flesh of horses and cattle. The Sikhs laid waste the whole territory with more than their ordinary vengeance, and their artillery levelled to the ground a great portion of the city walls. The city, being thus reduced, was given up to plunder, everything which the citizens possessed being forcibly wrested from them. Much barbarity was shown by the Sikhs towards the tender sex, many of whom committed suicide by strangling or throwing themselves into wells, thus preferring death to dishonour. Hundreds of women and children were carried away as slaves, and numerous helpless people were deprived even of their wearing apparel, and forced to go about naked. The outrages committed by the Sikhs on this occasion were more than ordinarily cruel, and are remembered by the people to the present day. Kutb-ud-dín shut himself up in the fortress of Kasúr. But internal seditions and broils completed the ruin of his family, and, at the end of March, he was compelled to surrender, and retire to his territory of Mamdot, on the opposite bank of the Sutlej, holding it in jágír, subject to his supplying 100 horsemen for service when required. This territory had been conquered by Kutb-ud-dín Khan and his brother, in the year 1800, from the Rai of Raikot, with the assistance of the Dográs, a turbulent Mussalmán tribe, inhabiting the neighbouring country. To Fatteh Dín Khan, nephew of the chief, and son of Nizám-ud-dín Khan, Ranjít Singh gave a jágír at Marup, in the Gurgáon district, subject to the same military conditions as were imposed upon his uncle. Kasúr, with the whole of the country adjoining it, lapsed to the kingdom of Láhore, and was temporarily assigned to Sardar Nehal Singh, Attariwálá.

Acts of devastation and violence committed by the Sikhs.

The conquest of Kasúr, 1807.

The Sikh soldiers are said to have greatly enriched themselves by plundering Kasúr, and the property of Kutb-ud-dín Khan in particular, which fell into the hands of the Maharájá, consisting of jewels, rich stuffs and fabrics, shawls, horses and camels, is said to have been enormous; while thousands of *Quráns* and Arabic and Persian books, plundered by the Sikhs, were sold at very cheap rates in the bazars of Láhore. On his return to Láhore, Ranjít held a great darbár in honour of the victory gained, and the cities of Láhore and Amritsar were illuminated to celebrate the occasion, a large amount of money and property being also sent to Amritsar to be presented at the Sikh Harmandar. Ranjít Singh next proceeded to Dipálpur, the fort of which he invested and reduced, making it over to the heir apparent as jágír. At Dipálpur he received *nazars* from the neighbouring chiefs and sardars, and he then marched to Multán, an expedition undertaken at the instigation of Abdul Samad Khan, the Baddozie chief, who had recently taken refuge at Láhore. He was at one time appointed Governor of Multán by Shah Zamán, but was at last defeated by Muzaffar Khan and dispossessed of his fort and jágírs. But excuses were not wanting, and the cause of the expedition was stated to be that the nawáb, after concluding his treaty in 1802, renewed in 1805-1806, by which he acknowledged his submission to the Maharájá, had given protection to his enemy, Ahmad Khan, the Siál of Jhang, providing him with men and money, and thereby enabling him to recover a considerable portion of his territories, and, secondly, he was suspected of intriguing with Kutb-ud-dín Khan, of Kasúr. On his way, he occupied and garrisoned various dependencies of the Multán Government, and in April he laid siege to Multán itself. The walled town was captured, but the citadel, into which the principal inhabitants had retired, with their valuables, offered a stubborn resistance. Ranjít Singh, who was unprovided with the means of carrying on a difficult and protracted siege, was glad to accept the payment of a *nazráná*, or tribute, of Rs. 70,000

Riches obtained by the plunder of Kasúr.

Rejoicings at Láhore.

Ranjít Singh proceeds to Dipálpur which he captures, 1807.

Third expedition to Multán, 1807.

The Maharájá retires on receiving a *nazráná*.

(half of which was raised by the nawáb from the inhabitants), and retired with credit. Having now crossed the river, the Sikh monarch made his sudden appearance in the territory of Nawáb Bháwal Khan, who was much alarmed at the approach of this devourer of small states. The nawáb sent his confidential agents to the Maharájá, and, terms having soon been arranged, the Sikh retraced his steps to Láhore, which he reached in May. Fakír Aziz-ud-dín, secretary to the Maharájá, was then sent to Báháwalpur, on his behalf with a rich *khilat* for Nawáb Bháwal Khan. Before the rains, Ranjít Singh sent a detachment of troops to reduce Adínanagar, the city of the famous Adína Beg Khan, at the foot of the hills, and exacted tribute and *nazránás* from all the Sikh sardars bordering on the Kangrá mountains, thus giving the first cause of annoyance to that talented lady, Sadá Kour, his mother-in-law, who had so materially aided him in attaining the enviable position which he then held, and to whom all these territories belonged, being dependencies of the Kánhia *misl*. This uncalled for interference on the part of the Maharájá was the beginning of a series of plots and counter-plots between the lady and her son-in-law, which eventually led to her ruin.

Báháwalpur threatened, but terms agreed to.

Ranjít's encroachments on the possessions of Sadá Kour below the Kangrá hills.

He is again invited to Patiala, 1807.

It is now necessary to return again to the affairs of the states on the other side of the Sutlej. The departure of Ranjít Singh from the scene of action was the signal for the contending parties, especially Rájá Sahib Singh, of Patiálá, and his wife Ráni Aus Kour (neither of whom had gained anything by their appeal to his arbitration) to renew their domestic feuds, which, as usual, they determined to decide by force of arms. The chiefs who had obtained the largest share of the prey on the last occasion of their quarrelling, again asked the assistance of Ranjít Singh, who was more willing to give, than they to solicit, his aid. Accordingly, in conjunction with the Patiálá, Jhínd, and Nabhá rájás, he crossed the Sutlej at Hariká Pattan, its juncture with the Biás, at the head of a large army, accompanied by his famous general, Mokham Chand, Fatteh Singh, Ahluwalia, and Ghirba Singh. He first visited Kot Kapurá, which he had reduced in the previous year, and then Bhador, from the chief of which he extorted a *nazráná*. Then, after visiting Nabhá, he appeared before Patiálá in September 1807. The Rájá of Patiálá had at this time invited a large number of sardars to his capital, among them being Sardar Bhanga Singh of Thanesar, and had collected a body of 15,000 troops there. All the chiefs had accepted his invitation, including Rájá Sahib Singh, and they received the Maharájá outside the town with great ceremony. The work of arbitration was now begun. The intriguing Ráni bribed the arbitrator, presenting him with a large sum of money, and, in addition, with a necklace of diamonds worth Rs. 70,000, and a brazen cannon belonging to the family, and known as the *Kárá Khan*, which was subsequently taken by the English in the Sutlej campaign. The arbitrator, pleased with these rich presents, settled upon the Ráni and her regent son a *jágir* worth Rs. 50,000 per annum. From all accounts, however, it appears that the influence exercised by the Rájás of Jhínd and Nabhá, Sardar Bhanga Singh of Thanesar, and Bhái Lal Singh of Kythal, contributed materially to bringing about this compromise between the Rájá and his Ráni. The rájá did not much relish the idea of parting with his gun and necklace, and would have evaded the delivery of them to Ranjít, had not the latter coolly informed him that he would prove his claim to them by recourse to arms. Sahib Singh now perceived that it would be advisable for him to yield with a good grace, which he accordingly did.* After settling the affair of Patiálá, Ranjít Singh proceeded to Ambála.

Crosses the Sutlej a second time, 1807.

Appears before Patiálá, September, 1807.

Acts as an arbitrator,

But accepts a large bribe from the Ráni.

The dispute settled.

---

* Rai Kánhia Lal here narrates the ridiculous story that, when peace was concluded between Rájá Sahib Singh and his Ráni, Maharájá Ranjít Singh took the little child, Karam

The Maharájá levies tribute from the chiefs of Sirhind, 1807.

Here Ráni Dia Kour, the widow of Sardar Gurbaksh Singh,* who held Ambála, presented him with a *nazráná*. He also exacted tribute from Bhái Lal Singh, of Kythal, Gurdit Singh, and Karam Singh, of Shahábád, Bhagwan Singh, of Buria, Jodh Singh, of Kálsia, and all the Sikh sardars of Sirhind, and bestowed *khilats* on each in return. He then marched to reduce Naraingarh, a strong fort between Ambála and the hills, held by Kour Kishen Singh, of Náhan. An attempt to carry it by storm having failed, the fort was closely invested. The besieged held out heroically for nearly three weeks, and repeatedly repulsed the enemy in their attempts to capture the fort, inflicting heavy losses upon them on each occasion. The fort was ultimately stormed and taken by the Maharájá's troops, led on by Fatteh Singh, Kalianwálá, Ranjít's famous general. This was the last fight in which he ever engaged, he being killed in the assault, though not until victory was assured. In this engagement, two other chiefs of the Maharájá where killed, Mohan Singh (commandant and sardár), and Dewa Singh, Bhandári, while, altogether, the Maharájá lost in this engagement about 400 in killed and wounded. After the capture, the Maharájá made over the territory to Sardar Fatteh Singh, Ahluwalia, on receipt of a *nazráná* of Rs. 40,000, the estate being worth Rs. 15,500 a year.

The siege of Naraingarh, 1807.

The place is captured and made over to Fatteh Singh, Ahluwalia.

The Maharájá seizes Ráhon.

The old chief, Tárá Singh, Gheba, once the leader of the Dalíwálá confederacy, who had followed the Láhore forces during the siege of Naraingarh, died before that town. His followers secretly sent his corpse for cremation to his fort at Ráhon, where the widow and the sons of the deceased lived. While the body of the old sardar was on the pyre, and the funeral obsequies were being performed, a detachment of Ranjít Singh's troops, who had been informed of the event, appeared suddenly and demanded the deceased's treasures and estates. The widow of the aged head of the Dalíwálá was, however, a spirited woman. She girded up her garments, and appeared, sword in hand, in the battle-field, but the battered walls of the fort of Ráhon soon gave way, and the place became the prize of the invaders. A certain sum was fixed

---

Singh, son of the Rájá of Patiálá, on his knee. The child, seeing the necklace of pearls on the Maharájá's neck, cried out: "This is the same necklace which I used to wear: give me this necklace." The child wept, and insisted upon having the ornament. On this, says the Rai, Ranjít Singh, out of pity for the child, gave the necklace to him, and never took it back. The *History of Patiálá*, by Khalifa Mohamed Hassan, and the *Panjáb Rájás*, by Sir Lepel Griffin, the best authories on Patiálá affairs, however, are silent on the subject. Moreover, the story is, upon the face of it, a pure invention, since Karam Singh, who was born in 1798, was not at that time a little child, but a boy about 10 years of age, and the Maharájá was hardly likely to cause a grown boy of that age to sit on his knee. Again, when the earnest supplications of the father had had no effect on the greedy Sikh monarch, it is ridiculous to suppose that the wailing of a child would avail to snatch so rich a prize from his grasp. On this subject Khalifa Mohamed Hassan writes as follows: "The Maharáj (Sahib Singh) had at first hesitated in making over these articles; but the Singh Sahib (Ranjít Singh) on 26th Assoj, 1864 Samvat, wrote an agreement, to which he affixed his seal, promising to give Ráipur and Gujarwál, together with the adjoining villages, to the Maharájá. Upon this, the Maharáj considered it advisable to deliver up the gun and necklace. Having secured these, the Singh Sahib marched to Ambála."—*History of Patiálá*, page 197. The agreement of 26th Assoj, 1864 Samvat, was, according to the same author, never fulfilled by the Maharájá. It is clear, then, that the story about the weeping child, and the return of the famous necklace to its owner, is incorrect.

* McGregor says, at page 159 of his *History*, that the *nazráná* was levied from Gurbaksh Singh. But the sardar had died twenty-three years before, namely, in 1783. The town and district of Ambálá had at first been conquered by Sangat Singh and descended to his brother-in-law, Dhian Singh. This latter appointed Gurbaksh Singh and Lal Singh as thanedárs in charge, and then removed to Singhwálá, in Ferozepur. On the return of Dhian Singh to Ambála, his thanedárs refused to deliver the place over to him, and so became masters of it themselves. On the death of Lal Singh, Gurbaksh Singh became the sole owner. Gurbaksh Singh died childless, and was succeeded by his widow, Dia Kour, in 1783. Ranjít Singh temporarily ejected her, but she was restored by General Ochterlony, and held it until her death in 1823, when it lapsed to Government.—*Panjáb Rájás*, by Sir Lepel Griffin, page 100.

by way of maintenance for the aged widow and her sons, but its payment was shortly afterwards discontinued. The Sikh monarch then took Noushera, the jágír of Tárá Singh, Gheba, expelling the officials of the old ráni, seized Morinda, south of the Sutlej, the jágír of Dharam Singh, from his son, who had refused to pay *nazráná* to the invader, and captured Báhlolpur and Bharatgarh from Bhag Singh's widow. During the same campaign, his general, Mohkam Chand, conquered the district of Wadni, in Ferozepur, which Ranjít, later in the year, gave to his mother-in-law Sadá Kour. The same year, the Maharájá divided his conquests in Ráipur, Ghamgrama, Sirhind, Zira, Kot Kapurá, and Dharmkot among his favourites, Sardar Fatteh Singh, Ahluwalia, Rájá Bhág Singh, of Jhínd, Jaswant Singh, of Nabhá, Mohkam Chand, the general and dewán, who was fast gaining favour, Gharba Singh, and Sardar Karam Singh, of Náglá. Lahangarh, in Ráhon and Dhanor in Parganá Rahímábád, the possessions of Tárá Singh's widow, were also given to Gharba Singh. Shergarh, in Parganá Thará, was given to Sardar Attar Singh. The Sutlej campaign was then closed by the levy of a tribute of 20,000 from Ranjít Singh, zemindár of Manauli, Rs. 30,000 from Gopál Singh, of Mani Májra, 15,000 from Sardar Hari Singh of Ropar, and Rs. 80,000 from the zemindárs of the Doábá.

Captures Noushera, Morinda, Báhlolpur and Bharatgarh.

Wadni conquered by Dewán Mohkam Chand.

The Maharájá's territorial rewards to his chiefs.

Tribute levied during the same campaign, 1807.

Ranjít Singh returned to Láhore in December 1807, when Ráni Mahtáb Kour, daughter of Sadá Kour, presented the Maharájá with Sher Singh, and Tárá Singh as her twin sons. In reality, however, she never bore any children to the Maharájá. Sadá Kour knew well that the only way of increasing her power with her son-in-law was through her daughter. Ráni Mahtáb Kour had been childless, and consequently not in very great favour with her royal husband. The mother-in-law, therefore, hit upon a plan by which the wife of the Maharájá was to become a mother. She had it rumoured about the country that Mahtáb Kour, the wife of the Maharájá was pregnant, and after some time had elapsed, she had it proclaimed, with great rejoicings, that the queen (her daughter) had given birth to twins. The Maharájá's absence favoured the mother-in-law's plans. The night previous to the proclamation being made public, of the queen having given birth to twins, two new-born babes were purchased, Sher Singh from his father Nehála, a chintz weaver, a native of Mokerian, in the Hoshiárpur District, which was then held as jágír by Mái Sadá Kour, and Tárá Singh from a Mahomedan woman, daughter of Manki, a slave girl of the Mái. Ranjít Singh was never deceived; but as he liked the idea of being called a father, he treated both as sons, and called them Shahzádás, or princes.

Birth of Sher Singh and Tárá Singh, reputed sons of the Maharájá, 1807.

Their true parentage.

In the beginning of 1808, Ranjít Singh reduced the fort of Pathánkot, at the foot of the hills, the possession of Sardar Jay Singh, Kánhia. The killadár fled and the sardar had to bear the loss with patience. He next marched to Jasrota, the rájá of which place surrendered and became tributary, having first paid a large *nazráná*. Having spent several days in hunting at Jasrota, the Maharájá set out to invade Chambá. He had not proceeded half way when the Chambá rájá, hearing of his approach was terrified, and sent his agents to settle terms. A large *nazráná* was paid by the rájá, besides a *ziyáfat*, or present of money, for the Maharájá, and the agents were dismissed with a rich *khilat* for their master. Basoli was next invaded, and Rs. 8,000 exacted from the rájá, as an annual tribute, besides a *nazráná*. While the Maharájá was extending his conquests in the mountainous districts north of the Panjáb, Dewán Mohkam Chand was busy in subduing the chiefs on the left of the Sutlej, formerly dependents of the Dalíwálá *misl* under Sardar Tárá Singh, Gheba. Most of these sardars were reduced, and, having transferred their allegiance to the new kingdom of Láhore, were confirmed in their possessions

Pathánkot reduced, 1808.

Jasrota rendered tributary.

Chambá and Basoli meet the same fate.

Conquests on the left of the Sutlej.

on promising to supply a contingent of horse, and to remain constantly in attendance upon the Láhore ruler.

Coming down to the plains, the Maharájá convened a grand meeting of all the sardars, in which he formally received *nazars* from the chiefs of the Panjáb who had acknowledged themselves to be his feudatories. All responded to the call, save Sardar Jiwan Singh of Siálkot and Sahib Singh of Gujrát, who refused to comply with the order, less from a spirit of rebellion than from fear of treachery. Ranjít Singh now marched against these chiefs to punish them for their audacity. An attack was made on Siálkot, and the city taken by storm, but Jiwan Singh, with a body of one thousand fighting men and four pieces of artillery, ably defended the fort, which was closely invested. The siege lasted seven days, when one of the gates of the fort was battered down by the fire of the besiegers, which enabled them to enter and occupy it. Jiwan Singh was put in chains, and, arrangements having been made for the administration of the district, the troops left for Gujrát. The Maharájá himself followed these troops, but before he reached his destination, Sahib Singh's agents met him and paid him a large sum of money as tribute, and, in addition, entered into a treaty acknowledging his allegiance to the Maharájá. Ranjít, being satisfied with these terms, withdrew. He then went to Akhnúr, the chief of which, Alam Khan, paid him *nazráná* and was reinstated.*

The insurrection of Jiwan Singh of Siálkot and Sahib Singh of Gujrát.

Siálkot invaded a second time, 1708.

The city and the fort are reduced.

The Maharájá marches to Gujrát.

Sahib Singh of Gujrát submits.

Akhnúr rendered tributary, 1808.

In January of the same year, 4,000 troops were sent, under Ghouse Khan, commandant of the Maharájá's artillery, and sardar Hakma Singh, to reduce Haran Minár,† otherwise known as Shekhupura, the chiefs of which place, Arbel Singh and Amir Singh, had greatly disturbed the public peace by their depredations throughout the country.

Troops sent to Shekhupura.

Prince Kharak Singh‡ was put in nominal charge of the expedition. Arbel Singh and Amir Singh vigorously defended themselves and their fort, and the Maharájá's troops had great difficulty in battering down the walls; this not being effected until the Bhangi *top* of Ahmad Shah (which had been captured at Amritsar from the possession of the Bhangis) was brought to bear against one of the gates of the fort. The gate was then broken in pieces, and the Láhore troops effected their entrance into the fort, which was reduced. Arbel Singh and Amir Singh were put in irons, and their fighting men were transferred to the Maharájá's service, and the reduced country was bestowed upon Prince Kharak Singh as jágír, with his mother Rání Nakáin as his guardian. The Rání lived in the fort until her death, and seldom came to Láhore.

Shekhúpura annexed to the Láhore territory, 1808.

In the end of Bysakh (April) of the same year, a *vakíl* of the British Government arrived at Láhore, with presents for the Maharájá from that Government. The object of his visit was to strengthen the relations of amity between the British Government and the Darbár of Láhore, which had been initiated by the mission of Eusaf Ali Khan, eight years before. The *vakíl* was honourably received, and on his departure a *khilat*, valued at Rs. 5,000, was presented to him, together with presents of valuable articles, the products of the country, for the British authorities.

Arrival of a British Agent at Láhore, 1808.

* Rai Kanhai Lal here mentions (page 194 of his work) that Daská was conquered by the Maharájá from Sardar Nidhán Singh. But Daská was reduced in the beginning of 1802, according to the Rai's own account, given at page 153 of his book.

† The hunting-ground of Jahangír, where that emperor constructed beautiful edifices, now the jágír of Rájá Harbans Singh, reputed son of Rájá Tej Singh.

‡ Prinsep says Dewán Mohkam Chand was put in command of this expedition. But he was at this time engaged in reducing the Anandpur Makhowál Valley, and had nothing to do with the Shekhúpura expedition, which was under the charge of Shahzada Kharak Singh. Compare Sohan Lal's diary with Bute Shah's history, and the memoirs of Dewán Amar Náth, all contemporary historians.

The fort of Govindgarh founded at Amritsar, 1808.

In the course of the same year, the fort of Gujar Singh, Bhangi, at Amritsar, having been rebuilt under the superintendence of Imám-ud-dín, brother of Aziz-ud-dín, the Secretary of the Láhore Darbár, the Maharájá gave it the name of Govindgarh. It was made the repository of the Maharájá's treasures, and was garrisoned by 2,000 troops, and had twenty guns of large calibre mounted upon its ramparts. The Nawáb of Multán having made some delay in remitting the promised tribute, orders were issued to Bábú Báj Singh, Jassa Singh, Bhangi, and Kutb-ud-dín Khan of Mamdot (late of Kasúr) to proceed to Multán forthwith at the head of 5,000 cavalry to levy the tribute due from the nawáb, and the zemindárs of that territory who had made their submission to the new Láhore Government. The expedition returned after three months, having collected the whole of the tributes, and Dewán Mohkam Chand arrived with a *nazráná* of six lakhs of rupees from the Doáb country. The campaign had been carried on during the rainy season, and the dewán succeeded in conquering the whole country from Anandpur Makhowál downwards, formerly ruled by Bhagel Singh and Tárá Singh, Gheba. The Maharájá was well pleased with the dewán's distinguished services.

Levy of tribute from Multán.

The country about Anandpur Makhowál subdued, 1808.

Bhowáni Das is appointed head of pay office and finance office, 1808.

In the same year, 1808, Bhowáni Das, a revenue officer of high standing under Shah Shujá, son of Thakur Das, the privy councillor, first of the celebrated Ahmad Shah, and then of Shah Zamán, having left the Kábul Court in disgust, came to Láhore, where he was well received by the Maharájá. He was an eminent financier. The revenue of the State of Láhore, at that time, was about thirty lakhs of rupees, and no system of treasury or State accounts existed. Revenue transactions were conducted by Ramá Nand, the Amritsar banker, to whom where also leased the Pind Dádan Khan salt mines. Bhowáni Das was made head of the Finance Department, and he, for the first time, introduced a system of accounts for the Civil and Military Departments. The following year he was joined by his brother Devi Das, the dewán of Wazír Sher Mohamed, son of Shah Wali Khan, chief minister of the celebrated Abdáli King. The seal of the Maharájá was, the same year, 1808, given into the custody of Karam Chand (formerly in the employ of Bishan Singh, Kalál), father of Rattan Chand, Darhiwálá, of Láhore.

Karam Chand is appointed Lord of Privy seal, 1808.

The Cis-Sutlej Sikhs ask British protection, 1808.

The systematic aggressions and usurpations of Ranjít Singh, and the warlike measures adopted by him, showed clearly that the king of all * the Sikhs, as he now called himself, was anxious to establish a Sikh monarchy extending from the Indus to the Jamna. The Sikhs of Malwa and Sirhind were filled with alarm, as they clearly foresaw their own ruin in the aggressive policy of the Láhore ruler. The alternatives left them were only two; either to submit to the yoke of the Láhore conqueror, or to seek the protection of the paramount power of Hindostán (a power before whom even the new Lord of the Sikhs trembled). At a meeting of the Sikh chiefs of Patiálá, Jhínd, and Nabhá, convened at Samána † for the purpose of considering which of these alternatives it would be better to adopt, it was unanimously resolved to choose the latter. Accordingly, a formal deputation, consisting of Rájá Bhag Singh of Jhínd, Bhái Lal Singh of Kythal, Sardar Chen Singh, dewán of Patiálá, and Mir Gholám Husain, the confidential agent of Nabhá, proceeded to Delhi, in March, 1808, to wait upon the British

* Ranjít Singh preferred to be called *Khálsaji*, signifying the whole body of the Sikhs, and in all public documents this word had the same signification as that of the *Maharáiá* or *Sarkar*. The fact is that Ranjít's great successes had led that monarch to entertain notions that he was the Lord of the whole Sikh nation.

† In Patiálá.

Resident, Mr. Seton, and implore the protection of the British Government. On the first of April, the members of the deputation presented a written memorial to Mr. Seton, in which the subject was dealt with at full length. It was pointed out in this document that the States of the Sutlej had always been under the protection of the sovereign of Delhi, and rendered him service in time of war. Thus, when the Durráni King, Ahmad Shah, waged war on the Emperor Mohamed Shah of Delhi, Rájá Ala Singh of Patiálá was present with his contingent of troops, in the train of Wazír Kamr-ud-dín Khan. Again, when Ahmad Shah conquered Delhi and made Nawáb Najíb-ud-doula his subadár at that capital, the Patiálá rájá supplied the nawáb with a contingent of 4,000 troops under Sardar Bhola Singh, to fight against Jawáhar Singh Rájá of Bharatpur, on the side of the nawáb. Other instances were also cited; but they need not be recapitulated here. Upon these grounds, the members of the deputation solicited the protection of the British Government, and the extension of the paramount power to all the States south-east of the Sutlej. The attitude of these States was unmistakeably friendly, and the Government of India had, on its part, assured the nawáb of Kunjpura, in Karnál, that his hereditary possessions would be respected, while the services of the Sikh chief of Sikri were considered worthy of recognition; yet the policy of the Government of India was to act cautiously with respect to its relations with the Cis-Sutlej States. The Resident held out no hopes to the deputies of the confederate Sikh chiefs of direct British interference in their relations with the Láhore ruler, but nevertheless they were led to hope that they had the best sympathies of the British authorities, and that, when the time came, a helping hand would not be denied them. The reply, though encouraging, was not decisive, and by no means sufficient to save the chiefs concerned from eventual ruin. In the meanwhile, news of the mission having reached Láhore, Ranjít Singh became anxious to prevent them from going over to the side of the English and deserting his own. He, therefore, proposed a meeting of these chiefs at Amritsar, where they went to settle their own terms with the acknowledged ruler of Láhore. Ranjít Singh received them with every mark of consideration and favour, and did everything in his power to allay their fears.

Their grounds for the request.

The British government does not accede to their request.

Ranjít Singh enters into terms with them.

While these transactions were pending, the political aspect of affairs in India underwent a material change, and the policy of non-interference inaugurated by Lord Cornwallis was totally abandoned by the new Governor-General of India, Lord Minto, a statesman of great promise, and of special experience at the Board of Control. The ambitious Napoleon Buonaparte, Emperor of France, now in the zenith of his power, who had won brilliant victories in Europe, and had just concluded a treaty with the Emperor of Russia, was believed to be meditating the invasion of India (in concert with the Turks and the Persians); and, to prevent his designs, Lord Minto determined to form a defensive alliance, not only with the powers beyond the Jamna and Sutlej, but also with those beyond the Indus. It was, accordingly, resolved to send ambassadors to the court of Shah Shujá, the King of Kábul, the court of the Shah of Persia, and of Ranjít Singh, the ruler of Láhore, whose authority had now been firmly established in the Panjáb, to negotiate with those monarchs, and to persuade them that their interests were identical with those of the British, and that, in the event of an invasion of this country by the French Government, the interest of the Sikhs would be the first to suffer; he therefore urged upon them the necessity of a policy of unity as the only means by which they could hope to keep the enemy at bay. Mr. Elphinstone was deputed to the Court of Kábul, Sir John Malcolm to the Court of Teheran, and in August 1808, Mr. (afterwards Lord) C. T. Metcalfe, a young

British policy towards the Sikhs modified, consequently on the suspected designs of the French on India.

The mission of Mr. Metcalfe to Láhore, 1808.

Bengal Civilian, one of Lord Wellesley's ablest pupils, who had already distinguished himself for political sagacity and firmness, was sent as the British plenipotentiary to the Court of Maharájá Ranjít Singh at Láhore. The aggressive policy of Ranjít Singh against the Cis-Sutlej States was, it need hardly be said, an additional motive for deputing the mission to Láhore.

Mr. Metcalfe at Patiálá, 1808.

Mr. Metcalfe reached Patiálá on 22nd August, and was received by Rájá Sahib Singh with great ceremony. In his first public interview with the envoy, the rájá delivered the State keys to him, meaning thereby, that he had thrown himself on British protection, and implored the restoration of these keys, as an assurance, that he was holding the charge of his State as a trust from the British Government. The British officer, though he declined the acceptance of the keys, assured the rájá of the good-will of the British Government towards him, remarking, at the same time, that the keys had long remained perfectly safe in the rájá's own hands, and that there was every prospect of their remaining so for a long time to come. The rájá now adopted measures to strengthen Patiálá and other forts against the threatened invasion of his territory by Ranjít Singh.

He assures the Rájá of the good-will of the British towards him.

Ranjít's power paramount in the Panjáb.

The Maharájá was, about this time, at Láhore, having in his train Rájá Bhag Singh of Jhínd, Rájá Jaswant Singh of Nabhá, Bhái Lal Singh of Kythal and Sardar Gurdit Singh of Ládwá. The rájá of Patiálá, the chiefs of Thanesar, Shahábád, Buriá, Basiá and Kálsia, were represented by agents. After the discouraging reply given to them at the Delhi conference, and the recent meeting of Mr. Metcalfe with Rájá Sahib Singh at Patiálá, wherein the latter was recommended to rely on his own strength, every chief was beginning to look on the court of Láhore as his asylum, and was disposed to trust more to the mercy of the Láhore ruler than to British countenance and support. Everybody had now seen the rising power and fortune of Ranjít Singh. He had conquered city after city and town after town, without being checked in any quarter in his ambitious career, which appeared to be unlimited. He had got the better of the strongest leagues which had been formed against him; he had broken the power of the united confederacies and humbled to the dust many proud families and tribes. His arms had conquered the countries between the old Hydaspes and the Biás, forming the Panjáb proper, and even penetrated beyond the limits of the Panjáb proper. The Afgháns, who were left in possession of the north-west portion of the Panjáb, the Saddozie family of Patháns, who held the province of Multán, and the hill rájá of Kangrá, had already felt the weight of his power, and were treated by him as ordinary vassals. His highest ambition now, as Maharájá of Láhore, was to unite all the Sikhs under one banner, and extend his sway from the banks of the Sutlej to the Jamna, and thus to absorb into his own dominions all the independent States encompassed by those rivers. Already his last two Sutlej campaigns had borne good fruit, and his successive inroads and victories had reasonably led him to hope that another season would see the whole country from the Sutlej to the Jamna annexed to his new kingdom of Láhore. He was munificent in his rewards and severe in his exactions. He was dreaded, if not loved, by his subjects, and respected by those around him. His power was absolute, and, from the chief of a State to the common soldier, every one implicitly obeyed him. The British envoy had personally observed how submissive the Cis-Sutlej rájás and other chiefs were to him. He had no cause to be attracted to the side of the English, whose interests he knew were adverse to his own, so far as the Cis-Sutlej States, the choicest object of his ambition, were concerned.

His ambitious views.

The British envoy was marching to Láhore, but, as he approached, the wily Maharájá moved to his newly acquired town of Kasúr, with the double object of preparing for his march beyond the Sutlej, and of preventing the envoy from seeing his chief cities, Láhore and Amritsar. Mr. Metcalfe reached Kasúr on 11th September. He was received at some distance from the town by Dewán Mohkam Chand, and Sardar Fatteh Singh, Ahluwalia, at the head of two thousand horse. He brought with him an English carriage and a pair of horses, three elephants, with golden embroidered howdahs, and trappings, shawls, &c., as presents for the Maharájá from the British Government. He was courteously received by the Maharájá, and had several interviews with him, but the latter studiously avoided all discourse on the subject of the negotiations. These were at length explained to him at a private interview. As might have been expected, the Maharájá expressed his great satisfaction at the prospect of a British alliance, but would not consent to the proposal to confine himself to the east of the Sutlej. As for the reported French invasion of India, he affected to be indifferent about the matter. The negotiations had not much advanced, when the Maharájá suddenly broke up his camp and made his third invasion into the districts south of the Sutlej, at the head of a large army, leaving instructions for Aziz-ud-dín to follow him with the envoy. The envoy was justly offended at the discourtesy shown him, but he possessed firmness and patience, and followed the Maharájá to Khai, where another interview between them took place, but with no better results. Having levied a *nazráná* at Ferozepur, the Maharájá sent his general, Karam Chand, Chábal, to seize Farídkot, which surrendered on the 1st of October without offering any resistance. The Maharájá himself followed Karam Chand, and, taking possession of all the treasures and assets of the deposed chief, put Dewán Chand at the head of affairs. The British envoy, who had submitted a draft treaty, was constrained to follow him. He then marched against the Pathán possession of Maler Kotla, held by Atá Ullah Khan, from whom he demanded a lakh of rupees as tribute. Most of his villages *en route* had been devastated, and he was now threatened with the plunder of his city, if the fine were not paid without delay. The Khan, pressed with the Sikh's extortionate demand, paid a portion of the fine in cash, and the balance was raised by a mortgage of the fort of Jamálpur, and three other strongholds to the rájá of Patiálá. The Pathán chief laid the matter before the British envoy, on his arrival in that territory, but Mr. Metcalfe, though expressing his sympathy with the oppressed chief, declined to interfere. The envoy, moreover, perceiving that the Maharájá was using him as a tool to further his own ends, made his stand at Farídkot, and objected to proceeding further with his camp. He remonstrated with the Maharájá for his acts of hostility in attacking those very chiefs who had solicited the protection of his Government, and deliberately declined his request that he would accompany him to Ambála. The envoy rightly urged that the object of his visiting the ruler of Láhore was to enter into negotiations of a nature which the Maharájá could only too plainly perceive, as was very evident from the fact of his studiously evading all discussions upon that head, and his acting in direct contravention of what, he was perfectly well aware, was the object of the mission. But the object of the Láhore ruler was to gain time and trick the envoy. Mr. Metcalfe has left a graphic account of his negotiations with Ranjít Singh; and the following passage from the envoy's description of an interview with the Sikh ruler will be found interesting:—

The meeting between the Maharájá and Mr. Metcalfe at Kasúr, 1808.

The Maharájá unwilling to accede to the proposals of the British envoy.

His third expedition across the Sutlej, 1808.

He captures Farídkot.

And marches against Maler Kotla.

The envoy remonstrates with the Maharája for his hostile proceedings.

"Reverting to the object of his wishes, the rájá said that the only little

His description of the interview.

doubt that remained in his mind, proceeded from his not being able to conceive why the Governor-General should hesitate to grant such a trifling request. He did not, he said, ask any country from the British Government; he only wanted to be left to carry on his concerns with the people of his own nation, his brethren, without interference. That they all acknowledged his supremacy, and that he merely wanted the Governor-General to say that he would not dispute what was acknowledged by all. That the British Government had given away territories, yielding large revenues on many occasions, and was known to make great sacrifices for friends; and that he was not able to account for the hesitation in complying with his small request. I remarked upon this that, if the object of his request was trifling, the earnestness with which he pursued it was surprising, and that, if it was important, he ought not to wonder that a certain degree of deliberation should take place upon it."

The views of Ranjít Singh evidently modified since his interview with Lord Lake in 1805.

But the Maharájá had himself proposed to Lord Lake, four years previously, that the river Sutlej should divide the two States, and his seriously taking up the question of the Sutlej States in 1808 could only be regarded as a breach of a stipulation entered into by himself, prompted, of course, as it was, by the rapid growth of his military power in the Panjáb. But, to revert, the envoy remained at Fattehábád on the banks of the Sutlej, until Ranjít Singh recrossed that river, and he had received further instructions on the point from his own Government.

The mission halts at Fattehábád.

In the meantime, Ranjít Singh continued his march to Ambála, which, with its dependencies, he seized from Ráni Dia Kour, widow of Sardar Gurbaksh Singh, and he also took possession of all the jewels and treasures of the unfortunate lady. The confiscated estates of this lady were made over to the chiefs of Nabhá and Kythal.

The Maharájá continues to prosecute his Sutlej campaign.

Ambála was made over to Gandá Singh, *Sáfi*, a favourite menial servant of the Maharájá, and 5,000 cavalry and infantry were placed under his command. He then seized Saniwál, Chándpur, Jhandar, Dhári and Bahrámpur, all worth Rs. 50,000 a year, and granted them to his favourite Dewán Mohkam Chand. Rahimábád, Machiwara, Kanna, Trúkot, Challowdi and Kylawar were next seized and made over to the favourite sardars around him, Karam Singh, Náglá, Fatteh Singh, Ahluwalia, and others. Tribute was then exacted from the sons of Sardar Karam Singh of Shahábád and the Chief of Thanesar.*

His interview with the rájá of Patiálá, November 1808.

At Shahábád the Maharájá proposed a meeting with Rájá Sahib Singh of Patiálá. The rájá did not relish the idea of accepting the invitation, but eventually was obliged to do so from fear. The interview with the Maharájá took place at Lakhnour, 20 miles east of Patiálá, on the Shahábád road on 24th November 1808, the presence there of Bábá Sahib Singh, Bedi, the revered descendant of Bábá Nának, having done much to allay the rájá's fears of treachery on the part of the Láhore ruler. The Maharájá appeared, at Lakhnour, at the head of a large army, which was employed in the reduction of the States south of the Sutlej. Each chief suspecting the other of treachery, the meeting took place in the Bedi's tents, when the Maharájá

* Rai Kanhai Lal mentions at page 200 of his work that, after levying *nazráná* from the Nawáb of Maler Kotla, Ranjít Singh took the fort of Bhatinda and the town of Sinám, in the territory of the Rájá of Patiálá, but restored these to the rájá after taking from him a *nazráná* of 50,000 rupees. There is no mention of the alleged incident in any of the works consulted by me. The *Panjáb Rájás* and the *History of Patiálá*, the best authorities on Patiálá, affairs say nothing about it. Sir Lepel Griffin writes in his work, previously alluded to: "But he (Ranjít Singh) was even more a diplomatist than a warrior. He preferred to attack those who were unable to defend themselves, and throughout his march he had scrupulously avoided injuring the territory of Rájá Sahib Singh. . . . He would have liked to attack the Rájá and annex his country, but he dared not do so." *Panjáb Rájás*, page 116.

received Rájá Sahib Singh with great kindness and cordiality. Ranjít Singh swore perpetual friendship with Rájá Sahib Singh, and exchanged turbans with him, as a sign of eternal brotherhood. The following day, formal treaties, duly sealed and signed by each chief, were executed, and, the farce being over, Ranjít Singh recrossed the Sutlej on 2nd December, having, in his train, Rájá Bhag Singh of Jhind, Bhái Lal Singh of Kythal, and other chiefs of the Cis-Sutlej States. He marched to Amritsar by forced marches, and, arriving there on 4th December, was joined by Mr. Metcalfe, the British envoy.

The Maharájá recrosses the Sutlej, December 1808.

The decision of the Governor-General was now communicated to Maharájá Ranjít Singh, that the Cis-Sutlej chiefs had been declared to be under the protection of the British Government, and that the State of Láhore must sever all its connection with it. The Government argued that these chiefs had long been considered under the protection of the Power in the north of Hindostán; that, by the issue of the war with the Mahrattas, the British Government became possessed of the power and right formerly exercised by that nation in Northern India; that at that time the Maharájá had no claim on the country between the Sutlej and the Jamna, and that in an early period of that contest, a communication was received from the Maharájá by the late Lord Lake, which proposed to fix the Sutlej as the boundary between the British Government and his, which was clear proof that the Maharájá, in those days, was well aware that the country, in question, was dependent on the power paramount in the north of Hindostán. "Since the British Government has come into this situation," wrote Mr. Metcalfe in his note of 12th December, "it has relieved the chiefs between the Sutlej and the Jamna from tribute, and that degree of subserviency which they were used to pay to the Mahrattas, and has allowed them to carry on their own concerns without interference or control. But this liberality on the part of the British Government was meant for the benefit of those chiefs, not for their injury. It was never intended that the forbearance of the British Government should be taken advantage of by another power to oppress and subjugate those whom the British Government wished to protect and relieve." It was on these grounds declared that the British Government could not consent to these chiefs being subjugated by the Maharájá or any other power, and announced that those chiefs, according to established custom, were, and should remain, under the protection of the British Government. The Maharájá was, therefore, called upon to restore all the places situated between the Sutlej and the Jamna, of which he had taken possession (since the period of the first reference of this question to the British Government), to their former possessors, and to confine his army to the right bank of the Sutlej.

The ultimatum of the British Government.

The Cis-Sutlej chiefs declared to be under British protection.

Ranjít Singh was very unwilling to relinquish his most cherished conquests of the countries between the Sutlej and the Jamna. He protracted the negotiations from time to time on various pretences, and he even affected to understand that the declaration of the Governor-General was not final. Being at length assured that the decision of the Government of India was unalterable, he made preparations for war with the English. Great activity was shown in making military preparations; troops were assembled from all quarters, and munitions of war and stores collected; the new fort of Govindgarh at Amritsar was put in a state of defence; guns were mounted on the ramparts, and a large quantity of supplies provided for consumption in case of a siege, for which the fort was well strengthened. Mohkam Chand, the favourite dewán of the Maharájá, and one of his best generals, was hastily recalled from Kangrá and posted at

Ranjít Singh delays the negotiations.

And prepares for war with the British.

Phillour on the Sutlej, opposite the town of Ludhiáná, at the head of a large force. In the meantime, Lord Minto determined upon advancing a detachment of British troops to the Sutlej to support the British envoy in his negotiations with the Láhore ruler, and effectually confine Ranjit Singh to the north of that river. This detachment, under command of Sir David Ochterlony, crossed the Jamna on 16th January, 1809, it having been formally declared that all the Sikhs on the south bank of the Sutlej were under the protection of the British Government. The General advanced by way of Buriá, Patiálá and Nabhá towards Ludhiáná, and was welcomed by all the Sirhind chiefs. He restored Ambála to Ráni Dia Kour, who waited on the British commander in person to thank his Government for the generous act done to her. Rájás Sahib Singh and Jaswant Singh received him with enthusiastic joy, and they were much pleased at seeing British troops marching through their territories. He then visited Maler Kotla, and reinstated the Pathán ruler in his dominions.

The British troops move to the Sutlej, January 1809.

Sir David Ochterlony in command of British forces.

He is hailed as a deliverer by the chiefs of Malwa and Sirhind.

The advance of the British troops somewhat discomposed Ranjít Singh, but he spared no device to evade compliance with the propositions of the envoy. In the meantime, General Ochterlony strengthened his position at Ludhiáná, which was occupied by British troops. While these transactions were going on, an incident occurred at Amritsar which, though trivial in itself, had yet the effect of inspiring the Láhore ruler with profound respect for the power of his English neighbours, and created in him an impulse to imitate European military discipline. It happened that, while Mr. Metcalfe was at Amritsar, the Moharram festival, sacred to the Mahomedans, was celebrated. The Hindostáni soldiers of that persuasion, in the suite and escort of the envoy, began to celebrate the festival with the rites and solemnities peculiar to the occasion. A procession of *táziás*, or a display of artificial tombs of Hassan and Husein, sons of Ali, was made, and the biers carried through the city with bands playing. As this noisy procession, with all its pomp, passed the quarters of the Akális, or immortals, of the Sikh military priests, attached to the Golden Temple, the fanatics looked upon it as an insult to their religion and their sacred city. They were headed by a fierce desperado, named Phula Singh, the Akáli who afterwards figured so prominently in the history of Ranjít's early exploits. As the Moslem procession advanced, these fanatics opened fire upon them with their matchlocks, and broke their model sepulchres to pieces. The Hindostáni soldiers, though greatly overmatched in numbers by the Sikhs, were not disposed to submit quietly to such treatment. They at once seized the arms of their assailants, and entered into a sort of regular engagement with them. A fierce struggle ensued, in which the Sikhs were completely routed by the mere handful of men which, though, in respect of numbers it comprised only two companies of native soldiers and sixteen troopers, was, nevertheless, composed entirely of disciplined soldiers, together with the escort of the British envoy. Ranjít Singh, who was then in his fort of Govindgarh, was a witness of this close contest, and of the defeat which his "immortals" sustained. Hearing of the tumult, he hastened from his residence in the fort while the fight was still going on, whirled his handkerchief as a sign for peace, and proceeded to Mr. Metcalfe's tent to apologize to him for the conduct of the Akális, some of whom were nominally punished. He complimented the envoy on the bravery displayed by the small band of his escort, and expressed his high admiration of their discipline and order. The Hindostáni sepoys were, with the envoy's permission, fully compensated for the damage done to them. The outrage was, of course, an outburst of Sikh fanaticism, and had no political significance, nor had the

Aversion of Ranjit Singh to comply with the envoy's proposals.

Attack on the British escort at Amritsar.

The fanatic Phula Singh, Akáli.

Behaviour of Ranjit Singh on the occasion.

Maharájá anything to do with it; but it taught the Maharájá the value of British discipline, and from that moment the Sikh monarch used every means in his power to introduce such discipline into his own army.

The Maharájá is strongly impressed with the value of British military discipline.

Ranjít Singh, now seeing the danger of further protracting the negotiations, and feeling that the British Government was in earnest, and in no way to be turned from its resolution, at length awoke to the necessity of a speedy settlement with that Power. He also saw that his own authority in the Panjáb could hardly be said to be yet firmly established, and was fully sensible that the still independent chiefs of the Panjáb might shake off their allegiance to him and go over to the side of the English at any moment. All chance of establishing an empire would then be lost, his lofty aspirations effectually humbled, and he himself involved in hostilities with a Power which he very well knew he was incapable of effectually opposing in the field. He, therefore, prudently made up his mind at once to withdraw his forces from the south of the Sutlej, as required by the British authorities. There can be no doubt that, had Colonel Ochterlony not been sent to the aid of the Cis-Sutlej States beyond the Jamna, backed up by British troops, another raid across the Sutlej would have established the Maharájá's power more firmly than ever, and would have enabled him to treat the dictating authority of the British Government with disdain. Thanks to this timely movement, and to Mr. Metcalfe's mission, conducted with diplomatic ability, patient firmness and determination, which never failed him, even under the darkest aspect of affairs, a treaty was concluded at Amritsar on 25th April 1809, by which Ranjít Singh agreed not to attempt conquest, or occupy territory south of the Sutlej, and to withdraw all claims of sovereignty over the Sikhs inhabiting that territory.* From this time until the annexation of the Panjáb by the British in 1845, the history of the Cis-Sutlej States merged into that of the Empire of Hindostán, and remained distinct from the new kingdom founded at Láhore by the restless ambition of Ranjít Singh, who found ample field for his aspirations in the

He withdrawns his troops from the south of the Sutlej,

And concludes a treaty with the British, April 1809.

---

* *Treaty between the British Government and Rájá Ranjít Singh of Láhore.*

Whereas certain differences which had arisen between the British Government and the Rájá of Láhore have been happily and amicably adjusted, and both parties being anxious to maintain the relations of perfect amity and concord, the following articles of treaty, which shall be binding on the heirs and successors of the two parties, have been concluded by Rájá Ranjít Singh on his own part, and by the agency of Charles Theophilus Metcalfe, Esquire, on the part of the British Government.

Treaty of 1809.

ARTICLE I.—Perpetual friendship shall subsist between the British Government and the State of Láhore. The latter shall be considered, with respect to the former, to be on the footing of most favoured powers; and the British Government will have no concern with the territories and subjects of the rájá to the northward of the river Sutlej.

ARTICLE II.—The Rájá will never maintain in the territory occupied by him and his dependents on the left bank of the river Sutlej more troops than are necessary for the internal duties of that territory, nor commit or suffer any encroachments on the possessions and rights of the chiefs in its vicinity.

ARTICLE III.—In the event of a violation of any of the preceding articles or of a departure from the rules of friendship on the part of either State, this treaty shall be considered to be null and void.

ARTICLE IV.—Relates to the ratification of the treaty by His Excellency the Governor-General in Council.

Seal and signature of C. T. METCALFE.

Signature and seal of RÁJÁ RANJIT SINGH.

Company's Seal.

(Sd.) MINTO.

Ratified by the Governor-General in Council on 30th May 1809.

north-west and south-west of his newly acquired dominions in the Panjáb proper.

The British envoy leaves Amritsar.

The treaty being concluded, the British envoy left Amritsar on 1st May, 1809. British officers on the frontier were warned to watch the proceedings of the Láhore ruler, and to see that the terms of the treaty were not infringed. It is, however, to the credit of Ranjít Singh that he observed his treaty with the British with fidelity until his dying day. This was due mainly to the shrewd monarch's well knowing the strength of the British Government, and his personal conviction that that Power was sincere in its professions of friendship and amity, and really desired to see him powerful and prosperous, for the extinction of his sway would unmistakeably have been followed by those convulsions, bloodshed and anarchy (on the borders of the British possessions) which had long continued a source of disgrace and misery, and a repetition of which would have ruined the Maharájá's Government.

What the British Government desired from the Cis-Sutlej chiefs in return for the protection extended to them.

It would appear that the advance of Colonel Ochterlony in the direction of the Sutlej was in strict conformity with the solicitations earnestly made by the chiefs of the Cis-Sutlej States. The British Government, in return for this trouble, desired nothing more from the protected chiefs than the stability and duration of their power and internal peace and harmony. No tribute was demanded and no kind of contribution asked for to defray the enormous charges incurred in conducting the negotiations with the Láhore ruler. The relations between these chiefs and the paramount power under whose protection they had now come, were defined in a separate treaty called *Ittilanámá*,* executed on the 6th May, 1809, and duly promulgated to all the chiefs concerned, who felt very grateful to the British Government for the successful issue of their prayer, and vied with each other in showing their deep sense of obligation to their patrons and protectors. Among themselves, however, the relations of these chiefs were most unsatisfactory. The more powerful chief was inclined to usurp the possession of the weaker chief, and feuds and quarrels, attended with much bloodshed and of loss of life, were the order of the day. A third proclamation was, therefore, issued on 22nd August, 1811, warning them that if any of the sardars had forcibly taken possession of the estates of others, or otherwise injured the lawful owners, it was necessary that, before the institution of any complaint, the proprietor should be satisfied. Should, however, delay occur in the restoration of such property, and the interference of the British authority become requisite, "the revenues of the estates," said the proclamation "from the date of ejection of the lawful owner, together with whatever other losses the inhabitants of

The relations of the chiefs among themselves how regulated.

---

* *Proclamation of protection to the Cis-Sutlej Chiefs against the State of Láhore.*

(After usual preamble) Be it known—

1. That the territories of Sirhind and Malwa had been taken under British protection, and Ranjít Singh had bound himself by treaty to exercise in future no interference therein.
2. That it was not the intention of the British Government to demand any tribute from the chiefs and sardars benefiting by this arrangement.
3. That the chiefs and sardars would be permitted to exercise, and were for the future secured in the rights and authorities they possessed in their respective territories prior to, and at time of, the declaration of protection by the British Government.
4. That the chiefs and sardars should be bound to offer every facility and accommodation to British troops and detachments employed in securing the protection guaranteed or for purposes otherwise connected with the general interest of the State, whenever the same might be marched into, or stationed in their, respective territories.
5. In case of invasion or war the sardars were to join the British standard with their followers, whenever called upon.
6. Merchants conveying articles, the produce of Europe, for the use of detachments at Ludhiáná, or of any other British force or detachment, should not be subjected to transit duty, but must be protected in their passage through the Sikh country.
7. In like manner, horses for the cavalry, when furnished with passports from competent officers, must be exempt from all tax.

that place may have sustained from the march of troops, should, without scruple, be demanded from the offending party; and for disobedience of the present orders a penalty, according to the circumstances of the case and of the offender, would be inflicted, agreeably to the decision of the Government."

British cantonment established at Ludhiáná, 1809.

After these transactions a British cantonment was established at Ludhiáná under the command of Colonel Ochterlony; and Bakhshi Nand Singh, *Bhandari*, of Batála, was appointed the Maharájá's Ambassador with the British General. Khushwakt Rai, a *Kayath*, was, in the meanwhile, deputed by the British Government as their news-writer in the court of Láhore.

CHAPTER II.

FROM THE TREATY OF THE SUTLEJ TO THE CONQUEST OF MULTÁN, KÁSHMÍR, AND PESHÁWAR, 1809 TO 1826 A.D.

Suspicion of the contracting parties against each other, despite their joint treaty.

ALTHOUGH a treaty of peace and amity had been concluded between the British Government and the ruler of Láhore, formal protestations had little or no effect in removing the suspicions which the two States entertained with respect to each other's real intentions. The Maharájá Sindhia, of Gwálior, the Mahratta Holkár, and the Rohilla chief, Amir Khan, had long cherished a hope that an alliance with the Sikhs of the Panjáb against the foreign conquerors of Hindostán was yet a possibility, and, with the view of furthering this aim, their agents continued to make their appearance at Láhore for a considerable time. It was further suspected that Ranjít Singh was forming plans for entering into a secret alliance with the Sikhs of the Cis-Sutlej States against the British. To meet any possible emergency, it was thought prudent to throw up defensive lines at Ludhiáná and collect supplies. Ranjít Singh, on the other hand, had his own fears; but, as time advanced, these apprehensions were removed, and, by degrees, the States began to regard each other with perfect confidence, as future events will show.

It is gradually removed.

The strengthening of the forts of Govindgarh and Phillour, 1809.

After the departure of Mr. Metcalfe, in May, 1809, the first business to which the Maharájá devoted his attention was the strengthening of the fort of Phillour, situated on the north bank of the Sutlej, opposite Ludhiáná, and the new fort of Govindgarh, at Amritsar, where he had deposited his treasures. The walls were rebuilt, and a deep ditch of scarped masonry was constructed round each of these strongholds. The old sarai at Phillour was also thoroughly repaired, and put in a condition of defence. Dewán Mohkam Chand was appointed kiladár, or commandant, of the fort of Phillour.

The Gorkhás again invade Kangrá.

As soon as these arrangements were completed, the Maharájá set out on his intended expedition to the hills. The Gorkhá commander, Amar Singh, Thápá, after his reverses of four years previously, had again laid close siege to Kangrá; and, the garrison being reduced to straits, and the dream of the aspiring Rájput prince, of a kingdom extending from the Jamna to the Jhelum, effectually dispelled, Sansár Chand, in the hour of extremity, deputed his younger brother, Fatteh Chand, as envoy to Láhore, to ask the Maharájá's aid in expelling the Gorkhás from his territory to the north-west of the Sutlej, the famous stronghold of Kangrá being offered him as the price of his assistance. The Maharájá gladly accepted the invitation, and advanced to Kangrá, at the head of a large army, by the Patiálá and Jawálá Mukhi road, having, in his train, his enterprising mother-in-law, Sadá Kour. On 28th May, he reached Pathánkot, where he seized the possessions of the Kánhia *misl*, and thence he marched to Jawálá Mukhi. At the latter place, he collected all the sardars, and made them take an oath of fidelity to his cause in the impending war against the Gorkhás. Having taken *nazránás* from the hill chiefs of Jasrota and Núrpur, he marched to the relief of the citadel of Kangrá. The reduction of this fort which had hitherto had the reputation, in India, of being impregnable, occupied three months. The supplies of the invaders were cut off by the forces of the confederate hill chiefs, and they were thereby considerably weakened, but the duplicity of Sansár Chand at this juncture, in entering into negotiations with the Gorkhás, and promising them the surrender of the fort in the event of himself and his family being permitted to withdraw unmolested, excited the anger of the Sikh ruler, who, in the meantime, had received offers, in money, from the Kathmandu General, equivalent in value to the famous hill fortress. Ranjít Singh, by his excessive craftiness, succeeded in making dupes both of the Rájput chief and of the Nepál commander. In August, he made a prisoner of the son of his Kangrá ally, then in attendance on him, while, with his pretented negotiations, he amused Amar Singh, Thápá, who had proposed a joint expedition against the mountain chief. Having learnt that the Nepálese troops had fallen short of supplies and ammunition, he suddenly made his appearance at the head of a chosen body of his troops, and demanded admission to the fort. His demand being rejected, he attacked the fort and the Sikh warriors, in their advance, suffered severely in a hand-to-hand conflict with their adversaries, but the place at last fell, and Ranjít Singh made his triumphant entry into it on 24th August, 1809. Thus did the Maharájá gain possession of fort Kangrá, the key of the valley of that name. Amar Singh, after this defeat, retired to Malákra, the fort of which he besieged, but was compelled by the pursuing Sikh army to raise the siege, and driven to Chár Bágh. An understanding was ultimately come to between the Maharájá and the Nepálese General, who procured the means of transport and retired across the Sutlej. Amar Singh long brooded over these reverses, and repeatedly proposed to Sir David Ochterlony and other authorities of the British Government to unite in an attack on the Panjáb, but he met with no success in any quarter. The war of 1814-15 between the English and the Gorkhás settled the fate of the latter, who, instead of being in a position to participate in Káshmír,* had to be content with their abodes in the hills of Kathmandu, the English becoming the neighbours of the Sikhs in the hills as well as in the plains.

The Maharájá marches to the relief of the Kángrá chief.

Duplicity of Sansár Chand.

A fierce engagement.

The Maharájá reduces the fort.

And compels the Gorkhá general to confine himself to the left bank of the Sutlej, 1809.

War between the English and the Gorkhás, 1814-15.

Desá Singh appointed to the charge of Kangrá and other Hill States.

Desá Singh, Majithia, was appointed kiládar, or commandant, of the fort of Kangrá, and Pahar Singh second in command. Desá Singh was also made Názim, or governor, of the hill states of Kangrá, Chambá, Núrpur, Kotla, Shahpur, Jasrota, Basoli, Mánkot, Jaswán, Sibá, Goler, Kolhor, Mandi, Suket, Kúlú and Datárpur. The Maharájá then proceeded to Jawálá Mukhi to perform his religious devotions there, and distributed large sums to the keepers

* Captain Wade was told by the Maharájá that the Gorkhás were anxious to participate in Káshmír, but that his own idea was to keep them outside the limits of the Panjáb.—Cunningham's *Panjáb History*, p. 156. Ranjít Singh was not, however, asked to give assistance in reducing the Gorkhá power.

of the sacred temple. Having received *nazránás* from the hill chiefs of Mandi, Suket and Kúlú, he returned to the Jalandar Doáb, where he wrested Hariáná from the widow of Bhagel Singh, who had recently died. At an interview which took place, about the same time, between Bhúp Singh, Fyzulpuria, and the Maharájá, the latter treacherously seized his person and confiscated all his possessions. The Maharájá then returned to Amritsar, where he celebrated the Holi festival with all the usual excesses.

Hariáná taken, 1809.

The possession of the Fyzul purias captured.

It was about this time that the Maharájá, for the first time, introduced the European system of drill into his army, and formed regular battalions after the British model. Preference was given to Purbiás, or natives of the Gangetic provinces, and the Cis-Sutlej Sikhs, bodies of whom were instructed by deserters from the English army, who received high wages under the Maharájá and were put in command of both infantry and artillery.

Introduction of the European system of drill into the Panjáb army, 1809.

Towards the close of the same year, Jodh Singh, of Wazírábád, died of dropsy. The Maharájá hastened in that direction to confiscate his estates, but Gandá Singh, the son of the deceased sardar, tendered his submission, and paid a lakh of rupees as *nazrána* to the Maharájá, and his cupidity having thus been satisfied, he refrained from annexing the sardar's territory, and returned, after conferring a rich shawl and a turban of investiture on the representative of the deceased chief. Hearing next of a dispute between Sahib Singh, Bhangi, of Gujrát, and his son, Ranjít Singh crossed the Chináb, to profit by the quarrel. Sahib Singh, who was at Islámgarh, hearing of the Maharájá's approach, fled to Jalálpur; and the fort of the former place was taken possession of by Ranjít Singh. The fort of Mahawár was then vacated by Goláb Singh, Bhangi, and occupied by the officers of the Maharájá. The Maharájá then proceeded to Jalálpur, in pursuit of Sahib Singh. The fort of Jalálpur was occupied without opposition, and Sahib Singh fled to Mangla, between Rohtás and the town of Mirpur Chonmukhia, and strengthened the Mangla fort against an attack. About the same time, Fakír Aziz-ud-dín, the Maharájá's able and trusted secretary, occupied the town of Gujrát without encountering any resistance. The humane Fakír prohibited the Sikh soldiers, who were greedy of plunder, from committing any ravages on the inhabitants, and great discontent, in consequence, prevailed among the troops that had assisted in the capture. Fakír Aziz-ud-dín thereupon levied a moderate contribution from the townspeople, and gave the money to the soldiers, who were thus pacified. All the treasure, valuables and other property belonging to Sahib Singh were confiscated to the State by the Fakír, who laid the spoils before his royal master at Jalálpur and congratulated him on the success of his arms. The Maharájá was greatly pleased, and showed his appreciation of the excellent services rendered by his secretary, by conferring on him a valuable *khilat*. Núr-ud-dín, the Fakír's younger brother, was appointed governor of Gujrát. The Maharájá then resolved to reduce the fort of Mangla, but, on the earnest representations of Sahib Singh's wife, who was related to Ranjít Singh on his father's side, abandoned his resolve. About the same time, Dewán Bhawáni Dás was deputed for the conquest of Jammú, at the head of an army, and, in a month's time, Jammú was conquered for the Maharájá, the Dográ chief, Dedú, who had obtained the ascendancy there, being expelled. The Maharájá next entered the country west of the Jhelum, as far as Khushháb, which he reduced, after worsting the sardars and chiefs, who were rendered tributary.

The Maharájá receives a *nazráná* from the heir of Wazírábád, 1809.

Conquers Islámgarh and Jalalpur.

Fakír Aziz-ud-dín captures Gujrát, 1809.

Núr-ud-dín is appointed governor of Gujrát.

Bhawáni Dás conquers Jammú, 1809.

The country west of Jhelum reduced.

In the midst of these operations, the Maharájá was informed, in the beginning of February, 1810, that Shah Shujá-ul-Mulk, with whom Mr. Elphinstone had just concluded a treaty against France, had been driven

Shah Shujá expelled from Afghanistan, 1809-10.

out of his kingdom, and was approaching to seek refuge in the Panjáb. Shah Zamán, who had twice invaded the Panjáb, had long ceased to be king of Afghanistán, he having been dethroned and his eyes put out by a brother, Shah Mahmúd, who, in his turn, was dethroned and imprisoned by Shujá-ul-Mulk, own brother of Shah Zamán. Between the years 1800 and 1809, the country of the Afgháns had been the scene of civil wars, about half a dozen revolutions having taken place. When the well-appointed British embassy reached the court, Shujá-ul-Mulk was seated on the throne. His success was principally due to the fact that he was in possession of almost all the jewels and other valuable property pertaining to the Crown which had been entrusted to him by his brother, Shah Zamán. The Court was then at Pesháwar, and the king, though seated on the throne, was not in possession of his own capital, a war of clans having spread havoc from the confines of Pesháwar to Kandahár. The gorgeous embassy was received at Pesháwar, and the distinguished ambassador had an interview with Shah Shujá-ul-Mulk. He describes his majesty as a handsome man, of about 30 years of age, of an olive complexion, and with a thick black beard. "The expression of his countenance," observes the learned ambassador, "was dignified and pleasing, his voice clear and his address princely. We thought, at first, that he had on armour of jewels; but on close inspection, we found this to be a mistake, and his real dress to consist of a green tunic, with large flowers worked in gold and precious stones, over which were a large breastplate of diamonds, shaped like two flattened *fleurs-de-lis*, an ornament of the same kind on each thigh, large emerald bracelets on the arms (above the elbow), and many other jewels in many places. In one of these bracelets was the *Kohinúr*, known to be one of the largest diamonds in the world."*

The embassy of the Honorable Mr. Elphinstone.

The Envoy's description of the Shah.

A treaty was concluded with Shujá-ul-Mulk, in which the co-operation of the Afgháns against the reported designs of the French was promised, the English, on their part, agreeing to recoup the Kábul king for any loss or expense which might be incurred by him in checking the progress of the French, or of any other enemy, to the borders of Hindostán. The embassy had hardly travelled four miles from Pesháwar, when a band of robbers plundered it of a mule which was carrying the richest shawls, given as a present by the Kábul king, and of cash amounting to Rs. 10,000. Soon afterwards, it was heard that Prince Mahmúd, who had been kept in close confinement by Shujá-ul-Mulk in the Bálá Hissár at Kábul, had effected his escape and, with the assistance of the gallant and talented Wazír Fatteh Khan, Barakzai, had given battle to Shujá, in one of the engagements the prince commanded in person, and Shujá, being again beaten, was compelled to fly. He crossed the Atak, with a handful of followers, in the vain hope of securing assistance, and the meeting between him and the Maharájá took place at Khusháb, on the 3rd of February, 1810. The Maharájá received the ex-king at Khusháb with all outward respect, and the ceremony due to his kingly rank. As the Shah alighted, a *ziyáfat* (or dinner) of Rs. 1,250 was sent to his tents, but the Shah was in a hurry to proceed to Ráwalpindi, to join his dethroned brother, Shah Zamán, and no decisive arrangements were come to between him and the Maharájá. The Shah's cause was not yet utterly

Shah Shujá crosses the Atak and meets the Maharájá at Khusháb, 1810.

But no arrangement come to.

* "Lord Minto had sent many splendid presents to the king. The Afghán officers who received charge of these presents, kept the camels on which some of them were sent, and even seized four riding camels which had entered the palace by mistake. They stripped Mr. Elphinstone's elephant drivers of their livery, and gravely insisted that two English footmen, who were sent to put up the chandeliers, were part of the Governor-General's present to the Shah. His Afghán majesty himself seems to have been craving, for, having admired the English silk stockings worn by Mr. Elphinstone, and the gentlemen of his suite, he sent a message desiring that some might be given to him."—*Elphinstone's Kábul.*

lost. The people of Pesháwar, and several powerful mountain tribes in the neighbourhood of that district, were firm in their allegiance to Shujá-ul-Mulk, who, being thus enabled to assemble a fresh army, and being, moreover, assisted with money, by the subadár of Káshmír, Ata Muhammad Khan, son of Wazír Sher Muhammad Khan, once more advanced against Shah Mahmúd. Shah Mahmúd was repulsed, and, being compelled to fly, took refuge in the fort of Atak. The clans of Afghán mountaineers who were friendly to Shujá, however, continued to harass him, and Shah Shujá, having returned to Pesháwar, was received there on the 20th of March, taking possession of the vast regions west of Pesháwar inhabited by the Afghán race; but the tide of fortune soon turned in favor of Shah Mahmúd, for, in the following September, Muhammad Azím Khan, brother of Wazír Fatteh Khan, inflicted a signal defeat on Shujá-ul-Mulk, and drove him across the Indus again.

The Shah makes a fresh attempt on Kábul.

But eventually fails, and is driven across the Sutlej.

As Mr. Elphinstone was returning to the British provinces through the Sikh country, he was overtaken by Shujá-ul-Mulk's fugitive harem, and among them was the exiled, dethroned and blind Shah Zamán. The ambassador, who was gifted with a good and generous heart, met the unhappy monarch, and treated him with the honour befitting a king. The interview, which was most affecting, is fully described in Mr. Elphinstone's excellent work on Kábul. The scene was heart-rending. A monarch, whose name was once the terror of Persia and India, and whose reputation had spread to the remotest confines of Asia, was now to be seen in the train of women, helpless, blind and dethroned. But Shah Zamán was a thorough Persian scholar, and familiar with the history of Asiatic nations. He possessed all the qualities of a king, and spoke of reverses and strokes of fortune as the common lot of princes. He spoke with much composure of the great calamities which had befallen kings, frankly narrating all that had happened to him. "Had he gone over all the history of Asia," observes Mr. Elphinstone, "he could scarcely have discovered a more remarkable instance of the mutability of fortune than he himself presented, blind, dethroned and exiled in a country which he had twice subdued."

Interview between Mr. Elphinstone and the blind Shah Zamán.

It was during the first interview of Maharájá Ranjít Singh with Shah Shujá-ul-Mulk that the Sikh ruler led the ex-king to hope that he might yet make an attempt to recover his lost provinces of Káshmír and Multán, with the co-operation of the Sikh troops, whose services the wily chief offered with apparent pleasure. The Shah's troops had made an attack on Multán, in 1803, but were repulsed by Muzaffar Khan. The latter chief had, more than once, offered an asylum to the Shah, and shown his anxiety to conciliate him, but the Shah wanted to conquer the city and province for himself. At the present juncture, the Shah had reason to distrust the Láhore ruler's sincerity, but no sooner had the ex-king recrossed the Atak, leaving Ranjít Singh to settle his affairs with the Mussalmán chiefs, east of that river, than he made preparations for a descent on Multán. The affairs of the recently-subdued district of Sáhiwál, however, precluded him for a short time from prosecuting his plans against Multán. The revenues of Sáhiwál now amounted to Rs. 1,50,000, and Fatteh Khan, its chief, had, in 1804, agreed to give Ranjít Singh 25 horses and 25 camels annually, as tribute. This tribute had, in January, 1809, been commuted for an annual payment of the sum of Rs. 12,000, and, the chief having recently failed to remit the tribute punctually, Ranjít Singh found a pretext in this act of default for invading his territory, and accordingly marched to Sáhiwál, at the head of his troops, in the spring of 1810, and

The politics of Multán.

Final conquest of Khusháb and Sáhiwál, 1810.

summoned the chief to his presence. The Biluch chief, suspecting treachery, sent his minor son, Lal Khan, with rich presents, to the Maharájá who received the boy with great cordiality and withdrew, apparently satisfied. Thence the Maharájá proceeded to Khusháb, which place was now finally reduced, after a siege of several days, the chief Zafar Khan being expelled. Having thus lulled the suspicions of Fatteh Khan, who thought himself secure, Ranjít Singh at once returned to Sáhiwál by night, when he immediately assaulted and captured the fort, having succeeded in completely taking its defenders by surprise. Fatteh Khan was put in chains and sent to Láhore with his family, his castle at Kachi, and all his estates being confiscated to the State. In the same month of February, an army was sent against Uch, the residence of the Sayads of Gilán and Bokhárá, whose religious sanctity, however, saved them from ruin, the Sayads waiting on the Maharájá, with a present of horses, and engaging to pay tribute.

Fatteh Khan chief of Sáhiwál is sent a prisoner to Láhore.

Fourth expedition to Multán, 1810.

Ranjit uses the Shah's name for purposes of his own.

After these transactions, the Maharájá hastened on his long contemplated expedition to Multán, and called upon Muzaffar Khan to surrender it to him in the name of the Kábul king, to whom the governor was bound. The nawáb sent his agents with an humble message, and promising to pay the stipulated subsidy, within a reasonable time, but, as the Maharájá was determined upon annexing this fertile province, no excuses were listened to, and, in a short time, the whole Sikh army was encamped before Multán, after having ravaged the surrounding country by the way. The nawáb made his preparations for defence, and provided the fort with an abundance of water, provisions and supplies. The Sikh army, which had reached Multán on the 24th of February, took possession of the city on the following day. The appearance of the Sikh army at Multán and their occupation of the town, spread alarm throughout the neighbouring country; Muhammad Khan, the chief of Leia and Bhakkar, bought off the invader by the payment of Rs. 1,20,000 as a ransom for his State, and the chief of Báháwalpur, Sadiq Muhammad Khan, though a friend of Muzaffar Khan's, offered a lakh as tribute, but, as the Maharájá wanted more substantial aid, the offer was not accepted. The Báháwalpur chief was, at last, compelled to furnish a contingent of 500 cavalry for service in the impending Multán campaign.

The Sikhs take possession of Multán city,

And lay siege on the citadel.

The citadel of Multán was now closely besieged by the Sikh army, but the Patháns offered a stout resistance, and the most strenuous attempts of the Sikh soldiers to carry the fort by assault signally failed. A heavy bombardment was kept up for several days, but without any effect. Batteries were then erected opposite the fort, and an incessant fire was maintained, but hardly any impression was made on the citadel. Recourse was at length had to mining; but the besieged successfully countermined. Ranjít Singh made the most solemn and lavish promises to the chiefs who should distinguish themselves in the action by the earliest effective advance. He personally reconnoitred the enemy's position, examined his posts and fixed his own, marking out the spots for the batteries, and assigning lines of approach to the different chiefs, whose sense of duty to their countrymen was appealed to with vehemence. Extensive transport arrangements were made both by land and water from Láhore and Amritsar, and the whole resources of the country were unreservedly placed at the disposal of the military authorities to secure this much-coveted possession.

The *zamzama* gun is brought to Multán.

The famous Bhangi *top*, named '*zamzama,*' was brought from Láhore to batter down the walls of the fort; but it made little impression on the besieged. It discharged a ball of two and a half maunds (*kacha*), or 80 lbs., in weight; but the appliances for working this huge piece of ordnance were wanting in the Sikh camp, while nobody possessed sufficient science and skill to make a proper use of it. Some little impression that was made on the ramparts of the citadel by the Sikh artillery had the effect only of redoubling the zeal of the besieged, who, in countermining, blew up the battery of Sardar Atar Singh, Dhari, close to the fort, killing the sardar and twelve others, and severely wounding many more, among whom were Sardar Nehal Singh, Attariwálá, and the youthful Hari Singh, Nalwa. Confused and panic-stricken, the assailants fled, leaving their dead close to the fort; but the high-minded Pathans sent the bodies to the besiegers, that of Atar Singh being wrapped in a pair of shawls. The siege lasted for two months, during which the Sikh army was greatly reduced, and its best soldiers and generals killed or incapacitated. The most conspicuous of these was Atar Singh, Dhari, a favourite companion and confidential sardar of the Maharájá.

The Sikhs fail to make any impression on the besieged.

Nor did the Sikh army meet with better success in other quarters. Dewán Mohkam Chand, who had been sent to reduce Shujá Abád, found the fort impregnable. A general assault was made, on the 21st of March, but the Sikh army was repulsed with considerable loss. The dewán became dangerously ill and the loss on the side of the Sikhs, in killed and wounded, was great. Another general attack was made on the 25th, but with no better result.

Failure of the Sikhs at Shujá Abád

These protracted military operations now caused a scarcity of provisions in the Sikh camp both in Multán and Shujá Abád, and the Maharájá, seeing his case to be hopeless, retired on the 19th of April, being forced to acknowledge himself completely foiled in his attempt, and having the additional mortification of finding himself compelled to accept now the very terms which he had on so many previous occasions rejected with scorn, namely, a tribute of two and a half lakhs of rupees, twenty chargers and a contingent in time of war. Of the amount of the ransom, Rs. 30,000 was paid in advance, while Abubakr Khan, brother-in-law of Muzaffar Khan, was delivered up as a hostage for the payment of the balance. The Maharájá's '*amour propre*' being in this way, to some extent, soothed, he returned to Láhore on the 25th of April, much depressed in spirits by the ill-success of his campaign, and throwing the blame on his sardars and officers.

The Maharájá is compelled to retire.

He is greatly mortified by the ill-success of his campaign.

After a few day's rest in the gardens of Shalámár, he turned his attention to the introduction of measures of reform in his military department, designed after the European fashion. A corps of horse artillery was organised under the superintendence of skilful generals. To the already existing Ghurchar *sawars* and Ghurchar *khas*, paid, respectively, in money and jágírs, were added orderly *khas*, or select orderlies, resembling a body-guard, on enhanced pay and emoluments, who were entrusted with the work of carrying State *dastaks*, or orders, to different chiefs and sardars, which proved to them a source of gain. The Multán Governor, Muzaffar Khan, in the meantime, opened a correspondence with the British Governor-General in Calcutta, and the Maharájá did the same with Colonel Sir David Ochterlony at Ludhiáná, proposing joint action against Multán, but both the chiefs were left to themselves, and told to settle their affairs as best they could.

Reforms in the Military Department.

The British decline to interfere in Multán affairs.

Gandá Singh, son of Jodh Singh, of Wazirábad, who, the year before, had received *khilats* of investiture, on his father's death, on the payment of a large *nazráná* to the Maharájá, did not long enjoy what had cost him so much. In June, 1810, a large force was sent to Wazirábád and all the estates of the deceased sardar were confiscated. A promise

Wazirábád finally annexed to the State of Láhore, 1810.

was indeed made that, when the minor sons of Jodh Singh should attain age of discretion, Wazirábád would be restored to them; but the promise was never fulfilled. A jágír of Rs. 10,000 in Thib, was allowed as subsistence to Amrik Singh and Gandá Singh, sons of the deceased sardar. About the same time, Ráni Rám Kour, widow of Sardar Bhagel Singh, was expelled from Bahádurgarh, which she had held as a jágír for her maintenance.

The widow of Bhagel Singh expelled from Bahádurpur, 1810.

The Dasahra being over, the Maharájá marched, in person, in October 1810, to Ramnagar, on the banks of the Chináb, and summoned Nidhán Singh, Hattú, so called on account of his courage (*Hat*), to his presence. This chief, whose head-quarters were in Maraka, a few miles below Láhore, on the Rávi, had risen, to eminence in the latter days of Mahá Singh, Sukerchakia, and was looked upon with jealousy, not only by the Sukerchakia chief, but also by Sahib Singh of Gujrát, Panjáb Singh of Siálkot, and Jodh Singh, of Wazirábád, with whom he had constant feuds. When Shah Zaman invaded the Panjáb, in 1797, Nidhán Singh was one of the few Sikh chiefs who welcomed the Shah's approach, and was honorably received by the Shah, on the banks of the Chináb, and confirmed in all his possessions. He kept the road from Láhore to Wazirábád open for the Kábul monarch, and rendered many other important services to his powerful ally. When Ranjít Singh invaded Multán, in the beginning of 1810, Nidhán Singh was, after some difficulty, induced to accompany the Maharájá, with a contingent of 250 horsemen, and, at the close of the campaign, he went to his fort at Daska, contrary to the Maharájá's instructions. Ranjít Singh summoned him to his presence; but the spirited chief refused to attend, except under the guarantee of a Sodhi, or Sikh priest. This conduct incensed the Maharájá, who, on the 17th of October, closely invested the fort, bringing against it the famous gun *zamzama*, which was brought to operate only on occasions of unusual emergency. The siege lasted a month, but no impression was made on the fort, after which resort was had to ill-treatment of the wives and families of the besieged who had fallen into the hands of the invaders; but this mode of revenge also failed to influence the garrison. At length, on a guarantee being given by Bábá Mulak Ráj and Jamiat Singh, *Bedis*, or high Sikh priests, and a promise made to him of a munificent jágír, the refractory old chief surrendered. He came into the camp of the Maharájá, who instantly put him in irons, unmindful of the solemnity of the engagement entered into with the priests, who were naturally highly indignant at this breach of faith.

Nidhán Singh, Hattú, chief of Maraka, reduced.

His fort of Daska is be sieged.

He is himself taken a prisoner, 1810.

In the month of November, Bhág Singh, of Hallowál, in the Richna Doáb, who, with his son, Sobha Singh, was present in camp, having incurred the displeasure of the Maharájá, was put in chains, all his estates being at the same time sequestered. The Maharájá then returned to Láhore, and sent his minister, Mohkam Chand, at the head of 5,000 horse, to bring Sultan Khan of Bhimbar, and the chief of Rájáuri, as well as other hill tribes who had become refractory, more fully under subjection. The Bhimbar chief offered a gallant resistance; but the fort was at length captured, Sultan Khan agreeing to pay Rs. 40,000 per annum as tribute. Ismail Khan, a relation of his, was left in possession of a large portion of the territory reduced by the Sikh general. The hill fort of Gang, in Katas, was then attacked. The besieged offered a desperate resistance, but the Maharájá cut off the only watercourse, called Choya Sedan Shah, which supplied water to the fort, and the besieged were consequently forced to surrender, upon which the fort was occupied by the Sikh troops. The month of December of the same year (1810) was marked by acts of royal favour and concessions. Mái Lachhmi, the mother of Sahib

Hallowália possessions in Richna Doáb seized, 1810.

The expedition of Dewán Mohkam Chand.

Capture of the forts of Bhimbar and Gang, 1810.

Singh, Bhangi, of Gujrát, interceded with the Maharájá for her son with such effect that the sardar, who had been expelled from his estates, was invited to return, and the territory of Bajwant, with a revenue of a lakh of rupees, was restored to him. Bhag Singh, Hallowalia, was also set at liberty, and endowed with jágírs. The Sikh high priests, Mulak Ráj and Jamiat Singh, sat in *dharna* * on Ranjít Singh, for the insult offered to them in arresting Nidhán Singh, after they had become personal guarantees for his safe conduct and good treatment, and the Maharájá found himself compelled to yield to this religious demonstration and set the prisoner at liberty. An offer of a jágír was made to Nidhán Singh, but the indignant sardar refused the offer and left forthwith for Káshmír, where he took employment under the Governor, Fateh Khan, Barakzai.

A jágír betowed on the head of the Bhangi clan.

Release of Bhag Singh, Ahluwalia, and Nidhan Singh, Hattú.

In January, 1811, Fateh Khan, the Sáhiwál chief who had been put in irons in the previous year, was also liberated, an Udási faqír having interceded with the Maharájá for his release. A jágír of Rs. 14,400 was given to this chief, at Jhang, on the condition of his supplying fifty horsemen to the State. He returned to Láhore in the year 1812, after a three years' absence from the court, and, finding that the wind had again ceased to blow in his favour, went to Mankera to live with the great Bilúch chief, Muhammad Khan. Ultimately he retired to Baháwalpur, where he died of grief, in the town of Ahmadpur, in the year 1820.

Release of Fatteh Khan of Sáhiwal, 1811.

His death, 1820.

Dharm Singh, the ejected chief of Dharmkot, in the Jalandar Doáb, which had been annexed in 1806, was again taken into favour and endowed with a jágír. In February, the Maharájá marched in the direction of the salt mines between the Jhelum and the Indus; and, in the vicinity of Pind Dádan Khan, captured three forts. At the close of the same month, intelligence was received of the advance of Shah Mahmúd of Kábul, at the head of 12,000 Afghans, in the direction of the Indus, which he had crossed, creating great consternation in the country visited. Ranjít Singh forthwith proceeded to Ráwalpindi and took up a position there. He also deputed his Secretary, Fakir Aziz-ud-dín, to the Shah's camp, to make enquiries as to the object of his majesty's expedition. The Shah had, however, already instructed his agents to state that his only object in visiting the country was to punish or overawe Ata Muhammad Khan, the governor of Káshmír, and the governor of Atak, for aiding Shah Shujá-ul-mulk in his late attack on Peshávar. The Maharájá's apprehensions being removed, a ceremonial interview between the two chiefs took place, in the course of which presents were exchanged and promises of friendship made. On his return to Láhore, the Maharája sent Dewán Mohkam Chand to reduce the country between Multán and the Mánjha, held by Kánh Singh, Nakai, who was charged with oppressing his Mahomedan subjects of Hujra Shah Mukim, under Shah Abdul Razak and Shah Dín. Prince Kharak Singh was put in nominal command of the expedition. The country having, without resistance, fallen before the active general, a jágír, valued at Rs. 15,000, was bestowed on Sardar Kanh Singh, in the neighbourhood of Bhairowal. The dewán was then sent to the hills north of Gujrát, from the Rájput chiefs of which he exacted Rs. 40,000. About the same time, Sardar Desá Singh, Majithia, was sent to reduce the fort of Kotla, in Iláka Tilok Nath, half way between Kangrá and Nurpur, the services of Ghous Khan, commandant of the Maharájá's artillery, being put at the disposal of the sardar. The fort was held by Dhian Singh, at one time wazír of the rájá of Goler, who, trusting to

The Maharájá visits the Salt mines.

Shah Mahmúd of Kábul crosses the Indus.

Ranjít Singh meets the Shah, 1811.

The country between Multán and Mánjaha reduced, 1811.

Capture of the fort of Kotla, 1811.

---

* *Dharna* means a way of threatening, or invoking the Divine wrath on a person who refuses to grant a favour asked by sitting at his doorway and refusing food. It is now punishable under the Indian Penal Code with imprisonment and fine.

his own strength, had assumed independence. The Maharájá promised the Majithia sardar half of the Tilok Nath estate as a jágír, if he succeeded in reducing the fort within a week, and the gallant sardar, having captured the fort within the appointed time, obtained from his royal master a jágír worth Rs. 7,000. Budh Singh, of the Fyzulpuria *misl*, whose possessions lay on both sides of the Sutlej, and who had uniformly refused personal attendance at Court, now showed a rebellious disposition, and the quick-sighted dewán, Mohkam Chand, promptly entered the Jalandar Doáb in Assoj (September,) at the head of a large number of troops, having, in his train, Jodh Singh, Ramgarhia, Fateh Singh, Ahluwalia, and other sardars. The fort of Phillour was garrisoned, and the city of Jalandar closely besieged. The refractory chief fled to Ludhiáná, to seek British protection; but his troops, actuated by an impulse of honour, made a desperate resistance. Their chief disadvantage was in the approaches to the town being open with no ramparts to afford protection against attack, and, after several days' hard fighting, the city fell into the hands of the besiegers, who plundered the inhabitants of all their property and reduced them to great straits. The forts of Jalandar, Patti and Hetpur were then reduced, and the whole of the territory belonging to the Fyzulpurias, valued at upwards of three lakhs of rupees, annexed to the State. All the valuables in these forts belonging to Sardar Budh Singh were confiscated. Horsemen were also sent in pursuit of the sardar, but he had crossed the Sutlej before they reached the bank. He was subsequently forced to content himself with the position of a protected chief under the British Government, subsisting on the possessions left to him east and south of the river. For his conspicuous services, Mohkam Chand was created a dewán, and a rich *khilat* was granted him, together with a sword set in diamonds and an elephant with a golden howdah.

Mohkam Chand seizes the possessions of the Fyzulpuria *misl*, Jalandar, Phillour, Patti and Hetpur, 1811.

He is created a dewán.

In December of the same year, Nidhán Singh son of Jay Singh, the great Kanhia chief, incurred the displeasure of the Maharájá, and was put in irons, his jágír of Hajipur and Phulwara being confiscated at the same time. The policy of Ranjít Singh was to abolish the system of feudal tenures altogether, and to reduce to subjection all chiefs and sardars having any pretensions to power and independence, or who attributed their rise to worldly distinction and fame, or to the warlike deeds of their ancestors. The old Sikh confederacies had either all been swept away by his systematic usurpations and grasping policy, or, like the Phulkia and the Nihang, had sought the protection of a power greater than his, by settling east of the Sutlej. The Kanhia, Ramgarhia and Ahluwalia *misls* ranged themselves under his banner and took pride in following him to the battle-field. Ties of affinity had no weight with a chief whose policy, was to leave no one in a position to defy his authority, or, in any way, to interfere with his vast schemes of conquest and ambition. For this he once received a sharp rebuke from Jodh Singh, Ramgarhia, who had just aided in the reduction of the Jalandar territory. Ranjít Singh ordered presents to be given him, as a mark of special favour, on his taking leave of the Court, to join the expedition. The old sardar, with his usual candour and frankness, begged to be excused from an honour of the permanence of which there was no certainty, for, he said, he would think himself most fortunate, if allowed, in these times, to keep his own turban on his head. Ranjít Singh, who always valued real merit and loyalty, and at times allowed great latitude to his courtiers, and was more familiar with them than with the rest of his sardars, passed over this outspoken remark as a jest, and, smiling, told the sardar, to persevere in his good work with the devotion that had throughout marked his career. He had made a vow of eternal friendship with the sardar, and,

Nidhán Singh, Kanhia, made prisoner.

The policy of Ranjít Singh one of systematic usurpations and forfeitures.

He receives a sharp rebuke from Sardar Jodh Singh, Ramgarhia.

His intimate friendship with the sardar.

in the holy temple of the Darbár Sahib at Amritsar, had, in his royal, illiterate way, stamped a leaf of the *Granth* with his open palm dyed with saffron. He was not particular as to keeping pledges, however solemn, but Jodh Singh proved such a devoted follower and ally that he had no excuse for annexing his territory, and feigned the greatest affection for him. The new fort of Govindgarh was built after the fashion of the one at Ramgarh, belonging to the Ramgarhia territory, where the Maharájá went almost unattended, to cajole his distinguished follower.

Khushhálá, a Brahmin adventurer of Hindostan.

He attracts the Maharaja's attention.

He rises daily in his master's favour.

Is created Lord Chamberlain.

Becomes a Sikh, and is called Khushhál Singh.

His nephew, Tej Ram, afterwards Tej Singh.

This period of the great Sikh leader's life was marked by the extraordinary favours lavished on a young Gaur Brahman, of Hindostán, named Khushhálá. He was the son of Har Govind, a poor Brahman shopkeeper of Ikri in the Sardhána parganá of the Mirath District, and, coming to Láhore to seek his fortune, in 1807, he enlisted as a soldier, on a salary of five rupees a month, in the newly-raised regiment called the Dhounkal Singhwálá. Through the influence of Gangá Singh and Jatri, the Maharájá's chamberlains, he became one of the body-guard of Ranjít Singh, and soon won advancement by his assiduous devotion to his duties and his smart and soldierly bearing. It is related that young Khushhálá, who possessed a fine voice, combined with a pleasing exterior, first attracted the Maharája's attention as he was singing one night, while keeping guard over his tent. He was raised to the trusted and much-coveted office of Lord Chamberlain, or *Deorhiwálá*, in 1811, with the title of jamadar, and was, soon after, created a rájá and endowed, besides, with extensive jágírs. The post was a lucrative and important one, for the Lord Chamberlain was master of ceremonies, regulated seats in the darbár, and arranged processions. No person, however high in rank, could be admitted to a private audience of the Maharájá without his mediation, and this became the means of young Khushhálá's enriching himself, for every one of note wished to obtain an interview with so celebrated a personage as the Sukerchakia chief had now become. In 1812, Khushhálá received the Sikh baptism, and came to be called Khushhál Singh. All household appointments were at his disposal, and he read daily reports of the army to the Maharájá. Khushhál Singh and his nephew, Tej Ram, whom Khushhál Singh had sent for from Mirath, to act as his deputy, were now placed on active service. This Tej Ram, who was the son of Niddha, the brother of Khushhálá, also became a Sikh, in 1816, and adopted the name of Tej Singh.

Shah Zaman repairs to Láhore, 1811.

His brother, Shah Shujá.

Their fruitless negotiations with the British Government.

In November, 1811, Láhore was visited by the dethroned, exiled, and blind king of the Afghans, Shah Zaman. He brought with him his family and dependants, and, for a time, took up his residence in the town; but the neglect he experienced at the hands of the Sikh monarch caused him to return to Ráwalpindi, where he had, some months previously, found an asylum. His brother, Shah Shujá, was equally unfortunate. After vainly attempting to obtain a reception at Multán, and reduce the country beyond the Indus, a desperate undertaking, in which he lost his ablest general, Akram Khan, he was compelled to take refuge in flight. The brothers then deputed Eunis, a son of Shah Zaman, to Ludhiáná, in the hope of securing British co-operation. The prince was received with due attention by Sir David Ochterlony, but was distinctly informed that the British Government was not disposed to meddle in domestic broils at Kábul, and that, by the treaty entered into with Shah Shujá in 1809, the British Government had only pledged itself to help in the defence of Afghanistán against the French, and not to take a part in internal feuds.

The marriage of Prince Kharak Singh, 1812.

Láhore was the scene of great rejoicings and festivities in the beginning of 1812, in connection with the marriage of the heir-apparent, Kanwar

Kharak Singh, with Chand Kour, the only daughter of Sardar Jaimal Singh, Kánhia, of Fatehgarh, near Gurdáspúr, the same who had been deprived of his Pathankot territory by the Maharájá, four years previously. The bride was then ten years of age. The marriage procession, with all its pomp and pageantry, moved with the Maharájá and the bridegroom to Fatehgarh, the residence of the bride. Sir David Ochterlony came from Ludhiáná, with a small escort, at the express invitation of the Maharájá, and brought with him a galloper gun which Ranjít Singh had expressed an earnest desire to inspect. The rájás of Jhind and Nabhá, the chief of Kythal, and other sardars, and, indeed, the whole Sikh nation, assembled at Fatehgarh to do honour to the occasion. Among the guests were also the agents of the king of Kábul, the nawáb of Multán, the subadar of Káshmir, and the chief of Thatta, who brought large sums as *tambol*, or wedding presents, from their respective masters. The Maharájá dressed all his troops in scarlet broadcloth and striped silk, and the scene, as the grand procession, with numerous elephants, horses and equipage, left Láhore for Majithia, was most imposing. The Kanhia chief spared no expense on the occasion, and entertained his numerous guests in a truly royal manner. Fifty thousand rupees were paid for the first day's *ziyáfat*. or entertainment, on the arrival of the guests at Fatehgarh, and Rs. 15,000 were paid daily in cash, by way of *ziyáfat*, to the Maharájá for as many days as he stopped there. The marriage was celebrated with the greatest spendour, on the 6th of February 1812, and the ceremonies were presided over by Brahmans, in accordance with the custom enjoined by the Shastras and Vedas. The procession then returned to Láhore with the bride, and the dowry, consisting of shawls, jewels, ornaments, slave girls, elephants, horses and other objects, valued at several lakhs of rupees, was displayed. Sir David Ochterlony, was treated with marked courtesy during his stay at Láhore. High officers of State were appointed to look after his personal comforts, and the Maharájá appeared to take great pleasure in spending several hours at a time in his company. All the suspicion and distrust that was so conspicuous at the time of Mr. Metcalfe's visit to the Panjáb, appeared to have been removed, and the Maharájá, with frank confidence, ordered a parade of his troops in honour of his visitor, to whose notice his newly-raised battalions were particularly brought. He showed him over the fortifications of Láhore, and the defensive works which were then in progress to connect the fort with the grand mosque of Aurangzeb. The minister, Dewán Mohkam Chand, tried to dissuade the Maharájá from placing implicit confidence in the foreigner, and pointed out that the knowledge thus imparted, might be turned to account against him, but the Maharájá was satisfied that there was nothing to apprehend, and the remonstrances of the cautious minister were of no avail. The British Agent was invited by the Maharájá to attend the Holi festival, which had then commenced, but the invitation was politely declined, though all the chiefs and sardars, who had attended the marriage ceremonies, and were at the time staying at Láhore, gladly accepted the honour.

Sir David Ochterlony is invited to Láhore as a guest.

Cordial relations between the Maharájá and the representative of the British Government.

After the nuptial ceremonies of the heir-apparent and the observances of the Holi festival had been duly gone through, military operations were resumed, and, intelligence having been received, in the spring of 1812, of the murder, by Sultán Khan, the chief of Bhimbar, of his relation, Ismail Khan (who had been placed in charge of a portion of the Bhimbar territory, in consequence of occurrences which had led to a campaign two years previously, under the command of Dewán Mohkam Chand), a portion of the Láhore army, consisting of four battalions of infantry, 500 horse, and a train of siege artillery, was detached under the command of Bhái Ram

Fresh Invasion of Bhimbar, 1812.

Singh, the tutor of the heir-apparent, to punish the refractory chief. Prince Kharak Singh accompanied the force in nominal command of the expedition. The Bhimbar chief offered battle from an elevated position, which he had chosen with great judgment. The action began with a brisk fire of musketry from both sides, which the Sikhs supplemented with their artillery, but the ground chosen by the Bhimbar chief, gave him the advantage throughout, and the Sikhs, notwithstanding the prodigious efforts they made to overcome the natural difficulties in their way, and their stubborn valour, were utterly routed, on the third day. When intelligence of this disaster was received at Láhore, Dewán Mohkam Chand was despatched in all haste to the scene of action with a fresh contingent from Gujrát. Sultán Khan had strengthened his position, but negotiations were opened through Sardhá Ram, the secretary to the dewán, and the Khan surrendered, on condition that he should be treated with honour, and have his territory restored to him by the Láhore darbár. He was conveyed to Láhore, and put in irons by Ranjít Singh, who did not scruple to break the solemn pledges of his generals. Sultán Khan was kept in captivity at Láhore for six years, and was then removed to Jammu, where he died. All his possessions, and property in Bhimbar were seized. In vain did the heirs of Ismail Khan, to restore whom the expedition had been ostensibly undertaken, clamour for a share of the estate; the policy of the Maharájá was the complete overthrow of the Bhimbar family. The dewán next visited Rájáuri, and, having levied tribute from the chief of that place, returned to Láhore. Kharak Singh, assisted by Bhái Ram Singh, completed the reduction of Jammu and Akhnúr, and the Maharájá was pleased to confer these territories, along with Bhimbar, as a jágír on the prince. Budh Singh, Bhagat, was, about this time, deprived of his possession of Sujánpur.

The Khan of Bhimbar surrenders.

His territory annexed to the Láhore kingdom, 1812.

Tribute levied from the chief of Rájáuri.

Further operations in Jammu and Akhnúr.

Capture of Sujánpur, 1812.

When the expedition against Bhimbar, under Prince Kharak Singh, was undertaken, two more expeditions were organized, one under Dal Singh for the levy of arrears of tribute from Muzaffar Khan, nawáb of Multán, and the other under Desá Singh, Majithia, for the renewal of operations against the hill chiefs near Kangrá, who had shown an inclination to re-assert their independence. Dal Singh entered the district of Mitha and Twána, in the Shahpur district, and Uch, in Baháwalpur, and having exacted tribute from the chiefs of those places, appeared before Multán. The balance of tribute due was Rs. 50,000, for which Abubakr Khan was kept as a hostage in Dal Singh's camp. The agents of the nawáb had gone to Delhi to dispose of jewels, and, they having returned with the money, the sum due to the Sikh chief was paid by Muzaffar Khan, and Abubakr Khan was set at liberty. Dal Singh then made an attack on Kot Kamália, which he subdued, and returned to Láhore, where the Maharájá, in appreciation of his services, honoured him with a valuable *khilat*.

Tribute levied from the chiefs of Mitha, Twána and Uch,

And from the nawáb of Multán, 1812.

Kot Kamália subdued, 1812.

Desá Singh, Majithia, who had gone to the hills, was soon followed by the Maharájá himself. He first visited Amritsar, and, having paid his respects at the Darbár Sahib, proceeded to Adínanagar, where he spent some days in summoning various hill chiefs and making fresh arrangements with them for the payment of increased tribute. The Maharájá then marched to Nurpur, from the rájá of which place, Rs. 40,000 was levied as *nazráná*. In Bysakh (April) of the same year, Dewán Mohkam Chand and Mian Mota Dogra, were sent, at the head of troops, to levy tribute from the rájás of Mandi, Suket, Kullú and other hill chieftains with whom the arrangements of the preceding January had remained incomplete. All these places were effectually reduced, and the dewán, having collected a *nazráná* of Rs. 1,90,000, returned to Láhore.

Expedition against the hill chiefs.

The Maharájá seizes the wealth of Jaimal Singh Kanhia, 1812.

In August, 1812, Jaimal Singh the father-in-law of prince Kharak Singh, died without male issue. The Maharájá sent Ram Singh on a pretended mission of condolence to the widow of the deceased sardar, but as soon as this officer was admitted, he seized the hoards which the sardar had accumulated during a long life of frugality. He had also lent money on interest to the mahajans of Amritsar, who were called upon to furnish accounts to the Láhore treasury. Three months later, the widow of Jaimal Singh gave birth to a son, who was named Chandá Singh, and the Maharájá released a portion of the confiscated estate, valued at Rs. 15,000, as a jágír for the maintenance of the heir.

Insurrection of the hill chiefs near Káshmír.

The heirs of Ismail Khan, the murdered chief of Bhimbar, who had recently been disappointed by the ruler of Láhore in their efforts to obtain the restoration of their estates, and Aiz Khan, chief of Rájáuri, raised the standard of revolt. This insurrection was countenanced by the governor of Káshmír and supported by the Mahomedan chiefs and sardars of the neighbouring country. Ranjít Singh, who had so often had occasion to try his strength against these Mussalman states, now marched in person to reduce them. He thought it the more necessary to do so to further his designs against Káshmír, as the possessions of the chiefs in question commanded the route to the Pir Panjal mountains. The confederate army of the chiefs was entirely routed, and the country finally annexed about the middle of November. The independent chiefs and jágírdars who had joined in the insurrection fled to Káshmír and were afforded protection by the governor, Ata Muhammad Khan.

Suppressed, 1812.

It was in the previous September, when the Maharájá was making his preparations for an expedition against the hill states of Bhimbar and Rájáuri, that the families of the two ex-kings of Kábul, Shah Zaman and Shujá-ul-Mulk, took up their residence at Láhore. The disastrous retreat of Shujá, after his ill-designed enterprise in September, has been already noticed. To add to the Shah's misfortunes, his person was seized by Jahándád Khan, the governor of Atak, who sent the royal prisoner to his brother, Ata Muhammad Khan, at Káshmír, where the unfortunate king was now kept in close confinement. The blind Shah Zaman brought both the families to Láhore, where the wily Sikh chief professed much concern for their afflictions, and even held out to the helpless Shah a hope of obtaining the liberation of his brother, and of replacing him on the Káshmír throne. He professed deep sympathy with the misfortunes of Wafá Begum, the wife of Shah Shujá, promising to do everything in his power to alleviate her distress, but expressing a hope that his services, when crowned with success, would be rewarded by the presentation to him of the famous diamond, the *Kohinur*, or 'mountain of light,' which had adorned the throne of the Moghal emperors. The object of these artifices was to inspire the distressed lady with confidence, and to induce her royal husband, by means of her representations, to believe that he had at least a sympathiser in the ruler of Láhore, and to repair to Láhore, where, of course, the possession of his person could be obtained without any difficulty.

The families of Shah Zaman and Shah Shujá at Láhore.

Ranjít's professions of sympathy for the distressed families.

His real motive.

His designs on Káshmír.

The plans of Ranjít Singh against the much-coveted valley of Káshmír were now approaching completion. His newly-married son, Kharak Singh, had subdued Jammu. His own personal exertions had ended in the complete overthrow of the Mussalman chiefs of Bhimbar and Rájauri, and the final annexation of these territories to those of the *Khálsá*. His Sikh sardars and generals had penetrated the various principalities in the hills south of Káshmír, and had, after repeated actions, rendered them tributary to the Láhore kingdom. It only remained now to make a general advance into the valley itself; and the friendship professed for the ex-kings of Kábul, and the most humane duty of relieving the unhappy monarchs from their pending distress, were ample excuses to justify an immediate advance. But another chief from beyond the Indus, quite as enterprising and ambitious as the ruler of Láhore, was making preparations for an attack on the 'paradise of the east,' as the happy valley is called. This was Fatteh Khan, the famous wazír of Shah Mahmúd of Kábul, who was advancing, in order to punish the brothers, Ata Muhammad Khan, governor of Káshmír and Jahándád Khan, governor of Atak, for having assisted Shujá-ul-Mulk, in his attempt to recover Pesháwar, and to recover the provinces for the Kábul Government. Eight thousand Afghan troops were already at Rohtas, while the wazír himself crossed the Indus, towards the end of November, at the head of a considerable army. The recent successes of the Sikh arms in territories so near that which the wazír now contemplated making the theatre of military operations, rendered it necessary for both chiefs, thoroughly to understand the views of each other before those operations commenced on one side or the other. The wise wazír perceived the necessity of securing the Maharájá's co-operation, or at least his sympathy, to ensure success in the task of conquering Káshmír, which would be rendered extremely difficult, if opposed by the Láhore ruler. He accordingly deputed his dewán, Gudar Mal, to the Court of Láhore, with suitable presents, inviting the Maharájá to unite with him in the invasion of Káshmír, and proposing a friendly meeting, with the view of facilitating negotiations. The Maharájá gladly accepted the proposal, and the chiefs met on the bank of the Jhelum, on 1st of December, when it was agreed that the Maharájá should assist the wazir with troops, and, at the same time, afford every facility for the march of the invading army through the passes recently subdued by him. The Maharájá demanded a substantial benefit, in return for the succour required, namely, a portion of the revenue of the valley, but the politic wazír offered a third of the spoil expected, which was eventually agreed upon. Upon these terms twelve thousand Sikh troops, under Dewán Mohkam Chand, were placed at the disposal of the Afghan commander, and the joint armies of the Sikhs and the Afghans marched from the Jhelum, while the Maharájá returned to Láhore. The Páthán chief had, however, no intention of allowing the Sikhs to take any prominent part in the reduction of the valley, or to claim the credit of conquering it. What he really wished was the neutrality of the Sikh ruler. A heavy fall of snow impeded the progress of the invading army, as it reached the Pír Panjál Range. The Sikhs, less accustomed to endure the severities of a mountain winter, than the hardy Afghans, were unable to move. Fatteh Khan, without waiting to consult the dewán, or even informing him of his intention, pressed forward his mountain troops by double marches. Mohkam Chand, seeing how the Afghan had tried to outstrip him, induced the chief of Rájáuri, by the promise of a jágír of Rs. 25,000, to show him a route which would enable him to reach the valley at the same time as the wazír. This the chief did, and the active dewán, with a handful of troops, under Jodh Singh, Kálsia, and Nehál Singh, Attári, penetrated into the valley, in time to be present at the siege of Shergarh and Hari Parbat, much to the amazement of the Kábul wazír. But the portion of the Sikh army which thus reached its destination, was exhausted by its march through the hills and by exposure to cold, and was consequently unable to render any material help. Ata Muhammad, the governor, fled after offering but a feeble resistance; the valley was reduced, and soon afterwards all the strongholds of the province were captured by the wazír, Fatteh Khan, without difficulty. Great was the rejoicing at Láhore

The valley is in the meanwhile invaded by Wazir Fatteh Khan, of Kábul, 1812.

He asks the Maharájá's co-operation in the task of reducing Káshmir.

Meeting between the Maharájá and the Kábul wazir.

The Maharájá agrees to the wazir's proposal.

Invasion of Káshmir by the joint armies of the Afgháns and the Sikhs, 1812.

The Kábul wazir outstrips the Maharájá and holds Káshmir for Shah Mahmúd, 1813.

when the news of the reduction of Káshmír reached the capital; but Wazír Fatteh Khan now declined to allow the Sikhs the third share of the plunder, as had been stipulated. In the meantime, Shah Shujá, availing himself of the confusion which followed in Káshmír, consequent on the invasion of the valley by Fatteh Khan, effected his escape from confinement and joined the camp of Dewán Mohkam Chand. The dewán, with the consolation of having secured the prize of the ex-king's person, if none other, returned to Láhore, with his troops, much fatigued by their mountain toils in an uncongenial climate. The Maharájá received Shah Shujá with every appearance of respect; but his wrath knew no bounds when he was informed that Mohkam Chand had returned empty-handed, and that Fatteh Khan had refused to give him the stipulated share of the Káshmír booty. He determined on revenge, and his expedient did not entirely fail him. Jahándád Khan, the Governor of Atak, and brother of Ata Muhammad Khan, the ex-Governor of Káshmír, finding that the party of Shah Mahmúd had gained the ascendancy in Káshmír, and that his own brother was driven from his position, was alarmed, and Ranjít Singh opened negotiations with him with the offer of a large jágír for the surrender of the fort of Atak, which commanded the passage to the Indus. Jahándád Khan, expecting little favour at the hands of the Kábul wazír, agreed to the Maharájá's proposals, and permitted Dia Singh, who was already present in the neighbourhood of Atak, with a detachment of Sikh troops, as a precaution against any possible emergency, to occupy the fort in the name of the ruler of Láhore. Fakír Aziz-ud-dín and Dewán Devi Das were sent, immediately afterwards, at the head of a strong force, to settle the surrounding country. Fatteh Khan remonstrated with the Maharájá with respect to this usurpation, accusing him of barefaced treachery. He demanded the immediate surrender of the fort, which Ranjít Singh, confident in his own strength, refused, until the promised share of the Káshmír plunder was given to him. Upon this Fateh Khan marched to Atak, after placing the affairs of Káshmír in the hands of his brother, Azím Khan. The fort of Atak was closely blockaded. Karm Chand, *Cháhal*, hurried up from Láhore, at the head of a body of troops, to relieve the fort, and was shortly after followed by Dewán Mohkam Chand from Burhan. The Afghan and Sikh armies lay opposite each other for a long time, and frequent skirmishes took place, in which the Sikhs lost heavily; but Dewán Mohkam Chand avoided a general action till the Afghans had exhausted their supplies, and the hot weather had set in. The province had also been visited by a famine. At length, the season having sufficiently advanced, the Dewán determined to make a move, and marched to Haidaru, on the Indus, five miles from the fort. The Afghan troops took up a position to oppose the further advance of the Sikhs, a portion of their cavalry being led by Dost Muhammad Khan, a brother of the wazír, afterwards the well-known Amir of Kábul, the Afghan troops being chiefly comprised of Mulkia Mussalmans, or men from the country. The dewán, fresh for action, drew up his Sikhs in order of battle, the cavalry being formed into four divisions, the only battalion of infantry then present forming a square, and the artillery, under Ghouse Khan, supporting the whole. Dost Muhammad first made a resolute cavalry charge, which was, however, repulsed by a heavy fire from the Sikh battalion. The Afghans rallied, and Dost Muhammad, making a general attack with his horse, threw the foremost Sikh troops into confusion, capturing some guns. The Sikhs were beginning to give way, but Mohkam Chand, coming up on his elephant with two guns, opened on the enemy with grape. The latter,

Shah Shujá falls into the hands of the Sikhs.

Ranjít Singh acquires Attock, 1813.

Fatteh Khan remonstrates with the Maharájá on his usurpation.

The battle of Haidaru.

Dewán Mohkam Chand defeats the Afghans in a pitched battle, 1813.

owing partly to the check thus received, and partly to the fierce heat of the sun, were compelled to retire, and the Sikhs recovered their lost guns. Fatteh Khan, believing that Dost Muhammad Khan had been slain, fled, and the victorious Sikhs pursued the Afghans, and drove them out of Khyrabád. The wazír retired to Kábul, leaving another brother, Yar Muhammad Khan, in charge of Peshàwar, Kohat, and Eusufzai, with Sultan Muhammad Khan as his *naib*, or second in command. Mohkam Chand, after relieving the fort of Atak, returned victorious to Láhore in the month of August. The battle of Haidaru was fought on the 13th of July, 1813, and was the first on record in which the Sikh troops, under the Láhore darbár, had beaten the Afghans, who from this time began to entertain a dread of their prowess. There were great rejoicings at Láhore in honour of this great and decisive victory, royal salutes being fired at all the principal stations in the Ráj, while the cities of Láhore, Amritsar and Batála were brilliantly illuminated. Two months were spent in Láhore in these rejoicings, at the end of which time, in Assu (September), the Maharájá himself paid a visit to his newly-conquered province of Atak, with the view of further intimidating the Pathans, as well as of consolidating his authority in those distant regions.

Fateh Khan retires to Kábul.

Rejoicings at Láhore.

In October, 1813, the Maharájá visited Jawálá Mukhi and Kangrá, *viá* Pathankot, and then joined the camp of Kanwar Kharak Singh at Siálkot. Thence, taking the Wazirábad and Gujrát route, he reached Bhimbar and encamped on the banks of the Jhelum. Preparations were made here on a grand scale for an expedition into Káshmír, and all the jágírdars and tributary hill chiefs were summoned to join the Maharájá's camp with their respective contingents. Sardar Desa Singh, Majithia, was appointed to collect the *nazráná*, and succeeded in levying Rs. 40,000 from the rájá of Nurpur, Rs. 50,000 from the rájá of Jasrota, and one lakh from minor hill chiefs. Special arrangements were made to improve the artillery and to make the camel battery more effective, and, when all the preparations were complete, the Maharájá crossed the Jhelum and entered Bhimbar and Rohtas. At Rájáuri he was joined by Rájá Agar Khan, chief of that place, who was honourably received by him. Thatta, seven *kos* from Rájáuri, was easily reduced; but at Bahram Kalla, five *kos* further, on the Pir Panjál route, the Káshmír troops, under Wazír Ruhulla offered a determined resistance. The place was difficult of access, being surrounded by streams which flowed in deep currents. The bridge over one of these streams, between Thatta and Bahram Kalla, was destroyed by order of the governor; but the chief of Rájáuri pointed out a different route which obviated the necessity of crossing the steam. A detachment of 30,000 troops was sent under Sardar Dal Singh, Dewán Ram Dayál, Jodh Singh, Kalsia, and Fateh Singh, Ahluwalia, and the pass was seized without difficulty by the Sikh troops, who were subsequently reinforced by Desá Singh, Majithia, Daya Singh, Jawand Singh, Hukm Singh, Chamni, and Dewán Bhawáni Dás, who reached the valley with their battery of camel artillery (zambúraks). The reduction of Bahram Kalla, one of the most difficult passes of the valley, was an occasion of great rejoicing in the Maharájá's camp, and orders were now issued to Sardars Mit Singh, Shám Singh, Rájá Agar Khan, Dhanna Singh, Malwai, and Namdar Khan, Thakkar, for an advance on the Pir Panjál Range. But heavy rains interfered with the further progress of the Sikh troops, and it was reported that the summits of the Pir Panjál were still covered with deep snow. Further operations were, therefore, suspended, and the Maharájá, having made arrangements for strengthening the newly captured passes beyond Rájáuri, and for collecting grain and stores in select places, returned to Láhore, *viá* Bhimbar and Rohtas, on the 26th of December.

Second expedition to Káshmír, 1813.

Ill success of the expedition.

Wazír Fateh Khan's progress towards Derajat on the Indus and Multán checked.

It was during the operations in the hills beyond Rájáuri that the Maharájá was informed of the appearance of Wazír Fatteh Khan at Kálá Bágh in the Deraját, west of the Indus. Nawáb Sar Buland Khan, of Dera Ismail Khan, had already welcomed the advent of the wazír by presenting him with a number of horses and camels, while Abdul Jabbár Khan, the Nazim of Dera Ghází Khan, had placed 30 boats at his disposal on the Indus. The wazír had designs on Multán, and Nawáb Muzaffar Khan, fearing an attack, sent his vakil, Ghulám Muhammad, to the Láhore Darbár, to ask for aid against the Kábul wazír. Kanwar Kharak Singh was immediately sent to Serae, in the neighbourhood of Multán, at the head of a large body of troops, with instructions to march to Multán as soon as the Kábul wazír should cross at Trimu Ghat. These opportune measures had the effect of checking the progress of the wazír in the direction of Multán, and of inducing him to retrace his steps to Kábul.

Annexation of Makhad territory, 1813.

About this time, reports having been received by the Maharájá of the excesses committed by Wali Khan, the Afghan chief of Makhad, Dewán Mokham Chand was ordered to proceed thither, to bring the refractory chief to his senses. The dewán, accompanied by Sardars Jodh Singh, Ramgarhia, Dal Singh and Pahar Singh, Mán, marched to Makhad, and Wali Khan engaged to pay a *nazrana* of Rs. 50,000; but, finding, subsequently, that his means would not allow him to fulfil the promise, he retired from the fort of Atak, and the whole of his territory was annexed to the Láhore State. Dal Sing having been left to settle the country, the dewán returned to Láhore. Soon after this, the Maharájá received the joyful news of the capture of the Haripur hill territory by Dewán Bhawáni Das, who had been sent on an expedition against that State. A royal salute was fired at Láhore in honour of the victory, and Bhúp Singh, the chief, who had been treacherously seized some time before, was now released from confinement and received a small jágír for his support.

Capture of Haripur, 1813.

The Maharájá invites Pandit Ganga Ram, of Delhi, to Láhore, 1813.

In March 1813, the Maharájá, having heard of the talented politician, Gangá Ram, invited him, on the recommendation of Bhái Lal Singh and Sardar Himmat Singh, Jallawasia, to come from Delhi to Láhore with the offer of an appointment. Gangá Ram's father, Kishan Das, was a native of Káshmír, and had emigrated to Hindostán during the commotions which had followed Ahmad Shah's conquest of Káshmír, in 1752. Gangá Ram had greatly distinguished himself under Colonel Louis Burquinen, a French officer in the service of Maharájá Sindhia of Gwalior, and his intimate knowledge of the politics of the Cis-Sutlej States was of great use to General Sir David Ochterlony, when that officer arranged the relations of the chiefs of those States with the British Government in 1809. Gangá Ram, on arriving at Láhore, presented the Maharájá with Ganges water, and, having been entrusted with the Maharájá's seal, was placed at the head of the military office and made paymaster of the irregular forces, the head of the department being Bhawáni Das.

The Pandit is appointed head of the military office.

Ranjit Singh extorts the Kohinur diamond from Shah Shuja, 1813.

We now come to an incident in Ranjít Singh's life, which has left a stain on his memory, as one of the most avaricious, uncivil and selfish of monarchs that have ruled over the destinies of this country. It has already been related that, during the operations against Káshmír, Shah Shujá-ul-Mulk, the ex-king of Kábul, was brought to Láhore by Dewán Mokham Chand. He was received by the Maharájá with all the honours due to his rank, the heir apparent, Kanwar Kharak Singh, having been sent to Shahdara to receive his majesty. The house in the city, known as the Mubarak Haveli, was placed at the disposal of the king, his family and followers. No sooner had the king taken up his residence in the city, than a demand was made on him and his principal wife, Wafá Begum, for the great diamond, the *Kohinur*, which had once adorned the throne of the Moghals. A large sum of money and a valuable jágír were promised to the Shah, in the event of his majesty surrendering the great diamond. The Shah denied being in possession of it, while Wafá Begum declared that it had been pawned, for a large sum of money, with the merchants at Kábul, to supply her husband with funds in his late expeditions. The Maharájá disbelieving these statements, placed a strong guard round the Shah's residence, no ingress or egress being allowed without strict search. Finding that the severity of mere restraint was of little avail in inducing the Afghan king to part with so rich a prize, Ranjít Singh had the baseness to resort to extortion. The king was subjected to absolute deprivation of food; for two whole days, nothing was cooked in his majesty's kitchen, and the Shah, with his wives, children and servants, suffered from actual hunger. The exiled family was proof even against this act of oppression, and Ranjít Singh, out of regard for his own reputation, had the prohibition of food removed. The expedients of restraint and deprivation of food proving unavailing, recourse was now had to artifices and tricks. Two forged letters, purporting to have been written by Shujá-ul-Mulk to Wazír Fatteh Khan, and declared to have been intercepted, were produced in the darbár. In these the sufferings of the Shah from ill-treatment at the hands of the Láhore ruler, were described, and the aid of the wazír and the Afghans was solicited to put an end to these persecutions. This afforded ample pretext for increased violence against the Shah, and the addition of a strong guard to his residence was now assumed to be indispensable. Two companies of Sikh infantry, from newly-raised regiments, were, accordingly, placed over the king's haveli in the city, in addition to the previous guards and the Shah was threatened with separation from his family, and told that he would be sent to Amritsar, there to remain a prisoner, in the fort of Govindgarh, if he did not comply with the demand for the diamond. Threats of personal violence were also conveyed to him, and every possible device resorted to in order to enforce the surrender of the precious jewel. The Shah, finding expostulations without effect, had resort to stratagem in his turn, and asked for two months' time, to enable him to procure the diamond, which, he said, had been pledged by him to certain bankers for a large sum of money, which would be required to redeem it. The Maharájá, with much reluctance, allowed the time solicited, and there was a temporary cessation of severities. But so impatient was the Sikh ruler to secure the object of his ambition, and so little did he rely on the Shah's promise, that, before long, the extortionate demands for the jewel were renewed. The Shah, wearied of the insults to which he was subjected by the rapacious ruler of Láhore, and seeing that, if the surrender of the diamond were longer delayed, the Sikh would not hesitate to deprive him even of his life, resolved, at last, to comply with his demand. The news was received with intense joy by the Maharájá, who, on 1st June 1813, deputed Fakir Aziz-ud-dín, Bhái Gur Baksh Singh, and Jamadar Khushhál Singh, to receive the jewel. The Shah having, however, expressed a wish that the prize should be taken by the winner in person, Ranjít Singh gladly availed himself of an opportunity to wait on the Shah, with his principal courtiers. The interview took place on the first day of June at the residence of the Shah, in Mubarak Haveli. The exiled king received the ruler of Láhore with due honour, and, both princes being seated, a solemn pause ensued, which lasted for about an hour. Ranjít Singh, at last, becoming impatient, whispered to one of his attendants to give the Shah a reminder regarding his promise. The latter, therefore, made a sign to one of his eunuchs, who retired, and, after a while, brought in a small roll, which he placed midway between his master and the Maharájá. Dewán Bhawáni Das was then ordered by the Maharájá to unfold the roll, and, the diamond, in all its effulgence, being disclosed and identified, the Sikh immediately took it and deposited it in his pocket. The king had had the brilliant diamond set in an emerald, which he used to wear on his arm, but it had been taken out and was now set in gold. Presents were then exchanged, and a jágír assigned to the king for his maintenance, a promise of aid in recovering Kábul being also made to him. The guard on the Shah was withdrawn, and he was left more at liberty to move about in the city, which he often did in a State palanquin. An unhappy event, however, occurred soon afterwards, which had the effect of creating an unpleasant feeling between the Maharájá and the ex-king. The kárdár of Gujránwálá forwarded a letter, purporting to have been written by Kází Sher Muhammad, one of the followers of his Afghan majesty, and to have been intercepted and taken from a Pathan. The letter was addressed to Muhammmad Azím Khan, the new governor of Káshmír, and proposed a joint attack on Láhore with the Wazír Fateh Khan, which would render the assassination of the Maharájá at Láhore an easy task, and would be arranged by the Shah's party in the town. Ranjít Singh, on this letter being read out to him, sent for one of the royal princes, and asked him to explain the contents to the ex-king. Shah Shujá left the Maharájá at liberty to deal with the kází as he should think fit, declaring, at the same time, his own innocence. The holy man was so severely beaten with sticks and shoes, by the guard, that he fainted under the blows, but, thanks to the hardness of the Pathan skull, the castigation was borne with patience, and failed to extort a confession of privity on the part of the Shah from the pious kází, who, to the last, declared his master's entire innocence. He was then committed to prison; but the Shah, some time after, purchased the release of his faithful follower by the payment of Rs. 20,000 to the darbár.

A plot against the Shah.

The punishment of Kázi Sher Muhammad, a follower of his majesty.

When the Maharájá, as already mentioned, moved towards the Indus to consolidate his power in the newly conquered province of Atak, and to watch the proceedings of the Kábul wazír, Fateh Khan, he took Shah Shujá in his train, with the object, apparently, of using him as a tool for his ultimate designs against Káshmír, as well as of establishing his authority in the territory beyond the Indus. The season being now far advanced, the Maharájá suddenly returned, and the ex-king slowly followed, but he had traitors in his own household, and was plundered of many valuables on the way. The Shah believed the plunderers were the Sikhs themselves, though the officer who had been sent by his majesty to conduct Mr. Elphinstone to Peshávar, is believed to have had much to do with the Shah's misfortunes on the journey. This man, Mir Abul Hasan, embezzled a great deal of his master's property, and was the person who originally informed Ranjít Singh of the safety of the great diamond and other valuables at Láhore. He was also the author of the plot against the king, which made it appear that his majesty, in concert with the governor of Káshmír, was devising plans to overthrow the Sikh monarchy, and, finally, he it was who created obstacles in the way of the exiled family making their escape from the capital of the Panjáb.

The Shah's further misfortunes.

Mir Abul Hasan, the Shah's faithless servant.

The next act of Ranjít Singh was still more disgracefully extortionate and oppressive. The information supplied by the traitor, Abul Hasan and confirmed, in part, by the late unhappy incidents of the Shah's journey from Atak to the Sikh capital, left a strong impression on the mind of the Sikh that the Shah had still a collection of jewels of rare value left with

Still more extortions from his Afghan majesty.

him. A demand for these was accordingly made, and, on the Shah's declaring that none were left, he sent Bhái Ram Singh with a party of females, to make a search in the interior apartments of the Shah's harem, and bring away any boxes or bundles containing precious stones that might be found there. The female searchers committed acts, which were grossly insulting, against the persons of the unfortunate royal ladies, who had to bear the treatment with patience: and every box and packet which was found in their possession was brought before the Sikh ruler. In addition to jewels, a large collection of swords, pistols and valuable property, including carpets of rare beauty, and rich dresses, worn by the ladies of the harem, were seized and brought before the rapacious sovereign. Ranjít Singh had these boxes opened by the king's head eunuch, and retained, for himself, all the jewels and other articles of exquisite beauty and great value. The Shah, who had been allowed a temporary residence in the gardens of Shalimár, was ordered to remove to the city, where he was again subjected to strict surveillance.

The Shah, divested of an article of inestimable value, as well as of all the treasures that once decorated the throne of the great Durráni family, conceived that, should he continue his stay longer in the Sikh capital, the next step of his rapacious host would be to take his life if a pretext could be found. He, accordingly, determined to effect his escape, with his family. The Sikhs on guard were bribed, and communications opened with Balak Ram, the treasurer, a native of Hindostán and the agent of Sugan Chand, the great banker at Delhi and treasurer of the British Residency in that town. The Begums of the Shah, having, one night, dressed as Hindu females, and taken their seats in a cart drawn by bullocks, passed out of the city, with the assistance of Balak Ram, and were conveyed to Ludhiáná, where they were received, with due courtesy, by the Assistant Agent, Captain Birch. The circumstance of the flight of the Shah's harem having been brought to the notice of Ranjít Singh, towards the end of November, his rage was irrepressible. He placed a strong guard of artillery over the Shah, who was threatened with personal violence, to induce him to declare where the ladies were. He denied all knowledge of their movements, and declared that he knew nothing of their intentions. A strict search was made in the city, and egress from it to veiled women was prohibited. All merchants possessing any property belonging to the Shah, or to any member of the royal family, were ordered to surrender it to the Láhore Treasury. It having been, at last, represented to the Láhore ruler that the Afghan ladies had effected their escape from the Sikh capital, through, the assistance rendered by the treasurer, Balak Ram, that official was seized at Amritsar, his residence, and made over to Hira Singh, Topi. His houses at Amritsar were seized, and he was compelled, to show his account books. All the property belonging to the Shah or his family in possession of the Hindu was seized, after which he was set at liberty.

Escape of the Shah's harem from Láhore.

The Shah himself made his escape, in disguise, on a dark night in April 1815. A breach having been made in the wall of the *farrash-khana* on the side facing the street, the Shah made his way through it, accompanied by two of his slaves, and the princes Haidar and Zafar. Finding the gates of the city closed, the Shah then effected his exit from the town through the drain of the Lahori Gate. Repairing then to the tomb of Dátá Ganj Baksh, outside the Bhati Gate, he washed his clothes, which had become soiled in the drain, and, having offered up his prayers before the tomb of the saint, he swam across the Rávi at about 2 A.M. The passage to the Sutlej was intentionally avoided to

The Shah's own flight from Láhore, 1815.

prevent detection, as Ranjít Singh's suspicion would have naturally fallen on Ludhiáná as the probable place of the Shah's asylum. The Maharájá, on being informed of the Shah's escape, disgraced the artillery guard who were on duty on the Shah's residence in the Mubárak Haveli, and offered a reward for the recovery of the royal prisoner. Sawars were sent out in every direction, but no trace of the escaped prisoner could be found. Jamadar Khushhál Singh was then appointed to make enquiry as to how the Shah had offected his escape, and what persons were responsible for his flight from the Sikh capital. The result of the inquiry was that Shádi Khan and Eusuf Khan, keepers of the City Gate, were banished to Amritsar, where they were put in confinement, while the old guards on the city gates were removed and new Sikh guards appointed in their stead. The Shah proceeded to Gujránwalá in a bullock cart, which he hired, and from thence to Jammu, *viá* Siálkot. From Jammú he repaired to Kistwar, where he was well received by the chief of that place, and joined by some Sikhs who were discontented with Ranjít Singh. Having, with the help of the Kistwar chief, collected a body of three thousand men, the Shah, in the winter of 1815, once more tried his fortune in the direction of Káshmír. The cold, however, prevented his crossing the Pir Panjál Range, and his attempt to penetrate into the valley having failed, his troops dispersed, and he was compelled to retreat. After this reverse, he resided for some time, with his zealous mountain host, and then marched through the Kullú mountains, and, by a long and circuitous route; and after experiencing great hardships, reached Ludhiáná, in September, 1816, where he rejoined his family, and placed himself under the protection of the British Government. The Shah was treated by the British authorities with becoming respect and consideration, and the annual sum of Rs. 18,000 which had been assigned for the maintenance of his family was, on his arrival, raised to Rs. 50,000, while a separate pension of Rs. 24,000 was allowed by the Government for his blind brother, Shah Zamán.

He collects troops and makes an attempt on Káshmir, but fails, 1815.

Settles in Ludhiáná with his brother Shah Zamán.

The misfortunes of the exiled Kábul princes having been described connectedly, it is now necessary to revert to our narrative of the events subsequent to 1813.

The Maharájá proceeds to Adínanagar.

Third expedition to Káshmir, 1814.

The Holi having been celebrated with the usual pomp and magnificence, the Maharájá bathed in the sacred tank at Amritsar, and, in April 1814, moved his army in the direction of Adínanagar, below the hills, to enforce the payment of tribute from the hill rájás about Kangrá. Towards the middle of the year, he determined on making a complete conquest of Káshmír, and military operations were accordingly commenced. All the hill chiefs, as well as those of the plains, were summoned to Siálkot, and the Maharájá having himself repaired thither in person, a grand review of the Sikh troops took place. The experienced Dewán, Mohkam Chand, remonstrated against this expedition, urging that the season was not propitious; that sufficient supplies had not been collected on the route; that it would be extremely desirable, if not absolutely necessary, to construct large depôts of provisions at Bhimbar and Rájáuri, so as to provide against the possibility of a determined opposition being offered, and that the hill chiefs were hostile. These warnings were, however, unheeded, and the Dewán, seeing that the Maharájá was determined on an advance, asked leave to accompany the invading army. Sickness, however, detained him at the capital, and he was left there to preserve order during the Maharájá's absence. His grandson, Ram Dayál, then only twenty-two years of age, who had already distinguished himself by his ability and bravery, accompanied the Maharájá, and was entrusted with the command of a division of the army. The troops moved to Bhimbar early in June, and, advancing slowly from that place, reached

The Maharájá marches in person to Káshmír.

Rájáuri, *en route* to the valley. The Mahárájá encamped at Shah Bágh, in Rájáuri, and received the respects of Rájá Agar Khan, the chief of that hill state. Here the army, having been disencumbered of its heavy baggage, was equipped for a march through the interior of the hills, and preparations were made to pass the famous Pir Panjál. An attempt to gain over Rájá Rúhulla Khan, of Punch, failed, as his son was already a hostage with Muhammad Azím Khan, the Kábul governor. Rájá Agar Khan, of Rájáuri, was then consulted as to the best route by which to invade the valley. He proved a treacherous ally, and not only misled Ranjít Singh as to the number and strength of the enemy, but advised a division of the army, the main body commanded by the Mahárájá in person, to pursue the Punch route by the Toshú Maidán Pass, the other detachment to enter Káshmír by the Bahram Galla route, *viá* Supín, in the valley. This advice was unfortunately followed, and the division intended for a diversion, having been furnished with provisions, was sent forward under Ram Dayál, grandson of Dewán Mohkám Chand, on the 15th of June. The Dewán was accompanied by Sardár Dal Singh, Ghouse Khan, commandant of the artillery, Mit Singh, Padhania, and several other sardars and jágírdars. Jamadar Khushhál Singh commanded the van, which was to clear the way of the enemy, while Hari Singh, Nalwa, and Nehál Singh, *Attaríwálá*, brought up the rear. The detachment appeared before Bahram Galla, on the 18th, and secured possession of the pass by bribing the defenders, who were retainers of the Punch Rájá. The following day, under the guidance of Námdár Khan, Thakkar, whose knowledge of the route was of great value, the advanced column of the Sikhs surmounted the lofty barrier of the Pir Panjál by the Sarai and Madpur Pass, occupying Hirpur, and dislodging the Afgháns who defended those places. Azím Khan, having heard of this defeat, sent a strong force to meet the invaders, and an action was fought on the 22nd of July, near Hirpur, when the Káshmírians, being defeated, were followed by the Sikhs to Supín. On the 24th, the Sikhs, under Dewán Ram Dayál, made an assault on Supín, but the town was strongly defended by Shakúr Khan. The Sikh van was led by Jíwan Mal, a brave man and commandant of Kharak Singh's troops, who boldly engaged the Afghán army. The Sikhs fought well, but were outnumbered. The place was, moreover, visited by a snowstorm, and the Sikhs, being quite unaccustomed to such an event, could make no stand. Muhammad Azím Khan's cavalry coming up, the Sikhs were completely routed, and many of their sardars killed, among them being the gallant Jíwan Mal and Fatteh Singh, Chháchi. The routed Sikhs met with greater disasters the following night, going from place to place over snow-covered hills and valleys, in order to escape from the relentless Afgháns, who hung close upon their rear. Ram Dayál retired to a village, close to Srinagar, where the wounded men collected round his tent. Those who were able to fly, fell back on the skirts of the Pir Panjál. The Sikhs had no reinforcements at hand, and their supplies now failed. Reinforcements were, therefore, as anxiously waited for as provisions.

The treacherous conduct of Rájá Agar Khan of Rájáuri.

The division under Dewán Ram Dayál.

The Bahram Galla Pass secured,

And the Pir Panjál surmounted.

The actions of Hirpur and Supín.

The Sikhs routed.

The section of the Sikh army at Punch.

The main body, however, of the Sikh army, under the Mahárájá, which had advanced in the direction of Punch, met with no better fortune. Heavy rains delayed its march from Rájáuri, and the army started for its destination on the 26th of June, exposed to wet and cold. Ranjít Singh reached Punch, on the 28th, only to find it evacuated. This was done by order of the Punch Rájá, whose people were directed to desert towns and villages on the approach of the Sikh army, leaving nothing behind for the invaders to plunder; to bury or remove the grain, and to harass the flank of the Sikh columns in small bands. The effect of such tactics soon began to be felt, for the supplies of the Sikh army were running short, and this necessitated a halt in Punch till the middle of July. Ranjít Singh then moved with his army to Mandi, and thence to Toshú Maidán, on the skirts of the valley. Here he found the troops of Muhammad Azím Khan drawn up to check the progress of the invading army. Rájá Agar Khan suggested to Ranjít Singh the advisability of an attack on the Káshmír troops; but the Maharájá, after reconnoitring the position of the enemy, deemed it advisable to refrain from taking the offensive. The Káshmír and Láhore armies took up a position facing each other, both remaining inactive for several days. Here the Maharájá was informed of the precipitate haste with which Dewán Ram Dayál had carried on operations beyond the Pir Panjál range, and deplored the critical position in which his troops were placed in that quarter. He forthwith despatched Bhái Ram Singh, with Dewán Devi Dás and Kutb-ud-dín Khan, of Kasúr, at the head of five thousand cavalry and infantry to assist Ram Dayál. The Bhái, hearing of the critical position of the latter, remained stationary at Bahram Galla. Muhammad Azím Khan, seeing everything in his favour, thought the time had come for offensive operations against the main army of Láhore, which had been long in view, and was now suffering from cold and sickness, and still more from desertion. A desultory fire was opened by Wazír Rúhullah Khan, the Punch Rájá, on the Sikhs, on the 9th of July, and resulted in disorganising the Sikh troops. The attack was resumed on the following morning with greater vigour and with worse result for the cold-stricken Sikhs. The Maharájá now found that he must retreat, and he accordingly fell back on Mandi, leaving Ram Dayál to his fate. The retreat soon became a hurried and disastrous flight. Heavy rain fell, the roads were all but impracticable, and, checked by Rúhulla Khan, and tormented with the wet and cold, the Sikhs were much harassed on the way by the hill tribes, who disputed the passage of the army. In the midst of these difficulties, the Maharájá continued his retrograde march, setting the town of Mandi on fire. The retreat was attended with the loss of many men and officers, among the latter being the brave Mit Singh, Padhania, the chief of the staff, Gur Baksh Singh, Dhari, and Desá Singh, Mán. Many were also disabled and many drowned in a stream, in the precipitation with which the columns under Desá Singh, Majithia, and Hukm Singh, Chamni, executed the retreat, and, had it not been for the guidance of Námdár Khan, who conducted the main army, by a less difficult route, to Punch, many more would have perished, owing to the severity of the climate, as well as the impracticability of the passes which were now covered with snow. Ranjít Singh, stripped of nearly all his baggage, and his army all but disorganized, reached Punch, which he set on fire. Taking then with him Rájá Sher Báz Khan, of Punch, he continued his flight to Kotli, the rájá of which place would have endeavoured to cut off his retreat, but was prevented from effecting his purpose by his rání, who was won over by the persuasions of Fakír Aziz-ud-dín, and who induced her husband to permit the Sikhs to pass. Thus did the Maharájá reach Bhimbar and make his way out of the hills, whence, taking the nearest route, and attended by only a few followers, and with still fewer comforts, he reached his capital on the 12th of August. The Maharájá ever afterwards expressed a horror of the snow and cold of Káshmír, and the subject was such a sore one to him, that he never touched upon it without denouncing Káshmír as a vile place.

Defeat of the Sikhs at Toshú Maidán.

Disastrous retreat of the Láhore army.

The Maharájá's return to Láhore.

The advanced detachment, under Dewán Ram Dayál, was terribly harassed after its retreat from Srinagar. It was followed by Muhammad

Azím Khan, who surrounded the Sikhs and cut off their supplies. The Dewán, at this juncture, acted with resolution, and held his own with such determination, that Muhammad Azím Khan was compelled to come to terms. He not only allowed him a safe conduct to the Sikh frontier, but, as a sign of homage, sent presents for the Sikh ruler, and, in a written document, admitted the supremacy of the Láhore Darbár.* Thus the whole expedition returned to Láhore, having lost its best officers and men, and being shorn of everything that constituted its strength and utility as a military body. The Maharájá lamented that in the campaign he could not avail himself of his aged dewán's determination and judgment, as well as of his skill and valour. Everything had come to pass exactly as the old dewán had predicted; and the ruler of Láhore sighed at the political blunder he had committed. But misfortunes never come singly, and the Maharájá, and, indeed, the whole Sikh nation, was about to lose one who was to them a sincere friend, and who combined the qualities of an able counsellor and brave general. Mohkam Chand never recovered from the illness which had prevented his accompanying his master on the Káshmír expedition. Soon after the return of the Maharájá, the dewán grew worse, and he died at Phillour † on 15th Kartik, 1871 Samvat (October 1814), much to the regret of the whole Sikh community, and the sorrow of the Maharájá, who owed so much of his success to his skill, valour and fidelity. His military skill was as great as his administrative genius, and in him the Maharájá lost his most devoted and loyal servant. In his private character, the dewán was upright, liberal and high-minded. He was most popular among the troops and enjoyed the confidence of all the sardars of the nation. On his death, the Maharájá appointed Moti Ram Dewán in his father's place, conferring on him also the governorship of the Jalandar Doáb, and the charge of the fort of Phillour. Ram Dayál, the grandson of the deceased, who had already distinguished himself for bravery in the Káshmír expedition, was made commander-in-chief of the Sikh army.

The wise policy adopted by Dewan Ram Dayál.

Death of Dewán Mohkam Chand, 1814.

Moti Ram, his son.

Ram Dayál, his grandson.

The Maharájá, after resting for a few days at Shalámár, repaired to Amritsar, to meet Abdul Nabi Khan, the vakíl of the British Government, who had come from Ludhiáná, with Raí Nand Singh, bringing friendly letters from the Governor-General of India and General Sir David Ochterlony. The agent was received with due honours, and presented, on his departure, with a costly dress of honour, consisting of valuable shawls, and a thousand rupees in cash.

Arrival of British Agent at Amritsar.

Returning to Láhore, the Maharájá turned his attention to the construction of a moat around the city, and the repair of the city wall. About the same time, Phula Singh, the Nihang Akália, raised the standard of revolt in the Malwa country across the Sutlej. He was assisted in his mischievous designs by Néhal Singh, the Attari chief. Dewán Moti Ram was ordered from Phillour to repair to Malwa at the head of troops, and both the rebellious chiefs, having been captured at Kot Kapúra, were brought to Láhore.

Repairs of the city of Lahore.

Revolt of Phula Singh, Akáli.

* Cunningham here says that the advanced detachment was spared by Muhammad Azím Khan, out of regard for Mohkam Chand, the grandfather of its commander. Murray seems to hold the same view. This was, however, not at all the case. Dewán Ram Dayál is admitted on all hands to have acted with such determination, that Muhammad Azím Khan had to remind him of the friendship that existed between him and his grandfather, and, but for that friendship, the dewán was determined to fight to the last. Already two thousand Afghans had been slain in the conflict, and Muhammad Azím Khan had seen the danger of allowing the Sikhs to prolong their stay in the valley.—Compare Amar Nath's History with *Panjáb Chiefs*, page 556.

† His tomb was erected in a garden at Phillour.

The war between the Gorkhás and the British, 1815.

In the beginning of 1815, the British Government was engaged in a war with the Gorkhás, who were commanded by Amar Singh, Thápá. Colonel, afterwards General, Ochterlony took the field against the Nepál Commander, who, for a period of six months, successfully baffled all the attempts of the British General to reduce the hill country lying between the Jamna and the Sutlej. The Maharájá deputed Fakír Aziz-ud-dín to Ludhiáná with offers of assistance, and sent Dewán Bhawáni Das and Mohar Singh to the Governor-General with presents of horses and valuables on a similar errand, but the offer was declined with thanks. The Nepál Agent, Prithi Bilás, reached Láhore at the same time, to ask for help against the British; but, being coldly received by the Maharájá, he had to return to his country disappointed. The British troops at last gained a complete victory over the Nepálese, who were driven out of the country west of the Ghághra, or, Káli, river. This was highly favourable to the views of the Láhore ruler, who began to enlist the Gorkhá men so well adapted for hill warfare, in the army which he was raising for the hill campaign now in contemplation.

The Maharájá sympathises with the British.

The Dasahra festivities being over at Láhore, orders were issued for the Sikh army to rendezvous at Siálkot, and a division was sent in advance, in October, under Dewán Ram Dayál, Dal Singh and Dewá Singh, Ramgarhia, to punish the refractory chiefs of Rájáuri and Bhimbar and to devastate the whole of the country this side of the Pir Panjál, which had shaken off its allegiance to the Láhore Darbár. The Maharájá himself followed by the Wazirábad route. At Nadaun, news having reached him of the death of Jodh Singh, Ramgarhia, he sent for Wazír Singh, Mahtáb Singh and Dewá Singh, cousins of the deceased, who had quarrelled among themselves over the estate left by him, the avowed object of the invitation being a settlement of the dispute. On arrival at Nadaun, the sardars were received, with great courtesy, in a reception tent, but, in the midst of conversation, the Maharájá suddenly left the tent, which was straightway surrounded with troops, and the Ramgarhias were made prisoners. All their vast possessions, including the fort of Ramgarh at Amritsar and other small forts, upwards of a hundred in number, were seized. Rájáuri was next sacked by the Sikhs, who threw down the city walls and levelled with the ground the edifices of the rájá, who fled to Kotli, leaving all he had to be plundered by the invaders. After the reduction of Rájáuri, the Sikh troops stormed the fort of Kotli, and occupied it, together with the neighbouring tract of country. Here an enterprising Rájput woman, Mussammat Biwi, who was the holder of a jágír, offered her services to the Maharájá, and, with her help, the Serochi fort was reduced. The forts of Serochi and Kotli were then bestowed by the Maharájá on Rájá Sher Báz Khan. Bhimbar was subjected to a similar fate, but Punch was saved from a like visitation owing to its greater elevation, and the setting in of the cold weather with its usual severity. Further operations were now suspended, the experience of the last campaign having taught the Sikhs how disastrous it was to attempt such operations during that season, and in such a country, with troops unaccustomed to hill warfare. The troops now marched to Noushera, and the Maharájá returned to Láhore about the end of December.

The insurrection of the chiefs of Rájáuri and Bhimbar.

Ramgarhia possessions seized.

Punishment of refractory hill chiefs.

Pandit Dína Nath invited to Láhore, 1815.

The same year, Pandit, afterwards Rájá, Dína Nath, whose father, Bakht Mal, held a subordinate civil post at Delhi, was invited to Láhore by Dewán Gangá Ram, a near relation of his, and then head of the State Office at Láhore. The Pandit soon distinguished himself by his energy and intelligence, and became privy seal, as well as head of the civil and finance offices.

Punishment of the hill chiefs of Núrpur and Jaswál, 1816.

In January 1816, the Maharájá was waited upon by Bír Singh, the rájá of Núrpur, who had failed to comply with the summons to present himself at the meeting of the sardars at Siálkot. He was subjected to so heavy a fine that he was quite unable to pay it, and he offered his *thakurs* or household gods of silver and gold, in lieu thereof, but even their value did not suffice to make up the amount required. At length he was subjected to the disgrace of being personally seized at the door of the hall of audience, and sent back in a palanquin to his State under charge of Missar Ralia Ram, there to witness the seizure of all his property. A small jágír was offered him for his maintenance, but he declined to accept it, and, after a fruitless attempt to recover his lost possessions by force of arms, fled across the Sutlej, and put himself under British protection. Umed Singh, the rájá of Jaswál, father-in-law of Bír Singh, was, for a similar offence, subjected to very much the same treatment, all his possessions and jágírs being confiscated. He, however, was content with the jágír offered to him for his support. Fakír Imám-ud-dín and Dewá Singh were sent with two hundred sawárs, and Nának Chand, Daftri, to establish the Sikh rule in the confiscated hill territories.

A tour in the country bordering the Chináb, 1816.

The Maharájá, being joined by Fateh Singh, Ahluwalia, moved in the direction of Multán and Báháwalpur, at the head of his troops, collecting tribute and exacting *nazránás* from the zemindárs on the way. At Pákpattan, Dewán Sheikh Muhammad Yár, the Sajjáda Nishin of the great mausoleum of that place, presented the Maharájá with a fine horse and a sword set with jewels. The district was at first placed in charge of Jemadar Khushhál Singh; but out of consideration for the sanctity of the saint, whose remains are deposited there, it was restored to the Sajjáda Nishin, on condition of his agreeing to pay a tribute of Rs. 9,000 per annum. Sube Rae and Kishan Das, vakíls of the nawáb of Báháwalpur, having then visited the Maharájá, a fresh agreement was executed by the nawáb to pay a *nazráná* of Rs. 80,000, and an annual tribute of Rs. 70,000. The Maharájá, marching by easy stages, next reached Harappa, where he was joined by Dayá Singh, Qutb-ud-dín Khan, Kasúria, and Missar Dewán Chand, who were returning with their advanced division from Báháwalpur, after the new agreement made with the nawáb. The Maharájá ordered them to Tolamba, where he himself arrived on the 15th Chet, 1873, Samvat. Here Sayad Muhsin Shah, vakíl of Muzaffar Khan, nawáb of Multán, brought presents of horses, shawls and carpets for the Maharájá, who demanded a lakh and twenty-thousand rupees as *nazráná*. The agent asked for time to pay the subsidy, offering to pay Rs. 40,000 in cash and the balance after two months, but the Sikh ruler, becoming impatient, laid siege to Ahmadábád, which was reduced without difficulty by the artillery of Missar Dewán Chand. Then, crossing the Chináb at Trimu Ghát, the Maharájá encamped at Sálar Wáhan with his troops. An advanced column of Sikhs reached Multán to enforce payment of the tribute; and Phula Singh, Akálí, intoxicated with *bhang*, suddenly stormed the town, at the head of a band of fanatics, with such impetuosity that the storming party gained possession of the outworks of the citadel. The nawáb, seeing that the Sikh ruler was determined to proceed to extremes if the subsidy was not soon paid, remitted Rs. 80,000 through Dewán Bhawáni Das, and promised, in a short time, to pay the balance of Rs. 40,000. The cupidity of the Láhore ruler being thus satisfied, he marched on to Mánkera. The van of the Sikh army, under Sardar Sundar Singh, Ahluwalia, proceeded down the Indus to beyond the Sindh border. Muhammad Khan, surnamed Múin-ud-doula, the chief of Bhakkar and Leia, whose family had been expelled by the present Mírs of Sindh, dying about the same time, the suc-

Dealings with the Sajjáda Nishin of Pákpattan,

The Nawáb of Báháwalpur

And of Multán.

Storming of the citadel of Multán, 1816.

The chiefship of Bhakkar.

cession devolved on Sher Muhammad Khan, with the consent of Khudá Yár Khan, younger brother of the deceased nawáb, and Hafiz Ahmad Khan, his son-in-law. Negotiations for a *nazráná* were opened by the Maharájá, through his agent Suján Rai, the agents on behalf of the nawáb being Raizáda Pindi Das, Sundar Singh and Mohan Lal. The Maharájá made a demand for Rs. 1,25,000, while the nawáb offered only Rs. 20,000. The Maharájá, considering himself affronted, ordered the Mánkera country to be devastated with fire and sword. The forts of Mahmúd Kot, Khangarh and Muhammadpur, were closely besieged and subjected to a heavy cannonade. Phula Singh, the notorious Akálí fanatic, committed the grossest atrocities on the Mussalmán population, and the garrisons, on coming out of the blockaded forts, were subjected to insults of a revolting description, notwithstanding the solemn pledges given that they would be secure from maltreatment. At length, Rai Pindi Das having arranged to pay fifty thousand rupees in cash, through Jamadar Khushhál Singh, and the heat of the weather being severely felt, the Sikh forces withdrew, leaving Sher Muhammad Khan to govern the country.

The country of Mankera ravaged, 1816.

The Maharájá proceeds to Jhang.

The Maharájá now proceeded to Jhang, where Ahmad Khan, the Siál chief, was summoned to his presence, and called upon to pay forthwith a large *nazráná*. He pleaded his inability to do so, on which he was seized and sent a prisoner to Láhore, together with Jawáyá Ram, his dewán, under a strong guard. The whole country, yielding a revenue of four lakhs of rupees, was confiscated and farmed to Sukh Dayál for Rs. 1,60,000, the civil government being entrusted to Suján Rai. Sardar Fateh Singh, Ahluwalia, was in the meantime sent to Uch, on the Chináb, and Kot Maharájá, which he seized, evicting the Sayads of Uch, whose possessions had hitherto been held by them, on account of their religious sanctity, and who were now provided with a jágír. Rajab Ali Khan, the chief of Kot Maharájá, was seized and sent a prisoner to the Sikh capital. At this time, Abdus Samad Khan, son of Nawáb Shah Muhammad Khan, of Déera Dín Panáh, having suffered great oppression at the hands of Háfiz Muzaffar Khan of Multán, fled, with Nawáb Muzaffar Khan, Saddozai, to Láhore, where they were received with consideration by the Maharájá.

Imprisons the Nawáb.

Makes arrangements of the country, 1816.

Capture of Uch and Kot Maharájá on the Chináb, 1816.

The proceedings of Wazir Fatteh Khan in the hills adjoining Káshmír.

The Maharájá, having finished his tour in the south, returned to his capital on the 20th of May. Here he was informed that Wazír Fatteh Khan, having crossed the Indus at Atak, had employed the season in marching across the Pakhli and Damtour hills. He had established his own authority in the valley, having defeated his brother Muhammad Azím Khan, and was returning by the same route. Dewán Ram Dayál was, about this time, engaged in quelling a disturbance raised by Muhammad Khan, zemindar of Dheri, and in settling the country round Atak. The Maharájá sent the dewán orders to remain at Kálá ki Sarae, until Fatteh Khan should leave Káshmír and re-cross the Indus.

The reorganization of the *nikka* country and the dismissal of Bhái Ram Singh from office of tutor to Prince Kharak Singh.

Domestic troubles now occupied the attention of the Maharájá. Bhái Ram Singh, the guardian of the heir-apparent, Kanwar Kharak Singh, had mismanaged the *nikka* country held in jágír by the prince, and grievously oppressed the people. Loud complaints reached the Maharájá's ears of the Bhái's misbehaviour and excesses. He had formed a close intimacy with the Kanwar's mother, the Maharájá's second wife, and his influence over that lady, as well as over the prince, was so great, that his will prevailed in all matters, public and private. The Maharájá gave the prince, who had reached the age of discretion, time for amendment and reform; but the active interference of the Bhái made anything like improvement utterly hopeless. The Maharájá was at length compelled to take more serious notice of the matter. The dewán was thrown into confinement and called on to account for his stewardship of the estates. The Kanwar's mother was removed to Shekhupura, and the prince himself reprimanded for allowing matters to fall into such reckless confusion, and Dewán Bhawáni Das, Peshawaria, was appointed manager of the Kanwar's estates, in place of Ram Singh. Uttam Chand, the banker, with whom Ram Singh had accounts, was then put in chains, and jewels and precious stones, valued at a lakh of rupees, together with four lakhs in *hundis* and cash, belonging to the deposed dewán, were confiscated to the State.

Formal installation of Prince Kharak Singh as heir to the throne of Láhore, 1816.

For the disgrace inflicted on Kharak Singh, the Maharájá made ample amends soon after. A grand darbár was held at Anarkali, with the object of installing the prince on the *gadi* of heirship to the Láhore throne. Astrologers were consulted as to the most propitious day for the ceremony of installation, and, at their suggestion, the 15th of Magh, 1873 Samvat, was fixed as the date of the ceremony. Tents and shamiánas were pitched on the plain of Anarkali, and invitations issued to rájás, chiefs, sardars and jágírdars to be present at the ceremony. The chiefs repaired to Láhore, in obedience to the summons, and, on the date fixed, the darbár was held with appropriate pomp and magnificence. The heir-apparent, seated on the *masnad*, received *nazars* from all the chiefs assembled to do him honour, and, the ceremony being over, all returned to their respective States well pleased with their reception at the Sikh capital, and the festivities on the occasion.

The Maharájá's tour in the hills of Kangrá, 1816.

Having celebrated the Dasahra at Láhore, in October, the Maharájá visited Amritsar, where he performed his ablutions in the sacred tank of the Sikh temple. Orders were given to cut a branch from the Madhopur canal to Amritsar, to convey water to the tank. Ranjít Singh then proceeded to Adínanagar, previously to going on a hill tour. There he was visited by the agents of the hill rájás, among whom was the agent of the Chamba Rájá, who presented him with a *hundi* for Rs. 40,000, in part payment of his tribute, together with a number of curiosities consisting of hill birds and porcelains. Dewán Moti Ram was ordered to proceed to Jawálá Mukhi with his troops, and the Maharájá himself left for Nurpur on the 14th of Maggar. The place had suffered greatly from the recent disasters which had followed the expulsion of Rájá Bir Singh, and the Maharájá adopted measures to repopulate the town, the traders and artizans being exhorted to return to their abodes and resume business. After these arrangements had been completed, the Maharájá reached Kangrá, where, having made offerings to the holy temple of Jawálá Debi, he collected his yearly tribute from the hill rájás. The rájá of Chamba offered Rama Nand, the banker, and Iláchigir Gosain, as sureties for the balance of the tribute due by him, and their security was approved. Rájá Isri Sen, of Mandi, paid Rs. 65,000 by way of tribute, and Rs. 30,000 as *nazráná*, and the rájá of Suket Rs. 10,000. Rájá Bikrama Sen, of Kullú, having died, the Maharájá thought it a fitting opportunity for interference. He accordingly repaired to Kullú, and, having received a *nazráná* of a lakh of rupees from Thakur Das, the younger son of the deceased rájá, placed him on the *gadi*, to the exclusion of the elder son and the legitimate heir, whose appeal to the justice of the Sikh ruler passed unheeded. Having then received a *nazráná* from Rájá Lal Deo of Jasrot, Ranjít Singh visited Nadaun, where he met his old ally, Rájá Sansar Chand, and then returned to the plains. On his way to Amritsar, he seized the remnants of the Ramgarhia possessions, including the fort of Miani, near Tanda, the repository of Jodh Singh's wealth, all of which fell into the hands

Seizure of the Ramgarhia estates, 1816.

of the Maharájá. The entire possessions of the Ramgarhia *misl*, which were seized by Ranjít Singh, were estimated to yield a yearly revenue of five lakhs of rupees. The Maharájá having returned to Amritsar on the 13th of December, the city was illuminated in honour of the occasion. The return of the sovereign to his capital was marked by the celebration of the Holi.

The Sikh troops worsted at Multán, 1817.

In the beginning of 1817, Fakir Núr-ud-dín was sent to settle the Ramgarhia territory, and in Magh (January) of the same year, Dewán Moti Ram, Bhawáni Das, Peshawaria, Hari Singh, Nalwa, and other sardars, were sent against Multán, with a large force, to enforce the payment of tribute. Misr Dewán Chand, commandant of the artillery, followed with a large number of guns. The Sikh army besieged the fort, but Muzaffar Khan made a gallant defence and compelled the invaders to raise the siege and retire. When the army reached Láhore, the Maharájá placed Bhawáni Das, who had conducted the siege, in confinement, besides imposing on him a fine of Rs. 10,000.

The expedition to Hazárá, 1817.

Troops were then sent, under Prince Sher Singh and Tárá Singh, against Muhammad Khan, of Hazárá, who had given trouble to Hukm Singh, Chimni, the Sikh governor of Atak. Thousands of people from the surrounding country flocked to the standard of Muhammad Khan, and a battle was fought which ended in the total rout of the Mahomedans, who dispersed in all directions. Muhammad Khan himself was killed in the battle and was succeeded by his son, Sayd Ahmad Khan. As a punishment, the amount of his tribute was raised from Rs. 50,000 to Rs. 75,000, and the Sikh troops were withdrawn. The same year, a treaty was concluded with the nawáb of Mánkera, through Raizáda Pindi Das, binding the nawáb to pay an annual tribute of Rs. 80,000 and to supply a number of horses and camels and a contingent of troops for service in Multán in case of war. During the latter part of the year, the Maharájá's attention was wholly absorbed in making military preparations for an expedition against Multán. A life devoted to toil and debauchery, each excessive in its turn, had seriously impaired the Maharájá's health, and he was obliged to subject himself to a course of *regimen*, prescribed by the *hákims*, which lasted for forty days. He was, however, not wanting in energy, and, as soon as his complaint was partially cured, he resumed his personal supervision of all the preparations, including the transport and commissariat arrangements. It was resolved to convey the provisions and war material by the Rávi and Chináb, and all the boats on these rivers were put under requisition. A large number of bullocks were procured to convey the heavy artillery to the intended seat of war. *Zamzama*, the famous gun, had been moved from Amritsar, and all the sardars of State were busy in collecting supplies and men from every quarter.

Muhammad Khan, the Hazárá chief, is slain

Treaty with the Náwab of Mánkeria, 1817.

Preparations for a fresh expedition to Multán, 1817.

The army marches from Láhore, 1818.

In January 1818, an army of 25,000 Sikhs marched from Láhore to the south-west frontier. The chief command of the expedition was given to Prince Kharak Singh, assisted by Misr Dewán Chand, who had risen from a low position to that of commandant of the artillery on account of his talents and activity, and who held the real command. He was also honoured with the title of Zafar Jang. Repeated excursions and continued exactions, the number of which had, each season, been enormously increased, had so strained the resources of the country, and spread such devastation over it, that the Maharájá saw the time had come when this long-coveted possession could be secured without any considerable difficulty. Yet he prepared himself for all possible contingencies, and was fully alive to the danger of a Musalman combination in the cause of their faith, against the people of his own religion, an apprehension, the correctness of which future events fully justified. Before undertaking this expedition, he released Ahmad

Release of Ahmad Khan, Sial.

Khan, the Sial chief of Jhang, who, for nine months previously, had been kept in close confinement, retaining Ináyat Khan, his eldest son, who had been recalled from Sindh as security for his good behaviour at Láhore. On Ahmad Khan a jágír of Rs. 12,000 was bestowed, for his subsistence at Mirowál, in the Amritsar District. An exorbitant sum was now demanded, together with five of Muzaffar Khan's best horses, and, this requisition not being complied with, the forts of Khangarh and Muzaffargarh, on the way to Multán, were stormed and captured. A proclamation was issued by the nawáb, calling on the faithful to draw the sword in the cause of Islám, and hundreds of Mussalmans gathered from the surrounding country and were supplied with arms by the nawáb. The Sikhs, under Dewán Moti Ram, closely besieged the town of Multán, which was defended by Nawáb Muzaffar Khan with great vigour. The siege lasted for several days, until, at length, several breaches having been effected in the walls of the city by the incessant fire from the Sikh batteries, the invaders took possession of the town in February, after a severe struggle. The bombardment of the fort now commenced. The citadel was ill-provisioned for a siege, and the nawáb had a garrison of only 2,000 men there. With such scanty means at his disposal, Muzaffar Khan made a defence so gallant, that the Sikhs had never before witnessed the like. The Sikhs established batteries on commanding positions, each held by a jágírdár, and entrenched themselves outside the ditch. From these positions they opened a steady fire from their guns and matchlocks on the fort. The besieged made several sorties, and many desperate encounters took place between detachments of the two armies, but the continuous fire of the Sikhs had the effect of making several breaches in the walls of the citadel, and, in the course of April, the upper works of the defences were almost all demolished. The following month the approaches close to the *fausse braye* of the works were carried. The bombardment went on till the 2nd of June. The great Bhangi *top*, or *zamzama*, before mentioned, was now in full play, and had been fired four times with effect. Other heavy guns, the number of which was large, were also well employed. Two practicable breaches were made in the wall, and the gates blown up, but the defenders raised mounds of earth behind them, and from these engaged in a hand-to-hand fight with their assailants. The Sikhs made several assaults, but the small garrison repulsed the attack each time, with severe loss to their enemies. Ranjít Singh, though absent, regularly forwarded his orders regarding the conduct of affairs connected with the siege. He repeatedly wrote to Misr Dewán Chand, forbidding him to run the risk of storming the fort, for which the Sikh troops were eager, the object of the Maharájá being to compel Muzaffar Khan to surrender at discretion, and agree to accept a jágír which had been offered to him. The nawáb was, however, obstinate in his refusal, and was determined to repel the enemy, or die. Desertions now began to take place on the side of the nawáb, for the Sikhs offered large bribes to his Pathan adherents, and few of them were able to resist the temptation. At length the defenders of the citadel were reduced to two or three hundred fighting men, for the most part the immediate dependents and connections of the nawáb. All the rest had either been killed, or gone over to the enemy. This devoted little band determined to hold out to the last extremity. While matters were in this stage, one Sádhú Singh, an Akáli fanatic, taking with him a few companions, as fanatical and reckless as himself, rushed, without orders, on the 2nd of June, into an outwork of the fort and fell suddenly on the Afghans. It was Friday morning, and the Mussalmans, who were resting after the care and toils of the night, were taken by surprise. The Sikh soldiers, seeing this from the trenches, made a

> The city of Multán is invested and captured.

> Bombardment of the Fort.

> The *zamzama* gun employed at the siege.

> The war tactic displayed by the Maharájá.

> Sádhú Singh the Akáli.

simultaneous advance on the spur of the moment, and the entire work was carried, the defenders being all slaughtered in a hand-to-hand fight. The whole Sikh force, flushed with this success, advanced to the assault of the fort and effected an entrance through the breaches, at the Khizri Gate, which were the result of four months' battering. Thus the very suddenness of the onset of a small band of Akáli fanatics, led to the capture of the citadel. The old Nawáb Muzaffar Khan, seeing this, dressed himself in green, and with the remnant of his followers, his own sons, kinsmen, and personal attendants, made a stand with drawn swords at the door of his residence near the Khizri Gate. This handful of heroes now rushed on their assailants, and so furious and desperate was the onset, that many fell beneath their swords. Cutting his way through the enemy, the nawáb, with his devoted little band, reached the tomb of Baháwal Hak. Here the nawáb determined on standing his ground to the last, and such was the terror inspired by the desperate valour displayed by him, that the Sikhs drew back and opened fire on them with their matchlocks. "Come on like men!" shouted the braves, "let us try our valour in a fair fight." This was, however, a challenge to which the Sikhs did not care to respond. Thus fell, the grey-bearded Nawáb Muzaffar Khan covered with wounds, but disdaining to the last to accept the protection of a hated foe, and with him fell his five brave sons, Shah Nawáz Khan, Mumtaz Khan, Ayáz Khan, Haknawáz Khan and Shah Baz Khan. There also were killed Nasrulla Khan, nephew of the nawáb, one of his daughters, and his councillors Khan Mahomed Khan, Khoda Yár Khan and Sahib Dad Khan. Zulfikar Khan, his second son received a severe wound in the face. Sarfaráz Khan, the nawáb's eldest son, who had for some years, during his father's absence at Mecca, been entrusted with the reins of Government, was found concealed in a cellar and taken prisoner, with the youngest son, Amir Baz Khan. Dewán Ram Dayál, taking Sarfaráz Khan with him on his elephant, conducted him to his tent with all honours. A few only of the garrison effected their escape. Nawáb Muzaffar Khan, with his son, Shahnawáz Khan, was buried by the shrine of Baháwal Hak, with due honour. The city and fort were now given up to be plundered by the Sikh troops. Great were the ravages committed by the Sikhs on this occasion. About 400 to 500 houses in the fort were raised to the ground, and their owners deprived of all they had. The precious stones, jewellery, shawls and other valuables belonging to the nawáb were confiscated to the State and kept carefully packed by Dewán Ram Dayál, for the inspection of the Maharájá. The arms were all carried away. In the town many houses were set on fire, and nothing was left with the inhabitants that was worth having. Hundreds were stripped even of their clothes. Outrages were committed on the women, many of whom committed suicide by drowning themselves in the wells, or otherwise putting an end to their lives, in order to save themselves from dishonour. Hundreds were killed in the sack of the city, and indeed there was hardly a soul who escaped both loss and violence. So great, in short, were the horrors inflicted upon the unfortunate inhabitants, that the terrible incidents attendant on the sack of Multán are recollected to this day, and still not unfrequently form the topic of conversation. When all was over, Prince Kharak Singh made his triumphant entry into the fort, and took possession of all the State property and treasures belonging to the nawáb. The fort of Sujábad was then captured and sacked, and booty, estimated at four lakhs of rupees, consisting of gold and silver utensils, and other valuables, fell into the hands of the victors.

Capture of the citadel.

The bravery displayed by Nawáb Muzaffar Khan.

He is killed with his five sons.

Plunder of the city and the fort.

Excesses committed by the Sikhs.

Capture of the fort of Shujábad.

The first man who brought intelligence of the capture of Multán to

Ranjít Singh, was a mace-bearer (*chobdar*) in the service of Sardar Fatteh Singh, Ahluwalia. The Maharájá presented him with a pair of gold bracelets and a sheet of rich *Kalabatun* (cloth made of twisted silk and gold threads), and, on the news being confirmed through official sources, great rejoicings were made at Láhore, which was the scene of festivities for eight days. The Maharájá, having taken his seat on an elephant, moved about the principal streets of Láhore, showering down rupees to be scrambled for by the crowd. A large offering in money was sent to the Darbár Sahib at Amritsar, as a thanksgiving for the victory won. The towns of Amritsar and Láhore were brilliantly illuminated, and money was sent as alms to every place of Hindu or Mahomedan worship at Láhore. The palace was the scene of festivities for several days, and a large number of gold bracelets, *kanthas* (necklaces) and shawls were sent by the Maharájá to Multán for distribution among those sardars and jágírdars who had distinguished themselves in the action. In the midst, however, of these rejoicings, and in strong contrast to his many acts of princely munificence, Ranjít Singh displayed, in one instance, a degree of avarice only too characteristic of him, and showing that to his intense thirst for conquest and territorial aggrandisement was added an equally intense passion for the accumulation of wealth. He had always considered the citadel of Multán a great repository of wealth, and had entertained exaggerated notions of the riches of the town. His share of the spoil being low beyond his expectations, he issued orders for the return of the whole army to Láhore, with the exception of such portion, under Jodh Singh, Kalsia, as was necessary to hold the place and conduct the administration of the country. On the return of the army, he issued a proclamation calling on all sardars, jágírdars, officers and soldiers to surrender to the State all they had obtained at Multán by plunder, and stating that if any one was found in possession of any article of spoil, or any money obtained from the sack after a certain date, his punishment would be death. This order brought into the treasury shawls, utensils, rich apparel, books, carpets, &c., worth five lakhs of rupees, though the Multán plunder was estimated at two millions sterling. Of the gold and silver in coin and jewellery, and the precious stones plundered by the soldiers, little was returned. The whole of the property surrendered by the troops was sent to the *toshukhana* or jewel office, and appropriated to the State. The Maharájá felt proud that his commands had not altogether been unheeded; but he was never satisfied with the result, and complained that he had got very little of the booty he had expected. Yet the incident furnishes a proof of the awe in which Ranjít Singh's authority was held by his troops. The Civil Government of Multán was entrusted to Sukh Dayál, Khatri, who had taken the farm of Jhang, and Babu Baj Singh was appointed killadar, or keeper of the fort. The *thána*, or police post, of Jamadar Khushhál Singh was established at Muzaffargarh, of Sham Singh, son of Nehal Singh, Attariwala, in Khangarh, and of Fatteh Singh, Ahluwalia, in Tolamba. Sarfaráz Khan, the nawáb's eldest son, for whom his father had procured a confirmation of the succession as nawáb from the court of Kábul, was carried a prisoner to Láhore by Dewán Chand, with his wounded brother Zulfikár Khan. The Maharájá received Sarfaráz Khan with due honour and sent him a *ziyáfat* of Rs. 2,500, through Dhuman Khan, who was appointed to look after his personal comfort. A jágír at Sharakpur and Nowlakha, afterwards commuted to a cash pension, was assigned for his subsistence, and a pension was given to Zulfikár Khan. Dal Singh, Nakheria, Jodh Singh, Kalsi, Dhanna Singh and several other sardars were sent to Multán, and the walls of the fort, the ditch and the city were repaired.

Rejoicings at Láhore.

Ranjít's passion for accumulating riches.

Arrangements for the government of the newly-conquered province.

Khushhál Singh falls into disfavour.

Jamadar Khushhál Singh, the Maharájá's chamberlain, upon whom unlimited bounties had been lavished, and who was in command at the tomb of Shams Tabrez, fell into disfavour soon after the capture of Multán. His brother, Ram Lal, who had joined him from Hindostán in 1816, had received an appointment in the body-guard. He was the great court favourite, the boon companion of Ranjít Singh, who had a personal attachment for him. The Maharájá wished Ram Lal to give up the Brahminical thread and receive the Sikh initiation of the *Páhal* of the Guru, as his brother had done; but the most seductive offers availed not to induce Ram Lal to comply with his master's wish. The Maharájá becoming urgent on the point, Ram Lal, with the connivance of his brother, fled to Hindostán across the Sutlej, and thus placed himself beyond the reach of the Sikh ruler. This incensed Ranjít Singh in the highest degree. Khushhál Singh was immediately put under restraint, and Ranjít Singh, acting on the advice of Misr Dewán Chand, was induced by Zaffar Jang, who had quarrelled with Khushhál Singh about the Multán booty, to remove the latter from his office of chamberlain and to appoint in his place Mian Dhián Singh, a young Rájput, who was now rising into favour. A fine of fifty thousand rupees was imposed on Khushhál Singh, and Ram Lal, seeing the consequences which his obstinacy had brought on his brother, returned to Láhore and took the *Páhal*, changing his name to Ram Singh. Khushhál Singh had retained all his jágírs, and he was now admitted into the council and put in command of four thousand irregulars, thus obtaining more real power than he had before. Ram Lal was made commandant of Chet Singh's battalions, and Tej Singh appointed general of the irregular forces under Prince Kharak Singh.*

Dhián Singh is appointed chamberlain.

Commotions in Afghanistán, 818.

The peace which followed the capture of Multán was productive of an event which had a material effect on the future fortunes of the ruler of Láhore. A plot was formed against Fatteh Khan, the able Kábul Wazír, whose bravery and political wisdom had raised Shah Mahmud to the Kabul throne. His energy and talents had forced the Sindhians to pay tribute, and he had conquered Káshmír and kept in harmony the discordant clans and turbulent tribes of which the kingdom of the Afghans was composed. Prince Kámrán, son of the imbecile Mahmúd, had become jealous of the unbounded influence which the wazír exercised over his father. A vain conceit had taken deep root in his mind that the experience and ability of the wazír could be dispensed with and the affairs of the kingdom conducted as well without him. The wazír had been sent to Herat to repel an attack of the Persians, and had in his train his brother, Dost Muhammad Khan, and a Sikh chief, Jai Singh Attáríwala, who had left the Panjáb discontented. The wazír vindicated the honour of the Afghan name, and obtained a complete victory over the Persians, who were repulsed with great slaughter. This procured universal applause for the talented wazír, who, however, formed a project to eject Feroz-ud-dín, a prince of the blood-royal, from the government of Herat, and place it under Mahmúd, so that it might be within his own grasp. Dost Muhammed and his Sikh ally, who were employed to despoil the prince governor, however, effected their object in a somewhat coarse manner. Not only was the property of the prince plundered, but the person of a royal lady was touched in the eagerness to possess her jewels. The affront offered to a female member of the Durráni family was made a pretext for revenge, and any attempt at open resistance against the power

* Mr. Murray has given 1817 as the date of this incident, but all accounts agree that Khushhál Singh lost the lucrative office of chamberlain after the capture of Multán in 1818.—Compare *Panjáb Chiefs*, page 31, and the *Memoirs of Moulavi Dín Muhammad.*

of the wazír being thought little likely to be productive of any practicable good; recourse was had to treachery. A grand banquet was given in honour of the wazír by Kámrán, and, in the midst of the festive entertainment, four hundred armed Kards, who had been concealed in a room close by, suddenly rushed out and seized the person of the wazír, who suspected no treachery. The first act of Kámrán was to blind Fatteh Khan with hot irons. His hands and feet were shortly after mutilated, and he was killed with all the tortures peculiar to a barbarous race.

Cruel murder of Wazír Fatteh Khan, 1818.

The murder of Wazír Fatteh Khan created a great sensation throughout the whole country of the Afghans. The wazír belonged to the powerful Barakzai tribe, and had fifty brothers, all governors of territories, or otherwise possessing influence and wealth. They, one and all, raised the standard of revolt, and one cry for vengeance rang through the length and breadth of the kingdom. Mahommed Azím Khan hastened from Káshmír, which he left in charge of a younger brother, Jabbar Khan. He inflicted a signal defeat on Kámrán, and, driving his forces out of Kábul, put Ayúb Shah, son of Tymúr Shah, on the Kábul throne. His original plan was to reinstate Shah Shujá; but, that prince being at the time beyond his reach, Shah Ayúb was proclaimed king. He then reduced Ghazní and Kandahar, so that in a short time only the city and the plains of Herat were left to be governed by the weak Shah Mahmúd and his rash and ill-advised son Kámrán. The rest of Afghanistán was all parcelled out among the members of the extensive Barakzai family, and converted into independent principalities.

Shah Ayúb proclaimed King of Kabul.

The commotions in Afghanistán were favourable to the views of Ranjít Singh, who conceived that the time had come to put his designs on Peshâwar, and the country beyond the Atak into execution, the more so as the Khatak Mahommedans had recently raised the standard of revolt and defeated a detachment of the Sikh troops. The troops were ordered to rendezvous across the Rávi, where the Maharájá encamped for fifteen days, personally supervising the military arrangements, and collecting supplies and war material. When all his arrangements were complete, he marched to Atak in October, sending Báwá Phaddi, his confidential agent, in advance of the troops. The Báwá was murdered by the rebellious Khattaks, to the great grief of the Maharájá, who forded the river on an elephant. A detachment under Phula Singh, Akálí, Mahtáb Singh, Nakheria and Gurmukh Singh, was sent to chastise the Afghans, and an action was fought in which the Afghans were defeated. Firoz Khan and Najib-ullah Khan, the Khatak chiefs, made their submission, and were pardoned, on payment of heavy *nazráná*. Ranjít Singh then reduced Khairábád, on the right bank of the Indus, and captured Jahángira, and the territory on the opposite bank of the river. At Naushera he ascertained from Dewán Sham Singh and others, who had been to Peshâwar, that the Afghans had no organised force with which to oppose him in the field. He then directed an advance on Peshâwar, which city he occupied on 20th November. Yar Muhammad Khan, the Afghan governor of Peshâwar, evacuated the town on the approach of the Sikhs, and fled to the Eusufzai hills. The Maharájá saved the city from pillage, but set the Bálá Hissar on fire, as also the village of Chamkanni, the residence of Sheikh Umar. To Dewán Sham Singh was entrusted the task of collecting *nazránás* from the Arbábs and leading men of Peshâwar, and Rs. 25,000 was realized under this head. The Maharájá stayed at Peshâwar with his army for three days, receiving the respects of the leading men of the tribes, and conferring dresses of honour upon them. On the fourth day he retired, placing his ally Jahándád Khan, Wazír Khel, brother of Ata Muhammad Khan, to whose treachery he owed the posses-

The disturbed state of Afghanistán favourable to the views of the Sikh ruler.

He marches to Peshâwar, 1818.

Garrisons Khairábád.

And occupies Peshâwar, 1818.

The Maharájá makes over Peshâwar to Jahándád Khan, 1818.

sion of Atak, and who had not yet been substantially rewarded for his services, in charge of affairs at Peshäwar. He was, however, left to his own resources and furnished neither with troops nor with money to maintain possession. The Maharájá carried with him fourteen guns, which he had captured at Peshäwar, and with them crossed the Atak, on his way back to his capital. About the same time, Dost Muhammad Khan, Barakzai, brother of Yar Muhammad Khan, sent his agents, Damodar Mal and Hafiz Ruhulla, to the Maharájá, offering to pay a bribe of one lakh of rupees per annum if allowed to retain possession of Peshäwar and its suburbs. The proposal was accepted and the agents were dismissed with *khilats* of honour. Shortly afterwards, however, intelligence was brought to him that the Barakzai Sardars, having come down to the plains with their mountain hosts, had taken possession of Peshäwar, expelling the powerless Jahándád Khan, who had sought refuge at Hasht Nagar. The Maharájá was greatly irritated, and forthwith sent Sardar Dal Singh at the head of 12,000 troops with orders to replace the expelled Governor Jahándád Khan. Dal Singh recrossed the Attak and was followed by Prince Kharak Singh and Mishar Dewán Chand Zafar Jang. The Kábul agents, Mirza Hasan, Háfiz Ruhullah and Damodar Mal, however, arrived, and presented Rs. 50,000 in *hundis*, and a number of horses, with fruits, on behalf of Dost Muhammad Khan. The presents were received, and the Sikh troops which were advancing on Peshäwar, recalled. The Maharájá, after bathing in the spring of Katas, returned to his capital in Pos, or December.

But the territory is eventually occupied by Dost Muhammad Khan, 1818.

Shah Shujá once more tries his fortune beyond the Indus, but fails, 1818.

The state of affairs in Kábul tempted the exiled Shah Shujá once more to try his fortune beyond the Indus. Jahándád Khan, Wazír Khail, having received a free pardon, joined his standard. The Shah, having collected some troops, reached Peshäwar, which he occupied, and was now in advance at Khaibar; but Muhammad Azím Khan, collecting his hillmen, defeated him, and he was compelled to withdraw. He then proceeded to Dera Ghází Khan, and, with the assistance of Nawáb Sadiq Khan, of Baháwalpur, was enabled to enlist a body of soldiers in his service. It having been reported to Ranjít Singh that the Shah was bent on establishing himself at Déera Dín Panáh and had put himself in communication with the Amirs of Sindh, he ordered Dal Singh, Killadar of Makhad, to proceed to Dera Ghází Khan, and expel him from that territory. Before, however, Dal Singh had crossed the Atak, the unfortunate prince made his way to Sindh, and after some fruitless negotiations with the Amirs and other dependants of the Afghan empire, now no longer existing, returned in safety to his old asylum at Ludhiáná, where he had been living with his family since 1812. His ill-starred fate, which had brought so many misfortunes on the Shah himself and on his family, never left him. Whatever enterprise he undertook, whether on the plains, or in the hills, in the distant north, or the far west, seemed destined to fail. He was not destitute of ability, or wanting in vigour, but he lacked that inherent power, that inborn energy, which might have inspired awe, or given confidence to those who rallied round his standard, or were otherwise disposed to embrace his cause. Jahándád Khan, hopeless of favour at the court of the Láhore sovereign, repaired to Herát, there to cast in his lot with the party of Shah Mahmúd.

Expedition to the hill country, 1819.

In February 1819, Desá Singh, Majithia, and Sansár Chand of Katoch were employed in an expedition undertaken to collect tribute from the hill rájás. The rájá of Kalhúr, whose territories extended north and west of the Sutlej, but whose capital, Bilâspur, was on the British side of the river, ventured to resist the demand made. The rájá was a friend of the Gorkhas, the determined enemies of the Katoch chief, who accordingly rejoiced that the opportunity had come to reduce his power. Desá Singh and Sansár Chand crossed the Sutlej and captured the forts of Pichrota, Makálgarh and Binoli Devi, belonging to the rájá, and in a few days expelled him from the whole territory on the right bank of the river. A detachment of troops was sent against Biláspur, and the rájá was reduced to extremities. These proceedings necessitated British intervention, and the Political Agent in the adjoining hills was instructed by the Resident at Delhi to repair to the spot and oppose any further advance of the Sikhs by force of arms. Alarmed at this promptitude, Ranjít Singh ordered the immediate recall of his troops, and even sent Desá Singh to offer his apologies in person to the British Agent. Before raising the blockade, however, Desá Singh succeeded in exacting Rs. 24,000 from the Rájá of Bilúspur. The danger of rupture being over, Ranjít Singh now thought of giving effect to his long-cherished scheme of finally annexing the Káshmír valley to his dominions. A circumstance which highly favoured his views of aggrandisement occurred at this juncture. Bir Dhar, the Minister of Jabbár Khan, the Káshmír Governor, having cause for dissatisfaction with his Afghan master, fled from Káshmír and sought an asylum with the Maharájá, at Láhore. He was a man of considerable influence, which he now used to further the plans of the Maharájá, supplying him with important information as to the strength of the Afghan forces at various points in the country to be invaded. Muhammad Azím Khan, the most energetic of the Barakzai brothers, was at this time absent from Káshmír, furthering his projects in countries remote from the valley, which had been divested of the most efficient of the Afghan troops, and on that account, was not in a position to help the brother whom he had left to govern the country in his absence.

A rupture with the British Government avoided.

Third invasion of Káshmír, 1819.

In the month of April the Sikh army moved from Láhore, under the command of Mishar Dewán Chand Zaffar Jang, the conqueror of Multán. Sardar Fatteh Singh, Ahluwalia, was, during the absence of the Maharájá left in charge of Láhore, and Rájá Sultan Khan, Bhimbar, having been released from a confinement of seven years, his services were placed at the disposal of Dewán Chand. A second division of troops was placed under Prince Kharak Singh, to support the advance column under the Mishar, while the Maharájá, with a third division as a reserve, halted at Wazirábad, to expedite the transit of the munitions of war and personally supervise the prompt despatch of stores and supplies to the seat of war. Experience had taught Ranjít Singh how disastrous it was to attempt an invasion of Káshmír in the cold weather, when snow rendered the passes to the valley impracticable, and he therefore wisely delayed the march until May 1819, when the hot weather had set in. Mishar Dewán Chand, leaving the heavy batteries at Bhimbar, and taking with him only light guns, reached Rájáuri, the rájá of which place, Aiz Khan, violating his oath of perpetual friendship on account of the excesses committed by the Sikh soldiers on his people, broke into rebellion. The Mishar ordered his arrest, and the rájá thereupon fled. His son, Rahimullah Khan, however, joined the Sikhs, and was sent by Dewán Chand to Wazirábad, to the Maharájá, who was pleased to create him rájá in place of his father.

The Sikh army marches from Láhore under the command of Dewán Chand.

The Maharájá himself follows.

The Maharájá, with his camp, moved to Gujrát, and from thence to Bhimbar. Mishar Dewán Chand, taking with him the pick of the Sikh cavalry, which marched over the mountains on foot along with the infantry; soldier reduced Rájáuri, on 23rd June, and entered Bairam Gala. Mir Muhammad Khan, the *thanedar* of Punch, tendered his submission to the dewán, and so did Muhammad Ali, the *thanedar* of Supín. Zabbar Dast Khan, the rájá of Punch, who had fled to his fort of Tari, having closed

Rájáuri reduced.

the gates of that stronghold, refused to attend before the Sikh general and offered resistance. Rájá Sultan Khan, whose knowledge of the country was of great value, was ordered to reduce the fort. The rájá, with the men under him, scaled the rampart, and a fight ensued, in which large numbers of the defenders were killed. Zabbar Dast Khan at length surrendered, and the fort was occupied by the Sikh troops. The governor of Basána was prevailed upon by Rájá Rahimullah Khan to swear allegiance to the Maharájá, and Namdar Khan, an influential zemindar, placed his entire resources at the disposal of the Sikh commander. The passage to the Pir Panjál being thus secured, Mishar Dewán Chand divided the army under him into three divisions, each of which was to reach the valley by a different route. He himself headed the detachment which had to cross the Pir Panjál, and crossing this barrier, descended into the valley. The Pathans opposed this advanced detachment, and an engagement ensued, which lasted the whole day. Many were killed on both sides, till, at length, the Sikhs charging with the bayonet, the Pathans fled in dismay, leaving their camp, which was plundered. On the 16th of June, the whole army of the Sikhs in the valley, 12,000 strong, took up a position at Serai Ali, on the road to Supín. The Maharájá then arrived at Shahábád and saw that his arrangements for supplies and reinforcements were complete. Sardar Jabbar Khan, with 5,000 Afgháns, took his stand on the plains of Supín. The sound of the bugles in the Sikh columns on the morning of the 5th of July was the sign for the Láhore army to advance, and, the Sikhs coming up, a severe fight took place between the two armies. The Afgháns fought splendidly, and succeeded at first in repulsing the invaders and capturing two of their guns. Upon this the Sikhs made a rally, and so desperate was their next onset that the Afghans, after a short struggle, gave way before superior numbers, and fled precipitately to Shergarh, leaving the valley to be occupied by the invaders. Many were killed in the action and in the pursuit which followed; among those killed being Sardar Mihr Dil Khan and Mir Akhor Samad Khan. Sardar Jabbar Khan was wounded, and had a narrow escape. Káshmír was now in possession of the Sikhs, who made a triumphant entry into the city. The following day the troops of the Maharájá occupied Shergarh. Jabbar Khan, with the remnant of his Afgháns, having crossed the mountains towards the Indus, went to Bhimbar, and eventually reached Peshávar. On entering Káshmír, the Sikhs commenced plundering the inhabitants according to their invariable practice, but they were stopped by Mishar Dewán Chand, and the city was thus saved from the rapacity of the invaders. The Sikhs then reduced Azimgarh, a fort difficult of access, from its being situated on the summit of high hills near Rájáuri, and strongly fortified.

The advance of the army into the interior of the valley.

The battle of Supín.

Defeat of the Afgháns.

The Sikhs occupy Káshmír, 1819.

The Maharájá, on receiving the news of the conquest of the important and fertile province of Káshmír, made great rejoicings, and, sending Fakir Aziz-ud-dín to make enquiries about the climate, and Dewán Devi Das to take charge of the assessment and revenues, returned to Láhore. As usual with him on such occasions, the Maharájá spent several days in rejoicings at Láhore in commemoration of the victory won by his troops. The cities of Láhore and Amritsar were illuminated for three nights. The Maharájá visited Amritsar, where he gave his benediction at the Darbár Sahib, and made a large offering of money at the temple. On his return to Láhore, he recalled Mishar Dewán Chand, and sent Dewán Moti Ram, son of the late Dewán Muhkam Chand, as his first governor of Káshmír. Dewán Moti Ram took with him Bir Dhur Pandit, whose intimate knowledge of the financial affairs of the country was of great value in settling it. The farm of Káshmír

Dewán Moti Ram is appointed first governor of Káshmír.

was given to the Pandit for fifty-three lakhs of rupees, and that of the shawl manufacture to Jawahir Mal for ten lakhs.

Settlement of the country about Káshmír, 1819.

The remainder of the year 1819 was occupied in making arrangements consequent on the annexation. The rájás of Punch and Rájáuri having become troublesome, Ram Dayál, the grandson of Dewán Mukham Chand was sent to reduce them to subjection. Zabbar Dast Khan, the Rájá of Punch, sent his son to the Maharájá and accepted the terms offered. Hari Singh, Nalwa, Sardar Dal Singh and Dewán Bháwani Dás, who had been sent to reduce the fort of Darband, in possession of Payenda Khan, and other strongholds in the valley, were successful in the complete subjugation of those places.

A tour in Multán and Báháwalpur.

After celebrating the Dasahra at Láhore, and bathing at the Maghi fair at Amritsar, the Maharájá, towards the close of the year, moved to Multán in person, at the head of an army. The object of this expedition was to ravage the country of the nawáb of Báháwalpur, and exact contributions from the Mirs of Sindh, as far as Sakkar. He first went by road to Pindi Bhattian, *viá* Kot Hassan Khan, and thence by river to Chiniot, after stopping at which place for some days he advanced to Multán. About this time, intelligence was brought to him of two sons having been born to his wives, Ráni Rattan Kour, and Ráni Daya Kour. His sons being born about the time of the conquest of Káshmír and Multán, the Maharájá, in commemoration of these events, gave the son of Rani Daya Kour, the name of Káshmíra Singh, and the son of Rattan Kour, that of Multána Singh. Káshmíra Singh was really the son of a Jammu Rájput, and Daya Kour, seeing how the plot of Ráni Mahtáb Kour, in putting forward Sher Sing, and Tárá Singh as twin sons, had succeeded, followed her example, and procured two boys at different times, giving them out to be her own. These were Káshmíra Singh, and Pishora Singh. They were acknowledged by the Maharájá to be his sons, and received a jágír in Siálkot worth Rs. 50,000.

Birth of Multána Singh, Káshmíra Singh and Pishorá Singh, reputed sons of Ranjít Singh, 1819.

Ráni Rattan Kour, the reputed mother of Multána Singh, was first the wife of Mul Singh of Duburji, then of Sardar Sahib Singh of Gujrát, and lastly of Maharájá Ranjít Singh. She purchased Multána Singh from a Mahomedan slave girl. The Maharájá acknowledged him as his son, and gave him a jágír of Rs. 20,000, in Ajnála, in the Amritsar district. The town of Siálkot, where these boys were represented to have been born, was illuminated in honour of the occasion, and alms were distributed in profusion to the poor.

Sawan Mal appointed head of Account Office, Multán, 1820.

It was during his stay at Multán that, the Maharájá having heard of the excesses committed by Sham Singh, Peshávaria, to whom the farm of that country had been given some time before, for six lakhs and fifty thousand rupees, the sardar was dismissed from his office and put in chains. Sawan Mal, son of Hushnák Rae, a Chopra Khatri of Akálgarh, whose abilities were well-known to the Maharájá, and who had worked with his brother, Nának Chand, under Dal Singh, was appointed head of the Accounts Office, on Rs. 250 a month, under the new governor, Bhái Badan Hazari, who was destitute of abilities and had nothing to recommend him except his sycophancy and servility.

Jamadar Khushhál Singh captures Dera Ghází Khan, 1820.

About this time Jamadar Khushhál Singh seized Dera Ghází Khan, a dependency of Kábul on the west bank of the Indus, expelling the Pathan Governor, Zamán Khan. The Nawáb Rukn-ud-doula, of Báháwalpur, had, two years before, successfully invaded the Durráni chief, and the farm of the newly-acquired district was given to him at a heavy rental.

The Maharájá secures the famous horse *Sufed Pari* from the chief of Mánkera.

Ranjít Singh returned to Láhore on 27th April 1820, after securing the famous horse *Sufed Pari*, or the 'White Fairy,' from Háfiz Ahmad Khan, of Mánkera, who had to part with it under threats of violence from Mishar

Dewán Chand. Ranjít Singh had a passion for possessing any thing noted for its beauty or excellence, and this feeling grew with age to such a degree as to amount almost to a monomania. In this instance, the horse was of a snow-white colour (hence the name), and was noted for its rare beauty and speed.

The Hazárá campaign, 1820.

About this time, intelligence was brought of a rising of the Musalman inhabitants of Hazárá, Pulki, Dhamtor and Tarbela. Bhái Makkhan Singh, who was sent there to restore order, was killed, and Hukma Singh Chimni, the new governor sent from Láhore, had made matters worse. His conduct had thoroughly exasperated the tribes, and the success which they had achieved against the Sikhs at different times had given them confidence. The Maharájá, on hearing this, wrote letters to Sardar Fatteh Singh, Ahluwalia, and Ráni Sadá Kour, asking them to march forthwith, with their respective troops, to the scene of rebellion. Dewán Ram Dayál, General Ilahi Bakhsh, commandant of artillery, Shám Singh, Atáríwala, Gandá Singh, Lammá, Sheva Singh and Ahír Singh were also sent forward, under Prince Sher Singh, who was put in charge of the whole expedition. Fatteh Singh, Ahluwalia, and other sardars of experience adopted moderate measures of punishment in reference to the refractory hill men, and the rising was pretty well suppressed, but Ráni Sadá Kour, coming from Makerian, took the most rigorous steps and determined on extirpating the principal tribes which had rebelled. One of these was the Ratias, who were considered to be the ring-leaders; and hundreds of the people belonging to this tribe were put to the sword by the Sikhs. The excesses committed by the Sikhs at this time were such that even peaceful peasants who had never left their abodes, or changed their ploughs for arms, were killed in cold blood. The hill people and the Afgháns of Miswari, Sri Kot, Tarbela, Eusafzai and Swat, seeing these outrages committed by the Sikhs, formed a grand combination, and mustered in large numbers from all quarters to give them battle and drive them out. Prince Sher Singh ordered General Ilahi Bakhsh to meet the coming storm. The General, with his artillery, engaged the tribes. A smart fight ensued; but the Sikhs were greatly out-numbered, and their columns surrounded on all sides by the hill men, who inflicted heavy losses on them. Dewán Ram Dayál, a dashing youth, seeing General Ilahi Bakhsh in great straits, forthwith went to his aid, with such of the detachments as were at his disposal. He had, however, to contend with enormous odds, and the fight continued with heavy loss on both sides till late in the evening, when the Sikhs, being completely worn out, retired within their entrenchments. Dewán Rám Dayál was the last to leave the field, and the Afgháns, seeing that he was separated from the rest of the army, suddenly fell upon him, in the passes near Gandgarh. The handful of Sikhs with the dewán fought with great valour, but the whole escort was cut off by the assailants, the dewán, it need hardly be said, being among the slain.* The Sikhs, struck with panic at the death of their general, broke up their camp and retreated in all haste from Hazárá. Thus was the career of this most promising of the Sikh generals cut short. His death was a source of deep regret not only to the Maharájá, who had entertained great expectations from him, as the worthy grandson of the illustrious Dewán Mukham Chand, but to the whole Sikh nation. Already the late dewán had distinguished himself in the Káshmír campaign of 1814, and had gained a reputation for ability and bravery as a leader of the

Dewán Ram Dayál killed, 1820.

* Murray makes it appear, at page 125 of his work, that Ram Dayál met his death while employed in petty operations against isolated chiefs of the Káshmír valley. This is not the fact. Ram Dayál was killed in the action against the Mussalmans of Hazárá and the neighbouring country. Compare *Panjab Chiefs*, page 567, with the works of Sohan Lal and Dewán Amar Nath.

Khálsá army, with whom he was extremely popular. His father, Dewán Moti Rám, was greatly afflicted on hearing of his son's death. True is the Persian saying:—

ازین بد چه باشد به عالم دگر
پدر خاک ریزد به گور پسر

"What greater sorrow can there be in the world than that a father should have to throw earth into the grave of his son."

Hari Singh, Nalwa, appointed governor of Kashmír, 1820,

Overwhelmed with sorrow at the untimely death of so promising a son, Moti Ram desired to give up the government of Káshmír and retire to Benares, there to spend the remainder of his life as a devotee. The Mahárájá being unwilling to permit him to retire from public life, he was recalled to Láhore, and a more soldierly chief was sent to Káshmír, in the person of Hari Singh, Nalwa, the most dashing soldier in the Sikh army, now that Ram Dayál was no more. Hari Singh was a Sikh jágírdar who had acquired a great reputation for courage and dexterity, having on one occasion killed a tiger single-handed and on horseback, though at the sacrifice of the horse. Although a good soldier, he proved a failure as an administrator, and ground the people of Káshmír with tyranny. He was therefore recalled after a year, and Moti Ram, who was a man of pacific and devotional habits, was re-appointed governor, and held the office until 1826.

But Moti Ram is again sent there.

The Mahárájá rewards the services of Guláb Singh in Káshmír.

The protracted operations in Hazárá ended with the payment of a *nazráná* by Muhammad Khan, chief of Guldheri, and Sar Buland Khan, zemindar of Tarbela, and the submission of certain other chiefs, after which Prince Sher Singh and the Sikh sardars returned to Láhore. In May, Rájá Aiz Khan, of Rájáuri, who had broken out into rebellion, and had fled on the approach of Mishar Dewán Chand to his territory, was seized and sent a prisoner to Láhore by Guláb Singh, brother of Mian Dhian Singh, the Deorhiwálá, or Lord of the Privy Chamber, of the Láhore Court. About the same time Guláb Singh reported the death, by a cannon shot, of Dedu, the notorious Dográ rebel, in an action which was fought against him. The Mahárájá, pleased with the services of Mian Guláb Singh, granted a jágír to the family in Káshmír, with which they had been long connected. Rájás Rahimullah Khan and Gharibullah Khan, of Rájáuri, obtained a jágír of Rs. 12,000 in Káshmír for their services rendered.

The traveller Moorcroft at Láhore, 1820.

In the same year the able and adventurous traveller, William Moorcroft, a native of Lancashire, visited the Court of Láhore. He was educated at Liverpool for the profession of a surgeon, but had finally settled in London as a practitioner of veterinary surgery, and came out to India as Superintendent of the East India Company's Military stud in Bengal. He had already the reputation of being an enterprising traveller, having five years before penetrated into Central Asia by way of Chinese Tartary. He was the first European who, having crossed the Himálayas, made his way to the great plain between those hills and the Kuenlun chain, the site of the sources of the Indus and Sutlej, and of the two remarkable lakes, Ráwan and Mansarowar. He was now coming from Jawálá Mukhi and Nadaun, on his way to Balkh and Bokhárá, where he was going to purchase horses. He had strenuously urged on the Government the introduction of the Turkomán, in preference to the Arab, horse for the native cavalry of India; and his conviction was that the cavalry horse of this country could be improved only by an infusion of the bone and blood of the Turkomán steed. He had also an idea of establishing commercial intercourse between the Trans-Himálayan Districts and British India. With these

His past travels.

His advanced views.

praiseworthy objects in view, he passed through the capital of the Sikhs, on his way to Ladákh and Yárkand, and he was received with much courtesy and attention at the Láhore Court. The Maharájá conversed with him freely on different topics, and gave him access to any quarter of the town, citadel or suburbs which he might desire to see. At his interview with the Maharájá, Mr. Moorcroft presented him with a pair of double-barreled and a pair of three-barreled pistols, a sword, the model of a cannon, white chauri tails, and bags of musk from the mountains. The Maharájá was much pleased with the pistols, and still more so with the cannon. He had his own horses passed in review before Mr. Moorcroft, who thought some of them splendid animals. Mr. Moorcroft had several interviews with the Maharájá, in all of which the latter conversed freely. The favourite themes were his military and stud arrangements and past exploits. He showed Mr. Moorcroft his two regiments, consisting of Sikhs, Hindostánis and Gorkhas, which he had had drilled after the model of the Company's troops. The Maharájá said they had been trained by a naik, a deserter from the Company's service. Moorcroft describes Ranjít Singh as very communicative. On all occasions he conversed with him, with an apparent absence of all reserve, upon a variety of subjects. Mr. Moorcroft recommended to the Maharájá a fixed scale of duties for British merchandise that came into his territories, but the consideration of the question was adjourned *siné die*. The Maharájá, however, readily consented to his proceeding through Mandi and Kulú to Ladákh, and his passing through Káshmír, and appointed an attendant to accompany him to Kulú. On his departure from Láhore, Mr. Moorcroft was presented with an honorary dress of valuable shawls.

His interview with the Maharájá.

The traveller leaves Láhore.

Mr. Moorcroft in Central Asia.

Mr. Moorcroft descended into the Káshmír valley by the Pir Panjál mountains and visited Kábul and Bokhárá. He remained at Bokhárá nearly five months and effected the purchase of a number of valuable horses. With these he proposed to return to India, and he crossed the Oxus on his way back, about the 4th or 5th August, 1825. He, however, now determined to go to Memana, where he understood he would probably be able to make important additions to his stock of horses. "Before I quit Turkistan," he writes from Bokhárá, "I mean to penetrate into that tract which contains probably the best horses in Asia, but with which all intercourse has been suspended during the last five years. The experiment is full of hazard, but *le jeu vaut bien la chandelle*." The country visited was highly malarious, and, though forewarned of the danger of visiting it in an unhealthy season, he relied too implicitly on his European remedies, and his own medical skill, and his life fell a sacrifice to his zeal. He was taken ill with fever at Audkho and died. Mr. Moorcroft was the bearer of a letter from the Russian Minister, Prince Nesselrode, to Maharájá Ranjít Singh, in which the Emperor of Russia was represented as a benignant sovereign, who sincerely wished other countries prosperity and was particularly the friend and well-wisher of the sovereign who ruled over the Sikhs. The Prince recommended a merchant to the favourable notice of Ranjít Singh, and expressed a desire to establish commercial relations between Russia and the Panjáb, assuring the Maharájá that any merchant from the Panjáb to his own country would be well received. The bearer of this letter, however, died before it could be delivered to the addressee.

His lamented death.

Apa Sahib, the Mahratta chief, at Amritsar, 1820

During the course of the same year, Mundaji Bhuslá, otherwise known as Apa Sahib, whom the bounty of the English had installed at Nagpur, but who was neither a grateful nor a creditable ally, having escaped from the custody of the British authorities, on his way to Allahabád, where he had been sent as a State prisoner, reached Amritsar. He was disguised as a faqír or holy mendicant and stroller; but Ranjít Singh, knowing him to be an irreconciliable foe of his English allies, ordered him to quit his territory. He retired to the hills and sought protection with Rájá Sansar Chand, of Katoch, and while there, entered into some intrigue with Prince Haidar, a son of Shah Zaman, having for its object the subjugation of the whole of India, a scheme in which the prince royal was to be the emperor and the Mahratta his wazír, with the Dekkan under him, as a dependency of the Durráni court at Delhi. The rájá had large sums of money placed at his disposal; but his dreams having been disclosed to the Katoch chief, who was bound to Ranjít Singh, he looked upon the Mahratta as an unwelcome visitor, and expelled him from his territory. Apa Sahib then repaired to Mandi, and received eventual protection, with the cognisance of the British Government, from the rájá of Jodhpur.

Disagreement between the Maharájá and Sadá Kour, his mother-in-law.

After performing his religious duties at the temple of Amritsar, the Maharájá visited Batála, the possession of Ráni Sadá Kour, and pitched his tents near the tank of Shamsher Khan, the Gokul Tash of the great Akhúr. He remained at Batála a month, spending his time apparently in recreation and pastimes, but in reality devising plans to deprive his mother-in-law of her extensive possessions and seize upon them himself. Sher Singh, the reputed son of Mahtáb Kour, daughter of Sadá Kour, had now reached manhood and was clamouring for a separate jágír and establishment, in order to maintain his position as the son of the Maharájá. After the Hazárá campaign, in which Sher Singh held the supreme command, Ranjít Singh not only recognised the claims advanced by the young prince, but encouraged him to press them, hoping this would induce Sadá Kour to assign a suitable jágír for her grandson from the possessions of the Kanhia *misl* under her control. Sadá Kour, on the contrary, wished to force on her son-in-law the recognition of Sher Singh, and to make him provide an estate for the prince independently of her own. Ranjít Singh, whose ulterior object was the usurpation of all the territories that once belonged to the powerful Kanhia confederacy, obstinately refused this proposal, and insisted on the setting aside of a jágír for the young man in the way proposed by himself. The wily Sikh ruler, in the prosecution of his object, fomented an estrangement between Sher Singh and his reputed mother; and his intrigues, in which he was much assisted by the tale-bearings of one Gáme Khan Khansáma, led also to a dispute between Sadá Kour and Bysakha Singh, an old and trusted servant of Jey Singh, Kanhia, who was in great favour with that lady. Seeing his designs so far matured, he thought the time had come to attain his object by force, and, in October 1820, he sent an order calling on Sadá Kour to set apart half of her own estates for the maintenance of the two princes, Sher Singh and Tárá Singh. That spirited lady remonstrated against the order, and threatened to cross the Sutlej and put the estate of Wadhni under British protection. On hearing this, Ranjít Singh wrote conciliatory letters to her, and desired an interview, with every profession of humility as a son-in-law. Thus petted and coaxed, Sadá Kour joined Ranjít Singh in his camp at Shahdára. Here she was compelled to execute a deed, agreeing to make the assignment required for the princes, and was removed to the fort. She, however, soon after plotted to effect her escape, and, coming out of the fort one evening, on the pretext of paying her respects at the shrine of Gúrú Arjan, at the western gate, fled in the direction of her territory in a closed carriage. Ranjít Singh, being informed of this, sent Prince Kharak Singh in pursuit, and she was captured on her way to Mukerian. She was now kept in close confinement in the palace, and Mishar Dewán Chand Zaffar Jang was sent to seize all her territory,

The lady is put in confinement.

Her possessions are captured.

and confiscate her valuables and other property. The Mishar first captured Batála and then Pathánkot, the ráni's troops stationed in these places offering no opposition. He next went to Mukerian, then called Atálgarh, the head-quarters of the ráni's dominions, and the repository of the wealth and riches belonging to the Kanhia *misl;* but a slave girl of the ráni, in possession of the fort, offered a determined resistance. All the attempts of the Sikh troops to reduce the fort having failed, Mishar Zaffar Jang had recourse to artifice. He asked Sadá Kour, who had been sent with him, a close prisoner, to affix her seal to a document permitting the killadar to surrender the fort, and, on her refusal to do so, ordered her food to be stopped. For two days the ráni suffered absolute deprivation with great firmness, but on the third day she assented to the fixing of the seal on the document, and, this being done, the ráni's troops retired from the fort. Immense property, including shawls, jewels and military stores, the hoardings of the Kanhia *misl,* fell into the hands of the Sikh general, and was brought to Láhore, where it became the property of the State. After these acts of resumption, the ráni was re-conveyed, under military escort, to Láhore, where she remained a close prisoner till her death. Thus fell, after having figured prominently in Panjáb politics for about thirty years, the high-spirited Sadá Kour, one of the most remarkable women in the history of the Panjáb. She had been the mainstay of Ranjít Singh's power, the ladder whereby that monarch had been enabled to reach the summit of his greatness. She was the companion of his toils, and to her energy, intrigues and influence he chiefly owed his success in his early exploits. She maintained an unbending disposition to the last, and her ruin was brought about by the course of events, not less than by the high tone she was in the habit of assuming and the independence of character she asserted, both of which the Sikh monarch had become incapable of tolerating by the growth of his power. She bore the calamity of her confinement with great restlessness and impatience, upbraiding and execrating her ungrateful son-in-law, beating her breast with vehemence, and renewing her curses and lamentations every day. The authority of the captive widow was maintained at Wadhni, south of the Sutlej, where she was regarded by the British agents as the representative of the interests of the Kanhia confederacy on their side of the river and legitimately entitled, so far, to the protection of the English. This was, however, not done until it was resolved to eject Ranjít Singh from Wadhni by force, and a detachment of troops had marched from Ludhiáná to restore the widow to the authority of the place. Batála was given as a jágir to Sher Singh, and the rest of the Kanhia possessions, including the territory adjoining the hills, were put in charge of Sardar Desa Singh, Majithia.

The part she played in the political history of the Panjab.

After the Dasahra, the Maharájá proceeded to Siálkot, where, in October 1820, a review of the Sikh army was held. The Nikka territory and Kalanaur, the jágírs of Prince Kharak Singh, were given in farm, the former for Rs. 85,000 to Dewán Sukh Dayál, and the latter to Moulavi Nazhar Hussain, of Hindostán. The Maharájá then, crossing the Chináb and skirting the hills, reached the Chub Bhao territory, the tribes of which had become turbulent. Dewa Batála, the seat of the rebellion, and many other villages were burnt, and severe chastisement was inflicted on the refractory tribes. Having next crossed the Jhelum, Ranjít Singh proceeded to Ráwalpindi, expelling the chief, Nand Singh, and annexing that place to his own dominions. Nának Chand Daftri was put in charge of the newly-annexed territory, and the Maharájá returned to Láhore on the 13th of December.

Ráwalpindi captured, 1820.

Birth of Nau Nehal Singh, 1820.

Phagun (February) 1821, witnessed the birth of a son to the heir-apparent Kharak Singh, by his wife Chand Kour, the daughter of Sardar

Jaimal Singh, Kanhia, of Fatehgarh, near Gurdaspur. The boy, after consultation with the astrologers, was named Nau Nihál Singh. The birth of a grandson to the Maharájá was the occasion of great rejoicings and festivities in the court of Láhore. The following chronology, giving the Samvat era of the birth of the prince, was composed by Dewán Amar Nath :—

چون عقل کل آن نہال دانش
درگلشن آفرینش آمد
تاریخ ولا دتش بجستم
گلدستۂ باغ دانش آمد

"When that sapling of complete wisdom made his advent into the garden of the world, I looked for the date of his birth and found it in the expression,* 'Nosegay of the garden of wisdom.'"

The Sikh troops about this time seized the territories of Kishtwar and Mánkot, which were annexed to the Láhore kingdom. *Kishtwar and Mánkot seized, 1820.*

After the Dasahra the Sikh army was ordered to rendezvous at Amritsar, and the Maharájá, taking the command in person, marched to the Indus, with the object of finally reducing the countries south of Multán. The resources of Hafiz Ahmad Khan, the nawáb of Mánkera, had been annually drained by extortions and forced contributions, as well as by the ravage and waste of his country, so that Ranjít Singh had hoped that his territory would fall an easy conquest. Having crossed the Indus at Mitha Tiwána, he was joined by Sardar Hari Singh, Nalwa, and sent Mishar Dewán Chand and Kirpa Rám, who had joined him at Khusháb, to reduce the Bhakkar fort and town. Sayád Imám Shah and Hákam Shah, agents of the Nawáb of Mankera, fled from Bhakkar on the approach of the Sikh troops, and the place was reduced without resistance. From this place Sardar Dal Singh and Jamadar Khushál Singh were sent, with a detachment of 8,000 troops, to reduce Dera Ismail Khan. Manak Rae, the Nawáb's governor at Dera Ismail Khan, offered resistance; the city was besieged by the Sikh troops, and, the governor having been seized, the Nawáb's forces dispersed. The whole of the property and war munitions belonging to the Nawáb fell into the hands of the Sikhs. Khangarh, Leia and Manjgarh were next successively reduced without opposition, and the whole Sikh army then marched to Mánkera. The Nawáb, having paid the arrears due to his troops, made preparations for a determined resistance. The city of Mánkera was surrounded with a mud wall, and the fort was of brick; but the invading army had to struggle against natural difficulties. The citadel and the town were situated in the midst of sandy deserts and on a cluster of sandhills. The entire absence of waterworks and wells in the country invaded, reduced the Sikh army to great straits. A detachment was advanced to invest the stronghold, and the place was blockaded. A supply of water was brought for the besieging army on the backs of camels, bullocks, horses and ponies from Manjgarh and other places, by land, at great trouble and expense. The Maharájá had heavy guns with him, and with these a continual fire was maintained against the besieged. But the Mánkerian troops had effectively secured every gateway and bastion, and provided the rampart with means of defence. They poured a hot fire of musketry and cannon on the besiegers, who had carried their works close to the ditch. In the meanwhile the followers of the Sikh

March of the Láhore army to the countries south of Multán, 1821.

The town and fort of Bhakkar reduced.

Dera Ismail Khan conquered;

Also Khangarh, Leia and Manjgarh.

The seige of Mánkera.

* In Arabic and Persian every letter of the alphabet has a numerical value, and the values of the letters of an expression or sentence added together give the date.

army, under the personal supervision of the indefatigable Maharájá, had succeeded in digging twenty wells in their camp, and a supply of fresh water was now at hand, to the great relief of the invading army. A further division now moved forward to complete the investment, Ranjít Singh himself superintending the conduct of the whole. The siege lasted for twenty-two days, during which the Nawáb held his own. But desertions now commenced on his side, and some of his principal sardars, having secretly come out of the fort, joined Ranjít Singh, and pointed out the spots at which an attack could be successfully made. The dispositions for the attack were accordingly changed; but the Nawáb, seeing treachery on all sides and conceiving that he had done enough to preserve the honour of his ancestors, sent his agents, Kazi Gul Muhammad and *Ali Jah* Sikandar Khan, to Ranjít Singh, to propose terms of capitulation. These were that the Nawab should be allowed a safe conduct from the citadel to his camp, bringing with him the whole of his family, men, arms and property, and that he should be allowed to retain possession of Dera Ismail Khan, and receive a suitable jágír. The Maharájá agreed to these terms. The Nawáb had studied well the Sikh character, and knew the Sikh ruler's ideas of good faith. He therefore wanted him to put the impression of his hand, with the fingers extended, on a blank piece of paper, with saffron, as a solemn pledge for the due execution of the agreement; and Ranjít Singh, anxious to give a new example of the *Khalsá* faith, no less than to close a costly campaign in a country so ill-provided with the means of prosecuting it, went through the formality. Rich dresses were sent to the Nawáb, who, his suspicions having been thus allayed, surrendered the fort, and came out with 300 followers, bringing with him all his property and arms. His camp was pitched within the lines of the Sikhs, and he had an interview with the Maharájá on the 20th. The Maharaja half stood up to receive him, and was seated close to him on the same masnad. The Nawáb implored his conqueror to save the city from plunder, and to provide his troops, who had proved faithful to him, with suitable employment. Both these requests were granted by the Maharájá, who, as a further proof of his friendship for the Nawáb, discarded those who had joined him as deserters from their now-vanquished sovereign. The Nawáb made over twenty-two guns, with a large quantity of ammunition, to the Maharájá, and, with the whole of his harem, family and attendants, was sent to Dera Ismail Khan under a sufficient escort. The country of Nawáb Háfiz Ahmad Khan, annexed by the Maharájá, was worth annually ten lakhs of rupees, and its acquisition was the source of intense pleasure to Ranjít Singh, who ordered the towns of Láhore and Amritsar to be illuminated in honour of the occasion. Sardar Amir Singh Sindhianwalia was appointed governor of Máukera, while Bhakkar and Leia were farmed to Ráj Kour, Khatri. The Bilúch Mahomedan chiefs of Tank and Ságar having been then reduced to subjection, the Sikh army marched to Dáera Din Panáh. From this place the army was sent by land to Multán, the Maharájá himself embarking on the Indus for Dera Ghází Khan. Here five lakhs of rupees were exacted from the Baháwalpur Nawáb, under pain of an invasion of his territory, and the rent of Dera Ghází Khan and Mithankot, held in farm by him, was increased. Joining then his army at Multán, the Maharájá returned to his capital on the 27thof January 1822.

The Nawáb surrenders, 1821.

Arrangements for the government of the conquered country.

Expeditions to Nárá and Sarae Saleh, 1822.

On his arrival at Láhore, the Maharájá heard of the murder of Sardar Amar Singh, Majithia, by the zemindars of Nárá, and the flight of Sardar Jai Singh, Attariwálá, one of his principal sardars, to Afghanistán, and he thereupon sent Mishar Dewán Chand to punish the Nárá zemindars, and Dewán Kirpá Ram to restore order at Sarae Saleh, the chief of which place, Sardar

Payenda Khan, had become troublesome. Pakhli and Dhandor in Káshmír were bestowed as a jágír on the gallant Hari Singh, *Nalwa*, in recognition of his services in that country.

Arrival of Monsieur Ventura and Allard at Láhore, 1822.

In March 1822, two European adventurers, Monsieur Ventura, an Italian by birth, and an infantry colonel in the French service, and Monsieur Allard, a Frenchman, who held a similar rank in the cavalry, arrived at the Court of Láhore, in search of military employment. The fall of Napoleon Bonaparte had inflicted a death-blow on the military aspirations of the youths of France, and these officers, after in vain seeking honourable employment in Persia, came overland to Láhore, through Kandahar and Kábul. They came dressed like Mussalmans of Persia, and met with a friendly and honourable reception, but the suspicious chief was at first unable to understand what could have induced the young men to leave their country and undertake so long a journey. They explained their views in Persian, but, this failing to satisfy the Sikh ruler, he asked them to explain them in their own language, and, this having been done, he sent the paper written by them in French, to the British Agent at Ludhiáná, to be translated into the vernacular. All his suspicions were allayed, on seeing the translation, and he employed them to organise his army on the French system as to drill and manœuvres. The tomb of Anarkhali was given to them for a residence, and high salaries were fixed for them. In a short time both these officers, by their ability and energy, won the Maharájá's entire confidence, and raised new regiments of dragoons, which they disciplined and drilled after the manner of European cavalry. They built a large house outside the town of Láhore, near Wazír Khan's garden, and laid out beautiful bazars. Four years afterwards they were joined by Monsieur Court (who had received his training at the Polytechnic Institution at Paris, and was at one time Aide-de-camp to Marshal Bessieres in Spain) and Monsieur Avitabile. Both these officers were made generals in the Sikh army, and Court brought the Sikh artillery and musketry to great perfection. The Sikhs have a spirit of adaptation, and, under European discipline and drill, the excellence of their character and the hardihood of their disposition developed. The drilling of his troops after the European fashion had been an object of the greatest desire with Ranjít Singh, ever since the first impression he had received of the excellence of European discipline in 1809, at Amritsar, where, as previously mentioned, a handful of Mr. Metcalfe's Hindostáni escort had beaten back a crowd of Akális. This, his favourite project, had been more or less perfectly carried out since, Ranjít Singh never having lost an opportunity of utilising the services of ex-naiks and deserting sepoys and native officers of the Company's service. It was not without considerable difficulty that Ranjít Singh induced his men to give up their customary weapons and order of battle. To encourage them to resign their old mode of warfare, he gave them good pay and rations. He paid personal attention to their drill and equipment and was the first to break through prejudice by himself wearing the strange dress, and going through movements and military exercises after the European fashion. With the aid of these officers, the Maharájá was soon enabled to form a tolerably well-disciplined army of 50,000 men, besides 100,000 regular troops, and cannon foundries, powder magazines and manufactories of small arms were established in Láhore and Amritsar.

They are employed to instruct troops in the European method of exercise.

MM. Court and Avitabile are made generals of the Sikh army.

Strange conditions with the European officers in the employ of the Maharájá.

Ranjít Singh wanted the Europeans who entered his service to engage not to eat beef, not to shave their beards and not to smoke tobacco. On their agreeing to the first two conditions, the third was dispensed with. Ventura and Allard disciplined the Maharájá's regular cavalry; General

Avitabile drilled his infantry, while General Court put his artillery into order. Their pay ranged from Rs. 2,000 to Rs. 3,000 a month each, besides a princely recompense in lands and money. Their sphere of action was extensive, and they enjoyed the confidence of the Maharájá, though they were never consulted in affairs of state, or in matters relating to the Court.

Muhammad Azím Khan threatens Khairábád,

Towards the beginning of April, Muhammad Azím Khan, who had succeeded to the authority of his brother Fatteh Khan, moved to Peshávar, accompanied by the fugitive Jágírdar Jai Singh, Attariwálá. His object was to keep Ranjít Singh on the left bank of the Indus, and he even threatened Khairábád, the principal station held by the Sikhs on the opposite bank. The Maharájá sent Mishar Dewán Chand to watch the movements of the Afgháns, and he was shortly after reinforced by detachments under General Ilahi Bakhsh and by Dhankal Singh's battalions. Several skirmishes took place between the Afgháns and the Sikhs, and these proceedings brought the Maharájá himself westward; but affairs at home compelled Muhammad Azím Khan to retreat, and the Maharájá, after visiting Akhnúr in the Jammú hills, returned to his capital in June.

But retires to Kábul 1822.

Golâb Singh is created rájá of Jammú, 1822.

Kassúr Singh, the father of Dhian Singh, Lord of the Privy Chamber, having died in the hills, the Maharájá sent for his eldest son, Guláb Singh, and created him rájá of Jammú in place of his deceased father. In the meantime the tribes of Pakhli and Dhamtor rebelled, and Sardar Hari Singh, Nalwa, to whom these places had been given in jágír, was sent at the head of the troops to punish the offenders. Hari Singh spread havoc in the invaded country, and put the population of the disaffected villages to the sword. Pakhli and Dhamtor were burnt, and thousands of people rendered homeless. After these acts of wanton barbarity, Hari Singh returned to Láhore.

Proceedings of Hari Singh, *Nalwa*, in Phakli and Dhamtor.

Muster of the Sikh army at Rohtas, 1823.

After the Dasahra, or in October 1823, a muster of the Sikh army took place at Rohtas. Ranjít Singh, on this occasion, took particular care to see that the jágírdars were present, with their contingents, and visited with severity any one who had failed to present himself in time with his quota of troops, or who had neglected to equip his men properly. Among those guilty of such negligence was Dal Singh Naherna, a jágírdar who had served with honour on previous occasions. Ranjít Singh gave him a severe reprimand and threatened him with a heavy fine, on which the old sardar, retiring to his bed at night, took a dose of poison and died. In December the Sikh army moved to Ráwalpindi, whence Fakir Aziz-ud-dín was sent to Peshávar to exact tribute from the Barakzai Governor, Yar Muhammad Khan. The sardar, being unprepared to resist the demand, sent a present of valuable horses to the Maharájá, and, this having satisfied him, Aziz-ud-dín was recalled. The Maharájá having then made a pilgrimage to Katás, returned to Láhore in January 1824.

Nazráná levied from the Barakzai sardars in charge of Peshávar, 1823.

Muhammad Azím Khan disapproves of this, and repairs to Peshávar, 1823.

Muhammad Azím Khan, who was in power in Kábul, did not approve of the action of his brother of Peshávar, and marched for Jallálábád, to take into his own hands the management of affairs beyond the Khaiber. He reached Peshávar on the 27th of January, and Yar Muhammed Khan, suspecting his designs, fled to the Eusafzai hills. The Maharájá, having heard of this movement, sent Prince Sher Singh, at the head of a detachment of cavalry, and the prince was followed by Dewán Kárpá Ram, Hari Singh, Nalwa, and Sardars Atar Singh and Dhannu Singh. The Sikh troops, having crossed the Atak, laid siege to the fort of Jahángira, which, after some loss on both sides, was occupied by the Sikhs, the Afghans retreating precipitately to the hills. The defeat sustained by the Afghans had only the effect of doubling their zeal. They collected in large numbers on the Teri hills, 18 *kos* to the west of Atak, and were joined by the Jehadis, or religious warriors, from Swat, Buner, and the country of the Afridis, and the Khattaks. Muhammed Azím Khan was still in Peshâwar, and had issued proclamations calling on all the faithful to draw the sword for the faith. The Maharájá, having heard of this grand combination, mustered his army at Shahdára across the Rávi, and, sending Prince Kharak Singh, and Mishar Dewán Chand forward, followed at the head of his troops. Muhammad Azím Khan, had now reached Naushera, between Peshâwar, and Atak, while the Afghans under Dost Muhammad Khan and Jabbar Khan, brother of Azím Khan, prepared to meet the Sikhs. The Maharájá at the head of 15,000 horsemen, forded the river on the 13th of March. The guns were carried across on elephants. The stream ran deep in some places, and the rash attempt to ford it, which was prompted by the exigency of the moment, resulted in no trifling loss to the Maharájá, as no fewer than a thousand men were drowned, among them being Moulavi Mazhar Husain, Hindostáni, who had obtained the farm of Kalanaur. On the fourth day Sardar Desa Singh, Majithia, Sardar Fatteh Singh, Ahluwalia, Amir Singh, Surianwálá, Rattan Singh, Ghirjagia, Dúlá Singh, Malwai, Sadá Singh, Nodh, and Sadá Singh, Naherna, crossed the river at *guzar* Ghaziwálá, at the head of a force, with some loss. The whole army entered Akhora, where Ranjít Singh was joined by Jai Sing, Atariwálá, who showed himself anxious for pardon, and was re-admitted into favour. Twenty thousand mountaineers of the Khatak and Eusafzai tribes, all volunteers in a holy war, and brought together by the influence of their *pirzádas*, or priests and devotees, assembled on the left bank of the river to fight for their faith against the infidel invaders, while Azím Khan, with the regular Afghan army, was encamped on the right bank. The Maharájá sent eight battalions and two batteries, under Generals Allard and Ventura, to keep Muhammed Azím Khan, in check, and with his main strength, fell upon the Ghâzis, who had taken up their position around the heights near Naushera, on the left bank of the river. A strong detachment of the Sikh forces was posted behind the Teri hills, on which the mountain levies had collected, and this was to move to the rear at a moment's notice. The Sikh forces, under Sat Gur Sahae, and Colonel Mahá Singh, Akália, made an advance on the hills, and were met by a body of Afghans under Muhammed Zaman Khan, nephew of Azím Khan, and Sadiq Khan, son of the deceased Firoz Khan of Khatak.* The latter made a furious assault in overwhelming numbers; and the fire of their matchlocks, coupled with a shower of stones from the hills, which they covered, resulted in much loss to the advancing Sikh columns. In the midst of this struggle, an Afghan, approaching Sat Gur Sahae, shot him in the head, killing him on the spot. Another Afghan mortally wounded Mahá Singh. A large number of Sikhs fell, and the Afghans compelled their assailants to retreat down hill. Upon this Phula Singh the Akáli desperado, made a furious charge with some horsemen as fanatical as himself. But the Mussalman infantry were equally fired with religious zeal and fervour, and were, moreover, advantageously posted. They rushed upon their assailants with such determination and fury, that the latter were completely routed and their leader slain. Thus fell this wild Akáli leader, who had obtained so much celebrity in the Sikh battles by his fanatical and sudden attacks at times when recourse to regular warfare had proved ineffectual.* Exultant at the success of the charge, the Afghans fell upon the

The battle of Naushera, March 1823.

Phula Singh, Akáli, killed in the battle.

* The Khatak territory was occupied by the Sikhs during the course of this campaign.

flying Sikh columns, and executed fierce vengeance on them. Ranjít Singh, with his reserve, now led the attack in person, and a promiscuous fire was opened on the enemy by his rallying battalions, as well as by the artillery, which had been drawn up in line opposite to them. The Ghâzis, though unprovided with supplies or provisions, and even defrauded of their promised pay, met the assault with extreme bravery and repulsed every attack until sunset, by which time about half their original number had perished. Ranjít Singh now brought forward his Najib and Gorkha battalions in support of the advanced columns, and placed a strong detachment at the base, with orders to shoot instantly any soldier of the Láhore army who should be found turning his back on the scene of action. At the same time orders were given to the troops posted on the other side of the hills, to advance to the rear and charge and dislodge the enemy from their position in that direction.

The position of the Gházis, who were ignorant of the art of war, was thus surrounded, and they found themselves between two fires. Sword in hand, they fell upon the Sikh artillery and engaged in a hand-to-hand fight. But by this time a great number of them had fallen, and the Sikhs dislodged them from their positions. The remnant of the Pathans cut their way through the enemy to the mountains in the darkness of night, but not before they had inflicted severe loss on the disciplined and professional soldiers of the *Khálsá* army. There fell in this battle, on the side of the Sikhs many brave men, among whom were Gharba Singh, Manas, Karm Singh, Cháhal, and Balab Dhar Singh a Gorkha General. The last-named officer had served the Nepal Government with great distinction in the war with the English, led by Generals Gillespie and Martindell, but, having in time of peace enticed away a married woman, he had fled from his native country, and found employment under Ranjít Singh in the Panjáb, where he died an honourable death. The Sikhs had in this battle not less than 24,000 fighting men present, and the loss on their side in killed and wounded was estimated by Captain Wade at 2,000. The number of Afghans killed exceeded 3,000. Notwithstanding their defeat with great slaughter, the brave and resolute mountaineers re-assembled the following day to renew the contest, under their leader Pirzáda Muhammad Akbar; but Muhammad Azím Khan, fearing lest his treasures and harem at Minchini which were a constant source of solicitude to him, might fall into the hands of the invaders, broke up his camp, and the Ghâzís, being without countenance or support, reluctantly dispersed. The Barakzai Sardar, when he heard of the discomfiture of his militia, was greatly distressed. He wept

Defeat of the Afghâns.

Casualties on both sides.

---

*The famous Phula Singh, erst an outlaw, and, already referred to in the preceding pages, was an Akáli, or Sikh of the ascetic class, and, as such, exercised great influence over his countrymen. He headed the Akális of the Amritsar temple, who attacked Mr. Metcalfe's party in 1809, and also Captain White, who was employed in surveying the Patiálá boundary line in the same year. In 1814 he espoused the cause of Partáb Singh, the rebel prince of the Jhind State, and, taking up his position in Nandpur Makhowál, defied the whole power of the *Khálsá* to expel him. The English pursued him from place to place, and the Maharájá tried for years to seize him, but he could not be captured. On the rebellion of Prince Partáb Singh, the Maharájá sent stringent orders for his troops at Phillour to drive the outlaw out of his territory. The troops marched against him as ordered, but when they approached, Phula Singh asked them whether it behoved the followers of the *Sat* Gúrú (true leader) to kill a Gúrú. The garrison would not offer violence to him, treating him as a wandering faqír. The whole force followed him for some two months to prevent his devastating the country, marching where he marched, thus serving more as a guard-of-honour than anything else. He was a remarkable man, and, though a robber and an outlaw, he was nevertheless a splendid soldier, and a brave and enthusiastic man. (*Pánjab Rájás*, page 350.) In 1820, he told Mr. Moorcroft at Amritsar that he was dissatisfied with Ranjít Singh, and expressed his readiness to join the English, carrying fire and sword wherever he should be desired. That distinguished traveller declined to listen to him, and recommended him to entertain more prudent and loyal purposes.—*Travels* I, 110.

and tore his beard, and inveighed vehemently against the treason of his brethren, who had brought so dire a calamity upon him. Generals Allard and Ventura were followed to Chan Káva, the camp of Muhammad Azím Khan, opposite the bank of the river, by Prince Sher Singh, Dewán Kirpa Ram and Hari Singh, Nalwa. Azím Khan, hastily collecting the wreck of his forces, and picking up his harem and wealth at Michini, crossed the Momand hills with precipitate haste, and regained the valley of Jallálábád, leaving the field clear for the Sikh monarch and his army. The following day the Maharájá proceeded against the fort of Hashtnagar and occupied it. Ranjít Singh made his entry into Peshávar on the 17th of March, and his Sikhs plundered the whole country up to the Khaibar Pass, though the town of Peshávar was saved from pillage. The feeling of the entire Mussalman population was intensely roused against their infidel invaders, and the united bands of these zealots cut off all the stragglers of the Sikh army, whose camp had to be watched continually every night to guard it against their predatory excursions. Ranjít Singh, finding that public feeling throughout the country was bitterly against him, did not think it prudent to retain it. He privately sent for Yar Muhammad Khan and Dost Muhammad Khan, who repaired to the Sikh camp from Dháka, bringing with them five horses, including the far-famed Gauhar Bár (or Shower of Pearls), which, by its exquisite beauty and smartness, particularly pleased the Sikh monarch. He rewarded their treason to their brother and their services to himself by wisely allowing them to retain Peshávar as tributary to the Láhore Darbár. He, however, took care so to divide the territory between the brothers that Dost Muhammad Khan was placed in an antagonistic position to Yar Muhammad and his brothers, the object of the wily chief being to create an occasion for future dissensions and strife among the brothers, which should place him in a position to support one party or the other, as policy might dictate. After effecting these arrangements, the Maharájá returned to his capital, on the 26th of April.

Flight of Muhammad Azím Khan.

The Maharájá's triumphant entry into Peshávar.

He leaves Peshávar as a dependency with Yar Muhammad Khan and Dost Muhammad Khan, 1823.

Muhammed Azím Khan died shortly afterwards, of dysentery. He died broken-hearted, and with his death was dissolved the union of the brothers who had governed the three provinces of Kábul, Kandahar and Peshawar. After the death of his famous brother, Wazir Fatteh Khan, Muhammed Azím Khan was looked upon as the head of the family. He had a reputation for indomitable personal courage and lavish generosity. He was munificent and dignified, fond of show and pleasure, but not at the expense of public business. He fell a sacrifice to the treason of his brothers. His death renewed the dissensions and quarrels among his numerous brothers and nephews, who acknowledged nobody as their head.

Death of Muhammad Azím Khan, 1823.

The return of the Maharájá to Láhore, after the victory won by him at Peshávar, was an occasion of great rejoicing. The towns of Láhore and Amritsar were illuminated and several days were spent in merry-making. It having been now resolved to enclose the town of Amritsar with a wall of masonry, the work was entrusted to the sardars, who each had a portion allotted them to build. The work was carried on with great vigour, Sardar Fatteh Singh, Ahluwalia, sending a thousand masons from his territory, and Dal Singh, Desa Singh, and other jágírdars, each furnishing their quota of men and materials from their respective jágírs. The Maharájá then proceeded to Dinanagar, and thence to Sujanpur, where he received the respects of the rájá of Bassoli in the hills, and collected three lakhs of rupees from the hills rájás, as *nazráná*. The Dasahra was celebrated at Láhore in October, and towards the end of the year the Maharájá marched to the Indus, to reduce the refractory Mahomedan jágírdars.

Rejoicings at Láhore.

Building of the city walls of Amritsar, 1823.

He visited Khushab, Lakki, Sanghar, Leia, Kachi and Dera Ghází Khan, levying tribute and *naeránás* from the Bíluchis and other jágírdars. He took a south-westerly direction, his object in this being to make an impression on the Amírs of Sindh, and to usurp Sikarpur, but his plans were not yet matured, and in the course of December he returned with his army to Láhore.

Foreign and protected princes.

Prince Ibrahim, son of Tymur Shah of Kábul, having come to Láhore, was honourably received, tents being pitched for his reception close to the mausoleum of Ganj Baksh. The guard placed over Nawábs Sarfaraz Khan and Zulfikar Khan of Multán was removed, and they were permitted to move about at pleasure.

Death of Rámá Nand of Amritsar, and Sansar Chand of Katoch, 1824.

Two persons of note died during the course of this year, the first being Rámá Nand, the great banker of Amritsar, who left eight lakhs of rupees, which was seized, and with which the wall of the city of Láhore was built, and the other, the famous Sansar Chand of Katoch, whose power was once a source of dread to the Maharájá himself. The Maharájá was, at the time, at Adinanagar, and a demand for two lakhs of rupees was made from his son, Anrodh Chand, as *nazráná*, on his accession to his father's *gadi*. The young chief demurred, on which Fakir Aziz-ud-din was sent to Nadaun, at the head of a regiment of cavalry, to take proceedings against him. Anrodh Chand, becoming alarmed, accompanied the faqír to Jawálá Mukhi, where the Court then was, and, one lakh having been paid, the rest was remitted and his succession recognised.

Anrodh Chand succeeds his father at Katoch.

Death of Mishar Dewán Chand, 1824.

At the close of this year Mishar Dewán Chand died of paralysis at Láhore, much to the grief of the Maharájá. The whole darbár joined in the funeral procession, and the remains of the Dewán were burnt with sandal-wood fire. The Maharájá, through Rájás Dhian Singh and Guláb Singh and Mihan Singh, commandant, sent for the deceased a shroud of brocade and rich shawls, together with Rs. 2,000 for distribution to the poor. Dewán Chand was the conqueror of Multán, Káshmír, Mánkera, and many other places, and had served the Láhore ruler ably and faithfully. He was possessed of military talents, and the Maharájá had the greatest confidence in his judgment, skill and energy. The Mishar was highly popular with the army, and his death was a source of deep regret, not only to the Maharájá, but to the whole Sikh nation. Sukh Dayál, his brother, was appointed dewán in place of the deceased.

Dewán Moti Ram and his sons Shiv Dáyál and Kirpa Ram, 1825.

In the winter of 1824-25, no military enterprise was undertaken. As already stated, Moti Ram, son of Mohkam Chand, was appointed governor of Káshmír in place of Sardar Hari Singh, Nalwa, whose tyranny had passed all endurance. Moti Ram was a man of peaceful habits, and, though liked by the people, was indolent and apathetic. While he was in Káshmír, his son, Kirpa Ram, was in charge of the Jalandar Doáb, and Shiv Dáyál, another son, managed the family jágírs in the Gujrát District. Rájá Dhian Singh, who was now rising into favour, was jealous of the power and wealth which the family enjoyed, and, on his representation, the Maharájá granted the Sikh fort and estate near Phillour, formerly the jágír of Mohkam Chand, to Ram Singh, the Rájá's brother-in-law, to whom the ex-rájá of Siba had now promised his daughter. Kirpa Ram was so much incensed at this treatment that, in defiance of the Maharájá's orders to bring with him his whole contingent on the occasion of the late Darband and Gandgarh expedition, he appeared with only fifty horsemen. Ranjít Singh was furious; he imprisoned Kirpa Ram and re-called his father, Moti Ram, from Káshmír. A fine of Rs. 70,000 was inflicted on Moti Ram. Bhima Singh, commandant, was at first sent as governor; but he was soon after superseded by Gurmukh Singh and Dewán Chuni Lal, to whom Káshmír was farmed for Rs. 27,50,000. Shiv Dáyál was also removed from office, and the fort of Phillour was made over to Fakir Aziz-ud-dín, and then to Sardar Desa Singh, Majithia.* The appointment of Gurmukh Singh and Chuni Lal proved a failure, as they were unable to remit the stipulated revenue; and, after a year and a half, the family of Mohkam Chand having again been taken into favour, Kirpa Ram was sent as governor of Káshmír. Kirpa Ram was a man of considerable ability. He possessed an affable and gentle disposition, and was fond of show, and the administration of the valley improved during his tenure of office. He laid out the gardens of Rám Bágh in Srinagar, where the monument of Rájá Guláb Singh now stands.

The marriage of General Ventura, 1825.

In the course of this year, General Ventura was married to a European lady at Ludhiáná. The nuptials took place at Láhore, according to the French form, the Maharájá presenting the bridegroom with ten thousand, and his courtiers and Omerahs with thirty thousand, rupees, as *tambol*.

After the Dasahra the Maharájá marched with his army on an expedition to Sindh, and the camp advanced as far as Pind Dádan Khan; but, it having been brought to his knowledge that the country was suffering from scarcity, he abandoned the project, and retraced his steps to Láhore, where he arrived on the 24th of November.

Ill-feeling between the Maharájá and Sardar Fatteh Singh, Ahlúwalia, 1825.

In December, 1825, Sardar Fatteh Singh, Ahlúwalia, the old ally and turban brother of Ranjít Singh, suspecting treachery at his hands, left Kapúrthalla, and fled to Jagráon, across the Sutlej, with the whole of his family. He became alarmed at the advance of two battalions of the Láhore army towards his territory, and had recently been constrained by his associate in arms to leave a masonry citadel unfinished. Choudhri Kadir Baksh, his agent in attendance at the darbár, sent him very unfavourable accounts of the views and policy of the Maharájá, and it is said he was also under the influence of his dewán, named Sher Ali, a Moghal of Jalandar.† But the sardar had personally studied the character of his old ally, and, however ill-founded or exaggerated his suspicions, none knew better than himself what little weight solemn declarations of perpetual friendship had with his "turban brother" when his own interests were concerned. He had witnessed the fate of the Ramgarhia chief, with whom the Maharájá had sworn eternal friendship, and he was not forgetful of the likelihood of his being similarly treated himself. How much afraid the chief was of his old associate will appear from the fact that, as early as 1811, he had desired the British authorities to acknowledge him as a chief separately connected with the English. On the present occasion his object was to obtain a guarantee from the British Government for the security of his territories north of the Sutlej. This was refused to him, on the ground that, under the treaty of 1809, the British Government had no excuse for interfering with the Maharájá's affairs on that side of the river, nor, indeed, were the entire Cis-Sutlej territories under the protection of that Government at this time. Jagráon, where the chief had sought refuge,

He asks British interference, which is refused.

---

* Prinsep, in his "*Origin of the Sikh Power in the Panjáb*" mentions, at page 143, that consequent upon this sequestration, Moti Ram was subjected to no indignity or diminution of favour, and that he was left in his government of Káshmír. This was not the case. Moti Ram was recalled from his government of Káshmír and the whole family fell into displeasure. Compare *Panjáb Chiefs*, p. 588, and Kanhia Lal's *Panjáb History*, p. 312 and Dewan Amar Nath's *History* (manuscript).

† Kadir Baksh sent sealed letters to his master, imputing bad motives towards the person of the sardar on the part of the Maharájá, and these letters were much coloured by Sher Ali, the sardar's dewán. Kadir Baksh was a crafty man, and escaped the vengeance of the Láhore ruler, though Sher Ali was put to such straits, that he died soon after the visit of the Maharájá to Kapurthalla.—Dewan Amar Nath's *History* (manuscript), page 80.

was, with Naraingarh, and the neighbouring villages, given by the Maharájá to Fatteh Singh, as a grant, on payment of a *nazráná*, and in respect of both these estates the supremacy of the Láhore darbár was acknowledged by the British Government. He was, however, assured of British protection in his ancestral estates in Sirhind, on the British side of the Sutlej. But the British authorities, while acknowledging his possessions, or those of his ancestors, held on the left bank of the Sutlej previously to his alliance with the Láhore Maharájá, and recognising even those acquisitions on the same bank of the river which were made at a time when the conquests of the sardar and Ranjít Singh were portioned on a footing of equality, advised the chief not to be influenced by vague suspicions, but to stand by the friendship which had so long subsisted between him and the Láhore ruler. Ranjít Singh, on the other hand, unwilling to permit his old ally to slip into the hands of the British, earnestly endeavoured to allay his fears. Faqír Aziz-ud-dín, under the orders of the Maharájá, occupied all the Trans-Sutlej possessions of the Ahlúwalia chief, and even expelled his garrison. The Ahlúwalia Katra, or quarter, at Amritsar was also seized and occupied by the Maharájá's men; but he expressed a great desire for a reconciliation, and promised to give every assurance for the security of the sardar's person and possessions, should he return to his capital. Báwá Atar Singh, Sodhi, was selected to conduct negotiations, and he went to Jagráon, with Dewán Saudagar Mal, and Amír Chand, vakil, to induce the fugitive sardar to return. Fatteh Singh, though he little believed in the professions and assurances of his old ally, thought it politic to return to his territory, which he did in 1827. Immediately on his return, all his possessions were restored, and he was honourably received at the darbár the same year. On appearing before the Maharájá, Sardar Fatteh Singh, having unsheathed his sword, laid it before His Highness with tears in his eyes. The Maharájá embraced him, and, having spoken to him kindly, returned his sword to its scabbard with his own hands, and dismissed him with a *khilat* of honour, consisting of an elephant with a silver howdah, a necklace of pearls, and some jewels and pieces of costly cloth. The suspicions of the Ahlúwalia chief having been thus allayed, Faqír Nur-ud-dín was sent to Kapúrthalla to withdraw the Maharájá's officials, and replace those of the sardar. As future events showed, the fears of the Ahlúwalia Sardar were much exaggerated, he being one of the few men for whom the Maharájá entertained any sincere feeling of regard.

The sardar is advised to stick to his alliance with the Maharájá.

Confidence between the two chiefs restored.

Cordial relations between the Maharájá and Sangat Singh of Jhind, 1826.

In the early part of 1826, the Court was visited by Rájá Sangat Singh of Jhind. The Maharájá sent some of his sardars to meet the rájá at Amritsar, and they conducted him with all honour to Láhore, where he was received with distinction by the Maharájá. Tents and shamianas were pitched for him on the plain of the Masti Gate, opposite the palace, and all necessaries were provided for him and his retainers at the expense of the State. He was present at the Holi festival, and the Maharájá made his officers pay *nazárs* to his guest. At the desire of the Maharájá, who seems to have contracted a great liking for Sangat Singh, the chief consented to go with him to Jawálá Mukhi, and waited at Dinanagar for the Maharájá's return. The Maharájá went to Hoshiarpur, and from thence to Una, where he had an interview with Sahib Singh, Bedi, and presented him with a *nazráná* of five thousand rupees. Nadaun was then visited, and Anrodh Chand, son of the deceased Sansar Chand, having paid his respects to the Maharájá, offered a number of fine horses as *nazráná*. The Maharájá then visited Jawálá Mukhi, where he offered a *chattar*, or canopy of gold, and evinced some interest in making enquiries about the visit of the Emperor

A tour in the hills of Kangrá, 1826.

Jahángír to the hills, and saw the places visited by the Moghal Emperor. At Kangrá, having alighted in the Srinagar gardens, he determined on the conquest of Tárágarh, a fortress deemed impregnable, on the snowy ranges adjoining Núrpur and Chambá; but Wazír Nathu, having, on the part of the Rájá, paid a *nazráná* of Rs. 25,000, the idea was abandoned. Jamadar Khushhál Singh, Dewán Kirpa Ram and Sardar Lahná Singh were now sent with troops to reduce the fort of Kotler, and the Maharájá returned to Adínanagar, having given orders for the Rájás of Bassoli and Jasrota to co-operate with Khushhál Singh in his expedition against Kotler. Kotler was a strong fort, and from its position well adapted to resist artillery fire or assault. Sardar Dhanná Singh, Malwái, was also sent to join Jamadar Khushhál Singh with a detachment of troops. After all the troops had collected, the fort was blockaded, and the stream of water which flowed into it, having its source in the hills beyond, was stopped. The supply of water being thus cut off, the besieged garrison were put to great straits, and, after several days' attempts to repulse the invading army, capitulated. The fort was occupied by the Sikhs, and the killádár put in confinement by Jamadar Khushhál Singh; but he was afterwards released at the intercession of the Sodhi of Kartárpur. The whole territory of Kotler was annexed to the *Khálsá*, and a jágír of Rs. 12,000 per annum allotted to the ex-Rájá Shamsher Singh, for his maintenance. Intelligence was received from Kanwar Kharak Singh from Kálá Bágh that the tribes of Bannú had been all reduced and a *nazráná* levied from them. The operations in Bannú having been brought to a close, the prince was directed to return to Láhore. Generals Ventura and Allard represented to the Maharájá that a number of Sikh sardars and soldiers had refused to serve under them, and were ready to oppose their authority with drawn swords. The reason for this refractory conduct on the part of the troops was their aversion to serving under foreigners. The Maharájá, at the head of a body of troops and with some guns, came out of the city to Anarkali, and ordered his tents to be pitched there. Many arrests were made, officers degraded, and the ringleaders fined. These prompt measures restored order among the troops, the Maharájá taking the utmost precaution to allay unfounded fears.

The expedition to Kotler, 1826.

The fort of Kotler is reduced, 1826.

Insubordination to French officers punished.

In the course of this year, Dewán Gangá Ram died. He was a man of considerable ability, and the administration of the country about Gujrát was entrusted to him in 1821, and was held by him for two years. He first organised the Abkári system, and made great improvements in the system of military accounts. He was succeeded as keeper of the seal, and in the account office of the Military Department, by Pandit, afterwards Rájá, Díná Náth.

Death of Dewán Gangá Ram, 1826.

He is succeeded by Pandit Díná Náth.

Intelligence having been brought of an insurrection raised by the zemindárs of Gandgarh, who had put in confinement Abbás Khan, Khatak, the Maharájá's kiláldár and agent at that place, Sardar Hari Singh, Nalwa, and General Ventura were sent with a force in that direction. A fight took place near Gandgarh, in which several hundreds of zemindárs were killed and the rest fled. The leaders of the revolt at length made their submission and released Abbás Khan, Khatak. Hari Singh and the French General next went to Srikot, the fort of which is situated on the summit of the hills in the vicinity of Pukli and Dhamtor. The Sikhs laid siege to the fort, and the Patháns offered a vigorous resistance. The siege lasted fifteen days, at the end of which time the Patháns, who had gallantly defended this strong citadel, were compelled to surrender, and the fort was occupied by the Sikhs. The Maharájá was much pleased to hear of the capture of Srikot, and directed the French General and Hari Singh to proceed to Pesháwar and demand tribute from Yár Muhammad Khan. Reinforcements were sent from Láhore, under Prince Sher Singh; and Mishar Sukh

The fight at Gandgarh, 1826.

Capture of Srikot, 1826.

Dayál, Mazhár Ali, Imám Shah and Sheo Parshád, artillery officers, were also sent. The Sikh troops crossed the Attak, but Yár Muhammad Khan, against whose sincerity suspicions were entertained, sent his agents to Prince Sher Singh with *hundís* for a lakh of rupees, and the Sikh troops withdrew.

Arrangements with the heirs of several deceased chiefs, 1826.

Several persons of note died during the course of this year. Sadiq Muhammad Khan, Nawáb of Báháwalpur, surnamed Rukn-ud-doula, died in April 1826, and was succeeded by his son, Rahím Yár Khan, under the title of Muhammad Baháwal Khan. The leases and engagements held by his father for the territory west and north of the Sutlej were renewed with the new nawáb, who paid Rs. 25,000 as *nazráná* on his accession. Háfiz Ahmad Khan, late Nawáb of Mánkeria and jágírdar of Dera Ismail Khan, also died. Shah Nawáz Khan, his son, assumed the jágírs in place of the deceased nawáb. The Court was now at Garhigalla, on the bank of the Chináb. At this place orders were issued to Kanwar Kharak Singh, who was at Pind Dádan Khan, to proceed with his troops to Dera Ismail Khan, and levy Rs. 25,000 from Shah Nawáz Khan, as *nazráná*, on his accession to his father's jágírs. The Maharájá returned to Láhore, and the prince, having levied the *nazráná* ordered, proceeded to Bannú. Rájá Zalim Sen, of Mandi, also died, and was succeeded by his nephew, Bír Sen, a natural son of Rájá Isri Sen. Rájá Suchet Singh was ordered to Mandi, to place the new rájá on the *gadi* and levy Rs. 50,000 from him as *nazráná*.

Bír Singh, ex-Rájá of Núrpur.

Bír Singh, the ex-Rájá of Núrpur, who had been expelled in 1816, made an attempt to recover his lost territory. Collecting a large body of hill-men, he assaulted the fort, but was defeated by Sardar Desá Singh, Majithia, and fled. He concealed himself in the garb of a faqír in a dharmsálá, but was arrested by Desá Singh and sent a prisoner to Láhore. In September, Qutb-ud-dín Khan, of Kasúr, fled across the Sutlej to seek British protection, on the ground of his holding Mamdot and Rumnawálá on the left bank of the Sutlej, but he was told that his feudatory relations were with the Láhore Government, and this forbade the British authorities to recognise him as an independent chief.

Qutb-ud-dín Khan, of Kasúr.

Ill-health of the Maharájá.

Towards the close of the year the Maharájá became ill, owing to excessive toil and his habits of intemperance. He was treated by Hakíms Azíz-ud-dín and Ináyat Shah; but his ailment increased, and, for several days, he was unable to transact the affairs of his Court. He applied to the British authorities for a European medical officer, and Doctor Andrew Murray, a surgeon in the British Indian army, was sent over from Ludhiáná to attend him. He was received at the Shalámár gardens by Fakír Azíz-ud-dín and Dewán Moti Ram, and on the first day of his arrival at Láhore the Maharájá presented him with Rs. 1,000 in cash, and a number of trays of fruits and sweetmeats, bottles of rose-water and *bédmushk*, as a *ziyáfat*. This officer was at the Court of Láhore for several days, receiving an allowance of one hundred rupees per diem; but the Maharájá trusted more to his own physicians, and the English doctor was kept more as an object of curiosity than anything else. Ranjít Singh seemed to take a great interest in the transactions of his powerful neighbours and allies, the English. He wished to know the precise object of the visit of Lord Amherst, the then Governor-General, to the northern provinces; he enquired how the Burmese soldiers had fought in the late war with the English, and what amount of money had been demanded by the victorious British Government from the defeated king; he asked inquisitively about the nature of the mutiny of the sepoys at Barakpur, and inquired with what success native troops had been employed in quelling the disturbance. On the Maharájá's recovery the Holi festival was celebrated at Láhore with great rejoicings.

He is attended by Doctor Murray, an English Surgeon, 1826.

CHAPTER III.

FROM THE RISE OF SYAD AHMAD, THE GHÁZI, TO THE CLOSE OF THE KÁBUL WAR, AND THE END OF THE MAHARÁJÁ'S LIFE, 1827-1839.

In the early part of 1827 a Mahomedan fanatic, named Syad Ahmad, having set himself up as a reformer, raised the green standard of the Prophet in the Eusafzai hills, between Peshâwar and Attak, and declared a religious war against the Sikhs. He belonged to a family of Syads in Bareli, in Upper India, and commenced life as a petty officer of horse in the service of the great mercenary leader, Amír Khan. After the termination of the war against the joint power of the Maharattas and Pindaris, resulting in the destruction of the military power of that chief by the British, and his recognition as an independent prince, the Syad, severing his connection with Amír Khan, took a fanatical turn, and, pretending to have received special revelations from heaven, went to Dehli. Here he associated with Moulvís Abdul Hai, Muhammad Ismail and Abdul Azíz, preachers of great sanctity in the city, in whom he found zealous supporters of the doctrines propounded by him. These were, strict obedience to the precepts of the *Qurán*, the recognition of nothing not inculcated by the word of God as contained in the *Qurán*, the recognition of the sayings of the saints as the mere outcome of pious men, without giving them undue importance, the abolition of corrupt forms of worship, including bowing before tombs of saints and paying benedictions to their memory, the celebration of the death of Husan and Husein during the month of Moharram, and a variety of other customs and usages which were denounced by the reformer as idolatrous. In 1822 he visited Calcutta, and the force of his eloquence, coupled with his religious fervour, and the sanctity attached to his declared mission, gained for him a large number of followers from among the Mahomedan population. He sailed for Mecca and Medina on a pilgrimage, and is believed also to have visited Constantinople. On his way back, he travelled through India, preaching his new doctrines, and returned to Delhi after an absence of four years. Here he was joined by his devoted followers, Moulvís Abdul Hai and Ismail, and a work known as "*Takviat ul Islám*," or "The Basis of the Faith of Islám," was published, setting forth the views of the reformer. In this large city numerous congregations flocked around the new saint, and he now declared his resolution to devote himself to the cause of his religion. He called upon the faithful to join him in a holy war against the infidel Sikhs, who, he said, had committed countless outrages on the followers of the Prophet, and must be extirpated. He was careful to avoid complications with the British authorities; and although funds were raised in aid of his declared designs in all parts of the British territories, he gave no cause of offence to the officers of that Government. He left Delhi with about 500 followers in 1826, and it was arranged that this band of zealots and fanatics should be followed by other bands, led by fixed leaders. He first repaired to Tonk, the chief town of his old master, Amír Khan, who being dead, the saint enlisted his son, the ruling nawáb, among the followers of the

The origin of Syad Ahmad.

He sets himself up as a reformer.

His doctrines.

He visits Calcutta.

Sails for Mecca and Medina.

Travels through India.

Returns to Delhi.

Calls upon his followers to join him in a holy war against the Sikhs.

Leaves Delhi, 1826.

reformed faith. The youthful disciple rendered his spiritual leader substantial aid in money, and, thus strengthened, he made his way, first to Shikárpur and then to Khairpur, through the deserts of Sindh. Here Mír Rustam Khan gave him an honourable reception, and, having been joined by the rest of the Gházis who were following him, he proceeded to Kandahár. His apostolic mission made little impression on the mind of the Barakzai sardars in possession of that country, and he therefore travelled northward, through the Ghilzai country, in search of better material to work upon. Having crossed the Kábul river in the beginning of 1827, he reached Punjtar, in the Eusafzai hills, and raised the green standard of the Prophet among the warlike Mussalmán population of the hills, with the object of waging a perpetual holy war against their persecutors, the Sikh infidels. The Eusafzais were at this juncture apprehensive of the designs of Yár Muhammad Khan, Barakzai, who had gone over to the side of their great enemy, Maharájá Ranjít Singh, and the Syad and his host of Gházis, or fighters for the faith, were hailed as deliverers, and Ahmad was acknowledged as the leader of the faithful.

His journey through the deserts of Sindh to Kandahár.

Repairs to the Eusafzai hills, where he declares a religious war against the Sikhs, 1827.

Ranjít Singh having heard of the organization of this formidable insurrection on the immediate border of his territory, sent a large force across the Attak to protect Khairábád and his interests in the adjoining country. A detachment of the Sikhs, under Sardars Budh Singh, Attar Singh and Lahná Singh, Sindhianwáliás, moved forward to Akora, a few miles above Attak, where they threw up works to strengthen their position. The Syad, at the head of a numerous, but ill-equipped host, attacked this force. The Sikh commanders fought from their entrenched positions, and by their superior discipline and equipment, were enabled to repel the assault of the tumultuous mountaineers, who lost several hundred in killed and wounded. The Syad, being completely defeated, retired with his hill rabble to the mountains, whence a desultory warfare was kept up against small bands of the Sikhs and their convoys, much to the annoyance of the latter.

The Maharájá sends an army against the Syad,

Who is defeated by the Sikhs at Akora, 1827.

It was about this time that Ranjít Singh became anxious to possess the famous horse Laili, which surpassed in beauty and excellence the renounded Gouharbar, which the Maharájá had already secured from the Barakzai family. This was the horse which Fatteh Ali Shah, Kachár, King of Persia, was most anxious to possess, and his offer of Rs. 50,000 in cash and a jágír worth Rs. 25,000 had been declined by the owner, Sardar Yár Muhammad Khan. Negotiations were opened with Sardar Yár Muhammad Khan for its surrender, but it was declared that the horse was dead. The wily chief discredited the report, and the declaration of the Afgháns having been subsequently proved to be false, the agents of the Maharájá extorted a written engagement from Yar Muhammad Khan, agreeing to deliver the horse. Prince Sher Singh and General Ventura were sent soon after to Pesháwar, at the head of a body of troops, to enforce the execution of the deed and secure the animal. Dewán Dhanpat Rai, the agent of Prince Kharak Singh, without orders, committed ravages on Pesháwar and seized some important places in the neighbourhood. Prince Sher Singh was highly incensed at the rashness of the dewán and remonstrated with him for this action on his part. The dewán, depending upon the superior position of his master, showed some disrespect to Sher Singh, upon which he was seized and flogged severely. All his tents and property were plundered, and he was sent a prisoner to Láhore. The Maharájá was so much displeased with him that he dealt him several blows on the face with his own hand, and sentenced him to a mulct of twenty thousand rupees.

Ranjit Singh desires to secure the famous horse "Laili,"

And sends an expedition to Pesháwar with that object, 1827.

Ravages committed by Dewán Dhanpat Rai on Pesháwar.

The Dewán's punishment.

At this time the fame of the Mahomedan reformer, Syad Ahmad, as a

The fame of Syad Ahmad

warrior in the name of God, was in the ascendant in the frontier mountain tracts, and his strength had considerably increased. Yár Muhammad, seeing the growing influence of the Syad, and the general attitude of the powerful Eusafzai tribe against him, thought it prudent to enter into an engagement with the heads of that tribe to respect their territories.

Yár Muhammad forms a coalition with the Eusafzais.

In the course of 1827, Dewán Moti Ram and Fakír Azíz-ud-dín were sent to Simla on a complimentary mission to the then Governor-General, Lord Amherst, who was staying there for the hot weather. A variety of valuable presents, such as horses, elephants and pashmíná, were sent on this occasion for the Governor-General, and a handsome tent of shawl, manufactured at Káshmír, for the King of England. The mission was received with honour, Captain Wade, the Governor-General's Agent at Ludhiáná, through whom the transactions between the Láhore Darbár and the Government of India were conducted, being specially appointed to look after the comfort of the members of the embassy. Shortly afterwards, some officers of the Governor-General's staff, accompanied by the Governor-General's Agent at Ludhiáná, were deputed by his Lordship, with a suitable retinue, as a return compliment, with nice presents. The Court was then at Amritsar. Prince Sher Singh and Fakír Azíz-ud-dín were sent to receive the mission at a distance of five *kos*, and on arrival at Amritsar, on 31st May, Rs. 5,000 in cash, 500 gold mohurs and 200 trays of fruits and sweetmeats, were sent as a *ziyáfat*. The next day the Maharájá had an interview with the distinguished members of the mission in the Rám Bágh. On this occasion all the troops of the Maharájá wore yellow (*Basanti*) uniform, and presented a picturesque appearance. Gifts sent by the Governor-General were presented to the Maharájá, who was much pleased with them. They comprised two fine horses, one elephant, with a silver *howdáh*, a sword set with diamonds, a gun, a revolver, two pearl necklaces, and a variety of pashmíná and kimkháb cloths. A sum of rupees 1,100 was given to the bearers of these presents. The next day a review of the Sikh troops was held, and the honourable guests were shown over the city and the Golden Temple by Rájá Dhián Singh. They beheld, with much interest, the Akálís of the Akál Bunga, who were not now as averse to the sight of the foreigners as they had been at the time of the visit of Mr. Metcalfe, 18 years before. The party returned to British territory much pleased with the reception accorded to them, Prince Sher Singh accompanying it to Jandiálá and Fakír Imám-ud-dín to Ludhiáná. The following year a vakíl was sent by the Maharájá to Simla, to offer a welcome to Lord Combermere, the British Commander-in-Chief.

Complimentary mission to the Governor-General at Simla, 1827.

British mission sent to Amritsar.

A review of Sikh troops.

Láhore was visited this year by a cholera epidemic, which carried off a large number of the inhabitants, among them being Sardar Budh Singh, Sindhanwáliá, who had recently fought so bravely against the Eusafzai Patháns. The Maharájá showed much concern for the sardar's health, and, hearing of his indisposition, sent immediately Hakíms Azíz-ud-dín, Hakam Rai and Jawadgír to attend him; but the patient died, much to the alarm of the Maharájá, who went to live at Shahderá, across the Rávi, during the days of the pestilence, leaving the city to be ravaged by the disease. Káshmír was about the same time visited by repeated shocks of earthquake, resulting in much damage to life and property. It is said that thousands of people were rendered homeless and thousands lost their lives.*

Cholera at Láhore and earthquakes in Káshmír, 1827.

The objects of special favour on the part of the Maharájá at the Láhore Darbár, at this time, were Mián Dhián Singh and his brothers Guláb Singh and Suchet Singh, who claimed descent from Ranjít Deo. Guláb Singh,

Mián Dhián Singh and his brothers Guláb Singh and Suchet Singh.

* According to Dewán Amar Nath, 1,48,000 people died of the pestilence.

the eldest brother, first entered as a horseman (*ghor-charah*) in the Sikh cavalry, under Jamadar Khushhál Singh. He sent for Dhián Singh, his younger brother, from Jammú, and both, having attracted the attention of Ranjít Singh, obtained employment as running footmen under the Maharájá's eye. It was little known at the time that these footmen were destined, at no distant date, to become the lords of the hills, and that their power would be supreme in the vast kingdom established by the warlike talents of Ranjít Singh. Dhián Singh was soon created Master of the Entry, superseding the Brahmin chamberlain Khushhál Singh, who, however, retained his jágírs and estates, while Gúláb Singh distinguished himself by quelling disturbances raised by Mahomedan petty chiefs in the neighbourhood of Jammú and Káshmír. His services were rewarded by the bestowal of Jammú on him as a jágír, and thus he continued his influence and power among the Rájputs of the hills, using his Sikh name for purposes of his own. Dhián Singh attached himself to the Maharájá's person, while Suchet Singh became a gay and polished courtier and a brave soldier, indifferent to affairs of State. The brothers were truly the architects of their own glory. They were, one after another, raised to the dignity of rájá. Dhián Singh was this year created wazír with the title of *Rájá-i-Rájgán Rájá Hindpat Rájá Bahádur*. The Maharájá was dotingly fond of the boy Hirá Singh, who was about twelve years of age, and the son of Dhián Singh. He was, in common with his father and uncles, created a rájá, and had the privilege of sitting before the Maharájá on a chair, while all others stood or sat on the floor. The Maharájá seldom suffered him to go out of his sight, and delighted in humorous conversation with him. Anrodh Chand, son of Sansár Chand, of Katoch, was present at Láhore, with his two beautiful sisters, on his way to join the nuptial ceremonies of the son of Fatteh Singh, Ahluwáliá, which took place about this time. The family of the Katoch Rájá held a high place among the hill chiefs on account of the antiquity of its genealogy, and Dhián Singh, seeing the rájá within his grasp, sought a matrimonial alliance between one of his sisters and his son, Hirá Singh. The pride of the hill chief was roused, for he thought the proposed marriage tie with the Jammú hillmen a degradation to himself. Pandits Mahdá Sudan and Ram Kishen, who held a high position in the Darbár, were selected to open negotiations with the hill chief, and the influence of the Maharájá eventually obtained a written engagement from Anrodh Chand, agreeing to the proposed marriage. The mother of the young women, more indignant than her son, contrived to make her escape with her daughters beyond the Sutlej, where she would be secure from the grasp of the Láhore ruler and his favourite Dográ ministers. Dilbágh Rai, the agent of Dhián Singh, and Gahi Khan, were sent to Anrodh Chand to remind him of the solemn pledge given by him by the impression of his hand with the fingers stretched, which he had made on a blank sheet of paper with saffron, to execute the agreement already made, and calling upon him to procure the return of his sisters. He, however, fled to the south of the Sutlej, leaving his estates and jágírs at the mercy of the Sikh rulers. In vain did he ask for British interference; for that Government had been always averse to meddling in the affairs of the Sikhs on this side of the Sutlej. The widow of Sansár Chand, proud of her high family descent, but bowed down with grief and sorrow, died, and her humbled son followed her to the grave with a broken heart. On hearing of Anrodh Chand's death, the Maharájá left Phagwárá for Nadaun, with the object of sequestrating the deceased chief's principality. At Nadaun he was joined by Radár Chand, the son of Fatteh Chand, the brother of Anrodh Chand.

Gúláb Singh and Dhián Singh are appointed running footmen to the Maharájá.

The rapid rise of the brothers.

Dhián Singh is created *Rájá-i-Rájgán*, 1828.

The boy Hirá Singh, son of Dhian Singh.

His privileges in the Darbár.

The Maharájá's attachment to him.

Proposed affiance of Hirá Singh with the family of Sansár Chand, 1828.

The negotiations.

Flight of Sansár Chand's widow south of the Sutlej.

British interference refused.

Death of the widow and her son.

The Maharájá proceeds to Nadoun and confiscates the estates of the deceased, 1828.

The forts of Tirah, Riah and Palhiar were reduced, and vacated by the late Rájá's troops, on a promise of their being given their arrears of pay, which had largely increased. Nigahia, killádár of Palhiar, was restored to his post. Fatteh Chand, his son Radar Chand, and nephews Dil Thamman, Devi Chand and Malak Chand, each obtained a suitable jágír. After these arrangements, the Maharájá proceeded to Jawálá Mukhi, to pay his adorations to the natural flames so sacred to the Hindus. Disappointed at the high tone and spirit shown by the legitimate heirs of the late Rájá Sansár Chand, even when reduced to extremities, Ranjít gratified his ambition by himself marrying two of the daughters of Sansár Chand, by a woman named Gadin, who was carried away from the hills with several children she had borne to the Rájá.* A son named Jodh Bír Chand, by this Gadin, was elevated to the rank of rájá, and given a valuable jágír out of his father's principality. The marriage of Hirá Singh was celebrated at Láhore in 1829, with great pomp, with a maiden of equal degree, and was attended by a large number of the Sikh chiefs, the members of the offended Kangrá family making themselves conspicuous by their absence.

He himself marries Sansár Chand's two daughters, though by a different wife.

The marriage of Hirá Singh, 1829.

In the year 1828 the Maharájá went to Siálkot to punish certain insurgent zemindárs. Sardar Attar Singh, Nakeria, was sent to Sanghar to make a demand for certain horses from Assad Khan, the governor of that place, who was reported to possess some beautiful animals. Attar Singh, Basáwá Singh, and Lahná Singh, Sindhianwáliás, having failed to remit the stipulated *nazráná* imposed up on them as the condition for retaining the late Sardar Budh Singh's jágírs, orders were passed for the sequestration of their estates.

Sequestration of Sindhianwálá estates, 1828.

In the course of 1829 an attempt was made to remove Syad Ahmad by poison, and the governor of Pesháwar, being suspected of the offence, the Syad again appeared in the field with his mountain hosts. An action was fought between the Pesháwar troops, under Yár Muhammad Khan and the Gházis under the Syad, in which the former were completely vanquished and their leader mortally wounded. Pesháwar was saved to the Barakzai family by the opportune presence there of Prince Sher Singh and General Ventura, with a small escort, which had gone to fetch the famous horse Laili, under the agreement for its surrender which had been made by Yár Muhammad Khan. The horse was secured, and the succession of Sultán Muhammad Khan, brother of Yár Muhammad Khan, to the governorship of Pesháwar having been recognized, the Sikh troops withdrew to the Indus. The fame of Syad Ahmad reached Káshmír, and the Mussalmán population between that valley and the Indus being unwilling subjects of the Láhore Darbár, the enterprizing Syad thought it a good opportunity to extend his influence in those quarters. Accordingly, he crossed the Attak, in June 1830; but his progress was frustrated by the Sikh troops under General Allard and Hari Singh, Nalwa. The Gházis under the Syad were routed, and the reformer was compelled to retire to the west of the Indus. After a few months, the Syad again made a descent into the plains of Pesháwar in great strength. Sultán Muhammad Khan moved out, with such troops as he could collect, to defend Pesháwar. An action was fought, in which the Barakzai sardar was defeated, his troops dispersed, and Pesháwar occupied

Syad Ahmad defeats Yár Muhammad, who dies of his wounds, 1829.

Ranjít Singh secures the famous horse "Laili," 1829.

Sultán Muhammad Khan succeeds as Governor of Pesháwar.

Syad Ahmad crosses the Indus, 1830,

But his progress is checked and he is compelled to fall back to the west of the river.

* One of these girls was intended for Rájá Dhián Singh's son, but Ranjít Singh, having been struck with the exquisite beauty of the sisters, married both of them himself. Their mother insisted on the Maharájá's going through all the nuptial ceremonies, such as the wearing of garlands on the head, the putting on of the bridal chaplet, &c. The gay Maharájá went through all these formalities with much pleasure.

The Syad defeats Sultán Muhammad and occupies Peshávar, 1830.

by Syad Ahmad and his host of Gházis. The power of the Syad was now at its height. Elated with success, and the sanctity of his declared mission, the destruction of the infidel Sikhs, he assumed the title of Khalif, and is believedto have struck coins in his name, bearing the inscription:—"Ahmad the Just, Defender of the Faith, the glitter of whose sword scattereth destruction among infidels."

The Maharájá marches from Láhore to take the field against the Syad.

The news of the fall of Peshávar and the destruction of the Barakzai troops by a fanatic chief was received with alarm at Láhore, and the Maharájá was induced to take the field in person in order to chastise the pretender. The Sikhs crossed the Attak, and appeared on the plains of Peshávar; but the Syad, on their approach, again fled to the hills, and the rebel forces, which had occupied Peshávar and the adjacent places, fled in all directions. Ranjít Singh, finding nothing tangible on which his vengeance could be wreaked, recrossed the Attak, after reinstating Sultán Muhammad Khan in his government of Peshávar, and leaving a detachment of troops to support him. No sooner, however, had the Sikh ruler turned his back than the Indian adventurer again appeared on the scene, with the insurgent forces, and, for the second time, carried Peshávar. Sultán Muhammad Khan, unable to expel the Syad, found it convenient to enter into terms with him. These were, the acknowledgment of the Syad's supremacy, the payment of Rs. 3,000 a month to him as *nazráná*, a free passage for men and money proceeding to join the Gházis, the administration of justice in Peshávar by the moulvís of the new faith established by the reformer, and implicit obedience to the doctrines propounded by him. Upon these conditions the government of Peshávar was restored to Sultán Muhammad Khan, who adhered to the agreement for some time, and paid the stipulated *nazráná*. But Syad Ahmad had no sooner retired to his hill fastnesses than a popular tumult broke out in Peshávar, and the kazi and the two moulvís, who had been left to administer justice on reformed principles, were slain by the populace. Peshávar was thus lost to the Syad, who, moreover, met with no better success in the hills. His Eusafzai hosts had become tired of his yoke, and began to look upon his authority as a burden. The peasants had paid him a tithe of their goods willingly enough, for such payment to a warrior in the name of God was in accordance with their religious notions; but the Syad gave them cause for extreme provocation, by passing a decree that all young women who had attained a marriageable age should be married to his Indian followers. The reformer's motives for this innovation were impugned, and the dissatisfaction against him was loud, for not only did the announcement and its partial enforcement interfere with the liberty which the wild mountaineers had hitherto enjoyed, but they thought a forced matrimonial alliance of their unmarried women with the needy Indians a disgrace to the tribes, who took a pride in the traditions of the bravery of their ancestors. His public preachings, declaring that no person professing Islám should bow before the shrines of saints, or pay benedictions to tombs, or offer food or money for the benefit of the souls of the dead, since such ceremonies could not profit them, his disbelief in the miracles of the saints, and his other doctrines, which he had imbibed from the Wahábí moulvís of Nejd, in Arabia, were particularly distasteful to the mulláhs, as they had a direct effect on their perquisites and emoluments as religious leaders. They unanimously declared the Syad to be an impostor, and he was soon compelled to leave the Eusafzai hills, with his immediate adherents, who had throughout followed his fortunes; but he continued to exercise an influence over the insurrectionary chief of Mozuffárábád and the hill Khans in the neighbourhood of Káshmír. Ranjít Singh

Temporary success. The Maharájá's return to Láhore.

The Syad enters into terms with Sultán Muhammad Khan.

Rising at Peshávar against the Syad's authority.

Peshávar lost to him, 1830.

His growing unpopularity among the Afghans.

His edict regarding compulsory marriage of Afghán young women.

His new doctrine distasteful to the mullahs.

He retires towards Káshmír.

sent a detachment of troops against the Syad, under Prince Sher Singh. The former kept up a desultory warfare against the Sikhs, and success for the most part attended him in the rugged mountains. In one of these conflicts he was, however, taken by surprise, together with his wazír, Muhammad Ismail, at a place called Bálákot, in May 1831, and both were slain by the Sikhs, who soon brought under subjection the insurrectionary Khans of the hills. The heads of the Syad and his wazír were sent by Prince Sher Singh to the Maharájá. Thus ended the career of Syad Ahmad, the impostor, who, in the garb of religion, had endeavoured to promote his own private ends and those of his followers. His existence as the supporter of the Wáhábí persuasion was as dangerous to the Mussalmán community who followed the precepts of the *Qurán* and the Hadis as propounded by the early writers of the faith, as it was to the non-Mussalmán public. Immediately after his death became known, his deputies were expelled from the hills on the frontier, his Gházis fled in disguise, and his family sought protection with its old master, the Nawáb of Tonk. The neighbourhood of Pesháwar was quiet after the Syad's death, and Ranjít Singh entered upon no military enterprise of importance after taking the field against this pretender.

Is surprised and slain, May 1831.

His memory is detested.

Peace restored and preserved.

The power of Ranjít Singh was now consolidated, and his fame at its height. He had brought into subjection the Mahomedan provinces of Káshmír, Multán and Pesháwar. He was lord of the hills and plains in the Panjáb proper, and he entertained designs on Ladákh and Sindh. Distant sovereigns sought his friendship. In 1826 Darvesh Muhammad vakíl of the Nizám of Hyderábád, waited on the Darbár of Láhore with presents, consisting of four horses, a sword, a cannon and several matchlocks, for the Maharájá and Kanwar Kharak Singh. The same year, Sef Khan, agent of Prince Kámrán, of Herat, arrived with presents. In 1829 agents from Bíluchistán came to Láhore with presents of horses for the Sikh ruler, who was asked to help in the restoration of the posts of Dajál and Harrand on the frontier of Dera Ghází Khan, west of the Indus, which had been usurped by the Báháwalpur Nawáb, a feudatory of Ranjít Singh. The following year he was invited to witness the nuptials of the young Maharájá Sindhiá, of Gwalior; but he declined the invitation, on the ground that Sindhiá was not at Láhore when the Maharájá's son was married. The English valued his friendship and watched his proceedings with interest, being not without a suspicion that he had opened a correspondence with Russia.

The power of Ranjít Singh at its height.

His friendship courted by distant sovereigns.

The English value his friendship.

The shawl tent manufactured at Káshmír, which the Maharájá had sent as a present for His Majesty King William was taken to England by Lord Amherst, on his return to Europe in 1828, and became an object of curiosity and admiration. In return for this present, it was resolved to send Ranjít Singh, on the part of His Majesty, a present of five horses, accompanied by a letter of friendship from Lord Ellenborough, the Governor-General, as His Majesty's representative in Hindostán. The ship conveying these horses arrived at Bombay in 1830, and Lieutenant Alexander Burnes, who then held a political situation in Katch, was, with the sanction of the Governor-General, selected by Major-General Sir John Malcolm, the Governor of Bombay, to proceed up the river Indus on a mission to the Sikh capital with these presents. The Indus was chosen as the route of this journey, as the authorities, both in England and India, were anxious to collect full and complete information, political and geographical, regarding that river. The only accounts that existed of a great portion of its course were drawn from Arrion, Curtius, and other historians of

Presents from His Majesty King William of England.

The mission of Lieut. Alex. Burnes, 1830.

The Indus selected as the route of his journey.

Reasons for such determination.

Alexander's expedition. Moreover, the successes of Russia in Persia, and the apprehensions lest that Power should entertain further designs against eastern countries, had made it highly desirable to extend the knowledge of the English people as to the state of the countries on the frontiers of India, and the facilities for military defence offered by that great river barrier, the Indus. The Amírs of Sindh evinced the greatest jealousy of Europeans, and declined to allow the mission to proceed beyond Hyderábád, their capital. Lieutenant Burnes was made the bearer of presents for the Amírs, and was at the same time charged with communications of a political nature. His instructions were to obtain information as to the depth of water in the Indus, the direction and breadth of the stream, the facilities it offered for steam navigation, the supply of fuel on its banks, the conditions of the people and princes bordering on it, together with any other particulars which the exploration might suggest. Lieutenant Burnes had in his suite a young and active officer, Ensign J. D. Leckie, of the 22nd Regiment, N. I., a surveyor, and a native doctor, and was provided with a suitable establishment of servants. He sailed from Mandvi, in Katch, with a fleet of five native boats, on the morning of 21st January, 1831. The Amírs of Sindh showed a strong repugnance to letting the fleet pass through their country on the grounds of the difficulty of navigation and the unsettled and distracted state of the country between Sindh and Láhore, which were of course very much exaggerated. After much unnecessary delay, the requisite permission was given, but not before Colonel Pottinger, the Political Agent at Katch, had written strongly on the subject to the Amírs, and convinced them that their refusal to give the required permission to the mission to proceed by the Indus route could be viewed in no other light than that of an act opposed to decency on the part of the ruling Mírs, and calculated to give offence to the British Government.

The attitude assumed by the Amirs of Sindh.

The scope of Lieut. Burnes' explorations.

The hindrance caused by the Sindh Amírs.

Lieutenant Burnes describes the intense curiosity with which the people on the banks of the Indus looked upon Englishmen. One man stopped the party and eagerly demanded that the "white-faces" should be shown to him, for they had never seen such faces in their life before. The welcome which the mission had received everywhere on the Indus induced the Englishmen to exhibit themselves to the man and the crowd of which he was the spokesman. They said they had seen Shah Shujá, the ex-king of Kábul, but never an Englishman. "*Bismilláh*" ("In the name of God") was the exclamation everywhere that the "white-faced" made their appearance. They were styled kings and princes, and the ladies expressed more astonishment at the sight of them than did their husbands.

Journey on the bank of Indus, 1831.

The wonder of the inhabitants at the sight of the English.

Their courtesy.

On the evening of 27th of May, the party entered the country of the Dáudpotrás, ruled by Nawáb Baháwal Khan, and were received with much distinction by Ghulám Kadir Khan, a person of high rank, who had been sent by the Nawáb to welcome them. The interview with the Nawáb took place at Uch with great ceremony, including a salute of eighty guns. The Khan was seated in an area spread with carpets and attended by about ten persons. He rose to embrace Lieutenant Burnes, and made particular enquiries regarding Mr. Elplinstone, who, he said, had founded a lasting friendship between the family of the Dáudpotrás and his own Government. Lieutenant Burnes describes Baháwal Khan as a handsome man of about thirty years of age, grave in his demeanour, but affable and gentlemanly. He held a rosary in his hand, but his conversation was not interrupted by the telling of the beads. He talked of the honour which had been conferred by the King of England on Ranjít Singh, by sending him presents. He did not touch on political matters, but talked about his favourite pursuit, the manner of hunting

Lieut. Burnes in the country of Nawáb Baháwal Khan.

Interview with the Nawáb.

deer, and produced his matchlock. He asked Lieutenant Burnes to give him the pleasure of his company at his residence in the desert. That officer expresses himself quite charmed with the kindness he received at the hands of the Khan, and the sincerity with which he showed it. A testimonial granted to his grandfather by the Honourable Mr. Elphinstone, which had been preserved with great pride, was produced, a proof of the high estimation in which the English character was held in this remote corner of India. On 5th June the Nawáb paid a return visit to his distinguished guest, and sat for about an hour putting numerous questions on the manufactures of Europe. He was of a mechanical turn of mind, and produced some guns, caps and fulminating powder which he had caused to be manufactured after European patterns, and which Lieutenant Burnes thought did credit to the artificers. He expressed himself highly pleased with the presents which had been sent for him, consisting of a brace of pistols, a watch, and some other articles. After the ceremonial visit was over, the mehmándár brought for the British officer, as presents from the Nawáb, two horses, richly caparisoned with silver and enamel trappings, a hawk and some very rich shawls and trays of Baháwálpur manufacture. In addition to these was sent a purse of Rs. 2,000 and a sum of Rs. 200 for the servants, and, last of all, a beautiful matchlock, "which," in the words of Lieutenant Burnes, "had its value doubled by the manner in which it was presented." "The Khan," said the messenger, "has killed many a deer with this gun, and he begs you will accept this from him, and when you see it, remember that Baháwal Khan is your friend." Lieutenant Burnes had an audience, for the purpose of taking his leave, in the evening, when he presented the Nawáb with a handsome percussion gun, assuring him that he would long remember his kindness and hospitality. Baháwal Khan embraced him and begged him to keep him informed of his welfare and command his services.

English character held in high esteem even in those early days.

The Nawáb of a mechanical turn of mind.

Exchange of presents.

Farewell audience.

Immediately on landing in the country of the Sikhs, the embassy was received in state by Sardar Lahná Singh, who came on an elephant with a numerous retinue. He was richly dressed and wore a necklace of emeralds, and armlets, studded with diamonds. He held in one hand a bow, and in the other two Persian letters from his master, Maharájá Ranjít Singh, appointing him and two others mehmándárs. He presented the bow to the British officer according to the Sikh custom, and at the same time, the letters congratulating him in the name of the Maharájá on his arrival. By the desire of his master he declared that the Maharájá was deeply sensible of the honour that had been conferred upon him by the King of England, and informed him that Sikh troops had been specially posted on the frontier to punish, at a moment's notice, the barbarians of Sindh, who had so long delayed the progress of the mission to the Sikh capital. Bags of money amounting to Rs. 1,400 were then placed at the feet of the British officer, as *ziyáfat*, and the party withdrew. The Sikh sardars had the strictest injunctions regarding the reception of the embassy, and these were implicitly obeyed. They were embodied in a *parwáná* * from the Maharájá, which we insert below, from the journal of Lieutenant Burnes, as showing the high distinction and respect with which the embassy was received in the territories of the Maharájá.

The British Ambassador in the country of the Sikhs.

The ceremony of reception.

Civilities.

Parwáná of Ranjít Singh.

---

* *The Maharájá's parwáná or command to his officers* :—

Be it known to Dewán Ajudhia Pershad, Monsieur Chevalier Ventura and the great and wise Sardars Lahná Singh and Lala Sáwan Mal, Subedár of Multán, that when Mr. Burnes reaches the frontier, you are immediately to attend to all his wants, and previously despatch 200 infantry and the lancers under Tej Singh to Jalálpur, that they may be ready on his arrival as an honorary escort, and you are at the same time to make known your own arrival in the neighbourhood. When Mr. Burnes approaches, you are immediately to despatch an elephant,

The language of the document is, in some respects, hyperbolic, after the fashion of the east, yet it affords abundant proof of the sincerity of the conduct of the Láhore ruler on the occasion, and of the confidence he reposed in the British officer, in allowing him the privilege of inspecting his strongholds, a concession particularly appreciated at a time when so much distrust and jealousy were evinced by most Indian chiefs. Intelligence of the arrival of the embassy in the Sikh territory having reached the Maháràja, he sent a pair of gold armlets, set with diamonds and emeralds, as a gift for the mehmándár. The Maharájá, it should be noted, was always munificent in his gifts to his nobles and sardars.

The party reached Chánga Mánga, about 25 miles from Láhore, on 15th July, and were waited on by a deputation from the Maharájá, consisting of Sardar Shám Singh, Fakír Núr-ud-dín and other sardars. They brought with them an escort of lancers and Sikh cavalry, the latter of which had just returned with Shám Singh from the campaign against Syad Ahmad.

The meeting between Lieut. Burnes and the Sikh embassy.

The meeting took place on elephants, Shám Singh presenting Lieutenant Burnes with a bow, and congratulating him, on the part of the Maharájá, on his arrival. The health of the King of England was enquired about on behalf of the Maharájá, and each sardar delivered a purse of money in gold and silver. The most flattering and pleasing expressions were used by the sardars, but the eloquence of the learned Fakír Núr-ud-dín, who enjoyed the trust and confidence of the Sikh ruler, was peculiarly attractive, not only for the words used, but also for the sincerity it manifested.

Eloquence of Fakír Núr-ud-dín.

"The seasons," said the Fakír, addressing Lieutenant Burnes, "have been changed, to aid your safe arrival; and when it should have rained, the sun shines; but it is the sun of England. You must now consider yourself at home, and in a garden, of which you are the roses; that such a friendship had now grown up between the British and the Sikhs, that the inhabitants of Irán and Rúm would hear it proclaimed in their distant dominions; that light had suc-

with a silver *howdah*, in charge of the Dewán, who is to state that the animal has been sent for his own express use, and then ask him to be seated thereon, which will be gratifying. as the friendship between the States is great. When Mr. Burnes has mounted the elephant then shall Sardar Lahná Singh and Sáwan Mal, seated on other elephants, approach, and have an interview with that gentleman, paying him every manner of respect and attention in their power and congratulating him in a hundred ways on his safe arrival from a long and distant journey, distributing at the same time 225 rupees among the poor. You are then to present a handsome bow, and each of you eleven gold Venetians, and conduct the gentleman to the bathing place, and there set before him 1,100 rupees and 50 jars of sweetmeats; you are then to supply the following articles: grass, grain, bran, milk, eggs, fowls, fat-tailed sheep (*dumbás*), curds, vegetables, fruit, roses, spices, water-vessels, beds, and every thing else that may be necessary, in quantities without stint, and be neglectful and dilatory in nothing. When you visit, you are to parade the two companies and the horse, and salute, and then place guards according to Mr. Burnes' pleasure. When you reach Shujabád, you are to fire a salute of eleven guns and furnish everything as before directed, and present 1,100 rupees, with sweetmeats and fruits, and attend to every wish that is expressed. If Mr. Burnes desires to look at the fort of Shujabád, you are to attend on him and show it, and see that there is no obstruction, and that no one even raises his voice.

On reaching Multán, you are to conduct Mr. Burnes with great respect, and pitch his tent in whatever garden he shall select; the Hazúri, the Begi, the Shísh Mahal or the Khas-wa-ám, or any other. You are then to present him with a purse of 2,500 rupees, and 100 jars of sweetmeats, and fire a salute of eleven guns from the ramparts of the fortress. When you have complimented him on his arrival, you are to suggest, for his consideration, whether he would not like to halt at Multán for five or six days after his long journey, and act entirely as he desires; if he wishes to view the fort, you three persons are to attend him and allow no one to make a noise, and take most particular care that the Nihangs, and such other wrong-headed people, are kept at a distance.

In quitting Multán, you are to load 100 camels with provisions for the supply of Mr. Burnes to Láhore, and Subádar Sáwan Mal is to attend him in person for the first stage, and, after taking leave, repair to the camp of Monsieur Chevalier Ventura. Sardar Lahná Singh and Dewán Ajudhia Pershad, together with Fatteh Singh, Ramgarhia, accompanied by an escort of two companies and the lancers, shall attend Mr. Burnes, and proceed by easy stages to Láhore, despatching daily notice of his approach. At Dera Syadwálá the Kárdár is to present 1,100 rupees with the usual sweetmeats; and you are all directed to remember, in every instance, and at all times, the great friendship which subsists between the two States."

ceeded darkness when the mission emerged from among the barbarians of Sindh, and that its general influence had changed the bud into the rose."

Entry into Láhore.

On the morning of 18th June, Lieutenant Burnes made a public entry into Láhore. He was received at a distance of three miles from Láhore by Fakír Azíz-ud-dín, the Maharájá's minister, and Rájá Guláb Singh, escorted by a guard of cavalry and a regiment of infantry. The party alighted in the house of Monsieur Chevalier Allard, outside the city, and the sardars on deputation withdrew, presenting Lieutenant Burnes with a large sum of money and a quantity of sweetmeats in the name of the Maharájá. The presentation at the Court was fixed for the 20th, when, at about 9 A.M., a deputation of the Maharájá's nobles, with a numerous escort, arrived to conduct Lieutenant Burnes and party to the palace. The streets were lined with cavalry, artillery and infantry, who saluted the British officer as he passed, seated on an elephant. The streets were thronged with spectators, who filled every balcony and window overlooking the street. As the party entered the first court of the palace, they were received by Rájá Dhián Singh, described as being a fine soldier-like person, dressed in armour, who conducted them to the door of the palace. While Lieutenant Burnes stooped to remove his shoes at the threshold, he suddenly found himself in the arms and tight embrace of 'a diminutive old-looking man,' the great Maharájá Ranjít Singh. Two of his sons accompanied him, and they likewise embraced Mr. Leckie and Lieutenant Burnes. The Maharájá conducted Lieutenant Burnes by the hand to the interior of the palace, where he saw Captain Wade and Doctor Murray, who had come from Ludhiáná to witness the presentation. Lieutenant Burnes and party were seated on silver chairs in front of the Maharájá. The latter wore a necklace, armlets and bracelets of emeralds, some of which were very large. All his nobles were likewise dressed with jewels and appeared in yellow, the favourite colour of the Sikh ruler, which had a striking effect. His Highness was profuse in his congratulatory and complimentary remarks, asked particularly after the health of His Majesty the King of England, and enquired after Sir John Malcolm. After the ceremonial speeches were over, Lieutenant Burnes announced to the Maharájá the fact of his having brought in safety to Láhore five horses as a present for His Highness from his most gracious Majesty the King of Great Britain, in consideration of the relations of friendship and concord subsisting between the two Governments, as also a carriage from the Right Honourable the Governor-General, as a mark of His Lordship's esteem. The friendly letter to His Highness from His Majesty's Minister having been then produced in a bag of cloth of gold, sealed with the arms of England, His Highness touched the seal with his forehead in token of respect, and commanded his minister, Fakír Azíz-ud-dín, to read aloud the translation of it in Persian, which was accordingly done in the presence of the whole Court. As the letter was being read the Maharájá ordered a salute to be fired from the ramparts of the citadel, in order to convey to his subjects the joyful news of the arrival of the letter from the King of Great Britain. Sixty guns accordingly sent forth their thunder, conveying to the citizens of Láhore the intelligence of this event. The Maharájá then inspected the presents, accompanied by the members of the mission and his Court. He was highly gratified at the sight of the horses, and their size, colour and general appearance were objects of special admiration on his part and that of the courtiers, the Maharájá remarking that they were little elephants. Lieutenant Burnes speaks very highly of the affability of the Maharájá, and the warmth he showed on the occasion. Every word came from his heart, and was indicative of the feelings of high esteem which he entertained for the

The Ambassador on his way to the Court.

Reception at the Court.

The dress of the courtiers.

The letter from the King of England read out.

Display of presents from the King of England.

British Government. The conversation between him and the British officer lasted for an hour and a half. The Maharájá put numerous questions about the navigation of the Indus, the depth of the water, the condition of the people living on its banks, and their importance from political and military points of view. His cupidity was aroused on being informed that Sindh was a rich country. He introduced Lieutenant Burnes to all the representatives of the neighbouring States, and ordered the horses of his stud to be passed in review before him. They were thirty in number, all most superbly and richly caparisoned, and some adorned with very valuable jewels. The Maharájá named each horse as it passed before him, describing its pedigree and points.

The Maharájá's stud.

Parade of Sikh troops.

The following morning a review of the Maharájá's forces was held on the parade ground, in honour of the arrival of the distinguished guest. His Highness sat on the terrace, a short distance from the city walls, and, as the troops were passing in review, he asked the opinion of Lieutenant Burnes as to their fitness and equipment. He talked freely on a variety of subjects. He mentioned that each of his muskets had cost him seventeen rupees, and, passing to the subject of the revenues of Káshmír, he said that he had just got 36 lakhs of rupees from it that year, which was an increase of six lakhs over the previous year's income. "All the people I send to Káshmír," continued the Maharájá, "turn out *harámzádás* [rascals]; there is too much pleasure and enjoyment in that country; I must either send one of my sons there, or go myself." Such was the style of Ranjít Singh's conversation, but it marked a strength of character and originality which cannot be too much admired. The party left him on observing preparations for breakfast. He usually took his meals in the open air, and, while out in camp, in the presence of his troops, and sometimes on horseback. Great was his passion for riding and long journeys, and on such occasions he preferred taking his meals in the saddle, like a good soldier. He was perfectly free from pomp and show, yet everybody dreaded him, and, of all the throng which surrounded him, not an individual dared speak a word without a sign. He was very inquisitive about the strength and resources of England, and sent privately for a native of Hindostán who was on the establishment of the mission, and who had been to England, and asked him about the resources of England, and particularly, whether the wealth and power of the British nation were as great as he had believed.

The Maharájá's passion for riding.

He enquires about the resources of England.

A meeting on the Parade grounds.

As Lieutenant Burnes and party were going, one morning, to examine the tomb of Jahángír at Shahderá, they found Ranjít Singh seated on the plain and surrounded by his troops. He sent for that officer and talked with him for a long time, giving him an account of the inroads of the Afgháns into the Panjáb, and informing him that the ground on which they were then seated was the site of the Afghán encampment. He talked of the invasions of Zamán Shah, the blind and exiled king at Ludhiáná, and of his designs against India.

Private audience.

Ranjít's favourite object of amusement.

On the evening of 25th July, he gave a private audience to Lieutenant Burnes, and was on that occasion seen to great advantage. The Court was ordered to be withdrawn; Ranjít Singh sat on a chair, attended by a party of thirty or forty dancing-girls of Káshmír and the adjacent mountains, dressed uniformly as boys. Their features were remarkably handsome, and their figures small, graceful and attractive. They were dressed in flowing silk robes with gems dark and bright, and carried each a small bow and quiver. "This," said Ranjít Singh, "is one of my regiments (*paltuns*), but they tell me it is one I cannot discipline." The remark was amusing to the English guest, and very pleasing to the fair ones, who were engaged in the sham fight. He then pointed out two of these ladies who held the rank of commandants in this branch of His Highness' service, and said they held two villages in jágír and were in receipt of an allowance of five and ten rupees a day, respectively. After their performances were over, these undisciplined troops were sent to their homes on elephants. Ranjít Singh then talked of his relations with the British Government, saying he had valued it from the outset, when he first formed the acquaintance of Sir John Malcolm in 1805. He was very curious as to the relative strength of the European powers, and asked whether France or England were the greater power. From this subject he passed to that of his French officers, and wished to know the opinion of the British officer on the state of discipline of his troops. He talked of his campaigns across the Indus against the Gházis, and praised the bravery of his nation, to whom, he acknowledged, he owed his successes in the mountains of Káshmír and the plains of Peshávar. He said his troops were devoted to their duty, and free from prejudice. They would carry eight days' provisions on their backs, dig wells where water was scarce, construct roads and build forts, duties which the natives of Hindostán would be unwilling to perform. He then talked of his munificence to his sardars and courtiers and of his gifts of Káshmír shawls, which he had in abundance. From this he passed on to the praises of his wines and strong drinks, assuring Lieutenant Burnes that his wines were made up of pearls and precious gems. Ranjít was throughout very talkative and communicative, and at the close of the interview a splendid bow and quiver were produced, as also a horse, richly caparisoned with a shawl cloth, a necklace of agate, and a heron's plume on his head. "This," said the Maharájá, "is one of my riding horses, and I beg your acceptance of it." Similar presents were made to Mr. Leckie. The Maharájá then sprinkled rose-water and sandal oil over his guests with his own hand, and the ceremony of presenting gifts was complete.

Waste of public money.

Conversations.

Presents to the envoy.

Next morning a review of the Maharájá's horse artillery took place on the parade ground. There were 51 guns, commanded by a native officer, and the movements were effected with considerable celerity. "Every gun which you now see," said the Maharájá, "costs me 5,000 rupees annually for the pay of the officers and men, and the keep of the horses. I have 100 pieces of artillery, exclusive of battering guns and mortars, and my French officers tell me I have too many."

Review of horse artillery.

The members of the mission had their farewell audience on the 16th August, when there was a display of the Maharájá's jewels and of the celebrated diamond, the *Kohinúr*, or "mountain of light," at the express desire of Lieutenant Burnes. It was about half the size of a hen's egg, and of the finest water, weighing $3\frac{1}{2}$ rupees. It was set on an armlet, having on either side of it a diamond about the size of a sparrow's egg. Among the jewels exhibited was a large ruby, weighing 14 rupees, with the names of several kings engraved on it, among them those of Aurangzeb and Ahmad Shah, Durráni, and a topaz of great size, weighing 11 rupees, and half as large as a billiard ball. The Maharájá then invested Lieutenant Burnes with a string of pearls; he placed a diamond ring on a finger of one of his hands, and one of emerald on the corresponding finger of the other. He gave him four other jewels, set with emeralds and pearls. He then girt round his waist a superb sword, adorned with a knot of pearls. A horse, richly dressed with cloth of gold, the saddle and bridle of which were worked with gold ornaments, was next presented. A *khilat*, or robe of honour, was also presented, consisting of shawls and other valuable cloths, the manufacture of Káshmír. Mr. Leckie was similarly presented with a *khilat*,

Farewell audience.

A display of jewels. The *Kohinúr*.

Presents to the envoy and the members of the mission.

and so were the other attendants, for distribution among whom a sum of Rs. 2,000 was sent. A friendly letter was then produced, enclosed in a silken bag, fastened with a string of pearls. It was addressed to the Minister of His Majesty the King of England, in reply to the one sent by him to the Maharájá. It was written in a very ornate style, in Persián. Lieutenant Burnes had the honour of being styled in it "the nightingale of the garden of eloquence, and the bird of the winged words of sweet discourse." "On beholding the shoes of the horses sent by the King of England," says the letter, "the new moon turned pale with envy and nearly disappeared from the sky." On presenting this letter, the Maharájá embraced Lieutenant Burnes, and asked him to convey to the Governor-General his high sentiments of esteem and regard. Lieutenant Burnes left Láhore the same evening, on his journey to Simla, where he had been summoned to give an account of his mission to Lord William Bentinck, the Governor-General.

Letter to the King of England.

The envoy's departure from Láhore.

Disposal of British gifts.

It may be worth while to note what became of the gifts which for a time so much engrossed the attention of the Láhore Court, after the mission, so splendidly received, had left. The stallion which accompanied the team of cart horses, and which was remarkable for its enormous head and massive legs, instead of being made use of for breeding purposes, for which it had been sent, was put into the hands of a breaker to be taught its paces. This unwieldy animal was an object of special curiosity with the Sikhs, and stood always in the palace yard, or before the Maharájá's tent, adorned with necklaces of precious stones and a golden saddle. The mares were quite neglected, and the carriage sent by the Governor-General, after being looked at for a few days as a novelty, was allowed to lie by, as a useless article, which was also the case with the highly ornamental carriage sent to the Maharájá by Lord Minto in 1810, which was already lying neglected in the great arsenal at Láhore.

The visit of Monsieur Victor Jacquemont to Láhore, March 1831.

In June, 1828, Monsieur Victor Jacquemont, Travelling Naturalist to the Royal Museum of Natural History of Paris, was deputed by the Council of that Institution on a scientific mission to the countries of the east, to investigate the natural history of India in all its branches, and collect materials wherewith to enrich the Museum and promote the progress of science. After travelling through various parts of India, this eminent naturalist reached the Panjáb in March 1831, with a view to paying a visit to the Sikh capital. He was received at Phillour on the Sutlej, by Shah Dín, the son of Fakír Azíz-ud-dín, with military honours. At Láhore he was received with similar honours, and a hearty reception was given him by his fellow-countrymen, Messrs. Allard, Ventura and Court. He alighted, as he describes in his travels, 'at the entrance of a delicious oasis, consisting of a large parterre of carnations, irises and roses, with walks of orange trees and jasmine, bordered with vases, in which a multitude of little fountains were playing.' This was the celebrated garden of Shalámár, laid out with great taste and elegance. He had several interviews with the Maharájá, and spent hours in conversing with him "*de omnibus rebus et quibusdam aliis.*" "His conversation," writes the traveller, "is like a nightmare. He is almost the first inquisitive Indian I have seen, and his curiosity balances the apathy of the whole of his nation. He has asked me a hundred thousand questions about India, the British, Europe, Bonaparte, this world in general and the next, hell, paradise, the soul, God, the devil, and a myriad of others of the same kind." Monsieur Jacquemont, describes Ranjít as an extraordinary man, a Bonaparte in miniature. The Maharájá was at this time about to quit Láhore, and had directed Monsieur Ventura to proceed to Multán, with ten thousand

He puts up in the gardens of Shalámár.

Interview with the Maharájá.

troops and thirty pieces of cannon, for the purpose of collecting tribute. The French traveller, after being most hospitably entertained for several days, took his leave on the 18th March, and was honoured with a *khilat* valued at 5,000 rupees in addition to a purse of 1,100 rupees. The services of horse and foot soldiers were placed at his disposal, to conduct him in safety to the borders of the Sikh dominions.

Leaves Láhore, 18th March 1831.

In April, 1831, a Sikh deputation, consisting of Dewán Moti- Ram, son of Mokham Chand, Fakír Azíz-ud-dín and Sardar Hari Singh, Nalwa, waited on His Excellency, Lord William Bentinck, Governor-General of India, with presents, to convey to His Lordship the Maharájá's complimentary wishes for his own welfare and the prosperity and good of the British Government. The deputation was received with much distinction by the Governor-General, who, observing the very favourable disposition in which the Sikh ruler seemed to be, proposed an interview between His Highness and himself. The rising fortunes of Ranjít Singh and the establishment of his power this side of the Indus were considerations which led the Governor-General to propose a formal meeting at a time when the probable designs of Russia against Persia, and the further advance of that power towards the East were subjects of warm discussion in political circles, and it was thought fit to give the world an impression that a complete unanimity existed between the two States. On the other hand, Ranjít Singh had considerations of his own in view, in forming an alliance with his British neighbours, for his power, though predominant in the Panjáb proper, was hardly consolidated in the country beyond the Indus, and he was anxious to lead the public to believe that he was acknowledged as the head of the *Khálsá* by the paramount power in India. Accordingly, the deputation of Captain Wade to the Sikh capital to thank His Highness for his attention, and to propose an interview between him and His Lordship, had its desired effect. The Maharájá, notwithstanding the adverse counsel of some of his courtiers, prominent among whom was the gallant Sardar Hari Singh, Nalwa, agreed to the interview, and Ropar, on the banks of the Sutlej, was fixed as the most convenient spot for the proposed meeting. On the 16th October, the Dasahra Darbár was held, with unusal magnificence in the Rám Bágh garden in Amritsar, when all the sardars presented *nazars*, and received *khilats* from their sovereign. The festivities being over, a *murásila* was sent to Rájá Sangat Singh of Jhínd, asking him to join the Maharájá at Jalandar, for the Ropar meeting, and the Maharájá, having made his preparations, himself marched in that direction, accompanied by his chiefs and sardars, and escorted by 10,000 of his best horse, 6,000 trained infantry, and two batteries of artillery. Everything was done at Ropar by the British authorities to give *eclát* to the occasion. The deep interest which the Maharájá had always taken in the mode of equipment of the British forces, his attention to European drill and mode of warfare, and his well-known inquisitive disposition on such occasions, led the heads of Government to make special arrangements for a display of as great a variety of troops as possible. The troops ordered up to Ropar were two squadrons of European lancers, a European regiment, two battalions of native infantry, two squadrons of Skinner's Irregular Horse, and the mounted band of H. M. 16th Lancers. The Maharájá's camp was laid out on the opposite bank of the Sutlej, and, immediately on his arrival in the camp, a deputation from the Governor-General, consisting of British officers of rank, among whom were Major-General Ramsay, Mr. Prinsep, Major Colvin and his Lordship's Chief Secretary, waited on His Highness to enquire after his health. They were received by the Maharájá under a salute, and presented a purse of 10,000 rupees as *Sar-*

A Sikh deputation waits on Lord Bentinck, the Governor-General, at Simla, April, 1831.

His Lordship proposes a meeting with the Maharájá.

The meeting desired by both parties for considerations of their own

The deputation of Captain Wade to Láhore.

Ropar fixed as the appropriate spot for meeting

The Maharájá starts, accompanied by a large force.

Preparations at Ropar.

Friendly deputations

*warna.** When they withdrew, each member of the deputation was presented with a *khilat* consisting of jewels, shawls and horses. Shortly after this, Khanwar Kharak Singh, accompanied by Rájá Sangat Singh of Jhínd, Rájá Goláb Singh, Sardar Atar Singh, Sindánwalia, Sardar Sham Singh, Atariwálá and Hari Singh, Nalwa, was deputed by the Maharájá to present his compliments to the Governor-General. They each presented His Lordship with a bow and 1,100 rupees as a *Sarwarna*, and returned to their camp after receiving *khilats*. It was arranged that the meeting between the two chiefs should take place the next morning, the 26th October.

The Maharájá's apprehensions.

Matters had progressed smoothly so far, when the Maharájá's mind underwent a sudden change. He suspected some treachery, or foul play, and his advisers told him he had acted unwisely in leaving his own territory for an interview with the representative of the British Government on foreign ground. He was advised to see the Governor-General at Amritsar, or to postpone the interview altogether. The suspicious Maharájá sent for Monsieur Allard, late in the night, to inform him that he would not attend the meeting of the next day. That officer did his best to allay his master's apprehensions, and even staked his head that nothing unpleasant would happen. He left the Maharájá unsettled in mind, and the astrologers were now summoned. After consulting their holy books, they declared that the British were sincere friends of the Maharájá, and that the meeting would be conducive to more intimate friendship between the two States, but they advised the Maharájá to hold an apple in each hand, on meeting the Governor-General, and to deliver to him one of these, as soon as he should see him, keeping the other himself. If the apple was received by His Excellency without hesitation, the result of the meeting would be highly favourable, and the proceedings might be continued without fear.

He sends for M. Allard and relates to him his distress of mind.

The astrologers consult their holy books.

An expedient to render the meeting prosperous suggested.

The next morning, a deputation from the Governor-General having waited on His Highness, preparations were made for the meeting. The Maharájá, early in the morning, sent 800 of Monsieur Allard's Dragoons in advance across the bridge, and they were followed by 3,000 of his best *Ghurchara* cavalry. When he had seen all these cross, he himself breakfasted and went over with his principal sardars, all being seated on elephants, and dressed in yellow, or *basanti*, like the Maharájá. After the whole had passed, he ordered that no others should be allowed to cross the river, and placed a strong guard on the opposite bank to enforce the order. Having crossed the open plain, the Sikh chief with his escort entered the Governor-General's camp, which commenced a short distance from it. A passage was formed, lined with British troops, and the Maharájá examined each corps minutely, putting a variety of questions regarding their formation and mode of drill. He enquired about every strange article that attracted his eye, and thus did he proceed slowly until he came to the middle of the street. Here he was met by the Governor-General, and the first thing which he did, after an exchange of compliments, as enjoined by his astrologers, was to present His Lordship with an apple, as the elephants of the two chiefs came nearer. The apple was forthwith taken. Delighted at this good omen, the Maharájá crossed into the howdáh of the Governor-General, and the chiefs proceeded together to the audience tents, followed by officers of the Governor-General's staff and the Sikh sardars of His Highness's suite. On alighting from the elephant, the Maharájá was conducted to an outer tent, where European gentlemen who had assembled for the occasion were presented to him, standing, as the

The Maharájá starts for the Governor-General's camp.

His minute examination of British corps.

Observance of the ceremony as enjoined by the Brahmins.

The interview between the two chiefs.

* *Sarwarna* is money to be distributed among the poor. It is the custom among the nobles of India to present a *Sarwarna*, as charity for the poor, on the occasion of an interview.

Maharájá passed to an inner tent. Chairs were provided in this further tent for the sardars of the Maharájá's staff and his officers. He took care to call out the name of each of his sardars himself, and did not enter the tent until all had gone in and taken their seats on the chairs provided for them. The Governor-General and the Maharájá then took their seats on State chairs, placed side by side. The whole presented a most picturesque appearance. Not only were the Sikh sardars dressed in *basanti*, the colour of spring, but their highly-polished armour was worn with scarfs, also of this colour, and this, combined with the diamonds, rubies, emeralds and other precious stones that decorated their heads, breasts and arms, rendered the scene a truly grand one. After a friendly conversation between the Governor-General and the Maharájá, presents for the Maharájá and his suite were brought and exhibited in the darbár. These consisted of fifty-one trays, in which were arranged a variety of fine manufactured stuffs from Calcutta, Dháká and Benares, jewels of value, pearl necklaces, *sarpeches* set with diamonds, a tuft or ringlet, armlets, a jewelled sword and a handsome matchlock. To these were added a fine Burmese elephant and two horses from the Hissár stud, which were passed in review before the Maharájá. Twenty-one trays with rich stuffs and jewels were laid out for the heir-apparent, besides a horse richly equipped with gold and silver ornaments. Dresses of honour were also laid out for the sardars. His Highness carefully examined each article of his own presents, and presented the tray-bearers and the bandsmen in attendance with a purse of two thousand rupees. The meeting then broke up, and the Maharájá returned to his own camp at about noon, apparently highly pleased with the meeting. As he passed through the street of British troops, he renewed his enquiries regarding the formation and equipment of various corps, stopping whereever he saw anything to attract or interest him. He did not, however, leave the British camp before talking with the Governor-General, even in this ceremonial visit, on that most favourite subject, his horses, and causing them to be paraded before His Excellency at the door of the reception tent. On arriving at his camp, the Maharájá sent three *kalamdáns*, or pen-cases, of Káshmír manufacture, and richly decorated with precious stones, to the Governor-General, through his confidential minister, Fakír Azíz-ud-dín. One of these was intended for His Lordship, the other for his lady, and the third for his Chief Secretary.

The Darbár.

Presents from the Governor-General.

Presentation of kalamdáns to the Governor-General.

His Excellency the Governor-General paid a return visit to the Maharájá on the following day. Grand preparations were made in the Maharájá's camp for his reception. Tents of embroidered Káshmír work were pitched at the place fixed for the interview, and from here to the banks of the river, facing the Governor-General's camp, a double row of troops was formed. When all was complete, the heir-apparent, Prince Kharak Singh, and Prince Sher Singh, crossed the river, to conduct His Lordship to the Sikh camp. His Lordship crossed the river escorted by the lancers, a body of mounted bandsmen preceding the cavalcade. He was met at the bridge-of-boats by the Maharájá himself, and, after an exchange of compliments, seated on the Maharájá's howdáh. When both the chiefs had seated themselves, the artillery in attendance thundered forth a royal salute, and the troops presented arms. His Lordship and the Maharájá proceeded slowly in the direction of the darbár tents, which had been tastefully laid out. The Maharájá was much struck with the appearance of the British troops, particularly of the band, which preceded them, and which he heard play with great interest and pleasure on the river bank, during the interval in which the suite was passing over the bridge. In the Sikh

The return visit.

The magnificence of the Maharájá's camp.

camp, the *kanats*, and *shamiánas*, of beautiful embroidered work, and tents occupied a large space. The *shamiánas* were all lined with Káshmír shawls, tastefully and beautifully worked. That under which the Governor-General and Maharájá were seated, was inlaid with pearls and jewels. The floor cloth was of embroidered silk, richly worked in gold and silver. On one side was a bedstead, with curtains of exquisitely fine gold cloth, and fringes decorated with pearls and rubies of great value. The Governor-General was provided with a seat on a throne, worked with gold thread. The Maharájá sat on the right of the throne, on a golden chair. When all were seated, the Maharájá had his officers and sardars of State presented in succession to the Governor-General, and each of these presented a *nazar* of a gold mohur to both His Lordship and the Maharájá, which was touched and remitted. These sardars were introduced by Captain, afterwards Sir, Claude Wade, Assistant Political Agent at Ludhiáná, who gave a brief account of each as he passed. The Maharájá's horses, magnificently equipped, were then brought and passed in review, His Highness, as usual, telling the names and merits of each. An hour was passed in lively conversation, and dancers were then brought in. The presence of these dancing-girls, clad in their holiday attire, added greatly to the picturesqueness and brilliancy of the scene. When the time of departure approached, the presents intended for the Governor-General and staff were brought forward. Those for His Lordship were arranged in 101 trays, and consisted of rich stuffs from Káshmír and other parts of the Panjáb, jewels and seven single diamonds of various sizes. There were also ten matchlocks, a sword, two bows with arrows and a shield, all set with precious stones, several gold and silver utensils and a *chapar khát*, or bedstead, with curtains of gold and silver cloth, completely furnished. To these were added two fine horses, with superb trappings, and an elephant with a silver howdáh. Presents of different descriptions and values were also given to the officers of the Governor-General's staff, and, after *attar* and *pán* had been served out to the distinguished visitors, the party broke up, and His Lordship returned to his camp, accompanied by Princes Kharak Singh and Sher Singh.

A display of the State horses.

Presents for the Governor-General.

The following four days were occupied in evening entertainments and reviews of troops. On the 31st of October, some artillery practice with grape and spherical case shot was witnessed by the Maharájá across the river. An umbrella was shot at with one of the six-pounders, after which the sardars in attendance on His Highness, exhibited feats of horsemanship and dexterity. First of all, Rájá Dhian Singh, who was a good sportsman, displayed his skill in horsemanship, shooting and sword exercise. He was followed in succession by Rájás Suchet Singh and Goláb Singh, Sardar Hari Singh, Nalwa, General Ilahi Bakhsh and Generals Ventura and Allard, who each displayed great skill and activity in the military feats performed by them. Last of all came the Maharájá himself, on horseback. A brass vessel was laid on the maidán, and three times did the Maharájá lift it with the tip of his drawn sword, the horse going at full speed. He also joined in the feats of horsemanship displayed by his own and Colonel Skinner's Horse. The feats performed by the Sikh sardars, and especially by the Maharájá, excited the applause of the European spectators. The Governor-General on this occasion presented the Maharájá with two five-pounder horse artillery guns with horses and equipment complete.

Sports and feat of horsemanship and dexterity performed by the Sikh Sardars.

Sports performed by the Maharájá.

Two artillery guns presented to the Maharájá.

The parting interview.

The parting interview between the Governor-General and His Highness took place in the evening of the same day (31st October) in His Lordship's camp. The Maharájá was, on this occasion, presented by the Governor-General with the model of an iron suspension bridge made in Calcutta specially with that object, and His Highness was intensely pleased with it. The Maharájá was in great spirits throughout the interview, and was very inquisitive regarding the management and drill of British troops, the pay of officers of different grades, the charge for the guns, and the weight of metal in each shot. He was greatly struck with the evolutions performed by the British troops. At the conclusion of all these ceremonies, and on the night in question, a fresh treaty of perpetual friendship between His Highness and the British Government was executed and signed by the parties concerned. This was merely the renewal of the 1809 treaty, with additional clauses relating to the navigation of the Indus. On the following morning, namely the 1st of November 1831, both camps broke up and commenced their return march.

A new treaty of friendship between the Government of India and the Maharájá. Signed 31st October, 1831.

The camp breaks up, 1st November 1831.

At the meeting at Ropar, Ranjít Singh invited to his camp two officers of rank, who, he believed enjoyed the Governor-General's confidence above all the rest. One of these was His Lordship's official secretary. He had a long conversation with these officers on the affairs of Sindh, and expressed frankly what his own views regarding that country were. He alluded. to the richness of the country, its immense resources, and the distracted state of the Government under the Mirs. He coveted its treasures which, he said, had been accumulated there since the invasion of Hindostán by Nádir Shah, and hinted that the country might be easily conquered, as it had no standing army and no soldiers. He also alluded to the recent conduct of the Mirs of Sindh in not allowing Lieutenant Burnes a passage through their country till after much demur, and after a strong representation had been made to them by the British Political Agent at Katch. He therefore proposed joint action with the British against the Mirs of Sindh. The Governer-General had, however, already deputed Colonel Pottinger on a political mission to the Court of Sindh, to open negociations with the Mirs for the opening of the lower portion of the river Indus to the commerce of Europe and India, and it was not thought proper to make any communication yet to the Maharájá, lest he should endeavour, by secret working, to counteract the peaceful and beneficial project of the British Government.

Ranjít Singh's designs regarding Sindh.

He proposes joint action with the British against that country.

The British Government refrain from divulging the tenor of their proposition in regard to Sindh.

On 9th November, the Maharájá reached Kapurthalla, where he was the guest of Sardar Fateh Singh, Ahluwalia. The sardar had made grand preparations for the Maharájá reception, and the Maharájá and his sardars freely indulged in the festivities which had been provided for them. After visiting Amritsar and performing his religious services in the temple there, the Maharájá returned to Láhore on the 16th, when orders were issued to Prince Sher Singh to go to Káshmír to look after the affairs of the valley. Prince Kharak Singh was at the same time deputed to Tank and Bannu to levy contributions and *nazránás* from the Maliks and Khans of these districts. The same year Mir Akhor, the agent of Sardar Purdil Khan, the governor of Kandahár, arrived at the court of Láhore, with a present of horses from his master, and received presents in exchange and a dress of honour on his departure to his country. Nawáb Sadiq Mahomed Khan of Báháwalpur, to whom the district of Dera Gházi Khan had been leased for two lakhs and twenty-five thousand rupees per annum, having withheld payment for two years General Ventura was sent to Báháwalpur, at the head of a force to enforce the tribute. The Nawáb still failing to remit the money, property belonging to him, to the amount of six lakhs of rupees, was confiscated.

The Maharájá's return to Láhore, 16th November 1831.

Arrival of the Kandahár Agent.

Forfeiture of Nawáb Baháwal Khan's property in default of payment of subsidy.

In December of the same year a communication was received at the Láhore Darbár from the Governor-General of India, expressing His

The scheme of opening the Sutlej and the Indus to commerce, 1831.

Lordship's delight at the enlarged views of the Láhore Maharájá, who had some time previously desired to see a steam-boat, thereby giving proof of his enlightened and advanced ideas, and proposing that the commercial relations between the two States might be drawn closer and established on a firm footing. Shortly after this, Captain Wade, the Political Agent at Ludhiáná, paid a formal visit to the Maharájá at Láhore, in order to explain to his Highness the object of Colonel Pottinger's mission to Sindh, and, in continuation of the same project, to propose to the Maharájá the free navigation of the Sutlej. The Government of India at this time entertained notions, not without foundation, of the great superiority of the rivers of the Panjáb, for navigation, over the Ganges, and this proposal was prompted by commercial, as well as by political, considerations, with reference to Russian influence in Persia, and the possibility of the further extension of their power east and south. The desirability of extending British influence in the countries west of the Indus, and of adopting means to extend British commerce over those countries, was therefore obvious to all interested in the safety and welfare of the empire of India, though it was neither necessary nor desirable to make a rival power, like that of the Sikhs, privy to these proceedings, especially when the interests of the two were so plainly conflicting. The Maharájá was not free from suspicions, and felt that the English had designs of their own against the territory which he had himself so long coveted. But he had learnt to respect the power of the English, and he would not avow his ulterior motives against Sindh. Yet he had represented to the Governor-General at the Ropar conference that the vakils of Sindh were in attendance in his camp, and had asked if he might introduce them to His Lordship. This question was answered in the negative; but everybody understood at the time what the wily chief of Láhore meant by the discourse. On the present occasion, he spoke to Captain Wade, in terms declaring his superior right to Shikarpur, and advancing arguments in support of his position as the paramount power of the Barakzais, Mohamed Azím Khan and his brothers, who, he said, had originally held the district as vassals of the titular king, Shah Ayub. His request to be allowed to co-operate with the English in a march against Sindh had not been heeded, and he knew that coercion formed no part of the scheme of the British Government in regard to the affairs of that country. He now made propositions to Mir Morad Ali of Hyderábád to farm Dera Ghází Khan to him. But all these projects failed; the course of the Government of India had long been determined upon, and Ranjít Singh did not think it either wise or convenient to thwart the peaceful measures of his allies, and he gave his unqualified assent to the opening of the Sutlej and the Indus for common navigation, the supervision of which was to be given to a British Officer to be located at Mithan Kot. But he did not affect to conceal from the British Officer the fact that the commercial projects of the British Government had compromised his political designs and operations west of the Indus.

The views of the Government of India based on commercial, as well as political, considerations.

Its views regarding Sindh.

Ranjít Singh asserts his superior right to Shikárpur,

But he finally yields to the propositions of the British Government, 1832.

Commercial treaty concluded between the British Government and the Mirs of Sindh, April 1832.

Four months after, or in April 1832, a treaty was concluded between the British Government and the Mirs of Sindh, through Colonel Pottinger, whereby the Mirs agreed to open a passage by the river and the roads of Sindh to the merchants and traders of Hindostán.

The second visit of Lieut. Alex. Burnes to Láhore, January, 1832.

In the early part of January, 1832, Lieutenant Alexander Burnes, the enterprising and able officer who had headed the embassy to the Court of Láhore in the preceding year, and who had gone to Simla to give an account of his transactions with the darbár of Láhore to Lord William Bentinck, arrived at Láhore on his way to Kábul, Kunduz, Balkh and Bokhara, where he was to go by way of the Hindu Kush. The object of his journey was to obtain a knowledge of the condition of these countries and of the route to them.* He was received with great distinction, and became the guest of the Chevalier Monsieur Allard. He had several interviews with the Maharájá, who received him with marked affability. The Maharájá expressed much satisfaction at the interview he had lately had, for the first time, with the Governor-General of India, and made enquiries regarding the scope and object of Lieutenant Burnes' approaching journey.

The parting entertainment.

The parting entertainment was given by the Maharájá to his distinguished guest in the Palace of Mirrors, or Summan Burj, at night, when the palace was superbly illuminated with wax tapers, bottles filled with water of different colours being placed near the lights, thus increasing the splendour of the show. From the great hall, the ancient seat of the Moghal emperors, which led in front to an arched colonade of marble, the traveller was conducted to a small apartment, the bedroom of the Maharájá, where the festivities of the night were to take place. The Maharájá's bedstead, which was placed at one end of the room, was entirely covered with gold, the canopy being one massy sheet of the same metal. It stood on golden stands, about ten inches high. The curtains consisted of Káshmír shawls, embroidered with gold, and from the posts and legs of this superb bedstead, to its branched candlesticks, everything was of gold. The chairs for the guests, among whom were Captain Wade and Doctor Murray, were of gold and silver. The royal entertainer freely circulated wine, distilled from the grapes of Kábul, which is described as being of a very fiery nature, and stronger than brandy. Ranjít became very entertaining in his cups, and gave the foreigners an interesting account of his early exploits, mentioning many circumstances connected with his private life. Three of his chiefs, he said, had, at different times, fallen by his side; there were two mutinies among his troops quelled by his own energy; and on one occasion he had to challenge his adversary to settle the dispute by single combat. The entertainment closed, long after midnight, with a sham fight among the dancing-girls and a rich supper.

Lieut. Burnes leaves Láhore, 10th February, 1832.

Lieutenant Burnes took leave of the Maharájá on the evening of the 10th February on the parade ground, where his troops were collected to show what progress they had made in throwing shells. He then dictated letters for the chiefs of Peshàwar and Kábul, as well as several other personages beyond the Indus, to ensure the British officer's protection and honourable treatment by the neighbouring chiefs and the marauding Khaibarís. He also issued orders to all the chiefs and sardars between his capital and the frontier, enjoining upon them the duty of treating the British officer honourably, and of providing him with all necessaries. Then, stretching out his hand from the elephant, he gave each member of the expedition a hearty shake and bade him farewell. He particularly requested Lieutenant Burnes to write to him often, and give him an account of the countries he might visit, describing their politics and customs, and never to forget him, in whatever region he might be. "Nor did we forget his request," says the adventurous and good-hearted Lieutenant Burnes, "when far from his territories. We received letters from Ranjít Singh himself in the deserts of Tartary and in Bokhara." "I never quitted," continues he, "the presence of a native of Asia with such impressions as I left this man: without education and without

His opinion of the Maharájá.

* Lieut. Burnes was accompanied on this occasion by Mohan Lal, a Hindu lad of Káshmír, who subsequently became known by the name of Aghá Hasan Ján, the Government pensioner at Ludhiáná. He was a student of the Delhi College, and his work, styled *Mohan Lal's Travels* is well known to the public. His companion in the travels was Mahomad Ali, who had received his education in the Engineering Institution of Bombay.

a guide, he conducts all the affairs of his kingdom with surpassing energy and vigour, and yet he wields his power with a moderation quite unprecedented in an eastern Prince." Such was the opinion entertained of the founder of the Sikh kingdom in the Panjáb by an accomplished English traveller. Chunni Lal, Jamadár, was sent at the head of body of *sawars* to escort Lieutenant Burnes and party to the Indus.

Death of Sardar Desa Singh, Majithia, April 1832.

While the Court was at Amritsar, the Maharájá, to his great regret, received news of the death of one of his oldest and ablest sardars. This was Desa Singh, Majithia, who held jágírs and grants from the Maharájá to the value of about 1,25,000 rupees yearly. He had fought successfully in the Kangrá and Multán campaigns, and had been, for a long time, the Maharájá's governor of the Hill States. His son, Lahná Singh, succeeded to all his estates and honours, and was honoured by the Maharájá, who conferred upon him the title of *Kasirul Iktidar*, or "chief of exalted dignity." A robe of honour, consisting of eleven pieces of valuable cloth, a *jigha* (an ornament of gold worn on the turban) and a *turra*, or tassel, and gold earrings, was sent by the Maharájá for Lahná Singh, and he was appointed governor of the hill territory between the Rávi and the Sutlej, which appointment he held till the beginning of 1844. The sardar, however, did not reside in the hills, but at Amritsar, or at Majithia, and made periodical tours in the states under his charge to examine accounts and make necessary arrangements. He was in charge of the Darbár Sahib, or the great Sikh temple of Amritsar, an office of great honour, which his father had held before him. For all these honours he had, of course, to pay a handsome *nazráná* to the Maharájá, who, in all matters of succession, levied large sums as presents or tribute.

He is succeeded by his son Lahná Singh as governor of the hill territory.

Asa Nand and Muhammad Darvesh, the vakíls of Mirs Rustam Ali, and Murád Ali, of Sindh, having received *khilats* for their masters, were permitted to return to their country. In the meantime, the Mir Akhor of Sardar Sultán Muhammad Khan, the governor of Peshâwar, and Shekh Núr Ahmad, the agent of Sardar Hari Singh, Nalwa, reached Láhore, with fifty horses, twenty-five mules and as many camels, sent as tribute by the Afghans of Eusafzai and Chuk Hazárá. Sultán Muhammad Khan had sent a fine horse, named *Parí-Parwáz*, for the Maharájá's own use, and His Highness was greatly pleased with its beauty. Zulfikár Khan, the son of Nawáb Asad Khan, of Sanghar, was sent a prisoner to Láhore by General Ventura. A large number of horses, mules, camels and military stores, belonging to the sardar had been seized, and, on arrival at Láhore, were made over to Misser Beli Rám, *Toshakhánia*.

Tribute from Eusafzai and Chak Hazárá, 1832.

Zulfikár Khan, son of the Khan of Sanghar, made prisoner, 1832.

Death of Kutab-ud-dín Khan of Kasúr, 1832.

Qutab-ud-dín Khan, Kasuria, who had come to Amritsar the previous year, after sustaining a signal defeat at the hands of his nephew, Fatteh Dín Khan, for the possession of Mamdot, and had been since living there, died during the course of this year, at Amritsar. Charat Rám, his vakíl, was directed to convey the body of the late Khan to Mamdot, to be interred there.

Troubles in the Eusafzai hills quelled, 1832.

The Eusafzais of the hills again became troublesome at the close of the year. A body of 15,000 of these hillmen, under Painda Khan and Fatteh Khan, having collected near Darband and Jahángírábád, had reduced the Sikh troops under Hari Singh, Nalwa, to great straits, and in a night attack on the Sikh camp had put a large number of them to the sword. The Maharájá, on receiving this news, at once ordered the Najíb battalions, under Sardar Fatteh Singh Mán, Dhanukal Singh and Ganga Singh, to march to the scene of action, and in a few weeks the disturbance was quelled, and the hill-men retired to their abodes, after receiving severe chastisement.

Hari Singh subsequently routed the Muhammadan tribes above Atak, and ensured their better obedience by building a fort on the right bank of the Indus.

The victory gained by Hari Singh, Nalwa, over the hill tribes.

At the close of the year Sadá Kour, who had been held a close prisoner since 1820, died at Amritsar. The Maharájá at once sent Misser Beli Rám to Amritsar to confiscate all the property and valuables left by the deceased. Her funeral ceremonies were performed by Prince Nou Nehal Singh, and the Maharájá himself repaired to Amritsar, and went to the deceased Ráni's house to condole with his relations. Mái Dasi, her principal slave girl, was then called upon to deliver up all her property and valuables, and, a close search having been made in the Ráni's private rooms, assets belonging to her, valued at two lakhs of rupees, were found and confiscated to the State. Among the confiscated jewels was a necklace of pearls valued at sixty thousand rupees.

The death of Sadá Kour, 1832.

The pleasant dream of an Afghán empire, extending from the border of Belochistán to the Kábul river, had not yet forsaken the exiled monarch Shah Shujá, who with his blind brother, was now living on the bounty of the English at Ludhiáná. In his leisure hours he brooded over schemes of conquest and territorial aggrandizement and opened a correspondence with Ranjít Singh, who, for a time, amused him with vain hopes. The relations between the two chiefs became more cordial in 1832, when the rumoured advance of the Persians against Herat gave further encouragement to the Shah to prosecute his designs against his lost kingdom. In return for assistance in men and money, the Shah proposed to Ranjít Singh the permanent relinquishment of all claims to the countries west of the Indus, conquered by the Maharájá, which were originally part and parcel of the Kábul kingdom of the Ḍuránís, and to deliver also an acquittance for the famous diamond, the *Kohinúr*. The Shah was at this time in the neighbourhood of Shikárpur, whence he sent a vakíl, Mulla Shakur, to remain in attendance at the Láhore Darbár, the Maharájá deputing his agent Alif Shah to remain in attendance on His Majesty. It is now necessary to explain how the kingdom of Afghanistán, as founded by the adventurous Durránís, was parcelled out among various principalities about this time, and how they stood in relation to one another.

The revived hopes of Shah Shujá.

Rumoured advance of the Persians against Herat, 1832.

Negotiations between the Shah and Ranjít Singh.

When Kámrán succeeded his father Shah Mahmúd on the Kábul throne, in 1819, the man in chief power in Afghanistán was the Barakzai Sardar, Muhammad Azím Khan, the brother and eldest survivor of the family of Fatteh Khan, the gallant Kábul Wazír, who had been cruelly put to death by Kámrán in 1818.* He had several brothers, all of whom rebelled against the new king, and Muhammad Azím Khan joined them to dethrone the murderer of his brother. He recalled Shujá-ul-Mulk from his exile, promising him the restoration of the throne of his ancestors, and sending the ex-monarch a *Qurán* under his own seal, as a guarantee for the due fulfilment of the condition. The Shah forthwith repaired to Peshâwar. After all his misfortunes, the Shah might have yet been reinstalled on the throne of his ancestors, and retained it, but fortune had always stood in the way of the success of this ill-fated monarch, and an unhappy incident now happened which prevented him from accomplishing his object. While Azím Khan was still absent from Peshâwar, Shujá assumed an air of royalty, and began to make a premature display of splendour. An Amir, a great friend of his benefactor's, while passing in a palanquin through the town, was insulted and compelled to descend, on a charge of encroaching on the dignity of the king.

The affairs of Afghanistán, 1832.

Sardar Muhammad Azím Khan, Barakzai, in chief power.

He calls Shah Shujá-ul-Mulk from exile, with a view to placing him on the throne.

* *Vide* page 415, *ante*.

He offends the Afgháns by his conduct.

This inconsiderate act inflamed the whole of the Barakzai family, who considered their honour involved in the affront, and it was now resolved to place a more complaisant master on the throne. Ayúb, a brother of Shujá, availing himself of the opportunity, advanced his own claims to the throne. Having entered the camp of Azím Khan, he assumed the demeanour of the most abject of slaves. "Make me but king," he exclaimed, "and permit money to be coined in my name, and the entire power and resources of the kingdom shall rest with yourself; my ambition will be satisfied with bread, and the mere title of king." His prayer was accepted, and he was installed on the throne. He was a mere tool in the hands of the wazír, who exercised supreme power, the puppet king implicitly obeying all his directions and acting on his counsel in all affairs of State. So debased was the condition of royalty in Kábul at this time, that even the robe of honour granted to the wazír on his installation in office was a portion of his own property and was privately sent to the king, who conferred it on the wazír, with all the pomp and show of royalty. Several young princes of the royal blood who aspired to sovereign power were made over to the new king, and put to death by him. Shujá immediately fled to Peshàwar, and thence made his way to Shikárpur.

Shah Ayúb is installed on the throne of Kábul.

Shah Shujá flies from Kábul to Shikárpur.

The battle of Noushera,* fought between the Sikhs and Afgháns in 1823, sealed the fate of Muhammad Azím Khan. The supremacy of the Sikhs was established over the whole country lying between the Indus and Peshávar, and Muhammed Azím Khan died of a broken heart immediately after his return to Kábul, in May of the same year. He left a treasure little short of three millions sterling in value, which was inherited by his eldest son, Habib-ulla Khan, who succeeded to the supremacy which Muhammad Azím Khan and Fateh Khan had both exercised. But the youthful sardar soon became an object of jealousy to the brothers of the deceased. A cabal was formed against him, and his mother was induced by the threat of having her son blown from the mouth of a cannon, to deliver up the treasure. Sher Dil Khan, a brother of Muhammad Azím Khan, carried away about half a million sterling, and established for himself an independent chiefship of Kandahár; another was formed at Peshávar, under Sultan Muhammad Khan, another of the brothers, and the vassal of Ranjít Singh; while Kábul itself, together with Ghazni and Jallálábád, fell to the share of the crafty Dost Muhammad Khan, also a brother of the late wazír. Balkh was annexed to the dominions of Bokhárá, and Herat was held by Kámrán, the son of Shah Mahmúd ,who had given his allegiance to the throne of Persia; and the Sindhians, observing that there was now no member of the family of Shah Mahmúd left who had power to enforce tribute from them, threw off the yoke of submission to the Kábul throne. Ayúb, the puppet king of Kábul, having lost his son in these scenes of anarchy, fled in the direction of the Panjáb, and, in 1822, found an asylum at the Court of Láhore. Thus fell the great Durráni family, which had been founded by the genius of Ahmad Shah, seventy-six years previously.

The battle of Noushera and the death of Muhammad Azim Khan, 1823.

Habibullah Khan, son of Muhammad Azim Khan.

The division of the country among the Barakzai family.

Balkh and Herat slip out of the kingdom of Afghanistán,

And Sindh becomes independent.

Shah Ayúb's flight to the Panjáb.

The dismemberment of the Durráni kingdom.

The Sikhs levied yearly tribute in horses and rice from Sultán Muhammad Khan, for the chiefship of Peshàwar, held by him. He shared its revenues with his two brothers Pír Muhammad Khan and Said Muhammad Khan. The net revenue about this time (1832 A.D.) was a little less than five lakhs of rupees.

The chiefship of Peshávar held by Sultán Muhammad Khan in the name of the Sikhs.

The same circumstances which dismembered the Durráni government, led to the establishment of Kábul as a distinct principality, and that territory, with its dependency of Ghazni and Jallálábád, fell, in 1826, into the

The chiefship of Kábul with its dependency Ghazni and Jallálábád held by Dost Muhammad Khan.

* *Vide* page 429, *ante.*

hands of Dost Muhammad Khan, who governed the principality with the aid of only a brother. The revenues amounted to eighteen lakhs of rupees, and the chief maintained a force consisting of 9,000 horse and 2,000 foot, with other auxiliaries, village troops and a park of 18 guns. Dost Muhammad Khan is described as having been unremitting in his attention to business, attending the Court-house daily with his Kázi and Mulláhs and deciding disputes according to law.

The chiefship of Kandahár held by Khush Dil Khan.

The chieftainship of Kandahár was formed, as already mentioned, by Sher Dil Khan from the spoils of his nephew, on his flight from Kábul to Kandahár. The Sardar is described as being a man of singular habits, and bearing a great resemblance to his brother Fatteh Khan, in courage and bravery. It is related of Sher Dil that he once lopped off the finger of one of his sons, to test the youth's courage, telling him, at the same time, that, if he cried or uttered a sound, he could not be his son, or a Barakzai. The young fellow bore the pain with great patience. Sher Dil Khan had been accompanied in his flight from Kábul by his four brothers. But he, as well as one of his brothers, was now no longer living, and Kandahár was governed by Kohan Dil Khan, assisted by his two surviving brothers, Rustam Dil Khan and Mehr Dil Khan. The revenue of the principality amounted to about eight lakhs, and the forces consisted of 9,000 horse and six pieces of artillery.

Herat governed by Prince Kámrán.

Herat, governed by Prince Kámrán, had, at this time, virtually become a dependency of Persia. The Persian troops had several times entered it and retired only on payment of a sum of money. This year (September 1832), it was again threatened by the Prince Royal in person, who demanded pecuniary payment, and also required that the name of the King of Persia be stamped on the coins.

Shah Shujá sets out from Ludhiáná for a fresh campaign in Afghanistán, February 1833.

Such was the state of the country west of the Indus when Shah Shujá was forming new plans for the recovery of the throne of his ancestors. Having bought two guns of the Rání of Thanesar, the Shah left Ludhiáná, in 1833, having engaged the services of an Anglo-Indian named Campbell, to whom he gave the command of six hundred men. The Shah went first to Maler Kotla, where he remained for a month. On the festival of *Id*, the Nawáb of Maler Kotla presented His ex-Majesty with 5,000 rupees and two horses. The Shah then moved on to Jagránwán, where Sardar Fatteh Singh, Ahluwalia, of Kapurthállá, sent him 2,000 rupees and a number of swords. A fortnight after, he went to Báháwalpur, receiving from the Nawáb 5,000 rupees, a gun, some camels and bullocks. The Shah next marched to Shikárpur, and at Kámpur, six miles from Shikárpur, was met by Husain Shah, the Hyderábád Vakíl, who presented him with 50,000 rupees, five or six horses, some swords and two tents. The Shah remained at Shikárpur for ten months, sending from here a present of a Persian horse and some tents to Maharájá Ranjít Singh, who sent him 1,25,000 rupees, together with a piece of artillery and 21 matchlocks, on the understanding that he should relinquish for ever his claims to the territories of Káshmír, Attock, Peshávar, Bannú and Deraját. The Sindhians, being joined by the Talpur Amir of Hydrabád, who had become jealous of the Shah's growing power, attacked him near Shikárpur, but were signally defeated on 9th January 1834, the Shah taking possession of four guns belonging to the Amir. Many of the Sindh Chiefs were killed in this battle, among them being Husain Shah. The Sindhians paid the Shah Rs. 5,00,000 in cash and gave a promise of future submission. Elated with his success, the Shah made preparations for a march to Kandahár, with a view to laying siege to that city. He sent letters to the Khan of Kelat

He is assisted by several chiefs with money and war ammunition.

Defeats the Sindhians, 9th January 1834.

desiring him to send him five lakhs of rupees, ten horses, and a number of camels. The Khan sent him a lakh, four horses and twenty camels. Bahadur Khan *Kákar*, chief of Salkhaneh, near Hyderabád, also joined him, with a lakh of rupees, five horses and twenty camels. Having now reached Kandahár at the head of several thousand fighting men, the Shah laid close siege to the town. An attempt to carry the place by assault failed. Dost Muhammad Khan, leaving his brother, Amir Muhammad Khan, in charge of Kábul, marched to assist his brothers at Kandahár in repelling Shah Shujá. Everything seemed now to favour the Shah's projects. He had command of a strong army and was the possessor of a large treasure and immense military stores, purchased by himself and contributed by different reigning chiefs. He had also the sympathy and good-will of the people of Kábul. The Ghulám Khana leaders had already declared in favour of the Shah, and resolved to secure the person of Amir Muhammad Khán. Gulistán Khan, the Hazárá chief of Kará Bágh, south of Ghazni, had rebelled against the authority of the Kábul Amir and boldly engaged and defeated the Ghazni troops that had been sent against him. The Shah was also in correspondence with Nawáb Jabbar Khan, a brother of the Dost, who believed that the Shah's operations against Kandahár were not without the indirect sanction of the British Government. The influence of the Nawáb secured a strong party in favour of the Shah, Nawábs Muhammad Zamán Khán and Muhammad Usmán Khán having bound themselves in regard to the Shah strictly as they might be directed by Jabbar Khan. The understanding between the parties was as follows:—Nawáb Jabbar Khan was to get the chieftainship of the Ghilzais, of which Dost Muhammad Khan had deprived him, and Nawáb Muhammad Zamán Khan was to receive Jallálábád, while Muhammad Usmán Khan was to be reinstated in his jagírs. So sanguine was the aged Jabbar Khán of the Shah's victory, that, at Ghazni, he entreated the Dost to permit him to repair to the Shah at Kandahár, in order to settle terms with him. To these entreaties of his brother the insidious chief replied "*Lálá!*" (a term of affection) "it will be time enough to consider that when we are defeated." In the meantime, he wrote a letter to Shah Shujá, stating ironically that his brothers of Kandahár were unscrupulous men, unfamiliar with the rules of decorum and decency to be observed on the visit of His Majesty; that he, fully knowing the respect due to the imperial diginty, was now on his way to do honour to the 'Asylum of the Poor' and to escort him, with due respect, to Kábul. So the Dost arrived by rapid marches in the neighbourhood of Kandahár, at the head of twenty thousand horse, five thousand foot and about 18 guns. The Shah had hitherto entrenched himself in a position resting upon the old town of Kandahár, built by Nádir Shah; and, had he continued in the same position, no effort would have been needed on his part to effect the complete ruin of his enemy. As it happened, however, the reverse was the case. Rejecting the counsels of his general, Samandar Khan, and other chiefs, and in spite of their warnings, he abandoned the entrenchments as soon as the Kábul army arrived, falling back to the northern extremity of the hill, and occupying the gardens at the base of the old town of Husain Khan. This was a disastrous move, the object of the pusillanimous monarch being to keep open his rear for flight; for it was well known that, whatever the chances of battle, the Shah always regarded his personal safety more than victory. The following morning, Dost Muhammad Khan arrived at Kandahár, and the next day his son, Muhammad Akbar Khan, came out of the town with 12,000 cavalry and four guns. On the arrival of this reinforcement, Dost Muhammad Khan, unsheathing his sword, directed a

Lays siege to Kandahár.

Dost Muhammad marches to meet him.

Sympathy expressed for the Shah throughout the country;

Nevertheless, Dost Muhammad is sanguine of his own success.

The Shah's irresolution.

And pusillanimity.

forward movement, but returned, after galloping some fifty yards. At about five o'clock in the evening, Shah Shujá ordered Mr. Campbell to attack the enemy, and that officer, by a skillful move, succeeded in carrying all before him, dispersing in succession the battalions of Abdul Samad Khan and the cavalry of Muhammad Akbar Khan and the Kandahár chiefs. But he was ordered to return to the lines for the evening. Early the next morning Dost Muhammad Khan drew up his forces in order of battle. Samandar Khan and Jahan Dád Khan, the Generals of the Shah's army, moved forward to the attack with twelve thousand horse. Mr. Campbell was sent forward with two battalions, but with no guns or cavalry to support him. The whole of the remaining force was ordered to follow. Anything like order or discipline was quite unknown to the Shah's troops, the several divisions of his army acting independently of one another. The upshot of the attack was that the Shah's troops were hemmed in between the high banks of a dry water-course, and fell into confusion. Shah Shujá, from his elephant, ordered Mr. Campbell to "*chapao*," or rush forward to the attack. The latter remonstrated and represented that the circumstances required a bold stand and steady fighting, and that it was no time for breaking the ranks. The Shah, however, was headstrong, and rashly repeated the words "*Chapao! chapao!*" but, to the astonishment of all, with the same breath that he urged his troops forward, he gave the order to his *mahauat* to turn his elephant round, which having been done, he fled panic-stricken. Mr. Campbell engaged the enemy for two hours, but was wounded and taken prisoner. Three hundred Hindustánís, who had been in the service of the East India Company, made a bold stand, but were overpowered by superior numbers. The triumph of the Barakzais was followed by horrible scenes of slaughter and plunder, and the whole of the artillery and military stores of the fugitives fell into the hands of the Afgháns. Even the records and correspondence of the fugitive Shah fell into the hands of the Kandahár brothers, who made them over to Dost Muhammad. Among the papers was found a copy of a treaty between Ranjít Singh and Shah Shujá and some letters bearing the seal of Captain Wade. The battle was fought on 1st July 1834. Had it not been for the inertness of the Shah and the irresolution and incapacity of his Generals, Samandar Khan and Jahan Dád Khan, the battle would not have terminated so disastrously for him. Mr. Campbell was kept in the house of Mehr Dil Khan, who had his wounds washed and had him treated by a Surgeon. A week after, Dost Muhammad Khan, accompanied by Nawáb Jabbar Khan and Mirza Abdul Sami Khan, his minister, paid a visit to Mehr Dil Khan. The Amir treated Mr. Campbell honourably and sent him on an elephant to Kábul, where he put him in command of the artillery on a salary of Rs. 400 a month.

Disorder among his troops.

He is defeated and put to flight, 1st January 1834.

The Shah, after his discomfiture at Kandahár, fled to Farah. Prince Kámrán, of Herat, sent him handsome presents and a letter offering to send his son, Shahzádá Jahangír, with four thousand horse and guns to assist him in another attempt on Kandahár, but the suspicious Shah fancied, though without grounds, that Jahangir would be instructed to seize him, and he fled from Farah to Lásh, whence he proceeded across the deserts of Sistán and thence to Kelat in Belúchistán. Here he was honourably received by Mehrab Khan, the Barohi Chief. Rahm Dil Khan of Kandahár sent word to him to seize the Shah and deliver him up to his men. The Khan, who was assisted in his resolution by his wife Bibi Gul Ján, thought it unworthy of a Beloch Chief to betray the trust which the Shah, in his misfortune, had placed in him, and sent him under proper escort to Zehri, whence His Majesty made his way to Bágh in Kachi. Here he

The Shah's flight to Farah,

And from thence to the deserts of Sistán and Kelát.

He travels to Hyderábád in Sindh.

But eventually returns to Ludhiáná, 1833.

made fresh attempts to raise an army, with a view to another invasion of Kandahár; but his General, Samandar Khan, fell suddenly ill and died. The Shah then went to Hyderábád in Sindh; but, seeing that the wind blew unfavourably for him in every quarter, he at last concluded that he could do no better than return to Ludhiáná, his old asylum in the Panjáb. He therefore returned to that place, divested of his army, but bringing with him two lakhs and fifty thousand rupees in cash and valuables.

Mulct imposed on a rich Banker's death at Amritsar, 1833.

In the beginning of 1833, Sheodial, a rich Khatri of Amritsar, having died, Commandant Sham Singh was deputed to confiscate all the property of the deceased. The three sons of the deceased, Rám Dás, Kishen Chand and Naráin Dás, who made some demur, were sent in chains to Láhore, where a lakh of rupees having been exacted from them, they were set at liberty.

The Maharájá marries Gul Bahár, 1833.

The Maharájá having taken a fancy to Gul Bahár,* one of the *demi-monde* of Amritsar, married her with great pomp and splendour in the course of this year. The marriage procession, headed by the bridegroom, who wore on his head the bridal chaplet, or wreath of flowers, went to the bride's house. Here Mamola, sister of Moran, a woman of the same class, who had been previously married to the Maharájá, adorned the bridegroom's neck with a necklace of pearls and sprinkled saffron water on his clothes. The ceremonies closed amid great rejoicings; and for many days Láhore and Amritsar were the scene of merriment and festivities.

Complete subjugation of the country about the Sulemán hill range, 1833.

About this time Prince Kharak Singh was sent to Sanghar at the head of an army, for the complete subjugation of the country about the Sulemán Range of hills. Asad Khan, the chief, on hearing of the approach of the Sikh troops, fled to the hills to form a union with the Afgháns of the mountains. The Maharájá, hearing of this, issued orders for Dewán Sanwan Mal, the Governor of Multán, to send reinforcements to Sanghar. The country was soon after occupied by the Sikhs and farmed to General Ventura for the sum of Rs. 1,50,000 annually, besides a *nazaráná* of a number of horses.

Administration of Káshmír.

Reports having been received of the mismanagement of Káshmír by Dewán Baisákha Singh, under Prince Sher Singh, who had been sent there as Governor, some time previously, the Dewán was sent to Láhore in chains and a mulct of five lakhs of rupees was imposed upon him. Jamadar Khushal Singh, Bhai Gurmukh Singh and Sheikh Ghulám Mohi-ud-dín were sent to Káshmír to examine the accounts of revenue and expenditure and to assist Prince Sher Singh in the administration of the country, in place of the deposed Dewán.

Famine in Káshmír, 1833.

Káshmír was about this time visited by so severe a famine that thousands of people fled from the country in different directions, and hundreds died from starvation and hunger. The shawl manufacture, which was so thriving in the time of Dewán Moti Rám and Kirpa Rám, had come to a standstill under the governorship of Prince Sher Singh, who spent all his time in drinking and debauchery, leaving his subordinates to act for him. Jamadar Khushal Singh, who had shortly before been sent to Káshmír, made matters worse, and many were the complaints against his oppression. Large firms had become bankrupt, and thousands of people who derived their income from the shawl trade had no business to pursue.

Suppression of the shawl trade.

This, combined with a severe drought, completed the ruin of the people. The streets of Láhore and Amritsar swarmed with bands of starving Kashmirís, who went about the streets and lanes crying for bread. Khuda Bakhsh, the Kotwál, or chief police officer of Láhore, reported daily to the Maharájá the number of

* She was called Rání Gul Begam. She died at Láhore in 1863, and was in receipt of a pension of Rs. 12,380 per annum till her death.

persons who had died from starvation. The Maharájá ordered the depository of corn in Fort Gobind Garh at Amritsar to be opened for the benefit of the famished Kashmirís there, and Sardar Lahná Singh and Mian Samdu were specially ordered to alleviate the prevailing distress by a daily distribution of flour and blankets among the emigrants, at the expense of the State. Similara rrangements were made at Láhore under Misar Beli Rám. The famine-stricken people, men and women, were lodged in the mosque of Wazir Khan and in some Hindu temples and Musalmán shrines, where flour was distributed to them daily. Such a famine had not visited the Káshmír valley for 200 years; and the many Kashmirí families now residing in Láhore, Amritsar, Ludhiáná, Núrpur, Patháukot and Dera Bábá Nanak, owe their existence there to the great scarcity of that period. The Maharájá recalled Jamadar Khushal Singh and Sheikh Ghulám Mohi-ud-dín from Káshmír, and sent General Mihan Singh as a deputy to Prince Sher Singh, for the management of the affairs of Káshmír. The General did much for the relief of the suffering population, and through his exertions the distress was greatly alleviated. The Maharájá was so much displeased with Jamadar Khushal Singh for the excesses committed by him in Káshmír that, for a period of one month, he was not admitted into his presence.

Relief arrangements made by the Maharájá.

General Mihán Singh is deputed to Káshmír.

It was ordered about this time that Rájá Dhian Singh be addressed in public correspondence as "*Rájá Kalán Bahadur*," or "chief rájá, the champion of the State." The Maharájá was also at this period so pleased with the manner and address of Captain Wade, the British Agent at Ludhiáná who frequently visited Láhore on business and was the sporting companion of the Maharájá in the field, that he conferred upon him the high title of "*Farzand-i-Dil Band*," or "well-beloved son." Tárá Chand, the son of Karm Chand, having been created a Dewán, was sent to Bannú to levy tribute from the Kháns and Maliks of that District. Rám Singh, the Kárdár of Sujánpur having died and it having been reported that he had left twenty thousand rupees with the bankers of Amritsar, orders were issued to Fakír Imám-ud-dín to confiscate the money forthwith and credit it to the State. The Court was at Amritsar at the time, and confiscation and exactions were the order of the day. Sheikh Ghulám Mohi-ud-dín was put in chains and a heavy mulct was demanded from him. Miser Rúp Lál was sent to Hoshiárpur to seize all the household property of the Sheikh there. The mode in which the hidden treasure of the Sheikh was discovered in his private residence there is interesting. A spacious tomb, said to be the burial-place of the Sheikh's *Pír*, or spiritual guide, was erected, and Mulláhs surrounded it, reading the *Qurán* and burning benzoin, as on the tombs of the saints. It was reported to the Miser that this so-called resting-place of the *Pír* was the depository not of his holy ashes, but of gold and silver, and, the place having been dug out, no less than nine and a half lakhs of rupees were found concealed in it. This having been communicated to the Maharájá, His Highness tauntingly said to the Sheikh: "The ashes of your *Pír* have been converted into silver and gold. He must undoubtedly have been a great saint." The Sheikh in vain swore that this was the money collected by his father, Sheikh Ujálá, in the service of Sardar Bhúp Singh. Ranjít Singh knew very well that Ujálá was no great Sardar and had never seen a lakh of rupees in his life. He was sure that the money had been squeezed from the starving Kashmirís by the Sheikh, while a lieutenant of Prince Sher Singh. The whole of the money was confiscated to the State and a fine of Rs. 25,000 imposed besides. Ranjít Singh had also an eye on General Ventura, whom he suspected of gaining a great deal of money from his lease of Dera Ghází Khan; but considerations of his good services and his excellent management of districts

Rájá Dhián Singh is created "*Rájá Kalán*."

The title of "Farzand-i-Dil Band" conferred on Captain Wade.

Forfeitures and resumptions by the State.

Sheikh Ghulám Mohi-ud-dín, late lieutenant of Káshmír, subjected to a heavy mulct.

General Ventura and his lease of Dera Ghází Khan.

on the frontier, prevented him from indulging vent to his cupidity against an officer who was honoured alike by the people, the officers and the Government.

The Maharájá confers a jágír on the grandsons of Sansár Chand, of Katoch, 1833.

Rai Rámbír Chand and Barmodh Chand, the sons of Anrodh Chand, of Katoch, having been introduced, through Rájá Suchet Singh, they presented 31 gold mohurs, a horse, an elephant and a sword as a *nazar*. The Maharájá gave the grandsons of Sansár Chand a cordial reception and conferred upon them a jágír of Rs. 50,000 in the Kangrá hills. The Maharájá was not by nature wantonly harsh, and, though avaricious in the extreme, his generosity was proverbial, and it was his policy never to reduce anyone to desperation. During the same year, Misar Beli Rám was ordered to have some fine shawls and other articles suited for presents manufactured, with a view to their being sent to Calcutta, for His Majesty the King of England.

Serious illness of the Maharájá 1833.

On his return from Amritsar to Láhore, at the close of the year, the Maharájá's health became seriously impaired. He was a great believer in the prayers of fakírs, and even dreaded them. There lived on the banks of the Ravi about this time, a Bairagi fakír, and Ranjít went to him, as a private individual, and besought his prayers in his behalf. He offered a pair of shawls, 1,000 rupees in money and 25 pieces of crystallized sugar as a *nazar*, but these were distributed among the poor, as ordered by the fakír. He next went to the mausoleum of Mian Wadda, in the vicinity of Láhore, and invoked the prayers of the blind *darveshes* who were in attendance on the Khangáh, presenting them with money and fruit. On the first day of the moon, alms were given out to the poor. The same day the Maharájá narrated a dream which he had had the previous night. He saw a band of Sikhs dressed in black, with dreadful features, speaking harshly to him. His Highness seemed quite perplexed at this, and Brahmins and astrologers were consulted as to the interpretation of the dream. They declared, after a reference to their holy books, that the Sikhs he had seen in his dream were the soldiers of God (*Nihangs*), who had come to tell him that he had relinquished the religion of the Guru by marrying a Muhammadan lady (Gul Bahár), and that, unless atonement was soon made, the displeasure of the Guru would not be averted. It was therefore resolved that the Maharájá should take the *páhal* afresh and renew the faith of his ancestors by doing penance for his sin. Atma Singh and Dewa Singh, the Sikh priests, were accordingly sent for, and the necessary ceremonies having been performed, the Maharájá was duly invested with the *páhál* of the Guru. Such was the superstitious belief of Ranjít Singh, who, however, in accepting the *páhal* a second time, had no intention of putting away his much-favoured Muhammadan wife. Following this event, a large number of prisoners were released, and orders were issued to the governors of provinces to set at liberty a fixed number of convicts under their charge. Some old State prisoners at Láhore were also released on this occasion, among them being Mian Bhúp Deo, of Jammú, who had been in confinement for fifteen years, Bir Singh, the Rájá of Núrpur, and Faiz Talab Khan, of Bhimbar. The services of Bhúp Deo were placed at the disposal of Kour Kharak Singh and those of Faiz Talab Khan at that of Sardar Atar Singh, Sindhianwalia. A lakh of rupees was demanded from Rájá Bír Singh, as a ransom, but 80,000 rupees only was realized. The Basant festival having arrived, Kour Kharak Singh was ordered to hold the usual Darbár at the mausoleum of Lál Husain, and receive the *nazaránás* from the sardars and chiefs.

His dream.

Its interpretation by the Brahmins.

They advise him to receive afresh the Sikh initiation into *páhal*.

The Maharájá goes through the ceremony.

Release of State prisoners.

A curious rite performed.

Pandit Madhosúdan and other Brahmins of the Court, after consulting the Shastras, gave it as their opinion that, in order completely to remove the effects of the unpropitious star from the Maharájá, it was necessary to make an effigy of gold, 51 tolahs in weight, and set it with rubies and sapphires. This idol, they said, should be given in alms to a Brahmin of Benares or Mathrá, who, being seated in a cart drawn by black she-buffaloes, should be sent across the Biás and the Sutlej. Miser Beli Rám was ordered to have the effigy made, and, this having been done on the fourth day, as required by the pandits, a native Brahmin of the towns named was searched for. A Mathrá Brahmin being at hand, oil was rubbed over his body, which was then blackened, after which he was clothed in black and made to ride on the cart drawn by the black she-buffaloes, with the golden image in his hands. A present was also made to him of rupees 5,000 and gold earrings (*bálás*), together with a black horse, which had on its back a saddle covered with black satin. Thus prepared, the Brahmin was sent across the Biás and Sutlej under a guard of soldiers. Doctor Murray also came from Ludhiáná to see the Maharájá, who, however, soon after recovered from his sickness.

Death of Dewán Bhawáni Das, 1834.

Early in 1834, Dewán Bhawáni Dás, the head of the Finance Department, died. He had fought successively in the Multán, Peshâwar and Eusafzai campaigns, and before that, as the chief dewán of Prince Kharak Singh, had taken a leading part in the reduction of the country of the Ramgarhia Sardars about Amritsar and Gurdáspur. He was an eminent financier, and had once been charged with embezzlement by Miser Beli Rám, the Treasurer, on which occasion Ranjít Singh, being highly incensed, struck the dewán with his sheathed sword in open darbár, and imposed a fine of a lakh of rupees upon him. He was then banished to a hill appointment, but, his services being too valuable to be spared, he was recalled and reinstated in his post, after a few months. On his death, he was succeeded by Pandit Dina Nath.

Pandit Dina Nath succeeds him as Head of Finance Department.

Rising of the Afghans on the borders of Bannú, 1834.

About this time the zemindars of Ghári Dilássá Khan, in the Bannú District, raised the standard of revolt. Bakhshi Tárá Chand and Sardars Shám Singh, Jai Singh, and Jagat Singh, Attariwallas, besieged the mutineers in the *garhi*, or mountain stronghold; but the besieged, some two thousand in number, made a sudden sally, killing three hundred Sikhs with the fire of their matchlocks and wounding five hundred more. The Sikhs were compelled to raise the siege and retire to a distance of a *kos* from the *garhi*. The Maharájá, on receiving news of this, forthwith ordered Rájá Suchet Singh to march to the scene of insurrection at the head of a force for the relief of the Sikh army. He was, however, much irritated at hearing of the disaster. Tárá Chand had been created a dewán a short time before, and placed in charge of Bannú, Tánk and Dera Ismail Khan. On the present occasion, he had with him the flower of the Sikh army. His force of eight thousand men and eight guns was led by the Chiefs of Atári, Nakka, and Batála, and his ignominious repulse, with the loss of so many brave men, was looked upon by the Maharájá as a disgrace on his official career and a stain on his military character. He was highly indignant, and fined the dewán and his brothers, Mangal Sen and Ratan Chand, 1,25,000 rupees. Tárá Chand also quarrelled with Rájá Suchet Singh, who was at this time in charge of the Derajját, and this brought on his subsequent ruin. Peace was, in the meanwhile, restored on the borders of Bannú, through the exertions of Rájá Suchet Singh.

Discomfiture of the Sikh troops.

Rájá Suchet Singh ordered to the scene of action.

Peace restored.

Ranjít Singh resolves on regularly annexing Peshâwar to his dominions.

The unsettled state of Peshâwar and the probability of its becoming tributary to Kábul under Dost Muhammad Khan, or Shah Shujá, in the event of a fresh war breaking out between the two for the sovereignty of Afghanistán, now induced Ranjít Singh to make an endeavour to annex that province permanently to his dominions. Soon after the Dasahra, orders were issued to Sardar Hari Singh, Nálwa, to proceed with all his

Prince Nau Nehal Singh is sent in that direction at the head of a force.

forces from the Eusafzai hills to Pesháwar, and there act as lieutenant to Prince Nau Nehal Singh, who was in the meantime sent from Láhore in that direction, accompanied by Generals Ventura and Court and a large body of troops. The force crossed the Indus at the end of April, and, on arriving in the vicinity of Pesháwar, an increased tribute in horses, rice, swords, &c., was demanded. The horses, &c., which were offered were rejected as unsuitable, the object of the Sikhs being to gain time. The Barakzai Sardars in possession of Pesháwar, apprehensive of the designs of the Sikhs, had already sent their families to Michni, north of the Kábul river, with their guns and other property. They themselves remained in Pesháwar with their horses ready to be saddled at a moment's notice. "It was ridiculous," writes an eye-witness, "about twice or thrice a day, to see the servants running out with the saddles on their heads and returning when they discovered that the alarm which had been given was a false one." Everything which was portable had been carried away, even to the doors and windows of their houses. This had, indeed, always been the custom at Pesháwar whenever there was a report of the Sikhs approaching its vicinity. The remnants of the old Ghulám Khána of Pesháwar who, on account of their being Shiás, were dissatisfied with the rule of the Barakzai brothers, opened a clandestine correspondence with Hari Singh, and so did the principal Hindu dewáns of the country. Hari Singh, finding everything in his favour, sent a message to the Barakzai Sardars, Sultán Muhammad Khan, his brother, Pír Muhammad Khan, and his nephew, Abdul Ghias Khan, the son of Nawáb Jabbar Khan, and Náib Haji Khan, to evacuate the city and retire to the garden of Ali Murdán Khan, as the Shahzádá Nau Nehal Singh desired to see the city. The Sikh force was, in the meantime, in motion, and Sultán Muhammad Khan, observing this with a spy-glass which he had always in his hand, made immediate preparations for flight. The horses were saddled and mounted in a trice. The houses were evacuated, as if by magic, and all fled to the adjoining hills, except Abdul Ghias Khan and his party. The Sikhs moved forward in regular order. The van was led by the young Shahzádá, seated on an elephant and followed by Hari Singh and a host of other sardars. Behind them came detachments of cavalry, and, last of all, the battalions of General Court, advancing in column in quick time. Some Afghans who had concealed themselves among the trees, were soon cleared out. The advance of the Sikhs was checked by Haji Khan's men, and a skirmish ensued, in which Khan Muhammad Khan, the brother of Haji Khan, was badly wounded and borne off the field. A smart fire was kept up on both sides, and instances of individual bravery were not wanting among the Afghans. One gallant fellow cut down six of his adversaries. The Sikhs, having now completed the circuit of the city, entered and occupied the Bálá Hissár, and, simultaneously with it, the town was occupied, on 6th May 1834. The discomfited sardars fled to Takkál and Shekhán, at the foot of the hills. Pír Muhammad Khan was afterwards reported to have retired to Kohát with treasure amounting to three lakhs of rupees, which he carried away from Pesháwar. Thus did the Sikhs make themselves masters of an important and productive country. There is no doubt that, had Sultán Muhammad Khan made the least attempt to defend the country, it would not have fallen so easy a prey to them as it did. As it was, however, the sardar had sent away the best part of his troops, and prohibited the town and country people from defending the city.

Confusion in Pesháwar.

March of the Sikh troops to the city.

The Sikhs occupy the town of Pesháwar and the citadel, 6th May 1834.

The Maharájá concentrates his troops on the frontier, and himself marches to Pesháwar.

Pesháwar was taken, but Ranjít Singh's mind was not at rest, and he concentrated his whole attention on frontier affairs. Troops were daily sent in that direction; Kanwar Káshmíra Singh was sent to Atak at the head of his troops, and Sardar Tej Singh to Peshâwar. Last of all, the Maharájá himself set out for Peshâwar, encamping for a month at Rohtás *en route*, and sending Rájá Guláb Singh in advance of his camp to Peshâwar.

Dost Muhammad Khan, greatly perplexed by the Sikhs annexing Peshâwar to their dominions.

He desires British interference which is refused, 1834.

The occupation of Peshâwar by the Sikhs had been a source of great trouble to Amir Dost Muhammad Khan, as he had always laid claim to it as a dependency of Kábul. In vain did the Amir solicit the mediation of the British Government to induce the Sikhs to retire from Peshâwar and to adjust the difference between him and the Láhore ruler; he was told that the Government was unwilling to meddle in the affair, though a plain declaration was made to Dost Muhammad and his brothers of the desire of the British Government to form a connection with them by an interchange of commercial facilities. Left thus to his own resources, and to settle his differences with the Láhore Government as best he could, the Amir made preparations for a march in the direction of Peshâwar. At the same time, through one Muhammad Husain, a native of Persia, who had for some years resided at Kábul, he opened a correspondence with the Shah of Persia. He had desired Nawáb Jabbar Khan, his brother, and a man of great influence at Kábul, to become a party to this correspondence, but the Nawáb refused to have anything to do with the affair, declaring that he had always advocated a connection with the British Government, and would continue to do so.

He opens correspondence with Persia.

He marches from Jallálábád to give the Sikhs battle, 1835,

At length the Amir broke up his camp at Jallálábád, and, by easy marches, reached Bassowal. The *Id Kurbán* festival was celebrated at Ali Bághán, and here the Amir offered up prayers for the success of his arms in the impending conflict. He exclaimed audibly, that he might be heard by those around, "Allah! I am but a weak fly, about to resist a huge elephant. Thy power is great, and on Thee this poor fly places its dependence. If it be Thy will, the fly will be triumphant in its encounter with the elephant. From Thee I beseech help and from Thee I implore victory." A host of Ghâzis, or warriors of the faith, also joined the Amir from the surrounding country. He assumed the proud title of *Ghâzi* or Champion of the Faith, and endeavoured to rouse the population generally to a sense of their duty, which he declared was to destroy the infidel invaders of Peshâwar. The Sikhs, on their part, endeavoured to gain over many of the Maliks or petty chiefs of the Khaibar, by assigning allowances to them; but these abandoned the cause of the Sikhs and joined the Amir, on the plea of religious feeling. Having passed the defiles of the Khaibar, the Amir encamped at Shekán at the foot of the hills. The news that the Afghans had actually taken up a position on the plains of Peshâwar, induced the Maharájá, who was loitering in the country east of the Indus, to accelerate his march to that place, where he soon arrived, restoring confidence among his troops. He was joined by Sardar Sultán Muhammad Khan, who lent his moral support, but was in no way in a position to render the Maharájá material aid. The personal attention and exertions of the veteran ruler of Láhore now effected an immediate change in the disposition of the army, which had hitherto been located in different positions to no advantage. The camp nearest the Afghan detachments remained stationary, as if no movements were in contemplation. Further time was gained by amusing the Kábul Amir with negotiations, the diplomatists on the part of the Afghans being Nawáb Jabbar Khan and Agha Husain, the latter being deputed to watch the proceedings of the former, who lacked the Amir's confidence. Subsequent events, however, showed that the Agha was no more honest a dependant of the Amir than his Barakzai colleague, he having accepted a large sum of money from the Sikhs, and promised to prevail upon his master to retrace his steps to Kábul. The time thus gained was made

And assumes the title of Ghâzi.

The Maharájá reaches Peshâwar.

He gains the moral support of Sardar Sultán Muhammad Khan.

Negotiations.

use of by the Láhore ruler in concentrating his troops and redistributing them, so as to completely surround the Afghan positions. The semicircle formed by the Sikh forces comprised five camps, their fronts being protected by cavalry, their rear by regular infantry, consisting of 35 battalions, and behind them being detachments of cavalry of various strength. While these arrangements for an attack were going on, the Maharájá deputed Fakír Aziz-ud-dín and Mr. Harlan, an Anglo-Indian who had lately entered his service, to the Amir's camp, with instructions to induce the Amir to retire. Sardar Sultán Muhammad Khan was also sent along with the envoys, to assist in carrying on the negotiations. These were, however, still pending when the Amir was informed, to his great surprise, that all his troops were surrounded by the Sikhs. He never perhaps meant to bring on an actual rupture, so soon at least, for he was conscious of the great superiority of the Sikh army over his own; but he now clearly saw that his choice lay between retreat and flight. If he remained stationary, there was the danger of his being deprived of his munitions of war, including his guns and military equipage. In his dilemma, he consulted Mirza Sámi Khan, his confidential minister, and the idea now suggested itself of arresting the Sikh envoys in the Amir's camp. Dost Muhammad Khan knew well that the presence of Fakír Aziz-ud-dín, the Maharájá's physician, who prescribed medicines for him and regulated the doses, was absolutely necessary for his existence, and it was conceived that the Maharájá would be compelled to cede Pesháwar in exchange for the indispensable Fakír, or that, at any rate, a large sum of money would be offered as ransom. To avoid, however, the disgrace which would attach to an action so opposed to international laws, it was resolved to involve Sardar Sultán Muhammad Khan in the proposed detention of the Sikh envoys. The Amir accordingly sent for the sardar, and, after an exchange of oaths on the *Qurán* as to secrecy, informed him of his resolution. It was suggested that, as the envoys had come with him, it would be most convenient and conducive to the interests of the parties concerned, if he carried them off, when, it was surmised, everything would be gained as desired. The sardar at once saw that the object of the Amir's policy was to bring about his ruin at the expense of his own reputation. He feigned to fall in with the scheme and promised compliance forthwith, swearing on the *Qurán*, but considering the oath to be made under circumstances in which it would not be legally binding. Dost Muhammad, thinking his point gained, summoned the Fakír and Mr. Harlan into his presence and reproached and abused them. On being somewhat appeased by the persuasive speech of the learned Fakír, he said that he had kept the envoys in the Afghan camp merely as hostages for the due fulfilment of the terms proposed, which were the surrender of half the territory of Pesháwar to his brother, Sultán Muhammad Khan, and the payment to himself of a few lakhs of rupees as *nálbandi*, literally, the cost of shoeing his horses. The Fakír urged that it was necessary for him and his colleague to return to the Maharájá to acquaint him with the Amir's propositions, but to this it was replied that this could be more conveniently done by letter. The Fakír then argued that the detention of the envoys was a direct infringement of the respect which, among the Afghans, as among all other nations, is attached to their person. To this the Amir replied that the Sikhs were *Káfirs*, or infidels, and not like other people, that they themselves broke oaths and treaties, and that with such people it would be only fair to act in a different manner. The envoys were then made over to the charge of Sardar Sultán Muhammad Khan. The latter, however, perceiving the evil designs of his brother against him, and finding an opportunity to gain the confidence of the Maharájá, instead of carrying off the envoys, escorted

Redistribution of the Sikh army.

The Amír's perplexity.

The Amir imprisons Fakír Aziz-ud-dín and Mr. Harlan, and makes them over to Sultán Muhammad Khan.

The Amir's proposals.

The Amir is duped by Sardar Sultán Muhammad Khan, who sends Fakír Aziz-ud-dín and Mr. Harlan to the Sikh camp.

them with all honour to his own camp, and eventually sent them to Michni, there to await the Maharájá's orders.

Retrograde movement of the Amir.

Dost Muhammad Khan now resolved on an orderly retreat; but the greater part of his army Bazár was plundered by the Gházi's. Late in the evening, he reached the heights of Chaghárí in the defiles of the Khaibar, when he heard the reports of the Sikh *salvœs* discharged in triumph at the flight of the Kábul troops. The Amir, however, consoled himself with the thought that he had outwitted the Sikhs in the matter of the arrest of Fakír Aziz-ud-dín and Mr. Harlan, whom he believed to be still in the custody of Sardar Sultán Muhammad Khan. In the meanwhile, he continued his retrograde movement to Shekhán, but was told at Jahárghi that his scheme for the capture of the envoys had failed, and that they were far beyond his reach. The Amir and his confidential minister, the Mirza, were much mortified and chagrined at having been duped by Sultán Muhammad Khan, in addition to the utter failure of their scheme. He ordered his forces to be concentrated at Jallálábád, a few battalions being sent in advance to Surkh Pál, where his soldiers took the guard by surprise and plundered it of its horses, arms, and ammunition. The Amir was unable to restore order among his troops, and retraced his steps to Kábul during the night. He shut himself up, through shame, in the Bálá Hissár Fort for three or four days, and admitted no one to his presence. His Wazír, Mirza Sámi Khan, likewise secluded himself in his house, and, in a fit of rage and remorse, broke to pieces his *kalamdán*, or writing case, and reviled the Amir for not following his advice in matters of war and politics.

He retraces his steps to Kábul, 1835.

The Maharájá builds a fort at Peshawar.

On the retreat of Amir Dost Muhammad Khan to Kábul, the Maharájá ordered a fortress of considerable strength to be constructed on the site of the old citadel. This order was carried into execution with great zeal by Sardar Hari Singh, Nálwá, and Rájás Guláb Singh and Suchet Singh. Other forts were also constructed by the Sikhs to protect the country. The Sikhs consolidated their power at Pesháwar, and where, in the level country of Dáman, west of the Indus, their agents only had resided, they now actually occupied the territory, extending their influence to the extreme limit of Bannú. The Maharájá remained at Pesháwar for several weeks. Here Abdul Ghias Khan, son of Nawáb Jabbar Khan, and other chief residents of the town, paid their respects to him. His Highness placed Rájá Guláb Singh at the head of the financial affairs of the country, while General Ventura was made head of the Military Department. Rájá Guláb Singh subsequently falling ill, General Avitabile was appointed in his place. After making these arrangements, the Maharájá returned to Láhore. A jágír of a lakh of rupees was conferred upon Prince Nau Nehal Singh, in recognition of his services at Pesháwar.

The Sikh power consolidated in the North-western frontier.

Arrangements for the administration of the newly occupied country.

The system of branding horses and camels introduced, 1834.

During the year, 1834, the Maharájá introduced the system of branding horses and camels in the military service, and, in accordance with an order passed, all such animals were branded. The presents for the King of England being now ready for despatch, Sardar Gujar Singh and Bhái Govind Jas were sent on a mission to Calcutta, in September, 1834, with letters for the King and the Governor-General. This was only a friendly mission, and had no reference to political affairs. A large number of shawls and Káshmír cloaks, the property of Sheikh Ghulám Mohi-ud-dín, were found in the possession of the sons of Kází Kamál-ud-dín of Sodhra* and confiscated to the State. After the Dasahra Darbár, which was held with the usual pomp

A friendly mission to Calcutta, 1834.

Tour in Batála, Siálkot and Jhelum.

* A town built by Malik Azaz, the favourite slave of Sultán Mahmúd Gházni. He had built a sarai at this place, called Sad-dara, from its having one hundred doors. Sodhra or Sadhora is a corruption of this name.

at Amritsar, the Maharájá proceeded to Batála, and pitched his camp on the bank of Shamsher Khan's tank. This being the jágír of Prince Sher Singh, his son, Kanwar Partáb Singh, in the absence of his father on duty at the frontier, offered a *nazar* of an elephant, two horses and Rs. 2,100, together with 101 trays of sweetmeats, to the Maharájá, which was accepted, and the prince was presented with a *khilat* of honour. The Maharájá next went to Siálkot, and having received there the respects of Prince Peshora Singh, he proceeded to Jhelum, and encamped in the neighbourhood of Rohtás.

Death of Rájá Sangat Singh of Jhínd, 2nd November 1834.

Here news reached him of the death of his ally, Rájá Sangat Singh, of Jhínd, which event occurred in Basia on the 2nd of November. The Maharájá was much grieved to hear of the rájá's death, as he was one of his most valued and trusted friends. The deceased was only twenty-three years of age when he died. At Rohtás certain sardars presented their swords to the Maharájá, and were ordered for service at Peshávar. The Maharájá then returned to Láhore. The year 1834 closed with the betrothal of Prince Nau Nehal Singh to the daughter of Sardar Shám Singh of Atári.

The betrothal of Prince Nau Nehál Singh, 1834.

Ladákh rendered tributary by the Jammú Rájas, 1834.

Early in 1834 Zoráwar Singh, Commander of Rájá Goláb Singh's forces in Kishtwár, taking advantage of dissensions which prevailed among the reigning family of Ladákh, deposed the rájá and set up his rebellious minister in his stead. A Sikh garrison was placed in Leh, the capital of Ladákh, and a tribute of Rs. 30,000 fixed. In vain did the deposed rájá complain to the Chinese Minister at Lassa; he was not inclined to interfere, as the rájá's successor continued to pay the fixed subsidy regularly. On his return to Jammú, Zoráwar Singh was sent to Láhore with presents, the products of the country reduced by him. The Maharájá was pleased to receive these presents and was amused to hear from the adventurous Zoráwar Singh that, if ordered by the Maharájá, he was ready to carry his arms to the borders of the Chinese empire.

The Maharájá again asserts his superior rights to Sindh, 1836.

The idea of supremacy in Sindh recurred to the mind of Ranjít Singh, on the discomfiture of the Amirs in that country by Shah Shujá, and that monarch's subsequent return to Ludhiáná, after being beaten at Kandahar by the Barakzai brothers. A promise to surrender Shikárpur was made to him by Núr Muhammad Khan, of Hydrábád, on condition of a guarantee being given against the designs of the ex-king. But Ranjít Singh had little confidence in the promise of the Sindhians, and his active interference in the affairs beyond the Indus continued unabated. Sawan Mal, the Governor of Multán, sent Malla Singh, the son of Jodh Singh, at the head of a force to punish the Mazárís of Rojhán, who had made raids on the Sikh posts, and, in an action fought between the Sikhs and the Mazárí freebooters, a hundred of the latter were killed. Náhar Singh was subsequently sent in the direction of Rojhán, at the head of a detachment of troops and one gun, to restore order on the Sikh frontier. The Maharájá also maintained Ghulám Shah Kolhára, a chief who was expelled by the Talpurs, to whom a jágír had been assigned from Kábul. A suitable pension was assigned to this representative of the Kolhára family by the Maharájá at Rojhán, the seat of the Mazárís. Ranjít Singh again urged upon the British Government his superior claims to Shikárpur, contending that it was a dependency of the chiefs of Khorássán, and hinting, at the same time, that the river below Mithan Kot was not a tributary of the Indus, but of the Sutlej, "the river of the treaty," and, in the words of the eloquent Fakír Aziz-ud-dín, "the stream which had so long given freshness and beauty to the emblematic garden of their friendship, and which continued its fertilizing way to the ocean, separating, yet uniting, the realms of the two brotherly powers of the

And punishes the Mazárís of Rojhán on the Sindh frontier for raids in Sikh territory.

East." Ranjít Singh's ambitious views were displeasing to the British, but their object was to act with discretion and moderation, and to remain on friendly terms with States having conflicting interests.

His ambitious views displeasing to the English, who nevertheless, act with discretion.

The Maharájá paid a second visit to Peshāwar during the course of this year and personally superintended military and financial arrangements which required immediate attention. At Peshāwar the Maharájá gave a jágír of three lakhs of rupees to Sardar Sultán Muhammad Khan, in Kohát and Hashtnagar, and of rupees 25,000 in Doába. On the return of the Maharájá to Láhore, the Sardar, with some of his sons, accompanied him, and was lodged in the mausoleum of the Emperor Jahángír on the banks of the Rávi.

The Maharájá's second visit to Káshmir.

Shortly before the Dasahra, the Maharájá had an attack of paralysis, which affected his tongue and rendered him unable to speak distinctly. Fakírs Aziz-ud-dín and Imám-ud-dín prescribed fomentations and liniments, which were freely used. Sardar Lahná Singh, *Majithia*, of Amritsar, and Sardar Ratan Singh, *Gharjagia*, the Adálati of Láhore, were ordered to set a number of prisoners at liberty. Two thousand rupees were placed near the Maharájá's pillow every night, and distributed as alms to the poor in the morning. Horses, cows, and cloths were distributed in charity to the Brahmins of Láhore and Amritsar, and offerings of large amounts of money were made at the temples of Jawálá Mukhi and Kangrá. Musicians and singers of hymns were sent for from Multán, and they amused the Maharájá with their performances, as advised by the physicians. In a few days the Maharájá regained the power of speech, and his health was restored. On the day on which the Maharájá bathed, after his recovery, 5,000 rupees were distributed to the Brahmins and faqírs. The Court being then at Amritsar, the Maharájá went from the Bárádari to the Rám Bágh garden on horseback, and there received the salutations of the grandees and nobles, all of whom offered money as *sarwárná*. Sardar Sultán Muhammad Khan presented a fine horse, and was promised permission to go to his jágírs after the Dasahra. Kanwar Nau Nehal Singh was ordered to proceed to Multán, to realize the yearly revenue from Sawan Mal, and the Maharájá, having celebrated the Dasahra festival at Amritsar, returned to his capital in Assauj.

The Maharájá attacked by paralysis.

Cured.

Láhore was visited, this year, by a number of distinguished persons, European and Asiatic. Among the former were Doctors McGregor, Harlan, an American adventurer, and Honigbergher, the German traveller, and one Ventun in the employ of the Begum of Simrú. Among the latter were Kishen Pandit, the Vakíl of the Maharájá of Nepál, Surjú, the Vakíl of the Rájá of Bikanir, and Rájá Bhím Kál, the brother of the reigning Rájá of Thibet.

Láhore visited by several distinguished Europeans and Asiatics.

During the same year, Nawáb Shah Nawáz Khan was ousted from his possession of Dera Ismail Khan by Kanwar Nau Nehal Singh and Sardar Atar Singh, Sindhianwália, who, under orders from the darbár, put the nawáb under arrest. The fort of Tank was also taken from Sarfráz Khan, and a police post established there, 30 guns and other war material which were found in the fort, being confiscated to the State. The Kanwar, however, did not meet with success at Garhi Yunis Khan, where, in an encounter with the Afghans, 250 Sikh soldiers were killed and two sardars wounded.

Kanwar Nau Nehal Singh occupies Dera Ismail Khan and the fort of Tank.

On the 1st of January, 1836, Sardar Sultán Muhammad Khan, who had been at the Court for some time, took his leave, to return to his country and look after the jágírs that had been granted to him. On the 7th of the following month, Sardar Basáwá Singh, Sindhianwálá, died. He was the own brother of Sardars Atar Singh and Lahná Singh, and the Maharájá was much grieved at the news of his death. About the end of March,

Sardar Sultán Muhammad Khan leaves Láhore for Peshāwar, 1836.

Death of Sardar Basáwá Singh Sindhianwália, 1836.

Return of the Sikh Embassy from Calcutta.

Victories gained over the Eusafzais of Panjtár and the Afridis of the Khaibar.

Exactions from Sardar Atá-Singh, Sindhianwálá.

Rai Gobind Jas and Sardar Gujar Singh, who had been sent on a mission to Calcutta, returned to Láhore with presents from the Governor-General, consisting of musical boxes, telescopes, pictures, maps of India, the Panjáb and Sindh, and a variety of rich stuffs. The Eusafzais of Panjtár, under Fatteh Khan, who had become troublesome, were chastised by Prince Sher Singh and Sardar Tej Singh. Their chief fled to Buner, while Panjtár was plundered and the neighbouring villages devastated. At Jamrúd, near the Khaibar, Hari Singh, Nalwá, routed a party of the Afridís. On receipt of the news at the darbár, a salute was fired in honour of the victories. About this time, Misar Rúplál was ordered to confiscate the jágírs of Sodlí Atar Singh of Anandpur. Bhái Ram Singh was, at the same time, deputed to levy 20,000 rupees from Atar Singh, Sindhianwálá, as *tambol* for the approaching marriage of Nau Nehal Singh, and 30,000 rupees as *nazráná*, to which the sardar became liable, consequent on the demise of Basáwá Singh and the succession of the family to his jágírs. Amir Khan, of Oda, having been brought in chains to Láhore, was produced before the Maharájá, charged with assisting Fatteh Khan, of Panjtár, in his revolt against the authority of the darbár. The Maharájá, after making enquiries about his conduct from Kází Husain Bakhsh, the confidential agent of Hari Singh, and Sardar Tej Singh, ordered that he should remain a close prisoner in the Bhati gate bastion of the city.

Exactions consequent on a royal marriage.

In consequence of the approaching marriage of Prince Nau Nehal Singh, it was ordered that a month's salary should be deducted by way of *tambol* from all the employés of the military departments, and a fee of two rupees per cent. levied from the zemindars in excess of the Government revenue. A tax of five rupees per head was also imposed on all the bankers of the towns of Amritsar and Láhore.

The Sikhs take possession of Rojhán, August 1836,

And of the fort of Kán.

Captain Wade comes to Láhore to explain personally to the Maharájá the views of the English regarding Sindh.

The Maharájá yields to the demand of the English in spite of the perverse opinion of his courtiers.

In August, 1836, Dewán Sanwan Mal, Governor of Multán, reported to the Maharájá that, in consequence of the repeated attacks of the Mazárís on the Sikh posts, he had taken formal possession of Rojhán. In October following, another action was fought between the Mazárís and the Sikhs, in which the former were defeated with heavy loss, and their fort, called Kán, was occupied by the victorious Sikhs. Both the Princes, Kharak Singh and Nau Nehal Singh, were about this time on the bank of the Indus with large armies. These demonstrations on the part of the Maharájá were distasteful to the English, whose interest it was to prevent the extension of the Sikh power along the bank of the Indus. Captain Wade came at last to Láhore, to explain personally to the Maharájá that he was incurring a great risk in acting in opposition to the declared policy of the British Government. Ranjít Singh yielded, out of deference, as he said, to his old allies. He destroyed the fort of Kán, but continued to hold Rojhán and the Mazárí country.

Yet the Maharájá continued by his conduct to show that he never relinquished entirely his claims to Sindh.

His courtiers endeavoured to dissuade him from submitting to the proposals of the English Government; but the Maharájá shook his head and pointed out the danger of a rupture with a power against whom the arms of the Mahrattas, with their two hundred thousand soldiers, had failed, and at whose feet now lay the empire of the great Moghals, with its vast resources. To show, moreover, how completely he had forgotten the check put on his ambitious views on the Sindh frontier by the English, he wrote a friendly letter to the Governor-General, inviting His Excellency to join in the nuptials of his grandson, on whom he had fixed his eye to conquer the much-coveted province of Sindh for him. Yet he kept his relations with the Amirs of Sindh on the old footing. Their agents were in attendance at his darbár, and they dreaded his power; neither did he condescend to make any distinct settlement regarding the boundary with the Amirs on the question relating to the supremacy of the Mazárís. Thus, though avoiding an open rupture with his powerful British allies, he, nevertheless, continued to entertain ideas of final supremacy in Sindh at some future date.

The return of General Allard from France, 1836.

In the course of this year, General Allard, who had gone to his native country on leave, returned to Láhore, bringing with him presents and a friendly letter from the King of France for the Maharájá. The General returned by way of Calcutta, and brought from his country a number of French cuirasses, which were worn with much pride by the Sikh sardars. So great a desire he seems to have felt to return to Láhore and pay his respects to his Sikh master that, on first seeing the Maharájá, on his return, he recited the following Persian verses, composed at his instance, as he said, by a Persian poet, and which he had learnt by heart for the purpose of repeating in prayer to the Almighty:—

الهی باد شاهم زنده بادا   فلک در خدمت او بنده بادا
بدر گاهش رسم اعزاز یابم   دهم جان گردن از حکمش بتابم
بود لاهور گر مدفن مزارم   بود تا بوت در غنچه انارم

"O God! May my king live long!—
May the firmament be as a slave in his service;
May I reach his royal court and be honoured;
And, should I ever disobey his commands, may death come on me.
When I die, let my grave be in Láhore,
And my remains be interred in Anarkali." *

The Maharájá was greatly pleased to hear his French Officer recite these lines; and he wished him a long life, and gave him the credit of being a loyal and able servant of the State.

The marriage of Prince Nau Nehal Singh, 1837.

The year 1837 commenced with grand preparations for the approaching marriage of Prince Nau Nehal Singh. The scene of the gay festivities was Amritsar, where the Maharájá had already sent most of his trusted sardars to make preliminary arrangements, and whither he himself now repaired. It was the Maharájá's intention to make the event memorable in the annals of the Panjáb for its splendour and magnificence, and both he and his officers made every effort that the festivities might surpass those of all previous occasions in the Panjáb. The Rájás of Patiálá, Jhind, Nabhá and Farídkot, the Nawáb of Maler Kotla, the Sardars of Kapúrthala, Kalsia, Naráingarh and Ládwa, the hill Rájás of Súket, Mandi, Chambá Núrpur, and most of the other Chiefs and Sardars from the Sutlej to the Indus, were summoned and took part in the marriage festivities. Ranjít Singh had also invited Lord Auckland, the Governor-General of India, Sir Charles Metcalf, the Governor of Agra, and General Sir Henry Fane, the Commander-in-Chief of the British Army in India, to be present at the nuptials, but the officer last named was alone able to attend.

Several distinguished native chiefs invited.

As also high British Officers.

Reception of Sir Henry Fane, the British Commander-in-chief, in the Panjáb.

His Excellency at Amritsar.

The cavalcade.

The General was received at Hari ká Pattan on the Sutlej by Prince Sher Singh and Sardar Lahná Singh, Majithia, followed by a numerous retinue of horse and foot. At a distance of five miles from Amritsar, His Excellency was met by the heir-apparent, Kharak Singh, and the Prime Minister, Rájá Dhian Singh, and Jamadar Khushal Singh, who congratulated the chief on his arrival, and, presenting him with a purse of Rs. 5,000 as *sarwárna*, conducted him to his camp. The deputation consisted of from 2,000 to 3,000 horsemen, all splendidly attired, and extending to half a

* Vide *History of Láhore* (manuscript) by Dewán Amar Náth.

mile on either side of the road. Both the prince and the officers of his suite blazed with jewels and cloth of gold and silver. The most striking figure of the deputation was the Prime Minister, described as being the most powerful man in the Panjáb. He was dressed with the utmost magnificence and covered with jewels, which hung, row upon row, about his neck, in his turban, on the hilt of his sword and dagger, and over the whole of his dress; while a French cuirass shone upon his breast. He was mounted on a large Persian horse, which curvetted and pranced, as if proud of his noble rider. The saddle and bridle were embroidered with gold, the saddle-cloth being of silver-tissue and extending to the horse's tail; the legs, up to the knees, and the lower half of the tail of the animal, were dyed red. Prince Sher Singh, who is described as a handsome man, with a black beard, had the most beautiful tiara of diamonds, emeralds, and rubies, some of the emeralds, in particular, being of an enormous size and great value. As the gorgeous procession passed the Fort of Gobindgarh, the repository of the Maharájá's treasures, the guns of the fort announced to the citizens the arrival of the "jangi lord," as the Commander-in-Chief was called. The camp of His Excellency was formed at Mouza Katháni, and at some distance from it were the tents of the Maharájá, each with a golden ball on the top, and with scarlet screens surrounding it, and a line of sentries drawn about it. On his arrival in the camp, Miser Ram Kishan, on the part of the Maharájá, presented His Excellency with 2,100 budkís of gold and 500 trays of sweetmeats, as a *ziyáfat*, after which the party withdrew.

Rájá Dhian Singh.

Prince Sher Singh.

The camp of the Commander-in-Chief.

At eleven o'clock the next morning (6th March), the meeting between Ranjít Singh and the British Commander-in-Chief took place at the Maharájá's garden house in Rám Bágh. The Maharájá's party met the British General half way. His Highness and most of his Court were dressed in yellow, and surrounded with a cloud of cavalry and infantry. The "Lion of the Panjáb" is described as being a diminutive, infirm-looking old man. His dress was very plain, consisting of a green Káshmír turban, coat and gloves, with single rows of large pearls down the breast. There was a single string of very large diamonds round his arms, and his neck, arms and legs were covered with rows of large pearls. The Maharájá's elephant was followed by numerous others, in gorgeous trappings, on which were seated the sardars of State, clad in cloth of gold and in yellow, green and crimson coloured silk, presenting a profusion of gold, silver and jewels as far as the eye could see. When the two personages met, their elephants were brought side by side, and Sir Henry, stepping from his own elephant on to that of the Maharájá, gave him a cordial English shake of the hand and took his seat beside him. The meeting took place in front of the Maharájá's house, under a canopy formed of beautiful Káshmír shawls, embroidered with silver and supported by silver poles. The floor was covered with rich Káshmír shawls. The grandees and Omerahs of the State were seated on chairs of gold and silver, each of which was inlaid with jewels to the value of several thousand pounds. But the most superbly dressed of the Omerahs was the Prime Minister's son, a beautiful lad, and the reigning favourite of the day. He was literally one mass of jewels; his neck, arms and legs were covered so thickly with necklaces, armlets and bangles, formed of pearls, diamonds and rubies, one above another, that it was difficult to discover anything between them. As usual with him on such occasions, the Maharájá put numerous questions to the Commander-in-Chief about the composition of the British regiments, from the colonel down to the privates, and the English mode of casting artillery and manufacturing other weapons of war. He asked the number of battles Sir Henry had fought in, and enquired about the

The Maharájá.

His Sardars.

Interview between the Maharájá and the Commander-in-Chief.

Rájá Hira Singh.

Numerous questions asked by the Maharájá.

strength of the Company's army and the number of English officers attached to each regiment. The presents for His Excellency were then brought out. These consisted of rich stuffs, jewels and other articles of value, and an offering of rupees 5,000 in money. The Maharájá's favourite horses, richly caparisoned, were then passed in review before His Excellency, who was presented with five horses of different kinds.

At the departure of the Commander-in-Chief and the other English Officers Ranjít Singh stood at the place of egress, shaking hands with every one as he passed.

The *Tambol* ceremony.

In the afternoon of the same day, the ceremony of presentation of *tambol*, or marriage presents, to the bridegroom, took place in a spacious house, where also Sir Henry Fane and staff were presented. Among the party collected, there were upwards of eighty dancing-girls, singing in sets of three or four at a time; but their songs were quite inaudible, so great was the noise of the assembled multitude. The Maharájá and the bridegroom, who was half covered with a golden veil, took their seats under a tree, laden with artificial oranges. All the chiefs and sardars present on the occasion presented their offerings to the bridegroom, one after another, Sir Henry Fane presenting 11,000 rupees and Rájá Dhian Singh 1,25,000, while Rájás Guláb Singh, Suchet Singh and others presented smaller sums, in proportion to their rank. The *tambol* from all sources amounted to fifty lakhs of rupees. The ceremony lasted two hours, after which the meeting broke up.

The ceremony of investiture of the bridegroom with the bridal chaplet.

On the morning of 7th March, the ceremony of the investiture of the bridegroom with the bridal chaplet, or wreath, took place at the Harmandar of the Darbár Sahib. A wreath of diamonds and pearls was tied with gold thread to the head of the bridegroom by the Maharájá himself, at an auspicious hour appointed by the Brahmins. This being done, 500 rupees was presented before the *Granth*, or Sikh holy book, with five pieces of crystallized sugar. One hundred and fifty rupees was presented to the Akal Bungá, and Rs. 125 each to other Bungás of the Darbár, while Rs. 500 was distributed among the Akális present. At three o'clock in the afternoon, the entire marriage partly started for Atári, the residence of the bride's father. Artificial parterres, temples, towers and whirligigs were carried along with the procession. As the Maharájá advanced, he threw money on all sides to the poor, to be scrambled for by them. The multitude assembled was unprecedented. The news of the marriage had brought people from almost all parts of the country; and it is estimated that not less than six hundred thousand persons were present. The crush to get near the Maharájá's elephant was very great, and several lives were lost. The crowding of the elephants one against another, and the curvetting and prancing of hundreds of horses, caused the greatest confusion. Add to this the noise of the multitude, the firing of cannon at intervals, the sound of musical instruments, pipes and trumpets, and the beating of drums, and the scene may be better imagined than described. As the procession reached the house of the bride's father, the old Sardar Sham Singh presented the Maharájá with 101 gold mohurs and five horses, richly caparisoned; Kanwar Khark Singh, with 51 gold mohurs and a horse, Kanwar Sher Singh, with 11 gold mohurs and a horse, and so on with all the chief sardars.

The party starts for Atári.

Great gathering of the people.

The marriage procession.

The scene at the bride's house.

The sardar lived in a large baronial-looking castle. On the roof was erected a large canopy, which looked down on the main body of the building, and under this His Excellency and the Maharájá took their seats. The spacious edifice was thickly covered with spectators, from the highest tower and balcony to the lower court. The bridegroom was now introduced into the assembly

The marriage ceremonies.

for the first time. His face was covered with the wreath, or veil, before-mentioned, made of strings of large pearls and diamonds. The religious part of the ceremony now commenced, and was finished at 9 o'clock, the hour declared to be propitious by the Brahmins. The ceremony being over, there was a grand display of fireworks, followed by a dance, which lasted the whole night. The Maharájá was seated on a chair of State, surrounded by his ministers and favourites, his knees resting on a highly embroidered gold stool. The Commander-in-Chief took his place on his right, on a spacious chair of gold. Ranjít's breast shone with rows of great pearls, as before mentioned, and his arm with the *Kohinur*, his great diamond, which he wore on State occasions. Ranjít Singh now ordered his favourite intoxicating liquor to be served, so liberally each time, and with such rapidity, that it astonished his English guests. He took particular care to see that the General really drank, and always looked into the glass himself, to see that this was done. The liquor he used was so fiery that even a very small quantity brought tears into the eyes of his English guests; but the Maharájá himself drank several small glasses, filled to the brim, without any visible effect. His Excellency the Commander-in-Chief freely took part in the festivities of the evening until a late hour, to the great satisfaction of the Maharájá and the whole assembly.

The night's entertainment.

The great "Bárá."

On the morning of the 8th, the great "*Bárá*," or enclosure with a circumference of five miles, was formed to distribute money among the poor. The entire circle was surrounded with troops, and had eighty gate-ways, guarded by mounted soldiers, to allow nobody to go out without receiving his reward, and to let no one in when he had once got out. The entire arrangements rested with Miser Beli Ram and Kour Kharak Singh. At each of the outlets was stationed an officer, who, as each individual was presented before himself by the gate-keepers, gave him a rupee, as a mark of the liberality of the Maharájá. The number thus paid exceeded a million.

Exhibition of the dowry

The dowry was then exhibited by the bride's father. It consisted of 101 horses, richly caparisoned with gold aud silver trappings, 101 cows, 101 she-buffaloes, 10 camels, 11 elephants, gold and silver ornaments valued at many thousands of rupees, gold and silver utensils, precious stones, rich stuffs, consisting of silks of Multán and golden and scarlet *kimkhab* of Benares, and 500 pairs of shawls. These last were the most beautiful, being the products of the unrivalled looms of Káshmír, while many of the jewels were very handsome and of great intrinsic value. The female attire alone covered a space of not less than an acre. There was also a complete set of dinner and washing utensils, all of silver, most beautifully carved. During the night there was another display of fireworks, which surpassed in magnificence even that of the preceding night. The whole night was spent in rejoicing and festivities. The meeting closed with the presentation of rich *khilats* from the bride's father to the Maharájá, the Commander-in-Chief, the Princes Royal and the principal sardars. The *khilats* for the Maharája, the Commander-in-Chief and the Princes consisted of jewels, rich stuffs and an elephant each, with trappings.

Entertainment in the "Shalámár" garden.

Decorations in the garden.

On the night of 12th March His Excellency the General and staff were entertained by the Maharájá in the Shalámár Garden of Láhore, which was tastefully decorated for the occasion. The whole garden was brilliantly illuminated with rows of oil lamps, arranged at proper intervals on the copings of walls, the ridges of roofs, and along the sides of the walks and fountains, reflecting their light in the waters below, to the intense pleasure of the wondering spectators. At every ten or twelve yards, beautiful lamps of different colors were placed, and the branches of the trees were adorned with hanging-lamps of the same colors, to imitate festoons of flowers. The whole scene presented a picturesque appearance, and rendered the garden more like a vision of fairyland. The meeting was also graced by the presence of English ladies, for whom a splendid tent had been erected on the flat roof of the marble house fronting the marble throne of the Emperor Shah Jahán, the founder of these most superb gardens. The scene was calculated to raise a sigh at the vicissitudes of fortune and the mutability of every thing which owes its origin to human art or skill. The days had gone when the great Moghal, the 'Asylum of the World,' as he was called by his flatterers, occupied this throne, surrounded by his Persian Omerahs and favourites. It was now the turn of the Sikh monarch to occupy the same place, as lord of the Panjáb, with his long-bearded courtiers and councillors. But there were changes for it yet in store! The pleasure-garden of the Great Moghal was destined, at no distant date, to become the property of an adventurous race inhabiting a country in the far west. Nobody of course could foresee the events of the morrow. Suffice it to say that the night passed in great rejoicings. As soon as the ladies had retired, the English guests entered the audience hall, and dancing was kept up till a late hour of the night. Throughout the *tamáshá*, the old 'Lion' was, as usual, plying the British veteran with liquor and asking questions.

Reflections on the change of time.

By Ranjít Singh's particular desire, Sir Henry Fane and staff joined him on the march, on the morning of the 13th, near his garden-house, to pay a visit to one of his country pavilions and several small gardens which the Maharájá had all along the road as resting-places during the hot season. "We supposed, by his asking Sir Henry," writes His Excellency's Aide-de-camp in his account of the journey, "to accompany him this morning, and coming himself, with scarcely an attendant, that he intended to show the British Chief to his people in his train, and wished us to ride with him through Láhore. But it proved afterwards that it was a sheer good-will and kindness, to show him his flower-gardens, which are gaily filled with stocks and poppies, and put one quite in mind of England with their scent." "Ranjít Singh," continues the writer, "has no regular residence where he constantly lives, but, instead, is continually on the move, either in the wars in which he is constantly engaged, or moving from one part of his territory to another. For this purpose he has single rooms, built along the lines of the great roads, so that, in case the heat is too great for tents, a cooler place is always at hand." True it is the Maharájá lived a soldier's life. His great passion for horses was due to his unquenchable thirst for long excursions, having in view territorial aggrandizement, and he would, while on the march, take his meals on horseback.

The Maharájá's country pavilions.

On the afternoon of the 14th, the Maharájá paid his official visit to Sir Henry Fane. He was surrounded by his troops and courtiers, and, as he passed through the British escort, the whole of which had been drawn up to receive him, he stopped many times, putting questions as to their equipment. From the moment he entered the darbár tent, he never ceased asking questions of Sir Henry:—"What was the strength of the Indian Army?" "Did the British General think that Russian influence was doing much harm to the English in Persia?" "Was it thought that Persia had sufficient power to give effectual aid to the Russians in the event of their coming in this direction?" and the like questions, which were put with the greatest acuteness, and many of which were not easily to be answered. After more than an hour of these questions and answers, the British General at last rose and conducted the Maharájá, whose head reached up to Sir

The Maharájá's visit to Sir Henry.

Henry Fane's waist, to a tent close by, in which were laid out the presents intended for him. These consisted of an elephant, eight horses, a double-barrelled gun, a rifle, a brace of pistols and 51 pieces of different kinds of stuffs. After these ceremonies, the Maharájá proceeded on his elephant towards the British Artillery, and again renewed his questions regarding their formation, and looked minutely at the harness and equipment, so that the smallest matter did not escape his eye.

Grand review of the Sikh army.

On the 16th there was a grand review of the Sikh army assembled at Láhore, in all about 18,000 men. They are described as having been all exceedingly well clothed and armed after the European fashion. The following morning there was a review of the British troops which formed the escort of the British General. These consisted of squadrons of the 16th Lancers and 4th Cavalry, one troop of Horse Artillery, 200 men of the 13th Light Infantry, and eight companies from the 18th, 20th and 17th Regiments of Native Infantry. "The extreme delight of the old man at the discipline of the men and the explanation the General gave him of the movements, and how they would act with a large body, surpasses belief. He rode through and looked at every gun, examined the appointments of the men, counted the number in each square, and quite gained all our hearts by the interest he took and the acuteness which he showed by his questions." Such is the description of the review given by an eye-witness, and it bears testimony to the great discernment of Ranjít Singh and his hearty appreciation of all that was really excellent from a military point of view. Speaking of the quality of the British troops, he said to the Commander-in-Chief, "I see what liars my French officers and others are who tell me that English discipline was nothing; and that, though so much was talked about it, still it was only outward show, and that, were they to come before an enemy, the thing would bear a different aspect. But now," said he, "I see what liars they are; you have shown me not only how troops can be moved, but also how these movements can be brought to bear upon a hostile force. It is now no matter of wonder to me that the English have always been victorious in the east." One feat, displaying the dexterity of the artillerymen, particularly astonished Ranjít Singh. A six-pounder from one of the batteries of Horse Artillery was dismounted from its carriage, thrown on the ground, taken to pieces and then quickly put together, remounted and placed in perfect working order, with the men on the horses and in full gallop, all within the short space of five minutes. Ranjít could not, in the first instance, be induced to believe that the gun had really been taken to pieces, and ascribed the interruption caused to some portion of the harness having broken, but a repetition of the same performance convinced him of what had really taken place. His delight at the sight of the men was immense; he obtained the Commander-in-Chief's permission to send a present in money for the soldiers, as a mark of his appreciation of their skill; and directly he got to his palace, he sent a purse of eleven thousand rupees to be divided among the soldiers.

Review of British troops.

A feat of military dexterity.

A show of artillery practice.

On the morning of the 18th there was a show of artillery practice with grape, round shot and shrapnel. The canvas targets erected were brought down many times with rounds of grape, to the great delight of the Maharájá. Having been put up again, they were pierced through with marked success. Prince Sher Singh, who was a good sportsman, and many other sardars, were present, and, dismounting from their horses, watched the pointing of the guns. An umbrella planted by Sher Singh was torn into ribbons at 400 yards at the 5th and 6th shots. The Maharájá was much pleased to see the practice, and, on going home, sent a purse of 1,200 rupees as a present to the artillerymen. For each of the officers who had pointed the guns, a shawl and gold bangles were sent. After this, the Court jewels were exhibited for the inspection of the Commander-in-Chief; and some of these are described as the finest in the world. There were a variety of swords, armlets, necklaces, bangles and other ornaments and jewels. Many of the swords were of very great value, their blades alone, in some instances, being valued at 10,000 rupees, and the gold and jewels upon their hilts and scabbards at five times that amount. Many of these belonged to the Durráni Emperors, who probably squeezed them out of the Emperor of Dehli, or his ministers and grandees. Ranjít in his turn, had extorted them from Shah Shujá-ul-Mulk.

Display of the Court jewels.

Reception of English ladies by Ranjít Singh's wives.

In the evening of 19th March, a grand entertainment was given by the Maharájá at the palace in honour of the English ladies. On the afternoon of the 20th, the ladies went to see Ranjít's wives. The entire edifice of the Summan Burj had been most superbly decorated for the occasion with garlands and wreaths of flowers. Maharání Nakáin, the mother of Prince Kharak Singh, with other Ránís and members of the Royal seraglio, came to the gate of the fort to receive their honourable guests, every male (except the Maharájá) having been carefully excluded from the scene. The Grand Signior, the old Lion, was found seated in the midst of his wives, who received the English ladies with great distinction. The meeting lasted for some time, after which the Sikh ladies presented their English sisters with some very handsome and most valuable presents.

The Holi Festival.

On the 22nd the Maharájá celebrated the Holi festival with great magnificence. Here, too, Sir Henry Fane was present, and the scene was interesting when the Maharájá, with his own hand, poured the red powder and yellow saffron over Sir Henry's head, the Prime Minister at the same time rubbing the General all over with gold and silver leaf mixed with red powder. All the sardars and chiefs sat on chairs with baskets of red powder, and little balls filled with saffron. These they freely threw at one another, perfectly regardless of the result. Many were the long beards that were dyed and many the eyes temporarily blinded with the red dust. Among the guests there happened to be an Afghan ambassador, Gul Muhammad Khan, an orthodox Mahomedan, who had just arrived from Kandahar. He had not the faintest idea of what would happen to him, but in a few moments his beautiful garments were coloured from head to feet, and his beard, which he had nicely combed, was turned to a bright saffron colour, while red dust was literally thrown in his eyes. The gallant, but abashed Khan, cast looks of astonishment all round, but, finding no attention paid to him from any quarter, since etiquette was for the nonce thrown to the winds, he took to his heels amidst roars of laughter from the whole assembly. Ranjít's favourite guard of Amazons, the dancing-girls, some thirty or forty in number, many of whom are described as being very pretty, were present all the time that the battle raged, and took no insignificant part in the combat.

The Commander-in-Chief's farewell visit.

The Commander-in-Chief paid his farewell visit to the Maharájá, in his garden-house, on the 27th. His Highness was seated on a *masnad*, attended, as usual, by his Court, with tame pigeons feeding on the carpet before him. After half an hour's complimentary speeches, farewell presents were brought for the General and his staff. Those for His Excellency comprised most magnificent shawls, a beautiful sabre, an elephant with a silver howdah and horses. On his departure, the Maharájá bade adieu to the British Chief, and gave him and his Military Secretary the new order which he had instituted on the plan of the Legion d' Honneur of France, called "the Order of the Auspicious Star of the Panjáb." "I am sure," says Mr. Fane, His Excellency's Private Secretary, "both he and almost every one present felt sincere sorrow at parting from the good natured, kind old man, whom we had all begun to consider as an old friend and to treat accordingly." Prince Sher Singh went to the river Biás to conduct the Commander-in-Chief on his journey back.

Visit of Sardar Pír Muhammad Khan.

During Sir Henry's stay at Láhore, the Court was visited by Sardar Pír Muhammad Khan, brother of Sardar Sultán Muhammad Khan, who came with an escort of 1,200 Afghans to pay his respects to the Maharájá. These Afghan soldiers were all dressed in chain armour, with large jackboots. Pír Muhammad Khan brought for the Maharájá the celebrated horse called the "Mountain of Light," which the Maharájá had for years tried to obtain, without success, and also a celebrated Khorásán sabre, valued at 10,000 rupees.

The Sikhs occupy Jamrúd, 1837.

In the winter of 1837, the Sikhs, under their veteran General Hari Singh, Nalwa, occupied the fortress of Jamrúd at the entrance of the defiles of the Khaibar. This was very unwelcome news for the Kábul Amir, Dost Muhammad Khan, who saw that the measure adopted by the Sikhs was a prelude to further aggressions, as from the Khaibar the roads lay open to Jallálábád. It was therefore thought necessary to make a display of force, if not to run the risk of actual collision; and while he himself remained at Kábul, the Amir deputed his confidential minister, Mirza Sámi Khan, to superintend the operations, and act as the exigencies of the moment might require. He was provided with money and instructed to secure the co-operation of the maliks of the Khaibar by the payment to them of their annual allowances. The army collected on this occasion was headed by five sons of the Amir, Mahomed Afzal Khan, Mahomed Akbar Khan, Ghulám Haidar Khan, Mahomed Azim Khan and Mahomed Akram Khan. With these were associated Nawábs Jabbar Khan, Mahomed Usmán Khan, Shujá-ud-daula Khan, son of Nawáb Mahomed Zamán Khan, and Shams-ud-dín Khan, the Amir's nephew. Mir Alam Khan of Bajaur and Sa'adat Khan of Momand, were sent with Haji Khan, and the levies from Bajaur and Momand, to invade the districts of Doábá and Hashtnagar, north of the Kábul river, where Sardar Lahná Singh, Sindhianwala, had joined the Sikh forces from Shab Kádar.

The Amir Dost Muhammad Khan sends a force against the Sikhs.

Battle of Jamrúd, 30th April 1837.

The temporary absence of Hari Singh from Jamrúd tempted Mirza Sámi Khan and the Amir's son to make an attempt to carry the castle by assault, and a cannonade was commenced upon the walls. The weak defences of the fort were destroyed in the course of two or three days, and the Afghans, becoming sanguine, were congratulating themselves on the success which had attended them at the outset, when Hari Singh suddenly appeared and made an attack on them, which resulted in their retreat. This occurred on 30th, April 1837. Hari Singh next fell upon the divisions of Náib Amir Akhúndzáda, Mulláh Momand Khan *naib*, and Zerín Khan Arz Begi, which he threw into confusion, their leaders being severely wounded and fleeing from the scene of action in great dismay. The divisions led by the Amir's sons and Nawáb Jabbar Khan, which had not hitherto been attacked, also dispersed and fled. The only detachment which stood firm in the field was that of Mahomed Afzal Khan, the Amir's eldest son, who, keeping together his body of two thousand men, showed a bold front. Hari Singh, finding him inflexible, unexpectedly wheeled round, and, observing the Amir's sons and the Nawáb occupying small eminences in the defiles of the Khaibar, fell on their divisions. The assault was furious,

Defeat and flight of the Afghans.

The division of Muhammad Afzal Khan.

and the Sikhs drove the Afgháns from their positions with much slaughter, capturing fourteen guns. The Sikhs, thinking the victory gained, pursued the enemy, in order to drive them into the plains, when their progress was checked by a large body of horse, led by Shams-ud-dín Khan, who was coming to join in the battle.

Afghán reinforcements under Shams-ud-din Khan.

The prompt arrival of this reinforcement induced those of the Afgháns who were retreating without having engaged in the contest to return, and these now, in their turn, made a desperate attack on the Sikh forces. Nawáb Jabbar Khan and Shujá-ud-daula Khan, who had taken to flight, also returned, and a successful charge made by them led to the recovery of two of the captured guns. At this crisis the brave Hari Singh, while gallantly rallying the retiring Sikhs, received a mortal wound, and was borne from the battle field. This accident spread consternation among the Sikh troops, who retired under the walls of Jamrúd, where they entrenched themselves. The Afgháns recovered in all eleven of the fourteen guns they had lost, and captured three more belonging to the Sikhs.

Successful charge of the Afgháns.

Hari Singh, *Nalwa*, killed in the action and the Sikhs defeated.

The Sikhs hardly acknowledged the defeat; the Afgháns were unable to capture Jamrúd, which was still strongly garrisoned by the Sikhs; but the loss of the latter, in the person of their general, was irreparable. The gallant Sikh leader expired on the same day, the gloomy evening of which witnessed the burning of his body. Hari Singh was an intrepid soldier and a dashing leader. His undaunted courage had frequently placed him in critical situations, and he at last fell a victim to his bravery. He was a deadly foe of the Afgháns, whom he held in great contempt, looking upon them as cowards, and saying that he knew well their worth. Such was the dread in which the Afgháns held him, that to this day the name *Hariá* is repeated by mothers in Pesháwar and its neighbourhood in frightening their little children.

The character of Hari Singh, *Nalwa*.

The defeat of the Sikh Army at Jamrúd and the death of Hari Singh, *Nalwa*, caused some anxiety at the Court of Láhore. The Sikh leader had been Ranjít's playmate in boyhood, and was born in the same town as himself. The Maharájá personally liked him, and was much affected by his death, for in him he had his most courageous and loyal lieutenant and an able and experienced counsellor. Great was the zeal displayed at this juncture at Láhore, the ruler of which now marched in person to Rohtás, sending Dhián Singh in advance to Jamrúd, where the active minister pushed on the work of constructing the fort with great vigour, working with his own hands on the foundations, and thus setting an example of energy and devotion to the cause of his sovereign. Field batteries were hurried up with great alacrity from Ramgarh on the Chináb, to Pesháwar, a distance of more than 200 miles, in the short space of two days. As soon as the Sikh reinforcement had arrived at Jamrúd the Afgháns were compelled to retreat precipitately to Dháka, whence they retired to the skirts of the Sofèd Koh.

The Active measures adopted by the Maharájá to retrieve his loss on the frontier.

The Maharájá himself marches to Rohtás.

The Afgháns retire.

It has been already stated that Haji Khan and some Afghán sardars had been sent from Hashtnagar to repulse Sardar Lahná Singh, Sindhianwálá. The Sikh sardar had entrenched himself close to the castle of Hashtnagar. The Afgháns, after long procrastination in the hills, at length appeared in the plains under Haji Khan, Mír Alam Khan, of Bajour, Sa'adat Khan, the Mohmand chief, and Syad Bábá Ján, of Khonar. An attack was made on the fort without success; the influence of Sardar Sultán Muhammad Khan, who was now at Láhore, in attendance on the Maharájá, with his brother, Pír Muhammad Khan, was secretly at work, and the Bajour, Khonar, and Eusafzai chiefs having deserted Haji Khan, he was compelled to retire,

The retreat of Haji Khan from Hashtnagar.

together with Sa'adat Khan Mohmand. The Sikh forces at Peshawar about this time amounted to nearly forty-thousand men.

Death of Sardar Fatteh Singh, Ahluwália, 1837.

In October, 1837, Sardar Fatteh Singh Ahluwália, the turban brother of Ranjít Singh, died, and was succeeded in his estates by Nehal Singh, his eldest son. About the same time, Dhari, the Wazír of the Rájá of Mandi, arrived at Láhore and submitted a proposal for the succession of Bal Bír Singh as the rájá of that principality, in consequence of the lingering illness of his uncle the rájá. A *nazráná* of Rs. 50,000 was demanded; but the wazír agreed to pay only Rs. 20,000, and the last-mentioned amount having been paid, the installation of Bal Bír Singh as rájá was formally sanctioned, and a *khilat* was sent him. The Court was, at this time, at Amritsar, and on the 1st of Farwardi the Maharájá went to the Harmandar, accompanied by Sardar Lahná Singh, Majithia, and Fakír Imám-ud-dín, the killadár of the fort of Govindgarh, and offered Rs. 1,100 before the *Granth* and Rs. 500 at Akál Bunga, while Rs. 11,000 was distributed among the Brahmins, together with a number of cows, buffaloes, two horses and an elephant. In the meantime news arrived of an insurrection raised in Tánk by Payanda Khan, who had gathered around him a large number of insurgents, chiefly from the hill country. Sardul Singh Mán and Chet Singh, Commandant of Prince Nau Nehal Singh's battalions, quelled the disturbance, assisted by Hafiz Mahomed Afzal Khan, agent of the Ahluwáliá chief. On the side of the insurgents one hundred persons were killed, while the Sikh loss was about half that number. The Kachi tract of country was farmed to Fatteh Khan Tiwáná for Rs. 65,000, eleven horses, 51 camels, and 21 greyhounds. The year 1837 closed with the death of Shah Ayúb, who had been forced to become an exile at Láhore, and who had been supported by a pension from Ranjít Singh.

Bal Bír Singh installed as Rájá of Mandi.

An insurrection in Tank quelled.

Death of Shah Ayúb at Láhore, 1837.

Prince Kámrán of Herat involves himself in a rupture with the Shah of Persia, 1837.

It has already been stated that one branch of the Royal Sadozái family of Afghanistán retained the government of Herat. Prince Kámrán, who assumed the sceptre of that fertile province, had allowed himself to become a vassal of the King of Persia; and the success of the Persian Prince, Abbás Mirzá, the son of Fatteh Ali Shah, had so much daunted the Sadozái ruler, that he consented to raze the strong fortress of Ghorián on the frontiers of Khorasán. The confusion which followed the death of Abbás Mirzá, and, subsequently, of his father, Fatteh Ali Shah, encouraged Shah Kámrán to evade the fulfilment of his engagements with Persia: the payment of tribute was refused, as also the dismantling of the fort of Ghorián, and permission for the return of the Persian families in Herat to their homes. Nor did the ruler of Herat stop here. Khorasán was invaded by his wazír, and twelve thousand persons, subjects of Persia, were carried away captive, with the object of being sold as slaves in Central Asia. Muhammad Shah, the young king of Persia, resolved to punish the perfidy of Kámrán by attacking Herat. The new king extended his claims to Ghazni and Kandahár, on the ground that they had formed part of the Persian monarchy in the time of Nadir Shah. Such was the aspect of affairs when Mr. Ellis, the British envoy, visited the Court of Teheran, on a mission of condolence to the king of Persia. He found Russian influence predominant in the councils of Teheran, and the Shah's claim to Herat as the ancient patrimony of his crown was due mainly to the counsel of the Russian ambassador, Count Simonich. Throughout Central Asia the expedition was considered to be the triumph of Russia, by whom it was instigated, over the influence of England, by whom it was deprecated, for the Persians could only be regarded as the advanced guard of the Russians, who would thus be brought

The Persians besiege Herat.

The mission of Mr. Ellis to Teheran, 1837.

Russian influence at the Court of Persia.

into close proximity to the most exposed frontier of India. A large Persian army was assembled for the siege of Herat, and the British Government thought it necessary to take prompt steps for the safety of its north-west frontier. Captain Alexander Burnes, who, after the mission to Ranjít Singh, in 1831, had proceeded to Kábul and then travelled into Central Asia as far as Bokhárá, returning to Bombay by way of Persia, was sent as an envoy by Lord Auckland to the Court of Dost Muhammad Khan, on a commercial mission. The object of the mission was to invite the aid of the *de facto* rulers of Afghanistán in the measures necessary for giving full effect to the treaties entered into by the British Government in 1832 with the Amírs of Sindh, the Nawáb of Báháwalpur and Maharájá Ranjít Singh, which had for their object the opening of the navigation of the Indus, to facilitate the extension of commerce, and to gain for the British nation in Central Asia that legitimate influence which an interchange of benefits would naturally produce. The original objects of Captain Burnes' mission to Kábul were of a purely commercial nature, though, as the British representative in Afghanistán, he was interested in watching the course of events under the new aspect of affairs. He reached Kábul in September 1837, and was hospitably received by the Amír, Dost Muhammad Khan. But the Dost, who had overthrown the dynasty of the Durráni Ahmad Shah, in avenging his brother's death, now aspired to complete independence in the whole of Afghanistán. He was eager to recover the valley of Peshávar from the Sikhs; and the object of his letter of 31st May 1836 to the Governor-General was to enlist the sympathy of the British Government in his schemes of territorial aggrandizement. His wants, he thought, were arms and ammunition, to drive the Sikhs out of Peshávar, and not bales of commodities from India. The treaty concluded between Lord William Bentinck and Ranjít Singh at Ropar in 1831 forbade the English from interfering with the ruler of Láhore in the country beyond the Indus; and all notions of succouring the crazy and distracted Afghán monarchy had been abandoned. After these engagements with the Maharájá, the Government of India was most unwilling to render the Kábul chief, who had recently assumed the title of Amír, and who was regarded as no more than a usurper, any material aid in the prosecution of his designs. The refusal of the British Government to give up the cause of their ally, the Maharájá, was highly honourable; and they stood firm in supporting the Maharájá's authority. Dost Muhammad, on his part, treated the envoy with the greatest attention and seeming cordiality, assuring him of his hearty co-operation in all measures tending to promote British trade in Kábul and Afghanistán, yet he persisted in his demand for aid against his formidable neighbours, the Sikhs. The British envoy's errand left him no loophole for a political treaty. Dost Muhammad sedulously filled the mind of the English envoy with apprehensions of Russian intrigue and warnings of the danger which threatened India from the Russian advance to the east. But the attacks made by the Amír on the Sikh forces, besides being sudden and unprovoked, were calculated to kindle the flames of war in the very regions into which the British Government was endeavouring to extend its commerce, and it was rightly thought that the beneficent purposes of that Government would be altogether frustrated if these attacks by the Afgháns were continued. In order to avert so calamitous a result, the Governor-General authorised Captain Burnes to intimate to Dost Muhammad Khan that, if he should evince a disposition to come to just and reasonable terms with the Maharájá, His Lordship would exert his good offices with His Highness for the restoration of an amicable understanding between the two powers. The Maharájá, with

The mission of Captain Alexander Burnes to Kábul, 1837.

The objects of the mission purely of a commercial nature.

Dost Muhammad's views of self-aggrandizement.

His anxiety to recover Peshávar.

But the English respect their treaty with the Maharájá.

the characteristic confidence which he had invariably placed in the faith and friendship of the British nation, at once assented to the proposition of the Governor-General. While these peaceful negotiations were going on, Captain Burnes was startled by the sudden appearance, on December 19th, 1837, of a Russian envoy, Captain Vincovich, an Aide-de-Camp of the Russian Consul-General at Orenburgh, with a letter from Count Simonich, the Russian ambassador at the Court of Teheran. No definite line of action had been laid down in this letter; but the expression, 'Trust him with your secrets,' and 'I request you will look upon him as myself, and take his words as if from me,' had a wide significance, and might mean a great deal.

Dost Muhammad leans to Russia.

Captain Burnes, who enjoyed the entire confidence of the Governor-General, and was held to be an authority on the affairs of Central Asia, addressed His Lordship with great urgency. The imminent danger of the negotiations that had been now advanced up to the very borders of India was pointed out, and it was urged that much more vigorous proceedings were necessary to counteract Russian intrigue in this quarter than had yet been exhibited. The jealousy and alarm of Russia which had been diffused in India had equally alarmed the British ministers in Downing Street, and the English diplomatists at the Court of Teheran were also excited. Lord Auckland wrote to Dost Muhammad Khan, requiring him to abstain from all foreign alliances and to dismiss from his Court his Russian visitors. But that crafty chief, impatient for glory and triumph, had ideas of his own importance based on the fact that his friendship was courted. The question of the Sikh invasion of Jallálábád and Kábul had already been warmly discussed in the councils of Láhore, and, had friendly assurances been given to the Kandahár brothers and a hint that the Sikhs were at liberty to indulge their desire for a march to Kábul, Dost Muhammad would have been able to form a correct estimate of his own insignificance. As it was, however, he threw himself into the arms of Russia, in order to intimidate the English, cause the surrender of Peshâwar, and secure a guarantee against Ranjít Singh.

Captain Burnes advises the adoption of more vigourous proceedings on the part of the Government of India in regard to the Afghán policy.

British negotiations with the Amir.

The Government of India now clearly saw that Dost Muhammad Khan, encouraged chiefly by a promise of assistance from a foreign Power whose interests were in direct conflict with their own, persisted, as respects his misunderstanding with the Sikhs, in using the most unreasonable pretentions, such as the Governor-General could not, consistently with justice and his regard for the friendship of the Maharájá, be the channel of submitting to the consideration of His Highness; that he avowed schemes of aggrandizement and ambition injurious to the security and peace of the frontiers of India; and that he now openly threatened, in furtherance of those schemes, to call in whatever foreign aid he could command. To crown all, it was clear that the Amír gave his undisguised support to the Persian designs in Afghanistán, of the unfriendly and injurious character of which, as concerned the British power in India, he was well aware. The Government of India was compelled, by these considerations, to recall Captain Burnes from Kábul, which he quitted on the 26th April 1838. The Russian plenipotentiary was now admitted into the Darbár at Kábul and caressed by the Amír. He at once engaged to furnish Dost Muhammad with an abundant supply of money, and even to propitiate Ranjít Singh.

Lord Auckland's opinion as to the conduct and pretensions of the Amir.

His Lordship recalls Captain Burnes from Kábul, April, 1838.

Captain Burnes arrived at Láhore, on his way to Simla, to meet the Governor-General, in July 1838, and was splendidly received by the Maharájá. The whole question of foreign intrigues in the affairs of Afghanistán was discussed at Simla, and it was considered evident that no further interference could be exercised by the British Government to bring about a good

Amicable settlement between the Maharájá and the Amír considered impossible.

The Government resolve to restore Shah Shujá to the Kábul throne.

Grounds for upholding the claims of Shah Shujá.

The policy of the British Government.

understanding between the Sikh ruler and Dost Muhammad Khan, and that the hostile policy of the latter chief showed that, so long as Kábul remained under his government, the English Government could never hope that the tranquillity of the neighbourhood of their Indian empire would be secured, or its interests preserved inviolate. With a view, therefore, of arresting the rapid progress of foreign intrigue and aggression towards the frontier of India, it was considered necessary to strike a decisive blow, to make a triumphant march through Central Asia, and to restore Shah Shujá to the throne of his ancestors as a dependent prince. The prince was, indeed, the rightful heir to the Kábul throne, and his popularity throughout Afghanistán had been proved by the strong and unanimous testimony of the best authorities. He had, moreover, while in power, cordially acceded to the measures of united resistance to external enmity that were at that time judged necessary by the British Government, which, on his empire being usurped by the Barakzai family, had afforded him an honourable asylum in its dominions. The Barakzai chiefs were, from their disunion and unpopularity, considered by the Government of India ill-fitted, under any circumstances, to be useful allies to the British Government, and to aid that Government in its just and necessary measures of national defence. So long as they refrained from proceedings injurious to British interest and security, that Government acknowledged and respected their authority. But a different policy appeared to be now more than justified by the conduct of these chiefs, and to be indispensable to the safety of the British empire in Hindostán. The welfare of the British possessions in the East required that the British Government should have on its western frontier an ally who was interested in resisting aggression and establishing tranquillity, in the place of chiefs ranging themselves in subservience to a hostile Power and seeking to promote schemes of conquest and aggrandizement. It was from these considerations of justice and policy that the Government of India espoused the cause of Shah Shujá-ul-Mulk. Its resolution was bold and judicious, and the vigourous policy adopted worthy of the British name. The policy in question has been assailed by some writers as a disastrous one; but those who knew what public opinion then was in India, and what a mischievous effect active foreign intrigue in the countries immediately bordering on India was calculated to produce, notwithstanding the presence of the friendly Sikh power this side of the Indus, cannot deny that the policy was the best that could, under the circumstances, be adopted. The rumours of a northern invasion had been diligently spread throughout India by its vanquished princes, and the whole country vibrated with hopes of the ascendancy of a Power from beyond the Hindu Kush. It would hardly have been wise to have allowed Russian influence to be established in full vigour at the Court of Kábul at such a time. Nor would it have been worthy of the position of Great Britain to abandon, without reason, the cause of their ally, Maharájá Ranjít Singh, whose sincerity towards the British Government had been established beyond doubt. The Barakzai usurper of Kábul had sought the British alliance against the Maharájá, a request which it was necessary emphatically to disallow. And when the Amír openly went over to the side of Russia and prepared to act in opposition to the declared policy of Government, it was wisely resolved, for the sake of consistency, to show to the world that the British Government was always ready to uphold a cause that was just and proper, and that it could in no way allow its prestigé in India to suffer by foreign machinations and intrigues. The project was bold and honourable, and there is no doubt that, had it been steadily adhered to and subsequent mistakes carefully avoided, it would have fulfilled the ends in view.

Mr. Macnaghten sent on a political mission to the Court of Láhore, 1838.

The scheme for the restoration of Shah Shujá was matured in the first four months of 1838, and, it being thought proper, in consideration no less of the position of Maharájá Ranjít Singh than of his undeviating friendship towards the British Government, that His Highness should be invited to become a party to the contemplated operations, a mission was sent to the Maharájá, in May of that year, to unfold to him the views of the British Government. The mission consisted of Mr. Macnaghten, Political Secretary to Government, Captain Wade, Political Agent at Ludhiáná, Captain the Honourable W. G. Osborne, Military Secretary to the Governor-General, Captain McGregor, Aide-de-Camp to the Governor-General, and Doctor Drummond, Surgeon to His Lordship. They left Simla in company with several of the Maharájá's chief officers and sardars. The embassy, escorted by two companies of the 20th Regiment, two Horse Artillery guns and a squadron of Hearsay's Horse, crossed the Sutlej, on the opposite bank of which it was met by Sardars Ajít Singh and Karam Singh. The Court was then at Adinanagar, the summer residence of the Maharájá. Two marches from the city, the party was met by Prince Partáb Singh, a boy seven years of age, the son of Prince Sher Singh and the grandson of the Maharájá.* He is described as a handsome youth, richly dressed, armed with a small ornamented shield, sword and matchlock, all in miniature, covered with jewels and precious stones, and escorted by a body of Sikh Cavalry and some guns. The horse on which he rode was white, but was dyed with *henna* to a deep scarlet.† One march from Adinanagar, this interesting boy took leave of the mission, when Mr. Macnaghten presented him with a gold watch and chain, as a token of remembrance on the part of His Excellency the Governor-General. The young prince expressed his thanks in most graceful terms, and concluded by saying: "You may tell Lord Auckland that the British Government will always find a friend in the son of Sher Singh." Then mounting his horse, covered with plumes and jewels, he gracefully raised his hand to his forehead and galloped off with his escort curvetting and caracoling round him in circles till he was out of sight.

Reception of the party near Dinanagar by Prince Partáb Singh.

Arrival in the camp at Dinanagar.

Five miles from the Court, the party was met by Rájás Sher Singh and Suchet Singh, seated on an elephant in golden *howdahs*, and escorted by a body of about 500 of the Maharájá's bodyguard, gorgeously clad in chain armour and rich silk jackets of every colour and variety. The tents of the deputation had been pitched in a grove of mango trees

* According to custom, Sher Singh ought to have come himself to receive the members of the embassy, as the district of Adinanagar was that Prince's jágír, but it was said he had been a little overcome at a drinking party with the Maharájá the evening before, and was in consequence too ill to travel.

† The Honourable Mr. Osborne gives the following account of this intelligent and good-looking boy, Partáb Singh: "He is one of the most intelligent boys I ever met with; very good-looking, with singularly large and expressive eyes. His manners are in the highest degree attractive, polished, and gentlemanlike and totally free from all *mauvais honte* and awkwardness so generally found in European children of that age. In the course of conversation, I asked him if his matchlock was a real one and if he ever shot with it. He jumped off his chair highly indignant at the question, and after rapidly loading his musket exclaimed, 'Now what shall I shoot'? I replied that I saw nothing in the camp at present it would be safe to shoot at, and asked him if he thought he could hit a man at a hundred yards' distance, to which he replied, without a moment's hesitation, pointing to a crowd of Sikh chiefs and soldiers, that surrounded the tent, 'These are all your friends; but show me an enemy to the British Government and you shall soon see what I can do.' His father is said to be dotingly fond of this boy; and when he was deputed last year by the Maharájá to escort Sir Henry Fane to the frontiers of the Panjáb, took him with him: but such is Ranjít's jealousy of Europeans that, before they had got three marches, a regiment of cavalry was sent after them, with orders from the Maharájá to bring Partáb Singh back with them in order that he might remain as a hostage until his father's return to the Court." During the whole of the march through the jágírs of Sher Singh supplies for the entire camp of the British officers were furnished at the expense of that Prince. *Court and Camp of Ranjit Singh*, pp. 58-59. At Mukerian a grand feast was given to the members of the embassy, who were much delighted with the reception accorded to them. *Memoirs of Moulvi Din Mahomed.*

on the banks of a canal, separated from the Maharájá's gardens by only a few hundred yards. On arrival at the camp, the park of Sultán Mahmúd's artillery thundered forth a royal salute. No pains had been spared by the Maharájá's officers to promote the comfort of the deputation. In addition to the spacious tents which had been pitched in green mango groves, small buildings had been constructed by the Maharájá's orders for the comfort and accommodation of the members of the mission, and these were cooled by means of *khas-khas tattis*, or blinds. Each of these buildings had been well furnished with bedsteads, having handsome silk coverlets and mattresses, embroidered quilts, &c. About the grounds were scattered a number of buildings,* including a *zenan-kháná* encircled by a large garden, with shady trees and a canal running between. Constant irrigation kept the banks and vicinity always green and fresh, and in the shade of these trees the Maharájá passed his hot weather, drilling and manœuvring his troops. Between the parade ground and the gateway, which opened on a fine level plain, was always pitched a small scarlet and gold embroidered shawl tent, entirely open in front. Here the Maharájá used to retire soon after dark to rest and take his sleep in the open air, guarded by his trusted *sipahis*. His sword and shield always lay by his pillow, and a horse, saddled, stood constanly ready in front of his tent. In the morning he was always to be seen either on horseback or on an elephant, inspecting the drilling of his troops, or supervising the artillery practice.

The Maharájá in his summer retreat of Adinanagar.

The members of the mission had their audience of introduction to the Maharájá on the morning of 29th May. They were escorted into the presence of the Maharájá by Rájá Suchet Singh and Sardar Ajít Singh. On their reaching the verandah, the Maharájá's minister, Rájá Dhián Singh, came forward and conducted the British Officers round the palace to the hall of audience. At the entrance of this hall stood the Maharájá himself, who, after a friendly embrace, led the officers to the upper end of the hall and gave them seats on gold chairs, opposite himself. After the Maharájá had taken his seat on a gold chair, all his chiefs squatted on the floor round him, with the exception of his Minister Dhián Singh, who remained standing behind his master. After the usual enquiries about health, the presents from Lord Auckland to the Maharájá were produced. They consisted of His Lordship's picture, set in a star of very handsome diamonds, suspended by a string of large pearls; a pair of gold-mounted pistols; a splendid Damascus sword, in a golden scabbard, inlaid with precious stones, and two thorough-bred Cape horses, with housings and accoutrements of gold, richly studded with turquoises and enamel. Ranjít Singh examined each of these articles very minutely, and seemed to count every pearl and jewel before he made them over to his treasurer. It was a mere ceremonial interview, and no business was transacted that day. The time was chiefly occupied in replying to Ranjít's numerous questions on a variety of subjects—riding, hunting, fighting, drinking, &c. On the 31st May, the mission was received at the Maharájá's palace for the purpose of transacting business. After a few enquiries and compliments, the Maharájá proceeded to his private apartment, and a few minutes afterwards the distinguished members of the mission were requested to follow him. The Maharájá was found seated cross-legged on a large silver chair, with the boy Hirá Singh sitting before him, and

The first audience of introduction.

The second interview, 31st May 1838.

* These no longer exist at what was the summer retreat of the 'Panjáb Lion.' What is now left is a neglected *baradari* on the bank of the canal, which reminds old residents of Adinánagar, of its past grandeur and magnificence. Mango trees still exist in abundance at the spot, the luxuriance of which has been maintained by means of canal works and drainage, and it is to this day a place of refreshment and enjoyment for the people in the burning heat of June and July.

the Minister Dhián Singh standing behind his master's chair. Rai Govind Jas, the Maharájá's agent at Ludhiáná, Fakír Azíz-ud-dín and Sardar Lahná Singh were sitting at his feet. The letter of Lord Auckland to the Maharájá was then read out to the latter by Mr. Macnaghten, who explained to the Maharájá the policy proposed by the Government to be adopted in regard to Kábul affairs. The Maharájá was invited to co-operate with the British Government in the expulsion of Dost Muhammad from Kábul and the restoration of Shah Shujá-ul-Mulk to the throne of his ancestors. It was explained that, should the Maharájá choose to undertake the expedition himself and rely on his own resources, he was at perfect liberty to do so. But, should he think British co-operation necessary, the Government would be glad to render every aid in their power for the attainment of the desired end. Dhián Singh, who was standing * behind his master, here showed much reluctance to an English alliance, and, though he had not courage enough to make any remark, yet by the expression of his countenance and by shakes of the head, he could not refrain from showing how hostile he was to the project which had been laid before the Maharájá for his consideration. Ranjít Singh, however, agreed to the scheme without the slightest hesitation and with manifest cordiality and eagerness, and, after an audience of two hours, the members of the mission took their leave, the minor details of the conference being deferred for settlement till a future time. After the mission had departed, the Maharájá's chiefs brought weighty arguments to persuade him to adopt his own independent course as regards the advance to Kábul, deprecating a British alliance, but the Maharájá told them he had made up his mind and wished to hear no further talk about the matter.

The business of the mission transacted.

The objects of the mission and the views of the English in regard to Kábul affairs explained to the Maharaja.

Ranjít Singh accedes to the British proposals.

The audience of leave, 13th July, 1838.

The members of the mission had their final interview with the Maharájá on the 13th July, at Láhore. A public darbár was held by the Maharájá on that date in his marble palace in the Hazúri Bágh, and each officer of the mission was presented with a dress of honour, consisting of a string of pearls, a *chelink* of diamonds, six pairs of shawls, several pieces of gold embroidered silk, a pair of diamond armlets, a sword and a horse, with gold and velvet housings and accoutrements. The men of the escort were presented with twelve hundred rupees, and the servants of the mission with the same amount. The Maharájá then warmly embraced all the officers, and, wishing them all health and prosperity, retired to the fort.

Mr. Macnaghten proceeds to Ludhiáná to meet Shah Shujá and explain to him the views of the English.

The object of the British mission to the Darbár of Láhore having been gained, Mr. Macnaghten repaired to Ludhiáná, to meet Shah Shujá and announce to him the change which was about to take place in his fortunes with the united help of the English and the Láhore ruler, and to make him a party to the treaty concluded at Láhore between the Maharájá and the British Government. The result of these negotiations was the conclusion of a triplicate treaty by the British Government, the Maharájá and Shah Shujá-ul-Mulk, whereby His Highness was guaranteed in all his possessions. Shah Shujá was to enter Afghanistán supported by his own troops, but was to be aided by a British force and by the Maharájá. Independence was guaranteed to the rulers of Sindh, while the integrity of Herat, in possession of Shah Kámrán, was to be fully maintained. Ranjít Singh was anxious to secure something substantial and tangible as his share of the gain of the operations in Afghanistán. He knew full well the objections of the British Government to his

The triplicate alliance.

* It is to be observed that Rájá Dhián Singh, through his profound respect for his master, never, in his life, sat in the presence of the Maharájá, but always stood, while his other grandees and sardars sat on the floor. The only person who had the privilege of sitting before the Maharájá on a chair was Hirá Singh, son of Dhián Singh. The Maharájá was dotingly fond of the boy Hirá Singh.

having Shikárpur, and he, therefore, hinted at his being allowed to retain Jallálábád as his share of the spoils. Shah Shujá, on his part, agreed to pay him a subsidy of two lakhs of rupees per annum in consideration of his stationing a force of not less than 5,000 Muhammadan cavalry and infantry within the limits of the Peshávar territory for the support of the Shah. The Shah also agreed to send to the Maharájá an annual present of 55 high-bred horses of approved colour and breed, 11 Persian scimitars, 7 Persian poignards, 25 mules, and a variety of fruits and other produce of Afghanistán.

Ranjit Singh hints at retaining Jallálábád as his share of the spoil.

Towards the close of November, 1838, the British armies assembled at Ferozepur. This was the celelerated "Army of the Indus," as Lord Auckland called it, and it was commanded by Sir Willoughby Cotton. Further *eclát* was given to the opening of this memorable campaign by a meeting which had been in the meanwhile arranged between the Governor-General and the Maharájá, and which took place at Ferozepur on 30th November. The Maharájá had recently been attacked with a severe and dangerous illness, and was in a very enfeebled state of health; yet he took the most lively interest in the object of the meeting, and displayed his wonted spirit and acuteness and perspicacity on the occasion. In the *champ de drap d'or* of Ferozepur, His Excellency Lord Auckland make his appearance with the pomp and magnificence of an Indian potentate. The appearance of His Lordship's camp was imposing and picturesque, and, though the jewels and chain armour of the Sikh chiefs and sardars eclipsed the plain uniforms of the viceregal staff, the immense retinue of the British chief and his escort of 15,000 men at once showed to the acutely observing Sikh ruler the solid strength and the unassuming character of the great British nation. An interchange of ceremonious visits had given *eclát* to the occasion, while the splendid illuminations of the great mosque and of the city of Ferozepur were remarkable for their attractiveness and magnificence. Various reviews of the troops of the two nations were held, but none made so superb a display as the body guard of the Maharájá. They were dressed in yellow satin, with gold scarves and shawls; some were clad in cloth of gold, scarlet, purple or yellow; their beards were enveloped in a drapery of gold or silver tissue, to protect them from the dust, and their arms were all of gold. Amidst all this display of grandeur and interchange of magnificent hospitalities, an unfortunate circumstance happened, which was looked upon by the Sikhs as an unpropitious omen. While the Maharájá was proceeding to inspect the highly-finished guns, which were part of the presents to be made to him, he stumbled and fell flat on his face before them. He was not hurt; but the omen was nevertheless considered an unlucky one.

The rendezvous of the British armies at Ferozepur, November, 1838.

The "Army of the Indus."

Meeting between Lord Auckland and Maharajá Ranjit Singh at Ferozepur, 30th November, 1838.

Reviews of troops.

An accident thought to be unlucky.

A contingent was raised by Shah Shujá, more for form than for use, and this was united to the British force. In the beginning of December the Bengal army, 9,500 strong, was ready to proceed without delay to Sindh. A reserved division, 4,250 strong, was at the same time located at Ferozepur, under Major-General Duncan. The Maharájá had engaged to maintain an army of observation of 15,000 men. A Sikh contingent, about 6,000 strong, was placed under the orders of Lieutenant-Colonel Wade, and marched from Láhore in January, 1839, accompanied by Shahzáda Timúr. This force was joined at Peshávar by another Sikh contingent, under Prince Nau Nehal Singh, the Maharájá's grandson. Shah Shujá was himself to march by way of Shikárpur and Quetta. He entered Kandahár at the head of troops, and, the Barakzai Sardars having fled on his approach, he was formally enthroned on 8th May, 1839. On this occasion the whole of the British army, numbering

The Indian army marches for Afghanistán.

Kandahár occupied, 25th April, 1839.

about 7,500 men, was drawn up in line, at dawn, in front of the town of Kandahár, to the north. In the midst of an extensive plain, a throne was raised. The Shah's departure from the palace at sunrise was announced by a royal salute fired from the ramparts of the citadel of the Bálá Hissár. On his ascending the throne, the park of artillery thundered forth a salute of 101 guns. Sir John Keene and Mr. Macnaghten, the envoy and minister on the part of Government of India at the Court of the Shah, offered presents on behalf of the British Government, and then the officers, British and Native, in the king's service offered *nazars*. The "Army of the Indus" then marched past in front of the throne.*

Shah Shujá installed as King of Afghanistán, 8th May 1839.

Ranjít Singh at the height of his greatness, but his mind distracted and health broken.

Ranjít Singh had now apparently reached the summit of his greatness, but, amidst all his glories and thirst for further power, his dissolution was approaching. Harassed in mind and enfeebled in body, he sighed at the recollection of the rich plains across the Indús, and at his being prevented from undertaking an expedition against Shikárpur and Sindh, which was his most cherished aspiration during the later days of his life. A greater power than his own, for whom he had every ostensible esteem, had set bounds to his ambition on the west, as it had already done on the south and east. While Lord Auckland's host at Láhore and Amritsar, he felt a difficulty in utterance. His health continued to decline; but he lived to hear of the fall of Kandahár in April.

DEATH OF RANJÍT SINGH.

The Maharájá was endowed with a vigorous and powerful frame, capable of enduring the toil and hardship to which his aspirations and his genius as a conqueror and leader of men necessarily exposed him. He was gifted with extraordinary powers of endurance, but, had he possessed a constitution of iron, it would have inevitably succumbed to the tremendous strain to which it was subjected. The internal affairs of his kingdom and the reduction of the numerous clans and principalities around him, taxed his mental and physical faculties to the utmost. But what tended above all to bring about his dissolution was his general intemperance and insatiable appetite for strong drink. The Maharájá was afflicted with paralysis in 1834, and so severe was the attack that he never afterwards perfectly regained the power of speech. He made himself understood by signs only, and was unable to utter a single articulate sound.

The Maharájá is attacked by paralysis.

His partial recovery.

He partially recovered under European treatment, but fell seriously ill again. The physicians of Peshâwar and Láhore, the astrologers and *jogís*, were invited to a consultation, presided over by Fakír Azíz-ud-dín, physician in ordinary to His Highness. They brought with them various voluminous treatises of Æsculapian art, Homœopathic, Allopathic, Hydropathic, and, we must admit, that works of quackery were not wanting, as will appear evident from the prescription administered. After consultation, they unanimously resolved to dose the patient with a *majun*, or electuary, of which the principal ingredients were pearls and precious stones. The *majun* was administered to the Maharájá by the Fakír himself, but in less than a fortnight he breathed his last. During one of his rallying intervals the Maharájá convened a meeting of all his principal sarders and officers, and, formally investing Kharak Singh,† his eldest son, with ruling powers, placed

Electuary medicine prescribed.

Formal investment of Prince Kharak Singh.

* Ghazni was stormed in July 1839, and Kábul captured, and Shah Shujá seated on its throne, on 8th August, 1839. For subsequent disastrous events in Afghanistán, see Kaye's "Afghán War," and other works on Kábul and Afghanistán.

† According to Smyth, Kharak Singh was brought into the presence of Ranjít Singh only when the old King was on his deathbed. He and Sher Singh were both carefully kept at a distance on the frontier while the influence of the Dográ family reigned supreme in the Court.

the *tilak*, or mark of royalty, on his forehead. Rájá Dhián Singh was, in the meantime, acknowledged as prime minister to the new Maharájá. Ranjít Singh placed his hand in that of Dhián Singh, thus making over to him the charge of his son and heir. He enjoined Dhián Singh to act as his guardian and tutor, and to look upon him as he would on himself. A dress of honour having then been bestowed on the Minister, he received the title of *Naib ul Sultanat-i-Uzma, Kháir Khahi Samímí Daulat-i-Sarkár, Wazir-i-Muazzim, Dastur-i-Makkarram, Mukhtár wa Mudarul Maham Kul.*

Rájá Dhián Singh is declared the prime minister.

The fact was officially communicated to the governors of Multán, Pesháwar, Káshmír and other places, and promulgated throughout the length and breadth of the kingdom.

The last moments of the Maharájá.

When the last moments of the Maharájá arrived, thousands of rupees were distributed * as alms among the poor. Rájá Dhián Singh prepared a raised platform of ten lakhs of rupees, and spread on it a number of shawls, of the aggregate value of ten thousand rupees. On this "platform," or "terrace," the Maharájá expired. According to the will of the Maharájá it was intended to bequeath the celebrated diamond, the *Koh-i-núr* to the temple of Jagannáth, or to the institution of Gurú Rám Dás, and Ranjít Singh was ready to throw water on it as a sign of having made the bequest. Jamadar Khushhal Singh and Rájá Dhián Singh sent for the diamond, but Misar Beli Ram, who was in charge of the *toshakhána* objected to its delivery, on the ground that it was the property of the Crown and should not be thrown away in alms.

Death of Maharájá Ranjít Singh, 27th June 1839.

The funeral ceremonies.

The Maharájá's body, having been bathed with fragrant waters and embalmed, was dressed in rich clothes and decorated with ornaments, as in life. Four of the Maharájá's Ránís and seven of his slave-girls, of their own free will and accord, prepared to burn themselves along with the body of their lord and husband, animated with the hope, given them by their religion, of entering paradise with their earthly master. One of the Ránís who burnt themselves alive on the Maharájá's funeral pile, was Raj Deví † daughter of the celebrated Sansár Chand, Rájá of Kangrá, whom the Maharájá had reduced to subjection. According to the tenets of the Hindu religion only childless wives burn themselves alive on the funeral pile of their husbands, and they undergo the horrid ceremony apparently in the hope of getting in the next world what has been denied them in this.

Self-immolation of the Maharájá's wives and slave-girls on his funeral pyre.

Dhián Singh swears fealty to the new Maharájá.

All the Ránís who had prepared themselves for the horrible sacrifice, standing at the head of the Maharájá's body, called the Minister, Rájá Dhián Singh, into their presence. The sacred book, "Siri Gitaji," was placed on the Maharájá's chest, and Dhián Singh, having touched the body of his royal master and the sacred book, swore fealty to the new Maharájá, Kharak Singh, and solemnly promised to use his best endeavours to keep both Kharak Singh and Nau Nehal Singh on friendly terms.

The heir.

The Maharájá's body was placed on a decorated bier (*bawán*), in shape like a ship. It was wrought with gold, and the sails and flags were made of the richest silk, embroidered with gold. The vessel was placed on a board on which the body of the Maharájá lay, and was carried by a number of men. Thousands of people accompanied the funeral, and the procession moved

The mourning procession.

* Rae Kánhia Lal, in his history of the Panjáb, says that 22 lakhs of rupees in cash, and 25 lakhs of rupees worth property, was distributed among the poor Muhammadans and Hindus in Moques, Dharmsalas and other religions institutions, and that 250 maunds of *ghi* was sent to Devi Mandar of Jwálá Mukhi on this occasion.

† Rájá Kánhia Lal in his book mentions that both the daughters of Sansár Chand, who were Ránís of the Maharájá burned themselves on the funeral pile. This is a mistake, as, according to Dr. Honighberger, who was an eye-witness to the scene, only one became the *satti*, the other had some time before died of consumption.

slowly from the interior of the fortress towards the funeral pile, where originally existed a small, but beautiful, garden.

As the funeral procession advanced, thousands of rupees were thrown among the crowd as alms, and scrambled for by the needy and poor. For the first time during their lives, the Ránís of the great Maharájá came out unveiled from the harem and meekly followed the corpse barefooted. They were dressed in pure white silk and wore no ornaments. They had distributed all their jewels and valuables among the poor before leaving the *zenáná*. One of the Ránís who could not distribute all she had with her, had the remainder of her valuables carried by a man who walked by her side, and she gave them away to the poor with both hands, as she went to the horrible altar. In front of each Rání, at a distance of two or three paces, walked a man with his face turned towards her and moving backwards. He held a looking-glass before the Rání, in front of whom he walked, that she might see that her features were unaltered, and that her resolution to sacrifice her life had no effect on her appearance.

The procession of the widows to the funeral pyre.

After the Ránís followed the seven slave-girls, also barefooted. Some of these appeared to be only fourteen or fifteen years of age. All seemed quite indifferent to the awful fate which awaited them, and which, indeed, they had themselves sought. Dr. Honighberger, who was a personal witness of this melancholy scene, observes, "Perhaps our hearts throbbed more at the view of the dismal train, than those of the poor victims themselves."

The slave-girls marching to the scene.

The drums beat mournfully, the musicians sang melancholy dirges, and the sound of their instruments spread gloom and sorrow throughout the whole assembly. This, combined with the murmuring of a vast mourning crowd, whose anxious faces bore testimony to the grief and affliction inwardly felt by them, and to their love for their departed master, whom they adored, and who had loved them, gave the whole scene a most melancholy aspect. The funeral pile was constructed of sandal wood and aloe, in the form of a square six feet high. Upon it were strewed inflammable substances, such as cotton seeds, &c. The bier having been brought close to it, its valuable ornaments and costly covering were given away to the mob. The Brahmins and the Gurús then recited passages from their holy books and offered prayers for the benefit of the departed soul of the Maharájá. This occupied about half an hour. The ascent to the funeral pile was by a ladder. The ministers and the sardars first ascended and helped in gently removing the royal body from the bier and respectfully placing it in the middle of the pile, together with the board on which it lay. The four Ránís, with death-despising intrepidity, then ascended the fatal ladder, one by one, according to their rank, and occupied a place at the head of their royal husband, holding the head with their hands. The slave-girls, with equal courage and contempt for death, then ascended the ladder and placed themselves at the foot of their lord. The *sattís*, having thus seated themselves round the royal corpse, were covered with reed mats, on which oil had been profusely poured. Rájá Dhián Singh, at this moment, approached the Ránís and begged them to offer prayers for the prosperity of the new Maharájá; but not a word was uttered by the Ránís, who, with eyes closed and hands stretched towards the head of the Maharájá, which they were holding, maintained a solemn silence in expectation of the fatal moment which was now near at hand. A strong thick mat of reeds was then brought and saturated with oil, with which all were covered. The Minister, Rájá Dhián Singh, and the sardars then came down. The Rájá seemed the most affected, and grief had so much overpowered him that he felt his own life a burden, and insisted on being burnt with the Ránís.

The gloomy scene described.

Affliction of Rájá Dhián Singh.

Twice or thrice he even attempted to force his way forward; and it was with some difficulty that he was persuaded to refrain from sharing the fate of the *sattis*. Oil, otto and ghee were then profusely thrown on the pile. This being done, Prince Kharak Singh lighted the pile at each corner, and in a moment the whole was a blaze, the flames of which ascended to a prodigious height. In almost the twinkling of an eye the unfortunate creatures who had been covered with the mats, had ceased to exist, and in a short time the whole mass was reduced to ashes.

The ashes of the Maharájá on the way to the Ganges.

The burning of the pile occupied two days. On the third day the bones and ashes of the dead were picked out by the members of the household and, having been put in separate urns, were placed in separate tents made of Káshmír shawls, the poles of which were wrought with gold and silver, and which had cost an enormous sum. Preparations were then made to send the bones to the Ganges. The remains of the Maharájá and those of the four Ránís were placed in separate richly-caparisoned palanquins and brought out in state from the fort. They were accompanied by costly presents, such as valuable shawls, richly decorated elephants and horses, gold and silver utensils, rich cloth, &c., all intended to be distributed as alms among the Brahmins that live on the banks of the sacred river at Hardawar. On the procession leaving the fort, a royal salute was fired from it. All the chiefs and sardars and the members of the Royal household accompanied it, some on foot, others on elephants and horses.

The scene in the city of Láhore.

The procession traversed the principal streets and bazars of Láhore, which were crowded with people. The streets, house-tops, windows and balconies, were all filled with spectators. Those who occupied the higher localities showered down wreaths of flowers on the palanquins as they passed below. The doors of the palanquin that contained the ashes of the Maharájá were open; those of the other four, containing the remains of the Ránís, were closed. The faithful Minister, Dhián Singh, walked close to the Maharájá's palanquin, on the right hand, holding in his hand a fan of peacock's feathers, with which he drove away the flies, thus showing his homage and respect to his departed patron and lord to the last. When the procession arrived outside the Delhi Gate, a final salute was fired from the ramparts of the fort and the walls of the city, which continued to deafen the ears for a considerable time. The royal salute was a signal for the chiefs and sardars to retire. This being concluded, all returned to the city, leaving the remains and presents to be conveyed by the guards to their final destination. As the remains of the Maharájá passed the head-quarters of districts in British territory and in native states, the same formalities of respect and salutation were observed as in the Maharájá's lifetime. Mourning was observed for thirteen days, the mourning costume being white. On the 13th day, the last funeral obsequies were gone through, and thousands of rupees lavished on the Brahmins and fakírs.

Tribute paid by the British Government to the memory of their ally the Maharájá.

The character of Maharájá Ranjít Singh.

As the reader is aware, Ranjít Singh had received no education and could neither read nor write in any language; nevertheless he entertained great respect for learning and learned men. His secretaries were in perpetual attendance on him, and he had the papers read out to him in Persian, Panjábí or Hindí, and saw that his orders were drawn up in due form and that the drafts met his views. He conversed in Panjábí with his own people, but spoke in Hindostání to his European visitors. He was small in stature and little indebted to nature for beauty of features, which was disfigured with small-pox and deprived of the left-eye from the same cause; yet his appearance was prepossessing, his manner and address were delightful, and his features were full of animation and expression. His remaining eye was large, quick and searching, and its fire and brilliancy, displayed at once the great acuteness and the energy of mind of its owner. He possessed a long flowing white beard, which gave additional grace to his countenance. He generally sat cross-legged on his chair, and, while he talked, one of his hands rested on his knee, while he employed the other in stroking his beard.

He possessed a lively imagination, and his habits were genial and quite unreserved. In dress he was exceedingly plain, yet he was fond of show and pageantry, paid the most rigid attention to the elegance of his court and took delight in seeing his grandees and sardars superbly dressed and decorated with jewels. He was not a bigot, but he performed his religious observances regularly, heard the *Granth* every day at the appointed time and munificently rewarded the Gurús, Bháis and Báwás who helped him in the performance of religious ceremonies. He had great power of dissimulation, and his caprice, as has been amply shown in the foregoing chapters, had no bounds. In his pursuit of ambition or pleasure he was indifferent alike to the pledges of friendship and to the ties of blood or affection. In his youth he was remarkably active and vigorous, and an excellent horseman and sportsman, well skilled in military feats. He was fond of show and lavish in his gifts to his courtiers; but his avarice grew with his age, and a desire for hoarding treasure became his ruling passion. His temper was irritated at times, as the result of a shattered constitution, and he was unable to ride on a horse without being lifted on to it. He took delight in military displays and parades, and evinced a lively interest in the equipment of his army.

Ranjít Singh remoulded the political condition of the Sikhs, and consolidated numerous dismembered petty states into a kingdom. His relations with the paramount power of India were of a most cordial nature, and, although he had some misapprehensions in regard to them at first, yet, having once recognized his situation, he faithfully observed his treaty with the Government and kept his word with that power until his death.

PART V.—PERIOD FOLLOWING THE DEATH OF RANJÍT SINGH.

CHAPTER I.

THE SUCCESSORS OF MAHARÁJÁ RANJÍT SINGH.

KHARAK SINGH.

Kharak Singh ascends the throne, 1839.

THE funeral solemnities of Ranjít Singh being over, Kharak Singh, his eldest legitimate son, ascended the throne and was acknowledged Maharájá of the Panjáb. He was a man of weak intellect, and was more addicted to opium than his father. He was in the habit of taking the drug twice a day, and passed the whole of the time in a state of semi-inebriety. Physiognomically he was the counterpart of his royal sire, but he possessed none of his diplomatic qualifications. One Chet Singh, who had hardly anything to recommend him but arrogance and sycophancy, attained such an ascendancy over the weak mind of the new Maharájá that he became a mere puppet in his hands. One of Kharak Singh's first acts was to deprive Rájá Dhián Singh and his son, Hirá Singh, of the privilege of free admission into the king's *zenána*, so that the minister was unable to make important representations on State affairs privately to the king.

Chet Singh appointed Prime Minister.

Chet Singh was raised to the dignity of wazír, and a plot was made to assassinate Dhián Singh. Chet Singh lived in the fortress with his master, Kharak Singh, and had recently raised two battalions of bodyguards, with whom he conspired to despatch Dhián Singh one morning as he entered the fort. The plot was known to Dhián Singh, who succeeded not only in preventing the accomplishment of the treacherous act, but, having won over Kanwar Nau Nehal Singh to his side, revenged himself on Chet Singh so completely that all his plans were frustrated, and he himself met a melancholy and fatal end. A rumour was set afloat that Kharak Singh had formed a with the British Government and had consented to acknowledge their league supremacy, to pay a tax of six annas per rupee, to disband the Sikh army, and to do away with the sardars, who were to be replaced by English officers. This rumour was soon circulated through the town, and became the chief topic of conversation in the markets and streets. The civil and military freely vented their indignation at this supposed treacherous compact. Kharak Singh was openly calumniated, and the soldiery began to look upon him as a traitor, unworthly of his position.

Nau Nehal Singh is recalled from Peshá-war.

Nau Nehal Singh, who for some time before his father's accession to the throne resided at Pesháwar, was hastily recalled, together with Rájá Guláb Singh. He entered the city the avowed enemy of his father. So strong was the feeling against Kharak Singh that even his wife, Chand Kour, the mother of Nau Nehal Singh, became his bitterest enemy, and gave her full consent and connivance to her husband's dethronement. A plot, which obtained the concurrence and support of the Minister's brothers and of the sardars of their party, was formed to assassinate Chet Singh and to depose and imprison the Maharájá.

Plot against the new Maharájá and his favourite Chet Singh.

The conspiracy was kept a strict secret until the plan was ripe for action. When the time for active measures had arrived, the Minister, with his two brothers, Guláb Singh and Suchet Singh, the Sindhianwálá Sardars and others, went to the fort, two hours before sunrise, and entered the sleeping apartment of Kharak Singh with drawn swords. On their way, they were met by two Bháis, whom they cut down; further on they met Kharak Singh's *gadwai*, or water-carrier, who was just returning after assisting his master in performing his ablutions, as Kharak Singh was in the habit of retiring for prayers at that early hour.

Seeing the armed ruffians, the *gadwai*, terror-stricken, ran in the direction of his master's apartment, but he was waylaid by Dhián Singh, who shot him dead with an English rifle with which he was armed. The party then advanced to the king's sleeping apartment. Chet Singh now perceived the danger with which he was threatened, and hastily concealed himself in the *khábgah*, a long dark room close to the royal apartment. Here the conspirators met the king's guards and two armed companies, who at first offered some slight resistance; but, when the brothers, Dhián Singh and Guláb Singh, shewed their faces, they were so much awed that they laid down their arms and allowed the party free admission to the king's retiring room. The conspirators were so infuriated that they would have put an end to the life of the monarch but for the timely presence of Nau Nehal Singh and his mother, Chand Kour, who both had enjoined on the party not to injure the person of Kharak Singh. The king was surprised and placed in custody. Search was then made for his favorite, Chet Singh, who was at last discovered concealed in the dark chamber of the *khábgah*, crouching in a corner of the room and grasping a drawn sword with both hands, but trembling the while with fear. On being discovered, he craved for pardon and wept like a child; notwithstanding which he was dragged into the presence of Dhián Singh, who, having identified him, stabbed him twice through the stomach with a long knife. Thus ended the life of this notorious intriguer. Chet Singh's relations and partisans were instantly searched for by the infuriated assassins, and, on being discovered, shared the same fate. This occurred on the 8th of October, 1839, and was the beginning of those numerous scenes of bloodshed and horror which have left an ineffaceable blot on the history of the Sikh regimé in the Panjáb.

Kharak Singh is put in custody.

Assassination of Chet Singh, 8th October 1839.

Kharak Singh deposed.

Subsequently to these horrible transactions Kharak Singh was permitted to abdicate and retire to his city mansion. He had reigned for a brief period of about three months.

NAU NEHAL SINGH.

Prince Nau Nehal Singh succeeds.

The Royal Prince Nau Nehal Singh, the only son and real offspring of the titular sovereign, was proclaimed ruler of the Panjáb, and assumed the reins of Government at the early age of 18. His features and disposition bore a striking resemblance to those of his illustrious grandfather, and he was exceedingly popular with the army in consequence of his having chosen the profession of arms at a very tender age. He possessed an ambitious and warlike spirit, which, combined with consummate forethought, a keen judgment, and a clear insight into business matters, qualified him thoroughly for the position to which he aspired. The great Ranjít Singh was dotingly fond of his grandson, and justly cherished the hope that he would one day rule the destinies of the vast kingdom founded by himself. He, too, had his weak points. He almost believed in the infallibility of his spiritual preceptors. He was entirely under the influence of the Brahmins, and placed implicit faith in all that they told him. The Brahmins, Báwás, and Fakírs persuaded him that he would sway the sceptre from the borders of Afghanistan to Pragia, the most sacred city of the Hindus (now known as Benares),

His whims and caprice.

including Delhi, the ancient metropolis of Hindostán. He was so convinced of the truth of all this that he is said to have actually given royal *sanads* to certain individuals assigning them jágírs and landed estates in the vicinity of Delhi and Benares, in anticipation of the fulfilment of these prophecies. He was quite forgetful of his father and his sufferings, and very seldom paid him a visit in his private residence at the Láhori Gate, and that only for the purpose of roundly abusing him for his supposed treacherous and pusillanimous conduct.

A strong guard was placed over the person of the deposed monarch, who was believed to be feigning illness in order to leave Láhore for British territory and protection.

Nau Nehal Singh detested the British, and he is reported to have even collected an army in the vicinity of Láhore with the ostensible object of waging war with them, but his mischievous designs were frustrated by the occurrence of domestic broils and Court intrigues, which left him no time to carry out his views. He sent an army against the Rájá of Mandi and reduced the fort of Kamálgarh. He is opposed to British interests.

Kharak Singh's intellect became impaired, and, broken-hearted and afflicted by the revolting and insulting conduct of his only son, he lingered on a bed of sickness for some nine months, suffering from colic (spasmodic affection of the limbs and bowels), during which time his son shewed the greatest possible indifference in regard to his treatment, and, with the design of hastening his end, committed him to the care of specially appointed quacks and mountebanks, who had their own parts to play in the tragedy. His ill-treatment of his father.

The young prince visited his father, the deposed monarch, once, and only once, on the day previous to Kharak Singh's demise, and, on that one occasion even, treated him with the greatest brutality and insolence. He professed to believe that his father's illness was only feigned, while in reality the malady had been engendered and increased by the use of nostrums administered by his pseudo-physicians to an already undermined constitution. The next day, 5th November 1840, Kharak Singh breathed his last at the early age of thirty-eight.

The dying monarch cherished the greatest affection for his unnatural son. In the agonies of death he called for his "dear and only son," that he might pardon him for the parricide, but those employed about his person represented these cries to the prince as the wanderings of a maniac and the curses of a dying father.

Thus was Nau Nehal Singh kept from being present at his father's deathbed. The news of Kharak Singh's death was conveyed to the prince at his favourite hunting-ground in Shah Biláwal, in the environs of Láhore, where he was at the time engaged in a shooting-party. He received the intelligence with open demonstrations of joy, and did not even condescend to leave his amusement for the full space of two hours after the tidings first reached him, when orders were quietly passed for the performance of Kharak Singh's funeral obsequies.

Two of Kharak Singh's ránís* and eleven of his slave-girls burnt themselves alive on his funeral pile. The ceremony took place in the open space, opposite the *samádh* of Maharájá Ranjít Singh, in the presence of Nau Nehal Singh and the Court. The young Maharájá appeared to look on with the utmost *sang froid*, and before the body of his father was half consumed, he retired from the scene, accompanied by his sardars, with whom

* One of these was a young and most beautiful lady of about twenty years of age.—*Smyth.*

he bathed in a *nallah*, a short distance from the pyre, the elephants and other paraphernalia of royalty following close behind. The party were not mounted, ostensibly out of reverence for the dead monarch. Having bathed, the prince with his suite made his way back to the fort. As he approached the archway of the northern gate of the Hazúri Bágh, close to the *samádh*, he took the hand of Mian Udham Singh, the eldest son of Guláb Singh and nephew of Dhián Singh. They continued walking on slowly, the prince making some humorous remarks to his companion, quite unconscious of the fatal moment which awaited him. As both entered the archway, a loud crash was heard, and it was found that a fragment of the upper wall had fallen and crushed the two young men, who were walking close under it.* Udham Singh died immediately. The prince, whose head was frightfully crushed, was taken up senseless by Dhián Singh, who placed him in a palanquin and conveyed him to the fortress. Sardar Lahná Singh, Majithia, attempted to follow the palanquin; but Dhián Singh stopped him. Other sardars tried to follow, but were prevented by the minister from entering the fort, the gates of which were at once closed. In vain did the Maharáni Chand Kour, the mother of the injured prince, beat her head against the gates of the fortress and raise heart-rending shrieks and cries to be allowed to see her beloved and only child. Admittance was refused to all. Nau Nehal Singh was kept in an inner apartment, in a state of insensibility, and strict secrecy was observed as to his condition, the only person attendant on him being the minister, two of his followers and a few chosen hillmen. The sardars who waited at the gates outside were informed that there was no reason to apprehend danger; that the prince would in all likelihood shortly recover, as he had received but a slight wound, which, having caused a severe shock to the brain, had rendered him unconscious for the time being; that he required a short repose, and that his rest should not be disturbed. He therefore ordered them quietly to retire and mind their own business.

The accident to Prince Nau Nehal Singh.

His death, 5th November, 1840.

Two hours afterwards Chand Kour was informed by the minister that her son had breathed his last, but that, if she desired to take the reins of government into her own hands (to attain which object the minister promised to exert himself in her favour), she must keep the matter a strict secret until such time as he considered it proper to announce it. He did not quit the lady before obtaining from her a solemn promise that she would act as desired. Thus the death of Nau Nehal Singh was kept a secret for three days. The minister availed himself of this interval to send for Shér Singh, with whom he had previously corresponded from Mukeria, and whom he intended to place on the vacant throne. Shér Singh having made his appearance, the death of the royal prince was made public, and preparations were made for his funeral ceremonies. The ceremony of cremation took place close to the spot at which he had witnessed the funeral obsequies of his grandfather. Two beautiful young ladies, the widows of the deceased, burnt themselves alive with the body of their lord. One female, twelve years of age, was prevented by Shér Singh from undergoing the fatal trial, on account of her youth and exquisite beauty.

It is concealed for a time.

Sher Singh summoned to Láhore.

Surmise as to the true nature of Nau Nehal Singh's accident.

Historians have differed as to the real cause of Nau Nehal Singh's death. Some think that he and his companion, Udham Singh, were accidentally

* Major McGregor, in his *History of the Sikhs*, writes that Udham Singh, the eldest son of Rájá Guláb Singh, of Jammú, who was on the same elephant, shared the same fate. This is not a fact. Both walked on foot, hand-in-hand, and, as they passed the covered gateway, a portion of the structure fell, killing the minister's nephew on the spot, and injuring the prince so seriously that he became senseless. This account fully agrees with the English, as well as the vernacular, texts.

crushed; others, that the whole plan was premeditated and the machination of wicked conspirators. I do not agree with those who maintain that it was the result of a design to remove Nau Nehal Singh from the scene. Doubtless, the Jammú brothers, who are suspected of committing the crime, were quite capable of designing and prosecuting such a plan, but they would have certainly spared the life of Guláb Singh's own son, who was loved by Dhián Singh, and it would have been easy to appoint another companion for the prince, who could even have left his side as the young Maharájá emerged from the passage. Moreover, the exact moment of the downfall of the huge mass of stones and tiles which formed the structure could hardly have been foreseen.

According to Dr. Honighberger, who was an eye-witness of the event, the minister's own arm was severely contused, an injury for which the learned Doctor himself attended him. Furthermore, it would have been easy to arrange for the prompt arrival of Shér Singh when the Maharájá had breathed his last, in order to place him on the throne without the loss of a moment, and three days would not have been wasted in appeasing the widowed Maharání Chand Kour, who was eventually raised to the supreme power. It may be that the partisans of Kharak Singh and Chet Singh were the authors of this plot, as they had robbed and cheated the imbecile Kharak Singh in a most perfidious way, and the prince had already determined to bring them to account.

It appears to me that the whole was a just retribution of Heaven for his manifold sins and wickedness. The prolonged booming of the guns which announced to the world that Kharak Singh was no more was the instrument in the hands of the Almighty which brought to a close the ephemeral reign of the young Maharájá. That the roaring of the cannon shook the old fort to its foundation, is very well known, and that a part of it should have fallen in at this particular juncture is not, I think, very extraordinary. That this monstrous prince should have met with his death in this singular manner, cannot, I think, be attributed to any other cause but that of the Divine wrath.

CHAND KOUR.

In vain did the Maharání, Chand Kour, now look upon Rájá Dhián Singh to fulfil his promise, to give her the sovereign authority; for the shrewd minister knew well that the party of the Maharání and the Sindhianwálás were his deadly foes, and, if raised to power, would be the first to seek his destruction and that of his family. He therefore urged on the sardars to place Shér Singh, the reputed son of Ranjít Singh, on the throne with all despatch, advancing, as his argument, that a woman necessarily lacks those abilities to govern a vast kingdom which are essentially necessary in a country like the Panjáb, and that the Sikh soldiery would not quietly submit to the rule of the Rání.

Dhián Singh advocates the cause of Shér Singh.

The party of Chand Kour, however, prevailed. She summoned Attar Singh, the Chief of the Sindhianwálás, who was at that time absent at Hardawar, to her assistance at the capital. She was also supported by other sardars, but mainly by the Sindhianwálás, who claimed common descent with Ranjít Singh. Thus strengthened, she distributed alms to the Brahmins most liberally, and was, by popular acclamation, installed as the Maharání of the Panjáb. The factions were distracted by a representation that her daughter-in-law was pregnant, that she was holding power only as regent for the child in the womb, but that, in the event of the Rání of Nau Nehal Singh giving birth to a female child, she would be willing to adopt the boy,

Chand Kour proclaimed sovereign.

Shér Singh withdraws to Batálá.

Attar Singh, Sindhianwálá, appointed Prime Minister.

Hirá Singh, as a son (inasmuch as the Maharájá had treated him as such during his lifetime), and by this means acknowledge his claims. The cunning Dhián Singh appeared pacified with the show of sincerity thus displayed by the queen, but the rude Shér Singh was bent on offering her armed resistance. Dhián Singh considered this an inopportune time for carrying on warlike preparations, and advised his protegé to withdraw quietly. The good-natured voluptuary accordingly withdrew to Batálá, and there enjoyed his favourite pastime to his heart's content. Dhián Singh, pretending to be ill, went to the Jammú hills for change of air. Chand Kour now exercised supreme power, under the designation of *Mai*, or mother, as regent for the expected offspring of Nau Nehal Singh. She bestowed a *khilat* of honour on Attar Singh, Sindhianwálá, whom she appointed her Prime Minister. A council of four sardars was established under Attar Singh, whose advice was sought in all State affairs.

Guláb Singh embraces the cause of the Maharání.

First report of Dulip Singh's birth.

Rájá Guláb Singh, at this juncture, allied himself with the queen, the deep policy of the Jammú brothers, who appeared to share in all important intrigues, being that, whichever party might win, their element would preponderate. Feeling, moreover, doubtful whether Shér Singh's claims would be recognised by the English Government, Rájá Dhián Singh had the news conveyed to that Government that Rání Jindán, a favourite wife of Maharájá Ranjít Singh, had given birth to a son, named Dulíp Singh, a few months before the confusion arose about the re-seating of Shah Shujá on the Kábul throne. Thus was the British Government, for the first time, informed of the existence of another heir to the throne of Láhore.

Rájá Dhián Singh remained at Jammú for about a month; but he had left emissaries at Láhore, who secretly kept him informed of all that was going on in the capital. They played with the *Khálsá* soldiery and their sardars so well, that assurances of allegiance and support were given by several corps, whenever the Royal Prince, Shér Singh, and Dhián Singh, should make their appearance before the walls of Láhore.

Shér Singh appears before Láhore.

Jawálá Singh the chief councillor of Shér Singh.

The *panches* of the army support the cause of Shér Singh.

He makes *Budhu-ká-áwá* his stand-point.

The time now being considered ripe for an advance on Láhore, Shér Singh, according to previous arrangements with Dhián Singh, marched from Mukeria, at the head of about 300 followers, and posted himself at the Shalámár gardens. To his great disappointment, however, he was informed that Dhián Singh, instead of joining him at the gardens as previously arranged, had not, up to that moment, even left his hill territory. This afforded an opportunity to Jawálá Singh, an ambitious sardar, and one of Shér Singh's principal councillors, who aspired to the wazírship, to instil into the mind of the credulous prince the idea that Dhián Singh cared little for his interests, and that his real sympathies where with his brother, Guláb Singh, who had openly espoused the cause of the Maharání. Shér Singh now permitted Jawálá Singh to negotiate directly with the soldiery, and the *Khálsá* troops stationed at Mián Mír were informed of the arrival of the prince. The troops expressed their readiness to assemble the following day at *Budhu-ká-áwá*, a lofty old brick kiln, near Láhore, on the top of which General Avitabile had constructed a *barádari*, known in after times as the *fatehgarh*, or the house of victory. The place was used as the rendezvous of the *panches*, or deputies, of the *Khálsá* troops, who in those times exercised great influence over the army and people. The following day, 14th January 1841, witnessed the arrival of Shér Singh at *Budhu-ká-áwá*, where were also assembled the *Khálsá* troops from Mián Mír and the surrounding places.

Shér Singh having taken up his position on this mound, his safety was ensured by four battalions of infantry and two of cavalry, with several pieces of artillery stationed around it. The *panches* of the army and most of the sardars of the *Khálsá* soldiery now approached, and, having paid their homage to him, publicly declared him the sovereign of the Panjáb.

His arrival is welcomed by the residents of Láhore.

Crowds came from the city and welcomed his arrival by the national cheer, "*Wáh Guru ji ki Fateh,*" long and continued. The intention of the soldiery to support Shér Singh was further announced by the booming of artillery, which now awakened the amazed citizens of Láhore from their long slumber and roused them to a sense of their danger. The queen, on being informed of the arrival of Shér Singh in the environs of Láhore, ordered the gates of the city to be closed, and convened a council of her ministers, consisting of Rájá Guláb Singh, Jemadár Khushál Singh, Sardar Tejá Singh, and the sardars of the Sindhianwálá family. Guláb Singh's own troops, who were at that time encamped at Shádera, across the Ráví, were immediately ordered to march on Láhore, and were posted on the parade ground north of the Summan Burj. It was intended to send them to oppose Shér Singh's troops, encamped in the immediate neighbourhood of Láhore, but Guláb Singh suddenly changed his plan and located the detachments in the fort, thus strengthening his own position for defence.

Active measures of Guláb Singh.

The troops, under Jemadár Khushál Singh, Sardar Tejá Singh, and other Sindhianwálá Sardars, entered the fort, and the services of all were placed at the disposal of Rájá Guláb Singh. Every bastion round the city, as well as the gateway, was now strengthened. Guláb Singh was indefatigable in his efforts to place the city in a state of defence, himself personally inspecting each post and giving all necessary orders. As he visited the different posts, he distributed money in handfuls to the soldiers, receiving from them, in return, strong assurances of fidelity. The rájá, on his return to the fort, assembled all the sardars, officers and men of the army, and personally administered an oath to each—to the Mahomedans on the *Qurán* and to the Hindus on the water of the Ganges—to stand firm in their allegiance to the Maharání Chand Kour and to resist Shér Singh to the utmost of their power. Four months' pay was then distributed to the soldiers as a gratuity, with promises of further favours and promotion in the event of the enemy being repulsed and the throne of Láhore secured for the Maharání.

Suchet Singh and General Ventura join Shér Singh.

While these events were in progress in the city and fortress, Shér Singh was joined by Suchet Singh and General Ventura, who acknowledged him as king. The troops under the prince now numbered 70,000, and their impetuosity had reached such a pitch that Shér Singh was unable to restrain them. He entered the city at eight o'clock at night, by a wicket gate which then existed between Mewá Singh's barracks and the western portion of the Bádsháhí Mosque, and soon afterwards his artillery first entered the city by the Yakkí and Delhi gates, and afterwards by the Tak-sálí and other gates, the guards and keepers of the gates, who had the day before sworn allegiance to Chand Kour, after receiving large sums of money as rewards, having been won over by Shér Singh, from whom they received rewards still richer and more valuable. Thus, before daybreak, Shér Singh was master of the principal parts of the town. He also arranged, by means of further bribes, to enter the gate leading to the Hazúrí Bágh; and his troops occupied the palace garden and quietly took possession of the Bádsháhí Masjid, where a large magazine, stored by the troops of Guláb Singh, fell into their hands.

The Prince occupies the city of Láhore.

Excesses committed by the soldiers.

The whole city was in a state of uproar and commotion throughout the night. The enraged soldiery plundered all the principal bazars. The shops of the merchants and traders, which were closed for the night, were broken open and their contents pillaged, and the Chatta Bazár was set on fire, the flames rising above the highest house in the city.

The siege of the fort.

As day dawned, the whole army of 70,000 infantry, with 50,000 followers, rushed infuriated in the direction of the fort, filling the air with the war-cry, "*Wáh, Guru ji ki Fateh,*" "*Wáh, Guru ji ki Khálsá-ji.*" The fort was densely surrounded on all sides by eager troops, who covered the space below the walls, like a swarm of bees. Batteries of artillery were posted all round the fort in such a manner as to enable them to keep up constant communication with each other. Even this continuous line, which comprised 230 pieces of artillery, was considered insufficient, and more guns were brought into action. The main strength of the besieging force lay at the Hazúri Bágh, where Shér Singh himself directed their movements, arranging their posts and assigning commands to the officers. With the exception of a few minutes rest in the palace barádari, his whole time was uninterruptedly employed in personally conducting the manœuvres of his troops. Twelve guns were placed opposite the marble summer house, facing the western gate of the fort, for the purpose of blowing it in.

The besieged consisted of the Dográ force of Guláb Singh, who had been ordered from Shadera, and a force of 1,200 Sikhs under Budh Singh, Man, who guarded the fort treasury called the Moti Mandar. They lined the walls of the fort, on which their batteries were mounted at different points.

The whole presented a strange and terrible spectacle. Elated with the hope of rewards, and still more of plunder and rapine, the wild *Khálsá* soldiery, directed by Shér Singh in person, formed one compact body, which reached to the very walls of the fort and assailed it with the impetuosity of the ocean when in the height of a tempest it angrily beats against a rock. The savage cries of the warriors and the loud sounds of their wild music were deafening. A volley was then fired from the batteries of the attacking force, in order to terrify the defenders, which completely stunned both besiegers and besieged, shaking to their very foundations the walls of the fort built by the Great Akber. This was all unreplied to by the defenders in the fort. The besiegers now became still more excited, and were clamorous in demanding the immediate opening of the gates. All this was unheeded. At length a terrible fire was simultaneously opened by the twelve guns which had been posted opposite the western gate of the fort, and the result was that the old gate fell down, with thirty-seven out of the thirty-nine men who, with two guns loaded with grape shot, were defending it. A band of 300 Akálís now rushed to the front to seize the guns, but the two surviving men discharged their pieces simultaneously, and in the twinkling of an eye a hundred of the assailants fell dead on the ruins of the gate, where the bodies of the fallen defenders lay. A large number of horses belonging to the besiegers were also killed. The Dográs on the walls and ramparts of the fort now promptly opened fire with their muskets, the result being that the twelve guns which had hitherto hurled destruction on the besieged were abandoned, and in about ten minutes the palace garden was cleared of the besiegers, who dispersed in all directions, leaving behind them, on the field, 300 killed and 100 wounded, besides 50 prisoners who had been captured by the Dográs in a sally.

The eastern gateway of the fort was bombarded under very much the same circumstances as the western gate had been, and with similar results for the besiegers, whose loss in killed and wounded, men and animals, was enormous.

The *Khálsá* force, being thus repulsed in the first assault, opened a heavy and general fire from the train of artillery which encircled the fort, and continued it with such violence and rapidity that it threatened the destruction of the old walls; but the fire of the Dográ garrison on the rampart was so well directed that in about an hour the artillery below was silenced, and the besiegers, falling back, sought protection in the houses of the city. About 146 guns were left on the plains, with no one to protect them. The dead bodies of men and carcases of horses and bullocks which were to be seen in numbers around them presenting a most ghastly spectacle.

Savage conduct of the besiegers.

At this juncture the *Khálsá* troops behaved in the most savage and brutal way. Seizing the women of private houses in the city, they compelled these unfortunate creatures to stand in front of their guns and around them. Many were forcibly bound to the wheels of the artillery. The object of the barbarians in thus forcing the tenderer sex to surround their guns and occupy a place in front of their own ranks was to divert the direct effect of the enemy's fire. The handful of Dográs, however, deserved the greatest credit for their cautious conduct, taking into consideration the disadvantages under which they were placed and the difficulties under which they suffered. With such skill did they direct their fire on the besiegers below that very few of the unfortunate women were struck, and the work of destruction in the ranks of the besiegers went on steadily to their profound amazement. As the best proof of their gallantry and humanity, as also of their skill as marksmen, it is stated that, of 1,200 women who had been thus barbarously exposed, only 19 fell victims to the atrocity of the Sikhs, while 200 of the artillerymen were found dead around their guns from the effects of the fire of the garrison.

The manly bearing of the besieged.

The bombardment of the fort.

In this manner the besiegers continued the bombardment for three days and nights, and the small garrison replied to the best of their ability and power. The Sikhs took up secure positions in and behind the houses in the city, and advantageously placed their guns close to the walls, directing their muzzles through embrasures made for the purpose. From these concealed batteries a tremendous cannonade was maintained at intervals. The fortress, which was originally intended by the Emperor Akber as a palace for the residence of the royal household, contained no embrasures, and the besieged, to overcome this defect, erected batteries of wood and earth within the fort, from which they returned the fire of the besiegers. The incessant and heavy cannonade kept up by the besiegers for three days resulted in several large breaches in the walls of the fortress, which afforded the Dográs the advantage of being able to make several sallies on the besiegers during the night. Shér Singh, on this occasion, hired the services of some forty *mochis*, who, hunters, or *shikaris*, by profession, were good marksmen, and whom he mounted on the *minars* of the Bádsháhí Mosque. The *mochis* were paid at the rate of Rs. 10 to Rs. 20 each, and their commanding position enabled them to inflict considerable loss on the garrison inside the fort, who were unable to reply effectually to their fire, since they commanded every corner of the palace with their weapons.

The siege lasted five days, during which time the besiegers once entertained the idea of blowing up the Bádsháhí Masjid, where Shér Singh had taken up his position, and which they knew to contain a magazine of 6,000 maunds of powder. They, however, desisted from exploding this magazine, fearing their own destruction by the explosion of subterraneous passages filled with powder which connected the Gulâb Khâná of Hazúri Bágh with the middle of the fort. On the evening of the fifth day news reached Láhore of the arrival of Rájá Dhián Singh from the Jammú hills at a place three or four miles from Shadera. Shér Singh ordered the cessation of hostilities, and entered into negotiations with Guláb Singh, but that Chief refused

The arrival of Rájá Dhián Singh at Láhore.

to accept any overtures until his brother Dhián Singh should act as the mediator. Shér Singh sent 500 *ghorcharás*, or cavalry, wit hseveral of his chiefs and sardars, to receive Rájá Dhián Singh with due honour, and bring him to Láhorę. Escorted by these troops and 500 of his own followers, who had accompanied him from Jammú, the rájá made his entry into the city on the sixth day of the siege, accompanied by his brother, Suchet Singh. He was met near the walls of the city by Shér Singh, who came out to receive him with a strong escort and a numerous retinue.

At the Tak-sálí gate of the city, thousands of people assembled to receive the rájá, and, as he made his appearance before the city walls, the soldiery greeted his arrival with long and continued cheers. Amidst these acclamations Rájá Dhián Singh entered the city, and, by his command, all further hostilities ceased. The Sikhs now began to burn or bury the dead, and the Hazúrí Bágh was cleared of the dead bodies of men and the carcases of cattle and horses with which it was filled. This work of clearing was carried on during the seventh and eighth days of the siege, and the returns showed that, on the side of the besiegers, the number of killed was 4,786 men, 610 horses and 320 bullocks, while the number of men killed on the side of the besieged garrison did not in all exceed 130. A sum of between four and five lakhs of rupees was expended by Shér Singh in rewards and presents to the *Khálsá* troops in the six days during which the siege lasted, while the Dográs of the garrison each received from Guláb Singh sums amounting in the aggregate to Rs. 100, as bounty, exclusive of the rewards to officers, which were still larger in amount. Nearly half the houses of the city were dismantled by the Sikh soldiery, on the plea of procuring wood for the purpose of erecting their batteries and works for the protection of their guns; and they committed other atrocities as indescribable as they were horrible. The dead were collected in large heaps and burnt like fuel. The flames of the piles mounted high, and the air was filled with the stench of burning flesh and bones. The savage troops were seen throwing wounded men on the piles. The cries of these unfortunate beings, as they were thrown, still living, into the flames, were intensely heart-rending. In vain did they cry for mercy; their entreaties merely elicited derisive laughter, it being asked if they were afraid to go to Heaven: "*Char Jáo, Bhai! char Jáo; khauf kás galda.*"—"Mount, brother, mount! what are you afraid of?" The object of committing atrocities so horrible was to secure the little property which the barbarous Sikh soldiers had found on the persons of their comrades. Negotiations for peace were now set on foot, and Rájá Híra Singh was deputed by Rájá Guláb Singh, on behalf of the Maharání Chand Kour, to arrange the terms of peace according to directions given. Híra Singh came out of the Summan Burj, with the Sindhianwálá sardars, on the seventh day of the siege, and peace was agreed to on the following terms:—The Maharání Chand Kour to surrender the fort of Láhore to Shér Singh, and to give up all her claims to the throne of Láhore. In return for this, Shér Singh was to give the ex-queen a jágír of nine lakhs of rupees, adjoining the Jammú hills, which should be managed by Guláb Singh, as her regent, or mukhtár; *secondly*, that Shér Singh was to refrain from his wish to marry the Maharání by the ceremony "*chadar-dalná;*" *thirdly*, that the Dográ troops should be permitted to leave the fort and capital unmolested; and, *fourthly*, that security should be furnished for the due fulfilment of the treaty.

Further hostilities ceased.

Savage conduct of the soldiers.

Peace negotiations.

The terms of peace.

Maharání Chand Kour abdicates the throne.

Rájá Guláb Singh carried away all the money and valuables belonging to the Maharání Chand Kour under pretence of keeping it safely for her. The night after the treaty was signed, the Dográ forces vacated the fort.

Wealth carried away by Rájá Guláb Singh to Jammú.

Rájá Guláb Singh carried off the accumulated treasures of Ranjít Singh which were in the fort. Sixteen carts were filled with rupees and other silver coins, while 500 horsemen were each entrusted with a bag of gold mohurs, and his orderlies were also entrusted with jewellery and other valuable articles. The costly *pashmínás*, and rich wardrobes, and the best horses in Ranjít Singh's stables, were all purloined by Guláb Singh on the occasion of his evacuating Láhore, an event which took place on the night following the cessation of hostilities. Before leaving for his native land, he paid his respects to the new Maharájá, whom he assured that all that had been done by him had been done in perfect good faith, and as the old servant of the old Maharájá; that it was, moreover, his duty to save the honour of the great Maharájá's daughter-in-law, who had entrusted herself to his care.

SHÉR SINGH.

Shér Singh succeeds, 1841.

On the 18th of January, 1841 (1892 *Samvat*), Shér Singh was seated on the throne of Láhore. All the sardars, with the exception of the Sindhianwálás, paid homage to him. Dhián Singh was again installed in the office of wazír, and a rich *khilat* was conferred on him by the new Maharájá. The pay of the soldiery was permanently raised by one rupee per mensem. All the jágírs and territories belonging to the powerful family of Sindhianwálá were confiscated to the State, and orders were issued for the arrest of Attar Singh, Sindhianwálá, and his younger brother, Lahná Singh.

Dhián Singh appointed Prime Minister.

The Sindhianwálá possessions seized.

Attar Singh, with his nephew, Ajít Singh, escaped across the Sutlej to British territory, while Lahná Singh, another principal member, who had till now remained with his division of troops, was made a State prisoner and conveyed in chains to Láhore. The soldiery, who had chiefly contributed to the rise of Shér Singh to power, now became intolerant and uncontrollable. They began to wreak their vengeance upon such of their officers as had in any way molested them, or defrauded them of their pay or prizes. The houses of several of these officers were burnt, and men suspected of any ill-feeling towards the soldiery were seized and put to death. The Europeans then living at Láhore in the employ of the Darbár were terror-stricken at the sight of the atrocities committed by the furious *Khálsá* soldiery. General Court, an officer of much distinction and reputation in the darbár, effected his escape, but a brave young Englishman, named Foulkes, was murdered in cold blood. Regimental Paymasters and Ministers living in the town were plundered in broad daylight, nor was the discontent of the soldiery confined to the capital. In Káshmír, General Máhán Singh was plundered and slain, while at Pesháwar General Avitabile was so hard pressed that he abandoned that town, to take safety in Jallálábád. The turbulence of the *Khálsá* army gradually subsided; but not until British intervention had been threatened.

The soldiery becomes uncontrollable.

The character of Shér Singh.

Shér Singh was addicted to pleasure, and had been in the habit of indulging in the use of spirituous liquors to an immoderate extent before he assumed the reins of Government. Firmly established in his kingdom, he gave himself up to his favourite pursuits, hunting and wrestling, paying but little attention to affairs of State, which were left entirely in the hands of his prudent Minister, Rájá Dhián Singh. He was brave, and of a mild and affable disposition. He, however, sometime after, became a complete libertine and an open drunkard, indulging especially in champagne. The marble palace garden, opposite the royal mosque of Aurangzeb, was his favourite resort of pleasure; and here he used to sit on his bed of roses, with wreaths of flowers hanging over the beautiful marble arches, and rose and musk water sprinkled on the ground, while bands of musicians discoursed sweet music. "Eat, drink, and be merry," was the maxim of the royal sage, Sardanapalus, of ancient celebrity, and the same maxim might with truth have been attributed to the voluptuous Shér Singh.

Whether in the palace garden of Hazúrí Bágh, or in the marble summer house of Shalámár with its luxurious baths, or the crystal palace of the Summan Burj, or the favorite Barádari of Shah Bilávwal, bands of musicians and beautiful damsels were always in attendance upon him. His excesses were not viewed with disgust by a people who measured the physical powers of a man by the quantity of liquor which he was able to consume at one sitting, and at a time when debauchery in all its forms was the order of the day, and, indeed, a mark of wealth and worldly distinction. Even for a common soldier, indulgence in wine and women was considered a social matter. It did not require any very great prophetic power to foretell the inevitable result of this debauchery of the king and his subjects. Shortly afterwards there commenced those civil feuds and broils which brought this corrupt and decayed monarchy to an end.

Jawálá Singh, the confidential agent of Shér Singh.

The crafty Rájá Dhián Singh had his eye on the ambitious Jawálá Singh, once his rival, and a candidate for the premiership, whom, it will be remembered, Sher Singh had promised to create his wazír, should he succeed in obtaining the throne of Láhore through his instrumentality, and without the aid of the Dográ chief. Jawálá Singh was a rich sardar, who exercised great influence over the *Khálsá* troops. At the siege of Láhore, when Dhián Singh arrived in the city from his hill territory, and when Shér Singh repented the ill-success of the campaign and ordered the cessation of hostilities, Jawálá Singh, feeling that the decision of Dhián Singh, would be law for both the contending parties, and that his own services would not be taken into account, saw his interest in continuing the war, the successful issue of which, without the intervention of Dhián Singh, would secure for him the much-coveted and promised rank of wazír. He persuaded the troops to stand firm in their resolution to obtain possession of the fort by force of arms, and for twelve hours the orders of Shér Singh to cease firing were disregarded. It was only by the combined efforts of Shér Singh and Dhián Singh, who personally appeared before the troops and explained matters to them, that they were induced to desist by the offer of gifts. All these matters rankled in the revengful heart of Dhián Singh, who poisoned the Maharájá's ears against Jawálá Singh to such a degree that he began to look upon his old and zealous servant as a dangerous and crafty antagonist. Jawálá Singh kept aloof with 5,000 of his *ghorcharhá* cavalry, at the Shálámár Gardens, and, when ordered by the Maharájá to appear in his presence, hotly refused to comply with the command. Upon this the Maharájá, attended by the minister, sallied forth from the city, at the head of an army, to chastise his perverse and disobedient agent, but Jawálá Singh, hearing of his approach, went forward to receive his angry master and threw himself at his feet. Jawálá Singh was brought into Láhore and at once heavily shackled. He was thrown into a dark and deep dungeon in May 1841. While in prison, he was flogged daily, after which he received his prison allowance of food, which consisted of half a measure of flour and an equal quantity of salt, mixed together. Hot irons were applied to the soles of his feet, as an additional punishment. Under these tortures he lingered for forty days, and expired in the fort of Shekhúpura, whither he had been removed ten days previously to his death.

The Maharájá begins to look upon him with distrust.

Jawálá Singh is imprisoned.

His cruel death.

Disagreement between the Maharájá and Ráni Chand Kour.

Though the freedom of Chand Kour from a matrimonial tie with Shér Singh formed one of the stipulations on which peace had been concluded between her and him, the Maharájá appears never to have given up the cherished idea of securing her hand by the custom of *chadar-andází.* The Rání might have accepted Shér Singh's protection and become one of his wives; but she was secretly assured by Guláb Singh that the Maharájá only desired it in order to work her destruction. The frail and confiding woman, therefore, left the fort and retired to the private house of her late son in the city. Shér Singh, burning with rage at her conduct, lost all command over his temper when he was further assured by Dhián Singh that the Rání despised him as the reputed son of Ranjít Singh, while she considered herself, as the daughter of Jaymal Singh, the great chief of the Kanhia *misl*, to be the descendant of a noble house. Enraged at these repeated misrepresentations, Shér Singh secretly resolved to put an end to the life of the widowed Maharání. Having bribed the slave-girls of Chand Kour to murder their mistress, he suddenly left for Wazírábád with his darbár. He promised a jágír of 5,000 rupees to each of four of the slave-girls, on condition of their carrying out his scheme. One day, while Shér Singh was absent from Láhore, these disloyal maid-servants, as they were dressing the hair of their royal mistress, smashed in her skull and dashed her brains out with bricks. The murder was perpetrated in June, 1842, in the house built by her son, Nau Nehal Singh, in the town where she was living at the time through fear of Shér Singh. Dhián Singh, in the absence of the Maharájá, proceeded to punish the assassins, and had their noses, ears and hands cut off publicly before the kotwáli, or chief police office in the town. Their tongues, however, were not mutilated, and they related the circumstances under which they had been tempted to perpetrate the horrible crime at the instance of both the Maharájá and his minister. What they uttered was, however, treated as the ravings of mad persons in extreme mental affliction, and they were banished to the other side of the river Rávi and were never heard of afterwards. The news of the death of this unfortunate princess was received with feelings of joy by both Shér Singh and Guláb Singh, inasmuch as by her death a claimant to the Láhore throne had been quietly removed, while to Guláb Singh it secured the peaceful and undisturbed possession of the whole of her immense property.

Her tragic death, June 1842.

After the successful conclusion of the Kábul campaign, in which the British Government was assisted by the Maharájá of the Panjáb, a grand review of the two armies took place at Ferozepur. Prince Partáb Singh, heir-apparent to the Láhore throne, attended by the Minister Rájá Dhián Singh, had an interview with the Governor-General, Lord Ellenborough, which resulted in more friendly relations being established between the Indian Government and the Láhore Darbár.

Lord Ellenborough meets the heir-apparent at Ferozepur, 1842.

In February 1843, Dost Muhammad Khan, the released Amír of Kábul, was received with distinction at Láhore; and a formal treaty of friendship was entered into between him and the darbár.

Dost Muhammad Khan at Láhore, 1843.

The cordial relations that existed between the Maharájá and his Prime Minister, Rájá Dhián Singh, were now drawing to a close. They began to hate each other in the most acrimonious manner. The Sindhianwálás, as our readers know, were descendants of the same stock as Ranjít Singh, and supporters of the claims of the late Mai Chand Kour. They were deadly foes of both Shér Singh and Dhián Singh, and, with their troops, fought against Shér Singh on the side of the Mai. There was a family of the Sikh spiritual leaders, known as the Bháis, who, on account of their religious sanctity, exercised considerable influence both at Court and in the king's zenáná. Foremost among these were Bháis Ram Singh and Gurmukh Singh, who were rivals for the favour of their sovereign and attached to parties whose interests were mutually opposed. Thus Bhái Ram

Distrust between the Maharájá and his Minister.

Bháis Ram Singh and Gurmukh Singh.

Factions formed at the Court.

Singh supported the party of the Dográ chiefs and of Rájá Lál Singh, and his family, while Bhái Gurmukh Singh and Missar Beli Ram were united in their policy, and were the deadly foes of the Dográ chiefs and Rájá Lál Singh. Shér Singh had put Lahná Singh, the chief of the Sindhianwálá family, in confinement, for the part he had taken against him before his accession to the throne. His brother Attar Singh, and the nephew of Ajít Singh, who were at large, had gone to live at Thánesar, across the Sutlej. Ajít Singh was even reported to have visited Calcutta for the purpose of laying his grievances before the British Governor-General. Shér Singh possessed an open and generous heart, and, from his tender disposition, was at times ready to forgive his worst enemies. On the intercession of Bhái Ram Singh, but chiefly through female influence, as the Bhái was secretly working on the favourite women of Shér Singh in his holy character, the Sindhianwálá exiled Sardars, Attar Singh and Ajít Singh, were recalled, and Lahná Singh was released from confinement. Their confiscated estates were restored, and fresh favours and honours were heaped upon them by the Maharájá. Attar Singh returned to his jágírs, but Lahná Singh and Ajít Singh, uncle and nephew, took their accustomed places at the Court. In the course of time the Sindhianwálá sardars obtained such an ascendancy over the mind of Shér Singh, that their advice was sought in all matters, political or domestic. They were found with the Maharájá day and night, in public and private. They became his boon companions; whatever they wanted was granted them, and nothing that they disapproved was insisted upon. Dhián Singh, to whom, in no small degree, they owed their rise and fortune, naturally became jealous of the unlimited power they exercised over their master, and the disregard which was shown to him by the Maharájá made him his secret and inveterate foe. Guláb Singh was privately called from Jammú by the wazír, and, during his short stay at the capital, the two brothers settled the line of policy which they determined to pursue under the circumstances existing at the time. Thenceforward the wazír began to show great consideration to the child Dulíp Singh, the reputed son of Maharájá Ranjít Singh, then five or six years of age. He treated the child as the legitimate and rightful heir to the throne, and showed him great respect. He used frequently to send for him and make a show of him as the issue of the great Maharájá by his highly-favoured queen, the Ráni Jindán. Such behaviour on the part of the wazír was, of course, very annoying to the Maharájá, who strove in many ways to reduce his power and get rid of him, but Dhián Singh was too strong to be crushed by even a man of Shér Singh's undaunted courage. The Sindhianwálá sardars, who ever cherished a deep-rooted and secret enmity towards the king, whom they considered an upstart and a usurper, and his minister, and whose spirit of resentment was never softened by the amends made by them, as had been amply evinced by their recent conduct, carefully watched all these events. They were unmindful of the favours which their master had shown them, and the confidence which he had reposed in them. Equally were they forgetful of the kindness which the prudent and favourite wazír had shown them, in arranging for their recall from banishment, and in bringing them to the favourable notice of the Maharájá. They now thought that an opportunity presented itself of wreaking their vengeance on both the Maharájá and the wazír, who were divided in opinion and hated each other, and of doing something for their own aggrandizement at the expense of both.

The Sindhianwálá sardars restored to favour.

Dhián Singh becomes jealous of their position.

The policy of the Sindhianwálá sardars, Lahná Singh and Ajít Singh.

Their great familiarity with the Maharájá.

The familiarity and feigned courtesy which existed between the Maharájá and the Sindhianwálá sardars was great. There were times of festive mirth and familiar jollity in which all were treated alike. The sardars quarrelled with the Maharájá, and harsh words were even exchanged between them; but all this was taken in good part. In these hours of revelry, Ajít Singh was known to have frequently threatened to take the life of the Maharájá; but the latter paid no regard to his threats. Shér Singh was repeatedly cautioned by his friends to be on his guard and not place too implicit confidence in the Sindhianwálás, but he took no heed of these warnings. When the plans of the sardars were completed, they at first waited on Shér Singh and held a private conference with him. They began with stories of their own fidelity to the person of the Maharájá and of their devotion to the State. As servants and loyal subjects it was, they said, impossible for them in any way to support or countenance the wicked machinations of Dhián Singh, who, they represented, had resolved to put an end to the Maharájá's life. They informed the Maharájá that the acquisition of worldly rewards was not their object in making these designs of Dhián Singh known to him, for they had, after all, to leave this world and account to the Creator for their acts. Had they cared for such wealth, they would, they maintained, not have deprived themselves of a jágír of sixty lakhs of rupees, which was promised them by Dhián Singh in the event of their taking the Maharájá's life. They assured the Maharájá that Dhián Singh had resolved to place the young Dulip Singh on the throne, and that they had a promise from him that they should act as regents during the minority of the young chief. All this was declared to Shér Singh in a spirit of apparent candour and strict confidence, and after the Maharájá had been prevailed upon to take an oath of secrecy. The Maharájá was further assured that they had been actually commissioned by the wazír to assassinate him. Shér Singh, who was a brave and intrepid soldier, was deeply affected by this information, and, with the bluntness usual to him, drawing his own sword, he offered it to the sardars, telling them: "Here is the sword, and here my throat; cut it, if you have been commanded to slay me, and are inclined to act as ordered. But forget not one thing; the day will not be far off when your own throats will be cut by the very men who now wish to make you their tools." Feigning to be startled at these prophetic remarks, the cunning Sindhianwálá brothers immediately stood up, joined their hands, and, with bent heads, protested: "Take the life of our lord and sovereign! What are our own heads for? These will be sacrificed first of all, should any designs be entertained by the ill-disposed on the precious life of our master, on which depend the happiness and the welfare of millions of people." Such was their display of sincerity and candour that the Maharájá was convinced of the treacherous designs imputed to the wazír and the loyalty and devotion of the sardars to his person. They proposed to the Maharájá that the perfidious minister should be immediately put to death, and took upon themselves the responsibility of carrying their proposal into effect. The Maharájá gave his full and unqualified consent to this; and the brothers obtained a *firman** under his signature, authorising them to act in the manner resolved upon, and exonerating them from all responsibility for an act which was

Their professions of friendship for him.

The grand tragedy.

The Maharájá signs the Minister's death-warrant.

* According to McGregor, "the Maharájá's signature was obtained to this writing at a time when, overcome by the effects of liquor, he was unconscious of what he was doing." This can hardly be the fact, as his seal was also subsequently obtained to this document, as will appear hereafter. The mode and the time of the intended murder were fixed, with only this difference, that the victim really designed was the Maharájá himself. The same programme was strictly acted upon the day of murder. All this could not have been arranged and consented to by the Maharájá in a state of unconsciousness, for he is shown to have *acted* according to the programme and received the Sindhianwálá sardars as had been arranged. The whole plan, it is clear, was well considered, and had received Shér Singh's full approval.

understood to be undertaken in the interests of the reigning family. It was then agreed that the Sindhianwálá sardars should retire for a while to their jágírs in Rájá Sansi, near Amritsar, and afterwards return with a body of their troops, all well armed and equipped, whom they were to draw up for inspection before the Maharájá at Shah Bilâwal, better known as the Házri, the usual place for reviews aud manœuvres of troops. These troops were to be ready with matchlocks and ammunition to perform their evolutions fully accoutred before His Highness, who was to call Rájá Dhián Singh and give him orders for their inspection. The rájá and his son, Hírá Singh, were then to be suddenly surrounded by the troops and shot.

Having made these preliminary arrangements and secured the possession of the document giving authority for the assassination of the wazír, the Sindhianwálá brothers went at once to Rájá Dhián Singh, and, the preliminaries being over, they showed him his death-warrant, signed by the Maharájá himself. The Rájá was too shrewd to accept at once, as a fact, what the Sindhianwálás narrated to him, or to believe in the genuineness of the document. He expressed his inability to believe that Shér Singh, his own protegé, whatever seeming difference might have existed between them, could act with such ingratitude towards him. He, in short, gave the sardars to understand that, unless both the seal and the signature of his master were attached, he would refuse to believe that he entertained designs against his life. Lahná Singh and his nephew lost no time in obtaining the Maharájá's own seal to the document. Rájá Dhián Singh, on seeing this, was incensed in the highest degree. Availing themselves of the effect produced on his mind, the cunning Sindhianwálá sardars suggested to him that, as a just punishment for his ungrateful conduct, the Maharájá should himself be treated in the manner in which he desired them to treat the innocent Rájá; that they shrank from polluting their hands with the blood of so wise, upright and innocent a minister as Dhián Singh, and that they thought they would be only doing their duty to their countrymen if they were to put an end to the shameful career of a usurper and debauchee who was at once unacceptable to the people and quite unworthy of the high office to which he had been raised, mainly through the instrumentality of the prudent wazír whose life he was now anxious to destroy. These sycophantic expressions made a deep impression on the Rájá's mind, and he gave his full consent to the assassination of his master, promising the Sindhianwálás great rewards in the event of their successfully carrying out their mission. They had a document executed by Dhián Singh, authorising them to put an end to the Maharájá's life, and obtained his signature on it just as they had done on that authorising the wazír's murder. This being over, arrangements were entered into with Dhián Singh to post such a number of troops about the palace, on the day appointed for the tragedy, as would tend to expedite the work in hand. The Sindhianwálás then, taking leave of the minister, marched for Rájá Sansi. Thus the Sindhianwálás played their double game so well that they insinuated themselves into the confidence of both the Maharájá and his wazír, and, without the knowledge of either, arranged to destroy them both. The game was devised so that the Maharájá and his minister were made the unconscious murderers of each other. Each of them believed, in his turn, that the blow was intended for his adversary, and finally it fell upon both of them.

And attaches his seal to it.

The minister signs the death-warrant of the Maharájá.

Rájá Dhián Singh now feigned illness, and retired to his private residence in the city. Friday was the day appointed for the execution of the tragedy, and it happened to be the first day of the Hindu month. Shér Singh left the city early on the morning of that day.* He was on horseback, attended only by Dhián Singh, Dewán Diná Nath, and his armour-bearer, Budh Singh, a brave man who was always in attendance on his person. He passed through the Roshnái gate of the city, and, taking the road leading to the parade ground, proceeded to his mansion at Shah Biláwal. He had no escort about him. In due time the firing of the matchlocks announced the arrival of the Sindhianwálás at Shah Biláwal. They presented themselves with a newly-raised levy and were attended by about fifty followers, who, like themselves, were well armed and equipped. It being the first of the Hindi month, or a *Sankrant* day, no darbár was held on that date. The Maharájá entered the house, and, having seated himself opposite a window of the Barádari, began to amuse himself with the wrestling of some athletes. This lasted a short time, and the Maharájá was dismissing them with presents, which he gave with his own hands, sitting in the window, when Ajít Singh reported the arrival of his new levy, which he arrayed before the window. The Maharájá ordered Dewán Diná Nath to enlist them as soldiers. As the athletes received presents from the Maharájá, they bowed before him and made their obeisances, the Maharájá receiving them freely and in a courteous manner. He reclined easily on his chair, little suspecting the fate which awaited him. While he was thus employed, Ajít Singh approached Shér Singh, and, exhibiting a handsome double-barrelled fowling-piece for his inspection, said with a smile: "See, what an excellent rifle I have bought for 1,400 rupees; I would not now part with it for even 3,000." The Maharájá stretched out his hand to take the gun, which was loaded with two balls in each barrel; and, as Ajít Singh handed it to the Maharájá, he discharged both barrels simultaneously into his breast? The Maharájá instantly fell back in his chair, exclaiming, "*Eh ki daghá?*" ("What treachery is this?") and expired immediately after.† As the Maharájá fell back a corpse, Ajít Singh, at one blow, severed his head from his body. Budh Singh, the armour-bearer of Shér Singh, came to the spot, immediately on hearing the report of the gun. This brave man cut down two of Ajít Singh's followers, and aimed a blow at Ajít Singh himself, but the sword snapped in two. He ran to procure another, but, his foot slipping, he fell down, and was immediately despatched by Ajít Singh's followers. The Sindhianwálá troops, who were arrayed before the window, fired a volley, through the window, at the men,

Ajít Singh assassinates Maharájá Shér Singh, 15th September 1843.

---

* According to Smith, Shér Singh on this occasion went to live in Shah Biláwal, three miles east of the city. All accounts, however, agree that he left the city the very day of his assassination.

† Speaking of this occurrence, Doctor Honighberger thus writes, in his *Adventures in the East*: "I was by accident not further than ten steps from the place, where the horrid crime was committed; and five minutes before his atrocious murder, I had spoken to the Maharájá in the garden under a tree, where he ordered me to remain until his return. The subject of our interview was a gun powder mill with a machinery which Dhián Singh had ordered me to make. Shér Singh had inspected that establishment four days previously (on a Sunday), and was so satisfied, that with his own hands he put on my arms two pairs of gold bracelets, and ordered Rs. 500 to be given to me as an additional sum to the Rs. 900 which I already received as my monthly salary. This having been only an oral promise, I went daily to the darbár in order to receive an authority in writing, and was with him on the fatal Thursday on which he was assassinated." The learned Doctor was an eye-witness to the horrible scene, and his statements of facts coincide with ours in the main. The story given by McGregor of the mode of Shér Singh's death receives no corroboration from any known authority. He writes: "While thus employed, Ajít Singh produced a handsome case containing a new English rifle, which he shewed to Shér Singh. The Maharájá inspected the box and its contents, and, raising the barrel and stock, adjusted the one to the other, and then tried the sight. Ajít Singh remarked that it was loaded, on which Shér Singh gave the rifle to one of Ajít Singh's attendants, and desired him to take aim and fire it off. His master gave the signal, and the contents of the rifle were lodged in the Maharájá's chest." This account, very improbable in itself, makes one of Ajít Singh's servants the murderer of the Maharájá, while all accounts agree that Ajít Singh himself was the assassin.

who surrounded Shér Singh. Then, entering the room itself, they commenced their work of destruction, and such of the Maharájá's servants as made the faintest show of resistance were at once either shot or cut down remorselessly.

The assassins then repaired to the garden close by, in search of the heir-apparent, Partáb Singh, a lad twelve years of age. The prince was engaged in his prayers and in giving alms * to the Brahmins in the garden, when the ferocious Lahná Singh advanced towards him, with a drawn sword in his hand. The boy was terrified, and trembling threw himself at the ruffian's feet and implored forgiveness, saying: "Spare my life, for God's sake; oh! uncle, I will serve as a menial for removing the dung of your horses." "An uncle at such a time?" was the reply of the bloodthirsty Lahná Singh, who, as he uttered these words, severed the boy's head from his body. The villainous soldiers then cut the boy's body to pieces with their sabres.

Lahná Singh at the same time kills the heir-apparent.

Having imbrued their hands in the blood of their common master and his eldest son, the conspirators took steps to extend their scheme of aggrandizement and bloodshed. A body of about 300 cavalry and 250 infantry were waiting outside the garden where this bloody affair was transacted. At the head of these troops, Ajít Singh hurriedly repaired to the city, which was now in a state of commotion. The inhabitants, fearing the savage soldiery, had shut themselves up in their houses. The shops were closed and business was suspended. While Ajít Singh went off quickly towards the city, Lahná Singh slowly followed him with about 200 horsemen. About half way to Láhore, Ajít Singh was met by the minister, who was just coming out of the fort after his usual prayers, and was proceeding at his ease towards Shah Biláwal, with a few followers, not anticipating so speedy an execution of the plan laid down by him in conjunction with the Sindhianwálá sardars. Ajít Singh saluted the Rájá and informed him that the job was done. The Rájá expressed his surprise and showed a disposition to doubt the correctness of the intelligence, upon which the heads of the murdered father and son were exhibited. Dhián Singh blamed the Sindhianwálá kinsmen for taking the life of the young prince; but Ajít Singh observed that what was done could not be helped. Ajít Singh now desired the Rájá to return to the fort with him, to make final arrangements regarding the administration of the country. The Rájá was dismayed, when, glancing at his escort, he saw that they were greatly out-numbered by the Sindhianwálá soldiers, and he had no alternative but to make his way to the fort in the company of Ajít Singh. The minister and the sardar, with all their followers, entered the outer gate of the fort; but, as the party arrived at the second gate, admittance was refused to the minister's attendants by the gate-keepers, while those of Ajít Singh, 500 or 600 strong, entered. Dhián Singh's suspicions were now confirmed, and he again looked around to see how many men were coming with him. He was, however, quite helpless, and though he felt, from the tone of Ajít Singh's conversation and the surrounding circumstances, that there was something wrong, yet he maintained an apparently calm attitude and continued to converse with Ajít Singh in as frank a manner as he could assume, manifesting nothing like fear or apprehension, conscious, of course, that any show of suspicion on his part would be of no avail. Yet he could not help asking the Sindhianwálá sardar who the men were who stood on the battlements of the fort. The sardar replied that "they were all friends." Ajít Singh then, bringing his

Alarm caused in the city.

* It was an eclipse day, and the prince was being weighed against silver and gold, which were to be given to the Brahmins as alms.

horse close to that of the minister, took him by the hand, and, with seeming frankness, asked, "Who is now to be the king?" to which question the Rájá replied, "There is no one better entitled than Dulíp Singh."* Ajít Singh rejoined, "And so he is to be made king and you become his wazír. What are we to get for all this trouble?" The Rájá was annoyed at these bantering remarks, and was about to move off. The old Bhái Gúrmukh Singh, who was near, observed, "Deeds are better than words. Despatch the Rájá as you have done Shér Singh and his son, and then your path will be clear." Ajít Singh thereupon made a signal with his fingers, and instantly the minister was shot dead from behind, as he was scanning the men who had taken up their position on the ramparts of the fort. The first shot was immediately followed by another from a blunderbuss, though the first had closed his career. No sooner had he dropped dead from his horse, than the mercenary soldiery hacked his body to pieces with their swords. A Mahomedan orderly of the minister, one of the few of his immediate attendants who had obtained access to the interior of the fort, made a show of resistance, but he was immediately despatched, and his body, with that of his master, was thrown upon a heap of rubbish in a gun foundry pit in the fort.

Dhián Singh is shot dead.

Shortly after these occurrences, Lahná Singh arrived with his followers. On learning what had happened during the brief interval of his absence, he remonstrated with his brother for his hasty conduct, as the plan of the Sindhianwálá brothers was to collect Rájá Dhián Singh, his son Rájá Hírá Singh, and brother, Rájá Suchet Singh, at one place, on some pretence, and to destroy them all together. As matters stood, the son and the brother of the late Rájá were at large, and, as they exercised considerable influence over the *Khálsá* troops, the object of the Sindhianwálás would not be attained as easily as it would have been had the scheme originally laid down by them been strictly followed out. This, however, did not dishearten them, and they resolved to accomplish, at any cost, the task they had already begun. An express was sent through Misr Lál Sing (who afterward became so conspicuous in the war with the British), to Rájás Hírá Singh and Suchet Singh at *Budhu-ká-áwá*, where they were stationed with their troops, in the minister's name, requesting their attendance at the fort for consultation on affairs of State. The rájás and their counsellors, the principal of whom was Rai Kesri Singh (who subsequently distinguished himself by deeds of valour, fighting on the side of his master Suchet Singh), were too acute to be deceived by the Sindhianwálás. They, therefore, asked for an order in the handwriting of Dhián Singh, or signed by him, calling upon them to attend the fort. The Sindhianwálás now sent 500 horsemen to compel the rájás to comply with their mandate; but the latter, collecting all their troops, presented such a threatening front that the Sindhianwálá cavalry deemed it prudent to return as quietly as it had come, without venturing to attack them.

The proceedings of the Sindhianwálá sardars.

The young Rájá, Hírá Singh, had heard of the death of Shér Singh, but he never suspected that his own father had shared the same fate. When Misr Lál Singh waited on him, and asked his attendance at the fort, Hírá Singh was addressing his troops and exhorting them not to mind the death of the Maharájá. He and his uncle had purposely retired to Monsieur Avitabile's house to keep aloof from the bloody scenes which they expected

Misr Lál Singh brings the news of his father's death to Hírá Singh.

* McGregor assumes that both Ajít Singh and Lahná Singh had accompanied Dhián Singh to the fort on this occasion, and describes this dialogue as having taken place between Lahná Singh and Dhián Singh; but Lahná Singh did not come to the fort until after the minister had been despatched.

to follow the consultation between Dhián Singh and the Sindhianwálá clan. In an hour afterwards the death of the wazír was made public, and the news fell upon the young Rájá Hírá Singh like a thunderbolt. He wept bitterly, and, throwing himself upon the ground, rolled and tossed in a violent manner, but the prudent Bhái Kesri Singh upbraided him for his childish behaviour and admonished him to stand firm in the cause of his lamented father and avenge himself on the authors of the catastrophe. The soothing words of the Bhái had the desired effect, and Hírá Singh now resolved to exert his influence with the soldiery to effect the destruction of those who had polluted their hands with the blood of their king, his innocent minor son, and his prudent wazír. He ascended the terrace of Avitabile's house, and, having seated himself there, sent messages to the several sardars, requesting their immediate attendance. The call was promptly obeyed; and the sardars, with their troops, assembled at the foot of *Budhu-ká-áwá*. Placing himself in front, and unbuckling his sword and shield, the young Rájá said: "You know the traitors have killed our sovereign, his innocent son, and my dear and brave father, who loved you as much as he loved me. We are deprived of our sovereign, and I am now fatherless. I now trust to your courage, your patriotism, and your loyalty to our lamented king. Either uphold me firmly, or kill me with this sword, as it is better to die with honour than to live in disgrace in the midst of enemies." He reminded them how he had been loved by the great Maharájá Ranjít Singh, from his infancy, how fondly he had been brought up by him as his adopted son, and how the traitors were now ready to cut his throat. He assured them that the Sindhianwálá sardars had made a traitorous alliance with the British, and wanted to place the government of the country in their hands, and urged that, if the British power were established in the Panjáb, disgrace would be the lot of the whole Sikh nation, and their great and glorious name would sink into oblivion. The Sikhs, who now took a pride in the profession of arms, would be compelled to seek an ignoble living by following the plough. He solemnly promised to increase their pay by one half, each foot soldier to receive Rs. 12 a month, and every horseman Re. 1 a day. This was enough for the mercenary soldiery; they would listen no more. The death of either the king or the wazír, both of whom they loved and honoured, was not pleasant news to them. The presence of the youthful Rájá who had just been rendered fatherless by the treachery of the obnoxious Sindhianwálás; his innocent and mournful appearance, his eloquence, and above all his promises of handsome rewards and permanent increase of pay made a strong impression on the minds of the *Khálsá*, who responded unanimously to the young Rájá's call and received his proposition with loud acclamations. An attack on the citadel, under the leadership of Hírá Singh, was resolved upon, the brave soldiery determining to conquer or die. Hírá Singh told them to be ready for action at a moment's notice, but at the same time urged upon them the necessity of waiting until he had matured his plans. But the troops were impatient and inflamed with anger, and would listen to no one. Although, at the time this resolution was arrived at, about half the troops were engaged in cooking and preparing their evening meal, they even left their cooking utensils and half prepared food on the plains where they were encamped, and responded to the call to arms made by the trumpeters and drummers. Those who proved dilatory were stimulated by the butt-ends of muskets, and forced to leave their cooking things and prepare for action. Thus, in an incredibly short time, about 40,000 troops were assembled, impatiently awaiting the orders of Rájá Hírá Singh to march against the enemy.

The grief of the latter.

He summons the sardars and their armies.

Hírá Singh's address to the soldiers.

They respond to his appeal, and promise him their support.

Their thirst for revenge.

While these arrangements were being made at *Budhu-ká-áwá* by Rájá Hírá Singh to avenge his father's death, the Sindhianwálá sardars shut themselves up in the fortress, and by beat of drum proclaimed Dulíp Singh, the youngest son of Ranjít Singh, as Maharájá, and Ajít Singh as his wazír. They made every effort to bribe the troops stationed in the city and around it, and to win them over to their side. They sent for the chiefs and commandants of the troops and artillery, and even obtained from them promises of support. But this was an unwise step. Had they personally appeared before the troops and exerted their influence on them, they, as true Sikhs, and as the Maharájá's own kinsmen, had a far better chance of winning the good will of the soldiery, than the foreigners, the Dográs. As it was, they failed.

Dulíp Singh proclaimed Maharájá and Ajít Singh his wazír, September, 1843.

Rájá Hírá Singh, with the *Khálsá* troops, foremost among whom were those of Generals Ventura and Avitabile, and about a hundred pieces of horse artillery, approached Láhore about an hour after sunset. He reached the Delhi Gate, followed by all the sardars and grandees, and made his entry into the city under the fierce war-cry, "*Wáh, Guru ji ki Fateh,*" which resounded through the city. In addition to this, the noisy sounds of their wild music and drums, and the tumult of the mob at midnight, dismayed and terrified the citizens, whose patience had already been exhausted, and their spirits damped by the recent atrocities and civil commotions. The fort was once more surrounded and blockaded. Its feeble and tottering walls were again subjected to the same fierce bombardment as on the former occasions. The besieged consisted of about a thousand or twelve hundred armed men; but they were not as well led as the Dográs in the siege of three years previously, and were themselves very inferior, as soldiers and marksmen, to the hill soldiers. The thundering of cannon lasted the whole night on both sides, but the besieged were greatly outnumbered by their assailants and could but ineffectually return their fire. By dawn of the following morning several breaches had been made in the walls of the fortress, but none were large enough to permit the entrance of troops. At this time Rájá Hírá Singh sent for all the officers of the artillery and promised them handsome rewards if they succeeded in effecting a practicable breach. He inflamed their passions still more by taking an oath that he would neither eat nor drink until he had seen at his feet the heads of those who had assassinated his father severed from their bodies. The widow of the murdered wazír was, in the meanwhile, preparing to mount the funeral pile of her late husband with her slave girls. Rájá Hírá Singh craftily induced her stepmother to delay the performance of this shocking ceremony until she had seen the murderers of her late husband duly punished, and their heads severed from their bodies. The widow and the slaves, the intending *sattis*, were kept waiting before the troops to inspire them with revenge, and the spectacle of their melancholy and dismal figures increased their fury a hundredfold. The soldiers had already been enriched by the presents lavished on them by Hírá Singh, and the plunder of the city. In addition to this they were now promised the plunder of the fort as soon as they should bring the corpses of the Sindhianwálá sardars to Hírá Singh. The result was that the gunners exerted themselves indefatigably to effect the desired breach in the wall of the fort, which they succeeded in accomplishing at about nine o'clock the following morning, through the south-west angle near the tower. The first soldier who mounted the battlements of the dismantled walls was a Spanish Colonel, in the service of the Sikhs, named M. Hurban. Immediately a body of forty or forty-five thousand infantry and dismounted cavalry clamour-

Hírá Singh enters the city,

And lays siege to the fort.

ously rushed forward and effected an entrance through the breach and swept everything before them. Bhái Kesri Singh, the principal adviser of Rájá Suchet Singh, mounted the tottering walls by means of scaling ladders, and thus effected the entrance of the detachment under him. The little garrison made a desperate resistance, but were borne down and almost annihilated by the superior number of the besiegers, and in about an hour all resistance was at an end. Ajít Singh, Sindhianwálá, with Mahar Ghasitá, his confidential agent, escaped over the wall by means of a rope, but they were observed by a Mussalmán soldier, who pursued them. Ajít Singh, being hard pressed, took the gold bracelets off his hands and threw them to the man, and made him lavish promises, hoping thereby to induce him to spare his life; but he and his comrade were immediately slain, and the Mussalmán soldier cut off Ajít Singh's head and hurried to Hírá Singh, to whom he delivered it as a trophy. The soldier was munificently rewarded. Valuable presents, money and *jágírs* were bestowed on all who had made themselves conspicuous in the siege and assault, while even common soldiers filled their pockets with silver and gold obtained as presents or spoil. The fort was now indiscriminately plundered by the soldiery. The house of Rání Chand Kour was pillaged, and vast quantities of clothes, shawls and jewels were carried away. The royal Toshakháná was also plundered, and everything that could be found taken away. Great depredations were committed on the citizens of Láhore. The merchants left their shops to save their lives. The inhabitants buried their valuables underground, and whatever was left unprotected was pillaged by the infuriated Sikhs. The noses of the common women in the streets were cut off, and whoever made the slightest show of resistance was forthwith despatched.

Capture of the citadel.

Ajít Singh, Sindhianwálá, is slain.

Plunder of the fort.

Commotions in the city.

The immolation of Dhián Singh's widow on the pyre.

The plundering, which continued for some time, was at length stopped by the orders of Rájá Hírá Singh, who brought Ajít Singh's head to his step-mother and laid it at her feet. On beholding it, the Rání exclaimed: "My mind is now at perfect ease, let the pyre be now prepared, and I will follow my lord in his journey to the next world." Addressing the youthful Hírá Singh, she said: "When I see your father I will tell him that you acted as a brave and dutiful son." The pile was in readiness; she talked with patience and perfect composure, distributing her valuables and jewels among the bystanders as alms, and giving orders regarding her affairs. Her last act was the placing of her late husband's *kalgi*, or the warrior's aigrette, in the turban of Hírá Singh. She then quietly and cheerfully ascended the fatal ladder which led to the pile, followed by her slaves. The women, thirteen in number, took their seats around their mistress. The lady then took her final leave of all with smiling and cheerful countenance, and, in a loud and dignified voice, ordered the torch to be applied. Her orders were immediately obeyed. In the twinkling of an eye the whole pile was in flames, and in a short time nothing remained but heaps of indistinguishable ashes.

A touching incident.

An interesting and touching instance of fidelity occurred on this occasion. A female child, ten years of age, a slave-girl of the Rání, and a native of the hills, was declared by all, including the Rání, to be too young to be sacrificed, and her mistress entrusted her to the charge of her step-son, Hírá Singh, strictly enjoining him to look well after her. But the child insisted upon perishing in the flames with her mistress. Three times did she throw herself on the pile, and was as many times forcibly taken away. At last, with a courage and zeal as surprising as they were extraordinary in one of her age and sex, she loudly protested by the murdered corpse of the Rájá that lay on the pile, that if the opportunity were now refused to her of destroying her life with that of her mistress, she would immediately after end her life by some other means. Seeing that the little girl was resolutely bent on sacrificing herself, the Ráni allowed her to share her own and her companions' fate, on which the girl joyfully mounted the funeral pile, occupying the place at the feet of her mistress, who now closed her eyes, with the head of her husband in her lap.

After the fight was over and the pillage had ceased, under the orders of Hírá Singh, a search was made for Lahná Singh, Sindhianwálá, whose body was not found among the slain, and who had disappeared.

Every nook and corner in the fort and around it was examined, but in vain. At length a sepoy, peeping through a subterranean drain, with the aid of a torch, discovered the sardar hidden in a dark cell, attended by a faithful follower, named Ráh Singh, a strong and muscular man, about fifty years of age. The sardar was found with a broken thigh, and was guarded by his gallant attendant, who stood at the entrance of the cell with a drawn sword. The infuriated soldiers rushed on this man; but he cut down thirteen with his own sword before he fell, covered with wounds, and shortly after expired. His dying request was that his master might not be molested, and the Sikhs, honouring his bravery, were inclined to take Lahná Singh alive; but one of their own number shot the sardar dead on the spot, observing: "Are we going to lose 10,000 rupees?" The sardar's head was immediately severed from his body and taken to Rájá Hírá Singh, who gave the soldiers the promised reward. The murder of Lahná Singh was the last event of the day, at the close of which the victorious soldiery returned to their quarters.* When the fort was completely in the possession of Rájá Hírá Singh, he first went to the young Maharájá Dulíp Singh, and kissed his feet in token of submission. He next went to the Hazúri Bágh, and, having seated himself in the marble *barádari*, ordered all the friends and relations of the Sindhianwálás then present at the capital, and who had taken part against him in the fight which had just closed, to be brought into his presence. The youthful avenger had them all murdered in cold blood, or shot in his presence, one by one. Among them were Bhái Gúrmukh Singh, the Granthi of the great Maharájá, and Miser Beli Ram, the treasurer, the latter of whom had instigated the late minister's assassination, and was believed to have connived at the death of his royal master, whilst the former had always been conspicuous in his opposition to the Dográ family, though he stood high in the favour of Maharájá Ranjít Singh.† One of the Sindhianwálás, who had concealed himself in a ditch or drain, was dragged out and his belly ripped up. The bodies of Ajít Singh and Lahná Singh were dragged through the city, and then mutilated and exhibited to the public gaze on the gates. The possessions and jágírs of the Sindhianwálás in Rájá Sansi and elsewhere were confiscated, and their houses razed to the ground. Attar Singh, who was coming to the aid of his brother and nephew, having heard of their defeat and death, retreated precipitately and sought the protection of Bábá Bír Singh, a celebrated Sikh priest. Hírá Singh's men pursued him, but Attar Singh, being apprised of

The murder of Lahná Singh.

Punishment of the rebels.

* McGregor makes Lahná Singh's death to have taken place prior to that of Ajít Singh. He mentions that "Lahná Singh was observed coming from the Hazúrí Bágh and going towards the Bádshâhi Masjid for ammunition. Kesri Singh took aim and the sardar fell mortally wounded, but was dragged through the gate into the sleeping apartments, where he died two days after." This account is wholly unconfirmed. Compare Smyth's *History of the Reigning Family of Láhore* with Rai Kanhia Lal's *History of the Panjáb.*

† Both, being religious men (one a Granthi or a reader of the holy *Granth*, and the other a Brahmin), were murdered concealed from the public view to avoid the excitement of the Sikh public. Miser Beli Ram was made over to Sheikh Imam-ud-dín, who despatched him privately.

this, crossed the Sutlej with all his retainers. All the Sindhianwálás were now punished with either death, confiscation of property, or banishment. The only Sindhianwálá sardar whose life was spared by Hírá Singh was Shamshér Singh, he being the known adversary of Ajít Singh and Lahná Singh.

Rewards to soldiers.

This done, all the troops were assembled in the fort, when Hírá Singh gave them a written agreement for one month's pay as gratuity, and renewed assurances of permanent increase of salary.

On the fourth day, a council of all the military officers was called, at which the *panches* or deputies from each company were present. The meeting was convened at Hazúrí Bágh, and was attended by all the sardars of the State. At this meeting of the civil and military officers, the public acclamations declared Dulíp Singh Maharájá of the Panjáb, and Hírá Singh his wazír. Hírá Singh hypocritically declined to accept the office of wazír, assigning, as his reason, that he had too many enemies in the State who hated him and his family, and might frustrate his designs, but he was assured by the soldiery that any person not well disposed towards him would be looked upon as the direct enemy of the State and summarily punished. As a proof of their sincerity, the sardars and *panches* then and there proposed the murder or imprisonment of certain officers and men who were suspected of being in league with the Sindhianwálás. Appearing to be satisfied with their honesty of intention, Hírá Singh, with seeming reluctance, accepted the office of wazír.

Dulíp Singh declared Maharájá and Hírá Singh his wazír, September 1843.

The soldiery all-powerful.

The soldiery were all-powerful at this time. They could make or unmake a king. The most extravagant desires of the military were acceded to; nothing which they coveted was withheld from them. They took away the best of Ranjít Singh's horses from the royal stable, without anybody daring to utter a word against their acts of spoliation. The whole of the old king's carriages, elephants and costly furniture, were scattered about in all directions, and what had cost the great Maharájá years of trouble and toil to collect was now at the mercy of the *Khálsá* troops. A sum of between 35 and 40 lakhs of rupees was surreptitiously abstracted from the treasury alone within a few weeks after Sher Singh's death; and yet it is positively affirmed that this, combined with other valuables lavished on the soldiery, was not equal to even one-eighth part of what Hírá Singh had appropriated to himself; not to mention the immense riches carried away by Guláb Singh to his mountain recesses before the accession of Shér Singh to the throne.

DULÍP SINGH.

The character of Hírá Singh.

Dulíp Singh was proclaimed Maharájá of the Panjáb in September 1843, and Hírá Singh installed in the high, but fatal, office of wazír. Hírá Singh was brought up under the care of the great Maharájá, and possessed talents and energies suited to the times in which he lived. He had received a good education and was able to read and write well. Having received his training in the school of the one-eyed monarch, and being in constant attendance on him, he had acquired the old king's habits of reflection and thoughtfulness, while in hypocrisy and shrewdness he resembled his father Dhián Singh. He knew well how to treat the sardars and behave to the troops, with whom he was very popular. He was excessively fond of wearing jewellery, and was rather effeminate in appearance, unlike his father, who was a tall, well-built and powerful man. But he was endowed with wit and genius, and his measures were prudent, and suited to the requirements of the occasion. He was in the prime of youth (being 25 years of age) when exalted to the rank of wazír. The young king, eight years old, had, therefore, a young minister who might have had a long political career before him had he not allowed himself to be influenced in State affairs by a crafty and fanatic Brahmin from the mountains, named Jállá *Missar*. This man exercised great control over the young wazír, who regarded him as a deity. He amused him with recitals of astrological dreams and false prophecies. A rancorous enmity existed between him and Rájá Suchet Singh, younger brother of Rájá Guláb Singh, having its origin in the rivalry that existed in the zenáná of the late Maharájá Ranjít Singh, to which both of them had free access. Rání Jindán, the mother of the infant Maharájá, wished to favour Rájá Suchet Singh, and induced him to aspire to the wazírát, to the exclusion of his nephew, Hírá Singh, who was regarded as a stripling, inexperienced in business and incapable of discharging the duties of the office entrusted to him. This brought the Rájá into collision with Jállá Pandit, who clearly foresaw his own ruin if his patron Hírá Singh were supplanted in power by his uncle. The ambitious views of Suchet Singh created a bitter jealousy between him and Hírá Singh, who saw his own position endangered, and on this account fully shared the feelings of Jállá Pandit. Suchet Singh had the full support of the Rání and was also countenanced by her eldest brother, Jawáhir Singh, and some of the sardars. Hírá Singh increased his popularity with the soldiery by adding 2½ rupees to the pay of the common soldiers, and discharging the arrears of pay due to them. He made them other lavish promises and rewarded them with a liberal hand. At this juncture he sent a message to his uncle, Rájá Guláb Singh, requesting his presence at the capital.

He falls entirely under the influence of a Brahmin, Jállá *Missar*.

Jealousy between the new minister and his uncle Suchet Singh.

Rání Jindán supports Suchet Singh.

Guláb Singh reached Láhore on 10th November and was honourably received. Through his influence, Lahná Singh, Majithia, who had been previously suspected by Hírá Singh of intrigue against him, was reconciled with the latter. The wily old chief was, however, cautious in his proceedings, and cared little whether his brother or his nephew held the title of wazír, as long as his own independence was recognised. In the meantime, Suchet Singh became impatient for the honours promised him by the Queen Jindán, and intrigued with Jawáhir Singh, the maternal uncle of Dulíp Singh, to inflict a sudden blow on the power of his nephew. At a review of the *Khálsá* troops, Jawáhir Singh was induced to mount an elephant, with the young Maharájá in his arms, and to complain to the troops of the harsh treatment to which the royal boy and his mother had been subjected at the hands of the minister and his party. He threatened the troops that, if prompt redress were not afforded him, he would, with his nephew, be compelled to seek protection with the British across the Sutlej. This course was adopted in the expectation that the *Khálsá* would pity the royal child thus exhibited to their view and by a unanimous voice elect Suchet Singh, or Jawáhir Singh, as the future wazír. It being late in the evening, and an unusual hour for a review, the troops suspected something wrong. The very idea of British protection was repugnant to them. They wanted time for deliberation, and for the night kept Jawáhir Singh and his young charge under a strong guard. The *Khálsá* troops were at this time under the command of Missar Jodha Ram, a Brahmin, father-in-law to Jállá, and he inflicted on Jawáhir Singh the utmost disgrace, giving him a blow in the face, for which he lost his nose when Jawáhir Singh was installed as wazír. During the night a council of *panches* was convened, and the result of their discussions was that Jawáhir Singh and Suchet

Guláb Singh's arrival at Lahore.

Jawáhir Singh the Rání's brother.

His unsuccessful appeal to the soldiery.

Missar Jodha Ram.

Singh were declared traitors to the State, as it was thought their real object was to place the young Maharájá under the protection of the British and to invite that Government to occupy the country. The prime minister, Hírá Singh, whose emissaries were busy at work the whole night, was informed of the line of action which the *Khálsá* had adopted, and this met his full approval. A rumour was afloat in the city that Jawáhir Singh intended to take the young Maharájá to Ferozpur and deliver him over to the British Government. Early the next morning the wazír rode out on horseback and brought both the fugitives back to the city. A salute of 101 guns was fired on this occasion from the fortress, as the young Maharájá made his entry into the city; and he was again delivered to his mother, to her profound joy and satisfaction. Jawáhir Singh was placed in close confinement and put in irons in the *haveli* of Maharájá Kharak Singh, in the town. His life was spared, at the request of the soldiery, as the maternal uncle of the young Maharájá. From this time Suchet Singh was looked upon as the enemy of the State, and strongly suspected of favouring the English. The dread of his power and influence and the presence of his elder brother, Guláb Singh at the capital, were, however, sufficient to protect him from personal injury. At any rate, under the orders of the wazír, the two battalions of infantry in the employ of Rájá Suchet Singh, which were quartered in the fort, and all the Rájá's men and dependants stationed there, were at once expelled, disarmed and otherwise disgraced. Orders were also issued prohibiting the entrance of Rájá Suchet Singh and his men into the fort without the wazír's special permission. The wrath of the Rájá at the ignominy thus inflicted on him at the hands of his nephew knew no bounds, but, being fully conscious of the wazír's power and influence over the soldiery, he feigned acquiescence. Guláb Singh, in the meanwhile, seeing an amicable settlement between the hostile uncle and nephew to be impossible, deemed it prudent to withdraw from the scene, taking with him his brother, Suchet Singh. Before going, he contrived to secure most of the valuables which Hírá Singh had hoarded up for himself, as well as all the property that belonged to his late brother, Dhián Singh. Thus loaded with abundant riches, he left for Jammú with Rájá Suchet Singh, accompanied by 2,000 of his troops. His first act, on reaching his territory, was to induce Suchet Singh, who was childless, to adopt one of his four sons as his legal heir and representative, and Suchet Singh, having gladly agreed to this proposal, Ram Bhir Singh, commonly called Mián Pino, the youngest son of Rájá Guláb Singh, was publicly declared the adopted son and heir of Rájá Suchet Singh. Thus did the crafty old Guláb Singh secure to himself the immense fortune of his childless brother, Suchet Singh.

He is put in confinement.

Suchet Singh suspected of intrigue with the British.

Guláb Singh and Suchet Singh retire to the Jammú hills.

About this time Jállá Pandit entered into a *liaison*, with a widow of the late Maharájá Sher Singh, and a conspiracy was set on foot to poison the young Maharájá and place the widow's son on the throne. Rání Jindán, however, being informed of this in time, the impending disaster was nipped in the bud.

It has already been noted that the late Maharájá Ranjít Singh had two reputed sons, Káshmíra Singh and Peshora Singh. The former held Siálkot as his patrimony from the Maharájá and the latter, Gujránwálá. There were certain individuals in the Panjáb who considered the claims of the boy Dulíp Singh to succeed to the throne of Láhore superior to those of Ranjít Singh's two adopted sons, Káshmíra Singh and Peshora Singh, and the minister, Hírá Singh, thought his position insecure as long as the brothers held aloof and were in power. Pretexts were therefore devised to entangle them in

The wazír's plot against the Princes Káshmíra Singh and Peshora Singh.

difficulties, and they were charged with complicity in the late plots of the Sindhianwálá brothers, which terminated in the assassination of the late king and his minister. Forged letters were produced, purporting to have been written by Káshmíra Singh and Peshora Singh, implicating them in the late bloodshed. Several disclosures were made by an old servant of Káshmíra Singh, named Kapur Singh, who held the office of kárdár at Siálkot. The villainous conduct of this man towards his master contributed much to aggravate the minister; but the *Khálsá* troops were averse to the reputed sons of the old Maharájá being subjected to ignominy. Rájá Guláb Singh, who, in compliance with orders received from the darbár, had put them in confinement and seized all their valuables, was, therefore, ordered to seize their persons and property. A fine of 50 lakhs of rupees was imposed upon them and their jágírs were confiscated. Only 20,000 rupees could be realized, and this was, under the circumstances, thought sufficient and the brothers were reinstated in their jágírs. A pardon was conferred upon them on the express condition that they would not molest the Kárdár Kápúr Singh, who had been the chief cause of their misfortune. Soon after their release, however, the princes had good reason to find fault with the conduct of their faithless servant, and had him beaten to death. This gave a fresh excuse to the Láhore Darbár for carrying out the diabolical designs of the minister against Káshmíra Singh and Peshora Singh, and as, by this time, the brothers had greatly strengthened their position at Siálkot and had, moreover, been joined by some mutinous troops from Pesháwar, it was considered necessary to reduce them by force of arms.

Rájá Guláb Singh marches against them to Siálkot.

Rájá Guláb Singh was ordered by the darbár to invade their territory and to bring them as prisoners of State to Láhore. The brothers made a desperate resistance, and, with the small number of troops at their disposal, inflicted a signal defeat on the contingent of the Jammú Rájá, who conducted the operations in person. Guláb Singh asked for reinforcements from Láhore, but the *Khálsá* troops, as usual, refused to operate against the reputed sons of the great Maharájá, or to become the instruments of their destruction. Only two Mahomedan battalions and some Dográ troops were sent to Siálkot, on the express condition that no personal injury should be inflicted on the persons of the brothers, but this contingent, dreading an engagement with the *Khálsá* troops, remained inactive on their arrival at Siálkot, and again fresh succour was demanded. This time the old battalions belonging to Dhián Singh, with 500 cavalry and six horse artillery guns, were despatched from Láhore as a reinforcement. Operations were commenced in the midst of heavy rains, and both the town and the fort of Siálkot were closely invested. The brothers made a vigorous resistance, but, before sunset, the town was in possession of Rájá Guláb Singh. The fort had, however, yet to be taken, and a heavy cannonade was kept up the whole night and until noon of the following day, when the besieged brothers yielded to superior numbers, and gave themselves up to the besiegers on condition of being allowed to go away unmolested with their family and property. This was agreed to, and after dark the brothers vacated the fort and left for the Mánjhá country, between the Rávi and the Sutlej, where they wandered about in reduced circumstances.

The Princes are defeated and escape to the Mánjhá country.

While the plans of Hírá Singh as regards the two reputed sons of Mahárájá Ranjít Singh were completely successful at Siálkot, the minister was himself undergoing all sorts of disgrace and ignominy in the capital, at the hands of the furious *Khálsá* soldiery. It has been already mentioned that the Sikh nation had the profoundest esteem for even the adopted sons of a man whom they universally revered, and that the great *Khálsá* were from the first averse to waging war with the reputed sons of the late Maharájá. The march of a contingent of troops to Siálkot against Káshmíra Singh and Peshora Singh on two different occasions was quite opposed to the wish of the *Khálsá*, who, from the moment that the second contingent left Láhore, began to annoy the minister in every conceivable way. They feared that the contingent from Láhore would not only reduce the fort and the city of Siálkot, but probably put the reputed sons of the old Maharájá to death. This caused a great commotion at Láhore, and the troops watched the movements of Hírá Singh with such vigilance that, for three or four days, he was not allowed to come out of his father's private residence in the city, and was, in fact, kept a prisoner there. The minister was not released until such time as the *Khálsá* troops were assured that the lives and property of the two princes were safe, and that the obnoxious Jállá Pandit would in future be prevented from taking any part in affairs of the State. A further condition was made by the wazír as the price of his ransom, *viz.*, that Jawáhir Singh, the brother of Rání Jindán, should be released from confinement. This was immediately acceded to. Rájá Suchet Singh who was checkmated by his nephew, Hírá Singh, in the affair of Jawáhir Singh and the *Khálsá* troops, which led to the withdrawal of the Rájá to the Jammú hills, still aspired to the office of wazír. He placed great confidence in the support of the young queen, Jindán, with whom he was a favourite. He watched with keen interest the affairs of the darbár and Panjáb politics generally, and his emissaries were constantly at work at Láhore. The difficulties of Hírá Singh were in the meanwhile increasing. The protracted civil wars carried on in the heart of the capital, the unusual expenditure incurred in maintaining the troops in order, and other heavy miscellaneous charges, had the effect of not only emptying the public treasury, but exhausting the resources of the kingdom. During the prolonged anarchy and confusion which spread through the country, no revenue could be realized, and the whole country was devastated.

(The sympathy of the *Khálsá* troops for the reputed sons of the great Maharájá. — They subject the minister to disgrace. — Release of Jawáhir Singh. — The minister's difficulties. — Condition of the Panjáb at this time.)

In the meantime, Fatteh Khan, a Tiwáná chief, the trusted and personal follower of Rájá Dhián Singh, who was suspected of being privy to the assassination of his master, and who designedly withdrew while Ajit Singh took the Rájá on one side, fled to Dera Ismail Khan, his native province, and there raised an insurrection. The son of Dewán Sanwan Mal, the Nazim of Multán, who owed large arrears of revenue to the darbár, became hostile and countenanced the Tiwáná chief, which caused great anxiety in the darbár. The affairs of Pesháwar were in an equally unsatisfactory state. Some of the troops there wanted an increase of pay, and, as there was no one to give it, rebelled and joined the rebel princes at Siálkot. Want of money was much felt in the darbár. The minister set Pandit Jállá, his right-hand man, to examine the financial accounts and to ascertain what money was due to the State by the Nazims, Kárdárs, Jágírdárs, lessees, &c. The accounts having been examined, large sums were found due by the grandees and others, among them being Rájás Guláb Singh and Suchet Singh. Those at or near Láhore were pressed for the money, and this added considerably to the unpopularity of the minister and his favourite Jállá. All the Europeans in the service of the State were dismissed, under the orders of Jállá Pandit, from economical motives. In the meanwhile, the *Khálsá* lost all patience with Hírá Singh in connection with the rebellion of Káshmíra Singh and Peshora Singh, and before his final release some of the battalions, with whom Rájá Suchet Singh's emissaries were at work, sent messages to the Rájá, inviting him

(Disaffection of certain chiefs. — The state of Pesháwar. — The unpopularity of Pandit Jállá. — The *Khálsá* troops invite Rájá Suchet Singh to Láhore.)

to come to Láhore, and promising him assistance against his nephew. He also received assurances of help from some of the members of the Láhore Darbár. The Rájá, accordingly, put in a sudden appearance at Shahdera on the Rávi on 26th March 1843, and sent a message to the troops and the sardars who had invited him, announcing his arrival. But nothing on earth was in those days susceptible of more constant change than the temper and disposition of the *Khálsá*. The tempest which threatened the destruction of the vast fabric constructed by Hírá Singh had now passed away, and the wazír was again looked upon by the whole *Khálsá* as their common leader. The reply sent to Suchet Singh was evasive; but, not discouraged by this, the sanguine and impatient chief crossed the river, leaving the main body of his troops at Shahdera, and accompanied by about 400 horse and foot and his principal adviser, Rai Kesri Singh, thinking that his presence before the troops would have the effect of enlisting their sympathies in his favour. A sort of jealousy existed between the cavalry portion of the army and the regular infantry and artillery, and the Rájá believed himself to be popular with the former. His expectations were, however, never realized. The very battalions which had invited him, advised him to withdraw, as they said they could do nothing contrary to the general wish of the *Khálsá*. Suchet Singh, who was a brave and determined soldier, resolved not to withdraw, but to hold his ground to the last. He accordingly set out at midnight for the mausoleum of Mián Waddá, in the neighbourhood of Láhore, and took up his quarters there, in an old mosque attached to the tomb, placing the small number of troops which he had brought with him, around the mosque. The rest of the night was devoted to the reading of long passages from the *Granth*, or the sacred book of the Sikhs, to Rájá Suchet Singh. It may now be interesting to narrate briefly what happened at Láhore after Suchet Singh reached Shahdera. Hírá Singh, on receiving intelligence of the arrival of his uncle on the banks of the Rávi, collected the *panches* of the army, and, standing before them, with folded arms and every sign of humility and submissiveness, addressed them in the following terms:—

They eventually give up his cause.

Suchet Singh takes up his position in the mausoleum of Mián Waddá.

> *Khálsá ji!*—The son of your old minister and the adopted son of your old Maharájá now stands in your presence as a suppliant. Tell him, I beg you, what fault he has committed, to punish which, you have invited his uncle, his greatest enemy and your own inveterate foe, being, as you are aware, a staunch ally of the *Feringi*. If you want to kill me, here is the sword, and I give you full liberty at once to sever my head from my body. It would be an honour to me to die at the hands of the brave *Khálsá*. But, for the Guru's sake, do not allow me to suffer a death of shame. If you have not called my uncle from the hills, and are not disposed to help him, support me and fight for my cause as good and brave soldiers, and you will receive the blessings of the Guru.

Hírá Singh's speech to the *Khálsá* soldiery.

This, coupled with the promise of a reward of one gold *butki* to each soldier, infantry and cavalry, and one gold *kantha* (necklace) to each officer, was enough to rouse the spirit of the *Khálsá*, who swore a fresh allegiance to the wazír and the extirpation of his uncle. The next morning witnessed the *Khanquah* of Mián Waddá besieged by the troops, 14 or 15,000 infantry, 3 or 4,000 horse and 56 pieces of artillery. This vast army was opposed to about 45 men, the chosen followers of Suchet Singh, the remainder of his troops having faithlessly deserted him over night. Before the *Khálsá* troops had assembled on the plains of Mián Waddá, the friends of Rájá Suchet Singh at Láhore sent him word advising him to make his escape to the neighbouring hills while there was yet time, but the brave Rájá could not for a moment harbour the idea of flight, for he considered such a course

Advance of the Láhore army against the Rájá's camp.

cowardice. He resolved to fight, happen what might. The passage from the Rávi was cut off, to prevent Suchet Singh's levies from the adjacent hills from joining him. At daylight a general assault was made on the devoted little band within the mosque, and a tremendous cannonade was opened on its walls. Amidst the continuous roar of artillery the brave Suchet Singh and his devoted adherents, with complete composure of mind, continued to hear the holy *Granth*. A school for the secular instruction of *darveshes* existed at the *Khanquah*, where also used to be fed, as now, a large number of destitute blind persons. When this fire was opened, about a hundred of these helpless *darveshes* and blind men were present at the *Khanquah*. Mián Sharaf Dín the *Sajjada-Nashin*, entreated Rájá Suchet Singh to leave the mosque, in order to prevent its destruction, promising to conduct him outside in safety, even at this, the eleventh hour; but the Rájá turned a deaf ear to the Mián's admonitions.

In a short time the old walls of the mosque were levelled to the ground. All the blind *darveshes* were killed, but the others effected their escape. The reader of the *Granth* now closed his book, and Suchet Singh and his followers rose, sword in hand, to meet their adversaries. Rájá Suchet Singh, with a dauntless courage, to which history knows few, if any, parallels, placed himself in front of the advancing column and addressed them in a stentorian voice as follows: "Relying on your good faith, I came to Láhore at your special invitation. You have forsaken me and have now come to kill me in such numbers. I beseech you at this moment to behave with me like true soldiers. Come on, my friends, come on, one by one, and let the world see the worth of a Rájput soldier," and, as the gallant soldier uttered these words, he advanced impetuously closer to the ranks of the enemy. This challenge, made by a person of Suchet Singh's ferocity and bravery, struck the front columns with such awe that, for a time, the soldiers remained as motionless as statues.

Suchet Singh's address to the soldiers.

His gallant behaviour.

In the meantime, Rai Kesri Singh, the Rájá's wazír, a brave and powerful man, pulled him back, and the devoted band placed their master in the midst of their small number, thus affording him momentary shelter and showing their fidelity to the last. The handful of brave soldiers then rushed sword in hand upon the foremost rank of their assailants, and so desperate was their assault that they actually drove back four battalions. More than thirty of the assailants in the front columns lay dead on the field, and the heroes continued to cut down those who approached them. The desperate valour displayed by the Rájá and his companions struck a panic through the *Khálsá* army, and the gunners fled in consternation; not a shot was fired, though Hírá Singh was close upon their heels, with a lighted torch in his hand, urging upon them to push on and fire. Rai Kesri Singh, with his own hand, cut down nine of the assailants in the foremost rank. Several who attempted to flee were killed by the bayonets of their own comrades. Bassant Singh, one of the Rájá's adherents, was another who stood conspicuous for his bravery. He slew no fewer than 17 Sikhs before he fell. But how long could a handful of heroes stand their ground when their destroyers numbered thousands! After a few minutes more had elapsed, the whole body of the besieged (excepting one, who survived badly wounded) lay dead on the field. The gallant Rájá Suchet Singh, it need hardly be said, was among the slain. He slew three men with his own hand before dying from the effect of two bullet wounds. Thus perished this brave Rájput soldier with 43 of his faithful adherents. The total loss of the *Khálsá* army in this memorable and deplorably unequal combat was about 160 men in killed and wounded.

The bravery of his comrades.

The Rájá is slain.

The troops were ordered back to their quarters, and Hírá Singh now visited the field of action, to behold with his own eyes the bodies of the fallen band. The first body which met his gaze was that of Rai Kesri Singh, whom few in the country equalled in gallantry and skill as a soldier. This brave man, before he fell, cut down some twenty of his adversaries. Several times did he fall down, but as often did he rise again and renew the bloody combat. Covered with wounds he fell at last, like a lion, but not before he had killed with his own hands the authors of his death-wounds. The Rai was in the agonies of death, when Hírá Singh stood at his head. The dying hero saluted the wazír by saying "*Jey deb*," and made signs for water, but received the brutal reply, that the best place for quenching his thirst was the hills, where there was plenty of clear cold water. He then looked disconsolately around him and expired. Hírá Singh was very much affected when he discovered the corpse of his uncle lying on the ground, mingled with dust and blood, among the heaps of slain. He could not help shedding tears on witnessing the melancholy and gloomy scene. He had the corpse removed in his own palanquin to the fort. The bodies of Rai Kesri Singh and Bhím Sen, the principal mukhtiar of Rájá Suchet Singh, were also honourably treated. The other bodies were disposed of according to rank and circumstances. Rájá Hírá Singh returned to the city in pomp, with drums beating and guns firing at intervals, as the procession advanced in celebration of the victory. The same day the body of Suchet Singh was burnt close to the mausoleum of Mián Udham Singh, son of Rájá Guláb Singh, the Rájá Hírá Singh and the Court being present at the funeral obsequies. The deceased Rájá's Ránís, five in number, ended their lives according to the rite of *satti*, having placed their deceased husband and lord's turban before them as a substitute for the body.*

Rai Kesri Singh.

Rájá Hírá Singh distributed the gold *butkis* and *kanthas* as rewards to the troops according to his promise.

The hostile proceedings of Sardar Attar Singh, Sindhianwálá.

He joins Báwá Bír Singh.

It will be remembered that Sardar Attar Singh, Sindhianwálá, the brother and nephew of the murderers of Maharájá Shér Singh, was still at large. He now aspired to the wazírát, and, having recrossed the Sutlej on 2nd May, 1844, joined Báwá Bír Singh, a holy man who had become famous in those days in the Mánjhá country, and maintained a force of 1,500 infantry and cavalry and two guns as a body-guard. He also afforded protection to such of the sardars and chiefs as had been disgraced at the darbár, and the combined forces of all these amounted to about 3,000 men and three guns. The holy Báwá declared that the kingdom of Láhore was virtually the kingdom of Gurú Gobind Singh, that the Máhárájá Dulíp Singh was yet a child, incapable of managing his own affairs, that therefore it behoved the *Khálsá* to have one of their own number at the head of the administration; that Hírá Singh had proved himself quite unworthy of his position, and that, for the sake of their own personal aggrandizement, he, and, before him, his father, had been instrumental in shedding the blood of thousands of Singhs, the true disciples of the Guru, and that it was high time that the ascendancy of the Jammú family should be brought to a close, and the claims of the kinsmen of the great Maharájá be taken into consideration by the *Khálsá;* that not one of his kinsmen was better qualified to hold this important office than Sardar Attar Singh, Sindhianwálá, and that the *Khálsá* would meet the wishes of the country and of the nation at large in acceding to his appointment to the office of

---

* Mr. McGregor mentions that these Ránís burnt themselves with the body of their husband. This is impossible, as the Rájá came from Jammú to Láhore *without* his Ránís and was burnt alone near the *sammádh* of his nephew.

wazír. Letters to this effect were secretly issued to the sardars of troops and the darbár, and intercepted by Hírá Singh.

Princes Káshmíra Singh and Peshora Singh join the standard of revolt, 1844.

The disaffected Káshmíra Singh and Peshora Singh also joined the standard of rebellion. A large force promptly marched from Láhore under the command of Generals Mahtáb Singh, *Majíthia*, Guláb Singh, *Calcutiá* (so named for his having, in the time of Ranjít Singh, accompanied a friendly mission to Calcutta), Mián Jawáhir Singh, younger brother of the minister, Sheikh Imám-ud-dín, governor of the Jalandar Doáb, and other sardars, to punish Sardar Attar Singh and the rebels under him. The *Khálsá* troops, before leaving Láhore, gave the Minister clearly to understand that they would not injure the holy Báwá, on account of his sanctity. Hírá Singh assured them that no one felt greater reverence for the holy man than himself. The whole expedition was put under the charge of Mián Lábh Singh, a relation of Hírá Singh. A conflict ensued, and in the general engagement and the confusion and uproar which followed, it happened that one of the first victims who fell was the holy Báwá himself, one of whose legs was carried away by a cannon ball. General Guláb Singh was shot dead by Attar Singh, who subsequently fell himself, with the Prince Káshmíra Singh and other sardars, in a hand-to-hand conflict. Hundreds of people on the side of the insurgents were drowned in the river in their attempt to escape. The Báwá had hoarded up immense riches from all quarters of the Panjáb, from his disciples and followers, who numbered thousands, so that his camp afforded a great temptation for a general plunder, which even the known sanctity of the Báwá could not prevent.

Fight at the Sutlej.

Attar Singh and Prince Kashmira Singh are killed in the action, 1844.

The troops returned victorious to the capital, with their General Mián Lábh Singh, though the *Khálsá* long remembered, with feelings of intense remorse the lamented death of their revered teacher, and gave General Court's battalions, which were believed to be guilty of the sacrilege, the nickname of *Guru Már* or destroyer of the Guru; and it was some time before their men were permitted to eat or drink with the *Khálsá*. Peshora Singh, the other reputed son of Maharájá Ranjít Singh, having witnessed the fate of his brother Káshmíra Singh, repaired to the Láhore Darbár and made his submission. His lands and jágírs were restored to him, and he retired to Gujránwálá, to lead a quiet life. Peace and tranquillity now reigned among the *Khálsá* troops, and Hírá Singh, the wazír, looked for better and more prosperous days for himself. Two of his powerful rivals and bitterest foes, Rájá Suchet Singh and Sardar Attar Singh, whom he always dreaded, were dead, and could no more disturb his peace of mind. A difference now arose between the minister and his uncle, Rájá Guláb Singh, regarding the division of the property left by the late Suchet Singh, and other matters, and it assumed so serious an aspect that twenty battalions of infantry, with a proportionate number of cavalry and artillery, were despatched to Jammú; but a peaceable termination of the misunderstanding between the uncle and nephew was brought about by the negotiations of Bhái Ram Singh, Dewán Díná Nath and Sheikh Imám-ud-dín, who had been subsequently deputed to Jammú on a special mission. To ensure the stability of the reconciliation effected, it was resolved that Mián Jawáhir Singh, the younger brother of Rájá Hírá Singh, should remain at Jammú as a hostage, while Mián Sohan Singh, the eldest son of Rájá Guláb Singh, should remain in the same capacity at the court of Láhore.

Submission of Prince Peshora Singh.

Relations between the Minister and Rája Guláb Singh.

The influence of Pandit Jállá excites the bitter jealousy of the Sikhs.

Hírá Singh had now apparently reached the zenith of his power; but he and his trusted family priest, Pandit Jállá, had made too many enemies both in the darbár at Láhore, and abroad, for them to retain their power very long in safety. The Pandit, a crafty and ambitious man, held the office of tutor to Dhián Singh's sons. Hírá Singh himself was nothing more than a tool in the hands of his designing and unprincipled priest and tutor, Pandit Jállá. This individual exercised such influence over him that all his ministerial measures, whether private or public, were dictated to him by this accomplished intriguer. The unlimited power which he still exercised, in the face of repeated remonstrances on the part of the *Khálsá*, gave rise to bitter jealousy and feelings of intense hatred against him. Prompted by arrogance, he tried to crush every chief, even the most powerful and respected among the sardars and nobles, without showing the slightest respect to any of them. The attitude assumed by him was offensive and insulting to everybody, and injured the feelings of all, high and low. Lahná Singh, *Majithia*, an able sardar, quitted the Panjáb in March 1844, under the pretence of performing a pilgrimage to Hardwár, and the only sardar who exercised any degree of influence, was Lal Singh, a Brahmin like Jállá himself, who owed his position, not to the wazír, or his favourite, the Pandit, but to the favours lavished upon him by the Queen Jindán, mother of the young Maharájá. The Pandit habitually treated Jawáhir Singh, brother of the Rání, with contempt, and, in his arrogance, ventured to use expressions of disrespect towards the Rání herself. In the meanwhile Jawáhir Singh, by his timely withdrawal from Láhore and his residence at Amritsar, the holy city of the Sikhs, was enabled effectually to sow the seed of disaffection towards the Láhore Darbár, as then constituted, among the Bháis, Akálís, Báwás, Gurus and other fanatics. On his return to Láhore he received promises of support from the sardars, the *Khálsá* troops and their deputies, who were all tired of the ascendancy of the Dográ family.

His arrogance.

The proceedings of Sardar Jawáhir Singh at Amritsar.

A plot formed to do away with the Dográ ascendancy.

The treasurer, Lál Singh, was the principal creature of Rájá Dhián Singh, to whom he owed his splendid position in the darbár. He was always in the society of Hírá Singh, and was his trusted and valued friend. He and Pandit Jállá had exchanged turbans in token of true amity. The cunning Rání Jindán and her lover, Lál Singh, entered into a conspiracy to overthrow the power of the Dográ element, and with it the ascendancy of the Misser Jállá. Hírá Singh and his idol, Jállá, were quite unconscious that a creature of their own would, in the garb of a friend, contribute materially to their destruction. Jawáhir Singh was supplied with money to allure the *Nihangs* and other fanatics to embrace his cause. In due time all the discontented regular troops were attached to his party.

The treason of Lál Singh.

It was the first day of the month, and Rání Jindán, as was usual with her on such a day, was distributing golden *butkis* as alms to the poor, to secure her son, the young Maharájá against misfortune, when Pandit Jállá, in a most insolent and abrupt manner, threatened and grossly abused her. The incensed queen and her injured brother appealed to the children of the *Khálsá*, whose rage at this uncalled-for and unwarranted insult to this relative of the great Maharájá, knew no bounds. Early one morning, at a review of troops on the parade ground opposite the fort, Jawáhir Singh, placing himself at the head of the troops that had openly embraced his cause, formally asked Rájá Hírá Singh to deliver over to him the person of Jállá Pandit. This he positively refused to do. An open rupture was, however, avoided, and both parties withdrew in peace, though secretly remaining enemies. Rájá Hírá Singh and Pandit Jállá now saw that their rule was fast drawing to a close, and that to remain at the capital any longer would in all probability cost them their lives. The Rájá at once made preparations for flight to the Jammú hills, and placing all his valuables on elephants, left his private residence in the town

Pandit Jállá gives fresh cause of annoyance to the soldiers.

The flight of Rájá Hírá Singh and Pandit Jállá from Láhore.

early on the morning of 21st December 1844, attended by Pandit Jállá, Mián Sohan Singh, Mián Lábh Singh and others, with three or four hundred horse and foot, under the pretext of inspecting the troops stationed at Mián Mír. His original plan was to leave the city at dark; but, owing to some delay in his preparations, he could not leave until the morning. The party had scarcely cleared the Taxali Gate of the city when trumpets were sounded from the quarters of the Sikh regiments, saluting Jawáhir Singh as wazír. On hearing the noise of the trumpets, the party acceleratad their speed and reached the banks of the Rávi, where the Sikh attendants of the Rájá separated from the rest, and the Dográ chiefs, accompanied by their own men and soldiers, crossed the river, and proceeding to Targar, dismounted for the purpose of taking rest in the old *barádari*. They had scarcely unsaddled their horses when they saw a large party of horsemen coming from the direction of the city at full speed, whereupon they forthwith remounted and renewed their march at a quickened pace. The body of cavalry rapidly advanced till they were close upon the heels of the fugitives. Hírá Singh, acting on the advice of the Pandit, his preceptor, moved quickly in the direction of the *ghorcharás* of Rájá Suchet Singh, who were at a short distance from him, hoping to receive protection from them. As the Rájá and his party approached nearer, the troopers pursued them, and, changing their direction, they made their way to the *sarai* of the Emperor Jahángír's mausoleum, in Shahdera, in expectation of assistance from some Pathans who were encamped there; but the Pathans repulsed them. The party, disappointed, proceeded to the main road with as much speed as possible, but were overtaken at a distance of less than 600 yards from the village of Shahdera. Hírá Singh opened his bags and scattered gold mohurs to divert the attention of the pursuing troopers by the hope of plunder; but Sardar Shám Singh, Attariwálá, and General Mewá Singh, Majithia, imperatively called upon the troops to press forward. "Slaughter the *súrs*," said they; "don't let them go." But gold has its charms for all, and the troopers were no exception to the rule. The time occupied by the troops in picking up the *ashrafís* was taken advantage of by the Dográ chiefs to make the best of their way out of their enemies' reach, and when the pursuers approached nearer, again the same device of emptying bags of *ashrafís* and scattering them on the ground was resorted to.

Jawáhir Singh is saluted wazír.

They are overtaken by the Sikh soldiers,

A running skirmish was kept up, and all the infantry of the fugitives was either cut down or dispersed. The flying Dográs, with a few of their adherents, had advanced 10 or 12 *kos*, when, at about midday, Pandit Jállá, completely exhausted, fell from his horse and was immediately cut to pieces by the pursuing Sikhs. A little distance further on there was a small village of some 20 houses, where Hírá Singh dismounted to quench his thirst. Jawáhir Singh now came up, with a body of General Ventura's Dragoons, and ordered the little village to be set on fire. This order was instantly complied with, the Sikhs surrounding the place and setting it on fire. Finding his life in danger, Hírá Singh, with his escort, remounted, but, in the attempt to escape, was cut down, with the whole of his party, with the exception of six soldiers, who owed their lives only to the swiftness of their horses. The whole of the valuables which the fugitive wazír was carrying with him, fell into the hands of his pursuers. This event occurred on 21st December, 1844.

And put to death, 21st December, 1844.

Sardar Jawáhir Singh, with the *Khálsá* troops in his train, at about noon, made his triumphant entry into the capital, where he was enthusiastically received. He brought with him, as trophies, the heads of Rájá Hírá Singh, his chief counsellor, Pandit Jállá, Sohan Singh, the minister's cousin, and Lábh Singh, who had so lately been hailed as a victorious commander. Every one hastened to present his *nazráná*, and to offer congratulations. Some of the Americans and Spaniards who were still quartered in the town did the same, and they were restored to their former offices. The heads of the sardars were the next morning hung up to public view at the several gates of the town. That of Hírá Singh was exhibited at the Láhori gateway, and that of Sohan Singh at the Mori gateway. Mián Lábh Singh was held in some esteem by the *Khálsá* troops, and General Mewá Singh, who had served under him, saved his head and body from being thus ignominiously treated. The memory of Pandit Jállá, once the idol of Hírá Singh, was bitterly execrated, and the fanatic Akális and the Nihangs treated his head with the greatest indignity. They would not allow it to be exposed at the gateways with the others, but carried it for some days about the city from house to house and shop to shop, procuring a few *cowries* from each spectator as payment for their trouble in exhibiting it. So great was the unpopularity of the Pandit, that even women, on seeing it, cursed his memory. "That is the rogue," exclaimed they, "who induced the young Hírá Singh to murder his uncle, the brave Suchet Singh, for which he wanted an army of 20,000 men, although his antagonist was only assisted by forty valiant mountaineers." When the head had thus been dragged and exposed through the whole city, it was thrown on a heap of rubbish and filth and allowed to lie there for weeks. The irritated passers-by spat on it, and, after being subjected to this horrible ignominy, it was, by orders of Jawáhir Singh, given to the dogs. The heads of Mián Sohan Singh and Hírá Singh, after being taken down, were thrown into a ditch outside the fort, whence, some days after, they were conveyed into the private rooms of Rájá Dhián Singh's house, where they were discovered by Guláb Singh about the middle of February 1846, when the latter came to Láhore, on a visit to the Governor-General, when His Excellency was advancing with the British army on the capital of the Panjáb. The bodies of Hírá Singh and Lábh Singh became a prey to the wild beasts and birds of the village which was the scene of their murder.

Ignominious treatment of the dead.

Those who have watched the progress of political events in the Panjáb at this critical period, cannot fail to notice the great want of discretion and judgment shown by the Sikh soldiery. Had they not acted under a mistaken notion of patriotism and blind zeal, much of the bloodshed and mischief which ravaged the country might have been averted. If, after the death of Sher Singh and Dhián Singh, the soldiery had espoused the cause of the Sindhianwálá brothers, and exalted Ajít Singh or Lahná Singh to the office of wazír, to the entire exclusion of the Jammú family, the kingdom would have maintained its power and stability, and party-spirit would have died a natural death. The Sindhianwálás, being the direct lineal descendants of the common ancestor, with the old Maharájá, were the best suited for the coveted office, and they had fully identified their interest with those of the young Maharájá Dulíp Singh, the acknowledged sovereign of the Panjáb. The extirpation of the Sindhianwálás and the restoration to power of the Dográ family, whose interests could never have been identical with those of the legitimate rulers, was a death-blow to the kingdom of the great Maharájá. Hírá Singh was quite indifferent to life when his father was assassinated, and had he been arrested, as the circumstances of the moment imperatively demanded, quiet would have been restored throughout the country, and not only would the lives of thousands have been saved, but the immense wealth and treasures of the kingdom which flowed to the Jammú hills, would have remained in the State, and proved a source of

Survey of events.

strength and honour to it. But, as affairs stood, the fate of the Panjáb was sealed. True is the saying, "*Quem Deus Vult perdere prius dementat.*"

THE WAZÍRAT OF JAWÁHIR SINGH.

Jawáhir Singh and Lál Singh attain power.

The worthies who now appear on the stage of the Láhore drama are, Sardar Jawáhir Singh, brother of Rání Jindán, the queen of the great Mahárájá, and her favourite Lál Singh, the Brahmin. One of their first acts was to increase their popularity among the *Khálsá*, conscious as they were of their unlimited power in the politics of the country. The golden utensils of the Royal Toshakháná, were all melted down and given to the goldsmiths for the preparation of golden *kanthás*, or bracelets, to be given to each soldier. The preparation of these *kanthás* occupied fully two months, and the *Khálsá* on receiving these golden prizes were elated with pleasure and pride. The soldiers now possessed immense riches. The anarchy which had prevailed during the last four years, and which had literally drained the resources of the country, was all to their advantage, since whatever faction came into power, owed its rise and strength to them alone, and gained the point with their countenance and support.

Bountiful rewards to the Sikh soldiers.

The army moves to Jammú, 1844.

The *Khálsá*, elated with their successes, marched to Jammú, several thousand strong, under the command of Shám Singh, Attaríwálá, General Mewá Singh, Majithia, Sultán Mahmúd Khan and Fatteh Singh, Mán, to reduce Rájá Guláb Singh. The darbár demanded of Guláb Singh three crores of rupees, as a fine, and the restoration of all the property belonging to the late Rájás Suchet Singh and Hírá Singh. In a fight which ensued at Jammú, Fatteh Singh, Mán, fell by the hands of the Dográs. He was a brave old chief of Ranjít Singh's time, and a great favourite with the *Khálsá* troops. His murder greatly incensed the *Khálsá*, who now pushed forward to Tavi, the river running below the walls of Jammú. The astute chief of Jammú, fully knowing the inferiority of his own troops, and dreading the excitement caused among the *Khálsá* by the murder of the Mán Sardar, brought all his arts into play.

The Dográs slay Sardar Fatteh Singh, Mán.

He expressed his grief at the death of the old sardar and disclaimed all participation in it. Taking with him his nephew Mián Jawáhir Singh, who was a great favourite with the *Khálsá*, he went to the troops himself, and, prostrating himself before the *panches*, declared that he and his family were, as they had ever been, their devoted servants, and that all the wealth which he had amassed was theirs. He distributed his money freely among the soldiery and sent three lakhs of rupees, laden on camels and elephants, as a *nazar* for the Láhore Darbár. His personal exertions and attention to the members of the *panchayats* averted the catastrophe which threatened him, of a sack of Jammú, and was so far successful that he partially gained over some of the brigades; but he was nevertheless carried to Láhore, under military surveillance, in April, 1845. Arrived at the capital, he was placed on an elephant and conveyed under a strong escort to the Summan Burj, to meet the Rání. He was honourably received by her, and so well satisfied her with the accounts given by him, that she offered him the office of wazír, which had not yet been formally bestowed on Jawáhir Singh, her brother. This greatly excited the jealousy of the latter, whose will prevailed, and he was formally installed as wazír on 14th May, 1845, Lál Singh receiving at the same time the title of rájá. Guláb Singh was present at this ceremony. He subsequently took part in the betrothal of the young Maharájá to a daughter of Chatter Singh, Chief of Attari, which took place on 10th July. Firmly established in power,

Guláb Singh is brought to Láhore, 1845.

Formal investment of Jawáhir Singh as wazír, 1845.

Jawáhir Singh now brought Guláb Singh to account for his recent conduct in the hills. Guláb Singh deemed it prudent to avoid a rupture, seeing that the wind had ceased to blow in his favour, and was anxious to leave Láhore.

Fine imposed on Guláb Singh.

He agreed to pay, in all, a fine of Rs. 68,00,000 to the darbár, to give up nearly all the territories which had belonged to his brother, Suchet Singh, and which the darbár claimed as the escheated property of a feudatory without male heirs of his body, as well as the property of his nephew, Hírá Singh. In short, he reserved only his own proper fiefs. The lease for the salt mines between the Jhelum and the Indus was also renewed, which deprived Guláb Singh of a large income, as also of his power over the Rohtás hills. Thus shorn of much of his real power, Guláb Singh left Láhore for his country about the end of August, after a sojourn of three or four months.

Múl Ráj succeeds his father Sáwan Mal at Multán, September 1844.

Sáwan Mal, the able and popular Governor of Multán, was assassinated in September, 1844, by a ruffian who was charged with marauding, and his son Mulráj was permitted to succeed him. The *Khálsá* demanded of him an increased term, or contract, which was evaded by the new-governor. He also objected to the payment of a large *nazráná* which, on his accession to the office of his father, he was required to pay. Displeased with his conduct, the darbár resolved upon sending a force against Multán; but the new governor, hearing of its warlike preparations, was induced to yield, and remitted to Court a sum of Rs. 1,80,000 as a fine or *nazráná*, which satisfied all demands, though some petty districts which he originally held, were taken away from him.

And agrees to pay a heavy *nazráná*, 1845.

The pretensions of Prince Peshora Singh.

Peshora Singh, the reputed son of the old Maharájá, who, after the assassination of his brother Káshmíra Singh, had been re-instated in his jágírs at Gujránwálá on conditions of leading a quiet and retired life, was now again persuaded to renew his claims to the throne of Láhore. He was encouraged by Guláb Singh, then safe in his hill country, who, at this juncture, played a double game, for, on the one hand, he promised his full support to the prince,—a vain person of inadequate capacity, with nothing but his relationship with the great Maharájá to recommend him,—and, on the other hand, he instigated Jawáhir Singh to exile him, or to put him out of the way as best he could, as he was his only foe and the rival of his young nephew. Peshora Singh, having received assurances of support from the troops, who had put in confinement Sardar Jawáhir Singh, on that chief declaring his readiness to take protection in British territory with the young Maharájá, repaired to Láhore, where he was received by military deputations with great pageantry. At the Rání's invitation, he also attended the darbár, and was received with open arms and treated with honour as the equal of Dulíp Singh, her own son. This engendered jealousy in the mind of the wazír, Her Highness' brother, who received the prince with coldness, and also showed him some slight in the darbár. The prince, disgusted at this treatment, withdrew from the town and put up in the house of General Avitabile, on the summit of *Budhu-ká-áwá*, outside the city, where his friends had advised him to take up his position, in the superstitious belief that some good fortune attached to it, as being the place where Sher Singh had been saluted by the *Khálsá* soldiery as king of Láhore. Peshora Singh was here surrounded by the *panches* of the army, who offered him their aid, which made him sanguine of success. The minister, on receiving these tidings, took immediate steps to confirm his authority and consulted his sister in the matter. The brother and sister having both agreed upon a line of policy, the most liberal promises were made to the troops to induce them to abandon the cause of the prince, the

He repairs to Láhore.

Is saluted by the deputies of the army.

claimant to the throne. A golden necklace of the value of Rs. 25 was, among other things, promised to each soldier. The *Khálsá* were greatly pleased with this liberality and advised Peshora Singh to withdraw to his principality, and there await a more favourable opportunity. The prince prudently withdrew, carrying with him the good wishes of the *Khálsá* and rich presents from the darbár of Láhore. The minister wreaked his wrath on the battalions who had invited Peshora Singh to the capital, by ordering the mutilation of the commander's nose and ears. The ruler of Jammú saw that his design of bringing about a rupture between the Láhore Darbár and Peshorá Singh had collapsed. He therefore urged the minister to hurry on the arrangements for the assassination of the prince, advancing, by way of argument, that, being the rival of the young Maharájá, his nephew, he would not fail to avail himself of the earliest opportunity to establish his own supremacy, and that, the sooner he was removed from the scene, the better it would be for the interests and stability of the kingdom of Láhore. The consideration which inspired the policy of the astute chief was that, if Jawáhir Singh was known to be the contriver of Peshora Singh's death, the *Khálsá* would avenge his death on him, and thus two great obstacles to the extension of his influence and power would be removed, and that without his being in the least suspected of complicity in the matter, as he was distantly situated from both. Peshora Singh at this time held Siálkot in fief, but was in very straitened circumstances, in consequence of his Sikh troops having deserted him. It was at this juncture that he put in an appearance, towards the end of July, at Atok. There he was joined by the Mahomedan Pathans of the neighbourhood, and, having surprised and seized the fort, he proclaimed himself Maharájá and entered into correspondence with Dost Muhammad Khan of Kábul. Troops were sent from Láhore to punish the insurgent prince; but such was the respect in which he was held, owing to his reputed relationship to the old Maharájá, that, on reaching their destination, they refused to fight. Not a shot was fired, and the rebel still remained at large, daily gaining ground and advancing in popularity.

Is advised to leave Láhore for the time being.

Guláb Singh urges the assassination of the Prince.

His deep policy.

The Prince repairs to Atok.

Army sent against him.

The Láhore minister was much disgusted and disappointed at receiving this news, and two confidential sardars of high rank were now sent, at the head of a body of troops to punish the prince, without the aid of the *Khálsá* troops of Láhore. Sardar Chattar Singh, Attaríwálá, the new father-in-law of the Maharájá, and Fatteh Khan, Tiwáná, a personal friend of the minister, were ordered to proceed to Atok at once. The former moved from Naushera, and the latter from Dera Ismail Khan, where they were on special duty at the time, settling some differences with the people of the hill country about Rájáuri and the upper Deráját of the Indus. Peshora Singh had so strengthened his position in the fort that, when the combined forces of these chiefs reached Atok, they saw that it would be a losing game for them to assume the offensive. The chiefs therefore resorted to negotiations, which lasted twelve days. Peshora Singh, conscious of his power and of his great popularity with the children of the *Khálsá*, at first refused to come to terms, but the sardars, with every show of sincerity, made large promises on behalf of the Crown, and the prince was at last induced to vacate the fort on 30th August. The terms of the capitulation were that he should leave the fort at the head of his troops with all the honours of war, and should be treated with the respect and distinction due to his position as the son of the great Maharájá; that, in addition to his previous jágirs in Siálkot, another fief, yielding an income of one lakh of rupees per annum, should be permanently assigned to him by the darbár (letters written by Sardar Jawáhir Singh

Sardar Chattar Singh Attaríwálá and Fatteh Khan, Tiwáná, ordered, to Atok.

being produced as authority for this); and that he should make his triumphant entry into the capital, escorted by his own troops. He was treated with the greatest cordiality and apparent respect. Having thus been put off his guard, he was treacherously made prisoner and thrown into a dark dungeon, or low tower, called *Kálá Burj*, in the fort of Atok, where he was strangled at night and his body thrown into the Indus. The day following this tragedy, the treacherous chiefs, not daring to go to Láhore to announce their success to the minister, through dread of the *Khálsá*, repaired to their respective destinations.

The Prince is seized and put to death, 1845.

The news of the death of Peshora Singh was received by the Láhore minister with profound joy. The ramparts of the fort thundered forth a royal salute, and the city was illuminated at night. In vain did Báwá Rattan Singh, and Bhai Chattú, the principal advisers of the minister, remonstrate with him for so indiscreet and dangerous an act.

The *Khálsá* soldiery become disgusted with Jawáhir Singh.

The fury and indignation of the *Khálsá*, on hearing of the tragical end of the prince, and still more on seeing the demonstrations made to celebrate the event, passed all bounds. The whole of the *Khálsá* troops made common cause, and swore to take vengeance on Jawáhir Singh, as the sole author of the horrible crime. The Dográ element was busily at work exciting the wrath of the Sikh soldiery at this juncture. Pirthi Singh, son of Mián Arbela Singh, and his party, were at the capital, and played their part with the troops so well that several divisions of the army withdrew to a place three or four miles from the city, on the road to Mián Mír, to concentrate the rest of their body there with the object of eventually seizing the person of Jawáhir Singh, or acting in any way which the urgency of the case might require. They were joined by the whole of the *Khálsá* troops, with the exception of the two battalions of Jawáhir Singh's bodyguard, stationed in the fort. The *panches* of the army now sent messages to Jawáhir Singh, demanding his presence before the *Khálsá*, but the sardar paid no attention to their demand, still hoping to win over the soldiery to his side by bribes and promises. Both he and his sister exerted all their energies to persuade the deputies of the troops to let the matter drop. They even gave written agreements, promising the troops an increase of pay in the event of Jawáhir Singh's offence being forgiven, but all their promises and declarations were ineffectual. The deputies had been bribed with ready money to a large amount by the Dográ faction, and would yield to no promises, however liberal, and to no entreaties, however humiliating. A part of the impatient and furious soldiery set itself in motion and took up its station opposite the Dehli gate. Another portion of the army marched to attack the fort. The sound of their drums and bugles startled the obnoxious minister from his slumbers. Jawáhir Singh now saw the danger of his position, and immediately proceeded to consult with his sister upon the matter. Taking her and her son, the young Mahárájá, with him, he left the fort at noon on the 21st September, 1845, escorted by about 1,000 men, and repaired to the spot where the main army was encamped. He had the young Mahárájá with him on his lap on the same elephant, while his sister, the queen-mother, followed on another, with the slave-girl Mangela, and other members of the *zenáná* and slave-girls followed on elephants. As the sardar advanced, with his party, he was everywhere saluted, the Rání at the same time being most lavish in her promises of rewards to the troops, which she now made personally, as she advanced, in the hope that her brother's life would be spared. Jawáhir Singh, on his part, entertained hopes of forgiveness after he had made his personal appearance before the soldiery, shielded, as he thought, he was, by

The deputies of the army demand his presence before them.

The perplexity of the minister.

the presence of the young Maharájá and of the queen-mother. He was further encouraged by the salutations which he received on all sides from the *Khálsá* soldiery, and to which he replied with an apparently cheerful countenance. But his fate was sealed, and the presence of his nephew and his royal sister could avail him nothing. While he was thus proceeding pompously and boldly, the bugles suddenly sounded, the drums beat, and the bands began to play, as a signal for action. A great tumult ensued and Jawáhir Singh's elephant was abruptly stopped by the troops, who compelled the driver to make it kneel. The fierce and infuriated soldiery surrounded the elephant on all sides, and the boy Dulíp Singh was roughly snatched from the arms of his uncle. Jawáhir Singh bowed before the troops, and, with folded arms, implored them to hear him for a moment, but they would not allow him to utter a word. He was stabbed with a bayonet on the left, and as he bent over on the right, a man sent a bullet through his brain. The wazír fell from the *howdah* a corpse, and his body was dragged from the elephant and mangled by the swords of those who surrounded it. Báwá Rattan Singh and Bhái Chettú, the councillors of Jawáhir Singh, were killed without any ceremony, immediately afterwards, on the same spot. The cash, in gold and silver coin, which Jawáhir Singh and the Rání had brought with them from the fort, was now plundered by the soldiers, and the Rání and her slave-girls were compelled to retire to the tents which had some days previously been pitched for their reception, the whole thing having been well premeditated and planned. The boy Dulíp Singh was separated from his mother for a while and kept with the soldiery, who feared that the Rání, in her rage and excitement, would destroy her own and her child's life; when these fears had subsided, the prince was again made over to his mother. The soldiers, however, kept a strict watch over Her Highness's tents the whole night, to prevent accident. She passed the night in fearful screams and shrieks, lamenting over the death of her beloved brother and cursing the *Khálsá*. As morning broke, she was permitted to see the mangled body of her brother, and her lamentations and painful cries were renewed with a violence which moved the bystanders to pity and melted even the iron hearts of those who had been instrumental in causing her brother's murder. Weeping bitterly, she threw herself and her child on the body of her brother, and when, partly by entreaties and partly by force, she was separated from the corpse, she rolled upon the ground, tearing her hair and her clothes. This heartrending spectacle touched the sympathies of the most callous spectators. The scene was terminated at noon, when the Maharání was, with great difficulty, persuaded to return to the city. The corpse of the murdered minister was also carried to the city, where his funeral obsequies were performed, the same day, outside the Masti Gate, in the presence of several sardars of the Court. Two of the murdered wazír's ránís and three of his slave-girls immolated themselves with his corpse as virtuous *sattis*. A guard of Sikh soldiers was in attendance at the horrible ceremony, and their behaviour towards the unfortunate women was marked by a cruelty and barbarity quite unequalled in the history of the nation. As these poor defenceless women were marching in solemn procession to the altar, with all their money and jewellery in open trays, carried by men on either side of them, for the purpose of distribution in charity, these armed ruffians remorselessly plundered them, and as the unfortunate women were mounting the funeral pyre, these villainous guards tore away their nose and ear-ornaments (which were worn in strict conformity with their religion) from their persons. The cries and remonstrances of the women at the indignities to which they were subjected were treated

He is condemned by the army and put to death, September 21st, 1845.

The lamentations of the Rání.

Brutal conduct of the soldiery towards the intending *sattis*.

by these monsters as if they had been the veriest ribaldry. Not satisfied with what they had already robbed, they actually snatched from the fire the trinkets and embroidery on their costly attire. The helpless victims, stretching their hands towards heaven, cursed the whole Sikh nation to which the savages belonged.

The Rání inconsolable.

Thus was the death of Peshora Singh avenged by the Sikhs. The Rání was quite inconsolable for many weeks after the catastrophe. She renewed her lamentations every day, and with her long dishevelled hair, accompanied by her slave-girls, walked through the streets of Láhore, exposed to the public gaze, to pay her visit to the tomb of her brother, in a garden outside the Masti Gate, across the parade ground, where she gave free vent to her tears.

The troops now sought to make their peace with the Rání. The different corps recriminated one another for the murder of the wazír. Those who were immediately concerned in the atrocity were declared by some to be alone deserving of punishment, while others maintained that every corps which had been present in the line had a full knowledge of the object for which they had been summoned. After a few days, the Rání convened a meeting of the *panches* and sardars at the Summan Burj, and when all had assembled, she declared that she would be satisfied if her enemies were seized and delivered up to her. Jawáhir Mal, formerly the dewán of Suchet Singh, who had been accessory to the plot and who was present at the time, was accordingly seized and made over to the Rání, and, as for Pirthi Singh and others of the Dográ party who had supplied the troops with the money, it was agreed that they too should be seized and delivered up to her. They were, however, allowed to leave the city for the hills, with a few horsemen, at night, and the Rání, seeing that she had no alternative for the present, kept quiet. The sardar most intimate with her about this time was Lál Singh, who was generally understood to be her paramour, and under his advice Jawáhir Mal was, after a few days, released.

The ringleaders of the late plot are surrendered to her.

The Rání now assumed charge of the administration and held daily darbárs, at which orders were passed. She was declared regent of the State after the Dasahra, and appeared frequently in public, consulting alternately Dewán Díná Nath, Bhái Ram Singh and Misser Lál Singh on State affairs. But the real power rested with the *panchayats*, or delegates of the army, who were disposed to place the wazírát in the hands of Guláb Singh, though that wily chief declined to accept the perilous honour. Tej Singh, nephew of Khushál Singh, who was at this time governor of Pesháwar, arrived at Láhore, and was offered the high office, but he, too, declined it. The Rání, ever anxious to promote the interests of her paramour Lál Singh, resorted to the expedient of solving the question of appointment by divination. Five slips of paper were prepared, each containing the name of a candidate, and the young Maharájá was allowed to draw the lot. By some accident or contrivance, the name of Lál Singh turned up; but the soldiery refused to recognise him, and the plan fell through. The Rání continued to carry on the affairs of State in her own name, as regent, assisted by Lál Singh as executive minister, and Teja Singh as Commander-in-Chief.

The Rání is declared regent of the State,

But the deputies of the army become all-powerful.

Lál Singh and Teja Singh.

The power of the *Khálsá* army was now at its height. Every one dreaded them, and the highest officers of State felt themselves in momentary danger of annihilation if the cupidity of the troops, which had no bound, was not satiated. The Rání saw her perilous situation. With an empty treasury and the resources of the kingdom exhausted, she was left in no position to feed the rapacity of the turbulent Sikh soldiers, who now openly talked of proclaiming the infant son of Shér Singh, Maharájá of the Panjáb. To

The Rání and her chiefs try to involve the Sikh troops with the British Government.

divert their attention in another direction, as also to break their union and power, the Rání and her friends originated the proposal of crossing the Sutlej to make war on the British Government. The troops, on hearing this, clamoured for munitions of war and military stores, and as these were not provided, the idea of an expedition to Hindostán seems to have been abandoned for a time. In the meanwhile, the Court moved to Amritsar, and all orders of State were passed from the palace of Rám Bágh. It returned to Láhore about the beginning of November, 1845, and for a while encamped in the Shalámár gardens. Rájá Lál Singh now openly assumed the duties of wazír, and conducted the business of State under the control of the queen-mother.

False reports regarding the advance of the British to the Panjáb.

Reports were now ingeniously circulated that the British army was advancing to the south and east of the Sutlej; and letters from the Sikh governors of the territories beyond that river were produced to show that British officers were actually interfering with the Sikh subjects and inflicting on them all sorts of annoyance and trouble. So successfully were these reports disseminated that the troops were thrown into a state of intense agitation, and great alarm prevailed in the city of Láhore. Early in November a council of the sardars, *panches* of the army and officers of State was convened by Rájá Lál Singh at the Shalámár gardens, and, when all had assembled, Dewán Díná Náth read them a letter, purporting to have been sent by the Sikh officers beyond the Sutlej, intimating that the British authorities were treating the subjects of the darbár as their own and demanding tribute from them. He informed them that there was no system of government in Kashmír and Pesháwar, which had ceased to remit a single rupee on account of Government revenue, and that confusion and anarchy reigned throughout the country. He reminded them that their sovereign was but a child, that the whole Sikh nation were, as loyal subjects, bound to defend his rights, and that, unless arrangements were speedily made for the maintenance of Sikh rule and power, its utter collapse would be the inevitable result. The Dewán then communicated to the assembly the wish of the Maharání to create Rájá Lál Singh wazír and Sardar Tej Singh Commander-in-Chief of the Sikh armies. This eloquent speech made such an impression on the *panches* of the *Khálsá* and the sardars assembled, that there was a unanimous cry for war, and the appointments proposed by the Maharání were acceded to with loud acclamations. Two or three days after this meeting, the young Maharájá, with his sardars, returned to the palace in Láhore.

The grand meeting of the Sikhs at Shalámár.

The speech of Dewán Díná Náth.

The deputies of the army resolve on war with the British.

The absorbing topic of conversation with all classes of the community at Láhore was an expedition to Hindostán, and the wild soldiery expatiated on the spoils they hoped to bring from Mathrá, Delhi and Benares; for nothing short of the subjugation of all India was boasted of as the project they had in view. Rájá Lál Singh and Sardar Tej Singh were formally installed at the *samádh*, or mausoleum, of Maharájá Ranjít Singh and the *panches* of the army and the sardars assembled there to do honour to the chiefs, as well as to receive orders for a march towards the Sutlej. Passages from the *Granth*, or the holy book, were first recited, and *karchá parshád*, or bread sweetened with sugar and raisins, was distributed. The *panches* and sardars were then requested to lay their hands on the sacred *Granth* and the canopy over the shrine of Ranjít Singh, as a pledge of fidelity to the young Maharájá Dulíp Singh, and obedience to Rájá Lál Singh, the wazír, and Sardar Teja Singh, the Commander-in-Chief. These ceremonies being over, war against the British Government was formally declared, and the march of the *Khálsá* army across the Sutlej ordered. The grounds alleged by the darbár for this fatal determination were four—*first*, the advance of

Lál Singh made Wazír and Teja Singh, Commander-in-Chief.

The meeting at the *Samádh* of Maharájá Ranjít Singh.

Formal declaration of war, 17th November, 1845.

Grounds for such resolution.

bodies of British troops towards the Sutlej and the adoption by the British of defensive measures, in anticipation of the outbreak of hostilities in the Panjáb, which were looked upon in the light of aggressive preparations; *secondly*, the refusal of the British authorities to restore eighteen lakhs of rupees in the Ferozepur treasury, claimed by the Sikh Government as the property of the late Rájá Suchet Singh; *thirdly*, the confirmation, by the British Government, of the escheat of the village Morwán to the Rájá of Nabhá; and, *lastly*, the refusal of the British Government to allow a free passage to the Sikh troops into the *Khálsá* possessions south of the Sutlej. It was also believed that the English were preparing boats at Bombay to make a bridge across the Sutlej, and that troops were being equipped in Sindh for an advance on Multán. All these allegations were, of course, mere pretexts to lead the uncontrollable and obnoxious *Khálsá* army into collision with a power which was sure to destroy their influence, if not their existence, and so make it possible to establish a Sikh government in the Panjáb unrestrained by the censorship of the army.

CHAPTER II.

WARS WITH THE BRITISH.

THE FIRST SIKH WAR.

The British authorities remain strictly on the defensive.

During the whole time that tumult and confusion were reigning in the Panjáb, the attitude assumed by the British Government was pacific and forbearing. It was, indeed, not thought probable that a nation, disunited, contentious and engaged in internecine feuds, would be so rash as to run the risk of invading the territory of its powerful, but inoffensive neighbour. Actuated by these considerations, the British authorities had remained strictly on the defensive. As early as June 1845, the Governor-General, Sir Henry Hardinge, expressed his determination to maintain a Sikh government in the Panjáb as long as possible; this declaration of policy being repeated in September and again in the early part of October. Provocation was repeatedly given, but it was invariably answered, not by arms, but by friendly advice, or timely warnings in the plainest terms, the Governor-General and the Commander-in-Chief (Sir Hugh Gough) maintaining the opinion, even up to the 14th of December, that the Sikhs would not cross the Sutlej.

The Sikhs cross the Sutlej, 8th December, 1845.

On 8th December, large detachments of Sikh troops made their appearance on the right bank of the Sutlej, and the influx continued in great numbers on the two following days. As they poured in, they discharged artillery, of which they had brought a numerous train. Considerable numbers of Sikh cavalry also crossed the river to the left bank, the plains opposite Ferozepur as far as Harí-ká-Pattan being covered with masses of Sikh troops. The exposed post of Ferozepur was then held by Sir John Littler, a brave and skilful officer, with 10,000 men and 31 guns. By the 13th, the Sikhs, having crossed the river in large bodies by a bridge of boats, passed about ten miles above Ferozepur. The Governor-General, in consequence of reports received from his agent, Major Broadfoot, met the Commander-in-Chief at Karnál, and then visited Ludhiáná, the other post on the frontier, at this time held by one European regiment, five regiments of native infantry, one regiment of native cavalry, and two troops of horse artillery. Up to the 8th no forward movement was made by the British troops, and the pacific policy of the British Government was manifest from the fact that, when the Sikhs marched towards the Sutlej, Sir Henry declared that that would in no way justify hostilities on its part, "unless the frontier should be actually violated." "The Láhore Government," observed the British statesman, "had as good a right to reinforce their bank of the Sutlej as we to reinforce our posts on that river." As soon, however, as he heard, on 8th December, that the Sikhs were bent on hostilities, he ordered prompt measures to be taken to oppose the invading army, and he was indefatigable in his exertions. A proclamation was issued on the 13th, declaring the policy of the British Government and setting forth its objects and views. The manifesto declared that the British Government had ever been on terms of friendship with that of the Panjáb, and had faithfully observed the conditions of the treaty concluded with Maharájá Ranjít Singh in 1809; that the same friendly relations had been maintained by the British Government with the successors of Maharájá Ranjít Singh; that, since the death of Maharájá Sher Singh, it had become incumbent on the Governor-General to adopt precautionary measures for the protection of the British frontier, in view of the disorganised state of the Láhore Government; that, notwithstanding many most unfriendly proceedings on the part of the Láhore darbár during the last two years, the Governor-General had shown, on every occasion, the utmost forbearance, and sincerely desired to see a strong Government re-established in the Panjáb; that the Sikh army had recently marched from Láhore by the orders of the darbár, for the purpose of invading British territory, and no reply had been given to the repeated demands for an explanation; that the Sikh army had now invaded British territory without any shadow of provocation; and that the Governor-General must, therefore, take measures for effectually protecting the British Provinces, for vindicating the authority of the British Government, and for punishing the violators of treaties and the disturbers of the public peace. The document then declared the possessions of Maharájá Dulíp Singh, on the left bank of the Sutlej, confiscated and annexed to the British territories.

Proclamation of 13th December, 1845.

Complaints against the Sikh Court.

The Sikh territories on the left bank of the Sutlej confiscated.

The intrigues of the Sikhs.

It was now ascertained that the aim of the Sikhs was to cause a general rising against the British Government. They had endeavoured systematically to tamper with the native army in the employ of that Government, and appealed to their religious prejudices. Intrigues had also been going on for some time with the object of inducing the chiefs of the protected Sikh States to join the *Khálsá* as soon as the Láhore army should cross the Sutlej.

The British army advances.

The whole of the Ludhiáná force, numbering 5,000 men and 12 guns, and the Ambálá force of 7,500 men, and 36 guns, made a forward movement, under the command of Brigadier Wheeler, and by a rapid march, reached Basian, at the junction of the Ambálá and Karnál roads, where Major Broadfoot had collected provisions and stores. Lál Singh, passing Sir John Littler near Ferozepur, had taken up an entrenched position at the village of Ferozshahr, about ten miles to the south-east, while a portion of his army had pushed on to Mudki, the whole exceeding 50,000 men, with 108 guns. Hearing that the British force advancing was small compared with his own, he advanced to meet it. The British troops had marched 150 miles in six days, and had had but little food or rest, for the intelligence of the passage of the Sutlej by the Sikhs had reached Ambálá only on 11th December, when a grand ball was to be given by the Commander-in-Chief.

The battle of Mudki, 18th December, 1845.

The first battle was fought at Mudki, twenty miles to the south-east of Ferozepur, on 18th December 1845, between the united Ambálá and Ludhiáná divisions, numbering about 11,000 fighting men, and the Sikh army under Lál Singh, estimated at 30,000 men, with 40 guns. According to an eye-witness, all was quiet in the British camp on that date, and nothing was heard of the enemy except the report that they were close upon the British, when suddenly, at about 4 o'clock P.M., the sounds of a heavy cannonade were heard. The Governor-General, an old and tried soldier,* instantly galloped into the field on horseback. The British soldiers, who were in a state of great exhaustion, were engaged at the time in preparations for dinner. The troops were immediately drawn up in order of battle. The Commander-in-Chief, Sir Hugh Gough, pushed forward at the head of cavalry and horse artillery, the infantry and field batteries being ordered to follow. The position of the enemy was two miles from the British camp, behind jungle, bushes and sandy hillocks, among which they had screened their artillery. Immediately on the British force coming in sight, the Sikh artillery opened a heavy cannonade, which checked the British advance in this direction, but a flank movement of the British cavalry turned the left of the Sikhs and swept along the rear of their infantry and guns, while the artillery silenced the enemy's guns. The Sikh infantry was then attacked by the British infantry under Sir John M'Caskill and Major-Generals Sir H. Smith and Gilbert. While the fight was going on with great fierceness on both sides, Lál Singh, in accordance with his original design, suddenly abandoned the field, leaving the Sikhs to fight as their valour might prompt. The hardy Sikhs, not discouraged by the treachery of their commander, continued the conflict with undiminished energy and devotion. Some of their cavalry men, dismounting from their horses, grasped their swords with both hands and rushed furiously on the British lines, but were repulsed with great slaughter. Sir Henry directed the movements of a part of the British force himself. Mr. Currie remonstrated with His Excellency for thus exposing himself; but Sir Henry disregarded his advice, as the great Macedonian monarch had done before him, on the same soil, when remonstrated with by his advisers, more than two thousand years previously. The Governor-General's presence inspired the troops with confidence, and the British soldiers fought with great courage. The Sikhs at last gave way before the determined valour of the British, and were driven from post to post at the point of the bayonet. The approaching darkness and the dust prevented the British force from pursuing them in the direction of the river, whither they had retreated, but before night, seventeen of their guns, some of them of heavy calibre, had been captured. The battle lasted until an hour and a half of dim starlight, amidst clouds of dust from the sandy plains. The victory was dearly purchased, and by it the British learnt the true character of their foe. The battle-field, after the fight was over, presented a terrible spectacle. An officer who was in the fight, has thus painted the scene:—"It was now growing dusk and the enemy appeared to be retreating. Underneath our feet, as we rode along, were scattered the bodies of men, horses and camels, some gasping and others dead, while the wounded were groaning piteously and calling out for help, which we could not give." The loss on the side of the British was 215 killed and 657 wounded. Amongst those killed were Major-General Sir Robert Sale, famous for his gallant defence of Jallálábád, and Major-General Sir John M'Caskill.

Sir Hugh Gough meets the enemy.

Defeat of the Sikhs.

The scene described by an eye-witness.

The British loss.

* During his campaigns in the Panjáb, Lord Hardinge was often seen sitting under a tree at a table, official papers and boxes before him, issuing orders and giving instructions. He disregarded ceremony, and did not so much as wait for his tents to arrive to dispose of business when its nature demanded prompt attention.

During the battle, the Sikhs had drums beaten to keep up their spirits. They had captured Captain Biddulph and kept him bound with a chain, until victory began to declare itself for the British, when they sent him back. The Captain was clothed in a long red garment which the Sikhs had put on him, while they had taken away his own clothes out of curiosity. Captain Biddulph, on coming back, furnished important intelligence as to the disposition of the Sikh troops, the number of their guns and their munitions of war..

The Sikhs concentrate at Ferozshahr.

After the action of the 18th, the Sikhs were incessantly employed in entrenching themselves in their position around the village of Ferozshahr, distant about ten miles both from Mudki and from Ferozepur. It was now resolved to make an assault on the great Sikh entrenchments in this locality, and, with that view, Sir John Littler effected a junction with the main body of the British army, bringing with him from Ferozepur 5,000 infantry, two regiments of cavalry and 21 guns. The British forces now numbered 16,700 men and 69 guns, while those of the enemy consisted of 33,000 of the flower of the Sikh army, with 108 guns of heavy calibre, vastly superior in weight of metal to those of the British. Sir Henry Hardinge offered his services to the Commander-in-Chief, as second in command, and they were gladly accepted.

The battle of Ferozshahr, December 21st, 1845.

The junction with Sir John Littler's division having been effected about midday on 21st December, at a distance of four miles from the Sikh entrenchments, an immediate attack on the enemy's position was resolved upon. The assault was commenced at about four o'clock in the afternoon, Sir Hugh Gough commanding the right wing, the Governor-General the left. The British army marched in even array, and their artillery opened a steady fire, which was replied to with such rapidity and precision by the enemy that the best efforts of the British soldiers to silence their guns were unavailing. In the midst of a storm of whizzing bullets, cannon balls, and shells, the British infantry, under Captain Pringle O'Hanlon, of the staff, advanced, and having gained a footing in the entrenchments, wrested some of the guns from the enemy, but the Sikh infantry, drawn up behind the guns, opened such a tremendous fire of musketry that the advanced force was hurled back, much shattered. The British troops renewed the assault, and by sunset a portion of the enemy's entrenchments was finally carried.

Attack on the entrenched position.

Major-General Sir Harry Smith's brigade captured the village of Ferozshahr, but was unable to retain it during the night, and had to withdraw. Her Majesty's 3rd Dragoons charged the enemy with great gallantry and took some of their most formidable batteries;

Severe fighting.

yet the enemy continued to hold a considerable portion of their position. Darkness now fell upon the scene ; the contest was raging everywhere, and the obstinacy and persistency with which it was carried on, threw the English into confusion and disorder.

The night of terrors.

The night that ensued was truly designated a "night of terrors." Thirst, cold and fatigue oppressed the weary soldiers, exhausted by over-exertion and reduced in numbers. Yet they were animated by an indomitable spirit, and the courage and tact displayed by them were truly worthy of British soldiers.

Its description by Sir Henry Hardinge.

Sir Henry Hardinge gave a vivid description of the events of that memorable night in his official despatches, which were read with great enthusiasm in the House of Commons by Sir Robert Peel.

Gallant conduct of the Governor-General.

"The night of the 21st December," wrote Sir Henry, "was the most extraordinary of my life. I bivouacked with the men without food or covering, and our nights were bitter cold. A burning camp in our front, our brave fellows lying down under a heavy cannonade, which continued during the whole night, mixed with the wild cries of the Sikhs, our English hurrah, the tramp of men and the groans of the dying. In this state, with a handful of men who had carried the batteries the night before, I remained till morning, taking very short intervals of rest by lying down with various regiments in succession to ascertain their temper and revive their spirits. I found myself again with my old friends of the 29th, 31st, 50th and 9th, all in good heart. My answer to all and every one of them was that we must fight it out, attack the enemy at day-break, beat him, or die honourably on the field. The gallant old General (Sir Hugh Gough) kind-hearted and heroically brave, entirely coincided with me." There was a proposal to fall back on Ferozepur during the night, but the dauntless spirit of Lord Gough and the intrepid courage of Sir Henry Hardinge were strongly averse to the adoption of such a course. In the midst of their difficulties, the spirit of the wearied soldiers was cheered by the genial temper and lofty bearing of the Governor-General. The Sikhs had provided themselves with abundant brush-wood, which they lighted during the night to warm their stiffened limbs. They continued to harass the British troops by the fire of their artillery, and the position of the English was one of great danger. Amid these difficulties, the night wore away. As soon as daylight broke on the 22nd, the British infantry formed into line with alacrity, and fire was opened from the centre by such of the heavy guns as remained effective, aided by a flight of rockets. The cold was so severe that it was with difficulty that the men could handle their muskets. Their thirst during the day was so intense that they were driven to drink putrid water which, at any other time, would have been rejected as poison; the horses almost went mad with fatigue and privation. Sir Hugh Gough and Sir Henry Hardinge advanced steadily, unchecked by the enemy's fire, and drove them rapidly out of the village of Ferozshahr and their encampment; then charging down on the centre, the British force swept through the camp, bearing down all opposition, and dislodged the enemy from their whole position. The line then halted, receiving its two leaders, as they rode along its front, with a gratifying cheer, and displaying the captured standard of the *Khálsá*. The English were masters of the field, and had captured upwards of 73 pieces of cannon. The Sikh army was in full retreat across the Sutlej, in the greatest confusion and dismay, having abandoned large stores of grain, camp equipage and ammunition. Their commander, Lál Singh, had fled at an early period, and his military chest was plundered by the exasperated soldiery.

Battle renewed in the morning of December 22nd, 1845.

Final advance and victory.

Disastrous retreat of the Sikhs.

But the toils and glories of the victors were not yet at an end. Téj Singh, who had commanded in this great battle, brought up from the Sutlej a fresh force consisting of 20,000 infantry, 5,000 cavalry and 70 guns. The sudden advance of a new Sikh army was looked upon with much concern by the British commanders at this juncture, for their ammunition of all sorts was nearly expended, while the troops were thoroughly exhausted, and had hardly had time to recover from their late privations. It happened, however, that after firing a few shots from their guns, the Sikhs, apparently panic-stricken at the movement of British cavalry, retired as they had come. Téj Singh had been advised by his zealous and faithful soldiery to attack the British column at daybreak; but he intentionally delayed, and did not appear on the scene until he had seen that Lál Singh's force was defeated at every point, his object being to disperse and overawe the turbulent *Khálsá* army. This completed the victory of the British.

Téj Singh's movements.

He suddenly retires.

The real object of his manœuvre.

Never before had a more severely contested battle, with so many attending perils, been fought on the plains of India since the British set foot on its soil. Their loss in this battle was great, being 694 killed and 1,721 wounded, or about a seventh of the whole British force engaged. Amongst those

Severe losses.

killed were Major Broadfoot, Political Officer, D'Arcy Todd, of Herat fame, and Brigadier Wallace. The whole staff of the Governor-General was disabled, the only exception being his son, Captain Hardinge. The loss of the Sikhs was estimated at 8,000; 73 fine guns and many standards fell into the hands of the victors. The victory of Ferozshahr was of great importance, inasmuch as it not only had the effect of completely disheartening the *Khálsá* army, but also deprived it of nearly all its artillery. Indeed, had the British chiefs known or credited, on the night of the 21st, the incapacity of Lál Singh, or the treason of Téj Singh, the thought of retiring upon Ferozepur could have never occurred to any one that night. After these transactions, Téj Singh, the Sikh commander, visited the British camp, and tried to open negotiations with the Governor-General, but His Lordship refused to transact any business with him until the British troops should reach the walls of the capital of the Panjáb.

The Governor-General's manifesto, 31st December, 1845.

On the 31st of December 1845, the Governor-General issued a proclamation from his camp at Ferozepur, declaring that the Láhore Government had, without any provocation, or a declaration of war, commenced hostilities against the British; that a large Sikh army, which had invaded the British territories, had been repulsed and driven across the Sutlej; and that it had become necessary for the British Government to take measures for punishing this unprovoked aggression, and for preventing similar acts of treachery in future by the Government and army of the Panjáb. It called upon all natives of Hindostán who had taken service under the Láhore Government to quit their service at once, and place themselves under the orders of the Governor-General of India. They were ordered to repair to the British side of the Sutlej, and to report themselves to the British authorities. If they failed to comply with this order, they were to be considered as having forfeited all claim to British protection, and to be treated as traitors to their country and enemies of the British Government.

While the British were reduced to a state of inactivity for want of heavy guns, ammunition, and stores, which were daily expected from Delhi, the enemy, towards the middle of January, made a further effort upon the upper Sutlej. A strong body of the Sikhs under Ranjúr Singh, *Majithia* (brother of Sardar Lahná Singh), crossed the Sutlej at Phillour, with a train of seventy pieces of artillery, and threatened the frontier station of Ludhiáná, then weakly garrisoned. He was joined by the Rájá of Ládwá, a petty chief, dependent on the English, who had proved a traitor to them. Sir Harry Smith was detached to the relief of Ludhiáná, at the head of a body of cavalry and eighteen guns. The fort of Baddowál into which Ranjúr Singh had thrown a small garrison, lay on his route, but before the British General could reach it, it had been reinforced by ten thousand Sikh troops. Sir Harry Smith tried to avoid the unequal combat, and continued his march to Ludhiáná, inclining to remain at a distance from the position occupied by the Sikhs; but the latter were resolved on fighting, and, as soon as the British troops came in sight, opened fire on them with their artillery. A sharp skirmish ensued, terminating in the defeat of the British, a portion of their baggage, and a number of beasts of burden falling into the hands of the Sikhs. Indeed, had it not been for the opportune help rendered by the cavalry under Brigadier Cureton, which was advancing from Dharmkot, and the dashing charges made by it on the enemy, the loss on the side of the British would in all probability have been far more severe than it actually was. Sir Harry Smith now effected a communication with Ludhiáná, which was relieved. The skirmish of Baddowál took place on 21st January 1846, the loss on the side of the British being about sixty-nine killed,

Ranjúr Singh crosses the Sutlej and threatens Ludhiáná, January, 1846.

The skirmish of Baddowál, January 21st, 1846.

sixty-eight wounded, and seventy-seven missing. Of the last, several were taken prisoners to Láhore, among them being Mr. Barron, an Assistant Surgeon.

Ranjúr Singh had by this time been reinforced from the right bank of the Sutlej by 4,000 regular troops, twelve pieces of artillery and a large body of cavalry, and he advanced to Jagráon, with the apparent object of intercepting the British communications by that route. The Sikhs, elated with their success at Baddowál, boasted of driving the British off the field. Guláb Singh arrived at Láhore on 27th January, 1846, and was immediately hailed as minister and leader. Simultaneously with the Sikhs, Sir Harry Smith was reinforced by a brigade under Brigadier Wheeler, and a junction was effected with the Ludhiáná troops, which raised the forces under his command to 11,000 men, with thirty-two guns. With this force he advanced at daylight on the 28th to attack the enemy, who had taken up an entrenched position at Aliwál, with an army estimated at 15,000, with fifty-six guns. Immediately on the British troops coming in view, the enemy opened a fierce cannonade along his whole line, and a brilliant action ensued, the gleam of the bayonets and swords having a most imposing effect. There was no dust, and the sun shone brightly. The British line was compelled to halt for a few minutes under fire, till the brigades on the right were brought up, and a rapid charge being made, the village of Aliwál was carried; but the Sikhs stood their ground on the field, and fought with much resolution. They sustained frequent hand-to-hand encounters with the British cavalry. In one charge of infantry upon the 16th Lancers they threw away their muskets, and advanced with sword and shield against the lances of their opponents. Their most resolute resistance, however, proved unavailing, the British troops, storming position after position, and capturing battery after battery; and although the enemy made repeated attempts to rally behind Bundi, they were at length completely hemmed in, and fled precipitately across the Sutlej, hundreds of them being drowned in the stream, and hundreds more perishing under the fire from the British artillery, directed with great precision against the enemy's boats. The spectacle of numerous corpses floating on the river was most horrible. The whole of the enemy's guns were either captured or spiked, or else were sunk in the river, and all his munitions of war, stores of grain and nearly everything that had been brought into the field, fell into the hands of the victors. The Commander-in-Chief, describing the successful issue of this memorable battle, thus exultingly remarks in his official despatch, "I am unwont to praise, when praise is not merited, and I here must avowedly express my firm opinion and conviction, that no troops in any battle on record ever behaved more nobly." The loss sustained by the English in this battle was 151 killed, 413 wounded and 25 missing.

Guláb Singh arrives at Láhore and is hailed as minister.

The battle of Aliwál, January, 1846.

Defeat of the Sikhs.

Loss on the side of the British.

The immediate effect of the victory gained.

The immediate effect of the opportune defeat of the Sikhs at Aliwál was the evacuation by them of all the forts garrisoned on the British side of the Sutlej, and the cession to the British Government of all the territory on the left bank of that river. Guláb Singh, who, on the exclusion of Lál Singh, had undertaken the office of minister, instead of rallying the vanquished troops, reproached them for the folly of hoping to succeed against the conquerors of Hindostán. He opened negotiations with the Governor-General; but, when told that the first demand of the British Government antecedent to the acknowledgment of a Sikh sovereignty in Láhore, was the immediate disbandment of the Sikh army, he declared that he was helpless to effect it, as he could not deal with the turbulent soldiery.

Negotiations.

Meanwhile, the Sikhs were not wanting in energetic preparations for

The Sikh position at Sobráon.

renewing the contest. They continued to hold their position on the right bank of the Sutlej, while on the left they constructed formidable entrenchments in front of the main army of the British. A skilful Spanish officer, Huerba, had been employed by the Sikhs in constructing these works, together with a remarkably powerful *tête-de-pont* at the village of Sobráon, about twenty miles from Ferozepur. Below the fords of Hariki, they threw a spacious bridge across the Sutlej, the flanks of which rested on the river and which was covered by a ditch in front. These great works had been repeatedly reconnoitred by a party of observation, and were found to extend over two-and-a-half miles, protected by powerful batteries, so as to command the passage of the river. The strength of the Sikhs was estimated at 35,000 fighting men, with 67 heavy pieces of artillery, united by the bridge to a reserve on the opposite bank. This reserve consisted of a considerable camp and some artillery, flanking the field-works on the British side. It was resolved by the British to delay the attack on the Sikhs' entrenched position until the arrival of a formidable siege train and ammunition from Delhi. These reached the camp on the 7th and 8th of February, and on the latter date the brigades which had been detached for the relief of Ludhiáná, rejoined the main army. The total strength of the British army now was 15,000 men, of whom 5,000 were Europeans.

The Sikhs were much depressed in spirit by the British victory at Aliwál. The British troops were full of confidence and exulted in anticipations of triumph. There was a sad want of unity among the Sikh commanders, and it was rightly said, that, while the soldiers did everything, the leaders did nothing. "Hearts to dare and hands to execute," observes Captain Cunningham, "were numerous, but there was no mind to guide and animate the whole." There was a flush of joy on the faces of the British soldiers and sepoys as they beheld, in stately array, the huge elephants dragging the heavy ordnance, and the Transport Department bringing abundant ammunitions and war stores from Delhi. There was now nothing to hinder an advance, and the 10th of February, or only twelve days after the victory of Aliwál, was fixed for storming the strong works of the Sikhs. Early in the morning of that day, under cover of a thick fog, the dispositions of the army were effected unnoticed by the enemy. The English heavy ordnance was planted in masses opposite the most commanding points of the Sikh entrenchments commanded by Téj Singh. Lál Singh with his cavalry lay higher up the stream. The sinking spirits of the Sikhs were revived by the capture of a British post of observation, which had been left unprotected at night. That experienced old man, Shám Singh, of Attari, lamented the choice of the Sikhs in daring to wage war with their colossal neighbour, but the admonitions of the hoary-headed chief were not heeded. The brave old soldier thereupon announced to the desponding *Khálsá* his resolution to die in the first combat with the enemy, as a sacrifice to the spirit of their martial Guru and the sacred commonwealth.

The battle of Sobráon, February 10th, 1846.

The declaration of old Shám Singh, the Attari chief.

About seven o'clock in the morning, the gloomy fog that had loomed over the scene rolled away. The English batteries opened fire on the enemy's entrenchments, and, for upwards of three hours, a tremendous storm of iron hail poured incessantly upon the general mass of the enemy, spreading death and destruction on every side; but the Sikhs returned the fire steadily from behind their huge batteries of earth, planks and fascines. Clouds of sulphurous smoke hung over the battlefield, presenting a strange contrast to the bright steel of the arms and the polished brass accoutrements. The formidable calibre of the English guns, mortars and howitzers, aided by the rocket battery, began to tell severely on the enemy, but the latter continued to

Description of the battle-field.

work their heavy batteries, from which shot and shell fell hissing in the British lines. The thunder of full 120 pieces of ordnance, which were employed on both sides, produced an appalling roar, the firing being very distinctly heard at Ferozepur, twenty miles off. It soon became evident that the issue of the contest must be left to the arbitrament of musketry and the bayonet. At nine o'clock the left wing of the British army under Brigadier Stacey, supported by a troop of horse artillery, advanced steadily to the attack. They were within 300 yards of the heavy Sikh batteries, but, notwithstanding the scientific mode of their assault, and the regularity of their movements, so deadly a fire of cannon, musketry and swivels was kept up by the enemy that the greater part of the division was driven back. The battle raged with inconceivable fury, but at length the persevering gallantry of the British triumphed. The assailants, who had been repulsed, rallied and dashed forward with great pertinacity, led on by Sir Robert Dick, an old and fearless commander, and, though the Sikhs offered a stubborn resistance and fought desperately, the gallant British soldiers leaped the ditch with great steadiness, and, after a fierce hand-to-hand struggle, swarmed up and mounted the ramparts amidst loud shouts of victory. The hardy Sikhs fought bravely, keenly contesting every inch of ground, but fortune had forsaken the *Khálsá;* their bravest efforts to retrieve the day proved of no avail, and destruction awaited them on every side. The fire of the Sikhs first slackened, and then ceased entirely. Thus were the formidable entrenchments of Subraon, which had bid defiance to the British, at length carried. Many had thought the position of the enemy, with his tremendous artillery, next to impregnable, but all was over now. The traitor, Téj Singh, as before, had fled on the first assault, and sank a boat in the middle of the bridge communicating with the opposite bank of the river. But very different was the conduct of the hoary-headed Shám Singh, the faithful friend of the *Khálsá*, who, remembering his vow to his countrymen, dressed himself in a garment as white as his long snowy beard, galloped forward, and cheering on his ardent followers, led them to the attack, reviving their spirits with the promise of everlasting bliss made to the brave by their great Guru. Thus fighting, thus encouraging his comrades and awakening them to a sense of their duty, thus scorning death to the last, did this veteran soldier fall a martyr, and his memory is held in the greatest esteem by his countrymen to this day. Terrible was the carnage on that day. The trenches were filled with the dead and the dying, and the parapets were covered with blood from one end to the other. Although so hard pressed by the victors, no disciple of the Guru asked for quarter, but everywhere showed a bold front. The Sutlej had risen high in the night, and the bridge-of-boats constructed by the Sikhs was swept away. The routed host tried to swim to the right bank, but the British horse artillery, coming up at a gallop, poured on the flying masses a deadly shower of grape and shrapnel, till the current of the stream was crimsoned with blood and choked with corpses. The battle had begun in earnest at nine o'clock; and by eleven o'clock, or, within the short space of two hours, nearly one-third of the total forces brought by the Sikhs into the field had perished. Hundreds fell under the deadly storm of grape and canister, while hundreds upon hundreds were drowned in attempting the passage of the swollen stream. "Their awful slaughter, confusion and dismay," observed the Commander-in-Chief, "were such as would have excited compassion in the hearts of their generous conquerors, if the *Khálsá* troops had not in the early part of the action sullied their gallantry by slaughtering and barbarously mangling every wounded soldier whom, in the vicissitudes

The British storm the Sikh position.

Gallant conduct of Shám Singh.

Victory of the British.

of attack, the fortunes of war left at their mercy." Sir Hugh Gough was himself heard to say that he was sure the bodies of the enemy lay so thick, that he "could have walked over to the other bank of the river by stepping from one to the other."

Sixty-seven pieces of cannon, upwards of 200 camel-swivels (*zamburaks*) numerous standards and vast munitions of war, seized by the troops, were the trophies of the British victory. By order of the Commander-in-Chief a part of the vaunted bridge constructed by the *Khálsá* was burnt. The victory was decisive; but it was not purchased without severe loss to the victors: 320 British soldiers were slain in the battle-field, including Major-General Sir Robert Dick, who was mortally wounded close to the trenches, while cheering on his brave men. He had served with distinction in the Peninsular War and was present on the field of Waterloo.* The number of wounded on the side of the British was, 2,083. The loss of the Sikhs was immense, no less than 8,000 being killed, wounded or drowned. Amongst those wounded was Téj Singh, the Commander-in-Chief. By this victory the Sikh army was irretrievably broken and scattered, with no hopes of being again able to take up arms. It is remarkable that, in the neighbourhood of Sobraon, the scene of the great English victory, a bloodly battle was fought by Alexander the Great upwards of two thousand years before. Little did the British heroes, who were engaged in that campaign, dream, in their school-boy days, in a country so remotely situated from India, that they would ever tread ground so famous in the history of the Macedonian conqueror! Nor is it less interesting to reflect on the motives which guided the Macedonian monarch and the British Governor-General, each in his turn, to invade the famous country of the five rivers. The one was influenced mainly by an unconquerable lust for conquest, while the other drew his sword in the cause of humanity, in self-defence against an aggressive foe! The one invaded, half conquered, the country and hastily departed, leaving it in a state of perplexity and confusion. The other came as a deliverer from violence and rapine, completely conquered the country and retained the conquest, giving the conquered inhabitants the blessings of peace, civilization and freedom, the greatest and most valued gifts that nations have ever enjoyed under an enlightened and beneficent Government.

The victory decisive.

Losses on the side of the victors

And on that of the vanquished.

Comparison of events that occurred at the same spot more than two thousand years before.

On the very night of victory, the advanced brigades of the British army were pushed across the Sutlej opposite Ferozepur; no enemy was visible to check their progress. By the 12th, a bridge-of-boats had been thrown across the Sutlej by Major Abbot with the materials furnished by Lord Ellenborough from Sindh a year before, and on the 13th, the whole of the British force, excepting the heavy train, crossed the river. Kasúr, 32 miles from Láhore and 16 miles from the river, was occupied by the van of the British force, on the 11th, on which day also envoys arrived from Láhore. The fort of Kasúr was occupied the following day without opposition. The Governor-General joined the Commander-in-Chief's camp on the morning of the 14th. It was ascertained that the Sikhs had re-assembled, to the number

The British cross the Sutlej.

The capture of Kasúr 11th February, 1846.

*The monument of this brave soldier is situated in the Ferozepur churchyard, and is covered with sandstone slabs. The marble tablet has the following inscription:—

"Here lies in the hope of a joyful resurrection, Sir Robert Henry Dick, of Tully Mett, Perthshire, N. B., Major-General, Knight Commander of the order of the Bath and of Hanover; Knight of the Austrian Military order of Maria Theresa, and of the Russian order of Vladimir; Colonel of H. M.'s 73rd Regiment.

"For his country he fought and bled in Egypt, at Maida, throughout the Peninsula, at Waterloo and in India. For his valour and skill at Fuentes d'Honor, Busaco, Salamanca and Waterloo, he received two medals and two honorary clasps. Born on 29th July 1787 A.D. He fell in the moment of victory on the 10th of February 1846 A.D., while cheering on H. M.'s 80th Regiment, having led his division in the assault on the entrenched camp of the Sikhs at Sobraon. Honoured and beloved he lived, honoured and lamented he died."

of twenty thousand, in the direction of Amritsar, but that they were not in a position to offer battle to the victors. On the same day the Governor-General issued a proclamation, announcing, that the British army had crossed the Sutlej and entered the Panjáb, declaring that the occupation of the Panjáb by the British would not be relinquished until ample atonement had been made for the infraction of the treaty of 1809, and the unprovoked invasion of the British Provinces, full indemnity paid for all expenses incurred during the war, and such arrangements made for the future government of the Láhore territories as would give perfect security to the British Government against similar acts of perfidy and aggression in the future; that military operations against the Government and army of the Láhore State had been undertaken by the Government of India from no desire of territorial aggrandizement, though the measures necessary for providing indemnity and security would involve their retention of a portion of the Láhore territories, the extent of which would be determined by the conduct of the Darbár, and by considerations for the security of the British frontier; that the Government of India would, under any circumstances, annex to the British Provinces the districts, hill and plain, situated between the rivers Sutlej and Biás, the revenues thereof being appropriated as a part of the indemnity required from the Láhore State; that the Government of India, as frequently declared by it, had never desired to subvert the Sikh government in the Panjáb; that, although the conduct of the Darbár had been such as to justify the most severe and extreme measures of retribution, nevertheless the Governor-General was still willing that an opportunity should be given to the Darbár and to the chiefs to submit themselves to the authority of the British Government, and by a return to good faith, and the observance of prudent counsels, to enable the Governor-General to organize a Sikh government in the person of a descendant of its founder, the late Maharájá Ranjít Singh, the faithful ally of the British. The Governor-General therefore called upon all those chiefs who were well-wishers of the descendants of Ranjít Singh to act in concert with him, in carrying into effect such arrangements as would maintain a Sikh government at Láhore, capable of controlling its army and protecting its subjects, and based on principles that would provide for the future tranquillity of the Sikh States, secure the British frontier against a repetition of acts of aggression, and prove to the whole world the moderation and justice of the paramount power of India. The Proclamation concluded with the declaration that if the opportunity then afforded of rescuing the Sikh nation from military anarchy and misrule were neglected by the Darbár, and hostile opposition to the British army renewed, the Government of India would make such other arrangements for the future government of the Panjáb as the interests and security of the British power might render just and expedient.

Proclamation of the Governor-General.

The Rání and the Darbár now urged Rájá Guláb Singh, their chosen minister, to proceed immediately to the British camp to implore mercy in the name of the Darbár, and endeavour to enter into negotiations. All the chiefs, sirdars and *panchayats* of the army solemnly pledged themselves to abide by such terms as the rájá might arrange with the British Government, on the basis announced in the Proclamation, of recognising a Sikh government in Láhore. On the 15th, the Governor-General was visited at Kasúr by Rájá Guláb Singh, Dewán Díná Náth, Fakír Núr-ud-dín and the Barakzai chief, Sardar Sultán Muhammad Khan. His Excellency received the Rájá and his colleagues as the representatives of an offending government, the formalities observed at friendly meetings being omitted and the proffered *nazars* refused. The Governor-General explained to the Sikh deputation how

The Láhore Darbár sues for peace.

unprovoked and unwarrantable the conduct of the Darbár and Sikh army had been towards the British Government, and the moderation and forbearance which had throughout characterised the action of that Government. He commended the conduct of the Rájá in keeping aloof from the hostile and perfidious transactions of the Sikh Government, and expressed his readiness to mark his sense of that conduct. As for the conditions on which the British Government would be prepared to make an adjustment with the Láhore Darbár, His Excellency referred the chiefs to his Chief Secretary, Mr. Currie, and to his Agent for the affairs of Northern India, Major Lawrence. The conference of the chiefs with these officers took place at night, and the terms of peace having been explained to them, they, after some discussion, signed a document conceding all the demands of the British. These included the recognition of Dulíp Singh as sovereign of Láhore, but required the cession in full sovereignty of all the country between the Sutlej and the Biás rivers, the payment of a crore-and-a-half of rupees, or a million-and-a-half sterling, to the conquerors, as indemnity for the expenses of the war; the disbandment of the present Sikh army and its re-organisation under the system and regulations with regard to pay which existed in the time of Ranjít Singh; an arrangement for limiting the extent of the force which might be henceforth employed to be determined on in communication with the British Government; the surrender of all the guns that had been pointed against the British; the cession to the English of the entire regulation and control of both banks of the river Sutlej, and such other arrangements for settling the future boundaries of the Sikh State, and the organisation of its administration as might be determined on at Láhore. It was further agreed that the young Maharájá, with Bhái Ram Singh and other chiefs who had remained at Láhore, should forthwith repair to the camp of the Governor-General and surrender themselves to him, and that, after personally tendering his submission to the Governor-General, the Maharájá should accompany him in his march to Láhore with all the Sikh chiefs.

Treaty with the Sikh Government.

The young Maharájá pays his respects to the Governor-General in His Excellency's camp at Luliáni.

Luliáni, about midway between the Sutlej and Ráví, was fixed on as the place of meeting, but the Maharájá with his chiefs, hastening from Láhore, before the Governor-General could reach the place, expressed his readiness to wait on His Excellency at once. Sir Henry, however, deemed it right to see the Láhore sovereign on the appointed day, and, accordingly, in the afternoon of 18th February, the Maharájá paid his respects to His Excellency in his camp at Luliáni attended by Rájá Guláb Singh, Bhái Ram Singh, Dewán Díná Náth, Fakír Núr-ud-dín, and ten or twelve other chiefs. They were all dressed in plain attire and came with the mien of humiliation suited to their condition. The interview took place in the Darbár tent, Sir Hugh Gough and staff being present on the occasion. No salute was fired on the arrival of the Maharájá, nor were other formalities proper to such occasions observed, the Governor-General causing it to be explained that, as no formal submission had yet been tendered, the young Maharájá could not be received as a friendly prince. The Maharájá accordingly tendered his submission in person and begged for the pardon and clemency of the British Government on such terms as might be dictated by the Governor-General. Sir Henry stated that, the conditions of peace having been duly announced to the minister and the sardars accredited with him, and they having, in the name of the Maharájá, acquiesced in all the terms imposed by the British Government, it was unnecessary to re-open the discussion, the more so then, as the Maharájá was of too tender an age to take part in such proceedings. He considered it right to treat the Maharájá, from the moment he had thrown himself on the mercy of Government, as a prince restored to the favour of the British Government, which extended its clemency to a prince the descendant of one who for many long years had been the faithful friend and ally of the British Power, as the representative of the Sikh nation, selected by the chiefs and the people to be their ruler, on the condition that all the terms imposed by the British Government, and previously explained to His Highness's ministers and sardars, should be faithfully executed. Some observations having been then made regarding the bearing of the late Maharájá Ranjít Singh towards the English, and a hope expressed that the young Maharájá would follow in the footsteps of his father, the meeting broke up. It was further settled that the Maharájá should not return to the Rání at Láhore forthwith, but should remain with the camp of the Governor-General and accompany His Excellency to the Sikh capital.

Alarm in the cities of Láhore and Amritsar.

While friendly negotiations were going on between the Governor-General and the young Maharájá at Luliáni, the greatest alarm and consternation prevailed in the cities of Láhore and Amritsar. The calamities experienced by the people in past times on the approach of a victorious army from a foreign country and State were remembered, and it was gravely apprehended that the British conquerors would form no exception to the rule. On this the Governor-General issued a Proclamation on the 18th February, from his camp at Luliáni, to the chiefs, merchants, traders, rayats and other inhabitants of Láhore and Amritsar, informing them that Maharájá Dulíp Singh had, on that day, waited on His Excellency and expressed the contrition of himself and the Sikh Government for their late hostile proceedings; that the Governor-General had every hope that relations of friendship would speedily be re-established between the two Governments; and that the inhabitants of Láhore and Amritsar had nothing to fear from the British army. The Governor-General assured the inhabitants of the Panjáb, that if the Láhore Darbár acted in good faith, and no further hostile opposition was offered by the *Khálsá* army, they would be perfectly safe in person and property from any molestation by the British troops. They were therefore called upon to dismiss all apprehensions, and to resume their respective callings with all confidence.

The Governor-General's manifesto.

Arrangements made at Láhore for the reception of the British army.

In the meantime Rájá Guláb Singh gave positive orders that the troops which had encamped at Raiwind, 18 miles east of Láhore, after their defeat at Sobraon, should remain stationary. The number of these troops was estimated at from 14,000 to 20,000 horse and foot, with about 35 guns, and they were under Sardar Téj Singh and Rájá Lál Singh. At Láhore the Mahomedan and Najíb battalions of the British army were placed in the fort and at the gates of the city, with strict orders that no armed Sikh soldier should be permitted to enter.

Láhore reached and occupied, 20th February, 1846.

Having advanced by easy marches, the British army appeared in sight of the ancient city of Láhore on the morning of the 20th February, and by noon its tents were pitched on the plain of Mián Mír, whence the *Khálsá* army had so lately issued on their rash expedition, boasting that they would conquer the countries between the Jamna and the Ganges, and hoping to enrich themselves with the spoils of Delhi, Mathra and Benares. The Maharájá was conducted to the citadel, his residence, the same afternoon, escorted by two regiments of European cavalry, two regiments of native cavalry, and two troops of horse artillery, all under the command of Brigadier Cureton. His Highness was accompanied by Mr. Currie, Chief Secretary to Government, Major Lawrence, Political Agent, Mr. C. Hardinge, Private Secretary, and other functionaries. On reaching the gateway of the palace, the escort withdrew, and the Maharájá was conducted to the

The Maharájá is conducted to the palace.

inner door by Rájá Guláb Singh. Mr. Currie then announced to the Maharájá, his ministers and sardars that, by order of the Governor-General, the Maharájá, escorted by British troops, had been brought to his palace, which he had left with the view of tendering his submission to the British Government, and of placing himself, his capital and his country at the mercy of the Governor-General, and that His Excellency had thus restored him to his palace, as a mark of favour which he desired to show to His Highness out of consideration for the memory of the late Maharájá Ranjít Singh. As the Maharájá entered the palace, a salute of 21 guns was fired by the horse artillery.

No troops were posted within the precincts of the palace, the residence of the families of the late Maharájá Ranjít Singh, but British troops were posted at the gateway of the citadel. Formal possession was also taken by the troops of the Bádsháhí Masjid (Royal Mosque) and the Hazúrí Bágh. In order that the inhabitants of the city might have time to gain confidence and to understand that the English had no intention of plundering or harming them, strict orders were issued that no European, except of course officials sent on public business, was, until further orders, to go into or near the city.

Proclamation of 22nd February, 1846.

On the 22nd of February, the Governor-General issued a Proclamation reviewing the events that had occurred, and describing the victories gained by the British troops over the enemy; dwelling with proud satisfaction on the fact that, in the short period of sixty days, they had defeated the flower of the *Khálsá* army in four battles, and wrested from them 220 pieces of artillery; that of their great army only 14,000 now remained; and that he was now dictating a treaty, the conditions of which would tend to secure the British Provinces from a repetition of a similar outrage to that committed by the Sikhs by their unprovoked attack on the English.

A grand dinner at Láhore, 5th March, 1846.

On the 5th of March, the Governor-General gave a grand dinner at Láhore at which all the officers of the army, including the Commander-in-Chief and Sir Charles Napier, were present. Toasts and speeches followed, in which the officers bestowed warm eulogies on one another, and on the army at large, for the bravery displayed in the field. Every face flushed with joy, and at the conclusion of the entertainment the outburst of "hip, hip, hip hurrah" was deafening.

Signing of the treaty, 8th March, 1846.

On the 8th March, the treaty between the British Government and the Láhore Darbár was signed by the Commissioners, Mr. Currie and Major Lawrence, representing the former, and Rájá Lál Singh, Sardar Téj Singh, Bhái Ram Singh, Dewán Díná Náth and Fakír Núr-ud-dín the latter. On this occasion the Sikh chiefs produced, on behalf of the Maharájá, a letter addressed to Major Lawrence, acknowledging the consideration, kindness and generosity which the Governor-General had evinced to the Láhore Darbár, and expressing an earnest desire that, as the Government was endeavouring to make a satisfactory settlement of affairs, and as it was necessary that effectual measures should be taken to prevent the recurrence of any disturbances, some British regiments with artillery and officers should remain at Láhore for the protection of the State, the Maharájá and the inhabitants of the city.

The Governor-General's Darbár for the ratification of the treaty.

On the afternoon of the following day, the treaty of peace was ratified by the Governor-General in his State tent, in the presence of the young Maharájá, who was attended by Rájá Lál Singh, Rájá Guláb Singh, Sardar Téj Singh and about thirty other sardars and civil officers, the Commander-in-Chief and staff, the Governor of Sindh (Sir Charles Napier) and staff, the Generals of Divisions, the Brigadiers, the heads of each department, and all officers commanding corps, with one native officer from every British regiment being also present. The Governor-General was, on this occasion, seated on the throne, with the Maharájá on another throne on his right, and Prince Waldemar, a distinguished guest, on his left. The British officers were ranged on one side of the tent and the Sikh chiefs on the other. The Governor-General's band played at intervals outside. On the treaty being duly ratified and duplicates executed and exchanged, the Governor-General addressed the chief, his speech being translated, sentence by sentence, by the Chief Secretary, Mr. Currie. In this address Sir Henry repeated his desire that peace and friendship might always subsist between the two Governments, and that a Sikh government might be re-established, capable of controlling its army and of protecting its own subjects, whilst respecting the rights of its neighbours. He commended the policy of Ranjít Singh towards the British Government as the model for their future imitation; and strongly enforced on them the desirability of "wisdom in council and good faith in fulfilling agreements." He declared that the British Government had no objects of aggrandizement by hostilities, and did not desire in any way to interfere in their internal affairs; that he had reluctantly consented, at the earnest solicitation of the Darbár, to leave a British force in the garrison at Láhore until the Sikh army was re-organised in accordance with the treaty, but adding that in no case should it remain longer than the end of the year. "If," observed His Excellency, "friendly assistance now afforded by the British Government were wisely followed up by honest exertions, the State might prosper, and his co-operation should not be wanting; but if they neglected this opportunity, no aid on the part of the British Government could save the State."

His Excellency's address to the Mahárájás, Chiefs and Sardars.

At the close of this speech, the chiefs present expressed their deep gratitude to His Excellency for all the kindness he had shown to the young Maharájá and the valuable advice he had given, and expressed their readiness to follow that advice.

Terms of the treaty, 9th March, 1846.

By the terms of the treaty of peace, the Maharájá renounced all claim to, or connection with, the territories south of the Sutlej, and ceded to the Honourable East Indian Company, in perpetual sovereignty, the whole country, hill and plain, between the rivers Biás and Sutlej. The Láhore Government being unable to pay the one-and-a-half crores of rupees as an indemnity for the expenses of the war, or to give security satisfactory to the British Government for its eventual payment, the Maharájá ceded to the Honourable Company, as an equivalent for one crore, his possessions in the hill countries between the Biás and the Indus, including the provinces of Káshmír and Hazárá, engaging to pay the remaining fifty lakhs on or before the ratification of the treaty. He engaged to disband the mutinous troops of the Láhore army, and to re-organize the regular, or *Ain*, regiments of infantry upon the system, and according to the regulations as to pay and allowances, observed in the time of the late Maharájá Ranjít Singh. The regular army of the Láhore State was not to exceed twenty-five battalions of infantry, consisting of eight hundred bayonets each, and twelve thousand cavalry, and the guns, thirty-six in number, which had been pointed against the British troops on the right bank of the Sutlej, were to be surrendered. The control of the rivers Biás and Sutlej, with the continuation of the latter river, commonly called the Garráh and Panjnad, as far as the confluence of the Indus at Mithankot, and from Mithankot to the borders of Bíluchistán was, with respect to tolls, to rest with the British Government. Free passage was to be allowed to the British troops through Láhore territories, and no European or American was to be employed by the Láhore Government without the sanction of the British. In consideration of the services rendered by Rájá Guláb Singh, of Jammú, to the Láhore State towards procuring the restoration of the relations of amity between the Láhore and British Governments, the Maharájá agreed to recognise the independent sovereignty of Rájá Guláb Singh in such territories and districts in the hills as the British might make over to him. No changes were to be made in the frontiers of the Láhore State without the concurrence of the British Government, and all its disputes were to be referred to that Government, which was not to exercise any interference in the internal administration of the Láhore State.

The above treaty, consisting of sixteen articles, was agreed to at Láhore, on 9th March 1846, by Mr. Frederick Currie and Major H. M. Lawrence, on the part of the British Government, and by Bhái Ram Singh, Rájá Lál Singh, Sardar Téj Singh, Sardar Chattar Singh, Atariwálá, Sardar Ranjúr Singh, Majithia, Dewán Dína Náth and Fakír Núr-ud-dín, on the part of the Maharájá Dulíp Singh, and ratified, the same day, by the seal of the Right Honorable Sir Henry Hardinge, G.C.B., Governor-General, and of His Highness the Maharájá Dulíp Singh.

The Governor-General's visit to the Maharájá.

On the 10th March, Sir Henry paid a State visit to the Maharájá in his palace or Summan Burj, which was tastefully decorated for the occasion, the floor being carpeted with Káshmír shawls, and a large *shamiáná*, outside, lined with shawls, protecting the inside from the sun. Rich shawls were spread upon the ground of the quadrangle. The Sikh chiefs were all dressed in their richest attire, and the variety of costumes presented a most picturesque spectacle. Dewán Díná Náth, on behalf of the Maharájá and the chiefs assembled, read an address, warmly thanking the Governor-General for the kindness and generosity shown by him towards the Maharájá in maintaining the State of Láhore, for the excellent advice given by His Excellency the day before, and for his compliance with the solicitation of the chiefs to leave a garrison of British troops in Láhore. At the conclusion of the address the great diamond called *Kohinúr*, in size about a pigeon's egg, was exhibited to the company, and the ceremony concluded with the presentation of shawls and swords.

His Excellency agrees to leave a British force at Láhore.

On the 11th March, 1846, articles of agreement were concluded between the British Government and the Láhore Darbár by which the Governor-General engaged to leave at Láhore, till the close of the year 1846, a British force, for the purpose of protecting the person of the Maharájá and the inhabitants of the city of Láhore during the re-organisation of the Sikh army, the Darbár, on its part, agreeing to pay to the British Government all the extra expenses in regard to the said force, which might be incurred by the Government in consequence of their troops being employed away from their cantonments and in foreign territory.

Guláb Singh is invested with the title of Maharájá.

On the 15th of March, the Governor-General formally invested Guláb Singh with the title of Maharájá at Amritsar. The new ally, on receiving this recognition, stood up with folded hands and expressed his warmest gratitude to His Excellency for the honour done to him, adding that he regarded himself as his *zarkharid*, or gold-bought slave.

Treaty between Guláb Singh and the British Government, 16th March, 1846.

On the 16th March, a treaty was concluded at Amritsar between the British Government and Maharájá Guláb Singh, by which the former made over to him all the hilly and the mountainous country east of the Indus and west of the Rávi, including Chambá and excluding Láhoul, being part of the territory ceded by the Láhore State to the British Government, the Maharájá, in consideration of the transfer made to him, stipulating to pay to the British Government £1,000,000; the limits of the territories of the Maharájá were not to be changed without the concurrence of the British

...s made an in-...nt sovereign of ...ir.

Government. The Maharájá engaged never to retain the services of any British subject, or the subject of any European or American State, without the consent of the British Government, and acknowledged its supremacy, in token of which he was to present annually to the British Government, one horse, twelve perfect shawl goats, and three pairs of Káshmír shawls.

Thus was the independence of the Sikhs as a nation broken, the monarchy formed by the genius of Ranjít Singh reduced to insignificance, and a contest brought to a close which, in its origin and results, has few parallels in history. Major, afterwards Sir Henry, Lawrence who had accompanied to Kábul the Sikh contingent attached to Pollock's forces, and served as British representative in the court of Katmandu in Nepál, was left in charge of affairs at Láhore. The captured Sikh guns, 250 in number, with their equipments, were sent to Calcutta under a guard of British troops, and were objects of interest to the inhabitants as they passed through the various stations on their way to their destination, where they were publicly received with all military honours.

Major Henry Lawrance is left in charge of affairs at Láhore.

The captured Sikh guns.

For the tact, foresight, and judgment which characterised this memorable campaign the greatest praise is due to Sir Henry Hardinge, who combined, in so uncommon a degree, the qualities of a statesman and a warrior. The previous increase of the army and the conveyance of the pontoon bridge to Ferozepur show that he was not unprepared for the contest, but that, while he omitted no measures of wise precaution necessary for the protection of the British frontier, he offered no provocation for the war, which commenced on the side of the enemy. To a mind just and magnanimous he added the utmost sagacity and wisdom, and his toleration and political honesty had their just reward in the great triumphs won by him over the enemy. In England the accounts of the British conquest were received with great enthusiasm. Both houses of Parliament passed votes of thanks to the army, and Sir Henry Hardinge and the Commander-in-Chief were raised to the peerage. Sir Henry Smith was created a baronet and the honour of the Order of the Bath was profusely bestowed on officers who had taken part in the campaign, while twelve months' batta was conferred on the army by order of the Government of India.

The services of Sir Henry Hardinge as Commander-in-Chief.

After the conclusion of the treaty, Rání Jindán was recognised as regent of the State, with Rájá Lál Singh as executive minister, the advice and direction of Major Lawrence being available on all occasions. The choice of the Rání, in selecting her own paramour for the office of minister, was another great suicidal blow struck at the life of the *Khálsá* kingdom. The perfidy of Lál Singh soon became manifest. He instigated Sheikh Imám-ud-dín, the Sikh Governor of Káshmír, to refuse to surrender that country to Guláb Singh according to the treaty by which the British had agreed to recognise him as its independent sovereign, the country having been ceded to the British Government by the Láhore Darbár. Several actions were fought between the troops of the insurgent Sheikh and those of Guláb Singh, and the Sheikh did not surrender until Major Lawrence himself went to Káshmír at the head of troops which had lately been fighting against the British forces. Lál Singh was tried in open Darbár on the 3rd and 4th of December, 1846, in a tent opposite the citadel, the Court of Inquiry consisting of Major-General Littler, Lieutenant-Colonel Lawrence, Lieutenant-Colonel Goldie, Mr. Currie and Mr. J. Lawrence. The accused was defended by Dewán Díná Náth, but when the charge was read out to him, he said nothing in his own defence. Sheikh Imám-ud-dín produced the very letters, in the handwriting of Puran Chand, the State *Parwáná Navis* or clerk, signed by Lál Singh, which he had privately sent to him enjoining him on no account to deliver up the

Rání Jindán acts as regent with Lál Singh as wazir.

The rebellion of Sheikh Imám-ud-dín in Káshmír.

He surrenders to the British.

Trial of Lál Singh, December, 1846.

territory to Guláb Singh. The guilt of Lál Singh was clearly proved. The decision of the Court was communicated to the sardars, who were requested to withdraw, and Lál Singh was left with the British officers. He was deposed from the office of minister, and was informed that he was not permited to enter the palace. He was escorted to his own house by Mr. Edwards, Assistant to Colonel Lawrence, surrounded by a guard, and was shortly after banished from Láhore to Benares on pension.

He is banished to Benares.

The Government of Láhore was now placed in the hands of Dewán Díná Náth, Sardar Téj Singh, Sardar Sher Singh, of Atari, and Fakír Núr-ud-dín, Major Lawrence, as usual, representing British interests in the Darbár. Before the time came for the withdrawal of the British troops from Láhore, according to the treaty of 11th March, 1846, the Sikh chiefs saw the necessity of asking the British Government for an extension of the period for which they had been located there, as they found it impossible to carry on the administration without a continuance of British assistance and direction. They accordingly solicited the Government to continue British protection until the Maharájá should attain his majority. Lord Hardinge, after fully considering the situation, gave a very reluctant assent to the proposed measure, and on 16th December, 1846, a new treaty was executed and signed by fifty-two principal chiefs of the Panjáb, by which the British were made virtual masters of the country. A convention was entered into for the administration of the Láhore Government by a Council of Regency at Láhore, consisting of eight Sikh chiefs, *viz.*, Dewán Díná Náth, Sardar Téj Singh, Sardar Sher Singh, of Atari, Fakír Núr-ud-dín, Sardar Ranjodh Singh, Bhái Nidhán Singh, Sardar Attar Singh, Kallianwállá, and Sardar Shamsher Singh, Sindhianwálá, to be directed by the British Resident. The Sikh Government, on its part, agreed to pay to the British Government twenty-two lakhs of rupees per annum for the maintenance of 10,000 British troops in the Panjáb, the arrangement to last till 4th September, 1854, on which date the minority of Dulíp Singh would end, and the Government be handed over to him. Colonel Lawrence was appointed British Resident at Láhore.

Subsidiary treaty, 16th December, 1846.

The Láhore Council of Regency.

The treaty was ratified in a public Darbár held at Láhore on the 26th December, the Commander-in-Chief being present. Lord Hardinge, seated on a throne, delivered an address explaining the object of the British Government to be the welfare of that of Láhore. Among the chiefs who were present was the famous Sheikh Imám-ud-dín. The speech was interpreted to the chiefs by Mr. Currie, and the Darbár closed with a profusion of *nazars* consisting of jewels, shawls, guns, etc.

The treaty ratified, 26th December, 1846.

CHAPTER III.

THE SECOND SIKH WAR.

REVOLT OF DEWÁN MÚL RÁJ.

The Sikhs dissatisfied.

THE expulsion of Lál Singh from the Panjáb was far from pleasing to Jindán, the queen mother of Dulíp Singh, a most artful and profligate woman, but the Sikh chieftains soon repented of their treaty of the 16th of December, 1846, and came to look on it with dismay; for though beaten, they were as yet unsubdued; their monarchy and their army of 80,000 disciplined troops, together with their park of artillery consisting of about 400 guns, the result of Ranjít Singh's organization, still remaining to them, while by the terms of the treaty their country was shorn of its most fertile provinces. The Court of Láhore was as dissolute in politics as in morals, and encouraged faithlessness to the British. Major Henry Lawrence, who had been left at Láhore with 10,000 British troops, laboured hard to keep order, but ill-health compelled him to leave the Panjáb in November, 1847, and his place was occupied for a time by his brother, Sir John, afterwards Lord Lawrence, and ultimately conferred on Sir Frederick Currie, formerly Chief Secretary to Government, who assumed charge on the 6th of April, 1848.

Múl Ráj, the Dewán of Multán.

Múl Ráj, the Dewán of Multán, a practised disciple of deceit and cunning, had succeeded his father Sáwan Múl in 1844. The province of Multán, as held by Múl Ráj in the spring of 1848, extended from the district of Kachi on the left bank of the Indus, on the north, to the eastern frontier of Sindh, on the south, and from Chicháwatni, on the Rávi and Tibbi, on the Sutlej, on the east, to the Sulaimán Mountains, Trans-Indus, on the west.* Sáwan Múl had strengthened the fort of Multán, by digging around it a broad and deep ditch faced with masonry, and throwing up a glacis, while within the ditch, was a formidable wall, 30 feet high. He aspired at sovereign power, and his eldest son, Múl Ráj, was reared up amid dreams of future independence. On Sáwan Múl's death, Múl Ráj was confirmed in the Governorship of Multán, on condition of paying thirty lakhs of rupees as *nazráná*, or a succession fee to the Darbár, and the enormous sum of ninety lakhs of rupees, hoarded by the old Dewán during a long period of 23 years, was divided by the new Governor with his brothers. Rájá Lál Singh, on the re-establishment of the Láhore Government, sent a force against Múl Ráj to secure the payment of the *nazráná*; but the troops were defeated near Jhang. The British Resident at Láhore intervened, and it was arranged that the district of Jhang should be removed from the jurisdiction of Múl Ráj, that the succession fee should be reduced to twenty lakhs and the revenue of the districts still left under his charge raised in amount by more than one-third. As observed by Sir John Lawrence, Múl Ráj "faithfully fulfilled his pecuniary engagements up to the time of his rebellion," but he proved himself grasping and avaricious, and rendered himself obnoxious to the trading and agricultural classes, who complained bitterly of his exactions. The old Dewán's popularity in the province which he governed was proverbial. Múl Ráj, who had inherited none of his liberal views or conciliatory qualities, deliberately broke up many of his wise institutions. Indeed, his character was sufficiently known to the people before the death of his father, and a proverb is still current in the district of Jhang, having reference to the Sikh times, to the effect that while Multán was blessed with *Sáwan* (or rains) Leia with *Karam* (kindness), Jhang was cursed with *Mulá* (an insect which eats the roots of the corn).†

The fortifications of Multán.

He renders himself obnoxious to the people.

The Darbár interferes.

The Darbár interfered with Múl Ráj's coercive measures at Multán, as they could not be tolerated so long as State affairs were under the supervision of a British Resident. Múl Ráj asked leave to come to Láhore, and, in his interview with the Resident, Sir John Lawrence, expressed his desire

* Edwardes.

† The old dewán, to relieve himself of some of the cares of Government, and accustom his sons to business, put the province of Jhang (then included in Multán) under charge of Múl Ráj and Leia under his second son Karam Narayan; he himself remaining in Multán.—*A Year on the Panjáb Frontier*, by Sir Herbert Edwardes.

to resign the charge of the Multán province, but his resignation was not accepted. On his return to Multán, he repeated his wish to resign his office into the hands of any authorised person sent to receive the trust. On this Sardar Kahn Singh was nominated governor of Multán, and two British officers were selected by Sir Frederick Currie to accompany the new Governor to his province. They were Mr. P. A. Vans-Agnew, a young Bengal civilian, who was Assistant to the Resident at Láhore, and was now charged with the principal duties, and Lieutenant W. A. Anderson, of the 1st Bombay European Fusiliers. Sir Frederick described the former as a "man of much ability, energy and judgment, with considerable experience in administrative duties;" and the latter as an "excellent oriental scholar, who was for some time Deputy Collector in Sindh under Sir Charles Napier, and has travelled through the whole of the Multán districts." Mr. Vans-Agnew was known to be most popular with the natives of the country, towards whom he carried his kindness almost to excess, and Lieutenant Anderson is described as an officer of "unusual achievements and of peculiarly conciliatory manners."

Múl Ráj resigns his office.

Sardar Kahn Singh appointed his successor.

Mr. Vans-Agnew and Lieutenant Anderson are sent to Multán.

They reach Multán.

To avoid the heat, the officers went by river, while Kahn Singh, with an escort of 600 Gurkhás, 700 cavalry and a troop of horse artillery, with six guns, went by land. They all met in the neighbourhood of Multán, on the 18th of April, and encamped at the Idgáh, a fortified enclosure, within cannon shot of the fort. Múl Ráj paid two visits to the British officers in the course of the 18th, and behaved with apparent candour and sincerity, and it was arranged that the fort should be made over to the new Governor on the following day.

Múl Ráj delivers up the keys of the fort to them.

Early in the morning of the 19th, Mr. Vans-Agnew and Lieutenant Anderson, with Sardar Kahn Singh, went to the fort, accompanied by Múl Ráj, who delivered up the keys to the British officers. Two companies of Gurkhás were placed in charge of the fort, and sentries were planted at various points. The former garrison having been mustered, their fears were allayed, and promise of service was made to them. All arrangements being complete, the British officers, who were unarmed, suspecting nothing, set out to return to the Idgáh, Múl Ráj riding by their side. As the cavalcade reached the gate, two of Múl Ráj's soldiers appeared standing on the bridge over the ditch. One of them, named Amir Chand, gazing at the Englishmen for a moment, struck Mr. Vans-Agnew with a spear and knocked him off his horse. Mr. Agnew resisted, whereon the ruffian, drawing his sword, gave him two severe cuts, but was himself knocked into the ditch by a horseman of the escort. Múl Ráj, either afraid of his own life, or indifferent to what had happened, instantly galloped off to his garden-house at the Am Khas, about a mile from the Idgáh. The wounded officer was with difficulty rescued from the mob, and carried back on an elephant to the Idgáh by Kahn Singh and Rang Ram, Múl Ráj's brother-in-law. Múl Ráj's personal sowars, pursuing Lieutenant Anderson, wounded him desperately and left him for dead. He was afterwards found by some of his Gurkhá soldiers, and carried into the Idgáh on a litter.

The British Officers assaulted and wounded.

Mr. Vans-Agnew had the courage, during the day, to write a report of the occurrence to the Resident at Láhore and letters to General Cortlandt at Derá Ismail Khan, and to Lieutenant Edwardes at Bannú, informing them of his peril. He also sent a letter to Múl Ráj, summoning him to his presence to account for the treachery, and asking him to seize the guilty parties and deliver them up, expressing at the same time a generous disbelief in the Dewán's complicity. Mr. Agnew, no doubt, displayed great composure of mind and bravery at this trying moment. A reply was

Mr. Vans-Agnew summons Múl Ráj to his presence.

received from Múl Ráj, stating that all the garrison was in rebellion, that he could neither give up the guilty nor come himself, and that the British officers had better see to their own safety. He was urged by the soldiery to declare his independence.

Evasive reply of Múl Ráj.

The dewán went to his mother and asked her advice. "Act like a man," said the widow of Sáwan Mal, "take counsel from your amírs (nobles) and come not to women for advice." Múl Ráj, having, thereupon, convened a meeting of his chiefs made up his mind for war. The Mahomedans set their seals to an oath of allegiance taken on the *Qurán*, the Hindus swore by the water of the Ganges, and the Sikhs by the holy *Granth*, to fight to the last. A war-bracelet was fastened by the Sikhs on the wrist of Múl Ráj himself. This was on 20th April, 1848. The men of the escort were now bribed, and the troops, horse, foot and artillery, all deserted and went over to Múl Ráj. Only Sardar Kahn Singh, with eight or ten faithful horsemen, and the domestic servants of the British officers, remained with them to the last. They formed a group around the beds of the wounded Englishmen, beneath the lofty centre dome of the hall.

He declares war against the British, 20th April, 1848.

That same evening a mob from the city, led by a company of Múl Ráj's *Mazbi* Sikhs, rushed into the Idgáh with loud cries. Sardar Kahn Singh begged Mr. Agnew's permission to wave a sheet and sue for mercy. Strength had forsaken Mr. Agnew, through loss of blood, but not the pride of an Englishman. His heart failed him not. Scorning the idea of asking for mercy, he replied: "The time for mercy has gone; let none be asked for. They can kill us two if they like, but we are not the last of the English; thousands of Englishmen will come down here, when we are gone and annihilate Múl Ráj and his soldiers and his fort." With frantic shouts the crowds now rushed in. Kahn Singh was made a prisoner. The two Englishmen, wounded and despairing of their lives, were bidding farewell to each other. Mr. Agnew was sitting by the bedside of his countryman, who had been badly wounded and had not strength enough to move, holding his hand, and both had resigned themselves to their fate. On came the furious mob, clamouring, shouting and scoffing, and pushing the servants aside with the butts of their muskets. Gudar Singh, a Mazhabi, then rushed on Mr. Agnew, with a drawn sword, and, after heaping insults on him, gave him two sword cuts on the neck and, with a third, cut off his head, after which another soldier discharged his musket into the lifeless body. Lieutenant Anderson was immediately despatched with sword cuts, and the two bodies, being then dragged outside, were slashed and insulted and left out in the open all night. Gudar Singh, the murderer, took Mr. Agnew's head to Múl Ráj, who rewarded him with an elephant, money, and the horse his victim had ridden. The head was thrown into the lap of Sardar Kahn Singh, now Mul Ráj's prisoner, and he was tauntingly told to take the head of the youth he had brought down to govern Multán. The sardar burst into tears, but Múl Ráj reproached him for his sympathy with the foreigners. The bodies of the murdered Englishmen were then laid in a hasty grave near the Idgáh, under the orders of the dewán; but they were not safe even there. Twice were they torn up by the people of Multán and stripped of the clothes in which they had been buried. A third time they were buried, and a guard placed over the tomb till the matter was forgotten.

Gallant conduct of the wounded British officers.

Kahn Singh made prisoner.

A touching scene.

The murder of Mr. Vans-Agnew and Lieutenant Anderson.

Their remains are insulted.

The news of this atrocity roused the strongest indignation, and the British Resident at Láhore, Sir Frederick Currie, immediately put troops under orders for Multán, but waited for the final orders of the Commander-in-Chief. The hottest period of the year had arrived, and it was thought expedient to defer the operations to a more convenient season. The proceed-

Action taken by the British Resident at Láhore.

ings of the Láhore Darbár were dilatory, and when the Resident told the Sikh Government that the rebellion of Múl Ráj must be put down, the chiefs professed their inability to undertake the task.

Lieutenant Edwardes marches from Bannú.

Lieutenant, afterwards Sir Herbert, Edwardes, raised a body of Mahomedan troops at Bannú, and with them crossed the Indus. He was supported by General Cortlandt, at the head of 4,000 troops, and by their efforts the rebellion on the right bank of the Indus was suppressed. The first action fought with the rebellious troops was at Dera Gházi Khan, on May 21st.

The rebellion of troops at Dera Ghází Khan.

Longa Mal, the Governor, hearing of the approach of General Cortlandt, who had been reinforced by the Suraj Mukhi regiment from Bannú, strengthened his position at Dera Gházi Khan, and was joined by Jalál Khan, Laghári, a powerful Tomandár of the Dera Gházi Khan district. His bitter enemy was one Kourá Khan, an equally powerful Tomandár of the Khosa tribe, who, fifteen days before, had offered his submission to Lieutenant Edwardes.

Kourá Khan the Tomandár Chief.

His son, Gholám Hyder Khan.

That officer conferred a rich *khilat* on Ghulám Hyder Khan, son of Kourá Khan, and made him over to General Cortlandt, who was then encamped at Daera Din Panah. This young Bíluch chief, having obtained the General's permission, marched in advance to Dera Gházi Khan at the head of his father's clan, determined to do or die. At Dera Ghází Khan he was joined by his father, Kourá Khan, and the two now prepared for a grand struggle with their hereditary enemies, the Lagháris, who had mustered in large numbers around Longa Mal.

The battle of Dera Gházi Khan.

The rebel governor had been joined by his uncle Chetan Mal, governor of Sangarh and Mangrota, and came out of the city with his whole strength and with one gun and five *zamburaks*. The Khosas drew nearer, in the last watch of the night, and were repulsed more than once by the Lagharis, who fought desperately.

Heroism displayed by Kourá Khan.

As morning dawned, old Kourá Khan, dismounting from his horse, drew his sword and called upon his men to follow him on foot if they were true Khosas, and to leave their horses for the enemy to fly on. His clan obeyed and made a furious assault on the enemy. The battle lasted three hours, when victory declared for the noble Khosas and the enemy was overpowered. Chetan Mal, with one of his nephews, fell on the field, Longa Mal was taken prisoner and the gun and five *zamburaks* were captured. The rebels left forty dead on the field and the Khosas lost fifteen killed, including Muhammad Khan, nephew of Kourá Khan. By the defeat of his troops at Dera Ghází Khan, Múl Ráj lost all his Trans-Indus dependencies.

Defeat of the rebel troops.

The reward of Kourá Khan.

For their conspicuous service and their gallantry in the field, the Láhore Darbár conferred on Kourá Khan and his son the coveted title of "*Alijah*," or of "high dignity." Lord Dalhousie subsequently showed his appreciation of the Khan's services by conferring on him a money pension, the perpetual grant of a garden in his native place, and the confirmation of his jágírs.

The battle of Kaneri, 18th June, 1848.

The next battle of importance was fought on the 18th of June, at Kaneri, on the banks of the Chináb. The troops of Múl Ráj, under Rang Ram, his General, numbered 7,000 strong, including Pathan cavalry, regular regiments, and the Gurkhás who had deserted Mr. Agnew and Lieutenant Anderson at Multán, and ten guns.

The contingent of the Nawáb of Baháwalpúr.

The British army under Lieutenant Edwardes consisted of a contingent of 5,000 men from the Nawáb of Baháwalpur and about an equal number of troops raised by Lieutenant Edwardes from among the frontier Mahomedan tribes, including Subhán Khan's regiment of regular infantry and General Cortlandt's Suraj Mukhi regiment, ten guns and 25 *zamburaks*. It was a pitched battle, and lasted nine hours, from seven o'clock in the morning till half-past 4 P.M. The hostile artillery commenced firing grape, and were steadily replied to by

Cortlandt's well trained artillery. Two of the enemy's guns were quickly silenced and the rest slackened their fire. Lieutenant Edwardes then ordered Subhán Khan's regiment to attack. Subhán Khan, a stout heavy soldier, himself led on his men, leaping over bushes with great dexterity. The men carried two more guns, which lay dismounted on the ground at the point of the bayonet. The whole of the British force now advanced towards the enemy, who rallied, and the artillery on both sides re-opened with full vigour. At half-past three o'clock, Lieutenant Edwardes, calling to the front General Cortlandt's well disciplined Suraj Mukhis and Subhán Khan's regiment of Musalmáns, took command of them himself and ordered them to charge the rebels. The order was at once obeyed, the troops rushing on the enemy with the most desperate and irresistible valour. A hand-to-hand fight ensued in which Subhán Khan, leading his men, carried one of the enemy's guns at the point of the bayonet. Confusion now fell upon the ranks of the enemy and, after a momentary struggle for the mastery, the rebels were put to flight. Rang Ram, their General, had fled long before, and now the rebels were hotly pursued by the victorious British troops. The camp of the enemy at Nimar, four *kos* from the Chináb, and all their ammunition, tents and stores, fell into the hands of the victors. Of the ten guns brought by the rebels into the field, eight were captured. On the side of the English, 247 men were killed or wounded, while the enemy left between 500 and 600 dead upon the field, their total loss, including the wounded, being about 1,000. By the battle of Kanerí the whole country between the Indus and Chináb, and nearly all that between the Chináb and Sutlej was lost to Múl Ráj.

Victory of Lieutenant Edwardes.

Losses on both sides.

Submission of the Killadár of Shujábád.

Early on the morning of the 20th June, the Killadár of Shujábád tendered his submission to Lieutenant Edwardes, and the chowdris and bankers, having presented themselves, begged for kind treatment, which the British officer readily promised. The troops of the Nawáb of Baháwalpur were now sent to take peaceful possession of the fort.

Bhái Maharáj Singh, the Sikh Guru.

In the meantime, Múl Ráj was joined at Multán by a Sikh Guru of great venerability, named Bhái Maharáj Singh, the disciple and successor of Bhái Bír Singh, who, it will be remembered, fell fighting at the Sutlej on the side of Attar Singh, Sindhianwálá, the uncle of Shamsher Singh, in the time of Rájá Hírá Singh. The presence of the Sikh pontiff in the midst of the Hindu fanatics at Multán, and his solemn blessings and prayers for victory, inspired them with confidence; and the wild cry of "*Dharm!*" was loud among all ranks of the rebel army. Múl Ráj personally was entirely under the influence of his religious adviser and private secretary, Mishar Kuljas, a high caste Brahmin, who was to him what Jállá Pandit had been to Hírá Singh, at Láhore six years before. On the morning of the 28th June, 1848, Lieutenant Edwardes, with the allied armies, advanced from Adiwálá Bágh to Suraj Kund, three *kos* from Multán, and, on the 30th he was joined by Sheikh Imám-ud-dín's division of 4,000 troops. The Sikh Guru, having consulted the stars with great ceremony, informed Múl Ráj that the 1st of July would be an auspicious day for a fight with the English, when he should command the army in person, and his army would be invincible. Inspired with this solemn assurance, the dewán resolved to fight, and, suddenly recalling his troops from the Suráj Kund bridge, where the attack had been expected, marched them to the other side of Wálí Muhammad's canal and emerged on a plain, a *kos* and a half in advance of the British camp. This was at noon on the 1st of July. The object of this manœuvre was to prevent the junction of Lieutenant Edwardes' force with that of Nawáb Baháwal Khan, and to attack the latter while moving to cover the passage of Lieutenant Edwardes' force over the Chináb.

Kuljas, the preceptor of Múl Ráj.

Múl Ráj's recourse to divination.

The battle of Saddasám, July 1st, 1848.

No sooner were the British officers informed of the approach of the enemy, than they ordered the men to fall in and form a line. The army then advanced in the following order:—The Baháwalpur force on the right, commanded by Lieutenant Lake; Sheikh Imám-ud-dín's troops on the left; Subhán Khan's Musalmán regiment and the Suraj Mukhis, with the guns, in the centre, commanded by General Cortlandt, the Pathan infantry levies on the left centre, flanked by Pathán cavalry, commanded by Lieutenant Edwardes. The enemy had in the field a force of 11,000 men and 10 guns, while the British officers had under them a force of not less than 18,600, with 22 guns. The enemy selected his ground at the village of Saddasám. Lieutenant Lake occupied a high mound with his Dáudputras, and from this commanding position poured a heavy fire on the enemy's left, which was as promptly returned. The centre and left of the English columns then advanced and silenced the enemy's fire, whereon the fight became general. The Sikhs stood their ground with much obstinacy, and fought with great

Victory of the British.

courage, but found it impossible to sustain the superior fire of the English artillery, and were compelled to retreat in irretrievable disorder. Múl Ráj, who commanded in person, was thrown from his elephant, owing to a shot striking the *howdah*, and, mounting his horse, fled precipitately in the direction of the city.

Losses.

The total number of killed and wounded on the side of the English was 281. Among the killed were some Pathans of note—Rahím Khan, Khudakka, a relation of the Nawáb of Dera, Hussan Khan, Musazie, and Fatteh Khan, of Khyssore. Captain Macpherson, in the service of the Nawáb of Baháwalpur, also fell at the head of his regiment. Several of the Pathan chiefs distinguished themselves in this battle by their reckless bravery, among them being Ghulám Sarwar Khan, Khakwáni, of Multán, a skilful swordsman and an intrepid soldier, styled by Lieutenant Edwardes the "pride of the border," who killed several Sikhs with his own hand, and Faujdár Khan, Alizai, the Adjutant-General, who were both wounded. The enemy suffered very heavy loss. The battle of Saddasám had the result of shutting Múl Ráj up in the city and fortress of Multán, whence he was unable to emerge except to resist the siege by the British force.

Rejoicings consequent on the victory.

On receipt of the news of the victory of Saddasám at Láhore, the Darbár caused a royal salute to be fired from the fort, and similar salutes were fired from the forts of Govindgarh, Attak and the cantonments of Hazárá, Pesháwar, Bannú and Dera Ismail Khan.

Sher Singh, Attáriwálá, marches towards Multán.

Meanwhile, Múl Ráj was not idle. With the assistance of the zealous citizens of Multán, he constructed an enormous rampart of mud outside the ditch which surrounded the city, and he recruited his army with disaffected Sikhs from Láhore. At this period Rájá Sher Singh, son of Sardar Chattar Singh, Attariwálá, the Sikh governor of Hazárá, advanced towards Multán with an army of 5,000 men, ten horse artillery guns and two mortars. In command of this army the Rájá had two colleagues, Sardar Shám Singh, Sindhianwálá, and Sardar Attar Singh, Kalewálá, who had charge of the cavalry, while the Rájá had special charge of the infantry and a troop of horse artillery. Various intrigues were set on foot by Múl Ráj to induce the army of the Rájá to join his standard, but they proved unavailing. The armies under Lieutenants Edwardes and Lake were at this time encamped at Tibbi, two *kos* from Multán, while the division of Sher Singh was in their rear. In this position the armies remained till the arrival, on the 18th of August, of

He is followed by General Whish.

General Whish, with a battering train and an army of 8,000 men of all arms.

The siege of Multán.

General Whish, reached Multán on the 4th of September and found it invested by Lieutenant Edwardes with 7,700 infantry and 4,000 cavalry besides Nawáb Baháwal Khan's army of 5,700 infantry and 1,900 cavalry, under Lieutenant Lake, and a Sikh army of 900 infantry and 3,800 cavalry, under Rájá Shér Singh. Thus, the total strength of the army on the side of the British was 32,000 men, with 45 guns and 4 mortars. To encounter these confederate armies, Múl Ráj had a force of only about 12,000 men, with 54 heavy guns and 4 mortars; but he had rendered the citadel of Multán one of the strongest forts in India, and it was not inappropriately styled a second Bhartpur. The siege operations commenced on the 7th of September, and an attempt was made on the 9th to take a village and garden near the walls, which had been strongly entrenched, but, after a spirited charge, and a stout resistance on the part of the enemy, the British column was driven back with considerable loss. On the morning of the 12th, another attack was made on the enemy's position in the suburbs of the town. Múl Raj's troops fought well, but they suffered heavily in a *dharmsálá* which they had strongly fortified. Within the walls of this enclosure 300 men were slaughtered. The British troops, by this success, were enabled to advance within battering distance of the city walls, and it was expected that the city would be reduced in a few days; but an event now happened which disappointed these expectations.

The insurrection of Sardar Chattar Singh at Hazárá.

Sardar Chattar Singh, Atariwálá, whose daughter was to be married to Dulíp Singh, was the Sikh governor of the Hazárá province, under the control of Major James Abbot, his counsellor and adviser. Early in August, the Sikh troops under him rebelled and murdered Colonel Canora, an American in the employ of the Sikh Government. The insurgent Sikhs then marched in the direction of Attak with the object of seizing the fort, which commands the passage across the river, but Lieutenant Nicholson, acting under the orders of Major George Lawrence, the British Assistant at Peshávar, succeeded in reaching that place before them, and the fort was saved from falling into their hands. Rájá Shér Singh, whose conduct had long been suspicious, at last cast in his lot with his father, and, early on the morning of 14th September, putting himself at the head of his troops, he ordered the *Dharam-ká-Dhosá*, or religious drum, to be beaten in the name of the *Khálsá* and joined the rebels. It was declared that "this war was not a war between Múl Ráj and the Darbár, but a strife of religion, and he who wished to go to heaven would die a martyr in defence of his faith." "*Wáh, guru ji ki Fateh!*" was the unanimous cry of the *Khálsá*, who bodily went over to the enemy. Shér Singh's two colleagues, Sardar Attar Singh and Sardar Shamsher Singh, abandoned him and escaped to Lieutenant Edwardes.

Shér Singh deserts and joins the rebels.

The arrogance of the Patháns.

Of the 20,000 men under General Whish, 13,000 were irregulars, composed chiefly of Patháns, whose false Oriental pride would not allow them to dig the ground for the benefit of others. Thus the effective force under General Whish was reduced to 5,800 British infantry and sappers. According to the laws of military science, a besieging army ought to be three times the number of the garrison besieged. Múl Ráj had 15,000 excellent soldiers after he had been joined by Shér Singh's force. Colonel Cheape, the Chief Engineer, who had witnessed the siege of Gwalior, expressed it as his opinion that the fort of Multán was too strong to be assaulted by the force at the disposal of the British General. The regular troops were diminished and a portion of Major Edwardes' troops had been posted at various stations to prevent their occupation by the rebels. Three thousand men had been despatched to protect the Bengal depôt at Shujábád and the Bombay depôt at Uch, and men had been detached to keep open the road between Multán and the Sutlej, and to watch the ferries on the right bank of the Chináb, to prevent recruits and supplies from reaching the garrison of Multán. Sheikh Imám-ud-dín was sent with a force of upwards of two thousand men and two guns against the rebels at Jhang under Naráin Singh, one of Múl Ráj's most active officers, and the Sheikh drove them out of Jhang and pursued them to Chiniot, where they subsequently surrendered to General Whish. All these circumstances combined led to a council of war, at which it was resolved to suspend, for the present, the siege of Multán. Accordingly, the British troops were recalled from the trenches and took up a position on the plains of Suraj Kund.

The operations of the siege are suspended.

The intrigues of Ráni Jindán.

Meanwhile, the Rání had been most active in her intrigues. In May a plot of considerable extent, inspired by her, was detected at Láhore, having for its object the defection of the native troops, and two of the ringleaders, General Kahn Singh and Bhái Ganga Ram, the confidential agent of the Rání, were executed. Being involved in several dangerous schemes, she was, on the 20th of August, induced to quit Láhore, and was, by the advice of the Darbár, and with the consent of the Governor-General, removed to Shekhúpura, twenty miles from the capital. She continued to embarrass the government by her intrigues, and, her presence in the Panjáb being found incompatible with the proper administration of the country, she was taken under a strong escort to Ferozepur and thence removed to Benares. Even in this exile she was not quiet. She sent an agent to Calcutta to engage the services of an attorney to plead her cause, and she contrived to send messages to native States in the Panjáb and westward of Delhi to induce the chiefs to subvert the power of the British in those countries. The whole of the Panjáb became a scene of covert disaffection. Both Major Abbot, the Political Officer of Hazárá, and Lieutenant Nicholson, in charge of the fortress at Attack, urgently required reinforcements to maintain their ground. In the beginning of November, Peshávar revolted. Major George Lawrence, the Political Officer with his lady and Lieutenant Bowie, escaped to Kohát, where the treacherous Afghán governor gave them up to Chattar Singh, who treated them with consideration and kept them as hostages. At Bannú, Colonel Holmes, a European officer of the Sikh army, was murdered by his own troops. A short time after, Malik Fatteh Khan, Tiwáná, who had been sent by Major Edwardes as Governor of Bannú, was besieged by the Sikh army in the fort of Dalípgarh. The rebels called on the Malik to surrender. Fatteh Khan, taking his sword and shield, ordered the gate of the fort to be thrown open. He then walked out and cried loudly to the mutineers, "I am Malik Fatteh Khan, Tiwáná! Do not shoot me like a dog, but if there are any two of you who are equal to a man, come on!" With frantic yells, the Sikh soldiery rushed upon him, calling out, "You are he who murdered our Prince, Peshorá Singh, and we will murder you." He was instantly pierced through by a hundred bullets, and fell. "Nobly, fatally," observes Sir Herbert Edwardes, "he had redeemed his pledge." "In the war of 1848-49," continues Sir Herbert, "I met with many instances of attachment and gratitude which raised my estimate of the natives of India, but none more truly touching than the death of Malik Fatteh Khan, Tiwáná, on the threshold of the fort he promised to defend."

She is removed to Benares.

The whole of the Panjáb teems with disaffection.

The insurrection at Bannú.

The spirited conduct of Fatteh Khan, Tiwáná.

He is slain.

Dost Muhammad, to whom Múl Ráj had sent his envoys, was raising a large army at Kábul, and had sent a part of it in advance to Jallálábád, with the view of eventually seizing Peshávar. He had also sent one of his sons, at the head of a force, to occupy Bannú. The chiefs of Kandahar had opened negotiations with Múl Ráj, while the wily chief of Káshmír, on whom the Panjáb conspirators had fixed their eyes for help, had the astuteness to keep on good terms with both parties. About the end of September, Múl Ráj suspecting Rájá Shér Singh of complicity with the British, the

Dost Muhammad sends troops to Jallálábád.

The duplicity of Guláb Singh.

Rájá left the Dewán in disgust, and formed a junction with his father near Wazírábád, where their united forces amounted to about 30,000 men. The Rájá had already issued inflammatory manifestoes and seditious letters to the Sikh community, reminding them that the *Feringís* had treated the Maharání, the widow of the great Maharájá Ranjít Singh, and the mother of the people, with undue violence, that the kingdom had lost its former repute, and calling on all the servants of the *Khálsá Ji*, of the holy Guru and of the Maharájá to sacrifice their lives and to murder all the *Feringís*, in return for which service, he said, they would receive the blessings of the holy Guru and be recompensed with higher rank and a distribution of rewards. His route, in marching to join his father, was marked by the plundering of villages, the defilement of mosques, the murder of priests, the oppression of merchants and other excesses characteristic of Asiatic warfare. Thus, the whole Panjáb was in a flame, and the seeds of dissension so deeply sown, sprung up vigorously in various quarters, and brought about circumstances which led to the final struggle for the mastery in the Panjáb. Dost Muhammad's dream of occupying Peshawar, or Bannú, was not destined to be realized. An effectual check was put on his troops by Lieutenant Taylor, while the expedition to Harrand from Kandahar had to be abandoned, as the assembled armies suffered severely from fever and ultimately dispersed. The siege of Multán was resumed on the 27th of December.

Shér Singh effects a junction with his father at Wazírábád.

His seditious manifestoes.

The siege of Múltán resumed, 27th December, 1848.

The Bombay division, commanded by Brigadier Dundas, reached Multán on the 21st of that month. Múl Ráj had by this time further strengthened the fortifications of the town and suburbs. The citizens, in their zeal for the "holy war," tore down their doors and shutters to be converted into traverses for the ramparts. But the forces under Múl Ráj were much reduced, and numbers deserted him to join the standard of Chattar Singh on the Jhelum, which locality was now becoming the focus of rebellion. Múl Ráj suffered from want of money and began to coin his store of gold. He had still at his command 12,000 fighting men within the fort. On the arrival of the Commander-in-Chief, hostilities were commenced, the forces under his personal command numbering upwards of 20,000 men, with nearly a hundred pieces of artillery.

Desertions on the side of Múl Ráj.

Sir Henry Lawrence, who had gone to England on sick leave, returned to Multán in time to witness the commencement of the second siege. He had not fully recovered his health; but his strong sense of duty outweighed all personal considerations, and, as Sir Frederick Currie's term of office had not yet expired, his services were placed at the disposal of Lord Gough in connection with the impending operations. On the 27th of December, one British column was sent to deliver an attack on the suburbs, which included Múl Ráj's own garden-house, Am Khas, while three other columns were ordered to make diversions, so as to distract the enemy. The irregular forces commenced the diversion at noon, and by 4 P.M. the whole line of the suburbs, including the tomb of Sáwan Mal, the blue mosque of the Saint of Tabrez, and the cantonments of the Am Khas, was in possession of the British. Brigadier Dundas captured, occupied and crowned with guns several important posts, while the Bombay Fusiliers, charging the enemy at the point of the bayonet, drove them towards the city, and the Bombay Native Rifles actually entered one of the city gates.

Sir Henry Lawrence returns from England.

Several important posts in the suburbs captured.

It was now resolved to take the city first and to attack the fort from the city, which was considered to involve less difficulty to the besiegers than if the attack were made on it from any exposed point outside. The irregulars under Major Edwardes and Lieutenant Lake were ordered to main-

Attack on the city.

tain possession of the long line of suburbs that had been seized, while the rest of the British force was left to prosecute the siege.

The bravery of a volunteer.

On the 29th, a body of the rebels, 2,000 strong, sallied out from the Delhi gate of the city, but after an hour and a half of hard fighting, were driven back within the walls. Great praise was won in this action by a volunteer named MacMahon, who cut down the leader of the Sikh infantry, a powerful man, dividing his head with one blow.

The magazine in the fort blown up.

On the 30th, the principal magazine in the fort, in which was stored 5,000 maunds of powder, was blown up by a shell from a mortar, destroying the great mosque, the lofty tower of which had long been the pride of the ancient town. Five hundred of the garrison perished in this explosion.

On the 2nd of January, two breaches were reported practicable, one in the Khuní Burj (or Bloody Bastion) of the city, and the other at the Delhi gate, and storming parties advanced and crossed the intervening ditch, but, to their surprise, found the city wall in front, which the hollow had hitherto concealed, to be about 30 feet in height, unbreached and totally impracticable. The division at this part of the city wall was therefore compelled to retire, and repaired to the Bloody Bastion, to assist the other division engaged there. The breach was easily surmounted, but on reaching the summit it was found that it was retrenched inside. A most bloody struggle ensued. The columns passed the trenches, pushed on to the ramparts, and planted the English flag on the very crest of the breach. The insurgents having been driven into holes and corners, the English became masters of the town. Terrible had been the carnage during the siege and frightful the effect of the British ordnance. The battered town of Multán, on the 3rd of January, 1849, presented the appearance of a vessel wrecked and broken by a tremendous storm which had driven it to an inhospitable shore. The streets were strewn with slain Sikhs, whose long locks, matted with gore, and beards, blown about by the wind, gave the dead a demoniacal appearance. Not a house or wall had escaped the effects of the English shells. All had been scorched and blackened by the bombardment. Múl Ráj retired to the citadel with more than 3,000 picked men; the rest all dispersed and fled. In vain did the Dewán make an endeavour to rally them. They were dispirited, and nothing was left for the garrison but to sally or surrender. Múl Ráj was now reduced to the last extremity. A constant storm of shell had reduced the interior of the fortress to a wreck. All the flour having been blown up in the explosion of the grand mosque, every soldier of the garrison was obliged to grind the wheat for his own food. Múl Ráj's chief advisers urgently pressed him to surrender, and he promised either to do this or take poison. Múl Ráj made overtures for peace, and, in one of his *arzis* to Major-General Whish, he said: "If you grant me my life and protection to my women, I surrender; otherwise it is better to die with honour than live with disgrace." "You are," said the rebel Dewán, "a sea of compassion; if you forgive me, I am fortunate; if you do not, I meet my fate with contentment." To this the British General replied: "I have neither authority to give your life, nor to take it, except in open war. The Governor-General can only do this. And as to your women, the British Government wars with men, not with women."

Capture of the city of Multan, 3rd January, 1849.

Horrible sight in the town.

Múl Ráj retires to the citadel.

The fort is stormed.

Múl Ráj sues for peace.

Múl Ráj yields unconditionally.

On the morning of the 22nd of January, the murderer of Agnew and Anderson gave himself up to justice. He came out of the citadel gorgeously attired in silks and riding a fine Arab steed. He was kept a prisoner in the tent of the Chief Engineer, and, the fortress being occupied by the British troops, the flag of Great Britain was seen waving in a fresh breeze from the highest bastion of the famous citadel. The garrison, between 3,000 and 4,000 strong, at the same time surrendered, laying down their

The citadel is surrendered.

arms to the columns under Brigadiers Hervy and Capon, which had been in orders for the assault of the citadel.

Thus the second siege of Multán was brought to a close, and the supremacy of British power completely vindicated. The loss of the British was 210 killed and 982 wounded.

The bodies of Mr. Vans-Agnew and Lieutenant Anderson were removed from their neglected grave, where they lay side by side, and, wrapped in Káshmír shawls, were carried by the soldiers of the 1st Bombay Fusiliers to their appointed resting-place on the summit of the citadel, where they were interred with military honours. The bodies of the faithful Kahn Singh and his son were found locked in each other's arms under the ruins of their prison.

The bodies of Agnew and Anderson are found and decently interred.

Múl Ráj was subsequently brought to Láhore, and tried by a military court, composed of two officers and a civilian, who found him guilty, but recommended him to mercy, as the "victim of circumstances." Lord Dalhousie accepted the recommendation, and Múl Ráj was banished beyond the seas, but the sentence was commuted to imprisonment for life, and not long after he died. Thus ended the life of Dewán Múl Ráj, the treacherous host, who murdered his two innocent English guests in the Idgáh; the despised and dastardly foe, who broke his faith with his own Government.

The trial of Múl Ráj.

He is found guilty and sentenced to imprisonment for life.

His subsequent death.

Lord Dalhousie bestowed a yearly pension of a lakh of rupees on Nawáb Baháwal Khan, for assisting the British with his whole military resources, and a lakh for every month his army kept the field.

The reward of the Nawáb of Baháwalpúr.

CHAPTER IV.

THE SECOND SIKH WAR (*concluded*).

LAST STRUGGLE OF THE SIKHS FOR INDEPENDENCE.

THE Multán rebellion was suppressed, but it served only as the prelude to a great national outbreak, and the whole of the Panjáb was seething with disaffection. The great body of the *Khálsá* army and the Sikh population had for their avowed object the total expulsion of the British from the Panjáb, and the restoration of *Khálsá* supremacy. The general belief of the sardars was that, as the British had abandoned Kábul, so they would give up the Panjáb. The theatre of the war which was about to begin, lay between the Chináb and the Indus. Shér Singh having joined the standard of his rebel father, Chattar Singh, fixed his head-quarters at Ramnagar, on the left bank of the Chináb, about half way between the source of the stream and its junction with the Indus. He now decided upon a separate line of action, and, with that view, occupied with a brigade an island situated in the middle of the river, at a bend opposite Ramnagar, and strengthened it by batteries commanding the ford. He issued the most inflammatory proclamations, calling on the *Khálsá* troops to assemble, and fight the foreigners for the independence of their country. A compact was formed between Chattar Singh and Dost Muhammad, whereby it was agreed that Peshávar, the wild aim of the Dost's life, should be delivered to him, if he aided the Sikhs against the British. Major, afterwards Sir, George Lawrence, after being taken to Kohát by the rebels, as previously stated, was brought back to Peshávar by Chattar Singh, and there confined. The whole of the Darbár troops at Peshávar, 8,000 strong, being treacher-

The Sikhs aim at expelling the British from the Panjáb.

Compact between Chattar Singh and Dost Muhammad.

Major Lawrence put in confinement.

ously seduced by Sultán Muhammad, brother of Dost Muhammad, joined Chattar Singh. Dost Muhammad, having proclaimed himself sovereign of Peshâwar, marched to the Indus, at the head of an Afghán force, and threatened Attak, which was lost to the Darbár on his approach. Lieutenant Herbert, in charge of Attak, made a spirited defence, but was compelled to surrender to Chattar Singh, who made him a prisoner.

The Sikh and Afghan alliance against the English.

Dost Muhammad despatched one of his sons, at the head of Durráni troops, to the camp of Shér Singh, and thus, for the first time, the Sikhs and the Afgháns, those old hereditary enemies, were arrayed against the British.

Lord Gough at the head of the British army.

The rendezvous of the armies at Ferozepur took place during October 1848. On 21st November, Lord Gough joined the grand army at Sahâran.

The action of Ramnagar.

He found Shér Singh encamped at Ramnagar, on the right bank of the Chinâb, at the head of 15,000 men, and a powerful force of artillery, with a strong force also on the left bank, covered by batteries. Brigadiers Campbell and Cureton, at the head of an infantry brigade and a cavalry division, were sent to drive the enemy across the river and capture their guns on the left bank. A forward movement was made, and small parties of the Sikhs were driven in. The British horse artillery was, however, rendered helpless by the deep sand, and, the enemy having brought their heavy guns to play on the left bank, the British gunners were obliged to retire from the conflict. The enemy, seeing this, sent a body of 4,000 Sikh cavalry across the ford. On reaching the left bank, they were repeatedly charged by the British cavalry, but the irregular nature of the ground and the clouds of dust deceived the cavalrymen. It was chiefly an artillery battle which arose from the flank movement of General Thackwell, and the attack was directed against a strongly fortified position under most disadvantageous circumstances.

Colonels Havelock and Cureton killed.

Lieutenant-Colonel William Havelock, of the 14th Light Dragoons, brother of the hero who afterwards won immortal renown in India, fell in this engagement. He had been a hero in many a Peninsular fight. A dashing soldier and a determined warrior, the desperate charges made by him swept the bank of the river, in a few minutes, of its swarthy occupants; but the last charge saw him in the midst of the enemy. With his left arm half severed from his body, he was dealing frantic blows with his sword with his right hand, when he was cut off. His last words were, "Follow me." A death such as this was worthy of a British soldier. General Cureton, of the Lancers, also fell in this battle, and many officers were mortally wounded.

Several desperate charges made.

The enemy having been driven from the left bank of the river, it was now resolved to attack his position from the right flank, and on the 2nd of December, Major-General Sir Joseph Thackwell crossed the Chinâb at Wizirábád, 24 miles higher up, at the head of 8,000 troops. He was subsequently joined by other troops, and various indecisive skirmishes took place. On 28th December, Lord Gough crossed the Chinâb with his army, and taking up a position on the right bank, opened a heavy cannonade on the island and batteries of Ramnagar. Brigadier Godby, with a brigade of infantry, crossed the river higher up and opened communications with General Thackwell. General Sir Walter Gilbert was moved across with a brigade of cavalry.

Sher Singh abandons his position at Ramnagar,

These manœuvres led Shér Singh to abandon his entrenchments at Ramnagar. At the head of a considerable force he marched to attack General Thackwell, whose forces he met at Sadullápúr, but, without attempting to close with him, he executed a rapid retreat to the Jhelum, carrying with him all his guns and equipment.

And retires to Rasúl on the Jhelum.

Shér Singh, having thus moved away from the Chinâb with impunity, took up his position at the village of Rasúl, a post of singular strength on the Jhelum, and Lord Gough, hearing that Chattar Singh was moving forward to join Shér Singh, resolved to force a battle with the latter before the junction could be effected. Shér Singh's troops, under one hundred chieftains of various ranks, now numbered forty thousand, all, or nearly all, drilled by English and French officers under Ranjít Singh and his successors, and in a high state of discipline, besides 62 guns of the heaviest calibre ever brought into the field. The manner in which Shér Singh, avoiding a collision with General Thackwell's division, had cut his passage clear to the Jhelum, and the judicious selection made by him of his position, evinced, in no small degree, his skill as a general. That position was protected on the left by a low ridge of hills, intersected with ravines, and by the main stream of the Jhelum, the right being posted in different villages, enclosed by a thick jungle, which served as a natural bulwark, entrenchments being thrown up at Chilianwálá, about three miles to the south of the ridge. The dispositions of their army were not understood, owing to natural difficulties, and sufficient time had not been obtained to reconnoitre the enemy's position. On the 13th, the British army reached the village of Loliánwálá, and, after some fighting, Lord Gough dislodged a strong picket of the enemy from an elevated mound. Ascending the mound, the Commander-in-Chief and staff obtained a full view of the surrounding country and beheld the *Khálsá* army forming themselves in majestic battle array along the furrowed hills. Their batteries were chiefly masked by bushes, and their compact infantry and well-marshalled cavalry were arranged and proportioned with scientific exactness. A part of the Sikh horse artillery, having advanced, opened fire on the British position, on which the Commander-in-Chief gave orders for immediate action. The British artillery advanced to an open space in front of the village, and the heavy English guns opened fire on the enemy's artillery. The British cannonade was vigorously replied to by the enemy's field batteries, and the British army, acting under the orders of the Commander-in-Chief, were drawn up in order of battle. The British brigades opened a sharp fire on the enemy's centre, where his guns were principally placed, but the enemy poured in a galling cross-fire of grape and musketry with such rapidity and exactness, that it proved most destructive to the British, 459 men with 23 officers being almost immediately killed or disabled. Brigadier-General Colin Campbell, afterwards Lord Clyde, Sir Walter Gilbert, Brigadier Mountain, who distinguished himself in China under Lord Gough, and Brigadier Pennycuick, each, in his turn, made the most desperate charges, and the timely arrival of a field battery and artillery reserves enabled the British to recover two out of the six guns captured by the enemy. The battle raged with great fury until night, and, when it was dark, the fire on both sides ceased. The Sikhs who had begun the engagement, gradually withdrew, leaving the scene of the contest in possession of the British, who, on that account, claimed the victory, though the Sikhs fired a salute of 21 guns in honour of what they conceived to be a victory won by them, and a similar salute was fired at Attak, the capital of Chattar Singh. The loss on the side of the English was heavy; 602 men killed and 1,651 wounded; three regiments lost their colours, and four horse artillery guns were taken. There were also many desertions of the Sikh soldiers under the command of Lord Gough. The Sikhs lost many a brave and old officer and soldier. They left a number of guns on the field, of which the English brought twelve into their camp after the close of the battle; the rest were recovered by the Sikhs under cover of night. The Sikhs barbarously murdered the helpless wounded, whom the British were unable to remove from the field before the close of the contest. This was the last great attempt of the army of Ranjít

Sikh entrenchments at Chilianwálá.

Bloody battle of Chilianwálá, January 13th, 1849.

The darkness of night causes a cessation of hostilities.

Heavy losses.

Singh to recover independence. They fought bravely and desperately, and the advantage of the bloody battle that had been fought was decidedly in their favour, for they continued to occupy, for a month, strategical positions from which the British were unable to dislodge them.

Public opinion respecting the carnage of Chilianwálá.

The carnage of Chilianwálá was the subject of severe criticism by the British public in England, whose ears had been so long wont to hear brilliant accounts of Indian victories. There was an outburst of popular indignation, and the generalship of the veteran Commander became the subject of open attack. There was a demand for the recall of Lord Gough, and the announcement of Lord John Russell, in the British Parliament, that Sir Charles J. Napier, the conqueror of the Bíluchís, would be appointed to the command of the Panjáb armies, was received with loud cheers. Before, however, Sir Charles Napier landed in India, Lord Gough had retrieved the honour of the British arms by winning the battle of Gujrát, which inflicted a deadly blow on the aspirations of the *Khálsá*.

The advance of General Whish to Jhelum.

After the suppression of the Multán rebellion, General Whish, at the head of twelve thousand men, moved up to reinforce the Commander-in-Chief at Jhelum. Guláb Singh, the newly-made Maharájá of Káshmír, sent ten thousand troops to the scene of war, but the wily chief, with his characteristic shrewdness, left his benefactors, who had so recently been the arbiters of his fate, to deal with their opponents as best they could, reserving to himself the opportunity of joining whichever side should prove victorious in the coming grand contest. Shér Singh, hearing of the approach of General Whish, moved towards Wazírábád, with the object of crossing the Chináb and marching on Láhore, but a strong detachment of British troops had been sent to Wazírábád to check his retreat in that direction, and a timely occupation of the fords of the Chináb by these troops prevented the Sikhs from crossing the river. Thus foiled, Shér Singh took up his position at Gujrát, where he was joined by his father, Chattar Singh, at the head of all his forces, and by Akram Khan, a son of Dost Muhammad Khan, with three thousand Afgháns. The concentrated forces, according to Lord Gough's estimate, numbered 61,500, with 61 pieces of ordnance. They encircled the town of Gujrát, strongly situated between the Jhelum and Chináb, but nearer to the latter. The British army under Lord Gough, numbering 25,000 men and one hundred guns, many of heavy calibre (and drawn by elephants, now used for the first time during the two campaigns) being reinforced by the Bombay column, under General Whish, began the attack.

Shér Singh retreats to Gujrát.

He is joined by an Afghán force.

The battle of Gujrát, 21st February, 1849.

Coolly and deliberately did the veteran British Commander fight out the great battle before him. He had to encounter the most formidable army that had yet appeared in the East to challenge the British arms; but he fought the battle, as a great battle ought to be fought, on the strictest principles of military science. In the early dawn of the 21st of February, Lord Gough began the action by opening a terrible cannonade on the Sikhs. The enemy replied to the fire with great steadiness, but, after two hours and a half of the severest contest of artillery, in which great havoc was done in his ranks and many of his guns and tumbrils were smashed along the lines, the fire of the Sikhs was nearly silenced, and, the fight becoming general, the British infantry made a brilliant charge. The Sikhs were dislodged from their entrenched positions and driven back. They rallied, and the combined Sikh and Afghán Horse, making a brisk attack on the British columns, were gallantly met by the famous Sindh Horse under Captain Malcolm and put to flight. The infantry flanks then, wheeling round the village of Gujrát, inflicted terrible losses on the Sikhs. By noon, the enemy were retreating in the utmost disorder, leaving their camp, baggage, stores

Lord Gough's great victory.

and ammunition to the victors. They were relentlessly pursued by the British cavalry and artillery, and a most fearful vengeance was exacted. The Afgháns, deserting the fallen fortunes of their *Khálsá* allies, retreated to the Khaibar, having lost more than half their number on the field of action or in the course of their flight. The loss on the side of the victorious British was small, being five officers killed and twenty-four wounded, with ninety-two privates killed and 682 wounded. The British captured 53 of the enemy's guns, with many standards. The loss of the Sikhs amounted to several thousands; and their great army was dispersed. Major Lawrence, with his wife and children, who were prisoners in the hands of the Sikhs, were sent back to the British camp, where they were welcomed with enthusiastic shouts. Rájá Shér Singh, with the wreck of his army, some 16,000 men, and all his guns, repaired to the British camp, at the great Buddhist monument of Manakyálá, and surrendered unconditionally, on the 12th of March, to General Gilbert. The spectacle on that memorable day was grand, awful and touching. The British lion had effectually humbled the power of the *Khálsá* and the last deadly blow had been inflicted on the empire of Ranjít Singh. All the aspirations, misguided though they were, of the valiant Sikh race were humbled to the dust, the remnant of the military power of the great *Khálsá* being broken, never again to unite. Foremost among the assembled chiefs was Rájá Shér Singh, who set the example of delivering up his sword to the British General. Then followed the other chiefs, who, one by one, laid down their swords at the feet of the General. Then came the Sikh soldiers, those brave warriors who had so long measured their arms with the victorious British. In gloomy silence did they advance, one after another, casting their arms on the heaps that received them. Some delivered up their arms with tears in their eyes, others with sighs and downcast looks. The soldiers, in performing this ceremony, had to pass through the lines of two native infantry regiments that had been appointed for the duty. The vanquished soldiers were graciously permitted to retain their horses, and received a rupee each to enable them to return to their homes. Fifty-one more guns were delivered up; the submission of the Sikhs to the British power was complete. In the emphatic words of Lord Dalhousie, "the victory gained was memorable, alike from the greatness of the occasion and from the brilliant and decisive issue of the encounter." The completeness of the victory "equalled the highest hopes entertained."

The Afgháns retreat to the Khaibar.

Major Lawrence is set at liberty.

Sher Singh surrenders, 12th March, 1849.

The Sikh chiefs and soldiers lay down their arms.

Generous treatment of the vanquished soldiers by the victors.

CHAPTER V.

ANNEXATION OF THE PANJÁB.

THE fate of the Panjáb could not long remain in suspense after the crowning victory at Gujrát. The British Government of India had throughout acted with the utmost forbearance and moderation in their relations with the Sikh Darbár, and the policy of the Governor-General had, from the outset, been wholly unaggressive, and entirely free from any taint of greed or ambition. He sincerely desired to see a strong government established in the Panjáb, able to control its army and protect its subjects, and willing to maintain friendly relations with the paramount Power in India. But the sinking fortunes of the Sikhs prevented that noble policy from being appreciated, and every endeavour made to give it effect

The policy of the Government of India wholly unaggressive, &c.

No middle course open now.

proved unavailing. It was therefore clear that there was no middle course open to meet the impending crisis, and, that the only measure, at once just and expedient, that could be adopted, was the annexation of the country to the British Empire. The boy-king had been already restored to power and placed under the control of a Council of Regency, selected from amongst the Sikh sardars themselves. That was the utmost which a considerate and humane Government could, in justice to the country, do for the declining Sikh State. It was hoped that by a return to good faith, and the observance of prudent councils, the Sikh Darbár and chiefs would be able to organise a Sikh Government under the young prince, but the experiment proved a failure after a fair trial, and all the good wishes of the Indian Government for the Láhore Darbár were destined to meet with disappointment. All indulgence had been shown, and everything possible done to preserve the independence of the country, but the representatives of the country would not allow its independence to be preserved. They had invited the struggle which had ended in their ruin, by their own acts of treachery and deceit. The consequences of a breach of faith on the part of the Sikhs had already been foreshadowed. "If this opportunity," said Lord Hardinge in his manifesto at the close of the first Sikh War, "of rescuing the Sikh nation from military anarchy and misrule be neglected, and hostile opposition to the British army be renewed, the Government of India will make such other arrangements for the future Government of the Panjáb as the interests and security of the British Power may render just and expedient." It was abundantly manifest that a repetition of the indulgence shown would have been inconsistent with sound policy and the true interests of the people, who had been impoverished by years of anarchy and misrule, and would have proved injurious to British prestige in the East. Few will, therefore, be disposed to question the wisdom and justice of the policy adopted by the Governor-General, in declaring that thenceforth the Panjáb was to form an integral part of the British dominions in India.

Lord Hardinge's warning had proved unavailing.

The Panjáb annexed to the British possessions of India, March, 1849.

The Darbár held at Láhore.

A Darbár was held at Láhore on the 29th of March, 1849, at which the following Proclamation of the Governor-General, announcing the annexation of the Panjáb, was read aloud in the presence of the young Maharájá and the remainder of the Sikh chiefs who had refrained from acts of open hostility towards the English:—

The Proclamation of 21st March, 1849.

For many years during the time of Maharájá Ranjit Singh, peace and friendship prevailed between the British nation and the Sikhs. When Ranjit Singh was dead and his wisdom no longer guided the Councils of the State, the sardars and the *Khálsá* army, without provocation and without cause, suddenly invaded the British territories. Their army was again and again defeated. They were driven with slaughter and in shame from the country they had invaded, and, at the gates of Láhore, the Maharájá Dulip Singh tendered to the Governor-General the submission of himself and his chiefs, and solicited the clemency of the British Government. The Governor-General extended the clemency of his Government to the State of Láhore, he generously spared the kingdom which he had acquired a just right to subvert, and, the Maharájá having been replaced on the throne, treaties of friendship were formed between the States. The British have faithfully kept their word, and have scrupulously observed every obligation which the treaties imposed upon them. But the Sikh people and their chiefs have, on their part, grossly and faithlessly violated the promises by which they were bound. Of their annual tribute no portion whatever has at any time been paid, and large loans advanced to them by the Government of India have never been paid. The control of the British Government to which they voluntarily submitted themselves, has been resisted by arms. Peace has been cast aside. British officers have been murdered when acting for the State; others engaged in a like employment have been thrown into captivity. Finally, the whole of the State and the whole Sikh people, joined by many of the sardars in the Panjáb, who signed the treaties, and led by a member of the Regency itself, have risen in arms against us and have waged a fierce and bloody war for the proclaimed purpose of destroying the British and their power. The Government of India formerly declared that it required no further conquest, and it proved by its acts the sincerity of its professions.

The conduct of the Sikhs described.

The Government has no desire for conquest now, but it is bound in its duty to provide fully for its own security and to guard the interests of those committed to its charge. To that end, and as the only sure mode of protecting the State from the perpetual recurrence of unprovoked and wasting wars, the Governor-General is compelled to resolve upon the entire subjugation of a people whom their own Government has long been unable to control, and whom (as events have now shown) no punishment can deter from violence, no acts of friendship can conciliate to peace. Wherefore the Governor-General has declared, and hereby proclaims, that the kingdom of the Panjáb is at an end; and that all the territories of Maharájá Ranjít Singh are now and henceforth a portion of the British empire in India. His Highness the Maharájá shall be treated with consideration and with honour. The few chiefs who have not engaged in hostilities against the British shall retain their property and their rank. The British Government shall leave to all the people, whether Mussalmans or Hindus or Sikhs, the free exercise of their own religion, but it will not permit any man to interfere with others in the observance of such forms and customs as their respective religions may either enjoin or permit. The jágírs and all the property of sardars and others who have been in arms against the British shall be confiscated to the State. The defences of every fortified place in the Panjáb which is not occupied by British troops shall be totally destroyed, and effectual measures shall be taken to deprive the people of the means of renewing either tumult or war. The Governor-General calls upon all the inhabitants of the Panjáb, sardars and people, to submit themselves peaceably to the authority of the British Government which has hereby been proclaimed. Over those who shall live as obedient and peaceful subjects of the State, the British Government will rule with mildness and beneficence. But if resistance to constituted authority shall again be attempted, if violence and turbulence be renewed, the Governor-General warns the people of the Panjáb that the time for leniency will then have passed away, and that their offence will be punished with prompt and most rigorous severity.

The kingdom of Láhore suppressed.

The Governor-General insures peace to all the lovers of tranquillity.

The policy initiated by the Governor-General's manifesto was crowned with success. By it the Sikhs were treated, not as conquered enemies, but as free subjects of the Crown, enjoying the same protection and privileges as the rest of the Queen's subjects. A pension of five lakhs of rupees was conferred on the young Maharájá Dulíp Singh, who was to come of age in 1854. All the State property was confiscated to the East India Company. The celebrated diamond, the *Kohinúr*, or Mountain of Light, one of the most precious and beautiful gems in the world, was surrendered to the British. It was presented to Her Majesty Queen Victoria by the Chairman and Deputy Chairman of the East India Company at a levée held on the 3rd of July 1850, and was subsequently exhibited at the Great Exhibition of 1851. All the Sikh chiefs who had not taken part in the late wars were endowed with pensions suitable to their rank and settled in their hereditary villages. The conquest of the Panjáb was a great military achievement for the British. By the acquisition of that vast province, the conquest of India by the British nation may be said to have been completed, and the empire of Hindostán brought within its natural boundaries, the Indus, that 'forbidden river,' the historical boundary of India, the stupendous Himálayas and the great Indian Ocean.

The Sikhs treated not as conquered enemies.

Dulíp Singh deposed.

The great diamond the *Kohinúr* surrendered to the Queen of England.

Pensions allowed to the Sikh chiefs.

The conquest of India completed by the conquest of the Panjáb.

The young Maharájá Dulíp Singh was placed under the tutelage of Doctor Sir John Logan, of the Bengal Army, and sent to the North-West Provinces, and afterwards to England, with his mother, the Maharání Chand Kour or Jindán. All his personal effects and jewels were made over to his guardians. The whole of the State property was put up to public sale. Although these measures were calculated to cause some excitement among the people, they were, nevertheless, carried out without any ebullition of feeling on their part. Under the wise ministration and guidance of Dr. Logan, Dulíp Singh embraced Christianity and became an English country gentleman, owning extensive estates in Suffolk. He conducted himself with dignity and prudence, and the Queen regarded him with sympathy and honoured him with invitations to select dinner parties. On public occasions he appeared in rich oriental costume and decorated with the richest gems. He was a frequent

Dulíp Singh is sent to England.

He embraces Christianity

visitor at Court and gained the esteem of statesmen and citizens. He married an Egyptian Christian lady, by whom he had issue. Thus for many years he continued to pass his life in peace and luxury, when a sudden change became perceptible in his temper. Having expressed a desire to visit his home, the Panjáb, he obtained the permission of the Government to make a journey to India. Immediately afterwards, he not only took the *Puhal* of the Guru and re-embraced his old religion, but opened a suspicious correspondence with certain old Panjáb sardars. The Government disapproved of this action on the part of one to whom it had shown the utmost consideration and favour, and who had been brought up on English bread, and ordered him to return to England, but he contrived to make his way to Russia and France, the Governments of which countries showed themselves quite indifferent to his fate. His Christian wife died in England of sorrow. His turbulent mother, the notorious Chand Kour (or Jindán), whose ambition and intrigues had mainly conduced to the rapid fall of the Empire of Ranjit, having become nearly blind, broken in heart and subdued in spirit, had previously died in England, in 1863, and found her last resting-place in a London suburb.

And marries an Egyptian wife.

His subsequent treacherous behaviour.

Death of Ráni Jindán in London, 1863.

But the most important, by far, of the victories achieved by the British in the Panjáb were victories of peace and civilization. The active mind of Lord Dalhousie mapped out a scheme of administration for the newly-annexed country which combined the advantages of both a civil and a military government. To ensure substantial justice, the protection of the law was extended to the people without its tedious formalities and intricate niceties, and if the system inaugurated was lax, compared with the strict procedure of the regulation provinces, it was thoroughly adapted to the condition of a people inured to war, recently deprived of power and accustomed to be ruled by a despotic, unconstitutional government. A Board of Administration was established at Láhore, with power to communicate directly with the Governor-General. The first seat at the Board was given to that soldier statesman, well known for the benevolence of his heart and the justice of his schemes, who had lately directed the affairs of the Láhore State in the name of the Maharájá. This was Colonel, afterwards Sir Henry, Lawrence, who, with high intellectual powers, combined indomitable personal energy. His colleagues on the Board were his brother, Mr. John, afterwards Lord, Lawrence, an officer of the Company's Civil Service, and Mr. Charles Grenville Mansel, also a Covenanted Civilian. The former had greatly distinguished himself in matters of revenue settlement under Mr. Thomason and his predecessors in the North-Western Provinces, and as Manager of the Jalandar Doáb in the Panjáb, and the latter had earned a high reputation as one of the ablest financiers in India. The functions of the Board were divided into Political, Revenue and Judicial, and the members had each special charge of one of these departments, though all worked jointly when any question of more than ordinary importance arose.

The policy of Lord Dalhousie towards the Panjáb.

Board of Administration established at Láhore, March, 1849.

Colonel Henry Lawrence first member of the Board.

His colleagues Messrs. John Lawrence and Mansel.

The functions of the Board.

Under the able guidance of these officers the great work of the pacification of the Panjáb by ameliorative measures was begun. To render the turbulent elements of the population harmless, the British army was wisely retained in the country. A general muster of the Sikh soldiery and the military retainers of the late Darbár was held at Láhore, when all were paid up and disbanded, the most promising of them being subsequently taken into British service, while the infirm and superannuated obtained pensions and gratuities. The ease and quiet with which large bodies of brave men, once so turbulent and formidable as to overawe their government and wield the destinies of the empire, laid down their arms and abandoned the profes-

A general muster of the Sikh soldiers and military retainers.

Pensions and gratuities allowed to them.

Sikh soldiery disbanded.

sion of war to adopt that of agriculture, was indicative of the wholesome effect produced by the British power, and the satisfaction with which the measures of that Government had been received by the people. All the forts, except those required for military purposes at principal stations, were dismantled, and such as were retained were repaired or rebuilt upon scientific principles.

General disarmament of the population.

A general disarmament of that part of the province lying between the Indus and the Sutlej was ordered and carried out quietly and systematically.

The Military Police and the Civil Police.

Two distinct bodies of police, the military and the civil, were organised: the former body, 8,100 strong, under the control of military officers, being charged with the duty of furnishing guards, patrolling the country, preventing crime and apprehending offenders; while to the latter, under civil officers, were entrusted the duties of watch and ward in towns and villages and the preservation of internal peace.

The constitution of the Panjáb Frontier Force.

A special force, called the Panjáb Frontier Force, was raised for service on the frontier and placed under the immediate control of the Board. Along the whole frontier line a chain of fortified posts was established, parallel to a military road.

Measures of improvement introduced.

One of the earliest works undertaken was the construction of a Grand Trunk Road between Láhore and Pesháwar, while cross-roads were commenced in all directions. The Bárí Doáb Canal was commenced, and many other works of public utility were undertaken. The entire British system and its institutions were introduced. The erection of public buildings at all the principal stations was taken in hand. The wooded wilds of the central doábs, the haunts of thieves and plunderers, were cleared and intersected by roads protected by police stations. Public schools, charitable dispensaries and jails were established in each district; all taxes weighing heavily on trade were remitted, and a system of regular settlements with land-owners and agriculturists as to the land revenue payable by them to the Government for the future was introduced. In the management of the land revenue, the maintenance of the village communities and the demarcation of boundaries, the rules then in force in the North-Western Provinces were observed. The resources of the country were developed; trade, agriculture and commerce fostered and river navigation promoted.

The abolition of the Board of Administration and the establishment of Chief Commissionership, 1853.

In February, 1853, the Board of Administration was abolished, and Sir John Lawrence was appointed the first Chief Commissioner of the Panjáb. He corresponded directly with the Supreme Government and was the recognised chief functionary in carrying out its orders and the head of the local executive administration in all civil and political departments.

The appointment of Judicial and Financial Commissioners.

Their respective functions.

Subordinate to him were appointed a Judicial Commissioner, the chief authority in the Judicial Department, and a Financial Commissioner, the head of the Revenue branch. The supervision of police, education and local and Municipal funds devolved on the Judicial Commissioner. The principal measures adopted by the Chief Commissioner were the abolition of the house tax, with the full preference of the people, and the substitution in lieu thereof of octroi duties in towns and large villages, the introduction of tea cultivation in the Kangrá hills, and of extensive operations in arboriculture throughout the province, and the virtual extermination of thuggi.

What the Government did for the Sikh aristocracy.

The British Government did all it consistently could to mitigate the reverses of the feudal nobility of the defunct Sikh realm. They received handsome pensions, their hereditary claims were recognised, and they were treated with consideration and regard by the officers of Government. Their retinue, still enormous, swelled public processions, though their city residences were less gay with gaudy equipages and visitors. Their retainers similarly enjoyed the bounty of Government. The numerous dependents of the late regime were also bountifully provided for; not only were handsome allowance granted to the royal widows, and their attendants cared for, but the office bearers of the court, chamberlains, mace-bearers, soothsayers, physicians, savants, musicians and men-in-waiting, were all inscribed on the pension rolls of the British State, according to the statistics furnished by Rájá Díná Náth from the records of the late Darbár. Thus, the multitude which surrounded the throne of Ranjít Singh and his successors, enjoyed substantial comfort under the English rule.

The priestly castes were respected,

Nor were the priestly castes and religious classes of the old regime neglected. They had every reason to be contented and happy under their new masters. The Sikh holy places were respected; Mahomedan religious and national institutions were maintained, and a large portion of the endowments allowed by the Sikh Government to the shrines of Derá Nának, Amritsar, Táran-Táran and Anandpur, was allowed to be retained by them. All religious characters, even mendicant friars and village ascetics, were liberally treated and allowed to retain their grants of land. Gratified with the treatment thus shown them, they blessed their English rulers, and their indirect influence on the mass of the population was enlisted on the side of the Government.

And all religious institutions maintained.

Universal contentment.

The agricultural classes.

Not less thankful for the protection afforded them were the agricultural classes, who had been ground with oppression by the tax-collectors and *kárdárs* of the old regime. The influence of *chaudhrís*, a species of local chiefs or leading resident gentry, who, under the Sikhs, aided in collecting the revenue and exacting forced labour (*begár*) from the villagemen, and enjoyed many privileges and immunities, was greatly reduced. Many of their just privileges were maintained to them; their legitimate position as representatives of the brotherhood was strengthened and defined, but their undue influence over the village communities was curtailed. The tenures of the village co-parcenary bodies were adjusted and their rights recorded. The change from the appraisement of the standing crop, or division of the garnered grain, to a regular money taxation, protected the peasant proprietors from Government interference and from the frauds of their more intriguing brethren, and gave a value to landed property previously unknown, whilst the harsher consequences of cash payments were averted by reduced taxation. The rights of the cultivators and the return for their labour, became more secure. The working classes, including day-labourers and artisans, prospered beyond all precedent, owing to the progress of cantonments and gigantic public works. The poorer classes were greatly benefited by the extraordinary cheapness of provisions, and the commercial and trading classes throve beyond expectation. In short, from the hardy yeoman and the sturdy peasant to the thrifty trader and the enterprising capitalist, all rose in robust prosperity, to become the casting and reliable bulwarks of the power which had extended protection to them.

Reduced taxation on land,

Security to cultivators.

Introduction of gigantic schemes of public works.

Their effect on the poorer classes.

The trading classes.

General prosperity.

The external face of the country changed by public works.

But, irrespective of the framework of society, the external face of the country also changed rapidly owing to the advance of vast public works, both for communication and for irrigation; fine cantonments everywhere sprang up and public buildings, both civil and military, added to the beauty of the country. This alteration of circumstances was not less apparent in towns than in the country. The aspect of the streets was, perhaps, less gay and brilliant than heretofore, but the improvements in drainage, in street conservancy, in the laying out of bazars, proved to the commonest observer that an era of solid comfort and cleanliness had commenced.

Improvements in towns.

Important State measures introduced.

Other important State measures adopted were the crusade against dacoity, the suppression of thuggi, the movement against infanticide, the tracking of criminals, the economic and hygienic reformation of the jails, the utilisation of prison labour, the elaboration of the revenue system, field measurement, the training of village accountants, the registration of rights, the interior professional survey, the census of the population, the preparation of statistics, the arrangements for the great highways, the erection of caravansarais and supply-depôts, the improvement of the breed of cattle, the planting of trees, the pursuit of agricultural science, geological researches, and, lastly, the supervision of finance. A civil code sufficient to meet the growing requirements of a commercial and agricultural population was compiled by the joint efforts of Messrs. Montgomery and Temple, and revised by the Chief Commissioner. A sanitarium was established in the hills for wounded or invalid soldiers, and for the worn out civilian to recruit his health. In short, within a brief period of five years, the Panjáb was quite changed. The whole face of the country told its own tale. In the force and vigour of its police, in the simplicity and precision of its civil justice and in the popularity of its municipal arrangement, the Panjáb vied with the best regulated provinces in India. Such were the improvements effected in the Panjáb by its first Chief Commissioner, Sir John Lawrence, with the help of his able coadjutors. Most of the schemes had been already inaugurated under the Board of Administration, but the credit of the working out of these measures was due to the able Government of Sir John Lawrence.

The Panjáb Civil Code.

A Sanitarium established in the hills.

The Panjáb becomes a model province.

The labours of Sir John Lawrence and his able colleagues.

Early in January 1857, Sir John Lawrence held a conference with Amír Dost Muhammad Khan of Kábul, at Jamrud near Peshávar. The Dost, with his venerable white beard, and clad in a garment of coarse camel's hair, entered the darbár tent, accompanied by two of his sons and his most trusted sardars. At this meeting a subsidy of twelve lakhs of rupees a year was guaranteed to the Amír so long as the war with Persia, then pending, should last, or it should please the British Government to continue it, the promise being accompanied with a present of 4,000 muskets. After the articles of agreement had been signed and sealed in the Amír's tent, His Highness exclaimed: "Witness it, *Alláh*, and His Prophet! I have now made an alliance with the British Government: come, what may, I will keep it till my death;" and he was as good as his word; for to the day of his death his pledge to the British remained unbroken. The Shah of Persia, observing the attitude of the ruler of Afghanistán and the renewal of his alliance with the British, renounced his pretensions to Herat, and withdrew his army from Afghánistán, and, the war being then speedily terminated, the necessity of an Afghán army meeting the Persians in the field was avoided. Meanwhile, the Panjáb prospered under the fostering care of the British statesmen on whom had devolved the pleasant, but onerous, duty of its administration. But an event now happened which not only engrossed the attention of the British Government, but which taxed the exercise of its energy and resolution to the utmost.

The conference of Sir John Lawrence with Amír Dost Muhammad Khan at Peshávar, January, 1857.

The Shah of Persia gives up his pretensions to Herat.

In May 1857, the storm of the great Sepoy Mutiny burst. The first intelligence of the revolt at Meerut and the massacre of the Europeans at Delhi was flashed to Láhore, the seat of the Panjáb Government, on the morning of the 11th. The Chief Commissioner was absent at Ráwalpindi, and the chief civil officer present at the capital of the Panjáb was Mr., afterwards Sir, Robert Montgomery, the Judicial Commissioner. He saw at once the immensity of the danger, and, with a wisdom and foresight equal only to his energy, came to the conclusion that the emergency admitted of no delay. Accordingly, he convened forthwith a conference of the leading civil and military officers of the station, *viz.*, Mr., afterwards Sir Donald, McLeod, Financial Commissioner, Mr. A. A. Roberts, Commissioner, Major Ommaney, Chief Engineer, Colonel Macpherson, Military Secretary, and Captains Lawrence and Hutchinson. At this meeting the Judicial Commissioner proposed

The Sepoy Mutiny of 1857.

The intelligence received at Láhore.

The action taken by Mr. Montgomery.

He holds a conference of the leading Civil and Military officers at Láhore.

that Brigadier Corbett, commanding the military cantonment at Mián Mír, should be moved to disarm the native corps stationed there. The proposal was unanimously adopted, and the Judicial Commissioner, accompanied by Colonel Macpherson, proceeded to Mián Mír and suggested the scheme to Brigadier Corbett, who accorded it his unqualified approval. The disarming of the sepoy regiments at Mián Mír, an act of great wisdom and decision, was preceded, as was the Battle of Waterloo, by a ball. The shadow of events had in no way been allowed to cast its gloom over society. On the evening of the 12th a ball and supper was given, while preparations were made in silence for the morning parade. The regiments to be disarmed had been famous for their achievements in the field, dating from Mysore and Seringapatam to Ferozshahr and Gujrát. At daybreak on the 13th, the troops were all paraded at Mián Mír. The native regiments to be disbanded were four in number, comprising 3,500 men, while there were but three hundred British soldiers, with thirteen guns, to perform the task. By a clever manœuvre these forces were brought face to face, the guns and muskets of the British being all loaded, unobserved by the sepoys. This manœuvre complete, the sepoys were ordered to pile arms. Nothing was left to them now but to obey. In an instant the danger of mutiny was averted, and the native soldiery were marched off without their arms. Nothing could have been effected in a more orderly or soldierlike manner.

Proposal to disarm the native corps at Mián Mír.

Parade of troops at Mián Mír.

The sepoys are disarmed.

This simple morning manœuvre was the turning point in the destiny of the Panjáb, and, indeed, of India itself. It was subsequently discovered that on that very morning the native regiments were to have seized the fort and magazine of Láhore. That this was part of a concerted plot, was almost certain; for, six hours after the regiments at Mián Mír had been disarmed, their comrades at Ferozepur broke into mutiny. The arsenal at Ferozepur contained vast military stores. An attempt was made to take it by the 45th Native Infantry, but it was defeated by Brigadier Jones, who occupied it with a British force consisting of H. M.'s 91st Foot and 300 European artillery. The 45th were successfully disarmed and turned out of the cantonment, but not before they had done considerable mischief to both public and private buildings by setting them on fire. The greater portion of the 54th then laid down their arms. The pursuit of the fugitive mutineers was carried out by the 10th Light Cavalry under Major Marsden, Deputy Commissioner. Numbers were brought in prisoners, and several were subsequently seized in Patiálá territory, but many escaped and joined the rebels at Delhi.

The salutary effect of the Mián Mír manœuvre.

Mutiny at Ferozepúr.

Disarming of the native troops at Ferozepúr.

Damage done to private and public property.

The pursuit of the fugitive mutineers.

Amritsar, the Sikh Benares, was forthwith made safe. The great fort of Govindgarh had been abundantly stored. Timely succours were sent from Jalandar to Phillour on the Sutlej, where there was another great magazine. Peshâwar was in the hands of men who knew what they were about,—Major Edwardes, Brigadier Cotton and Colonel Nicholson. All mutiny there, whether by armed or disarmed regiments, was put down with lightning speed and effect. There was a rising of disarmed soldiers at Jalandar, who, after much confusion and plunder, marched to Delhi, being joined at Phillour by the rebel 3rd Native Infantry. On the 2nd of May, the 55th Native Infantry rose at Mardán and fled to independent territory, but the insurgents were betrayed by the hillmen of the border, or hunted down in pursuit by Major Edwardes' police. Numbers were brought afterwards into British territory, and shot or blown from the guns. The outbreak at Ludhiáná was suppressed by the prompt measures adopted by Mr. Rickets, Deputy Commissioner, of the Civil Service. At a general parade of troops held at Multán by Major Crawford Chamberlain, he commanded the 62nd and 69th Regiments of Native Infantry, suspected of contemplating an outbreak, to surrender their

Measures adopted at Amritsar and Phillour.

Proceedings at Peshâwar.

Rising of disarmed soldiers at Jalandar.

Native Infantry at Mardán.

Outbreak at Ludiáná.

The Multán troops disbanded.

arms forthwith. The former piled arms at once. The 69th wavered, but, under the menace of the guns, they, too, yielded. The disarmament of the disaffected troops restored confidence to the inhabitants, who waited on the Commissioner, Major Hamilton, and thanked him for the renewal of peace and security in Multán. The inhabitants who had left the city in terror, at once returned and resumed business. In the first week of July, the native troops at Jhelam and Siálkot mutinied, but were met and defeated, the mutineers from the latter station being destroyed to the last man.

Peace restored at Multán.

The mutiny at Jhelam and Siálkot suppressed.

By the adoption of vigorous measures, 13,000 native troops were disarmed in the Panjáb by the end of July. Nor is it less gratifying to observe that, although the Bengal sepoys in the Company's service manifested a disloyal and rebellious spirit throughout the Panjáb, the statesmen who guided its affairs, were, within a week after the announcement of the outbreak at Meerut and Delhi, in a position to rely upon the loyalty of the Sikhs on either side of the Sutlej and of the Muhammadans on both sides of the Indus. The calm, stern energy displayed, deeply impressed the Panjáb population with a sense of British power, and they at once became the staunch allies of the British. Into the new regiments raised at Láhore the Sikhs of the interior and the Muhammadans of the border equally flocked, and within the short period of four months, eighteen new regiments were raised in the province to supply the place of those sent down from time to time to Delhi, the seat of war. Regiment after regiment was sent across the Sutlej to help in the siege of Delhi. Seven thousand men, forming the contingents of the Rájás of Patiálá, Jhínd and Nabhá, accompanied the regular troops to the scene of the grand contest. To this was added a contingent of 2,267 infantry, 190 cavalry and 140 artillery furnished by the Maharájá of Káshmír, together with the movable column which had recently crushed the Siálkot mutineers under Brigadier-General John Nicholson, and a heavy siege train from Ferozepur. There then remained, to hold the Panjáb, 4,500 Europeans, including the sick. Now was the crisis. Every eye was turned in the direction of Delhi, the focus of rebellion, which, before the arrival of the reinforcements from the Panjáb, had been besieged by General Anson with but a small force.

The loyalty of the Sikhs and of the Muhammadans on both sides of the Indus.

New regiments raised in the Panjáb and sent to Delhi, the seat of war.

The contingents of the Native States.

The crisis.

All eyes turned to Delhi.

In the meanwhile, the old King of Delhi, a mere puppet and the sole representative of the race of Timúr, for whom the bounty of the British Government had provided a munificent pension, and who had lived peacefully in the palace of the Great Moghal, not as a hereditary claimant, but as a dependent of the British crown, assumed the sovereignty of India by proclamation, an ancient silver throne being placed in the marble hall of audience, and the mock King taking his seat on it, under a salute of 21 guns, and thence commencing to issue royal mandates. One Bakht Khan, a subadár of artillery, better known for his personal prominence than for his military qualifications, was appointed Commander-in-Chief under the King's son, Mirzá Moghal. Poets sprang up, and the subject of one of the earliest emanations of their muse, intended for coinage, was the following:—

Affairs at Delhi.

Proceedings of the old King.

He assumes sovereign authority.

One Bakht Khan is appointed Commander-in-Chief.

The new coinage.

"Siráj-ud-dín, Bahádur, the conqueror of England and of Hind, has issued a new currency."

Intelligence was brought to the King from Lucknow that Qudratullá Beg, son of Mendú Khan, had placed the son of Wájid Ali Shah, late King of Oudh, on the throne of his father, subject to the approval of the Emperor, and that he had commenced coining money with the following inscription:—

بزر زد سکهٔ نصرت طرازی — سراج الدین بهادر شاه غازی

"Siráj-ud-dín the Ghází (Conqueror) has established a gold coinage as the emblem of Victory."

Prognostications of Hindu astrologers.

Hindu Pandits, with painted foreheads and garlands of flowers in their hands, flocked round the chief actors in the drama, and, opening their bulky books, rich in occult lore, prophesied that *Sanichar*, or the God of Vengeance, had descended on the heads of the English, that by the grace of Rámchandar, their camp should be destroyed by fire like Lanka (Ceylon), and that in an action, the date of which was fixed, should be fought as great and as bloody a battle as that described in the Mahabharat, the horses' hoops should be steeped in blood; and that after that the sepoy forces should be dominant all over India."* Bigoted and haughty *mulláhs*, the disgrace of Islám, forgetting, in their mistaken frenzy, the manifold blessings of British rule, raised the green standard of the Prophet at the Jumma Masjid, calling on the faithful to fight for a cause which they falsely pretended to be that of religion. The roughs of the city, the representatives of the class who, a century and a quarter before, had caused the sword of the hardy Nádir to be drawn against the population, joined the pretenders, though, as before, in the hour of danger, they and their false moulvis were the first to keep out of the way.

The bigoted *mulláhs*.

The fall of Delhi.

On the 16th of September, Delhi fell. The palace of the Moghals was captured, and the king, with his favourite wife, Zinat Mahal, and two sons and a grandson (Mirzá Moghal, Mirzá Kuresh Sultán and Mirzá Abu Bakar, son of the late heir-apparent), the chief inciters of the late atrocities, who had betaken themselves to the mausoleum of Humáyún, surrendered themselves to Captain Hodson, who, with his own hand, shot the princes dead on the way back to Delhi and ordered their bodies to be conveyed to the kotwáli, the mayor's court, where they were thrown on the *chabútra*, or raised terrace, and exposed to the scoffs and jibes of the gallant soldiers and the avenging Sikhs, for on that self same spot, 180 years before, Tegh Bahádur, one of the two martial gurús of the latter, had fallen a victim to the relentless hatred of Aurangzeb, and the fervent hope of the disciples of the Guru had long culminated in a prophecy that the day of retribution was not far distant. The longed-for day had at length arrived; as in the Hebrew story of old, the headless bodies of the descendants of Alamgír lay exposed until, for sanitary considerations, they were removed from the scene where they had directed and themselves witnessed the massacre of the helpless English women and children. The king was tried by martial law and found guilty of waging war against the Queen and of the massacre of British residents who had fallen into his hands. His life was spared by Lord Canning; but he, with his son, Jawán Bakht and wife, Zinat Mahal, who had been chiefly instrumental in the revolt, and was the rival, in treacherous intrigue, of Chand Kour (or Jindán) of Láhore notoriety, was banished to Rangoon. Thus ended the royal line of Bábar, of which, however, since the days of Shah Alam, nothing more than the title had remained.

The King surrenders.

The rebel princes are shot dead. Scene at the mayor's court, Delhi.

Contrast with the events that occurred at the same spot 180 years before.

The trial of the King.

He is banished to Rangoon.

The lamented death of Brigadier-General Nicholson.

To the intense sorrow of the army and of the public, Brigadier-General Nicholson, who had been mortally wounded when gallantly leading a column of attack at the assault of Delhi, on the 14th, died of his wounds on the 23rd. The choice of the brothers Lawrence was fully justified by the event. He possessed some of the highest qualities of a soldier, being at once bold, resolute and devoted to his profession. When news of the death of this inestimable man reached Láhore, "Sir John," writes his biographer, "burst into tears." "We have lost," said he to Sir Neville Chamberlain, "many good and noble soldiers, but none of them to compare to John

* See the address of the Pandits to the rebel troops at pp. 169 and 206 of Cooper's *Crisis in the Panjáb*, edition of 1858.

Nicholson. He was a glorious soldier; it will be long before we shall look upon his like again." The gallant John Nicholson, who was not unworthy to be compared with Nelson and Wolfe, is dead, but his fame cannot die so long as the British power in India shall last.*

The behaviour of British soldiers.

It is to the honour of the English nation that, in the midst of victory, when the British soldiers made their triumphant entry into the city and the palace, no children or women, and few, if any, of the inhabitants suffered at their hands.

Heavy losses.

The loss on the side of the victors, from the beginning of the investment of Delhi to the close of the siege, was great, being 3,837 killed and wounded; that of the besieged will never be known.

Chief Commissioner's acknowledgment of the services of the army.

In honour of the capture of Delhi a royal salute was fired at all the principal stations in the Panjáb, and the services of the gallant army were thus deservedly acknowledged by the Chief Commissioner, whose own indefatigable exertions in supplying troops and munitions of war had contributed so much to the achievement of this most important victory:—

> All honour to the noble army which, under command of Major-General Wilson, has effected the most important conquest by which the widespread rebellion of the mutinous Bengal army has received a complete defeat in Upper India. The days of Clive and Lake are again revived among us. Neither the devastations of that terrible scourge, the cholera, nor the deadly stroke of an Indian summer sun, which so grievously thinned the ranks of our small army, during the past three months, the harassing and almost incessant duties of the camp, the ever-recurring combats with a highly trained and veteran enemy, who out-numbered us by thousands in men and hundreds of guns of all calibres, the stubborn and desperate resistance offered by the mutineers, during and since the assault of the 14th instant, nothing has abated the ardour of our troops, European and Native, nor equalled that indomitable courage and persevering energy which take no denial and will brook nothing short of success.
>
> It will be for a grateful Government to acknowledge, as they deserve, the services of Major-General Wilson and his army to the British empire in India; but the Chief Commissioner cannot refrain from offering them the warm tribute of his heart-felt admiration.

Divine service held in the palace of the Moghals.

On the Sunday after the occupation of the city, divine service was held in the throne room of the Moghals, in thanksgiving for the final victory gained by the British arms, and from every grateful heart and every lip flowed the sweet yet humble acknowledgment—

"Not unto us, O Lord, not unto us, but unto Thy name be the praise!"

The joy of the soldiers.

At the same place, at a fitting opportunity, the British officers and soldiers, flushed with joy, drained goblets of wine to the health of Her Majesty the Queen, when a thousand triumphant voices filled the air with the strains of their beloved National Anthem, "God save the Queen!"

The Panjáb saved India.

Thus, cool, resolute and prepared, did the Panjáb save India. Not only did the five classical rivers run clear of the revolt, but head and hand ready to devise and carry out measures for maintaining the prestige of British arms in the East, the Panjáb became a nursery of troops for the reconquest of the North-Western Provinces. The honour of an empire was at stake when General Wilson held his ground before Delhi with an insufficient number of troops, resting his hopes of succour on the Panjáb and his hopes of success on the inherent bravery of the British soldier. The position was critical, but the Panjáb proved itself a tower of strength to India.

---

* An obelisk at the head of the Margalla Pass (Peshäwar) was erected to his memory. The monument is seen from long distances in all directions. Within the basement is the following inscription:—

This column is erected by friends, British and Native, to the memory of Brigadier-General John Nicholson, who, after taking a hero's part in four great wars for the defence of British India; Kábul, 1840; 1st Sikh war, 1845; 2nd Sikh war, 1848; Sepoy Mutiny, 1857; and being as renowned for his civil rule in the Panjáb as for his share in its conquest, fell mortally wounded on 14th September, in leading to victory the main column of assault at the great siege of Delhi, and died 23rd September, 1857, aged 34, mourned by the two races with an equal grief.

The energy and resolution displayed by its administrators.

Never were the great virtues of energy and determination more signally displayed than during that great crisis in the Panjáb by its British administrators. Never had such a spectacle of vigour and greatness of soul been witnessed as was then displayed by its Government.

The loyalty of the Panjáb never overrated.

It has been argued by some that the Panjáb had been recently conquered, that the memory of the British victories was still fresh, that the country was chiefly inhabited by antagonistic races, Mahomedans and Sikhs, neither of which cared to see the other in power to the exclusion of the British, who had given peace to both, and that there was no general desire for change. It should, however, be remembered, that the first Sikh war, though executed with much vigour and attended with brilliant success for the British arms, was insufficient to overawe the turbulent Sikhs, who preferred plunging into a second war, and that, although the Sikh power had been crushed for the time, the military spirit of the nation was not dead, that Mahomedans and Sikhs might have united on common ground in pursuance of the same considerations which had weighed with the Hindu and Mahomedan soldiers in the Company's service, and that the peaceful pursuits of life were of secondary importance to a nation inured to war and active life. To keep the turbulent element of the population in check and enlist the sympathy of the people in general on the side of the rulers during the high tide of the *Purbia* mutiny deserved to be reckoned among the most solid and brilliant achievements in Indian history. Great praise is due to the administrative efforts of the statesmen who faced and overcame the difficulties of the crisis. There is not perhaps in the annals of India a grander page than that which records the salvation of the Panjáb, or one which more brightly illustrates the best characteristics of the English race.

The divisions of Delhi and Hissár incorporated with the Panjáb, 1858.

In February, 1858, the divisions of Delhi and Hissár, having been separated from the Regulation Districts, were formally incorporated with the Panjáb and placed under the able administration of Sir John Lawrence.

The generous views of Sir John Lawrence.

After the restoration of peace there was a proposal to plough up Delhi and to destroy the grand mosque; but, to his great credit, Sir John Lawrence saved both. As regards the proposal to demolish the mosque, he said, "I will on no account consent to it. We should carefully abstain from the destruction of religious edifices, either to favour friends or annoy foes." He advocated an open trial of all persons suspected of treason during the late crisis, and, subject to the observance of due precautions, brought back to the city of Delhi the starving citizens who had been driven from their homes. His merciful views were fully shared by Her most Gracious Majesty the Queen, who wrote to the Governor-General as follows:—

They are fully shared by Her Majesty the Queen.

Her Majesty's autograph letter to Sir John.

> To the nation at large, to the peaceable inhabitants, to the many kind and friendly natives who have assisted us, sheltered the fugitives, and are faithful and true, there should be shown the greatest kindness. They should know that there is no hatred to a brown skin, none; but the greatest wish on the Queen's part is to see them happy, contented and flourishing.

Sir John Lawrence's opinion regarding the Mutiny.

The opinion of Sir John Lawrence regarding the Mutiny was that—

> It had its origin in the army itself; it is not attributable to any external or antecedent conspiracy whatever, although it was afterwards taken advantage of by disaffected persons to compass their own ends. The immediate cause was the cartridge affair, and nothing else.

Rewards to the Panjáb Chiefs for services rendered.

Reward of the Maharaja of Patiálá.

For their services the Panjáb chiefs were munificently rewarded by the British Government. The Narnaul division of the Jhajjar territory, valued at two lakhs of rupees, was granted in perpetuity to the Maharájá of Patiálá, together with jurisdiction over the small State of Bhador, which His Highness had long desired to obtain, and a remission of the annual commutation tax to which he was then subject, amounting to Rs. 5,265.

Of the Rájá of Jhind.

To the Rájá of Jhind was assigned the hereditary title to the Dadri territory, estimated at Rs. 1,03,000 per annum, with thirteen villages in the Kularan Pergannah, with a rental of Rs. 13,810 per annum.

The Rájá of Nabhá.

On the Rájá of Nabhá a portion of the Jhajjar territory, valued at Rs. 1,06,000 per annum, was bestowed in perpetuity.

In return, the chiefs were bound thenceforth to render civil and military service when required by Government.

The Maharájá of Káshmír.

In acknowledgment of the aid afforded by the Maharájá of Káshmír, jewels and horses to the value of one lakh of rupees were presented to His Highness; the Maharájá sending for the acceptance of Her Majesty a costly selection of the choicest fabrics of Káshmír.

The Rájá of Kapúrthalá.

To the Kapúrthalá Rájá, who had taken a force of 2,000 men to Oudh, under his personal command, and had borne his part in six different actions, a considerable estate in that territory was allotted, and he himself became a principal talúqdár in Oudh.

Lord Canning's Darbár at Allahábád, 1858.

On the 1st of November, 1858, Lord Canning held a grand darbár at Allahábád, in which he published the most gracious proclamation of Her Majesty, Queen Victoria, the true Magna Charta of the Indian people, announcing the assumption of the Government of India by the Queen. Thus the rule of the East India Company, which had lasted for upwards of two centuries and a half, was brought to an end, and the entire administration of the country was taken over by the Crown. India was thenceforward to be governed by the Queen of England through one of her principal Secretaries of State, assisted by a Council of fifteen members. Lord Canning, the Company's last Governor-General, became the first Viceroy of the Queen. The Royal Proclamation was published at Láhore on the same date. By it all existing usages and customs, rights and dignities, treaties and covenants were confirmed; religious toleration was extended to all ranks of society; peace was proclaimed to all, and an amnesty granted to all except those who had taken a direct part in the murder of British subjects.

Assumption of the Government of India by Her Majesty the Queen.

Lord Canning becomes the first Viceroy of India.

Publication of the Royal Proclamation at Láhore.

Constitution of a Lieut.-Governorship in the Panjáb, 1859.

Sir John Lawrence the first Lieutenant-Governor.

From the 1st of January, 1859, the Panjáb and its dependencies were constituted a Lieutenant-Governorship, Sir John Lawrence, who had hitherto held the office of Chief Commissioner, and had been intimately associated with its politics, from the beginning of the British connection with it, being appointed the first Lieutenant-Governor. On the 8th of February, 1859, the ceremony of turning the first sod of the Panjáb Railway from Amritsar to Multán was performed by its first Lieutenant-Governor, who had so long advocated its construction. The silver shovel presented to Sir John Lawrence for the occasion bore the appropriate motto, "*Tam bello quam pace.*" One of the latest acts of Sir John, before resigning his office, was destined to compose the long-standing feud between Maharájá Guláb Singh and his cousin Rájá Jawáhir Singh, son of Rájá Dhián Singh, long Prime Minister of the Láhore Darbár, mainly through whose influence Guláb Singh had risen to sovereign power in the hills. Jawáhir Singh received from the Maharájá an allowance of a lakh of rupees per annum, on condition of his residing at Ambálá, or anywhere to the east of it.

The ceremony of turning the first sod of the Panjáb Railway.

Settlement of the dispute between Maharájá Guláb Singh and his cousin, Jawáhir Singh.

Sir John Lawrence resigns his office.

Sir John Lawrence was compelled by ill-health, brought on by over-exertions, to vacate his office at the end of February, and to leave for England. On the eve of his departure from Láhore an address was presented to him by the civil and military officers and gentlemen, in which, referring to Sir John's services during the Mutiny, they said :—

The Panjáb address to Sir John Lawrence.

All those among us who are military officers know how, when the Panjáb was imperilled and agitated by the disturbances in Hindostán, you, preserving a unison of accord with the military authorities, maintained internal tranquillity and held your own with our allies and subjects both within and without the border; how, when the fate of Northern India depended on the capture of Dehli, you, justly appreciating the paramount importance of that object, and estimating the lowest amount of European force with which the Panjáb could be held, applied yourself incessantly to despatching men, material and treasure for the succour of our brave countrymen engaged in the siege; how, indeed, you created a great portion of the means for carrying on that great operation and devoted thereto all the available resources of the Panjáb to the utmost degree compatible with safety. . . . . And, lastly, all of us, of whatever class or profession, are conscious of the untiring energy, unflinching firmness and unswerving honesty of purpose, with which you have devoted yourself to promote the public service. We all believe from personal knowledge or common fame that you have been an instrument in the hand of Providence for the preservation of British rule in Upper India, by your good management and resolute bearing during a period of unexampled difficulty. Indeed, there are many who feel a debt of gratitude to you for the preservation of themselves and their families during that terrible time.

Sir John Lawrence thanked the assembly for the genial terms in which it had acknowledged his services in the Panjáb. Adverting to his services in the Mutiny, he said :—

Sir John's reply.

When the great mass of the native army in Hindostán first gave signs of its intentions to mutiny, when disaffection spread from station to station, until almost all the Hindostáni troops in the Panjáb became infected, and only waited the opportunity for rising in revolt, I had to look with anxious eyes for the means of maintaining British supremacy in the Panjáb. In the quality of the civil and military officers under my control; in the excellence of the Panjáb force which had been raised, trained and disciplined under the civil Government; in the general loyalty of the chiefs and people, as much as in the valour of our British troops did I find the means of securing public tranquillity here and of rendering assistance in Hindostán.

Sir Robert Montgomery succeeds him as Lieut.-Governor of the Panjáb, February, 1859.

On the 26th of February, 1859, Sir John Lawrence left for England, making over charge of the office of Lieutenant-Governor to his successor, Sir Robert Montgomery.

Opening of the Bári Doáb Canal.

The auspicious rule of Sir Robert Montgomery commenced with the bringing in of water into the Bári Doáb Canal. On the 11th of April 1859, seven and a half years after the first sod had been turned, water was for the first time admitted into its channel. The total length of the canal and its branches as projected, from the head to the point, about 56 miles above Multán, where it rejoins the Rávi, was 466 miles, and the total estimate of cost amounted to 1,35,85,502 rupees.

The Viceregal darbár at Ambálá, January, 1860.

The Hindore State restored.

On the 18th of January, 1860, Lord Canning held a darbár at Ambálá, which was attended by all the chiefs of the cis-Sutlej States. At this darbár the Viceroy was pleased to restore the Hindore State, in the Simla hills, to Ugger Singh, an illegitimate son of the late raja, in consideration of the services of the head of the family (one of great antiquity) during the Gurkhá War of 1814. The State had lapsed to the British Government, but, in accordance with the wishes of the home authorities, the Viceroy restored the sovereignty in the person of the recognised heir, subject to the payment of an annual tribute of Rs. 5,000. His Lordship also granted an increase of territory to the Maharájá of Patiálá and the Rajas of Jhind and Nabhá, in lieu of debts and *nazrána*.

Concessions to the Chiefs of Patiálá, Jhind, and Nabhá.

The year was memorable for the gracious concession, on the recommendation of the Governor-General, by the Queen's Government to the independent Sikh and Hindu chiefs of the Panjáb, as well as to those of all India, of their long-cherished custom—

Adoption of a successor to chiefships acknowledged.

That, on a failure of natural heirs, their adoption of a successor according to Hindu law, and to the customs of their race, will be recognised, and that nothing shall disturb the engagement thus made to them so long as their houses are loyal to the crown, and faithful to the conditions of the treaties which record their obligations to the British Government.

To the Muhammadan chiefs also, the assurance was given—

That the paramount power desires their governments to be perpetuated, and that any succession to them which may be legitimate according to Mahomedan law and consistent with the claims of primogeniture will be upheld.

The Governor-General announced the future policy of the British Government towards the Independent States of India in the following words:— Policy of the Government towards Independent States.

Notwithstanding the greater purity and enlightenment of our administration, its higher tone, its sure promise of future benefit to the people as compared with any Native Government, I still think we have before us a higher and more pressing duty than that of extending our direct rule; and that our first care should be to strengthen that rule within its present limits, and to secure for our general supremacy the contented acquiescence and respect of all who are subjected to it. Our supremacy will never be heartily accepted and respected so long as we leave ourselves open to doubts which are now felt, and which our uncertain policy has justified, as to our ultimate intention towards Native States. . . . The safety of our rule is increased, not diminished, by the maintenance of native chiefs well affected to us.

Setting aside the well-known services rendered by Sindhia, and subsequently by the Mahárájás of Rewá, Charkari and others, over the wide tract of Central India, where our authority is most broken upon by Native States, I venture to say that there is no one who remembers the condition of Upper India in 1857 and 1858, and who is not thankful, that in the centre of the large and compact province of Rohílkand there remained the solitary little state of Rámpur, still administered by its Muhammadan prince; and that, on the borders of the Panjáb and of the districts above Delhi the chief of Patiálá and his kinsmen still retained their hereditary authority unimpaired.

In the time of which I speak, these patches of Native Government served as breakwaters to the storm which would otherwise have swept over us in one great wave. And in quiet times they have their uses. Restless men, who will accept no profession but arms, crafty intriguers bred in native courts, and others who would chafe at our stricter and more formal rule, live there contentedly; and should the day come when India shall be threatened by an external enemy, or when the interests of England elsewhere may require that her Eastern Empire shall incur more than ordinary risk, one of our best mainstays will be found in these Native States. But to make them so we must treat their chiefs and influential families with consideration and generosity, teaching that, in spite of all suspicions to the contrary, their independence is safe, that we are not waiting for plausible opportunities to convert their country into British territory, and convincing them that they have nothing to gain by helping to displace us in favour of any new rulers from within or from without.

True it is that the British Government has faithfully observed the just and wise policy enunciated by Lord Canning, and the chiefs of India have proved well worthy of the confidence reposed in their loyalty to the Crown.

Famine in the Panjáb, 1860-61.

In 1860-61, the Panjáb suffered from the dire effects of a famine which spread desolation throughout the country. A Relief Committee was organized by the Panjáb Government, of which Mr., afterwards Sir Donald, McLeod, the Financial Commissioner, was nominated President. For some months, in 1861, the average number of persons fed daily ranged between 90,000 and 116,000. The distress was intensely felt in the neighbourhood of Delhi, the city that was the focus of the great rebellion a few years before. The authorities showed the deepest sympathy for the hungry multitudes who clamoured for bread, and the distress was greatly alleviated. The number of persons relieved is estimated at half a million, and the expenditure by Government at about three-quarters of a million sterling. The help rendered at that critical period to the starving population of Delhi was a true exhibition of Christian love, to return good for evil, for we all know what had been done in that city a few years before.

Relief operations.

True exhibition of Christian love.

Death of Amir Dost Muhammad Khan, of Kábul, 1862.

On the 9th of June 1862, Amír Dost Muhammad Khan, of Kábul, closed his eventful life at Herat, and was succeeded by his son Sher Ali Khan, who had been appointed heir-apparent during the lifetime of his father.

The grand mosque at Delhi restored, 1862.

On the the 28th of November 1862, the grand mosque at Delhi, which had been closed as a place of worship since the capture of the city in 1857, was restored to the Mahomedans, on certain conditions, calculated to provide against the outbreak of disputes and injury to the interests of Government. The celebrated Idgáh of Multán, which in, 1848, was the scene of the murder of Mr. Vans-Agnew and Lieutenant Anderson by the Sikhs, was also restored to the Mahomedans in February, 1863. It had been confiscated by the Sikhs, when they took the town of Multán by assault and were exasperated by the resistance of the Patháns. At the time of the murder of the European officers, it was not in the possession of the Mahomedans, who fought conspicuously on the British side in the war that followed the death of those officers. It was quite clear that this place of worship had never been confiscated through any misconduct towards the British Government on the part of the Mahomedans of Multán, and, in deference to these considerations, its restoration to the Mahomedans was ordered.

The Idgáh of Multán restored, 1863.

Lord Elgin, Viceroy of India, 1862.

In March, 1862, Lord Canning was succeeded in the office of Viceroy of India by Lord Elgin, who had been employed as H. M.'s Ambassador Plenipotentiary in China; but Lord Elgin's reign was of short duration. On his return from Simla, he died at Dharamsálá, on the 20th of November, 1863. During his Viceroyalty a conspiracy was discovered to exist between the Wahábi fanatics of Patna in Bengal and, the Hindostánis of Sittáná and Mulkhá on the borders of Afganistán, having for its object a coalition of all the Afgháns of the mountains against the British power and an invasion of the Panjáb. The centre of operations was Patná, which supplied some of the principal leaders of the colony, as well as money, with the object of prosecuting a religious war. From thence natives of Bengal were recruited and sent up, in parties of five or six at a time, to join the camp in the independent hill territories. At Thánesar they were received by a Rain *lambardár* named Jaffar, a disciple strongly imbued with Wahábi tenets. Another principal agent in the Panjáb was Mahomed Shaffi, a contractor for the supply of meat for Europeans in all the cantonments from Ambálá to Naushera. Captain Parsons was specially deputed to Patná to investigate the case, and the individuals before mentioned, with some of the principal ringleaders, were brought to trial before Sir Herbert Edwardes, Commissioner of Ambálá, and sentenced to transportation for life.

His death, 1863.

The Wahábi fanatics of Patna and their conspiracy with the Afgháns of the Panjáb border.

The trial of Muhammad Shaffi.

The ringleaders are transported for life.

The Ambeyla Campaign, 1863.

The campaign against the Sittáná fanatics, called the Ambeyla Campaign, from the mountain pass of that name, was conducted with much vigour by General Neville Chamberlain. The fanatics resided chiefly in the district and town of Malkhá, north of a mountain which divides the Indus from the Kábul River. There was much actual hand-to-hand fighting, and in one of them General Chamberlain was badly wounded. The enemy collected in large numbers, and reinforcements were sent. On 15th December General Garmack, who had succeeded to the command, made an attack on Lálú, a position strengthened by the enemy, who had collected in thousands. It was taken by storm, and the enemy fled. The next morning, Ambeyla was assaulted and taken after a desperate fight, when the Afgháns fled to the hills.

Capture of Malkhá.

The Boners submitted, and Malkhá, the chief town of the fanatics, having been captured, the houses were burnt and the powder factory found there blown up. After inflicting this merited chastisement, the British troops marched back to the plains on Christmas-day, 1863.

The first exhibition of arts and manufactures at Láhore, 1864.

The first exhibition of arts and manufactures was held at Láhore during 1864, under the auspices of Sir Robert Montgomery, and remained open for about six weeks. The collection of the products of the Panjáb and Káshmir was very complete, contributions being received from all the neighbouring

States, as well as from British districts, and the number of visitors of all classes was large.

Sir John Lawrence succeeds as Viceroy, 1864.

Sir John Lawrence, who, on the death of Lord Elgin, had been appointed Governor-General and Viceroy of India, landed at Calcutta on the 12th of January, 1864. He was enthusiastically received by all ranks, European and native. After remaining at Simla for the hot season, he arrived at Láhore in October, and had the gratification of seeing himself once more in the midst of his Panjábí friends, after a separation of six years. The accomplished biographer of Sir John Lawrence has devoted an entire chapter to his visit to Láhore. It is full of interest and gives a vivid account of the proceedings in that city during the week His Excellency stayed there. At Amritsar he was greeted by his old friends and associates in work, Sir Robert Montgomery, Lieutenant-Governor, Mr., afterwards Sir Donald, McLeod, Financial Commissioner, and Mr. Arthur Roberts, Judicial Commissioner. On arrival at the Láhore railway station, the chiefs, sardars, and notable men of the Panjáb gave their old chief a hearty reception. There were present the young Maharájá of Patiálá, blazing with diamonds, the young Maharájá of Jhínd and the Maharájá of Kapúrthalá, who was to receive from his hands, a day or two afterwards, the most exalted Order of the State of India, in recognition of his distinguished services as well as his personal worth.

His Excellency's visit to Láhore.

His reception at Amritsar

And at Láhore.

"The friends of the Governor-General," writes Mr. Bosworth Smith, "saw at a glance—they never could have thought otherwise—that he was quite unchanged by the change in his condition." "He wore," says an eye-witness, the same simple dress. There was the same vigorous movement of his limbs and head, and the same determined mode of expression enforced by considerable action."

Opening of the Lawrence Hall.

Grand darbár at Láhore.

On the evening of the 17th of October, the Lawrence Hall, erected by his Panjáb friends to commemorate his services in the province, was formally opened in the presence of an enthusiastic assemblage, and on the following day, the 18th, a grand darbár was held for the reception of the princes, chiefs, and nobles of the Panjáb. It was attended by the Kábul envoy and the ambassadors from Kokand. On the right of His Excellency was the Maharájá of Káshmír, and, next to him, other rájás and princes, in order of precedence. On his left were Sir Robert Montgomery, Sir Henry Maine, Mr. Donald McLeod and the Commissioners of various Divisions. As the booming of the last gun ceased, Sir John Lawrence rose and addressed the assembled chiefs in Hindostáni as follows:—

Speech of Sir John Lawrence.

Maharájás, Rájás, and Chiefs,—Listen to my words. I have come among you after an absence of nearly six years, and thank you for the kindly welcome you have given me. It is with pleasure that I meet so many of my old friends, while I mourn the loss of those who have passed away. Princes and Chiefs, it is with great satisfaction that I find nearly six hundred of you assembled around me in this darbár. I see before me the faces of many friends; I recognize the sons of my old allies; the Maharájás of Káshmír and Patiálá, the Sikh Chiefs of Malvá and the Manjhá, the Rájput Chiefs of the hills, the Mahomedan Maliks of Peshávar and Kohát, the Sardars of the Deráját, of Hazárá and of Delhi. All have gathered together to do honour to their old ruler.

Interest taken by Her Majesty the Queen in the welfare of her Indian subjects.

My friends, let me tell you of the great interest which the illustrious Queen of England takes in all matters connected with the welfare and comfort and the contentment of the people of India. Let me inform you, when I returned to my native country and had the honour of standing in the presence of Her Majesty, how kindly she asked after the welfare of Her subjects of the East. Let me tell you, when the great Queen appointed me Her Viceroy of India, how warmly she enjoined on me the duty of caring for your interests. Prince Albert, the Consort of Her Majesty, the fame of whose greatness and goodness has spread through the whole world, was well acquainted with all connected with this country, and always evinced an ardent desire to see its people happy and flourishing. My friends, it is now more than eighteen years since I first saw Láhore. For thirteen years I lived in the Panjáb. For many years, my brother, Sir Henry Lawrence, and I governed this vast country. You all knew him well, and his memory will ever dwell in your hearts as a ruler who was a real friend of its people. I may truly say that from the day we exercised authority in the land, we spared neither our time nor our labour, nor our health in endeavouring to accomplish the work we had undertaken, we studied to make ourselves acquainted with the usages, the feelings and the wants of every class and race, and we endeavoured to improve the condition of all. There are few parts of this province which I have not visited, and which I hope that I did not leave in some degree the better for my visit. Since British rule was introduced taxation of all kinds has been lightened, canals and roads have been constructed and schools of learning have been established. From the highest to the lowest the people have become contented and have proved loyal. When the great military revolt of 1857 occurred, they aided their rulers most effectively in putting it down. The chiefs mustered their contingents, which served faithfully, and thousands of Panjáb soldiers flocked to our standards and shared with the British troops the glories as well as the hardships of that great struggle. Princes and gentlemen, if it be wise for the rulers of a country to understand the language and appreciate the feelings of its people, it is as important that the people should have a similar knowledge of their rulers. It is only by such means that the two classes can live happily together. To this end, I urge you to instruct your sons, and even your daughters. Among the solid advantages which you have gained from English rule I will now only advert to one more. It has given the country many excellent administrators. Some of the ablest and kindest of my countrymen have been employed in the Panjáb. Every man, from the highest to the lowest, can appreciate a good ruler. You have such men as Sir Robert Montgomery, Mr. Donald McLeod, Mr. Roberts, Sir Herbert Edwardes, Col. Lake and Col. John Beecher, officers who have devoted themselves to your service.

I will now only add that I pray the great God, who is the God of all the races and all the people of this world, that He may guard and protect you and teach you all to love justice and hate oppression, and enable you, each in his several ways, to do all the good in his power. May He give you all that is for your real benefit! So long as I live, I shall never forget the years that I passed in the Panjáb and the friends that I have acquired throughout this province.

How the Viceregal speech was received by the hearers.

The words of the Governor-General went straight to the hearts of his hearers, who had been addressed in their own language. They were simple and sweet, and told them in the plainest terms their duty towards their rulers and towards themselves. They were replete with paternal admonition and showed what genuine happiness the great speaker felt in seeing himself surrounded by men for whose benefit he had laboured so long and officers who had been associated with him in his great work. All gazed upon his commanding form, his rugged face and steady bearing. The earnest philanthropy and the genial courtesy displayed by him delighted all. His thankful remembrance of glorious past events, his bright anticipations and hopes for the future, and, lastly, his prayer for the happiness and prosperity of those present, moved every heart. His addressing the chiefs assembled in the vernacular was due to genuine feeling, not less than to high policy; and his speech will not soon be forgotten by those who heard it.

The district of Montgomery constituted.

When the railway between Láhore and Multán was under construction, it was considered desirable to move the head-quarters of the Gugairá District to some point on the line in regard to which Gugairá was not conveniently situated. The place selected for the head-quarters of the district, together with the district itself, was named Montgomery, after the Lieutenant-Governor.

Advance of female education.

Gardens laid out around Láhore.

Under the administration of Sir Robert Montgomery female education advanced in the Panjáb. It was in his time that the beautiful gardens which now surround the city of Láhore, were planted, and the canal which flows on its margin was excavated. Lord Canning in, reviewing the work that had been done in the Panjáb during the time of Sir John Lawrence, said:—

Next, but not inferior to any man, in his claims to the gratitude of his country is

Mr. Montgomery, the present Lieutenant-Governor of the Panjáb. I know but one opinion of the value of his prompt and courageous counsels, tempered, as they always have been, with the soundest and most generous judgment.

Sir Robert Montgomery resigned his office on the 10th of January, 1865. Three days before this, an assembly of native chiefs and gentlemen, at a public darbár held to bid him farewell, presented him with an address expressing their gratitude for the benefits conferred by his administration of the province and for the interest he took in their welfare. After his departure to England they raised a magnificent memorial in his honour, which took the form of the Montgomery Hall, now standing by the side of that which bears the name of Sir John Lawrence. Before he left Láhore, Sir Robert was entertained in the Lawrence Hall by English officers and gentlemen. At this meeting, Mr. Arthur Roberts, his successor in the office of Judicial Commissioner, in an appreciative speech, recounted his brilliant services, and all joined in doing honour to their departing ruler.

Sir Robert Montgomery resigns his office, 1865.

The Montgomery Hall founded.

Sir Robert Montgomery was succeeded in the office of Lieutenant-Governor by Sir Donald McLeod, a highly gifted ruler, who had played an important part in the administration of the Panjáb ever since it became a British province. He joined the Panjáb in 1849 from Benares as Commissioner of Jallandar, for which post he had been selected in succession to Sir John Lawrence, who had obtained a seat at the Board. God-fearing and by nature of a mild disposition, the feelings with which Sir Donald entered upon the duties of his office may be gathered from the following extracts from a letter, dated the 1st of January 1865, and written a few days after the event:—*

Sir Donald McLeod succeeds as Lieut.-Governor, 1865.

The feelings with which he entered his new office.

> Truly, when I look back to the past and the present, how can I but feel amazed, and, I may add penetrated, with conflicting feelings, in which humiliation bears a large part, that one so full of weaknesses and failings should have been elevated to such a post, the post in which the strong and vigorous Sir Henry and Sir John Lawrence won their first renown, the post which Sir Robert Montgomery has graced during the past five years by virtues rarely combined in one individual, and which has been filled by all of these with an ability, energy and success which render the task of their successor doubly onerous and responsible. In my consciousness of weakness and the prayers of many good men lies my only strength; and well do I know, deeply do I feel, that if I should ever cease to look above for guidance and for strength, I must fail. God grant that it may never be so! I have felt much more solemnized than gratified by the position in which I find myself. . . . I will not allow myself to doubt that it has been brought about in the decrees of an All-wise Ruler for the welfare of this very interesting province.

In the year 1865, the office of Judicial Commissioner was abolished, and a Chief Court, consisting of two judges, was created with final appellate authority in civil and criminal cases. In subsequent years the staff of the court was strengthened by the addition of more judges. The first civilian judge was Mr. H. A. Roberts, who had been Judicial Commissioner, and a Barrister-Judge, Mr. Charles Boulnois.

Establishment of the Chief Court of the Panjáb, 1865.

Mr. A. A. Roberts and Mr. Ch. Boulnois first Judges of the Chief Court.

The succession of Sher Ali Khan to the Kábul throne, after the death of the Amír Dost Muhammad Khan, was contested by Muhammad Afzul Khan and Muhammad Azím Khan, Sher Ali's brothers, and a series of civil wars broke out in Afghanistán, resulting in the defeat of Sher Ali, and the accession of Afzul Khan to the throne. On the 7th January, 1867, in an engagement near Khilat-i-Ghilzai between the troops of Sher Ali Khan and the Kábul army under Sardar Muhammad Azím Khan and Abdul Rahmán Khan, son of Muhammad Afzul Khan, Sher Ali was again disastrously defeated with the loss of eighteen guns, and retired to Herát, and on the

The civil war in Afghanistán, 1866.

The defeat of Sher Ali Khan and the accession of Afzul Khan to the Kábul throne.

* *Life of Sir Donald McLeod*, a Record of forty-two Years' Service in India, by Major-General Edward Lake, C. S. I.

26th of January, Kandahár, the western capital of Afghanistán, came into the possession of the victors.

Muhammad Afzul Khan lost no time in announcing to the British Government the important success he had achieved. Sir John Lawrence, in reply, congratulated His Highness the Amír Muhammad Afzul Khan, Wali of Kábul and Kandahár, upon an event which seemed likely to bring about peace and the establishment of a strong government. At the same time the Governor-General frankly intimated that he personally felt pity for the broken fortunes of Sher Ali Khan, who had given no cause of offence in his relations with the British Government; and that while, in the pursuance of a strictly neutral policy, His Excellency recognised him (Muhammad Afzul Khan) as the *de facto* ruler of Kandahár and Kábul, and offered him, as such, the peace and good-will of the British Government, in like manner, so long as Sher Ali Khan should hold Herát and maintain friendship with the British Government, he would recognise him as ruler of Herát and reciprocate his amity.

Azím Khan succeeds Afzul Khan to the Kábul throne, 1867.

On the 1st of October, 1867, Afzul Khan died, and was succeeded by his brother Muhammad Azím Khan. Meanwhile Sher Ali Khan, who still retained his footing in Herát, not disheartened by his continued ill-success, made active preparations for a renewed attempt on Kábul. He attacked the Kábul troops at Panjshahr, and obtained a complete victory on 26th August, 1868. Azím Khan fled to the north, and Sher Ali Khan entered Kábul in triumph on the 8th of September, 1868.

He is defeated by Sher Ali, who ascends the throne, 1868.

The Black Mountain Expedition, 1868.

In September, 1868, an expedition was undertaken against the tribes occupying the Black Mountain and other hills lying to the north-west of the Panjáb, near the locality of the Ambeyla Campaign. Hostilities were commenced by the Hasanzai tribe, who attacked a frontier police station, and as no disposition to submit to the demands of Government for reparation was evinced, it was considered necessary to inflict chastisement. An expedition was organized under General Wylde, and the British troops having advanced to Oghi in October, several engagements took place, in which the tribes were uniformly routed and many of their villages destroyed. The chiefs of the tribes, finding further resistance hopeless, tendered their submission, and the British troops were withdrawn.

The law of hereditary occupancy in land defined, 1868.

The year 1868 was also remarkable for the introduction of the first Tenancy Act in the Panjáb (XXVIII of 1868). By this Act the tenures of hereditary occupants of land, which had hitherto been undefined, were legally secured and recognized. Under a settled Government whose assessment on land was moderate, the value of land was enhanced, and to prevent friction between the conflicting interests of the landlord and the tenant, it was necessary to introduce a law defining the tenant's status. With the landlord and tenant, each contented in his place and working harmoniously for their mutual advantage, the most beneficial results for landed property were expected; and the legislation then introduced has since fully realized these hopes. The introduction of the Panjáb Tenancy Act was the last legislative measure of Sir John Lawrence in the Council for regulating laws. This Act was superseded by Act XVI of 1887.

The Panjáb University College established, 1868.

In 1868, the Panjáb Government submitted a proposal to the Supreme Government to establish a university at Láhore. After a considerable correspondence, the Supreme Government was pleased to sanction the establishment of an institution, to be styled the 'Láhore University College,' with a governing body, or Senate, consisting of the Lieutenant-Governor of the Panjáb, President, certain *ex-officio* members appointed by the Government, and members nominated by the Lieutenant-Governor of the Panjáb on the

The constitution of the Senate.

ground of their being eminent benefactors and original promoters of the institution, or persons distinguished for attainments in Literature or Science. The Senate so constituted was empowered to expend the income at its disposal in the foundation of fellowships and scholarships; in making grants-in-aid to educational institutions conducted in accordance with the principles of the movement; granting rewards for vernacular translations of European standard works, and for the encouragement of the enlightened study of Oriental literature; to grant "certificates of proficiency" after examinations to be conducted under rules framed by the Senate on certain accepted principles, the general object of which was to encourage the diffusion of Western literature, as far as possible, through the medium of the vernacular, but where this was not possible, through the medium of English. Further, the Senate was to be, with the educational officers of Government, the "Council of Education," or consulting body, in matters relating to education for the province. In support of the institution, Government granted an equivalent to the income from subscriptions and endowments, up to Rs. 21,000 per annum. Lastly, while disallowing, for the present, the title of "University," and declining to grant power to confer degrees, the Supreme Government intimated its readiness to re-consider this portion of its decision, should the institution prove itself worthy of the superior status of a University. The idea of the improvement and extension of vernacular literature generally, and of the encouragement of the enlightened study of Eastern classical languages and literature, originated with Sir Donald McLeod, who addressed the Director of Public Instruction on the subject, fully expressing his views as to the development of the scheme. These were communicated by the Director to the *Anjumán-i-Panjáb*, a society established at Láhore for the diffusion of useful knowledge, under the presidency of Dr. Leitner. That body and its learned president took up the subject warmly, and at many busy meetings which were held by the members, European and native, and with which are associated many distinguished names (such as Sir Charles Aitchison and Sir James Lyall), the scheme of Sir Donald McLeod developed itself into a University movement, and hence it has been rightly said, that the University in the Panjáb owes its origin to the *Anjumán-i-Panjáb*.

The powers of the Senate.

The Senate a consulting body in matters of education.

The idea of the improvement of the Eastern classical languages originated with Sir Donald McLeod.

The Anjumán-i-Panjáb gave birth to the Panjáb University.

To carry out the policy of the University College, the Senate established an Oriental school and college at Láhore, endowed lectureships, literary fellowships and scholarships, and held public examinations in the various subjects of study which it was desired to encourage.

The Láhore Oriental School and College.

Amír Sher Ali Khan had already expressed his desire to have an interview with the Viceroy of India, but obstacles of an insuperable nature precluded Sir John Lawrence from meeting the Amír on the frontier of the two countries. When Lord Mayo assumed the Viceroyalty of India, the Amír again expressed his wish for an interview with the representative of the Queen. This request was readily accorded by His Excellency, and it was arranged that the place of meeting should be Ambálá. The Amír entered British territory on the 3rd of March, 1869, accompanied by his young son Abdullá Ján, his Secretary, Sayad Núr Muhammad Shah, the Chamberlain, Sherdil Khan, Shah Ghází, and others. He was received by the Lieutenant-Governor about two miles from Láhore and escorted under royal salute to the State apartments in the fort, where he was sumptuously entertained for five days. A darbár was held in his honour, in the Montgomery Hall, at which native chiefs and nobles from all parts of the Panjáb were present, and a splendid fête was given in the Shalámár Gardens, which were gorgeously illuminated. On the afternoon of the 27th

Meeting between Amír Sher Ali Khan and Lord Mayo at Ambálá, 1869.

The Amír at Láhore.

The Ambálá darbár.

Sher Ali acknowledged sovereign of Afghanistán.

of March, the Viceroy received the Amír at a public darbár at Ambála, which was attended by officers, feudatory chiefs and native gentry. Sher Ali was recognised as Amír of Afghanistán, and received, besides presents of great intrinsic value, the promise of a money subsidy of twelve lakhs of rupees per annum. Following the policy of his predecessor, Lord Mayo assured the Amír that the British Government looked upon him as the lawful as well as the *de facto* sovereign of Afghanistán, and, while it had no wish to see a new competitor attempting to deprive him of his power, it would on no account allow itself to be involved in domestic feuds and civil broils in that country. After a week of reviews, soirees and other entertainments, the Amír returned to Kábul, having previously telegraphed to Her Majesty the Queen his gratification at the splendour and hospitality of his reception.

Yet the Government of India were averse to meddling in the domestic broils of the Afgháns.

The visit of His Royal Highness the Duke of Edinburgh, 1870.

In February 1870, the Panjáb was honoured by a visit from His Royal Highness Prince Alfred, Duke of Edinburgh, the second son of Her Majesty Queen Victoria. A reception worthy of a Royal visitor was accorded to him, and the occasion was marked by splendid festivities, rejoicings and demonstrations of personal loyalty to the crown. His Royal Highness reached Delhi on the 5th of February, when the city was brilliantly illuminated. On the 7th he received an address of welcome from the inhabitants, and visited the fort, palace and grand mosque, and the position of the British army during the siege of Delhi in 1857. The following day he visited the ruins at the Kutab and the tomb of Humáyún, and reached Láhore on the 9th. Here His Royal Highness was received by the Lieutenant-Governor, the civil and military authorities and the principal feudatories and chiefs of the province, *viz.*, the Maharájá of Jammú and Káshmír, the Maharájá of Patiálá, the Nawáb of Báháwalpur, the Rájás of Jhind, Nabhá, Kapúrthalá and others, all of whom gave the illustrious visitor a most hearty welcome.

His Royal Highness at Delhi.

Arrival in Láhore.

During His Royal Highness' stay at Láhore, he received addresses from the European and Native residents, paid a State visit to the city, fort and palace, accompanied by the princes, rájás and nawábs and the civil and military authorities, and opened the Soldiers' Workshop Exhibition at Mián Mír.

Opening of the Soldiers' Workshop Exhibition, Mián Mír.

There was a grand review of troops at Mián Mír, a provincial ball at the Montgomery Hall, and a conversazione at Government House. On the 12th, His Royal Highness proceeded to Amritsar, where he received an address from the inhabitants, and visited the Sikh temple and the sacred tank, which were profusely illuminated in honour of his visit. Next morning His Royal Highness proceeded to Saháranpur.

His Royal Highness at Amritsar.

Departure.

Impressions of the Royal visit.

The enthusiasm which prevailed on the occasion of his visit among all classes of people, Europeans and natives, was great, and his address, courtesy and affable demeanour, won for him the esteem and admiration of all. The moral effect of the visit on the people can hardly be overrated. Their hearts were gladdened by the sight of the son of their most august and gracious sovereign. They now beheld with their own eyes the person of a prince of the Royal blood of England, and their thoughts were concentrated on the blessings extended to them by the benign rule of the Queen of England. Scholarships and fellowships to be called after His Royal Highness were founded in connection with the Panjáb University College, by the Nawáb of Báháwalpur, the Maharájá of Patiálá and the Rájás of Jhind and Nabhá, to commemorate his visit to the Panjáb.

The munificence displayed by the Chiefs of the Panjáb on the occasion.

The beneficent measures introduced by Sir Donald McLeod.

Sir Donald McLeod carried out with vigour the policy inaugurated by his predecessors, of developing the resources of the Panjáb by constructing canals, roads and railways. He took an active interest in the culture of products new to the province, such as cinchona, silk, China grass and teas of good quality. He took measures for the improved culture of cotton, flax, hemp and other articles. As President of the Agri-Horticultural Society of the Panjáb, he had not only plants and trees sent from one part of India to the other, but also from Kábul, and even from countries as far distant as England and Australia, and distributed a portion of them among the chiefs and nobles of the Panjáb. He caused also specimens of rare trees and plants to be sent to England. His extreme delight was in the works of nature, and he took a warm interest in improving the products of the country, acting on the motto that he who makes two blades of grass grow where nothing has grown before, is a benefactor of his race.

His interest in products new to the country.

His taste for Horticulture.

Sir Donald also took the most lively interest in the working of the Medical College, Láhore, and of the dispensaries established in the province, and in the extension of vaccination. It was in his nature to exert himself to the utmost of his power for the alleviation and mitigation of the sufferings of his fellow-creatures, and every measure calculated to facilitate this end received his hearty attention and co-operation. He established municipalities in more than three hundred places with the view of training the people to manage their own affairs and to give them a voice in the educational system of the country. The rules of the system of grants-in-aid to schools were applied by him in a liberal spirit. His inexhaustible energies for the good of the public received the commendations of all who took a real interest in the advancement of the country, and he wrote many able papers on a great variety of subjects touching the welfare of the Government and people. The following extracts from a Despatch of his, dated September 5th, 1867, on the relative merits of native and British rule, may prove interesting:—

His interest in the medical training of the people and the dispensaries of the province.

His working of the municipal system.

And of the grants-in-aid to schools.

> I do not think that any one who really knows India will attempt to deny that the security, both in person and property, the freedom from violence and oppression of every kind, the stability of established order, the encouragement to trade and progress and facilities for accumulation and utilization of capital afforded under British rule, are infinitely preferred by the bulk of the people to the comparative lawlessness existing in the Native States by whom we are surrounded.
>
> Where an Englishman has shown a warm and rational sympathy with the people, they invariably respond in a manner which is unmistakeable, regarding him with feelings nearly akin to affection; and in the case of the Government, the same result would, I feel assured, follow from the same cause, for the people already fully appreciate and admire its love of justice, its honesty of purpose and its stability, and would, I believe, be quite prepared to accord to it their devoted loyalty, if they could perceive in its principles of action that spirit of sympathy which it is easy to invoke, but very difficult to describe. The more, in short, we study the people, consult their wishes and feelings and take them into our confidence, the more shall we soften or remove that alienation which difference of race at present begets.

His views regarding the relative merits of native and British rule.

In January, 1870, the five years' term of Sir Donald McLeod having expired, he was requested to remain for a further period of six months. At the conclusion of this period he resigned office on the 1st of June. On the 5th of May a grand farewell banquet was given in his honour in the Montgomery Hall, presided over by His Excellency the Viceroy. On this occasion high encomiums were passed on the retiring Lieutenant-Governor by the Viceroy and by Lord Napier, of Magdala. Little did those present think that, of the distinguished guests who honoured the banquet with their presence on that occasion, three would lose their lives within a comparatively short time—Lord Mayo by the knife of an Afghán assassin, Sir Henry Durand and Sir Donald McLeod by frightful accidents. After his departure, the European residents of the Panjáb raised a "memorial fund" in token of the respect and affection they entertained for the retired Lieutenant-Governor. With the money raised, they were enabled to place an excellent picture of

He resigns his office, June, 1870.

Farewell banquet.

Founding of the McLeod Prize Medal.

Sir Donald in the Public Hall, among other Panjáb administrators, and to found a medal called the "McLeod Prize Medal," which was open for competition annually to all the students of the Panjáb, and was to be awarded to the one passing the best examination in the Oriental Classics, combined with a competent knowledge of English. The medal bears on the obverse the likeness of Sir Donald, and on the reverse the words: "McLeod Prize. Oriental Classics and English." The Maharájá of Jammú gave Rs. 31,000, to be expended in the foundation of a fellowship in the Láhore University College, to be held in the name of Sir Donald McLeod.

The death of Sir Donald McLeod, November, 1872.

After his return to England, Sir Donald took a deep interest in the proceedings of the Geographical, Asiatic and other public Societies having for their object the diffusion of knowledge. He evinced the deepest sympathy for the distressed condition of the poorer classes in the east of London, and was on his way to attend the meeting of a charitable institution on the 28th of November, 1879, when, in his attempt to enter a train in motion, to ensure, as he thought, his punctual attendance, for the furtherance of a cause which he had so much at heart, the terrible accident befell him, which cost him his life.*

Sir Donald was born in Fort William, Calcutta, on the 6th of May 1810. He was, therefore, in the 63rd year of his age when he died.

Sir Henry Durand succeeds.

Sir Henry Davies assumes the reins of Government, 1872.

The Kúká outbreak, 1872.

Bálak Singh founds the sect, 1847.

Its religious tenets.

Sir Donald McLeod was succeeded in the office of Lieutenant-Governor by Sir Henry Marion Durand, who, however, met with a fatal accident in Tánk seven months afterwards. His successor was Sir Henry Davies.

In January, 1872, an outbreak of the Kúká sect occurred in the District of Ludhiáná. The founder of the sect was one Bálak Singh, a resident of Hazro, in the Ráwalpindi District. He founded the religion in 1847. The Kúkás are an orthodox sect of the Sikhs. The principles of their teaching are monotheistic and moral, and the tents of their religion prohibit idol worship and an observance of the distinction of caste. They permit the marriage of widows, prohibit the receiving of money in lieu of a daughter or a sister, and enjoin morality and abstinence from the use of spirits and other intoxicating liquors. The insignia of the sect were a woollen rosary, an untwisted turban and a staff, and each convert was enjoined to carry about him a knife and a small axe. Mahomedans were permitted to become members of the new sect; but the converts were chiefly Hindus and Sikhs of the lower classes. On the death of Bálak Singh, in 1863, Ram Singh, his principal disciple, became the gurú of the sect. Ram Singh was a man possessed of considerable intellectual ability. He was the son of a carpenter of Mauzá Bheni, in the Ludhiáná District. By degrees he acquired a great reputation among his followers for piety and sanctity. The number of his disciples largely increased, and with them his influence. The conduct of the sect was, at first, in general orderly and peaceable, but individual Kúkás subjected themselves to punishment by the courts of law for destroying

Bálak Singh is succeeded by Ram Singh as spiritual leader of the sect, 1863.

The members of the sect pacific at first.

---

* A touching account of his closing hours, written by a loving relative, who was with him to the last, is given in the little work of Major-General Lake, from which we extract the following :—

His left arm, which was much bruised, was removed while he was under the influence of ether. He was then placed in a bed in a small room, the Surgeon pronouncing the case hopeless, and that he was sinking rapidly, and would not survive more than half an hour. (He lived more than two hours after this.) While the operation was being performed, I had gone to fetch his sister, Mrs. Hawkins, and on returning to the hospital with her, we received this dreadful announcement. On being conducted to his room, we found him lying quietly in bed with his eyes closed, surrounded by his father-in-law, Sir Robert Montgomery, a young friend who was staying with him, the Lady Superintendent, a nurse and the Surgeon. . . Presently I said, "I have no doubt you can say, 'Into Thy hands I commend my spirit, for Thou hast redeemed me, O Lord God of truth."' He replied, "Most certainly!" And you can say, 'Come, Lord Jesus, come quickly?" He repeated the text, adding, "I shall then be free from sin and sorrow, and for ever with the Lord," or words to that effect. He then engaged in prayer almost inaudibly; but the last words were, "Praised be His holy name for ever and ever!" These were his last words. He now rapidly sank. He died in less than five hours after the accident. "O Death, where is thy sting? O Grave, where is thy victory?"

kúkás and demolishing graves and tombs, things which the members of the sect regard as objects of idolatrous worship, and, on occasions of religious assemblies, those present were frequently (like some revivalists) worked up into a religious frenzy. Suspicions having been aroused that the objects of Ram Singh and his disciples were not merely religious, but that, under the guise of a religious reformer and a teacher of moral precepts, he harboured deep political designs, the Guru was, for some years, detained under strict surveillance in his village; but, no tangible proof of disloyalty having been adduced against him, he was released from his quasi-imprisonment, and allowed the same religious freedom which the leaders of all well-conducted sects enjoy under the British Government. For some time after obtaining his liberty, Ram Singh behaved well, but, as he gained more importance by making converts, his teachings became more political in their nature. His followers assumed an air of arrogance, and instances were not wanting in which they disturbed the public peace at fairs and public gatherings by their intolerant behaviour. The first proofs of their being a dangerous sect appeared in June and July, 1871, at Amritsar, and at Rái Kot in the Ludhiáná District, when some Mahomedan butchers being found to have been murdered on account of the slaughter of kine, the investigation and trial that followed showed that the instigators and perpetrators of the murders were Kúkás. On 14th January, a party of 200 Kúkás attacked the town of Malodh, and after doing some damage and wounding a Sikh sardar, against whom they appear to have entertained some degree of animosity, they proceeded to Malerkotla, their numbers having in the meantime been augmented. They attacked the town and rushed through the streets to the treasury, but, after a sharp fight, were repulsed by the Nawáb's men, and driven out of the town. British troops were immediately sent to the scene of strife, but the outbreak had, in the meantime, completely collapsed. The rebels, discouraged by their repulse at Malerkotla, fled to the forest, where they were hunted down by the troops of the Patiálá State, and all either slain or captured. The Kúká sect remained under surveillance for some time after, but the restrictions which it had been considered expedient to place upon it at the time of the outbreak, were gradually withdrawn. Ram Singh, the leader of the sect, who had been seized and removed to Allahabad, was sent to Burmah, where he subsequently died.

But seemed subsequently to entertain political notions.

They become disorderly.

A party of them attack Malodh,

And proceed to Malerkotla.

The outbreak is suppressed.

Rám Singh is removed from the Panjáb.

His death.

In January, 1876, the Panjáb was honoured by a visit by His Royal Highness the Prince of Wales. Never before in the annals of India had there been a more passionate outburst of loyalty than on the occasion of the visit of the heir-apparent to the crown of England. The people and the chiefs of India felt that they were united by a firmer tie to the English people, and that their country was incorporated with the vast and splendid empire ruled over by Her Majesty the Queen.

Visit of His Royal Highness the Prince of Wales to the Panjáb, 1876.

The joy of the people unprecedented.

His Royal Highness with his suite, consisting of the Duke of Sutherland, Sir Bartle Frere, Lord Suffield, Lord Alfred Paget, Earl of Aylesford, Major-General Probyn, Mr. Sydney Hall, and Secretaries, and Aide-de-camps, arrived at Delhi on January 11th. The entry of His Royal Highness the Prince within the ancient capital of Hindostán, the scene of so many dramatic episodes in the history of India, and the site of a multitude of monuments and other historical reminiscences, was attended with a pomp and magnificence suited to the occasion and the place. The entire way from the Railway Station to the Royal Camp was lined with troops. Great was the enthusiasm displayed by the people on seeing the heir-apparent to the throne of England and India, and every face flushed with joy. As His Royal Highness came in sight of the Jummá Masjíd, in front of which were

His Royal Highness at Delhi.

The Jummá Masjíd.

the 5th regiment and 28th Panjábis, the immense multitude which had crowded over the steps leading to the grand mosque, rose to salute him. At the Royal Camp the members of the municipality, having been admitted to the honour of an interview, presented His Royal Highness with an address, in which they expressed the joy and honour they felt at the privilege allowed them of expressing their feelings of profound loyalty and devotion to the person and rule of Her Most Gracious Queen and on behalf of the whole community, of whatever race or creed, offered to His Royal Highness a most hearty welcome to their ancient city. Since the happy announcement of the intended Royal visit had been made by His Excellency the Viceroy, they had anxiously looked forward to that auspicious day, and they thanked God for having had the honour of beholding the Royal Prince at last. They dwelt on the historic interest and monuments of antiquity possessed by Delhi, which, for upwards of a thousand years, was the seat of great dynasties, which in succession rose, flourished and passed away, leaving behind them traces of their grandeur and civilization in superb mosques, splendid palaces, tall minarets, lofty towers, chaste tombs and picturesque temples. Though no longer the capital of the Empire, it was flourishing and prospering under the sway of the British. Three railways converged to it, tending materially to develop its resources by trade and industry. It was still the home of the polished Hindostáni language and a seat of learning. They expressed their earnest wish that His Royal Highness might retain pleasant recollections of his visit, and that the remainder of his tour might be as full of interest as the commencement had been.

The Municipal address.

The Prince's reply.

The Prince thanked them for the reception they had accorded him, and said it had been a pleasure to him to visit their ancient capital, which abounded in architectural monuments of great beauty and splendor, and was associated with events of the greatest historical interest. The position their city naturally enjoyed in the centre of India, where so many lines of railway converged, must ever render it one of the most important possessions of the Indian empire. He was glad to meet them there, and much gratified in being able to convey to Her Majesty the Queen assurances of the appearance of reviving prosperity in a city so famous and beautiful.

Review of troops at Delhi.

On 12th January, a grand review of troops of all arms took place at Delhi. The Prince was, on this occasion, dressed in the uniform of a Field Marshal. As His Royal Highness appeared on the parade ground, the royal standard was hoisted and a royal salute thundered forth along the line; a shout of welcome went up from the great multitude and handkerchiefs from the dense line of carriages fluttered in the air. The bands played the National Anthem and the colours were lowered. The Prince rode across the line from right to left, and back again. A signal being given, the troops began to move; and for an hour and a half the stream of horses, foot and artillery flowed past the royal party. There was then the march past by the whole force, and, after a royal salute, the various detachments marched off towards their respective lines.

Visit to the Qutb and other ancient monuments.

On the 13th, His Royal Highness visited the Qutb Minar, the highest column in the world, measuring 238 feet in height. Mounting the summit of the tower, he had a view of the ruined cities, mosques, palaces, and tombs which stretch around for miles. The same day, he visited the mausoleum of Humáyún, described by Mr. Russell as 'sombre, massive, vast, one of the grandest piles of the kind in the world;' the magnificent mausoleum of Nizám-ud-dín and the beautiful tomb of Safdar Jang. There were grand illuminations at night, and with a sham fight of troops, the following day, the Delhi pageant came to an end.

Early on the morning of 18th January, His Royal Highness reached Láhore by special train. He was received on the platform of the Railway Station by the Lieutenant-Governor of the Panjáb (Sir Henry Davies), the chief civil and military officials of the province, and a very large assemblage of Europeans. The royal cortége, in passing round the city, had a full view of the encampments of the ruling chiefs of the Panjáb, which were pitched on the parade ground, north of the citadel. Each Rájá had his separate ground assigned to him, and a banner which waved before each encampment, marked the spot. The tramp of horses, fantastically decorated with embroidered saddle-cloths, the trumpeting of elephants, richly caparisoned with gold and silver howdas, the roll of drums and the roar of artillery, gave a thoroughly eastern character to the scene. Each prince vied with his neighbour in magnificence. Their infantry soldiers, armed with shields and matchlocks, and troops of cavalry, clad in chain armour, and armed with lance and sword, with shining breastplate and morion, presented a most picturesque appearance. The chiefs who had assembled to pay homage to the heir and representative of their august Sovereign, belonged to different nationalities and races, and their armed retainers consisted of the flower of Panjáb chivalry. The regular and irregular troops of these chiefs lined the roads and saluted the Prince as he passed.

Visit to Láhore.

The camps of the ruling chiefs.

At Government House, His Royal Highness received the address* of the Municipality. This was followed by a grand levee of European officers, after which the ruling chiefs of the Panjáb were introduced to the Prince, in the order of their precedence. The Prince, with his staff, next drove to the citadel, and, mounting the high tower of the *Shish Mahal*, or Palace of Mirrors, had a full view of the surrounding country—the luxuriant plains with their rich foliage of trees on one side, the densely populated city with its spacious houses, lofty minarets, gilded domes and elegant temples on the other, and the placid river, like a silvery streak, flowing to the north-west. It was the place where the "Lion of Láhore," as Ranjít Singh was called, used to watch the rising sun, and survey at his ease the movements of his troops on the plains below, as well as the bustle of life in the city. The palace sparkles with the glittering of myriads of tiny mirrors, and is historically interesting as the place where the sovereignty of the Panjáb was formally ceded by the Sikhs to the British Government. In the armoury, the Prince saw the weapons employed by the Sikhs, and the arms used in warfare by Govind, their martial Guru. His attention was attracted by a tiny cannon, mounted on a revolving frame, which was said to have been used as a toy by Dulíp Singh, when he was a little boy. At the desire of His Royal Highness the toy was sent to Bombay, to be conveyed to England as an object of interest.

The Láhore Municipal address.

Visit to the Fort.

The Palace of Mirrors.

The armoury.

On the forenoon of the 19th, His Royal Highness opened the Soldiers' Industrial Exhibition at Mián Mír, where some hillmen exhibited some very fine falcons, hunting eagles, short-winged hawks, shaggy deer-hounds, and Thibetan mastiffs. In the evening a grand fête was given in the Shalámár Gardens, which were brilliantly illuminated.

Opening of the Soldiers' Industrial Exhibition, Mián Mír.

Fête in the Shalámár Gardens.

On the 20th January, the Prince paid a visit to Jammú. The Mahárájá had constructed a splendid palace, on the summit of a ridge above Jammú, expressly for the reception of His Royal Highness, at an enormous cost. It was gorgeously decorated, and carpeted with the richest pashmína. The Mahárájá received his royal guest with the greatest honour. There was a Darbár and a display of fireworks, the festivities ending with a sporting expedition, in which His Royal Highness took part. On his return to Wazírábád, the Prince

Visit to Jammú.

* *Vide* Appendix I.

The opening of the Alexandra Bridge over the Chenáb.

Return to Láhore.

The conversazione.

opened the great bridge over the Chináb, which was named the Alexandra Bridge, after Her Royal Highness the Princess of Wales. On the return of the Prince to Láhore, the citadel, public buildings and streets were illuminated. A conversazioue was held in the spacious hall of the Láhore College. His Royal Highness took his seat on a dias covered with a carpet of gold embroidery, and placed at the end of the central hall. On the right was a full-length portrait of Her Royal Highness the Princess of Wales, and on the left a portrait of the Prince, both works of great artistic merit executed by order of the Maharájá of Patiálá to commemorate the restoration of the Prince's health. The walls were decorated with the coats-of-arms, flags and emblazoned shields of the Panjáb chiefs, under each shield being a Panjábi, armed and standing on a pedestal, representing the district in which he was born. About a hundred and twenty chiefs from all parts of the Panjábi were introduced to His Royal Highness on this occasion, and a number of them received successively from his hands commemorative medals, ribands and rewards. The ceremony being over, the Prince witnessed a display of fire-works from the roof of the college, and round the great bonfires was exhibited the sword dance peculiar to the frontier people.

The sword-dance.

Visit to Amritsar.

On his way to Agra, the Prince visited Amritsar, the sacred city of the Sikhs, and surveyed the celebrated golden temple from the terrace, crowds of people making their salutations as they passed before him. His Royal Highness generously made donations at the mausoleum of Ranjít Singh, at Láhore, and the Darbár Sahib at Amritsar. At the former place an interesting ode * was presented to him. At Rájpurá station, His Royal Highness received the respects of His Highness the Maharájá of Patiálá, and, at a splendid banquet, the Maharájá proposed the health of the Queen, and the Prince of Wales. The Prince bade good-bye to the delighted Maharájá under a royal salute, and continued his journey down country. The visit of His Royal Highness was followed, a year after, by another act of royal grace, which became a turning point in the annals of British India. This was the assumption by Her Majesty Queen Victoria of the title of "Empress of India." *(Indiæ Imperatrix.)* With a view of proclaiming to the Queen's subjects throughout India the gracious sentiments which had induced Her Majesty to make to Her Sovereign style and titles an addition specially intended to mark Her Majesty's interest in this great dependency of the Crown, and Her Royal confidence in the loyalty and affection of the princes and people of India, His Excellency, Lord Lytton, Viceroy and Governor-General of India, held an Imperial Assemblage at Delhi on the first day of January 1877, an occasion which will ever be remembered by the Indian nations under British sway, as inaugurating a new epoch in the history of their country. Eighteen years had elapsed since the direct sway of Her Majesty's Eastern dominions had passed to the Crown. To assume the title then would have been inopportune, as tending to perpetuate the memory of the direst events in the annals of British India, and associating it with stories of treason and treachery. The Imperial Assemblage was a festival of peace, the natural outcome of an age of prosperity and contentment. The event owed its significance to those historial changes which had moulded India into a mighty British Empire. The assumption by the Queen of the title of "Empress of India" at this time was most opportune and in perfect accord with the feelings of all classes of the people. It bound the Indian chiefs and people by closer ties of devotion and loyalty to the Crown of England, and the event, following so soon after the visit of their Royal Highnesses the Prince of Wales and the Duke of Edinburgh, was proof of the increased

His Royal Highness at Rájpurá.

The Queen proclaimed "Empress of India," 1st January, 1877.

The Imperial Assemblage at Delhi.

India moulded into a mighty British Empire.

Moral effect of the Assemblage on the princes and people of India.

* *Vide* Appendix II.

interest which Her Imperial Majesty took in the affairs of this her great dependency. It brought the reigning princes of Hindostán and its people into closer communion with their British rulers. It strengthened the bonds of friendship between the Chiefs of North and South India, all of whom, with an enthusiasm unparalleled in history, joined in doing homage to the representative of their most august Sovereign. It served, on the one hand, to establish the reality of the British Empire in the minds of the people of India, while, on the other, it identified the governing race with their true interests. It was the crowning event in the history of British India; all hearts were cheered, all felt the beneficent suzerainty of the Queen, all were proud and grateful for an act of Royal favour which had brought them closer to the throne of Great Britain.

The gracious intentions of Her Royal Majesty.

His Excellency, Lord Lytton, addressed the assembled chiefs and people in a speech in which he explained the gracious intentions of Her Majesty in adding the title to the style and dignity of her ancestral Crown.

His Lordship then communicated the gracious message which the Queen had addressed to him in her own Royal and Imperial name, and which he had received that morning from Her Majesty.

The Royal message.

> We, Victoria, by the Grace of God, of the United Kingdom, Queen-Empress of India, send through our Viceroy, to all our officers, civil and military, and to all princes, chiefs and peoples now at Delhi assembled, our Royal and Imperial greeting, and assure them of the deep interest and earnest affection with which we regard the people of our Indian Empire. We witnessed with heart-felt satisfaction, the reception which they have accorded to our beloved son, and have been touched by the evidence of their loyalty and attachment to our house and throne. We trust that the present occasion may tend to unite in bonds of yet closer affection ourselves and our people; that from the highest to the humblest all may feel that under our rule the principles of liberty, equity and justice are secured to them; and that to promote their happiness, to add to their prosperity and advance their welfare, are the ever present aims and object of our Empire.

Honours conferred on the chiefs of the Panjáb on this occasion.

In connection with the assumption of the Imperial title by Her Majesty, the salutes of the Jammú, Jhínd, Nabhá and Malerkotla chiefs were each increased by two guns, as a personal distinction. The additions of "Indar Mahandar Bahádur," and of "Sipar-i Sultanat," were made to the title of the Maharájá of Káshmír, and that of "Mashír-i-Kesur-i-Hind" both to his titles and to those of the Rájá of Jhind. Maharájá Rambír Singh of Káshmír was also endowed with the honorary rank of General in the British army.

Sir Robert Egerton succeeds as Lieutenant-Governor, 2nd April, 1877.

Famine in Káshmír, 1878-79.

On the 2nd of April, 1877, Sir Robert Eyles Egerton succeeded Sir Robert Henry Davies as Lieutenant-Governor of the Panjáb. During the years 1878 and 1879, Káshmír was visited by a terrible famine, and the mortality among the suffering classes, chiefly Mahomedans, was great. The distribution of grain ordered by the Maharájá was generally either not made or made inequitably; the poorer Mahomedan classes being unable to obtain sufficient to maintain life with, while the richer pandit and official classes were allowed to embezzle enormous quantities, reducing the general stock and securing large profits for themselves. The desolation caused by famine in the valley and town of Káshmír was terrible. A number of the chief valleys to the north were utterly deserted; whole villages lay in ruins; some of the suburbs of the city were tenantless; the city itself was half destroyed; the grave-yards were filled to overflowing; the river was full of the corpses thrown into it; death everywhere did its destructive work. Some 20,000 persons made their way into Jammú and the Panjáb, and several thousands fled to the north. Of the hundreds who perished on the road, no accounts will ever be published. The shawl and the silk trade of Káshmír were almost destroyed, owing to the almost total cessation of the European demand for Káshmír shawls and *pashm* work.

The havoc caused by the famine.

A blow to the Káshmír shawl trade.

The Afghán war, 1878.

In November, 1878, a war with Amír Sher Ali Khan broke out. It was ascertained that he had been favouring Russian intrigues, and while an embassy from the British Government was refused admission into the country, a Russian mission (under a Russian officer named Stolietoff) was received with marked cordiality. The Amír having acted in direct contravention of an express understanding between him and the British Government, war was declared against him. The British army invaded Afghanistán by three different routes, the Khaibar, the Kuram and the Bolán. The good-will and active loyalty of the Panjáb chiefs was shown by their unanimous expression of a desire to assist the Government by every means in their power during the operations. The services of contingents from Patiálá, Baháwalpur, Nabhá, Jhind, Kapurthálá, Faridkot and Náhan, amounting to about 3,000 infantry and 1,000 cavalry, with thirteen guns, were accepted by the Government, and the forces put under the command of Brigadier-General Watson. They were supplied by the Government with the new sniders, and after being carefully instructed in their use, the forces were reviewed at Láhore on the 17th of December 1878, by the Viceroy, previous to their departure to the front. The contingent of the Bahawálpur Nawáb was sent to the Dera Ghási Khan frontier, while those of the other chiefs performed guard and watch duty on the borders of Bannú and the Kohát Districts, thus relieving the Kuram Division of the British forces of very onerous duties. The conduct of these forces received the commendation of General Watson and other military officers, who had an opportunity of seeing their work and bearing.

The British Army invades Afghanistán by three different routes.

Contingents from Native States.

The British troops succeeded in occupying the passes without much opposition. Sher Ali fled to Afghani-Turkistán, and entered into negotiations with the Russians for that assistance against the British power which General Kaufmann had led him to expect, but he met with disappointment in that quarter, and died of a broken heart at Mazar-i-Sharif. A treaty of alliance was concluded at Gandamack between Yákúb Khan, son of the late Amír, and the British Government, by which the British frontier was extended to the further sides of the passes, and it was agreed that a British officer should remain at Kábul, as the envoy and minister plenipotentiary at the court of the Amír. Sir Louis Cavagnari, formerly Deputy Commissioner of Peshawar, an officer of great natural force of character and energy, who had for a long time successfully transacted border affairs, being nominated to the office, was sent to Kábul with a suite and escort. His suite consisted of Mr. W. Jenkyns, of the Bengal Civil Service, distinguished for his linguistic attainments, who was appointed Political Assistant at the Kábul court; Lieutenant W. R. P. Hamilton, V.C., of the Guide Corps, and Doctor A. Kelly, of the same regiment. The British embassy had been only a few months in Kábul when it was treacherously attacked by the Afghans. The British Resident and his staff were all massacred in cold blood, and the escort was cut down. Yákúb Khan being suspected of complicity or connivance, was deported to India, and a second war became necessary.

Flight of Sher Ali to Afghani-Turkistán.

His death at Mazar-i-Sharif.

The treaty of Gandamack.

Sir Louis Cavagnari appointed British envoy at the Court of Kábul.

Massacre of the British Embassy at Kábul.

Yakúb Khan deported to India.

In April, 1880, Lord Lytton laid down the reins of Government, consequently on the defeat of the Conservative ministry in England, and was succeeded by the Marquis of Ripon. In the same year a detachment of British troops was cut to pieces by the Afghan forces under Ayúb Khan, between Kandahar and the river Helmund; but General Sir Frederick Roberts, the present Commander-in-Chief, made a brilliant march from Kábul to Kandahar, and near this town totally routed the troops of Ayúb Khan, on the 1st of September, 1880. The British were now masters of the whole country of Afghanistán, but, as the Government did not propose

The second Afghán war, 1880.

The march of Sir Frederick Roberts from Kábul to Kandahár.

The total rout of Ayúb Khan's army, 1st September, 1880.

to retain the country as a British dependency, Abdul Rahman Khan, the eldest surviving member of the family of Dost Muhammad Khan, whose father, Mahomed Afzul Khan, had been Amír of Kábul, was installed as Amír.

Installation of Abdúl Rahmán Khan as Amir of Afghanistán.

In September 1880, the British army which had been in occupation of northern Afghanistán, returned to India through the Khaibar Pass. Garrisons were for a time maintained at Landi Kotal and Ali Masjid; but they were ultimately withdrawn. The British troops vacated Kandahar as soon as Amír Abdul Rahman Khan had established his authority in southern Afghanistán. Soon after this, Ayúb Khan, descending from Herat, defeated the Kábul troops and captured Kandahar; but his success was not of long duration. Abdul Rahman Khan, marching from Kábul at the head of his troops, inflicted a disastrous defeat on Ayúb Khan, who was compelled to fly, Kandahar being re-occupied by the troops of the new Amír. Ayúb Khan, after his defeat at Kandahar, fled to Persia, but afterwards surrendered to the British, by whom he was deported to India and detained at Ráwalpindi, a liberal pension being allowed to him and his family and dependents who followed his fortunes in his exile to India.

The British troops vacate Afghanistán.

Abdul Rahman Khan defeats Ayúb Khan at Kandahar.

Ayúb Khan surrenders himself to the British.

At the close of the year 1881, an Exhibition of Industrial Arts was held at Láhore, with the twofold object of ascertaining the progress made in this respect since the last Exhibition in 1864, and of encouraging the production of genuine native work of original oriental designs. Specimens of indigenous art and industry, and works chiefly of a domestic character, bearing the mark of the individuality which only hand labour can bestow, from the tissue wrought by the peasant's needle to the jewelled ornament worn by the noble, were brought together. The Exhibition was formally inaugurated by Sir Robert Egerton on the 24th of December, 1881. In the course of his address to the assembled chiefs, sardars and nobles, Sir Robert said:—

The Exhibition of Industrial Arts at Láhore, 1881.

> In a frontier province like this, where, in former times, the professions of arms and agriculture chiefly occupied the attention of the people, it is essentially desirable to foster arts and manufactures, for, in a period of peace and security, such as India enjoys under the rule of Her Majesty the Queen-Empress, these have an opportunity of development which did not in former times exist. The rapid increase of the population renders it necessary to seek in every direction for some means of employment besides agriculture, which will bring money into the country and support its people; and one great means of providing such employment is to encourage a demand for local manufactures, which can best be done by making what our workmen can do more widely known; and I have reason to hope that this, which is one great object of the present exhibition, will be in some degree accomplished.

Sir Robert Egerton's views regarding local manufactures.

Selected artisans were sent from the leading towns in the Panjáb to the Exhibition, to obtain, by a comparison of the articles displayed, a correct idea of what was best in style and execution, and the Exhibition was an unqualified success.

Sir Charles Umpherston Aitchison assumed the office of Lieutenant-Governor of the Panjáb on the 2nd of April, 1882.

Sir Charles Aitchison succeeds as Lieutenant-Governor, 2nd April, 1882.

In November, 1882, His Excellency the Viceroy personally opened the great Sirhind Canal, designed to irrigate a vast extent of country. The main line of this canal has been completed as well as the Abohar branch and the Sutlej navigation channel. The Bari Doáb Canal, the Sirhind and Western Jamna canals are great works which mark the efforts of Government to bestow the boon of fertility upon waste tracts. Further west, the Chináb Canal and several other works, undertaken at enormous outlay, have conferred immense benefit on the country. The Swát river, Sidnai, and Chináb canals which have been opened, have fertilized nearly a million acres. The construction of the Jhelum Canal, has received the approval of the Government of India and the sanction of the Secretary of State. These

The opening of the Sirhind Canal, 1882.

Progress of works of irrigation in the Panjáb.

measures are calculated to afford an outlet to the inhabitants of congested districts; and the means of improving their material condition, and developing the wealth and resources of their country.

The Panjáb University established, October, 1882.

The Panjáb University Act (XVII) was passed in 1882, and, in accordance therewith, the Panjáb University came into existence on the 14th of October of that year. The Viceroy consented to become the patron of the institution, the Lieutenant-Governor was appointed *ex-officio* Chancellor, and the members of the Senate were designated Fellows.

The Russo-Afghán Boundary Commission, 1884.

The Russian Cabinet having urged, in 1884, that the North-Western boundary of Afghanistán should be demarcated, to prevent disputes arising regarding the Afghan territory lying on the borders of Russian Turkistán, a Commission was appointed by the British Government, with the consent of the Amír, to determine the line of frontier, in conjunction with Russian Commissioners deputed for the purpose. The Intelligence, Survey, Geographical, Botanical and other departments were represented in the Commission, which was escorted by a strong guard of cavalry and infantry, comprising three hundred sabres of the 11th Bengal Lancers, and two hundred and forty bayonets of the 20th Panjáb Infantry. The command of the whole mission, until the arrival of Sir Peter Lumsden from London, was given to Colonel Sir Joseph Ridgeway. The other members of the Commission were Captain C. E. Yate, Lieutenant the Honourable M. G. Talbot, R.E., Captain Maitland (Bombay Staff Corps) of the Intelligence Branch, Doctor Charles, in medical charge, Doctor Owen, Major Bax of the 11th Bengal Lancers, Captain Heath, Lieutenant Drummond and Major Hill, R.E., the head of the Survey party, Doctor Aitchison, the Naturalist and Botanist, Major Meiklejohn of the 20th Panjáb Infantry, Captain Cotton, Lieutenant Rawlins, Mr. Merk, Personal Assistant to Colonel Ridgeway, Captain Gore of the Survey, Major Rind, Assistant Commissary General, Lieutenant Burne, 23th Pioneers, in charge of transport, Captain Peacock, R. E., of the Intelligence Branch, Lieutenant Wright, Colonel Prinsep, Major Holdich, Lieutenant Peatson, Captain Griesbach, the Geologist, Captain DeLaessoe, and Mr. Barnes, C.S. The Native *attachés* accompanying the mission were Risaldar-Major Baha-ud-dín of the Central India Horse, Subadár Muhammad Husain Khan of the 2nd Sikhs, Sardar Sher Muhammad Khan, an Extra Assistant Commissioner in the Panjáb, and son of the late Governor of Kandahar, Sardar Muhammad Aslam Khan, Commandant of the Khaibar Jazelchis, Khan Bábá Khan, Extra Assistant Commissioner, Mirza Ghulam Ahmad, Risaldar-Major Muhammad Husain Khan, 7th Bengal Cavalry, Kazi Muhammad Aslam Khan and Aziz-ulla Khan. Mirza Ghulam Ahmad accompanied the Sistan Mission of 1872, and Aziz-ulla Khan was with Lord Blandford (now Duke of Marlborough), when he travelled in India. He was with His Lordship in his voyage round the world, and, on arrival in England, took employment under His Royal Highness the Prince of Wales, with whom he remained for two years. In 1878 he was appointed a Lieutenant in the army of the Sultán of Turkey, and was present at the siege of Kárs. In recognition of his services during the war, he received the fifth class of the order of Medjidi from the Government of the Sultán. Returning to the Panjáb, he was appointed jamadar of the 5th Panjáb Cavalry and, for service in the late Afghan war, received a medal and clasp.

The departments represented by the Commission.

Sir Joseph Ridgeway in temporary command. The members of the Commission.

Native *attachés*.

The demarcation of boundaries.

The mission, thus composed, left India in September, 1884, and arrived in the valley of Herat in November of the same year. A well-defined boundary was fixed between Russian-Turkistán and Afghanistán, by which the frontier line between the Hari Rud and the Murgháb was conceded to Russia, and that from the Murgháb to the Oxus settled.· The Zulfikar Pass was retained for the Amír, and, on the whole, Russia got very much less than she claimed. The proceedings on the part of Russia were conducted by General Komeroff, the Governor and Commander-in-Chief of the Russian forces in the Trans-Caspian Province, whose head-quarters are at Ashkabad, which was conquered by the Russians under General Skobeleff in 1880-81. Colonel Alikhanoff was, at this time, the Russian Governor of Merve, which included Panjdeh and other tracts of Afghan country ceded to Russia. A small part of the work of demarcation, which could not be finished by the Commission, was gone through subsequently, and the frontier settled as far as the And-Khui territory. Most prompt and effectual aid was throughout given to the mission by the Amir's officials, who spared no pains in providing supplies and the means of transport, which materially tended to facilitate the arduous work of the Commission. The labours of the Commission have added materially to our knowledge of the countries it visited. The defences of Herat have been improved under the superintendence of Captain Peacock. The Intelligence Department under Captain Maitland, explored the routes between Nushki and the Helmand, which are of great strategical importance. The country from Maru Chak on the Murgháb to Kilif on the Oxus was surveyed, and the routes to the Khanets of Maimena, And-Khúi, Shibarghan and Akhcha were explored. Independently of the Afghan Boundary Commission, the routes from Yarkand to Charshambá, across the Pamir and of Chitral, Kafristán, Badakshán and Dardistán were explored by Mr. Nevy Elias and Colonel Lockhart. The Survey Department of the Commission under Captains Gore and Talbot surveyed almost the whole of western and northern Afghanistán, including Khorasan east and south-east of Mashhad. A valuable collection of botanical specimens was made in western and northern Afghanistán, while, in the natural history branch, many birds, beasts and reptiles were collected. In the geographical surveys, important contributions were made by Captain Griesbach, while Captain deLaessoe made interesting discoveries in the Archæological Department, which he represented. He opened up an extensive series of ancient cave dwelling in the valley of the Murgháb near Panjdeh, and Captain Yate had similar cave dwellings excavated near Kiláhi-nou. Old coins and other antiquities were also collected by Captains Durand, Talbot and other members of the Mission.

Friendly attitude of the Amír.

Political and scientific results of the Boundary Commission.

The Amír Abdul Rahman Khan has been very energetic in improving the lines of communication throughout his territory. He has linked Kábul to Balkh and Herat by good roads; and the road from Kábul to Herat and the Hazáráját has been improved. The Amír has also strengthened the garrison of Afghan Turkistan. On the return of the Mission from Central Asia, the Amír gave a sumptuous entertainment to the members in his new palace at Kábul, and expressed himself highly pleased with the result of their labours.

Improvements of means of communication in Afghanistán under the new Amír.

In April, 1885, the Viceroy, Lord Dufferin, received a visit from His Highness Abdul Rahman Khan, Amír of Afghanistán, at Ráwalpindi. A grand assemblage took place which was attended by seven ruling chiefs of the Panjáb. His Royal Highness the Duke of Connaught, His Excellency the Commander-in-Chief of the army in India, the Commanders-in-Chiefs of Madras and Bombay, the Lieutenant-Governors of the North-Western Provinces and the Panjáb, and the members of the Executive Council, also took part in the proceedings.

The Ráwalpindi Assemblage, 1885. The meeting between Lord Dufferin and Amír Abdul Rahman Khan.

On the morning of 6th April, a grand military review took place, when 20,000 British troops of all arms, and contingents from the States of Patiálá, Baháwalpur, Jhind, Nabhá, Kapurthálá and Faridkot, forming a total of

The grand military review.

upwards of 3,000 troops, paraded. His Highness the Amír rode beside Lord Dufferin to the parade ground, and remained on horseback throughout the proceedings. He wore a white coat, begirt with a bossed belt, light trousers, with a broad gold stripe, and long riding boots. On his head he wore his usual flat cap of grey brown fur. Gholám Haidar Khan, the Commander-in-Chief of the Afghan army, wore a black helmet. The sight of the British troops in arms created in the mind of the Amír a feeling of respect for the British power, and he saw, for the first time, that he must depend on the friendship of the British, than whom a better ally, or one more able and willing to render him effectual help, it would be in vain to seek. A grand darbár was held on the morning of 8th April, at which were present the notables before mentioned. It was a magnificent spectacle. The ceremony comprised the presentation of valuable gifts to the Amír, and a short conversation between the Viceroy and the Amír. When the gifts had been formally laid out in the Darbár the Amír rose and spoke as follows in Persian :—

The Viceregal darbár.

The Amír's speech.

> I am greatly obliged for the kindness shown me by the Viceroy and the favour shown by the Queen. In return for their kindness, every possible service shall be rendered by me. As regards my army and people, as England has declared her intention of beating off any enemies of Afghanistán, therefore the Afghan nation will join in the firmest manner, and will stand side by side with the British Government.

The presentation of sword to the Amír.

In presenting the sword of honour to the Amír, Lord Dufferin said, it was given to the Amír as a token of the Viceroy's personal regard. It was a gift which he hoped would be acceptable to so distinguished a soldier, who was at the same time a powerful ruler, and who had just declared himself the friend and ally of England. The Amír said in reply: "He hoped with this sword to cut down any enemy of the British Government." At the conclusion of his speech in the darbár, the Amír was understood to say that his words had been uttered after due consideration and before all; so that all present might bear witness to what he had said. The Viceroy gave a banquet in honour of the Amír in the Viceregal camp. In responding to the toast of his health, Abdul Rahman rose and delivered a short speech in Persian, in which he expressed a hope that Afghanistán might continue to prosper like England in future, and that the English arms, would be victorious wherever they went. The assemblage was a great success. It was graftiying to observe the sincerity and depth of good feeling towards the British, which one and all evinced on the occasion. Many chiefs made voluntary offers of service which were gratefully acknowledged by the Government.

The banquet given to the Amír.

Delhi manœuvres, 1885.

In the winter of 1885, the Government of India determined to hold the most extensive peace manœuvres which had ever been undertaken by a British army, and it will not be out of place if we consider what benefits were likely to be gained in return for the expense to be incurred. In cantonments all arms of the service carry out the instructions proper to each separate branch. In larger cantonments all the arms are combined for instruction, so as to obtain the mutual support and assistance in the field which each may expect from the other. But this was not all that was required, and to give a real idea of the requirements of active service, it was necessary to call together as large a number of troops as could conveniently be assembled.

The object of the manœuvres.

Total strength of the armies collected.

This being the object, a large force, consisting of about sixty thousand men of all ranks, and divided into two armies, called respectively the northern and southern force, was assembled in the vicinity of Ambálá in the early part of December 1885, the troops composing the southern force marching to their ground around Gurgáon and Delhi.

It was naturally to be expected that the collection and movements of so large a force would cause destruction to the crops of the districts through which they marched, and instructions were issued to the district officers of the districts, which came within the scope of the manœuvres, to send returns of the loss caused, for which liberal compensation was given by Government.

Compensation for losses to agriculture.

The programme of the manœuvres was that the two armies should meet at Pánipat, north of Delhi, and that the southern, which was to be the defending army, should be beaten and retreat on Delhi, defending it against the northern, or investing army. Delhi was ultimately captured, and the manœuvres ended in a grand review of all the troops comprising the two armies. The northern force commenced its advance on the 30th December, and came in contact with the southern force, as had been arranged, at Pánipit, the historical battle-field of western India, between Karnál and Delhi. In this engagement the southern force offered a vigourous resistance to the northern attack, but finally fell back rapidly on Delhi, closely and vigorously pursued by the northern force. The latter army advanced at an average rate of twenty-five miles daily, leaving behind their transport and taking with them nothing but food for several days and a small quantity of bedding. The hardships undergone by the armies were great, especially as heavy rain fell along their route.

The programme.

When the camp of exercise was first proposed, the neighbourhood of Láhore was mentioned as the probable scene of operations, but it was subsequently abandoned in favour of the districts around Delhi, on the ground of the scarcity of fodder.

Reason of the choice of Delhi.

For the first time in Indian history, representatives of foreign European Powers visited India to witness the manœuvres of the British army. These were Colonel Descharmes and Commandant de Torey the representatives of France; Major Von Hagenow and Major Baron Von Hainingen of Germany, Colonel Timber and Colonel Prince Odviewsky Malsoff of Russia; Lieutenant-Colonel H. M. Lazelle, and Captain S. M. Mills, of the United States of America, Brigadier-General Saletta and Captain Valleris of Italy and Lieutenant-Colonel Prince Louis Esterhazi of Austria.

The representatives of foreign European powers present at this military show.

No army in the world contains so great a number of different races as the British army in India. No doubt a very beautiful spectacle was presented to the foreign visitors by the variety and brilliancy of colouring and the diversity of uniform; but what these trained representatives of foreign Powers chiefly regarded was the harmony and blending of the heterogeneous elements. They were interested in the spectacle, and wrote valuable accounts of what they had seen of the might of the British in India. This was the problem about which the military Governments of Europe especially desired information. They knew that the British army had performed miracles in India, that they had won battles against enormous odds, and had snatched victory out of defeat. They knew that an army of native soldiers had been formed that could be sent to distant shores and uphold British prestige against savage foes; and they recognised that the Indian army had become an integral part of the disciplined forces of the British Empire. What they desired to know was the value of this army when opposed to soldiers of a European Power. The foreign representatives were men chosen for their military fitness; and it is to be hoped that they saw enough to convince them that, not only the Indian army, but the Indian princes and chiefs are able and prepared to resist to the last any invasion by a foreign Power, and that the British Empire in India is maintained, not only by her large and disciplined army and lines of communication and fortresses, but also by the

What they recognised in the spectacle.

The loyalty and gratitude of the people the main strength of the British Empire in India.

loyalty and gratitude of all the races of India. The representatives of Russia also made a tour of the North-West Frontier, accompanied by a British officer; and doubtless saw enough to convince them that all necessary measures had been taken to make that frontier secure.

The Panjáb Chiefs' College established, 1886.

The Panjáb Chiefs' College, a sort of Panjáb Eton, was established at Láhore for the education of the sons of ruling chiefs, of titular and other prominent native gentlemen, and of minors under the Court of Wards, and in the new institution the Wards' School, of Ambálá, was incorporated.

The Mayo School of Arts, Láhore, 1882.

The Mayo School of Art at Láhore has done excellent service in the cause of technical education in the Province. The building, which was finished in the Spring of 1882, was constructed from funds raised by a subscription for founding a memorial to the late Lord Mayo; and the object of the school is to convey instruction in drawing and designing.

The Veterinary School, Láhore, 1882.

A Veterinary School was established at Láhore, in May, 1882, for the improvement of horse-breeding and instruction in that subject. The course of study prescribed for the school is practical, embracing veterinary medicine, surgery, anatomy, physiology and chemistry, bovine pathology, clinical lectures on the diseases of cattle and horses, and shoeing. The students are made to work in the forage, and handle lame and diseased animals. The large numbers of horses and cattle which have been placed in the hospital attached to the school, furnish proof of the popularity and success of this important institution. Mule-breeding also has been attended with much success in the Panjáb; the Government Cattle Farm at Hissár has supplied excellent bulls to most of the districts, and the breeding of rams at Hissár has been attended with useful results.

Results gained from the Institution. Mule breeding. The cattle farm at Hissar.

The Panjáb Public Library, established, 1885.

The Panjáb Public Library was opened by Sir Charles Aitchison, its founder, on the 31st of December, 1885. The want of a large central house of literature which should be available to any student, had been long felt in the Panjáb, and to supply the want this useful institution was established. Its object is "to aid the intellectual progress of the people of all classes by placing within their reach all that is best in the literature of the west and of the east." The extensive library bequeathed to the Local Government by the late Mr. T. W. H. Tolbort, C.S., and the Library of the Director of Public Instruction, have been incorporated in the new Library, which gives promise of material help to the researches of the learned and the moral and intellectual development of the people.

The Public Service Commission, 1886.

Towards the middle of December, 1886, the Public Service Commission met at Láhore, under the presidency of Sir Charles Aitchison, to enquire into the question of the conditions under which the natives of India should be employed in posts ordinarily reserved for the Covenanted Civil Service, and the questions relating to the admission of natives of India and Europeans, respectively, to those branches of the Uncovenanted Service which are directly engaged in the executive and judicial administration of the country. The witnesses examined by the Commission represented various views and interests. No person desirous of giving evidence on any point falling within the scope of the enquiries was excluded. Twenty members of the Civil Service, including five Statutory Civilians, twenty members of the Uncovenanted Service, and forty members of the general public, including Societies and Editors of newspapers, were examined. After making the most searching inquiry into the conditions of the Service in the different public departments, the Commission submitted their report to the Government of India; and it is hoped that the recommendations of the Governor-General on the report made to the Secretary of State will, if carried out, have, in the words of Lord Dufferin, "the effect of throwing open to the natives of each province

Witnesses examined by the Commission.

Recommendations of the Government of India on the report of the Commissioners.

more of the higher administrative posts, and of opening out to them a career which will satisfy their aspirations."

India owes a debt of undying gratitude to Lady Dufferin for organising a scheme having for its object the supply of medical aid to the women of India. Gifted by nature with a philanthropic mind and a charitable and benevolent disposition, this noble lady inaugurated the National Association, having for its object three different ends, namely, medical tuition, medical relief, and the supply of trained nurses.

Lady Dufferin's scheme for supplying medical aid to the women of India.

The National Association, Calcutta.

Its objects.

The unanimity expressed as to the desirability of the objects of such a scheme, and the support it has met with from one end of India to the other, have been most encouraging. All over India various centres of medical aid have been established, and every endeavour is being made towards the accomplishment of the scheme by giving a liberal training to women, to enable them to serve as female doctors and render effectual medical relief to the zenáná population. The Lady Aitchison Hospital at Láhore will, besides the relief given to in-door female patients, serve, in connection with the Medical College, as a school in which women will receive a thorough medical training and be fitted to carry relief to other districts, and to work in other hospitals which it is intended to establish, as the work of the National Association in Calcutta progresses. Wherever female hospitals have been established, female doctors and trained nurses have been employed, and the multiplication of female wards in such hospitals, and the remarkable proficiency displayed by native ladies in the studies they have undertaken, show that the scheme is warmly appreciated by those whom it concerns. The result arrived at has been particularly gratifying to the noble lady who so deservedly shared the honours of her distinguished husband.

Centres of medical aid established throughout India.

The Lady Aitchison Hospital, Láhore.

"It was," said His Excellency, "inexpressibly gratifying, for it shows how, even in the unchanging east, where improvement is so readily supposed to knock vainly at the gates of cast-iron tradition, if only sympathy, kindness and practical good sense inspire the effort, the doors fly open and joyfully admit the train of blessings that follow the advance of all sound and well-considered national progress."

Lord Dufferin's views of the scheme.

The National Association will prove a lasting memorial of the good done to millions of women by Her Excellency Lady Dufferin, who, on her leaving the shores of this country, was followed by the prayers of thousands upon thousands of Her Majesty's Indian subjects.

One of the most brilliant achievements of Lord Dufferin's term of Viceroyalty has been the pacification of Upper Burmah. The Burmese are Mongol in race and Buddhist in religion. Their country had, for generations, been a prey to internal strife and commotions, which threatened to embroil the British with one of the great military powers of Europe. The Government was, therefore, compelled to have recourse to arms. The country was invaded by British troops, and, in the course of a fortnight, the Burmese army surrendered to the victors; their king was captured, and Mandalay, his capital, occupied. The country, which was in a complete state of disorganisation, has been tranquillised; quiet has succeeded to disorder, the formidable dacoit bands have been dispersed and their leaders disposed of. Vast and impracticable jungles are now being reclaimed, roads are under construction, military posts and telegraphic communication have been established, and all the appliances of a civilised country introduced. Burmah now forms an integral part of the British dominions. Its industrious inhabitants, freed from the pest of dacoity, have applied themselves to the arts of peace, and every hope is entertained that the Province will develop into one of the most prosperous parts of Her Majesty's Indian Empire, and add materially

The annexation of Burmah.

to its strength and resources. Had the Government of India not acted with vigour and decision in regard to this province, it would have been menaced by dangers and difficulties which it would have been no easy matter to face and surmount. It is to the interest of the subjects of Her Majesty to make Imperial India compact and strong, to see its resources developed and its influence and power increased. The true interests of the people and of the Government are closely interwoven; they are inseparable—they are, in fact, identical. Every well-wisher of the country feels sincerely grateful for the stroke of policy adopted by Lord Dufferin with reference to Burmah; and the people rejoiced when the news came that the Imperial Government of Her Majesty the Queen-Empress had not been slow in showing its recognition of the services of His Lordship in connection with the annexation, and that Her Most Gracious Majesty had been pleased to confer the title of the *Marquis of Ava* on Lord Dufferin, a distinction to which his services eminently entitled him.

What the interests of Imperial India dictate.

Jubilee of Her Majesty the Queen Empress, 16th February 1887.

The Jubilee of Her Majesty the Queen-Empress was celebrated on the 16th February, 1887. It was ushered in, at all the principal stations of India, by an imperial salute of 101 guns. A more prosperous reign or a more beloved sovereign the world has never seen. The 50th year of Her Majesty's auspicious reign was celebrated with the greatest enthusiasm in the Panjáb, which, fifty years ago, was still ruled by Ranjít Singh. Festivities and rejoicings and gaiety were everywhere the order of the day. Darbárs for the reception of the nobility were held at the head-quarters of all the districts; there was a presentation of addresses, breathing a spirit of fervent loyalty to the person and throne of Her Majesty, and a review of troops was held at every military station. Over two thousand convicts were released in the Panjáb, in honour of the event; nor were the poor forgotten on the happy occasion; charitable and public buildings were opened or founded; and there were general illuminations and social entertainments of every description. The Lieutenant-Governor laid the foundation stone, which was of Naushera marble, of the Victoria Jubilee Hall at Láhore, and received congratulatory addresses from fifteen societies and local bodies, including the Panjáb University, the Khálsá Dewán, the Indian Association and the Mahomedan Association. Following the precedent established at the Imperial Assemblage, certificates bearing the signature of the Honourable the Lieutenant-Governor of the Panjáb were presented to some four hundred native gentlemen throughout the Province, as an acknowledgment of their good services and loyalty. The Government had left the initiative of rejoicings to the people, and the public demonstrations of joy exhibited throughout the length and breadth of the empire were of a marked character. At the Jummá Masjíd, in Dehli, special prayers for the welfare of Her Majesty were offered up. At Pesháwar an enterprising Hindu (Lorindá Mal) gave a lakh of rupees to found a poor-house and home for the sick and incurables. A Mahomedan gentleman (Ghulám Rasúl Khan) gave 60,000 rupees to build new gates for the city and shops, the income of the latter to be devoted to charitable purposes. At Amritsar, Hindus, Sikhs and Mahomedans, assembled in masses at their respective places of worship and offered up prayers for Her Majesty. At Bannú the Mahomedan Maliks, Khans, Arbábs and officers assembled in the grand mosque, and special prayers were offered for the long life of Her Majesty.* At Ráwalpindi the members of the Ahluwáliá Singh Sabhá offered a beautifully wrought needle work-box and *phulkári*, worked by the ladies of their

Public festivities and rejoicings.

Release of convicts.

Congratulatory addresses from public bodies.

Public prayers for Her Imperial Majesty.

* The speech made on the occasion by the author was most enthusiastically received by the Patháns and Maliks of the independent hill country. Khan Bahadur, Khan Baba Khan, Extra Assistant Commissioner, a member of the late Boundary Commission, made an impressive speech in Pusthú.

zenánás for Her Imperial Majesty. A public meeting of the chiefs, tomándárs and citizens was held at Dera Gházi Khan, at which a large sum was subscribed for the erection of a free *serai* to be called the *Shahi Serai*. At Ludhiáná a Jubilee commemorative hospital for women was established. At Kangrá there were national mountain dances by torch-light. Thanksgiving services were held in cathedrals and churches throughout India. At Jalandar the Commissioner unveiled a bust of His Royal Highness the Prince of Wales, presented by Bikráman Singh and Suchet Singh, the Ahluwáliá Sardars. At Wazírábád the Mahomedans illuminated their mosques and offered special prayers for the Empress. The women of Gujránwálá inaugurated a memorial of the Jubilee by raising a subscription for a Jubilee female school, the expenses of which were to be defrayed entirely by their subcriptions. The ruling chiefs of the Panjáb vied with each other in their exhibition of loyalty to the Queen-Empress. The Nawáb of Baháwalpur held a State reception in his Palace of Núr Mahal, which was tastefully decorated. In Náhan water-works were instituted in honour of the Jubilee, to be named the Kaisar-i-Hind Water-Works, at a cost estimated at a lakh of rupees. The Rájá of Nabhá remitted 10,000 rupees to the Imperial Institute in London. At Kapurthálá the Rájá held a Darbár with the object of laying the foundation-stone of an hospital, to be called the Victoria Hospital, for women and children. The Maharájá of Patiálá, at a public darbár held by him, announced donations aggregating Rs. 54,000 in commemoration of the Jubilee year. A gold medal was founded, to be given annually to the best student in the Female Medical School at Láhore. A large guest-house was to be founded at Patiálá in commemoration of the event, while the course of instruction in the Mahandar College was raised to the B. A. standard. This was all proof of the deep attachment of the people to the British rule and to the throne of the Queen-Empress, of which wisdom, justice, piety and duty have been the guardians and which have been the companions of her daily life. With each returning year, the foundations of her mighty realm have become more firmly established, while the loyalty and devotion of her subjects have grown more tender and more intense.

Loyal demonstrations by the ruling chiefs of the Panjáb.

The Nawáb of Baháwalpur.

The Rájá of Náhan.

The Rájá of Nabhá.

The Rájá of Kapurthálá.

The Maharájá of Patiálá.

At a meeting held at Láhore to commemorate the Queen-Empress' Jubilee, it was resolved to establish a "Technical Institute" in that city. The Institute is to be established in connection with the School of Arts, itself a technical educational institution of great utility. The Government has granted a central site, close to the Panjáb Public Library and the School of Arts for the Institute, which will contain spacious halls for the exhibition of art, industrial and economic specimens, as well as antiquities and ethnographic models. Accommodation will also be provided for chemical laboratories and for class or lecture rooms, for a library and for an engine room, where steam-power can be provided when wanted. A work of a very practical nature is going on at the Railway Workshops, where apprentices can learn the use of tools, machinery and the properties of metals and materials. In the new institute, practical demonstrations of chemistry, of dyeing and cotton-printing, food stuffs, leather tanning and many other trades will be given. The amount available for expenditure on the Victoria Jubilee Institute is about Rs. 93,000, collected from subscriptions, and a further sum of Rs. 20,000 will be received from Government, in part representing the price of the old Museum building.

Victoria Jubilee Technical Institute.

Sir Charles Aitchison was succeeded in the office of Lieutenant-Governor by Sir James Broadwood Lyall of the Civil Service, on the 2nd April, 1887. For the special encouragement of Mahomedans, the Government sanctioned a certain number of Jubilee Scholarships, tenable in High Schools and

Sir James Broadwood Lyall succeeds as Lieutenant-Governor, 2nd April, 1887.

Establishment of Jubilee Scholarships.

Colleges, and local bodies were authorized to award similar scholarships tenable in Middle Schools. Under the able guidance of Sir James Lyall, an expedition against the Black Mountain tribes on the north-western border, was brought to a successful termination. These tribes had, on various occasions, made raids on British territory, burning the villages on the border and murdering British subjects. For their hostile conduct they were adequately punished and made to feel that, though slow to avenge, the power of the British Government to inflict punishment was great. Their principal tower was blown up, and Pokál, their chief village, with many other villages, was set on fire. At Pokál there were about sixty houses substantially built, many of them with carved doorposts. All these were destroyed, and the troops burnt the outlying houses, together with stacks of corn belonging to the villagers, as they retired up the hills. Very little plunder of any value was obtained from the sacked villages, the principal thing being honey, of which a large quantity was found everywhere. A number of chairs, with carved wooden backs were carried off as trophies. The tribes were compelled to submit, and sued for mercy; and it is hoped that the lesson given them will prove a sufficient guarantee for the security and future tranquillity of the border.

The Black Mountain Expedition, 1888.

Lord Dufferin's visit to Láhore, 1888.

Towards the middle of November, 1888, the capital of the Panjáb was honoured by the presence of His Excellency Lord Dufferin and Ava. His Excellency was greeted at the railway station by the chiefs of the Panjáb and the Municipality, to the address of which body he replied in befitting terms. A splendid evening party was given at Government House, at which some of the ruling chiefs of the Panjáb were present, besides a large number of leading notables. The following morning (15th November), His Excellency received deputations from various public bodies at Láhore, and, with a courtesy and kindness which will never be forgotten by those who had the honour of seeing him that day, he replied to each separately. The addresses presented referred, in an extremely loyal tone, to the various measures of reform passed during His Lordship's tenure of office. His Excellency's reply to the address of the *Anjuman-i-Islámiá* of Láhore was clearly delivered in Persian, and was highly appreciated by the members of the deputation. The same day the Lady Aitchison Hospital for native women was formally opened by Lady Dufferin. After the address from the Managing Committee of the Institution had been read, the Marchioness rose and said: "I declare the Hospital open, and may God's blessing rest upon it." Lord Dufferin and Sir Charles Aitchison made speeches, which were most enthusiastically received by the chiefs and nobles who were interested in the Institution.

Address of the *Anjuman-i-Islámiá.*

Lady Aitchison Hospital opened.

Lady Dufferin's visit to zenáná ladies.

Her Excellency visited the zenáná ladies assembled in the room set apart for them, where some very interesting ceremonies took place. A native lady * read Hindi verses which she had composed for the occasion. Her Excellency and suite were decorated with garlands of flowers, which they wore throughout the ceremony. Some choice articles of female industry, such as baskets, hair chains, &c., were laid before Her Excellency. The Marchioness and party, on taking their leave, shook hands with the native ladies, expressing a hope that they would continue to sympathise with a work which was for the good of their own sex.

Brief as was the stay of Lord Dufferin at Láhore, His Excellency's courteous demeanour, and the gracious and affable way in which he received the several deputations of public bodies there, won all hearts. His words had a charming effect and impressed his hearers. His final words to the deputations were deeply touching and produced genuine regret at the departure from the country of a ruler possessed of so high a spirit, and of

* She was the wife of our fellow-citizen, Rai Bahádur Brij Lal Ghose.

such political and administrative wisdom and generous views. His farewell to the citizens of Láhore was thus worded:—

Lord Dufferin's farewell to the Panjáb.

And now, gentlemen, I will bid you farewell. You have always received me with kindness. You have judged my conduct with indulgence, and have never withheld your generous appreciation of the endeavours of my Government to do its duty. As long as I live, I shall always retain a most affectionate recollection of the brave and high-minded races of the Pánjáb, with so many of whose chiefs and leading men I have formed ties of personal friendship. May every blessing that Providence has in its gift rest upon you and yours for many a generation.

No words could have been more touching; and Lord Dufferin proved by his actions that his were not empty words, but that his desire to advance the interests of the people of the country and to foster all their just and legitimate aspirations was most genuine.

Patiálá festivities.

On his return from Láhore, His Excellency, accompanied by Sir James Lyall, paid a visit to Patiálá, where the festivities on the occasion of His Highness the Maharájá's marriage were most imposing. To commemorate the Viceregal visit, the Maharájá established a Zenáná Hospital in the capital of his State. The hospital is to be built at a cost of thirty thousand rupees, and ten thousand rupees is to be set aside by the State as the annual cost of its maintenance. A public darbár was held in honour of the Viceroy's visit, at which an eloquent speech was delivered by the Governor-General, in which His Excellency congratulated the Maharájá on the auspicious occasion of his marriage, and wishing him and his house all the happiness and prosperity this world can bestow. He then presented His Highness with a magnificent necklace and presents valued at thirty thousand rupees, including a fine sword of Damascene work, a gun and rich cloths; also five thousand rupees, as an equipment for the elephant and horse, which were not presented. "When His Highness comes into the possession of power," said Lord Dufferin, "I feel convinced that he will worthily maintain the honour of his ancestral house, and take a high place among the Princes of India as a loyal and brave feudatory of Her Majesty the Queen-Empress, as well as a conscientious and enlightened ruler."

The Maharájá establishes a Zenáná Hospital in his capital.

His Highness has since been invested with full powers over his extensive dominions, and it is gratifying to know that he has proved himself thoroughly worthy of the confidence reposed in him by the talented Viceroy of India.

In 1885, when war between England and Russia seemed imminent, the ruling princes of India, in both the south and the north, in a spirit of loyalty unparalleled in history, came forward to place at the disposal of the Imperial Government the entire resources of their states. War was happily averted; but the feelings displayed by the chiefs not only made a very favourable impression in England, but produced a most desirable effect in other countries. Again, in the year of the Jubilee of Her Most Gracious Majesty the Queen-Empress, the princes of India availed themselves of the opportunity for a fresh display of loyalty, and made very liberal offers to contribute towards the frontier defences of the empire. Foremost among the ruling chiefs on both occasions were those of the Panjáb, whose forces had on different previous occasions fought side by side with British troops to maintain British prestige in the East. The Government of India, knowing well the sincerity of the motives which had prompted the chiefs to make these loyal offers, and appreciating their sense of duty to the paramount Power in matters involving their common interest, devised a scheme by which their offers might be turned to advantage. The Darbár of Patiálá seemed to the Governor-General to afford a fitting opportunity for the public inauguration of that scheme which was made in the following terms:—

Government scheme for utilizing the offers of the native Princes for co-operation in the frontier defences.

The Government of India did not think it necessary, nor, in all respects, desirable to accept from the Native States of India the pecuniary assistance which they had so freely tendered, but in one very important particular the Government wished to enlist their co-operation. The armies of Native States were strong in numbers, but at present of various degrees of efficiency. It was proposed to ask those chiefs who possessed specially good fighting material in their armies to raise a portion of those armies to such a pitch of general efficiency as would make them fit to go into action side by side with the Imperial Troops; for this purpose some extra exertions would, it was thought, be necessary, as troops at the present day, to be thoroughly fit for service, require very complete arrangements in the way of arms, transport, equipment and organisation generally. To help the chiefs in setting on foot and maintaining the troops selected for service, it was resolved to appoint a few English officers as advisers and inspectors. The officers will have their head-quarters at some central point in British territory, and will visit the several States in turn. Capable native drill instructors will also be lent to the states from the British regiments.

The selected troops will be armed with breech-loading weapons presented to the several states by the British Government; there will be carbines for the cavalry and Snider rifles for the infantry, and, in addition to this, each Panjáb chief will receive a battery of four guns. Thus, while each force is to remain a purely State force, recruited in the territories of its chief and serving within them, the troops composing it will gradually be made so efficient as to enable the Imperial Government to use them as part of its available resources to meet any external danger.

Having thus explained the views of the Government, His Excellency said:—

I trust that the chiefs selected will in any case regard the acceptance of their offers as an honourable distinction, while those whose armies it is not found possible to utilise in the same manner, will understand that if they cannot usefully contribute to the fighting strength of the Empire, they can, in other ways, render service equally meritorious and equally sure to win the approval of Her Majesty the Queen-Empress.

Retirement of Lord Dufferin, 1888.

Early in December, 1888, Lord Dufferin resigned the office of Viceroy and Governor-General, and was succeeded by the Marquis of Lansdowne. The retired Viceroy had fully justified the anticipations which had been formed of his great administrative capabilities when his appointment was first announced, and great was the regret among all classes of people, European and Native, when the time came for his retirement. A complete master of the art of diplomacy and politics, he brought with him a high reputation as a ruler of men, and his keen insight into the wants of the country over whose destinies he was called upon to rule, and the great measures introduced by him for strengthening the empire of India internally, as regards its own affairs, externally, as to its relations with foreign countries, as well as the calm perseverance and energy with which he applied himself to the accomplishment of his great task, gained for him universal confidence and admiration. When he first came to India, the Empire was on the verge of war, on the North-Western Frontier, with one of the greatest military Powers of Europe. By the wise policy adopted by the Governor-General, not only were the war and its concomitant calamities averted, at a moment when the British were the least prepared to face the tempest, but effectual measures were adopted to strengthen the Frontier by the construction of military post and forts, the laying out of cantonments, the construction of new lines of railway and the improvement of the means of communication by extending the system of roads to the hitherto comparatively inaccessible parts of the border. These active measures had the effect of soon restoring the strength and security of the Empire, and this at a time of special financial difficulty, as there was a great drain on the resources of the country, consequent on the loss on exchange and a decrease in the opium revenue. With due regard to economy, and at a cost which is infinitesimal, compared with the expenditure on similar schemes in Europe, the whole of the North-Western Frontier has been put into such a state of defence as will enable the culti-

India on the verge of war with a European military Power.

The danger averted.

Strengthening of the frontier defences.

vator to till his fields in peace and contentment. The native chiefs of the Panjáb showed their appreciation of these schemes by offers of co-operation in carrying out the policy of Frontier defence, by placing at the disposal of the Government the entire resources of their dominions and by making offers of large sums of money, as their contributions towards the outlay to be expended on the scheme. Never was there a more spontaneous outburst of loyalty; and the offers made were indubitable proof of the deep interest which the feudatories took in maintaining British supremacy and of the extent to which they had identified themselves with the true interests of the paramount power.

Loyalty displayed by the ruling chiefs of the Panjáb.

Lord Dufferin fostered education and afforded encouragement to training in technical subjects. With reference to this last subject, His Excellency said, at Láhore, in reply to an address presented to him by the National Mahomedan Association, on the occasion of his visit to the capital of the Panjáb, in November, 1888, that his attention had been particularly struck by the fact that the present system of popular education in India was too exclusively liberal in its aims, and failed to produce young men able to earn their living by devoting themselves to the arts, handicrafts and sciences. "Endeavours are now being made," said His Excellency, in addressing the assembly, "to remove this reproach against our present practice, by the introduction of a system of technical education which shall run in parallel lines with, and be supplementary to, the literary course."

The services of Lord Dufferin.

His Lordship on the subject of technical education.

As observed by Lord Dufferin, a considerable advance towards bringing a scheme of this nature into operation has already been made in the Panjáb. Lord Dufferin took a keen interest in Municipal reforms. He was a friend of the Local Self-Government scheme, and was anxious to give full play and every advantage to the working of those Municipal institutions which his illustrious predecessor had so liberally enlarged and strengthened. He insisted on sanitary and prison reforms, instituted careful enquiries with a view to the amelioration of the condition of the people, granted facilities for emigration and made beneficial recommendations for the re-organisation of the public service.

On the 23rd of November, 1889, the capital of the Panjáb was honoured by a visit from His Excellency the Marquis of Lansdowne, Viceroy and Governor-General of India. His Excellency was welcomed at the Railway Station by some of the ruling chiefs of the Panjáb and a large concourse of ladies and gentlemen. The Municipal Committee presented him with an address of welcome, to which his Lordship replied in terms suitable for the occasion. "After a somewhat protracted 'tour,'" observed His Lordship, "throughout the Frontier Districts of this Province, it afforded pleasure to him to find himself in its capital city, which, from its historical associations in the past, and from the position which it occupied to-day, was the centre of the political life of the Panjáb, and entitled to the utmost respect of those who were concerned in the Government of India."

The visit of Lord Lansdowne to Láhore, 1889.

On the 25th, His Excellency formally declared open the buildings of the Láhore Mission College. In reply to an address read to His Excellency by the Principal of the College, Lord Lansdowne felt there was every reason for looking forward with confidence to the future of the Institution, and believed that "the foundations upon which it was built were sure and solid."

The opening of the building of the Láhore Mission College.

The same day, Lady Lansdowne performed the ceremony of laying the foundation-stone of a new Female Students' Boarding-house, in course of construction in connection with the work of the Countess of Dufferin Fund. The Managing Committee of the Panjáb Branch of the Countess of Dufferin Fund has already done good work in the Province. It has assisted the

Laying of the foundation-stone of the new boarding-house for female students.

Lady Aitchison Hospital, Láhore, by providing scholarships for female students, and helped the Municipalities of Gurdáspur and Delhi and the women's ward of the Ripon Hospital at Simla. A hospital has been built at Kapurthállá and opened for work, and another at Patiálá is under construction.

Convocation of the Panjáb University, 1889.

At noon the following day, the Chancellor, Vice-Chancellor and Fellows of the Panjáb University, met in convocation for the purpose of conferring degrees. The meeting was held in the Government College Halls, Láhore, which were tastefully decorated for the occasion. His Excellency the Viceroy, Patron of the University, and his Honor Sir James Lyall, the Chancellor, took their seats on a raised dais, the Vice-Chancellor, W. H. Rattigan, Esq., taking his seat to the left of the Chancellor. The Fellows of the University were ranged on each side, right and left, of the dais, the body of the hall being thronged by the donors and subscribers to the University, University graduates, habited in academic robes, and a large gathering of the visitors. The Senate having previously decided that His Excellency, by reason of his eminent position and attainments, was a fit and proper person to receive the degree of Doctor of Literature, His Excellency was, amidst great applause, invested with the said degree *honoris causá.** Lord Lansdowne, having honoured the University with the acceptance of the degree offered to him, delivered an important address. The same day there was a brilliant conversazione in the Montgomery Hall, at which His Excellency and Lady Lansdowne were introduced to numerous visitors, European and native. There was also a Chrysanthemum Exhibition in the Lawrence Gardens, and the festivities ended with a visit to the City and the principal ancient buildings of the station.

Degree of D. L. conferred on Lord Lansdowne.

Conversazione in the Montgomery Hall.

Visit of His Royal Highness Prince Albert Victor of Wales, to the Panjáb, 1890.

The visit to India, in the beginning of 1890, of the grandson of Her Imperial Majesty the Queen-Empress was a further indication of the interest taken by our most Gracious Sovereign, and by the Heir-Apparent to the throne, in her vast Indian Empire. The people of this country regarded the presence in their midst of a representative of the Royal House of England with the highest appreciation, and great was the joy felt by the people of all classes and races throughout the length and breadth of the Empire when the illustrious visitor honoured the country with his august presence. His Royal Highness landed at Calcutta on Friday, the 3rd January, 1890, and, after visiting Lucknow, Cawnpur, Benares and Agra, arrived in Láhore on Saturday morning, the 25th of January, and was received with general demonstrations of loyalty and rejoicings. He was welcomed at the railway terminus by a distinguished civil and military company, the former headed by Sir James Lyall, the Lieutenant-Governor, and the latter by Sir Hugh Gough. There was a brilliant gathering of native princes and nobles. As the train conveying His Royal Highness entered the station (brightened by decorative festoons and flags) a royal salute was fired from the ramparts of the fort. His Royal Highness, who bears a striking likeness to his uncle, the Duke of Connaught, was dressed in the uniform of the 10th Hussars. The introductions over, His Royal Highness was conducted to the portico, and thence outside the station, where the Panjáb Volunteer Rifles, who furnished guards-of-honour, and a Company of 19th Panjáb Infantry, presented arms, the bands simultaneously striking up the National Anthem. The scene in front of the Railway Station was instinct with life and movement. The

* Up to the present the roll of the University bears six names among its honorary graduates, Lord Ripon, Lord Dufferin, Sir Charles Aitchison, the Reverend V. French, the late Lord Bishop of Láhore, and Doctor Leitner. Each received the honorary degree of Doctor of Oriental Learning. All, except the first, are oriental and classical scholars, and the degree of Doctor of Literature was most appropriately conferred on His Excellency the present Viceroy.

road to Government House was gaily decorated with Venetian masts, shields, arms, drapery and flags, and picturesquely lined by the 17th Bengal Lancers. The roads leading to the station and its precincts were thronged with crowds of spectators, whose enthusiasm at seeing the grandson of their beloved Sovereign was unbounded. At noon His Royal Highness received the chiefs of Baháwalpur and Nabhá, who are both Grand Commanders of the Star of India, and in the afternoon he returned their visits. The native contingents of Jhind, Patiálá, Baháwalpur and Nabhá, recently instructed by the officers of the Bengal Army, were then inspected at Government House.

Interchange of visits with native chiefs.

The same day, at 4-45 P. M., His Royal Highness, accompanied by His Honour the Lieutenant-Governor and staff, visited the city, mounted on elephants. At the Delhi Gate, an arch bore the legend :

Visit to the city.

"Welcome to our beloved Prince Victor of Wales."

Passing the Golden Mosque and through the streets, His Royal Highness visited the *samádh* of Ranjít Singh, where he was pleased to hear a beautiful hymn sung by the priests, welcoming the grandson of the English Maharání to the land of the five rivers. The party next visited the great Bádsháhí Mosque, which they entered bareheaded. The fort was then entered, and the *Shish Mahal*, or Palace of Mirrors, and the soldiers' quarters, inspected. At seven o'clock, the fort and the environs were lighted up, and the huge motto, "Loyalty, Fidelity, Obedience," blazed out in variegated letters. A magnificent display of fireworks followed, after which the procession set out to return to Government House, inspecting on the way the illuminations in Anárkali and the environs, which were most effective.

At night a brilliant conversazione was held at the Montgomery Hall, in which a large company of Europeans, native chiefs and the officers of native regiments, were introduced to His Royal Highness. The Prince having then been conducted to the dais, Sir Meredyth Plowden read to him the Panjáb address, in which the assembly, as representative of all classes, official, non-official, European and native, of the community of this frontier province, offered His Royal Highness a loyal and hearty welcome to its capital. Fourteen years had passed since Láhore had been visited by His Royal Highness's illustrious father, and during this period the Panjáb had made rapid strides. By the completion of railway communication between Láhore and Karrachi, the province had obtained a natural outlet for its sea-borne trade, and the extension of the railway to Pesháwar, the pacification of the turbulent tribes of the Khaibar, and the improvement of communications along the Deráját border, had tended materially to secure the North-Western Frontier of India against foreign aggression. Amongst peaceful pursuits, the advance made in education had been marked by the establishment of an independent provincial University at Láhore. The tour planned by His Royal Highness would afford an opportunity of seeing the chief cities of the Panjáb, while, in the military camp of exercise at Muridki, would be found assembled several regiments of the army, which is so largely recruited from the various warlike races of this Province. The Panjáb could not boast of possessing in its plains the beauties of natural scenery presented by other provinces through which His Royal Highness had lately passed. But it contributed to the Empire a population noted for manly qualities, in the enjoyment of a high degree of agricultural prosperity, which, while composed of many different tribes, of various religions, Sikh, Hindu and Mahomedan, was united by the common bond of devoted loyalty and attachment to Her Most Gracious Majesty, our beloved Queen-Empress.

The conversazione.

The Panjáb address.

His Royal Highness made a suitable reply, of which the following is the text :—

His Royal Highness's reply.

Sir Meredyth Plowden and Gentlemen,—I tender you my warmest thanks for the very cordial address which has been just read to me; an address which, coming as it does on behalf of the community of the Panjáb, gives me peculiar gratification and interest, inasmuch as it shows how united is the vast and varied population of this province in their loyalty and devotion to Her Majesty the Queen-Empress; and it will be a most pleasing duty to me to repeat to Her Majesty the terms in which your heart-felt sentiments of attachment to Her Majesty have been communicated. I feel I cannot give you a better idea of the immense interest and sympathy which exist in the mind of our beloved Sovereign towards her Indian subjects, than by telling you that, notwithstanding her inability to visit her Indian Empire, a fact she never ceases to deplore, Her Majesty has, by the greatest diligence, acquired some knowledge of the Hindostáni language.

Interest taken by Her Imperial Majesty towards her Indian subjects.

Other Provinces of India may be richer than the Panjáb; some may present scenes of greater beauty; but there is no province in India that can boast, as the Panjáb can, that it is the bulwark of defence against foreign aggression, or that can be termed with the same significance, the guard-room of our Eastern Empire.

As the Panjáb is one of the greatest recruiting grounds, so it is also the home, or place of service, of a large portion of the army in Northern India; and it is particularly gratifying to me to think that it is here, in the soldiers' land, that I shall see, at Muridki, a force of cavalry such as is seldom brought together in any part of the world.

At Láhore itself, I have observed to-day much that has interested and impressed me; side by side, at this, one of the most ancient capitals of India, I see the signs of prosperity and vigorous civilisation, in the new buildings which are opening up on every side and in the loyal demeanour of a contented and manly population.

Let me, Gentlemen, once more thank you, and, through you, all classes of the Panjáb, for the gratifying address and hearty welcome you have given me to-day.

The Muridki cavalry camp of exercise, 1890.

On Sunday, the 26th of January, the Royal party took train for Muridki, where a grand review of the troops assembled there, was held in honour of His Royal Highness. The manœuvres were executed on the plains to the west of the Commander-in-Chief's camp. The Government of India had of late recognised the necessity of instructing each branch of the army in its own particular duties before it could be expected to work in combination with other arms. The fact was also recognised, that, in the case of cavalry, Commanders should acquire the power of handling large bodies of horsemen with skill and rapidity. The breech-loader had, as observed by Sir Frederick Roberts, no doubt, increased the power of infantry most materially, while the introduction of smokeless powder was, in all probability, calculated to revolutionise modern warfare still further. Occasion had been taken by the Commander-in-Chief to exhort infantry soldiers to learn how to use their rifles effectively, while, addressing artillerymen lately, he had pointed out the necessity for their being able to make the utmost of their guns. It was equally important, maintained Sir Frederick Roberts, to impress on cavalry soldiers how essential it was that they should excel in the use of the sword and lance. "There is only one method," argued His Excellency, "by which a cavalry soldier can become thoroughly expert in the use of his weapon and also in the management of his horse, and that is by practising mounted combat."

The object of the manœuvres.

The essential requisites of cavalry soldiers.

The practice of mounted combat.

With this object, camps of instruction had been sanctioned during the last few years, and there had been artillery camps at Unáo, Gurgáon and Pur, and cavalry camps at Lawrencepore and Delhi, while at the head-quarters of each of the larger districts a considerable force of infantry had been collected for some weeks every cold season. The cavalry camp of exercise at Muridki had for its object the attainment of the same military discipline. Instructive work had been carried on for some days previously, and there were competitions for the assault of arms, rendezvous formations, sham-fights and other manœuvres. On the morning of 29th January, the whole of the huge forces of cavalry being on parade, they formed themselves up in two lines. The first line, extending for two miles, was composed

Work done at the camp of exercise.

The grand parade of 29th January, 1890.

of two batteries of Royal Horse Artillery, ten regiments of Native Cavalry and three of Dragoon Guards, the five Lancer regiments being in the centre, and the sabre regiments occupying the flanks. The second line consisted of nine squadrons of the Native States troops. The Prince, accompanied by Sir James Lyall, the Lieutenant-Governor, Sir Frederick Roberts, the Commander-in-Chief, and a numerous staff, was shortly afterwards seen rounding the left flank of the line. As the procession reached the saluting base, the general salute was given by the whole line, His Royal Highness and the Chief advancing and acknowledging it. The inspection of the two lines being over, the march-past commenced, led by General Luck and his staff, and followed by the Royal Horse Artillery and the two cavalry divisions. Squadron after squadron passed, and, no sooner had the last brigade disappeared, than the artillery advanced again. The whole force trotted past, and, the front being cleared by counter-marching and deploying to the right, each regiment galloped past in line. The galloping-past being over, the two divisions formed up in line of squadron columns at deploying interval, and the order to advance was given. The entire line, two miles in length, breaking into a gallop, charged up to within fifty yards of where His Royal Highness was standing. The halt was then sounded, and, the whole line giving a general salute, the review came to an end. General Sir Frederick Roberts then, riding forward to the saluting base, delivered a most able speech to the British and Native officers assembled. He expressed his pleasure at the success which had attended the late manœuvres, and the steadiness with which the movements had been performed. This was, in a great measure, due to the systematic and careful manner in which squadron training had been carried on, and His Excellency desired that the officers assembled might be assured that their efforts had been thoroughly appreciated.

The march-past.

The galloping-past of artillery.

The speech of the Commander-in-Chief.

After the conclusion of the speech, His Excellency announced to the officers of the 1st Panjáb Cavalry that Her Majesty the Queen-Empress had been graciously pleased to approve of the regiment being named after His Royal Highness Prince Albert Victor of Wales, and that it was henceforward to be called "Prince Albert Victor's Own." This is an honour which will certainly be appreciated, not only by all the ranks of the 1st Panjáb Cavalry, but by the whole of the Panjáb Frontier Force. At 2-30 P.M. His Excellency dismissed the parade, and the Muridki cavalry camp of 1890, comprising the largest number of civilised cavalry ever collected in India, came to a conclusion.

Honour conferred on 1st Panjáb Cavalry.

Leaving Muridki for Peshâwar, His Royal Highness reached the latter station on the morning of the 30th January. He drove through the city, accompanied by the Commissioner, and, on arrival at Gor Kotri, was introduced to the Municipal Commissioners, who had all assembled at that point to do him homage. A splendid garden party was held in his honour, and the following day His Royal Highness, accompanied by Sir Edward Bradford and his private staff, started for Jamrúd, driven in a Royal Artillery drag. At Jamrúd, 200 men of the Khaibar Rifles received the Prince with a royal salute. His Royal Highness presented medals for the Black Mountain expedition of 1888 to Major Aslam Khan, native officers and those who had received Orders of Merit for the expedition. He commended their conduct in the campaign and their bravery in action, which had won for them the respect and appreciation of all the Generals and Commanders with whom they had been brought in contact. He expressed his pleasure at having, on the occasion of his first visit to the Khaibar, had this chance of seeing the Khaibar Rifles, of observing their soldierlike

His Royal Highness's visit to Peshawar

And Jamrúd.

Presentation of medals to the officers and men of the Khaibar Rifles.

bearing, and of delivering to the men with his own hands their well-earned medals.

Visit to Lundi Kotal.

The Royal party then rode to Lundi Kotal, where His Royal Highness received the respects of the chiefs of the Shinwaries. *En route*, the Prince was met by a section of the Zaka Khyles, who welcomed him to the Khaibar. His Royal Highness and party then returned to Ali Masjid, and started at midnight for Ráwalpindi.

The Prince at Ráwalpindi.

On 1st February, 1890, the Prince reached Ráwalpindi, and there was a grand parade of troops on the plains of Khana. His Royal Highness was greatly interested in the different regiments passing by, which consisted of Gurkhás, Sikhs, Pattians and Dográs, besides many exceptionally fine British Corps.

The laying of the foundation-stone of the new Jubilee Museum and Technical Institute, Láhore, 1890.

On Monday, the 3rd of February, His Royal Highness laid the foundation-stone of the New Jubilee Museum and Technical Institute in Anárkali, Láhore. This is intended to serve as an auxiliary to the greater Indian Institute in London, and is to be constructed at a cost of over a lakh-and-a-half of rupees. The address having been read by Mr. J. L. Kipling, Curator of the Museum and Principal of the Mayo School of Art, His Royal Highness made an impressive and eloquent reply. The real military spirit and the real military material were so conspicuous in this province of action, that he could count on military brevity being acceptable that day. He had heard of the cunning wood-carving and of the beautiful embroideries of the Panjáb before he came to India, and he had a special reason for being delighted to take a part in a scheme which had the double object of forming a great Museum and Sample-house of the products of this interesting country, and of affording technical education to those whose career must lie in other paths than those of the plough and the sword. They knew how his father had laboured to establish in England a splendid and lasting institution which would teach mankind the power and reality of the great British Empire, and this Museum and Technical Institute of the Panjáb embraced precisely the same objects as those aimed at by the Imperial Institute. The pleasure His Royal Highness the Prince of Wales would feel on learning that the Panjáb was to have an Institute based on the lines of the Institute in London, would, the Royal speaker felt sure, be shared by the Queen-Empress; for the loyal offerings poured in by the chiefs and people of the province, could have found no more appropriate or useful object than that of an institution for the promotion of trade and agriculture and for the encouragement of art among the people of the Panjáb.

The speech of His Royal Highness.

His Royal Highness, having then performed the usual ceremonies, was pleased to declare the foundation-stone well and truly laid.

The opening of the Town Hall.

The Prince then proceeded to the new Victoria Jubilee Hall, where, the Municipal address having been read to him, His Royal Highness said, in reply, that it afforded him great pleasure to be present that day. The Victoria Jubilee Hall, which they had invited him to declare open, was a worthy and useful memorial of the fiftieth year of the reign of the Queen-Empress, and he trusted that it might be the scene of many quiet and wise debates of pure and loyal counsels, and, as in other countries, it was the highest ambition of the citizen to win esteem in his own city, so here the men of Láhore and of its district might find an appropriate Temple of Fame, where their names would remain honoured and revered. Possibly, hereafter, too, on the walls of this hall their features might be handed down to posterity in truthful portraits by Indian artists. His Royal Highness then thanked them for the kind sentiments they had expressed towards himself, and said he had much pleasure in declaring the Hall open.

Garden party at Shalámár.

A brilliant garden party at Shalámár, or the House of Joy, given by Sir James Lyall, in which both Europeans and natives took part, and a public ball at the Montgomery and Lawrence Halls, which was both brilliant and unique, closed the festivities connected with the Royal visit to the capital of the Panjáb.

The Royal visit to Amritsar.

On the 6th of February, His Royal Highness visited Amritsar. Grand preparations had been made there to receive the Prince. The road decorations were most effective, and the triumphal arch near the Hall Gate was a grand work of decorative art. Inside the city, from the Kaisari Bágh to the Golden Temple, the fronts of the houses were literally covered with Káshmír shawls and other rich cloths, while arches of shawls had been erected at convenient intervals. The bye-streets and house-tops were filled with crowds of enthusiastic spectators. His Royal Highness, after being greeted at the railway platform by a distinguished company of officers and European and native gentlemen, stepped into a magnificent carriage specially provided for him, which was drawn by a team of four Artillery horses, and two drivers, who rode postillion. He drove first to the Golden Temple, where the Royal party was received by the Managing Committee of the Darbár Sáhib. The members of the party, after putting on gold embroidered cloth shoes, which had been previously provided for the occasion, entered the Temple and were shown round. At their departure, His Royal Highness and the members of the party were decorated with garlands of flowers by the priests. The party having then driven to the beautifully decorated Town Hall, the Prince received the respects of the native gentlemen and officials of the district present. The presentations over, His Royal Highness adjourned to an adjoining room, where a large and varied assortment of magnificent articles of local manufacture was displayed. He inspected closely a large number of articles, and showed great interest in what he saw. The Carpet Factory of Amritsar was then inspected, and, after a drive through the Rám Bágh, historically famous as the Court House of Ranjít Singh, and a short respite, His Royal Highness left by special train for Kapurthállá.

Visit to the "Darbár Sáhib."

The Town Hall.

Inspection of local manufactures.

The Royal visit to Kapurthállá.

At Kapurthállá His Royal Highness was magnificently received by the Rájá, the whole city and the main approaches being profusely decorated. The Prince was entertained by an exhibition of some good wrestling and Sikh athletic sports, which were highly appreciated. The city was illuminated and the handsome Darbár Hall lighted up by electricity.

And Patiálá.

On the 7th of February the Royal party arrived at Patiálá. Grand preparations were made by the Maharájá to receive his illustrious guest; the railway station and the roads, as well as the town, as far as the camp at Moti Bágh, were profusely illuminated, the principal streets were tastefully embellished and the Darbár rooms handsomely decorated. At a grand Darbár held by the Maharájá in honour of the Royal visit, His Highness made an eloquent speech, replete with loyal sentiments and good wishes for the Royal Family of England. In commemoration of the joyful and auspicious event, the Maharájá expressed his intention of founding a scholarship in the Panjáb University, to be called the Albert Victor Patiálá Scholarship, to be awarded to the most distinguished scholar in the Panjáb.

The Maharájá of Patiálá founds a scholarship in commemoration of His Royal Highness's visit to his capital.

His Royal Highness, in reply, cordially thanked His Highness for the splendid reception accorded to him. He expressed his pleasure at making His Highness's acquaintance, and thanked him for the handsome manner in which his visit was to be commemorated. The Prince departed for Delhi on the 9th, leaving behind him a recollection which Patiálá will ever proudly cherish.

Character of the reception of His Royal Highness by the Princes and people of this country.

The popular manifestation and out-burst of joy on the arrival in this country of the Heir-Presumptive to the crown of England and India, the wide-spread interest felt in his visit in all parts of the province, and the spontaneous demonstration of loyal feelings made everywhere, are undoubted proof how deep is the hold Her Majesty the Queen-Empress has on the affections of her Indian subjects, and how sincere and hearty is their loyal devotion to her person and throne.

The cordial union and good will which animated all sections of the community on this happy occasion, and the display of loyalty and devotion to the throne which it evoked, were not confined to the great centres of civilisation, but manifested themselves in all parts of the Empire, from the Khaibar to the Jamna, from the distant south to the furthest north. The people of this outlying province will ever gratefully remember that the Royal Prince, having travelled many thousand miles, came to see them as they are, and did them the honour of visiting them in the country of their birth, while it is hoped the knowledge gained by His Royal Highness from his visit will be of special use to him when, in his turn, he ascends the throne of this great Empire and wields its sceptre.

Dera Ghází Khan protective works.

The river Indus having made encroachments in the direction of the town of Dera Ghází Khan, and cut away the foreshore to within less than 3,000 feet of the town, and almost as far as the banks of the Kasturi Canal, which serve as a sort of defence against floods, the Government resolved to construct a protective embankment along the line of road encircling the city. The embankment was formed of rough stone brought from the Warcha quarries in the Salt Range and from Sakhar in Sindh. This was piled against the embankment, so that on the land being cut away by the erosive action of the stream, it gradually fell into the river, till a natural bank revetted with stone was formed. Similar arrangements proved successful in connection with the new Chináb Bridge protective works at Sher Shah, and it is a matter for congratulation that the scheme worked out had the result of saving an important town of the Panjáb from destruction. The estimated cost exceeded seven lakhs of rupees, provided equally by the Government of India, the Panjáb Government, and a Municipal loan.

The Jammú Railway.

The Jammú Railway was completed in the beginning of the year 1890; the first locomotive was run into Jammú in January of that year, and the line was opened for traffic soon afterwards.

New canal projects.

Besides the perennial canals already mentioned, the inundation canals in operation in the Panjáb, which contribute materially to the development of the wealth of the country, are the Lower Sohág and Para Canal, the Sidhnai Canal, the Upper Sutlej series, the Lower Sutlej and Chináb series, the Indus series, the Imperial canals in the Shahpur District and the Mozaffargarh series. The sanction of the Secretary of State has been received for a project for the Sirsá Branch of the Western Jamna Canal, and the work is to be proceeded with at once. Projects are also before the Government for the construction of subsidiary canals from the Ráví, above the Sidhnai weir, while surveys are in progress for the following canals, *viz.* :—

(*a*) A canal taking its supply from the left bank of the Indus near Dera Ismail Khan, to irrigate the lower half of the Sindh-Sagar Doáb.

(*b*) Inundation canals from the Chináb river, to irrigate the *Khadar* lands in the Shahpur District, and in Gujrát in the vicinity of Kadirábád.

(*c*) Inundation canals from the left bank of the Chináb to irrigate the *Khadar* lands in the northern part of the Jhang District.

(*d*) A canal to take out of the Kábul river near Michni fort and to extend to Pesháwar.

Extension of railway communications.

The survey of the Bhatinda-Bháwalpur Railway was in progress in 1888-89, and the field-work was finished by the end of January, 1889. The project of this railway forms a link which, in connection with the Patiálá-Bhatinda Railway, will shorten the distance between Ambálá and Karrachi by 122⅜ miles.

The work of the Patiálá-Bhatinda Railway was taken in hand in April 1888. The first engine, with permanent way material, ran through to Nabhá, 15½ miles, on the 17th March, 1889, and the line was opened for public traffic in October, 1889.

A reconnaissance to connect Delhi with Karrachi, *viá* Kotri, was carried out in 1888-89. The route for an extension of the North-Western Railway from Pesháwar to Jamrúd, for military purposes only, has been surveyed and estimated for.

The Queen-Empress's Indian servants.

The employment of natives of India by the Queen-Empress as Her Majesty's domestic servants, to which His Royal Highness Prince Victor of Wales referred in one of his eloquent speeches at Láhore, has created a deep impression in the minds of the people of the country, and has gone far towards confirming them in the conviction that Her Royal Majesty cherishes the most sincere affection for India and her Indian subjects. Some of Her Majesty's Mahomedan servants who lately visited their homes on leave, spoke in the warmest terms of the high virtues and queenly qualities which distinguish the "Mother of India," as Her Majesty is designated by her Indian subjects out of their deep reverence for her august person and throne.

Death of Maharájá Ranbir Singh of Káshmír.

He is succeeded by Partáb Singh.

On the 12th of September, 1885, Ranbir Singh, the Maharájá of Káshmír, son and successor of Maharájá Golab Singh, to whom it will be remembered the Government of India had made over the beautiful and fertile valley of Káshmír for a price, breathed his last.* The deceased Maharájá was succeeded by his eldest son Partáb Singh. The Government of India took the opportunity of informing the new Maharájá that, in future, the status of the "British officer on special duty in Káshmír"

* A picturesque account of his death is given by Sir Oliver St. John. He had, twenty-four hours before, recalled a Brahmin exiled many years previously for cursing him. This pious act gave him no relief, and he made up his mind that death was imminent. He abolished a liquor contract, restored the old prohibition against the liquor traffic, abolished certain obnoxious taxes, gave his sons good advice, and then, being removed from his bed to the floor, he breathed his last. Next day his body was burnt on the banks of the Taví in the presence of a large multitude. The body is said to have been enveloped originally in forty coverings of shawls and other rich stuffs interspersed with gold coins and jewels of great value placed there by the women of his harem, though thirteen of the wrappers only were taken off by the attendant Brahmins before the body was placed on the pile. The whole of the Maharájá's wardrobe, jewels and riding horses, with seven elephants, and a number of cattle, besides a very large sum in cash, the whole estimated at from five to ten lakhs of rupees, were set aside for distribution among the Brahmins, or to be sent to the holy men in the neighbourhood. Business was suspended, the shop-keepers dealing only through one leaf of their shop-doors. The Government employees, including the soldiers, shaved their heads and faces, excepting only Sikhs, Mahomedans, Brahmins and Rájputs connected with the Maharájá by marriage. White garments were worn by all, and ornaments of every description laid aside. The period of mourning extended over thirteen days. On the 25th September, the new Maharájá took his seat in darbár, after he had performed the ceremony of tying on his turban which is supposed to mark the close of the period of acute grief. The morning was spent in distributing gifts to the Brahmins on the spot where the Maharájá's body had been burnt. In addition to a large sum of money, these gifts consisted of thirteen sets of everything that had been used by the Maharájá in this world, including horses, cows, and other domestic animals, but only one elephant. The remainder of the Maharájá's effects, with a sum of five lakhs from his private treasury, were retained to be added to the fund consecrated by him to the perpetual use of the temples, which fund already amounted to fifteen lakhs.

would be changed to that of "Political Resident." The new Maharájá not only proved a very weak and indolent prince, but systematically opposed every measure of reform that was introduced. "My impression," wrote Sir Oliver, "as regards the new Maharájá is that, though entirely wanting in the quick wit of his father, he has inherited a full share of his obstinacy and cunning. He will, I fear, offer as much opposition as he dares." In spite of the significant appointment of a British Resident, the country continued to be badly managed, and the sufferings of the people passed all bounds. In March, 1888, the new Resident, Mr. Plowden, wrote in much the same tone as Sir Oliver St. John. He said, "The Government should be under no illusion as regards Maharájá Partáb Singh. From first to last I have failed to discover in him any sustained capacity for governing his country, or any genuine desire to ameliorate its condition, or to introduce those reforms which he has acknowledged to be necessary. More than two years have passed since his succession, but not only has he achieved nothing, but he has opposed beneficial measures proposed by others. I do not believe he is loyal, but fortunately he is powerless to carry his country with him."

Misgovernment in Káshmír.

Lord Ripon, in a despatch written in 1884, complained bitterly of the misgovernment of Káshmír, declaring it to be his opinion, that a condition of things such as existed in that tributary country, could not be indefinitely tolerated, and suggesting that a favourable opportunity of dealing with it would arise on the occurrence of a fresh succession.

The papers relating to Káshmír presented to the British Parliament showed how serious was the mal-administration of Káshmír and Jammú, and revealed an amount of injustice and oppression which may be best measured by the fact that, in the course of half a century, the population had considerably diminished in numbers. It was evident that so long as the Maharájá remained in power, no reforms could be carried out, for he opposed even those which he himself considered necessary. So gross had been the mismanagement of the customs revenue collections, that, while the poorer raiyats were unfairly taxed on rice, the richer men paid only comparatively, light duties on a profitable staple like cotton.

Appointment of a Council of Regency in Káshmír.

After a patient delay of many years, the Government of India, as the protector of the people against oppression, found it their plain duty, in the interest of the subject populations, to put a stop to this state of things. Indeed, the intervention of the paramount Power in behalf of the oppressed population had been already too long delayed.* Accordingly, Maharájá Partáb Singh was required to withdraw, for a time, from active participation in the government of his State, and the sovereignty of the country was entrusted to a Council of Regency composed of the Maharájá's own brothers, and a few chosen native officers of proved ability and integrity under the Government, whose services were lent to the State.

* A friend who had visited Káshmír a short time before the establishment of the Council of Regency there, narrated to us a heartrending story of the exteme poverty and indigence of the Káshmírians. He was taking his meals in a country village, not far from Srinagar, when a dozen of destitute men and women, with dejected looks and their persons half covered with rags, surrounded him, hoping to receive the refuse of the meals. Thrilled with compassion at the sight of these hungry creatures, the visitor in question determined to distribute the loaves to them; but he had hardly moved his hand with that object when, to his great astonishment, the number of hungry people was more than doubled, each crying vehemently for "*Nán, nán*," ("Bread, bread"). The beggars vied with each other as to who should receive the bread first, and the visitor, to do justice to all, gave a morsel to each, who, as he got it, retired quite thankful as if he had won a great victory. He said, and what he told us is fully borne out by the testimony of other visitors to the valley, that men waited on a visitor for a morsel of bread as dogs wait on a traveller partaking of food in an Indian *serae*. Many harrowing stories of the sufferings of the people in Káshmír are told, but we need not dilate on the subject here. The extreme indigence of the Káshmírians and their miseries and sufferings before the present arrangement came into force, are too well known to everybody in the Panjáb, to need any detailed description from us here.

As pointed out by Sir J. Gorst in the British Parliament, there was no desire on the part of the Government to interfere with the rights of the chiefs of India; "but there was one right," said the Honourable Member, "more sacred than even the rights of oriental despots, and that was the right of the people living under the protection of the military power of Great Britain to a just and upright government." Nor would it be just to attritube the action of the Government of India to a desire to possess Káshmír as a good frontier, for the mighty mountains of the Himaláyas have placed an insuperable barrier between India and the countries beyond them. What has been done was determined on simply because a reform urgently needed in the interests of the people could not otherwise be carried out.* Debates in Parliament.

It should be remembered that the present era of British administration in India is one of material advancement and development, not only from a social, but also from a political point of view. An age of darkness, the outcome of despotism, intoleration and cruelty, has been succeeded by an age of enlightenment, justice, toleration and liberty. The paramount power considers it its bounden duty to see that the subjects committed by Providence to its care, are contented and happy, that justice is brought to the door of the meanest of them, and that all, of whatever creed or nationality, are equally benefited by its wise institutions and sheltered by its just laws. To see the subjects of the Crown happy and contented, the chiefs and Princes of India prosperous and their country and people flourishing, is the highest aim of the British rulers of India. Policy of the Government towards its subjects.

Experience has fully taught us how readily our rulers show their appreciation of whatever is really good, how heartily true loyalty to the Crown is acknowledged, and how munificently it is rewarded, though, in showing loyalty to the Government which has protected us from oppression, and given us the valued gift of freedom, we have in truth, done no more than our duty to ourselves and to our countrymen. The liberal views of the Government;

But it must not be forgotten, that while the Government have thus shown by their acts the genuine interest they take in everything that tends to our material advancement, and how warmly they acknowledge whatever they deem worthy of approbation, their keen sense of honour, dignity, duty and justice, qualities inherent in all Englishmen, impels them, also to take serious notice of any wilful disregard of what is the plain duty of those who seek honour at their hands, in their individual capacity, or as representatives of sections of the community, and who, despite the knowledge of their position and responsibility, and in the face of repeated warning, allow themselves to be led away, either by their own whims and caprices, or by the pernicious councils of their subordinates. On all occasions of such emergency, the Government would fail in their duty if they did not at once stretch out a helping hand for the relief of the suffering millions whose lives, as the paramount Power, they are bound to protect, and whose interests it is their duty to preserve. Nevertheless, it takes serious notice of wilful disregard of duty on the part of native chiefs.

Under the Council of Regency, with the advantage of the advice of a British Resident, the administration of Káshmír has already shown unmistakeable signs of improvement. Schemes for water-supply, roads and railways, have been successfully introduced; and, while every department of State is thriving, it is gratifying to see that the annual Budget shows Improvements under the Council of Regency in Káshmír.

---

* Speeches of Sir Richard Temple and Mr. W. H. Smith in Parliament. Sir Richard Temple observed, with reference to the question raised by Mr. Bradlaugh, that he was well acquainted with Káshmír, and had enjoyed the acquaintance of the father and grandfather of the deposed Maharájá, and that he repudiated the idea that England had looked with greedy eye upon this territory.

a growing surplus. All this is indubitable proof of good and honest work done, and it is hoped that, under the beneficial influence of the Council of Regency, the "Happy Valley" will, at no distant date, reach that degree of real happiness and prosperity which nature intended for it, and to which it is the birthright of the humblest Káshmíri subject to aspire.

Lawrence Memorial Asylum, Murri.

About two-and-a-half miles from the Church at Murri, at an elevation of 6,398 feet above the sea-level, is the useful institution known as the Sir Henry Lawrence Memorial Asylum, Murri. The Asylum was founded in 1860, by public subscription, to perpetuate the memory of Sir Henry Lawrence. The object of the institution is to provide for the children of soldiers serving, or having served, in India. It is supported by the interest from the endowment, a Government grant-in-aid, and by public subscription. The institution comprises a High School, Middle School and Upper Primary and Lower Primary Departments. The girls are taught geography, history, arithmetic, algebra, euclid, Shakespeare, physiology, and Indian vernaculars, and are, besides, thoroughly trained in every-day domestic life, such as making beds, scrubbing floors and making the clothes for both boys and girls. The institution is doing substantial and good work, and does great credit to the British army in whose behalf it was founded and is maintained.

The Káshmír Railway scheme.

In the year 1890, the Káshmír Darbár re-opened communications with the Government of India regarding a proposal to connect the Káshmír Valley with the Indian Railway system. Several alternative routes were suggested, and General de Bourbel, Chief Engineer to the Káshmír State, issued an interesting report on the practicability of these routes. The route most welcome to the military authorities would go *viâ* Abottabad, to join the North-Western Railway at Hassan Abdál. The other would start from a point at or near Ráwalpindi, and, passing four or five thousand feet below Murri, which would be left at a distance of a few miles, would proceed direct to the fine new cart road to Kohálá, or on the further side of the Jhelum river, taking in the Punch traffic *en route* from Kahuta to Ráwalpindi. The survey made has resulted in a most favourable report, and a definite scheme is now under consideration. The proposed capital is thirty lakhs, and the traffic returns are estimated at twenty lakhs annually. The Káshmír Council have expressed their willingness to lodge Government securities to guarantee four-and-a-half per cent. interest for fifteen years on the Káshmír portion, which would form about two-thirds of the whole line, and it is hoped the Government of India will do the same for the British portion of the line. Strategically, the line would add materially to the strength of the frontier. The interests of the Empire demand that the Káshmír frontier should be permanently garrisoned by British troops, as in the case of Quetta, and that every facility should be provided for the conveyance of troops in that direction. It is hoped that the new line will be worked by the North-Western Railway at fifty-five per cent. of the gross earnings to cover the expenses of working.

Road from Srinagar to Gilgit.

Communications between Srinagar and Gilgit have been improved by means of a road which is now under construction between these places. Mr. Johnson, Executive Engineer, submited a scheme for diverting the road from a point selected by him, and carrying it across the Indus on a suspension bridge. The scheme is calculated to afford facility in crossing the Indus in times of flood, and to improve the means of communication with Gilgit. The greater part of the new road from Bunji, on this side of the river, will be on the level, while, as far as Pári, thirteen miles to the other side, the ground will also be found to be good. The road will be a great boon to travellers and merchants, and is calculated to afford then special facilities of communication with India and Central Asia.

The trade of the Province with Afghanistán and Central Asia is improving, owing to the increased facilities of communication now afforded, and the general tranquillity in Afghanistán. The increase, according to Mr. D. C. Johnstone's report, is chiefly in piece-goods, and the Indian and European cotton traffic. The trade with Central Asia would be susceptible of further improvement, but for the well-known hostility of the Russian fiscal system, and the heavy imposts laid on British merchandise passing through Afghanistán.

Trade with Afghanistán.

The scheme for the proposed railway from Karrachi to Delhi, has been lately before the Government of India, to whom Mr. Croudace submitted his report on the survey and estimated cost of the line. Although the construction of the proposed line would be abnormally expensive, it would be valuable, as affording special facilities for the concentration of troops at that strategical point from three converging lines, Peshâwar and Rāwalpindi, Delhi and southern and eastern India, Karrachi and Europe, and would add materially to the strength of the Frontier Railway system. It is, moreover, calculated to bring the commercial town of Delhi into direct communication with the great and rising port of Karrachi. As pointed out by Lord Lansdowne in his reply to the Address of the Delhi Municipality in November, 1890, there is no prospect of this project receiving direct assistance from the Government in the immediate future. But "the scheme," observed His Excellency, "was one, for which, if it was based upon sound commercial principles, a large amount of private support might he anticipated," and should this be the case, His Excellency hoped, "the Government of India would not deny the promoters any facilities which they could reasonably expect."

The Karrachi Railway scheme.

Another subject of importance under the consideration of the Government in connection with the scheme of defences for the North-West Frontier, is the proposed Karrachi-Láhore route. Under instructions from the Naval Commander-in-Chief, a minute inspection of Karrachi harbour was made towards the close of 1890, with a view to using the port for the embarkation and debarkation of troops to and from England. It was found that the channel, although comparatively narrow, was still easily navigable, and that troops could be landed more expeditiously and in far greater numbers than they could even at Portsmouth. The improvements already made in the harbour have made it accessible to vessels of the largest tonnage. The wharf accommodation has been largely increased, and the means of landing cargo by the use of modern appliances have been greatly improved; but as the natural terminus of the Panjáb Railway and the natural outlet of its commerce, the harbour possesses still further capabilities of improvement. It is proposed to establish a large depôt at Landi, about ten miles from Karrachi, with four rest camps between Landi and Láhore, namely, Mián Mír, Shershah, Reti and Dadu. It is hoped that the new route, when completed, will not only prove economical to the public and beneficial to the mercantile classes, drawing to Karrachi, as the natural seaport of North-West India, a great bulk of the direct trade of foreign countries with Northern India, but that, Karrachi being the nearest port for reinforcement from England to the front, it will contribute, in no small degree, to the development of the Indian military organization. The recent completion of the Khojak Tunnel by the boring of the Khwája Amran Range, has brought the Railway from Karrachi within easy distance of Candahar, and the measure may, it is hoped, result in better acquaintance with the countries of Afghanistán.

The proposed Karrachi Láhore route.

Karrachi as a harbour for troops.

The Khojak Tunnel.

The gigantic works at the Khojak and the piercing of the hills were undertaken by the British, strictly as measures of precaution and defence against any possible aggression from outside, and although they caused some anxiety at first to the Amír's Governor at Candahar, His Highness has been fully convinced that the measures adopted by the British Government were of imperative necessity for the safety of his own kingdom, as well as the better security of the British frontier in that part of the country.

Frontier Railway surveys and projects.

The Quetta-Candahar defences, which have been completed at enormous outlay to Government, may be regarded as the inauguration of what is called the scientific frontier system. The impregnability of Quetta is unquestionably a source of great military strength to India in that outlying position, while the occupation of the Zhob Valley, the extension of the railway to new Chaman, the storing of immense railway materials for a line onwards in the direction of Candahar, the securing of both ends of the Gomal Pass, and the reconciliation of many independent tribes hitherto hostile, and establishment of British supremacy in their countries, display a policy on the part of the Government at once vigorous and opportune. The works of the Gomal Railway and the Zhob Valley Railway are being actively pushed on. The survey from the Quetta end is complete, and all that remains is to select the line to be finally adopted from among the two or three trial lines which have been surveyed.* Much has also been done towards the renewing and improving of the Harnai line, and an enormous sum spent on the Bolán Railway, to maintain its strategical position as an alternative route to the Peshin plateau. The survey of the Kábul River Railway route, was sanctioned, and placed under Mr. Upcott. The survey of the line between Pesháwar and Jamrúd was finished in 1889-90, and an improvement of the alignment on the Sindh-Peshin Railway was effected. In March, 1890, Sir James Browne reconnoitred the entire route from the Gomal, through the Kajuri Kach and Aparzai, to Quetta. The completion of these and certain other surveys in connection with the proposed extensions of the North-Western Railway, marks an era of enterprise, activity and forethought, having for its object the safety of the empire, and to provide it with adequate means of defence against any possible foreign aggression.

Gigantic schemes of frontier defence.

The Imperial Service Corps.

We have observed before how spontaneously the Feudatory Chiefs of India, acting under the impulse of duty, came forward to assist the Imperial Government in its beneficent measures connected with the frontier defences, by offering to contribute, each in his degree, to the defence of the Empire. The conquerors of the east, whose soldiers have fought successfully in the remotest parts of the known world, hardly stand in need of help from the ruling chiefs of India; but the far-sighted policy of the Government, in accepting the loyal offers of its feudatory chiefs, is to enlist the martial spirit of the country on the side of loyalty to the Crown, and generously to allow the chiefs a share of the glories and honours which its own gallant soldiers are capable of winning single-handed.

Inspection of the Panjáb States Imperial Service troops.

Lord Lansdowne, during his recent visit to Patiálá, took the opportunity of inspecting the Imperial Service Corps on the 24th of October, 1890, accompanied by Sir James Lyall, Lieutenant-Governor of the Panjáb. The whole of the contingent, consisting of 2,416 men (1,600 cavalry and the

* A correspondent writing to the *Civil and Military Gazette*, Láhore, on the state of the country says: "The country is very poor, and there is comparatively very little cultivation. Water is obtained in rather a curious way, quite peculiar to this part of the world. Shafts are sunk where water is likely to be found—how they choose the particular spot, I cannot tell—sometimes over a hundred feet in depth; these are connected below by a channel along which the water flows, and which gradually brings it out to the surface and conveys it to their fields. These 'Karais,' as they are called, are made by regular professionals at this sort of thing who come from Ghizni, and who make a very good thing by it."—*Civil and Military Gazette*, October, 1890.

equivalent of six battalions of infantry), were brought in review on the parade-ground under the command of Lieutenant-Colonel H. Melliss, Chief Inspecting Officer, Native States troops; and both His Excellency and His Honour were pleased with the efficiency of the ranks. The material, both as regards men and horses, was admitted on all sides to be excellent, and the physique of all grades fine. Two years previously, as we have observed, the policy of utilizing the military spirit of the native chiefs and developing in their territories an Imperial Service Corps, was formally inaugurated by Lord Dufferin, and it is gratifying to see that it has been vigorously pursued by his successor.

Investiture of the Rájá of Kapurthállá with the power of administration.

On Monday, the 24th of November, 1890, His Highness Rájá Jagat Jit Singh, Rájá of Kapurthállá, having completed his eighteenth year, was formally invested with full powers of administration in his State, by the Honourable Sir James Lyall, Lieutenant-Governor of the Panjáb. A brilliant incident of the festivities on the occasion was a banquet given to the distinguished guests on the night of the 24th November. The toast of the Queen-Empress having been loyally responded to, Sir James Lyall, in proposing the Rájá's health, made an eloquent speech, in which he dwelt, in terms of warm appreciation, on the cordial relations existing between the State and the British Government, and described graphically the gallant and loyal behaviour of the people of the Panjáb towards the paramount Power. Speaking of the late Rájá's services, His Honour said:—

The banquet.

Speech of Sir James Lyall.

> Rájá Ranbhir Singh's services to the British Empire in the critical times of the Mutiny were of the most splendid kind. He most promptly and loyally led his army in person to fight in line with the Queen's troops; and he and his brother, the late Kanwar Bikarma Singh, C.S.I., displayed a personal gallantry in the field worthy of the best Sikh traditions. May our recollections of such services never grow cold! How warmly we recognized them at the time can perhaps hardly be realized by those who were not then in India I came to the Panjáb in those days, and the feeling between Englishmen and Panjábis, was then of the most cordial kind. The soldiers of both races had been fighting splendidly side by side, as they have done since in Afghanistán and elsewhere; and we were proud to be fellow-subjects with them of the same great Empire.

The allusion made by Sir James Lyall to the mutual respect and good-feeling that prevailed among the people of this province and their rulers in the time of the Mutiny, is an instance of that strong sense of justice and keen appreciation of everything worthy of admiration, which forms one of the essential characteristics of the British nation. Well may our country be proud of those manly acts, deeds of distinguished bravery in the field and of valour prompted by loyalty to the Crown, which have admittedly made the Panjáb a model province.

His Honour's speech at the Darbár of investiture.

The speech of His Honour at the darbár of investiture was full of sentiments of kindness and expressions of the profoundest regard for the welfare of the ruling chief, and his illustrious family and the happiness of his subjects. Read in its entirety, it is a series of admonitions, such as an affectionate father might give to his son just entering upon active life, and shows what real interest the Government has taken in the advancement of the territory of this chief during the long period of his minority—an interest which has had the result of materially benefiting the State. On the subject of the capabilities of the young chief, Sir James Lyall said in the course of his speech: "It is often said that the period of minority for Ruling Chiefs in India is dangerously short, and no doubt there is truth in the remark; but in your case, Rájá, I have such confidence in your judgment and character, and in the ability and honesty of your excellent staff of State officials, that I feel no apprehension." His Honour exhorted the Rájá to "recognize the fact that, without steady perseverance and punctuality in despatch of business, the best intentions and the greatest cleverness will not secure good government." In conclusion, His Honour expressed his hope that the honourable and prudent disposition and kind temper which the Rájá had hitherto always displayed would make him a just and considerate ruler of his subjects in the Panjáb, and a liberal landlord of his great estates in Oudh, from which he had derived so splendid an income. His Honour closed his most impressive speech by reminding the Rájá of the words of an English poet which had been addressed more than 200 years ago to a king of England, and which were specially admired and often repeated by him :—

"The glories of our birth and state,
Are shadows, not substantial things :
There is no armour against fate,
Death lays his icy hands on kings :
Sceptre and Crown must tumble down,
And in the dust be equal made
With the poor crooked scythe and spade :
Only the memory of the just
Smells sweet and blossoms in the dust."

Pardon of Maharájá Dulíp Singh by the Queen-Empress.

Among the unconsidered trifles of history may be recorded the profession of penitence made to the Queen-Empress by that eccentric personage, Maharájá Dulíp Singh, who, not content with the princely allowance of £40,000 a year, which had been provided for him in England by the bounty of the British, had, it will be remembered, gone over to Russia, in 1885, hoping to gain the favour of the Czar, by representations, however false, that he still exercised influence over the Sikhs of the Panjáb, and was capable of turning the scale of affairs in that country. But the damp squib which, after his abortive journey to India and return from Aden, he persistently endeavoured to light, failed to ignite. As was expected, the Czar treated him coldly, and the Maharájá, finding his pretensions of no avail, and seeing that he was no welcome guest at St. Petersburgh, thought it his best policy to profess repentance to the Queen. He had been sufficiently long in obscurity to be almost forgotten, and the Queen, after his notorious intrigues, might well have turned a deaf ear to his appeal for mercy. Gifted, however, as Her Royal Majesty is by nature, with a noble and a magnanimous heart and a philanthropic disposition, she was most graciously pleased to extend her pardon to him, and permitted him to return to England. His pension, which the British Government had been compelled to discontinue, was generously restored, and the arrears discharged. It being the Queen's personal command that Dulíp Singh's return to his former position in England should be made as easy and gentle as possible, his subsequent prayer to be restored to the order of the Star of India, as a G.C.S.I., was also graciously granted. There never was a case of a man more wilfully and wantonly bringing misfortune upon himself. As pointed out by a Continental journal, "he would have led a happier life, upon the whole, if he had continued to entertain shooting parties at Thetford Hall, instead of running about all over Europe with a bee in his bonnet." But the lesson which has been taught the Maharájá in the school of adversity to which he chose to go for it, has profited him, for he has now come to know that, after all, he is not so important a personage as he imagined himself to be, and that his life in the country of his first adoption was infinitely more agreeable than his subsequent experiences have been.

As the reader is aware, the scandal would probably have never occurred, but for the intrigues of a Sindhianwálá sardar, a maternal relation of the Maharájá, who, later on, closed his disgraceful career in Pondicherry. His Excellency the Governor-General was pleased to extend pardon to the sardar's sons who had been the companions of their father in his mysterious flight from the Panjáb, and they have been permitted to reside in Delhi. All honour to the Queen-Empress whose mercy and forbearance, of which we see no parallel in the history of the nations, saved the reputed son of Ranjít Singh, the staunch ally of the British, from ruin, and restored to him his *status quo.* This country has never shown any concern for the affairs of the reputed son of the deceased Maharájá; but none the less it expects him to be loyal to a sway under which he, in common with themselves, enjoys the privileges of a free subject, and looks on his return to more prudent counsels, and the renewal of his loyalty, with as unmixed a satisfaction as it regards the royal clemency extended to him by their Lady Sovereign with a sense of the profoundest gratitude.

Vaccination in the Panjáb.

The extension of the Vaccination Act to the municipal towns of Amritsar, Simla and Ambálá, and to the cantonment of Kassauli, and the general results achieved by the Vaccination Department during the past few years, constitute altogether a gratifying record of good work and progress. The practice of inoculation for small-pox is gradually dying out, and inoculators, as a class, are either taking to vaccination, or giving up their old calling. Arm-to-arm vaccination with human lymph proved unpopular with the people. Close superintendence of the operations being impossible, petty acts of oppression and high-handedness on the part of the vaccinators became the cause of complaints. But the introduction of animal lymph has been attended with great success, and already a large number of persons have been vaccinated from the calf. As remarked by Dr. Stephen, the Sanitary Commissioner of the Panjáb, in his report on the vaccination operations of the province, the employment of a special agency in conducting the operations has been attended with favourable results. Thus the employment of a high caste Brahmin in the Kangrá District contributed much to the success and popularity of the scheme among the Hindu population there, while the appointment of a Mahomedan of position to conduct the operations cannot fail to be equally acceptable among the Mahomedan populace.

The early Sikhs.

It has been shown in the previous chapters that the mission of Nának was to bring peace to the world; but the state of affairs in the country in the time of the tenth martial Guru, Govind Singh, had the effect of converting a religion of peace into a religion of the sword. The votaries of the Guru turned their rosaries and ploughs into implements of war, and the keeping of steel in some shape by every male adult was made a sacred obligation. The wearing of the long hair and beard was enforced, and an initiation into the *Páhal* of the Guru, or the "baptism of the sword," as it is called, made the votaries *Singhs*, or "lions" of the race. The pages of history shine with the heroic deeds of this martial race, and the examples of self-devotion, patriotism and forbearance under the severest trials, displayed by the leaders of their community, are excelled by none in the annals of the nations. The race of men who prided themselves on these deeds, and who paved the way for the future greatness of the Sikhs as a nation, having played their part honourably and well, disappeared. The theocracy of Singhs which had roused the slumbering spirit of the subdued Hindu nations of the Panjáb, converting rude herdsmen and yeomen into successful soldiers and warriors, merged into feudal States, each aspiring to power. How all these States, or *misls*, developed themselves into one strong monarchy, guided by the genius of Ranjít Singh, has been fully described in the foregoing pages. Before their monarchy collapsed, the Sikhs fought hard for their hearths and homes, but they had finally to submit to the great Power with which, under the influence of unwise counsels, they had themselves invited war.

The Sikh confederacies or *misls*.

The brave Sikhs, true to their country and faithful to their nation, cheerfully accepted the British rule, and an experience of nearly half a century has now shown how conspicuous their loyalty to their new rulers and masters has been. Under the banners of the British they have fought gallantly, side by side with Englishmen, in the remotest regions of the earth.

The Sikhs of the present day.

But the high aspirations after conquest, and the glories of war have ceased to inspire the *Khálsá.* The Sikhs of to-day are gradually losing those qualities which were once the essential characteristics of their race. Beyond their excellent physique and an inborn bravery which, under a system of proper discipline and training, is capable of being turned to useful account, there is little in the Sikhs of the present time, looked on as a whole, to attract special attention. Sikhs of course there are who have faithfully preserved the glorious traditions of their forefathers, and who entertain the most implicit reverence for the teachings of their great Gurus. But admirable as this spirit is in its way, it is not all that the exigencies of the time require. The present is an era when education serves as the readiest passport to success. Like the Mahomedans, they have suffered themselves to be thrown far behind the less manly, but more intelligent, of the Hindu races in the field of competition for progress which Western education has thrown open to all the people of this country. The quick-witted Bengali and the thrifty Hindu have eagerly seized the opportunities for advancement afforded by British civilization, which the Mahomedan and the Sikh has each in his turn neglected. The hard lessons of adversity, learnt by the Mahomedans, have at length awakened them to a sense of their duty, and they have paid such attention to the subject of education as the urgency of the times required, establishing a college of their own at Aligarh, and holding conferences in the great centres of civilization in India, in which education forms the sole subject of their deliberations. Nothing can be more befitting the honour of the Mahomedan community, than that the leaders of public opinion among them, avoiding all concern with political matters, should devote their heart and soul to endeavouring to raise their less fortunate brethren in the scale of civilization, and afford them such educational facilities as shall equip them for the struggle of life. It is believed they have thoroughly realised the fact that it is education on sound principles alone that will better their position in the future. Slowly, but surely, they are working their way to progress, and, if they avoid pitfalls, there is good reason to hope that their old prestige in the learned world may gradually be regained

The Bengali. The Hindu.

The Mussalman.

The Aligarh Mahomedan College.

The *Khálsá* Dewán.

The leaders of the Sikhs represented by the "*Khálsá* Dewán," a body of the Sikhs whose aim is to spread enlightened and advanced ideas among the members of their community, recognizing the truth of the motto that "union is strength," brought themselves early to public notice by presenting petitions to Government praying for certain concessions and privileges which they considered would improve the condition of their co-religionists. These first signs of change were hailed by all well-wishers of the country with feelings of satisfaction.

Early signs of improvements among the Sikhs.

Their petitions received due consideration ; but it was apparent, nevertheless, that, however much it might desire to advance the prosperity of its subjects, a Government could not do everything for them, and that it was only proper and reasonable that, before they could expect help from Government, they should help themselves, and adopt some such definite scheme as would justify their solicitations. Accordingly, the "*Khálsá* Dewán" in the name of the Sikh community, set on foot a truly national movement, and one which, judging from the nobility of its aims, gives promise of a vast and brilliant future, well worthy of the aspirations of the manlier races of the Panjáb, and opening to them a new sphere of activity and intellectual advancement. The movement is to take the form of a Central *Khálsá* College, to be established on the lines of the Mahomedan College at Aligarh, worked in connection with a system of schools in the outlying districts, for which it will serve as a feeder. The proposed college aims at giving its pupils education in Western learning, combined with the advantage of instruction in the teachings of the Gurus, thus affording them an opportunity of keeping pace with the more zealous of their countrymen in educational progress and the development of their mental powers, and at the same time preserving the tradition of their forefathers, and maintaining their own individuality as the faithful disciples of their Gurus. Thus, the object is to give the Sikhs an education suited to the spirit of the age, which shall not only make them better scholars, but, by fostering the national sentiments, also make them better Sikhs, and enable them to retain the more valuable characteristics of their race. The subsidiary schools which it is intended to open, will bring education within the reach of the masses of the Sikh community. It is clear that nothing but a rigid observance of the religious rules laid down by their leaders, and of the tenets of their faith, can keep the Sikhs together as a class, and that, with the laxity now prevailing among the generality of the Sikhs in the observance of these rules, the characteristic of their race would be gradually lost, the military spirit of the nation would die out, and Sikhism would insensibly lapse to Hinduism with which it is surrounded, or be irretrievably lost in the unfathomable gulf of time.

The proposal for a Central *Khálsá* College.

Its aims and objects.

As pointed out by the "*Khálsá* Dewán" in their appeal for help to their Sikh brethren, even "the few *Khálsá* students who come forth from the recognized colleges of the Panjáb exhibit a tendency to despise and abandon the religious and civil traditions of their fathers." The result equally applies to the other sects receiving education in Government educational institutions. The typical educated native assumes a spirit of hostility towards the religion of his forefathers; he considers himself free from social restraints, and looks on his elders with contempt; he shuns the society of those who, with nobler sentiments and finer aims, represent the true aristocracy of the country; he imitates the European in mode of living, dresses himself as a European, and in every walk of life assumes a European air, but he remains, after all, a native. He imitates few European virtues, but the habits which in his arrogance he adopts, estrange him from his own countrymen, nay, from his own kinsmen. The result is, of course, due to a disregard of religious instruction and moral precepts. But, however deplorable such a state of affairs may be, Government is not responsible for it. Government has provided a system of education purely non-religious, which shall suit equally the circumstances of all its subjects. If it were to provide instruction in the *Qurán*, or *Hadis*, in one of its educational institutions for a Mahomedan, the Hindu would claim instruction in his *Vedas* and the Sikh in his *Granth*. This would create controversies, which the Government, as at present constituted, would be the last to engender or tolerate. So far, therefore, as the action of Government in the matter of education is concerned, it is manifest that it has done for us all it could, consistently with justice to each race and to itself as a Christian Government.

The typical educated native.

On the 7th of September, 1890, a deputation of the *Khálsá* College Committee waited on the Maharájá of Patiálá, and presented His Highness with an address, fully explaining the aims and objects of the proposed movement, and appealing to his liberality to lend a helping hand to the institution. The Maharájá made the munificent donation of a lakh and

Munificence of the Maharájá of Patiálá and Nabhá.

sixty thousand rupees in aid of the *Khálsá* College scheme, and the officials under him made large donations besides. The grant made by the Maharájá is in the highest degree liberal, and proves, beyond doubt, the deep interest His Highness, as the natural leader of the Sikh community, takes in the welfare of his countrymen. On Friday, 26th December, 1890, the Maharájá of Nabhá received a deputation of the *Khálsá* College Committee, which had waited upon him at his request, and His Highness was pleased to make the magnificent donation of one lakh and eleven thousand rupees to the *Khálsá* College Fund, with the promise of an additional gift if a further appeal to him should be necessary. Additional subscriptions were also received, and the amount now subscribed by His Highness the Maharájá and State officials has reached the handsome figure of two lakhs and eighty thousand rupees. It is hoped that other Sikh chiefs of the Panjáb will follow the noble example set by the enlightened chiefs of Patiálá and Nabhá, by joining hands with them in the advancement of a scheme fraught with the greatest educational advantages for the Sikh nation, and that not only they, but every true disciple of the Guru, will consider it his paramount duty to assist the laudable movement with all his heart. Lord Lansdowne, Sir Frederick Roberts and Sir James Lyall have each shown their sympathy with the movement by subscribing sums of money in aid of it. The scheme has been launched, and we trust to hear that the initiation taken by the liberal-minded chiefs of Patiálá and Nabhá, will be followed by other Sikh princes and people, with a generosity worthy their own name as well as of the noble examples before them.*

Sympathy shown by British statesmen in the Sikh national movement.

Improvements in Delhi.

The residents of Delhi, through their Municipal Corporation, availed themselves of the honour of the presence in their midst, on 17th November, 1890, of His Excellency the Marquess of Lansdowne, to present an address of welcome to His Excellency on the occasion of his visit to their historical and ancient city. After alluding to the position which their city enjoyed under the ancient dynasties, as the capital of India and the seat of learning and science, and adverting to the fact that, though no longer the seat of Government, it was still the commercial capital of northern India, the memorialists stated that they considered the Viceregal visit the more welcome and memorable, in that it afforded them the opportunity of expressing their sense of the remarkable advance in trade, in the arts and sciences, in schemes for the material development and prosperity of the country, in plans for the improved sanitation and the like, which had been so intimately associated with the period of His Excellency's rule in this country. The Municipality of Delhi had succeeded in laying down a tramway which would greatly improve the sanitary condition of the city, and was busy in carrying out a most important water-works scheme, which, by supplying the citizens with fresh and wholesome water, would, it was believed, remove one of the worst evils from which the city had for a long time suffered, and thus contribute materially to the health and strength of the inhabitants.

Among the tokens of material progress were instanced the foundries, the cotton presses, the flour mills and the factories for spinning and weaving cotton which have been lately established, and the Delhi-Ambálá-Kalka Railway, now on the point of completion.

The religious dispute of 1886 in Delhi.

In conclusion, the Corporation referred to the unfortunate disputes which arose in 1886, between the followers of different religions, and rejoiced that they had totally disappeared.

---

* Since the above was written the Rájá of Jhind has subscribed Rs. 81,000, and the Rájá of Kapurthállá one lakh of rupees towards the proposed *Khálsá* College. The State officers of Nabhá have given Rs. 30,000 more. The question of the locality of the college is still unsettled.

The Viceroy congratulated the members of the Corporation upon the success of their efforts to improve the sanitation of their city and its water-supply. The duty of seeing to this was one specially incumbent upon Indian municipalities, for not a month passed without bearing witness to the fatal results which followed the neglect of this obligation.

His Excellency expressed the satisfaction with which he had listened to the vigorous condemnation by the municipality of those religious animosities in Delhi which at one time promised to gain for its neighbourhood an unenviable notoriety. He rejoiced to see that the leading men of both parties had, since the year in which these discreditable incidents occurred, united for the purpose of maintaining harmony and peace, and that their efforts had been so far successful. The Government had a right to expect that all Honorary Magistrates and members of municipalities would exert themselves for this purpose, and trusted that, as holders of honourable offices under Government, they would recognize the obligation which rested upon them. "These disputes" observed Lord Lansdowne, "are a survival of intolerance which should have no place in a civilized community. Government can do something to repress the commotions to which they have given rise, and you may depend upon our doing our duty without flinching, should this become necessary." "It is, however," His Excellency pointed out, "upon the influence of public opinion, rather than upon that of repressive measures, that I should much prefer to rely; and I believe that, if that opinion is wisely directed by those who have the right to lead it, and if the authors of these disturbances are made plainly to perceive that they are offending not only the law of the country, but the honest convictions of the great majority of their fellow-citizens, these regretable incidents will entirely cease to disfigure the records of your city."

The views of the Government of India in regard to these dissensions.

We have taken occasion to record at some length the views of His Excellency the Governor-General on the subject of religious and tribal differences among the natives of our country, with the twofold object of showing, first, how severely our rulers reprobate quarrels among ourselves, and how sincerely they wish us to unite in every cause that is just and really conducive to the happiness and well-being of the people, and, secondly, of impressing on our countrymen that, however actuated some of them may unluckily be by misguided sentiments, Government will not allow itself to be slothful in doing its duty in regard to their conduct, and will not be found backward in bringing the offenders to justice.

Duties of the natives of India to the Government and their own countrymen.

It is the duty of the leaders of public opinion in this country to cement friendly relations between the two great communities of India—the Hindu and the Mahomedan,—and, as the main result of a settled Government and enlightend rule, it is the right of those in authority to have the satisfaction of seeing that mutual good-will and confidence among the different races of India, and the cordial relations existing between them, tend not only to promote the happiness of the people, but make them vie with each other for the foremost place in devotion to the Crown. Where communities are thus united in fidelity to the Crown, where race jealousies and factious hostilities have been subordinated to the more manly and more noble qualities of patriotism, and a desire for concord and harmony among the people, and a healthy emulation of all that is excellent in our daily dealings in life, there the blessings of heaven will ensue and make the people happy and prosperous. It has been rightly said that loyalty to the rulers is a plant of indigenous and perennial growth in the Panjáb, and it is to be hoped that by the effectual effacement of hostile differences, and by assiduous application to the cause of social reform, political enterprise and commercial activity, our countrymen of the Panjáb will show that to maintain and strengthen the traditions of their forefathers in this respect is the highest aim which a Panjábi can recognise.

The Attock camp of 1890.

In the months of November and December, 1890, troops were assembled at Attock, with the twofold object of illustrating the facilities for attack and defence offered by the Attock position, and of furnishing practical experience of the operations of the war in a difficult country. As notified by His Excellency the Commander-in-Chief at the conclusion of the manœuvres, the results in both respects have been extremely valuable, and Sir Frederick Roberts was pleased to record his appreciation of the soldier-like keenness, and cheerful spirit and steadiness, displayed by all ranks in carrying out their arduous duties on the occasion.

The preliminary movements of the Cavalry Brigades afforded useful examples of the work they would be expected to perform in a campaign. The march of the Akora division through the Kunna Khyal Pass, the dispositions of the defending forces, and the field-firing with service ammunition, were all that could be desired. The British Commander-in-Chief was glad to welcome at Attock representatives of the armies of Australia, Madras, and Bombay which was proof of the interest taken in the working and organization of the Panjáb armies in such distant parts of the Empire.

The Black Mountain Expedition, 1891.

With a view to effecting the permanent pacification of the Hassanzie and Akazie clans of the Black Mountain, which have lately been in a state of declared hostility to the British Government, it has been decided to send a force of British troops to inflict effectual chastisement on the people of the clan. A notification was issued by the Honourable the Lieutenant-Governor of the Panjáb in February last, warning the public, generally, that they are forbidden to pass, otherwise than on public service, across the frontiers of the districts of Hazárá and Peshávar into the territories of the Hassanzie and Akazie clans, and the clans adjoining them on the Indus River. The projected expedition will have also for its object the construction of such roads and outposts as may appear to be necessary. The total strength employed is to be 6,800 fighting men and 1,900 followers.

The Age of Consent Bill.

To the beneficent measures of our humane Government, we mainly owe the abolition of that repugnant custom of the Hindus known as *Satti*, or the self-immolation of widows on the funeral pile of their husbands, which had obtained deep root in India, as also the suppression of infanticide, which was so prevalent in the Mánjhá and Cis-Sutlej country at the time of the annexation of the Panjáb by the British. The Bill relating to the lawful age of consent for the marriage of females which was under the consideration of the Government in the Legislative Department has been finally passed into law, and it is gratifying to see that, so far as the Panjáb is concerned, the beneficial measure of the Government aiming at a higher limit of age, has been welcomed by all classes of the people, Hindus and Mahomedans.

The Cesarewitch in the capital of the Panjáb, 13th January, 1891.

The visit of His Imperial Highness the Cesarewitch, the Czar's eldest son, to the Panjáb and its capital, after a sojourn in other principal towns of India, and the exceptionally brilliant reception given him at Láhore by the Honourable the Lieutenant-Governor of the Panjáb and the Chief Civil and Military Officers of the station, is particularly interesting, as affording proof of the relations of amity and concord existing between the two great Powers of England and Russia. That Russia and England, two great rival European Powers in Asia, and the subverters of many a mighty monarchy founded by the legions of Changez Khan, the Tartar, and the arms of Tymúr, the Gorgan, should, for the first time in the annals of the East, thus furnish evidence of their mutual trust, is a matter of no small political significance. Our own Government, guided, as it invariably is, by a liberal policy and broad views, not only towards its own subjects but in its relations with the foreign powers, heartily welcomed the arrival of the Russian Prince on the soil of India, and allowed him access to all parts of the country which he desired to see. The royal visitor was pleased with the reception accorded him everywhere, and it is hoped that the impressions which he carried away with him from India of a loyal, contented and happy people, and a prosperous and flourishing country, will be a useful guide to him in his dealings with Asiatics when, in course of time, he ascends the throne of his ancestors.

The opening of the Ambálá-Kálka Railway, March, 1891.

The opening of the new Delhi-Ambálá and Kálká Railway was celebrated in the Darbár Hall, Delhi, on 7th March, 1891, amid great rejoicings. The completion of a line of railway to the foot of the Simla hills, is the result of private enterprise, and is likely to prove a real boon to the country.

The line beyond Kálká has also been surveyed, and it is hoped that the Directors of the new railway will meet with sufficient encouragement to induce them to complete the line to the summer capital of India, and that a year or two will see Simla and the great military stations of Dagshai, Sabathu and Jatogh connected by railway with the rest of India.

The construction of the Chínab bridge.

The completion of the Chínab bridge, early in 1890, resulted in connecting the last link of the Sindh-Sagar Railway with the North-Western system. The structure comprises seventeen spans of two hundred feet, with a headway of fourteen feet above high flood level. The cost of construction, including the outlay spent on the military defences of the bridge, was forty-two and three-quarter lakhs of rupees.

THE END.

APPENDIX I.

LÁHORE MUNICIPAL ADDRESS, PRESENTED TO H. R. H. THE PRINCE OF WALES.

We beg humbly to express our thanks that it has pleased the heir-apparent of the throne to honour with his presence this distant portion of Her Majesty's dominions: for we see in this auspicious visit, following that of His Royal Highness the Duke of Edinburgh, another proof of the warm interest taken in our welfare by our Gracious Sovereign and the members of the Royal Family.

Though distant from the Capital of England, and among the youngest sons of Her Great Empire, we claim, in common with our countrymen, a foremost rank among the loyal subjects of the Crown; for, placed at the north-western door of India, on the borders of regions untraversed by Europeans, and mindful of our own past history, we are in a position to appreciate, even more than others, the benefits of British rule.

For those great benefits we hope ever to evince in acts, as we now express in words, the gratitude of a faithful people.

APPENDIX II.

THE ADDRESS OF THE GUARDIANS OF THE MAUSOLEUM OF RANJÍT SINGH, PRESENTED TO H. R. H. THE PRINCE OF WALES.

We, the Managers of the Mausoleum, beg to approach your Royal Highness with feeling of the deepest loyalty, and offer our cordial welcome for the visit paid to this edifice, consecrated to the relics of the departed royalty of this country. We never expected such an unusual honour, ever since the memorable visit of His Grace the Duke of Edinburgh. It is, however, realized. We rejoice in it, and once more pay our homage to Your Royal Highness for the honour done.

We are really immaculated to have a personal appearance of a Royal Prince. We are in duty bound to adore our Lord सम्राट the Emperor, for according to Hindu Shastras, Bhugbutgellah 11, Section, 27 verse नरानाचं नरा धिपा "Nurranuncho Nuradheephann," also adage देलश्वरो श्वरवा जगदीश्वर "Delhisuro bah Jugodisoro" and the Mahomedan expression ظل الحي "Zillúl-Hy," the Emperor is shadow of the Almighty. This Mausoleum was erected by the Rájá Khurk Singh, son of Maharájá Ranjít Singh, in the year 1839, nearly thirty-six years ago.

Though Láhore is far inferior to other Presidencies your Royal Highness has visited, the fidelity and loyalty which we feel warm in our bosom will for ever remain unchanged for your Royal Highness and Her Majesty the Queen of Britain. We sincerely pray for health, happiness, and safe journey of your Royal Highness through this country, and remain

With the greatest respect Your Royal Highness's
Most obedient and devoted subjects and humble servants,

THE GRINTHIANS.

January, 1876.

APPENDIX III.

DEPENDENT STATES OF THE PANJÁB.

The dependent and feudatory States of the Panjáb are thirty-six in number, *viz.* :—Jammú and Káshmír, Patiálá, Baháwalpur, Jhind, Nabhá, Kapurthálá, Mandi, Sarmur (Náhan), Malerkotla, Faridkot, Chambá, Suket, Lohâru, Patoudi, Dujáná, Kalsia and twenty other petty Hill States. Of these the first (Jammú and Káshmír) is, politically, under the Government of India, the others being under the control of the Panjáb Government. The total area of these States amounts, approximately, to 104,000 square miles, their population (1891) to 6,780,534 ; their revenues to about Rs. 18,000,000 per annum ; their military forces, exclusive of mere armed retainers, to about 50,000 men ; the total tribute received from them to Rs. 2,80,000 per annum.

The relations of two of the dependent States, *viz.*, Káshmír and Baháwalpur, with the British Government, are regulated by treaties ; those of Patiálá, Jhind and Nabhá by *sanads* or charters of the Governor-General. A *nazráná*, or tribute, is payable to the British Government by the chiefs of the last three States on the succession of collaterals to the chiefship, and the chiefs are bound to dispense justice and promote the welfare of their subjects, to prevent *satti*, slavery, and female infanticide ; to co-operate with the British Government against an enemy ; to furnish supplies to troops ; and to grant, free of expense, land required for rail-roads in their States as well as for imperial lines of road. On the other hand, the British Government guarantees them full and unreserved possession of their territories. They differ from the remaining feudatories in the fact that they have been granted full power of life and death over their subjects, from whom the British Government has undertaken not to receive any complaints whether muafidars, jagirdars, relatives, dependents, servants or other classes.

The remaining feudatories have not the power of life and death over their subjects, all capital sentences passed by them requiring the confirmation of the British Agent ; they are not, moreover, exempt from enquiry into complaints made by their subjects or dependents ; and all but two or three of the minor States, pay tribute in cash to the British Government.

It is only necessary to give here a brief description of the more important States—

KÁSHMÍR.

The area of Káshmír, including Jammú, is 80,900 square miles, with a population of 2,523,857 persons, according to the estimate of 1891. The State comprises Punch, Ladakh, Gilghit and the districts of Dárdistan, Baltistan, Leh and others. The State extends to the Karakorum mountains on the north, Chinese Tibet on the east, and the Panjáb Districts on the south and west. The revenue is estimated at Rs. 80,75,782. The military force consists of about 19,000 men. By the terms of the treaty with the British Government, the Maharájá is bound to refer all disputes with neighbouring States to its arbitration, to assist British troops, when required so to do, and never to retain any British subject, or the subject of any European or American State, except with the consent of the British Government. The Maharájá pays to the British Government an annual tribute of a horse, twenty-five pounds of pashm or fine wool, and three pairs of shawls.

The chief is a Dogra Rájput, whose grandfather, Goláb Singh, commenced his career as a horseman in Maharájá Ranjít Singh's service. Maharájá Goláb Singh furnished a contingent of troops and artillery to co-operate with the British forces against Delhi during the Mutiny. He died in 1875, and was succeeded by his son, Maharájá Ranbir Singh, who died on 12th September, 1885, being succeeded by his son Partáb Singh, the present Maharájá. Since the accession of the new chief, a British Resident has been located at Káshmír. The State is now under the management of a Council of Regency.*

The chief of Káshmír is entitled to a salute of 21 guns, and has been granted the right of adoption.

The first inhabitants of Káshmír were Indo-Aryans who worshipped the the Sun-god. Budhism then triumphed over Brahmanism, and spread its influence in all directions till, after centuries of struggle, it finally gave way to the religion of the Hindus. The old Hindu sovereignty was subverted by the Mahomedans, during the reign of Shams-ud-dín Altamsh, in the fourteenth century, when the Queen of the last Hindu sovereign, after upbraiding the Mahomedan usurper, stabbed herself; but Káshmír had been, long before (1012 A. D.), attacked and ravaged by Mahmud of Ghazni. Akber conquered the country in 1586, and the Afghans, under Ahmed Shah, in 1752. The Sikhs conquered it in 1819, and Goláb Singh, who ruled it, in the name of the Sikh Darbár, was acknowledged its independent sovereign by the British, in March 1846, on payment of 75 lakhs of rupees.

Sultán Baber mentions, in his Memoirs, that the hill country along the upper course of the Hindus (Indus) was, in old times, inhabited by a race of men named *Kás*, from whom the country came to be known Kás-*mír*, the denomination *mír* or *mere* being added to it to signify *town* or *habitation*, as is found in *Ajmere, Jesalmere*, &c., well known towns of Hindostán.

The whole of Káshmír, writes Abul Fazl, represents a garden in perpetual spring, and the fortifications with which nature has furnished it are of astonishing height. It rains and snows here at the same season as in Tartary and Persia. Violets, roses, narcissus, and innumerable other flowers grow wild.

The Persian poet Rafi-ud-dín writes in praise of it :—

I have seen Irak and India, Khorassán and Persia, but no place equal to Káshmír in beauty and excellence of climate. The air, tempered by gentle showers, has all the mildness of spring; there are flowers and green herbage, plains and running streams, palaces, cupolas, and public buildings, beautiful to view. On every side are rising grounds, crystal springs and lofty trees, amid mountains covered with nut trees, apple trees and fig trees. But how shall I describe the lovely damsels of that country? For, in my opinion, the young moon is not equal to them in beauty; with lips sweet as sugar, in stature like the graceful pine, fragrant as jasmine; from whatever point of view you look at those nymphs, they appear like the sun or moon. They are charming as houris; all fresh, young and blooming.

The valley of Káshmír is celebrated throughout the eastern world for its romantic beauty, the fertility of its soil and the salubrity of its climate. Urfi, the poet-laureate of Akber's Court, has sung in its praise :—

هر سوخته جانیکه بکشمیر در آید — گر مرغ کباب است که با بال و پر آید

"Any person suffering from vexation of mind who may visit Kashmír
Is sure to be endowed with the wings and feathers (of health) even if he is a roasted bird."

The surface of the country is generally flat, yielding abundant crops of rice, which forms the staple food of its inhabitants. Fruit trees of all kinds abound, and there is an abundance of grapes and herbs peculiar to cold countries. Water-nuts *(singháras)* growing in the lakes form a considerable portion of the food of the poorer classes, and a superior sort of saffron is cultivated in the plains.

Káshmír is famous for the manufacture of shawls, the wool from which they are manufactured being brought from the high table-lands of Thibet. The original colour of the wool is dark grey, but it is bleached by means of a preparation of rice-flour.

Sulphurous springs exist in many parts of the valley, and earthquakes are of not uncommon occurrence. In 1886, the valley was visited by most terrible shocks, causing enormous loss of property. Many thousand lives were lost, and thousands more were rendered homeless. On account of the frequent visitations of earthquakes, the houses are built of wood, or of light bricks and mortar, with a large intermixture of timber. Many of the houses are two or three storeys high. On the wooden roof a convering of earth is laid, which contributes to the warmth of the house during the winter, and, in the summer, is planted with flowers. The streets are narrow and filthy. The city enjoys a mild salubrious climate, and a river flows through its centre, along the banks of which are covered floating baths.

---

* *Vide* page 622.

The lake of Káshmír, provincially named Dal, has long been celebrated for its beauties. It is situated on the north-eastern side of the city, and is reached by a canal. The northern and eastern sides are bounded by green and lofty mountains, which slope down to the margins, affording a charming view. In the centre of the plain, as it approaches the lake, is the spacious garden of Shalámár, constructed by the Emperor Jahángír. The garden is 590 yards long and 207 yards broad, and is surrounded by a brick and stone wall, ten feet high. It consists of four terraces of equal dimensions, each furnished with numerous pavilions, fountains, and waterfalls. The chief objects of interest in the valley are the floating gardens, the *jhúla*, or suspension bridge, the ruins of ancient buildings, rocks, springs, lakes and natural scenery, which abound everywhere.

Iron abounds in Káshmír. It is worked near Sapur, Rampur and Islamabad. Lead, sulphur and copper exist in various parts. The other products of the country are timber, shawls, saffron, borax and cereals. Káshmír is also noted for its paper manufacture. The paper is of very superior quality, as compared with other papers of Indian manufacture, and is extensively used in copying books.

The first Europeans who visited Káshmír were Saint Francis Xavier, a Spanish Jesuit, and Goez, who accompanied the Emperor Akber to the valley in 1594. Bernier, the French physician, visited the country in 1663, in the suite of Aurungzebe. He has left a most interesting and romantic description of the valley and the city.

PATIÁLÁ.

This State is under the political superintendence of the Panjáb Government. The Rájá belongs to the Phulkia family, and is a descendant of Rama, the second son of Phul, their common ancestor. The rájás of Nabhá and Jhind, being the descendants of Taloka, the eldest son of Phul. The three States of Patiálá, Jhind and Nabhá form thus the Phulkia family.

The area of the State is 5,887 square miles, with a total population of 1,583,803, according to the census of 1891. The estimated gross revenue of the State is Rs. 46,89,560. The military force consists of about 2,750 cavalry, 600 infantry, and 288 artillery men, with 31 field and 78 other guns. The Maharájá is entitled to a salute of 17 guns. Maharájá Narandra Singh, who rendered excellent service to the British Government during the Mutiny, died in 1862, and was succeeded by his son, Mahander Singh, who, dying in 1876, was succeeded by his infant son, Rájander Singh, the present Maharájá.

Within the boundaries of the State are situated a slate-quarry, near Simla, and a lead mine, near Sabatu. In Narnoul, there are also marble quarries and copper mines.

A broad-gauge line of railway from Rájpura, on the Sindh-Panjáb and Delhi (now the North-Western) Railway, to the capital of the State was opened in 1882. This was the first line of railway constructed in the Panjáb at the expense of a native State.

BAHÁWALPUR.

The area of this State is 15,000 square miles, of which 9,880 square miles are desert. The population, according to the census of 1891, is 648,900. The gross revenue of the State is estimated at sixteen lakhs of rupees. Its military force consists of 300 cavalry, 2,493 infantry and police, and 99 artillerymen, with 12 guns. The nawáb ranks third, in order of precedence, among the Panjáb chiefs, coming next to the Maharájá of Patiálá, and is entitled to a salute of 17 guns. The principal towns in the State are Baháwalpur, the capital, Ahmadpur, Khanpur, Kherpur and Minchinabad.

The chief of Baháwalpur is of the Dáúdputra tribe, a descendant of Baháwal Khan, who acquired independence on the dismemberment of the Durráni empire, after the death of Shah Shuja. The tribe claims descent from Abbas, uncle of the Prophet Mahomed. Sultan Ahmad II, the ancestor of the tribe, having migrated from Egypt, invaded Sindh at the head of ten thousand horse. Sindh was then ruled by a Hindu Rájá named Ráe Dhourang, who, after some faint show of resistance, submitted to the Sultan's authority, and gave his daughter to him in marriage. Mobarak Khan was the last of the family, who died in peace in Shekarpur in 1726 A. D. His successor Sadiq Muhammad Khan, the founder of the present monarchy, after repeated invasions by Khodayár Khan *Khilora*, was compelled to abandon Shekarpur, and, with all his family, settled in a place called Bet Dabli, now in the Dera Ghazi Khan District. By the force of his arms he reduced to obedience many tribes living in the neighbourhood of Uch, and Nawáb Hayátulláh Khan the Moghal Governor of Multán granted to him the lease of the Parganá of Choudhri now in the *Kardarí* of Khanpur. He also founded Allahábad and other towns and reclaimed a great area of waste land.

Dáúd Khan, after whose name the Dáúdputras are called, was the twelfth in descent from Abbas. The Purjani, named after Purji Khan, *alias* Feroz Khan, is a clan of this tribe, from whom his present Highness is descended. The descendants of the tribes who migrated to Baháwalpur with Sadiq Mahommed Khan, the first Nawáb, have spread throughout the Baháwalpur territory, and bear the names of their respective ancestors, such as Marufanís, or descendants of Máruf Khan, Arbanis of Arib Khan, Golanis of Gúl Mahomed Khan, Achranis of Achar Khan, and so forth.*

Nawáb Baháwal Khan rendered excellent service to the British Government in the siege of Multán, in 1847-48, and was rewarded by the grants of the districts of Sabzal Kot and Bhoung, together with a life pension of one lakh of rupees per annum. He was a staunch ally of the British, and entered into an alliance with that power so far back as 1809, by which, while retaining independent jurisdiction within his own borders, he acknowledged the supremacy of the British Government. At the close of 1852, Baháwal Khan died, and in accordance with a wish expressed by him previous to his death, his third son, Saádat Khan, succeeded to the chiefship. The Dáúdputras, the dominant clan in Baháwalpur, headed by Haji Khan, eldest son of the late Nawáb, however, disputed his succession. Saádat Khan was deposed, and brought to Láhore with his family. The successful chief, Haj Khan, was recognised by the Governor-General in Council, and received a *khilat* of investiture. Saádat Khan, no longer remembering the condition from which he had been rescued by the British intercession, aspired to the recovery of his power, and had even the effrontery to solicit the interference of the British Government in his behalf. He was placed under arrest in the Summan Burj Palace of the fort, and was informed that he would not be released until the Government was satisfied as to his future good behaviour. The ex-nawáb died in 1862. Four years after, Haji Khan, the reigning nawáb, died, and was succeeded by his son, Sádiq Mahommed Khan, the present ruler.

After a long minority, Sádiq Mahommed Khan was invested with ruling powers on 28th November, 1879. The British Government had, during the period of the Nawáb's minority, taken the management of the country into their own hands, at the earnest and repeated request of the leading chiefs of Baháwalpur, the counsellors and ministers of the Nawáb, and the members of his own famliy. The State for years, had been a prey to anarchy. The revenue, which could not be collected in 1865, rose, in the next year of settled rule, to 14 lakhs, and had reached the annual average of 20 lakhs, when charge of the administratiron was made over to the Nawáb. Roads, bridges and public buildings had been constructed, ancient canals had been enlarged and repaired and new ones dug ; while a quarter of a million of acres had been added to the irrigated area. The British Government administered the estate of its ward carefully and wisely, and took great care in educating the chief so as to imbue him with ideas essential to success as the ruler of an important Mahomedan State. Sir Robert Egerton, to whom is justly due the credit of giving the Nawáb an excellent training, and of devising schemes which materially tended to the prosperity of his State, thus expressed his opinion, in regard to this chief :—

> The Lieutenant-Governor trusts that the young Nawáb of Baháwalpur, who possesses many excellent, generous and manly qualities, may have the strength and courage to resist the influence of evil counsellors, and, by the just rule of his territory, may sufficiently repay the Government for the care which has been for so many years expended on it.

These expectations were fully realized. During the Afghan campaign of 1878-80,

* *Vide* the *Doulati Abbasia*, a manuscript history of Baháwalpur.

the Nawáb placed the entire resources of his State at the disposal of the British Government, and furnished a contingent of troops, which rendered good service on the Dera Gházi Khan frontier, in keeping the communications open.

There is a silk manufactory at Baháwalpur. The State is noted for the manufacture of fine *lungis, suf* and silk goods, and produces indigo, cotton and cereals. Things have, of late, considerably improved. There is a department of Public Instruction, a stud farm for the improvement of the breed of horses and cattle, and a forest establishment to provide a supply of fuel. Railway communication has been established, and new lines and canals have been opened out throughout the country.

JHIND.

This is one of the Phulkian States of the Panjáb. It has an area of 1,232 square miles, and a population (1891) of 284,303 souls. The revenue is between six and seven lakhs of rupees. The Rájá supplies 25 horsemen for general service in British territory. The military force consists of 1,600 infantry, 392 cavalry, and 234 artillery, with 6 horse and 6 mule guns. Rájá Sawarup Singh supplied a contingent of troops to aid the British against the mutineers at Delhi, and received, as a reward, additional territory yielding Rs. 1,16,810 per annum.

NABHÁ.

The Rájá of Nabhá is descended from the same branch as the Rájás of Jhind and Patiálá, and the three families are known as the Phulkian House. The area of the State is 928 square miles, the population (1891) 282,756, the gross revenue Rs. 6,50,000 per annum. The State maintains a military force of 1,250 infantry, 560 cavalry and 50 artillery, with 12 field and 10 other guns. The Rájá is entitled to a salute of 11 guns. Rájá Bhurpur Singh displayed conspicuous loyalty to the British Government during the Mutiny of 1857, and was rewarded by the grant of territory valued at more than a lakh of rupees. He died in 1863, and was succeeded by his brother, Bhagwan Singh, who died, without issue, in 1871. Híra Singh, a jágírdar of Jhind, and a descendant of Phul, was, thereupon, elected Rájá by the two other Phulkian chiefs, and a representative of the British Government, according to the treaty of 6th May 1860, which provided that, in case of failure of male heirs to any one of the three Phulkian chiefs, a successor should be chosen from among the descendants of Phul. Rájá Híra Singh has proved an able and energetic ruler.

KAPURTHÁLÁ.

This State covers an area of 620 square miles, and has a population (1891) of 299,593 persons. The revenue is about ten lakhs of rupees, subject to a charge of 1,31,000, payablo to the British Government as commutation for military services. The Oudh estates, awarded to Rájá Randhir Singh for his services during the Mutiny, yield, in addition, about eight lakhs per annum. The military force consists of 186 cavalry, 926 infantry, 303 police, 9 field and 4 fort guns. The Rájá receives a salute of 11 guns, and has been granted the right of adoption. The principal towns in the State are, Kapurthálá, Phagwárá and Sultánpur. The chief of Kapurthálá is a Kalál, and his ancestor, Jassa Singh, rose to importance about the middle of the last century.

Rájá Randhir Singh was a good English scholar, and could speak and write that language fluently. He died at Aden, on his way to England, in 1870, and was succeeded by his son Kharak Singh.

The death of Rájá Kharak Singh occurred in the summer of 1887, from brain disease, and he was succeeded by his infant son, Jagat Jít Singh.

The State was under the direct management of the British Government during the minority of the Rájá, but the Rájá has lately been invested with governing powers.*

The police force has been re-modelled on the principle of the Panjáb Police Force, and the procedure and substantive law administered by the courts are nearly identical with the law and procedure in force in the Panjáb. The Randhír Hospital, in the capital of the State, is very popular. Education is liberally supported by the

* *Vide* page 627.

State, which maintains a High School at Kapurthálá, two Anglo-Vernacular Middle Schools, and thirty-one schools for primary education.

In December, 1890, the Government of India was pleased to raise the status of the Rájá of Kapurthálá in the matter of complimentary *khilats*, which will in future be valued at Rs. 6 000 instead of Rs. 4,500 as heretofore. This honor has been granted in consideration of the State's loyal services in the Afghan war, and of its good administration during the minority of the present Rájá.

MANDI.

The estimated area of Mandi is 1,000 square miles, with a population (1891) of 166,921, and an approximate revenue of Rs. 3,60,000, of which one lakh is paid as tribute to the British Government. The military force consists of seven hundred infantry and twenty-five cavalry. The Rájá is entitled to a salute of 11 guns. The Rájá belongs to the Mandiál family, and claims descent from the Chandar Bansi Rájás. The country is mountainous. There are salt mines in the State, the income from which furnishes about one-fourth of its revenue. Iron in small quantities is found, and gold is obtained in small particles by washing.

There is a well furnished dispensary at Mandi, under the management of a hospital assistant, lent by the Government. There is also a school in which English, Persian, Sanskrit and Hindi are taught. The Rájá takes some interest in this, being himself a Sanskrit scholar. The chief has constructed a handsome suspension bridge over the Biás at Mandi, with a clear span of 240 feet. It was opened for traffic in 1878, and named by the Rájá the "Empress Bridge of Mandi."

SIRMÚR.

Sirmúr is one of the sub-Himaláyan States of the Panjáb, and is also called Náhan, from the name of its chief town. The area is 1,077 square miles, with a population (1891) of 124,224 souls. The estimated revenue of the State is Rs. 2,10,000. The Rájá pays no tribute, but is bound to furnish a contingent of troops to the British Government when called upon. He receives a salute of 11 guns, and maintains a force of 300 infantry, 55 cavalry and 20 artillery, with 10 field guns. The State abounds in wild elephants, tigers, leopards, bears and hyænas, which live in dense forests. There are extensive quarries of slate, a mine of mica, abundant iron ore and a lead mine.

The present Rájá, Shamsher Par Kash, born about 1843, is a prince of very liberal views. Sirmúr, in respect of its administration, holds first rank among all the Hill States. The roads are broad and maintained in excellent order. The forests are preserved upon sound principles, while the Rájá's capital, in point of conservancy and general appearance, might set an example to many municipalities in British territory. The State contains 65 schools, the police are properly accoutred and controlled by a European officer; and a medical officer retired from the British service superintends the State dispensaries and the sanitation of the capital.

MALERKOTLA.

The State of this name has an area of 164 square miles, and a population (1891) of 75,755 souls. The estimated gross revenue is Rs. 2,84,000, and the military force of the Nawáb consists of 200 infantry, 67 cavalry, and 16 artillery, with 8 field guns. He receives a salute of 11 guns.

The chief of Malerkotla is the head of an Afghan brotherhood, originally natives of Kábul, whose ancestors held positions of trust in the Sirhind Province, under the Moghal empire, and gradually became independent, as the Moghal dynasty sank into decay.

FARIDKOT.

The area of the State is 612 square miles, and the population (1891) 115,040. The estimated revenue is three lakhs per annum, and the military force consists of 200 cavalry, 600 infantry and police and 3 field guns. The Rájá is entitled to a salute of 11 guns, and the right of adoption has been accorded to him by the Government.

The founder of the Faridkot family was one Bhullan, who rose to importance in the time of Akber.

Pahár'Singh, the grandfather of the present chief, rendered good service to the British Government on the outbreak of the Sikh war, in 1845. As a reward for his services, he was created a Rájá, and his territorial possessions were increased. He was succeeded by his son Wazír Singh, who served on the side of the British during the Second Sikh War, in 1849, and also distinguished himself during the Mutiny. For the services rendered, he was liberally rewarded by the Government. In April 1874, Wazir Singh died, and was succeeded by his son, Bikrama Singh, the present ruler, who was born in 1842.

Rájá Bikráma Singh has established a firm rule in his dominions, taking on himself the functions of Judge in all departments, with a Magistrate and Civil Judge under him. Criminal cases of a serious nature are regularly prepared in the Magistrate's Court and submitted to him, as Sessions Judge, for formal orders ; and the proceedings are marked by a regular procedure, His Highness' judgments being fully and carefully recorded.

Railway communication has been established through the territory of the Faridkot State, in which four stations are situated.

CHAMBÁ.

Chambá is an ancient Hindu principality to the north of the Kangrá and Gurdáspur districts.

The estimated area of the State is 3,180 square miles, and the population 118,637* according to the census of 1891. During the minority of the present Rájá the administration was carried on by a British officer, aided by native officials. The revenue rose from Rs. 1,20,000, to Rs. 1,73,000, during 8 years, and, by 1882, to Rs. 2,40,000, exclusive of Rs. 50,000 revenue free grants. The military force of the State consists of one hundred and sixty men and police and a gun.

The forests of Chambá form an important source of supply for timber, and are leased to the British Government, yielding annually from one to two lakhs of rupees to the State. The soil is suited for tea cultivation. Copper and iron ore are found in the hills, and slate quarries exist all over the country. The State is a favourite resort of sportsmen. Musk-deer are found in the Barmaor Parganá of the State and *barasingha* (stags), wild sheep, hill leopards, brown bears, ghural and ibex (*banbakri*), in the mountain ranges.

The Rájá is of Khatri descent. He takes a personal interest in the management of his territory and his administration reflects credit on him.

SUKET.

The area of the State is 474 square miles, and the population (1891) 52,426. The estimated revenue is a lakh of rupees per annum, of which eleven thousand rupees are paid as tribute to the British Government. The Rájá is entitled to a salute of 11 guns, and maintains a small force of 365 infantry and 40 cavalry. The ruler of the State is Rájá Dasht Nikandar Sen, who came of age in 1884. He rules the State with firmness and vigour.

LOHARU.

This State has an area of 285 square miles, with a population (1891) of 20,123. The estimated revenue is Rs. 69,000. The chief is bound to furnish a contingent of 200 horse to the British Government when required. The chiefs of Lohárn, Patoudi and Dojaná are descendants of Afghan adventurers, on whom the estates were conferred by the British Government in reward for services under Lord Lake, in the beginning of the present century. The founder of the State was Ahmad Baksh Khan. His son, Amin-ud-dín Khan, died in 1869, and was succeeded by his son, Ala-ud-dín Khan, who received the title of nawáb in 1874, on condition of faithful allegiance to the British Government. He also received a *sanad* of adoption.

Ala-ud-dín Khan was an accomplished Arabic and Persian scholar. He died in October, 1884, and was succeeded by his son, Amir-ud-dín Ahmad Khan. The condition of the finances has been embarrassed by the extravagances of the late chief, but the present chief is careful, and hopes are entertained of his eventually rescuing the State from its financial difficulties.

* Except Pangi and Lahul, of which the census has not yet been ascertained.

INDEX: